TITLE4B 1980

BRITISH AUTHORS

of the

Nineteenth Century

THE AUTHORS SERIES

AMERICAN AUTHORS: 1600-1900

BRITISH AUTHORS BEFORE 1800

BRITISH AUTHORS OF THE NINETEENTH CENTURY

EUROPEAN AUTHORS: 1000-1900

TWENTIETH CENTURY AUTHORS

TWENTIETH CENTURY AUTHORS: FIRST SUPPLEMENT

THE JUNIOR BOOK OF AUTHORS

MORE JUNIOR AUTHORS

THIRD BOOK OF JUNIOR AUTHORS

BRITISH AUTHORS

of the

Nineteenth Century

Edited by

STANLEY J. KUNITZ

Associate Editor

HOWARD HAYCRAFT

COMPLETE IN ONE VOLUME WITH
1000 BIOGRAPHIES AND
350 PORTRAITS

NEW YORK

THE H. W. WILSON COMPANY

NINETEEN HUNDRED THIRTY-SIX

BRITISH AUTHORS OF THE NINETEENTH CENTURY

Copyright 1936
By The H. W. Wilson Company
Copyright renewed © 1964
By The H. W. Wilson Company

First Printing, 1936
Second Printing, 1940
Third Printing, 1948
Fourth Printing, 1955
Fifth Printing, 1960
Sixth Printing, 1964
Seventh Printing, 1973

PRINTED IN THE UNITED STATES OF AMERICA

International Standard Book Number 0-8242-0007-1

Library of Congress Catalog Card Number 36-28581

4786

Preface

THE purpose of this work is to provide in a single volume brief, readable accounts of the lives of the major and minor British authors of the nineteenth century concerning whom students and amateurs of English literature are likely at any time to desire information. More than a thousand authors of the British Empire (including Canada, Australia, South Africa, and New Zealand) are represented by sketches varying in length from approximately 100 to 2500 words, roughly proportionate to the importance of the subjects. Reproductions of portraits illustrate almost 350 of the sketches. Eligibility has been restricted, as a rule, to British writers of books who published a major portion of their work between 1800 and 1900, but some liberties have been taken with this chronological formula where reasons of literary association or historic connection supervened. In general, however, it may be said that few authors earlier than William Blake or later than Aubrey Beardsley have found a place in this volume. No living authors are included. Preference has been given, in the main, to writers of *belles lettres,* although an effort has been made to summarize, if only briefly, the lives of the more eminent figures in all departments of knowledge (including science, philosophy, travel and exploration, jurisprudence, political economy, sociology, and education) whose written works, though hardly classifiable as literature, have proved valuable in their respective fields.

In the writing of these sketches concision has been a prerequisite, but contributors have not been encouraged to cultivate the bristling encyclopedic style. Current bio-critical research into nineteenth century English literary history has been consulted and, it is hoped, assimilated.

The nationality of an author is mentioned in the opening descriptive phrase only when he is not a native Englishman. Following each sketch is a list of the principal works of the author in question, with dates of original publication. (In the case of dramatists, the dates given in the list of works are, unless otherwise stated, dates of production.) Source material about the author is listed as a suggestion for further study.

The work of the following contributors, whose talent and industry are largely responsible for what value this production may have, is signed with their initials:

Dorothy F. Atkinson, Donald Cummings, Miriam Allen deFord, Peter Gray, Herbert B. Grimsditch, Dorothy Homans, Robert Molloy, Virginia Mussey, George E. Novack, J. B. Orrick, Barbara Damon Simison, Paula Bayne-Spencer, Robert Woodman Wadsworth.

Special acknowledgment is gladly made to Wilbur C. Hadden, editorial assistant, for his long, patient, and invaluable assistance in the preparation of manuscripts.

In a work of this scope involving so much detail, it is inevitable, despite the most scrupulous care, that some errors should occur. Hoping that they are few and pardonable, the Editors will none the less be thankful for having them brought to their attention.

August 1936

British Authors of the 19th Century

ABBOTT, EVELYN (March 10, 1843-September 3, 1901), scholar, historian, and biographer, was born in Nottinghamshire, the son of a gentleman farmer. He was educated at Lincoln Grammar School, Somerset College (Bath), and Balliol College, Oxford, which he entered in 1862. There he distinguished himself equally in classical studies and in athletics. In 1866 he fell in a hurdle race and injured his spine; complete paralysis of the legs resulted and he never walked again. For a while after leaving the university he took private pupils. In 1873 he returned to Balliol at the invitation of the famous master Benjamin Jowett and remained there the rest of his life. He taught Greek, Latin, and history and held a number of college offices. He died unmarried.

As a writer Abbott is best known for his scholarly three-volume history of Greece, his life of Pericles, and his biography (with Lewis Campbell) of his friend and benefactor, Jowett. In addition to his original writing he did a good deal of translating and editing. His works are characterized by independent thinking; his style is simple and clear.

PRINCIPAL WORKS: History of Greece, 1888-1900; Pericles and the Golden Age of Athens, 1891; Life of Benjamin Jowett (with L. Campbell) 1897.
ABOUT: Foster, J. Alumni Oxonienses.

A BECKETT, GILBERT ABBOTT (February 17, 1811-August 30, 1856), humorist, editor, playwright, and barrister, was born in London of an old Wiltshire family that claimed descent from the father of St. Thomas à Becket. He was educated at Westminster School. In 1831, at the age of twenty, he founded a successful comic journal, *Figaro in London,* from which he withdrew in 1834.

When the famous humorous magazine *Punch* was founded in 1841, à Beckett became a member of the staff and a regular contributor. The most popular of his contributions was a series dealing with the ludicrous adventures of a young barrister named "Mr. Briefless." His most successful works, however, did not appear in the magazine itself, but were published by the *Punch* office in monthly numbers, after the fashion of Dickens' novels. His *Comic History of England* and *Comic History of Rome,* published in this manner, and illustrated by John Leech, had a very considerable vogue in their time. *The Comic Blackstone,* similarly issued, with illustrations by Cruikshank, was also popular.

Simultaneously with these activities à Beckett contributed to several other journals, wrote and produced for the stage, and pursued an

GILBERT ABBOTT A BECKETT

active legal career. At the age of thirty-eight he was appointed a metropolitan police judge and held the office until his death. He died of typhus fever at the age of forty-five at Boulogne, France, where he had gone for a holiday.

À Beckett was genial but dignified, quiet, reserved, abstemious, and a prodigious worker. Dickens and Thackeray were among his close friends. He is little known today; his writings, though competently done, were too topical to survive their era. They are now of interest only for their illustrations.

Two of à Beckett's sons followed in his footsteps as humorous writers and staff members of *Punch.* ARTHUR WILLIAM À BECKETT (1844-1909) achieved popularity with the letters of "A. Briefless, Jr." GILBERT ARTHUR À BECKETT (1837-1891) was best known as a writer of plays, notably *The Happy Land* (1873) in collaboration with W. S. Gilbert.

PRINCIPAL WORKS OF GILBERT ABBOTT À BECKETT: The Comic Blackstone, 1844-64; The Quizziology of the British Drama, 1846; The Comic History of England, 1847; The Comic History of Rome, 1852.
ABOUT: À Beckett, A. W. The à Becketts of *Punch*; À Beckett, A. W. Recollections of a Humourist; Newton, A. E. The Amenities of Book-Collecting; Spielmann, M. H. The History of *Punch*; Quarto Club Papers, 1930.

ABERCROMBIE, JOHN (October 10, 1780-November 14, 1844), Scottish physician and popular philosopher, was born in Aberdeen, the son of a clergyman. He received

1

a medical degree from Edinburgh University in 1803 and started practice in Edinburgh in 1804. A few years later he began writing the semi-philosophical works which made him famous during his lifetime. In 1835 Oxford gave him an honorary M.D. and the following year he became Lord Rector of Marischal College, Aberdeen. For a period he was Scottish physician-in-ordinary to the king. He died of an unusual form of heart disease. His brain was examined after death and found to weigh sixty-three ounces—almost the largest on record. Abercrombie had little originality as a writer, and his works, though popular in their day, had no lasting philosophical value.

PRINCIPAL WORKS: Inquiries Concerning the Intellectual Powers, 1830; The Philosophy of Moral Feelings, 1833; Essays and Tracts, 1847.

ABOUT: Edinburgh Medical and Surgical Journal 42:225 1844; The Witness November 23, 1844.

ABERIGH-MACKAY, GEORGE ROBERT (1848-1881), Anglo-Indian satirist, was born and lived most of his life in India. His father was a Bengal chaplain. He was educated at Magdalen College School and at Cambridge and then returned to India, where he joined the Education Department of Central India. In 1873 he became professor of English literature at Delhi College; in 1876 tutor to the Rajah of Rutlam; and in 1877 principal of Rajkumar College, Indore. His only work, *Twenty-one Days in India: Being the Tour of Sir Ali Baba*, was first published in *Vanity Fair* in 1878-79, and was well received. *The Academy* said, "His humor and satire possess a rare charm." He died too young, however, to fulfill the literary promise of this early work.

ACTON, LORD (John Emerich Edward Dalberg, First Baron Acton) (January 10, 1834-June 19, 1902), historian, was by birth and rearing a cosmopolitan—"never more than half an Englishman." His mother was a German baroness from Bavaria, his father, the seventh baronet, was in the diplomatic service, and their only child was born in Naples. Of old Roman Catholic families on both sides, Acton could not follow the usual educational course of the well-born Englishman; Cambridge refused him admittance because of his religion—an ironical situation in view of his later history—and he was educated in schools at Paris, Edinburgh, Oscott (where the future Cardinal Wiseman, later his enemy, was headmaster), and finally at Munich. There he both lived with and worked under the great historian von Döllinger, one of the prime influences of his life. From Döllinger he learned his historical method, laid the foundation of his immense erudition, and imbibed the "unflinching and austere liberalism" which became his outstanding characteristic.

His father died in the son's early childhood, and when he was only six his mother married the famous Liberal, Earl Granville, who became a second father to him. With Granville, also a diplomat, he traveled first to the United States, where he became an ardent advocate of state's rights, then to Russia, to the coronation of Alexander II, where his own liberalism was confirmed by observation of autocracy. He then retired to Aldenham, in Shropshire, the family seat of the Actons, and began his life-work as an historian. There he collected the valuable historical library of 59,000 volumes ("Books are made from books," he once remarked) which after his death was bought by Andrew Carnegie and presented to Lord Morley, who in turn gave it to Cambridge. In 1859 he was elected a Member of Parliament as a Whig from Carlow, and sat till 1865, but with no great success, for he was a scholar, not a debater. He then stood for his own town of Bridgnorth, was elected by a majority of one, and on a recount was unseated. This ended his parliamentary career; its one benefit was his meeting with Gladstone, whose disciple and close friend and advocate he became. It was through Gladstone's influence that he was later elevated to the peerage.

The mainspring of Acton's life and work was his effort to liberalize Catholicism, and to bring it into consonance with modern thought. In this cause he became part owner and sometimes editor of successive publications: *The Rambler*, which died finally under the displeasure of Cardinal Wiseman, and gave birth to the famous Papal Encyclical condemning liberalism; *The Chronicle*; and the *North British Review*. To all of these he contributed numerous historical articles and reviews. In 1868 he stood for Parliament once more, but lost. The next year came the great struggle of his career—his valiant last stand against the promulgation of the dogma of papal infallibility. The months he spent in Rome were one long battle, in the end a losing one, which brought him near to excommunication, and permanently injured his health.

From 1879 Acton was obliged to spend his winters in Cannes, his autumns in Tegernsee, Bavaria (which belonged to the family of his wife, Countess Marie Arco-Valley, of Munich, by whom he had one son and three daughters), and only a few spring or summer months in London. Nevertheless his real career was still in the making. His historical work spread his reputation, especially after he helped in 1886 to found the *English Historical Review*; already beneficiary of an honorary doctorate from Munich, in 1888 he became honorary LL.D.

LORD ACTON

from Cambridge, in 1889 honorary D.C.L. from Oxford, in 1891 was elected an honorary fellow of All Souls, and in 1892 was appointed Lord in Waiting to the queen.

Finally, in 1895, Cambridge, which had rejected him as a student, made him regius professor of modern history and honorary fellow of Trinity. Acton was like a boy in his delight over his college rooms and associations. He threw himself into his work, in spite of failing health, and his lectures drew large classes. The great *Cambridge Modern History* was the child of his brain, and exists as a monument to him, though he did not live to see its first volume published. The strain of the work done on it in 1899 and 1900 was too much for him; he suffered a stroke, and was taken to Tegernsee, where in 1902 he died and was buried.

During his life Acton published only articles in periodicals, separate lectures, and letters. He was perhaps the most learned man of his day, able to write in German, French, Italian, or Spanish as fluently as in English, and he is said to have read habitually an octavo volume daily. Always a devout Catholic, he was equally a settled enemy of the papal government and dogma, with "a passionate faith in individual liberty and political righteousness." His essays are really monographs, partisan, bent on proving a thesis. His style is not an easy one; it is brilliantly epigrammatic, full of allusions, assuming much on the part of the reader, dignified and aloof as he himself was. He has been condemned for barren learning, yet Sir A. W. Ward calls him "the very type of modern historical learning in its mature development." His chief fault was a lack of

planning ability which left his greatest work incomplete.

Lord Acton was externally a man of the world, with an ironic humor, beloved by his few close friends, rigidly Puritanical in his life and outlook, but patient and courteous with intellectual ignorance. He was the very fruit of his time and his background.

M. A. deF.

PRINCIPAL WORKS (all posthumous): Correspondence With Mary Gladstone (ed. by H. Paul) 1904; Lectures and Essays on Modern History, 1906; Historical Essays and Studies, 1907; The History of Freedom and Other Essays, 1907; Lectures on the French Revolution, 1910; Correspondence (ed. by J. N. Figgis and R. V. Laurence) 1917.

ABOUT: Bryce, J. Studies in Contemporary Biography; Drew, M. G. Acton, Gladstone, and Others; Morley, J. Life of Gladstone; Christian Century 51:161 January 31, 1934; Commonweal 20:247 June 29, 1934; Dublin Review 194:169 April 1934.

ADAMS, FRANCIS WILLIAM LAUDERDALE (September 27, 1862-September 4, 1893), Anglo-Australian poet and novelist, was born in Malta. His father was a well-known zoologist and professor at Queen's College, Cork, and his grandfather was a physician and classical scholar. He was educated at private school in Shrewsbury, and then from 1878 to 1880 in Paris. For two years thereafter he was assistant master at Ventnor College; then he married and moved to Australia. After some hardship he joined the staff of the Sydney *Bulletin*, and also contributed stories, articles, and essays to many magazines. His autobiographical novel, *Leicester*, went through several editions in England after its first publication in Australia; and his poems, *Song of the Army of the Night*, were a *succès de scandale* because of their outspokenness in a prudish age. He returned to England about 1890, but by this time it was apparent that he was a victim of tuberculosis, of which his brother had already died in Australia. In a period of depression and despair because of his physical condition he committed suicide by shooting, three weeks before his thirty-first birthday. He was married twice, but left no children.

Adams was a man of great personal charm and of precocious and original talent. He suffered, however, from a lack of discipline as a writer. His finest work was his play *Tiberius*.

PRINCIPAL WORKS: Leicester, 1885; Australian Essays, 1886; Songs of the Army of the Night, 1888; The Melbournians, 1892; Australian Life, 1893; Tiberius, 1894.

ABOUT: Adams, F. W. L. Tiberius (see Introduction by W. M. Rossetti); London Times September 5, 1893; Saturday Review July 21, 1894.

ADAMS, SARAH FLOWER (February 22, 1805-August, 1848), poet and hymn-writer, was born Sarah Flower at Great Harlow, in Essex, the daughter of Benjamin Flower, a political journalist. In her twenty-ninth year she was married to William Bridges Adams, inventor and pamphleteer, who wrote on scientific and technical subjects. She was a devout Unitarian, and her piety found expression in religious verse. Her most ambitious work was a long dramatic poem dealing with the life of the early Christians, *Vivia Perpetua*, which contains some impressive passages. But her finest works were her hymns, set to music by her elder sister Eliza Flower and used in the services at Finsbury Chapel, London. The most famous of these is "Nearer, My God, to Thee."

Richard Garnett described Mrs. Adams as "a woman of singular beauty and attractiveness, delicate and truly feminine, high-minded, and in her days of health playful and high-spirited." She died at forty-three, leaving no children.

PRINCIPAL WORKS: Nearer, My God, to Thee, 1840; Vivia Perpetua, 1841.

ABOUT: Adams, S. F. Vivia Perpetua (see Memoir by E. F. Bridell-Fox in 1893 ed.); Nearer, My God, to Thee (facsimile ed.; see notes by J. Julian).

ADAMSON, ROBERT (January 19, 1852-February 5, 1902), Scottish philosopher, was born at Edinburgh, the fifth child of a solicitor. He was educated at Daniel Stewart's Hospital, Edinburgh, and at Edinburgh University, where he took first-class honors in philosophy. For three years after graduation he continued his studies at Edinburgh, while serving as assistant to a professor of philosophy. Then followed two years on the staff of the *Encyclopaedia Britannica* (9th edition) to which he contributed articles that established his reputation as a philosophical critic and historian.

Adamson at twenty-four became professor of philosophy at Owens College, Manchester, in which position he remained for seventeen years (1876-93). From Manchester he went to the University of Aberdeen chair of logic for two years, and thence to Glasgow, where he spent the last seven years of his life as professor of logic and rhetoric.

He died of enteric fever at Glasgow, and his body was cremated at the Western Necropolis. He was survived by his wife, Margaret Duncan of Manchester, and their two sons and four daughters. Mrs. Adamson presented his large philosophical library to Manchester University, where an Adamson Lecture was founded in his memory.

Adamson's literary productivity was greatest during his early years at Manchester, when he published an address on Roger Bacon, a small volume on the philosophy of Kant, a monograph on Fichte, and wrote a short history of Logic which did not appear in book form until after his death. Though he lived to the age of fifty, he published no books after his twenty-ninth year, partly because his time was increasingly taken up with lecturing and academic affairs, and partly because his philosophical views underwent a radical change. His early work was idealistic, his later work realistic and naturalistic. The later point of view, though never as fully developed as the early one, was revealed in his posthumous collection of lectures, *The Development of Modern Philosophy*.

PRINCIPAL WORKS: Roger Bacon: The Philosophy of Science in the 13th Century, 1876; On the Philosophy of Kant, 1879; Fichte, 1881; The Development of Modern Philosophy, With Other Lectures and Essays (ed. by W. R. Sorley) 1903; The Development of Greek Philosophy (ed. by W. R. Sorley & R. P. Hardie) 1908; A Short History of Logic (ed. by W. R. Sorley) 1911.

ABOUT: Adamson, R. The Development of Modern Philosophy (see Memorial Introduction); Mind July 1902; Mind January 1904.

AGUILAR, GRACE (June 1816-September 16, 1847), novelist, was born in Hackney of a Sephardic (Spanish) Jewish family. She was always very frail, and all her education was at home. Her family, however, moved about a great deal in her girlhood, and she traveled all over England, living for the most part in Devonshire. She began writing very early, her first interest being in the history and religion of the Jewish people, a subject to which she devoted several works. Although she was most devout, she was liberal in her tendencies and advocated some loosening of the bonds of orthodoxy.

Miss Aguilar is best known, however, for her novels. Only one of these, *Home Influence*, was published during her short lifetime; the others were edited by her mother and published posthumously. The year her first book was issued also witnessed the final wreck of her always delicate health, and she was a semi-invalid or worse for the remainder of her few years. In 1847 she went to Frankfort, Germany, to visit her brother, who was studying music there. Almost at once she became very ill, and a few days later she died. She is buried in the Jewish Cemetery in Frankfort. She is not known to have had any love-affairs or to have contemplated marriage, and her life is almost devoid of outward interest. Her few close friends spoke of her as amiable, sweet-natured, and markedly charitable.

All these characteristics appear in her books, which were very popular eighty years ago. They are sentimental, domestic, and pious, but they have a tenuous charm, especially the two historical novels—one a narrative of Scotland, the other of the Jews in Spain in the days of Ferdinand and Isabella. When in 1925 Edith Wharton published a novel called *A Mother's Recompense*, Grace Aguilar was still enough of a living name for the modern novelist to acknowledge having used a title which belonged originally to the novelist who died in 1847.

PRINCIPAL WORKS: The Spirit of Judaism, 1842; The Women of Israel, 1845; Home Influence, 1847; A Mother's Recompense, 1850; Woman's Friendship, 1851; The Days of Bruce, 1852; The Vale of Cedars, 1853.

ABOUT: Hall, S. C. Pilgrimages to English Shrines.

AINGER, ALFRED (April 9, 1837-February 8, 1904), humorist, biographer, and divine, was born in London, the son of an architect. His mother died when he was two, and his father soon remarried and added a second set of brothers and sisters to the first four. At school Ainger's classmates were Dickens' sons; Dickens became interested in him, coached him in amateur dramatics, and at one time had the boy's mind made up to be an actor.

A stronger influence, however, was Frederick Denison Maurice, the founder of Christian Socialism, under whose aegis Ainger deserted Unitarianism for the Church of England. At King's College he became interested in literature and music; from there, in 1856, he went to Cambridge, where he was in close touch with Maurice. He received his B.A. in 1860, his M.A. in 1865.

Ainger had been intended for the law, but his father's death made it necessary for him to pursue a more immediately remunerative profession. He took holy orders and became a curate in Staffordshire. He preferred teaching, however, and from 1864 to 1866 was assistant master at a school in Sheffield. In the latter year he was made reader at the Temple, a position he held until 1893.

In 1867 a dearly beloved sister died (his hair is said to have turned white from grief) and left four orphan children, whom Ainger reared. In 1887 he was made canon of Bristol. In 1893 he retired for reasons of health, but a year later became Master of the Temple, and the following year was made chaplain to Queen Victoria (and later to Edward VII). A severe attack of influenza in 1903 caused him to resign his Bristol post, and the next year he died of pneumonia at his niece's home near Derby.

Ainger was renowned as a wit and humorist. He was the intimate of literary circles, and the friend of Tennyson and George du Maurier. His chief literary interest was in Lamb, but his work as editor and biographer is marked rather by sympathy than by scholarship, and he is guilty of emasculating his hero's work when he found details which he considered inconsistent with his ideal picture of his subject.

PRINCIPAL WORKS: Lamb, 1882; Crabbe, 1903; Lectures and Essays (ed. by H. C. Beeching) 1903.

ABOUT: Sichel, E. The Life and Letters of Alfred Ainger; Tollemach, L. Old and Odd Memories.

AIKIN, ANNA LETITIA. See BARBAULD, ANNA LETITIA AIKIN

AIKIN, JOHN (1747-1822), physician and author, was born at Kibworth Harcourt, Leicestershire, the only son of John Aikin, D.D., and younger brother of Anna Letitia Aikin (later famous as Mrs. Barbauld). His mother's father was also a clergyman, and it was therefore quite natural that John should have been intended for the ministry.

He was educated by his father until the latter accepted the position of tutor at the Noncomformist (Unitarian) Academy at Warrington, where he continued his education. In the course of his upbringing it was discovered that his voice was weak—a fatal defect in an intended minister. Besides, he showed keen interest in medicine, and his parents therefore decided that he should become a physician.

During his school-days he amused himself by writing verses and essays, some of which appeared in a London magazine. When he was about eighteen, he wrote to his sister, "I have a strong notion of becoming an author some time or other."

He studied medicine at Edinburgh and surgery in London under Dr. William Hunter, the first great anatomy teacher in England, and then practised as a surgeon at Chester and Warrington. Finally, on a trip to Leyden, Holland, in 1780, he took his degree of Doctor of Medicine.

He married his cousin, Miss Martha Jennings. Oddly enough, his father too had married his own cousin, also a member of the Jennings family. On November 6, 1781, John Aikin's daughter Lucy (later known as a historian, and her father's biographer) was born. He also had two sons, one of whom

DR. JOHN AIKIN

was adopted by Mrs. Barbauld (who wrote for him the famous *Easy Lessons*).

In 1784 Aikin moved his practise to Yarmouth, which was "at that time exceedingly hostile to dissenters." In 1790 there was great excitement over the repeal of the Corporation and Test Acts (imposing strict adherence to the Church of England on all office-holders). Aikin, being a Unitarian, was of course a religious and political dissenter. He wrote to a friend, saying that he had no intention of becoming "the hero of a cause," but at his age it would be "trifling not to have a character, and cowardly not to avow and stick to it." He therefore published anonymously two fiery pamphlets, whose authorship, becoming known, made it impossible for him to go on living and practising in Yarmouth. He then (1792) removed to London, where he found a congenial circle of dissenters at Hackney.

He devoted his leisure to literature, and when paralysis ended his medical career he retired to Stoke Newington, and spent all his time writing. He is more famous as a writer than as a doctor; his literary fame rests on such works as *Biographical Memoirs of Medicine in Great Britain*, *England Delineated* (a sort of illustrated geography), and biographical and critical prefaces to *Select Works of the British Poets*, but most firmly of all on the six volumes of *Evenings at Home*, written between 1792 and 1795 with the help of his sister, Mrs. Barbauld. He was also the excellent editor of the *Monthly Magazine*, and later of *The Athenaeum*.

E. V. Lucas says of *Evenings at Home*, "The best stories are still well worth reading"; to which F. J. Harvey Darton adds, "It is only the manner and visible purpose of the book which makes it seem out of date."

V. M.

PRINCIPAL WORKS: *Biography*—Biographical Memoirs of Medicine, 1780; General Biography, 1799-1815; Lives of John Selden and Archbishop Usher, 1812; Select Works of British Poets, 1820. *Essays*—Essay on Song Writing, 1772; Essay on the Plan and Character of Thomson's *Seasons*, 1788; Critical Essay on Pope's *Essay on Man*, 1792; Critical Dissertation on Goldsmith's Poems, 1805; Essay on Poetical Works of John Milton, 1805. *Juvenile*—Evenings at Home (6 vols., with Mrs. Barbauld) 1792-1795. *Miscellaneous*—Calendar of Nature, 1785; Geographical Delineations, 1806.

ABOUT: Aikin, J. Evenings at Home (see Preface by Sara Hale to American ed. of 1847); Aikin, L. Memoir of John Aikin; Darton, F. J. H. Children's Books in England.

AIKIN, LUCY (November 6, 1781-January 29, 1864), historian, biographer, and writer of children's books, was the daughter of Dr. John Aikin and the niece of Anna Letitia Aikin Barbauld. Her mother, Martha Jennings, was first cousin once removed to her own husband. Lucy was born at Warrington, Lancashire, where her father taught in a Nonconformist academy, and was carefully educated by her parents. Her paternal grandmother (who was also a Jennings) called her "little dunce" because, unlike her aunt, she was unable to read at the age of two. Lucy suffered under this smart for many years. Although not precocious, she was an authoress from her seventeenth year.

Under the pseudonym of "Mary Godolphin" she edited classics in words of one syllable. She did *Robinson Crusoe, Aesop's Fables,* and the popular work by her father and aunt, *Evenings at Home*, in this style. Her *Aesop's Fables* was put into shorthand by Isaac Pitman in 1873, and was generally a favorite text for shorthand manuals. She wrote or edited several other books for children, but "her work in this direction," says F. J. Harvey Darton, authority on English children's books, "was not memorable," even including her collection of *Poetry for Children*.

It was rather as an historian that she won some repute, especially with her *Memoirs of the Court of Queen Elizabeth*. This was so popular that it was followed by other court memoirs. She was an authority on Addison, and wrote a life of him. Her memoir of her father was sympathetic; a short sketch of Mrs. Barbauld, her more gifted aunt, was less so. Besides these books, she contributed a great many articles to reviews and magazines, among them the *Annual Register*.

Her life was singularly quiet and uneventful. Her most exciting adventure was a six-day removal trip to Yarmouth two hundred and forty miles away, near the end of which her grandmother died of cold and fatigue. She lived in London for five years, and then in Stoke Newington until the death of her father. The last twelve years of her life were spent at Hampstead in the family of her niece.

V. M.

PRINCIPAL WORKS: *History and Biography*—Memoirs of the Court of Queen Elizabeth, 1818; Memoirs of the Court of James I, 1822; Memoirs of John Aikin, 1823; Memoir of the Court of Charles I, 1833; The Life of Joseph Addison, 1843. *Juveniles*—Poetry for Children, 1803; Juvenile Correspondence, c. 1816; An English Lesson Book, 1828; Holiday Stories, 1858. *Novel*—Lorimer: A Tale, 1814. *Miscellaneous*—Epistles on Women, 1810. *Editor*—The Works of Anna Letitia Barbauld, 1825; numerous one-syllable books for children under the pseud. of "Mary Godolphin."

ABOUT: Darton, F. J. H. Children's Books in England; Le Breton, P. H. Memoirs, Miscellanies, and Letters of Lucy Aikin.

AINSWORTH, WILLIAM HARRISON (February 4, 1805-January 3, 1882), novelist, was born in Manchester, the son of a prosperous lawyer.

The boy was sent to the grammar school in his native city, where he was popular, precocious, and highly respected by teachers and students. At sixteen he was apprenticed to a prominent solicitor, and upon the death (1824) of his father he proceeded to London to study law with a member of the Inner Temple. Instead, however, of following his profession, he turned to publishing and to writing, having already contributed to magazines, published some poems and tales, and even started an unsuccessful periodical of his own, *The Bœotian.* Among these early efforts were some original "fragments" from "old dramas," with which the young man succeeded in deceiving even the poet Campbell. In London he met John Ebers, an operatic manager and a publisher, who issued for him his first novel, *Sir John Chiverton,* and whose daughter Anne Frances he married in the same year (1826).

Faced with the necessity of choosing a vocation, Ainsworth became for a brief time a publisher, but gave this business up after a year and a half. Still anxious for a literary career, he was unsettled in his plans as late as 1830, when he made a Continental journey, visiting Switzerland and Italy.

In the next year, however, he began to write *Rookwood,* which appeared in 1834 and made the author famous. He became the darling of society, and was admitted to the august and respectable company of Holland House, where Lord and Lady Holland, the leaders of society in the Whig Party, entertained many of the literary and political leaders of the time.

Crichton (1837) followed, and in 1839 Ainsworth became editor of *Bentley's Miscellany* to which he had been contributing and which he owned from 1854 to 1868, selling it in the latter year to the founder for a small fraction of the amount which he had paid for it. *Ainsworth's Magazine,* founded in 1842, he left in 1845 to take over the editorship of the *New Monthly Magazine,* which he had bought. In addition to his editorial duties he continued to write novels with amazing industry.

By this time his success and his influence were great; he was an important figure, not only in literature, but in society as well, and he entertained brilliant men at his home near London. With the progress of time, however, his novels grew less profitable financially, and, although the author was granted a pension, he did not die a wealthy man. His old age was honored, and in 1881 he was given a banquet by the Mayor of Manchester, in recognition of his services to literature and of his eminence as a native of the city. At this time, however, Ainsworth was feeble and bent with age, and in the next year he died at Reigate, on the third of January.

A very handsome man, almost too dandified in appearance, Ainsworth had a pink and white complexion and wavy scented hair. He dressed very carefully, and in his youth his

WILLIAM HARRISON AINSWORTH

taste ran to gorgeous and rather lavish costume. He was vain of his personal beauty and had an admiration for men of title that on one occasion caused Thackeray to express irritation in *Punch.* Impetuous, generous, but likely to become irritable, Ainsworth was possessed of the temperament commonly described as "artistic." His first marriage resulted in a separation, and the second was also unfortunate. Very popular, he numbered Dickens, Lamb, Scott, Wordsworth, and Thackeray among his many friends.

Unfortunately he lacked his father's business ability. He was, however, a model for magazine-editors, prompt in paying and courteous to his contributors. He gave personal attention to their manuscripts and often advised them of possible markets for those which he could not himself accept. "If he had been content to concentrate upon either authorship or magazine proprietorship as a single occupation, he might have spent most of his life in leisure and affluence; combining the two functions, he worked with incredible energy, inspired only to greater effort by financial losses, and died in harness, a poor man," writes Malcolm Elwin. . . . "He was a sanguine, full-blooded man, built for the big occasion—a bit of a buccaneer, perhaps, with his puerile love of the limelight and his predilection for sonorous names, but too transparently sincere to be charged as a charlatan."

Ainsworth's novels are noteworthy, not for character-analysis or sublety of motivation, but for their vivid pageant of scenery and historical accuracy. Thanks partly to the serial publication of most of his novels, little plot is to be found in any of them. The dialogue is often artificial and unnatural, and the characters are stereotyped. His art consisted in the picturing of crowded scenes and times from history, as in *The Tower of London* and *Old St. Paul's*. Unlike his contemporary, Dickens, he failed to develop his powers; and his novels retain to the end a naiveté of order and motive that reminds one of books for boys. The humor is either broadly farcical or characterized by such obvious devices as puns. "His foot on the paths of literature is sometimes sure and firm, it is occasionally even swift; but it is always flat—fit only for progress on the lower levels," wrote Francis Gribble.   R. W. W.

PRINCIPAL WORKS: *Novels*—Sir John Chiverton (with J. P. Aston) 1826; Rookwood, 1834; Crichton, 1837; Jack Sheppard, 1839; The Tower of London, 1840; Guy Fawkes, 1841; Old St. Paul's: A Tale of the Plague and the Fire of London, 1841; The Miser's Daughter, 1842; Windsor Castle, 1843; Modern Chivalry (with C. F. Gore), 1843; St. James's: or, The Court of Queen Anne, 1844; Lancashire Witches, 1848, 1849; Star Chamber, 1854; The Flitch of Bacon: or, The Custom of Dunmow, 1854; Spendthrift, 1856; Mervyn Clitheroe, 1857; Ovingdean Grange: A Tale of the South Downs, 1860; Constable of the Tower, 1861; The Lord Mayor of London, 1862; Cardinal Pole, 1863; John Law the Projector, 1864; The Spanish Match: or, Charles Stuart in Madrid, 1865; Myddleton Pomfret, 1865; The Constable de Bourbon, 1866; Old Court, 1867; The South Sea Bubble, 1868; Hilary St. Ives, 1869; Talbot Harland, 1870; Tower Hall, 1871; Boscobel, 1872; The Manchester Rebels: or, The Fatal '45, 1873; Merry England, 1874; The Goldsmith's Wife, 1874; Preston Fight: or, The Insurrection of 1715, 1875; Chetwynd Calverley, 1878; The League of Lathom: A Tale of the Civil War in Lancashire, 1876; The Fall of Somerset, 1877; Beatrice Tylderley, 1878; Beau Nash, 1880; Stanley Brereton, 1881. *Poems*—Poems by Cheviot Tichburn, 1822, 1825; Ballads: Romantic, Fantastic, and Humorous, 1855, 1872. *Miscellaneous*—Considerations on the Best Means of Affording Immediate Relief to the Operative Classes in the Manufacturing Districts, 1826; Letters from Cockney Lands, 1826.

ABOUT: Ellis, S. M. William Harrison Ainsworth and His Friends; Elwin, M. Victorian Wallflowers; Horne, R. H. A New Spirit of the Age; Joline, A. H. At the Library Table; Locke, H. A Bibliographical Catalogue of the Published Novels and Ballads of William Harrison Ainsworth; Fortnightly Review 83:533 March 1905; Manchester Quarterly 2:136 April 1882.

AIRD, THOMAS (August 28, 1802-April 25, 1876), Scottish poet and journalist, was born at Bowden, Roxburghshire, and educated at the parish school of Bowden and at Edinburgh University. He began publishing poetry at twenty-four, and achieved popular favor with his collected poems, published in his forty-sixth year. According to Carlyle, "he found everywhere a healthy breath as of mountain breezes." Besides Carlyle, his many friends included De Quincey, William Motherwell, and A. P. Stanley. For twenty-eight years he edited the *Dumfriesshire and Galloway Herald*. After his retirement at sixty-one he lived quietly in Dumfries, taming

birds for recreation. He died unmarried at seventy-three.

PRINCIPAL WORKS: *Poetry*—Poetical Works, 1848. *Prose*—Old Bachelor in the Scottish Village, 1845.
ABOUT: Aird, T. Poetical Works (see Memoir by Rev. J. Wallace in 1878 ed.).

ALBEMARLE, LORD (George Thomas Keppel, Sixth Earl of Albemarle) (June 13, 1799-February 21, 1891), soldier and author of reminiscences, was the second son of William Charles Keppel, fourth earl, and grandson of George Keppel, third earl of Albemarle. Educated at Westminster School, he joined the army at sixteen in time to be present at the Battle of Waterloo. Subsequently he was aide-de-camp to the governor-general of India. He returned to England from India by way of Persia and Russia, a route seldom traveled in those days, and wrote an interesting narrative of the trip. He sat in the first reformed parliament for East Norfolk (1832-35) and for Lymington (1847-49). On the death of his brother, the fifth earl, he succeeded to the title in 1851. By his wife, Susan Trotter, he had one son and four daughters. He died at his London residence at the age of ninety-one. His best known work is his autobiography.

PRINCIPAL WORKS: Journey From India to England, 1825; Fifty Years of My Life, 1875.

ALBERY, JAMES (May 4, 1838-August 15, 1889), dramatist, was born in London. Schooled privately, he went to work at fourteen in an architect's office. Upon the death of his father when James was twenty-one, he joined his mother in conducting a rope and twine business. In his twenty-eighth year he began a career as playwright in London. His greatest success was achieved with a three-act comedy, "Two Roses," played by Sir Henry Irving in 1870. He made many successful adaptations, but in his later works failed to fulfill his early promise. His wife was Mary Moore, an actress. He died in London at the age of fifty-one.

None of his plays was ever published in a book entirely his own. Two plays, "Pink Dominoes" (adapted from the French of Hennequin and Delacour) and "Two Roses," appeared in *Lacy's Acting Edition of Plays* in the collections of 1878 and 1881 respectively.

ALEXANDER, CECIL FRANCES (1818-October 12, 1895), Irish hymn-writer and poet, was born Cecil Frances Humphreys in County Wicklow, Ireland. She died in her seventy-seventh year at the bishop's palace in Londonderry, North Ireland, leaving two sons and two daughters. She is best known as the author of "Jesus Calls Us O'er the Tumult," "There is a Green Hill Far Away," and nearly 400 other hymns. Her sacred poem "The Burial of Moses" was admired by Tennyson. Notable also are her Irish national songs, "The Siege of Derry" and "The Irish Mother's Lament," the latter being one of the most poignant lyrics of its kind. In addition to her poetical works she wrote tracts for the Oxford movement.

Her husband, WILLIAM ALEXANDER (1824-1911), Protestant archbishop of Armagh, primate of all Ireland, and one-time professor of poetry at Oxford, was the author of delicately spiritual poems dealing with Irish scenery. At the time of their marriage in 1850 he was rector of Termonamongan in Tyrone. Subsequently he served as rector of Upper Fahan on Lough Swilly and bishop of Derry before his elevation to the primacy in 1896, the year after she died. His poems were collected in 1887 as *St. Augustine's Holiday and Other Poems*.

PRINCIPAL WORKS OF CECIL FRANCES ALEXANDER: Verses for Holy Seasons, 1846; Hymns for Little Children, 1848; Moral Songs, 1849; The Legend of the Golden Prayers and Other Poems, 1859; Poems, 1896.

ABOUT: Alexander, C. F. Poems (see Biographical Preface); Alexander, E. J. Life of Primate Alexander.

ALFORD, HENRY (October 10, 1810-January 7, 1871), Biblical scholar, was born in London, the son of a clergyman. As a student at Trinity College, Cambridge, he belonged to the serious-minded group that gathered round Tennyson. After graduation he was successively vicar of Wymeswold in Leicestershire (1835-53), minister of Quebec Chapel in London (1853-57), and dean of Canterbury (1857-71). During the last five years of his life he served as the first editor of the *Contemporary Review*. By his wife, Fanny Alford, who was his cousin, he had two sons (deceased in childhood) and two daughters.

His critical edition of the New Testament in Greek—the first to gather the commentaries of the best Continental critics—was for many years the standard work in England and is still a valuable source, although it has been largely supplanted by subsequent research. Several of his hymns are popular, notably "Forward Be Our Watchword" and "Ten Thousand Times Ten Thousand." He also wrote poetry, sermons, tracts, and translations—forty-eight volumes in all.

PRINCIPAL WORKS: The Greek Testament (ed.) 1849-61; The Odyssey (tr.) 1861.

ABOUT: Alford, F. A. The Life of Dean Alford by His Widow.

ALISON, SIR ARCHIBALD (December 29, 1792-May 23, 1867), Scottish historian, was born in Shropshire, the son of Archibald Alison, noted clergyman. The family moved to Edinburgh in 1800 and most of his life was spent in Scotland. He studied law at the University of Edinburgh and was called to the bar in 1814. Thanks to the influence of friends, he was immediately successful and soon became very prosperous. His leisure he spent in travel, being an enthusiastic tourist, with a system of traveling of his own; when he became an historian his trips were always made in connection with the current phases of his writing.

He was appointed advocate-depute in 1822, with the prospect of soon becoming solicitor-general, but in 1830 the Tory ministry fell, several of his most important clients failed in business, and Alison became an historian—his enforced leisure he spent in writing the history of Scottish criminal law.

In 1834 he was made sheriff of Lanarkshire, and the next year moved to Glasgow, where he lived for the remainder of his life. In 1825 he had married Elizabeth Glencairn, and they had several children, whose education he conducted. His life was so full that he had to regulate it literally by time-table. An extreme Tory, he was noted for his prosecution of strikers and his opposition to the efforts of workers to better themselves. In 1852 he was made a baronet. He became Lord Rector of Marischal College, Aberdeen, in 1845, and in 1851 of Glasgow University. During the American Civil War he was a strong Confederate sympathizer, since he believed in slavery as a social system. He was ill only one day before his death at seventy-five, working up to the day before. Nearly 150,000 persons attended his funeral. Despite his Toryism, he was personally amiable and a popular figure in Glasgow.

Alison said that he wrote his *History of Europe* "to show the corruption of human nature and the divine superintendence of human affairs." From its beginning in 1833 until his death new volumes and new editions, revised by himself, were constantly in preparation. At first the work received no attention, but gradually became a huge success. If his prejudices are discounted, it is still a concise summary, of value as a work of reference.

PRINCIPAL WORKS: History of Scottish Criminal Law, 1832-33; History of Europe, 1833-42; Life of Marlborough, 1847; Essays: Political, Historical, and Miscellaneous, 1850; Lives of Lord Castlereagh and Sir Charles Stewart, 1861; Some Account of My Life and Writings, 1862.

ABOUT: Alison, A. Some Account of My Life and Writings.

ALLEN, GRANT (February 24, 1848-October 28, 1899), Canadian novelist, philosopher, and scientific writer, whose full name was Charles Grant Blairfindie Allen, was born near Kingston, Canada. He was the second son of Joseph Antisell Allen, a minister of the Irish Church, and Charlotte Catherine Ann Grant, daughter of the fifth

GRANT ALLEN

Baron de Longueil, holder of an ancient French title recognized in Canada.

He was educated by his father at first. When the family removed for a time to New Haven, Connecticut, he was put under the care of a Yale tutor, after which he attended the Collège Impériel at Dieppe and King Edward's School at Birmingham. A post-mastership enabled him to study at Merton College, Oxford, where he won a first class in classical moderations and was graduated in 1871 with the degree of B.A. These were hard years for Allen; he had married a wife whose invalidism made it imperative for him to earn money while pursuing his college course, and considering the fact that his own health was delicate, his efforts were heroic. He spent three years teaching at Brighton, Cheltenham, and Reading, and in 1873 was appointed professor of mental and moral philosophy in a newly founded university for Negroes at Spanish Town, Jamaica. Only some half dozen students were recruited, and these were totally unprepared for such a subject as he was supposed to teach. The death of the principal led to the abandonment of the project in 1876, and Allen returned to England determined to make writing his profession.

As a boy, he had been interested in birds and flowers, and he had carried his scientific interests so far as to have formed, during his stay in Jamaica, an evolutionary system of philosophy based on that of Spencer. A study of Anglo-Saxon, too, made it possible for him to write later such a work as his *Anglo-Saxon Britain* (1881). In 1877 he published his *Physiological Aesthetics,* and although not a success, the work opened up a market for his writing. He assisted in the compilation of the Imperial Gazetteer of India and worked for a while on the staff of the *Daily News,* contributing also to magazines and newspapers. A number of "popular" scientific works followed, culminating in importance with *Force and Energy* (1888), a statement of dynamics which Allen had formed. The work did not have the reception he had anticipated from scientists, but he seems to have considered it his best work.

Under various pseudonyms, particularly that of "Cecil Power," he had begun to write fiction, often of a startling quality, and his *The Devil's Die, Strange Stories,* and *Philistia,* a satire on socialism, attracted popular attention. A serious novel of purpose, *The Woman Who Did,* published in 1895, brought him more condemnation than anything else, because of his treatment of the sexual question. He published a modest volume of poetry in 1894 and his *Evolution of the Idea of God* in 1897. During the closing years of his life he became interested in art, and wrote excellent guide books to the cities of Belgium, and to Paris, Florence, and Venice.

Poor health had forced him to spend his winters in the South for a number of years. He died at his country home in England, of an illness not diagnosed until after his death. He was survived by his second wife, the former Ellen Jerrard, whom he had married in 1873, and by their son.

Allen had many friends, attracted by his conversation, his amiability, and his sincerity. "He was the most sincere man I have ever known," said Richard Le Gallienne, who knew him well. He was rather frail in appearance but seems to have had unbounded energy and to have utilized his time with great efficiency. His Irish temperament occasionally led him to overstatement, but he was very modest about his writing.

His best work was done in the field of popularized science, in which he wrote clearly and brightly and with an exactness attested by the praise given his *Colin Clout's Calendar* by Darwin and Huxley. His essays are individual in flavor and unassuming in tone. The fiction he wrote belonged to the class of well-written pot-boilers, but he told a story well and had a powerful imagination upon which to draw.   R. M.

PRINCIPAL WORKS: *Fiction*—Strange Stories, 1884; Philistia, 1884; The Devil's Die, 1888; The Woman Who Did, 1895; The British Barbarians, 1896. *Poetry*—The Lower Slopes, 1894. *Essays*—Falling in Love and Other Essays, 1889; Post-prandial Philosophy, 1894. *Science and Philosophy*—Physiological Aesthetics, 1877; The Colour Sense, 1879; Vignettes From Nature, 1881; An Evolutionist at Large, 1881; Colours of Flowers, 1882; Colin Clout's Calendar, 1883; Flowers and Their Pedigrees, 1883; Force and Energy, 1888; The Evolution of the Idea of God, 1897. *Miscellaneous*—Anglo-Saxon Britain, 1881.

ABOUT: Clodd, E. Grant Allen; Bookman 10:293 December 1899; Critic ns 33:38 January 1900; Fortnightly Review ns 96:1003 December 1, 1899.

ALLEN, JOHN (February 3, 1771-April 10, 1843), political and historical commentator, was born at Redfoord, near Edinburgh, Scotland. Educated as an M.D. at the University of Edinburgh, he accompanied the third Baron Holland to Spain as physician, 1801-05 and 1808, and lived thereafter with the baron's family at Holland House in England. He was a prominent figure in social life, and was called by Macaulay "a man of vast information and great conversational powers." From 1811 on he was associated with Dulwich College, first as warden and after 1820 as master. To the *Edinburgh Review* he contributed many historical articles, notably two criticisms (1825-26) of John Lingard's *History of England* which caused Lingard to issue a *Vindication*. His *Inquiry Into the Rise and Growth of the Royal Prerogative in England* became the standard treatise on its subject. He died at Lady Holland's residence in London at seventy-two.

PRINCIPAL WORKS: Reply to Lingard's Vindication, 1827; Inquiry Into the Rise and Growth of the Royal Prerogative in England, 1830.
ABOUT: Allen, J. Inquiry Into the Rise and Growth of the Royal Prerogative in England (see Biographical Notices in posthumous eds.).

ALLINGHAM, WILLIAM (March 19, 1824-November 18, 1889), Irish poet, was born at Ballyshannon, Donegal, the eldest child of William Allingham, a merchant and banker, and Elizabeth (Crawford) Allingham.

His education was all too brief, and of a quality hardly likely to appeal to a sensitive youth. From a Ballyshannon school, where only Latin was taught, and where Allingham kept up with the class in its routine while he proceeded to read widely on subjects of greater interest to himself, he went to a boarding-school at Killeshandra, County Cavan, which was even more distasteful to him; and, despite a quick mind and a body active in various sports, the boy in 1838 was put to work in his father's bank.

His tasks were not congenial to him, and he bitterly regretted the loss of educational opportunity. Accordingly he studied and read widely; and he made such good use of his time that he managed, in the course of a busy life, to master Greek, Latin, French, and German. His interests naturally made him turn toward London, and in 1843 he made the first of a great many visits to the metropolis.

A civil-service vacancy occurred in 1846 which made it possible for Allingham to leave the bank, and he accepted it, becoming Principal Coast Officer of Customs. For many years he lived at Donegal, Ballyshannon, and other Ulster towns, and he heard the Irish girls singing ballads. Many of these he rearranged and completed or perfected, printing them and selling or giving them away in the neighborhood. In recognition of his services in the cause of popular education in this manner Allingham was given, in 1864, a Civil List pension of £60, which was later augmented to £100.

In the course of a visit to London in 1847 he met Leigh Hunt, who was very friendly and introduced him to Carlyle, of whom Allingham became a close friend. On a subsequent visit in 1849 he met Coventry Patmore, by whom he was later introduced to Tennyson, an admirer of Allingham's poems, and to Dante Gabriel Rossetti and others of the Pre-Raphaelite group.

Except for a brief attempt in 1854 to live by his pen in London, in the course of which he found journalism, with its petty annoyances and details, trying, and decided that he preferred the country to the city, Allingham remained continuously in the Customs service until 1870, living most of the time at Ballyshannon until 1863, when he was transferred to Lymongton in Hampshire. By this time his career as a poet had begun. *Day and Night Songs* (1854) was successful enough to warrant a reissue in the next year with a new title-poem, "The Music Master." The volume included woodcuts by Rossetti and Millais. During this period Allingham edited collections of poetry and issued his ambitious if not-too-successful epic of Irish agricultural life, *Laurence Bloomfield*.

For a considerable time he had contributed to *Fraser's Magazine;* and in order to assume the sub-editorship (under James Anthony

WILLIAM ALLINGHAM

Froude) of that journal, he resigned his position in the civil service in 1870, removing to London. In 1874, the year of his marriage, at fifty, to Miss Helen Peterson, a water-color painter, he became the editor of *Fraser's*, and he retained this position until 1879. It was because of his intimacy with Carlyle that the latter's *Early Kings of Norway* appeared in that journal in 1875.

Chiefly for the sake of his wife and children, Allingham removed to Witley in Surrey in 1881. Several years later, however, the necessity of securing educational advantages for his children induced him to remove to Hampstead in 1888. Here his health, which had been injured by a fall from his horse, gave cause for alarm, and, after a decline of some protraction, he died in November 1889.

Allingham's opinions on poetry seem to have been respected; William Michael Rossetti pronounced him a shrewd critic, and his verdicts were sought by Dante Gabriel Rossetti and Coventry Patmore. His own talent as a poet, however, is best seen in rather isolated selections. His muse was not one of sustained vigor; much of his later work was revision of what already had been written. He was great in small things, as the short lyrics, "Lovely Mary Donnelley" and "The Fairies." *Laurence Bloomfield*, an attempt, somewhat in the manner of Crabbe and Goldsmith, to set forth, in heroic couplets, a picture of society in Ireland, failed, in spite of its fine descriptive passages, to rise to prolonged elevation. In his ballads and Irish verse Allingham attempted to convey the Irish peasant speech, at least in flavor, without the actual employment of ungrammatical or corrupt Irish expressions. His poetry is not Irish in a political sense. Indeed, he lacked any organized scheme of thought in his writings, and in no real sense was he a major figure of his period. "He was the poet of little things and little moments," wrote William Butler Yeats. "The charm of his work is everywhere the charm of stray moments and detached scenes that have moved him. . ."

R. W. W.

PRINCIPAL WORKS: *Autobiography*—William Allingham: A Diary, 1907. *Editor*—Nightingale Valley, 1860; The Ballad Book, 1864. *Letters*—Letters of William Allingham to Robert and Elizabeth Barrett Browning, 1914; *Poetry*—Poems, 1850; Peace and War, 1854; Day and Night Songs, 1854; The Music Master, 1855; Laurence Bloomfield in Ireland, 1864; Fifty Modern Poems, 1865; Songs, Ballads, and Stories, 1877; Evil May-Day, 1882; The Fairies, 1883; Blackberries Picked off Many Bushes, 1884; Irish Songs and Poems, 1887; Rhymes for the Young Folk, 1887; Flower Pieces and Other Poems, 1888; Life and Pantasy, 1889; Thought and Word, 1890. *Play*—Ashby Manor, 1882. *Miscellaneous*—Rambles in England and Ireland by "Patricus Walker," 1873; Sketch of the Life of Thomas Campbell, 1875; Varieties in Prose, 1893; By the Way, 1912.

ABOUT: Allingham, H. Letters to William Allingham; Allingham, W. William Allingham: A Diary; Edwards, M. B. B. Friendly Faces of Three Nationalities; Graves, A. P. Irish Literary and Musical Studies; Miles, A. H. The Poets and the Poetry of the Century; Rossetti, D. G. Letters . . . to William Allingham (see Introduction by George Birkbeck Hill); Yeats, W. B. Letters to the New Island; Philological Quarterly 12:290 July 1933; Studies in Philology 31:567 October 1934.

ANDERSON, ALEXANDER (April 30, 1845-July 11, 1909), Scottish labor poet known as "Surfaceman," was born at Kirkconnel in Upper Nithsdale, the son of a quarryman. After attending the village school at Crocketford in Kirkcudbright, he began working at seventeen as a surfaceman, or platelayer, on the Glasgow and Southwestern railway in his native village. For eighteen years he labored twelve hours a day with pick and shovel at a wage of 17 shillings a week. In the evenings he wrote dialect poems of railway life and of child life in humble Scottish homes. These brought him a certain literary reputation which eventually resulted in his being relieved of manual labor and given the more leisurely position of assistant librarian of Edinburgh University in his thirty-fifth year; but he wrote little thereafter. He died unmarried in Edinburgh at sixty-four. His work is represented in most anthologies of Scottish verse, and several of his poems are popular recitations.

PRINCIPAL WORKS: A Song of Labour and Other Poems, 1873; The Two Angels and Other Poems, 1875; Songs of the Rail, 1878; Ballads and Sonnets, 1879; Later Poems of Alexander Anderson, Surfaceman, 1912.

ABOUT: Anderson, A. Later Poems (see Biographical Preface).

ANDERSON, ROBERT (February 1, 1770-September 26, 1833), poet, was born at Carlisle in Cumberland. After attending charity and Quaker schools, he began earning his living at ten as assistant to a calico printer in Carlisle. Later he became a pattern drawer. His desire to write poetry was stimulated by hearing songs at Vauxhall during a five year period of work in London. "Lucy Gray," his first poem, is believed to have suggested Wordsworth's "She Dwelt Among the Untrodden Ways." His ballads in the Cumbrian dialect pictured with realistic detail the life of the peasants in his native district, who esteemed his humor but feared his satire. He grew intemperate in his last years and died penniless in Carlisle at sixty-three.

PRINCIPAL WORKS: Cumbrian Ballads, 1805; Poetical Works, 1820.

ABOUT: Anderson, R. Poetical Works (see Autobiographical Sketch).

ANSON, SIR WILLIAM REYNELL (November 14, 1843-June 4, 1914), author of legal works, was born at Walberton, Sussex, and educated at Balliol College, Oxford.

From 1874 he was teacher of English law at All Souls College, Oxford, and from 1881 he was warden of the college, the first layman to hold that office. He helped to found the Oxford school of law. As a member of Parliament from Oxford University, he performed services of lasting value to the development of public elementary education in England. He is remembered chiefly for two widely used and highly esteemed works of legal literature, of which *Principles of English Law of Contract* remained long a standard introductory textbook in both England and America. He died unmarried in Oxford at the age of seventy.

PRINCIPAL WORKS: Principles of the English Law of Contract, 1879; The Law and Custom of the Constitution, 1886-92.

ABOUT: Henson, H. H. A Memoir of Sir William Anson; The Times June 5-6, 1914.

APPERLEY, CHARLES JAMES (1779-May 19, 1843), English sportsman and sporting writer, known as "Nimrod," was born at Plasgronow, Denbighshire, the second son of Thomas Apperley, of a well-to-do and old Herefordshire family.

When eleven he was sent to Rugby, where, according to his own account, the boys were a rowdy lot, indulging in excessive drinking and boasting of acts of insubordination. On leaving school at nineteen, he joined a regiment of cavalry and served in the suppression of the Irish rebellion. At the close of the war, his regiment was criticized for unnecessary cruelty; and in later years Nimrod, who was an essentially humane man, was reluctant to write of the affair.

A friend commenting on his young manhood, emphasized his great charm and attractive appearance and called him "a truly sunny person." A recent biographer suggests that in Nimrod's case, charm was a good substitute for force of character. Nimrod's father stammered excessively, and he himself was afflicted with stammering until he reached maturity.

He returned to England in 1801, married Winifred Wynn of Peniarth in Merionethshire, and tried to settle down to the life of a country squire at Hinkley in Leicestershire. Three years later he moved to a property once owned by Joseph Addison near Rugby, and from there moved to Bitterly Court in Shropshire and then to Berwood in Straffordshire and to Beaurepaire House in Hampshire. He served for a while as captain of the Nottinghamshire militia and lost most of his capital with a farming venture in Hampshire.

Wherever he lived, he hunted a good deal, went to races, frequented all manner of sporting events and associated with prominent sportsmen and sporting enthusiasts such as

CHARLES JAMES APPERLEY

Henry Alken, George Tattersall, R. S. Surtees, and John Mytton. He was a phenomenally sound judge of horses and hounds, and, in fact, a remarkably good all-round sportsman. Such qualities—which too many sporting writers lack—combined with his natural charm and wit and some culture to make him the first great sporting writer in England.

Before his time no gentleman in good standing wrote for sporting papers, and it was with some misgiving that he allowed his initial effort, an article on "Foxhunting in Leicestershire," to be published in the *Sporting Magazine* for January 1822. The article, however, was received enthusiastically; and his subsequent writings for the same paper made his pseudonym of Nimrod a byword, gained him a generous salary and a stable of hunters, and trebled the paper's circulation.

In 1830, on the death of the editor, *Sporting Magazine* got into financial difficulties involving Nimrod, and he was forced to remove to Calais. While in France he joined the staff of the *Sporting Review* and wrote several volumes of reminiscences and the famous articles on "Melton Mowbray," "The Road," and "The Turf" which appeared in the *Saturday Review* of 1835.

In 1842, the year before his death, he returned to England. The same year, the first instalments of "My Life and Times" appeared in *Fraser's Magazine*. He avoided in these papers his earlier faults of discursiveness, occasional awkwardness, and a too liberal decoration with Latin quotations and classical references; but he repeated much material from his former books, and displeased the editor, who refused to publish further instalments. In 1927 *My Life and Times* appeared first in book form, well edited and illustrated.

Nimrod's two best-known works are his autobiographical *The Life of a Sportsman* and his *Memoirs of the Life of John Mytton.* The latter is the story of a heroic sportsman who was also a diseased and insane drunkard; and the biographer's difficult task was performed with admirable judgment.

Many of Nimrod's numerous children and grandchildren became accomplished sportsmen.

The avowed purpose of his writing was the promotion of sport, and he accomplished it to a high degree. Sportsmen still read his books for enjoyment and information and still respect his sporting standards. Collectors value his books because of his unique position and for the admirable illustrations by Henry Alken.   P. G.

PRINCIPAL WORKS: *Sporting*—Remarks on the Condition of Hunters, 1831; Nimrod's Hunting Tours, 1835; The Chace, the Turf, and the Road, 1837; Sporting Illustrations of British Field Sports, 1838; Nimrod's Northern Tour, 1838; Nimrod Abroad, 1842; The Horse and the Hound, 1842; Hunting Reminiscences, 1843. *Biography*—Memoirs of the Life of John Mytton, 1837; The Life of a Sportsman, 1842; My Life and Times by Nimrod (ed. with additions by E. D. Cuming) 1927. ABOUT: Apperley, C. J. The Life of a Sportsman; My Life and Times.

ARBER, EDWARD (December 4, 1836-November 23, 1912), antiquary, was born in London, the son of an architect. Educated at private schools, he entered the civil service at seventeen as a clerk in the Admiralty office in London, remaining twenty-four years. His leisure hours were devoted to the study of English literature.

At forty-one he resigned from the Admiralty and obtained an appointment as English lecturer at University College, London, under Henry Morley, whose lectures many years before had stimulated his literary studies. After three years he went to Mason College, Birmingham, as professor of English. Thirteen years later, at fifty-seven, he retired from teaching and settled in London to devote his remaining years to research. A few days before his seventy-sixth birthday, he was run over by a taxicab in London and instantly killed. He left two sons, by his wife, Marion Murray.

Arber's best known literary works were three series of reprints of latter-day English authors which he edited, with critical and historical introductions, in response to a need for reliable English texts at reasonable prices. "English Reprints" (30 volumes) appeared while he was in the Admiralty office; "An English Garner" (8 volumes) and "The English Scholar's Library" (16 volumes) ran concurrently during his years of teaching. Some of these reprints remained for many years the only easily available texts.

Regarded as Arber's most valuable contributions to English studies, however, are his *Transcript of the Registers of the Company of Stationers of London* and his *Term Catalogues.* These two works, comprising much hitherto inaccessible material, were edited from the quarterly lists of booksellers. The first was completed in the year of his retirement; the second, his final work, occupied the later years. All these volumes were privately printed and distributed by Arber himself.

PRINCIPAL WORKS EDITED BY ARBER: English Reprints (30 vols.) 1868-71; An English Garner (8 vols.) 1877-96; The English Scholar's Library (16 vols.) 1878-84; Transcript of the Registers of the Company of Stationers of London 1554-1640 (5 vols.) 1875-94; Term Catalogues 1668-1709 (3 vols.) 1903-06.

ARBLAY, MADAME D'. See BURNEY, FANNY

ARGYLL, DUKE OF (George Douglas Campbell, Eighth Duke of Argyll) (April 30, 1823-April 24, 1900), Scottish statesman and writer on science, was born at Ardencaple Castle, Dumbartonshire, the son of John Campbell, seventh duke. He won fame as an orator in the House of Lords and held several public offices, including lord privy seal, postmaster-general, and secretary of state for India at the time of the outbreak of the second Afghan war. A leisure-time student of science, he engaged boldly in controversies with Darwin, Huxley, and Herbert Spencer on the subject of evolution. His writings on scientific questions were of little value in themselves, but did much to stimulate public interest in these questions and to effect advancement in the fields which were the targets of his criticism. He also wrote on politics and a variety of other subjects. Three times married, he had five sons and seven daughters, all by his first wife, Lady Elizabeth Leveson-Gower. His eldest son, the Marquis of Lorne, married Princess Louise, daughter of Queen Victoria.

PRINCIPAL WORKS: The Reign of Law, 1866; Primeval Man, 1869; The Unity of Nature, 1884; The Unseen Foundations of Society, 1893; Organic Evolution Cross-Examined, 1898; Autobiography and Memoirs (ed. by his widow) 1906. ABOUT: Argyll, G. D. C. Autobiography and Memoirs.

ARNOLD, SIR ARTHUR (May 28, 1833-May 20, 1902), radical writer, was born at Gravesend, Kent, England, a brother of Sir Edwin Arnold the poet. He was educated at home. In his leisure time as surveyor and land agent he wrote a pair of sensational novels. His best known work, a popular *History of the Cotton Famine,* was written while he was a government inspector in charge of the employment of destitute cotton operatives for road-building and other public works in Lancashire. Subsequently he edited *The Echo,* an evening newspaper, for a few years, traveled in Persia, contributed articles to reviews on social and farm problems, was a radical member of Parliament for Salford, and served as alderman of the London County Council. He was knighted in 1895. Eight days before his sixty-ninth birthday he died in London, leaving his wife, Amelia Hyde.

PRINCIPAL WORKS: *Fiction*—Ralph: or, St. Sepulchre's and St. Stephen's, 1861; Hever Court, 1867. *Non-Fiction*—History of the Cotton Famine From the Fall of Sumter to the Passing of the Public Works Act, 1864; Through Persia by Caravan, 1877; Social Politics, 1878.

ARNOLD, SIR EDWIN (June 10, 1832-March 24, 1904) poet, journalist, and Orientalist, was born at Gravesend, the second son of Robert Coles Arnold.

He was educated at King's School, Rochester, Kings College, London, and at University College, Oxford, from which he was graduated in 1854 with the degree of B.A., receiving the degree of M.A. in 1856. His interest in Greek literature inspired the poem *Belshazzar's Feast* with which he won the Newdigate Prize in 1852.

For a brief while Arnold taught at King Edward's School in Birmingham, until in 1856 he received an appointment as principal of Deccan College at Poona. He was honored with a fellowship by Bombay University, studied the Indian languages, Persian, and Turkish, and won the commendation of the Indian government for his conduct as principal during the Mutiny.

In 1861 he returned to England, and secured a position as writer for the *London Daily Telegraph,* with which his association lasted forty-odd years. He became chief editor in 1873 after a brilliant period of writing for the journal. Under his editorship the paper sponsored the expedition of George Smith to Assyria in 1874, and was associated with the *New York Herald* in promoting the expedition of Stanley. Despite his productivity as a journalist, he had published numerous works, including a history of Dalhousie's administration (1862), his translation of *The Book of Good Counsels* and of French and Italian verse, Musäus' *Hero and Leander,* etc.

Arnold defended Turkey's part in the Russo-Turkish War of 1877, and was decorated by the Sultan for his support. He was made C.S.I. in 1877 and Knight Commander of the Indian Empire in 1888; he also held a Persian decoration.

In 1888 he traveled with his daughter to Japan and the Pacific coasts, and wrote picturesque and interesting accounts of his travels. His fame as author of *The Light of Asia* (1879) and other works of an Oriental cast enabled him to undertake a successful lecture tour of the United States in 1891. It is said that the confusion in the American mind between Matthew and Edwin Arnold was often the cause of embarrassment for both.

During the last ten years of his life, Arnold was troubled by failing eyesight, but he continued to write and added materially to the already long list of his works, his last, *Ithobal,* being published in 1901, three years before his death.

He was survived by his third wife, Tana Kuro Kawa of Sendai, Japan. He had previously married, in 1854, Katharine Biddulph, who died in 1864, and Fannie Channing of Boston, Massachusetts, who died in 1889.

Arnold was a strongly built man of good height, with heavy, strong features and a wide forehead and an expression of eternal good humor. "Never for one instant have I seen a dark cloud overshadow Edwin Arnold's bright and attractive countenance," wrote Clement Scott, who adds that he was one of the best talkers he had ever met. Major Pond, who managed his lecture tours, said that he was lovable and entertaining. He had a remarkable memory and a literary facility that made it possible for him to write at any time and under any circumstances.

The fame Arnold acquired during his lifetime, and his immense popularity, can be understood, although his literary reputation has had a swift descent. He wrote exotic verse that was fluent and arresting, and captured the popular fancy with his poetic interpretation of the life and teachings of Buddha, *The Light of Asia.* Its luxuriant

EDWIN ARNOLD

blank verse seems over-rich and pompous now, and scholars do not regard the interpretation as either complete or correct. A similar work about Jesus, *The Light of the World,* dealing as it did with more familiar matter, was a failure. Yet such a critic as Stedman said of Arnold: "He is not a creative poet . . . [but] he has zest, learning, industry, and an instinct for color and picturesqueness," and other critics of his day were extravagant in their praise. It is generally agreed that the poem "He and She" is free from the usual defects of his work. In prose he wrote entertainingly of things he had seen, and his translations of Eastern works served a good purpose.   R. M.

PRINCIPAL WORKS: *Poetry*—Belshazzar's Feast, 1852; Poems Narrative and Lyrical, 1853; Griselda, 1856; The Wreck of the Northern Belle, 1857; The Light of Asia, 1879; Pearls of the Faith, 1883; The Secret of Death, 1885; Lotus and Jewel, 1887; With Sa'di in the Garden, 1888; Poetical Works, 1888; The Light of the World, 1891; Potiphar's Wife, 1892; The Tenth Muse and Other Poems, 1895; The Voyage of Ithobal, 1901. *Prose*—History of the Marquis of Dalhousie's Administration (2 vols.) 1852, 1865; India Revisited, 1886; Seas and Lands, 1891; Japonica, 1892; Adzuma, 1893; Wandering Words, 1894; East and West, 1896; The Queen's Justice, 1899. *Translations*—The Book of Good Counsel, 1861; Political Poems by Hugo and Garibaldi, 1868; Poets of Greece, 1869; Musäus' Hero and Leander, 1873; Indian Song of Songs from the Jayadeva, 1875; Indian Poetry, 1881; Indian Idylls from the Mahabharata, 1883, 1885; The Chaura Panchasika, 1896; Sadi's Gulistan: I-IV, 1899. *Grammar*—A Simple Transliteral Grammar of Turkish, 1877.

ABOUT: Pond, J. B. Eccentricities of Genius; Wilkinson, W. C. Edwin Arnold as a Poetizer and as Paganizer.

ARNOLD, MATTHEW (December 24, 1822-April 15, 1888), poet and critic, was born at Laleham on the Thames, the eldest son of Thomas Arnold, historian and great headmaster of Rugby, and of Mary (Penrose) Arnold.

He was educated at Winchester; Rugby, where he won a prize for a poem on "Alaric at Rome"; and Oxford, to which he went as a Scholar of Balliol College in 1841, and where he won the Newdigate Prize for "Cromwell, A Prize Poem," and received a Second Class in *litterae humaniores,* to the regret though hardly to the surprise of his friends. Always outwardly a worldling, he had not yet revealed the "hidden ground of thought and of austerity within" which was to appear in his poetry. "During these years," writes Thomas Arnold the younger in *Passages in a Wandering Life,* "my brother was cultivating his poetic gift carefully, but his exuberant, versatile nature claimed other satisfactions. His keen bantering talk made him something of a social lion among Oxford men, he even began to dress fashionably."

In 1845, however, after a short interlude of teaching at Rugby, he was elected Fellow of Oriel, accounted a great distinction at Oxford since the days of Keble, Newman, and Dr. Arnold himself.

The record of his private life at this period is curiously lacking. It is known that his allegiance to France was sealed by a youthful enthusiasm for the acting of Rachel, whom he later said he followed to Paris about this time and watched night after night, and that he visited George Sand at Nohant on one occasion and made on her the impression of a "Milton jeune et voyageant." It seems not improbable, from the poems to the mysterious Marguerite and a veiled reference in an early letter to his intimate friend Arthur Hugh Clough, that his French allegiance was further strengthened by a less intellectual bond.

In 1847 he became private secretary to Lord Lansdowne, who in 1851 secured him an inspectorship of schools, which almost to the end of his life was to absorb the greater part of his time and energies, and may have been partly responsible for the smallness of his poetical output. But it shortly enabled him to marry Frances Lucy Wightman, daughter of Sir William Wightman, a Judge of the Queen's Bench.

His literary career—leaving out the two prize poems—had begun in 1849 with the publication of *The Strayed Reveller and Other Poems by A.,* which attracted little notice—although it contained perhaps Arnold's most purely poetical poem "The Forsaken Merman"—and was soon withdrawn. *Empedocles on Etna and Other Poems* (among them "Tristram and Iseult"), published in 1852, had a similar fate.

Arnold's work as a critic begins with the Preface to the *Poems* which he issued in 1853 under his own name, including extracts from the earlier volumes along with "Sohrab and Rustum" and "The Scholar-Gipsy" but significantly omitting "Empedocles." In its emphasis on the importance of subject in poetry, on "clearness of arrangement, rigor of development, simplicity of style" learned from the Greeks, and in the strong imprint of Goethe and Wordsworth, may be observed nearly all the essential elements in his critical theory. He was still primarily a poet, however, and in 1855 appeared *Poems, Second Series,* among them "Balder Dead."

Criticism began to take first place with his appointment in 1857 to the professorship of poetry at Oxford, which he held for two successive terms of five years. In 1858 he brought out his tragedy of *Merope,* calculated, he wrote to a friend, "rather to inaugurate my Professorship with dignity than to move deeply the present race of *humans,*" and chiefly remarkable for some experiments in unusual—and unsuccessful—metres.

In 1861 his lectures *On Translating Homer* were published, to be followed in 1862 by *Last Words on Translating Homer,* both volumes admirable in style and full of striking judgments and suggestive remarks, but built on rather arbitrary assumptions and reaching no well-established conclusions. Especially characteristic, both of his defects and his qualities, are on the one hand, Arnold's unconvincing advocacy of English hexameters and his creation of a kind of literary absolute in the "grand style," and, on the other, his keen feeling of the need for a disinterested and intelligent criticism in England.

This feeling, a direct result of his admiration for France, finds fuller expression in "The Function of Criticism at the Present Time' and "The Literary Influence of Academies," which were published as the first two of the *Essays in Criticism* (1865), in which collection the influence of French ideas, especially of the critic Sainte-Beuve, is conspicuous, both in matter and in form—that of the *causerie.* The *Essays* are bound together by a scheme of social rather than of purely literary criticism, as is apparent from the Preface, written in a vein of delicious irony and culminating unexpectedly in the well-known poetically phrased tribute to Oxford.

After the publication in 1867 of *New Poems,* which included "Thyrsis" and "Rugby Chapel," elegies on Clough and on Dr. Arnold, and in 1868 of the *Essay on the Study of Celtic Literature,* a stimulating but illusory excursion into dangerously unfamiliar realms of philology and anthropology in imitation of Renan and perhaps of Gobineau, Arnold turned almost entirely from literature to social and theological writings. Inspired by a fervent zeal for bringing culture and criticism to the British middle class, beginning with the challenging *Culture and Anarchy,* Arnold launched by dint of sheer repetition most of the catchwords associated with his name; such as "Sweetness and Light," borrowed from Swift, and the term "Philistine," borrowed from the Germans through Carlyle. He felt himself to be like the poet earlier described in his "Stanzas from the Grande Chartreuse":

Wandering between two worlds, one dead,
  The other powerless to be born

and in an attempt to reconcile traditional religion with the results of the new higher criticism, he fell back on the idea of God as a "Stream of Tendency," a phrase derived from Wordsworth.

To the relief of a good many of his contemporaries, a volume appeared in 1878 called *Last Essays on Church and Religion;* and the next year was published *Mixed Essays*—"an unhappy title," says Mr. Herbert Paul, "suggesting biscuits." Worthy of par-

MATTHEW ARNOLD

ticular mention are the two essays on the French critic Edmond Scherer and his writings on Milton and Goethe, and that on George Sand, who had influenced him strongly in his youth.

In 1883 Gladstone conferred on Arnold a pension of £250 a year, enabling him to retire from the post in the exercise of which he had not only traveled the length and breadth of England, but made several trips abroad to report on continental education. These reports were published in book form, and together with his ordinary reports as a school inspector had an important effect on English education.

With his increased freedom, he set out on a lecture tour in the United States, spreading Sweetness and Light as far west as St. Louis. There, however, he began "to recognize the truth of what an American told the Bishop of Rochester, that 'Denver was not ripe for Mr. Arnold.'" The three lectures on "Numbers," "Literature and Science," and "Emerson," which he delivered to American audiences in 1883-84, were afterwards published as *Discourses in America*—the book, he told George Russell, later his biographer and editor of his *Letters,* by which, of all his prose writings, he should most wish to be remembered.

At this time an American newspaper compared him, as he stooped now and then to look at his manuscript on a music stool, to an elderly bird picking at grapes on a trellis; and another described him thus: "He has harsh features, supercilious manners, parts his hair down the middle, wears a single eyeglass and ill-fitting clothes."

He crossed the Atlantic again in 1886 on a visit to his daughter who had married an

American. When she returned the visit in 1888, he went to Liverpool to meet her, and there, while running to catch a tramcar, suddenly died.

Essays in Criticism: Second Series which he had already collected, appeared shortly after his death. This volume, introduced by the essay on "The Study of Poetry," with the celebrated discussion of poetry as "a criticism of life," contains together with *Essays in Criticism: First Series* the prose work by which Arnold is best known. His best-known poems are probably "The Scholar-Gipsy"; "Thyrsis," considered one of the finest elegies in English; and "Sohrab and Rustum," a narrative poem, in tone a blend of the Homeric with the elegiac, based on an episode from the *Shah-Nameh* of the Persian poet Firdausi.

Matthew Arnold "was indeed the most delightful of companions," writes G. W. E. Russell in *Portraits of the Seventies*; "a man of the world entirely free from worldliness and a man of letters without the faintest trace of pedantry." A familiar figure at the Athenaeum Club, a frequent diner-out and guest at great country houses, fond of fishing and shooting, a lively conversationalist, affecting a combination of foppishness and Olympian grandeur, he read constantly, widely, and deeply, and in the intervals of supporting himself and his family by the quiet drudgery of school inspecting, filled notebook after notebook with meditations of an almost monastic tone. In his writings, he often baffled and sometimes annoyed his contemporaries by the apparent contradiction between his urbane, even frivolous manner in controversy, and the "high seriousness" of his critical views and the melancholy, almost plaintive note of much of his poetry. "A voice poking fun in the wilderness" was T. H. Warren's description of him.

A deeper inconsistency was caused by the "want of logic and thoroughness of thought" which J. M. Robertson noted in *Modern Humanists*. Few of his ideas were his own, and he failed to reconcile the conflicting influences which moved him so strongly. "There are four people, in especial," he once wrote to Cardinal Newman, "from whom I am conscious of having learnt—a very different thing from merely receiving a strong impression—learnt habits, methods, ruling ideas, which are constantly with me; and the four are—Goethe, Wordsworth, Sainte-Beuve, and yourself." Dr. Arnold must be added; the son's fundamental likeness to the father was early pointed out by Swinburne, and has been recently attested by Matthew Arnold's grandson, Mr. Arnold Whitridge. Brought up in the tenets of the Philistinism which, as a professed cosmopolitan and the Apostle of

Culture he attacked, he remained something of a Philistine to the end.

In his poetry he derived not only the subject matter of his narrative poems from various traditional or literary sources, but even much of the romantic melancholy of his earlier poems from Senancour's *Obermann*. His greatest defects as a poet stem from his lack of ear and his frequent failure to distinguish between poetry and prose. His significant if curious estimate of his own poems in 1869 was that they represented "on the whole, the main movement of mind of the last quarter of a century."

It is perhaps true, however, that as Sir Edmund Chambers says, "in a comparison between the best works of Matthew Arnold and that of his six greatest contemporaries . . . the proportion of work which endures is greater in the case of Matthew Arnold than in any one of them." His poetry endures because of its directness, and the literal fidelity of his beautifully circumstantial description of nature, of scenes, and places, imbued with a kind of majestic sadness which takes the place of music. Alike in his poetry and in his prose, which supplies in charm of manner, breadth of subject-matter, and acuteness of individual judgment, what it lacks in system, a stimulating personality makes itself felt. He was chiefly valuable to his own age as its severest critic; to ours he represents its humanest aspirations.

J. B. O.

PRINCIPAL WORKS: *Poetry*—Alaric at Rome, 1840; Cromwell, 1843; The Strayed Reveller, 1849; Empedocles on Etna, 1852; Poems, 1853; Poems: Second Series, 1855; Merope, 1858; New Poems, 1867; Poems (2 vols.) 1869; Poems (2 vols.) 1877; Selected Poems, 1878; Poems (3 vols.) 1885. *Critical, Political, and Theological Writings*—England and the Italian Question, 1859; On Translating Homer, 1865; Essays in Criticism, 1865; On the Study of Celtic Literature, 1867; Culture and Anarchy, 1869; St. Paul and Protestantism, 1870; Friendship's Garland, 1871; Literature and Dogma, 1873; God and the Bible, 1875; Last Essays on Church and Religion, 1877; Mixed Essays, 1879; Irish Essays, 1882; Discourses in America, 1885; Essays in Criticism: Second Series, 1888; Civilization in the United States, 1888. *Educational Writings*—Popular Education in France, 1861; A French Eton, 1864; Schools and Universities on the Continent, 1868; Higher Schools and Universities in Germany, 1874; A Special Report on Elementary Education Abroad, 1888; Reports on Elementary Schools, 1889. *Letters and Note-Books*—Notebooks (ed. by Mrs. Armine Wodehouse) 1902; Letters (2 vols., ed. by G. W. E. Russell) 1895; Unpublished Letters (ed. by Arnold Whitridge) 1923; Letters of Matthew Arnold to Arthur Hugh Clough (ed. by H. F. Lowry) 1932.

ABOUT: Harvey, C. H. Matthew Arnold: A Critic of the Victorian Period; Kingsmill, H. Matthew Arnold; Paul, H. Matthew Arnold; Russell, G. W. E. Matthew Arnold; Saintsbury, G. Matthew Arnold; Sells, E. Matthew Arnold and France: The Poet; Sherman, S. Matthew Arnold and How to Know Him; Smart, T. Bibliography of Matthew Arnold; Cornhill Magazine 3ns60:

133 March 1926; Nineteenth Century 113:498 April 1933; Times Literary Supplement August 12, 1920; ibid. April 13, 1922; ibid. December 21, 1922; Yale Review 22:782 June 1933.

ARNOLD, THOMAS (June 13, 1795-June 12, 1842), historian, ecclesiastic, and great headmaster of Rugby, was born at East Cowes in the Isle of Wight, the son of William Arnold, a collector of customs, who died suddenly when his son was six years old, and Martha (Delafield) Arnold.

While his education was still the care of his aunt Miss Delafield he gave evidence of a precocious memory, a love of history, and a talent for geography which was later to give its chief value to his edition of Thucydides. In 1803 he went to Warminster and in 1807 to Winchester, where he was called "poet Arnold," more for his habit of reciting ballads than as a tribute to his own long poem on Simon de Montfort. In 1811 when sixteen years old he became a scholar of Corpus Christi College, Oxford. After three years, a "first" in classics led to an Oriel fellowship in 1815, in which year and in 1817 he won the chancellor's prizes for Latin and English essays. Although, as an early member of the Attic Society, which developed into the Oxford Union, he is described as "an embarrassed speaker," he was an eager conversationalist remarkable for his flashing eye, his keen intelligence, and his energetic views. Though somewhat frail in appearance and not fond of games, he took a delight in walks and cross-country runs which, as with his dislike of early rising, he never outgrew.

Very soon, however, he overcame his restlessness and religious doubts. Ordained deacon in 1818, he settled the next year at Laleham on the Thames to take private pupils. There he married in 1820 Mary Penrose, daughter of the Reverend John Penrose. Their eldest son was Matthew Arnold, the poet and critic.

In 1827, on the recommendation of the provost of Oriel who predicted that "he would change the face of education all through the public schools of England," Arnold was elected to the headmastership of Rugby, and having been ordained priest the following year began his real life's work, in the course of which—as an anonymous correspondent of the *Times Educational Supplement* has lately summed it up—"he altered Rugby and English education, not by any striking reforms or changes but because he lived there for fourteen years." "Throughout," wrote his pupil and biographer Stanley, "whether in the school itself, or in its after effects, the one image that we have before us is not Rugby, but *Arnold*." In pursuance of his main purpose of making Rugby a place of Christian

education, as the first headmaster to assume the duties of chaplain also, he made his Sunday evening sermons the high point of the school life. His insistence on religion and his inculcation of moral earnestness through the prefectorial system are more frequently remembered than the fact that he added mathematics, history, and modern languages to the curriculum.

Holding views considerably in advance of his time on many subjects besides education, he earned for himself the reputation of a dangerous radical by championing the cause of the Irish Catholics, founding a newspaper to call attention to the dire consequences for the working classes and the nation of the unregulated growth of industrial exploitation, and urging what he regarded as the Christianity of Christ as opposed to that of the majority of Englishmen and churchmen. For long in disfavor at Oxford as one of the principal opponents of the Tractarian Movement, the appointment of the broad-church Hampden to the professorship of divinity, paved the way to his appointment in 1841 as regius professor of modern history. In his notes on Thucydides and in the *History of Rome* at which he had been working for some years and which he did not live to complete, he introduced into England the scientific method of historical research. "What his general admiration for Niebuhr was as a practical motive in the earlier part of his work," says Stanley, "that his deep aversion to Gibbon, as a man, was in the latter part."

The expectations aroused by his inaugural lecture at Oxford and his stimulating and suggestive introductory course were never fulfilled. He died suddenly at Rugby of

THOMAS ARNOLD

angina pectoris, on the eve of his forty-seventh birthday.

Arnold's impression on those who came into contact with him was partly due to his appearance and manner—of more than average height, vigorous though never robust, with a prominent underlip, deep piercing eyes, heavy eyebrows and curling black hair, his stern countenance grew terrifying when he was angry, but gleamed radiantly when, as oftener, he was interested or pleased. But, as Lake has said, his effect was produced "in the main by the union of reality and simplicity of character with a constant freshness and liveliness of intellect almost amounting to poetry."

As a writer he has an admirable prose style and compels interest by originality of illustration, integrity of purpose, and consistency of reasoning.

Remembered solely as a schoolmaster by most people, Dr. Arnold, in the words of his great-grandson, Arnold Whitridge, "has fared better at the hands of posterity than most schoolmasters. He has inspired a great biography, a great elegy, and the best novel of school life that has ever been written; more recently he has provided a brilliant essayist with an excellent opportunity of displaying his talent for caricature. . . It is not easy task to take the measure of a man who could win the devotion of a delicate scholar like Dean Stanley, of a poet and man of the world like Matthew Arnold, of a vigorous country gentleman like Thomas Hughes, and who although only a schoolmaster was eminent enough to excite the irony of Mr. Lytton Strachey."   J. B. O.

PRINCIPAL WORKS: *Theological and Religious Writings*—Sermons (3 vols.) 1829-34; The Principles of Church Reform, 1833; Two Sermons on the Interpretation of Prophecy, 1839; The Christian Life: Its Course, Its Hindrances, and Its Helps, 1841; The Christian Life: Its Hopes, Its Fears, and Its Close, 1842; Fragment on the Church, 1844; Sermons, 1845. *History*—Thucydides (ed. 3 vols.) 1830-35; History of Rome (3 vols.) 1838-43; Introductory Lectures on Modern History: With Inaugural Lecture, 1842; History of the Later Roman Commonwealth (2 vols.) 1845; The Second Punic War, 1886. *Miscellaneous*—Thirteen Letters on Our Social Condition, 1822; Miscellaneous Works, 1845.

ABOUT: Arnold, M. Rugby Chapel; Bradby, G. F. The Brontës and Other Essays; Campbell, R. J. Thomas Arnold; Fitch, Sir J. F. Thomas and Matthew Arnold; Hughes, T. Tom Brown's School Days; Stanley, A. P. Life and Correspondence of Thomas Arnold; Stanley, A. P. Sermon Preached in Rugby Chapel on the Death of Arnold; Strachey, L. Eminent Victorians; Whitridge, A. Dr. Arnold of Rugby; Times Educational Supplement July 9, 1927.

ARNOLD, WILLIAM THOMAS (September 18, 1852-May 29, 1904), historian, was the son of Thomas Arnold, teacher and author of a *Manual of English Literature*. He was the grandson of Thomas Arnold, the famous historian and headmaster of Rugby;

the nephew of Matthew Arnold, the poet and critic; and the brother of Mrs. Humphry Ward, the novelist. Born in Hobart, Tasmania, where his father was for a time inspector of schools, he was taken to England at the age of four and educated at Rugby and at University College, Oxford. After graduation he remained at Oxford doing private coaching and literary work. In his twenty-seventh year he won the Arnold Prize with an essay on *The Roman System of Provincial Administration* which established his reputation as a historian and was accepted as the English authority on the subject. His best known work was the editing of the concluding part of his grandfather Thomas Arnold's *History of Rome* (dealing with the Second Punic War). For seventeen years he wrote on politics for the *Manchester Guardian*. He died in London at fifty-one, survived by his childless wife, Henrietta Wale.

PRINCIPAL WORKS: The Roman System of Provincial Administration to the Accession of Constantine the Great, 1879; Thomas Arnold's History of Rome: The Second Punic War (ed. with notes) 1886; Studies in Roman Imperialism (ed. by E. Fiddes) 1906.

ABOUT: Arnold, W. T. Studies in Roman Imperialism (see Memoir by E. Fiddes); Ward, Mrs. H. & Montague, C. E. Memoir of William Thomas Arnold.

ASHE, THOMAS (1836-December 18, 1889), poet, was born in Cheshire. His father, formerly a Manchester manufacturer and amateur artist, later took holy orders, his own son preparing him for ordination.

Thomas Ashe received his B.A. from St. John's College, Cambridge, in 1859. The same year he was ordained deacon, and was ordained priest in 1860. He was for a time a curate in Northamptonshire, but gave up the incumbency to become a teacher. First at Leamington College and then at St. Elizabeth's School, Ipswich, he taught mathematics from 1865 to 1879. As soon as he was financially able to do so, he resigned, and after spending two years in Paris, went to London in 1881. He spent the remainder of his life there, engaged in a purely literary life. He never married.

Ashe edited editions of several poets, chiefly of Coleridge, and gave occasional lectures on literature. He was a prolific poet, bringing out a volume every few years, appearing often in magazines and reviews, and occasionally writing poetic drama. He was reticent and retiring, and little is known of his personal life. He died rather suddenly, at fifty-three, in London, and is buried at Macclesfield.

As a poet Ashe has charm but no vigor, a deficiency which is most obvious in dramas like *Hypsipyle* and narrative poems like *Edith*. His shorter lyrics are graceful, and some of them are enshrined in anthologies. He was an exceedingly minor poet, however, and there is no outstanding verse of his which has any life today.

PRINCIPAL WORKS: Poems, 1859; Dryope and Other Poems, 1861; Pictures and Other Poems, 1863; The Sorrows of Hypsipyle, 1867; Edith: or, Love and Life in Cheshire, 1873; Lectures and Notes on Shakspere, 1883; Best Collected Poems, 1885; Songs of a Year, 1888.

ABOUT: Ellis, H. Poets and Poetry of the Century (Vol. 6).

ASHWORTH, JOHN (July 18, 1813-January 26, 1875), social reformer and story writer, was born near Rochdale, the eighth child of poor weavers. The family's poverty was increased by the father's intemperate habits; as a child Ashworth's only clothing was made of wool sacks. He had no education except what he could secure in Sunday School, and he was married before he was twenty. Yet by 1850 he had taught himself, by study at night, sufficiently well to permit him to become a dissenting preacher, and from weaving had worked himself up to the position of a prosperous manufacturer.

Keenly interested in the condition of the destitute weavers from whom he sprung, Ashworth in 1858 founded at Rochdale (the home of the cooperative movement) a chapel and a sort of settlement for the benefit of poor workers. Religiously he was extremely orthodox, but he was liberal politically and he did a tremendous amount of good. He was a strong teetotaller and his preaching helped to reform his own father.

In the course of his life Ashworth traveled once to Palestine and once to the United States, and wrote books on both journeys. His reputation as an author, however, rests upon two books of simple stories which were written for the edification, amusement, and instruction of his flock in Rochdale. They are really classed incorrectly as fiction, since most of them are founded on real persons and occurrences. Ashworth never pretended to literary style, and his writing is simply plain, clear narrative with a forceful moral attached to each tale. He was primarily a social reformer, and his writing is merely incidental to his labors among the poor.

PRINCIPAL WORKS: Strange Tales From Humble Life, 1863; Simple Records, 1865.

ABOUT: Calman, A. L. Life and Labours of John Ashworth.

ATHERSTONE, EDWIN (April 17, 1788-January 29, 1872), poet, began his chief work, *The Fall of Nineveh,* at the age of forty and spent twenty years writing its thirty volumes, which were published in three installments. He also wrote prose romances, and worked in friendly rivalry with the painter John Martin, one of whose canvases was entitled "The Fall of Nineveh" after Atherstone's poem. In the closing years of his life he received an annual pension of £100. He

died at Bath, England, at the age of eighty-three. His poems attracted some attention in their time by their grandiosity; but they are now forgotten.

PRINCIPAL WORKS: *Poetry*—The Last Days of Herculaneum, 1821; A Midsummer Day's Dream, 1824; The Fall of Nineveh (30 vols.) 1828-1868; Israel in Egypt, 1861. *Romances*—The Sea Kings in England, 1830; The Handwriting on the Wall, 1858.

AUSTEN, JANE (December 16, 1775-July 18, 1817), novelist, was born at Steventon, Hampshire, seventh of the eight children of the Rev. George Austen. Her mother was Cassandra Leigh, a niece of the famous Rev. Theophilus Leigh, master of Balliol College, Oxford. The situation of the Austens, a large family of gentle lineage and no fortune, was similar to that bestowed by Miss Jane upon some of her own characters. Like many clergymen of the time, Mr. Austen supplemented his income by farming and tutoring.

The Steventon parsonage is described as having been more commodious than most, but, with eight children in addition to the small boys who were taken to board, it cannot have seemed so to its inhabitants. It may have been exigencies of space which caused Jane, aged six, and Cassandra, aged nine, to be sent away to a school at Oxford, later to Southampton, in 1782. Here both girls fell dangerously ill of fever. They were next placed under Madame Latourelle, an old lady with a cork leg who conducted the Abbey School at Reading. Like the school in *Emma,* it was a place "where girls might be sent to be out of the way, and scramble themselves into a little education without any danger of coming back prodigies." This experiment lasted but a short time and thereafter the Austens educated their daughters at home.

It was a lively, cheerful family, given to novel-reading and charades. Mr. Austen's children took part in the theatrical entertainments which were given before his pupils went home on vacation. In the eighteenth century a parson's family was not limited in its enjoyment of whatever worldly diversions were available, but roads were bad and balls few enough so that on the whole country life was quiet at best. Jane had plenty of time to wield her pen for her own amusement. Copy-books from her fourteenth year, containing sketches and stories which precociously shadow forth the splendid vein of irony she was later to develop, are most remarkable in the sure critical sense which they display. The youthful essays of genius are commonly slavish imitations of current favorites. Jane Austen recognized and pilloried the faults of the popular novel before she was fifteen. *Love and Friendship* is the most brilliant of the *juvenalia*.

Between 1795 and 1798 she had completed three novels. A London publisher, Cadell by name, has achieved a certain immortality by his refusal of *First Impressions*. It was ultimately called *Pride and Prejudice*. Too much stress has perhaps been laid upon the placidity of Jane Austen's life and the fact that she could not have worked in any other genre than the one she created. It cannot be said, however, that the stirring events of her period did not touch her. Two of her brothers were naval officers who saw active service, and living with the family from Jane's tenth year was her cousin, the Comtesse de Feuillade, whose husband was guillotined in 1794. But it is true that Miss Austen never trifled with situations outside her own experience. She advises her niece, who is writing a novel, "Let the Portmans go to Ireland, but, as you know nothing of the manners there, you had better not go with them." There was one element in Miss Austen's life which might have been grist to another writer. This was her second brother George, "mental invalid," who lived over sixty years. He is usually not mentioned in biographies of the novelist, but his existence may have contributed to her impatience with the vogue for treating insanity as an ingredient of romance, and it certainly added to the financial burdens of the family.

Jane Austen was never a bluestocking. In her youth at Steventon she is described as having been something of a flirt. She was tall, slender, and graceful, "a clear brunette with a rich color, hazel eyes, fine features and curling brown hair" whom no one outside her immediate family suspected of having literary ambitions. The only authentic portrait of her, from the pencil of Cassandra, while of rather indifferent composition shows a primly elfin face with a small, determined mouth that is quite appealing. She dearly loved a ball and was as impatient of poor dancing as she was of poor sense. She did exquisite needlework and had other practical domestic virtues. "I always take care to provide such things as please my own appetite, which I consider as the chief merit in housekeeping."

The years after 1798 seem to have been particularly quiet and contented ones. Mr. Austen gave up his school and the parsonage expanded enough to allow the devoted sisters a sitting-room of their own. Here were Jane's piano and writing materials and Cassandra's drawing implements. This felicity, however, did not long endure. In 1801 Mr. Austen made the Steventon living over to his eldest son James, and prepared to settle with his wife and daughters at Bath. It may have been because these daughters were

JANE AUSTEN

unmarried that the elderly retired clergyman elected to spend his declining years in this populous and expensive watering-place. Jane was twenty-six at the time, Cassandra, twenty-nine, and both doomed to spinsterhood unless something immediate was accomplished. Jane had had several romantic attachments while at Steventon, but nothing serious had ever developed. Cassandra had been engaged to marry a former pupil of her father's, Thomas Craven Fowle. He went out to the West Indies as chaplain to his cousin Lord Craven's regiment and died there of yellow fever.

During the summer of 1801 the Austens toured South Devon and Jane is reported to have met and fallen in love with a clergyman named Blackall. The attraction was mutual, but before it reached a formal engagement the gentleman died. This tragedy not only prevented Jane's acceptance of another unnamed eligible who offered himself the following year but caused a break in her literary productivity. Told many years after Jane's death by Cassandra, this touching story suffices well enough for those of the author's admirers who insist upon a serious love affair for their darling, but it bears a strange resemblance to the account of Cassandra's own broken heart.

It was in 1802 that Jane had the felicity of selling her first manuscript. *Susan*, posthumously published as *Northanger Abbey*, was sold to Crosbie of London for £10. The Gothic novel which it parodied was still too popular for Miss Austen's treatment of it to be appreciated and Crosbie failed to publish. *The Watsons* was begun about this time, dropped, and never finished.

Mr. Austen's death in 1805 left his wife and daughters with an income of only £210 a year between them. This was raised by the brothers to £450, a sum barely adequate in a day when living costs were high, and niggardly, considering that Mrs. Austen's brother and one of her sons were extremely wealthy. Jane had no need to draw upon imagination for her portrayals of rich relatives and their attitude toward less fortunate kinsfolk. Further to economize it was decided that the ladies should go to live in the recently established household of Francis Austen at Southampton. It cannot have been a comfortable situation for any one concerned. Francis Austen, himself barely a year older than Jane, was called to sea, leaving his young wife to anticipate an infant in company with newly acquired female relatives whose ages ranged from thirty to seventy.

Happily for Jane the arrangement did not last many years. In 1808 the wealthy brother Edward lost his wife and by reason of this bereavement had his attention turned toward his own family. He offered them then the use of a house on his estate at Chawton near Alton. Here after eight unsettled years Jane could compose her mind to write. Revising *Elinor and Marianne*, she sold it as *Sense and Sensibility*. Published in 1811, it was an immediate success. Encouraged by this and the further popularity of *Pride and Prejudice*, she wrote, almost as if she knew her time was short, *Mansfield Park, Emma*, and *Persuasion* in rapid succession. Domestic pursuits and the entertainment of her multitude of nephews and nieces occupied her as usual betimes. She used the common sitting-room as her work place, making as her sole stipulation that the squeak should not be taken out of the swinging door because it gave her warning in time to conceal her manuscript.

In 1815, while Jane was in London correcting proof on *Emma*, Henry Austen whom she was visiting there fell dangerously ill. This was Jane's fourth and her favorite brother. His wife, the aforementioned Eliza de Feuillade, was dead and it was Jane who nursed him back to health.

In 1816 Henry Austen bought back *Northanger Abbey* for £10, the amount originally paid Jane in 1802. She had written Crosbie in 1809, urging him to publish the book, and his only reply had been a threat to sue if the manuscript was offered elsewhere. It must have been with considerable satisfaction that Henry concluded the interview by informing the publisher that the manuscript he had just relinquished was by the author of *Pride and Prejudice*!

Now at the fullness of her powers Jane's health began to decline. Cassandra took her to Winchester to be under the care of a doctor friend of the family, but her ailment was never properly diagnosed. Some sprightly verses, written a day or two before her death, show that her sense of humor never failed. She died in her sister's arms and was buried in Winchester Cathedral.

Generations of readers have marveled at the modernity of her work. Excepting an occasional quaintness of phraseology, the savor of Jane Austen's novels is as vivid today as it was when they were new. Regiments of critics have idolized her. Macaulay places her "among the writers who have approached nearest to the manner of the great Master" [Shakespeare]. Her creations have come alive for others than Macaulay. Tennyson, on a visit to Lyme Regis, scorned its historical associations, saying "Don't talk to me of the Duke of Monmouth. Show me the exact spot where Louisa Musgrove fell!" Professor Saintsbury said that "not even Scott's or Thackeray's characters dwell in the mind more securely." Her portraiture, "distinctly satirical . . . has even been accused of a touch of cruelty; but this only gives flavor and keeping quality. . . . She is the mother of the English nineteenth century novel as Scott is the father of it."

P. B. S.

PRINCIPAL WORKS: *Novels*—Sense and Sensibility, 1811; Pride and Prejudice, 1813; Mansfield Park, 1814; Emma, 1814; Northanger Abbey, 1818; Persuasion, 1818. *Fragments and Juvenalia*—Love and Friendship and Other Early Works, 1922; The Watsons, 1923; Fragment of a Novel [Sanditon] 1925; Plan of a Novel, 1926.
ABOUT: Cornish, F. W. Jane Austen; Leigh, W. A. Jane Austen: Her Life and Letters; Leigh, J. E. A Memoir of Jane Austen; Mitton, G. E. Jane Austen and Her Times; Rawlence, G. Jane Austen; Thomson, C. L. Jane Austen.

AUSTIN, ALFRED (May 30, 1835-June 2, 1913), poet laureate, was the son of a wool stapler of Leeds, and nephew of a member of Parliament. The Austin family being Roman Catholics, he was educated at Stonyhurst and Oscott Colleges, but received his B.A. from the University of London in 1853. By his family's wish he read at the Inner Temple, and was called to the bar in 1857, joining the northern circuit, but the next year he abandoned law for literature, and never practised thereafter.

His first writing was critically received, but he managed to gain a place as a political journalist. He tried also to make a career in politics, standing for Parliament as a Conservative in 1865 and again in 1880, but without success. From 1866 to 1896 he was leader writer for *The Standard*, and was their correspondent abroad, at the Vatican and in Germany, on several occasions; he also wrote frequently for the *Quarterly Review*, chiefly on foreign affairs. He was a disciple of Disraeli, all of whose views and prejudices he shared—though he was quite innocent of the Tory premier's brilliance. This, how-

ALFRED AUSTIN

ever, would never have occurred to Austin, who was profoundly convinced of his own genius.

In 1883, with William J. Courthorpe, he founded and edited the *National Review*, being its sole editor from 1887 to 1893. From 1863 onward he also contributed literary criticism to various reviews, becoming known as the champion of Byron and Scott and the enemy of every poet after them. In 1865 he married Hester Homan-Mulock. It was a childless but happy match. In 1867 he settled at Swinford Old Manor, Kent, and returned to his earliest love, the writing of poetry, producing some twenty undistinguished volumes between 1871 and 1908.

In 1895 to the surprise, consternation, and ridicule of all England, Austin was appointed poet laureate to succeed Tennyson—as someone has said, "appointed over the heads of abler men because of the sins he had not committed." (Swinburne and Kipling, the logical candidates, were unacceptable to Queen Victoria.) As laureate he was completely mediocre and frequently banal.

Austin's best work is found in his prose "garden diaries," *The Garden That I Love* being his only truly popular book. His vast vanity and self complacence kept him from ever realizing his actual negligible position as a poet. The only real poetry, he said, must be epic or dramatic, and must deal with love, patriotism, or religion. He dealt with all three with pomposity, obviousness, and solemn sentimentality. His mind was entirely provincial, and he has been called "the last minstrel of Toryism," who attained fame "without being read," among those who admired the views he voiced. The laureate who could think "He is no worse, he is just the same" a poetic line was a strange successor to Tennyson and Wordsworth (both of whom he detested); and his "jolting lines and strained metaphors" made him the butt of critics. The best that can be said of him is that he sometimes attained to "creditable mediocrity," and that he had a real feeling for the more placid aspects of nature. His autobiography is almost incredible in its calm assumption that its writer was a great genius; it may survive his poems as a document portraying the vagaries of human self-deception.

M. A. deF.

PRINCIPAL WORKS: *Poetry*—Randolph, 1854; The Season, 1861; My Satire and Its Censors, 1861; The Human Tragedy, 1862 (incorporated in it in later editions: Madonna's Child, 1873; Rome or Death, 1873); The Golden Age, 1871; Interludes, 1872; The Tower of Babel, 1874; Leszko the Bastard, 1877; Savonarola, 1881; Soliloquies in Song, 1882; At the Gate of the Convent, 1885; Prince Lucifer, 1887; Love's Widowhood, 1889; English Lyrics, 1890; Lyrical Poems, 1891; Narrative Poems, 1891; Fortunatus the Pessimist, 1892; England's Darling, 1896; The Conversion of Wincklemann, 1897; Songs of England, 1898; A Tale of True Love, 1902; Flodden Field, 1903; The Door of Humility, 1906; Sacred and Profane Love, 1908. *Novels*—Five Years of It, 1858; An Artist's Proof, 1864; Won by a Head, 1866. *Miscellaneous Prose*—A Vindication of Lord Byron, 1869; The Poetry of the Period, 1877; Russia Before Europe (Tory Horrors) 1876; England's Policy and Peril, 1877; Hibernian Horrors, 1880; The Garden That I Love, 1894 (2nd ser., 1907); In Veronica's Garden, 1895; Lamia's Winter Quarter's, 1898; Spring and Autumn in Ireland, 1900; Haunts of Ancient Peace, 1902; The Poet's Diary, 1904; The Bridling of Pegasus, 1910; Autobiography, 1911.

ABOUT: Austin, A. The Autobiography of Alfred Austin: Poet Laureate; Broadus, E. K. The Laureateship in Modern Times; Sherman, S. P. On Contemporary Literature; Literary Digest 46: 6:1334 June 14, 1913; Nation 93:360 October 19, 1911; 96:578 June 5, 1913; Outlook 104:311 June 14, 1913.

AUSTIN, JOHN (March 3, 1790-December, 1859), jurist and writer on jurisprudence, was born at Creeting Mill, in Suffolk. After serving five years in the army, he practised law in London for a while and was six years professor of jurisprudence at London University. For about ten years he lived abroad —on the island of Malta (where he investigated the government), in Germany, and in Paris. The last ten years of his life were spent at Weybridge, Surrey, and he died in obscurity at sixty-nine. A brilliant talker, he was a friend of John Stuart Mill and Jeremy Bentham.

He was never satisfied with his work and wrote little, the only book that appeared in his lifetime being scarcely noticed. He rose to posthumous fame with his *Lectures on Jurisprudence,* which became a standard text in England and the United States. His writing was redundant and dull as to style, but its content gave a new precision to the meanings of legal terms and laid the foundations for modern analytical jurisprudence.

His wife, SARAH TAYLOR AUSTIN (1793-1867), was a gifted translator of work in German and French. Their only child was Lucie, Lady Duff-Gordon, author of travel letters.

PRINCIPAL WORKS OF JOHN AUSTIN: The Province of Jurisprudence Determined, 1832; Lectures on Jurisprudence: or, The Philosophy of Positive Law (ed. by his widow) 1863.

ABOUT: Austin, J. Lectures on Jurisprudence (see Biographical Preface by Mrs. Austin); Brown, W. J. Austinian Theory of Law; Holland, T. E. Elements of Jurisprudence; Mill, J. S. Autobiography.

AVEBURY, LORD (Sir John Lubbock) (April 30, 1834-May 28, 1913), naturalist, was born in London. His father, who succeeded to the baronetcy when Lubbock was a child, was a well known banker, and treasurer of the Royal Society. This scientific interest, and the fact that the family moved to Downe, in Kent, when the boy was six, were the determining factors in Lubbock's life; for Downe was the home of Darwin, who took an interest in the boy and fostered his bent for natural history.

Lubbock was sent to Eton at only eleven, but he did not proceed to a university. Instead, in 1849, he was taken from school and put to work in his father's bank. For the remainder of his life he pursued three simultaneous careers, and gained distinction in all of them—as banker, as scientist, and as a public official.

In 1856 he married Ellen Hordern, who died in 1879, leaving three sons and three daughters. In 1884 he was married again, to Alice Pitt-Rivers, daughter of a famous archaeologist; by her he had three sons and two daughters. In 1865 his father died and he succeeded to the baronetcy, and in 1900 he was elevated to the peerage.

From 1870 until he entered the House of Lords as a peer, Lubbock served in the House of Commons, where he was active in securing numerous banking and social reforms. He was the father of the English August Bank Holiday, and he brought about the passage of the Early Closing Act. In 1890 he was Privy Councillor. He served as Vice-Chancellor of London University, Principal of the Workingmen's College, trustee of the British Museum, and Rector of St. Andrew's University.

It is as a naturalist of the old school, taking all natural science for his province, that Lubbock earned his chief fame. He did research in and writing on botany, geology, and anthropology, but his principal contribution is to the study of insect life and of animal psychology. Outside of science, he is best known as the compiler (in 1891) of a list of the "hundred best books." He was a mild liberal in politics, heterodox religiously but distinctly reverent, and in everything an optimist. His scientific writing at least is still of value, and his style is pleasing and lucid.

PRINCIPAL WORKS: Prehistoric Times, 1865; The Origin of Civilization, 1870; Ants, Bees, and Wasps, 1882; The Pleasures of Life, 1887; On the Senses, Instincts, and Intelligence of Animals, 1888; The Beauties of Nature, 1892; The Use of Life, 1894; Peace and Happiness, 1909; Marriage, Totemism, and Religion, 1911.

ABOUT: Duff, Mrs. A. G. The Life-Work of Lord Avebury; Hutchinson, H. G. Life of Sir John Lubbock.

AYTOUN, WILLIAM EDMOND-STOUNE (June 21, 1813-August 4, 1865), Scottish poet and novelist, was born in Edinburgh, son of a writer to the signet. He came of an old Scottish family on both sides, and his mother, a close friend of Sir Walter Scott, taught him ancient ballads from his infancy. A seventeenth century ancestor was a famous balladist.

After schooling at Edinburgh Academy and the University of Edinburgh, Aytoun read law for one winter in London, but decided against this profession. He then studied German literature at Aschaffenburg. But his family was not wealthy enough to allow him to live by literature alone, and so in 1835 he was admitted as writer to the signet in his father's office. In 1840 he was called to the Scottish bar, which he disliked less than the English.

He began translating from the Greek and the German, and became a constant contributor to *Blackwood's Magazine*, on whose staff he secured a place in 1844. The next year he became professor of rhetoric and belles lettres at the University of Edinburgh. His lectures were very popular, the attendance rising from 30 students in 1846 to 1,850 in 1864.

W. E. AYTOUN

In 1849 he married the youngest daughter of the famous critic John Wilson ("Christopher North"). The marriage, though childless, was very happy. His wife's death in 1859 almost killed him, and he never really recovered from it, though out of sheer loneliness he remarried in 1863.

In 1852, when a Tory government came in, Aytoun was made Sheriff of Orkney—largely an honorary office. In 1853 he received an honorary D.C.L. from Oxford. He died at fifty-two, at Blackhills, near Elgin, where he had gone for his health.

Aytoun was almost a great satirist. His best known poem, *Firmilian*, was intended as a caricature of the so-called "spasmodic" school (Aytoun himself invented the term), high-flown and bombastic, of Philip James Bailey and his followers, but it got away from him and turned into serious poetry. He was a splendid parodist, especially of the "spasmodics," and of Tennyson and the Brownings. Genial, playful, and the most loyal of friends, he made fewer enemies than any satirist known to history. His friend Theodore Martin collaborated with him in many of his parodies, most of which were published under various pseudonyms. His lays and ballads have the authentic ring, and constitute his claim to lasting reputation. The best known of them is "Edinburgh After Flodden."

His only novel, *Norman Sinclair*, was largely autobiographical, and gave a good picture of life in Scotland during his youth, in the early part of the nineteenth century. He also wrote one unimportant historical work, and with Martin translated the poems and ballads of Goethe.   M. A. deF.

PRINCIPAL WORKS: *Poetry*—Poland, Homer, and Other Poems, 1830; Bon Gaultier's Ballads (with T. Martin) 1845; Lays of the Scottish Cavaliers and Other Poems, 1848; Firmilian: or, The Student of Badajoz, 1854; Bothwell, 1856; Ballads of Scotland, 1858; Nuptial Ode to the Princess Alexandria, 1863. *Prose*—Life and Times of Richard I, 1840; Norman Sinclair, 1861.

ABOUT: Masson, R. Pollok and Aytoun; Living Age 279:742 December 20, 1913.

"B. V." See THOMSON, JAMES

BABBAGE, CHARLES

BABBAGE, CHARLES (December 26, 1792-October 18, 1871), mathematician, inventor, and writer on science, was born near Teignmouth in Devonshire, the son of a banker. Educated at Trinity College, Cambridge, he spent thirty-seven years and about £6,000 in an attempt to perfect a wide-range arithmetical calculating machine, which was finally abandoned for lack of funds but laid the groundwork for future developments. For eleven years he occupied the Lucasian chair of mathematics at Cambridge, but never lectured. His outspoken criticism of the Royal Society

(of which he was a member) was a material factor in the foundation of the British Association for the Advancement of Science.

During the seventy-eight years of his life he wrote, by his own count, more than eighty works, mostly pamphlets or short treatises, lively and useful, but unfinished. Regarded as his one complete achievement is the *Economy of Machinery and Manufactures*, a widely-reprinted study of the British mechanical art. Best known to literature, however, is his autobiographical *Passages From the Life of a Philosopher*, which is highly revealing of his eccentric genius.

PRINCIPAL WORKS: The Comparative View of the Various Institutions for the Assurance of Lives, 1826; Table of Logarithms of the Natural Numbers From 1 to 108000, 1827; Economy of Machinery and Manufactures, 1832; Ninth Bridgewater Treatise, 1837; The Exposition of 1851: or, Views of the Industry, the Science, and Government of England, 1851; Passages From the Life of a Philosopher, 1864.

ABOUT: Babbage, C. Passages From the Life of a Philosopher; Royal Astronomical Society Monthly Notices (Vol. 32).

BAGEHOT, WALTER

BAGEHOT, WALTER (February 3, 1826-March 24, 1877), writer on economics and related subjects, was born at Langport, in Somersetshire, the son of a banker.

He was sent to school in Bristol, where Dr. Prichard, his mother's brother-in-law, exerted a strong influence upon him. As he could not enter Oxford without passing a doctrinal test (his father was a Unitarian), the boy went to University College, in London. He did well in mathematics, and revealed a taste for poetry, metaphysics, and history. He took his B.A. degree at the University of London in 1846, with a scholarship in mathematics; and in 1848 he took the M.A. degree with a gold medal in intellectual and moral philosophy and political economy. At this time his health broke down.

Bagehot turned first to the law, and he was interested particularly in special pleading, a phase of the profession which soon came into disuse. While in 1852 he was called to the bar, he did not follow law as a profession, but, in the same year, entered his father's ship-owning and banking business. Then he proceeded to London to direct the metropolitan business of Stuckey's Banking Company, with which his father was connected.

Before entering this service, however, Bagehot had made a trip to Paris, and he had seen the arbitrary seizure of power by the President, Louis Napoleon. He was much impressed, and shocked English friends by taking the side of the President. His political views as expressed in his works reflect a somewhat similar attitude.

In 1855 he became an editor of the *National Review*, and in 1860 the editor and manager of *The Economist*, a free-trade organ founded

WALTER BAGEHOT

by the Right Hon. James Wilson, whose eldest daughter, Elizabeth, Bagehot had married in 1858. Failing of election to Parliament (1866), he continued to hold this second position until his death at Langport, in 1877; and the history of the rest of his life is simply that of his productions.

Rather delicate, and with a tendency to absent-mindedness, which may partially explain his editorial carelessness with proofs, his pages containing many errors in punctuation and grammar as well as misprints, Bagehot had great charm as a conversationalist, possessing wit and lucidity. Although he appeared rather spirited, he had at the same time an expression of reserved detachment. Swift in grasping ideas, he was slow to accept beliefs.

In his critical essays Bagehot showed perception into character, and was not superficial in his analyses, but he tended to substitute insight for learning. The truth seems to be that he gave himself more readily to economic subjects than to literary ones. Hugh Walker writes of him, "As he did not choose to concentrate himself upon literature, his criticism, though brilliant, remains fragmentary." His merits are well stated by Woodrow Wilson, who disagreed with him on some issues: "Occasionally, a man is born into the world whose mission it evidently is to clarify the thought of his generation, and to vivify it; to give it speed where it is slow, vision where it is blind, balance where it is out of poise, saving humor where it is dry—and such a man was Walter Bagehot. When he wrote of history, he made it seem human and probable; when he wrote of political economy, he made it seem credible, entertaining—nay, engaging

even; when he wrote criticism, he wrote sense." R. W. W.

PRINCIPAL WORKS: *Economics and Politics*—Count Your Enemies and Economise Your Expenditure, 1862; The English Constitution, 1867; Physics and Politics, 1872; Lombard Street: A Description of the Money Market, 1873; Articles on the Depreciation of Silver, etc., 1877; Economic Studies, 1880; Essays on Parliamentary Reform, 1883; Postulates of English Political Economy, 1885; Practical Plan for Assimilating English and American Money as a Step Toward Universal Money, 1889. *Miscellaneous*—Literary Studies, 1878; Biographical Studies, 1881.

ABOUT: Bagehot, W. & Wilson, E. Love Letters; Barrington, E. I. The Works and Life of Walter Bagehot; Baumann, A. A. The Last Victorians; Birrell, A. Essays and Addresses; Read, H. The Sense of Glory; Stephen, L. Studies of a Biographer; Wilson, W. Mere Literature and Other Essays.

BAILEY, PHILIP JAMES (April 22, 1816-September 6, 1902), poet, was the son of Thomas and Mary (Taylor) Bailey of Nottingham. His father was an ardent poetaster and stimulated the boy's interest in poetry. Educated by tutors and at Glasgow University, where he matriculated at the age of sixteen, young Bailey first planned to enter the ministry and later changed to law. He was admitted to the bar in 1840 but never practiced.

Before his legal studies were completed he had published *Festus* at the age of twenty-two. This poem met with great success. It was first published anonymously. When the age of the author was discovered by the critics a great future was predicted for him. But *Festus* remained his one great work, and critics generally agree that it was best in the original version. Bailey continued to revise and add to it most of his life, so that what had originally been a poem of 10,000 verses, acquired in its later form some 40,000 verses.

Festus was obviously inspired by Goethe's *Faust*, which it follows closely in the main episodes. But Bailey's inspiration was prompted by a different philosophical viewpoint. This difference lay chiefly in his attitude toward evil, which he considered a purifying experience that purges mankind of the dross of humanity.

To appreciate the furore created by *Festus* it is necessary to realize the state of English literature during the preceding decade. In a reaction against the disciples of Byron, "the mere luxuries of poetry" had been discredited and the function of poetry was held to be purely didactic. *Festus*, with its high moral purpose and religious theme, evaded the censure of critics of the prevailing school while at the same time it expressed the feelings of those who craved more passionate, imaginative, poetical expression.

Bailey's first admirers were found in professional literary circles, but their enthusiasm

PHILIP JAMES BAILEY

cooled with time. However, a wider audience had been attracted and the popularity of *Festus* continued upon moral and religious, if not upon artistic, grounds. In the 'fifties a brief stir was created by a group of writers who took Bailey as their model. They copied his ecstatic style but not the moral earnestness. William Aytoun refered to them derisively as "Spasmodists" and the name stuck. Bailey was at great pains to deny any connection with this spasmodic school. Contrasting Bailey with these imitators Gosse says: "His was a mind of greater weight and fuller body. . . He was often redundant and sometimes nebulous, but there was always something definite behind the colored cloud. *Festus* appeals to the non-literary temperament . . . , those who love it appreciate its imagery, its large music, its spacious landscape, but they value it mainly for its teaching."

If Bailey had died soon after *Festus* was first published he would always have been mourned—like Chatterton—as a lost genius. Instead he lived to the age of eighty-six—a prolonged anti-climax. The popularity of *Festus*, however, continued unabated for many years. In America there were thirty pirated editions by 1889. The author never received a penny from American publishers.

Bailey was compelled to divorce his first wife, by whom he had a son and daughter. In 1863 he married Anne Sophia Carey of Nottingham. They were a devoted couple until her death in 1896. Bailey lived most of his life in the country or in small towns in various parts of England. In 1864 he settled on the Island of Jersey from which he made frequent trips to the continent. He next moved to Lee in Devonshire in 1876, and in 1885 again moved to Blackheath. At length he retired to his native city of Nottingham, where he died.

In 1856 Bailey was honored by his government with a pension of £100 in recognition of his literary work, and a year before he died, Glasgow University conferred upon him the honorary degree of LL.D.

Gosse, who had known Bailey for the last thirty years of his life, describes the poet as: ". . . a sort of prophet or bard, with a cloud of voluminous white hair and silver beard. As the years went by his head seemed merely to grow more handsome, almost irritatingly so, like a picture of Connal, 'first of mortal men,' in some illustrated edition of Ossian. . . . He had an attitude of arrested inspiration, as if waiting for the heavenly spark to fall again, as it had descended from 1836-39. . . But the beauty of Mr. Bailey's presence, which was so marked as to be an element that cannot be overlooked in any survey of what he was, had an imperfection in its very perfectness. It lacked fire. What the faces of Milton and Keats possessed, what we remember in the extraordinary features of Tennyson, just this was missing in Mr. Bailey, who, nevertheless might have sat to any scene-painter in Christendom as the type of a Poet." D. C.

PRINCIPAL WORKS: *Poetry*—Festus, 1839; The Angel World, 1850; The Mystic, 1855; The Age, 1858; The Universal Hymn, 1867; Nottingham Castle, 1878; Causa Britanica, 1883; *Prose*—The International Policy of the Great Powers, 1861.

ABOUT: Gosse, E. W. Portraits and Sketches; Nicoll, W. R. Literary Anecdotes of the 19th Century; Ward, J. Philip James Bailey: Personal Recollections; Winter, W. Old Friends.

BAILLIE, JOANNA (September 11, 1762-February 23, 1851), Scottish playwright and poet, was born in Lanarkshire of an old family which claimed descent from the Scottish hero, Sir William Wallace. Her father was a Presbyterian minister, and she led a sternly repressed childhood. Bright in mind but slow in her studies, she was sent at ten to school in Glasgow, where she was particularly interested in music, drawing, composition, and, rather strangely, mathematics.

In 1776 the father was appointed professor of divinity at the University of Glasgow, but two years later he died. At first Joanna continued to live in Glasgow with her mother and older sister. But in 1783 the family went to London to join the brother, MATTHEW (1757-1823), who was later to become a well known physician and the author of *Morbid Anatomy;* at this time he had just been left by his uncle, the famous medical pioneer, Dr. William Hunter, the use of his house and collections. They lived together until Matthew Baillie was married, in 1791, when the mother and sisters moved together to Hampstead. In 1806 the mother died, and the sisters rented a house on Hampstead Heath which continued to be their home for the rest of their long lives. (The sister, Agnes, lived to be over a hundred and Joanna herself almost to ninety.)

It was a queer environment to produce a dramatist, but one day in 1790, when she was already thirty-six and had written nothing except a few poems, it suddenly came to Joanna Baillie as she sat sewing that she could produce a series of plays, each based on the operation of a single passion on human nature and life. No sooner thought of than started; the first series of *Plays on the Passions* saw publication shortly after.

They created a literary furore, and (since they were published anonymously) one critic thought they were by Sir Walter Scott. This allegation caused an acquaintance with Scott himself, which ripened into a lifelong friendship. Since Miss Baillie had no practical experience of the theatre, her plays for the most part were what is called "reading plays," unsuitable for stage presentation. Nevertheless the famous actor John Kemble and his still more famous sister Mrs. Siddons thought so highly of one of them, *De Montfort*, that they produced it at Drury Lane in 1800 and it was later revived. Miss Baillie's later plays, not so exclusively harping on a single string, were more actable. Her *Constantine Paleologus*, under the name of *Constantine and Valeria*, was produced with success in London, Liverpool, Edinburgh, and Dublin; in the same year the younger Kemble put on *The Separation* at Covent Garden and *Henriquez* was produced at Drury Lane (though neither ran very long); and the production of *The Family Legend* at Edinburgh in 1810, with a prologue by Scott, was a real triumph.

Meanwhile the series of published plays continued to appear, interspersed with volumes of verse. It is probable that the adulation she received went a little to Miss Baillie's head, for in 1836 she brought out three more volumes of *Miscellaneous Plays*, explaining that she had originally intended these to be posthumous but could no longer resist the temptation to publish them! Two of her plays, *The Martyr* and *The Bride,* had the unusual distinction of being translated into Cingalese by Sir Alexander Johnston, chief justice of Ceylon, so that the natives might learn the virtue of forgiveness!

The Baillie sisters kept open house, and were literary lionesses—or a lioness with an unliterary but leonine sister—for many years. In 1814 Joanna sent out notices asking that henceforth she be known as "Mrs." Baillie, as was then the custom with unmarried middle-aged ladies of dignity; Scott retorted that one might as well speak of "Miss" Sappho! Byron and other leading writers of the day spoke of her with the most exag-

JOANNA BAILLIE

gerated praise, and she was ranked as a dramatist "second only to Shakespeare." Reading her plays now, all this enthusiasm is hard to understand; it is probably accounted for on three grounds—the lady's own wit and geniality; the lack of competition in an undramatic period; and the fact that she was the darling of exclusively literary circles rather than of the reading public as a whole, and that authors are always good "log-rollers" for their friends.

Joanna Baillie's life was thus an unmitigated triumph, punctuated only by the sorrow of family deaths. Small and slender, she was a charming old lady, hospitable and wideawake. She had besides both simplicity of nature, unbounded charity, and marked moral courage and integrity. In her religious views she became a Unitarian, and wrote a book on the nature of Jesus which almost lost her the friendship of Scott. She died finally by a sort of mental suicide: at eighty-nine she was tired of life, said so, went to bed, and died.

She had already largely outlived her reputation, but her work is not negligible. She wrote mostly in a sonorous blank verse, and she had real power, though not much sense of the dramatic. Her lyric poetry is delicately beautiful, and her songs in the Scottish dialect will probably outlast all the rest of her writing. Many persons even today know such songs as "Woo'd and Married and A'," "Saw Ye Johnnie Comin'," or "Oh Swiftly Glides the Bonny Boat" who have never consciously known the name of Joanna Baillie.

M. A. deF.

PRINCIPAL WORKS: *Poetry*—Fugitive Verses, 1790; Metrical Legends of Exalted Characters, 1821; A Collection of Poems Chiefly Manuscripts and from Living Authors (anthology) 1823; Fugitive Verses (new ser.) 1840. *Plays*—Plays on the Passions, 1798 (Second Series, 1802, Third Series, 1812); Miscellaneous Plays, 1804 (three more volumes, 1836); The Family Legend, 1810; The Martyr, 1826; Athalya Baee, 1851 (privately printed, 1849). *Miscellaneous*—A View of the General Tenour of the New Testament Regarding the Nature and Dignity of Jesus Christ, 1831.

ABOUT: Carhart, M. S. The Life and Work of Joanna Baillie; Carswell, D. Sir Walter; Gilfillan, G. Galleries of Literary Portraits.

BAIN, ALEXANDER (June 11, 1818-September 18, 1903), Scottish philosopher, was born in Aberdeen, the son of a small farmer and weaver who was a strict Calvinist. His mother died when he was a small child, and his sister mothered him and protected him from his father's severity. He left school at eleven to work as a weaver, but studied at home (mostly mathematics) and in evening school and at the Mechanics' Institution. At eighteen, he secured influence which enabled him to enter Marischal College as a bursar, and in 1840 he was graduated with the highest honors. He was already contributing to the *Westminster Review*, and a year later he was made assistant to the professor of moral philosophy. His application to this and other colleges for an appointment as professor was refused on the grounds of his lack of religious orthodoxy. Meanwhile, in 1842, he had visited London and had met such men as John Stuart Mill, Carlyle, George Grote, and George Henry Lewes. In 1848 he returned there as assistant secretary of the Metropolitan Sanitary Commission, and remained in this position for two years. He lectured also at the Bedford College for Women.

In 1855 Bain married Frances Wilkinson; she died in 1892 and the next year he married Barbara Forbes. There were no children by either marriage. He moved to Richmond and supported himself by writing. He edited Grote's posthumous works and Paley's *Moral Philosophy*. In 1860, against strong opposition, he was appointed by the crown as professor of logic and English in the United Universities of Aberdeen. For his students he wrote three grammars and a book on composition and rhetoric. He was the founder, financial supporter, and first editor of the psychological journal, *Mind*. His health failed in 1880 and he resigned his position as professor, but later served as Lord Rector for two three-year terms. He received a civil list pension of £100 in 1895.

Bain was an educational reformer, advocating the teaching of science and modern languages, and one of the earliest of the physiological psychologists. He distrusted metaphysics, and was in all essentials a materialist. His work is still worth reading, for he had a real talent for clear and methodical exposition.

PRINCIPAL WORKS: The Senses and the Intellect, 1855; The Emotions and the Will, 1859; Mental and Moral Science, 1868; Logic, 1870; Mind and Body, 1874; Education as a Science, 1879; James Mill, 1882; John Stuart Mill, 1882; Autobiography, 1904.

ABOUT: Bain, A. Autobiography; Mill, J. S. Dissertations and Discussions; Ribot, T. La Psychologie Anglaise Contemporaine.

BAKER, SIR SAMUEL WHITE (June 8, 1821-December 30, 1893), explorer and travel author, was born in London, the son of a West India merchant. After being privately educated, he hunted big game and explored in Ceylon for eight years, explored the Nile tributaries of Abyssinia, traveled up the Nile, and in 1864 discovered Lake Albert, great basin of the Nile. For his valuable exploits he was given the gold medal of the Royal Geographical Society and was knighted in 1866. In 1870 he established an administration in the Equatorial Nile basin, the area of his discoveries, and he served four years as its governor general, suppressing the slave trade and opening up the lakes to commerce. The last twenty years of his life were spent in travel and in quiet residence on his English estate, Sandford Orleigh, in South Devon, where he died at seventy-two. Twice married, he had seven children by his first wife.

He is known to literature for the personal accounts of his hunting expeditions in Ceylon and his explorations in Africa; also by a popular adventure tale. He wrote easily and swiftly, and his works were many times reprinted.

PRINCIPAL WORKS: *Travel*—The Rifle and Hound in Ceylon, 1853; Eight Years' Wanderings in Ceylon, 1855; The Albert Nyanza, Great Basin of the Nile, and Explorations of the Nile Sources, 1866; The Nile Tributaries of Abyssinia, 1867; Ismailia, 1874. *Fiction*—Cast Up by the Sea, 1868.

ABOUT: Murray, T. D. & White, A. S. Sir Samuel Baker: A Memoir. See also Baker's own works.

BALFOUR, FRANCIS MAITLAND (November 10, 1851-July 19, 1882), Scottish biologist and writer on embryology, was born in Edinburgh, a younger brother of Arthur James Balfour, the noted statesman. After attending Harrow and Trinity College, Cambridge, he spent three years at the Stazione Zoological in Naples, and made some important discoveries in the history of the elasmobranch fishes. His findings were recorded in a monograph which added much to existing knowledge of the development of urogenital and other organs in the vertebrates. From 1876 until his untimely death he lectured on animal morphology at Cambridge, where he gathered about him an enthusiastic group of students. The results of his researches were embodied in a complete two-volume textbook of embryology, which was the outstanding work on its subject in that day. At the age

of thirty he was killed while attempting to climb an unscaled mountain near Cormayeur, Switzerland. Burial was in his boyhood home of Whittinghame, East Lothian, Scotland.

PRINCIPAL WORK: A Treatise on Comparative Embryology, 1880-81.

BALL, SIR ROBERT STAWELL (July 1, 1840-November 25, 1913), Irish astronomer, mathematician, and expositor of science, was born in Dublin, the son of Robert Ball, a well-known naturalist. After winning scholastic prizes at Trinity College, Dublin, he served successively as professor of applied mathematics and mechanism at the Royal College of Science, Dublin (1867-74); professor of astronomy in the University of Dublin and royal astronomer of Ireland (1874-92); and professor of astronomy at Cambridge (1893-1913). Between 1877 and 1906 he wrote thirteen popular books on astronomy, and these, together with his wide-spread lectures, did much to arouse public interest in heavenly phenomena and to bring him world fame as an astronomer. Among scientists, however, he made his greatest reputation as a leisure-time mathematician with two scholarly treatises on the theory of screw motions and their relation. Knighthood was conferred upon him in 1886. By his wife, Frances Elizabeth Steele, he had four sons and two daughters. He died in Cambridge at seventy-three.

PRINCIPAL WORKS: The Theory of Screws: A Study in the Dynamics of a Rigid Body, 1876; The Story of the Heavens, 1886; The Story of the Sun, 1893; Great Astronomers, 1895; A Treatise on the Theory of Screws, 1900; The Earth's Beginnings, 1901; Popular Guide to the Heavens, 1905; Treatise on Spherical Astronomy, 1908.

ABOUT: Ball, W. V. Reminiscences and Letters of Sir Robert Ball.

BALLANTINE, JAMES (1808-December 1877), Scottish artist and poet, was born in Edinburgh. His first occupation was that of house-painter. After studying drawing at the Trustees' Gallery in Edinburgh, he revived the art of glass-painting, published a treatise on it, and headed the firm of Messrs. Ballantine, glass stainers, in Edinburgh. The stained-glass windows in the House of Lords were executed by him. Late in life he visited Jamaica for his health; he died in Edinburgh in his sixty-ninth year.

He is known as the author of "Ilka Blade o' Grass Keps Its Ain Drap o' Dew" and other popular Scotch songs, some of which appear in his prose volumes The Gaberlunzie's Wallet and The Miller of Deanhaugh.

PRINCIPAL WORKS: The Gaberlunzie's Wallet, 1843; The Miller of Deanhaugh, 1845; Essay on Ornamental Art, 1847; Poems, 1856; One Hundred Songs, With Music, 1865; The Life of David Roberts, R. A., 1866.

BALLANTYNE, ROBERT MICHAEL (April 24, 1825-February 8, 1894), Scottish author of stories for boys, was born in Edinburgh, a nephew of JAMES BALLANTYNE (1772-1833), the editor and publisher of Scott's works, and a brother of JAMES ROBERT BALLANTYNE (d. 1864), the Orientalist who made Hindu philosophy accessible to European readers.

Between the ages of sixteen and twenty-two he was a clerk with the Hudson Bay Fur Company in Canada, and during this time accumulated a store of fur-trading experiences which later served as the basis for some of his most successful tales. Before beginning (at thirty) his career in fiction, he worked seven years in the printing and publishing establishment of Thomas Constable in Edinburgh.

His first few books dealt with adventures in frozen Canada; later he befriended such colorful characters as lifeboat coxwains, lighthouse keepers, firemen, and Cornish miners, and traveled in Norway and Africa to gather material. In less than forty years he produced over eighty books which were widely popular, despite their instructive aim and the rivalry in the same field of Jules Verne, G. A. Henty, and others. His home in late years was at Harrow, England, and he died at the age of sixty-eight during a visit to Rome.

PRINCIPAL WORKS: The Young Fur Traders, 1856; Ungava: A Tale of Eskimo Land, 1857; The Coral Island, 1857; The World of Ice, 1859; The Dog Crusoe, 1860.

ABOUT: Ballantyne, R. M. Hudson's Bay: or, Life in the Wilds of North America; Ballantyne, R. M. Personal Reminiscences of Book-Making.

BANIM, JOHN (April 3, 1798-August 15, 1842) and BANIM, MICHAEL (August 5, 1796-August 30, 1874), Irish novelists, were born in Kilkenny, the sons of a prosperous farmer and trader.

The two boys were educated in their native city, Michael, the elder, studying for the bar, and John, who had artistic aspirations, leaving Kilkenny College in 1813 for Dublin, where he entered the Academy of the Royal Dublin Society. Here he worked hard and was successful, and for a time (1815-20) taught drawing in Kilkenny, but an unfortunate love-affair, ending in the death of the lady, rendered him so unhappy that he returned to Dublin, where, after a short artistic career, he transferred his activities to literature. Michael, in the meanwhile, had been obliged to give up his studies and to assist his father, who had suffered financial reverses. Thanks to the hard work of the son, the family was again made comfortable materially.

In 1822 the younger brother, who had already written a long poem, The Celt's Paradise, regarded favorably by Scott, and

JOHN BANIM

had produced a successful play, *Damon and Pythias*, suggested collaboration in the production of a series of Irish national tales; and accordingly the "O'Hara" collection was begun. The aim was to do for the Irish what Scott had done for his own people, and to represent them, not as a butt for ridicule or a subject of humor, but as a human folk, in all the tragedy of their existence. The first series, published in 1825, included *Crohoore of the Bill-Hook, The Fetches,* and *John Doe,* and the second was issued in the following year.

By this time John, who in 1822 had married a Miss Ellen Ruth of Kilkenny, was settled in London, and writing for magazines. His career, from this point on, was one of ill health, poverty, and struggle. He lost a child, and suffered from a spinal disease which resulted in the loss of use of both legs. After living for a while in Boulogne, he returned to Ireland, where he was honored publicly by his countrymen in 1835, making his home near Kilkenny until his death in 1842. His fortunes were assisted by subscription and by government pension.

Michael, who had been fairly prosperous, lost his money shortly after his marriage, in 1840, to a Miss Catherine O'Dwyer, and suffered in addition a serious illness. After a brave fight he recovered sufficiently to work on *Father Connell*. In 1852 he was given an appointment as postmaster in Kilkenny, which, despite ill health, he kept until 1873, when his health gave out completely. With his family he removed to Booterstown, on the coast of the County of Dublin, where, even with an allowance from the Royal Literary Fund, his last years were spent in hardship.

Upon his death the widow was given a pension on the Civil List.

While their struggles and disappointments do not make pleasant reading, the career of the Banim brothers is the record of a beautiful attachment and a warm mutual regard. On Christmas the toast was made regularly in the home at Kilkenny, "Health and long life to poor John and Ellen far away!"; and a similar one was made in London. "My creed," wrote Michael to the younger brother, who demurred at accepting aid, "is that one brother should not want while the other can supply him." John, less successful financially than his brother, was no less generous. It was largely thru his efforts that the artists of Dublin became incorporated and received a government grant; and in London he was a friend in need to the Irish novelist Gerald Griffin when the latter came there to embark upon his brief literary career. His own last hard years were sweetened by the affection and care of his brother.

In their work, as in their lives, the two were closely associated, and they examined and criticized each other's writings. The "O'Hara" tales, the greatest and most characteristic achievements of the Banims, are marked by intimacy with and insight into the Irish national character, especially that of the peasant class. Mary Russell Mitford, the essayist, referred to the character of Father Connell as "the portrait of a parish priest so exquisitely simple, natural, and tender, that in the whole range of fiction I know nothing more charming," and the same figure has been compared to that of Dr. Primrose in Goldsmith's *The Vicar of Wakefield*. While fault has been found with the overstrained and strong writing characteristic of the Banims, and with their tendencies toward melodrama and "horror," critics have praised the realism of their tales. The relative shares of the two authors in their collaborations have never been exactly determined; the younger has received more attention, possibly because of a superior poetic strain in his work, and, it is exceedingly likely, because of the self-effacing nature of his senior.

R. W. W.

PRINCIPAL WORKS OF JOHN BANIM: *Essays*—Revelations of the Dead-Alive, 1824. *Novels*—The Fetches, 1825; Boyne Water, 1826; The Nowlans, 1826; The Anglo-Irish of the Nineteenth Century, 1828; The Disowned, 1826; The Denounced, 1830; The Smuggler, 1831. *Plays*—Damon and Pythias, 1821; Turgesius, c. 1821; The Prodigal, c. 1823; The Sergeant's Wife, 1827. *Poem*—The Celt's Paradise, 1821.

PRINCIPAL WORKS OF MICHAEL BANIM: *Novels*—Crohoore of the Bill-Hook, 1825; The Croppy, 1828; The Ghost-Hunter and His Family, 1833; The Mayor of Wind-Gap, 1835; Clough Fion, 1852; The Town of the Cascades, 1864.

JOHN AND MICHAEL BANIM: *Novels*—John Doe, 1825; Peter of the Castle, 1826; Father Connell,

1842. *Poetry*—The Chaunt of the Cholera, 1831. *Miscellaneous*—The Bit o' Writin', 1838.

ABOUT: Murray, P. J. Life of John Banim; Read, C. A. The Cabinet of Irish Literature; Williams, A. M. The Poets and Poetry of Ireland; Irish Quarterly Review 4:270, 527, 825 June, September, December 1854; 5:24, 221, 477, 823 March, June, September, December 1855; 6:66 March 1856.

BARBAULD, ANNA LETITIA AIKIN

(June 20, 1743-March 9, 1825), writer of children's books, poet, critic, and essayist, was born at Kibworth Harcourt, Leicestershire, the only daughter of John Aikin, D.D. and Jane Jennings Aikin, also the daughter of a clergyman. She was educated at home by her parents. Her mother wrote that Anna was as eager to learn as to be taught, that at two she could read "without spelling," and that at two and a half "she could read as well as most women." Although her father too was proud of her uncommon capacity, for a long time he refused to teach her Latin and Greek. But Anna won, and learned both. Her childhood and early youth were not the happiest, but when she was fifteen her father moved to Warrington to teach in a Nonconformist ·(Unitarian) school. Here she lived happily for fifteen years, and began her literary career. She made lasting friends of Dr. Priestley, the famous chemist, and Dr. Enfield, later co-author with her brother John, and their families, and celebrated the academy in her poem "The Invitation."

It was to her brother that she owed her literary début and lifelong encouragement. He sent off her first poems to the printer when she hesitated. The same year (1773) she collaborated with him in a successful volume of prose pieces. Between the two from this time on there existed a remarkable friendship.

Shortly after this, while she was engaged to the Reverend Rochemont Barbauld (whom she married in 1774), a friend and admirer wanted her to start a college for young ladies, but Miss Aikin refused on the ground that young women would then not be "good wives or agreeable companions," and that "the best way for a women to acquire knowledge is from conversation with a father, or brother, or friend." In the meantime the Rev. Dr. Barbauld accepted the dissenting congregation of Palgrave in Suffolk, and decided to open a school. Mrs. Barbauld's reputation and her active part in the school were largely responsible for its immediate and continued success. She taught English, geography, and dramatics, and for the benefit of her pupils wrote and compiled books. Among these was the famous *Hymns in Prose for Children*. She adopted her brother's son Charles, and for him she wrote, in 1781, *Early Lessons*, another of the books on which her fame rests.

Even from the titles of these books it is evident that her object was to instruct first and delight afterwards. She agreed with Rousseau that a child "should steadily contemplate Nature," but added "that by so doing he will be led to contemplate the traditional God." Her children's books were translated into French and Italian and *Early Lessons* caused Mr. Richard Edgeworth, who was interested in children's education, to begin *Harry and Lucy* "to carry on Mrs. Barbauld's good work."

After teaching eleven years in Palgrave the Barbaulds took a vacation in southern France; then returned to Hampstead, where Mrs. Barbauld tutored two girls. Her brother felt that she was wasting her time and genius, and addressed a sonnet to her to induce her to write. This evidently had its effect, for she wrote her *Epistle to Mr. Wilberforce on the Rejection of the Bill for Abolishing the Slave Trade*, contributed fourteen pieces to her brother's first volume of *Evenings at Home*, and wrote several critical essays. In 1802 she and her husband moved to Newington Green, so that Mrs. Barbauld and her brother could be together. In 1804 she published her most successful book of literary criticism, criticism of selections from the *Spectator, Tatler, Guardian,* and *Freeholder,* and began editing Richardson's letters, on which our knowledge of his life largely rests. She continued writing to the end of her life. One of her poems, "Life," is in English anthologies; another, "Eighteen Hundred and Eleven," was the last of her separate publications.

Personally she was charming and friendly, and in her niece's words "was possessed of great beauty" of which "traces remained to

MRS. BARBAULD

the end of her life." She was fair and slender, and had shining dark blue eyes. She was devout, and wanted the young "to connect religion with a variety of sensible objects."

Of her literary work everybody from Lamb to Harvey Darton had something to say. Lamb objected because "Mrs. Barbauld's stuff has banished all the old classics of the nursery. . . " Samuel Johnson said that of all his imitators she had done it best; "for she has imitated the sentiment as well as the diction." (This was said of "On Romances" in *Miscellaneous Pieces*.) Critics agree that her verses "are not contemptible." Harvey Darton calls her critical essays "capable," and says of her juveniles, "Language like that [*Hymns in Prose*], so simple yet almost majestic, is worth giving to children. . . Mrs. Barbauld's masterly command of English has been rivalled by few other writers for children; . . . and if words alone sufficed, she would have achieved for all time her purpose in exciting wonder and delight in things seen."

V. M.

PRINCIPAL WORKS: *Juveniles*—Lessons for Children, 1780; Hymns in Prose for Children, 1781; Evenings at Home (6 vols., with J. Aikin) 1792-6; The Arts of Life (with J. Aikin) 1802. *Essays*—Miscellaneous Pieces (with J. Aikin) 1773; Devotional Pieces, 1775; Epistle to Mr. Wilberforce, etc., 1791; Remarks on Mr. Gilbert Wakefield's Inquiry, etc., 1793; Essay on Akenside's Pleasures of Imagination, 1795; Essay on the Odes of Collins, 1797; A Selection From the Spectator, Tatler, etc., 1804. *Editor*—Richardson's Correspondence, 1804; Collections of British Novelists, 1810. *Poetry*—Poems, 1773; The Female Speaker, 1811; Eighteen Hundred and Eleven, 1811.

ABOUT: Barbauld, A. L. The Works of Anna Letitia Barbauld (see Memoir by Lucy Aikin); Ellis, G. A. A Memoir of Mrs. Anna Letitia Barbauld; Darton, F. J. H. Children's Books in England; LeBreton, A. L. Memoir of Mrs. Barbauld.

BARHAM, RICHARD HARRIS (December 6, 1788-June 17, 1845), English humorist, novelist, and clergyman, was born at 61 Burgate, Canterbury. He was of the family for whom a village and the range of downs between Dover and Canterbury had been named. His father was an alderman, a bon vivant, and enormously fat; his mother was vivacious and fun-loving. Both were Kentish. Barham, then, was by birth as well as by sympathy and over thirty years' residence a man of Kent, and many scenes in *The Ingoldsby Legends* are unmistakably Kentish.

He received his preliminary education in Canterbury, and in 1797 went to St. Paul's School, London, where he became a friend of his future publisher, Richard Bentley. He was encouraged by the headmaster to write speeches, and was invited by the headmaster's wife to gatherings of literary women. For two years he was "captain" of St. Paul's. "Barham describes himself as 'a fat, little, punchy concern of sixteen' in these days—a description which held good all his life, for he was short in person, broadly built and deep-chested," wrote S. M. Ellis.

He next went to Brasenose College, Oxford, where he was just an average undergraduate, extravagant and wild. After receiving his B.A. he returned to Canterbury and founded, according to Ellis, "the convivial Wig Club whose members in masquerade took part in burlesque debates in the summer-house in Barham's gardens." In 1813 his mother died, and he suffered a severe illness. As a result his views and conduct changed. He gave up all thought of the law to enter the ministry. In 1814 he was curate of Westwell, Kent, when he married Caroline Smart, a daughter of a captain of the Royal Engineers. He next got the living of Snargate and the curacy of Warehorne in the dreary Romney Marsh. His parishioners were smugglers who commandeered the church belfry to store their contraband tobacco. He broke a leg in a gig accident, and wrote his novel *Baldwin* in a few weeks while recovering. In 1821 he was elected a minor canon of St. Paul's. He moved to London with his wife and three children, and in his leisure wrote light tropical articles and poetry for *John Bull*, the *Literary Gazette*, the *Globe and Traveller*, and *Blackwood's Magazine*, edited the *London Chronicle*, and contributed about two-thirds of *Gorton's Biographical Dictionary*. In three years he was appointed Priest-in-Ordinary to the Chapel Royal, and shortly afterwards received the gift of the livings of St. Mary Magdalene and St. Gregory by St. Paul. It was during these next fifteen years that he reached his peak in society and in the literary world. He had an astonishing number of clever and witty friends, among them Theodore Hook, the

RICHARD HARRIS BARHAM

practical joker and novelist, Harrison Ainsworth, novelist, Sydney Smith and Edward Cannon, the witty priests, and Mr. and Mrs. Hughes, grandparents of the author of *Tom Brown's Schooldays.* His diary is full of references to these people, and jammed with the stories they told. To Mrs. Hughes he owed most. It was she who sent the unfinished script of his novel *My Counsin Nicholas* to Blackwood, the publisher, who accepted it, thus compelling Barham to finish it. It was she too who gave him some of the ghost stories and legends that produced *The Ingoldsby Legends,* for, as he said, "give me a story to tell, and I can tell it in my own way; but I can't invent one." The *Legends* were first published in *Bentley's Miscellany,* then edited by Charles Dickens, and the first of the series was "The Spectre of Tappington" in the January 1837 issue. In 1840 *The Ingoldsby Legends* by Thomas Ingoldsby were first published in book form. Thomas Ingoldsby was soon discovered to be Richard Barham, and Barham enjoyed the success. He ridiculed (because he dreaded) all signs of Popery creeping into the Established church, and this (besides a sometimes vulgar humor) is why some hostile criticism has always existed against the *Legends.*

Barham wrote easily or not at all, at night, and often with the aid of gin. He was devoted to cats; one or two sat on his table or his shoulder as he wrote.

The last five years of his life he was inconsolable over the loss of his favorite son Ned; some of the sorrow went into the poem "As I Laye a-Thynkynge"; a second shock was the death of his good friend Theodore Hook. Barham died at the age of fifty-six, aftei having "made careful disposition of everything—even the cats."

"His career," wrote George Saintsbury, "was one of unostentatious, but real, work in his profession, varied by the writing of some novels (whereof the chief is *My Cousin Nicholas*) and of the famous verses by which he is still known. . . He had good humor, good feeling, good breeding, an immense sense of fun and an inexhaustible fund of rhymes and rhythms, . . . and in the kind of burlesque poetical narrative I am quite sure that Thomas Ingoldsby never has had a superior, and I think it extremely improbable that he ever will have one."

Barham is remembered only for *The Ingoldsby Legends.* There was a time when every schoolboy knew them by heart, so great was their popularity.   V. M.

PRINCIPAL WORKS: *Novels*—Baldwin, 1820; My Cousin Nicholas, 1841. The Ingoldsby Legends, 1840-1847.

ABOUT: Barham, R. H. D. The Life and Letters of Richard Harris Barham; Saintsbury, G. Essays in English Literature (2nd ser.); The Bookman 112:51 January 1917; The Manchester Quarterly 187:38 January 1919.

BARING-GOULD, SABINE (January 28, 1834-January 2, 1924), novelist, essayist, and miscellaneous writer, was born in Exeter, eldest son of the squire of the 3,000 acres of Lew-Trenchard, North Devon, and grandson of an admiral. He secured his B.A. and M.A. from Clare College, Cambridge, which later made him an Honorary Fellow. Before taking orders he made an extended tour to Iceland in 1861. Immediately after being ordained priest, in 1864, he became a curate at Horbury, Yorkshire.

This was a mill town, and the wealthy, aristocratic young clergyman fell madly in love with Grace Taylor, a beautiful mill-hand. He paid for her education at York, and in 1868 married her. The marriage was ideally happy until her death in 1916.

In 1866 Baring-Gould became vicar at Dalton, Yorkshire, and in 1872 rector at East Mersea, Essex. In 1872 his father died, and he inherited Lew-Trenchard, to which he retired for the remainder of his long life. The estate had a living in its gift, held at the time by Baring-Gould's uncle. The uncle died in 1881, and Baring-Gould presented himself as vicar, serving until his death. He was also the local justice of the peace. Baring-Gould has been called "the last of the squarsons," a word coined from the combination of "squire" and "parson."

He was a writer of simply dizzying prolificity. The mere list of his published works is exhausting. He poured forth religious homilies, travel books, novels, and verse, often several volumes in a year, and he kept on writing (though not quite so voluminously) until a year before his death from old age, less than a month before his ninetieth birthday.

S. BARING-GOULD

Naturally the great majority of these almost innumerable volumes were mere hack work; they could be nothing else, written at such speed. Occasionally, however, he rose to greater heights, in such *curiosa* of literature as *The Book of Were-Wolves* and *Historic Survivals,* or in his rather stodgy, "dated," and pious novels. Perhaps in the end his name (which he always signed as S. Baring-Gould) will be remembered for some simple verses—the words of the two well-known hymns, "Onward Christian Soldiers" (music by Sir Arthur Sullivan) and "Now the Day is Over."

M. A. deF.

PRINCIPAL WORKS: *Religious Works*—The Path of the Just, 1854; Post-Mediaeval Preachers, 1865; Origin and Development of Religious Belief, 1869-70; The Golden Gate, 1870; The Silver Store, 1870; In Exitu Israel, 1870; Legendary Lives of Old Testament Characters, 1871; A Hundred Sermon Sketches for Extempore Preachers, 1872; Secular *v.* Religious Education, 1872; Lives of the Saints, 1872; Village Conferences on the Creed, 1873; The Lost and Hostile Gospels, 1874; Some Modern Difficulties, 1875; Village Sermons for a Year, 1875; The Mystery of Suffering, 1877; Sermons to Children, 1879; The Preacher's Pocket, 1880; The Village Pulpit, 1881; Village Preaching for a Year, 1884; The Seven Last Words, 1884; The Passion of Jesus, 1885; The Nativity, 1885; Our Parish Church, 1886; The Resurrection, 1888; Our Inheritance, 1888; Conscience and Sin, 1890; History of the Church in Germany, 1891; A Study of St. Paul, 1897; The Sunday Round, 1898; Virgin Saints and Martyrs, 1900; The Restitution of All Things, 1907; The Church Revival, 1914; The Evangelical Revival, 1920. *Travel*—Iceland: Its Scenes and Sagas, 1862; Germany: Present and Past, 1879; Germany, 1886; In Troubadours' Land, 1890; The Deserts of Southern France, 1894; A Book of the West, 1899; A Book of Dartmoor, 1900; In the Roar of the Sea, 1892; A Book of North Wales, 1903; In Dewisland, 1905; A Book of South Wales, 1905; A Book of the Riviera, 1905; A Book of the Rhine, 1906; A Book of the Pyrenees, 1907; A Book of the Cevennes, 1908; The Land of Teck, 1911; Cliff Castles and Cave Dwellings, 1911. *Fiction*—Mehalah, 1880; John Herring, 1883; Court Royal, 1886; Red Spider, 1887; The Gaverocks, 1887; Richard Cable, 1888; Eve, 1888; The Pennycomequicks, 1889; Arminell, 1889; Urith, 1890; Mrs. Curnenven, 1893; Cheap Jack Zita, 1893; The Queen of Love, 1804; Old Fairy Tales Retold, 1894; Noemi, 1895; The Old English Fairy Tales, 1895; The Broom Squire, 1896; Guavas the Tinner, 1897; Bladys, 1897; Domitia, 1898; Pabo the Priest, 1899; Furze-Bloom, 1899; The Crock of Gold, 1899; Winefred, 1900; In a Quiet Village, 1900; The Frobishers, 1901; Miss Quillet, 1902; Chris of All Sorts, 1903. *Verse*—Church Songs, 1884; Songs of the West, 1891; A Garland of Country Song, 1894. *Miscellaneous*—Book of Were-Wolves, 1865; Curious Myths of the Middle Ages, 1866; Historic Oddities, 1889; Old Country Life, 1889; Curious Survivals, 1892; Napoleon Bonaparte, 1896; A Book of Ghosts, 1904; A Memorial of Nelson, 1905; Devonshire Characters, 1908; Cornish Characters, 1909; Family Names, 1910; Early Reminiscences (1834-64) 1923.

ABOUT: Baring-Gould, S. Early Reminiscences; Literary Digest 80:4:33 January 26, 1924; Outlook 136:90 January 16, 1924.

BARNARD, CHARLOTTE ALINGTON

December 23, 1830-January 30, 1869), writer of ballads under the pseudonym of "Clari-

bel," was educated in music and singing by private teachers and was married at twenty-four to Charles Cary Barnard. In her twenty-eighth year she began to compose drawing-room songs, and during the eleven years that remained of her life she produced about a hundred ballads which enjoyed great popularity in their time but were (most of them) quickly forgotten. Usually she wrote both words and music. She published three collections of her songs and verses, and died in Dover, Kent, England, at thirty-nine.

PRINCIPAL WORKS: Thoughts, Verses, and Songs; Songs and Verses.

BARNES, WILLIAM (March 20, 1801-October 7, 1886), poet, came of an old line of yeomen who had tilled the soil of northern Dorsetshire for centuries. He was the son of John and Grace (Scott) Barnes who leased a farm in the Vale of Blackmore-Rushay in the parish of Bagbere.

This beautiful, secluded valley, through which runs the river Stour, is the inspiration of most of his dialect poems. So "far from the madding crowd" was this little corner that in William Barnes' boyhood it still retained the modes and manners of the 17th and 18th centuries to a greater degree than did most parts of rural England.

He attended a school in the village of Sturminster until 1815, when a local solicitor came to the school to find a boy "clever enough with the quill" to copy deeds in his office. William was selected, and thus was opened to him greater opportunities for study than would ordinarily have come the way of a farm-boy of his time and country.

Three years later young Barnes moved to Dorchester where greater opportunities for study were opened to him by the rector, John Richman. His particular interest was philology, and he acquired extensive knowledge of a surprising number of languages and dialects.

The first of his poetical efforts to get into print appeared in the local weekly paper. Some of these were "Verses to Julia," the daughter of a local exciseman, to whom Barnes became engaged in 1822—the same year in which his first book was published.

The following year (1823) his self-education had progressed sufficiently to enable him to obtain the mastership of a small school at Mere in Wiltshire. Here he remained for twelve years.

The study of languages was his greatest interest and the extent of his knowledge ranged from Hindustani to Welsh, from Italian and French to Persian, Hebrew, Russian, and early Saxon. But his interests were unlimited. He took up engraving and woodcutting, illustrating several books. Gardening was one of his chief delights. He was an

WILLIAM BARNES

archeologist whose contributions to various journals were given serious consideration. He was an inventor, a musician, and an abstract mathematician. He assisted General Shrapnel with calculations for his famous shell. All of his writing was not in poetry, and all of his poems were not in dialect, yet, oddly enough, it is for these dialect poems almost exclusively that William Barnes is remembered today.

In 1835 Barnes returned to Dorchester with a boarding school of his own, which prospered sufficiently to require larger quarters within two years. Signing up at St. Johns College, Cambridge, as a ten year man in 1838, he was ordained by the Bishop of Salisbury in 1847 and made pastor of Whitcombe, three miles from his school. He discharged his new duties without relinquishing his school. The new dignity, in fact, brought the school into greater favor. In 1850 he graduated from Cambridge with the degree of Bachelor of Divinity.

During this period (1835-50) he contributed many articles and poems to periodicals, and the first volume of *Poems of Rural Life* had appeared in 1844. He was also engaged with his philological researches, particularly in Anglo-Saxon and related Teutonic tongues. These resulted in the publication of a number of learned volumes. In 1860 he was given a pension from the civil list, at the unsolicited instigation of Lord Palmerston; and in 1862 he became rector of Winterbourne Came church where he remained until his death.

Thomas Hardy, writing his obituary notice for *The Athenaeum* said: " . . . people who have seen him only in latter years, since the pallor and stoop of old age overcame him, cannot realize the robust, upright form of his middle life, the ruddy cheek and the bright quick eye. The last, indeed, dimmed but slightly, and even on his death-bed his zest . . . was strong as ever." And John Drinkwater tells how the old poet upon his death-bed, awoke one morning feeling rather better and wrote a poem, "and a very good one, out of lightness of heart."

Of his poetry, Thomas Hardy says: "Unlike Burns, Beranger, and other poets of the people, Mr. Barnes never assumed the high conventional style; and he entirely leaves alone ambition, pride, despair, defiance, and other of the grander passions which move mankind, great and small. His rustics are, as a rule, happy people, and very seldom feel the sting of the rest of modern mankind—the disproportion between the desire for serenity and the power of obtaining it. . . . Their pathos, after all, is the attribute upon which the poems must depend for their endurance. . . ."

D. C.

PRINCIPAL WORKS: *Poetry*—Poems of Rural Life in the Dorset Dialect, 1844; Homely Rhymes, 1859; Poems of Rural Life (third collection) 1862. *Philology*—A Philological Grammar, 1854; Tiw: or, A View of the Roots and Stems of the English as a Teutonic Tongue, 1862; A Grammar and Glossary of the Dorset Dialect, 1863.

ABOUT: Baxter, L. Life of William Barnes; Drinkwater, J. A Book for Bookmen; Hewlett, M. Extemporary Essays; Powys, L. Thirteen Worthies; Woodberry, G. E. Literary Memoirs of the 19th Century.

BARRETT, WILSON February 18, 1846- July 22, 1904), actor-manager and dramatist, was born William Henry Barrett in Essex, England, the son of a farmer. At twenty he was married to Caroline Heath, a leading actress, eleven years his senior, and together they successfully toured the provinces for many years. Subsequently he operated several theatres in London. When his wife retired in ill health, he presented Madame Helena Modjeska to the English public and started her towards fame. His own acting triumphs were in Henry Arthur Jones' *The Silver King* and George R. Sims' *Lights o' London*; he also won popularity with *Hamlet*. He frequently appeared in his own plays, of which the most successful was *The Sign of the Cross*, a religious melodrama that played a year in London. More often than not he wrote in collaboration; Hall Caine was a frequent collaborator. Six times he took his company on tour of America. He died of cancer in London at the age of fifty-eight, leaving two sons, a daughter, and an estate of £30,000.

PRINCIPAL PLAYS: Hoodman Blind (with H. A. Jones) 1885; Sister Mary (with Clement Scott) 1886; Clito (with Sydney Grundy) 1886; The Lord Harry (with H. A. Jones) 1886; The Golden Ladder (with G. R. Sims) 1887; Ben-My-Chree (with Hall Caine) 1888; The Good Old Times (with Hall Caine) 1889; Nowadays, 1889; The People's Idol (with Victor Widnell) 1890; The

Sign of the Cross, 1896; The Daughters of Babylon, 1897; Man and His Makers (with Louis N. Parker) 1899; Quo Vadis? (adapted from Sienkiewicz's novel) 1900; The Christian King, 1902; Lucky Durham, 1905.

BARROW, SIR JOHN (1764-November 23, 1848), secretary of the British Admiralty and author of travel works, was born in the village of Dragley Beck, parish of Ulverston, in Lancashire. With only a grammar school education, he became private secretary to George Macartney, noted diplomatist, and accompanied him on government missions to China (1792-94) and to South Africa (1796-98). Beginning in 1804, he was for forty years second secretary of the Admiralty, in which capacity he made a distinguished record as the promoter (and historian) of Arctic exploration. Point Barrow, Cape Barrow, and Barrow Strait were named in his honor; and he was created baronet in 1835. He was the founder of the Royal Geographical Society. In literature he is best remembered for his accounts of travel in China, particularly the observations of Oriental life recorded in his interesting *Autobiography*. Notable, too, is his *Life of Lord Macartney*, which Southey called the most skillfully written book of its kind he had ever read.

PRINCIPAL WORKS: Travels to the Interior of South Africa, 1801-04; Travels in China, 1804; A Voyage to Cochin-China, 1806; Life of Lord Macartney, 1807; Chronological History of Arctic Voyages, 1818; Life of Lord Howe, 1838; Voyages of Discovery and Research Within the Arctic Regions From 1818 to the Present Time, 1846; Autobiography, 1847.

ABOUT: Barrow, J. Autobiography; Staunton, G. Memoir of Sir John Barrow.

BARTON, BERNARD (January 31, 1784-February 19, 1849), poet, was born in London, the son of John Barton, a Quaker manufacturer, and Mary (Done) Barton, who was likewise a member of the Society of Friends. His mother died a few days after his birth and John Barton was married a second time to Elizabeth Horne, who brought up the three children as her own. When Mr. Barton died at Hertford, where he was engaged in the malting business, Mrs. Barton moved to her father's house at Tottenham, taking with her her own son and her step-children.

Bernard was educated at a Quaker school in Ipswich, although when he was fourteen he was apprenticed to Samuel Jesup, who was a shopkeeper at Halstead in Essex. In 1806, however, he went to Woodbridge, where he not only married Jesup's niece, Lucy, but also entered into the coal and corn business with her brother (1807).

The next year his wife died, leaving an only daughter named for herself. Barton left town almost immediately to go to Liver-

BERNARD BARTON

pool as a tutor in the home of Mr. Waterhouse, a merchant there. A year later he returned to Woodbridge to take the position of managing clerk in Messrs. Alexander's bank, where he worked until his death.

His father is said to have been "of a literary turn." So it is not surprising that in 1812 the son published a first book of poems, which he entitled *Metrical Effusions*. About the same time, too, Barton began his long correspondence with Southey as well as his friendship with the Scottish poet, James Hogg. Two other volumes appeared in 1818, the anonymous *Convict's Appeal* and *Poems by an Amateur*, which were followed by *Poems* and *Napoleon*.

His success in these ventures gave him the idea that he would like to devote his life to literature. In his youth he had, he confessed, scribbled verses on the sly. But in the bank he was compelled to "keep verses at arm's length." So he decided to quit the bank. His good friend, Charles Lamb, however, prevented him from taking this rash step, and he continued his clerking in spite of the fact that in 1824 the Society of Friends made him a gift of £1200.

The bank business kept him in Woodbridge, where he lived, first in lodgings at the house of the Quakeress, Ann Knight, and later in the home of his employers. Only occasionally did he go to London to see Lamb or to Whitehall to look in on Sir Robert Peel, who granted him a pension of £100 a year. His life in the country was sedentary, for, when he was not writing verse for the annuals in his leisure, he was not taking exercise. Instead he spent his time sitting in the grass watching the ebb and flow of the tide.

This kind of life, perhaps, more than anything else, had a bad effect on his health. He was never "dangerously ill," said his son-in-law, "till the last year of his life." But on the evening of February 19, 1849, he was found dying by his daughter (who edited his works and afterwards married Edward Fitzgerald).

Although Barton was called the "Quaker poet" he was not a "stiff Quaker." He wore the dress of his sect, but it was a modified costume, and he dropped the customary "thees" and "thous" when out in society. Indeed, he was "dressed in sober brown," but "his face was plump and florid; and over a steaming tumbler he was far more jocose than a Quaker usually chooses to be." Charles Lamb nicknamed him "B.B.," and it is for his association with Lamb that Barton is chiefly known.

In his own day, however, he was famous as a poet. Jeffrey reviewed him favorably. A Suffolk ship-owner named his vessel "The Bernard Barton." His work was usually of "a domestic and religious cast," and his style was always easy and natural. But to the modern critic the very fluency constitutes a fault, and Barton's poems are condemned for their lack of polish.   B. D. S.

PRINCIPAL WORKS: *Poetry*—Metrical Effusions, 1812; Convict's Appeal, 1818; Poems by an Amateur, 1818; A Day in Autumn, 1820; Poems, 1820; Verses on the Death of Percy Bysshe Shelley, 1822; Napoleon and Other Poems, 1822; Poetic Vigils, 1824; A Missionary's Memorial, 1826; Devotional Verses, 1826; A Widow's Tale and Other Poems, 1827; A New Year's Eve, 1828; The Reliquary, 1836; On the Signs of the Times, 1838; Household Verses, 1845; Sea-Weeds, 1846; A Memorial of J. J. Gurney, 1847; Birthday Verses at Sixty-Four, 1848; Ichabod, 1848. *Prose*—A Brief Memorial of Major E. Moor, 1848.

ABOUT: Barton, B. Selections From Poems and Letters (see Memoir by Edward Fitzgerald); Lamb, C. Letters; Lucas, E. V. Bernard Barton and His Friends; Good Words 36:236 April 1895; Knickerbocker 39:514 June 1852; Living Age 61: 195 1859.

BATES, HENRY WALTER (February 8, 1825-February 16, 1892), naturalist and travel author, was born in Leicester, England, the son of a hosiery manufacturer. Educated briefly at a boarding school, he was apprenticed at thirteen to a local hosier and later worked for a time as office clerk at Burton-on-Trent. In his twenty-third year he went with Alfred Russell Wallace to Brazil, where he remained eleven years and discovered more than 8,000 entomological species new to science. As a result of his observations, he offered the first plausible explanation for the protective coloring of animals and insects. Upon his return to England he wrote (at Darwin's suggestion) an account of the expedition, *Naturalist on the Amazons,* his only book, which is ranked as one of the outstand-

ing travel works in English literature. He edited a number of works on natural history and topography, and served twenty-eight years as assistant secretary of the Royal Geographical Society. He died of bronchitis at sixty-seven, survived by his wife Sarah Ann Mason of Leicester and their three children.

WORK: Naturalist on the Amazons, 1863.
ABOUT: Bates, H. W. Naturalist on the Amazons (see Memoir by Edward Clodd in 1892 reprint); Clodd, E. Pioneers of Evolution.

BAYLY, THOMAS HAYNES (October 13, 1797-April 22, 1839), songwriter, novelist, and dramatist, was the only child of a well-to-do and influential family of Bath. On his father's side he was a cousin of the Earl of Stamford and Warrington, while his mother's connections included Viscount Middleton, the Countess of Errol and Baroness Le Despencer.

At the age of seven his mother found him dramatizing a tale from one of his story-books, and this precocious literary bent continued to manifest itself throughout his school days. At Winchester he wrote a weekly newspaper chronicling events of the classroom and playground.

When he was seventeen his father made a brief attempt to attract young Bayly to his own profession—the law. But his mind turned inevitably toward gayer and more amusing work, the writing of humorous articles for periodicals. About this time the publication of a small volume, *Rough Sketches of Bath,* brought him favorable notice from the public.

He next decided upon a career in the Church, and to that end he entered Oxford. He remained three years at St. Mary Hall, but did not apply himself very diligently. Dur-

THOMAS HAYNES BAYLY

ing the latter part of his stay at Oxford, Bayly fell in love with a young woman of Bath, but owing to the fact that he was entirely dependent upon his father, who refused or was unable to make a settlement upon him, the girl's family would not consent to the match.

To forget his unhappy love affair he traveled about Scotland and Ireland. In Dublin he mingled with the most brilliant society and distinguished himself in private theatricals, as well as writing some successful ballads. Returning to England in 1824, Bayly determined upon a literary career instead of the church. This proved to be profitable, and in 1826 his income was sufficient to make him seem a desirable match—not only to Miss Hayes but to her mother as well.

While on their honeymoon Bayly wrote the song "I'd Be a Butterfly," which had a great popular success. This was followed shortly by a novel, *The Aylmers*. In all, Bayly wrote some thirty-six dramatic pieces and several hundred songs of the "drawing room ballad" type. Many of his plays enjoyed considerable popularity. *Perfection,* which came to be regarded as the best of these, was written during a stagecoach journey from Bath to London.

Bayly was also one of the chief conductors of the political paper *John Bull.* This sheet was threatened with libel actions so frequently that the contributors, including Bayly, were forced to remain prudently anonymous.

Bayly's reputation has faded steadily since the vogue for sentimental ballads of his era has gone out of fashion. In this respect he suffers by comparison with Praed, whose style he often imitated. The *Cambridge History of English Literature,* while referring to the whole school of lesser poets of his class as "twitterers," says: "Perhaps contempt might be qualified by a little affection if they (Bayly's songs) were more read, for there is pathos and (independently of the famous composers who 'set' him) music in Bayly. But it is too often, if not invariably, frittered away."

D. C.

PRINCIPAL WORKS: *Prose*—Rough Sketches of Bath, c. 1816; The Aylmers, 1827; *Drama*—Perfection, 1836; *Poetry*—Parliamentary Letters and Other Poems, c.1820; Kindness in Women; Weeds of Witchery, 1837; Songs, Ballads, and Other Poems, 1844.

ABOUT: Bayly, J. H. Songs, Ballads, and Other Poems (see Memoir).

BAYNES, THOMAS SPENCER (March 24, 1823-May 31, 1887), philosopher and editor, was born at Wellington, in Somerset, the son of a Baptist minister. Through his mother, he was a descendent of John Ash, eighteenth century lexicographer. At Edinburgh University he studied logic under Sir William Hamilton and later assisted him in his classes for a time. He was successively

editor of the *Edinburgh Guardian* (1850-54), assistant editor of the London *Daily News* (1858-64), and professor of logic, metaphysics, and English literature at St. Andrews (1864-87). His death occurred at sixty-four in London.

He is known chiefly for his exposition of Sir William Hamilton's views in an essay on logic which won the prize in Hamilton's class when he was twenty-three. His other works include studies throwing new light on Shakespeare. The ninth edition of the *Encyclopaedia Britannica* was edited by him (1873-87).

PRINCIPAL WORKS: An Essay on the New Analytic of Logical Forms, 1850; Arnauld's *Port Royal Logic* (tr.) 1851; Shakespeare Studies and Other Essays, 1894.

ABOUT: Baynes, T. S. Shakespeare Studies (see Memoir by Lewis Campbell).

BEACONSFIELD, LORD. See DISRAELI, BENJAMIN

BEARDSLEY, AUBREY VINCENT (August 21, 1872-March 16, 1898), illustrator and writer, was born at Brighton of a family in reduced circumstances that (without satisfactory evidence) claimed descent from the great Pitt. His earliest education was at Brighton and Hurstpierspoint; then, as the boy's health already caused concern (he was showing tubercular symptoms at the age of nine), he was taken to Epsom; but by the time he was twelve he was back in Brighton as a day pupil at the Grammar School.

This was all his schooling. In 1888, at sixteen, with less than ten years of life still before him, he was apprenticed to an architect. His few months there, together with a still shorter time later at a London art school, gave him all the formal training in art he ever received.

Beardsley's enormous erudition in literature likewise was achieved by his own endeavors. So was his proficiency in music, his natural talent for which was so great that when he was only eleven, he and his sister Mabel (later an actress) were billed together in concerts as "infant musical prodigies." Only his overwhelming genius for drawing, which attracted attention even in his school-days, saved him from a fatal versatility.

For two years, from 1889 to 1891, Beardsley, who had now moved to London, earned his way as clerk in the Guardian Life and Fire Assurance Company—surely the strangest insurance clerk who ever lived. In every spare hour he was drawing, and the quality of his work brought him the friendship and counsel of artists as different as Burne-Jones and Puvis de Chavannes. But his great friend and guide was Frederick Evans, a publisher and bookseller, who introduced the boy around and secured him his first good commission, the illustrations for an edition of Malory's *Morte d'Arthur* being brought out by Dent and Company. Beardsley was able to abandon commerce forever and to devote himself entirely to his art.

In 1893 he burst upon the London world like a sky-rocket. His strange and bizarre drawings became the rage, the center of heated controversies, attacks, and defenses equally impassioned. His single line work with its mass of black, subtly Japanesque and daringly perverse, was the very expression of his age. As Holbrook Jackson says, "his appearance at any other time would have been inopportune," and his limited and local art was "archaic before he died." He founded no school, left no followers; he was unique, the flower of his mannered, artificial epoch.

Beardsley was chosen by Henry Harland to be the art editor of the famous *Yellow Book*, and so acted for the first four numbers (1894-95). But Harland was trying to draw too many disparate fish into his literary net. One of his "big names," William Watson, refused to allow his poems to appear if Beardsley's drawings were to be in the same magazine; and he had the support of Mrs. Humphry Ward, who carried behind her conservative protests the weighty prestige of the Arnold family. Harland gave way; the original fifth issue (April 1895, the month of the Wilde trial) was canceled, and Beardsley was dropped. In January 1896, when Arthur Symons founded *The Savoy*, he invited Beardsley to become its art editor.

Not only did Beardsley draw for *The Savoy*, but he contributed to it his only published writings. These were three short poems and a highly embellished and erotic prose version of the Tannhäuser story. This rococo romance appears never to have been finished; its author called it "Venus and Tannhäuser," but the abbreviated and expurgated fragment which was published in *The Savoy* was entitled "Under the Hill." Even in its emasculated form it is a gem of brilliant decadence, "a mosaic of artificiality" which "creates life out of cosmetics and aberrations" (Holbrook Jackson). Beardsley is perhaps the only man whose claim to representation in a dictionary of literature rests on so slender an array of published work.

Disaster, regeneration, and the end were close upon his heels. The man whose magnificent, decorative illustrations of *The Rape of the Lock, Mlle. de Maupin,* and Dowson's *Pierrot of the Minute* had made him a storm-center, the quintessence of the decadent school which so curiously polished off the age of Victoria, seemed the logical illustrator of Oscar Wilde. In fact, he illustrated only *Salome,* and his drawings for that play, though Wilde himself thought them too Japanese for his

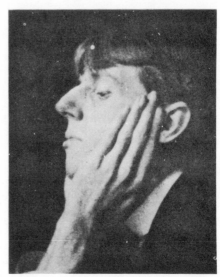

AUBREY BEARDSLEY

Byzantine style, are justly among his most celebrated. But in the fall of Wilde others were dragged down who had the merest hold on the hem of his garments. Beardsley had no share in Wilde's sexual perversion, he did not even like Wilde personally, but he had long been fair game and the outraged herd turned on him, glad of so ornamental a victim. The precedent of the *Yellow Book* was remembered; John Lane, who had been Beardsley's regular source of publication and commissions, now dropped him abruptly; again Mrs. Humphry Ward seems to have been among the orthodox who used their drawing-power as a weapon against him.

Beardsley was shocked to the depths by this treacherous injustice. Embittered, he plunged for a while into dissipation, went about denying charges that no one had ever made against him who knew him at all. He fell into the hands of a new and dubious publisher, a man who specialized in erotica, and for whom he did a number of drawings—notably the illustrations for *Lysistrata*—that were technically superb but almost unprintable. In the midst of this turmoil his lifelong tendency to tuberculosis flared up. Sick in body and mind, he underwent a profound religious experience, from which he emerged a totally different man for the short time left to him. In March 1897, with only a year to live, he was received into the Roman Catholic Church.

In 1895 he had spent a summer in Dieppe with Symons and other friends. As his illness progressed he returned there, with his mother and sister. As late as September 1897 he had hopes of full recovery. But in March 1898, at Mentone, he died. Almost his last act was to write—in vain—to his publisher, imploring him—"in my death agony"—to destroy "all obscene drawings."

This gay and gracious boy, loved by all who knew him, this adorer of social life, this indefatigable worker who joyed in his work and was full of a fine vanity utterly without conceit, this marvelous conversationalist and light-hearted poseur, died in the odor of sanctity. But it is the Beardsley who was actual, not one who was potential, who must be considered in any estimate of his work as artist or writer. His emaciated figure, his pale hatchet face, his mop of straight fine brown hair tumbling over his green eyes, have been immortalized in Rothenstein's drawings and Beerbohm's caricatures; his lovable and generous spirit, varnished over with a veneer of debonair affectation, lived on in the hearts of his friends to hide the gentle saint who might have been.

Outside of three poems—charmingly mannered, artificial, "naughty"—and a dialogue begun with William Rothenstein but never finished, all that Beardsley wrote was *Under the Hill*. He has been called "the most literary of modern artists," and he was among the most artistic of all modern litterateurs. Every phrase he wrote was conscious, precocious, gracefully elegant, almost too polished, instinct with an exaggerated urbanity, with the "ennui of sin." Most of this was an excited boyish pose, to *épater les bourgeoises*—a pose by which nature became the only abnormality. Huysmans was the spiritual father of "Under the Hill"—and Huysmans followed later the same path to Golgotha and to Rome. But this unfinished fragment is a masterpiece of literary eroticism, the very final flower of the age of decadence which forced and fostered Beardsley's exotic art.

As stated above, the only publication of Beardsley's writings during his lifetime was through the medium of *The Savoy* in 1896. In 1903—five years after his death—these fragments, together with some others previously unpublished, were collected in book form as *Under the Hill and Other Essays in Prose and Verse*. Some years later an unexpurgated version of "Under the Hill" was printed privately as *The Story of Venus and Tannhäuser*. In 1904 *The Last Letters of Aubrey Beardsley* made its appearance. This completes the record of Beardsley's published literary work. In addition, several collections of his drawings (*Early Work, Later Work, Uncollected Work*, etc.) have appeared in book form.　　　　　　　　M. A. deF.

WORKS: see paragraph above.
ABOUT: Beardsley, A. V. Later Work (see Biographical Note by H. C. Marillier); Beardsley, A. V. Uncollected Work (see Introduction by C. L. Hind); Jackson, H. The Eighteen Nineties; Ross, R. Aubrey Beardsley; Rothenstein, W. Men and Memories; Symons, A. Aubrey Beardsley.

BECKFORD, WILLIAM (October 1, 1760-May 2, 1844), writer of Oriental tales and travel-books, was born at Fonthill-Gifford, Wiltshire, son and namesake of a famous and very opulent ex-Lord Mayor of London, the descendant of a shoemaker, and his wife, Maria, daughter of the Hon. George Hamilton, of the titled Hamilton family. Owing to Mrs. Beckford's prejudice against formal instruction William was not sent either to school or university. A clergyman called John Lettice was his general tutor: he learned French from a native, music from Mozart, and architecture from Sir William Chambers.

As a youth he evinced considerable originality and sensibility. Lord Chatham, his godfather, pronounced him to be "all air and fire," and felt it necessary to warn him against reading the *Arabian Nights*. In 1776 he went to stay with relatives in Geneva and remained there for some eighteen months. His first book, *Biographical Memoirs of Extraordinary Painters*, appeared in 1780. It is a high-spirited production, written partly as a burlesque of the Fonthill housekeeper's descriptions of the pictures there, and partly as a satire on certain schools of painting, notably the Dutch and Flemish.

In 1783 he married Lady Margaret Gordon, who, after bearing him two daughters, died in 1786. In April 1782 he had finished a work of travel called *Dreams, Waking Thoughts, and Incidents,* written up from notes made during a journey through Holland, Germany, Austria, and Italy, taken with Lettice in 1780. For reasons which have never been satisfactorily determined he suppressed this book, and only six copies came into circulation. So late as 1834 he issued it, drastically revised, as *Italy: With Sketches of Spain and Portugal.*

In January 1782, inspired by a devotion to Orientalism, and influenced by the suggestion of the Rev. Samuel Henley, a Harrow master, he began to write an Eastern tale. He went abroad the following May, and corresponded at length with Henley about the progress of the tale, which was called *Vathek,* and written in French. The story of *Vathek's* having been written at one sitting of three days and two nights was invented by Cyrus Redding in his *Memoirs of William Beckford*—why, no one knows. Though it is still frequently cited, it was exploded so long ago as 1893 in Richard Garnett's introduction to his edition of the book. Henley had the manuscript for translation, and, in spite of strict instructions not to publish the English before the French had appeared, he perversely did this very thing, in July 1786, and even went so far as to suppress Beckford's name and to issue the work as a translation from the Arabic. His reasons (like so much in Beckford's life) remain a mystery. Beckford then issued the French at Lausanne (1787) and another version in Paris in the same year. The question of priority has been much debated, but the present writer chooses the Lausanne as the first (for reasons set out in his edition of 1929). This book is Beckford's chief title to celebrity. Though it contains reminiscences of earlier work, it is a *point de repère* in the history of the Oriental tale, and shows remarkable knowledge of the East in one who had never traveled there. It is distinguished by great richness of description, buoyant humor, and teeming imagination, and its final scenes in the Hall of Eblis have a grandeur hard to match in this type of fiction. Professor Oliver Elton wrote: "The wit and passion, and the sombre sense of fatality and mortal tragedy, are wonderfully harmonious with the externals, and the result is a classic." Henley's translation is turgid, and contains many inaccuracies. In 1929 the present writer (Herbert B. Grimsditch) issued a new translation, from the definitive text of 1815, which differs from both the aforementioned texts. The *Episodes*, admirably translated by Sir Frank Marzials, were printed in 1912.

Beckford's other writings are *Modern Novel Writing* (by "The Right Hon. Lady Harriet Marlow") and *Azemia* (by "Jacquetta Agneta Mariana Jenks"), skits on the minor novelists of the day; *Al Raoui*, a short Oriental tale; and *Recollections of an Excursion to the Monasteries of Alcobaça and Batalha*. *Liber Veritatis*, a caustic examination of the pedigrees of various English "noble" families —inspired by his own unsuccessful quest for a peerage—was not published until 1930.

The whole nobility-ancestry question played a part in Beckford's life that should not be underestimated. In fact, it may be said without exaggeration to have been the strongest single motivating factor in his unique career. To begin with, he was extremely sensitive on the subject of his own genealogy. He resented any reference to his plebeian origin on his father's side and never missed a chance to emphasize his Hamilton descent, through his mother. Added to this, he had a consuming lifelong ambition to acquire a baronetcy of his own. In his stubborn and imprudent pursuit of this end he frequently got himself into humiliating, sometimes serious, predicaments. After one scandal he was forced to flee the country for some months. But the longed-for patent was never granted and he died a commoner. He did succeed, however, by the most determined maneuvering and unashamed use of his vast wealth, in engineering a match which made one of his daughters the Duchess of Hamilton. His plans to buy a similar title for his other daughter were wrecked when

WILLIAM BECKFORD

she made a runaway marriage with a perfectly respectable—but untitled—young army officer. Beckford never forgave her.

Beckford's private life has been the subject of endless anecdote and not a little calumny. He was abroad a great deal until near the end of the century. Thereafter he spent most of his time at Fonthill Abbey, a fantastic "folly," with a huge tower, which he had built for himself. He put a great wall all round his estate to exclude fox-hunters and unwelcome visitors. He played amazing pranks on uninvited guests who intruded on his privacy. He collected pictures and *objets d'art*. Rumor made him a monster of iniquity, probably on no surer grounds than the undoubted fact of his wide deviation from the usual type of country gentleman. He was a Member of Parliament for many years, but seldom went near the House. In his dealings with publishers and persons of a social grade inferior to his own he was often brusque and high-handed, though this trait has probably been over-stressed by biographers.

By 1822 Beckford's income (though still huge) was so much reduced by his extravagance and by the depreciation of his properties in the West Indies that he was forced to vacate Fonthill and sell part of his collection. He moved to Lansdown Tower, Bath, where he lived in the main a tranquil life—broken only by his periodic efforts to obtain a title— until his death twenty-two years later at the age of eighty-four.

In person Beckford was well set-up, tall and handsome. His longevity is no bad index to the temperate life he led, and he was active and healthy to the end.

As an author he showed in *Vathek* a talent not far below genius; and even his travel-books, infused as they are with esthetic sensibility, are noteworthy for their age. The belated publication of *Italy* has robbed it of its true claim to a place in the Romantic Movement. As a collector his taste was erratic and fanciful, but Hazlitt's very strong condemnation of it, as it was displayed in the goods at the Fonthill sale, must be discounted by the fact that Beckford had already removed his most valued treasures, while the auctioneer, following the custom of the day, had added trash from other sources.

"Beckford," wrote Oliver Elton, "like Blake, was a dreamer, as defiant, as full of stubborn vitality; but he was ironical and divided in soul, knowing the pain of curious pleasures, and reveling in things that are strange and costly and transitory. . . Of [his] wealth his genius seems a sort of exhalation, having the faults that attend—one almost says that beseem—such a nature. . ." Richard Garnett called him: "The most brilliant amateur in English literature."   H. B. G.

PRINCIPAL WORKS: *Oriental Tales*—Vathek (1st English text, as "An Arabian Tale from an Unpublished Manuscript," 1786, 1st French text, 1787, 2nd French text, 1787, 3rd French text, 1815, 2nd English translation, 1929); The Story of Al Raoui: A Tale From the Arabian, 1799; The Episodes of Vathek (trans. by F. T. Marzials) 1912. *Works of Travel*—Dreams, Waking Thoughts, and Incidents, 1783; Italy: With Sketches of Spain and Portugal, 1834; Recollections of an Excursion to the Monasteries of Alcobaça and Batalha, 1835. *Miscellaneous*—Biographical Memoirs of Extraordinary Painters, 1780; Popular Tales of the Germans (trans. [by Beckford?] from J. C. A. Musaeus) 1791; Modern Novel Writing: or, The Elegant Enthusiast, 1796; Azemia, 1797; The Vision and Liber Veritatis (ed. by G. Chapman) 1930.

ABOUT: Beckford, W. Liber Veritatis (see Introduction by G. Chapman); Beckford, W. Vathek (see Introductions to the various editions by S. Mallarmé, R. Garnett, and H. B. Grimsditch); Chapman, G. and Hodgkin, J. A Bibliography of William Beckford of Fonthill; Conant, M. P. The Oriental Tale in England in the 18th Century; Elton, O. A Survey of English Literature: 1780-1830; May, M. La Jeunesse De William Beckford et la Genèse de son Vathek; Melville, L. Life and Letters of William Beckford; Oliver, J. W. Life of William Beckford; Redding, C. Memoirs of William Beckford; Sitwell, S. Beckford and Beckfordism; Zeidler, K. J. Beckford, Hope, und Morier als Vertreter des Orientalischen Romans; London Mercury 14:509 October 1926; Temple Bar 120:182 June 1900; Quarterly Review 51:426 June 1834 and 213:377 October 1910.

BEDDOES, THOMAS LOVELL (June 30, 1803-January 26, 1849), poet, dramatist, and physician, was born at 3 Rodney Place, Clifton, near Bristol. He was the son of Dr. Thomas Beddoes, well-known physician, scientific writer, and founder of the Pneumatic Institute for curing diseases by inhalations, and Anna (Edgeworth) Beddoes, sister of Maria Edgeworth, the novelist. Though

Dr. Beddoes died in 1808, leaving his five-year old son to the guardianship of Davies Giddy, afterwards Sir Davies Gilbert, President of the Royal Academy, who had been associated with him in his rather odd experiments (there is a legend that they included bringing a live cow into a patient's bedroom to try the effect of its breath on the sufferer's condition) he had had time to make a lasting impression on the future poet.

It was a remarkable boy who, after three years at the Bath Grammar School, entered Charterhouse in 1817. He excelled at once, though without effort, as a student, as a ringleader in all sorts of disturbances, and as a budding writer. His fag, Charles Dacres Bevan, in some reminiscences sent years later to Beddoes's friend and editor, Thomas Forbes Kelsall, recalled that "the expression of his face was shrewd and sarcastic, with an assumption of sternness, as he affected the character of a tyrant and bully, though really not much of either; but a persevering and ingenious tormentor, as I knew to my cost. . . He had a great knack at composition in prose and verse, generally burlesque—and a great notion of dramatic effect. . . He knew Shakespeare well when I first saw him, and during his stay at the Charterhouse made himself master of all the best English dramatists. . . Though his voice was harsh and his enunciation offensively conceited, he read with so much propriety of expression and manner, that I was always glad to listen; even when I was pressed into the service as his accomplice, his enemy, or his love, with a due accompaniment of curses, caresses, or kicks, as the course of his declamation required."

Before going up to Pembroke College, Oxford, in 1820, Beddoes had twice won prizes for Latin Essays and once for Greek, written *Scaroni: or, The Mysterious Cave*, and had a poem on "The Comet" (Halley's) printed in the *Morning Post*.

At Oxford Beddoes continued to write, publishing *The Improvisatore* in 1821. When *The Bride's Tragedy* appeared in the following year, this production of an eighteen-year old undergraduate received, principally on account of the exquisite lyrical gifts it revealed, the unusual recognition of long and favorable reviews from nearly all the principal reviewers of the day, among them Bryan Waller Proctor ("Barry Cornwall") who became the poet's intimate friend and correspondent. He now made the acquaintance, too, of the young lawyer, Kelsall, spending much time with him at Southampton, and writing in the intervals of these two years *The Last Man, Love's Arrow Poisoned, Torrismond*, and *The Second Brother*.

In the midst of his examinations at Oxford in 1824 Beddoes was called to Florence by the illness of his mother, who died before he arrived. On his return to England he spent several months first with Kelsall at Southampton and then with his cousins, the Kings, at Clifton. Only a year later did he take his B.A., with no special honors.

He had now reached a turning point in his life. A translation of Schiller's *Philosophic Letters* in the *Oxford Quarterly Magazine* showed where his interests were tending, and in July 1825 Beddoes left England for Germany, and Oxford for Göttingen and a lifelong wandering from university to university in Germany and Switzerland. He applied himself in earnest to the study of anatomy and the composition of *Death's Jest Book*.

For four years he remained at Göttingen, except for a short visit to England in 1828, when he completed the first manuscript of the "Gothic-styled tragedy" which he regarded as the real test of his powers. The unfavorable criticism, especially from Proctor, of the second version which he sent home a year later, contributed to a growing depression which culminated in an attempt at suicide, followed by expulsion from the University for being drunk and disorderly.

Accordingly, in October 1829, Beddoes matriculated at Würzburg where, in 1831, he took his degree of M.D. But now his restlessness began to find an outlet in political activity. Two articles in the *Volksblatt*, and fiery speeches at a banquet in honor of Poland and later at a revolutionary meeting, provoked the King of Bavaria to order him deported in July 1832. After a week in prison for debt he left by way of Strasbourg for Zürich, where he matriculated in 1833, to remain for six years.

His residence was broken by a visit to England via Brussels in 1835, and punctuated

THOMAS LOVELL BEDDOES

by his recommendation to an anatomical chair in the University later in the same year, and his appearance in the character of Hotspur in Shakespeare's *Henry IV* in 1838, for which he hired the theatre for one night. In 1839 the radical government of Zürich, with whose members he was closely allied, was forced to resign, and his intimate friend Hegetschweiler was killed in the rioting. A few months later Beddoes suddenly left Zürich and reappeared in London where he lectured unsuccessfully on the drama at the Polytechnic Institute in Regent Street, soon departing for Berlin where he matriculated. Having returned to England for a month in 1842 he then seems to have divided his time for several years largely between Baden in Argau, Zürich, and Frankfort, with many short journeys, including one to Berlin in 1844 to attend the opening of the Kroll Opera House. In 1846-1847 he spent nearly a year in England where he shocked his friends by the alteration in his appearance and the violent singularity of his behavior, attempting on one occasion, it is said, to set fire to Drury Lane Theatre with a five-pound note.

An infection caught while dissecting at Frankfort on his return very seriously affected his already poor health as well as his spirits. In July 1848 he went to Basle where an attempt at suicide by opening an artery in his left leg necessitated its amputation. He was apparently recovering; but on January 26, 1849, he died. A note was found: "I am food for what I am good for—worms . . . I ought to have been among other things a good poet; Life was too great a bore on one peg and that a bad one." He had taken poison.

The cause of his death was concealed by his family and friends, and disclosed only in 1890 by Edmund Gosse after an interview with Browning, to whom Kelsall had bequeathed a box of Beddoes papers, subsequently missing. The lack of positive proof still left some doubt, and no less a medical authority than the late Sir William Osler believed that Beddoes might well have died from the after-effects of amputation. The researches of his latest editor and biographer, Henry Donner, have now, however, established the suicide beyond question.

Beddoes was a good poet, but he has had to wait for full recognition. His name was revived and the foundations of his future fame were laid by Kelsall's publication of *Death's Jest-Book* in 1850 and of *Poems Posthumous and Collected* in the following year. Kelsall's labors were carried further by the editions of Gosse; but like so much of the pioneer work for which we are indebted to that critic they contained many inaccuracies and omissions. To a large extent these gaps were filled and the errors corrected by Donner in 1935.

The decree of the Bavarian Government, of July 10, 1832, expelling Beddoes, fortunately included this description, as given by Donner in his biography: "Height 5′ 7″, hair light-brown, forehead high, eyebrows fair, eyes dark ["You must fancy him looking out of the picture thro' two very clear, decidedly brown eyes," wrote Kelsall in 1868 when sending Browning a portrait of his friend], nose fairly long and pointed, mouth big, chin rather prominent, face oval, complexion pale, build slight, neglected clothing, light-grey coat, white breeches, and either in English fashion or as German hero of Hambach one boot black, the other red and on one of them a gold or gilt spur, speaks bad German, fair moustache, bad teeth." At 21 he was said by Proctor, Taylor, and "an intelligent man who had lived at Hampstead" to resemble Keats. At 44, when he had let his beard grow during his illness at Frankfort, he looked like Shakespeare to Degen, a young baker ambitious to become an actor, to whom he was much attached at the time.

From allusions in his poems it would appear that Beddoes's undoubted homosexuality was responsible for many unhappy experiences, as it was also responsible for much of his dissatisfaction, restlessness, and unconventionality, his self-imposed exile from family and friends in E gland, the turn which his revolutionary tendencies took, and his unwillingness, lacking the spur of pecuniary necessity, to follow any one line of endeavour to complete fulfillment. The sharpened sensibility of his type showed itself in his poetry in the alternation of extreme delicacy of feeling with grossness, as well as in the peculiar subtlety and intensity of his lyrical expression. Called by Lytton Strachey "The Last Elizabethan," Beddoes in his dramas approaches most nearly to Webster and Tourneur by his violent plots, his sardonic phraseology, and his preoccupation with death. He is closer to the German Romantic notion of the Elizabethans than he is to the Elizabethans themselves. His two finished tragedies, compounded of the tragic, the Rabelaisian, the macabre, and the lyrical, lack a sense of character and form. As Donner says: "...his real experience forced its own expression in lyrical poetry. His poems of the last twenty years of his life possess the rich associative power which reproduces the experience out of which it was created, mostly sorrowful, but often lightened up by wit and humor, ranging from grief unutterable, to exuberant joy, varied in mood from the elegiac to the burlesque, but always complex and always genuine." J. B. O.

PRINCIPAL WORKS: Poetry—The Improvisatore, 1821; The Bride's Tragedy, 1822; Death's Jest-Book: or, The Fool's Tragedy, 1850; Poems Posthumus and Collected, 1851; Poems, 1907. Letters—Letters (ed. by E. Gosse) 1894. Collected Works—Complete Works (ed. by E. Gosse) 1927; Works (ed. by H. W. Donner) 1935.

ABOUT: Blunden, E. Votive Tablets; Donner, H. W. The Browning Box; Donner, H. W. The Life of Thomas Lovell Beddoes; Snow, R. H. Thomas Lovell Beddoes: Eccentric and Poet; Strachey, I. Books and Characters; Modern Philology, 1923.

"BEDE, CUTHBERT." See BRADLEY, EDWARD

BELL, HENRY GLASSFORD (November 8, 1803-January 7, 1874), Scottish poet, was born in Glasgow, the son of an advocate. Educated at the University of Edinburgh, he became a youthful friend of Hogg, Lockhart, and John Wilson ("Christopher North") in whose Noctes Ambrosianae he figured as "Tallboys." He established (at twenty-five) and for three years edited the Edinburgh Literary Journal. Called to the bar, he was for twenty-eight years sheriff substitute of Lanarkshire and for seven years—succeeding the historian Sir Archibald Alison—sheriff principal. (A sheriff in Scotland at that time exercised judicial powers.) He took an interest in Glasgow civic institutions, patronized fine arts, made occasional trips to the Continent, and was chess champion of west Scotland. Twice married, he had six children by his first wife. He died at seventy and was buried in the nave of St. Mungo's Cathedral, Glasgow.

The best known of his works is a narrative poem, "Mary, Queen of Scots," popular as a recitation; it appears in his volume Summer and Winter Hours. His brilliant prose defense of Mary Stuart, in the form of a biography, was widely read in its day but was supplanted by later research.

PRINCIPAL WORKS: Poems, 1824; Life of Mary, Queen of Scots, 1828-31; Summer and Winter Hours, 1831; My Old Portfolio, 1832; Romances and Minor Poems, 1866.

"BELL, PAUL." See CHORLEY, HENRY FOTHERGILL

BELZONI, GIOVANNI BAPTISTA (1778-December 3, 1823), Italian archaeological explorer who wrote in English, was born in Padua, Italy, the son of a barber. He was educated in Rome. In 1803 he went to England, where he earned a livelihood by exhibiting feats of strength. In 1815 he traveled to Egypt to introduce a hydraulic machine of his own invention. Financed by Henry Salt, the British consul-general in Cairo, he remained four years, excavating many tombs and pyramids, including the famous grotto-sepulchre of Seti I (known as "Belzoni's Tomb"). One of his achievements was the removal of the colossal bust of Rameses II from Thebes to Alexandria for shipment to the British Museum. After his return to England in 1819 he wrote an account of his discoveries which created wide interest as the first contribution to English research in Egypt. He died of dysentery at Gato, Benin, West Africa, in his forty-fifth year, while on a journey of exploration to Timbuktu. He ranks higher as a discoverer than as a scholar.

PRINCIPAL WORK: Narrative of Operations and Recent Discoveries Within the Pyramids, Temples, Tombs, and Excavations in Egypt and Nubia, 1820.
ABOUT: Belzoni, G. B. Narrative of Operations, etc. (see his own Introduction).

BENNETT, WILLIAM COX (October 14, 1820-March 4, 1895), song writer, was born in the borough of Greenwich (a London suburb), son of a watchmaker. When he was nine years old his father died, and he left private school to assist his mother in carrying on the business. Grown up, he took active part in effecting borough reforms in Greenwich and in electing Gladstone to parliament in 1868. His other activities included serving on the London council of the Education League, writing editorials and art criticism for the *Weekly Dispatch*, and contributing to the London *Figaro*. He died at seventy-four at his final home, Eliot Cottages, Blackheath, a suburb of London. Of his several collections of songs and poems, *Songs for Sailors* was set to music by John Liptrot Hatton.

PRINCIPAL WORKS: Poems, 1850; War Songs, 1855; Songs for Sailors, 1872; Baby May: Home Poems and Ballads, 1875; Songs of a Song Writer, 1876; Prometheus the Fire-Giver: An Attempted Restoration of the Lost First Part of the Promethean Trilogy of Aeschylus, 1877.

BENT, JAMES THEODORE (March 30, 1852-May 5, 1897), explorer and archaeologist, was born at Baildon, in Yorkshire, and educated at Wadham College, Oxford. He conducted archaeological investigations in the Greek islands of the Aegean Sea (1885-87), the west coast of Asia Minor (1888-89), the Bahrein Islands in the Persian Gulf (1889), Cilicia Tracheia in Asia Minor (1890), Mashonaland in British South Africa (1891), Abyssinia (1893), and the Arabian peninsula (1893-97). His wife, Mabel Hall-Dare, an expert photographer, assisted him in his work. Between journeys, he visited England and wrote valuable accounts of his findings. His book on *The Ruined Cities of Mashonaland* made the ruins at Great Zimbabwe well known to English readers, and his record of explorations in the Hadramut region of Arabia added greatly to the knowledge of this uncharted land. He died in London at forty-five, of pneumonia resulting from malarial fever contracted in Southern Arabia.

PRINCIPAL WORKS: The Cyclades: or, Life Among the Insular Greeks, 1885; The Ruined Cities of Mashonaland, 1892; The Sacred City of the Ethiopians, 1893; Southern Arabia, Soudan and Sokotra (completed by Mrs. Bent) 1900.
ABOUT: The Times May 7, 1897. See also Bent's works.

BENTHAM, GEORGE (September 22, 1800-September 10, 1884), botanist and logician, was born at Stoke, near Plymouth, the son of Sir Samuel Bentham, naval architect and engineer. Educated by private tutors, he lived twelve years in France and was for six years secretary to his uncle Jeremy Bentham, the philosopher, in London, before he began, at the age of thirty-two, to devote his life to botany.

His crowning achievement, which occupied him more than twenty years, was the monumental three-volume *Genera Plantarum*, in collaboration with Sir Joseph Hooker, defining every genus of flowering plant and its geographical distribution. But British botanists knew him best by his *Handbook of the British Flora* (many times reprinted) and similar handbooks of the flora of British possessions. In the realm of philosophy he made an impression at an early age with his *Outline for a New System of Logic*, which stated for the first time clearly the doctrine of quantification of the predicate. He died in London twelve days before his eighty-fourth birthday.

By virtue of his works, he ranks as one of England's greatest systematic botanists.

PRINCIPAL WORKS: Outline of a New System of Logic, 1827; Handbook of the British Flora, 1858; Flora of Hongkong, 1861; Flora Australiensis, 1863-78; Genera Plantarum (with J. D. Hooker) 1862-83.
ABOUT: Jackson, B. D. Life of George Bentham; Nature October 2, 1884.

BENTHAM, JEREMY (February 15, 1748-June 6, 1832), philosopher and economist, was born in London. His great-grandfather was a pawnbroker, and his father, though an attorney by profession, gave more attention to what would now be called his real estate business; he was decidedly "on the make," and looked forward (vainly, as it happened) to profiting by the achievements of his brilliant son. For Jeremy was a child prodigy; he read Latin and Greek at three, like John Stuart Mill, and at five was known as "the philosopher." His parents tried to keep him from all sports or light reading—an ambition happily thwarted by summers spent with his grandmother near Reading. At seven, a sensitive, shy, undersized child, he was sent to Westminster School, and at twelve he entered Queen's College, Oxford. There his first religious doubts made him reluctant to sign the Thirty-nine Articles, as was required for enrollment.

Bentham detested Oxford. Nevertheless he attained his B.A. in 1763, was entered at

JEREMY BENTHAM

Lincoln's Inn, and succeeded to his M.A. in 1766, leaving Oxford finally the following year. As late as 1817 he was called to the bar, but he hardly made a pretence of practising law. Instead he experimented in chemistry, and began, with more fruitful results, to interest himself in politics and the theory of jurisprudence. His inimical commentary on Blackstone (the *Fragment on Government*) was almost the sole accomplishment of his professional legal career.

For a time Bentham became depressed, and perhaps because of his extreme precocity, already felt himself to be a failure. An acquaintance, which speedily grew to intimacy, with Lord Shelburne (the first Lord Lansdowne) restored his self-esteem; as an habitué of Shelburne's house he met most of the men who were later to become his followers—not the least one Étienne Dumont, his disciple and translator. A less fortunate result was a meeting with a lady, whose name is unknown, but who inspired a lifelong unrequited passion in Bentham, and kept him a bachelor all his days.

Before 1780 Bentham had already worked out the details of his utilitarian philosophy (afterwards to be known also as philosophic radicalism), and had written, though he had not published, his most famous book, *An Introduction to the Principles of Morals and Legislation.* In a sense all that he did afterward was in the nature of a commentary. Its main thesis, set forth by him with force and brilliance, is that men act only to attain pleasure or to avoid pain, and that this should be the objective of the moralist and the legislator. Punishment is evil, and should be resorted to only to avoid a greater evil. The seeds of this philosophy are in Hume

and Helvetius, but the developed creed is Bentham's own. It made him the founder of a peculiarly English philosophical and ethical school.

In 1785 Bentham went to visit a brother who was, strangely enough, an official of the Russian government. His observations in White Russia led him to an intense interest in penology, and particularly in a device—a sort of watch-tower and control-post in the midst of a factory or a prison—called the "Pantopticon." Bentham espoused the Pantopticon ardently for twenty-five years; he almost persuaded the British government to adopt it, and to dispense with deportation to Botany Bay; but in the end all he achieved was a refund of his expenses.

In 1792 his father died and left him independently wealthy. In the same year the French revolutionary government made him an honorary citizen, in recognition of his friendship, for from his original Toryism he had gradually become a radical. His health failed and he thought of going to Mexico. Instead he settled at Ford Abbey, near Chard. There little by little he became a recluse, a sage whose disciples sat reverently, although infrequently, at his feet.

His labor was indefatigable, and his production enormous, but his methods of work were most peculiar. As someone said, he was "always running from a good scheme to a better." He carried out several projects at once, wrote voluminously on scraps of paper, rewrote books before they were finished, and in fact for the most part simply turned out masses of notes which Dumont, James Mill, and others reduced to order. Most of his books were privately printed long before their general publication.

Bentham's last public action was in helping to found the liberal *Westminster Review* in 1824. Even in his old age he worked with passion, as if to do all he could for humanity. When feebleness at last overcame him, he died as calmly as he had lived. He left his body to be dissected for the benefit of science, and his skeleton, dressed in his usual rather eccentric clothes, is still in the possession of University College.

Bentham's interests extended to ethics, jurisprudence, logic and political economy. His style, once witty and powerful, became in the end dry and formal, with clarity its only virtue. He was fond of inventing new words; one which has survived is "international." Immense masses of his notes and manuscript are still unpublished. He influenced almost every thinker of his time. He himself remained entirely unspoiled, serene, even-tempered, and genuinely a lover of his kind.   M. A. deF.

PRINCIPAL WORKS: Fragment on Government (anonymous) 1776; View of the Hard Labor Bill,

1778; A Defence of Usury, 1787; Introduction to the Principles of Morals and Legislation, 1789; Pantopticon, 1791; A Protest Against Law Taxes, 1795; The Pantopticon versus New South Wales, 1802; A Plea for the Constitution, 1803; Scotch Reform, 1808; An Introductory View of the Rationale of Evidence, 1812; A Table of the Springs of Action, 1817; Papers Upon Codification and Public Institution, 1817; Swear Not at All, 1817; Church of Englandism and Its Catechism Examined, 1818; On the Liberty of the Press, 1821; The Analysis of the Influence of Natural Religon Upon the Temporal Happiness of Mankind (under name of Philip Beauchamp) 1822; Not Paul but Jesus (under name of Gamaliel Smith) 1823; Codification Proposals, 1823; A Book of Fallacies, 1824; Rationale of Reward, 1825; Rationale of Evidence, 1827; Rationale of Punishment, 1830; Constitutional Code, 1830; Deontology: or, The Science of Morality (posthumous) 1834; Collected Works (9 vols., posthumous) 1838-1843.

ABOUT: Bowring, J. Life (in Bentham's Collected Works); Everett, C. W. The Education of Jeremy Bentham; Ogden, C. K. Bentham's Theory of Fictions; Stephen, L. The English Utilitarians; Contemporary Review 142:213 August 1932; Queen's Quarterly 39:658 November 1832.

BERNARD, WILLIAM BAYLE (November 27, 1807-August 5, 1875), dramatist, was born a British subject in Boston, where his father (an English actor who had come to America in 1797) was managing a theatre. In his thirteenth year he was taken to England to remain permanently. Educated at a school in Uxbridge in Middlesex, he worked for a time as clerk in the army accounts office before becoming a professional dramatist in his twenty-third year. He produced a total of 114 plays, many of them written for American audiences. Less than half of his works were ever printed; the best known pieces are to be found in the collections *Lacy's Acting Edition of Plays* and *The Acting National Drama.* He was rated a sound critic and scholar, a playwright of inventive and literary skill. His death occurred at Brighton, Sussex, when he was sixty-seven.

PRINCIPAL PLAYS: Rip Van Winkle, 1832; Marie Ducange, 1837; The Round of Wrong, 1846; The Passing Cloud, 1850; The Doge of Venice, 1867.

BERRY, MARY (March 16, 1763-November 20, 1852), the friend and literary heiress of Horace Walpole, was born at Kirkbridge, Yorkshire. She was the daughter of Robert Berry, who in spite of wealthy mercantile connections was in very moderate circumstances. Mary's sister AGNES was a year younger than herself and was her constant companion throughout life. Their mother died when Mary was three and the girls were sent to their maternal grandmother's.

When Mary was twenty, their father's income having been improved by the gift of an annuity of £1000 a year, the girls were taken to the Continent. It was then that Mary began her *Journals and Correspondence,* which constitute her greatest claim to literary fame.

MARY BERRY

In October 1788 Horace Walpole met the Berry sisters. He was over seventy, but he fell in love with Mary, even as Madame du Deffand had fallen in love with him in *her* old age—twenty-three years earlier. Although Walpole tried to disguise the situation by pretending that he was equally fond of both sisters—and in spite of the fact that after coming into the title of Earl of Orford he offered to make either of them his countess so that he might settle the estates upon her—it is nevertheless certain that Mary was the real object of his adoration. But both sisters were in love—Mary with General O'Hara, Governor of Gibraltar; and Agnes with a wealthy cousin. And in the end neither of them ever married.

The girls, with their father, were persuaded by Walpole to occupy a small house near his estate of Strawberry Hill, and much of their time was spent with the old dilettante. He entertained them with the accumulated anecdotes of a lifetime spent in the most brilliant society of 18th century Europe. He also wrote his *Reminiscences* for their amusement. He introduced them into the highest literary, political, and social circles of England where they at once became popular.

Mary was called by Madame de Staël "by far the cleverest woman in England." She became the center about which the wittiest and most fashionable gathered, whether in England or on the continent. She had some literary ambitions and wrote a play, *Fashionable Friends,* and a book, *Social Life in England and France,* but as Strachey says, "her style failed to express the force of her mentality, so that her careful sentences are today unreadable."

Robert Berry and his daughters inherited all of Walpole's printed books and manuscripts with the express provision that they were to edit and publish the latter for their own profit. Mary edited the five volumes of Walpole's works published in 1798 and the *Letters of Madame du Deffand.*

The Berry sisters are important because they formed a living link between two very dissimilar ages. Active to the end of their days (Mary lived to be 89) they were able to give to such representatives of the Victorian era as Thackeray and Macaulay, a glimpse of the salons of the 18th century.

Mary Berry was a forerunner of the modern feminists. "Had she been a man," says Strachey, "she would not have shone as a writer, but as a political thinker or an administrator; and a man she should have been; with her massive, practical intelligence, she was born too early to be a successful woman."

D. C.

PRINCIPAL WORKS: *Editorial*—The Works of Lord Orford (5 vols.) 1798; Letters of Madame du Deffand; 1810; Letters of Rachael: Lady Russell, 1815; *Prose*—A Comparative View of Social Life in England and France, 1828-31; Complete Works. 1844.

ABOUT: Lewis, T. (ed.). The Journal and Correspondence of Miss Berry; Melville, L. (ed.). The Berry Papers; Strachey, L. Portraits in Miniature.

BESANT, SIR WALTER

(August 14, 1836-June 9, 1901), novelist, was born in Portsea, the fifth child of William Besant, a merchant, and Sarah (Ediss) Besant.

After some education at home, where he read through his father's library, he was sent to grammar schools at Portsea and Stockwell, proceeding to King's College, London, and, in 1856, to Christ's, at Cambridge, where his career was distinguished, and from which he was graduated in 1859.

Having been unsuccessful in journalism in London, and having definitely rejected the Church as a future, Besant, who had been an instructor in mathematics at Leamington College, accepted (1861) the senior professorship at the Royal College, Mauritius. He spent his vacations studying French and writing essays.

The fruit of these efforts was to appear in a few years. In 1867, having refused, because of ill health, the rectorship of the Mauritius college, Besant returned to London to embark upon a literary career. His first book, *Studies in Early French Poetry,* was successful enough to induce him to continue his writing on French literature, and, in addition, he formed a Rabelais Club in 1879 for the discussion of that author's works.

From 1868 to 1886 he was secretary of the Palestine Exploration Fund. In the course of this connection he collaborated with Professor E. H. Palmer on *Jerusalem: The City of Herod and Saladin.*

As a contributor to *Once a Week,* Besant had made the acquaintance of the editor, James Rice, who had asked him to collaborate on a novel. *Ready-Money Mortiboy,* 1872, the result, was successful, and the partnership continued until 1881, when illness forced Rice to stop his work. Besant, who in the course of this time had written but one novel (*When George the Third Was King*) by himself, proceeded to issue novels with great frequency for the next twenty years, many of them historical in their setting, and two of them, *All Sorts and Conditions of Men* and *Children of Gibeon,* definitely sociological.

In accordance with the ideals expressed in *All Sorts and Conditions of Men,* Besant worked actively in the founding of a "People's Palace" in London for the recreation and improvement of the poor. The institution, actually opened in 1887, contained schools, a gymnasium, a library, and similar features. Eventually the educational branches of the "Palace" grew into a part of London University.

Besant was the moving spirit also of the Society of Authors, formed in 1884 to improve copyright laws and to protect authors against exploitation by publishers; and it was in this cause that he wrote *The Pen and the Book.* His attitude was that of a business man: that the author, like any other producer, is entitled to a fair return on his product.

What he considered his greatest work, a survey which was to deal with modern London as Stow's survey had done with the city of the time of the Tudors, Besant was obliged to leave unfinished, although he did publish

SIR WALTER BESANT

some studies before his death at his home in Hampstead in 1901.

A genial, warm-hearted man with a mathematical kind of efficiency, Besant was zealous in all causes that he espoused, and often indiscreet in his enthusiasms. Thus, in his statements about publishers and their practices, he offended prominent members of that profession by his undiscriminating charges of unethical methods; and his remarks upon organized religion, to which he was opposed, and upon literary reviewers, whom he denounced with fervor, were somewhat excessive. His greatest personal interest was his city, and he was thoroughly acquainted with its background as well as its general topography. Besant's kindness was extended to young authors, to whom he gave aid and advice. In 1874 he married Mary Forster-Barham, of Bridgwater, by whom he had two daughters and two sons.

His importance as a man somewhat overshadows his rank as a writer, which is not with the greatest. His novels, while ingenious and well-made, are not subtle or profound. On the other hand, despite eccentricities that may be attributed to the influence of Dickens, they have qualities of humor and common-sense, are decidedly readable and pleasant, and certainly enjoyed great popularity. His treatment of the social evils of the East End of London was of great influence, although here his purpose operated against his artistic success. In general, the novels written with Rice are superior to those that Besant wrote himself. It is, in the main, for his efforts at social improvement and for his championing of the rights of the author that Besant is entitled to literary fame.   R. W. W.

PRINCIPAL WORKS: *Autobiography*—Autobiography of Sir Walter Besant, 1902. *Biography*—Gaspard de Coligny, 1879; Sir Richard Whittington (with J. Rice) 1881; The Life and Achievements of E. H. Palmer, 1883; The Eulogy of Richard Jefferies, 1888; Captain Cook, 1889; The Story of King Alfred, 1901. *Editor*—The Literary Remains of C. F. T. Drake, 1877; The Survey of Western Palestine (with E. H. Palmer) 1881-83; Readings in Rabelais, 1883. *Essays*—As We Are and As We May Be, 1903; Essays and Historiettes, 1903. *History*—Jerusalem (with E. H. Palmer) 1871; Constantinople (with W. J. Brodribb) 1879; The Rise of the Empire 1897; *London*—London, 1892. The History of London, 1893; Westminster, 1895; South London, 1898; East London, 1901; Westminster (with G. E. Mitton) 1902; The Strand District (with G. E. Mitton) 1902; London in the Eighteenth Century, 1902; Holburn and Bloomsbury (with G. E. Mitton) 1903; The Thames, 1903; London in the Time of the Stuarts, 1903; London in the Time of the Tudors, 1904; Mediaeval London, 1906; Early London, 1908; Shoreditch and East End, 1908; London in the Nineteenth Century, 1909; London City, 1910; London North of the Thames, 1911; London South of the Thames, 1912. *Novels*—Ready-Money Mortiboy (with J. Rice) 1872; When George the Third Was King, 1872; My Little Girl (with J. Rice) 1873; With Harp and Crown (with J. Rice) 1875; This Son of Vulcan (with J. Rice) 1876; The Case of Mr. Lucraft (with J. Rice) 1876; The Golden Butterfly (with J. Rice) 1876; Such a Good Man! (with J. Rice) 1877; The Monks of Thelema (with J. Rice) 1878; By Celia's Arbour (with J. Rice) 1878; The Seamy Side (with J. Rice) 1880; The Chaplain of the Fleet (with J. Rice) 1881; The Ten Years' Tenant (with J. Rice) 1881; All Sorts and Conditions of Men, 1882; The Revolt of Man, 1882; All in a Garden Fair, 1883; The Captain's Room, 1883; Children of Gideon, 1884; Dorothy Forster, 1884; Uncle Jack, 1885; Katharine Regina, 1887; The World Went Very Well Then, 1887; Herr Paulus, 1888; For Faith and Freedom, 1888; The Inner House, 1888; The Bell of St. Paul's, 1889; The Doubts of Dives, 1889; Armorel of Lyonesse, 1890; The Demoniac, 1890; St. Katharine's by the Tower, 1891; The Ivory Gate, 1892; Verbena Camellia Stephanotis, 1892; The Rebel Queen, 1893; Beyond the Dreams of Avarice, 1895; In Deacon's Orders, 1895; The Master Craftsman, 1896; The City of Refuge, 1896; A Fountain Sealed, 1897; The Changeling, 1898; The Orange Girl, 1899; The Alabaster Box, 1900; The Fourth Generation, 1900; The Lady of Lynn, 1901; *Plays*—Ready-Money Mortiboy (with J. Rice) 1874; Such a Good Man! (with J. Rice) 1879; The Balladmonger (with J. Rice) 1887; The Charm and Other Drawing-Room Plays (with W. H. Pollock) 1906; *Studies*—Studies in Early French Poetry, 1868; Rabelais, 1879; The French Humourists From the Twelfth to the Nineteenth Century, 1873. *Tales*—'Twas in Trafalgar's Bay, 1879; To Call Her Mine, 1889; The Holy Rose, 1890; A Five Years' Tryst, 1902; No Other Way, 1902. *Miscellaneous*—A Book of French, 1877; The Art of Fiction, 1884; Twenty-one Years' Work: 1865-86, 1886; Fifty Years Ago, 1888; Correspondence on the Distribution of Pensions to Literature, 1890; Thirty Years' Work: 1865-95, 1895; The Queen's Reign and Its Commemoration, 1897; Alfred, 1898; The Pen and the Book, 1898.

ABOUT: Besant, W. The Autobiography of Sir Walter Besant (see Prefatory Note by S. S. Sprigge); Besant, W. & Rice, J. Ready-Money Mortiboy (see Preface to library ed., 1887); Athenaeum June 15, 1901; The Author 12:20 July 1901; Forum 34:150 July 1902; Outlook 68:383 571 June 15, July 6, 1901.

BETHAM-EDWARDS, MATILDA BARBARA (March 4, 1836-January 4, 1919),

novelist and writer on French life, was born at Westerfield, Suffolk, England, the daughter of a farmer named Edward Edwards. She took her mother's maiden name, Barbara Betham, as part of her own. Amelia Blandford Edwards, the Egyptologist, was her cousin. She attended school only a short while, educating herself largely by reading and extensive travel in rural France. Beginning at the age of twenty-one, she wrote voluminously for sixty years, mostly interpretations of France and its people or novels based on her recollections of Suffolk. She lived for some time in London and spent her declining years in retirement at a villa in Hastings, Essex, where she died two months before her eighty-third birthday.

PRINCIPAL WORKS: *Novels*—The White House by the Sea, 1857; Dr. Jacob, 1864; Kitty, 1869; Lord of the Harvest, 1899. *Books on France*—French Men, Women, and Books, 1910; Twentieth Century France, 1917.

ABOUT: Betham-Edwards, M. B. Reminiscences; Mid-Victorian Memories.

BETHUNE, ALEXANDER (July, 1804-June 13, 1843), Scottish poet, was born at Upper Rankeillor, in the parish of Monimail, Fifeshire, the son of an impoverished farm worker. He attended school only a few months, being employed as an outdoor laborer most of his life from the age of fourteen. Twice he was injured by explosions of gunpowder which permanently mutilated his body. His poems depicting Scottish character among the lower classes were published first in local newspapers of the village of Lochend, near the Loch of Lindores, where his family lived. At thirty-four he won fame with his first book of verse, but he is best known for his last book, published shortly before he died of pulmonary consumption in Newburgh at the age of thirty-eight.

PRINCIPAL WORKS: Tales and Sketches of the Scottish Peasantry, 1838; The Scottish Peasant's Fireside, 1842.

ABOUT: McCombie, W. Life of Alexander Bethune.

BIGG, JOHN STANYAN (July 14, 1828-May 19, 1865), poet and journalist, was born at Ulverston in Lancashire, England. He was educated at the old Town Bank School in Ulverston and at a boarding school in Warwickshire. In his twentieth year he published *The Sea King,* a metrical romance in six cantos, and six years later he brought out his most important work, a dramatic poem called *Night and the Soul.* After editing the *Ulverston Advertiser* for a time, he went to Downpatrick, Ireland, where he edited the *Downshire Protestant* for several years and was married to Miss R. A. H. Pridham. Returning to Ulverston, he served as editor and proprietor of the *Advertiser* from 1860 until his death at the age of thirty-seven. He belonged to the so-called "spasmodic school" of poets, burlesqued by W. E. Aytoun in *Firmilian.*

PRINCIPAL WORKS: *Poetry*—The Sea King, 1848; Night and the Soul, 1854; Shifting Scenes and Other Poems, 1862. *Novel*—Alfred Staunton, 1860.

BIRD, ISABELLA. See BISHOP, ISABELLA BIRD

BISHOP, ISABELLA BIRD (October 15, 1831-October 7, 1904), travel author, was born Isabella Lucy Bird at Boroughbridge Hall, Yorkshire, the daughter of a clergyman. At the age of forty-nine she was married to Dr. John Bishop, an Edinburgh physician, ten years her junior; in five years she was left a widow. Chronic spinal trouble, missionary zeal, a restless nature, and repeated family deaths caused her to travel extensively from the time she was twenty-two. Her experiences in America, the Sandwich Islands, Japan, the Malay Peninsula, Tibet, Persia, Kurdistan, Korea, and China were recorded in nine books, the most valuable of which were those dealing with the Asiatic countries. These works brought her a reputation as one of the outstanding travelers of her day. In Asia she founded five hospitals in memory of her husband, sister, and parents. A daring horsewoman, undaunted by ill-health, she rode a thousand miles in Morocco at the age of sixty-nine. She died in Edinburgh eight days before her seventy-third birthday.

PRINCIPAL WORKS: Unbeaten Tracks in Japan, 1880; Journeys in Persia and Kurdistan, 1891; Among the Tibetans, 1894; Korea and Her Neighbours, 1898; The Yangtze Valley and Beyond, 1899.

ABOUT: Stoddart, A. M. The Life of Isabella Bird.

BLACK, WILLIAM (November 15, 1841-December 10, 1898), Scottish novelist, was born at Glasgow, the son of James Black, a merchant.

A rather retiring boy, Black was educated in private schools and sent to the government School of Art at Glasgow. After a short time he felt that he was a failure at landscape painting, his chosen profession, and the death of his father in 1855 made it necessary for him to earn a living. Accordingly he turned to his pen, which never in his life failed to keep him above actual want.

He began to contribute youthful criticisms of the leading writers of the day to a Glasgow newspaper, and proceeded next to write essays and even poetry for the *Glasgow Weekly Citizen.* In 1864 was published his first novel, *James Merle,* which was a decided failure; and in the same year, having had an unhappy love-affair with an actress older than himself, he left Glasgow for London, to accept a clerkship in a counting-house.

There he was befriended by Robert Buchanan, the poet, and before very long joined the staff of the *Morning Star.* On April 8, 1865, he married Miss Augusta Wenzel, a German girl who had been in England for about a year, and they settled at Hounslow, thirteen miles from London. In May of the following year Mrs. Black died of a fever, leaving her husband with a son, who died five years later.

In the same year (1866) Black's newspaper work with the *Star* took him to Germany, to write letters on the subject of the war between Prussia and Austria. This experience strengthened and reinforced his already strong sympathies and admiration for German literature, song, and music, as well as for the German national character.

In the autumn he established himself in Clapham, a London suburb, with his mother and his little boy, and wrote for the *Star* and for magazines, and edited the *London Review.* From the *Star* he proceeded in 1870 to the *Daily News,* of which he was assistant edi-

WILLIAM BLACK

tor. He enjoyed the work of writing upon literature, but detested his editorial duties and the necessity for preoccupation with politics. A few years later he was enabled to retire altogether from journalism because of his success as a novelist. *A Daughter of Heth, The Strange Adventures of a Phaeton,* and *A Princess of Thule* established him with the public, and from this time forth he was relatively free to amuse himself with yachting, fishing, and traveling. In 1874 he married Miss Eva Simpson, daughter of George Wharton Simpson, a journalist, and in 1878 removed to Brighton, where he spent his years in the dispensing of hospitality and the enjoyment of the society of his friends. In 1876 he made a visit to the United States where he had many admirers. His death in 1898 was widely mourned because of his popularity in the literary society of his time, and to his memory the William Black Memorial Beacon, first lighted in 1901, was erected by subscription at Duart Point, Sound of Mull.

The novelist was a man of humor, sincerity, and directness, incapable of dissimulation. An able journalist, he, in one emergency, translated a state dispatch and wrote a leading article (which was highly regarded) of editorial comment upon it, all in an hour and a quarter. In his novel-writing he was methodical, industrious, and thorough as to detail. He planned his books carefully before writing them, and kept regular hours of work on the days devoted to the actual writing. He was able to detach himself completely from his surroundings, losing himself in his work. His kindness is apparent in his giving up an offer of a desirable newspaper appointment, transferring it to a sick

friend, for whom he did the actual writing himself. A comparable instance of generosity is his finishing a novel for Charles Gibbon, when the latter was ill and unable to work. Black was unspoiled by his own success, and cared nothing for the lionizing for which he was eligible.

His permanent place in literature is not among the gods, but, despite faults in plot and character, his novels are remarkable for minute description. Aside from his skill in description, particularly evident in *The Strange Adventures of a Phaeton,* Black is noteworthy for his heroines. "His chief success and his most praiseworthy characteristic," declared a writer in *The Athenaeum,* "consisted in the skill with which he drew women who were at once natural and lovable. Indeed, his men are far inferior, as human beings, to his girls and women." Black's best stories are those with settings in the mountains or along the Scottish coast.

R. W. W.

PRINCIPAL WORKS: *Biography*—Goldsmith, 1873. *Novels and Tales*—James Merle: An Autobiography, 1864; Love or Marriage, 1868; In Silk Attire, 1869; Kilmeny, 1870; The Monarch of Mincing-Lane, 1871; A Daughter of Hath, 1871; Mr. Pisistratus Brown, 1871; The Strange Adventures of a Phaeton, 1872; A Princess of Thule, 1873; The Maid of Killeena, 1874; Three Feathers, 1875; Lady Silverdale's Sweetheart, 1876; Madcap Violet, 1876; Green Pastures and Piccadilly, 1877; Macleod of Dare, 1878; White Wings, 1880; Sunrise, 1880; The Beautiful Wretch, 1881; The Four Macnicols, 1881; The Pupil of Arelius, 1881; Adventures in Thule, 1883; Shandon Bells, 1883; Yolande, 1883; Judith Shakespeare, 1884; White Heather, 1885; The Wise Woman of Inverness, 1885; Sabina Zembra, 1887; The Strange Adventures of a House-Boat, 1888; In Far Lochabar, 1888; Nanciebel, 1889; The Penance of John Logan, 1889; The New Prince Fortunatus, 1890; Stand Fast, Craig-Royston! 1890; Donald Ross of Heimra, 1891; Wolfenberg, 1892; The Magic Ink, 1892; The Handsome Humes, 1893; Highland Cousins, 1894; Briseis, 1896; Wild Eelin, 1898. *Miscellaneous*—With the Eyes of Youth, 1898.

ABOUT: Reid, T. W. William Black: Novelist; Athenaeum December 17, 1898; Harper's 66:15 December 1822; National Quarterly Review 41:190 July 1880.

BLACKIE, JOHN STUART (July 28, 1809-March 2, 1895), Scottish classical scholar, was born in Glasgow. His education was obtained at Edinburgh and Aberdeen Universities, and by travel in Germany and Italy. Though he studied for the ministry and the bar, he became professor of Latin at Marischal College, Aberdeen, remaining eleven years. Thereafter he was for thirty years professor of Greek in Edinburgh University, where he helped to found and endow the Celtic chair. By his wife, Eliza Wyld, he had no children. A genial eccentric, he took a prominent part in the literary life of Edinburgh and was popular as a public lecturer. He remained active and healthy in old age, and died in Edinburgh at eighty-five.

His chief works were metrical translations of *Faust*, Aeschylus' plays, and the *Iliad*, besides an effective discourse on the Homeric question and a hymn "Angels Holy, High and Lowly." He wrote some forty volumes, including verse and essays on moral and religious philosophy.

PRINCIPAL WORKS: Goethe's *Faust* Translated Into English Verse, 1834; The Lyrical Dramas of Aeschylus Translated Into English Verse, 1850; Lays and Legends of Ancient Greece, With Other Poems, 1856; Homer and the *Iliad*, 1866; Life of Robert Burns, 1887; Selected Poems (ed. by his nephew A. Stodart Walker) 1896.

ABOUT: Blackie, J. S. Letters; Notes of a Life; Selected Poems (see Appreciation by A. Stodart Walker); Kennedy, H. A. Professor Blackie: His Sayings and Doings; Stoddart, A. M. John Stuart Blackie: A Biography.

BLACKMORE, RICHARD DODD-RIDGE

(June 7, 1825-January 20, 1900), novelist, known throughout the English-speaking world as the author of *Lorna Doone*, was born at the village of Longworth, Berkshire, where his father was curate. Owing to his extreme secretiveness, relatively little is known about his life. Even Edward Marston, one of his publishers, who knew him well, refrained at his request from writing his life.

He came of a long line of clergymen. He once wrote, "Before I was four months old, my mother was taken to a better world, and I started crookedly." At any rate, he went to live with his grandmother in Glamorganshire, Wales, a country which was the background for some of his best stories.

The shyness which accompanied him through life made him the victim of bullies at Blundell School, in Tiverton (where he was sent at eleven), although he was a scholastic success. Here his tendency to epilepsy was first apparent. His life at Exeter College, Oxford, was, on the other hand, very happy. He won a scholarship, and began his literary career with some poems written under the name of Melanter. It was fortunate that before these appeared he had begun to support himself by the law, entering the Middle Temple, London, as a student in 1849, and being called to the bar in 1852, since the poems showed no particular ability.

He soon gave up the law for teaching, however; shortly after this, poor health and an inheritance combined to allow him the pursuits of gardening and writing at Teddington, near London. He married while a law student, and although his wife was an invalid, her death after 36 years was a lasting grief to him.

For a picture of Blackmore we can quote Edward Marston, his publisher: " . . . he was very tall, and of a large muscular frame, but not so broad-chested and portly as he became in after years. He dressed very plainly, and

RICHARD D. BLACKMORE

altogether looked very much like what he was by choice, a gardener and vine-grower. His voice was gentle, deliberate, almost timid, and yet manly." This was the impression he created in 1862, when he first visited Marston with a volume of translations of Virgil's *Georgics*.

Two years later he wrote his first novel, *Clara Vaughan*, and a second, *Cradock Nowell*, came before *Lorna Doone*, which made his fame and fortune. Although subsequent generations have acknowledged the excellence of *Lorna Doone*, it "languished for a year and a half" before achieving success—which, when it finally came, was largely the result of an erroneous popular belief that the story had something to do with the family of the Marquis of Lorne, who had just married (1869) a daughter of Queen Victoria.

Novel followed novel, even though he wrote only a page (in his tiny handwriting this mounted up to six printed pages) a day. His real joy, however, was working outdoors in his beautiful garden full of rare plants. He took great pride in his orchard of *standard* peaches, then a novelty in England. He lived a simple life, shielded from publicity. He was self-reliant, but had the rare gift of self-criticism, and once wrote: "Thank heaven, I have plenty of self-confidence, simply because I know good work when I see it, and pretty soon condemn work—though my own—when it is scampish." And again, "In none of my books have I satisfied myself. There is something rather childish in *Lorna Doone*, I think. Perhaps, taken altogether, *Alice Lorraine* is the best."

From his novels we learn more about him and his background than from any other source. His father is the clergyman in *Perly-*

cross. His nearest approach to autobiography is in *Tales From the Telling House* and in *Christowell*. His books are full of high adventure, high romance, and drama—not to say in some instances melodrama. On the incidental characters, which are the best, he lavishes humor and telling detail. He has been called "the Walter Scott of Devonshire."

He died after a long illness at the age of 75. Four years later his admirers, including such men of letters as James Barrie, Hall Caine, Thomas Hardy, and Rudyard Kipling, put up a memorial window in Exeter Cathedral. At the unveiling of the window Eden Phillpotts said, "His manliness, insight, . . . humor, were a tonic to the mind, and heartened a man at every page. . . . Absolutely fearless, he answered only to his own ideals, and not the most arrogant critic of literature dared to handle his work as severely as he did himself." 　　　　　　　　　　V. M.

PRINCIPAL WORKS: *Poetry*—Poems by Melanter, 1854, 1855; *Novels*—Clara Vaughan, 1864; Cradock Nowell, 1866; Lorna Doone, 1869; Maid of Sker, 1872; Christowell, 1880; Perlycross, 1894; Tales From the Telling House, 1896; Dariel, 1897. *Miscellaneous*—Translation of the Georgics, 1862.

ABOUT: Marston, E. After Work; Snell, F. J. The Blackmore Country.

BLACKWOOD, FREDERICK H. T. See DUFFERIN, LORD

BLACKWOOD, HELEN SELINA. See DUFFERIN, LADY

BLAKE, WILLIAM (November 28, 1757-August 12, 1827), poet and artist, was born, lived, and died in London. His father was a prosperous hosier, who, early observing his son's artistic bent, sent him at ten to the best drawing school of its day. He bought casts for him to work from, and gave him an allowance which permitted him while he was still a child to become in a small way a collector of prints—"my little connoisseur," one dealer used to call him. At fourteen the boy was apprenticed to an engraver for seven years. This was really a continuation of his art training, for his master sent him in summer to draw monuments in old London churches, particularly in Westminster Abbey, which he engraved in winter. From him Blake learned the rudiments of the technique which made him one of the greatest engravers of English history.

In 1781, his majority attained and his apprenticeship over, Blake studied for a short time at the newly founded Royal Academy. But his strong individualism at once asserted itself and made his connection with the orthodox academy very short; when his teacher recommended his copying Rubens instead of Michelangelo, as being more "finished," Blake retorted that what had never been begun could not be finished, and quit the school. He ceased thenceforth to draw from living models, and his work became increasingly abstract, though it was only later on that his vivid imagination conjured hallucinatory models for him out of thin air.

He began to make his living by engraving for booksellers, and his work soon became popular and assured him of a steady income. In 1782, at twenty-two, he fell in love with a girl who laughed at his proposal of marriage. Telling this at a dinner-table with friends, another girl present, Catherine Boucher, said that she pitied him. "Do you indeed?" he replied. "Then I love you for it." Shortly afterwards they were married. Catherine was totally illiterate, and had to sign the marriage register with her mark, but she became a more than devoted helpmate. Blake taught her to read and write, and she became his assistant, taking off prints and helping him to color his engravings. They were inseparable companions, and she echoed his every thought and opinion, but it is doubtful if their marriage was ever consummated; certainly it was childless, in a prolific age. It is probable that Blake's young passion frightened Catherine into what would now be called a permanently neurotic state, though some of the stories told of their relation are certainly apocryphal. What is beyond doubt is that they were lifelong comrades and coworkers.

In 1784 Blake started in business for himself as printseller and engraver, with a partner; and his favorite brother, Robert, came to live with them. In 1787 Robert died. Heartbroken, Blake gave up the shop and in 1793 he moved with Catherine to Lambeth, where they lived until 1800, and where much of his most significant work was done.

From his boyhood Blake had written poetry, with a talent as precocious as for drawing. Some of his best known poems were written when he was only twelve to fourteen years old. His first volume had already appeared, *Poetical Sketches*, published in 1783 through the financing of two wealthy persons interested in his career. Now he had another volume (to be known as *Songs of Innocence*) ready for publication, but he could find no publisher. In a dream his dead brother appeared to him and suggested a method (which, however, he had already partly worked out in his waking hours). He and Catherine together literally made the book, by a sort of etching process; the poems were printed by hand on copper plates, with decorations and embellishments, and the prints were colored. Thenceforth nearly all of Blake's work appeared in this technique—a fact which, together with his custom of adding short poems or bits of poetic prose to his published drawings, makes it almost impossible to present any complete bibliography of his writings.

He had made the acquaintance of the celebrated artist Flaxman, whom Blake regarded as a dear friend, but who in turn treated Blake rather scurvily and with patronizing contempt. Already the poet and mystic were overcoming the adaptable engraver in Blake, and he was finding it increasingly difficult to earn a livelihood. Through Flaxman, he was induced in 1800 to go to Felpham, Sussex, as a sort of tame artist for William Hayley, a wealthy squire who fancied himself as a poet. There, in a little cottage, he lived for three years, at first with naive delight in the country, but after a while with increasing discontent, when he found that he was to be called upon to illustrate all the inanities of Hayley's relatives and friends, and to officiate also as a sort of resident butt and court jester. The atmosphere of "elegant triviality" disgusted him, and though outwardly he remained on the politest of terms with Hayley, he gave vent to his feelings in numerous private journal entries and satirical verses; he said bitterly that he had become a mere "likeness taker." The climax came in a row with a drunken ex-soldier who claimed to have been employed as his gardener, and who when thrown out bodily had Blake arrested on a charge of sedition. This was not so grotesque as it sounds; Blake had been known as a Jacobin, a sympathizer with the French Revolution when all its earlier English advocates had deserted it; he had been involved (accidentally) in the Gordon Riots, and later in the disturbances in consequence of which Priestley's house was burned and the scientist forced to migrate to America. It was only for a short period that Blake had been an intimate of the Paine-Godwin-Wollstonecraft circle; but he had walked the streets of London wearing the red cap of the French Revolutionists, and he was a fair target for anyone who wished to attack him on the ground of disloyalty to the state. However, it was easy to prove the foolishness of the charge in this instance, and Hayley seems to have made some efforts in his behalf; he was tried and acquitted, and immediately afterwards he left Felpham and returned to London for the remainder of his life.

The last quarter century of Blake's existence was marked by increasing poverty and neglect. Flaxman was a false friend, and he had few others, though one (Captain Butts) remained a faithful patron. During his earlier years he had exhibited regularly at the Royal Academy, in spite of his abrupt leaving of its school; but after 1785 his pictures were accepted only twice, the last one in 1808. Yet during the first period of his return to London from Felpham he continued to receive and execute commissions for engravings, and some of his most famous plates were made during this time. His poetry had descended from its first simple, passionate lyricism to the confusion and unintelligibility of the *Prophetic Books*, but he had not yet reached the stage where he drew angels and the famous dead as they appeared in space before him. A double instance of treachery and injustice gave the final blow to his career as a working artist. An unscrupulous dealer named Cromek ordered a series of drawings from him at a guinea apiece, with the distinct understanding that he was to do the engraving; instead of which Cromek gave it to a popular artist named Schiavonetti. The only notice of the series was in *The Examiner,* which praised Schiavonetti's work and cried down Blake's. Then Cromek went to Blake's friend Stothard, and suggested his doing a series (*The Canterbury Pilgrims*) already proposed and begun by Blake; Stothard innocently went ahead with the idea, and a permanent breach was caused between the friends. Blake involved himself also in a futile row with *The Examiner* and in an unsuccessful exhibit of his works; he was no meek and mild sufferer under injury, and in his manuscript writings, if not publicly, indulged in the severest utterances about Cromek, and in less justified invectives against Stothard.

Naturally all this did not increase Blake's desirability to the booksellers (who were also the purveyors of engravings), and the injustice he smarted over drove him also more and more into himself. Gradually he ceased to receive orders or to do any work except that suggested by his own imagination—work technically superb but incomprehensible to the ordinary observer. He was rescued from the most abject poverty only by the devotion of a group of young artists, and of a slightly older but almost equally poor artist named Linnell, who from their own scantily furnished pockets drew funds to pay for drawings they commissioned Blake to make for them. That was the only paid employment he had during his last years; he continued to print (or etch) his poems by his private method, but they had no circulation and were scarcely offered for sale. Much of his later work still remains in manuscript.

Yet he, whose moods in better times had oscillated between exaltation and extreme melancholy, remained unceasingly happy and contented in these years of destitution and obloquy. He painted and drew his "spiritual portraits," he wrote his strange prophetic poems, and he lost himself in the inner life created for him by his fancy. Many of his contemporaries and more of his followers have considered Blake actually insane in his later years. It is a nice question. He was a pronounced mystic, and perhaps there is a

WILLIAM BLAKE

a shadow of the world of eternity." His early ethic was a doctrine of love, but of love in liberty; no valid law, he felt, existed external to man. He believed mightily in the authority of passion, in the righteousness of revolt. His earliest poems are pictures of a world of peace and harmony; as life taught him increasingly of the prevalence and power of evil, he felt that rebellion was no longer enough, and turned to prophecy for consolation. Unfortunately his poetry was hurt by his growing philosophy; he drank too deeply of the "windy rhetoric" of Ossian and the Ossianic school, and ruined his lyric beauty by bombast and didacticism.

He came to think of himself as the prophet of a new ethical system; he said, whether he felt it as an objective truth or not, that the spirit of Milton had entered into him. If so, the spirit of Swedenborg—though he never accepted the Swedish mystic as a guide—had entered into him also, and the mixture was a deplorable one. It is not in the *Prophetic Books,* but in the pure beauty of *Songs of Innocence,* and of some at least of the poems in *Songs of Experience,* that the true expression of Blake's poetic genius is to be found. On the other hand, much of his difficult symbolism was deliberate; he had no patience with uncomprehending readers, and believed that the reader owed to the writer the duty of cultivating his own imagination until he could understand what was offered to him. Whole libraries of interpretation have been built up in the attempt to accept this challenge, and yet much of the symbolism was perhaps not clear to Blake himself, and the symbols sometimes change their nature in the midst of their creation. Two are unchanging, the God and Satan of his mythology—Urizen, who represents legality, restrictive morality, who is the Jehovah of the Bible, and who in Blake's system fell instead of Lucifer, and Orc, the liberator, the prototype of human passion, identified by Blake with the spirit of young America and resurgent France.

tinge of insanity in all mysticism, but his life was disciplined and controlled, there were no overt evidences of lunacy in any of his actions, and it may be doubted whether even his hallucinations were actually real to himself. He said that intense concentration on the exercise of a vivid imagination could produce images so strong that they appeared to have genuine existence, and yet it is questionable whether he himself did not always realize that they were purely subjective. He led the quietest of existences; a few months before his own end, Flaxman died, and Blake remarked that death was merely going from one room into another. For him it was indeed that; his heart failed him and he had to take to his bed, still drawing and writing in spite of his illness; for a day he lay singing softly to himself (he had always loved music, and his earliest poems he set to unwritten tunes and used to sing to groups of admirers), and then he quietly faded out of life. As J. P. R. Wallis said, "He died singing." He had lived so too, first singing and then prophesying.

The truth was, that Blake, like so many geniuses, was born out of time and place. With Lord Acton, and with greater approximation to truth, he could say that he "had no contemporaries." Most of his work was done in the classical eighteenth century, yet he was the first of the romanticists. His affiliations are with Burns and Coleridge before him, with Keats and above all with Shelley after him. "Only imagination is real," he said, and "imagination is my world." He despised experimental science and the scientific spirit. "This world," he held, "is

In a word, Blake was a genius. Like all geniuses, he was neurotic, with violent transitions from joy to despair and back again. He felt himself to be under the daily guidance of angels, who appeared to him and guided his pencil. He was a born rebel who sublimated his rebellion into mysticism; he could not remake the world externally, so he reconstructed it from the inside out. Ill treated and neglected by men, he went to live with angels; yet he took mankind with him, and in a flash of half-insane understanding he said "all are men in eternity." Like Shelley, he was not entirely human, if humanity implies material grossness, but was himself a bit of an angel. Osbert Burdett has said the concluding word on Blake: "His life was noble, but his work sublime."

M. A. deF.

PRINCIPAL WORKS: [Much still in ms., chiefly in the W. M. Rossetti collection: e.g., The Four Zoas (former title, Vala) 1797-1800; An Island in the Moon (circ. 1784); The Everlasting Gospel, 1818. Most of his other work appeared first not in print, but in Blake's own hand-made format. Books actually printed are starred.] Poems—*Poetical Sketches, 1783; Songs of Innocence, 1789; The Book of Thel, 1789; A Song of Liberty, circ. 1792; Prospectus, 1793; The Gates of Paradise, 1793; Songs of Experience, 1794; Prophetic Books: *The French Revolution, Book I, 1791 (seven books projected but unwritten); Visions of the Daughters of Albion, 1793; America: A Prophecy, 1792; Europe: A Prophecy, 1794; The First Book of Urizen, 1794; The Book of Los, 1795; The Song of Los, 1795; The Book of Ahania, 1795; Jerusalem, 1804; Milton, 1804; The Ghost of Abel, circ. 1822. Prose—There Is No Natural Religion, 1790; All Religions Are One, 1790; A Marriage of Heaven and Hell, 1793; *Descriptive Catalogue, 1809; On Homer's Poetry (no date, late); On Vergil (no date, late).

ABOUT: Bruce, H. William Blake in This World; Burdett, O. William Blake; Chesterton, G. K., William Blake; Clutton-Brock, A. Blake; Damon, S. F. William Blake: His Philosophy and Symbols; Gardner, C. William Blake: The Man; Gilchrist, A. The Life of William Blake; Jenkins, H. G. William Blake: Studies of His Life and Personality; Murry, J. M. William Blake; Symons, A. William Blake; Wilson, W. The Life of William Blake; Wright, T. The Life of William Blake; Sewanee Review 43:210 April, 1935.

BLANCHARD, EDWARD LITT LAMAN (1820-September 4, 1889), playwright, was born in London, son of the popular theatrical comedian William Blanchard. Educated at Brixton, Ealing, and Lichfield, he began to write plays at nineteen. London and country theatres paid him often no more than 10 shillings an act for his work. For thirty-four years he supplied the Drury Lane with pantomimes, of which he produced altogether about a hundred, known for their prettiness and fancy. He wrote dramatic criticism for newspapers, contributed to comic journals, and engaged in miscellaneous journalism. His works included a pair of novels and many illustrated guides to London and other places. Twice married, he died in London of creeping paralysis in his sixty-ninth year. His countless plays have never been collected, and very few of them have ever been printed.

PRINCIPAL WORK: Faith, Hope and Charity, 1845.

ABOUT: Scott, C. & Howard, C. The Life and Reminiscences of Edward Laman Blanchard.

BLANCHARD, (SAMUEL) LAMAN (May 15, 1804-February 15, 1845), poet, essayist, and journalist, was born at Great Yarmouth, in Norfolk, the only son of a painter and glazier. Educated in London at St. Olave's School, he worked in youth as clerk, actor, proofreader, and secretary to the Zoological Society. To the detriment of his

health, he engaged industriously in journalism as editor of a succession of liberal organs, notably The Constitutional and The Courier. In his last years he was a contributor to The Examiner. His many literary friends and admirers included Douglas Jerrold, Thackeray, Bulwer-Lytton, and Letitia E. Landon, whose Life and Literary Remains he published. Two months after the death of his wife, Ann Gates, he died by his own hand in a fit of delirium at the age of forty, leaving three children.

He was the author of light and serious verse which was popular in its day and has been compared to the work of Hood, but is not credited with lasting value. His Lyric Offerings was dedicated to Charles Lamb.

PRINCIPAL WORKS: Poetry—Lyric Offerings, 1828; Poetical Works (ed. by B. Jerrold) 1876. Essays—Corporations Characters, 1855; Sketches of Life (ed. by E. Bulwer-Lytton) 1846.

ABOUT: Blanchard, S. L. Poetical Works (see Memoir by B. Jerrold); Blanchard, S. L. Poetical Works (see Memoir by E. Bulwer-Lytton).

BLESSINGTON, LADY (Marguerite Power Farmer Gardiner, Countess of Blessington) (September 1, 1789-June 4, 1849), diarist, novelist, and beauty, was born Margaret Power at Knockbrit, County Tipperary, Ireland, the daughter of Edmund Power, an improvident country squire of dissolute and violent character. Her early life held little happiness. Before her fifteenth birthday, scarcely more than a sensitive child, she was literally sold into marriage with Captain Maurice St. Leger Farmer, a carnal and sadistic Irish army officer, from whom she fled after three terrible months. Michael Sadleir, her modern biographer, believes that the shock of this brutal experience destroyed her normal feminine instincts and thus holds the psychological key to her later life.

At the age of eighteen, to escape further persecution by her father, she accepted a liaison of convenience with a dull but kindly English army officer, Captain Thomas Jenkins. Under his roof she lived quietly for ten years, educating herself by wide reading. When she was twenty-eight Farmer was killed in a drunken brawl. This cleared the way for her marriage to Charles John Gardiner, Earl of Blessington, a wealthy, good-natured widower, who had been attracted by her beauty and by the social and intellectual graces which she had assiduously developed. Blessington paid Jenkins £10,000 as "reimbursement."

Thus Margaret Farmer became Marguerite, Countess of Blessington. In London, where the Blessingtons made their home for the next four years, her beauty, charm, and shrewdness, coupled with genuine kindness and generosity, quickly established her as one of the noted hostesses of the day. The at-

LADY BLESSINGTON

tendance at her salon was almost entirely masculine, however; "ladies" shunned her because of her past.

In 1822 Lady Blessington made her literary début with three volumes of sketches and essays, her only publications for a decade. In the same year she and her husband began a protracted Continental tour, which included a long stay at Genoa, in daily contact with Lord Byron.

In 1829 Lord Blessington died suddenly in Paris from an apoplectic stroke. Thenceforth to the end of her days Lady Blessington lived with Alfred, Count d'Orsay, the estranged husband of her stepdaughter. A charming, penniless, selfish French nobleman, twelve years her junior, he was known as "the last of the dandies" and was reputed to be the handsomest and best-dressed man of his times. Their relationship was probably platonic; in fact, not unlike that of an indulgent mother and a spoiled son. After two years' residence in Paris, they returned to London, where, despite the scandal attached to her name, Lady Blessington again established herself as hostess to the first rank of social, literary, and political celebrities, entertaining on a prodigal scale. Virtually every noted man of the day was her guest at one time or another.

In the meantime, however, the income from Lord Blessington's estate had begun to dwindle at an alarming rate, and to meet expenses Lady Blessington turned again to authorship. Her most successful work was her *Journal of Conversations With Lord Byron*, which is still considered an invaluable source of personal information about the poet. Her first novel, a *roman à clef* called *The Repealers*, was also widely read. Of

varying success and worth were her travel diaries and later society novels, written under increasing financial pressure. She even edited two popular "annuals" for several years.

But the effort was futile. Although her writing at one time brought in more than £2,000 yearly, expenses (particularly d'Orsay's) were far in excess of this amount. Finally her inherited income ceased entirely, and early in 1849 she became bankrupt. After a weary tragi-comedy of creditor-dodging, d'Orsay fled from England. Lady Blessington remained behind to auction her effects and then followed him to Paris, where within two months she died of apoplexy complicated by heart disease, in her sixtieth year. She was buried in the village of Chambourcy, near St. Germain-en-Laye, not far from Paris. D'Orsay survived her by only three years and was buried by her side.

Lady Blessington's books are today chiefly of interest to the social historian. They reveal keen observation, but are otherwise undistinguished as literary products. Their author is better remembered for the drama of her own life. Ambitious, over-fond of luxury, heedless of proprieties, she was nevertheless "more sinned against than sinning" and had what she termed in a letter to Bulwer-Lytton late in life "a sort of silent respect" for herself.   H. H.

PRINCIPAL WORKS: Sketches and Fragments, 1822; The Repealers, 1833; The Journal of Conversations With Lord Byron, 1834; The Two Friends, 1835; The Idler in Italy, 1839-40; The Idler in France, 1841.

ABOUT: Madden, R. R. The Literary Life and Correspondence of the Countess of Blessington; Molloy, J. F. The Most Gorgeous Lady Blessington; Sadleir, M. The Strange Life of Lady Blessington (English title: Blessington d'Orsay).

BLIND, MATHILDE (March 21, 1841-November 26, 1896), poet, was born Mathilde Cohen at Mannheim, Germany, the daughter of a banker. Upon her mother's second marriage, to Karl Blind, a well-known political writer, she changed her name to Mathilde Blind. Her stepfather was a leader in the Baden revolt of 1848-49, and when the insurrection was put down, he and his family were forced to leave Germany. They found refuge in London, where Mathilde was educated from the age of eight. She grew up an English woman, although her German stepfather's house was frequented by foreign exiles and she maintained close contact with Continental literature and life by frequent travel.

Miss Blind made her literary début at the age of twenty-six with a volume of *Poems* published under the pseudonym of "Claude Lake." Her chief works were three long poems. *The Prophecy of St. Oran, The Heather on Fire,* and *The Ascent of Man.* The first two grew out of a visit to Scotland

and the third, her most ambitious work, was an epic on Darwin's theory of evolution.

In addition to her poetic work, she made translations of D. F. Strauss's *The Old Faith and the New* (1873) and *The Journal of Marie Bashkirtseff* (1890)—both famous Continental works in their time—and wrote biographies of George Eliot (1883) and Madame Roland (1886).

While writing the two biographies, in the early 'eighties, she lived for the most part in Manchester, where she could be near the painter Ford Madox Brown and his wife, for whom she had high regard. Later she traveled widely in Italy and Egypt, searching for healthful climates and indulging her love of nature and ancient relics. These travels were reflected in her *Dramas in Miniature, Songs and Sonnets,* and *Birds of Passage.* Her final poetic work was done at Stratford-on-Avon, where the scenery and the Shakespearian landmarks inspired the sonnets which are her best remembered work.

She died in London at fifty-five, leaving her property to Newnham College, Cambridge. Four years after her death Arthur Symons made a collection of her poetical works, with a memoir by Richard Garnett.

PRINCIPAL WORKS: The Prophecy of St. Oran, 1881; The Heather on Fire, 1886; The Ascent of Man, 1888; Songs and Sonnets, 1893; Birds of Passage: Songs of the Orient and Occident, 1895; The Poetical Works of Mathilde Blind (ed. by A. Symons) 1900.

ABOUT: Blind, M. The Poetical Works of Mathilde Blind (see Memoir by R. Garnett).

BLOOMFIELD, ROBERT (December 3, 1766-August 19, 1823), poet, was born at Honington in Suffolk, the son of a tailor, George Bloomfield, who died before the child was a year old.

From his mother, Elizabeth (Manby) Bloomfield, who, in order to support her six children, taught the village school, the little boy gained a rudimentary knowledge of reading; and for a few months he attended a school in Ixworth, where he learned to write. Upon his mother's remarriage, however, he was taken from school, and, a few years later, sent to work on the farm of a Mr. Austin, his mother's brother-in-law.

Here he was treated kindly, and acquired the familiarity with farm life that was to stand him in such good stead. His small physique, however, was not adequate to his tasks, and his mother, who was so poor that she found it difficult to keep the boy clothed, wrote to two elder sons, asking for their aid. His brother George, a shoemaker, offered to teach him the trade, and Nathaniel, a tailor, to keep him in clothes; in June 1781, accordingly, Robert came to London, escorted personally by his anxious mother.

Living in a garret with his brother George and four other men, Robert made himself useful by running errands, and by reading the newspaper to the others. As he had difficulty with the words, he improved his knowledge of language with the aid of a small dictionary, and by attendance upon the sermons of a non-conformist minister, a Mr. Fawcett. At his brother's suggestion he sent to the *London Magazine* some verses, which were accepted and published.

Thanks to a Scotchman named Kay, who allowed Robert the use of his books, the boy was enabled to read *Paradise Lost* and Thomson's *Seasons.*

After a brief visit to Mr. Austin's farm, where he renewed his acquaintance with rural life, Bloomfield returned to London to work as a shoemaker for his brother, who left the city in 1785, Robert remaining to ply his trade. It was about this time that he learned to play the violin.

In 1790, as he wrote his brother, he sold his fiddle and got a wife, Mary Anne Church. He was wretchedly poor; and it was in a garret where others were at work that he wrote his poem, *The Farmer's Boy,* almost half of which had been composed before a line was written.

The publication of the poem, with wood cuts by Thomas Bewick, was due to the influence of a Mr. Capel Lofft, who lived near the poet's birthplace. The work, which resembles Thomson's *Seasons,* met with wide popularity, and the publishers, who had given the author a relatively small flat price, voluntarily gave him £200 of their profits. In better circumstances, Bloomfield removed to a small house in the City Road.

ROBERT BLOOMFIELD

From this point, however, his fortunes declined. His health forced him to relinquish his appointment as Undersealer of Writs in the Seal Office, which he had received through the influence of the Duke of Grafton, who gave him a small allowance. For a time he made Aeolian harps, and apparently was fairly successful. His next venture, however, was in the book trade, in which he failed and went bankrupt.

From this time his health declined, and, after a tour in Wales in 1811 (*The Banks of Wye*) and a short trip to Canterbury and Dover in 1814, Bloomfield, half-blind from the violent headaches to which he was subject, and a hypochondriac, retired to Shefford, Bedfordshire, where he died, in poverty, in 1823, leaving a widow and four children.

The poet was a man of gentle instincts and affections, but a fragile and perhaps undisciplined nature, and a mind which, never powerful, might eventually have become insane.

His verse, like the man, was unsophisticated and distinctly rustic, although cast in a classical form. ". . . A racy strength, a temperament that savors of the people, is warped and weakened through the medium of an acquired style, a studied elegance, a commonplace regularity," writes Louis Cazamian. His work is notable, not for suggestion or depth of reflection, but for realistic description of country scenes. Unlike Wordsworth's realism, Bloomfield's leaves nothing between the lines. While he wrote with fluency, he lacked profound thought or humor. Lamb complained of his "poor mind," and Hazlitt said that his muse was not only rustic but menial. Yet, for truth and faithfulness of description of country life of the times, his poetry deserves a place, if not a high one, in English literature of the period.   R. W. W.

PRINCIPAL WORKS: *Letters*—Selections from the Correspondence of Robert Bloomfield (ed. W. H. Hart) 1870. *Play*—Hazelwood-Hall, 1823. *Poetry*— The Farmer's Boy, 1800; Rural Tales, Ballads, and Songs, 1802; Good Tidings, 1804; Wild Flowers, 1806; The Banks of Wye, 1811; May Day With the Muses, 1822. *Miscellaneous*—The History of Little Davy's New Hat, 1817; The Remains of Robert Bloomfield, 1824.

ABOUT: Craik, G. L. The Pursuit of Knowledge Under Difficulties; Winks, W. E. Lives of Distinguished Shoemakers; Academy 68:663 June 24, 1905; Leisure Hour 21:196 March 30, 1872; Westminster Review 169:226 February 1908; also memoirs in various editions of Bloomfield's works.

BLUNT, WILFRID SCAWEN (August 14, 1840-September 10, 1922), poet and political writer, was born in Sussex of a wealthy Roman Catholic family. He was educated at the two principal Catholic colleges, Stonyhurst, and St. Mary's College, Oscott. From 1858 to 1870 he was in the diplomatic service, being attached to embassies or ministries in

WILFRED SCAWEN BLUNT

Greece, Turkey, France, Spain, South America, and Germany.

In 1869 Blunt married Lady Anne Noel Baroness Wentworth, daughter of the Earl of Lovelace, and Byron's granddaughter, her mother being the poet's only legitimate child, Ada. One daughter was born to the Blunts. Though at first she idolized him, Lady Anne gradually became estranged from her husband and they lived apart, a reconciliation taking place just before her death in 1917.

In 1872 Blunt's older brother died and he succeeded to the 2,000-acre family estate, Crabbet Hall, Sussex. He resigned from the diplomatic service at this time. From 1877 to 1881 he and his wife traveled in Arabia, Syria, Persia, and Mesopotamia. He became a strong advocate of Egyptian independence, violently opposed to British policy in the Sudan, and was active in the Egyptian nationalist movement in 1881 and 1882. The next year he spent in India.

He stood twice for Parliament, as a Tory Home Ruler in 1885, as a Liberal Home Ruler in 1886, but each time without success. He then became deeply involved in the Irish Home Rule movement, and active in Parnell's Irish Land League. As a result he came into collision with the British government, and was imprisoned in Ireland in 1888, the first Englishman to go to jail for Irish freedom.

Blunt belonged to the great group of English eccentrics, of the order of Trelawny, Burton, Doughty, and T. E. Lawrence, all of whom were strongly attracted to the East. He bought a home in Egypt and spent his winters there during most of his life. At home his chief interest was in the breeding of Arab horses; unfortunately, after his wife's death, this led to a bitter law-suit against his own daughter. He changed his religion frequently, being in turn a devout Catholic, an Orientalist interested in the reform of the Mohammedan religion, and an avowed Atheist. He was a bundle of contradictions—a natural Tory always at outs with his fellow-Tories, a vain man capable of unselfish, obscure service in a cause in which he believed. Tall, impressive, with a long beard, he greatly resembled the Arab sheiks among whom he sometimes lived.

As a writer, Blunt was the *enfant terrible* of his time. In his *Secret History* he gave away private conversations and letters with the shameless indiscretion of a child. His diaries are full of vivid, cruel characterizations of his contemporaries—and he knew everybody of importance. They are invaluable source-books for the period; T. P. O'Connor says "there is scarcely a line in any of them that is not worth reading." His political poems, full of fierce indignation, are Byronic in derivation, though he denied the influence. His love poems are superb in their honesty of emotion. His poetry is irregular, often substituting assonance for rhyme, but full of force and passion.   M. A. deF.

PRINCIPAL WORKS: *Poetry*—Love Sonnets of Proteus, 1880; The Wind and the Whirlwind, 1883; In Vinculis, 1889; Esther, 1892; Stealing of the Mare, 1892; Griselda, 1893; Satan Absolved, 1899; Seven Golden Odes of Pagan Arabia, 1905. *Prose*— The Future of Islam, 1882; Ideas About India, 1885; A New Pilgrimage, 1889; Secret History of the English Occupation of Egypt, 1907; India Under Ripon, 1909; Gordon at Khartoum, 1911; The Land War in Ireland, 1912; My Diaries, 1919-20.

ABOUT: Blunt, W. S. My Diaries; Catholic World 116:357 December 1922; Living Age 315:157 October 21, 1922; Nation 113:600 December 7, 1921; 114:60 January 18, 1922; North American Review 217:664 May 1923; Poetry 22:337 September 1923.

BOHN, HENRY GEORGE (January 4, 1796-August 22, 1884), publisher, bookseller, and compiler, was born in London, the son of a bookbinder and second-hand book dealer. After leaving school, he learned the book trade by working many years in his father's establishment. At thirty-five, upon his marriage to Elizabeth Simpkin, he started an independent business of his own, his father having refused to make him a partner.

The next ten years were taken up mainly with collecting valuable old books and compiling *The Guinea Catalog of Old Books,* his chief work, descriptive of 300,000 titles. Published in 1841, this 2,000-page opus brought him immediate fame and preeminence as a second-hand bookseller.

It was as a publisher of cheap editions, however, that Bohn made his greatest reputation. Beginning in 1846 with "Bohn's Standard Library," he brought out numerous popular series—the "Antiquarian," "Scientific," "Classical," "Illustrated," "Ecclesiastical," "Philological," and other "libraries"—all containing books of an instructive nature. Together with the various additional "Bohn's Libraries" which appeared after he had given up his publishing business, these reprints filled more than six hundred volumes.

A man of tremendous energy and capacity for work, Bohn not only supervised every detail of his business but did much of the editing and compiling himself. His contributions to the "libraries" included translations, handbooks, biographical notices, and prefaces. He also performed numerous other editorial tasks, notably the enlarging and revising of William Thomas Lowndes's *The Bibliographer's Manual,* with prefatory notes.

Bohn sold his business for a handsome sum in 1864, and lived twenty years longer, devoting himself to cataloging his books, collecting rare shrubs, roses, and works of art, and giving entertainments on his estate at Twickenham. Active even in extreme old age, he worked on a catalog of his art collection until two days before his death at the age of eighty-eight.

PRINCIPAL WORKS COMPILED OR EDITED BY BOHN: *Popular Series*—Bohn's Standard Library, 1846; Bohn's Extra Volumes, 1846; Bohn's Antiquarian Library, 1847; Bohn's Scientific Library, 1847; Bohn's Classical Library, 1848; Bohn's Illustrated Library, 1849; Bohn's Shilling Series, 1850; Bohn's Ecclesiastical Library, 1851; Bohn's Philological Library, 1852; Bohn's British Classics, 1853. *Other Works*—The Guinea Catalogue of Old Books, 1841; W. T. Lowndes's The Bibliographer's Manual, 1857; Dictionary of Quotations, 1867.

ABOUT: The Times August 25, 1884; Athenaeum August 30, 1884; Bookseller September 1884; Bibliographer October 1884.

"BOLDREWOOD, RALPH." See BROWNE, THOMAS ALEXANDER

BOOLE, GEORGE (November 2, 1815-December 8, 1864), mathematician, logician, and author of textbooks, was born in Lincoln, England, the son of a small tradesman. Educated at a national school in Lincoln and at a commercial school, he began teaching at sixteen. In his twentieth year he opened his own school in Lincolnshire, and from the age of thirty-four until his death he was professor of mathematics at Queen's College, Cork, Ireland. By his wife, a Miss Everest, he had five daughters. He died suddenly at forty-nine, of lung congestion contracted while walking in the rain.

His best known work was a treatise on *The Laws of Thought,* which laid the foundations of modern logical calculus. He also wrote two valuable and widely-used textbooks on pure mathematics.

PRINCIPAL WORKS: The Mathematical Analysis of Logic, 1847; An Investigation of the Laws of Thought, 1854; Differential Equations, 1859-65; Calculus of Finite Differences, 1860. Some of his most important works are fugitive papers to be found in the *Philosophical Transactions of the Royal Society.*

ABOUT: British Quarterly Review July 1866.

BOOTH, CHARLES (March 30, 1840-November 23, 1916), writer on social questions and shipowner, was born in Liverpool, England, the son of a corn merchant. Educated at the Royal Institution School of Liverpool, he had a long and prosperous career in the shipping business, first as partner with his brother in Alfred Booth & Company, engaged in Brazil trade, and later as chairman of the Booth Steamship Company. He died at the age of seventy-six at his home in Whitwick, Leicestershire. By his wife, Mary Macaulay, he had three sons and four daughters.

Turned author when he was past forty, he devoted sixteen years to compiling (with the aid of Beatrice Webb, Graham Balfour, Ernest Aves, and other sociologists) his chief work, *Life and Labour of the People in London,* an exhaustive, eighteen-volume social survey of urban conditions, which was notable as the first study of its kind. Through his writings, he did much to bring about passage of the Old Age Pension Act.

PRINCIPAL WORKS: Occupations of the People, 1886; Life and Labour of the People in London, 1891-1903; Old Age Pensions, 1899; Poor Law Reform, 1910; Industrial Unrest and Trade Union Policy, 1913.

ABOUT: Booth, M. M. Charles Booth: A Memoir.

BOOTHBY, GUY NEWELL (October 13, 1867-February 26, 1905), Australian novelist, was born in Adelaide, South Australia, the son of a member of the South Australian house of assembly. He was educated in England (1874-83) and lived again in Australia (1883-94) while he wrote unsuccessful plays and acted as secretary to the mayor of Adelaide. In 1894 he settled in England, and he devoted the remaining eleven years of his life to writing novels and stories of adventure, of which the best were based on his extensive travels in Australia. His works were sensational, exciting in plot, and widely popular, but hastily and carelessly written. (He produced more than fifty volumes during his brief career.) He died suddenly of influenza at his home near Bournemouth at the age of thirty-seven, leaving his wife, Rose Alice Bristowe, and their three children.

PRINCIPAL WORKS: A Lost Endeavour, 1895; A Bid for Fortune: or, Dr. Nikola's Vendetta, 1895; A Beautiful White Devil, 1896; Dr. Nikola, 1896; Bushigrams, 1897; Billy Binks, Hero, and Other Stories, 1898; Dr. Nikola's Experiment, 1899; Farewell Nikola, 1901.

ABOUT: The Times February 28, 1905.

BORROW, GEORGE HENRY (July 5, 1803-July 26, 1881), was born in East Dereham, Norfolk, the son of Captain Thomas Borrow, a Cornish man who had risen from the ranks, and Ann Parfrement, an actress of French Protestant descent. The exigencies of his father's career as a recruiting officer kept the family constantly on the move until 1816. Thus during the first thirteen years of his life young Borrow shifted about England, Ireland, and Scotland attending a variety of schools, including the high school in Edinburgh.

From 1816 until his father's death in 1824 the family lived in Norwich. Here George attended the grammar school until at the age of seventeen he was articled to a solicitor, with whom he remained until 1824. But the most important influence upon Borrow's life during this period was his association with William Taylor.

Taylor was a well-to-do scholar, the translator of Goethe and other German poets, and a man of advanced and liberal views. He taught Borrow German and encouraged his literary efforts. When, at the age of twenty-one, Borrow went to London to try his fortunes, Taylor gave him letters of introduction to Sir Richard Phillips and Thomas Campbell. Taylor wrote to his friend Southey (the poet): "A Norwich young man is construing with me Schiller's *Wilhelm Tell* with the view of translating it for the Press. His name is George Henry Borrow, and he has learnt German with extraordinary rapidity; indeed he has the gift of tongues, and though not yet eighteen, understands twelve languages—English, Welsh, Erse, Latin, Greek, Hebrew, German, Danish, French, Italian, Spanish and Portuguese. He would like to get into the Office for Foreign Affairs, but does not know how."

In 1824 Borrow left for London and there encountered the usual difficulties of budding authors. He was engaged by Sir Richard Phillips in various hack-writing jobs, among which was compilation of part of the *Newgate Calendar.* But by the latter part of 1825 he had quarreled with Sir Richard and was in very straitened circumstances. The publication of his *Romantic Ballads* (translated from Danish) in May 1826 was not a financial success.

Borrow's activities from 1825 to 1832 remain generally obscure. It was during this period that many of the adventures and gypsy episodes described in *Lavengro* and *Romany Rye* are supposed to have occurred. But it is impossible to tell, with certainty, where accurate autobiography leaves off and fiction begins in these books.

At last in 1833, at the age of thirty, Borrow was recommended to the British and Foreign Bible Society by a Norfolk vicar whom he had

GEORGE BORROW

met through Mrs. Clarke—the widow he married seven years later. His first assignment was to translate the New Testament into Manchu, the court language of China. Borrowing a few books, including a Manchu-French Dictionary and the Gospel of St. Matthew in the Manchu-Tartar dialect, he retired to the country to study this new language. After two or three weeks' study he wrote to the secretary of the Bible Society: "I can already . . . translate Manchu with no great difficulty . . . had I a (Manchu) Grammar, I should in a month's time be able to send a Manchu translation of Jonah." Nineteen weeks after starting the study of Manchu, Borrow passed an examination in the language and was soon thereafter sent to Russia to begin work on the translation. At this time Russia was the only European country which had a minister at the court of the Chinese Empire, and this in addition to the fact that certain material was available in the libraries of Petrograd made it necessary to do the work there. After about two years in Russia his task was completed and he returned to London in September 1835.

By November of that year Borrow was in Lisbon, Portugal, ready to start the adventures related in *The Bible in Spain*. His travels in Spain and Portugal continued intermittently until 1839. His work of distributing tracts and Bibles in these Catholic countries was undoubtedly sincere, but it appears to have been prompted more by hatred of the Roman Catholic Church than by a deep religious feeling.

In 1840 Borrow married Mrs. Clarke and settled on Oulton Broad, on an estate of which Mrs. Clarke had been part owner. With the income from his writings they purchased full title to the property. *Gypsies in Spain*, published in 1841, and *The Bible in Spain*, published two years later had a tremendous popular sale—particularly the latter—many people in that sanctimonious age buying the book under the impression that it was a religious tract.

But the popularity of these two books was only that of a current best-seller. During his lifetime, Borrow was never rated among the important literary figures of his day. On the contrary, *Lavengro* and his later works were discredited by contemporaries who did not care for such robust literature.

There is no doubt that Borrow was the victim of both snobbery and prudishness. His resentment toward the self-satisfied arbiters of morals and good taste often led him into giving boorish rebuffs to well meant advances, as when Agnes Strickland offered to send him a copy of her book *The Queens of England*, he replied ungraciously: "For God's sake, don't, madam; I should not know where to put them or what to do with them!" He was an outsider to the polite society in which most of his contemporary writers moved. But at his estate on Oulton Broad he was a generous host. Here gypsies were free to camp and he welcomed all whom he called friends.

There has been much mystery hung about Borrow's life, particularly those portions of it about which he has written the most. Practically all his original writings (as distinguished from his translations) are autobiographical, but they are so full of romantic adventure, it is obvious they cannot be entirely true. But Borrow was himself such a remarkable person that it would be difficult to be sure where truth ended and fiction began. Augustine Birrell says, "Few things are more comical than to hear some douce body, unread in Borrow, gravely inquiring how far his word may be relied upon. The sole possible response takes the exceptionable shape of loud peals of laughter. And yet, surely, it is a most reasonable question. . . So it is; but after you have read your author you won't ask it—you won't want to. The reader can believe what he likes and as much as he likes."

The great enthusiasm for Borrow began to develop some time after his death. Clement Shorter remarked, in an address on the occasion of the Borrow Centenary in 1903, that: "There are hardly any good and distinctive appreciations in print of Borrow's works." Yet, since that time there has been an ever increasing body of "Borrovians" and a corresponding bibliography of criticism and appreciation. One enthusiast writes: "A single chapter of Borrow is air and exercise." And again: "If one was in search of a single epithet most properly descriptive of Borrow's effect upon his reader, perhaps it would best be found in the word 'contagious.' He is one of the most catching of our authors."

Compare these impressions gained from Borrow's writing with descriptions left by two of his intimates and it becomes evident that the true man is revealed in his books no matter how much fiction he mixed with autobiography. In a letter written September 12, 1848, W. B. Donne says: "We have had a great man here—and I have been walking with him—George Borrow—and what is more we fell in with some gypsies and I heard his speech of Egypt . . . Borrow's face lighted up by the turf fire of the tent was worth looking at. He is ashy-white now, but twenty years ago, when his hair was like a raven's wing, he must have been hard to discriminate from a born Bohemian. Borrow is best on the tramp: if you can walk four and a half miles per hour . . . and can walk fifteen of them at a stretch . . . then he will talk Iliads of adventures even better than his printed ones. He cannot abide Amateur Pedestrians who saunter, and in his chair he is given to groan and be contradictory. But on Newmarket Heath, in Rougham Woods he is at home, and specially when he meets with a thorough vagabond like your present correspondent." And his publisher, John Murray, describes Borrow as: ". . . tall, broad, muscular, with very heavy shoulders, he was a figure which no one who has seen him is likely to forget. I never remember to have seen him dressed in anything but black broadcloth, and white cotton socks were generally distinctly visible above his low shoes. I think that with Borrow the desire to attract attention to himself, to inspire a feeling of awe and mystery, must have been a ruling passion."

D. C.

PRINCIPAL WORKS: *Translations*—Romantic Ballads, 1926; Targum: or, Metrical Translations From Thirty Languages and Dialects, 1835; New Testament (Luke) in Romani, 1837. *Prose*—The Zincali: or, Account of the Gypsies in Spain, 1841; The Bible in Spain, 1843; Lavengro, 1851; The Romany Rye, 1857; Wild Wales, 1862; Romano Lavo-lil, 1874.

ABOUT: Birrell, A. Collected Essays and Addresses; Borrow, G. Letters; Hearn, L. Life and Literature; Jenkins, H. G. Life of George Borrow; Knapp, W. I. Life, Writings and Correspondence of George Borrow; Saintsbury, G. Essays in English Literature (Series 1); Shorter, C. K. Immortal Memories; Shorter, C. K. George Borrow and His Circle; Thomas, E. George Borrow: The Man and His Books; Watts-Dunton, T. Old Familiar Faces; Wise, T. J. Bibliography of the Writings of George Borrow.

BOSWELL, SIR ALEXANDER (October 9, 1775-March 27, 1822), Scottish poet, was born in Ayrshire, the oldest son of the famous James Boswell, the biographer of Dr. Johnson. After an education at Westminster and Oxford, and the "grand tour" of Europe then fashionable among the wealthy, Boswell returned to the family estate at Auchinleck, Ayrshire, which remained his permanent home.

He was a great admirer of Burns, and in imitation of him and of Allan Ramsay wrote a vast amount of verse in the Scottish dialect. It was by his efforts that a monument was erected to Burns on the banks of the Doon in 1820. He was also a bibliographer and antiquary; he established a private press and reprinted by hand a number of fifteenth and sixteenth century Scottish works. He was poet laureate of the Harveian Society of Edinburgh.

Boswell, as a Scottish squire, acted as magistrate, and was also deputy lieutenant of Argyllshire and lieutenant colonel of the Ayrshire cavalry. From 1818 to 1820 he served in Parliament as a conservative. He was made a baronet in 1821. He married a distant cousin whose maiden name was Montgomery, and had several children.

High-spirited, amiable, and jovial, Boswell unfortunately was also a bit overbearing and too fond of ridicule. It was a fatal trait. In several papers he had anonymously attacked and satirized a writer named James Stuart who was supposed to be his friend. When Stuart found out the author he challenged Boswell to a duel. Several attempts at securing an apology were unsuccessful, and Stuart's second shot caused Boswell's death the next day. Stuart was tried for murder and acquitted.

Boswell's verse is graphic, highly humorous, often coarse, but full of life. In English poetry he was more rhetorical than poetic. He had by no means his father's great talent; he was really only a Tory squire who amused himself by writing dialect songs and printing them on his own press.

PRINCIPAL WORKS: Songs Chiefly in the Scottish Dialect, 1803; The Spirit of Tintoc, 1803; Clan Alpin's Vow, 1811; The Tyrant's Fall, 1815; The Wo'-creel, 1816.

BOSWORTH SMITH, REGINALD (June 28, 1839-October 18, 1908), biographer and historian, was born at West Stafford in Dorset, England, where his father Reginald Southwell Smith (later canon of Salisbury) was then rector. At Corpus Christi College, Oxford, he took first-class honors in the classics, and at Trinity College he tutored and lectured three years on a fellowship. For thirty-six years he was classical master at Harrow School in Middlesex. After his retirement he lived at Bingham's Melcombe, Dorset, where he died at sixty-nine. His wife, Flora Wickham, and nine of their ten children survived him.

He is best known as the biographer of the first Lord Lawrence, contemporary military general in India, whose Afghan policy he had defended in letters to *The Times*. A useful historical monograph on Carthage and the Carthaginians also stands to his credit. He made a life-long study of birds and wrote two books on the subject.

PRINCIPAL WORKS: Carthage and the Carthaginians, 1878; Life of Lord Lawrence, 1883.

ABOUT: Grogan, E. F. Reginald Bosworth Smith: A Memoir

BOUCICAULT, DION(YSIUS) LARDNER (December 26, 1820?-September 18, 1890), Anglo-Irish dramatist and actor, was born at Dublin, the youngest son of S. Boucicault (or Bourcicault) a merchant of French extraction, and Anne Darley. He was the ward and namesake of the famous educator, Dionysius Lardner, and was educated under his influence at Dublin, at Bruce Castle, and at London University. In his school days he is said to have displayed the ready wit which was afterwards to be so characteristic of him.

At the age of seventeen or eighteen, he began a career as actor under an assumed name in London, and in 1841 his first play, *London Assurance,* was produced with great success and with the added distinction of being the first English comedy in modern attire. G. H. Lewes, the critic who was George Eliot's husband, was of the opinion that it was the very best of Boucicault's plays. From this time until the very end of his life Boucicault continued to write, act in, and produce successful plays, his most acclaimed work being perhaps the adaptation of Irving's *Rip Van Winkle,* in which Joseph Jefferson, the distinguished American actor, appeared repeatedly over a long period of years. In 1872 he produced in London *Babil and Bajou,* said to have been the most expensive spectacle mounted up to that time. After 1876 the plays of this busy author were produced by him in New York, where he took up residence in that year.

Boucicault was considered an excellent actor. "A slight, graceful figure; very brilliant eyes, and a clear and powerful voice" reads a contemporary description. It is said that in his adaptation of the French comedy *La Joie Fait Peur* he was the equal of the most polished actors of his day. It may be added that, in general, Boucicault's plays were little more than adaptations, being taken from French, Spanish, and Italian originals, and often from sources nearer home—Mayne Reid's novel *The Quadroon* becoming Boucicault's play *The Octoroon,* for example. These plays were well constructed and the characterizations were fair, although much of the dialogue, witty and pointed as it is, seems absurd to us today. The Irish plays, in which Boucicault came to be the consummate type of stage Irishman, were tremendously popular. He was also the founder of the sensational

DION BOUCICAULT

play and many of his productions were salted with rescues, escapes, and other types of thrills. *After Dark,* one of his old melodramas, was revived in the late 1920's at Hoboken, New Jersey, just across the river from New York City, and enjoyed a successful and amusing run. Boucicault was in many respects an innovator of stage technique, being the first to employ carpets, moving scenery, and such properties as real flowers.

He had married, in 1853, Agnes Robertson, a remarkably beautiful young actress, for whom many of his later plays were frankly vehicles. The author himself was content with smaller rôles. Six children were born to them, one of whom, Dion, became known as an actor. In 1883 the aging playwright, now in the United States, declared that he had never been legally married to Miss Robertson, and married Louise Thorndyke, a member of his company, who, with two children, survived him. Agnes Robertson's divorce suit and the public feeling it aroused against Boucicault were injurious to his popularity, and he died practically a poor man, deeply hurt by his decline and by the lack of managerial interest in his last play, *The Tale of a Coat,* which he never finished.

Clement Scott, the English poet, describes Boucicault as a charming man and as one of the wittiest of all talkers. He was constantly embroiled in controversy, mainly of a professional nature, with the one important exception of his attack on Disraeli regarding the Irish question, and doubtless derived great satisfaction from the ensuing notoriety.

Boucicault was the author of the words of the Irish song "The Wearing of the Green." R. M.

PRINCIPAL WORKS: *Plays*—London Assurance, 1841; The Colleen Bawn, 1860; Arrahna-Pogue,

1865; After Dark, 1868; Led Astray, 1874; The Shaughraun, 1875; The O'Dowd, 1880; The Jilt, 1886.

ABOUT: Men of the Time (12th ed.); Athenaeum 96:426 September 27 1890; New York World March 5, 1916.

BOURINOT, SIR JOHN GEORGE (October 24, 1837-October 13, 1902), Canadian historian and political scientist, was born at Sydney, Cape Breton Island, Nova Scotia, the son of a member of the Canadian senate. Educated at Trinity College, Toronto, he held various parliamentary offices from youth, finally serving as clerk of the Canadian House of Commons during the last twenty-two years of his life. He made early and authoritative studies of Canadian government, parliamentary procedure, and constitutional history. His writings also include a popular history, The Story of Canada, and miscellaneous works on Canadian life. One of the original members of the Royal Society of Canada, he contributed many of his writings first to its Transactions. He received numerous honors, was three times married, and had five children. His death occurred in Ottawa eleven days before his sixty-fifth birthday.

PRINCIPAL WORKS: The Intellectual Developments of the Canadian People, 1881; Parliamentary Procedure and Practice in Canada, 1884; Local Government in Canada, 1887; A Manual of the Constitutional History of Canada, 1888; Federal Government in Canada, 1889; How Canada Is Governed, 1895; The Story of Canada, 1897; Canada Under British Rule, 1900; Builders of Nova Scotia, 1900.

BOWDEN, JOHN WILLIAM (February 21, 1798-September 15, 1844), ecclesiastical poet, essayist, and biographer, was born in London. He received his education at Harrow and Trinity College, Oxford. As John Henry Newman's intimate friend and supporter in the tractarian movement, he collaborated with Newman (at twenty-three) on a poem in two cantos called St. Bartholomew's Eve, wrote six of the 178 hymns in Lyra Apostolica (signing his work with the Greek alpha), supplied five numbers for the Tracts for the Times, and contributed four important articles to the British Critic. His wife, whom he married in 1828, was Elizabeth Swinburne. He served as commissioner of stamps for fourteen years until ill health compelled him to resign, and he died in London at the age of forty-six.

PRINCIPAL WORKS: St. Bartholomew's Eve: A Poem (with J. H. Newman) 1821; Tracts for the Times (with others) 1833-35; Lyra Apostolica (with Newman, J. Keble, and others) 1836; Life of Gregory the Seventh, 1840; Thoughts on the Work of the Six Days of Creation, 1845.

ABOUT: Bowden, J. W. Thoughts on the Work of the Six Days of Creation (see Biographical Preface by J. H. Newman).

BOWLES, CAROLINE ANNE. See SOUTHEY, CAROLINE BOWLES

BOWLES, WILLIAM LISLE (September 24, 1762-April 7, 1850), poet, antiquary, critic, and cleric, was born at King's Sutton, Northamptonshire, his father's vicarage.

Bowles was educated at Winchester School under Dr. Joseph Warton, going thence to Trinity College, Oxford, in 1781. Here in 1783 he won the Chancellor's prize with his Latin Calpe Obsessa. He left Oxford in 1787, taking his M.A. in 1792. In this year he was ordained and became curate, first at Donhead St. Andrew, Wiltshire, and later vicar of Chickdale.

Fourteen Sonnets, his best known poetry, was published in 1789; it is filled with the melancholy of the eighteenth century, but in this case the grief appears sincere, springing from two unhappy courtships. The second had closed with the lady's death. Bowles composed these poems as he toured the British Isles and the continent, using the older, purer sonnet form. Coleridge, a mere youth at the time, greeted the volume with delight and in eighteen months made forty transcripts of it for his friends.

Bowles in 1797 became vicar of Dumbleton, Gloucestershire. In the same year he married Magdalene Wake, daughter of a Westminster prebendary. He transferred, in 1804, to Bremhill, Wiltshire, where he remained until his death at The Close, Salisbury. He became also prebendary (1804) and residentiary canon (1828) of Salisbury Cathedral, and in 1819 was appointed chaplain to the Prince Regent.

Bowles published some valuable antiquarian studies, a letter on crime and education, much

W. L. BOWLES

verse including some hymns, an edition of Pope, and many critical pamphlets. In his essays on the *Poetical Character of Pope* he called Pope second-rate, holding that "all images drawn from what is beautiful or sublime in the works of nature are more beautiful and sublime than any images drawn from art, and they are therefore *per se* (abstractedly) more poetical. In like manner those passions of the human heart, which belong to nature in general, are *per se* more adapted to the higher species of poetry than those derived from accidental and transient manners." This re-opened the "Pope controversy," which absorbed Bowles for years. At once, on many fronts, the battle raged. Pope's defenders included Gifford, Octavius Gilchrist, Thomas Campbell, Byron, Isaac D'Israeli and others. Hazlitt and *Blackwood's* supported Bowles. Confused and ineffective as Bowles the controversialist was, his cause was victorious, for the age was that of the return to nature. His position is that almost of *provocateur*. To him Coleridge dedicated his poetry; Southey acknowledged a great debt to him; Tom Moore admired him; Wordsworth was deeply influenced by him. Henry Hallam placed Bowles' sonnets "among the first fruits of a new era in poetry." Nevertheless, Bowles is not a great poet, though he possessed tender feeling, imagination, and a gift for pure diction.

His pictures show him tall and well-built, with a high forehead and grave expression. Absent-minded and eccentric, he was also genial, lovable, impulsive, and humane.

D. F. A.

PRINCIPAL WORKS: *Poetry*—Fourteen Sonnets, 1789; Verses to John Howard, 1789; Coombe Ellen and St. Michael's Mount, 1798; The Battle of the Nile, 1799; The Sorrows of Switzerland, 1801; The Picture, 1803; The Spirit of Discovery, 1804; Bowden Hill, 1806; Poems, 1809; The Missionary of the Andes, 1813; The Grave of the Last Saxon, 1822; Ellen Gray, 1823; Days Departed, 1829; St. John in Patmos, 1832; Scenes and Shadows of Days Departed, 1837; The Village Verse Book, 1837. *Antiquities*—Hermes Britannicus, 1828; The Parochial Library of Bremhill, 1828; Annals and Antiquities of Lacock Abbey, 1835. *Criticism*—The Poetical Character of Pope, 1806; The Invariable Principles of Poetry, 1819; A Reply to an Unsentimental Sort of Critic, 1820; Letters to Lord Byron, 1821; An Answer to Some Observations of Thomas Campbell, 1822; An Address to Thomas Campbell, 1822; A Vindication of the Late Editor of Pope, 1825; A Final Appeal to the Literary Public, 1825; Lessons in Criticism to William Roscoe, 1826. *Biography*—Life of Pope, 1806; Life of Bishop Ken, 1830. *Sermons and Miscellaneous*—A Sermon, 1804; Ten Parochial Sermons, 1814; The Plain Bible, 1818; Vindiciae Wykehamicae, 1818; A Voice from St. Peter's and St. Paul's, 1823; Paulus Parochiales, 1826; Letter to Sir James Mackintosh; A Few Words to Lord Chancellor Brougham, 1831; Sermons Preached at Bowood, 1834; Further Observations, 1837; St. Paul at Athens, 1838; The Cartoons of Raphael, 1838.

ABOUT: Beers, H. A. A History of English Romanticism; Bowles, W. L. Scenes and Shadows of Days Departed (see Introduction); Bowles, W. L. Poetical Works (see Memoir by G. Gilfillan); Byron, G. G. N. English Bards and Scotch Reviewers; Byron, G. G. N. Letters to John Murray; Coleridge, S. T. Sonnet in *The Morning Chronicle* December 21, 1794; Hallam, H. Address to the Royal Society of Literature; Maclise, D. The Maclise Portrait Gallery; Moore, T. Memoirs, Journal, and Correspondence.

BOWRING, SIR JOHN (October 17, 1792-November 23, 1872), statesman, traveler, and anthologist, was born in Exeter, Devonshire. Educated privately, he visited Spain, France, Belgium, Holland, Russia, and Sweden as a mercantile trader, and later performed missions for the British government in Switzerland, Italy, Egypt, Syria, and Germany. He promoted free trade as twice-member of Parliament, and served briefly as British consul at Canton, China, and governor of Hongkong, receiving the knighthood in 1854. Twice married, he died in Exeter at the age of eighty.

His place in literature is made chiefly by his reminiscences of travel in Siam and the Philippines (undertaken in 1855 and 1858 respectively) and his numerous translations and collections of European and Oriental verse. (He claimed that he knew 200 languages and could speak 100.) He is remembered also as the first editor of the *Westminster Review* (founded in 1824), and the friend and biographer of Jeremy Bentham. His thirty-six works include original poems and hymns, and political pamphlets.

PRINCIPAL WORKS: *Anthologies*—Russian Anthology, 1820-23; Batavian Anthology, 1824; Ancient Poetry and Romances of Spain, 1824; Servian Popular Poetry, 1827; Specimens of the Polish Poets, 1827; Sketch of the Language and Literature of Holland, 1829; Poetry of the Magyars, 1830; Cheskian Anthology, 1832. *Travel*—The Kingdom and People of Siam, 1857; A Visit to the Philippine Isles, 1859.

ABOUT: Bowring, J. Autobiographical Recollections (with Memoir by his son Lewin Bowring); Bowring, J. Memorial Volume of Sacred Poetry (see Memoir by Lady Bowring); Moor, L. Bowring, Cobden, and China: A Memoir; Nesbitt, G. L. Benthamite Reviewing.

BOYD, ANDREW KENNEDY HUTCHINSON (November 3, 1825-March 1, 1899), Scottish essayist, autobiographer, and divine, was born in Auchinleck Manse, Ayrshire, Scotland. He was educated at King's College and Middle Temple, London, and the University of Glasgow. As parish minister, he served successively Newton-on-Ayr, Kirkpatrick-Irongray near Dumfries, St. Bernard's in Edinburgh, and finally St. Andrews in Edinburgh, where he remained twenty-five years. He died in Bournemouth, England, at the age of seventy-three, when he mistook a poisonous acid for his medicine. His second wife and six children by his first wife survived him.

He first became widely known at thirty-four with a series of essays called *Recreations of a Country Parson,* contributed to *Fraser's Magazine.* There followed more than thirty works, notably several volumes of personal reminiscence full of shrewd observations, lively anecdotes, and candid comments on people.

PRINCIPAL WORKS: Recreations of a Country Parson, 1859, 1861, 1878; Graver Thoughts of a Country Parson, 1862, 1865, 1875; Critical Essays of a Country Parson, 1865; Twenty-five Years of St. Andrews, 1892; St. Andrews and Elsewhere, 1894; Last Years of St. Andrews, 1896.

ABOUT: Boyd, A. K. H. Sermons and Stray Papers (see Biographical Sketch by W. W. Tulloch). See also Boyd's autobiographical works.

BRADDON, MARY ELIZABETH (Mrs. John Maxwell), (October 4, 1837-February 4, 1915), novelist, was born in London. Her father, a solicitor and writer on sports, was of an old Cornish family; her mother was Irish. Her brother became premier of Tasmania.

Miss Braddon was educated entirely at home, but her training was thorough. Her first writing was done in 1856, when a Yorkshire printer offered ten pounds for a story "combining Dickens and Marryat." The story which he bought from her was scarcely that, and he failed before it could be published.

In 1861 John Maxwell, then publisher of *Robin Goodfellow,* bought the serial rights of *Lady Audley's Secret.* Again the magazine failed, but the story was transferred to the *Sixpenny Magazine.* The next year it appeared as a book. Few first novels have ever been such an overwhelming success. Miss Braddon was made rich for life by the proceeds. So far as her reputation was concerned, the enormous acclaim was bad for her, for the book was melodramatic and is decidedly her poorest work, yet all her subsequent eighty novels were judged by it and it "placed" her definitely in the public mind. In 1874 she married the publisher Maxwell, and had by him three sons and two daughters; two of the sons, W. B. Maxwell and Gerald Maxwell, have become well known novelists.

Miss Braddon, as she continued to be known in her work, was a prolific writer. Besides her almost innumerable novels, she wrote poems and plays, and edited several magazines, including *Temple Bar* and *Belgravia.* She bought a home at Richmond, Surrey, where she died at seventy-eight.

Her name has become a synonym for the lurid, sensational novel; yet men like Thackeray and Stevenson were admirers of her books. She was no semi-literate hack, but a clever, cultured woman with a great zest for life, a keen eye for natural beauty, and a vivid style. She was attacked ridiculously for "making crime attractive" and "teaching immorality." Quite the contrary; virtue always triumphs, and her heroes and villains are pure white and unredeemed black. Her work was ephemeral, but at its weakest was never contemptible.

PRINCIPAL WORKS: Lady Audley's Secret, 1862; John Marchmont's Legacy, 1863; The Doctor's Wife, 1864; Birds of Prey, 1867; Charlotte's Inheritance, 1868; Strangers and Pilgrims, 1873; Dead Men's Shoes, 1876; Vixen, 1879; Asphodel, 1881; Phantom Fortune, 1883; Ishmael, 1884; All Along the River, 1893; Sons of Fire, 1895; London Pride, 1896; Rough Justice, 1898; The Rose of Life, 1905; The Green Curtain, 1911.

ABOUT: James, H. Notes and Reviews; Jay, H. Robert Buchanan.

BRADLEY, EDWARD (March 25, 1827-December 12, 1889), humorous author known as "Cuthbert Bede," was born at Kidderminster, in Worcestershire. After attending University College, Durham, he served successively as curate of Glatton-With-Holme in Huntingdonshire, vicar of Bobbinton in Staffordshire, rector of Denton-With-Caldecote in Huntingdonshire, rector of Stretton in Rutlandshire, and finally vicar of Lenton-With-Hanby near Grantham in Lincolnshire, where he died at the age of sixty-two. He left two sons by his wife, Harriet Amelia Hancocks.

His best known work was *The Adventures of Mr. Verdant Green,* a humorous description of Oxford life in the manner of Dickens, in which he caricatured several university officials. (He had studied for a year at Oxford, though he had never matriculated.) Of his twenty-odd miscellaneous works in prose and verse, many were illustrated by himself and originally contributed to *Punch, All the Year Round,* and other periodicals.

PRINCIPAL WORKS: The Adventures of Mr. Verdant Green, 1853-56; Shilling Book of Beauty (ed.) 1856; Tales of College Life, 1856; Fairy Fables, 1858; Glencreggan: or, A Highland Home in Cantire, 1861; Fotheringay and Mary Queen of Scots, 1886.

BRADLEY, FRANCIS HERBERT (1846-September 18, 1924), philosopher, was the son of the vicar of Glasbury, his half-brother later becoming Dean of Westminster. He was reared in an atmosphere of narrow piety which unconsciously effected all his later work. After schooling at Cheltenham and Marlborough, he entered University College, Oxford. There (like another freshman at University College nearly half a century earlier, Percy Bysshe Shelley) he was known as a rebel against university authority; and he was graduated with nothing better than a second class in *litterae humaniores,* though this slighting estimate of his ability was belied by his immediately winning an open fellowship in Merton College.

A severe illness at the end of his school-days, which left him all his life practically an invalid, limited Bradley's existence and forbade any active participation in the affairs of the world. He remained at Merton for the most part until his death, still holding the fellowship. He never lectured and seldom taught classes, giving all his time to study and writing in his chosen field. The only magazine to which he contributed was *Mind*, the psychological quarterly. He was not, however, entirely withdrawn from interest in life outside his library; for example, he was a strong opponent of Home Rule for Ireland, a thorough conservative who hated Gladstone and could always be aroused to anger on that subject. He took an active part in the management of the business of the college, and when his health compelled him to spend most of his time in winter in the south of England or the south of France, he frequently traveled back to Oxford to participate in some meeting or discussion, though the result might mean weeks in bed as a consequence of the journey. To his pupils, who came to him for tutelage as individuals—he never had any disciples or founded a school of thought—he was noted for his kindness and patience.

Had Bradley not been afflicted with incurable illness, he might by nature have led a much more active life. He had the normal English interest in sport, and had yearnings, necessarily unfulfilled, for either a military career or the adventures of an explorer. He was obliged instead to do his fighting and exploration both within the confines of a college study. He was a tall, handsome man, with fine features and a keen gaze, though the general impression he gave to strangers was of aloofness and austerity. Partly this was deliberate, for he did not suffer fools gladly, and was often caustic in getting rid of bores. He was a brilliant conversationalist, with a wide knowledge of British and French literature, especially in the field of historical memoirs. He never married, and his personal relationships were limited to a few friends and the companionship of his beloved dogs. He received the Order of Merit in June, 1924, but did not live long to enjoy it. He died at 78, still full of plans for revision and expansion of his former publications. Curiously, he died, not of the disease from which he had suffered for sixty years (probably a pulmonary ailment), but of blood poisoning following an accident. His extreme reticence concerning himself makes it difficult to fill out the details of a life in any event devoid of much outward incident.

Bradley has been called "the thinker's thinker." He was the last of the English philosophers on the grand scale, who considered it their function to regard the meaning of the universe as a whole. He was an idealist, equally opposed to Pragmatism,

which says (to put it crudely and roughly) that a thing is true if it works, and to philosophical Realism, which considers phenomena to have real objective existence. In his philosophy there is a profound dualism between thought and feeling. Though he was highly unorthodox, he continued to describe himself as a Christian, and even as an Anglican; however, he was a lifelong foe of "the idolatry of the Church for the Biblical text." He wanted, indeed, a revival of the religious spirit, and he was essentially non-scientific and even anti-scientific. The keynote of his theory lies in his statement: "All humanly obtainable truths are unreal and all errors are somehow partial truths."

In style, Bradley has been attacked as inconsistent and unintelligible, and praised as lucid: certainly he avoided the cant jargon of many philosophers. He claimed that "German philosophers should write in French," and this impatience with long-windedness and lack of clarity had its influence on his own style. A "terrible thoroughness" fought with a tendency to ambiguity throughout his work. He is difficult reading, though he is eloquent and often brilliant; he influenced every English thinker of his time, yet never had one complete follower.

Bradley is not to be recommended to the general reader; his place in a history of literature is small, in spite of the incisiveness of his style: but in a history of philosophy, however alien he was to the dominant spirit of the scientific age, he must be reckoned with as the great enemy of hedonism in the field of ethics, and of the utilitarian empiricism of John Stuart Mill and his school.

M. A. deF.

PRINCIPAL WORKS: The Presuppositions of Critical History, 1874; Ethical Studies, 1876; Mr. Sidgwick's Hedonism, 1877; The Principles of Logic, 1883 (revised, with Commentary and Terminal Essays, 1922); Appearance and Reality, 1893; Essays on Truth and Reality, 1914.

ABOUT: Campbell, C. A. Scepticism and Construction; Reid, S. B. The Rôle of Logical Form in Propositions About Existence; London Quarterly Review 143:94 January, 1925; London Times September 20, 1924; Mind 34:1 January, 1925; Monist 44:238 July, 1934; Nature 114:546 October 11, 1924; New Republic 44:148 September 30, 1925; New Statesman 23:284 June 14, 1924; Publications British Association for the Advancement of Science 11:458 1924-25; Spectator 133:500 October 14, 1924.

BRADLEY, KATHERINE HARRIS. See "FIELD, MICHAEL"

BRASSEY, ANNA (or ANNIE) (Baroness Brassey) (October 7, 1839-September 14, 1887), travel author, was born Anna Allnutt in London. In 1860 she was married to THOMAS BRASSEY (1836-1918), a wealthy statesman, who later held high civil offices in the British admiralty and was created baron. He compiled a valuable encyclopedic work, *The British Navy,* and inaugurated the widely-used *Naval Annual.* By him she had one son and four daughters.

She assisted her husband in his political career and accompanied him on yearly voyages in their yacht "The Sunbeam." Several of these cruises she described in books originally written for private circulation among her friends and later published with great success. Most popular was *The Voyage in the Sunbeam,* describing their world tour of 1876-77. During her travels she collected natural and ethnological curiosities which formed a museum in her home.

She died at sea near Brisbane, Australia, while making a long cruise for her health, at the age of forty-seven. A year before her death she became Baroness Brassey.

PRINCIPAL WORKS: The Voyage in the Sunbeam: Our Home on the Ocean for Eleven Months, 1878; Sunshine and Storm in the East: or, Cruises to Cyprus and Constantinople, 1880; In the Trades, the Tropics, and the Roaring Forties, 1885; The Last Voyage (ed. by M. A. Broome) 1889.

ABOUT: Brassey, A. The Last Voyage (see Memoir by Lord Brassey).

BRAY, ANNA ELIZA (December 25, 1790-January 21, 1883), novelist, was born Anna Eliza Kempe in the parish of Newington, Surrey, England. She was married in 1818 to Charles Alfred Stothard, well-known artist, who was killed three years later by a fall from a ladder in the church at Beerferris, Devonshire, where he was making drawings of a stained-glass window for his book *The Monumental Effigies of Great Britain.* The work was completed by his widow and her brother Alfred John Kempe. About 1823 she was married to the Rev. Edward Atkyns Bray, vicar of Tavistock in Devonshire. After his death in 1857 she removed to London, where she died at the advanced age of ninety-three.

She wrote popular romances of an historical nature, accounts of her European travels, biographies of her first husband and his noted artist-father, tales for children, and (most notably) a series of letters to Robert Southey on the legends and superstitions bordering the rivers Tamar and Tavy in the vicinity of Tavistock, where she had lived for more than thirty years.

PRINCIPAL WORKS: The Borders of the Tamar and the Tavy, 1836; Life of Thomas Stothard, R. A., 1851; A Peep at the Pixies: or, Legends of the West, 1854.

ABOUT: Bray, A. E. Autobiography.

BREWER, JOHN SHERREN (1810-February 2, 1879), historian, was born at Norwich. He was the son of a Baptist schoolmaster, but reverted to the Church of England while a student at Queen's College, Oxford, from which he was graduated with first class honors. His marriage in 1832 lost him

a fellowship, and he supported himself by private tutoring and by the preparation of an edition of Aristotle's *Ethics.*

In 1837 Brewer went to London, where he took deacon's orders and was appointed chaplain of the workhouse of two parishes. A disciple of the High Church "Oxford Movement," he taught the inmates of his workhouse to sing psalms in Gregorian Chant.

Within a year, because of a difference of opinion with the rector, he resigned, and secured employment in the British Museum. In 1839 he became lecturer in classical literature at King's College, where Frederick Denison Maurice, the leader of the Christian Socialism movement, became his friend. It was through Maurice's influence that he first taught at and then acted as principal of the Workingmen's College. In 1855 he was appointed professor of the English language and literature and lecturer on modern history at King's College. A great deal of his time was given to journalism, and for a while he was editor of the *Standard.*

In 1856 Brewer's real life-work began, with his commission by the Master of the Rolls to prepare a calendar of the state papers of Henry VIII. Most of the remainder of his life was given over to this work. In 1877 he was given the crown living of Toppesfield, Essex; he took his duties seriously and they indirectly caused his death, for he caught cold while visiting a sick parishioner and never recovered. The immediate cause of his death was heart failure.

Brewer edited Bacon, Hume, and other writers, but his chief work was the laborious and exact compilation and collation of the Tudor state papers. His prefaces to the various volumes of the calendar were published posthumously as a book. He was trustworthy and careful, and his compilation has been of the greatest value to all succeeding English historians.

PRINCIPAL WORKS: Lectures to Ladies on Practical Subjects, 1855; English Studies, 1861; The Reign of Henry VIII (ed. by J. Gairdner) 1884.

ABOUT: Brewer, J. S. English Studies (see Memoir by H. Wace).

BREWSTER, SIR DAVID (December 11, 1781-February 10, 1868), Scottish scientist, was born in Jedburgh, the son of the rector of the local grammar school. His mother died when he was nine.

His interest in science came very early; when only ten he constructed a telescope. He entered the University of Edinburgh in 1793, at twelve years of age, and was graduated before he was seventeen. He received his M.A. in 1800. In 1802 he became editor of the *Edinburgh Magazine,* and continued as such for twenty years, under its later names of the *Edinburgh Philosophical Journal* and the *Edinburgh Journal of Science.* To earn a living unprovided by this service, he acted as tutor in two families from 1799 to 1807.

In 1804 Brewster was licensed to preach in the Established Church, but his career as a minister was very short; the strain of speaking caused him to faint in the pulpit. A more satisfactory way of living was found in 1807, when he was made editor-in-chief of the *Edinburgh Encyclopaedia*, a position which he retained until 1829. In 1810 he married Janet Macpherson (illegitimate daughter of James Macpherson, supposed discoverer—and probably author—of the "ancient Scottish odes" of Ossian). She died in 1850, and in 1857 Brewster married Jane Kirk Purnell, by whom he had one daughter.

Brewster sent his first paper on physics to the Royal Society in 1813. In 1815 he was made a Fellow, and subsequently received the Copley, Rumford, and Royal medals for his researches on the polarization of light. He was the inventor of the kaleidoscope, introduced the stethoscope, and in rivalry with the French astronomer Fresnel proposed improvements in lighthouses. In 1831 he was a founder of the British Association for the Advancement of Science, of which he was president in 1851. In 1839 he became principal of a college in the University of St. Andrews, a position he nearly lost four years later during the disruption of the Established Church which led to the establishment of the Free Church. He contributed to the *North British Review* and the *Quarterly Review*, in 1860 was vice-chancellor of the University of Edinburgh, and was an honorary M.D. of the University of Berlin. An accident almost cost him his sight, but he continued to work until 1864. He was an invalid for the last four years of his long life.

Brewster was a sound scientist and a great influence on the thinkers and writers of his time. His work, however, is outdated and he is no longer read. The *Edinburgh Encyclopaedia* is his most lasting monument.

PRINCIPAL WORKS: Treatise on New Philosophical Instruments, 1813; Treatise on Optics, 1831; Memoirs of the Life, Writings, and Discoveries of Sir Isaac Newton, 1831; Martyrs to Science, 1841; More Worlds Than One, 1854.

ABOUT: Gordon, Mrs. The Home Life of Sir David Brewster.

BRIDGES, JOHN HENRY (October 11, 1832-June 15, 1906), positivist philosopher, was born at Old Newton, Suffolk, where his father CHARLES BRIDGES, author of religious writings, was vicar. Educated at Rugby and Wadham College, Oxford, he served as metropolitan medical inspector in London for twenty-eight years. He died at Tunbridge Wells, in Sussex-Kent, at the age of seventy-two, survived by his second wife Mary Alice Hadwen.

Under the influence of Richard Congreve, he studied Auguste Comte's philosophy and became a leader of the positivist movement in England. He translated some of Comte's works, wrote on the positivist doctrine, contributed a hundred articles to the *Positivist Review*, and lectured to the Positivist Society for thirty years. His miscellaneous writings dealt with health questions, history, science, and social reform.

PRINCIPAL WORKS: Comte's *General View of Positivism* (tr.) 1865; The Unity of Comte's Life and Doctrine: A Reply to J. S. Mill, 1866; Comte's *System of Positive Polity* (tr. with Frederick Harrison) 1875; Five Discourses on Positive Religion, 1882; Roger Bacon's *Opus Majus* (ed.) 1897; Essays and Addresses (ed. with L. T. Hobhouse) 1907; The Life and Work of Roger Bacon, 1914.

ABOUT: Bridges, J. H. Essays and Addresses (see Biographical Introduction by F. Harrison); Bridges, M. A. H. Recollections of J. H. Bridges.

BRIGHT, WILLIAM, December 14, 1824-March 6, 1901), church historian, was born at Doncaster in Yorkshire, a son of the town clerk. After taking first-class honors in classics at University College, Oxford, he remained at the college as fellow and tutor until his forty-fourth year, with the exception of a seven-year interval at Trinity College in Glenalmond, Perthshire, Scotland, where he tutored in theology and lectured in ecclesiastical history. The last thirty-three years of his life were spent as regius professor of ecclesiastical history and canon of Christ Church, Oxford. There he died at seventy-six.

He is remembered for his diligent studies in the church history of Great Britain, particularly *A History of the Church* which became the standard textbook for theological students. He is also known as a writer of hymns.

PRINCIPAL WORKS: A History of the Church, A.D. 313-451, 1860; Hymns and Other Poems, 1866; Chapters of Early English Church History, 1878; The Roman See in the Early Church and Other Studies in Church History, 1896.

ABOUT: Bright, W. Selected Letters.

BRIGHTWEN, ELIZA (October 30, 1830-May 5, 1906), naturalist, was born Eliza Elder at Banff in Banffshire, Scotland. Brought up in the vicinity of London by her uncle Alexander Elder, a founder of the publishing house of Smith, Elder & Company, she read much in natural history but had no regular education. In her twenty-fifth year she was married to George Brightwen, a banker. The rest of her life was spent at Stanmore, not far from London, in Middlesex, where she made zoological observations on their large, wooded estate called "The Grove." Widowed in 1883, she began writing in her sixtieth year and by virtue of her books became one of the most popular naturalists in her time. She died childless at Stanmore at the age of seventy-five.

PRINCIPAL WORKS: Wild Nature Won by Kindness, 1890; More About Wild Nature, 1892; Inmates of My House and Garden, 1895; Glimpses Into Plant Life, 1898; Rambles With Nature Students, 1899; Quiet Hours With Nature, 1903; Last Hours With Nature (ed. by W. H. Chesson) 1908.

ABOUT: Gosse, E. (ed.). Eliza Brightwen: The Life and Thoughts of a Naturalist.

BRIMLEY, GEORGE (December 29, 1819-May 29, 1857), critic, was born in Cambridge, educated at Cambridge University, and died in Cambridge at the age of thirty-seven of an incurable disease from which he suffered most of his life. From the time he took his degree at twenty-five until a few weeks before his death he served as college librarian.

He began his journalistic career with notable contributions to the *Cambridge University Magazine* while attending Trinity College. During the last six years of his life he wrote criticisms of Byron, Wordsworth, Thackeray, Bulwer-Lytton, and other distinguished Victorian authors for *The Spectator* and *Fraser's Magazine*. His best critical piece, and the only one to which he signed his name, was an essay on "Tennyson's Poems" in the *Cambridge Essays* of 1855. These essays, posthumously gathered in a small volume, have given him a distinct (though not great) place in English criitcism.

"His power," according to Stanley T. Williams, "lay in this: he penetrated with unusual insight into the enduring qualities of his contemporaries. . . . In almost every case, in spite of moral bias and verbiage, his verdict is that of posterity. In the babel of critcism in the 'fifties his was one of the few voices to speak the truth."

WORK: Essays (ed. by W. G. Clark) 1858.

ABOUT: Brimley, G. Essays (see Prefatory Memoir); Williams, S. T. Studies in Victorian Literature.

BRONTË, ANNE (January 17, 1820-May 28, 1849), novelist, was the youngest and least gifted of the three celebrated Brontë sisters. In contrast to Charlotte's driving energy and Emily's fierce and reserved inner storms, Anne's history seems mild and almost featureless. Like her sisters in early youth, she had no formal education; her only schooling was a few months at Miss Wooler's school at Roe Head in 1835. In April 1839 she went as governess to the Inghams at Blake Hall; this engagement, involving the care of "an unruly, violent family of modern children," lasted only until Christmas of that year, but she remained as governess at the Robinsons', in Thorp Green, from 1841 to 1845. Then, when her brother Branwell was dismissed from his post as tutor to the Robinson children because of discovery of his violent

ANNE BRONTË

and deluded passion for Mrs. Robinson, Anne too resigned. Her position was hardly tenable under the circumstances, but she set a Brontë record nevertheless for tenure of office. (It was about this time that she fell in love with her father's curate, William Weightman, but nothing came of this unreciprocated fancy.)

Agnes Grey, Anne's first novel, was written during the winter of 1845-46, at the same time as Emily's *Wuthering Heights* and Charlotte's *The Professor*. It was published with *Wuthering Heights* in December 1847, and the publisher seems to have treated the two young authors very unfairly. Anne's only previous literary venture was a few negligible poems in the joint volume by her sisters and herself published in 1846. For the chronicles of the imaginary Gondal cycle, written by herself and Emily, were all destroyed either by herself, or by Charlotte after Anne's death, so that they can hardly be counted in a record of her work. Her second novel, *The Tenant of Wildfell Hall*, came out under the aegis of Charlotte's publishers in 1848, and went into a second edition the same year. All of Anne's work was published under the pseudonym of Acton Bell.

It is probable that the tuberculosis which killed Anne was of long standing—Charlotte had been worried about her health as early as the school days at Roe Head. Her fine, clear complexion, her abundant hair, and her lustrous violet eyes should have attracted suspicion of this disease from her childhood. In any event, she failed rapidly after Emily's death in December, 1848, and died in May of the next year. More of her life had been spent at the family home, her father's parsonage at Haworth, Yorkshire, than that of either of her sisters; but she alone died away from home—she had insisted on being taken to Scarborough for the sea air, but lived only two days after arriving there with Charlotte. Her only previous journeys of any extent (for her governess positions were only a few miles away from home) were one trip with Emily to York, and one with Charlotte to London, to prove to the publishers that "Currer, Ellis, and Acton Bell" were not all one and the same person.

"Dear, gentle Anne," she is always called, but there must have been more than sweetness and yielding in her nature to make her the one close companion of that deep, wild spirit, her sister Emily. She had a touch of melancholy from birth, and was the most religious-minded of the three; indeed her best poems are those of a religious nature. It is probable that without the example of Charlotte and Emily she would never have thought of writing, but it was impossible to be a Brontë and not write. *Agnes Grey* is a quietly realistic account of a governess' life, autobiographical except in detail. *The Tenant of Wildfell Hall* is more dramatic—not to say melodramatic; it is the story of a marriage ruined by the dissipation and extravagance of the husband. It appears that earlier critics who thought Anne's brother Branwell the model for this villainous hero were mistaken; Anne would never have exposed her brother to public scorn, and the real model seems to have been a curate whose wife had told her bitter troubles to Anne's father.

Anne's books are of most interest because she was Charlotte's and Emily's sister; however, they have an historical importance of their own, from their picture of middle-class country life in England in the early nineteenth century.   M. A. deF.

PRINCIPAL WORKS: *Verse*—Poems by Currer, Ellis, and Acton Bell, 1846; Complete Poems, 1920. *Novels*—Agnes Grey, 1847. The Tenant of Wildfell Hall, 1848.

ABOUT: Clarke, I. C. Haworth Parsonage; Dimnet, E. The Brontë Sisters; Romieu, E. & G. Three Virgins of Haworth; Sangster, A. The Brontës; Sugden, K. A. R. A Short History of the Brontës; Willis, I. C. The Brontës; Wise, T. J. & Symington, J. A. The Brontës: Their Lives, Friendships, and Correspondence (includes Shorter, C. K. The Brontës); Wright, J. C. The Story of the Brontës.

BRONTË, CHARLOTTE

BRONTË, CHARLOTTE (April 21, 1816-March 31, 1855), novelist, was the oldest surviving child of Patrick Brontë and Maria Branwell, and oldest of the three famous Brontë sisters. The father was a rector, son of an Irish peasant (the family name was originally Brunty or Prunty), who had raised himself by his own bootstraps to Cambridge and Holy Orders; he was eccentric, domineering, and hypochrondriacal. The mother, of a Methodist family of Penzance, Cornwall, died of cancer in 1821, a year after they had moved from Thornton, where Charlotte, Emily, and Anne were all born, to Haworth, that isolated Yorkshire village which was their home thereafter. Soon after the mother's death her sister, Elizabeth, came to care for the children—six of them then—and remained until her death in 1842. But she was aloof, fault-finding, and tyrannical, and all the real mothering the younger ones had was from the oldest child, Maria, then only seven.

The children received no real schooling, but they associated with their elders exclusively, read newspapers and magazines assiduously, and had a precocious grasp of world-affairs. From "Tabby," the old servant, they garnered wild folklore and melodramatic gossip of the neighborhood. For the rest, they ran wild on the moors, or wrote their "magazines" and their miniature library based on the imaginary cycle-saga of "Verdopolis" and "Angria." Charlotte and her brother Branwell being the chief progenitors of this game which fed their fancies through the dull domestic days in the stone house overlooking the graveyard.

In 1824 Mr. Brontë took the fatal resolution of entering all the girls except Anne, the baby, in a cheap boarding school for poor clergymen's daughters at Cowan Bridge. Maria and Elizabeth, the two oldest, died in consequence of the malnutrition and lack of sanitation; Charlotte and Emily were brought home only just in time. The next school venture was Charlotte's; at the beginning of 1831 she went to Miss Wooler's school at Roe Head (afterwards moved to Dewbury Moor). There she met her lifelong friends, Ellen Nussey and Mary Taylor. She left in summer of the next year, but in July 1835 she returned as assistant teacher, taking Emily with her as pupil. Emily endured only three months of what to her was painful imprisonment; Charlotte brought her home and took Anne back with her instead.

Though Miss Wooler was her good and constant friend, Charlotte was most unhappy as a teacher at the school, as she was later as governess in private families. She disliked children, hated the monotony and drudgery, and the contrast was too great between her actual life as a plain, poverty-stricken governess and her dream-life of beauty and love and fame and wealth. Besides, she was going through a period of morbid religiosity which for a while drove her close to the border of insanity. She picked a quarrel with Miss Wooler over Anne's health, and though finally she was persuaded to stay on after Anne went home again, she did not remain much longer.

It was necessary, however, that all the girls do something to increase the family income.

CHARLOTTE BRONTË

The pride and hope of the family was the only brother, Branwell, a year Charlotte's junior; he was to be a great artist and then support them all, but meanwhile he must have funds for his training. There was nothing in those days for a "lady" to do to earn her livelihood except to teach, and so, reluctant as she was, Charlotte had to find another teaching position. This time she went as governess to the Sidgwicks, related to the celebrated Benson and Sidgwick families of English authors today. She detested them and they did not like her; she lasted barely a few months. Another breathing-spell at Haworth, and then, in 1841, she became governess to the children of a Mr. and Mrs. White. This time, though they were very kind to her, Charlotte, who was a bit of a snob, was irked by their lack of birth and breeding; as a matter of fact no subservient position could have failed to irritate one as ambitious and as conscious of her powers as was Charlotte Brontë.

Back again to Haworth she came, this time with a grand scheme for herself, Emily, and Annne to establish a private school of their own, their aunt having gone so far as to offer to lend them £150 for capital. Miss Wooler was thinking of giving up her school at Dewsbury Moor, and there was some talk of their taking it over, but this plan fell through. Then it occurred to Charlotte that what they needed most before undertaking such an enterprise was more training in foreign languages. Charlotte was always quick to rationalize her longings; Mary Taylor was traveling on the continent and Charlotte too dreamed of foreign experience. Actually Miss Branwell furnished the money, and February 1842 found Charlotte and Emily as pupils at the *Pensionnat Héger* in Brussels.

The nine months of this residence were pure torture for Emily, and Charlotte too had by no means a happy time. They were ten years older than the rest of the pupils in M. Héger's fashionable school, and their insular prejudices were offended at every turn. In October "Aunt Branwell" died, and the girls came home again. Each of the sisters inherited about £100 from their aunt, and now they proposed starting their school on the premises. Advertisements were printed and sent out, but not even one inquiry or application was made.

Things seemed to be at a standstill, and then M. Héger, who had thought highly of Charlotte's intelligence, offered her a position as English teacher at his school. She accepted, and went back to Brussels in January 1843, for a whole year. Poor Charlotte! She had had every other misfortune, so now she fell in love with her employer, who had a wife of his own, was most proper and decorous, and besides had no emotional interest in the small, homely, badly dressed English Miss. Charlotte suffered tortures, which only the letters she wrote M. Héger afterwards—and never sent—disclosed when they were made public after her death.

Finally she could endure the situation no longer, and returned to Haworth. There the family circumstances were becoming increasingly more distressing. Branwell, the brilliant, petted boy of whom so much was expected, was not turning out well; he was given to drink, and lost every post he obtained, from tutoring to clerking on a railroad. In 1845 he went to his last position, that of tutor to the Robinsons, at Thorp Green, where Anne was governess; there he fell in love with Mrs. Robinson, who was seventeen years his senior, and when he was dismissed in disgrace fell into actual madness, believing that Mrs. Robinson returned his passion and that only her husband separated them. He drank more than ever, and took to opium besides; Charlotte, who had been closest to him of his sisters, turned on him in righteous wrath, and he slid rapidly downhill until his death in September 1848.

Meanwhile the brief and glorious period of the flowering of the Brontë genius had begun. In 1845 Charlotte accidentally discovered the manuscript of Emily's poems. At once, recognizing their power, and knowing that she herself and Anne had also indulged in secret (and vastly inferior) versification, it occurred to her that they should issue a joint volume. It was a difficult task to persuade Emily, outraged at violation of her fiercely defended privacy; but once that was done the rest was easy. *Poems by Currer, Ellis, and Acton Bell* appeared in 1846. The girls paid £50 for publication of the volume, and exactly two copies were sold during the first year.

Nothing daunted, the three set to work, each on a novel. Charlotte's was *The Professor,* founded on her Brussels experiences. Emily's and Anne's novels found a publisher, but not Charlotte's. (It remained unpublished until after her death.) But she received so kind a letter from the publisher, that she took heart and labored at completing *Jane Eyre,* her most famous work. This was published in October 1847 and, in spite of some scathing criticism in the style of the day, was a success from the start. Indeed, it was so great a success that the reviewers jumped to the conclusion that all three novels were by the same author, and Charlotte was obliged to give up her cherished anonymity to prove the opposite.

Then came a year of death. Branwell died in September 1848; Emily in December; Anne the following May. Charlotte was left alone with her aging father, slowly growing blind, and her bitter memories. Lonely and grief-stricken she did not succumb. She went to London more than once, and in spite of her shyness became something of a lioness. She set herself to writing as a cure for sorrow, and produced two more novels—*Shirley,* in which she tried to give some (not too accurate) characterization of Emily, in 1849; *Villette,* also a reminiscence of Brussels, in 1852.

In 1854 Charlotte married—married her father's curate, Arthur Bell Nicholls, whom she had once derided heartily. She had had three other proposals, but small temptation to accept them. The marriage was calmly happy, but it did not last long. On March 31, 1855, she died; the exact cause of her death is not established, but it was complicated by pregnancy, and probably was a flare-up of the Brontë tubercular tendency. Mr. Nicholls stayed on with old Patrick Brontë until the latter died in 1861.

Charlotte Brontë's is not an altogether sympathetic character, but it is an admirable one. She was keenly conscientious, a "managing" type whose urge for running the lives of others was accentuated by the responsibilities her family placed upon her. Her emotions were strong and deep, but masked by a painful shyness. Her talent was of very nearly the first order; she had a remarkable power of observation, and since her novels are all founded on experience they are highly realistic. She had also a native gift for powerful and moving description, and in *Jane Eyre* particularly she has produced scenes and passages that make this one of her novels, at least, immortal.　　　　M. A. deF.

PRINCIPAL WORKS: *Novels*—Jane Eyre, 1847; Shirley, 1849; Villette, 1852; The Professor, 1857; [Early "Angrian" chronicles:] The Twelve Adventurers and Other Stories, 1925; The Spell, 1931;

Legends of Angria, 1933. *Verse*—Poems by Currer, Ellis, and Acton Bell, 1846; Complete Poems, 1924.

ABOUT: Benson, E. F. Charlotte Brontë; Birrell, E. Life of Charlotte Brontë; Gaskell, E. C. The Life of Charlotte Brontë; Goldring, M. Charlotte Brontë: The Woman; Langbridge, R. Charlotte Brontë: A Psychological Study; Shorter, C. K. Charlotte Brontë and Her Circle. (See also Bibliography for Anne Brontë.)

BRONTË, EMILY JANE (July 30, 1818-December 19, 1848), novelist and poet, was the middle in age of the three famous Brontë sisters, two years younger than Charlotte, a year and a half older than Anne. Like them, she was born at Thornton, Yorkshire, and moved in early childhood to Haworth, where she spent most of the remainder of her short life.

With Charlotte and her two oldest sisters, she was sent in 1824 to the Clergy Daughters School at Cowan Bridge which cost the lives of Maria and Elizabeth, and from which Emily and Charlotte were rescued just in time. A schoolmate remembered that Emily was the pet of the school, and she does not seem to have been any unhappier there than were the rest of them. She was only three at her mother's death, and Emily retained no memory of her. It must have been some time between 1825 and 1835 (whether occasioned by shock from being locked in the room where her mother died, or simply the result of the strange surroundings of all the Brontës in their childhood) that Emily developed that almost-mania against restraint, that agony under regimentation, which made schools and governess' positions alike, torture and imprisonment to her thereafter.

In any event, when Charlotte took Emily with her as a pupil to Miss Wooler's school at Roe Head in 1835, three months of it almost finished her. She had to be brought back before she died of the experience. Again, in 1837, she acted as governess to a family in Halifax for six months, which was all that she could endure; the position besides was an onerous one, and she was supposed to be on constant duty for sixteen hours a day.

In 1842, when the three sisters planned to establish a private school of their own (strangely enough even Emily indulged in pleasant day dreams of that enterprise, which in actuality they would all have hated), she went with Charlotte to the *Pensionnat Héger* in Brussels, and stayed for nine months. She was older now, and managed somehow to live through what must have been an unmitigated nightmare, but she made no friends. When Charlotte returned, after their aunt's death, to Brussels as an English teacher, Emily might have gone too, to teach piano, but she could not contemplate the ordeal. The rest of her life, except for a brief trip to York with Anne, was passed at Haworth.

(There is a possibility that in 1838 Emily kept house for her brother Branwell in Bradford, but the evidence is only internal, from the dating of some of her poems.)

It was in 1845 that Charlotte discovered a manuscript volume of Emily's carefully guarded poems, and insisted on their publication with her own and Anne's verses. Some of these were "Gondal" poems, this being the imaginary saga which Emily and Anne conducted together, in the style of Branwell's and Charlotte's "Angria" cycle of ten years before. But some of them were the inmost expressions of Emily's hidden and secret self, and she never entirely forgave Charlotte for the outrage. She gave in, however, to Charlotte's persistency, and the *Poems by Currer, Ellis, and Acton Bell* were published in 1846.

During the months preceding and following, Emily produced her only prose work (for all her and Anne's Gondal stories were destroyed)—a blazing torch in the broad daylight of fiction, *Wuthering Heights.* It was published in the same volume as Anne's *Agnes Grey* in December 1847—just a year before Emily died.

Emily, too, had had her ambitions for fame, and she suffered under the neglect and misjudgment that greeted her violent creation. Perhaps she suffered, secretly, the more when Charlotte's *Jane Eyre* became so instant a success that the novels by the other sisters were ascribed to "Currer Bell." But far beyond this was Emily's terror at the thought that anyone—even her father—should know her as the author of *Wuthering Heights,* or that her personality should be revealed or exploited in any fashion. Branwell Brontë was by this time undergoing the last dreadful phase of his wasted life—a drunkard and drug addict, almost an outcast from the family with whom he was still forced to live, and on or over the verge of madness. The rash critics who have guessed that he had any hand at all in *Wuthering Heights* have read very little of either his or Emily's other work. Branwell was a hollow shell as a writer as well as in his painting; he was incapable of writing a page of his sister's book. If he hinted that the book was his, that is no more remarkable than his obsession that his former employer was madly in love with him and would have married him after her husband's death except for a (purely imaginary) stipulation in the husband's will. As a matter of fact, Charlotte states explicitly that he never even knew of the publication of the novels of any of his sisters; and though Charlotte is sometimes inaccurate, this time there is supporting evidence that she was right. Branwell died

EMILY BRONTË

in September 1848 and Emily was to follow him in less than three months.

Emily probably caught cold at Branwell's funeral, and her cold turned into inflammation of the lungs. It is doubtful if she wanted very much to live. Her pride and obstinacy kept her from yielding to any pain—the same pride and obstinacy that had made her, the wild genius, take upon herself most of the worst drudgery of the household for many years. She would not go to bed, she would not have a doctor, she would not even take any home remedies; she simply ignored the dereliction of her dying body, until at last she fell dead before her sisters, in the very act of trying to stand erect.

Emily Brontë is an almost indescribable person. No labels fit her. One may say that she was fiercely reserved and taciturn, wholly introverted, suffering damnably all her life long for the love she could not give or attract, diabolically proud, the grimmest of stoics—and all these things are true, yet they do not make up the sum of Emily. As a person, in one sense, she hardly exists—we hear that she had beautiful, liquid, grey-blue eyes; we know she was a fine musician; we feel the strong masculine strain in her, the affinity with the desolate moor country and its wasting winds; but still, as in life she eluded those who sought to pin her down or hold her, she eludes our curious scrutiny now.

She is, as Rebecca West has said, an artist who transcends the limitations of her medium. Her poems are "on the edge of greatness," and sometimes they overstep the edge. She carries expression beyond the limits of expressibility, and we have always an uneasy feeling that one moment more, and we shall see before us divinity or madness.

And *Wuthering Heights* is almost as indescribable as is its author. On the framework of a melodramatic story (in part a reminiscence of a tale by the German romanticist Hoffman), Emily Brontë has built up a living thing. She has told the story twice, in one novel—first as it was in the depths of her soul (for "Romer Wilson" has shown plainly enough that Heathcliff, the terrible hero of the book, is in essence the hidden Emily herself), then as it might have been, relieved of the dreadful shadow of Heathcliff. It is a tale of usurpation, revenge, and a devilish, preternatural passion that tamer beings can scarcely recognize as love. It has all the deficiencies of a book written by a woman living in isolation, half educated, inexperienced in any world except the world of imagination. It is a wild prose commentary on the more direct (and therefore more jealously secreted) revelations of Emily's personal poems. As Professor A. A. Jacks has remarked, *"Wuthering Heights* bears the same relation to *Jane Eyre* that Webster bears to Shakespeare, if one could imagine Webster greater than Shakespeare." Charlotte was an immensely talented person; Emily is pure genius.

There is perhaps no other author in English literature who has produced so little and yet has so high a rank. Emily Brontë is no minor author of a dozen great poems and one unique novel; she is a major figure who poured all of herself into a narrow mould. One cannot even say that she died too soon to complete her work; her work was already completed, and she died of its completion. Her death is next door to suicide. She had given birth to the most awful exposition of a hidden self that ever found its way into words, and life after that profound shattering of a terrible lifelong secrecy was no longer possible. From her childhood Emily never spoke her secret thoughts. When the iron repression broke and she spoke them at last, she died of the cataclysmic shattering.   M. A. deF.

PRINCIPAL WORKS: *Poetry*—Poems by Currer, Ellis, and Acton Bell, 1846; Poems of Emily Brontë, 1906; Complete Poems of Emily Brontë, 1923. *Novel*—Wuthering Heights, 1847.

ABOUT: Duclaux, A. M. F. R. Emily Brontë; O'Brien, F. R. M. W. ("Romer Wilson"). All Alone: The Life and Private History of Emily Jane Brontë; Simpson, C. W. Emily Brontë; Southern Atlantic Quarterly 34:202 April 1935. (See also Bibliography for Anne Brontë.)

BROOKE, STOPFORD AUGUSTUS

(November 14, 1832-March 18, 1916), Anglo-Irish clergyman, essayist, critic, and biographer, was born at Letterkenny, County Donegal, Ireland, son of Richard Sinclair Brooke and Anna Stopford.

He was educated at Kidderminster, Kingstown, and matriculated at Trinity College, Oxford, where he had a distinguished schol-

STOPFORD BROOKE

astic career, winning several prizes, and being graduated in 1856. Ordained in 1857, he occupied two curacies in London before becoming, in 1863, chaplain to the Princess Royal at Berlin. He held this post for two years, and found leisure to complete *The Life and Letters of the Late Frederick W. Robinson,* a document which proved his broad church tendencies and caused a considerable stir among partisans and opponents.

In 1866 Brooke was called to St. James' Chapel, where his fame as a preacher grew rapidly. He became Royal Chaplain in 1872 and was appointed to Bedford Chapel, Bloomsbury, in 1875. This chapel was secured for his proprietary use in 1876 by the generosity of friends. With a brilliant church career seemingly open to him, Brooke in 1880 quietly withdrew, without undue publicity, from the communion of the Church of England, because he could no longer accept the doctrine of the resurrection. The ideas of the Unitarians attracted him, but he could not bring himself to subscribe to any body of dogma, and continued to preach independently. He served as principal of Men's and Women's College from 1881 to 1884.

Brooke had several published volumes to his credit when he produced, in 1876, the *Primer of English Literature,* a text that sold some 500,000 copies up to the time of his death. For this work, said Israel Gollancz, the teaching of English literature owed more to its author than to any man of his time. The *History of Early English Literature* (to the Norman Conquest), published in 1894, is another work of solid scholarship and understanding.

Always an enthusiast in matters pertaining to Ireland, Brooke contended bravely against the treatment meted out to that country, and never tired of calling the attention of the English speaking world to the importance of its literature. One of his last lectures, of which he delivered a brilliant series (1900-05) at University College, London, was entitled *On the Need and Use of Getting Irish Literature Into the English Tongue.* He published *A Treasury of Irish Poetry in the English Tongue* in 1900.

Brooke was a tireless student and critic of literature, and published various volumes of biography and criticism during his long career. In about his sixtieth year, he felt that his physical powers were flagging, and rested for a time from preaching and other work, but his vitality was restored to such an extent that he lived on with his faculties unimpaired, and even began the study and practice of painting, in his late years, with considerable success. His last work was *Four Poets,* 1908. He died at Ewhurst in his eighty-fourth year.

He was married in 1858 to Emma Beaumont, who died in 1874.

Brooke's personal charm and his sweet dignity were part of the man himself, but he owed much of his popularity to eloquence, a handsome presence, and a fine delivery. The esteem in which he was held had much to do with the success of such undertakings as his campaign for the preservation of Wordsworth's home, in aid of which his *Dove Cottage* (1890) was written. The *Quarterly Review* said of him that "his fine voice, a ready turn of speech, a very courteous wit, a love of gallant manners, and a fearless regard for the truth . . . made him one of the most notable and welcome figures in the more thoughtful social world of his long day." "He was," said Chesterton, "in an exact and rather exceptional sense, a Liberal, a champion of Liberty; and all the more a Liberal for being always something of an aristocrat."

As a man of letters, Brooke occupies a solid position. Matthew Arnold gave high praise to his *Primer,* and John Drinkwater has written that if Brooke's qualities had been less disturbed by conflict, he would have been one of the greatest men of his age. The influence of Ruskin, whom he admired, is marked in his work.   R. M.

PRINCIPAL WORKS: *Poetry*—Poems, 1888; *Criticism*—Theology in English Poets, 1874; Primer of English Literature, 1876; History of Early English Literature, 1894; Tennyson, 1894; The Poetry of Robert Browning, 1902; Ten Plays of Shakespeare, 1905; Studies in Poetry, 1907; Four Poets, 1908. *Biography*—The Life and Letters of the Late Frederick W. Robinson, 1865; The Life and Writings of Milton, 1897. *Sermons and Religious Studies*—The Freedom of the Church of England, 1871; Sermons, 1868-77; A Fight of Faith, 1877; Spirit of the Christian Life, 1881; The Unity of God and Man, 1886; The Early Life of Jesus, 1887; God and Christ, 1894; Jesus and Modern Thought, 1894; The Old Testament and Modern Life, 1896;

The Gospel of Joy, 1898. *Miscellaneous*—Riquet of the Tuft: A Lyrical Drama, 1880; Dove Cottage, 1890; A Treasury of Irish Poetry in the English Tongue, 1900; The Need and Use of Getting Irish Literature into the English Tongue, 1905.

ABOUT: Jacks, L. P. Life of Stopford Brooke; Arnold, M. A. Guide to English Literature; Dial 65:404 November 16, 1918; Hibbert Journal 16:377 April 1918; Quarterly Review 229:526 April 1918.

BROOKS, (CHARLES WILLIAM) SHIRLEY (April 29, 1816-February 23, 1874), editor of *Punch,* playwright, and novelist, was born in London the son of an architect. After studying law, he wrote parliamentary summary in the *Morning Chronicle* for several years and was married to Emily Margaret Walkinshaw of Naparima, Trinidad. At thirty-five he joined the staff of *Punch.* His contributions, which continued until his death, included humorous poems and a well-known series of weekly satirical summaries of parliamentary debates called "The Essence of Parliament." In 1870, upon the death of Mark Lemon, he became editor of *Punch,* a position which he held for the remaining four years of his life. He died in London at the age of fifty-seven.

He was the author of popular novels, and of several short burlesques and farces which were successfully produced in London.

PRINCIPAL WORKS: *Plays*—Anything for a Change, 1848; The Daughter of the Stars, 1850; The Exposition, 1851. *Novels*—Aspen Court, 1855; The Gordian Knot (ill. by John Tenniel) 1860; The Silver Cord, 1861; Sooner or Later (ill. by George du Maurier) 1868. *Verse*—Wit and Humour: Poems from *Punch* (ed. by R. S. Brooks) 1875.

ABOUT: Layard, G. S. A Great *Punch* Editor: Being the Life, Letters, and Diaries of Shirley Brooks.

BROUGHAM, LORD HENRY PETER (First Baron of Brougham and Vaux) (September 18, 1778-May 7, 1868), Scottish statesman and historian, was born in Edinburgh. From seven to thirteen he attended the Edinburgh High School, and in 1792 entered the University of Edinburgh. His first interest was in physics and he sent a paper to the Royal Society at eighteen.

He passed advocate in 1800 and took the northern circuit, but he disliked the law, and was an eccentric and unconventional lawyer. He was one of the founders of the *Edinburgh Review,* and was for most of his life a voluminous contributor to it. His articles showed enormous versatility, but they were supeficial and frequently unjust.

In 1803 he was admitted to Lincoln's Inn, but did not go to London until 1805. There he supported himself mainly by his articles, and became an habitué of the Whig circle of Lord Holland. In 1806 he was secretary of a mission to Lisbon. His interest in the anti-slavery movement began at this time. In 1808 he was called to the bar and practised in the northern circuit. He first became a Member of Parliament in 1810.

Brougham was defense attorney for Leigh Hunt and his brother in the libel suits against their paper, *The Examiner*, both when they were acquitted in 1811 and when they were convicted in 1812. After a brief retirement, he was returned to Parliament in 1815, where he became prominent in the Whig opposition. In 1821 he married Mary Anne (Eden) Spalding, a widow, by whom he had two daughters; she died in 1865.

He was advisor and attorney to the Princess of Wales, later Queen Caroline, and his defense of the popular queen (when she was accused of adultery by her husband, George IV) made him famous. In 1825 he was Lord Rector of Glasgow University. He became noted as an orator—brilliant, sarcastic, but severe and extravagant. His great achievements were marred by lack of tact, boastfulness, and exhibitionism.

In 1830 Brougham was raised to the peerage and made Lord Privy Chancellor. He continued his career as reformer and "muck raker." He was much interested in education, and helped to found the London University in 1828. He was enormously popular; an instance is his name, which has come down as the name of the carriage (brougham) he used.

In 1835 he was eliminated as Chancellor, and retired to Scotland. He emerged in 1839 to lead the opposition in the House of Lords. After 1840, when his second and dearly beloved daughter died, he spent several months yearly at Cannes and gradually withdrew from politics. In 1850 he returned to his interest in science, and for six years was president of the Social Science Association. In 1850 he was Chancellor of the University of Edinburgh. In 1860 he received a second patent of peerage, with reversion to his brother.

From 1867 Brougham's mind, weakened by age, gave way completely. He died at nearly ninety, in Cannes, in the house he had named for his daughter.

Brougham was a man of great energy, wide intellect, and real reforming spirit, but jealous, bitter, and excitable. He is better remembered as an individual than as an author. In his writings he was seldom thorough and his style is slovenly. He was at his best in his speeches, his letters, and his biographical sketches.

PRINCIPAL WORKS: An Enquiry into the Colonial Policy of European Powers, 1803; Practical Observations on the Education of the People, 1825; Speeches Upon Questions Relating to Public Rights, 1838-43; Historical Sketches of Statesmen . . . in the Time of George III, 1839; Lives of Men of Letters and Science . . . in the Time of George III, 1845-46; Life and Times of Henry, Lord Brougham, 1871.

ABOUT: Aspinwall, A. Lord Brougham and the Whig Party; Bagehot, W. Biographical Studies; Brougham, H. P. Life and Times of Henry, Lord Brougham; Garratt, G. T. Lord Brougham.

BROUGHTON, RHODA (November 29, 1840-June 5, 1920), novelist, was born the daughter of a clergyman near Denbigh in North Wales. Her childhood was spent in an Elizabethan manor house at Broughton, Staffordshire, England, one of the ancient residences of her family. (This provided the background for some of her novels.) She was educated in English poetry by her father, who died in her twenty-third year. Her mother being already dead, she lived for the next twenty-nine years with her sister Mrs. William Charles Newcome, first in North Wales at Upper Eyarth and then in England at Oxford. After her sister's death she made her home with a cousin at Headington Hill, near Oxford, until her own death at the age of seventy-nine.

She won a wide audience in her twenty-seventh year with two novels that were considered quite audacious at that time. These were followed by more than fifteen amusing if shoddily written books, picturing country residence life in the latter nineteenth century.

PRINCIPAL WORKS: Cometh Up as a Flower, 1867; Not Wisely But Too Well, 1867; Good-bye, Sweetheart, 1872; Nancy, 1873; Joan, 1876; Belinda, 1883; Doctor Cupid, 1886; Foes-in-Law, 1900; A Waif's Progress, 1905.

BROWN, GEORGE DOUGLAS ("George Douglas") (January 26, 1869-August 28, 1902), Scottish novelist, was born at Ochiltree, Ayrshire, Scotland, son of George Douglas Brown and Sarah Gemmel, who was of Irish origin.

He first attended the village school and the Coylton parish school, where he proved himself a ready student. Some subsequent tutoring at Cronberry and Ochiltree was followed by two years' work as a coal picker. He then went to Ayr Acadamy, where he did well, failing to win the school's first award only because of a natural deficiency in mathematics.

In 1887 he matriculated at Glasgow University, winning a scholarship in the Bursary competition. He studied Greek under Professors Jebb and Murray, and after his graduation in 1890 was for a while assistant to the latter. He won his M.A. with first honors in classics and took the Eglinton fellowship and the gold medal, thus returning for further classical study. In 1891 he won the Luke Historical Prize and the Snell Exhibition fellowship, enabling him to go to Balliol College, Oxford. There he was a good, if not brilliant student, and passed his examinations with a first in classical moderations and a third in *litterae humaniores*, being

GEORGE DOUGLAS BROWN

handicapped in the latter by illness resulting from the strain of his mother's invalidism and death. He had been poor during all his college years, and he afterwards said that his four years at Oxford had been the most miserable period of his life. He mixed very little with the younger students, and it is significant that, although he had passed his examinations, he left without being graduated.

He went to London in 1895 to make his living as a free lance writer, formed a literary partnership with friends, read for a publishing house, and published articles, short stories, and a boy's book (under the pseudonym of "Kennedy King"). It was not until he had published, in 1901, under the pseudonym "George Douglas," his novel *The House With the Green Shutters,* that he won recognition.

This novel, praised by Andrew Lang, was well received in England and the United States and aroused great expectations for the future of its author. Brown, however, did not allow his success to turn his head, but rented a small cottage at Haslemere and set to work with his plans for a novel of the time of Cromwell and a study of *Hamlet,* visiting London only occasionally. His royalties in the summer of 1902 brought him the only financial ease he had ever known.

On August 25, 1902, he went to the house of his friend Andrew Melrose at Muswell Hill, London, where he was stricken ill. He grew steadily worse, and died on the morning of the 28th, of liver disorder and other complications. His friends, who describe him as a hale, hearty man, were stunned by the suddenness of his death, although they had been aware of his complaint.

His reputation rests upon his single novel, which is a powerful, tragic picture of Scot-

tish life. *The House With the Green Shutters* was in part a protest against the sentimentality of the "kailyard school" of Scottish novelists —Ian Maclaren, Samuel R. Crockett, Barrie, and numerous lesser writers; so named because of their excessive use of dialect. But Andrew Lang felt that the form of Brown's novel stemmed from the classical Greek tragedy in which its author was naturally steeped. It is a forthright, vivid picture of cottage life in a Scotch village, told in a strong, direct style, with excellent atmosphere, fine character drawing, and grim power. Critics have compared its effect with that of Balzac's *Père Goriot* and the peasant humor has been likened to that of Hardy. Some felt, indeed, that the grimness of the tale had been overdone, and that no village would have held such a group of unsavory and forbidding characters; but the general impression of excellence does not seem to have been questioned. Of this novel J. P. Millar says: "Never has a certain side of cottage life in Scotland been portrayed with a more vigorous and faithful hand."

Brown, according to friends, was a hearty man, good-humored, loyal, and frank. He was devoted to his mother and family and friendly with the people of his native village. His acquaintances insisted that, despite the impression created by his novel, he was not a misanthrope. R. M.

WORK: The House With the Green Shutters, 1901.

ABOUT: Lennox, C. George Douglas Brown: A Bibliographical Memoir; Millar, J. P. A Literary History of Scotland; Parker, W. M. Modern Scottish Writers; Bookman 14:547 October 1902; Critic 40:202 March 1902; McClure's Magazine 20:101 November 1902.

BROWN, DR. JOHN (September 22, 1810-May 11, 1882), Scottish essayist, best remembered for his dog story, *Rab and His Friends,* was born in Lanarkshire, the son of a minister who was a noted Biblical scholar. In 1826 he entered the arts course at the University of Edinburgh, and in 1828 began the study of medicine, being a pupil of the great surgeon Syme. He received his M.D. in 1833, and all his practice was in Edinburgh.

Brown was above all things a physician, who wrote primarily on non-technical subjects related to medicine and to the problems of the doctor. His interests outside of his profession were in children, dogs, poetry, art, and nature. He was married and had a son, but was always a good deal of a recluse, though he became the friend of such men as Thackeray and Ruskin.

Modest, unaffected, tender, practical, and wise, Brown was a sort of Scottish Charles Lamb, lovable and beloved, with the same faculty of putting himself into his writings, the same naiveté and humor. He had real insight, and genuine interest in and sympathy for all humanity. As with many gifted with humor, he was also congenitally melancholy; this characteristic grew upon him until it became actual melancholia, and finally he ceased to practice and withdrew entirely from society. In his last six months he seemed to be improving, when at attack of pleurisy brought his life to an end. By popular subscription a plaque was erected to his memory in St. Giles Church, Edinburgh.

Brown's principal work was the three volumes of *Horae Subsecivae* (Hours of Leisure), the first volume on medical, the other two on general, subjects. From it have been abstracted as separate volumes his two most famous essays—the one on Rab the dog and the other on Marjorie Fleming, the little friend of Sir Walter Scott who died as a child. All the volumes deserve reading—they are full of penetrating comment on writers and other notables; but these two essays are in their way immortal, and in themselves have made their author so.

PRINCIPAL WORKS: Horae Subsecivae, 1858-62; Rab and His Friends, 1859; Marjorie Fleming, 1863; John Leech and Other Papers, 1882.

ABOUT: Brown, J. Collected Works (see Biography by E. T. McLaren); McLaren, E. T. Dr. John Brown and His Sister Isabella; Shairp, J. C. Studies in Poetry and Philosophy.

BROWN, OLIVER MADOX (January 20, 1855-November 5, 1874), novelist, was the son of Ford Madox Brown, the distinguished painter, by his second wife Emma Hill. Born at Finchley, in Middlesex, he grew up a strange, brooding boy who kept a pet rat and went off on night walks alone or with his young friend the blind poet Philip Bourke Marston. He was called "Nolly."

The Pre-Raphaelites, with whom his father was closely associated, encouraged (and saw great promise in) his precocious writing and painting. He began to write poetry at thirteen, and during the next few years exhibited several water-colors in London galleries. *Gabriel Denever*, his first prose story—and the only one to appear during his lifetime—was published in his eighteenth year. He died suddenly at nineteen, poisoned, it was learned later, "by the air of a subterranean stable." (according to Evelyn Waugh).

His literary remains, including two unfinished novels, several short stories, and poems, were edited in two volumes by William M. Rossetti and Francis Hueffer, husbands respectively of his half-sister Lucy and his sister Catherine.

PRINCIPAL WORKS: Gabriel Denever, 1873; The Dwale Bluth, Hebditch's Legacy, and Other Literary Remains (ed. by W. M. Rossetti and F. Hueffer) 1876.

ABOUT: Brown, O. M. The Dwale Bluth, etc. (see Memoir); Ingram, J. H. Oliver Madox Brown: A Biographical Sketch, Waugh, E. Rossetti.

BROWN, ROBERT (December 21, 1773-June 10, 1858), Scottish botanist, was born in Montrose, the son of a minister, and educated at Aberdeen and Edinburgh Universities. He spent 1801-05 in Australia as naturalist to the famous expedition under Captain Matthew Flinders, and recorded his findings in *Prodromus Florae Novae Hollandiae*, a botanical work notable for its philosophical treatment. From 1810 to 1820 he was private secretary to Sir Joseph Banks, who bequeathed him his plant collection, his library, and his London house. Brown discovered the vibratory movement of minute particles suspended in a liquid (known as the Brownian Movement) and was the first to observe the nucleus of the vegetable cell. These and other important scientific discoveries he described in papers contributed to periodicals and posthumously collected in two volumes. He died at the age of eighty-four.

WORKS: Prodromus Florae Novae Hollandiae, 1810; Miscellaneous Botanical Works, 1866-68.

BROWN, THOMAS (January 9, 1778-April 2, 1820), Scottish philosopher, was born at Kilmabreck, the son of a clergyman. He was educated in philosophy and medicine at the University of Edinburgh. After practicing with an Edinburgh physician for a time, he spent the remaining ten years of his short life as professor of moral philosophy (in association with Dugald Stewart) at the University of Edinburgh. His lectures were extremely popular. A man of simple tastes, he lived quietly with his mother and sisters. He died at forty-two in London, whither he had taken a voyage for his health.

He made valuable and largely original contributions to philosophy, notably on the subjects of causation, sensation and touch, and "relative suggestion." His lectures, hastily written and never revised, were published after his death. The doctrines therein set forth earned the praise of John Stuart Mill and the severe criticism of Sir William Hamilton. Brown himself cared most for his poetical works, which are scarcely remembered.

PRINCIPAL WORKS: Observations on the Zoonomia of Erasmus Darwin, 1798; Inquiry Into the Relation of Cause and Effect, 1817; Lectures on the Philosophy of the Human Mind, 1820.

ABOUT: Brown, T. Lectures on the Philosophy of the Human Mind (see Memoir in eds. subsequent to 1820); Welsh, D. Account of the Life and Writings of Thomas Brown.

BROWN, THOMAS EDWARD (May 5, 1830-October 30, 1897), poet, was born at Douglas, Isle of Man, the fourth son of Robert Brown, a minister, and Dorothy (Thompson) Brown.

Until he was about fifteen the boy was tutored by his father and a parish schoolmaster. In 1846 he went to King William's

THOMAS E. BROWN

College, and, having received a servitorship, proceeded to Christ Church College at Oxford, matriculating in 1849. His position as servitor placed him in a socially inferior class and meant almost complete exclusion from student society. ("Servitors," receiving certain financial aids and privileges in living expenses and fees, originally had acted as menials for their more fortunate fellowstudents, and even at this time were obliged to dress differently from them and to take their meals at different times.) The humiliation was bitter for the brilliant boy, who made a splendid scholastic record and was elected a fellow of Oriel College in 1854.

In the next year he returned to the Island as Vice-Principal of King William's College; and in the same year he was ordained deacon. In 1857 he married a cousin, Emilia Stowell.

In 1861, having lost hope of effecting reforms in King William's, he accepted a headmastership at the Crypt School, Gloucester. The position, however, was unsatisfactory, and he removed, in 1863, to Clifton as the head of the modern departments of the new Clifton College.

There he remained until 1892, while the school flourished and the boys became devoted to "T. E. B." At the same time he served as curate of St. Barnabas, Bristol (1884-93). Ill health finally necessitated his removal from his active work, and he retired to the Island, continuing to live there quietly until his sudden death in 1897, which occurred on a visit to Clifton.

Brown's personality had Celtic fire and sensitiveness to beauty, but it was vigorous and hearty. He never was completely reconciled to his position as schoolmaster, but he was a strikingly vivid teacher and highly

respected and admired by the boys under him. He seems to have had an extraordinary capacity for entering into the joys and enthusiams of his friends, and he could meet humbler folk on their own levels. His powerful personality acted as a tonic upon his own acquaintances. W. E. Henley, a pupil, wrote of him:

> You found him cynic, saint,
> Salt, humourist, Christian, poet; with a free
> Far-glancing, luminous utterance; and a heart
> Large as St. Francis's: withal a brain
> Stored with experience, letters, fancy, art,
> And scored with runes of human joy and pain.

His poetry is interesting first of all for its national significance as an expression of Brown's fervent love for his native island. Much of it is written in Manx dialect. The poet shows gifts of narrative, of description, and of character-analysis, although he tended to go too far to extremes either of a sobbing pathos or a Rabelaisian mirth. He suggests Burns in many respects. As Saintsbury has indicated, he belongs to the mystic poets, although he is often realistic in subject and presentation. He was technically adept enough generally to fit his dialect and his forms to the subject-matter with ease and appropriateness. His works have appealed to a wider circle of readers with the passage of time. "A rugged tenderness is their most characteristic note; but the emotion, while almost equally explosive in mirth and in tears, remains an educated emotion, disciplined by a scholar's sense of language," writes Sir Arthur Quiller-Couch. "They breathe the fervour of an island patriotism . . . and of a simple natural piety."   R. W. W.

PRINCIPAL WORKS: Poetry—Fo'c's'le Yarns, 1881; The Doctor and Other Poems, 1887; The Manx Witch and Other Poems, 1889; Old John, 1893; Collected Poems, 1900. Letters—Letters of Thomas Edward Brown, 1900.

ABOUT: Simpson, S. G. Thomas Edward Brown: An Appreciation; Strachan, L. R. M. The Poet of Manxland; Thomas Edward Brown: A Memorial Volume; Macmillan's Magazine 82:401 October 1900; New Review 17:632 December 1897.

BROWNE, FRANCES (January 16, 1816-1879), Irish story teller and poet, was born at Stranolar in Donegal, North Ireland, daughter of the village postmaster. She was seventh in a family of twelve children. An attack of smallpox at the age of eighteen months left her permanently blind. At twenty-one she left home to make her way in the literary world, and after five years in Edinburgh she went to London. A strong imagination and a retentive memory enabled her to write eighteen books dealing with many lands, things, persons, and periods. The most popular of her stories for children was *Granny's Wonderful Chair*, which has been reissued a great number of times, illustrated by such well-known artists as Katharine Pyle and Emma L. Brock. In her reading and writing she was assisted by a sister and, when the sister left to get married, by a secretary. She contributed to the support of her mother and the education of a sister. A gift from the Marquis of Lansdowne relieved her of privation in late years. She died at the age of sixty-three.

PRINCIPAL WORKS: Lyrics and Miscellaneous Poems, 1848; Pictures and Songs of Home, 1856; Granny's Wonderful Chair and the Tales It Told, 1857 (reissued by Frances Hodgson Burnett as The Story of the Lost Fairy Book, 1887).

ABOUT: Browne, F. Granny's Wonderful Chair (see Prefaces to various editions); Browne, F. My Share of the World: An Autobiography.

BROWNE, THOMAS ALEXANDER

(August 6, 1826-March 11, 1915), Australian novelist who wrote under the pen-name of "Rolf Boldrewood," was born in London. In his fourth year he was taken to Australia where his father, Captain Sylvester Browne. helped to found the city of Melbourne. He was educated at Sydney College in New South Wales, and married in 1861 to Margaret Maria Riley. From his varied experiences as stock-farmer, pioneer squatter, police magistrate, and warden of the goldfields in New South Wales, he wrote some thirty novels and tales of Australian adventure which won wide popularity. The best known of his works was *Robbery Under Arms*, depicting life in the bush and the goldfields. He prided himself on his fidelity to local color and descriptive detail. *A Squatter's Dream* and *A Colonial Reformer* are regarded as the best pictures extant of the squatter's life. He died at the age of eighty-eight.

PRINCIPAL WORKS: Old Melbourne Memories, 1884; Robbery Under Arms, 1888; The Miner's Right, 1890; A Colonial Reformer, 1890; The Squatter's Dream, 1890; A Sydney-Side Saxon, 1891; Nevermore, 1892; A Modern Buccaneer, 1894; A Canvas Town Romance, 1898; Ghost Camp, 1902.

BROWNING, ELIZABETH BARRETT

(March 6, 1806-June 30, 1861), poet, was born Elizabeth Barrett Moulton. In her early childhood her father changed his name for reasons of inheritance from Moulton to Barret. She was born in Durham, the oldest of eleven children, but the family soon moved to Herefordshire, to the Moorish-style house known as Hope End, where she spent her childhood and girlhood. There, though she was small in stature, Elizabeth was healthy and active. She was also amazingly precocious, reading Greek at eight and writing poems in imitation of her favorite authors. Her father had her juvenile epic, *The Battle of Marathon*, privately printed when she was only twelve.

A fall from her pony at fifteen caused a spinal injury, but she was not yet an invalid. Elizabeth never was sent away to school, but studied and read at home and lived a fairly normal life until, when she was twenty, her mother died, and at the same time her father became involved in financial difficulties, which ended in his selling his home and moving first to Sidmouth, then, two years later, to London. After a short residence elsewhere, the family moved to 50 Wimpole Street, to be one of the most celebrated addresses in London until the house was torn down in 1936.

The well-known story of Elizabeth Barrett begins in this period—the viciously tyrannical father, insanely jealous of all his children and especially of his first-born; the favorite brother who was drowned at Torquay while he was visiting his sister there and caused years of psychic shock; the half-real, half-enforced invalidism which finally kept her a prisoner in a darkened room, while at the same time her writings gradually made her a nationally-known figure; and then her liberation at the hands of Robert Browning.

It was in 1846 that her staunch friend, John Kenyon, one of the few her father allowed her, succeeded in bringing to call on her the young poet whose work she had already admired greatly. Browning was in love with her almost before he saw her, and it was not long before she returned his feeling. But any closer relation seemed impossible, under the conditions of her life. Then the doctor said that she must leave England for the winter, and her father refused to allow her to go. More, when he became suspicious of the love between her and Browning, he arranged suddenly to move the whole family to the country, to prevent their further meetings. This was the last provocation. On September 12, 1846, she managed to slip from the house and she and Browning were married at St. Marylebone Church. She returned home immediately, but a week later, at night, she left the house secretly with her faithful maid Wilson and her spaniel Flush, met Browning, and they departed at once for Paris. Her father never forgave her, never saw her again, returned her letters unopened. A few years later one of her sisters took the same desperate step and received the same treatment. Although the Brownings were in England again four times before Edward Barrett's death, so far as the father was concerned his favorite daughter died in 1846.

Instead of actually dying, however, her marriage wrought what seemed a miraculous cure. She was never robust, but in spite of her frailness she managed to live a normal social life, to produce half a dozen more volumes of poetry, in 1849 (after a miscarriage in 1847) to bear a healthy son with no ill effects to herself, and to reach the age of fifty-five.

The Brownings paused briefly in France, then went to Italy, first to Pisa and then to

Florence, which was their home until Mrs. Browning's death. They had a floor in the Palazzo Guidi (the famous "Casa Guidi" of Mrs. Browning's poems), and the building bears now a memorial tablet to her set up by the municipality of Florence. Their small circle of friends was gradually enlarged, until it included most of the English celebrities who visited or lived in Italy. Both the Brownings became immensely concerned in the struggle of Italy to free herself from Austrian domination, and most of Mrs. Browning's later poems relate to public, especially Italian, affairs. In later years also she became very much impressed by spiritualistic phenomena, especially as demonstrated by the medium Daniel Home—much to the distress of her husband. All her life, however, she remained a devout member of the Church of England, much more orthodox than was Robert Browning.

An uneventful outer life, punctuated by occasional trips to Rome, Paris, and London, and a rich and varied inner life (the marriage of the Brownings remains the type of the perfect union) gradually drew to a quiet close. Mrs. Browning's literary reputation continued to spread, and was in fact much greater than her husband's during her lifetime. When Wordsworth died she was seriously considered for the poet laureateship. *Aurora Leigh,* published in 1857, and thought by herself to be her most mature work, was an immense popular success, though there are few willing now to wade through this long didactic novel in verse. She did some prose writing also, mostly critical essays or translations from the Greek, which were later collected from magazines into a volume. The Brownings had always had an adequate income, aside from returns from their books; and when their devoted old friend, John Kenyon, died in 1856, he left £4500 to Mrs. Browning and £6500 to her husband (he had all along sent them £100 a year so that they might be free from financial worry.)

In 1859 Mrs. Browning was very ill, and made worse by excitement over political events. She recovered, however, and by 1861 was in fairly good health. The death of Cavour, the great Italian patriot, in June distressed her immeasurably, and affected her health painfully. Nevertheless, when she died quietly and suddenly in her husband's arms on June 30 (her last word was "Beautiful!"), there had been no inkling that her death was so near. She was buried in the English cemetery at Florence.

Elizabeth Barrett Browning was a tiny person ("I am little, and like little things," she said of her famous miniature library), pale, with thick dark ringlets and deep, dark eyes. Her voice was low, with a curious musical tone. As one of her friends said,

ELIZABETH BARRETT BROWNING

she "seemed all her life something of a spirit." She died of tuberculosis, and this seems to have been the real cause of her lifelong illness.

As a poet, her chief gift is lyrical, and what will live in her work is chiefly certain lyrics—"The Rhyme of the Duchess May," "The Cry of the Children," some of the Italian songs of liberty, and above all the marvelous if uneven *Sonnets From the Portuguese.* These, among the most exquisite love poems in English, are an instance of how her love for Browning, who came like the sun and the free air into her darkened life, transformed her poetry as well as herself. Her faults as a poet are many—pedantry, diffuseness (nearly all her poems are too long), chaotic confusion, didacticism. As Kathleen Conyngham Greene puts it, she was "a teacher and preacher, eager, exuberant, sometimes distressingly complacent." But to offset these defects she has deep tenderness, nobility, and in her best work a real magnificence.

Criticism of a woman poet is always hampered by the tendency of critics to consider her as a woman first and as a poet afterwards. For this reason, Elizabeth Barrett Browning has been compared to many incomparable poets, from Sappho to Christina Rossetti. She was not in the least like either, or like most of the others to whom she has been likened. She was distinctly a child of her age, as is evidenced by her great contemporary popularity. Had she been able to live a more normal life during her first forty years, she would probably have written far less verse, but what she wrote might have reached a higher average level. On the other hand, her natural tendency to diffuseness, which often reduces her longer poems to mere verbiage, and the lack of literary self-discipline arising from her self-education, might have kept her as painfully articulate as ever and might have deprived us of those fine and beautiful lyrics wrung from her by her long imprisonment, which thrust her upon her inner self for poetic sustenance. One thing is certain, and that is that we have Robert Browning to thank, not only for his own great poetic output, but also for most of the best work of the wife he adored, and whom he considered a finer poet than himself. M. A. deF.

PRINCIPAL WORKS: *Poetry*—An Essay on Mind and Other Poems, 1826 (anonymous); Prometheus Bound (translated) and Miscellaneous Poems, 1833 (anonymous); The Seraphim and Other Poems, 1838 (by E. B. Barrett); Poems by E. Barrett Barrett, 1844; A Drama of Exile and Other Poems, 1845; Poems by E. B. Browning, 1850; The Runaway Slave at Pilgrim's Point, 1849; Sonnets From the Portuguese, 1850 (privately printed as Sonnets by E. B. Browning, 1847); Casa Guidi Windows, 1851; Two Poems, 1854; Aurora Leigh, 1857; Poems Before Congress, 1860; Last Poems, 1862 (ed. by Robert Browning); *Prose*—The Greek Christian Poets, and the English Poets, 1863 (ed. by Robert Browning); Letters of Elizabeth Barrett Browning to R. H. Horne, 1877; Letters to Various Correspondents, 1895-6 (ed. by T. J. Wise); Letters of Elizabeth Barrett Browning, 1897 (ed. by F. G. Kenyon); Letters of Robert Browning and Elizabeth Barrett Barrett, 1899; Letters to Her Sister, 1929 (ed. by L. Huxley); Twenty-two Unpublished Letters of Elizabeth Barrett Browning and Robert Browning, 1936.

ABOUT: Baynes, D. J. Andromeda in Wimpole Street; Boas, L. S. Elizabeth Barrett Browning; Burdett, O. The Brownings; Clarke, I. C. Elizabeth Barrett Browning; Loth, D. G. The Brownings: A Victorian Idyll; Lubbock, P. Elizabeth Barrett Browning in Her Letters; Shackleton, M. H. Elizabeth Barrett Browning: R. H. Horne—Two Studies; Willis, I. C. Elizabeth Barrett Browning; Cornhill Magazine 74:331 March 1933.

BROWNING, OSCAR (January 17, 1837-October 6, 1923), historian and biographer, was born in London, the son of William Shipton Browning. Educated at Eton and at King's College, Cambridge, he was a master at Eton for fifteen years (1860-75) and a history lecturer at Cambridge for thirty-three years (1876-1909).

He published more than thirty works which, in the words of A. C. Benson, "were seldom serious contributions to literature; they were written in a readable style, but they were scrappy and inexact... It must, however, be admitted that between the ages of forty to fifty he did a great deal of pioneer work in history." His most notable achievement was as a teacher rather than as a writer: he founded a school of history at King's, and by extra-curricular activities and social gatherings in his rooms he stimulated a large number of students.

Admired for his Rabelaisian wit, abundant energy, and good humor, he was nevertheless severely criticized for an incurable egotism and a fondness for publicity and celebrities.

His last years were spent in Rome, where he died unmarried at the age of eighty-six.

PRINCIPAL WORKS: England and Napoleon in 1803, 1887; History of England, 1890; Dante: Life and Works, 1891; Wars of the Nineteenth Century, 1899; History of Europe, 1814-1843, 1901; Guelphs and Ghibellines, 1903; Napoleon: The First Phase, 1905.

ABOUT: Benson, A. C. Memories and Friends; Browning, O. Memories of Sixty Years at Eton, Cambridge, and Elsewhere; Browning, O. Memories of Later Years; MacCarthy, D. Portraits (Vol. 1).

BROWNING, ROBERT (May 7, 1812-December 12, 1889), poet, was born in Camberwell, the son of an interesting father. The older Robert Browning had been sent by *his* father as a young man to manage the family estates in Jamaica (also, by coincidence, the birthplace of Elizabeth Barrett Browning's father, and the source of the wealth of the Brownings' great friend, John Kenyon). There the young man promptly liberated all the slaves, and distributed farms to them. His outraged father sent him a bill for all the expenses he had ever incurred on his behalf, including those incident to his birth! These the son dutifully paid. It was perhaps, from him that the poet inherited his horror of debt and his instinctive economy. Certainly they were not the result of experience in wage-earning; Robert Browning the younger (really the third in succession) received an allowance from his father up to middle age, benefited by the generosity and the legacy of his friend Kenyon, and was able to refuse ever to send his poems to magazines, on the theory that no one should read them who did not wish to do so voluntarily!

There were only two children in the family, Robert and his younger sister Sarianna. The mother was part Scotch and part German, and was as much of a "character" as the father. The father, after his idealistic youthful escapade, became a clerk in the Bank of England, though all his life he dabbled in painting. Robert was educated privately, except for some classes in Greek at the University of London at seventeen (and a dame's school in Peckham in early childhood, because he was so boisterous and unmanageable at home!). His father molded his mind, and encouraged his precocity. The child's first drawing was executed at two, and by twelve he had produced a book of poems, which he destroyed afterwards. From fourteen to sixteen he expected to make musical composition his lifework. But when, at seventeen, the question of his future was to be decided, he asked if the family income permitted his leading "a life of pure culture," and when told it did, set out consciously to be a poet.

Browning's earlier poems were all published at the expense of his father. He was long in coming into his own. It was not until after publication of *The Ring and the Book*, in 1868, that he was very widely read, though from the beginning he had staunch and discriminating admirers. His first published volume, *Pauline*, was the result partly of a youthful love, and partly of the interest and leisure of a visit to St. Petersburg (Leningrad) in 1833 and 1834 as the guest of the British consul-general. In 1834, 1838, and 1844 he made prolonged visits to Italy, the land which was to become his second home, and scene of the most vital period of his inner life. The publication of *Paracelsus,* his second book, in 1835, brought him the friendship of Carlyle, Landor, and Hunt, and later of Dickens and Wordsworth. *Sordello,* in 1840, merely mystified the critics, and left the public indifferent. From it dates the myth of Browning's obscurity based on the compression of his style. (In this respect he might almost be called a poetic Carlyle or Tacitus.)

A friendship with the famous actor Macready turned his attention to writing for the stage. Three of his plays were produced, with some, though not great, success: *Strafford* at Covent Garden in 1837, *A Blot on the 'Scutcheon* at Drury Lane in 1843, and *Colombe's Birthday* at the Haymarket in 1853. The chief non-dramatic poems of this period, *Bells and Pomegranates,* were issued originally as eight separate brochures, from 1841 to 1846, and then republished as a single volume.

In 1846 he was introduced by John Kenyon to Elizabeth Barrett, the cloistered invalid whose poems he had so much admired and whom he already loved by description. Their elopement followed in September, the beginning of sixteen years of the happiest marriage on record. For most of this time they lived in Florence, with occasional trips in France and Italy or back to England. Their only son, Robert Wiedemann Barrett Browning (usually known as "Pen"), who grew up to be a not very important sculptor and painter, was born in March 1849. The same year saw the first collected edition of Robert Browning's poems. It saw also his first great grief, the death of his mother a few days after the birth of his son—the source of months of deep depression.

But the deep and ineradicable blow of his life came with his wife's death in 1861. For two years, back in London (he never could bring himself to return to Florence), he gave himself up to anguish, in the deepest seclusion, writing nothing. Then suddenly he came to feel that this was pure morbidity, and that for his child's sake he must face life again. The deep optimism and will to live that are Browning's most prominent charac-

teristics reasserted themselves. He re-entered society, and became in time an indefatigable diner-out, an indispensable figure at every literary gathering. But inwardly he was Elizabeth Barrett Browning's widower all his life. (It is true, as has lately been discovered, that in 1869 he proposed marriage to Lady Ashburton, telling her plainly it was for the sake of her fortune, so as to be able to provide properly for his rather incompetent son! The lady, not unnaturally, refused him curtly and became his bitter enemy and calumniator.) Other losses were to follow—that of his dearly beloved father, and of his sister-in-law, Arabella Barrett, to whom he had been much attached. After the father's death, Sarianna Browning kept house for her brother and her nephew. In 1862 he had bought a house in London, in which he lived for twenty-five years, selling it and buying another in 1887, two years before his death, because of a (false) threat to run a railroad in front of it.

From about 1868 onward Browning gradually became, with Tennyson, the most noted contemporary English poet. In that year he received an honorary M.A. from Oxford and an honorary fellowship at Balliol College. Three times he refused the lord-directorship of St. Andrews University. From 1879, with the publication of the *Dramatic Idylls,* his fame was universal, as was evidenced by the formation of the Browning Society in 1881—an enterprise with which Browning sympathized, but with which he would not cooperate, for fear of ridicule.

His summers he spent in Scotland or France until 1878, when he forced himself to return to Italy, though never to Florence. A great part of his time thereafter was spent in

ROBERT BROWNING

Venice, where his son made his residence after his marriage. After 1883 Browning's great physical strength began to decline, though he continued to write up to the last autumn of his life. In 1884 he was made an honorary L.L.D. of Edinburgh University, and in 1886 was appointed foreign correspondent of the Royal Academy: his interest in both painting and music, so very evident throughout the body of his poetry, continued unabated through his lifetime.

A series of attacks of bronchitis culminated in pneumonia, and he died at his son's home in Venice in December of 1889. After a public funeral in the Italian city, his remains were taken to England and buried in Westminster Abbey, in the Poets' Corner.

In person, Browning presented a vivid contrast to his pale, shy, fragile little wife. He was not more than medium sized, but his great animation and robust physique gave the impression of greater stature. He was dark in coloring, with long black hair later streaked with grey, and with vivid dark eyes. His voice was loud and his gestures emphatic; everything about him spoke of energy, health, and buoyancy of spirit. Yet this bouncing aggressive personality could be tenderness itself—not only to his worshiped wife, his parents, his son, but to friends like the aged Walter Savage Landor, whom he took in (after the old poet had severed from his family in one of his explosions of temper) and comforted, cared for, and watched over to Landor's death. Browning could sympathize, perhaps, with the old man's explosiveness if not with his crotchiness, for he himself was given to sudden outbursts of anger, over before their echo died. He had much of the temperament of Theodore Roosevelt, with a far better mental equipment—the perpetual boyishness, the hearty enthusiasms, the noisy ebullience, the invincible optimism, the graciousness and personal charm. He had also, however, many characteristics peculiarly his own—a deep metaphysical bent, an enormous tolerance for anything in the world except deliberate cruelty, a genuine humility which made him, as someone has said, "the least self-centered of poets." His volubility hid a stubborn reserve and a profound reticence. In the agonized years when he was devoting himself to editing his wife's literary remains, he protested in torment against the invasion of the public into their cherished privacy, and cried that he would himself furnish every printed word concerning her that it was any of the world's business to know. It is ironic that few men have so had their inner life spread open to the public gaze, when they were dead and helpless. The most intimate letters of Robert and Elizabeth Browning have, by their son's consent, been laid out for all to read.

As has been said, the charge of obscurity laid against Browning as a writer is chiefly due to an elliptic compression, a discipline self-imposed because of his natural fluency. His thought frequently runs ahead of his words, but the words will catch up with it if the reader be patient. He has been called a "psychological monologist," a devoted observer of human minds, a conversationalist on paper concerning the conclusions drawn from his passionate curiosity about other people's emotions and thoughts. In another period he might well have been a novelist of the "stream of consciousness" school, endeavoring to put into words the half-formed cerebration of his subjects' inmost lives. And yet, though he has not the soft felicity of a Tennyson, he is indubitably a poet, and a great poet. His lyrics are as poignant as a bird's song, and he went to school well to his earliest masters, Keats and above all Shelley.

Perhaps the only thing which keeps Browning from being completely in accord with our later era is his ebullient and militant optimism —"God's in His heaven, all's right with the world." But Browning's optimism is not the shallow philosophy of a Pollyanna. It is courage "in spite of hell and high water": he is above all "one who never feared the future, but faced forward." Impulsive and violent as he often was—and what Browning himself was appears in his poetry in every line—he was steadfast always in that, always a yea-sayer to life. His place in literature is secure. Often harsh in style, often allusive, occasionally irritating to the later reader with the irritation inseparable from the Victorian assumption that "surely we are the people, and wisdom will die with us"—nevertheless, these are mere sun-spots. The essential Browning is a poet for all time, who will reward his disciples the more, the more they immerse themselves in him.   M. A. deF.

PRINCIPAL WORKS: *Poetry*—Pauline, 1833; Paracelsus, 1835; Strafford, 1837; Sordello, 1840; Bells and Pomegranates, 1841-6; Poems, 1849; Christmas Eve and Easter-Day, 1850; Poems (in Two Poems, by E. B. Browning) 1854; Men and Women, 1855; Dramatis Personae, 1864; The Ring and the Book, 1868-9; Balaustion's Adventure, 1871; Prince Hohenstiel-Schwangau: Saviour of Society, 1871; Fifine at the Fair, 1872; Red Cotton Nightcap Country, 1873; Aristophanes' Apology, 1875; The Inn Album, 1875; Pacchiarotto and How He Worked in Distemper: With Other Poems, 1876; La Saisias: The Two Poets of Croisac, 1878; Dramatic Idylls: First Series 1878, Second Series 1879; Jocoseria, 1883; Ferishtah's Fancies, 1884; Parleyings With Certain People of Importance in Their Day, 1887; Asolando: Francies and Facts, 1890; New Poems by Robert Browning and Elizabeth Barrett Browning (ed. by F. G. Kenyon) 1914. *Prose*—An Essay on Percy Bysshe Shelley, 1852; Letters of Robert Browning (collected by T. J. Wise, ed. by T. L. Hood) 1933. Letters of Robert Browning and Elizabeth Barrett, 1899; Twenty-two Unpublished Letters of Elizabeth Barrett Browning and Robert Browning, 1936.

ABOUT: Axson, S. Browning: His Time, His Art, His Philosophy; Browning, F. B. Some Memories of Robert Browning; Cary, E. L. Browning: Poet and Man; Chesterton, G. K. Robert Browning; Duckworth, F. R. G. Browning: Background and Conflict; Gosse, E. W. Robert Browning: Personalia; Griffin, W. H. Life of Robert Browning; Russell, F. T. One Word More on Browning; Shairp, W. Life of Robert Browning; Sim, F. M. Robert Browning: The Poet and the Man; Sim, F. M. Robert Browning: Poet and Philosopher; Symons, A. An Introduction to the Study of Browning; Yale Review 22:152 Autumn 1932.

BRUNTON, MARY (November 1, 1778-December 19, 1818), Scottish novelist, was born Mary Balfour on the island of Barra, off the West coast of Scotland. Her father was Colonel Thomas Balfour of Elwick. She had no regular education but studied French, Italian, and music while supervising her father's household. At twenty she was married to the Rev. Alexander Brunton, with whom she lived five years in the parish of Bolton in East Lothian, Scotland, and thereafter in Edinburgh, where he was minister of the Tron Church and professor of oriental languages in the University of Edinburgh. She died at the age of forty in Edinburgh, twelve days after giving birth to a stillborn son.

Mrs. Brunton wrote two novels popular in their day and left an unfinished story which was posthumously published. It was her great purpose in the novel, she declared, "to procure admission for the religion of a sound mind and of the Bible where it cannot find access in any other form."

WORKS: Self-Control, 1810; Discipline, 1814; Emmeline (ed. by A. Brunton) 1819.

ABOUT: Brunton, M. Discipline (see Memoir of her life and writings in 1832 ed.); Emmeline (see Biographical Memoir by A. Bruton).

BRYCE, JAMES (Viscount Bryce of Dechmont) (May 10, 1838-January 22, 1922), historian and travel writer, was born in Belfast, the son of James Bryce, LL.D., a Scottish schoolmaster, and Margaret (Young) Bryce, the daughter of a Belfast merchant. When the boy was eight the Bryces moved to Glasgow, the original family home, and there Bryce attended the Glasgow Grammar School and the University of Glasgow. He then entered Trinity College Oxford, where he received his B.A. in 1862, being made a fellow of Oriel College in the same year. In 1863 he studied at Heidelberg University, and in 1867 was called to the bar, practising law until 1882. In 1870 he was appointed regius professor of civil law at Oxford, but did not live there. In 1889 he married Elizabeth Ashton.

His travels began early, and encompassed nearly the whole world. His political career started when he was elected to Parliament in 1880. From 1886 to 1892 he was Foreign

JAMES BRYCE

Under-Secretary, in 1892 Chancellor for the Duchy of Lancaster (with a seat in the Cabinet), and in 1894 President of the Board of Trade. From 1905 to 1907 he· acted as Chief Secretary for Ireland. In the latter year he was appointed British Ambassador to the United States, which he had already visited four times and knew well. He was a remarkably popular and able ambassador during his six years of incumbency, and is said to have visited every state in the Union, besides Hawaii. He resigned in 1913, having reached the age of seventy-five.

His active life was by no means over, however, for five of his books were published after that date. (His first book had appeared in 1859.) During the summer of 1921 he lectured in America, and he addressed the Historical Association only two weeks before his death, which occurred at Sidmouth where he and his wife had gone for a vacation. He was working on a translation of Homer when he died peacefully in his sleep. He retained his keenness of intellect to the very moment of his decease.

An ardent mountain-climber (he was president of the Alpine Club), Bryce was slight, spare, and wiry, with piercing eyes under bushy brows. He was a typical nineteenth century Liberal of the best sort, a true democrat, and what is called a "good mixer." He was genuinely a "citizen of the world." His memory was very retentive and he had an encyclopedic mind; in fact, his chief fault as a writer is discursiveness from his very wealth of material. His honorary degrees and similar recognitions were innumerable.

A good classical scholar, his writing was always inductive, concrete, and practical, like his mind. In his more popular works his style approached the lively. At least two of his works, *The American Commonwealth* and *The Holy Roman Empire* (actuated by a university prize essay on the same subject), are permanent classics of history. He was the special champion of the Armenians (Mount Ararat was among the many mountains he had climbed), and he opposed the Boer War. His special advocacy of small nations made him Belgium's defender and Germany's bitter enemy during the World War. He was one of the founders of the League of Nations, though he took little part in its actual proceedings. He was perhaps the best liaison officer between Great Britain and the United States who ever lived.

He wrote a good deal for periodicals, being a contributor to *The Nation* (New York) for over forty years. His interest in science was also great, particularly in geology and botany, and he was a Fellow of the Royal Society. As a historian—which he was above all the other interests of his versatile mind—he was sound and conscientious, and primarily an educator. Few men have had better equipped intellects or more thoroughly useful careers.   M. A. deF.

PRINCIPAL WORKS: The Flora of the Island of Arran, 1859; The Holy Roman Empire, 1864; Report on the Condition of Education in Lancashire, 1867; Transcaucasia and Ararat, 1877; The Trade Marks Registration Act, 1877; The Predictions of Hamilton and DeTocqueville, 1887; The American Commonwealth, 1888; The Migrations of the Races of Men Considered Historically, 1893; Impressions of South Africa, 1897; William Ewart Gladstone, 1898; Studies in History and Jurisprudence, 1901; Studies in Contemporary Biography, 1903; The Hindrances to Good Citizenship, 1909; South America: Observations and Impressions, 1912; University and Historical Addresses, 1913; Essays and Addresses in War Time, 1918; Modern Democracies, 1921; International Relations, 1922; The Study of American History, 1922; Memories of Travel, 1923.

ABOUT: Fisher, H. A. L. James Bryce; English Historical Review 37:219 April 1922; London Quarterly Review 138:234 October 1922; Nation 114: 113 February 1, 1922; Nation (London) 30:650 January 28, 1922; Nature 109:113 January 26, 1922.

BUCHANAN, ROBERT WILLIAM (August 18, 1841-June 10, 1901), Scottish poet, novelist, and playwright, was born at Caverswall, in Staffordshire, England, the son of Robert Buchanan, socialistic lecturer and journalist. Educated in Scotland at Glasgow High School and University, he began his literary career in London at nineteen and was married a year later to Mary Jay.

In 1871 he achieved notoriety with a pseudonymous article in the *Contemporary Review* attacking Dante Gabriel Rossetti and the Pre-Raphaelites as "The Fleshly School of Poetry." After a bitter controversy, he withdrew his charge and made amends by dedicating his novel *God and Man* to Rossetti.

As dramatist, he had a highly successful career. Many of his plays were adaptations. In 1884 he visited America for the production of his popular melodrama, *Alone in London,* written in collaboration with his sister-in-law, Harriett Jay, who cared for him after the death of his wife. His dramatic and literary works brought in large sums of money which were lost in imprudent speculation, and he died in poverty at Streatham (near London) at the age of fifty-nine.

He is remembered today chiefly for his poetry, which was voluminous and unequal but contained such outstanding pieces as "The Vision of the Man Accurst," "The Ballad of Judas Iscariot," and "Ratcliffe Meg."

PRINCIPAL WORKS: *Poetry*—Undertones, 1863; London Poems, 1866; North Coast and Other Poems, 1867; White Rose and Red, 1873; Balder the Beautiful, 1877; Ballads of Life, Love, and Humour, 1882: The City of Dream, 1888; The Outcast, 1891; The Wandering Jew, 1893; Poetical Works, 1901. *Novels*—The Shadow of the Sword, 1876; A Child of Nature, 1881; God and Man, 1881; Father Anthony, 1898. *Plays*—A Nine Days' Queen, 1880; Lady Clare, 1883; Storm-beaten, 1883; Alone in London (with Harriett Jay) 1885; Sophia, 1886; A Man's Shadow, 1889; The Charlatan, 1894.

ABOUT: Jay, H. Robert Buchanan: Some Account of His Life; Symons, A. Studies in Prose and Verse; Walker, A. S. Robert Buchanan.

BUCKINGHAM, JAMES SILK (August 25, 1786-June 30, 1855), editor and author of travel works, was born a farmer's son at Flushing, near Falmouth, in Cornwall. His youth was spent at sea. In India he established the *Calcutta Journal,* through which he made such outspoken criticisms of the Indian government that the paper was suppressed within five years and he was expelled from the country. Later the East India Company gave him a pension of £200 yearly by way of acknowledging the injustice of its action. In London he founded and briefly edited several journals, notably *The Athenaeum,* which made its début in January 1828. For five years he served Sheffield as a member of Parliament. He died in London at sixty-eight, survived by his wife, Elizabeth Jennings, and several children, including LEICESTER SILK BUCKINGHAM (1825-1867), a successful dramatist, who made adaptations of French comedies.

Buckingham's varied travels in the Near East, America, and Europe filled nearly twenty volumes. His most notable works were those dealing with the Orient. In addition he wrote an autobiography and more than thirty pamphlets advocating temperance and social reform. His greatest reputation was as a lecturer.

PRINCIPAL WORKS: Travels in Palestine, 1822; Travels Among the Arab Tribes Inhabiting the East of Syria and Palestine, 1825; Travels in Mesopotamia, 1827; Travels in Assyria, Media, and Persia, 1830; America: Historical Descriptive, and

Statistic, 1841; The Slave States of America, 1842; The Eastern and Western States of America, 1842; Canada, Nova Scotia, New Brunswick, and Other British Provinces of North America, 1843; Tour Through Belgium, the Rhine, and Holland, 1845; Tour Through France and Italy, 1847; Autobiography, 1855.

ABOUT: Buckingham, J. S. Autobiography.

BUCKLAND, FRANCIS TREVELYAN
(December 17, 1826-December 19, 1880), naturalist, was born at Christ Church, Oxford, where his father, geologist and future dean of Westminster, was then canon. Educated at Christ Church College and St. George's Hospital, London, he was nine years an army surgeon. Spare-time researches in zoology led to his becoming in 1856 a writer on natural history (fishes in particular) for the magazine *Field*. In 1866 he founded a similar publication, *Land and Water*, which was the vehicle for most of his writings. From 1867 until his death he served as inspector of salmon fisheries in England. In the South Kensington Museum he established a permanent collection illustrative of fish culture, the first of its kind, which eventually was expanded into the Fisheries Exhibition of 1883. His writings were widely popular, despite their tendency to inaccuracy and looseness of style. He died in London two days after his fifty-fourth birthday.

PRINCIPAL WORKS: Curiosities of Natural History, 1857-72; Fish Hatching, 1863; Logbook of a Fisherman and Zoologist, 1875; Natural History of British Fishes, 1881; Notes and Jottings from Animal Life, 1882.

ABOUT: Bompas, G. C. Life of Francis Trevelyan Buckland.

BUCKLE, HENRY THOMAS (November 24, 1821-May 29, 1862), historian, was born at Lee, but merely during his mother's visit to relatives; in actuality he was all his life a Londoner. His father was a shipowner with a large and prosperous business, a pronounced Tory of the old nineteenth-century type, his mother a severe and devoted Calvinist. Buckle was from birth exceedingly delicate; so much so that his parents thought it useless to educate him, since he would surely die before manhood. In consequence when he was eight he could scarcely tell his letters, and up to eighteen is said to have read but three books. In his fourteenth year he was sent to school, but with instructions that he was to study only what he wished. His attention being attracted to arithmetic, he spent all his time on mathematics and won a prize; his father offered him a further reward, and he asked that it be his removal from school! That was the end of his formal education.

When he was seventeen, since he was still alive, his father insisted that he enter the shipping business, which he detested. A few months later, providentially, the father died,

leaving him with an independent fortune. The shock of his death caused a fainting fit in the boy, and these continued with such severity that there was no question of his continuing a commercial career. Instead, he started on a tour of the continent with his mother and sister, and always maintained thereafter that travel was the best and only real means of education. By 1850 he could read in nineteen languages and speak fluently in seven, though with an execrable accent.

Gradually the youth who had been reared a Tory and a Calvinist became a political radical and a free-thinker, and so remained. He determined to be an historian and devoted himself to preparation of a grandiose history of civilization. He undertook another long foreign journey, living and studying chiefly in Munich; there he overworked so badly that he became a victim of rheumatic fever, and his mother was obliged to go to Germany and bring him home.

Until her death in 1859 Buckle lived the quiet life of a scholarly bachelor in London with her—both his sisters having married. Twice in his boyhood he had fallen in love with cousins who rejected him; the fiancé of one of them he challenged to a duel, but was refused with laughter. He seems to have had no love affairs afterwards; he said that he would not marry until he possessed an income of £3000, twice that which he had, and appears never to have been tempted to break the resolution. His mathematical bent made him one of the greatest chess players of his time, and that was his chief recreation.

In 1857, after fifteen years of labor, the first volume of his *History of Civilization in England* was published. The second volume

HENRY THOMAS BUCKLE

came out in 1861. In spite of the title, the first volume contained no more than preliminary articles and an outline of the projected work, the second illustrated his proposed method by a history of the Spanish intellect from the fifth to the nineteenth century, and of Scotland and the Scotch mind to the eighteenth. The work as a whole was never completed, and it was all the integrated or comprehensive writing he ever did.

His mother's death was a profound shock to him. In spite of it, he remained in the home he had shared with her until publication of his second volume. Then he started on a tour of Egypt and Palestine with the two young sons of his friend Huth, one of whom later became his biographer. In Palestine he became ill with an ulcer of the throat. In Damascus his condition grew much worse. An American physician arrived too late to be of any help. On May 29, 1862, he died in Damascus and was buried in the Protestant Cemetery there.

In spite of the enormous work Buckle did, he remains a brilliant amateur. He was a disciple of Mill and Comte, believing that history was made and deflected by the operation of physical laws, and that "the historian is inferior to the scientist." Though he was receptive to the new evolutionary ideas, he was too early to come (as he would almost certainly have done) completely under the influence of Darwin and Spencer. What he left was little more than an introduction to what he had planned. His chief difficulty was that he really did not have sufficient knowledge for the huge task he had undertaken. But his vigorous, racy, incisive style made his work exceedingly popular, and gave him a reputation, not beyond his deserts, but beyond his actual accomplishment.

Buckle was a bit of an eccentric, as is indicated by his story. He was extremely thrifty, and had a name for meanness, yet he was most generous to others; for himself he begrudged spending all money except for books and for cigars, of which he was an incessant smoker. Perhaps he valued money primarily because it was his way to freedom and to the student life. He had very few intimate friends, and spent most of his time in study and writing, with a daily solitary walk for exercise. He was opinionated but never quarrelsome, and with his frail health he was obliged to conserve his strength for the work to which he had dedicated himself. As a man he was what used to be known as a "character"; as a writer what little he finished was an augury of powers which fate never allowed to come to fruition.

M. A. deF.

PRINCIPAL WORKS: The History of Civilization in England, Vol. I, 1857, Vol. II, 1861; Miscellaneous and Posthumous Works, 1872.

ABOUT: Huth, A. H. The Life and Writings of Henry Thomas Buckle; Nature 128:931 December 5, 1931.

BUCKSTONE, JOHN BALDWIN (September 14, 1802-October 31, 1879), actor-manager and dramatist, was born in London. He began his acting career at nineteen, becoming one of the most popular of low comedians in the London theatre of his time. As manager of the Haymarket for more than twenty years, he presented such famous players as E. H. Sothern, Mr. and Mrs. W. H. Kendal, and Eva Cavendish in the plays of W. S. Gilbert, Planché, Tom Taylor, and T. W. Robertson, besides his own, in which he usually appeared. His daughter, Lucy Isabella Buckstone, was an actress.

Beginning at twenty-four with Luke the Labourer, he wrote about 150 plays, of which scarcely one was a failure and many were great successes. "Adelphi melodrama" and "Adelphi screamers" (or farces) were familiar terms originating largely from his works produced at that theatre. The plays of Buckstone were highly sentimental and full of flowery language, but dramatically well constructed (though often of borrowed plots). Some were printed in The Acting National Drama or in Duncombe's Edition of the British Theatre, and they retained their popularity till the end of the century.

PRINCIPAL PLAYS: The Bear Hunters: or, The Fatal Ravine, 1829; Ellen Wareham, 1833; The Green Bushes: or, A Hundred Years Ago, 1845; The Flowers of the Forest, 1847; Damon and Pythias, 1871.

BULLEN, ARTHUR HENRY (February 9, 1857-February 29, 1920), poet, essayist, and editor, was born in London. His father was keeper of printed books at the British Museum. The boy was educated at City of London School, Worcester College, and Oxford. In college he was already noted for his knowledge of Elizabethan and nineteenth century writers, especially Lamb and Swinburne, and for his marvelous memory and facility in reciting poetry.

For a while he taught at a school in Margate but soon left and devoted himself entirely to literature. He wrote many articles for the Dictionary of National Biography on sixteenth and seventeenth century authors. Between 1881 and 1890 he edited nearly fifty volumes of old English plays and Elizabethan and Caroline lyrics.

In 1889 Bullen lectured at Oxford and applied in vain for the chair of English at University College, London. Disappointed in this, he became a publisher with a partner named Lawrence, issuing the Muses' Library, from 1891 to 1907. In 1904 he established the Shakespeare Head Press at Stratford-on-Avon, and brought out the Stratford Town Shakespeare. In 1906 he became editor of the revived *Gentleman's Magazine* (published by Lord Northcliffe). In 1879 he had married Edith Goodwin, by whom he had two sons and three daughters. He died in Stratford.

Bullen was a notable textual critic. He is credited with the rediscovery and rehabilitation of many forgotten poets, most celebrated of whom was Thomas Campion. He was a constant encourager of younger men, and had an immense influence on the scholarship of the late nineteenth and early twentieth centuries. His own writings are graceful and scholarly rather than powerful; his great work was as critic, editor, and publisher.

PRINCIPAL WORKS: *Edited*—John Day, 1881; Old English Plays, 1882-84; Selection From the Poems of Michael Drayton, 1883; Carols and Poems From the Fifteenth Century, 1884; Lyrics from Elizabethan Song Books, 1886; More Lyrics, 1887; England's Helicon, 1887; A Christmas Garland, 1885. *Original*—Weeping-Cross (poems) 1921; Elizabethans, 1924.

ABOUT: Brett-Smith, H. F. B. Memoir (in 3rd edition Shakespeare's Sonnets, 1921).

BULWER, EDWARD GEORGE EARLE LYTTON. See BULWER-LYTTON, E. G. E. L.

BULWER, EDWARD ROBERT. See LYTTON, LORD

BULWER, SIR HENRY (William Henry Lytton Earle Bulwer, Baron Dalling and Bulwer) (February 13, 1801-May 23, 1872), diplomatist and author of historical and biographical works, was born in London, elder brother of the novelist Bulwer-Lytton. He was educated at Harrow and Cambridge.

As secretary of embassy at Constantinople (1837-38) he negotiated an important commercial treaty; as ambassador to Madrid 1843-48) he arbitrated peace between Spain and Morocco; as ambassador to Washington (1849-52) he completed the Bulwer-Clayton treaty, which promised neutrality of the proposed canal across Central America; and as ambassador to Constantinople (1858-65) he fulfilled Palmerston's Eastern policy. He was twice member of Parliament, 1830-37, and 1868-71. Elevated to the peerage in 1871, he died a year later in Naples at the age of seventy-one, leaving no children. His wife was Georgiana Charlotte Mary Wellesley, daughter of the first Baron Cowley, and a niece of the Duke of Wellington.

The writings of Sir Henry were largely the outgrowth of his diplomatic career. His two volumes of *Historical Characters* contained well-balanced sketches of Talleyrand, William Cobbett, George Canning, and Sir James Mackintosh.

PRINCIPAL WORKS: An Autumn in Greece, 1826; France: Social, Literary and Political, 1834-36; Life of Byron, 1835; Historical Characters, 1868-70; Life of Palmerston (unfinished) 1870-74.

ABOUT: Athenaeum June 1, 1872; The Times June 3, 1872.

BULWER-LYTTON, EDWARD GEORGE EARLE LYTTON (First Baron Lytton) (May 25, 1803-June 18, 1873), novelist, poet and dramatist, was born in London, the third son of General William Earle Bulwer and Elizabeth Barbara (Lytton) Bulwer. Both the Bulwers and the Lyttons were among the oldest and most respected of county families. When Edward was four his father died at his estate, Heydon Hall, Norfolk, and the widow settled in London.

Young Edward was something of an infant prodigy, but his education was rather irregular. After a few years at private schools, he was sent—at his own request—to a tutor instead of to Eton. During this period he published a book of verse and had a romantic love affair in which the girl was forced by her father to marry another man.

Entering Trinity College, Cambridge, Bulwer became one of the group of bright young speakers of the Union Debating Society, among whom W. M. Praed (the poet) and Macaulay were particularly notable. He won some academic honors and graduated in 1826, subsequently earning a Master's degree and receiving honorary degrees from both Oxford and Cambridge in later years.

Before graduation Bulwer had established a reputation in the society of London and Paris as a dandy. He was an accomplished rider, boxer, fencer, and whist player. He published some poems written in the Byronic manner, but had made no serious pretensions to a literary career prior to his marriage in 1827.

Bulwer's marriage to Rosina Doyle Wheeler profoundly affected his entire career. She was the beautiful but rather ill-bred daughter of an inpecunious Irish officer. Bulwer's mother had opposed the match from the first and after the marriage she stopped her son's allowance of £1000 a year. This left the young couple with such meager means that they were forced to find a new source of income at once. Hence Bulwer turned to writing.

His first novel, *Falkland*, was published the year of their marriage and the following year *Pelham*, a study of the fashionable life of the period, was a marked success. Society gossip was busy trying to identify the characters in the book with people in real life. Bulwer's literary industry was amazing, and even more amazing is the fact that everything he wrote sold like hot cakes, even his poetry, which was decidedly second-rate. *Pelham* was followed by *The Disowned* in the same year and after that came many other novels at the rate of about one or two a year.

EDWARD G. E. L. BULWER-LYTTON

His earlier novels were didactic efforts to correct and reform faults of the day. Although other popular writers, such as Dickens and Thackeray, had individual successes which out-sold any one novel of Bulwer's, no other author was so uniformly popular.

For the first two years of their married life, Edward and Rosina Bulwer were extravagantly happy, and wildly extravagant. Their expenditures averaged about £3000 a year, and this sizeable sum was earned with the pen. But the strain began to tell. The author became extremely irritable. His wife no longer pleased him. His mother exasperated him. His health began to fail.

Yet—in spite of all this—he not only continued his writing in undiminished volume, but in 1831 he became a member of Parliament on Bentham's reform ticket. About the same time he became editor of the *New Monthly*, which post he held for about a year. He remained in parliament until 1841, when he was defeated by his failure to support, in full, the liberal policies.

In 1836 the Bulwers were legally separated and from this time forward, Bulwer was the object of his wife's bitter hatred. She attacked him in the courts and at political meetings. Eventually she was adjudged insane and placed under restraint for a brief period. She also became a novelist, writing *Cheveley: or, The Man of Honour,* in which Bulwer was caricatured. The two children lived chiefly with their father after the separation.

Bulwer had greatly resented the ridicule which his novels had suffered at the hands of the critics, though such criticism failed to diminish their sales. He used his position as editor of the *New Monthly* to answer his

critics. His editorial work brought him into contact with Disraeli, Dickens, and John Forster who became his good friends.

Throughout his first ten years in parliament Bulwer had continued to write, producing some of his most popular novels and plays. It is noteworthy that he was the most successful playwright of his time, and the only one whose plays held the stage for long periods—even after the death of the author. *The Lady of Lyons, Richelieu,* and *Money* were the greatest successes. His best known novels of this period were *The Last Days of Pompeii* and *Rienzi.*

In 1838 Bulwer had been made a baronet. Upon his mother's death in 1843 he inherited her father's estate of Knebworth in Hertfordshire and added the name Lytton. Until he was returned to Parliament in 1852 (this time as a conservative), Bulwer-Lytton divided his time between Knebworth and travel on the continent, where he gathered materials for his later historical novels and took the cures at various spas.

He was appointed colonial secretary in Lord Derby's ministry (1858-59) and in 1866 was raised to the House of Peers as Baron Lytton of Knebworth. After this he ceased to take an active part in politics.

A contemporary critic, in the *Edinburgh Review,* said of Bulwer-Lytton that he has "a style vigorous and pliable, sometimes strangely incorrect, but often rising to touching eloquence." Garnett and Gosse in their *History of English Literature* say: "What has shattered the once-glittering dome of his reputation is a reaction against what early readers of *Zanoni* called his 'fearfully beautiful word painting,' his hollow rhetoric, his puerile horrors. . . . His latest works are his best."

Michael Sadleir closes the foreword to his *Bulwer: A Panorama* with this summary: ". . . . Bulwer . . . has become a legend, half-impressive, half-absurd, to a posterity which can see his faults and read the satire of his enemies, but cannot appreciate wherein lay his power over his age, nor understand why, if he was the great man he must have been, he was not greater still."   D. C.

PRINCIPAL WORKS: *Prose*—Falkland, 1827; Pelham, 1828; The Disowned, 1828; Devereux, 1829; Paul Clifford, 1830; Eugene Aram, 1832; Godolphin, 1833; England and the English, 1833; The Last Days of Pompeii, 1834; Pilgrims of the Rhine, 1834; Rienzi, 1835; Athens: Its Rise and Fall, 1837; Alice: or, The Mysteries, 1838; Leila: or, The Siege of Granada, 1838; Calderon the Courtier, 1838; Night and Morning, 1841; Zanoni, 1842; Eva, The Ill Omened Marriage, and Other Tales, 1842; The Last of the Barons, 1843; Confessions of a Water Patient, 1845; Lucretia: or, The Children of Night, 1846; A Word to the Public, 1847; Harold: or, The Last of the Saxon Kings, 1848; The Caxtons, 1850; The Coming Race, 1871; Kenelm Chillingly, 1873; *Poetry*—Ismael, 1820; Weeds and Wildflowers, 1825; O'Neill, 1827; Siamese Twins, 1831; Poems & Ballads Translated From Schiller, 1844; The New Timon, 1845; King

Arthur, 1848-9; *Plays*—The Duchesse de la Valliere, 1836; The Sea Captain: or, Birthright, 1837; The Lady of Lyons, 1838; Richelieu, 1838; Money, 1840.

ABOUT: Collins, N. Facts of Fiction; Cooper, T. Lord Lytton; Cromer, E. B. Political and Literary Essays (2d ser.); Ellis, S. M. Mainly Victorian; Escott, T. H. S. Bulwer Lytton: An Exposure of the Errors of His Biographers; Feiling, K. G. Sketches in 19th Century Biography; Frost, W. A. Lord Lytton: The Man and the Author; Gosse, E. W. Some Diversions of a Man of Letters; Jackson, H. Great English Novelists; Lytton, V. A. G. R. The Life of Edward Bulwer; McCarthy, J. Portraits of the Sixties; Sadleir, M. Bulwer: A Panorama.

BURCKHARDT, JOHN LEWIS (November 24, 1784-October 15, 1817), Swiss explorer, who ranks as an English author by virtue of his travel works written in English, was born Johann Ludwig Burckhardt in Lausanne. After attending German universities at Leipzig and Göttingen, he spent between two and three years in England, learning English and studying Arabic at Cambridge.

In his twenty-fifth year he was sent by the African Association to explore the interior of Africa. Posing as a Mohammedan trader, he traveled extensively in Egypt, Syria, Palestine, and Arabia. So thorough was his knowledge of the Arabic tongue and religion that he was accepted as a true believer and was permitted to visit the holy city of Mecca. He died of dysentery at thirty-two in Cairo, where he was buried in the Mohammedan cemetery under his Moslem name of Pilgrim Ibrahim ibn Abdallah.

The lively records of his travels were posthumously published in England by the African Association. He left his valuable collection of 800 volumes of Oriental manuscripts to the library of Cambridge University.

PRINCIPAL WORKS: Travels in Nubia, 1819; Travels in Syria and the Holy Land, 1822; Travels in Arabia, 1829; Notes on the Bedouins and Wahabys, 1830; Arabic Proverbs, 1830.

ABOUT: Burckhardt, J. L. Travels in Nubia (see Biographical Memoir); Hogarth, D. G. The Penetration of Arabia.

BURGON, JOHN WILLIAM (August 21, 1813-August 4, 1888), religious biographer, was born at Smyrna in Turkey, the son of a well-known British merchant, Thomas Burgon. When he was a few months old he was taken to England. After attending private schools and London University, he spent eleven years in his father's counting house before its collapse permitted him to fulfil an ambition to study for holy orders at Worcester College, Oxford. A succession of brief curacies was followed by a thirteen-year period as vicar of St. Mary's in Oxford and finally by twelve years as dean of Chichester, succeeding Walter Farquhar Hook. Shortly before his death he completed his best known

work, *The Lives of Twelve Good Men,* containing biographies of leaders in the Oxford movement. He also published controversial sermons and Bible criticism marked by independence of judgment. He died unmarried at the Chichester deanery, seventeen days before his seventy-fifth birthday, and was buried in Oxford.

PRINCIPAL WORK: Lives of Twelve Good Men, 1888.

ABOUT: Goulburn, E. M. Life of Dean Burgon.

BURNAND, SIR FRANCIS COWLEY (November 29, 1836-April 21, 1917), editor, playwright, and humorist, was born in London, the son of a stockbroker. At Eton he showed a lively interest in the stage, and wrote a farce which was acted professionally; at Trinity College, Cambridge, where he went in 1854, his chief interest was in theatricals, and he founded the Amateur Dramatic Club.

Unexpectedly enough, Burnand then went to Cuddesdon Theological College to study for holy orders (a living in the family's possession was the motive), but there he was converted, in 1858, to Roman Catholicism. Manning, the great theologian, wanted him to become a priest, but he retorted that he had more "vocation for the stage." Nevertheless he studied law and was called to the bar in Lincoln's Inn in 1862; he practised, however, very little.

Burnand became not a dramatist, but a playwright—an adapter of other men's work and a voluminous writer of burlesques—nearly a hundred of them. He contributed also to numerous magazines, and with H. J. Byron helped to found the humorous journal *Fun.* In 1863 he sent his first contribution to *Punch,* and almost immediately was asked to join its staff. He was its editor from 1880 to 1906, and gave it its reputation for geniality and tolerance. In his own writing he was at his best in parody. He was too much given to punning for modern taste, but he had occasional flashes of brilliance. He wrote many plays which Sir Arthur Sullivan set to music.

In 1860 Burnand married Cecilia Victoria Ranoe, who died in 1870, leaving five sons and two daughters. In 1874 he married Rosina Jones, a widow, who added two sons and four daughters more to the family. He was knighted in 1902—the first writer for *Punch* to receive this honor. In 1906 he resigned his editorship because of his age, but continued writing to the end, which came at Ramsgate when he was over eighty. He edited the *Catholic Who's Who and Year Book* during his last years.

Burnand never took himself too seriously as a writer, and need not be so considered. His lasting work was as an editor; his plays and humor were alike pleasant but ephemeral.

BURNEY

PRINCIPAL WORKS: Black-eyed Susan, 1866; Happy Thoughts, 1866; New History of Sanford and Merton, 1872; The Colonel, 1881; Records and Reminiscences, 1904.

ABOUT: Burnand, F. C. Records and Reminiscences; Spielmann, M. H. The History of Punch.

BURNEY, FANNY (Madame D'Arblay) (June 13, 1752-January 6, 1840), novelist and diarist, was born at King's Lynn, Norfolk, daughter of Dr. Charles Burney, a musician and musical historian. Her mother was Esther Sleepe, of French Huguenot extraction, who bore six children, Fanny being the second daughter and fourth child. Mrs. Burney died in 1761, shortly after the family moved to London. Dr. Burney had wit and unusual charm and was welcome in the London society which first discovered him in the rôle of fashionable music-master.

Among the bright and talented Burney children Fanny, inordinately shy, short-sighted, and plain, was considered a dunce. She was eight years old before she learned her letters, but at ten she began "scribbling almost incessantly." Many of the notables of the day were received at the Burneys, and these were grist to the mill of the shy and unnoticed Frances, to whom writing was the recreation most people derive from reading.

Like Jane Austen, Miss Burney was constrained to bow to the public opinion of novels and novelists and write in secret. Her step-mother is described as a sensible woman, but the diaries of the girls indicate that they bore her no great affection. It was at her instigation that Fanny burned her manuscripts and the private journal was her compromise between duty and an insuperable urge to write. Thus her earliest work (and this, having been extensively edited, is not genuine *juvenalia*) is in the diary which was begun in 1778 and continued to her death.

Some months after the tremendous success of *Evelina: or, A Young Lady's Entrance Into the World* Miss Burney relinquished anonymity and became quite a thorough bluestocking, an intimate of the Thralès and a life-long pet of Dr. Johnson, who called the attractive little authoress a "sly rogue," undoubtedly recognizing the implications of "le sourire ingénument malicieux de ses grands yeux gris," and declaring there were passages in her book which might "do honor to Richardson." Although singularly successful in portraying affectation in either sex, Miss Burney got no life into her heroes. These epitomes of perfection are bloodless, but her heroines are progressive portraits of Fanny herself, and Evelina is a combination of sensitivity, moralizing and vapors, and eighteenth-century coarseness.

Society in general, delighted with the picture which one of its own, realistically but without malice, ironically but without lack of

FANNY BURNEY

proper reverence, had made of it, took her to its heart. It was only after a kind of genial abduction, engineered and executed by "Daddy" Crisp and Dr. Burney, that the socially-whirling Fanny was gently but firmly constrained to finish *Cecilia: or, Memoirs of an Heiress.* The book, which appeared in 1782, while enthusiastically reviewed, did not enjoy the mad success of *Evelina.* Less unstudied, with greater polish, and a "literary quality" which gave rise to the report that Dr. Johnson had corrected it, *Cecilia* gives a more realistic record of the "ton parties" of society, but lacks the delightfully irreverent caricature of the more spontaneous first novel.

Her popularity continued. She published nothing further, Crisp having died in 1783 and Johnson in the following year. Her chief sources of encouragement were gone, and Fanny's statement to the king that she believed she had exhausted herself contained but a part of the whole truth. It cannot therefore be said that the position at court, which she accepted in 1786, interrupted her literary activity.

Despite her own fundamentally snobbish nature, Fanny would not but for her father have taken a step which cut her off from normal existence. This somewhat shallow man, whom Fanny adored, saw in the appointment an immense advance socially for his own comparatively anomalous position in society. Monetary consideration was important, too, and the post carried a salary of two hundred pounds a year. It was soon apparent that Fanny, vivacious, gregarious, physically delicate, inconveniently near-sighted, and possessing a proper pride in her own accomplishments, was just in doubting her fitness for a rôle in the dull Germanic court, where no visitors but immediate family were allowed, where ladies in waiting sometimes stood five continuous hours in the queen's presence, where Fanny herself had to answer a bell like any servant, "cook snuff" for the queen and toilet her majesty's lapdog.

But if her years at court were not happy ones, it was chiefly because of her superior, the first keeper of the robes. Fanny, never as subservient as this querulous, bad-tempered, ignorant old bully wished, was compelled by her position to be with her almost constantly, and her treatment of Fanny, replete with abuse and insults in ridiculous broken English, was always humiliating and on occasions downright brutal. Miss Burney made no complaints while at court, but Mrs. Schwellenberg lives in her diary.

In 1791 her father was prevailed upon to join with Fanny in petitioning the queen for leave to resign. Miss Burney's memoirs give a far more indulgent picture of George III and his wife than do most of her contemporaries and only from Macaulay do we learn that the queen was incredulous at the impertinence of any one who preferred living away from court to dying with the privilege of folding her majesty's dresses.

With a pension of a hundred pounds a year Fanny retired to live with her father in Chelsea. She now became acquainted with a number of French exiles, including Madame de Staël, Talleyrand, and Narbonne. The attractions of one of these, a former adjutant of Lafayette, occasioned Miss Burney's first breach of filial piety, and on the thirty-first of July, 1793, General Alexandre D'Arblay wrested Fanny with her hundred pounds a year from Dr. Burney's unwilling arms.

The marriage was highly successful and seems to have stimulated Fanny's creative faculties, for in 1793 she published *Brief Reflections Relative to the Emigrant French Clergy*. In quick succession appeared a son, Alexandre, born December 18, 1794, and a tragedy in blank verse, *Edwy and Elgiva*, which not the combined efforts of Sheridan, Mrs. Siddons, and the Kembles could inspire with the breath of life for more than one night. This abortive work, unpublished like several essays into the field of drama made by Madame D'Arblay (as she was then known), was the only one to achieve even momentary production.

Camilla: or, A Picture of Youth appeared in 1796. The book is dull, moralizing, and the simplicity of *Evelina* nowhere apparent. Nevertheless it netted its author the convenient sum of two thousand pounds.

The D'Arblay family was caught in France by a renewal of hostilities with England, and Fanny remained "in Paris among what was left unguillotined of the best French society" from 1802 to 1812. She published nothing until 1814, when *The Wanderer: or, Female Difficulties* was brought out in England. Here the tendencies to fustian are apparent to a greater degree. Infinitely duller than *Camilla*, it is said to have realized seven thousand pounds. In the same year Jane Austen's *Mansfield Park* appeared without fanfare.

Before Louis XVIII returned to France, Madame D'Arblay was presented to him, and he gave her the title of Countess. There followed the most exciting period of her life. Having refused to desert her husband during the Hundred Days, she was placed as an Englishwoman and wife of an officer of Louis XVIII in a most precarious position, and her account of Brussels during Waterloo almost achieves her original spontaneity. She worked among the injured, and spent an anxious time waiting news of her husband. Wounded and weakened in health, General D'Arblay now received permission to settle in England.

Inconsolable after his death in 1818, Madame D'Arblay lived in London, working on a life of her father, which, presented in 1832, did not meet with unqualified approval. The critics, particularly Croker, whose attack was actuated by personal malice, showed no respect for the years of the author of this singularly egocentric work. In 1837 Alexandre, recently nominated minister of Ely Chapel, Holborn, died of influenza. And in January 6, 1840, at the age of eighty-eight, Madame D'Arblay followed her son, and was buried at Bath.

In 1842 was issued the first volume of *The Diary and Letters*, edited by Madame D'Arblay's niece, Charlotte Frances Barrett, and the vicious attack of Croker in the *Fortnightly Review* drew forth Macaulay's celebrated defense. Saintsbury characterizes Fanny Burney as the most important, though far from the most gifted novelist of the later years of the century. Modern readers still enjoy *Evelina* and, to a lesser extent, *Cecilia*, and find the *Diary* an "inexhaustible storehouse of amusement and information as to the manners and customs of the eighteenth century." Fanny Burney's talent was largely a precocious one and, while it may be regretted that a few years of her long life could not have been forfeited to such as Jane Austen, she is nevertheless, as Seeley remarks, "the best representative of a worthy and amiable family who had been trained in the school of Dr. Johnson."   P. B. S.

PRINCIPAL WORKS: *Novels*—Evelina: or, A Young Lady's Entrance Into the World (3 vols.) 1778; Cecilia: or, Memoirs of an Heiress (5 vols.) 1796; The Wanderer: or, Female Difficulties (5 vols.) 1814. *Pamphlet*—Brief Reflections Relative to the Emigrant French Clergy, 1793. *Biography*—Memoirs of Dr. Burney, 1832. *Diary*—The Diary and Letters of Frances D'Arblay (7 vols.) 1842-

1846; The Early Diary of Fanny Burney (edited by Mrs. Anne Raine Ellis) 1889.

ABOUT: Dobson, A. Fanny Burney; Johnson, R. B. Fanny Burney and the Burneys; Macaulay, T. B. Essay on Mme. D'Arblay; Overman, A. A. An Investigation Into the Character of Fanny Burney; Seeley, L. B. Fanny Burney and Her Friends; Contemporary Review 130:183 August 1926; Revue des Deux Mondes January 15, 1904.

BURNEY, JAMES (1750-November 17, 1821), naval officer and chronicler of navigation, was the son of Charles Burney, eighteenth century musical historian, and the brother of Madame d'Arblay, the novelist. Entering the British navy in his fourteenth year, he sailed round the world with Captain James Cook on the latter's second and third voyages of exploration, and progressed to the rank of rear admiral. After dramatically rushing a warship to the aid of Sir Edward Hughes, admiral, in time for the final encounter with the French in the East Indies in 1783, he retired from the navy in ill health and devoted the rest of his years to writing. His five-volume *Chronological History of the Discoveries in the South Sea* became the standard work on its subject.

He died suddenly in his seventy-first year. According to Muriel Masefield, he "had a downright temperament not quite in the Burney tradition, but no lack of vitality—Charles Lamb had a keen memory of his 'flashes of wild wit.'"

PRINCIPAL WORKS: A Chronological History of the Discoveries in the South Sea or Pacific Ocean, 1803-17; A Chronological History of North-eastern Voyages of Discovery and of the Early Eastern Navigations of the Russians, 1819; An Essay on the Game of Whist, 1821; History of the Buccaneers of America (section from A Chronological History of the Discoveries in the South Sea) 1902.

"BURTON, ALFRED." See MITFORD, JOHN

BURTON, JOHN HILL (August 22, 1809-August 10, 1881), Scottish historian and biographer, was born in Aberdeen. His father was a retired army lieutenant who died when the boy was ten; his paternal grandfather, driven insane by grief for his wife's death, detested his own children. It was not a promising ancestry, and it had its repercussions. However, Burton managed to attend the University of Aberdeen, and then went to Edinburgh to read law, accompanied by his mother, who had sold her home to pay his expenses. He never made a living as an advocate, and had to do hackwriting for years—chiefly elementary histories, under the pseudonym of White.

His espousal of the philosophy of Jeremy Bentham introduced him to the *Westminster Review* and the *Edinburgh Review;* he also was one of the editors of Bentham's posthumous works, and in 1843 became editor of *The Scotsman.* His life of Hume, in 1846 was his first considerable success, partly because he had access to hitherto unpublished papers and letters of the Scottish philosopher In 1867 he became Historiographer Royal of Scotland; he received honorary degrees from Edinburgh, Aberdeen, and Oxford.

Burton's first wife died in 1849, after only five years of marriage. Like his grandfather, he was prostrated by grief, and thereafter had a lifelong aversion to society, in spite of the fact that he remarried (a Miss Innes) in 1855.

For nearly forty years Burton was a constant contributor to *Blackwood's;* he was a great pedestrian, and wrote much for the magazine on his solitary walking tours abroad and in England. From 1880 he was often ill; realizing that his death was near, he sold his library, which he estimated not by number, but by weight—eleven tons!

Burton was a man of letters, a jurist, and a social scientist, but hardly distinguished in any field. He was accurate, but his style is journalistic and undignified. His biographies are his best work, though he was hampered even here by lack of sympathetic imagination. Ultra-sensitive and irascible, he was yet at heart generous and kindly. He was a hard worker, writing up to two hours before his death.

PRINCIPAL WORKS: Life and Correspondence of David Hume, 1846; Manual of Political and Social Economy, 1849; Narratives of Criminal Trials in Scotland, 1852; History of Scotland, 1853-70; The Book Hunter, 1860; The Scot Abroad, 1862.

ABOUT: Burton, J. H. The Book Hunter (see Memoir by Mrs. Burton to 1882 ed.); Blackwood's Magazine 130:401 September 1881.

BURTON, SIR RICHARD FRANCIS (March 19, 1821-October 20, 1890), explorer, archaeologist, and translator, was born at Torquay in Hertfordshire. Though his father was born in Ireland, he was of English stock, and his mother transmitted to him the wild blood of the MacGregors.

Taken abroad at the age of five by parents who roamed about Europe, Burton received very little formal education prior to entering Trinity College, Oxford, in 1840. But as a boy he learned half a dozen languages and fencing. After a bit more than one year at Oxford he managed to get himself rusticated in order to enlist in the army instead of the church for which his parents had destined him.

In 1842 he was gazetted to the 18th Bombay Native Infantry as an ensign and remained nominally attached to this regiment until 1861, rising to the rank of captain. Because of his exceptional linguistic abilities he was appointed an assistant in the Sind survey where for three years he held a commission to wander through the country making reports upon the native life. This he accomplished by traveling disguised as a wealthy Mohammedan merchant. So successful was he that neither natives nor brother officers recognized him. During these years he became proficient in some dozen or more oriental languages.

Burton's work in the deserts of Sind had injured his health and after two years sick leave, during which he traveled to Goa, he returned to England in 1849. The next four years were spent in England and on the continent recruiting his health and writing a great many books and papers upon a great variety of subjects. It was during this period too that he met his future wife at Boulogne, though they did not become engaged until 1856.

In 1853 a request for three years additional leave in which to explore the unknown Arabian peninsula was refused by the East India Company. However they granted him an additional twelve-month furlough "that he might pursue his Arabic studies." Leaving England in April of that year he joined the pilgrim caravan at Cairo, disguised as a Pathan hajj, and returned to Egypt late in September, having in the mean time visited all the sacred shrines of Medinah and Mecca. Further exploration was made impossible by ill health and when his furlough expired he sailed to India, sending the manuscript of his famous *Personal Narrative of a Pilgrimage to El-Medinah and Mecca* to London. A friend acted as editor and in that capacity deleted much of what he considered unprintable matter from the foot-notes.

After a few months duty in India Burton again got leave, this time to explore Somaliland. He first made a journey alone to

SIR RICHARD BURTON

Harar, the inland capital which was forbidden to white men. After entering the city disguised as an Arab he announced himself to the Emir. Returning to the coast, he organized a larger expedition. But of four Englishmen in this party, one was killed and Burton and Speke were seriously wounded by natives before they got well started. They were forced to return to England on sick leave.

On Burton's next expedition to discover the sources of the Nile, Speke was his second in command. This expedition discovered Lakes Tanganyika and Victoria Nyanza. On the return from this expedition Burton was delayed at Aden by sickness. Speke hurried back to England and reported the discoveries. Speke obtained support for a new expedition and when Burton got back to England in 1859 he found that he had been double-crossed by his second in command. This ended Burton's career in East African exploration.

In the summer of 1860 Burton visited the Mormons in Salt Lake City. Upon his return from America in January 1861 he was married to Isabel Arundell without the knowledge of her parents. Her family soon accepted him however and always afterward exerted their influence in his behalf in government circles.

The following March Burton took the post of consul at Fernando Po on the West Coast of Africa, where he remained four years. During this period he explored the western portion of Africa. In 1865 he was transferred to the consulship of São Paulo, Brazil, where another four year period was spent. Here again he made extended trips into the interior and crossed the Andes into Peru and Chili.

In 1869 he was transferred to Damascus. This was by far his most congenial post and one for which he was excellently fitted, but in less than two years he was suddenly dismissed. The causes for his dismissal were never made public, but it is known that it was caused in part by his refusal to help usurious money lenders collect from the poor natives. The British Foreign Office is said to have admitted that Burton was in the right.

After a year without a post, during which he traveled to Iceland, he was appointed to the consulship of Trieste, which he held until his death. But until about 1880 he continued to obtain extensive leaves during which he explored and prospected in Italy and Egypt. This was also the most fruitful period of his literary career. Here he completed his translations of Camoens and of the Arabian Nights as well as writing a number of books about his later travels. Even in his last years when under constant medical care, he continued to travel and write.

It is said of him that "those who knew him best admired him most." Frank Harris compares him to Sir Walter Raleigh but finds Burton the greater man, and says ". . . he carried himself like a young man in spite of his sixty years . . . He looked like a prizefighter. . . . 'Untamed'—that is the word which always recurs when I think of Burton." And Lord Derby once remarked of Burton that before middle age he had crowded into life "more of study, more of hardship, and more of successful enterprise and adventure than would have sufficed to fill up the existence of half a dozen ordinary men."

As a writer he was most prolific, publishing some fifty large works in addition to innumerable contributions to periodicals. His writing has not been greatly praised for style, but he was so observant and curious that his works are crammed with facts. But there appears to be unanimous agreement among critics that his translation of the Arabian Nights was as nearly perfect as a translation can be.

Burton's hatred of sham and pretence did not endear him to the smug and prudish society of Victorian England. Even his wife, in spite of their great mutual affection, never fully understood the man. She acted as his literary executor and as such she burned some of his manuscripts and also his private diaries after she had used them in preparing his biography. In her own will she forbade the publication of any of his works without the sanction of the secretary of the National Vigilance Society. Thus a vast store of valuable information about the man and his travels has probably been lost and many aspects of his life remain shrouded in secrecy.   D. C.

PRINCIPAL WORKS: *Grammars*—A Grammar of the Jataki or Belochki Dialect, 1849; A Grammar of the Multani Language, 1849; Critical Remarks on Dr. Dorn's Chrestomathy of Pushtu: or the Afghan Dialect, 1849; *Prose*—Sind: or the Unhappy Valley, 1851; Sind and the Races That Inhabit the Valley of the Indus, 1851; Goa and the Blue Mountains, 1851; Falconry in the Valley of the Indus, 1852; A Complete System of Bayonet Exercise, 1853; Personal Narrative of a Pilgrimage to El-Medinah and Mecca, 1855; First Footsteps in East Africa, 1856; The Lake Regions of Equitorial Africa, 1860; The City of the Saints, 1861; Wanderings in West Africa, 1863; Abeokuta and the Cameroons, 1863; A Mission to Gelele, King of Dahome, 1864; Explorations of the Highlands of Brazil, 1869; Letters From the Battlefields of Paraguay, 1870; Gorilla Land: or the Cataracts of the Congo, 1875; Unexplored Syria (in collaboration with C. F. T. Drake) 1872; Inner Life of Syria, 1875; Etruscan Bologna, 1876; Sind Revisited, 1879; To the Gold Coast for Gold, 1883; The Book of the Sword, 1884; The Jew, The Gipsy, and El Islam, 1897; *Translations*—Wit and Wisdom From West Africa, 1865; Gerber's Province of Minas Geraes, 1875; The Lusiads, 1880; The Book of a Thousand Nights and a Night, 1885-6; Supplemental Nights, 1887-8; The Pentamerone, 1893; Catullus, 1894; *Poetry*—The Kasidah.

ABOUT: Burton, I. The Life of Sir Richard Burton; Downey, F. Burton: Arabian Nights Adventurer; Hitchman, F. Richard F. Burton: His Early Private and Public Life; Richards, A. B. A Sketch of the Career of Richard F. Burton; Stisted, G. M. The True Life of Captain Richard F. Burton; Wright, T. The Life of Sir Richard Burton.

BURY, LADY CHARLOTTE SUSAN MARIA (January 28, 1775-March 31, 1861), diarist and novelist, was born in London, the youngest daughter of John Campbell, fifth duke of Argyll. At twenty-one she was married to Colonel John Campbell, who died thirteen years later, leaving her with nine children. Her second husband was the Rev. Edward John Bury, rector of Lichfield in Hampshire, by whom she had two children and was widowed after fourteen years. In the nine-year interval between her two marriages, she served as lady-in-waiting to the Princess of Wales, afterwards Queen Caroline. An intimate and unflattering diary of the royal household, believed to have been written by her during this time, was anonymously published after the Queen's death. It is chiefly by this work that Lady Bury's name is remembered, though she wrote several light novels which were popular in their time. After a prolonged second widowhood, she died in London at eighty-six.

PRINCIPAL WORKS: *Novels*—Flirtation, 1828; Separation, 1830; The Disinherited and the Ensnared, 1834; The Devoted, 1836; Love, 1838; The Two Baronets, 1864. *Memoirs*—Mrs. C. F. Gore's Memoirs of a Peeress (ed.) 1837; Diary Illustrative of the Times of George the Fourth, 1838 (republished as The Diary of a Lady-in-Waiting, 1908).

ABOUT: Bury, C. S. M. The Diary of a Lady-in-Waiting (see Introduction by A. F. Steuart).

BUTCHER, SAMUEL HENRY (April 16, 1850-December 29, 1910), Irish classical scholar, was born in Dublin, the son of Samuel Butler, future bishop of Meath. He was educated at Marlborough and Trinity College, Cambridge, winning numerous scholastic honors. After brief periods of teaching at Eton and his own college, he was for six years tutor at University College, Oxford, and for twenty-one years professor of Greek in the University of Edinburgh, Scotland. In the latter position he succeeded John Stuart Blackie. In 1904 upon the death of his wife, Rose Trench, daughter of Richard Chenevix Trench, he gave up academic work and removed to London, where his last years were full of varied activity. He succeeded Sir Richard Jebb as unionist member of Parliament for Cambridge University in 1906, and he was president in turn of the English Classical Association and the British Academy. He died in a London nursing home of an internal hemorrhage at the age of sixty and was buried in Edinburgh.

His prose translation of the *Odyssey*, done in collaboration with Andrew Lang, and his published lectures on Greek civilization are standard texts.

PRINCIPAL WORKS: The Odyssey of Homer Done Into English Prose (with A. Lang) 1879; Demosthenes (Classical Writers' Series) 1881; Some Aspects of the Greek Genius, 1891; Aristotle's Theory of Poetry and Fine Art: With a Critical Text and a Translation of the Poetics, 1895; Greek Idealism in the Common Things of Life, 1901; Demosthenis Orationes (ed.) 1903, 1907; Harvard Lectures on Greek Subjects, 1904.

BUTLER, ARTHUR JOHN (June 21, 1844-February 26, 1910), classical scholar, was born in Putney, a suburb of London, eldest son of William John Butler, a curate who eventually became dean of Lincoln. Educated at Eton and Trinity College, Cambridge, he worked seventeen years as examiner under the board of education in London, seven years in the publishing business, and finally twelve years as professor of Italian language and literature at University College, London. He died at Weybridge in Surrey, aged sixty-five, leaving his wife, Mary Humphrey, and their seven children.

A distinguished spare-time scholar, he made pioneer contributions to the study of Dante and the *Divine Comedy*. He also translated French and German works. His hobby was mountain-climbing: he had unparalleled knowledge of the Oetzthal Alps and for three years edited the *Alpine Journal*.

PRINCIPAL WORKS: Dante's *Purgatory* (tr.) 1880; Dante's *Paradise* (tr.) 1885; Dante's *Hell* (tr.) 1892; Dante: His Times and His Work, 1895; Calendars of Foreign State Papers, 1901-09; The Forerunners of Dante, 1910.

BUTLER, FRANCES ANNE. See KEMBLE, FANNY

BUTLER, SAMUEL (December 4, 1835-June 18, 1902), philosophical and miscellaneous writer, was born at Langar Rectory, near Bingham, Nottinghamshire, eldest son of the Rev. Thomas Butler, Rector of Langar and later Canon of Lincoln, and Fanny Butler, daughter of P. J. Worsley, sugar refiner, of Bristol. He was the grandson of Dr. Samuel Butler, Headmaster of Shrewsbury School, and later Bishop of Lichfield and Coventry.

The childhood of Ernest Pontifex in *The Way of All Flesh,* is a portrait of his own; and nearly all its characters are drawn directly from his relatives. At the age of eight he was taken to Italy. In 1848, after two years at a preparatory school at Allesley, he was sent to Shrewsbury. At about the age of thirteen he first heard the music of Handel, a composer whom he worshipped wholeheartedly all his life. Thus the foundations of his two great enthusiasms—for Italy and for Handel—were both early laid.

In the autumn of 1854 Butler went to St. John's College, Cambridge, graduating in 1858.

His family took it as a matter of course that he should proceed to ordination in the Church of England, and he did go far enough to become a lay assistant. But his was a mind that could take nothing on trust. It is characteristic of his practical mentality that what finally determined him to refuse ordination was the discovery that a large number of unbaptized boys in his class seemed to be no worse in manners or morals than those who had been baptized. His father was deeply shocked and grieved. Butler returned to Cambridge to seek pupils; and kept up his musical studies and learned drawing. By May 1859 Canon Butler had flatly refused to allow his son either to remain at Cambridge or to adopt art as a profession. It was decided that he should be a sheep-farmer in New Zealand, and early in 1860 he took up residence on a sheep-run in the Rangitata district of Canterbury Island.

His work as a sheep-farmer was very successful, and in the period of nearly five years during which he was in New Zealand he practically doubled the £4,000 capital with which he had started. Nor were his intellectual interests neglected. He read *The Origin of Species* soon after its appearance in 1859, and in December 1862 published a "Dialogue" thereon in *The Press* of Christchurch. In the same journal (June 1863) he published "Darwin Among the Machines," a paper containing a basic idea afterwards developed in *Erewhon*. His letters to his father were made by the Canon into a book called *A First Year in Canterbury Settlement* (1863).

It was in New Zealand that he met Charles Paine Pauli, who so greatly impressed him by his charm of manner that he agreed to lend Pauli his passage home and subsidize

SAMUEL BUTLER

him to the tune of £200 a year for three years while he studied for the Bar. Matters so sorted themselves, in fact, that Butler continued to make Pauli this allowance until the latter's death in 1897; and it was only then, after twenty-three years, that he discovered that the barrister had been for long earning from £500 to £900 a year by his profession. Back in London in 1864, his fortune safely invested, Butler took up residence at 15, Clifford's Inn, Fleet Street, and remained the tenant of these rooms for the rest of his life.

He now settled down to painting, writing and music; and took lessons at Heatherley's famous art-school in Newman Street. In 1865 he published anonymously a pamphlet, *The Evidence for the Resurrection of Jesus Christ As Given by the Four Evangelists Critically Examined,* wherein he came to the conclusion that Jesus had not died on the cross, but swooned, and had been revived by Joseph of Arimathea. A copy was sent to Charles Darwin, and a friendly correspondence ensued.

Though painting was his main business, Butler began, before 1870, to weave certain articles and sketches into a connected narrative which was published anonymously, at his own expense, in 1872, as *Erewhon: or, Over the Range.* This, the most famous of all his books, attracted a good deal of attention at the time, and since Butler's death has taken a high place as the wittiest and most penetrating satire in English since the days of Swift. Its main theme is the discovery of a country wherein manners are the reverse of those in England; where poverty and ill-health are prosecuted as crimes and theft is met by hospital treatment. The inhabitants have abolished all machines, lest machines should become their masters; and the chapter called "The Book of the Machines" is a masterly exercise in specious and persuasive argument purposely vitiated by a logical flaw. The book's chief weakness is its lack of coherence, caused by the manner of its composition.

In 1873 he published *The Fair Haven,* which purported to be by "John Pickard Owen," a clergyman, with a memoir by his brother, "William Bickersteth Owen." Written with the tongue in the cheek, this book professes to be an account of a mind assailed by religious doubt and eventually overcoming it. It was widely accepted as an exercise in apologetics, and was read in many pious households into which it would never have been admitted if its rationalistic tendency had been suspected.

The same year he began his novel, *The Way of All Flesh.* He also transferred his £8,000 from New Zealand and invested it in various companies promoted by one Henry Hoare. By March 1874 Hoare had failed

and most of Butler's money was lost in the *débacle.* He made two journeys to Canada to try to save something from the ruin, but his financial embarrassment remained very great until the death of his father in 1886. Before crossing the Atlantic he saw his picture, "Mr. Heatherley's Holiday" hung on the line at the Royal Academy: it is now in the Tate Gallery. While in Montreal he wrote the lacerating "Psalm of Montreal" which amazingly enough was later printed in *The Spectator* (May 18, 1878).

Life and Habit (1877) was the first of a series of books in which Butler applied his critical and constructive powers to the theory of evolution. The others were *Evolution: Old and New* (1879), *Unconscious Memory* (1880), and *Luck or Cunning As the Main Means of Organic Modification?* (1886). Broadly speaking, the theses developed in these works were that the Darwinian theory of evolution was too mechanistic, that it gave insufficient credit to such predecessors as Buffon, Lamarck, and Erasmus Darwin, and that "unconscious memory" was in itself a prime factor in the production of organic change and in the modification of behavior. The quarrel which arose between Butler and Darwin was not the direct outcome of the former's expression of these views, but a by-product arising from a feeling on both sides that there had been disingenuousness in controversy.

Butler's deep love of Italy, nurtured by numerous visits, found expression in *Alps and Sanctuaries of Piedmont and the Canton Ticino* (1881) to which was added in 1888 *Ex Voto: An Account of the Sacro Monte or New Jerusalem at Varallo-Sesia.*

The year 1889 was largely occupied in the writing of *The Life and Letters of Dr. Samuel Butler: Head-Master of Shrewsbury School,* which was not published, however, until 1896.

In his last years Butler turned his attention to the Homeric problem, on which he left (as on everything he touched) the impress of a fresh and unconventional outlook. Not only did he produce prose versions of the *Iliad* (1898) and the *Odyssey* (1900), but he believed that in Trapani and Mount Eryx, in Sicily, he had discovered the true setting of the *Odyssey.* The view put forward in *The Authoress of the Odyssey* (1897) is indicated by its title. The identification of Sicily as the site of the *Odyssey* had already been advanced in the *Rassegna Della Letteratura Siciliana* in 1893, and the year before he had delivered a lecture on "The Humour of Homer."

Concurrently with his Homeric studies, Butler was turning his mind to the mystery of Shakespeare's *Sonnets,* and in 1899 he issued *Shakespeare's Sonnets Reconsidered.*

The last book published during his lifetime was *Erewhon Revisited* (1901), a more connected story than *Erewhon*, chiefly existing to show how easily a religious cult may grow out of a supposed miracle. It has far less tang and force than the other work.

Butler died on June 18, 1902. The next year was published *The Way of All Flesh*, a novel dealing with his own childhood and youth. It ranks among the great novels of the period, and remains a blistering indictment of the worst kind of Victorian religiosity. In 1912 appeared selections from his copious *Note-Books*, pungent and witty commentary on diversified subjects. Further extracts were published in 1934.

No account of Butler could be considered complete without a word on his friendships. His amazing generosity to the worthless Pauli has been recorded. Two other friends, of a very different order, were Miss E. M. A. Savage and Henry Festing Jones. Butler never married. He met Miss Savage at Heatherley's in 1870, and their correspondence up to her death in 1885 is spirited and friendly, but on Butler's side at least there was never any question of more than friendship. Festing Jones, a solicitor, he met in 1876, and the two became boon companions to the day of Butler's death. Among their many common interests was a devotion to music (and especially to Handel) and they jointly published several musical compositions, including *Gavottes, Minuets, Fugues* (1885) and a burlesque oratorio, *Narcissus* (1888). Jones wrote Butler's life in 1919.

Butler's many-sided talent was never fully recognized while he was alive, and he lost money on every book save *Erewhon*, but in the years just prior to the European War he reached a high pitch of reputation. In the England of his day fresh consideration of ethical and philosophic problems from first principles was not encouraged; and the very moderation of his statement no doubt militated against his success. The British faculty for compromise is well exemplified by his attitude. In religion he quarreled with the orthodox without enlisting under the banner of Huxley. In science he again fell out with Darwin, the high priest, and his acceptance of evolution was a qualified one. The very diversity of his interests made him suspect, as a *dilettante* in every camp. However, he has now taken his place among the major English satirists, and, by virtue of his one remarkable novel, as an important influence in modern fiction. His "unconscious memory" theories are regarded as serious and weighty contributions to the subject, though often expressed (as was his way) with humor and paradox. Essentially a practical-minded man, he combined a canny sense of the value of money with a real integrity and idealism. In the preface to *Major Barbara* Bernard Shaw put on record his deep debt to Butler's ideas; and in a review of Gilbert Cannan's *Samuel Butler,* in *The New Statesmen* (May 8, 1915), the same writer said: "He had the supreme sort of style that never smells of the lamp, and therefore seems to the kerosene stylist to be no style at all."

H. B. G.

PRINCIPAL WORKS: *Topographical*—A First Year in Canterbury Settlement, 1863; Alps and Sanctuaries of Piedmont and the Canton Ticino, 1881; Ex Voto, 1888. *Satires and Theological*—The Evidence for the Resurrection of Jesus Christ As Contained in the Four Evangelists Critically Examined, 1865; Erewhon: or, Over the Range, 1872; The Fair Haven, 1873. *Scientific*—Life and Habit, 1877; Evolution: Old and New, 1879; Unconscious Memory, 1880; Luck or Cunning As the Main Means of Organic Modification? 1886. *Classical*—The Humour of Homer, 1892; L'Origine Siciliana Dell' Odissea, 1893 (English trans. same year); The Authoress of the Odyssey, 1897; The Iliad Rendered Into English Prose, 1898; The Odyssey Rendered Into English Prose, 1900. *Novels*—The Way of All Flesh, 1903. *Miscellaneous*—The Life and Letters of Dr. Samuel Butler, 1896; Shakespeare's Sonnets Reconsidered, 1899; Essays on Life, Art and Science, 1904; The Note-Books (ed. by H. Festing Jones) 1912; Further Selections From the Note-Books (ed. by A. T. Batholomew) 1934.

ABOUT: Bekker, W. G. An Historical and Critical Review of Samuel Butler's Literary Works; Cannan, G. Samuel Butler: A Critical Study; Garnett, R. S. Samuel Butler and His Family Relations; Harris, J. F. Samuel Butler: The Man and His Work; Hoppé, A. J. A Bibliography of the Writings of . . . and About . . . Samuel Butler; Joad, C. E. M. Samuel Butler; Jones, H. F. Samuel Butler: A Memoir; Lange, P. J. de. Samuel Butler: Critic and Philosopher; Shaw, G. B. Major Barbara (see Preface); Stillman, C. G. Samuel Butler: A Mid-Victorian Modern; Fortnightly Review 112:904 December 1919; Monist 32:307 April 1922; North American Review 208:277 August 1918; Monthly Review 8:137 September 1902; Quarterly Review 220:152 January 1914.

BUTLER, SIR WILLIAM FRANCIS

(October 31, 1838-June 7, 1910), Irish soldier and author of personal narratives, was born at Suirville in Tipperary. At twenty he began his long and distinguished career in the army which took him to many lands. In Canada he performed missions to the Red River settlement and to Saskatchewan. In Africa he took part in Sir Garnet Wolseley's expedition against the Ashanti, and in the Zulu war and the Egyptian war (including the campaign of Tel-el-Kebir). Retired at sixty-seven with the rank of lieutenant-general, he spent his last years at Bansha Castle in Tipperary, where he died at seventy-one. Surviving him were his wife, Elizabeth Thompson, a well-known painter of battle-scenes, and their five children.

He wrote books descriptive of his experiences in various parts of the world, besides biographies of three military men of his time. The noted poet and essayist, Alice Meynell, his wife's sister, assisted in the preparation of his posthumous autobiography.

PRINCIPAL WORKS: *Personal Narratives*—The Great Lone Land, 1872; The Wild North Land, 1873; Akim-Foo: The History of a Failure, 1875; Far Out: Rovings Retold, 1880; The Light of the West: With Some Other Wayside Thoughts, 1909; Autobiography, 1911. *Bibliography*—Charles George Gordon, 1889; Sir Charles Napier, 1890; Sir George Pomeroy Colley, 1899.

ABOUT: Butler, W. F. Autobiography.

BYRON, LORD (George Gordon Noel Byron, Sixth Baron) (January 22, 1788-April 19, 1824), poet, was born at Holles Street, London. His father, John Byron, was a Guards officer, known as "Mad Jack Byron," and the poet was the only offspring of his second marriage, to Catherine Gordon of Gight, a Scottish heiress. There was wild blood in the ancestry on both sides, and "Mad Jack" himself soon ran through Catherine's fortune, and died at Valenciennes in 1791, leaving his widow and son in comparative indigence. Byron was born with a deformity of one foot. His early days were passed in Aberdeen, and he attended the grammar school there from 1794 to 1798.

In 1794, by the death of the fifth baron's grandson, he unexpectedly became heir to the peerage, succeeding in May 1798. Shortly afterwards mother and son removed to the family mansion of Newstead, Nottinghamshire, then in a semi-ruinous condition; and the boy was put to school first at Nottingham and later at Dulwich, London. His youth was clouded by innumerable wrangles with his mother, a volatile and violent character, who, when angry, even went to the length of reviling him for his infirmity. Byron's lameness, his unhappy domestic life, and his early and unexpected succession to a peerage were all of paramount importance in the shaping of his character. There was a heavy vein of racial pride in his nature, and it is recorded that when he heard the appellation *dominus* added to his name at a Harrow roll-call he wept with emotion.

He went to Harrow School in the summer of 1801 and did not distinguish himself there. In 1804 he fell violently in love with his cousin, Mary Anne Chaworth (afterwards Mrs. John Musters) who, however, looked upon him as no more than a schoolboy. This precocious passion was celebrated in his first volume of poems, and, as late as 1816, in "The Dream." From school, in October 1805, he went on to Trinity College, Cambridge. His attendance was very irregular, and, though he read a great deal of solid matter, he had some contempt for academic learning and preferred to blossom as a *bon vivant* and man of fashion. He rode, shot, boxed and gambled, became a great swimmer and cultivated the acquaintance of "Gentleman Jackson," a celebrated pugilist. A more important

and enduring friendship made at this time was that with John Cam Hobhouse (later Lord Broughton) who became a lifelong intimate.

Byron took his M.A. degree in 1808. But before this, at the end of 1806, he had published a small volume of *Fugitive Pieces.* In the following January this was re-issued, revised and expanded, as *Poems on Various Occasions.* Only 100 copies were run off, and Byron's first real appeal to the public was *Hours of Idleness,* which appeared later in 1807. It was a production not much above the average of verse written by nineteen-year-old boys, though there are passages which give some foretaste of the power which was later to be known. It is chiefly notable for an indirect effect. In January 1808 it was attacked with contumely in the *Edinburgh Review* (probably by Brougham) and it was this attack which caused Byron to adjust a partly-written manuscript, *British Bards,* making it into *English Bards and Scotch Reviewers,* which came out in March 1809. Byron was always a warm admirer of Pope, and this vigorous, hard-hitting satire was written in the Popeian heroic couplet. It was often evil-tempered and unjust, and heaped invective alike on those who deserved it and many who did not; but it showed the appearance of a new poetic force that had to be reckoned with; it had passages of true satiric skill; and it sold in thousands. Byron came in due course to regret its intemperateness, and suppressed it in 1811.

Since leaving Cambridge he had divided his time between Newstead and London, and had begun a course of life which alternated between bouts of dissipation and periods of extreme abstemiousness, when he lived on soda-water, bread, and vegetables. In July 1809 he went on his first foreign tour, with Hobhouse, visiting Portugal, Spain, Malta, Athens, Smyrna, and Constantinople. It was two years before he returned to England. In August 1811 his mother died. He had returned to a state of great financial embarrassment; and this condition persisted for some time. Except in childhood Byron was never "poor" in the sense that Blake or Chatterton or Lamb were poor, but he had constant difficulties regarding property, and for many years refused to accept a penny in royalties from his poems.

With the publication of the first two cantos of *Childe Harold's Pilgrimage,* in March 1812, Byron, in the well-known phrase, "woke one morning and found himself famous." A descriptive and philosophic poem in the Spenserian stanza, it revealed a serious challenger to the pre-eminence of Scott in the field of the long poem. It had a color and an actuality that Scott's work lacked; and if its design was badly integrated and its spiritual

LORD BYRON

apprehension uncertain, it displayed a conscious mastery over subject-matter and no inconsiderable skill in the management of a difficult metre. Byron rose at once to immense renown, and was courted by the famous and lionized at fashionable parties.

Childe Harold was published by John Murray, whose house has ever since been inalienably associated with Byron's work. In November 1811 he had begun another famous association—with Thomas Moore, his future biographer, who was introduced to him at a dinner-party given by Samuel Rogers. The two found much pleasure in each other's company, and friendship was soon established. Other acquaintances made in the next few years were those of Leigh Hunt and Mathew Gregory Lewis.

The years 1813 and 1814 were fruitful poetically, the former producing *The Waltz, The Giaour,* and *The Bride of Abydos;* and the latter *The Corsair* and *Lara. Hebrew Melodies* followed in 1815 and *The Siege of Corinth* and *Parisina* in 1816. These poems varied in merit, and it has often been said that most of them dramatized the person of the author. They introduced, at any rate, an Oriental verve and coloring that had not been seen in English poetry hitherto.

Meanwhile, in 1812-13, had occurred a furious love-affair with Lady Caroline Lamb, who, after at first stigmatizing the poet as "Mad, bad, and dangerous to know," became the most infatuated of his idolaters. Towards the end of the affair Caroline became a nuisance; and after violent scenes she was withdrawn by her people to Ireland. In March 1812 Byron met her cousin by marriage, Anne Isabella Milbanke, a cold, formal-

minded but not unattractive young woman, whom he was later to marry. But before this another *liaison*—with Jane Elizabeth, Lady Oxford—intervened. After one rejected proposal, Byron married Miss Milbanke on January 2, 1815, and settled at Piccadilly Terrace, London. In December of the same year a child was born, and christened Augusta Ada. A month later Lady Byron went to the country with her child, and, after causing enquiry to be made into her husband's mental state, she refused to see him again and insisted on a separation.

The reasons for this drastic step remain a matter of controversy. The pair were obviously ill-assorted; but (though to the end Byron professed ignorance of the charges against him) it is generally accepted that Lady Byron believed him guilty of incestuous relations with his half-sister, Augusta Leigh, daughter of John Byron by his first wife. On the one hand, there exist letters from Byron to Augusta couched in extravagantly affectionate terms, and other testimony too long to set out here; on the other, there is ample evidence of great friendship between Augusta and Lady Byron herself; and Mrs. Leigh lived through a long married life with her husband, Colonel Leigh, and had a large family by him. The extreme case against Byron is set out in Lord Lovelace's *Astarte,* while John Drinkwater, in *The Pilgrim of Eternity,* examines the whole matter judicially (perhaps with a sympathetic bias towards Byron) and arrives at a verdict of "not proven."

Whatever the truth of the matter, Byron's social life was irretrievably ruined. Where lately he had been courted and fêted he now met with cold looks and ostracism. On April 25, 1816, he left England, never to return. In June he took the Villa Diodati, on the south bank of the Lake of Geneva. Here he wrote the third canto of *Childe Harold* and *The Prisoner of Chillon.* Here also he met Shelley and Mary Godwin, with whom was Jane (or, as she called herself, Claire) Clairmont, Mary's step-sister. This woman had already made a "dead set" at Byron; and when she now encountered him in Switzerland she immediately succeeded in her aim of becoming his mistress. A woman of parts and spirit, her determination was the equal of Caroline Lamb's, and it led her to sorrow. In January 1817 she gave birth to Byron's daughter, Allegra. There was much controversy as to the custody and upbringing of the child, Claire constantly endeavoring to use her as a means of approaching Byron anew when he would have none of her. The ill-fated Allegra was eventually sent to Byron in Venice. In 1821 she was placed in a convent near Ravenna; and in April 1822, to the poet's great grief, she died of a fever. Byron persisted in his refusal to see Claire.

Here may be interpolated a description of Byron in 1816 from the *Dictionary of National Biography.* "Dark brown locks, curling over a lofty forehead, grey eyes with long dark lashes, a mouth and chin of exquisite symmetry are shown in his portraits, and were animated by an astonishing mobility of expression, varying from apathy to intense passion. His head was very small; his nose, though well formed, rather too thick; . . . his complexion was colorless; he had little beard. . . . He had a broad chest, long muscular arms, with white delicate hands, and beautiful teeth."

From November 1816 Byron took up residence in Venice. Here two more *liaisons* followed in quick succession, the first with Marianna Segati and the second with Margarita Cogni ("the Fornarina"). His outward life seems to have combined a great deal of dissipation with much swimming, riding, and other healthy exercise. Yet his poetic output was prolific, and in the period between October 1816 and July 1819 he produced *Manfred,* canto 4 of *Childe Harold, Beppo, Mazeppa,* the first two cantos of *Don Juan, The Lament of Tasso,* and the *Ode on Venice.* As Mr. Drinkwater cogently argues, this bulk of some 9,000 lines of verse (mostly of a high order) produced in two-and-a-half years, is enough to discredit the wilder legends of his Venetian depravity.

From the middle of 1819 Byron was under the sway of the last and most famous of his mistresses, Teresa, Countess Guiccioli. She had been married at sixteen to a nobleman more than forty years her senior; and, by a convention well-recognized in Italian society at the time, the connection with Byron was tacitly connived at by the husband. Countess Guiccioli was a far from unintelligent woman; and she provided an influence which was in every way salutary.

Wanderings to Ravenna and elsewhere cannot here be followed in detail. Byron saw a good deal of the Shelleys; was pestered by correspondence from Claire; and in September 1821 settled in a palazzo at Pisa. He befriended Leigh Hunt, and helped him to start *The Liberal,* persisting in his generous conduct despite the fact that Hunt arrived in Pisa with a wife and six ill-behaved children, whom he installed in Byron's house.

Early in 1823 Byron decided to throw in his lot with the Greek rebellion against the Turks, which was in preparation. His life was disorientated; his advanced political views had made him suspect to the Italian police; the cause was one which held out the strongest appeal to his liberal sentiments; and he supported it not only with money and advice but with his actual presence at the seat of operations. In July, accompanied by E. J. Trelawny, Count Pietro Gamba, and others,

he set sail for Greece. After much delay, caused by indecision and inefficiency in the Greek camp, the party arrived at Missolonghi on December 30, 1823. The pestilential climate and rough conditions at this place brought about the final tragedy. On April 19, 1824, after ailing for some time, Byron died, and the event was a grievous shock to the whole of cultivated Europe and a national calamity to the Greeks. His body was taken to England and interred in the family vault at Hucknall Torkard, Nottinghamshire.

With Wilde, Shakespeare, and Dickens, Byron remains the most famous of British writers outside Great Britain itself. One obvious reason for this is extra-literary—the power and attraction of his personality. His unusual beauty, his rank, his innumerable adventures in living, his breathless career of love-making, his gloom and *saeva indignatio* (sometimes affected but often real enough) have combined with his poetic genius to create a figure in real life far more interesting and complicated than most heroes of fiction. He typified the romantic movement in literature, and on the political side his patrician attitude was combined with a genuine and burning liberalism which was a torch for the democratic movement of the century. "The king-times are fast finishing," he wrote. "There will be blood shed like water and tears like mist, but the peoples will conquer in the end." For this ideal he gave his life.

In poetry his reputation has suffered some diminution since his death. Seldom or never does he attain to anything like the pure mastery of Keats, Shelley, or Coleridge at their best. He wrote quickly, and this speed left its mark in glaring faults of diction, of taste, and even of grammar. His blank verse (in the poetic dramas) is very uneven and often flat. But when all has been said, when his carelessness and frequent theatricality have been duly taken into account, he is still a major poetic figure. His supreme achievement is *Don Juan,* the best comic poem in English. Using the *ottava rima,* which he learned from John Hookham Frere's "Whistlecraft" and from the Italian poets, Berni, Pulci, and Casti, he turns it to the most amazing variety of purposes, from pathos to the wildest farce, and he maintains his workmanship with unflagging skill. In *Childe Harold* there is rich description of the Near East, true feeling for historic association and for nature, and much philosophic reflection—though Goethe qualified his high praise by adding: "As soon as he reflects, he is a child." His letters are among the best in the language. He is not among the major lyrists, though even here there are things like "She Walks in Beauty" which only just miss the supreme rank. Matthew Arnold placed him high, saying: "Wordsworth and Byron stand, it seems to me, first and pre-eminent in actual performance, a glorious pair, among the English poets of this century." Few critics would now go so far, yet few would contest Byron's place among the first six poets in the story of English literature. **H. B. G.**

PRINCIPAL WORKS: *Poems*—Hours of Idleness, 1807; English Bards and Scotch Reviewers, 1809; Childe Harold, 1812-18; The Curse of Minerva, 1812; The Waltz, 1813; The Giaour, 1813; The Bride of Abydos, 1813; The Corsair, 1814; Ode to Napoleon Buonaparte, 1814; Lara, 1814; Hebrew Melodies, 1815; The Siege of Corinth, 1816; Parisina, 1816; Poems, 1816; Poems on His Domestic Circumstances, 1816; The Prisoner of Chillon, 1816; Monody on the Death of Sheridan, 1816; Manfred, 1817; The Lament of Tasso, 1817; Beppo, 1818; The Curse of Minerva, 1818; Mazeppa, 1819; Marino Faliero, 1820; The Prophecy of Dante, 1821; Sardanapalus, The Two Foscari, Cain, 1821; Werner, 1822; The Age of Bronze, 1823; The Island, 1823; The Deformed Transformed, 1823; Don Juan, 1819-24. *Letters and Journals*—Letter on the Rev. William Lisle Bowles's Strictures on Pope, 1821; Correspondence of Lord Byron With a Friend (3 vols. ed. by A. R. C. Dallas) 1825; Letters and Journals: With Notices of His Life by Thomas Moore (2 vols.) 1830; Letters and Journals (6 vols. ed. by R. E. Prothero) 1898-1901; Lord Byron's Correspondence, Chiefly With Lady Melbourne (2 vols. ed. John Murray) 1922.

COLLECTED WORKS: Among many collected editions the following are notable—The Works of Lord Byron: With His Letters and Journals and His Life by Thomas Moore (17 vols.) 1832-35; (7 vols., including bibliography, ed. by E. H. Coleridge) 1898-1904.

ABOUT: Blessington, M. Conversations of Lord Byron With the Countess of Blessington; Byron, G. G. N. Poetry: Chosen and Arranged by Matthew Arnold (see Arnold's Introduction); Brandes, G. Shelley und Lord Byron; Dallas, R. C. Recollections of the Life of Lord Byron; Drinkwater, J. The Pilgrim of Eternity; Fox, J. C. The Byron Mystery; Edgcumbe, R. J. F. Byron: The Last Phase; Galt, J. The Life of Lord Byron; Gamba, P. A. Narrative of Lord Byron's Last Journey to Greece; Guiccioli, T. Lord Byron Jugé par les Temoins de sa Vie; Hunt, J. H. L. Lord Byron and Some of His Contemporaries; Jeaffreson, J. C. The Real Lord Byron; Leigh, E. M. Medora Leigh; Lovelace, R. G. N. M. Astarte: A Fragment of Truth Concerning George Gordon Byron; Mauroise, A. Byron; Mayne, E. C. Byron; Medwin, T. Journal of the Conversations of Lord Byron; Moore, T. Life of Lord Byron; Nicolson, H. Byron: The Last Journey; Parry, W. The Last Days of Lord Byron; Polidori, J. W. Diary; Prothero, R. E. & Others. Lord Byron and His Detractors; Quennell, P. Byron: The Years of Fame; Stowe, H. Lady Byron Vindicated: A History of the Byron Controversy; 1870; Trelawny, J. W. Records of Shelley, Byron, and the Author; Winwar, F. The Romantic Rebels; Wise, T. J. A Bibliography of the Writings in Verse and Prose of George Gordon Noel, Baron Byron.

BYRON, HENRY JAMES (January, 1834-April 11, 1884), playwright and actor-manager, was born in Manchester, England, the son of Henry Byron, one-time British consul at Port-au-Prince, Haiti. He studied medicine and law, and was the first editor of *Fun* before entering upon a career in the theatre. First jointly, and then on his own

account, he managed various London theatres, producing (and often acting in) his own plays. These were of many kinds, ranging from burlesque to serious drama, and they included some of the most popular stage pieces of the day. His greatest success was *Our Boys,* a domestic comedy, which had an unprecedented run of four years at the Vaudeville Theatre, beginning in 1875. His own producing ventures were almost invariably disastrous, however, and he retired in ill-health a few years before his death in London at the age of fifty.

Though he filled his dialogue with puns and his plots with inane situations, he is given a place among nineteenth century dramatists by virtue of his cleverness and ingenuity. Some fifty of the countless plays of Byron are scattered through the volumes of *Lacy's Acting Edition of Plays.*

PRINCIPAL WORKS: *Plays*—Cyril's Success, 1868; Uncle Dick's Darling, 1869; Our Boys, 1875; The Upper Crust, 1880. *Novel*—Paid in Full, 1865.

BYWATER, INGRAM (June 27, 1840-December 17, 1914), classical scholar, was born in London, the only son of a clerk in the Customs. After attending Queen's College, Oxford, he served twenty-one years as fellow and tutor at Exeter College, nine years as reader in Greek at Oxford, and fifteen years as regius professor of Greek at Oxford (succeeding Benjamin Jowett). Upon the death of his wife in 1908, he resigned his professorship and retired to his London house, where he died at the age of seventy-four. He had no children.

His critical editions of Greek texts made him a noted authority on Aristotle and one of the outstanding scholars of his time. The most important of his works was his commentary on Aristotle's *Poetics.* He edited the *Journal of Philology* from 1879 until his death. His valuable collection of rare Greek works was left to the Bodleian Library of Oxford.

PRINCIPAL WORKS EDITED BY BYWATER: Fragments of Heraclitus, 1877; Works of Priscianus Lydus, 1886 Aristotle's Nicomachean Ethics, 1890; Contributions to the Textual Criticism of the Nicomachean Ethics, 1892; Aristotelis de Arte Poetica Liber, 1897; The Erasmian Pronunciation of Greek and Its Precursors, 1908; Aristotle on the Art of Poetry: With Translation and Commentary, 1909.

ABOUT: Jackson, W. W. Memoir of Ingram Bywater.

CAIRD, EDWARD (March 22, 1835-November 1, 1908), Scottish philosopher, was born in Greenock, the son of an engineer. He was the fifth of seven sons, the younger brother of the philosopher John Caird. The father died in 1838, and the boy was reared by an aunt.

He was educated first at the University of Glasgow and St. Andrews. Being considered too delicate to become a minister, he then went to Balliol College, Oxford, where, being older than the other students, his personal associations were with the dons. He received his B.A. with a first class in the Classical Moderations, in 1863. He taught philosophy privately for a year, and was then made fellow and tutor at Merton College. In 1866 he became professor of moral philosophy at Glasgow, and serve with great success until 1893. In 1867 he married Caroline Wylie; they had no children.

In 1893 Caird was called as master of Balliol. He resigned because of failing health in 1907, and died the next year.

Caird was a lifelong liberal, a special devoté of Abraham Lincoln. He was pro-Boer during the Boer War, and did much for various liberal causes, including the higher education of women. His philosophy was constructive, based on an all-embracing unity of being, and his writings were marked by originality and continuity of thought. Like the man himself, his writing is calm, simple, and frank.

PRINCIPAL WORKS: The Critical Philosophy of Immanuel Kant, 1877; Hegel, 1883; The Social Philosophy and Religion of Comte, 1885; Essays in Literature and Philosophy, 1892; Evolution of Religion, 1893; Evolution of Theology in the Greek Philosophy, 1904.

ABOUT: Benn, A. W. English Rationalism in the Nineteenth Century; London Times November 3, 1908.

CAIRD, JOHN (December 15, 1820-July 30, 1898), Scottish philosopher, was born in Greenock, the older brother of Edwin Caird. At fifteen he went to work in his father's engineering firm, then attended Glasgow University. The father died in 1838 and Caird took over his business for a year, then returned to the university from 1840 to 1845. He received a license to preach, and became parish minister at Newton-on-Ayr, then from 1847 to 1849 was a minister in Edinburgh, where he was known as a pulpit orator. Worn out from his duties at twenty-nine, he took a country parish in Perthshire from 1849 to 1857, where he studied divinity and German. He then returned to Glasgow. In 1858 he married Isabella Glover; the marriage was childless.

In 1860 Caird was made honorary D.D. by the University of Glasgow, and in 1862 became its professor of theology. In philosophy he was an Hegelian idealist, but in politics and economics, like his brother, he was a pronounced liberal. In 1873 he became principal of the university. In 1884 the University of Edinburgh conferred an honorary LL.D. upon him. He suffered a paralytic stroke in 1896, but recovered partially and was able to continue in his post. He died at his brother's home in Oxford, one day before the date set for his retirement as principal.

The essence of Caird's philosophy is the contention that Christianity is not contrary to reason, but that it is based on sound philosophical principles. In spite of the technical nature of his writing, he has been called "a master of style." His published sermon, Religion in Common Life, was exceedingly popular in its day.

PRINCIPAL WORKS: Religion in Common Life, 1857; An Introduction to the Philosophy of Religion, 1880; University Sermons, 1899; University Addresses, 1899; The Fundamental Ideas of Christianity, 1900.

ABOUT: Caird, J. The Fundamental Ideas of Christianity (see Memoir by E. Caird).

CAIRD, MRS. MONA HECTOR (1858-February 4, 1932), novelist, was a celebrated reformer of her day. Not much is known of her private life. She was an only daughter, her maiden name being Hector. In 1877 she married James A. Henryson-Caird, who pre-deceased her. She traveled widely and frequently on the Continent, and wrote several books on her journeys.

Mrs. Caird was an early advocate of "woman's rights." Her book Is Marriage a Failure? had a sensational success and aroused much controversy. Her chief social interest, however, was in the anti-vivisection movement, of which she was one of the pioneers. She was also active in temperance propaganda.

She is chiefly known, however, for her novels, which were didactic, sometimes sentimental, and frequently sensational, but which in their time were very popular. She continued her reform activities, but ceased to write several years before her death at seventy-four.

PRINCIPAL WORKS: The Wing of Azrael, 1889; A Romance of the Moors, 1891; The Daughters of Danaus, 1894; Beyond the Pale, 1896; The Stones of Sacrifice, 1915.

CAIRNES, JOHN ELLIOT (December 16, 1823-July 8, 1875), Irish economist, was born in County Louth, his father being a brewer. The clergyman who tutored him said he was too dull for college, and sent him home. Originally a Calvinist, he read Gibbon and was stimulated to both skepticism and study. After a quarrel with his father, he set off for Trinity College, Dublin, on an inadequate allowance. There, specializing in chemistry, he secured a B.A. in 1848 and an M.A. in 1854. While at work in an engineer's office in Galway he became interested in political economy, and studied it so thoroughly that he secured by examination the post of Whately professor of political economy at Dublin University. In 1857 he was made professor of political economy and jurisprudence at Queen's College, Galway. He was called to the bar the same year, but never practised.

In 1860 Cairnes married Eliza Charlotte Alexander, daughter of a judge in the Indian service. They had three children. A hunting accident that year ruined his health and finally crippled him. In 1865 he moved near London, and in 1866 became professor of political economy at University College. An operation in 1868 failed to help him, and from that time on he was a hopeless invalid, but still continued to write. In 1870 he moved near Blackheath. His last honor came in 1874, an honorary LL.D. from Dublin.

Cairnes was considered the chief economist of his day, though he was for the most part a disciple of John Stuart Mill. He was an ardent advocate of the Union cause during the American Civil War. An original and powerful thinker, these attributes infuse his writings.

PRINCIPAL WORKS: The Character and Logical Method of Political Economy, 1857; The Slave Power, 1862; Political Essays, 1873; Essays on Political Economy, 1873; Some Leading Principles of Political Economy Newly Expounded, 1874.

ABOUT: Fortnightly Review August 1875; London Times July 8, 1875.

CALDWELL, MRS. ANNE MARSH-
(1791-October 5, 1874), novelist, was the daughter of a deputy lieutenant of Staffordshire. She married Arthur Cuthbert Marsh, a banker, and had seven children by him; her husband died in 1849. In 1858, on the death of her older brother, she succeeded to the family estate, and had her name changed by royal license to Marsh-Caldwell. She was a friend of Harriet Martineau, the writer on economics, who encouraged publication of her novels. Of these, all issued anonymously, she produced eighteen between 1836 and 1867. Her work shows dramatic power, but is heavily didactic and very smug. Besides her novels, she wrote two historical works dealing with the Huguenots.

PRINCIPAL WORKS: Two Old Men's Tales, 1834; Mount Sorel, 1845; Emilia Wyndham, 1846.

ABOUT: Athenaeum 2:512 1874.

CALL, WATHEN MARK WILKS (1817-
1890), poet, was educated at Cambridge and took holy orders. He served as a curate until 1856, when, under the influence of the French philosopher Auguste Comte, he become converted to Positivism, the rationalistic philosophy of which Comte was the founder. His conscientious scruples then impelled him to retire from the clergy, and he devoted the remainder of his life to literature. Except for a translation of Comte's work, the bulk of his writing was in verse. He was also the author of two novels, which have been praised for their skill in characterization, but are thin, tenuous, and plotless. His verse was of the same order: the *Saturday Review* summed it up by saying that his poems were "carefully worked protests in behalf of culture."

PRINCIPAL WORKS: Lyra Hellenica, 1842; Reverberations, 1849; Golden Histories, 1871.

CALVERLEY, CHARLES STUART
(born Blayds) (December 22, 1831-February 17, 1884), humorous poet and translator, was born at Martley in Worcestershire, son of the Rev. Henry Blayds and Miss Meade. The original name of the family, Calverley, had been changed to Blayds, but was readopted in 1852.

He was educated by private tutors, spent three months at Marlborough, and entered Harrow September 9, 1846. A capable but lazy student, Calverley early astonished his fellows and masters by an extraordinary gift for mastering the classical languages, and especially by the finish and adroitness of his Latin verses. He spent four years at Harrow, where he was acclaimed as classical student and as a jumper of great daring and prowess.

A hastily written Latin poem, scarcely more than an improvisation, won for Calverley a scholarship at Balliol College, Oxford, where he matriculated in 1850. For some youthful prank in infringement of the strict regulations, Calverley was obliged to leave Oxford, and went to Christ's College, Cambridge, where he seems to have had no serious trouble with the disciplinary rules. At Cambridge he took numerous prizes and honors, always displaying the careless ease for which he was noted and never appearing to do any hard work at all.

After he was graduated, Calverley remained at Cambridge, tutoring and lecturing, and was awarded a fellowship in 1858. In 1865, because of his marriage to his first

CHARLES STUART CALVERLEY

cousin, Ellen Calverley, he forfeited his fellowship, took up the study of law, and was admitted to the bar, 1865. He seemed to have an honorable career, if not a brilliant future, in prospect, when, while skating during the winter of 1866-67 he suffered a fall. This injury was neglected, and it became apparent that Calverley had undergone concussion of the brain. He was soon obliged to abandon his profession, and was practically an invalid, with steadily declining physical powers, until his death from Bright's disease in 1884.

Calverley's first volume, *Verses and Translations,* appeared in 1862, and his last in 1872, save for the *Literary Remains* published after his death. He had continued, during his years of illness, to occupy himself with light literature, but produced little.

His personal qualities seem to have impressed his friends more than his literary abilities. All unite in declaring that he had an excellent disposition and a remarkable wit. Sendall, later the Governor of New Guinea, says in his memoir that Calverley was kind, considerate though independent, and completely charming, and adds that a certain "infirmity of will" was his only major weakness. Calverley was also a fairly able caricaturist and a capable amateur musician.

The very ease with which Calverley learned and produced was doubtless the handicap that prevented his attaining to greater heights in literature. In his field, that of parody and humorous verse, he has not been equaled for the remarkable power of imitation, ease of versification, and excellent taste he displayed. It has been said that "his humor shines rather than sparkles." The parodies he wrote impress the reader not by their skilful burlesque of any single work of an author, but by the clever assumption of a remarkable similarity of style and feeling. The translation of Theocritus is a smooth and satisfying rendering, and the Latin parodies of Tennyson and Milton are the work of a master of Latin diction.   R. M.

PRINCIPAL WORKS: Verses and Translations, 1862; Translations Into English and Latin, 1866; Theocritus Translated Into English Verse, 1869; Fly Leaves, 1872; Literary Remains, 1885; Complete Works, 1901.

ABOUT: Calverley, C. S. Literary Remains and Complete Works (see Memoir in each by Walter J. Sendall); Ince, R. B. Calverley and Some Cambridge Wits of the Nineteenth Century; Athenaeum 2:533 October 24, 1885.

CAMBRIDGE, ADA (Mrs. George Frederick Cross) (November 21, 1844-July 20, 1926), novelist, was born in Norfolk and educated at home. She lived in Norfolk and Staffordshire until 1870, when she married the Rev. George Frederick Cross and went with him to Australia. They lived at first in Victoria, mostly in the bush districts where he was a missionary, then near Melbourne, and finally in Melbourne itself. Mr. Cross died in 1917. They had one son and one daughter.

Mrs. Cross's novels of Australia, though unpretentious, are of value as giving a picture of life in the Antipodes fifty years ago, when comparatively little of the sort was written. Her *Thirty Years in Australia* has the same interest in the background it presents.

PRINCIPAL WORKS: A Mere Chance, 1882; The Three Miss Kings, 1891; A Marriage Ceremony, 1894; Materfamilias, 1898; Sisters, 1904; The Hand in the Dark, 1913.

ABOUT: Cambridge, A. Thirty Years in Australia.

CAMPBELL, GEORGE DOUGLAS. See ARGYLL, DUKE OF

CAMPBELL, JAMES DYKES (November 2, 1838-June 1, 1895), Scottish biographer, was born in Port Glasgow. He received only an elementary education, and at fourteen was at work in a merchant's office. His father died in 1854, and the family moved to Glasgow. There Campbell worked in the office of a pottery firm, and spent his leisure in studying English literature. In 1860 he was sent by his employers to Toronto, Canada, and stayed there for two years. He then returned to Glasgow and went into business for himself. In 1866 he went to Bombay, and soon after accepted a position in Mauritius. By 1873 he was a partner in the leading mercantile business in the island. In 1875 he married Mary Sophia Chesney, daughter of the commanding general; they had no children. With his wife, Campbell visited England in 1878, touring the Lake District.

By 1881 he had accumulated a sufficient competency to retire from business. After a visit to Italy, he settled in Kensington and devoted himself to study and writing. He became a close friend of Robert Browning's, and was honorary secretary of the Browning Society. He was also a special student of Tennyson, with less happy results; during his Canadian days he published privately a volume containing suppressed passages in Tennyson's poems, and Tennyson secured an injunction to prevent its circulation.

Campbell's chief interest, however, was in Coleridge. He wrote a great deal concerning the poet, chiefly in *The Athenaeum,* and in 1893 brought out a new and valuable edition of Coleridge's poems. The memoir prefixed to this was enlarged and published the next year as a full-length biography.

In 1889 he moved to St. Leonards for his wife's health. She outlived him, however, and it was his own health which failed. He went to Tunbridge Wells in the hope of recovery, but died there soon after. He was a cordial, sympathetic man, a sound and thorough scholar, and possessed of excellent critical sense.

PRINCIPAL WORK: Samuel Taylor Coleridge: A Narrative of the Events of His Life, 1894.

ABOUT: Campbell, J. D. Samuel Taylor Coleridge (see Memoir in 1896 ed. by L. Stephens); Athenaeum June 8 and 15, 1895; Illustrated London News June 8, 1895.

CAMPBELL, LORD JOHN (September 15, 1779-June 22, 1861), legal biographer, was himself primarily a jurist, having been Lord Chief Justice and Lord Chancellor. He was educated at St. Andrews University (he entered at the age of eleven) and, though intended for the church, prevailed upon his family to allow him to read law instead. He entered Lincoln's Inn in 1800, and was called to the bar in 1806. In 1821 he married a Miss Scarlett, afterwards created Baroness Stratheden in recognition of her husband's services to the country.

Campbell entered Parliament in 1826, and was raised to the peerage in 1841. He was an able judge, but vain and easily flattered, and gifted with the diplomatic "art of getting on." His writing is readable and lively, but rough, careless, and incorrect. He is frequently guilty of misquotation, misrepresentation, and downright plagiarism.

PRINCIPAL WORKS: Lives of the Lord Chancellors, 1846-47; Lives of the Lord Chief Justices, 1849-57; Lives of Lord Lyndhurst and Lord Brougham, 1849-57.

ABOUT: Campbell, J. Autobiography, Diary, and Letters, edited (as Life of Lord Campbell) by his daughter, Mrs. Hardcastle.

CAMPBELL, JOHN FRANCIS (December 29, 1822-February 17, 1885), Scottish story writer and essayist, was born at Islay of an old family, the grandson of an earl. He was educated at Eton and the University of Edinburgh. He then became successively a groom in waiting to the court, secretary of the lighthouse commission, and secretary of the coal commission. He was keenly interested in meteorology, and invented the sunshine recorder which indicates the varying intensity of the sun's rays. His other great interest was in Scottish folklore, especially among those still speaking Gaelic, with which he was familiar. He made visits to the Highlands during which he lived with the inhabitants as one of them and took down the stories he heard. In 1875 he began to issue a series of Gaelic texts, which were unfinished at the time of his death. His style has no particular distinction, but the research he did in folklore is of the highest value. He visited the United States during the Civil War, and wrote afterwards an account of his travels with the singular title, *A Short American Tramp.*

PRINCIPAL WORKS: Popular Tales of the West Highlands, 1860-62; Frost and Fire, 1865; Thermography, 1883.

ABOUT: Academy 27:151 1885; Athenaeum 1:250 1885.

CAMPBELL, LEWIS (September 3, 1830-October 25, 1908), Scottish Hellenist, was born in Edinburgh, son of a Commander in the Royal Navy, and cousin of Robert Campbell, the poet. He was educated at Edinburgh Academy and the University of Glasgow, where he received the medal in Greek, and then at Trinity and Balliol Colleges, Oxford. He received his B.A. in 1853 with a first class in the Classical Moderations. In 1855 he became a fellow of Queen's College. From 1856 to 1858 he was a tutor at Queen's, and was ordained deacon in 1857 and priest in 1858. He then married Frances Pitt Andrews (they had no children) and gave up his fellowship to become vicar at Milford, Hampshire. In 1863 he was named as professor of Greek at St. Andrews. He resigned in 1892 and went to live in Alassio, Italy, but returned in 1894 as a lecturer. Thereafter he gravitated between the two localities, dying at Alassio at seventy-eight.

Campbell was a nervous, excitable, irritable man, but a really fine classical scholar. Besides editing Plato's *Dialogues* (1861-67) and the plays of Sophocles (1875-8), he translated Sophocles (1883) and Aeschylus (1890) into accurate though undistinguished English verse.

PRINCIPAL WORKS: The Christian Ideal, 1877; Life of James Clerk Maxwell (with W. Garnett) 1882; Guide to Greek Tragedy, 1891; Life of Jowett (with E. Abbott) 1897; Nationalisation of the Old English Universities, 1900; Tragic Drama in Aeschylus, Sophocles, and Europides, 1904.

CAMPBELL, THOMAS (July 27, 1777-June 15, 1844), Scottish poet, biographer and historian, was born in Glasgow, the youngest of the eleven children of Alexander Campbell and his wife, Margaret, also named Campbell. Shortly before the boy's birth his father had suffered, in connection with the American War, great losses in the Virginia trade, and the family was reduced to near-poverty.

The youth was educated at the Glasgow Grammar School and at the university of the same city, where he studied 1791-95, showing promise not only in poetry but also in classical scholarship and in debate; he took prizes, and was popular and highly regarded by professors and students. Although he had taken some thought of a career in the Church, Campbell was obliged, by his father's legal misfortunes, to leave college and to rely upon tutoring as a means of support. He went to Edinburgh to study law, and did hackwork and teaching to maintain himself.

The publication, in 1799, of *The Pleasures of Hope* brought the writer instant popu-

THOMAS CAMPBELL

larity, but he failed to capitalize on it, perhaps because of a fear, which seems to have haunted him throughout his life, of inability to re-attain his early level of achievement; instead he traveled on the Continent in 1800-01, staying much of the time at Hamburg, and going to Munich, Ratisbon, Leipzig, and Altona, where he spent the winter, working hard on poetry.

On his return to England he established himself in London. To help his mother and his sisters (his father having died) he began to write for publication, producing his *Annals* and some of his poetry. Thanks partly to the efforts of Lord Minto, he met the best literary society in London, where he made his home until almost the end of his life, taking, however, several trips abroad.

In 1803 he married Matilda Sinclair, a cousin; and he began to think of writing *Specimens of the British Poets,* his critical writing having shown his fitness for the task. While his slow methods delayed the production of the book, he was enabled, by a Crown pension of two hundred pounds given him in 1805, by the success of *Gertrude of Wyoming* (1809) and a subscription edition of his poems, and by his work as translator of foreign news for *The Star,* to better his financial condition.

He was seriously upset by the loss, in 1810, of his second son, who died of scarlet fever, but he recovered himself and delivered (1812) for the Royal Institution a series of lectures on poetry which, despite their technical nature, were decidedly successful. Aside from a brief visit to Paris in 1814 and the business connected with a legacy of four thousand pounds which fell to him in the next year, Campbell's existence at this period was, for the most part, one of steady work. He

spent much time on the *Specimens,* which finally were published (in seven volumes) in 1819.

The rest of his life was relatively unfruitful as to fine literary production; he occupied himself largely with editing. From 1820 to 1830 he was in charge of the *New Monthly Magazine,* and, in 1831-32, of the *Metropolitan Magazine,* which was a failure. He lacked the methodical and orderly qualities for the duties of an editor, and the loss in 1828 of his helpful wife was a severe blow, coming after the discovery of the insanity of his one remaining son.

Two causes Campbell espoused with great enthusiasm. Especially dear to his heart was that of Poland, and in 1832 he founded the Polish Association. And he was a leader in the movement to found a university in London, and lived to see the successful culmination of this agitation, which he regarded as the greatest experience of his life. In recognition of his services to education and his prominence as an author he was thrice elected Lord Rector of Glasgow University, the third time in preference to Sir Walter Scott.

His last years were marked by failing health, and in 1843 he bade his friends farewell and left England, going to Boulogne, where, after considerable suffering, he died in the next year.

Few poets have been so unfortunate in the personal descriptions handed down by their contemporaries. One must conclude, after the perusal of even a part of the chorus of abuse which his fellow-men bestowed upon Campbell's character and person, that he was not only a peculiar individual but, at least on occasion, an extremely unpleasant one. In physique "a small thin man, with a remarkably cunning and withered face, eyes cold and glassy, like those of a dead haddock" (the description is from a discreetly anonymous Irish magazine article), Campbell seems nevertheless to have been jealously vain, even to the extent of dying his whiskers to match his wig. Carlyle said of him: "There is a smirk on his face which would befit a shopman or an auctioneer. . . . His talk is small, contemptuous, and shallow." And Harriet Martineau observed philosophically when telling how he left her society for ever, ". . . I was not very sorry, for his sentimentality was too soft, and his craving for praise too morbid to let him be an agreeable companion." Campbell apparently lacked control: while he could set forth an argument, he was likely to lose his temper in answering one. Although an excessively slow and careful writer, he was utterly unmethodical personally and so absent-minded that on one occasion, having been invited to dinner at a house near the *Green Man* at *Dulwich,* he proceeded to *Greenwich,* where he made vain inquiries for the sign of the *Dull Man.* While he possessed some power of humor, it was inadequate when applied to himself.

Against these disagreeable traits must be placed his intense sympathy for Poland, and his labors in behalf of the patriots, including the generous breakfasts which he gave to Polish exiles. The news of the fall of Warsaw is said to have affected Campbell visibly. And the fact remains that he did have friends, among them Fox and the elder Schlegel.

His fame as a writer is due, not to *The Pleasures of Hope* and his attempts to preserve the traditions of the classical school of the eighteenth century, but to the *Specimens of the British Poets* and to his lyrics, especially to such ringing war-songs as "Ye Mariners of England" and "Hohenlinden." The *Specimens* consist of selections and short lives of the poets, preceded by a critical essay on poetry revealing the writer's considerable acumen. Campbell's other volumes of prose are, in the main, unimportant. His relatively slight production may be attributed to some extent to his slow methods and to his misfortunes. His views on poetry, in an age of Romanticism, were semi-conservative, approximating to some degree those of Byron. "Campbell cannot be numbered among the greatest poets of the Naturalistic School; but in his lyrics there is a simple, powerful, and melodious pathos which reminds us of the old Greek elegiac poets," wrote G. M. C. Brandes. ". . . In his best verse there is a spirit, a swinging march time, and a fire that entitled him, if only for the sake of half-a-dozen short pieces, to a place among great poets."   R. W. W.

PRINCIPAL WORKS: *Biography*—Life of Mrs. Siddons, 1834; Life of Petrarch, 1841. *Editor*—Specimens of the British Poets, 1819; The Scenic Annual, 1837; The Dramatic Works of William Shakespeare, 1838; Frederick the Great: His Court and Times, 1842-43. *History*—Annals of Great Britain From the Ascension of George III to the Peace of Amiens, 1807; History of Our Own Times, 1843-45. *Poetry*—The Pleasures of Hope, 1799; Gertrude of Wyoming, 1809; Theodric, 1824; The Pilgrim of Glencoe, 1842. *Miscellaneous*—Letters From the South, 1837.

ABOUT: Beattie, W. Life and Letters of Thomas Campbell; Gilfillan, C. First Gallery of Literary Portraits; Hadden, J. C. Thomas Campbell; Hall, S. C. Retrospect of a Long Life; Redding, C. Literary Reminiscences and Memoirs of Thomas Campbell; Saintsbury, G. Essays in English Literature; 1780-1860 (second series).

CAMPBELL, WILLIAM WILFRED

June 1, 1861-January 1, 1918), Canadian poet, was born in Berlin (now Kitchener), West Ontario. He claimed descent from the family to which the poet Thomas Campbell and the novelist Henry Fielding belonged.

Campbell was graduated from Wycliffe College, Toronto, and the Episcopal Divinity School, Cambridge, Massachusetts. He was ordained in 1885, his father being a clergyman before him. For three years he served

in churches in New England, then returned to Canada, where he was rector at St. Stephen, New Brunswick. In 1891 he retired from the ministry.

He then became connected with the Dominion Archives Bureau in Ottawa, a civil service position which he held for many years. In 1893 he became a fellow of the Royal Society of Canada, and served as secretary, vice-president, and president of its English section. For some time he helped to edit a department of literary criticism in the Toronto *Globe*. In 1906 he compiled the *Oxford Book of Canadian Verse*. In 1884 he married Mary Louise Dibble, who outlived him.

Campbell wrote historical novels and plays as well as poetry. As a poet he is distinguished by his love of nature—he was known as "the poet of the lakes." He was a strong imperialist, a prejudice which also appears prominently in his work. There is a mystical strain in his verse, a sort of minor mixture of Poe and Wordsworth. He died near Ottawa, in his fifty-seventh year.

PRINCIPAL WORKS: Lake Lyrics, 1889; The Dread Voyage, 1893; Beyond the Hills of Dream, 1898; Ian of the Orcades (novel) 1906; Political Tragedies, 1908.

ABOUT: Campbell, W. W. Poetical Works (see Memoir by W. J. Sykes).

CANNING, GEORGE (April 11, 1770-August 8, 1827), statesman and satirist, was

born in London. His father died when he was only a year old, and his mother (who remarried twice and outlived three husbands) went on the stage until her son pensioned her in 1801. He was reared by his paternal uncle.

At Eton Canning edited a magazine *The Microcosm*, of which a publisher thought highly enough to pay fifty pounds for its copyright. He received his B.A. from Christ Church, Oxford, in 1790.

The French Revolution changed Canning from a Whig to a Tory, and it was as a Tory than he entered Parliament in 1794. From 1796 to 1801 he was under-secretary of state for foreign affairs. From 1799 to 1801 he, with George Ellis and others, edited the *Anti-Jacobin*, a magazine devoted to ridicule of radicals, to which he contributed satire in verse and prose. This, with his published speeches, constitutes Canning's claim to consideration as an author.

In 1800 he married Joan Scott, a great heiress and sister of the Duchess of Portland; they had three sons and a daughter.

Canning was a follower of the great statesman Charles Pitt, and followed him in and out of office as party fortunes changed. From 1804 to 1806, when Pitt died, he was treasurer of the navy. In 1807 the Tories were back again, with Canning's brother-in-law, the Duke of Portland, as prime minister, and

Canning became foreign minister. A disagreement with Lord Castlereagh, then secretary-at-war, led to a duel in which both were slightly wounded. In 1809 Portland resigned, and Canning was out of the cabinet for thirteen years.

As an intimate friend of Scott, Canning helped to found the *Quarterly Review* in 1808. In 1814 he was ambassador extraordinary to Lisbon, then stayed in the south of France till 1816. He returned to England to be president of the board of control, but retired in 1820 and again went abroad. In 1822 he was made governor general of India, but before he could sail the Tories came into office again and Canning returned to the foreign office. In 1827 he became prime minister; his coalition with the Whigs caused many of his former friends to attack him, and embittered his last months. Early in the year he had caught cold at the Duke of York's funeral, and never really recovered, dying in August.

Canning was a noted orator, eloquent and persuasive. Eloquence and a sometimes brilliant wit are the chief characteristics of his written style.

PRINCIPAL WORKS: Collected Poems, 1823; Collected Speeches, 1828 (ed. by R. Therry); The Rovers (play, with J. H. Frere and G. Ellis) 1887; Poetry of the Anti-Jacobin· (ed. by L. Rice-Oxley) 1924.

ABOUT: Bagot, J. George Canning and His Friends; Brougham, H. P. Statesmen of the Reign of George III; Hill, F. H. George Canning; Phillips, W. A. George Canning; Stapleton, A. G. Political Life of Canning; Temperley, H. W. V. George Canning.

CARLETON, WILLIAM (March 4, 1794-January 30, 1869), Irish story-teller, novelist, and journalist, was born at Prillisk, Clogher County, Ireland, the fourteenth child of James and Mary Kelly Carleton. The father, a tenant farmer, was remarkable for his knowledge of Irish folklore, and the mother was locally famous for an exquisite voice.

Educated in the hedge-schools and at the classical school at Donagh from 1814-16, Carleton early showed remarkable ability and familiarity with Irish folklore. His promise was such that he was destined for the priesthood, but poverty prevented his being educated. Forced to seek work, he tried stone-cutting, etc., and finally became tutor in the family of a wealthy farmer. Six months of tutoring persuaded him to try his fortune in Dublin. At nineteen he had gone on a religious pilgrimage, the story of which he tells in *The Lough Derg Pilgrim*. This experience not only dissuaded him from entering the priesthood, but prompted him to turn Protestant. Therefore in Dublin he became clerk of a Sunday School Society. He gained a moderate living by supplementing this work with teaching and journalism. However, a pension

WILLIAM CARLETON

of £200, secured from Lord John Russell in 1848, was welcome.

Carleton married, about 1822, Jane Anderson. Of their children two later went to New Zealand. Carleton lived on in Dublin, dying at Sandford County, Dublin.

At thirty-six Carleton was established in the front rank of Irish novelists by the first series of *Traits and Stories of the Irish Peasantry*. "There never was any man of letters who had an opportunity of knowing and describing the manners of the Irish people so thoroughly as I had," he wrote later. His intention was to be the "historian of the peasants." As might be expected, he drew heavily upon his experience, taking characters and situations from life. The realism for which he became so well known results largely from this autobiographic material, and is missing in such work as does not deal with the Irish scene. Much of his work appeared in the *Christian Examiner*, after 1828, and in the *National Magazine*, the *Dublin University Magazine*, etc. This work was collected later for publication.

Carleton was associated with nearly all aspects of Irish life and thought, and was variously regarded by his contemporaries. Many despised him for his realism, many for his unwillingness to write for both disputants in a controversy. His rank is that of a supremely gifted narrator whose work lights up the entire Celtic revival. He has the Irish humor, buoyancy, melancholy, and love of folk-tales. There is a large amount of self-confidence in his work.

By nature indolent and erratic, he was adventurer enough to make his way by his wits and to gain the friendship of great and small all over Ireland. His high forehead, penetrating glance, and prominent nose gave him an interesting appearance.

Perhaps his most characteristic work is found in his *Autobiography* and in *Traits and Stories of the Irish Peasantry*.   D. F. A.

PRINCIPAL WORKS: *Stories*—Traits and Stories of the Irish Peasantry (first series) 1830; Traits and Stories (second series) 1833; Tales of Ireland, 1834; Fardorougha, 1837; Father Butler and the Lough Derg Pilgrim, 1839; The Faun of Springvale, 1841; Traits and Stories (with autobiographic Introduction) 1843-4; Going to Maynooth, 1845; Rody the Rover, 1846; Parra Sastha, 1846; The Emigrants of Ahadarra, 1847; Art Maguire, 1847; Jane Sinclair, 1849; Three Tasks, 1851; The Clarionet, The Dead Boxer, and Barney Branagan, 1852; Phelim O'Toole's Courtship, 1853; Phil Purcell, 1853; Poor Scholar, 1853; Alley Sheridan, 1857; Tales of Irish Life, 1859; The Evil Eye, 1860; The Double Prophecy, 1862; Redmond, 1862; The Silver Acre, 1862; The Fair Emyvale and the Master and Scholar, 1870. *Novels*—Valentine M'Clutchy, 1846; The Black Prophet, 1847; The Tithe Proctor, 1847; The Red Hall, 1852; Willy Reilly, 1855; The Squanders of Castle Squander, 1852.

ABOUT: Carleton, W. Traits and Stories (see autobiographic Introduction to 1843-4 ed.); O'Donoghue, D. J. Life of William Carleton; Blackwood's Magazine 179:273-7 February 1906.

CARLILE, RICHARD (December 8, 1790-February 10, 1843), Rationalist philosopher, was born in Devonshire of a working class family. His father died when he was four. He learned to read at the village free school, then worked in a chemist's shop, and was apprenticed to a tinman who treated him cruelly. As a journeyman tinman he first read Thomas Paine, and became a radical and free thinker. In 1817 the Habeas Corpus Act had been suspended. Carlile circulated the forbidden journals, then opened a publishing house for the production of radical works by himself and others. He was prosecuted and persecuted from the start. In 1819 he was sentenced to three years' imprisonment in Dorchester, plus a £1500 fine which he had to work out in prison. His plant was raided, all his goods seized, his wife, sister, and assistants served prison terms, and he was in prison for six years altogether; but all the time, from his cell, he published his paper, *The Republican*. The Duke of Wellington headed the list of donors to a fund to prosecute his firm; the Czar of Russia forbade his books entry to the country; he was obliged finally to sell books by a clockwork device to keep his shopmen from arrest.

After his release he published two other papers, *The Gorgon* and *The Lion*. In 1830 a new free speech fight began. Once more his house was raided when he refused to pay church rates, and he served three years more in prison. Other shorter terms brought his total imprisonment to nearly ten years. All the money he made or received from sympathizers he spent for propaganda on free thought, republicanism, and birth control. He came very near to deportation to Australia.

Mrs. Carlile had stood by him through resentment at the injustice shown him, but they were ill-mated and from 1819 agreed to separate. It was not until 1832 that he was able to settle money on her and their children so that they could live apart. He died finally of excitement from a hunt for a lost child, and left his body for anatomical purposes to St. Thomas's Hospital.

Carlile established freedom of the press in England. Abstemious, mild, modest, heroic, he is one of the great names in the history of liberty. His deeds exceed his achievements as a writer.

PRINCIPAL WORKS: The Political Litany, 1817; Every Man's Book: or. What Is God? 1826; The Gospel According to Richard Carlile, 1827; A New View of Insanity, 1831; Church Reform, 1835.

ABOUT: Holyoake, G. J. Life and Character of Richard Carlile.

CARLYLE, THOMAS (December 4, 1795-February 4, 1881), Scottish historian, critic, and sociological writer, was born in the village of Ecclefechan, Dumfriesshire, eldest child of James Carlyle, stonemason, and Margaret (Aitken) Carlyle. The father was stern, irascible, a puritan of the puritans, but withal a man of rigid probity and strength of character. The mother, too, was of the Scottish earth, and Thomas' education was begun at home by both the parents. From the age of five to nine he was at the village school; from nine to fourteen at Annan Grammar School, where he showed proficiency in mathematics and was well grounded in French and Latin. In November 1809 he walked to Edinburgh, and attended courses at the University till 1814, with the ultimate aim of becoming a minister. He left without a degree, became a mathematical tutor at Annan Academy in 1814, and three years later abandoned all thoughts of entering the Kirk, having reached a theological position incompatible with its teachings. He had begun to learn German in Edinburgh, and had done much independent reading outside the regular curriculum. Late in 1816 he moved to a school in Kirkcaldy, where he became the intimate associate of Edward Irving, an old boy of Annan School, and now also a schoolmaster. This contact was Carlyle's first experience of true intellectual companionship, and the two men became lifelong friends. He remained there two years, was attracted by Margaret Gordon, a lady of good family (whose friends vetoed an engagement), and in October 1818 gave up schoolmastering and went to Edinburgh, where he took mathematical pupils and made some show of reading law.

During this period in the Scottish capital he began to suffer agonies from a gastric complaint which continued to torment him all his life, and may well have played a large part in shaping the rugged, rude fabric of his philosophy. In literature he had at first little success, a series of articles for the *Edinburgh Encyclopaedia* bringing in little money and no special credit. In 1820 and 1821 he visited Irving in Glasgow and made long stays at his father's new farm, Mainhill; and in June 1821, in Leith Walk, Edinburgh, he experienced a striking spiritual rebirth which is related in *Sartor Resartus.* Put briefly and prosaically, it consisted in a sudden clearing away of doubts as to the beneficent organization of the universe; a semi-mystical conviction that he was free to think and work, and that honest effort and striving would not be thwarted by what he called the "Everlasting No."

For about a year, from the spring of 1823, Carlyle was tutor to Charles and Arthur Buller, young men of substance, first in Edinburgh and later at Dunkeld. Now likewise appeared the first fruits of his deep studies in German, the *Life of Schiller,* which was published serially in the *London Magazine* in 1823-24 and issued as a separate volume in 1825. A second garner from the same field was his version of Goethe's *Wilhelm Meister,* which earned the praise of *Blackwood's* and was at once recognized as a very masterly rendering.

In 1821 Irving had gone to London, and in June 1824 Carlyle followed, in the train of his employers, the Bullers. But he soon resigned his tutorship, and, after a few weeks at Birmingham, trying a dyspepsia cure, he lived with Irving at Pentonville, London, and paid a short visit to Paris. March 1825 saw him back in Scotland, on his brother's farm, Hoddam Hill, near the Solway. Here for a year he worked hard at German translations, perhaps more serenely than before or after, and free from that noise which was always a curse to his sensitive ear and which later caused him to build a sound-proof room in his Chelsea home.

Before leaving for London Irving had introduced Carlyle to Jane Baillie Welsh, daughter of the surgeon, John Welsh, and descended from John Knox. She was beautiful, precociously learned, talented, and a brilliant mistress of cynical satire. Among her numerous suitors, the rough, uncouth Carlyle at first made an ill impression; but a literary correspondence was begun, and on October 17, 1826, after a courtship that was in some sort a battle of strong wills, the two were married and went to live at Comely Bank, Edinburgh, starting with a capital of £200. Francis Jeffrey, editor of the *Edinburgh Review,* was a cousin of the Welshes. He accepted Carlyle as a contributor, and during 1827 printed two important articles—on

"Richter" and "The State of German Literature."

The *Foreign Review* published two penetrating essays on Goethe; and in 1827 a cordial correspondence was begun with the great German writer, who backed Carlyle (unsuccessfully) for the vacant Chair of Moral Philosophy at St. Andrews. Another application for a university chair, this time at the new University of London, failed equally. An attempt at a novel was destroyed.

In May 1828 the Carlyles moved to Craigenputtock, an isolated farm belonging to the Welsh family, which was their permanent home until 1834. Carlyle lived the life of a recluse and scholar, and his clever wife, immersed in household duties and immured in solitude, led a dull and empty existence. Jeffrey, who paid visits in 1828 and 1830, said: "Bring your blooming Eve out of your blasted Paradise, and seek shelter in the lower world," but Carlyle was lacking in consideration for his partner, and would not. Jeffrey even thought of Carlyle as his successor in the editorship of the *Edinburgh,* when he gave it up in 1829, but the matter could not be arranged. A memorable visit, in August 1833, was that of the young Ralph Waldo Emerson, who was kindly received and became a fast friend.

At Craigenputtock was written the first of Carlyle's great commentaries on life in general, *Sartor Resartus,* which appeared in *Fraser's Magazine* between November 1833 and August 1834. The idea of a philosophy of clothes was not new; there are debts to Swift, Jean Paul Richter, and others; but what *were* new were the amazing, humorous energy, the moral force, the resourceful (if eccentric) command over English. It was damned by the press, and was not issued in book-form until 1838; but it is now numbered among his most significant works. Other notable writings of this time were essays on Voltaire, Novalis, and Richter (a new paper) in the *Foreign Review.*

After visits to Edinburgh and London, and an unsuccessful application for a professorship of astronomy at Edinburgh in January 1834, Carlyle decided to set up house in London, settling at 5, Cheyne Row, Chelsea. His struggle to live was made more severe by his refusal to engage in journalism: even an offer of work on *The Times* was rejected; and instead a grandiose history of the *French Revolution* was begun. In the spring of 1835 occurred one of the great heroisms of literature. The manuscript of the first volume of the new work had been lent to the philosopher, J. S. Mill, who in his turn had lent it to a Mrs. Taylor. An illiterate housekeeper took it for waste paper, and it was burnt. Mill was inconsolable; Carlyle behaved with the

THOMAS CARLYLE

utmost stoicism and nobility, and was only with difficulty induced to accept £100 as a slight pecuniary compensation.

The *French Revolution* was re-written, and its publication in January 1837 brought the praise of Thackeray, Southey, Hallam, and others of weight, and consolidated Carlyle's reputation as one of the foremost men of letters of the day. Even so, it sold slowly, and he had to resort to public lecturing (arranged by Harriet Martineau) to raise funds; and it was only in 1842, when Mrs. Welsh died and left them an annuity, that the Carlyles were able to rid themselves of financial worry.

Of outward event Carlyle's life contains little. From his establishment in London his history was one of enormous work and the gradual building up of a literary fame that became world-wide. In the 'forties and onward he became more and more sought after by men of letters, statesmen and the aristocracy, and his friends included such names as Monckton Milnes, Tyndall, Peel, Froude, Grote, Browning, and Ruskin. One friendship, with the clergyman, John Sterling, was close and warm, and left its record in the *Life* published in 1851. Another, with Lady Harriet Ashburton, caused grave dissension in the Carlyle home, being strongly disapproved by Mrs. Carlyle, though there was no suggestion of anything more than high mutual regard.

In literature Carlyle moved more and more away from democratic ideas. *Chartism, On Heroes, Past and Present,* and *Cromwell* all developed his thesis that the people need a strong and ruthless ruler and should obey him. *Latter-day Pamphlets* poured out all his contempt on the philanthropic and humanitarian tendencies of the day. His last monumental exaltation of strength was a six-volume history of *Friedrich II of Prussia: Called Frederick the Great.* Following his custom, he paid two visits to Germany to survey the scene (in 1852 and 1858), and turned over great masses of material. The first two volumes appeared in the autumn of 1858, were at once translated into German, and were hailed as a masterpiece. The remaining volumes appeared in 1862, 1864, and 1865. In this last year Carlyle was made Lord Rector of the University of Edinburgh. While he was still in the north, after delivering his inaugural address, he learned of the sudden death of his wife, from heart disease, and was thereby plunged into the deepest distress.

Thenceforward a gradual decadence supervened. In the autumn of 1866 Carlyle joined the committee for the defense of Governor Eyre, of Jamaica, who had been recalled for alleged cruelty in the suppression of a rebellion. The next year he wrote the tract, *Shooting Niagara,* against the Reform Act (which had introduced improvements into the British franchise system). He sided with the Prussians in the war of 1870-71; in 1874 he was awarded the high Prussian order "Pour le Mérite," and the same year refused Disraeli's offer of a Grand Cross of the Order of the Bath and a pension. He died on February 4, 1881, and was buried at Ecclefechan.

Carlyle's personal character and his philosophy are alike full of contradictions and hardly susceptible to summary exposition. The most high-minded devotee of the ideal, he could yet be in the last degree churlish and uncharitable to the work and personalities of others—even to such a man as Charles Lamb. An apostle of courage and endurance, he was yet the most vociferous and ungracious of grumblers. His love for his wife was deep and abiding, yet her life with him was often a torment. While he abhorred philanthropy and liberal legislation along utilitarian lines, and came more and more to admire despotism, he could be scathing about the "game-preserving aristocracy" and in his personal life was quick to relieve distress.

No coherent body of philosophy can be extracted from his teachings: it is rather as a prophet and a seer that he has his place. He was blind to the greatest phenomenon of his age—the rise of science as an interpreter of the universe—and spoke insultingly of Darwin. Formal economics also incurred his censure. His theological attitude is hardest of all to define. At an early age he found himself unable to subscribe to any of the orthodox creeds, but he was even more condemnatory of atheism than of the Kirk, and never ceased to believe passionately in a personal God. His central tenet was the worship of strength; and, after beginning as a radical, he came to despise the democratic system and increasingly to extol the value and necessity of strong and stern government, in which the people themselves should have no share.

In literature he was the pioneer who explored and made known the work of modern Germany. His literary judgments were penetrating, and (when he had a congenial subject) just; and on men like Voltaire, Burns, and Johnson he gave verdicts that approached finality. At a historian he is in the highest rank. Bating certain unimportant errors of detail, he illumined the past with astonishing insight and made his personages actual and his scenes dramatic. His style is an extraordinary farrago, leaping not flowing, coining strange words and performing extravagant evolutions; yet cumulatively it impresses as a great style, suffused with humor, irony, and passion; impossible to imitate, utterly personal, burning, and convincing.

"Carlyle's genius," wrote Hector Macpherson, "was many-sided. He touched and ennobled the national life at all points. He lifted a whole generation of young men out of the stagnating atmosphere of materialism and dead orthodoxy into the region of the ideal. With the Master of Balliol, we believe that 'no English writer has done more to elevate and purify our ideas of life and to make us conscious that the things of the spirit are real, and that in the last resort there is no other reality.'"   H. B. G.

PRINCIPAL WORKS: *History*—The French Revolution, 1837; On Heroes, Hero-Worship, and the Heroic in History, 1841; Oliver Cromwell's Letters and Speeches, 1845; History of Friedrich II of Prussia: Called Frederick the Great (6 vols.) 1858-65; The Early Kings of Norway, 1875. *Biography and Criticism*—The Life of Friedrich Schiller, 1825; Critical and Miscellaneous Essays, 1839; The Life of John Sterling, 1851; Inaugural Address at Edinburgh, 1866; Reminiscences, 1881; Reminiscences of My Irish Journey in 1849, 1882. *Sociology*—Sartor Resartus, 1838; Chartism, 1840; Past and Present, 1843; Latter-Day Pamphlets (8 nos.) 1850; Occasional Discourse on the Nigger Question, 1853; Shooting Niagara, 1867; Mr. Carlyle on the War (letters from "The Times") 1871; Last Words of Thomas Carlyle, 1882. *Translations*—Legendre, A. M. Elements of Geometry and Trigonometry (with chapter on Proportion by Carlyle) 1824; Goethe, J. W. von. Wilhelm Meister's Apprenticeship, 1834; German Romance: Specimens, 1827. *Letters*—The Correspondence of Thomas Carlyle and Ralph Waldo Emerson, 1883; Early Letters, 1886; Correspondence Between Goethe and Carlyle, 1887.

ABOUT: Arnold, M. Discourses in America; Birrell, A. Obiter Dicta; Carlyle, J. W. Letters and Memorials; Conway, M. D. Thomas Carlyle; Emerson, R. W. Lectures and Biographical Sketches; Froude, J. A. Thomas Carlyle: A History of the First Forty Years of His Life; Froude, J. A. Thomas Carlyle: A History of His Life in London; Garnett, R. Life of Thomas Carlyle (with bibliography); Gould, G. M. Biographic Clinics: The Origin of the Ill-Health of De Quincey, Carlyle (etc.); Horne, R. H. H. A New Spirit of the Age (Vol. 2); Hunt, J. H. L. Autobiography (Vol. 3); Lowell, J. R. My Study Windows; Macpherson, H. A Century of Intellectual Development; Mazzini, J. Life and Writings (Vols. 4-5); Mill, J. S. Autobiography; Morley, J. Critical Miscellanies; Nichol, J. Thomas Carlyle; Robinson, H. C. Diary; Scherer, E. Études sur la Littérature Contemporaine; Schmidt, J. Portraits aus dem Neunzehnten Jahrhundert; Shairp, J. C. Aspects of Poetry; Smith, A. Last Leaves; Sterling, J. Essays and Tales (Vol. 1); Thackeray, W. M. Sultan Stork (etc.); Thoreau, H. D. A Yankee in Canada; Whittier, J. G. Prose Works (Vol. 2).

CARPENTER, EDWARD (August 29, 1844-June 28, 1929), poet and essayist, was born in Brighton, one of ten children in a family of Cornish descent. He was educated at Brighton College and at Trinity College Cambridge, where he was graduated in 1868 as tenth wrangler, his interest then being chiefly in mathematics and physics. Before going to Cambridge he had spent five months at Heidelberg, where he wrote his first poems —in German.

Carpenter became a fellow of Trinity and a lecturer at the college, and then took holy orders. He served for a while as curate to Frederick Denison Maurice, the famous liberal clergyman, founder of Christian Socialism. But in 1874 his religious views underwent a change, and he could no longer continue in the church, even in association with so liberal a man as Maurice. Until 1881 he made his living by lecturing throughout the north of England (living at Bradway), his subjects being science and music. (All his life he composed music, and was the author of one of the best known labor songs, "England, Arise.") At Bradway he wrote *Towards Democracy*, which he called "the starting point and kernel of all my later work."

With the feeling that as a real democrat he should share in the manual work of the masses, in 1883 he bought a small farm at

EDWARD CARPENTER

Millthorpe, near Sheffield, where with a friend he worked and supported himself by sale of the farm products. He had become active in the labor movement, was connected with the Fabian Society, and called himself a socialist, though temperamentally he was always much more of an anarchist. In 1886 he helped William Morris to found the Sheffield Socialist Society.

After 1888, he turned over most of the actual farm work to his friend, and devoted himself to writing. This was a source of expense, not of income, for all his earlier works were paid for by himself and had very little circulation. He described his life at this time as consisting of "literary work, sandal-making, the Socialist movement, and street-corner propaganda." The Fabians were dress-reformers as well, and all of them wore Carpenter's stout leather sandals.

Carpenter lived in Millthorpe until 1919, when he moved to Guilford, Surrey, his last home. A thorough disciple of Whitman, in 1884 he made a pilgrimage to America to visit the poet, and spent several months with him. In 1890 he visited Ceylon, and become much interested in eastern philosophy, though he never again adhered to any formal theology. He was by nature a mystic. Starting as a scientist, he turned completely anti-scientific, with a strong tinge of Spiritualism. He was not, however, a mere dreamer or eccentric, but possessed plenty of common sense, a strong business capacity, and immense courage. It took a brave man to publish a pamphlet on homo-sexuality at the very time that Oscar Wilde's trial was being conducted. He was never molested, however, though it was common knowledge that his advocacy of the superiority of "the intermediate sex" had its basis in his own nature.

Besides editing two anthologies, *Ioläus: An Anthology of Friendship* (1902) and *Chants of Labour* (1888), Carpenter translated from Apuleius the myth of Eros and Psyche.

When Carpenter was buried at Guildford, at the age of eighty-five, a friend wrote of him that he was "a writer of distinction, a man of most individual charm, and a reformer of the first importance." First Shelley, then Whitman, then the Theosophical writers, influenced his thought and his style. His poetry is Whitmanesque, though less rugged than Whitman's; it is a flowing free verse, often of limpid beauty. The world passed beyond his reforms, but he remained a passionate natural rebel, urging his views in powerful, lucid prose. *England's Ideal, Civilization: Its Cause and Cure,* and *Love's Coming of Age* were landmarks of their time and text-books for the young inclined to heterodoxy in the 'nineties. They have their place still in the literature of protest and revolt. M. A. deF.

PRINCIPAL WORKS: *Poetry*—Narcissus and Other Poems, 1873; Moses: A Drama, 1875; Towards Democracy, 1883-1905; Sketches From Life in Town and Country, 1908. *Prose*—The Religious Influence of Art, 1870; England's Ideal, 1887; Civilization: Its Cause and Cure, 1889; From Adam's Peak to Elaphanta, 1892; Love's Coming of Age, 1896; Angel's Wings, 1898; The Art of Creation, 1904; Prisons, Police, and Punishment, 1905; Days With Walt Whitman, 1906; The Intermediate Sex, 1908; The Drama of Love and Death, 1912; Intermediate Types Among Primitive Folk, 1914; The Healing of Nations, 1915; The Story of My Books, 1916; My Days and Dreams, 1916; Towards Industrial Freedom, 1918; Pagan and Christian Creeds, 1920; The Psychology of the Poet Shelley (with E. Barnefield) 1925.

ABOUT: Carpenter, E. The Story of My Books; My Days and Dreams; Crosby, E. Edward Carpenter: Poet and Prophet; Dickinson, L., Ellis, H., Housman, L. & Others. Edward Carpenter: In Appreciation; Ellis, Mrs. H. Three Modern Seers; Jackson, H. All Manner of Folk; Lewis, E. Edward Carpenter: An Exposition and an Appreciation; Swan, T. Edward Carpenter: The Man and His Work; Bookman (London) 76:238 August 1929; Nation 129:114 July 31, 1929; Saturday Review 151:598 April 25, 1931.

"CARROLL, LEWIS" (Charles Lutwidge Dodgson) (January 27, 1832-January 14, 1898), the author of *Alice in Wonderland,* of mathematical treatises, and of a quantity of stories and poems, serious and humorous, was the son of a churchman and the eldest of eleven children. His mother and father were first cousins, and unusually religious. At the time of his birth, his father, Dr. Dodgson, was the vicar of Daresbury, Cheshire (he later was presented with the Crown living of Croft, Yorkshire, and subsequently became Archdeacon of Richmond and one of the Canons of Ripon Cathedral), and was a distinguished scholar whose favorite study was mathematics.

Daresbury was isolated, but there was no want of children, so Charles invented games to amuse himself and his brothers and sisters. He made a train with railway stations in the Rectory garden; he did conjuring in a brown wig and a long white robe; he made a troupe of marionettes and a stage with the aid of the family and a village carpenter; he wrote all the plays for it himself, and manipulated the strings. The most popular was *The Tragedy of King John.* He also made pets of snails and toads, and tried to promote modern warfare among earthworms by giving them small pieces of clay pipe for weapons.

Until he was twelve his father educated him, and then he went to Mr. Tate's school at Richmond. He was the butt of a few jokes as a new boy; later, however, he became the champion of the weak and small, and earned the reputation of "a boy who knew how to use his fists in a righteous cause." He contributed one story to the school magazine, probably a mystery, called *"The Unknown One,"* which is unknown. Dr. Tate wrote to

"LEWIS CARROLL"

Dr. Dodgson that Charles had "a very uncommon share of genius," and "you may fairly anticipate for him a bright career." From Richmond he went to Rugby under Dr. Tate, and again acquitted himself more than creditably of his work. He always "went home with one or more prizes." Indeed, the whole of his academic career was an endless series of excellent marks, prizes, and congratulations.

In the holidays between 1845 and 1850 he edited a number of magazines for his own amusement; the most entertaining of these was *The Rectory Umbrella*, which he illustrated as well as wrote. In this were the first nonsense rhymes and humorous drawings. "Seldom," says Walter De La Mare, "has any child shown himself so clearly the father-to-be of the man."

On May 23, 1850, he matriculated at Christ Church College, Oxford, his father's college; in January the following year he became a resident of that college, and "from that day to the hour of his death—a period of forty-seven years—he belonged to 'the House,' never leaving it for any length of time. . ." Again he distinguished himself with first class honors in mathematics, second class in classics, and the Butler Scholarship. He wrote, "I am getting tired of being congratulated on various subjects; there seems to be no end of it. If I had shot the Dean I could hardly have had more said about it." After receiving his B.A. degree he was made "Master of the House" and sub-librarian. According to the terms of the scholarship, or studentship, he was to remain unmarried, and proceed to holy orders. At this time, 1855, he began contributing poems and stories to *The Comic Times*, until its editor, Edmund Yates, founded *The Train*. It was Yates who chose from three names

Dodgson submitted the *nom de plume* Lewis Carroll, and Lewis Carroll was first signed to a poem, "Solitude," which appeared in *The Train* in 1856.

The year 1855 was eventful; he received the further appointment of lecturer in mathematics at Christ Church College, a position which he held until 1881. Six years later he was ordained a deacon, but he never proceeded to priest's orders, probably because he stammered. He did, however, preach from time to time, often to the servants of the college, but he enjoyed most preaching to children.

From this time until his death in 1898 the story of Lewis Carroll is the story of his literary work, of his child friends, of his hobbies and inventions, and the story of Charles Lutwidge Dodgson, mathematician, lecturer, and scholar, is secondary. (A trip to Russia with Dr. Liddon in 1867 was the only real interruption in the quiet routine of his life. *The Russian Journal* is his diary of this trip.)

On July 4, 1862, Lewis Carroll wrote in his diary, "I made an expedition *up* the river to Godstowe with the three Liddells, we had tea on the bank there, and did not reach Christ Church till half-past eight." Somewhat later he added, "on which occasion I told them the fairy tale of *Alice's Adventures Underground*, which I undertook to write out for Alice." The Liddells were the daughters of the dean of Christ Church College. Alice, the second daughter, lived to celebrate the centenary of Carroll's birth. Subsequently the book was called *Alice's Hours in Elfland*, but when it appeared in 1865 it was *Alice's Adventures in Wonderland*. The first edition both Tenniel, the illustrator, and Carroll condemned because the pictures were printed poorly. Some of these 2000 copies were given by Carroll to hospitals and institutions where he thought the book might be enjoyed and some were sold in America. It was six years later that *Through the Looking Glass* was published.

In the meantime Carroll had settled down in a spacious apartment on the northwest corner of Tom Quad, where he remained the rest of his life, and where he had a photographic studio. Here he made portraits of a great many of the celebrities of his day, as well as of his child friends. The pictures are clear and sharp and altogether remarkable for their time. It was here that Carroll did a great deal of entertaining. He made charts of where his guests sat at table, and kept track of menus in his diary, so that "people would not have the same dishes too frequently." He was by now a confirmed and exacting bachelor, who labeled and filed all his papers and letters; who asked perfection of the artists who illustrated his books, and even requested one of them, E. Gertrude Thomson, not to do any work for him on Sundays; who rose early every morning, and worked hard all day. But he was also the child-lover who kept "for the amusement of his child guests a large assortment of musical boxes and an organette which had to be fed with paper tunes," clock-work bears, mice, frogs, games and puzzles of all sorts.

While the fame of Lewis Carroll increased daily, Dodgson was turning out and publishing a quantity of mathematical works, but, as Harvey Darton puts it, "no one who ever wrote for children is more completely assured of unacademic immortality." Dodgson shied away from publicity, and "declined to welcome any tribute to Lewis Carroll." In fact he wrote, "Mr. C. L. Dodgson. . . neither claims nor acknowledges any connection with any pseudonym or with any book not published under his own name." But Dodgson has a good deal of fun even under his own name. He ridiculed the new belfry at Christ Church in a pamphlet; he wrote skits on Oxford subjects, and published a book of parodies, mostly of Tennyson and Longfellow. He invented a system of mnemonics for remembering names and dates; poetical acrostics; a system for writing in the dark; and he improved the game of backgammon. The later works of Lewis Carroll never reached the popularity of the Alice books. *Sylvie and Bruno* is full of the ideals and sentiments "he held most dear," though it contains also a good deal of nonsense.

Carroll was tall, thin, and dark, with delicate features, smooth skin, and "thick curly hair." He "was, at sight, a much odder figure than an effervescent country vicar" with his jerky step.

Toward the end of his life he began to have "a very peculiar, yet not very uncommon, optical delusion, which takes the form of seeing moving fortifications." He needed rest badly, but he kept on working, though he saw fewer people, and went to the theatre (which he liked exceedingly) almost never. He knew everybody of importance: writers—Ruskin, Tennyson, the Rossettis; actresses—the Terry sisters; scientists, churchmen, and men of affairs. He died at Guilford of influenza, but his memory is appropriately kept alive by perpetual public endowment of a cot in the Children's Hospital, Great Ormond Street, London.

Carroll "was an interesting but erratic genius," as Henry Holiday, the illustrator of *Sylvie and Bruno,* said. He was full of ingenious ideas even in his youth, when he liked "the *look* of logarithms"; he wrote on horse-race betting odds; he was constantly inventing puzzles and corresponding with strangers about mathematics. He was full of a tremendous reverence for sacred subjects, and would leave a theatre if a joke on such matters was made in the play. He is almost the only male

writer to have written for girls; *Sylvie and Bruno* was his only concession to boys, of whom he was very wary. *Alice in Wonderland* has been universally praised because it "changed the whole cast of children's literature, but he founded, not followed, a gracious type. . . " It was "a spiritual volcano of children's books." (Harvey Darton). Perhaps the most penetrating analysis of *Alice's* position in children's literature is the novelist Sir Walter Besant's remark that "it admits us into a state of being which, until is was written, was not only unexplored but undiscovered."   v. m.

PRINCIPAL WORKS: *Juvenile*—Alice's Adventures in Wonderland, 1865; Through the Looking Glass, 1871; The Hunting of the Snark, 1876; Rhyme? and Reason? 1883; A Tangled Tale, 1885; Sylvie and Bruno, 1889 and 1893. *Mathematical*—Syllabus of Plane Algebraical Geometry, 1860; Elementary Treatise on Determinants, 1867; Euclid, Book Five, Proved Algebraically, 1874; Euclid and His Modern Rivals, 1879; Curiosa Mathematica 1888.

ABOUT: Collingwood, S. D. The Life and Letters of Lewis Carroll; Darton, F. J. H. Children's Books in England; De La Mare, W. Lewis Carroll; Dodgson, C. L. The Russian Journal (see Introduction by J. F. McDermott).

CARRUTHERS, ROBERT (November 5, 1799-May 26, 1878), Scottish biographer and editor, was born in Dumfries, son of a farmer. With little formal education, he was apprenticed to a bookseller, and later became master of a national school at Huntindon. While there, he wrote the only history of the town, in 1824. In 1828 he became editor of the *Inverness Courier,* a position he retained for the remainder of his life—or for half a century. He became proprietor of the paper in 1831, and made it a highly popular journal. In politics he was a moderate liberal. He was a figure of note in his time and was given a public funeral.

Though Carruthers wrote most of the original matter in Chambers' *Cyclopaedia of English Literature* (1843-44), and many biographies for the eighth edition of the *Encyclopaedia Britannica,* his chief interest as a writer was in the poet Pope. He edited Pope's works, made many corrections in and additions to former editions, and wrote the standard biography of the poet.

PRINCIPAL WORKS: A Highland Note-book, 1843; Life of Alexander Pope, 1857.

"CARTON, R. C." See CRITCHETT, RICHARD CLAUDE

CARY, HENRY FRANCIS (December 6, 1772-August 14, 1844), poet, cleric, and translator, was born at Gibralter where his father, an army captain, was stationed. His paternal grandfather was Mordecai Cary, bishop of Killala.

The family settled at Cannock, Staffordshire, and Henry Francis attended several grammar schools, including Rugby (1783-85), Sutton Coldfield, and Birmingham. At the age of fifteen he published an ode to Lord Heathfield on his defence of Gibralter. This began his literary career and led to his becoming a contributor to the *Gentleman's Magazine*, after 1788. In the next year appeared his first volume, *Sonnets and Odes*. In April 1790 he entered Christ Church College, Oxford, from which he was graduated A.B. in 1794. He took his M.A. in 1796 and was ordained.

He married, in 1796, the daughter of James Ormsby of Sandymount, near Dublin. In the next year he received the living of Abbott's Bromley, Staffordshire, a place he held until his death. Three years later he moved to Kingsbury, Warwickshire, where he held the living and where he began his famous translation of the three books of Dante's *Divine Comedy*.

In 1805 his translation of the *Inferno* appeared and soon afterwards Cary moved to London, where he became reader at Berkeley Chapel. Somewhat later he was lecturer at Chiswick and curate at the Savoy. The death in 1807 of his youngest daughter caused a nervous disorder which bordered on insanity; it was to afflict him at intervals throughout his life. In May 1812 he finished the complete Dante translation. As *Divina Commedia* it appeared in 1814, published at Cary's expense because the *Inferno* had not proved a good investment. The *Divina Commedia* was already selling almost as slowly as the earlier volume when an accident changed the course of its sale and of Cary's literary name. Vacationing at Littlehampton, Sussex, Cary was in the habit of declaiming and discussing Homer with his son on their morning walks along the beach. One morning a stroller stepped up to Cary and said, "Sir, yours is a face I *should* know: I am Samuel Taylor Coleridge." The walk ended later at Cary's dinner table. There Coleridge heard of the Dante and borrowed a copy to take home. Returning it next day, he was able "to recite whole pages." In 1818 Coleridge lectured in London on Dante, and he read freely from Cary's translation. The result was a second edition in 1819 (two more came during Cary's lifetime). Another fortunate circumstance aided the book to take its present high place in literature. This was Tom Moore's kindness in bringing the attention of Samuel Rogers to the work. Rogers took care to supplement Ugo Foscolo's review in the *Edinburgh Review*.

Through Coleridge, Cary met Charles Lamb and became intimate with his circle and that of the publisher, John Taylor. From 1823 to 1834 Lamb's letters are strewn with jocular

HENRY FRANCIS CARY

notes and invitations to Cary, and echoes of many conversations. Through these associations Cary became a contributor to the *London Magazine*, his essays in it including his work on the early French poets. For these Cary collected material in France in 1821. In 1824 his translation of *The Birds* (Aristophanes) appeared, and his *Odes* of Pindar followed ten years later.

Meanwhile, in 1826, Cary was appointed assistant-librarian at the British Museum, and held the place eleven years. His position gave him residence at Montague House, and it was from this house that Lamb made his intoxicated departure for which he so gracefully apologized in a letter to Cary. His duty at the Museum was chiefly the cataloging of new purchases and "acquisitions by copyright," a congenial enough task for one with so deep a love of books and so intense a diffidence. In his leisure he continued to write, edit, read, and translate, keeping a meticulous journal of his occupations. As time went on, he felt slighted at his failure to become Keeper of the Printed Books, the appointment being his in the normal sequence of promotions. But a foreigner, Antonio Panizzi, was appointed, and Cary was hurt. His health was not equal to the work involved, for he had had a severe attack of delirium in 1832 at his wife's death and had not entirely recovered his health after traveling abroad. But his discomfort was increased by the fact that his retirement did not bring a pension. A Crown pension of £200, secured chiefly through Samuel Rogers, brought timely appreciation of Cary's work.

Cary died at Willesden and was buried in Westminster Abbey, lying next to Samuel Johnson.

He was gracious and kindly, sympathetic of expression, sensitive and shy, slow in his movements, preoccupied a little with his work. He was a voluminous reader in many languages, painstaking and thoughtful.

Cary's place in literature is high in the nineteenth century Dante revival. His literary reputation rests almost entirely upon his translation of Dante, a project whose inception can be traced to 1796 at Christ Church. In a letter to Anna Seward, "the Swan of Lichfield," he reveals the embryo of his lifelong devotion to Dante. At college he was absorbed in the subject and in the language, and he gave a full twelve years of his leisure to the translation, using English blank verse. Popular recognition came slowly, but it has been substantial. C. E. Norton points out that most Dante translations see one edition, whereas Cary's had twenty-seven before 1900. Coleridge, Rogers, Moore, Foscolo, the *Edinburgh* and the *Quarterly* reviews helped the work to find its place. Other translations are perhaps as good, but Cary's was the first to preserve Dante for the English reader in excellent verse. It is not a translation that will serve the research scholar, but it is a work of great talent and spiritual (if not verbal) accuracy. Cary's interpretation of Dante is remarkably penetrating, though he did not achieve equally happy results with other poets whom he edited. He left unfinished a book of poems and a translation of Valerius Flaccus.   D. F. A.

PRINCIPAL WORKS: *Poetry*—Ode to General Kosciusko, 1797; Sonnets and Odes, 1799; The Vision, 1805; Divina Commedia, 1814; The Birds, 1824; Odes of Pindar, 1834; Dante's Vision of Hell, 1871. *Prose*—Lives of the Early French Poets, 1846; Lives of English Poets: Johnson to Henry Kirke White, 1846.

ABOUT: Cary, H. C. Memoirs of the Rev. Henry Francis Cary; Edwards, E. Lives of the Founders of the British Museum; Hall, S. C. Retrospect of a Long Life; Lamb, C. Letters; Macaulay, T. B. Criticisms on the Principles of Italian Writers; Saintsbury, G. A History of Nineteenth Century Literature.

CHALMERS, THOMAS (March 17, 1780-May 30, 1847), Scottish divine and philosopher, was born in Fifeshire, the sixth of fourteen children of a merchant. He was educated at the University of St. Andrews, where at first he was noted more for his high spirits and idleness than for his studiousness. A passion for mathematics made a student of him. He had always wanted to be a minister, but in 1803, in his first church, at Kilmeny, Fife, he preferred science to divinity, and lectured on chemistry at his alma mater. His other great interest was in the condition of the poor.

From 1810 Chalmers became much more devout, and a strong evangelical; he had gone through a religious crisis, brought about partly by his writing of an article on Christianity for the *Edinburgh Encyclopaedia*. In 1815 he became minister of Tron parish, Glasgow, in a slum district. Here he became both famous and the fashionable rage as a preacher, while at the same time he organized his parish according to his system of dividing it into districts, with the church as the focus, giving relief by voluntary charity instead of a dole, and undertaking education through the church. In 1840, as minister of St. John's Parish, largest and poorest in Edinburgh, he further extended this system.

In 1816 Chalmers received an honorary D.D. from the University of Glasgow. From 1823 to 1828 he was professor of moral philosophy at the University of St. Andrews, and established the department of ethics. In the latter year he became professor of theology at the University of Edinburgh. In 1843 the Free Church arose as a schism from the Established Church of Scotland (over the issue of the election of ministers by the congregation) and Chalmers went out with other dissidents. He left the university and became principal of the New College (Free Church), Edinburgh.

In 1830 Chalmers became chaplain in ordinary at the Scottish Chapel Royal; in 1834 he became a fellow of the Royal Society of Edinburgh (he was vice-president the next year); and in 1835 received an honorary D.C.L. from Oxford. He died suddenly in his sleep, and half the population of Edinburgh is said to have attended his funeral.

His writings, largely published tracts and sermons, are vigorous, inspirational, and often brilliant. It was as a man and a preacher, however, that he achieved his fame.

PRINCIPAL WORKS: Commercial Discourses, 1817; Astronomical Discourses, 1817; Christian and Civic Economy of Large Towns, 1826; Political Economy, 1832; The Adaptation of External Nature to the Moral and Intellectual Constitution of Man, 1833; Institutes of Theology, 1846; Posthumous Sermons (ed. W. Hanna) 1847.

ABOUT: Blaikie, W. G. Thomas Chalmers; Hanna, W. Memoirs of Thomas Chalmers; Masson, D. Memories of Two Cities: Edinburgh and Aberdeen; Oliphant, M. O. Thomas Chalmers: Preacher, Philosopher, and Statesman.

CHAMBERS, ROBERT (July 10, 1802-March 17, 1871), poet, essayist, scientist, and publisher, was born at Peebles, the son of James and Jean (Gibson) Chambers.

A slight lameness (later overcome) inclined Robert to study, and in the local schools he showed unusual promise. He said, "At twelve I was deep not only in poetry and fiction, but in encyclopedias." In 1813 the family moved to Edinburgh and for three years Robert attended school and learned some Latin. Poverty made further education impossible, and in 1816, on leaving school, he

ROBERT CHAMBERS

relinquished all idea of entering the church. This period of his life he later called the "dark ages."

He taught a little, secured and lost two clerical positions, and finally at sixteen set up a bookstall in Leith Walk, moving later to better locations. William, the older brother, had been in this business since 1819, and, eventually, the two combined to form the publishing house of W. and R. Chambers.

Within ten years Chambers was well enough established to marry Anne Kirkwood (December 7, 1829). She died in 1863 and in 1867 he married the widow of his friend, Robert Frith. He traveled in the United States and made geologic tours in Canada and Scandinavia. But his large family of six daughters and three sons prevented his taking a prominent part, as did his brother, in local affairs and charity. However, his place was ultimately recognized by his election to the Athenaeum club of London and by an honorary degree from St. Andrews University. It was at St. Andrews that he died.

As publisher his "highest claim to distinction" was his success in giving a healthy tone to cheap literature. As writer, versatility was perhaps his greatest quality. Early in life he had become acquainted with Scott through his antiquarian works on Edinburgh. His life of Smollett was described by Carlyle as "vastly superior to anything that had ever been written about him before." His life of Burns was a real contribution to knowledge. But his greatest literary work was *Vestiges of the Natural History of Creation,* published anonymously in Manchester. The purpose of the anonymity (finally lifted in 1884) was to avoid financial disaster for his own firm and to escape the notoriety which such heterodox

views might have brought. Darwin's praise of the book as a pioneer in the subject of evolution was sincere. Other scientists viewed the work variously, but the tentative ascription of it to Lyell and others indicat s the success with which Chambers worked in a technical field. The heterodox views were probably sincere, for Chambers rented pews in two Edinburgh churches so that he might always be credited with attendance at the other.

Fair and striking in appearance, he was still grave enough to be taken in London for a clergyman. This mistaken conception of his profession used to "tickle him exceedingly." Though the first impression was not always genial, Chambers was well loved for his dry humor, his canniness, his kindly hospitality. He was conscientious almost to a fault, his devotion to the writing of his *Book of Days* nearly killing him. D. F. A.

PRINCIPAL WORKS: *Antiquities and History*—Fires Which Have Ocurred in Edinburgh, 1824; Traditions of Edinburgh, 1825; Walks in Edinburgh, 1825; History of the Rebellion: 1638-1660, 1828; History of the Rebellion of 1745, 1829; History of the British Empire, 1845; Book of Days, 1862-4. *Literature and Biography*—Illustrations of the Author of Waverly, 1822; Popular Rhymes of Scotland, 1826; Land of Burns, 1840; Cyclopedia of English Literature, 1844; Romantic Scotch Ballads, 1844; History of English Language and Literature, 1845; Life of Robert Burns, 1851; Edinburgh Papers, 1861; Songs of Scotland, 1862; Life of Smollett, 1867; Life of Scott, 1871. *Scientific*—Picture of Scotland, 1828; Vestiges of the Natural History of Creation, 1855; Explanation: A Sequel to Vestiges, 1845; Ancient Sea Margins, 1848; Tracings of the North of Europe, 1851; Tracings of Iceland and the Faröe Islands, 1856; Domestic Animals of Scotland, 1859-61; The Thrieplands of Fingask, 1880.

ABOUT: Chambers, R. Vestiges of Creation (see Preface by Alexander Ireland); Chambers, W. Memoirs of Robert Chambers; Payn, J. Some Literary Recollections; Walker, H. The Literature of the Victorian Era.

CHAMIER, FREDERICK (1796-November 1, 1870), novelist, was the son of a member of council for the Madras presidency. His maternal grandfather was an admiral, and he himself followed the sea. He entered the Royal Navy in 1808, and was made lieutenant in 1815, serving in the Mediterranean and the West Indies. In 1826 he was appointed commander of the sloop Britomart, but after bringing his home in 1827 he received no further commands, and was put on the retired list in 1833. In 1856 he was given the rank of captain. In 1832 he had married Elizabeth Sloane, by whom he had one daughter.

After retiring from the navy, Chamier settled near Waltham Abbey and devoted himself to writing. He produced a number of sea stories, once very popular, especially among boys, which are open imitations of Marryat, very far behind their model. He also edited and continued James' *Naval History,* and wrote on the French revolution of 1848 and on his Continental travels—this last in a heavily facetious style.

PRINCIPAL WORKS: The Life of a Sailor, 1832; Ben Brace, 1836; The Arethusa, 1837; Jack Adams, 1838; Tom Bowline, 1841.
ABOUT: London Times November 2, 1870.

CHEADLE, WALTER BUTLER (October 15, 1835-March 25, 1910), physician and travel writer, was born in Lancashire, where his father was a vicar. He was educated at Gonville and Caius College, Cambridge, receiving his B.A. in 1859, his M.B. in 1861. He also studied medicine at St. George's Hospital, London.

In 1862 Cheadle went as physician with the expedition of William Fitzwilliam, Viscount Milton, to explore western Canada. The trip lasted two years, and the trail then blazed is now the route of the Canadian Pacific Railway. The book produced jointly by Cheadle and Viscount Milton (but all the actual writing done by the former), *The North-West Passage by Land,* is Cheadle's only nonmedical writing. It is a classic of its genre, describing vividly the hardships of the expedition and the courage of its members.

In 1865 Cheadle, back in England, received his M.A. and M.D. from Cambridge, and became a member of the Royal College of Physicians (fellow in 1870). He rose in his profession until he became dean of the medical school of St. Mary's Hospital, and was on its staff, chiefly as dermatologist, until 1904. He was married twice, in 1866 to Anne Murgatroyd, by whom he had four sons, and, after her death, to Emily Mansel in 1892. She also predeceased him. In 1884 he went to Canada for a meeting of the British Association for the Advancement of Science, and contracted dysentery. He was never well again, though he continued to practise until near his death.

Cheadle was a reserved and dignified man, a thorough liberal, especially active in the cause of woman doctors. His chief writing, outside his one travel book, was in the field of children's diseases.

PRINCIPAL WORK: The North-West Passage by Land (with Viscount Milton) 1865.
ABOUT: British Medical Journal April 9, 1910; Lancet April 2, 1910.

CHESNEY, SIR GEORGE TOMKINS (April 30, 1830-March 31, 1895), novelist, was born in Devonshire in a family of army officers—his father, his brother, his uncle, and himself. He was educated in private schools and intended for a medical career, but on receiving an Indian cadetship he entered the military college of the East India Company, at Addiscombe, in 1847. He became a second lieutenant in the Bengal engineers in Decem-

ber, 1848, and gradually advanced in rank until 1892, when he was made a general.

In 1850 he went to India, and was in the mutiny which culminated in the siege of Delhi, at which he was wounded. He then became president of the engineering college at Calcutta. In 1855 he married Annie Louisa Palmer, of Bengal, four sons and three daughters being born of the marriage. In 1868 Chesney helped to establish the Royal Indian Civil Engineering College, at Staines. He was recalled from India to be its first president in 1871. In 1880 he returned to India as secretary of the military department, and from 1886 to 1891 he was a member of the governor-general's council. He was made Knight Commander of the Bath in 1890. The next year he returned to England permanently, and entered Parliament as a conservative in 1892.

Chesney's first fiction, *The Battle of Dorking,* appeared in *Blackwood's* and later was published as a book. It is an imaginary account of an enemy raid on England, and advocates a volunteer army for national defense. His best known novel is *The Dilemma,* which recites the story of the mutiny which he himself experienced. He died in London, suddenly, of angina pectoris, at sixty-five.

PRINCIPAL WORKS: The Battle of Dorking, 1871; The True Reformer, 1874; The Dilemma, 1876; The New Ordeal, 1879; The Private Secretary, 1881; The Lesters, 1893.
ABOUT: London Times April 1, 1895.

CHEYNE, THOMAS KELLY (September 18, 1841-February 16, 1915), Biblical critic, was born in London, where his father was master at Christ's Hospital. He was educated at the Merchant Tailors' School, at Magdalen and Worcester Colleges, Oxford, and at the University of Göttingen. He took holy orders in 1864, and became vice-principal of St. Edmund Hall. From 1868 to 1882 he was a fellow of Balliol; in the latter year he married Frances Godfrey, who died in 1907. In 1911 he married again, his second wife being Elizabeth Gibson. There were no children by either marriage.

Cheyne was rector at Tendring, Essex, from 1880 to 1885, when he became Oriel professor of the interpretation of Scripture. He held this position until 1908. In 1884, with other scholars, he engaged in a revision of the Old Testament, and his special interest in this field dates from that time. He was in charge of the Biblical department of *The Academy,* and contributed to the ninth edition of the *Encyclopaedia Britannica.* He was co-editor of the *Encyclopaedia Biblica* from 1899 to 1903, producing a reference book still standard and unique in its province.

Cheyne was the initiator of the so-called higher criticism of the Bible in England. He was an extreme modernist, and did pioneer work of the utmost importance. About 1880, however, his views changed, and he grew increasingly evangelical, becoming a propagandist rather than a scientific critic. In the end he was practically an adherent of the Bahaist cult. The work he had already done, however, still stood, and is the foundation of a vast body of learning amplified by later commentators.

PRINCIPAL WORKS: The Book of Isaiah Chronologically Arranged, 1870; The Prophecies of Isaiah, 1880-81; Job and Solomon, 1887; The Book of Psalms, 1888; The Founders of Old Testament Criticism, 1893; Jewish Religious Life After the Exile, 1898.

ABOUT: London Times February 17, 1915.

CHORLEY, HENRY FOTHERGILL

(December 15, 1808-February 16, 1872), musical critic, poet, and novelist, was born in Lancashire of a Quaker family, his father being a lock manufacturer. The father failed in business and died soon after, and the boy was sent to live with his uncle, Dr. Rutter, in Liverpool. He was put to work in an office, but gave all his spare time to the study of music and literature, and some sympathetic cousins enabled him to try his hand at living by writing. In 1830 he began to contribute to the *Athenaeum*, and in 1833 he joined its staff as literary reviewer and musical director.

As a critic he was good but not great; his style was mannered and his tastes commonplace, but he was high-minded and made a serious effort to be unbiased. He was supersensitive and became irascible and churlish under the effect of constant failure of his plays, poems, and novels, all of which really showed high talent but never achieved any popularity. He ended up as an alcoholic, a disappointed man who had alienated most of his friends. He retired from *The Athenaeum* in 1868, and died very suddenly four years later.

Many of Chorley's books were written under the pseudonym of "Paul Bell." He was a prominent librettist for current operas. Both his verse and prose are graceful and witty, but highly artificial.

PRINCIPAL WORKS: Music and Manners in France and Germany 1841; Pomfret, 1845; Roccabella, 1859; The Prodigy, 1866.

ABOUT: Chorley, H. F. Autobiography (ed. by H. G. Hewlett); Chorley, H. F. Thirty Years' Musical Recollections.

CHURCH, RICHARD WILLIAM (April

25, 1815-December 9, 1890) essayist, biographer, historian, and cleric, was born at Lisbon, Portugal, the eldest son of John Dearman Church and Bromley Caroline Metzener Church. Until 1828 the family lived in Florence, Italy, removing after the father's death to Bath. Church was educated at Leghorn, Exeter, Redlands, and Wadham. His mother's marriage to Thomas Crokat of Leghorn brought Church into association with

RICHARD WILLIAM CHURCH

George Moberly, later bishop of Salisbury, whose influence on Church's life was enormous. Graduated in 1836, Church two years later became fellow of Oriel and was ordained. "There is such a moral beauty about Church," a friend said in this year.

In 1835 Church had met Keble and Newman; he now became a definite disciple of the latter, who was actively associated with the Tractarian movement. In 1841 Church resigned the Oriel tutorship and made a translation of St. Cyril for Pusey's *Library of the Fathers*. His junior proctorship is significant chiefly for the brave refusal to censure Ward's *Tract 90*. In 1846 Church, with some friends, started a newspaper, *The Guardian*; Church's contributions to this were later collected and published as *Occasional Papers*. The next year he went abroad, writing articles for the *Christian Remembrancer* (collected as *Essays and Reviews*).

Upon his return he again held the Oriel tutorship, but resigned to marry (July 5, 1853) Helen Frances Bennett, a niece of Moberly's. He took the living of Whatley, Somersetshire, where he remained until 1871, refusing a crown appointment to a canonry at Worcester. He preached periodically at Oxford, and in 1869 became chaplain to Bishop Moberly.

In 1871, on Gladstone's nomination, Church became Dean of St. Paul's. It was a difficult task, at first entirely uncongenial to Church, who hated official business and ceremony, preferring rural quiet and study. His success in waking St. Paul's "from its long slumber" and in administering his office was so remarkable that in 1882 he was considered for the Archbishopric of Canterbury. His health prevented acceptance of the appointment, but he continued to hold the confidence of leading statesmen until his death at Dover. Three children survived him, the only son, Frederick, having died in 1888. Church's outlook was cosmopolitan and tolerant, his judgment remarkably profound, his piety "passionate." His style, formed largely, he said, by translating, was simple, vigorous, masterly in its control of details. His biography of Spenser is still a classic, but his literary masterpiece is undoubtedly his history, *The Oxford Movement,* a record, as he said, "that one who lived with them, and lived beyond most of them, believed in the reality of their goodness and height of character, and still looks back with deepest reverence to those forgotten men as the champions to whose teaching and example he owes an infinite debt." Newman was his spiritual and literary father.

Church was tall, but slightly stooped; his long thin hair accentuated a delicate face. He was sensitive, devout, genial, and extremely magnetic, drawing statesmen and parishioners alike to him in sympathetic personal relationships.　　　　　　　　　　　　D. F. A.

PRINCIPAL WORKS: *Biography*—Life of St. Wulfstan, 1844; Saint Anselm, 1870; Spenser, 1879; Bacon, 1884; Elizabeth, 1888: *Essays and Lectures*—Essays and Reviews, 1854; Montaigne, 1857; Civilization Before and After Christianity, 1872; On Some Influences of Christianity Upon National Character, 1873; The Sacred Poetry of Early Religions, 1874; Pascal, 1875; Bishop Andrewes, 1877; Human Life and Its Conditions, 1878; Essay on Dante, 1878; The Gifts of Civilization, 1880; The Relation Between Church and State, 1881; The Discipline of the Christian Character, 1885; Occasional Papers, 1897. *History*—The Beginning of the Middle Ages, 1877; The Oxford Movement, 1891. *Sermons and Miscellaneous*—Sermons Preached Before the University of Oxford, 1869; Advent Sermons, 1886; The Christian Church, 1887; Miscellaneous Writing, 1888; Cathedral and University Sermons, 1892; Village Sermons (3 vols.) 1892-7; Message of Peace, 1895; Pascal, 1895.

ABOUT: Cecil, A. Six Oxford Thinkers; Church, M. C. Life and Letters of Dean Church; Donaldson, A. B. Five Great Oxford Leaders; Holland, H. S. Personal Studies; Lathbury, D. C. Dean Church; Illustrated London News 97:740 December 13, 1891; Review of Reviews 3:20 January, 1891.

CLARE, JOHN (July 13, 1793-May 20, 1864), poet, was born in the village of Helpston in Northamptonshire, the son of a poor farmer named Parker Clare, who could scarcely read. His mother, formerly Ann Stimson of the nearby town of Castor, did not even know her letters. John's twin sister died shortly after birth, as did another sister, Elizabeth, although a third, named Sophy, lived to grow up along with John. As children John and Sophy spent long hours in the woods and fields together, playing with boats made of mushrooms, gathering cowslip greens, or talking of fairies. John, was fond too, of listening to tales of witches told by his mother on winter evenings.

His education was limited to three months of the year, first in a dame-school in the village, afterwards at a school in Glinton, where he was taught by a Mr. Seaton. The remaining months he spent on the heath tending the geese and the sheep. While he was still in school he became infatuated with Mary Joyce, daughter of a well-to-do Glinton farmer, who broke off the affair. Clare, however, never forgot this first love of his. When he was twelve he was obliged to give up day-school to learn a trade, though he did attend a night-school.

He began work as a team-leader on the farm of John Turnill, who helped the boy with his lessons. In his spare time he wrote verses any extra money he spent on books. At fourteen he stopped going to night school and worked here and there in the hayfields until finally he found a job at Blue Bell Inn tending cattle for Francis Gregory, the owner. This work lasted for a year, and, since Gregory was rather indulgent, Clare was able to continue his studies and his writing of verse. Thomson's *Seasons* was his favorite reading. At the end of his term at the inn Clare secured a job as gardener for the Marquis of Exeter at Burghley House. Here he fell in with drunken companions. But he soon tired of his work and in nine months went off with a companion, one George Cousins, to Newark, where he tried, unsuccessfully, to join the militia. Eventually he returned to his father's cottage at Helpston, although he actually did enlist in the army for a short period before 1814.

Such a wandering and desultory life fostered his gift for poetry. He liked, he said, to work in the fields because he had more time for thinking. He used to write down

JOHN CLARE

the thoughts upon the crown of his hat. He made friends, too, with the gypsies, and turned poacher for a time. Formerly he wrote simple poems about nature. Now he composed drinking songs. And an affection for Elizabeth Newbon followed his love for Mary Joyce.

Meanwhile Clare's father was relying on "parish bounty" for support. Clare tried hard to find permanent employment. At one time he found work in a lime-kiln in Rutlandshire; at another he was gardener at the New Inn, Casterton, where he wrote his "Elegy on the Ruins of Pickworth," and fell in love again, this time with Martha (or Patty) Turner.

With the publication of his first book, which was entitled *Poems Descriptive of Rural Life and Scenery,* "by John Clare, a Northampshire peasant" (1820) Clare found himself famous over night. The book created a veritable furor. Admirers swarmed into the country, curious to see the new "peasant poet." Through the book Clare met his future patron, Lord Radstock, and Mrs. Emmerson of London, who became a life-long friend. He was praised in no small terms by such journals as the *Quarterly Review* and the *London Magazine.*

In March 1820 Clare set out for his first trip to London, where he was royally entertained. He just missed hearing Madame Vestris sing his poem, "The Meeting," but he met J. H. Reynolds, the poet, and H. F. Carey, the translator of Dante. And he sat for a portrait by Hilton, the painter. On March 16 he was married to Martha Turner, for, through the instrumentality of his patron, Lord Radstock, he was now assured of a settled income. His second volume of verse, *The Village Minstrel,* came out the next year.

Married life, however, brought its difficulties. His family grew rapidly. A first daughter was born in June, 1820; another daughter followed in 1822. He needed money badly and he had frequent quarrels with his publishers. Such were the worries that served to heighten his melancholy, to stir up fears and phantasies in his mind. Nevertheless, he made a second trip to London in 1822. This time he met Lamb and Hazlitt, who were fellow authors on the *London Magazine,* to which he was a regular contributor. A first son, Frederick, was born in January 1824, shortly before Clare made a third trip to London, this time in search of health. He enjoyed sightseeing with the artist Edward Rippingille whom he had met in 1822. His health, however did not improve either in town or back at home among his books or at work in his garden, where he was an enthusiastic naturalist. But he still found strength enough to write, and he kept the annuals supplied with his verses. His next volume of poetry, *The Shepherd's Calendar,* came out in 1827.

But the book was not a financial success. His health was growing steadily worse. His family was larger. Two more children were born. In order to make ends meet he took to hawking his poems from house to house. In 1832, however, his luck changed when he was offered a cottage in Northborough. Clare's hopes for the future were brighter. But even in this new house he experienced strange visions in which his old love, Mary Joyce, figured large. The attacks did not stop, and in June 1837 Clare entered Dr. Matthew Allen's asylum in Epping Forest as a mental patient. Since Allen was a man of enlightenment, Clare was allowed to continue his writing and to work in the fields. Under such care he seemed to show improvement, but he grew homesick. In July 1841 he escaped and found his way home on foot. By December of the same year, however, he was again committed, this time to an asylum in Northampton, where he spent his last years receiving visitors and writing a great mass of so-called "asylum poems." But he grew less and less robust as the years passed, until, finally, on May 10, 1864, he suffered a stroke. Ten days later he died and was carried back to Helpston for burial.

In appearance Clare was short, "with keen, eager eyes, high forehead, long hair, falling down in wild and almost grotesque fashion over his shoulders." Indeed, to an urbane man like Bryan Waller Procter, the poet, he was "thoroughly rustic." To Charles Lamb, the essayist, on the other hand, he was "Clarissimus" and "Princely Clare." But to all he was the "peasant poet."

As such he achieved his fame, which, however, dwindled toward the close of his life only to rise again after his death and continue to the present. His poetry has been compared with that of Robert Burns, but actually his work was more than mere imitation, for his poems are filled with his own minute and exact descriptions of nature. Often he worked out his own rhyme schemes and his own rhythm; it is for such observation and such originality that he is known today. B. D. S.

PRINCIPAL WORKS: *Poetry*—Poems Descriptive of Rural Life and Scenery, 1820; The Village Minstrel and Other Poems, 1821; The Shepherd's Calendar, 1827; The Rural Muse, 1835; Poems (ed. by A. Symons) 1908; Poems Chiefly From Manuscript, 1920; Madrigals & Chronicles, 1924; Poems (ed. by J. W. Tibble) 1935. *Prose*—Sketches in the Life of John Clare, 1931.

ABOUT: Cherry, J. L. Life and Remains of John Clare; Clare, J. Poems (see Introduction by A. Simons to 1906 ed.); Clare, J. Poems Chiefly From Manuscript (see Introduction by E. Blunden); Martin, F. The Life of John Clare; Tibble, J. W. & A. John Clare.

"CLARIBEL." See BARNARD, MRS. CHARLES

CLARKE, EDWARD DANIEL (June 5, 1769-March 9, 1822), collector and travel writer, was the son of a clergyman who was also a noted traveler and author, and the grandson of an antiquary. He was educated at Jesus College, Cambridge, taking his B. A. in 1790 and his M.A. in 1794. He became a private tutor and companion, traveling with his charges, and beginning in 1792 his famous mineral collection. In 1798 he came back to Jesus College as a fellow, but in 1799 began a tour of three years in Russia, Scandinavia, Palestine, and Greece, constantly adding to his collection. In 1805 he became senior tutor at Jesus, and remained there for a year, when he married Angelica Rush, by whom he had five sons and two daughters. He was appointed to two college livings, at Harlton and Yeldham, Essex, and held both until his death. In 1807 he lectured on mineralogy at Cambridge, and the next year was made professor of mineralogy. In 1817 he became librarian of Cambridge, but his health failed and he resigned the office, though he continued to lecture until 1821. His mineral collection was bought by Cambridge at his death for £1,500; his manuscripts had already been sold to Oxford. He was a competent but not distinguished writer.

PRINCIPAL WORKS: The Tomb of Alexander, 1803; Travels in Europe, Asia, and Africa (11 vols.) 1810-23; The Gas Blowpipe, 1819.

ABOUT: Otter, W. Life and Remains of E. D. Clarke.

CLARKE, HENRY BUTLER (November 9, 1863-September 10, 1904), historian, was born in Staffordshire, the son of a clergyman. He was privately educated in Yorkshire and at St. Jean-de-Luz, on the Spanish border, where his father was English chaplain. Being a very delicate child, he was thought too frail for school. In 1883 he traveled in Germany with a private pupil. In 1885 he entered Wadham College, Oxford. From 1890 to 1892 he was Taylorian teacher of Spanish at Oxford. In 1891 he built a house at St. Jean-de-Luz, and though in 1894 he was made a fellow of St. John's College, he spent half the year there henceforth, and the other half at Oxford. He was unmarried.

Keenly interested in Spanish from boyhood, he resolved to give twenty years to the study of the early history of Spanish civilization. But his career was nearly at an end. Handsome, charming, a brilliant conversationalist, Clarke was nevertheless a lifelong neurasthenic, with occasional spells of actual melancholia. In 1904, while at St. Jean-de-Luz, he suffered one of these seizures, and shot himself.

His *History of Spanish Literature* is a valuable critical work, and his *Modern Spain* was at the time of its writing the best work on the subject. Had his nervous organization been less deranged, he might have become the foremost English historian of Spain, for he was only forty-one at the time of his suicide.

PRINCIPAL WORKS: Spanish Grammar, 1892; History of Spanish Literature, 1893; The Cid Campeador, 1897; Modern Spain, 1906.

ABOUT: Clarke, H. B. Modern Spain (see Memoir).

CLARKE, MARCUS ("Andrew Hislop") (April 24, 1846-August 2, 1881), novelist, and dramatist, was born in London, the only child of a barrister. He went to Victoria in 1863, and remained in Australia for the rest of his life. In 1867 he joined the staff of the *Melbourne Argus*, and eventually became its dramatic critic. In 1868 he married Marion Dunn, daughter of a well known comedian.

Clarke wrote many plays, the best known of which is *Plot*, and annual pantomimes for the Melbourne theaters. One of them, *Twinkle, Twinkle, Little Star*, has been called "the best ever given in Australia." The work which brought him his widest celebrity, however, was the novel, *For the Term of His Natural Life*, a powerful, sympathetic book portraying the lot of an Australian convict, and a strong indictment of the transportation system. He also published several volumes of verse.

PRINCIPAL WORKS: The Peripatetic Philosopher, 1868; Long Odds, 1869; For the Term of His Natural Life, 1874.

ABOUT: Mackinnon, H. The Marcus Clarke Memorial Volume.

CLARKSON, THOMAS (March 28, 1760-September 26, 1846), anti-slavery writer, was born at Wisbeach, where his father was headmaster of the grammar school. He was educated at St. Paul's School and at St. John's College, Cambridge, where he received his B.A. in 1883. A prize for a Latin essay against slavery aroused his lifelong interest in abolition, intensified by meeting William Wilberforce, chief of the anti-slavery forces. In 1787 he became one of a committee, nearly all Quakers but himself, for the suppression of the slave trade. He was ordained deacon, but gave all his time to his cause and seldom preached. He traveled throughout England and France investigating and speaking, and spent most of his fortune. His health failed and he had to retire. Wilberforce raised a subscription fund for his support, and in 1803 he was back at work again. In 1808 the slave trade was abolished, but slavery was not wiped out in all British territory until 1833. In 1818 Clarkson visited Russia for the cause. He became blind from cataracts, but recovered his sight by an operation in 1836. In 1839 he was admitted to the freedom of the city of London. His last public appearance was in 1840 at an anti-slavery convention. He had already retired to Ipswich, where he lived till his death at eighty-six. He was married, his wife's maiden name being Catherine Buck. Their only son, a police magistrate, was accidentally killed in 1837.

PRINCIPAL WORKS: Essay on the Slavery and Commerce of the Human Species, 1786; History of the Rise, Progress, and Accomplishment of the Abolition of the African Slave Trade, 1808; Memoirs of the Private and Public Life of William Penn, 1809; The Cries of Africa to the Inhabitants of Europe, 1812.

ABOUT: Taylor, T. Biographical Sketch of Thomas Clarkson; Elmes, J. Thomas Clarkson.

CLERKE, AGNES MARY (February 10, 1842-January 20, 1907), Irish scientific writer, was born in County Cork. Her father was a bank manager, a classical scholar, and an amateur astronomer, who first interested both Agnes and her older sister ELLEN MARY (later a poet and novelist) in the study of the stars. She was educated entirely at home, but better educated than in many a school. In 1861 the family moved to Dublin, and in 1863 to Queenstown. She spent 1866 and 1867 in Italy, contributing from there the first of many articles to the *Edinburgh Review,* her subject being "Copernicus in Italy." In 1877 the Clerkes (the name was pronounced "Clark") moved to London. Miss Clerke's first book, the *Popular History of Astronomy,* had a wide circulation. It filled a great need and at once became a standard work. It was not until 1888, however, that she had any practical experience of astronomical methods, during a visit to the observatory at the Cape of Good Hope. She contributed articles on astronomy to the *Encyclopaedia Britannica,* and lives of astronomers to the *Dictionary of National Biography.* In 1892 she won a £100 prize from the Royal Institute, and in 1903 was one of the few women to be made honorary members of the Royal Astronomical Society. She never lost her interest in general literature, publishing *Familiar Studies in Homer* in 1892, and she was a talented musician. She never married. She died in London of pneumonia at nearly seventy-five.

PRINCIPAL WORKS: Popular History of Astronomy, 1885; The Systems of the Stars, 1890; Problems in Astrophysics, 1903.

ABOUT: Huggins, Lady. An Appreciation of Agnes Mary and Ellen Mary Clerke (Foreword by A. St. J. Clerke).

CLIFFORD, WILLIAM KINGDON (May 4, 1845-March 3, 1879), philosopher, was born at Exeter. He was a very precocious child, showing his mathematical genius in early youth. In 1860 he entered King's College London, and in 1863, Trinity College, Cambridge. Before he was twenty he was engaged in independent research. He was a markedly fine gymnast. In religion, originally a high churchman, his views were turned by study of Darwin and Spencer, and he was active in the early Darwinian controversies.

In 1868 Clifford became a fellow of Trinity, and remained in residence till 1871, though in 1870 he went as a member of the English Eclipse Expedition that was wrecked off the coast of Catania. In 1871 he was made professor of applied mathematics at University College, London. An excellent lecturer and extemporaneous speaker, he was also active in the Sunday Lecture Society. In 1874 he became a Fellow of the Royal Society, having modestly refused an earlier nomination. From 1874 he was a prominent member of the Metaphysical Society. In 1875 he married Lucy Lane, of a Barbados family, and had two daughters by her.

It was soon apparent that Clifford was suffering from tuberculosis. Most of the time he worked purely "on his nerves." In 1876 he had to take six months' leave of absence in Algiers and Spain, and in 1878 another collapse sent him to the Mediterranean. He returned to England in August, but within a month was obliged to give up again. His chair was held for him, and he went to Madeira, but he died there the following March. He is buried in Highgate Cemetery, London.

Vivacious, unassuming, affectionate, almost childlike in his naiveté, Clifford was a most lovable character. Sometimes he was accused of levity, but his kindliness won him universal friendship. He was not a materialist, but an "idealist monist" of the school of the great philosopher Spinoza. The two foundations of his philosophy are what he called "mindstuff" and "the tribal self." In English mathematics he marked an epoch. He is unusually readable for a philosopher, though most of his best work was left unfinished. After his death his widow, as MRS. W. K. CLIFFORD, became a well known novelist and dramatist.

PRINCIPAL WORKS: Seeing and Thinking, 1879; Lectures and Essays (ed. by F. Pollock and L. Stephen) 1879; Elements of Dynamics, 1879-87; Mathematical Fragments, 1881; Mathematical Papers (ed. by R. Tucker) 1882; Common Sense and the Exact Sciences (ed. by K. Pearson) 1885.

ABOUT: Clifford, W. K. Lectures and Essays (see Life by F. Pollock); Clifford, W. K. Mathematical Papers (see Introduction by J. S. Smith).

CLIVE, CAROLINE ARCHER (June 24, 1801-July 13, 1873), poet and novelist, was the daughter of the member of Parliament for Worcester, but was born in London. Her maiden name was Meysey-Wigley. She was educated at home, and in 1840 married the Rev. Archer Clive, by whom she had one son and one daughter. She was an invalid for many years before her death, but continued to write. She died horribly when her clothing caught fire as she sat surrounded by books and papers.

Most of Mrs. Clive's work was published under the pseudonym of "V." Her poems are graceful but negligible. Her best known novel, *Paul Ferrol*, was a great popular success, and aroused so much controversy that she published a sequel; it is powerful and imaginative, and highly sensational.

PRINCIPAL WORKS: IX Poems by V, 1840; Paul Ferroll, 1855; Why Paul Ferrol Killed His Wife, 1860; Poems by V, 1872.

ABOUT: Athenaeum July 19, 1873; London Times July 16, 1873.

CLOSE, JOHN ("Poet Close") (1816-February 15, 1891), versifier, was the son of a butcher and Methodist preacher living at Gunnerside, Swaledale.

While still a boy, and apparently with no known formal education of any kind, Close began to issue little paper tracts of verse, and, although he had begun a career as a butcher, in 1846 he became a printer at Kirkby Stephen, in the Lake Country. His writings, while worthless, were numerous, and he honored his influential neighbors in them. Thanks to the influence of Lord Lonsdale, Lord Carlisle, and others, he was awarded (1860) a Civil List Pension of £50.

Close's utter incompetence and inadequacy as a poet were so obvious that this grant caused a scandal. The ridicule of the newspapers induced most of the "poet's" patrons to withdraw their support, and in 1861 the pension was stopped. In the same year, however, Close was given £100 from the royal bounty.

The "Poet Laureate to His Majesty the King of Grand Bonny," as Close called himself, was considerably disgruntled by his treatment at the hands of the government, and spent the rest of his life issuing and selling trashy verse, and complaining of his wrongs. He ran a stall convenient to the summer-tourist travel in the Lake Country, and he made money from sales to visitors, receiving also many letters of sympathy from all over England.

Close's comic-opera antics and general imbecility suggest a subnormal mentality. He circulated his verses through the mail. When the recipients made favorable comments and sent him money, "Poet Close" responded with praise. To others he applied ridicule. His animadversions, however, were not always legitimate; he used slander too freely, and on one occasion was held liable to the extent of £50 (despite the amazing allegation of his lawyer that Close's written statements were so obviously untrue that he should be acquitted) for damages he had inflicted upon a lady's character. When the plaintiff offered to waive the claim to money for a printed retraction, Close characteristically accepted the offer and made the public apology, then

JOHN CLOSE

complained of the injustice he had had to suffer because of his telling the truth. He seems not to have grasped the point of the merriment made over his doggerel; according to the obituary in the *Illustrated London News*, "He believed himself a poet to the last, and died an injured man." Close left a widow, two sons, and a daughter.

His works are the merest balderdash. "He had not a spark of literary talent of any kind," wrote Thomas Seccombe. "He may be termed a survival of the old packman-poet in the last stages of his degradation."

R. W. W.

WORKS: See above.

ABOUT: Close, J. Poet Close and His Pension; Close, J. The Wondrous Story of a Poet's Life!!; Hansard's Parliamentary Debates (3rd ser. Vol. 164); Illustrated London News 98:239 February 21, 1891; The Times February 17, 1891.

CLOUGH, ARTHUR HUGH (January 1, 1819-November 13, 1861), poet, was born at Liverpool, the second son of James Butler Clough, cotton merchant, and Anne (Perfect) Clough. His father, the first member of a distinguished family of Welsh origin to engage in commerce, moved when Arthur was four years old to Charleston, South Carolina, where the family resided until June 1836. On a visit to England in 1828 Arthur was left at school in Chester, whence he proceeded in the summer of 1829 to Rugby, then under Dr. Arnold, whose influence, nearly always overwhelming on impressionable pupils, was doubly powerful in Clough's case because home ties were absent.

He became the Doctor's favorite pupil. Though his two principal cares were "associating with fellows for their good" and "the publication and telling abroad of the merits

ARTHUR HUGH CLOUGH

of the school by means of the magazine," he won a scholarship open to the whole school at fourteen, became head of the Fifth Form at fifteen so that he had to wait a year to enter the Sixth Form, and was the only boy in the history of the school to win all the honors Rugby had to offer. Dr. Arnold was moved to break his rule and address Clough by name on Prize Day. In November 1836 the prize pupil crowned his career by winning the Balliol Scholarship. His perfections, moreover, extended to swimming and running, and he was declared in William Arnold's *Rules of Football* to have been the best goalkeeper on record. He preserved to the last the modesty and sweetness of disposition which were his most striking characteristics; more incredible still, he had a sense of humor.

At Oxford, where he went in October 1837, Clough was easily acknowledged foremost in a particularly brilliant group of Balliol scholars, soon to be joined by Dr. Arnold's son Matthew, whose *Thyrsis* commemorates his friendship with Clough. But the Oxford curriculum seemed only a continuation of the subjects to which he had applied himself so strenuously at Rugby; and the atmosphere of the Tractarian Movement, brought close to him by an intimacy with the brilliant Balliol tutor, William George Ward, leader of one of the two eventually "Romanizing" branches of the High Church party, was calculated to unsettle so earnest a Rugbeian; and in 1841 he shook the faith of the University in the reality not of his own gifts, but of academic honors, by receiving only a Second Class.

Having failed also to obtain a Balliol fellowship, Clough redeemed himself in the following year by passing the highest intellectual test in Oxford at that time and winning an Oriel fellowship, one of Dr. Arnold's last satisfactions before his sudden death in June. This severe blow was made heavier for Clough by the deaths of his brother George in America in October and of his father in the summer of 1843.

As tutor as well as fellow of Oriel, Clough passed five years in active teaching at Oxford until the vague dissatisfaction which had lingered since his undergraduate days came to a head over the question of subscribing to the Thirty-Nine Articles in the Book of Common Prayer. In 1848 he resigned, though without other means of support.

When it became known that a small volume by Clough would soon be published, Oxford expected an *apologia*. Instead appeared a seemingly frivolous production, *The Bothie of Toper-na-Fuôsich* (afterwards *Tober-na-Vuolich*), "A Long-Vacation pastoral" describing, in what Oxford unwillingly accepted as English hexameters, a reading party in Scotland.

Taking advantage of his new freedom, Clough now went abroad. After a month in Paris with Emerson whom he had recently met, he went on to Rome where he witnessed Mazzini's brief triumph and the siege by the French. The fruit of this sojourn was his long poem "Amours de Voyage," first published some years later (February-May 1858) in the *Atlantic Monthly*.

In the meantime he had been appointed Head of University Hall, a residence for students at the University of London, and took up his post in October 1849. After three years of a life which was not altogether congenial and not very remunerative, he resigned in October 1852 to emigrate to Cambridge, Massachusetts, where Emerson and other American friends urged him to try his fortune at tutoring and writing. Early in the following summer, however, an appointment as Examiner in the Education Office called him home. He began his duties in July 1853 and the following June was able to marry Miss Blanche Smith to whom he had long been engaged.

For the next six years Clough worked hard and apparently contentedly, varying his routine labors by a trip abroad in 1856 as secretary to a commission for reporting on military schools on the continent and spending himself freely to help in the work of Florence Nightingale, his wife's cousin.

Overwork, followed by the death in 1860 of his mother, to whom he had always been bound by strong ties of sympathy, hastened a decline in health. In February 1861 he went to Freshwater in the Isle of Wight, but failing to benefit, was advised to spend most of the following months abroad, first in Greece and then in the Pyrenees. In the autumn his wife joined him in Paris and they proceeded to Italy. By the time they reached Florence Clough was seriously ill with malarial fever. A stroke of paralysis ensued and on November 13 he died.

"Clough was five feet ten in height," writes William Allingham, "well made, inclining to burliness; he had a handsome frank face, dark-eyed, full-chinned and ruddy-complexioned, the nose being straight and rather short; his head, which was early bald, ran deep from front to back, and showed a graceful domed outline."

It is most often remembered that "his piping took a troubled sound"; but together with the natural gaiety so evident in *The Bothie* went a great sense of humor and a deep vein of satire. The Devil in his *Dipsychus* has been compared to Butler's Hudibras and Byron's Don Juan, and even suggests Goethe's Mephistopheles.

No full reproduction of the ms. of *Dipsychus* has yet been published, and many evidences in Clough's other poems of his satirical gifts and his humanity were omitted or altered by his wife in her edition, according to a note in the recent *Oxford Anthology of English Poetry* by Mr. H. F. Lowry, to whom Clough's descendants have now entrusted the whole of the poet's papers. Probably no Victorian poet was so free in his direct references to sex, to judge from samples of the omitted passages already published. Always the most responsive of friends, Clough's exaggerated demand for the complete sympathy of those to whom he was attached, which appears indirectly from Matthew Arnold's recently uncovered letters to him, sets his character in a more emotional light. Transparently sincere, unworldly, intensely high-minded and conscientious, and of an unusually independent intelligence, the root of his inaction seems not religious doubt, as so often stated, but moral certainty—a clear perception of the shams of the age and a refusal to compromise with them.   J. B. O.

PRINCIPAL WORKS: *Poetry*—The Longest Day, 1836; The Bothie of Toper-na-Fuôsich, 1848; Poems, 1862. *Prose*—Letters and Remains, 1865. *Works*—Poems and Prose Remains, 1869.

ABOUT: Allingham, W. A Diary; Arnold, M. Thyrsis; Arnold, M. On Translating Homer; Ehrsam, T. G. & Deily, R. H. Bibliographies of Twelve Victorian Poets; Lowry, H. F. The Letters of Matthew Arnold to Arthur Hugh Clough; Lowry, H. F. & Thorp, W. An Oxford Anthology of English Poetry; Shairp, J. C. Glen Desseray and Other Poems; Waddington, S. Arthur Hugh Clough: A Monograph; Ward, W. William George Ward and the Oxford Movement.

COBBE, FRANCES POWER (December 4, 1822-April 5, 1904), Irish writer on religion and philosophy, was born in Dublin. She was educated at home, except for two years in school at Brighton. Her family were strict evangelical Protestants, but she was unorthodox from girlhood, and for a time was an agnostic. Later she became a deist.

Her father died in 1856, and she traveled for two years in Italy and Greece. She made frequent visits to Italy thereafter, and was Italian correspondent of the London *Daily News*. Most of her life, however was given to philanthropy. In 1858 she worked with Mary Carpenter in Bristol in the "ragged schools" and the reformatories; from 1859 she devoted herself to workhouse philanthropy and the care of girls, which were her chief interests. She was also an early suffragist, a worker for university degrees for women, and an ardent anti-vivisectionist. From 1868 to 1875 she was on the staff of *The Echo*. She edited the works of the American abolitionist and preacher, Theodore Parker.

PRINCIPAL WORKS: The Theory of Intuitive Morals, 1855; Broken Lights, 1864; Studies of Ethical and Social Subjects, 1865; Dawning Lights, 1868; The Final Cause of Women, 1869; Doomed to Be Saved, 1874; The Scientific Spirit of the Age, 1888.

ABOUT: Chappell, J. Women of Worth; Cobbe, F. P. Life.

COBBETT, WILLIAM (March 9, 1762-June 18, 1835), political writer and reformer, was the son of a Surrey farm laborer, of pure peasant stock. His entire education was self-attained by reading. At thirteen he ran away from home to Windsor, where he worked in the gardens of George III. Returning to his home at Farnham four years later, he worked in the fields until 1783, when a sudden whim sent him to London, where he became a lawyer's clerk. No occupation could have been less suitable, and it is not surprising that after a year he had had enough of it and enlisted in the army.

He was sent with his regiment to Nova Scotia, where he rose to be sergeant major. There also he saw a pretty girl of thirteen, daughter of another non-commissioned officer's daughter, whom he determined to marry. Her name was Ann Reid. When her father's regiment was ordered home, Cobbett gave her all his savings, a hundred and fifty pounds, to ensure her comfort. (Soon after another pretty Canadian girl tempted him sorely, but he resisted the temptation and remained true to Ann.) When he too returned to England to be discharged, in 1791, he found Ann slaving as a servant, with his money untouched. They were married the next year, their long and fruitful union the only peaceful episode in Cobbett's stormy career.

During his army days he gave every spare minute to study, particularly of grammar. He also observed the graft indulged in by his officers, and no sooner was he discharged than he accused them of peculations and had them court martialed. He further aroused official wrath by being (though he denied it) undoubtedly part-author at least of a pamphlet, *The Soldier's Friend*, which advocated higher pay for privates. He soon found he had struck a wasps' nest; he himself was threatened with arrest, and he fled to France with his bride.

There he studied French, but the French Revolution was too much for his confused but very British views, so in 1792 he went to America, to Philadelphia, where he lived by teaching English to French refugees. No sooner was he there than he began to mix in politics, on the Federalist side, attacking Franklin and Paine in his two little magazines, *The Censor* and *Porcupine's Gazette* (his very appropriate pseudonym being "Peter Porcupine"). Unfortunately his extremely forthright journalism lacked common discretion, and involved him in so many libel suits that in 1800 he deemed it wise to return to England.

In London Cobbett founded a new paper, *The Porcupine*, violently anti-French. This lasted only a year, and was succeeded by the famous *Cobbett's Political Register*, which with one short interruption was published until his death, with fluctuating success and influence. At the same time he published reports of Parliamentary Debates and State Trials, and on the side ran a model farm near London.

By 1804 Cobbett's views, originally radical, then Tory, had become radical again. A consideration of the Irish question had persuaded him that he was wrong. He now became an ardent democrat. His paper (entirely self-written) expressed his change of views and proved something of a thorn in the side of the conservatives. When he published a particularly violent article against the flogging of soldiers, they took advantage of the opportunity and had him arrested. He was fined a thousand pounds and sentenced to prison for two years. Like Leigh Hunt with *The Examiner*, he was able to continue the publication of the *Register* from his cell. It must be confessed, however, that he first offered to give up the paper in exchange for remission of his sentence, and was refused. Friendly biographers have suggested that perhaps the offer was made because his farm was dearer to him than his journalism. (The farm became bankrupt during his time in prison.)

In 1816 Parliamentary reforms enabled Cobbett to extend his influence. He could reduce the price of his paper from a shilling to twopence, and it became the popular organ of the new group of industrial workers. But when habeas corpus was suspended in 1817 he found it well to go to America again, and spent two years on Long Island, farming and publishing the *Register* from there. He brought back with him for reverent burial the bones of Thomas Paine, whom once he had reviled. On his return he found himself again in financial difficulties, but he pulled himself once more out of bankruptcy, and by 1821 was owner of a seed farm in Kensington.

In 1832, thanks to various laws amending eligibility to Parliament, Cobbett found himself a member of the House of Commons. But Parliament, where for three years he labored valiantly in the workers' interests, was his undoing; for overwork brought on a throat inflammation which proved fatal. He died and was buried at Ash, near his birthplace of Farnham.

Six feet one and very sturdy, a typical rustic in appearance, Cobbett is best understood if it is realized that he was always primarily a peasant. It was an accident that made him the voice of the factory workers; his whole endeavor was to restore to England the "good old days" of his own rural youth. He loved to picture pre-industrial England, and never understood that economic change had killed it forever. This was the permanent consistency behind his seeming shifts of opinion. He was a born teacher, a reformer, a "muckraker." Extremely vain and self-confident, prodigiously industrious, hard-headed and opinionated, intensely moral, he loved a fight for the fight's sake, and his honest indignation often degenerated into vituperation. As a writer he never advanced beyond polemic journalism, except in *Rural Rides*, a heart-felt description of the countryside that bred him and that he so loved, and in his very lively *Grammar*. For the rest, over-emphasis makes much of his work hard

WILLIAM COBBETT

reading. But perhaps Ebenezer Elliott, "the Corn Law rhymer," had the best last word when he said of him: "For Britons honor Cobbett's name, Though rashly oft he spoke."

M. A. deF.

PRINCIPAL WORKS: Observations on the Emigration of Dr. Joseph Priestley, 1794; Le Tuteur Anglois, 1795; Porcupine's Works, 1801; Letters on the Peace With Bonaparte, 1802; The Political Proteus, 1804; Paper Against Gold, 1815; Letters on the Late War Between the United States and Great Britain, 1815; Mr. Cobbett's Address to his Countrymen, 1817; A Grammar of the English Language, 1818; A Journal of a Year's Residence in America, 1818-19; The American Gardener, 1821 (revised as The English Gardener, 1829); Cobbett's Sermons, 1822; Cobbett's Collective Commentaries, 1822; Cottage Economy, 1822; A French Grammar, 1824; History of the Protestant Reformation, 1824-27; The Woodlands, 1825; The Poor Man's Friend, 1826; A Treatise on Cobbett's Corn, 1828; Advice to Young Men, and Incidentally to Young Women, 1829; The Emigrant's Guide, 1829; Rural Rides, 1830; History of the Regency and Reign of George IV, 1830; Eleven Lectures on the French and Belgian Revolutions, 1830; A Spelling Book and Stepping Stone to English Grammar, 1831; Cobbett's Manchester Lectures, 1832; A Geographical Dictionary of England and Wales, 1832; Cobbett's Tour in Scotland, 1833; A New French and English Dictionary, 1834; Life of Andrew Jackson, 1834; Three Lectures on the Political State of Ireland, 1834; Legacy to Labourers, 1835; Legacy to Parsons, 1835; Selections From Cobbett's Political Works (ed. by J. M. & J. P. Cobbett) 1835; Legacy to Peel, 1836; The Doom to the Tithes, 1836; Legacy to Lords (ed. by William Cobbett, Jr.) 1863.

ABOUT: Benjamin, L. S. ("Lewis Melville"). The Life and Letters of William Cobbett; Carlyle, E. I. William Cobbett: A Study of His Life; Chesterton, G. K. William Cobbett; Cole, G. D. H. The Life of William Cobbett; Lodge, H. C. Studies in History; Smith, E. William Cobbett: A Biography; Contemporary Review 147:708 June 1935; Dublin Review 197:84 July 1935; English Review 61:185 August 1935; Nineteenth Century 117:735 June 1935; Queen's Quarterly 42:171 May 1935; Spectator 154:1009 June 14, 1935.

COBDEN, RICHARD (June 3, 1804-April 2, 1865), political writer, was born of yeoman stock on the western border of Sussex, the fourth of eleven children. From 1814 to 1819 the child was sent to a brutal Yorkshire school of the type of Dickens's "Dotheboys Hall." At fifteen he became a clerk in his uncle's warehouse in London, then a traveling salesman. In 1828, with some friends, he set up a calico business on borrowed money, working on commission. The business prospered and they began printing their own calicoes in Lancashire. From 1832 Cobden lived in Manchester. In his leisure hours he studied intensively, giving himself an excellent education.

In 1835 he traveled in the United States, in 1836 in the near East. He wrote books on both these journeys, and contributed letters on economic topics (he was an ardent free trader) to the *Manchester Examiner*. In 1838, with John Bright, he founded the Anti-Cornlaw League, and was its leader until 1846. (The corn laws were a tax on wheat, unbearable to the poor.) After an unsuccessful attempt in 1837, he was elected to Parliament in 1841. Sir Robert Peel, then prime minister, accused him of using bad language in debate, and made an enemy of Cobden, who admittedly caused Peel's subsequent defeat. Later Peel was obliged to deal with him in a more friendly manner.

In 1840 Cobden married Catherine Anne Williams; they had several daughters, but their only son died at fifteen. In 1845, just as the anti-cornlaw cause was triumphing, Cobden's business failed. By public subscription £80,000 was raised for him, which paid his debts and bought him a home in Dumford, Sussex; in 1860 another subscription brought him £40,000 more. From 1846 to 1847, worn out with his political labors, Cobden rested on the Continent, but he was still active for free trade. Back in Parliament, he supported all reform measures, attacked the Crimean War in 1854, and opposed the Chinese War in 1857. In consequence he lost his seat for two years. In 1859 he visited the United States again. In 1860 he brought about a low tariff agreement with France, and acted as its chief commissioner. He declined cabinet posts and a baronetcy. He died of bronchitis, in London, at sixty-one.

Independent, forthright, a true reformer, Cobden is said never to have made a personal enemy. His writing is now chiefly of historical interest; it was as a parliamentarian that his greatest work was done.

PRINCIPAL WORKS: England, Ireland, and America, 1835; Russia, 1836; 1792 and 1853, 1853; What Next? 1856; The Political Writings of Richard Cobden, 1867.

ABOUT: Axon, W. E. A. Cobden as a Citizen; Bagehot, W. Biographical Studies; Bowen, I. Cobden; Gowing, R. Richard Cobden; Hobson, J. A. Richard Cobden, the International Man; Morley, J. Life of Richard Cobden.

COCHRANE, THOMAS. See DUNDONALD, LORD

COCKBURN, LORD HENRY THOMAS (October 26, 1769-April 26, 1854), Scottish biographer, was born in Edinburgh, of an old Tory family, though he himself became one of the most prominent Whigs of his time. He was educated at the University of Edinburgh, and admitted to the Faculty of Advocates in 1806. He rose rapidly in his profession, becoming, with Lord Jeffrey, his great friend, the leader of the Scottish bar. In 1830 he was made solicitor general for Scotland and in 1834 appointed judge as Lord Cockburn. From 1831 he was lord rector of the University of Glasgow. He was a contributor to the *Edinburgh Review*.

Cockburn was a small, handsome, genial man, highly popular in society. His writing is like his personality—sympathetic and agreeable.

PRINCIPAL WORKS: Life of Lord Jeffrey, 1852; Memorials of His Time, 1856; Journal and Letters, 1874.

ABOUT: Cockburn, H. T. Memorials of His Time; Journal and Letters, 1831-34.

COCKTON, HENRY (December 7, 1807-June 26, 1853), novelist, was born in London. Very little is known of his antecedents, education, or personal life. He married Ann Howes, by whom he had one son. He made a good deal of money by his novels, particularly by *Valentine Fox*, the most successful, but lost it all by investing in the malting business, of which he knew absolutely nothing. He died at forty-five of tuberculosis.

Besides his humorous novels, by which he is best known, Cockton wrote several romances in the sentimental style of his period. His talent, however, was for broad humor and heavy satire, and his writings in this vein were extremely popular. Some of them may have influenced the earlier work of Dickens.

PRINCIPAL WORKS: The Life and Adventures of Valentine Fox, 1840; George St. George Julian, 1841; Sylvester Sound, 1844.

ABOUT: Gentleman's Magazine 40:212 August 1853.

COLE, SIR HENRY ("Felix Summerley") (July 15, 1808-April 18, 1882), artist and children's writer, was born in Bath, son of a captain in the army. He was educated at Christ's Hospital. He acted as clerk to Sir Francis Palgrave, the anthologist, and then was a subcommissioner under the Record Commission. At the same time he studied water color and began to exhibit at the Royal Academy. He was a friend of the novelist, Thomas Love Peacock, who encouraged his artistic interests.

In 1838 Cole became senior assistant keeper at the Record Office, the Commission having been abolished. Interested in postal reform, he worked out the present postage stamp system. He became especially concerned with medieval art, and particularly with industrial arts and crafts, studying engraving and etching to increase his knowledge. He prepared and published handbooks of design, and also wrote *Felix Summerley's Home Treasury*, a long series of juvenile books illustrated by woodcuts by famous artists. Another outgrowth of this work was Summerley's Art Manufactures, chiefly displayed in dishes and household furnishings. His interest in the subject went so far as to make him founder of a cooking school. He engineered various exhibitions of arts and crafts, leading up to the Great Exhibition of 1851, for which he was on the executive committee.

From 1851 to 1873 he was secretary of the School of Design, and was the designer of the Albert Memorial—not an altogether favorable monument to his artistic taste. He also helped to found the National Training School for Music. From 1849 to 1852 he edited the *Journal of Design*. In 1833 he married Marian Fairman; they had three sons and five daughters. He was made Knight Commander of the Bath in 1875.

Cole's only writing was in the *Home Treasury*—simple, unpretentious, without any claim to distinction.

PRINCIPAL WORK: Felix Summerley's Home Treasury, 1841-55.

ABOUT: Fifty Years of Public Work of Sir Henry Cole.

COLENSO, JOHN WILLIAM (January 24, 1814-June 20, 1883), Biblical critic, was born in Cornwall, where his father was mineral agent. The father lost his fortune in the mines and Colenso had to earn his own education. His youth was one long struggle. In 1831 he was assistant at a school in Dartmouth where he taught from 5 a.m. to 8 p.m., then did his own studying! He then entered St. John's College, Cambridge, as a sizar. In 1839 he became mathematics tutor at Harrow, but returned to St. John's, of which he was now a fellow, and was a tutor there from 1842 to 1846. He then married Sarah Frances Bunyon, and was a vicar in Norfolk until 1851. Meanwhile he wrote text books on arithmetic and algebra, mathematics having been his first love.

In 1853 he was named as Bishop of Natal, and went to Africa. An intimate friend of Frederick Denison Maurice, the founder of Christian Socialism, Colenso nevertheless went to Natal entirely orthodox in his theology. The questions asked him by his native converts first caused him to regard the Bible critically. He became an ardent advocate of justice for the Zulus, and earned the ill will of all their exploiters. When in 1861 and 1862 his powerful and revolutionary critical analyses of the Scriptures appeared, those who hated him for other reasons had a good weapon with which to attack him. Moreover, his ultra-heretical views lost him even his friendship with Maurice.

In 1863 Colenso was excommunicated by Bishop Gray, the metropolitan of Capetown, and his bishopric was declared vacant. The privy council declared the excommunication null and void. It was a contest of the South African prelates against the British law, and the question of whether Colenso was or was not still bishop was never settled. To add to the bitterness of the situation, he sided with the natives in a major dispute which culminated in the persecution of a Zulu chief. In 1875 he went to England in their behalf and secured redress for them; but the strain he had undergone broke his health, and he died a few years after his return to Natal.

PRINCIPAL WORKS: Commentary on St. Paul's Epistle to the Romans, 1861; The Pentateuch and Book of Joshua Critically Examined, 1862-79.

ABOUT: Cox, G. W. The Life of J. W. Colenso.

COLERIDGE, (DAVID) HARTLEY

(September 19, 1796-January 6, 1849), poet, was the oldest child of the famous poet Samuel Taylor Coleridge. He was born at Clevedon, Somersetshire, but since his parents were estranged while he was very young, and finally separated before he was fourteen, he spent most of his childhood with his uncle Robert Southey, the poet (husband of his mother's sister), at Keswick. After school at Ambleside, he went on a scholarship, in 1815, to Merton College, Oxford.

Hartley was a beautiful, precocious child, petted and indulged as the "genius" of a highly talented family. He remained just that throughout his life. His university experience blasted a life easy to tear from its moorings. He was second in Greats at Merton, and won a fellowship in Oriel College in 1826. But this involved teaching, for which Hartley was always unfit. He was afraid of his pupils, melancholy and introspective, and he took refuge in intemperance. In consequence his year of probation ended with his dismissal. There was no formal charge, and he received a "solatium" of £300, so he could not have been in utter disgrace; but he never recovered from the blow.

For the remainder of his life, though he tried feebly to secure private pupils, and twice acted as assistant at Sedbergh Grammar School, Hartley Coleridge was a charge on his relatives and friends, living mostly at Ambleside or Grasmere in the Lake Country. He contributed occasionally to magazines, edited an edition of Massinger and Ford, the Elizabethan dramatists, and it was by no fault of his own that his only considerable work, a series of biographies of "northern worthies," was left incomplete by failure of the publisher. But his ordinary life was one of occasional writing, much aimless wandering, and harmless dependence on others. In his youth there was an obscure love affair, which he renounced because it was hopeless to think of his ever supporting a wife.

In Hartley, his father's "fatal paralysis of will" was exaggerated to a psychic disease. He was fitted only for a life of ease and study, which he had forfeited, and his sensitive, self-reproachful, childlike nature kept him from any other fulfilment of the great promise of his youth. All who knew him loved him, and he could be as merry as any other child, delighted with simple things. He died finally of bronchitis, a white-haired old man at fifty-two.

HARTLEY COLERIDGE

Hartley had a vast, unorganized learning, and a fine critical faculty. Like his father, he was a great annotator of the margins of books, but his more extensive prose is diffuse and labored. In both prose and verse he was happiest in limited forms, since he had no power for continued effort, and his sonnets are the finest of his poems. His brother Derwent and his sister Sara, also his cousin Henry Nelson Coleridge (who married Sara), were all literary—editors, critics, and minor writers—but Hartley it was who inherited most of his father's genius—and most of his father's weaknesses as well.   M. A. deF.

PRINCIPAL WORKS: Poetry—Poems, 1833; Poems by Hartley Coleridge, 1851. Prose—Biographia Borealis, 1833; The Worthies of Yorkshire and Lancashire, 1836; Dramatic Works of Massinger and Ford (ed.) 1840; Essays and Marginalia, 1851.

ABOUT: Bagehot, W. Estimates of Some Englishmen and Scotchmen; Coleridge, H. Poems (see Memoir by Coleridge, D.); Drinkwater, J. A Book for Bookmen; Graham, H. Splendid Failures; Griggs, E. L. Hartley Coleridge: His Life and Work; Hartman, H. W. Hartley Coleridge: Poet's Son and Poet; Towle, E. A. A Poet's Children.

COLERIDGE, ERNEST HARTLEY (De-

cember 8, 1846-February 19, 1920), literary editor, was the son of Derwent Coleridge, and therefore the grandson of the poet, Samuel Taylor Coleridge. His sister, Christabel, became a popular novelist.

Coleridge was educated in Sherborne School and at Balliol College, Oxford, where he received his M.A. in 1880. He was an Honorary Fellow of the Royal Society of Literature. In 1894 he was secretary to the Lord Chief Justice.

Besides editing his grandfather's poems and letters, he edited Byron's poems. He wrote nothing in book form of his own. He was a fair critic and a competent scholar, but was not known as an original thinker. In 1876 he married Sarah M. Bradford, who died in 1917.

COLERIDGE, MARY ELIZABETH (September 23, 1861-August 25, 1907), poet, novelist, and critic, was born in London, the daughter of Arthur Duke Coleridge and Mary Anne (Jameson) Coleridge. Her father's grandfather was an elder brother of Samuel Taylor Coleridge.

Her education was at home, and she was much influenced by her father's friend, William Johnson Cory, the poet. The girl wrote verse and romantic stories, showed talent in drawing, and at twenty began to contribute to periodicals. Her first novel, *The Seven Sleepers of Ephesus,* appeared in 1893. While it was not successful, it was praised by Robert Louis Stevenson; and her first volume of poems, *Fancy's Following* (1896), received the commendation of Robert Bridges.

Apparently as a result of reading Tolstoy, Miss Coleridge felt impelled to help the poor; and she exercised her gifts as a teacher with working-women at her home. She gave instruction in English literature at the Working Women's College from 1895 to 1907. Her entire life was spent with her family. She lost her mother in 1898, but continued to live, unmarried, with her father and her sister, dying, after a sudden illness, at Harrogate in August 1907.

Miss Coleridge, whose personality has been described by Robert Bridges as "one of those rare combinations of character and intellect whose presence is everywhere beneficent and welcome," was a woman of strong enthusiasms and emotions, easily swayed in mood.

In her youth more desirous of being a painter than of becoming a writer, she was casual in her attitude toward her literary efforts, and found it difficult to take them seriously; she was very unwilling to speak of them. Her warmth of emotion and the selflessness that often made her fail to perceive the essential shallowness of pretentious egotists, made her a delightful friend; and in later life she overcame her youthful shyness and enjoyed society. Her labors in behalf of the poor were undertaken, not in a missionary spirit, but because of conscience, and a hunger (not satisfied) for personal companionship, as well as a conviction of the reality of a spiritual democracy among men. Her intellectual spontaneity and lack of consistency allowed her to feel great admiration for Ibsen and Wagner, despite her old-fashioned character; and she had great respect for Browning, Tennyson, and the Pre-Raphaelites. The pupils at the Working Women's College refused to go on with the class after her death, so much had her success in imparting enthusiasm to tired minds been one of individual personality and force.

"Like all true poets, and more vividly than most of them, Mary Coleridge felt the sense of 'moving in worlds not realized,' the contrast between the dreamy unreality of the visible and the reality of the invisible," wrote Bernard Holland. It is thus, perhaps, not surprising that her reputation in literature rests, not upon her charming essays, nor upon her novels, which, though they reflect a glamour peculiar to a Coleridge, are marked by some intricacy and perversity of plot, but upon her poems. Even Saintsbury, who objects to what he considers their sustained mood of gloom, admits that they have variety of note, if not of key. Of her early verses Robert Bridges said, "They are both beautiful and original, and often exhibit imagination of a very rare kind, conveyed by the identical expression of true feeling and artistic insight." In an effort to appraise her work, made soon after her death, the same poet and critic wrote, "It is the intimacy and spontaneity of her poems that will give them their chief value."   R. W. W.

PRINCIPAL WORKS: *Biography*—Holman Hunt, 1908. *Essays*—Non Sequitur, 1900. *Novels*—The Seven Sleepers of Ephesus, 1893; The King With Two Faces, 1897; The Fiery Dawn, 1901; The Shadow on the Wall, 1904; The Lady on the Drawing-Room Floor, 1906. *Poems*—Fancy's Following, 1896; Fancy's Guerdon, 1897; Poems Old and New, 1907; Last Poems, 1905; Gathered Leaves, 1910.

ABOUT: Baring, M. Punch and Judy & Other Essays; Coleridge, M. E. Gathered Leaves (see Memoir by E. Sichel); Contemporary Review 93: Literary Supplement, June 1908, p. 11; Cornhill Magazine 96:594 November 1907; Nation 85:227 September 12, 1907; National Review 51:100 March 1908.

MARY ELIZABETH COLERIDGE

COLERIDGE, SAMUEL TAYLOR (October 21, 1772-July 25, 1834), poet, critic, and philosopher, was born at Ottery St. Mary, where his father was vicar and master of the grammar school. He was the last of ten children of his father's second marriage.

The father died when Coleridge was only nine, and a few months later he was admitted to Christ's Hospital, London, as a charity pupil. One of the other pupils was Charles Lamb, who became his lifelong friend. The boy was exceedingly precocious, especially in the classics, his first interest. Medicine succeeded this as his next passion (his brother was studying to be a physician), then metaphysics, and then, at fifteen, poetry. In each of these subjects he immersed himself eagerly; incidentally, by overstudy and lack of care, ruining his health for life. He was disabled frequently by rheumatic fever, and the obscure pains from which he suffered always thereafter may probably be traced to this early period.

SAMUEL TAYLOR COLERIDGE

Coleridge left Christ's Hospital in 1790, and the following year entered Jesus College, Cambridge, as a sizar (the equivalent to "working his way through college"). There his early interest in the classics revived, and he was awarded a medal for a Greek ode. But his university life was not happy. His debts piled up, his expression of his highly individual variety of radical thought made him unpopular, and he was in love with a girl, Mary Evans, who apparently did not return his affection. At the end of 1793, deeply depressed and in the throes of a temporary period of intemperance, he suddenly ran away to London. There he managed to sell a few sonnets to the *Morning Chronicle,* but found no other means of livelihood; and a few weeks later he enlisted in the Fifteenth Light Dragoons under the name of Silas Tomkyn Comberback.

He soon sickened of life as a soldier—few young men could have been more inept in such a rôle—but it was not until the following April that his family managed to have him discharged and sent him back to Cambridge, where he was publicly disciplined. In June, on a visit to Oxford, he met Robert Southey, another budding poet of about his own age, with whom Coleridge's life was deeply intertwined for years to come. In Bristol he also met Southey's fiancée and her sisters, one of whom, Sara Fricker, was to become his own unloved wife. In fact, before the summer ended he was engaged to her: ungallantly he remarked afterwards that this was the result of carrying a flirtation too far!

Coleridge left Cambridge, without taking a degree, at the end of 1794, but, ignoring his Sara, he went to London, and Southey had to go after him and force him to return to Bristol. For a while he supported himself by giving lectures; then Joseph Castle, a bookseller, subsidized both him and Southey to write a volume of poems. Sure now of an income, he took the leap and in March 1795 married Miss Fricker. She was two or three years his senior, and they seem to have had little in common. Then and for a long time afterward, Coleridge was still in love with the unresponsive Mary Evans. However, the young couple settled at Clevedon, and two sons and a daughter were born to them before the end of the century.

It was in these years that Coleridge's dream of "Pantisocracy" was born and died. This was to be an ideal colony, on the banks of the Susquehanna in Pennsylvania (chosen for its romantic sound), the colonists to be Coleridge, Southey, and a few other young men and their families. In any real sense, Coleridge never was a radical; he was a bitter enemy of the extremists of the French Revolution. But he was also a bitter enemy of the Tories and die-hards of his own day in England, and the colony was to be more a retreat of choice souls from the tyrannies and injustices of the Old World than a model or example of a new social system. Southey's abandonment of the scheme caused a temporary estrangement between the friends; but Lovell, another of the group, died, and the whole idea was finally given up.

At the end of 1796, Coleridge moved back to Bristol, where he undertook the publication of a new magazine, called *The Watchman,* which had a life of ten months. Occasionally he preached in Unitarian chapels, and at one time thought of becoming a regular Unitarian minister. About 1797 occurred the most momentous meeting of his life—that with

139

Wordsworth and his sister Dorothy. Wordsworth brought out the latent poetic genius in Coleridge; in fact, when their closest association was over, he ceased gradually to be a poet. The first fruit of their friendship was the celebrated *Lyrical Ballads*, a pronunciamento for a new and simpler, more realistic type of poetry, to which Coleridge contributed chiefly *The Rime of the Ancient Mariner*. Strange to say, this poem, one of the most famous in English, was misunderstood and disliked, and helped to keep the book from success; it was not acknowledged as Coleridge's until much later.

It was soon after this (about 1798) that the sons of the great potter, Josiah Wedgwood (Darwin's cousins, and the family where he found his wife) settled an annuity upon Coleridge, that he might devote himself to poetry and philosophy. Feeling that he was weak in the modern phases of the latter subject (then chiefly represented by the various German schools of thought), Coleridge spent the next year in Germany with Wordsworth and his sister. It was during this period that he first became a contributor to the London *Morning Post*. His family had been left at Keswick, in the Lake Country always associated with his name and Wordsworth's, and he rejoined them in 1800. Although many of his poems did not appear in book form for a number of years to come, he was almost at the end of his sustained poetic effort; after 1802 or so he became, increasingly, first the critic and lecturer, then the philosopher.

He was almost at the end of his marriage also. He saw as little as possible of his wife after 1804, and separated finally from her in 1810. Although he loved his children dearly, he had little feeling of responsibility for them, and their care and education fell largely on the shoulders of Southey, their uncle by marriage. The fact is that at this period the darkest phase of Coleridge's life had begun— his addiction to opium. He was constantly in pain, and to ease the pain he took to laudanum. This in turn exaggerated all his weaknesses—his lack of will power, his procrastination, his indolence, and his irresponsibility. For years he took two quarts of laudanum a week, at one time even consuming one quart in a day. Against this habit he struggled desperately but vainly.

In 1804, hoping to improve his health, he went to Malta. There for a year he acted as secretary to the governor. When the regular secretary returned to his post, in 1805, Coleridge went to Sicily and then to Italy. Some of his polemic writings against Napoleon had reached that despot's ears, and Coleridge was probably not falsifying matters when he said that he was obliged to escape from Italy secretly and at the risk of his life.

He returned to England, but not to his family. Always Coleridge had good friends— DeQuincey, another opium addict and therefore a sympathizer, prominent among them— who assisted him financially and saw that he was not homeless or adrift. He began another series of lectures, which for a time were very popular. As a lecturer Coleridge was undependable; his fine critical ability made his discourses valuable in printed form, but when they were actually delivered, he was at times unable to give them properly, at other times not to be trusted to appear at the stated time at all. For the second time he began publication of a short-lived magazine, *The Friend*; at this period he was living with Wordsworth at Grasmere, while his family was at Keswick. (The best of his articles in both *The Friend* and *The Watchman* were later published among his essays.) He went to London, where he lived with various friends, lecturing, and writing for *The Courier*. In 1811 the younger Josiah Wedgwood withdrew his half of the annuity, on the ground that Coleridge was not fulfilling the duties on the basis of which it had been given. Coleridge made over the remainder of it to his wife, in perpetuity, and made shift to exist by his writing and by the philanthropic interest of his friends. One of his plays, *Remorse*, was put on at Drury Lane and ran for twenty nights, netting him a fair sum. Finally in 1824 he was made a "Royal Associate" of the Royal Society of Literature, receiving £100 a year until the death of George IV, when the pension was abandoned. (William Godwin, the radical philosopher, another "Royal Associate," was more fortunate; in his case the sum was continued to his own death.)

By 1816 Coleridge realized that his attempts to cure himself of the opium habit were hopeless, and that he was growing worse instead of better. At the solicitation of a physician, he was admitted to the household of a surgeon, James Gilman, in Highgate, London. He remained there for the rest of his life, an unpaying guest. The Gilmans became his devoted friends, and he made their house a literary center. Coleridge was a prodigious and tremendous conversationalist, of the type of "table talker" to which Dr. Samuel Johnson also belonged. His conversations were works of art in themselves, really informal lectures, for the hearers were not supposed to do more than keep him going by occasional question or dissent. To his discursive mind and vast though unorganized knowledge, this and his marginal annotations on his books (he was an omnivorous reader) were probably his most grateful forms of creative work.

He continued, while at the Gilmans', to write constantly and even to lecture occasionally. He was never entirely cured of the opium habit, but he submitted himself freely to the strictest discipline, and brought his vice down to an irreducible minimum. As late as 1828 he was well enough to travel with the Wordsworths on the Rhine. But he gradually grew weaker, until in 1834, at nearly seventy-two, he died. An autopsy revealed no organic reason for his lifelong pain.

Lamb summed Coleridge up well in his famous statement that he was "an archangel, a little damaged." In appearance he was un-attractive after his first and very handsome youth; he became heavy, and owing to a difficulty in breathing his mouth was always open, giving him an "idiotic expression" in repose. But he had a fine forehead and brilliant, beautiful eyes. He was a man who either attracted others powerfully and permanently, or else irritated them beyond endurance. His mind was profound and penetrative; he is doubtless the only man in English literature who was absolutely of first rank as a poet, a critic, and a philosopher. But his curse was an incurable weakness of will, which would have nullified any gifts less tremendous than those with which he was endowed. As it was, his genius overrode his defects, and they had no power except to make him a most unhappy man.

As a critic, notably in *Biographia Literaria,* that masterpiece of flashing insight and intense confusion, Coleridge took all literature for his province. There are few men of whom it can be said that their scribblings on the margins of books constitute, when collected, valuable critical volumes. The same is true of his published lectures.

As a philosopher, he was an anti-utilitarian; without being exactly a mystic, he was deeply religious (though heretically so), and the sworn enemy of systems based on the exclusive use of reason and common sense. He did a great service in introducing German philosophy to English thinkers. (Carlyle for one profited by that bounty.) He fancied himself greatly as an economist, but in that realm of thought he was really weakest; his private brand of radicalism was too personal and too confused for him to become the founder of a school. Indeed, his chief weakness as a philosopher is that he had no sustained power. He could not construct a system; he remained in essence a critic of philosophy, as he was of literature.

It is as a poet that Coleridge is greatest. Compared with many others—with his bosom friend Wordsworth, for instance—his output is very limited, with perhaps not more than twenty pages of the first order. But these— principally the *Ancient Mariner, Christabel,* and *Kubla Khan*—should be printed, it has been said, "in pure gold."

M. A. deF.

PRINCIPAL WORKS: *Poetry*—Poems on Various Subjects, 1796; The Vision of the Maid of Orleans (with Southey's Joan of Arc) 1796; Ode to the Departing Year, 1796; Fears in Solitude, 1798; Lyrical Ballads (with Wordsworth) 1798; Christabel (with Kubla Khan and The Pains of Sleep) 1816; Sybilline Leaves, 1817; Poetical Works, 1828; The Devil's Walk (with Southey; anonymous) 1830. *Plays (verse)*—The Fall of Robespierre, 1794; Wallenstein, 1799-1800; Remorse, 1813; Zapolya, 1817. *Criticism and Philosophy*—Conciones ad Populum, 1795; Omniana, 1812; The Statesman's Manual, 1816; A Lay Sermon, 1817; Biographia Literaria, 1817; Aids to Reflection in the Formation of a Manly Character, 1825; On the Constitution of Church and State, 1830; Specimens of Table Talk, 1835; Confessions of an Inquiring Spirit, 1840; Literary Remains (4 vols.) 1836-38; Essay on Method, 1845; Notes and Lectures Upon Shakespeare, 1849; Essays on His Own Times, 1850; Notes Upon English Divines, 1853; Seven Lectures on Shakespeare and Milton, 1856. *Miscellaneous*—Letters of S. T. Coleridge (with selections from his notebooks) 1846; Letters, 1895; Unpublished Letters, 1932.

ABOUT: Charpentier, J. Coleridge: The Sublime Somnambulist; Fausset, H. l'A. Samuel Taylor Coleridge; Garnett, R. Coleridge; Lowes, J. L. The Road to Xanadu; Muirhead, J. H. Coleridge as Philosopher; Traill, H. C. Coleridge; Contemporary Review 146:49 July 1934; English Review 59:53 July 1934; Quarterly Review 263:94 July 1934; Saturday Review 157:862 July 21, 1934.

COLERIDGE, SARA (December 22, 1802-May 3, 1852), poet and literary worker, was born at Greta Hall, near Keswick, the daughter of Samuel Taylor Coleridge and Sarah (Fricker) Coleridge. Because of her father's wanderings, his opium habit, and his gradual drifting away from his wife, she was educated with the help and service of Robert Southey, who allowed her the use of his library. She studied assiduously by herself, and succeeded in gaining an acquaintance, before she was twenty-five, with the best Greek and Latin authors, as well as a background in French, Italian, German, and Spanish. She showed great sensitiveness to nature, and absorbed Wordsworth's ideals and Southey's views of conduct.

In 1822 she issued a translation of Martin Dobritzhofer's *An Account of the Abipones* which showed knowledge of Latin and ability to write fine English. A few years later she published a translation, from the medieval French, of the "Loyal Servant's" memoirs of the Chevalier Bayard.

Miss Coleridge married in 1829 a cousin, Henry Nelson Coleridge, a lawyer with strong scientific interests. The couple became the centre of a refined circle of friends, living first at Hampstead and later in Chester Place, Regent's Park. In the course of educating her children Mrs. Coleridge composed little verses designed to facilitate and to make pleasant the lessons, and some of these were published in 1834 as *Pretty Lessons in Verse for Good Children. Phantasmion,* her best work, a romantic fairy-tale, followed in 1837.

Upon the death, in 1843, of her husband, who had been Samuel Taylor Coleridge's

SARA COLERIDGE

literary executor, the duties of editorship fell upon Mrs. Coleridge, who issued editions of, and annotations upon, her father's works, including also some original essays of her own. These labors occupied her for most of the rest of her life. In 1850 her health broke down, and, after considerable suffering, she died in 1852.

A devoted wife and mother, and a modest but thorough literary worker, Mrs. Coleridge has been praised as a saint. Her mental qualities, despite her femininity of personality, were distinctly masculine, and prove her to have been a child of her father, for whom she kept a pathetic reverence. Like him, she was much occupied with abstract questions of philosophy and religion, and these matters take up a large part of her published correspondence, the record of a powerful mind. "The chief impression left by the letters," wrote C. E. Norton, "is that Sara Coleridge's existence was far too much intellectualized. The sweet feminine soul was starved by the claims of the restless and dissatisfied intelligence."

The fact that Mrs. Coleridge produced nothing of the greatest literary importance is probably due to her tireless work as literary executrix. The ability revealed in her translation of *An Account of the Abipones* was the source of great satisfaction to her father. *Phantasmion*, however, is her claim to renown. The story is built on a plan perhaps too large for a fairytale, but is noteworthy for charm of fancy and excellence of diction, and especially for the verses appearing in the course of the narrative. "The little lyrics scattered through its pages," wrote Richard Garnett, "confer upon her a secure though a modest place among English poetesses."   R. W. W.

PRINCIPAL WORKS: *Autobiography and Correspondence*—Memoir and Letters of Sara Coleridge, 1873. *Editor*—Notes and Lectures Upon Shakespeare and Some of the Old Poets and Dramatists (by S. T. Coleridge) 1849; Essays on His Own Times (by S. T. Coleridge) 1850; Poems (by S. T. Coleridge) 1852. *Fairy-Tale*—Phantasmion, 1837. *Poetry for Children*—Pretty Lessons in Verse for Good Children, 1834. *Translations*—An Account of the Abipones (by M. Dobritzhofer) 1822; The Right Joyous and Pleasant History of the Feats, Gests, and Prowesses of the Chevalier Bayard (by "The Loyal Servant") 1825.

ABOUT: Adams, W. H. D. Celebrated Englishwomen of the Victorian Era; Coleridge, S. Memoir and Letters of Sara Coleridge; Towle, E. A. A Poet's Children: Hartley and Sara Coleridge; Edinburgh Review 139:44 January 1874; Penn Monthly 4:828 December 1873.

COLLINS, CHARLES ALLSTON (January 25, 1828-April 9, 1873), novelist and essayist, was the son of a painter and the brother of Wilkie Collins, the novelist. He showed much talent for painting and was trained in the school of the Royal Academy. He was an early member of the Pre-Raphaelite group, of which Dante Gabriel Rossetti was the leader. After 1858 he deserted art, though his work had shown great promise and some achievement, and devoted himself to writing. In 1860 he married Kate, the youngest daughter of Charles Dickens; and most of his essays appeared originally in Dickens' *Household Words*. Collins was an invalid for years before his death. He was a modest, sensitive, self-deprecating man, who might nevertheless have approximated his brother's fame had not so much of his energy gone to overcoming the handicap of poor health, for his essays show subtle observation, delicate humor, and charm. His novels are weak and of no moment.

PRINCIPAL WORKS: A Sentimental Journey, 1859; The Eye Witness, 1860; A Cruise Upon Wheels, 1862.

COLLINS, JOHN CHURTON (March 26, 1848-September 5, 1908), essayist, biographer, and critic, was born at Bourton-on-the-Water, Gloucestershire, the eldest son of Henry Ramsay and Maria Churton Collins. The father, a medical practitioner, died in 1858, and Collins was entrusted to a maternal uncle, John Churton, of Chester.

In 1863 Collins entered King Edward's School, Birmingham, going in 1868 to Balliol College, Oxford. His career was not remarkable, though he took a degree in classics and another in law and history. His mediocre record and disinclination to take orders disappointed his uncle and after 1872 Collins found himself entirely self-dependent. He began at once a literary career, writing articles for the *Globe*. At Oxford, and subsequently at London, he found work as a tutor, and spent the long vacations at Oxford in reading.

Out of his projected edition of Cyril Tourneur came a thirteen-year friendship with Swinburne, who had great confidence in Collins' critical judgment. A rift occurred when, in 1885, Collins attacked Swinburne's prose in a *Quarterly* article. Swinburne replied the next year in the *Athenaeum,* and only a prearranged meeting in 1900 restored relations. Other friends were Carlyle, Froude, and Browning.

On April 11, 1878, Collins married Pauline Mary Strangways, by whom he had seven children. A government pension of £100 was granted her in 1909. Journalism filled the years, but in 1880 Collins began a new task which he followed with great success for twenty-seven years. As lecturer for the London University Extension Society he traveled to Hamburg, Germany, and the United States, where he had large audiences and excellent press comments. He also lectured at the Royal Institution.

Collins had hoped for academic appointment, and in 1885 was keenly disappointed not to receive the Merton professorship at Oxford. From this and another similar disappointment in 1901 grew his writing on education and his attack upon the "medieval spirit" in the teaching of English literature in English universities. His criticism brought practical results in 1893 when the final honors school was established at Oxford. Recognition of his work came with his appointment to the chair of English literature at the new University of Birmingham, 1904.

Collins was also interested in spiritualism and criminology. In 1906 he assisted Sir Arthur Conan Doyle in the solution of a case, securing the release of the accused.

JOHN CHURTON COLLINS

Constant overwork caused a nervous breakdown in 1898; melancholia in 1901 and later nervous illnesses sent him, in 1908, to his physician at Oulton Broad. Here, in peculiar circumstances, he was found dead in a ditch. An inquest pronounced death accidental. Burial was at Oulton Broad.

As textual critic Collins was not successful, but as social and interpretative literary critic his work had considerable value. He was a relentless and outspoken writer, an interesting and inspiring speaker. His style has been described as fascinating and trenchant. Naturally modest, unaggressive, generous, and impulsive, he was embittered by overwork and disappointment, and became irritable and morbid. His pioneer work was his extension lecturing. He contributed voluminously to the journals. D. F. A.

PRINCIPAL WORKS: *Essays and Criticism*—Sir Joshua Reynolds, 1874; Bolingbroke and Voltaire in England, 1886; The Study of English Literature, 1891; Dean Swift, 1893; Essays and Studies, 1895; Ephemera Critica, 1901; Studies in Shakespeare, 1904; Studies in Poetry and Criticism, 1905; Voltaire, Montesquieu, and Rousseau in England, 1905; Memories, 1908; Greek Influence (ed. by Michael Macmillan) 1910; Posthumous Essays (ed. by L. C. Collins) 1912.

ABOUT: Collins, L. C. Life and Memoirs of John Churton Collins; Letters From Algernon Charles Swinburne to John Churton Collins, 1873-1886; Harper's Weekly 38:114 February 3, 1894.

COLLINS, MORTIMER (June 29, 1827-July 28, 1876), novelist and poet, was born at Plymouth, the only child of a solicitor who dabbled also in mathematics and poetry. He was educated entirely in private schools. His ambition was to be a journalist, but at his mother's pleading he became a tutor in private families instead. For several years he was mathematics master at Queen Elizabeth's College, Guernsey. From 1856 he was able to devote himself entirely to a literary life.

In 1849 Collins married Susannah (Hubbard) Crump, the widow of a clergyman; they had one daughter. In 1862 he moved to Knowl Hill, Berkshire, and there in 1867 his wife died. He married again the next year, his second wife being Frances Cotton. He died at Knowl Hill of heart disease at forty-nine, in spite of his book on *The Secret of Long Life*!

Though he was known as "king of the Bohemians," Collins was actually unconventional only in dress and manners. He was an old-fashioned die-hard Tory, highly religious, and detester of free-thinkers and free-livers. A typical English country squire, he was athletic, a great pedestrian, a lover of dogs and birds. He was a fine chess-player and never lost his interest in mathematics.

His verse, powerful and vigorous, ranges from humorous doggerel to light lyrics. His novels, though spirited, are carelessly written.

He was a good classicist, but there is little evidence of this (except perhaps in the satiric *British Birds*) in his now generally forgotten writing.

PRINCIPAL WORKS: *Verse*—Idyls and Rhymes, 1855; Summer Songs, 1860; The British Birds: A Communication From the Ghost of Aristophanes, 1873. *Prose*—Who Is the Heir? 1865; Sweet Anne Page, 1868; The Vivian Romance, 1870; The Secret of Long Life, 1871; Princess Clarice, 1872; Squire Sylvester's Whim, 1873; Sweet and Twenty (with Frances C. Collins) 1875.

ABOUT: Collins, F. C. Mortimer Collins.

COLLINS, (WILLIAM) WILKIE (January 8, 1824-September 23, 1889), novelist, was born in Tavistock Square, London, eldest son of the painter William Collins, R.A. The name Wilkie, by which he was always called, was derived from his father's good friend and fellow academician Sir David Wilkie.

Young Collins' education does not appear to have been very seriously considered by either himself or his family. It consisted of some years at Highbury, where Collins says that he was perpetually getting punished as a "bad boy" and "the master used to turn me to moral account, as a means of making his model scholars ashamed of their occasional lapses into misconduct: 'If it had been Collins I should not have felt shocked and surprised. Nobody *expects* anything of *him*. But YOU!!'" The school years were followed by two years with his parents in Italy.

When he was seventeen, Wilkie Collins was apprenticed to a firm engaged in the tea trade. While serving this apprenticeship he wrote his first novel. (Some believe it was *Antonina*, an historical novel of ancient Rome, built upon knowledge gained during his Italian residence. This book was not published until 1850.) The elder Collins was so pleased that he allowed young Wilkie to leave the tea trade and study law at Lincoln's Inn. He was called to the bar in 1851, the same year in which he first met Charles Dickens.

Collins had at this time three published books to his credit—though not greatly to his literary credit. They were a biography of his father, *Antonina*, and *Rambles Beyond Railways*, a book resulting from a vacation spent in Cornwall. This last volume had considerable success, going into several editions. This combination of circumstances comprised the deciding factors in Wilkie's choice of a literary career. Prior to this he had considered following his father's footsteps and had already exhibited a canvas at the Royal Academy.

The meeting of Collins and Dickens is of real significance to the history of English literature, as well as to their own individual careers. T. S. Eliot remarks: "To anyone who knows the bare facts of Dickens' acquaintance with Collins, and who has studied the work of the two men, their relationship and their influence upon one another is an important subject of study." Critics do not agree precisely as to the benefits of this mutual influence. Eliot, for example, claims that Dickens' best novel, *Bleak House*, is the one in which he most closely approaches Collins; and *The Woman in White*, Collins' best, or at least best remembered, novel is the one in which he most closely approaches Dickens. Swinburne, on the other hand, while considering *The Moonstone* among the best of Collins' novels, claims that its imperfections are due to Wilkie's ". . . illusions . . . that he might do good service, as Dickens had done . . . in the line of didactic fiction and reformatory romance."

Whatever conflicting opinions are held by the critics, there are certain points upon which all seem to agree. Dickens, a master of characterization, was distinctly inferior to Collins in the matter of plot. Collins had the power of devising a plot and controlling the mechanism of incident to a superlative degree, but his characters lacked life. In their mutual admiration it was but natural that each man should have been influenced by the obvious superiorities of the other.

Collins became one of Dickens' most intimate friends and a regular contributor to his publications. In 1855 they spent the winter in Paris, where they planned and collaborated upon several works. After this they frequently worked together. Some of their collaborations are: *The Lazy Tour of Two Idle Apprentices, The Perils of Certain English Prisoners,* and *No Thoroughfare.*

In 1873-74 Collins came to the United States (as Dickens had done before him) to give readings from his works. Ten years

WILKIE COLLINS

later his play *Rank and Riches* had a very successful run in this country, although it had been a failure when produced in London.

Collins had suffered from "rheumatic gout of the eyes" for many years, but his agony increased in later years so that he became more and more of a recluse. The heroism of the man in continuing his work is illustrated in a conversation reported by his friend William Winter: "My suffering was so great when I was writing *The Moonstone* that I could not control myself and keep quiet. My cries and groans so deeply distressed my amanuensis, to whom I was dictating, that he could not continue his work and had to leave me. After that I employed several other men, with the same result: no one of them could stand the strain." So he engaged a young woman, and to his surprise, she proved capable of working through the most trying seizures when: "I was blind with pain, and I lay on the couch writhing and groaning. In that condition . . . I dictated the greater part of *The Moonstone*." This is the work which T. S. Eliot calls "the first and greatest of English detective novels."

Almost every essayist or critic who writes of Wilkie Collins comments upon the strange lack of biographical material about him. The only attempt at a full length biography is "an insignificant German book" published in 1885. Malcolm Elwin (in *Victorian Wallflowers*) suggests that this may have been due, in part, to the fact that he was a bachelor and left no dutiful child to publish a "reverential memoir." This, plus the fact that Dickens destroyed his side of their correspondence as a matter of principle to prevent the "improper use of confidential letters," has left a paucity of material about the man's life.

Moreover, Collins, like his other intimate friend Charles Reade, was subject to some degree of social ostracism because of his rather Bohemian bachelor hall. Consequently he does not figure so importantly in the circumspect memoirs of his contemporaries. A friend records: "His eye seems to have roved in search of romance whenever he crossed the threshold of his home to set foot in London streets." To one such romantic encounter is attributed the conception of *The Woman in White*. Wilkie, his younger brother, and the artist Millais were walking home one evening when they were startled by a woman's scream coming from behind a garden wall. As they stopped, considering what to do, the iron gate flew open "and from it came the figure of a young and very beautiful woman dressed in flowing white robes . . . she paused for a moment in an attitude of supplication and terror. Then suddenly seeming to recollect herself, she moved on and vanished in the shadows. . ." Without a word, Wilkie Collins dashed after her, and that was the last his two companions saw of him that night. The next day, however, they were told a romantic tale of how the young lady had been held prisoner by a man living in Regent's Park. She had been kept there many months "under threats and mesmeric influence." And it was claimed, in later years, by Dickens' daughter—the wife of Wilkie's younger brother—that "this Woman in White was the same lady and henceforth lived with him."

As the father of the English detective story, if on no other score, Wilkie Collins is entitled to a significant place in the history of English literature. "He is," as Michael Sadleir says, "a writer for tired minds, capable . . . of holding the interest without calling on the emotional reserves of his readers. His influence on the novel of sensation has been enormous. It is the least of his due that a generation brought up on the mystery stories of his disciples should find time to turn over the principal works of the master himself."

D. S. C.

PRINCIPAL WORKS: *Novels*—Antonina, 1850; Mrs. Wray's Cash Box, 1852; Basil, 1852; Hide and Seek, 1854; After Dark, 1856; The Dead Secret, 1857; A Plot in Private Life, 1859; The Queen of Hearts, 1859; The Woman in White, 1860; No Name, 1862; Armadale, 1866; The Moonstone, 1868; Man and Wife, 1870; Poor Miss Finch, 1872; The New Magdalen, 1873; Miss or Mrs.? 1873; The Frozen Deep, 1874; The Law and The Lady, 1875; Two Destinies, 1876; A Shocking Story, 1878; The Haunted Hotel, 1879; A Rogue's Life, 1879; Jezebel's Daughter, 1880; The Black Robe, 1881; Heart and Science, 1883; I Say No, 1884; The Evil Genius, 1886; The Guilty River, 1886.

ABOUT: Dickens, C. Letters to Wilkie Collins; Eliot, T. S. Selected Essays; Ellis, S. M. Wilkie Collins, LeFanu and Others; Elwin, M. Victorian Wallflowers; Forster, J. Life of Dickens; Phillips, W. C. Dickens, Reade & Collins; Sadleir, M. Excursions in Victorian Bibliography; Swinburne, A. Studies in Prose and Poetry; Wolzogen, E. L. von. Wilkie Collins.

COLMAN, GEORGE ("The Younger") (October 21, 1762-October 17, 1836), dramatist, is so called to distinguish him from his father, a celebrated eighteenth century dramatist and lessee of the Haymarket Theater. His mother was an actress. Like his father, Colman was educated for the law. He was an idle pupil, more interested in amateur theatricals than in study; he had brief careers in Westminster School; Christ Church, Oxford; and King's College, Aberdeen. He kept a few terms at Lincoln's Inn but was never called to the bar.

He began by writing farces for his father's theater, and when the older man was incapacitated by a stroke the son took over the management of the Haymarket (in 1789). The father died in 1794 and the son bought the Haymarket patent.

In 1784 Colman was married secretly to Clara Morris, an actress; they were remarried openly in 1788. There are rumors of a later marriage after his wife's death, but they cannot be authenticated.

In 1820 Colman was appointed lieutenant of the Yeomen of the Guard, an honorary post which George IV later allowed him to sell. In 1824 he was made examiner of plays, and proved to be an absurdly squeamish censor, though he himself had frequently been guilty of extreme obscenity, especially in his comic poems, such as "My Nightgown and Slippers" (1797). He wrote many songs which were set to music for his plays.

Colman was a contentious man and conducted a long feud with the critics; he was always involved in litigation with someone. He was extravagant, and constantly in debt, making and losing fortunes. His best play is *John Bull.* Most of his writing is broad farce. Many of his plays held the stage for years after his death.

PRINCIPAL WORKS: Inkle and Yarico, 1787; The Heir at Law, 1797; John Bull, 1803.

ABOUT: Colman, G. Random Records; Peake. Memoirs of the Colman Family.

COLQUHOUN, JOHN (March 6, 1805-May 27, 1885), Scottish sporting and nature writer, was born in Edinburgh. His father was a baronet, his mother a well known writer on religion. He was educated at the University of Edinburgh.

In 1828 Colquhoun joined the 33rd Regiment in Connaught, Ireland, and the next year was gazetted to the Fourth Dragoon Guards. In 1834, on his marriage, he bought out of the army. He married Frances Sarah Maitland, who published several volumes of poems; they had four sons and five daughters.

Colquhoun's chief interest was in natural history and sport, on both of which he had exceptional knowledge. He was an authority on fishing and hunting in Scotland. Besides his books, he published two lectures, *On the Ferae Naturae of the British Islands,* 1873, and *On Instinct and Reason,* 1874.

PRINCIPAL WORKS: The Moor and the Loch, 1840; Lochs and Rivers, 1849; Salmon Casts and Stray Shots, 1858; Sporting Days, 1860.

ABOUT: Colquhoun, J. The Moor and the Loch (see Preface to 5th ed.); Fraser, W. The Chiefs of Colquhoun and Their Country.

COLTON, CHARLES CALEB (1780-April 28, 1832), poet and essayist, was educated at Eton and at King's College, Cambridge, taking his B.A. in 1801 and his M.A. in 1804. He was rector at Tiverton (a college living), and later at Kew and Petersham. He was an eccentric from the beginning, more interested in hunting and fishing than in his clerical duties, and he finally went to London and became a wine merchant. There he lived in a queer, half-miserly style, spending most of his substance on gambling. Harassed by debt, and frightened by his association with a convicted murderer, he fled England in 1823, going first to the United States and then to Paris. In 1827 he returned and calmly claimed his living again, but a successor was appointed against his protests, and he disappeared once more, first to America, then to France. He spent the rest of his life in France, committing suicide in a friend's house at Fontainebleau in terror of a threatened surgical operation (not so surprising or cowardly an act then as now, since there were no anaesthetics and most operations were fatal).

Colton's poems are of no interest, and he is best known through the collection of aphorisms he called *Lacon.* These are concise and forceful, though necessarily much of their content is borrowed from other writers.

PRINCIPAL WORKS: Hypocrisy: A Satire, 1812; Lacon, 1820-22; Lines on the Conflagration of Moscow, 1822; Modern Antiquity and Other Poems, 1835.

ABOUT: Colton, C. C. Modern Antiquity and Other Poems (see Introduction by M. Sherwell); Gentleman's Magazine 1:564 1832.

COMBE, GEORGE (October 2, 1788-August 14, 1858), Scottish moral philosopher, was born in Edinburgh, son of a brewer. He was delicate from infancy, and his home surroundings were very poor. He secured some education, however, attending the Edinburgh High School and taking some courses at the university from 1802 to 1804. In the latter year he was articled to a writer to the signet (he himself became a writer to the signet in 1812), and began really to study. All his life, however, he was half-educated and his writings show plainly the defects of his training.

In 1817 Combe became a phrenologist, then a more respectable connection than now, and from 1822 he was a lecturer for this cause. He became a leader in phrenological teaching in Great Britain, and an associate of Spurzheim, with Gall one of the two founders of this pseudo-science. In 1836 he retired from business and devoted all his time to writing and lecturing, his greatest interest outside of phrenology being in education. In 1833 he had married Cecilia, daughter of the celebrated actress Mrs. Siddons, having determined their fitness for each other by examining their cranial contours! (She was also a beauty, and an heiress.) The marriage was childless, but, as he predicted, happy.

From 1838 to 1840 Combe lectured on phrenology in the United States, and in 1842 in Heidelburg. He was a free thinker and a liberal, and his writing is like himself—sincere, but dull and didactic. He was personally unpopular, as a bore and a fanatic, but his works were extremely successful and he did much to increase interest in real science by his devotion to the scientific half-world of phrenology.

PRINCIPAL WORKS: Essays on Phrenology, 1819; Elements of Phrenology, 1824; Essay on the Constitution of Man, 1828.

ABOUT: Capen, R. Reminiscences of Spurzheim and Combe; Gibbon, C. Life of George Combe.

COMBE, WILLIAM (1741-June 19, 1823), satirical poet and miscellaneous writer, was born at Bristol, as the son of a merchant—though doubt·has been thrown on his paternity, and some suppose the Alderman Alexander to have been his father.

He was educated at Eton and entered Oxford about 1860, where he failed to take a degree. A legacy from his uncle, Alderman Alexander, whose protegé (and some say son) he was, enabled Combe to travel on the continent and to return to England for a life of extravagance which gained for him the nicknames of "Count Combe" and "Duke Combe" and swiftly resulted in bankruptcy.

Combe is thought to have engaged in menial occupations after this, and to have spent several years as cook in Douai College, as waiter, and as private in the French army. He set up as a teacher of elocution for a while, and almost became the tutor of the little girl who was later to be famous as Mrs. Siddons. Her mother's objections to Combe's character and past prevailed against this appointment.

There is some mystery surrounding Combe's first marriage, but there seems reason for the belief that he was tricked into marrying the mistress of Lord Irnham by the promise of a settlement, which was not made as agreed. This resulted in one of Combe's first writings, a squib directed at the behavior of the nobility. He had begun to write, evidently as a last resort, in 1771 or 1772. In 1779 appeared the anonymous *Letters Supposed to Have Been Written by Yorick to Eliza*, in imitation of Sterne, whom Combe had met on his travels.

Before 1780, Combe was heavily in debt, and had been for some time under the rules of the Kings Bench Prison. All his life he was in a precarious financial situation, and all his work was published anonymously or pseudonymously in order that he might escape seizure of the proceeds. He was pensioned by Pitt, evidently to reward him for political pamphleteering, but upon that minister's retirement lost his pension, and we find him employed on the staff of *The Times* in 1803.

In 1812 the publisher Ackermann had commissioned Thomas Rowlandson to execute a series of plates portraying an itinerant schoolmaster, and applied to Combe for the text. Working independently of the artist, Combe

WILLIAM COMBE

wrote the narrative, in doggerel verse, under circumstances similar to those prevailing when Dickens began the *Pickwick Papers*. Reprinted in book form in 1812 as *The Tour of Dr. Syntax*, the work was sufficiently successful to have two sequels, published between 1812 and 1821.

During the last period of his life, Combe had worked for Ackermann, with whom he had an open account from which he might draw at any time; and Ackermann was fearful lest all trace be lost of the vast amount of writing he had done, since circumstances had prevented his signing any of it. For this reason, before Combe's death, he asked the author for a list of what he had written, and the latter granted the request. This catalog of Combe's writing runs to eighty-six numbers. Nearly all that he produced was hackwork, and included, in addition to his longer works, some two hundred biographical sketches and seventy-three sermons, as well as numerous editions from his hand.

After the death of his first wife, Combe remarried in 1814, the second bride being Charlotte Hadfield. Whether this second marriage was a happy one is not definitely known. There were no children born to the couple.

There is considerable difference of opinion as to the merit of Combe's work. His continuation of Lesage's *Diable Boitu*, published in 1790 as *The Devil on Two Sticks in England,* has earned him the epithet of "the English Lesage"; and the *Cambridge History of English Literature* says: "Dr. Syntax is still a good companion." However, *Chambers' Encyclopaedia* remarks that "the humor is at best very thin—drearily Philistine in conception and frequently spiritless and pointless in execution." Much of Combe's hack work must have been no more than competent.

The character of this author is also open to question. He is described as having been of engaging manner as well as of striking appearance, and it is notable that he was a teetotaler in a time not remarkable for instances of abstemiousness. Ackermann, too, seems to have had considerable respect for him. On the other hand, he has been charged with dishonesty, and one report has it that he was once asked to leave a nobleman's house when a certain amount of money could not be found. It is fairly certain, too, that he was somewhat licentious. Of vicious tendencies in his writings, however, there has been little indication, despite his frequent employment as pamphleteer and the fact that he is known to have written on both sides of a question.

R. M.

PRINCIPAL WORKS: *Fiction*—Letters Supposed to Have Been Written by Yorick to Eliza, 1779; The Devil on. Two Sticks in England, 1790. *History*—History of Westminster Abbey, 1812. *Poetry*—The Tours of Dr. Syntax, 1812-21.

ABOUT: Combe, W. Dr. Syntax's Three Tours (see Biography by J. C. Hotten); Dyce, A. Recollections of the Table Talk of Samuel Rogers; Campbell, T. Life of Mrs. Siddons; Gentleman's Magazine 295:162 August 1903.

CONGREVE, RICHARD (September 14, 1818-July 5, 1899), essayist, was born in Warwickshire. He attended Rugby when the great Dr. Thomas Arnold was headmaster. He then went to Wadham College Oxford, receiving his B.A. in 1840, his M.A. in 1843. Until 1855, except for one term when he was a master at Rugby, he was a fellow and tutor at Oxford. In 1848 he visited Paris and met August Comte, the philosopher. It was the turning point in his life. Comte converted him to Positivism, his system of rationalistic philosophy, and Congreve left Oxford in 1855 and founded the Positivist Community in London. At the same time he studied medicine, becoming a member of the Royal College of Physicians in 1866. In 1878 he broke with Comte's chief disciple, Pierre Lafitte, the leader of the Positivist movement, and created a schism, of one branch of which (growing increasingly more ritualistic) he became the head. He remained so until his death in Hampstead at nearly eighty-one. Congreve was married, his wife's maiden name being Mary Berry.

Congreve was an earnest, high-minded man, but high-handed as well. He was left in comparative isolation after his disagreement with Lafitte, since most of the more distinguished and celebrated Positivists remained with the earlier faction. No one ever doubted his sincerity, however, or his devotion to the cause, which had been unquestioned since he

first translated Comte's *Catechism of Positive Religion* in 1858. As a writer he was sincere and downright, but unusually dull.

PRINCIPAL WORKS: The Politics of Aristotle, 1855; Roman Empire of the West, 1855; Gibraltar: or, The Foreign Policy of England, 1857; Italy and the Western Powers, 1862; Essays, Political, Social, and Religious, 1874; Human Catholicism, 1876.

ABOUT: Mozley, J. B. Letters; Athenaeum July 15, 1899.

CONINGTON, JOHN (August 10, 1825-October 23, 1869), classicist and translator, was born in Boston, Lincolnshire. His father was a clergyman. He went to Rugby, and then to Magdalen College, Oxford, in 1843; three years later he transferred to University College. In 1849 he began to read law, but found himself unsuited for the profession, and after six months gave it up and went back to Oxford for the remainder of his life. In 1854 he became professor of Latin and held the position till his death.

Except for an interest in politics, and a secret—and vain—hope of some day entering Parliament, Conington was the typical Oxford don, near-sighted and with a hesitation in his speech. He had an extraordinary verbal memory, and could recite long passages from Latin and Greek authors. In his youth he had radical leanings, and during his year in London, in 1849-50, wrote for the *Morning Chronicle*, but all his remaining work consisted of editions and particularly of translations of Latin writers. (He edited Aeschylus, but most of his attention was given to the Romans, not the Greeks.) In 1852 he began, with Goldwin Smith, an edition of Virgil on which he was still engaged at his death.

Conington was an eccentric, who classified his friends by their degree of intimacy with him, and appointed hours for them to walk with him, being much offended if they missed the engagement. He had much dignity, more human sympathy than was apparent on the surface, and some humor. His translations are vigorous, and show close knowledge and rhetorical ability, but he was no creative poet, and they give the effect of hasty writing and are frequently prosy and commonplace. He put Virgil into the measures of Scott's *Lady of the Lake*, with rather unfortunate results. All his translations have long ago been superseded by much better ones from other more gifted (though not more scholarly) writers.

PRINCIPAL WRITINGS: *Translations*—Horace, Odes, 1863; Virgil, Æneid, 1866; Horace, Satires, Epistles, Ars Poetica, 1869. *Original*—Miscellaneous Writings (ed. J. A. Symonds) 1872.

ABOUT: Conington, J. Miscellaneous Writings (see Memoir by H. J. S. Smith); Journal of Philosophy II, 1869.

"CONWAY, HUGH." See FARGUS, FREDERICK JOHN

CONYBEARE, WILLIAM DANIEL (June 1787-August 12, 1857), geologist, was the son of a clergyman. His older brother, JOHN J. CONYBEARE, was, like him, a geologist. He was educated at Westminster and at Christ Church, Oxford, where he was graduated first in classics and second in mathematics. While at the university he became interested in geology and an authority on the region. He received his M.A. and was ordained, leaving the university, on his marriage in 1814, for a curacy in the country. In 1823 he was vicar in Glamorganshire, Wales, and later curate at Banbury. He helped to found the Bristol Philosophical Institution and Museum, and through the interest of the great French scientist Cuvier was made a correspondent of the French Academy. In 1836 he presented himself to the family living of Axminster, but resigned in 1844 to become dean of Llandaff, Wales. He made a visit to Madeira during which he studied the volcanic phenomena of the district. In 1857, at the death-bed of his oldest son, he suffered an apoplectic stroke from which he died. He was a fellow of the Royal and Geological Societies.

Conybeare was an early palaeontologist. Considering his era and his clerical training, he was unusually open-minded and advanced. He gave its name to the Plesiosaurus, one of the early reptilian forms. His work is outdated, but it was well done and of great value in its day.

PRINCIPAL WORK: Outlines of Geology (with William Phillips) 1822.
ABOUT: Lyell, C. Principles of Geology.

COOK, ELIZA (December 24, 1818-September 23, 1889), poet, was born in London, the youngest of eleven children of a brasier. In 1827 the father retired from business and went to a farm in Sussex. Eliza was entirely self-educated, though her mother encouraged her studious turn of mind. She wrote verses from the age of fourteen, and published her first volume at seventeen; indeed, some of her best work is her very earliest. She sent her poems anonymously to papers, mostly to the *Weekly Despatch*. This paper published a request for her name and address, and when they had received them made her a regular contributor. In 1849 she became editor and publisher of *Eliza Cook's Journal*, but though its appeal was to the same sort of persons with whom her verses were so popular, she was a poor business woman, and in bad health as well, and the magazine failed in 1854. In 1863 she received a civil list pension of £100 a year. Her popularity and the merit of her work both declined in later life, and for a number of years before her death she was a confirmed invalid.

Miss Cook's best known poem is "The Old Arm Chair," written in memory of her beloved mother. She was extremely popular with the semi-educated, but often deserved a better audience; her work is simple, unpretending, and highly moral, but displays good sense and some humor; her verses are domestic but never mawkish.

PRINCIPAL WORKS: *Poetry*—Lays of a Wild Harp, 1835; Malaia and Other Poems, 1838; New Echoes and Other Poems, 1864. *Prose*—Jottings From My Journal, 1860; Diamond Dust, 1865.
ABOUT: Cook, E. Jottings From My Journal; Eliza Cook's Journal; Illustrated London News October 5, 1889.

COOPER, EDITH EMMA. See "FIELD, MICHAEL"

COOPER, THOMAS (March 20, 1805-July 15, 1892), poet and essayist, was born in Leicester, son of a working dyer. His father died in 1808 and the mother went to Gainesborough, where she lived by dyeing and box making. Cooper went to a bluecoat (charity) school till fifteen, then after one voyage as a sailor was apprenticed to a shoemaker. He studied Latin, Greek, and Hebrew by himself. After a serious illness in 1827 he gave up shoemaking and opened a school, two years later becoming a Methodist preacher as well. He led a roving life for several years, failing in his enterprises and moving on to Lincoln, London, Greenwich, and Leicester, working for a book seller, editing a paper, and finally in 1840 joining the staff of the *Leicestershire Mercury*.

He had now become a chartist (the chartists were the radical labor group of the period) and the *Mercury* promptly discharged him when they discovered it. He then edited the chartist organ, the *Midland Counties Illuminator*. In 1842 a coal strike gave rise to riots, and Cooper, who was giving speeches to and on behalf of the strikers, was three times arrested, for inciting to riot, for arson, and for sedition; the third time he was convicted and sentenced (1843) to two years in the Stafford jail.

While in prison he quarreled with the chartist leaders and left the movement. On his release he became a lecturer on history and education for radical and free thought groups. In the middle of a lecture in 1856 he shocked the audience by suddenly announcing that he had been converted to Christianity. For the remainder of his life he was an itinerant evangelist and anti-free thought agitator. In 1867 his friends raised an annuity by which he lived thenceforth. He had been married in 1834; his wife died in 1880.

Cooper's verse is uneven but often powerful. His earlier prose has directness and vigor; his later work is frequently mere ignorant rant. His autobiography, however, is interesting.

PRINCIPAL WORKS: *Poetry*—The Purgatory of Suicides, 1845; Poetical Works, 1877. *Prose*—Land for the Laborers, 1848; The Bridge of History Over the Gulf of Time, 1871; Life of Thomas Cooper: Written by Himself, 1872; Thoughts at Fourscore, 1885.

ABOUT: Cooper, T. Life of Thomas Cooper: Written by Himself; Thoughts at Fourscore.

COPLESTON, EDWARD (February 2, 1776-October 14, 1849), satirist and economist, was born in Devonshire of a very old West of England family. His father was a clergyman. He was educated at home until he entered Corpus Christi College, Oxford. There he was noted for his proficiency in Latin poetry. He received his B.A. in 1795, remained as a fellow, and was given his M.A. in 1797. He stayed on at the university (at first as a tutor) until 1810, in 1802 being appointed professor of poetry.

In 1814 Copleston was made provost of Oriel College, in 1826 dean of Chester, and in 1828 bishop of Llandaff, Wales, and dean of St. Paul's. He busied himself in church building—he built twenty new churches in his diocese—and in restoring the ruined cathedral. He learned Welsh in his fifties so as to get in closer touch with his parishioners. He died in Llandaff and was buried in the cathedral.

Copleston published nothing except pamphlets and letters. The best known of these were his satirical letters to the *Edinburgh Review* in defense of classical teaching, and his series of pamphlets addressed to the prime minister, Sir Robert Peel, on pauperism, the currency, and education. He was a noted satirist, and an erudite economist, but his style has been called "more Coplestonian than Ciceronian." He was a high churchman and a Tory, but with some liberal leanings.

PRINCIPAL WORKS: A Reply to the Calumnies of the Edinburgh Review, 1810; Letters to Peel, 1819.

ABOUT: Copleston, W. J. Memoir of Edward Copleston.

"CORNWALL, BARRY." See PROCTOR, BRYAN WALLER

COURTHOPE, WILLIAM JOHN (July 14, 1842-April 10, 1917), poet and biographer, came of an old Sussex family. His father, a clergyman, died in 1849 and the boy was brought up by an uncle. He was educated at Harrow and at Corpus Christi and New Colleges, Oxford, where he won the Newdigate Prize and the Chancellor's Prize for an English Essay, and was graduated with a first class in Classical Moderations. In 1870 he married Mary Scott, daughter of the inspector-general of hospitals in Bombay; they had four sons and two daughters.

Courthope was called to the bar, but never practised. In 1869 he became an examiner in the Educational Office, and in 1887 a civil service commissioner. He was senior commissioner from 1892 to 1907. From 1895 to 1901 he was professor of poetry at Oxford, and an honorary fellow of New College.

He was a scholarly editor, particularly interested in the literature of the eighteenth century. His poetry is satiric, and not very successful.

PRINCIPAL WORKS: *Poetry*—Ludibria Lunae, 1869; The Paradise of Birds, 1870; The Country Town and Other Poems, 1920. *Prose*—Life of Addison, 1882; Life of Pope, 1889; History of English Poetry, 1895-1909; Life in Poetry, Law in Taste, 1901.

CORY, WILLIAM (JOHNSON) (January 9, 1823-June 11, 1892), poet and classicist, was born William Johnson, in Devonshire. His mother was a grandniece of the famous painter, Sir Joshua Reynolds. He went to Eton at seven as King's Scholar, and was Newcastle Scholar ten years later; after a brilliant career at Eton he went to King's College, Cambridge, on a scholarship in 1842. There again he garnered scholarships and medals, and in 1845, the same year in which he received his B.A. degree, was appointed to a fellowship that he held until 1872.

In 1845 he also became assistant master at Eton. He remained there, as classical master, for over a quarter of a century. Such celebrated statesmen as Rosebery and the older Balfour were among his pupils, and he was rated as "the most brilliant tutor of his day."

In 1872, after he had inherited a small estate, he retired, simultaneously resigning his Cambridge fellowship. At this time, for reasons of inheritance, he dropped the name of Johnson and took that of Cory, by which he is more generally known. After a tour through Egypt and the Mediterranean with the Countess of Winchelsea and her children, he settled down as a country squire in Devonshire. In 1878, for reasons of health, he moved for four years to Madeira. There, in his middle fifties, rather to the surprise of his friends, the quiet ex-schoolmaster married Rosa Guille, the daughter of a Devonshire rector. When the couple returned to England they settled in Hampstead, where Cory lived for the remainder of his life. His only son was born in 1879.

In Hampstead Cory amused himself by giving free lessons in the classics to a group of woman acquaintances, writing a good deal, talking much more, and laying out his small fortune in modest benefactions. He died there at nearly seventy.

Today Cory is known almost entirely as the author of a single lyric—the lovely "Heraclitus," adapted from a poem by the Greek Callimachus. His only official volume of poetry was *Ionica*, published anonymously in 1858, and reprinted with (largely unfortu-

WILLIAM CORY

nate) additions the year before he died. Others of his poems, however, are well worth knowing—notably "Mimnermus in Church," "Amaturus," and "Reparabo." From the titles, the dominantly classical turn of his mind may be seen. His poems are about equally divided between translations from, adaptations of, and imitations of Greek and Latin models, and expressions of his devotion to and pleasure in his profession of teaching. Some of his Latin verses were called by H. A. J. Munro, the great classicist, "the only good imitations of Horace."

Cory was a prodigious talker, with a love for conversation as a fine art, a voluminous writer of letters and journals (these have been published since his death), and a keen and opinionated critic of his world and his time. As a curious side-line of character in a man apparently ordained by heaven to be a schoolmaster, he was not only an ardent and highly prejudiced patriot, but even had soldierly leanings. From any actual military career he had been debarred from the beginning by near-sightedness so extreme that he once noted with delight in his journal the only time he had ever actually seen a bird on the wing! His prose, as revealed in his letters and diaries, is racy and entertaining, but paradoxical in the highest degree. For example, he rated the nineteenth century French drama above either Shakespeare or the Greeks; considered Shelley an over-rated and subversive writer; and had contempt for Burns, Goethe, and Dickens. Tennyson was his literary idol, and he cherished his master's praise of a Latin translation of "Hesperus."

For his own lyrics, exquisite as some of them are, he had small respect. He recog-

nized that he possessed (in Drinkwater's words) a "slight and desultory genius," and said of his poetry, "the little slender vein is worked out." The three text-books he published, two of them on the method of writing Latin and Greek verses, respectively, are of interest only because of his original illustrations of that art. His one essay in general prose, a *Guide to Modern English History*, he left uncompleted, covering only the period from 1815 to 1835, and displaying no particular reason why it should have been continued. More than most, he is a player on a single string—a metaphor which would have pleased him, for music was his deepest passion.

Cory was of a type perhaps peculiarly English, the gifted amateur, the lover of his time and country, the schoolmaster secretly disappointed not to be a man of affairs, the country squire with scholarly leanings. He was fitted as few writers are to have done just the one thing he could and did accomplish—the production of English verse firmly grounded in the tone and style of the epigrams of the Greek anthology, but instinct with the temper of the nineteenth century in England.   M. A. deF.

PRINCIPAL WORKS: *Poetry*—Ionica, 1858 (republished with additions, 1891). *Miscellaneous*—Nuces, 1869; Lucretilis, 1871; Iophon, 1873; Guide to Modern English History, 1882; Extracts From the Letters and Journals of William Cory, 1897.

ABOUT: Cory, W. Extracts From the Letters and Journals of William Cory; Drinkwater, J. A Book for Bookmen; Esher, R. Ionicus; Paul, H. Stray Leaves.

COSTELLO, LOUISA STUART (1799-April 24, 1870),

poet, novelist, and essayist, was born in Sussex, but in 1814 her father died and she and her mother went to live in Paris. She showed great talent as a miniaturist and by her brush she helped support her mother and educate her brother (later a naval officer), even at this early age. Later she supplemented her miniature paintings by copying illuminated manuscripts.

Miss Costello's life was a long history of devotion to her mother and brother, neither of whom seems to have been particularly grateful. She never married (though she was very attractive in appearance), and had no private life aside from her work and her domestic affections. Both her relatives predeceased her, and she went to live alone at Boulogne, where she died of cancer.

Her work, especially her descriptions of French scenes and life, was highly popular. It is anecdotal and agreeably written. Her poems are graceful lyrics, best described as "pretty." Her novels, semi-historical in nature, were widely read.

PRINCIPAL WORKS: The Maid of the Cyprus Isle and Other Poems, 1815; Songs of a Stranger, 1825;

A Summer Among the Bocages and the Vines, 1840; The Queen's Poisoner, 1841; Béarn and the Pyrenees, 1844; Jacques Coeur, 1847.

ABOUT: Athenaeum May 7, 1870.

COX, SIR GEORGE WILLIAM (January 10, 1827-February 9, 1902), cleric, historian, and miscellaneous writer, was born in Benares, India, where his father was a captain in the East India Company; his mother was a native of the West Indies. He was sent to school in England, first at Bath and Ilminster, then to Rugby, then to Trinity College, Oxford, where he received his B.A. in 1859. He was active in the high church "Oxford Movement" of his time, and was ordained, in 1850, by one of its leaders, Wilberforce.

After acting as curate at Salcombe Regis, he was appointed English chaplain at Gibraltar. The bishop, however, disapproved of his views, and he went to Natal in 1853 with the famous J. W. Colenso, later Bishop of Natal, and one of the first of the "higher critics" of the Bible. Colensó influenced him toward a half-rationalism that made him most unpopular with the church dignitaries. However, in 1854 he was again a curate, this time at St. Paul's Exeter. From 1859 to 1860 he was master at a school in Cheltenham, and he did not return to clerical duties for twenty years.

In 1850 Cox married Emily Stirling, by whom he had five sons and two daughters. He claimed for himself a baronetcy created in 1706, as heir of the eighth son of the first baronet; another claimant proved he was a descendent of the eldest son, and Cox's claim was disallowed, though he continued to use the title. From 1861 to 1885 he was literary adviser of Longmans and Company, the publishers. In 1880 he became a vicar in Berkshire, and from 1881 to 1897 held a crown living in Yorkshire. In 1886 Bishop Colenso's faction in the church chose Cox to be successor to Colenso, but Archbishop Benson refused to consecrate him, so he never held the post. He died at Walmer and was cremated and his ashes buried there.

Cox's historical books, mostly popular compilations, are now out of date. His best work was in the study of mythology, a field in which he became something of an authority. He also wrote poems, stories, and miscellaneous works of many varieties.

PRINCIPAL WORKS: Poems Legendary and Historical (with E. A. Freeman) 1850; Tales From Greek Mythology, 1861; The Great Persian War, 1861; A Manual of Mythology, 1867; Latin and Teutonic Christendom, 1870; The Mythology of the Aryan Nations, 1870; A History of Greece, 1874; The Crusades, 1874; The Greeks and the Persians, 1876; The Athenian Empire, 1876; An Introduction to the Science of Comparative Mythology, 1881; Lives of Greek Statesmen, 1886; A Concise History of England, 1887.

ABOUT: London Times February 11, 1902.

COXE, WILLIAM (March 7, 1747-June 16, 1828), historian and biographer, was the son of the physician to the king's household. He was educated at Eton and at King's College, Cambridge, where he was a fellow in 1768. He was ordained deacon and became a curate, then a private tutor to titled families. In all he made four continental tours with his noble pupils. Through the influence of their titled fathers, his rise in the church was rapid. At one time he held four good livings at once, and was prebend of Salisbury besides. In 1804 he was made archdeacon of Wiltshire. In 1803 he married a widow, Eleonora (Shairp) Yeldham, daughter and wife of British residents in Russia.

Coxe's work is valuable for the facts it contains, since he had access to documents usually difficult for historians to obtain. He was a careful and laborious worker, but painfully dull, and his writing is of no value except as a source-book for later historians.

PRINCIPAL WORKS: Memoirs of Sir Robert Walpole, 1798; The House of Austria, 1807; Memoirs of the Duke of Marlborough, 1818-19.

COYNE, JOSEPH STIRLING (1803-July 18, 1868), Irish playwright, was born in King's County, Ireland, where his father was port surveyor of Waterford. He was educated at Dungannon School. He was intended for the bar, but, encouraged by the publication of his literary articles in Dublin magazines, he decided on literature as his career. In 1836 he went to London, where he contributed to the magazines and joined the staff of the Morning Gazette, the first cheap daily newspaper. He wrote farces for the Adelphi and the Haymarket, and for a short period at the beginning of its history was on the staff of Punch. He was drama critic of the Sunday Times, and secretary of the Dramatic Authors' Society. In 1840 he married Anne (Simcockes) Comyns, a widow.

Coyne wrote some fifty-five plays in all, besides collaborations. Many of them were adaptations from the French. His best dramas are The Hope of the Family, The Secret Agent, and The Black Sheep. Some of his plays are still occasionally performed. His writing had verve, vigor, and real humor. Few of his plays were published, but he wrote several non-dramatic works, chiefly in a humorous vein.

PRINCIPAL WORKS (non-dramatic): Scenery and Antiquities of Ireland, 1842; Pippins and Pies, 1855; Sam Spangle, 1866.

ABOUT: Sunday Times July 26, 1868.

CRABBE, GEORGE (December 24, 1754-February 3, 1832), poet, was the eldest child of George Crabbe, a collector of customs at Aldeburgh, Suffolk.

Although his father, observing his bookish inclinations, sent him to school, first in Bungay and later at Stowmarket, the boy's education was chiefly self-administered. He worked in a warehouse and in 1768 was bound as apprentice (farm-laborer and errand-boy) to the village doctor at Wickham Brook. From 1771 to 1775 he was apprenticed to a surgeon at Woodbridge, where he met Sarah Elmy, his future wife and the "Mira" of his poems. He began to write, publishing anonymously *Inebriety*.

Upon his return home he again went to the hated warehouse, but managed to continue his pursuit of medicine; and he went to London to learn surgery. He returned in less than a year, having exhausted his slender resources, and became assistant to a village surgeon, succeeding him in his practice. He made very little money; his health was bad; and his fiancée refused to marry without some assurance of support. So Crabbe, with almost nothing, set out again for London, hoping to earn money by his writing.

The Candidate was published in 1780, but with no profit to the writer. He appealed for assistance to Lord North, Lord Shelburne, and Lord Thurlow, and received nothing except a chilly letter from the last, who later became a friend and admirer. From Burke, however, to whom he wrote to explain his desperate need, he received aid and comfort. At Burke's instance *The Library* was published in 1781, and he made a home for Crabbe and helped him to enter orders in the same year. In 1782 Crabbe became curate at Aldeburgh.

As the neighbors were not particularly disposed to respect a clergyman who had so obviously risen from circumstances as humble as their own, Crabbe was not very happy in his own town, and, again through Burke's friendship, he was offered a chaplaincy to the Duke of Rutland, which he accepted in 1782.

Although he never felt completely comfortable in the splendor to which the Duke and Duchess were accustomed, he was kindly treated, and in 1783 he published a short memoir of the Duke's brother, who had been killed in battle.

In the same year appeared *The Village*, Crabbe's most famous and most successful work, praised and admired by Dr. Johnson. And also in 1783 came the poet's long-hoped-for marriage with Miss Elmy, to whom he had been engaged for many years.

After the publication in 1785 of *The Newspaper*, Crabbe remained silent for twenty-two years, although he wrote industriously. The next few years are mainly the record of changes in livings. In 1789 he made his home at Muston. When his wife's uncle died in Parham, 1792, Crabbe, his executor, went there as a curate. His agricultural neighbors prospered in a time of high prices because of the

GEORGE CRABBE

current war with the revolutionary government in France; and, as he felt no great enthusiasm for the war, Crabbe was not very popular.

In addition to this difficulty he suffered domestic troubles, losing five children and seeing his wife decline into a nervous depression. His own health necessitated the taking of opium, which helped him considerably. He occupied himself with literary and scientific writing, although little of it ever saw print.

In 1805 it was necessary for Crabbe to return to his own living at Muston. When he arrived, he found that in his absence dissenters from the Anglican Church had thrived. Not only were the Wesleyans well established, but a more radical group was gaining a foothold. Although he preached warmly against dissent, he succeeded only in irritating himself and his hearers.

Mrs. Crabbe, after a breakdown, died in 1813, and in the next year her husband, who himself had undergone a serious illness, went to Trowbridge in Wiltshire. Although hard feeling greeted him at first, because of the popularity of a rival candidate, Crabbe succeeded eventually in gaining respect.

By this time he was well known, and in 1817 he went to London and was received at Holland House. The sale of *Tales of the Hall* and his copyrights brought him £3000. In 1822 he met Scott, and a bond of warm friendship was formed between them. It is suggested in his son's biographical study that Crabbe was not unsusceptible to the attractions of feminine society, and that on one occasion, at least, the family would not have been surprised had he remarried.

His old age was quiet and uneventful. His son John and his family lived with him, and

153

the poet continued, until his death in 1832, to perform service and to occupy himself with his plants and other natural specimens of various sorts, in which he had always taken great interest. After his death his parishioners erected a monument in the Trowbridge church.

Described by Byron as "Nature's sternest painter, yet the best," Crabbe was, it is strangely true, greatly admired by the Romantic writers, with the exception of Hazlitt. Throughout his verse are evidences of the heritage of Pope and the classical writers of the couplet in the eighteenth century, whose characteristic form Crabbe uses; it was the conventional one when he began to write, and he chose the conventional as the least artificial. "Between the publication of Crabbe's first work and of his last, a revolution had come over English poetry," writes Harold Child. "Poetry took on a hundred new or revived forms; yet he clung, with very few remissions, to his couplets. In spite of all, his work was read and admired by the very men who were trying to set poetry free from the shackles in which he continued to labor."

But it is his realism for which Crabbe is most noted; and the grim pictures of rustic life given in *The Village* are in marked contrast to the glorifying treatment of the same theme found in Goldsmith's *The Deserted Village*. "The truth of his [Crabbe's] pen pictures is harsh and incomplete," writes Louis Cazamian, "but within its own limits is unrivaled; his pathos is sombre, crushingly painful at times, but this only makes it more telling." In his tales in verse he shows powers of narrative and of character-drawing. At the same time he lacked the greatest finesse in his writing, and has been described as "a Pope in worsted stockings." In the words of Saintsbury, "He sees his subject steadily, and even in a way he sees it whole; but he does not see it in the poetical way." And, while great critics and writers of his own time admired him—Jane Austen, in an effusive moment, remarked that she could consider even marrying him—he is not widely read today.   R. W. W.

PRINCIPAL WORKS: *Poetry*—Inebriety, 1775; The Candidate, 1780; The Library, 1781; The Village, 1783; The Newspaper, 1785; The Parish Register, 1807; The Borough, 1810; Tales, 1812; Tales of the Hall, 1819; Poetical Works, 1834. *Miscellaneous*—Character of Lord Robert Manners, 1783.

ABOUT: Ainger, C. Crabbe; Crabbe, G[eorge, Jr.]. The Life of the Rev. George Crabbe; Evans, J. H. The Poems of George Crabbe; Huchon, R. George Crabbe and His Times; Kebbel, T. H. The Life of George Crabbe; More, P. E. Shelburne Essays (second series); Annual Biography and Obituary 17:11 1833.

CRACKANTHORPE, HUBERT MONTAGUE (May 12, 1870-November 1896), short story writer, was the son of a Queen's

HUBERT CRACKANTHORPE

Councillor and Doctor of Civil Law, and of a mother who was a writer of sociological essays. (One of her essays, "The Revolting Daughters," attracted wide attention in the Victorian 'eighties.) The father had changed his name, for reasons of inheritance, from his original name of Cookson. He also wrote frequently for the more serious periodicals on eugenics and other social questions.

Richard LeGallienne, who knew Hubert Crackanthorpe, says that "hardly another writer of his generation had so thoroughly equipped himself for his calling of novelist by so adventurous a study of human life." But Rothenstein, who perhaps knew him better, remarks that he belonged to a good, solid family, and lived a quiet life in a workman's flat in Chelsea. He could scarcely have done much "adventuring" in any case, for he died at twenty-six.

In 1893 Crackanthorpe was married to Leila Macdonald, a descendant of the famous Flora Macdonald who saved the life of "Bonnie Prince Charlie," and a granddaughter of Sir William Grove, the chemist. She too dabbled in writing, some of her contributions appearing in the *Yellow Book* and *The Savoy*. Both she and her husband belonged, however quiet and orderly their daily life, to the Bohemian, decadent group gathered around these magazines; and in 1896 she proved her allegiance to it by running away with another man.

Her desertion broke her husband's heart. He went to Paris, where he had lived for much of his early youth (the scenes of many of his stories are laid in France), and there, some time in the late autumn, he threw himself into the Seine. When his body was recovered, about the end of the year, it had been in the water for six weeks or so, and was so badly disfigured that his brother identified him only by his cuff-links. His tragic death excited small comment: *The Critic* remarked that he "had done literary work of a strange sort," and a less restrained commentator said that his suicide was "the judgment of God for adoring French idols"!

Crackanthorpe's stories (he never wrote a novel, though he was undoubtedly a novelist in the making) were indeed of a "strange sort" for the era in which he lived. They are entirely outside the current of the sentimental and evasive fiction of the period. Like the early Stephen Crane, he wrote often of prostitutes and kept women; he had gone to school to the French naturalists and to Maupassant, and endeavored, twenty years before the time was ripe, to present life on the fringes of respectability with humanity and without moralizing. Symons called his stories "dreary," but there is in them an understanding and a tenderness far beyond his years. His work was no mere reporting, but was instinct with imaginative intelligence and a precocious maturity. He was in fact an early impressionist, consciously a pupil of his French masters, and willing and able to defend strongly the frankness and realism which won him so many bitter attacks during his lifetime.

For the rest, Crackanthorpe was a normal young Englishman, fond of sports and outdoor exercise, social, deeply interested in his fellow creatures, and for a while at least youthfully flattered by the attention of such writers as Symons, LeGallienne, and Henry James. He was included in the first number of the *Yellow Book,* but though he was widely acquainted among them, none of the Harland-Beardsley group seems to have been his close friend or to have done much to preserve his memory.

Had disaster and early death not overtaken Crackanthorpe, he would have lived (for his work was constantly growing in power) to see himself hailed as a pioneer, instead of damned and forgotten as a too early anticipation of the trend of English fiction.

M. A. deF.

PRINCIPAL WORKS: *Short Stories*—Wreckage (Seven Studies) 1893; Sentimental Studies and a Set of Village Tales, 1895; Last Studies (posthumous) 1897. *Essays*—Vignettes, 1896.

ABOUT: Harris, F. Contemporary Portraits (Second Series); James, H. Last Studies, 1897; Starrett, V. Buried Caesars, 1923; Symons, A. Studies in Prose and Verse, 1904; Critic 30:29 January 9, 1897; Sewanee Review 36:462 October 1928.

CRAIG, ISA (Mrs. John Knox) (October 17, 1831-December 23, 1903), Scottish poet, was born in Edinburgh, where her father was a hosier and glover. Both her parents died early, and she was reared by her grandmother. She was taken from school at nine, but did much reading at home. She began contributing verses to *The Scotsman,* and in 1853 joined its staff. In 1857 she went to London as secretary of the National Association for the Promotion of Social Science, and remained in this position until 1866, when she married her cousin, John Knox, an iron merchant. In 1858 she won a £50 prize for the best centenary poem on Burns, and this ode remains her finest work. She contributed frequently to various magazines, and for a short time edited *The Argosy.* Her verse shows lyric charm, but on the whole is rather slight. She wrote a prose work for children, *The Little Folk's History of England* (1872), which was very popular. She died in Suffolk at seventy-four.

PRINCIPAL WORKS: Poems by Isa, 1856; Esther West, 1870; Songs of Consolation, 1874.

ABOUT: Wilson, G. Poets and Poetry of Scotland.

CRAIGIE, PEARL MARY TERESA ("John Oliver Hobbes") (November 3, 1867-August 13, 1906), Anglo-American novelist and dramatist, was born Pearl Richards in Chelsea, Massachusetts, the eldest child of John Morgan Richards, a New York merchant, and Laura Hortense (Arnold) Richards. As, within a week of the child's birth, her father was called to London to conduct a manufacturing chemist's business and Pearl and her mother followed early in the next year, Mrs. Craigie was, by breeding if not by birth, an Englishwoman.

Her education was in a boarding-school at Newbury, Berkshire, and in private day schools in London. She was fond of stories and read widely; and, with the encouragement of a Congregational preacher, Joseph Parker, a friend of the family, she early attempted literary composition. At the age of nine she contributed stories to Parker's newspaper, *The Fountain.* She had other aspirations as well, and in 1885 studied music in Paris, becoming a pianist of considerable skill.

After a visit to America in the winter of 1886-87, she married Reginald Walpole Craigie. Her marriage was unfortunate, and, after the birth of a son in 1890, she left her husband. In 1895 she was granted a divorce and custody of the child, after a public trial which caused her considerable suffering. Her distress and her naturally mystic frame of mind resulted in her embracing the Roman Catholic faith, to which she was admitted in 1892; at this time she assumed the additional names "Mary" and "Teresa."

By this time she already had contributed criticisms and articles to a periodical; but her ambitions were higher, and she began serious study, plunging eagerly into the subject of

PEARL MARY TERESA CRAIGIE

Greek, Latin, and English literature, which she pursued at University College, London. Her career as an author began in 1891 with the appearance of *Some Emotions and a Moral,* issued under the pseudonym "John Oliver Hobbes," which she kept throughout her literary career. This first novel, popular for its wit and cynicism, established a reputation, and the author wrote in the next few years several novels which did little to add to it.

Next she turned her attention to drama, with varied success. *The Ambassador,* a four-act comedy (1898), won the audience, and ran for a full season, thanks largely to the wit of the dialogue. Her other efforts, however, with the exception of *The Bishop's Move* (written in collaboration with Murray Carson), were not received with great or sustained popular favor.

Despite poor health Mrs. Craigie was active in London society and the world of fashion, entertaining at her father's home a large group of literary and musical friends, and going to theatres and concerts. On occasion she withdrew for religious meditation to the Convent of the Assumption, Kensington Square. She was interested in philanthropic and literary work, and served as president of the Society of Women Journalists in 1895-96.

After a visit to India in 1903, she planned in 1905 to make a lecture tour in America, but ill health forced her to abandon the plan. In England she spent her time at her father's house in London and his residence at Ventnor, Isle of Wight; and near Ventnor she rented a small house, where she could retire for work. It was immediately after her return to London from Ventnor in August 1906 that she died very suddenly of heart failure.

"Handsome, widely read, and an excellent conversationalist, Mrs. Craigie was a favorite in society, which did its best to spoil her," declared an obituary notice. "That she was unaffected by success cannot be said, but she bore that hard test well on the whole." She was a strange combination of religious mysticism and worldly sophistication.

While she attempted various forms in literature, the novel is Mrs. Craigie's most characteristic medium. Her philosophical vagueness operated against her being considered a profound thinker. Although good at description, she tended to give her novels over to a witty brilliance of a rather steely glitter which provoked a caustic criticism in verse:

> John Oliver Hobbes, with your spasms and throbs,
>   How does your novel grow?
> With cynical sneers at young Love and his tears,
>   And epigrams all in a row.

Mrs. Craigie's most successful work was done in the vein of satire and cynical humor suggested above, and her novels are notable more for wit and for musical suggestiveness of style than for plot or for lifelike character. "She could paint a scene concisely, analyze character pungently, and deal neatly with the ironies of life," commented *The Athenaeum.* "Her limitation was that she hardly ever dealt with anything else. . . . A bitter sweetness is the leading characteristic of her novels. . . . Her work cannot be relished every day, though it is tonic in its way, or rather like some rare liqueur."   R. W. W.

PRINCIPAL WORKS: *Novels*—Some Emotions and a Moral, 1891; The Sinner's Comedy, 1892; A Study in Temptations, 1893; A Bundle of Life, 1893; The Gods, Some Mortals, and Lord Wickenham, 1895; The Herb-Moon: A Fantasia, 1896; The School for Saints, 1897; Robert Orange, 1900; The Serious Wooing, 1901; Love and the Soul Hunters, 1902; The Vineyard, 1904; The Dream and the Business, 1906; The Flute of Pan, 1905; Saints in Society, 1907. *Plays*—Journeys End in Lovers Meeting, 1894; A School for Saints, 1896; The Ambassador, 1898; Osbern and Ursyne, 1899; A Repentance, 1899; The Wisdom of the Wise, 1900; The Bishop's Move (with Murray Carson) 1902; The Flute of Pan, 1904. *Miscellaneous*—The Note-Book of a Diner-out, 1888-89; The Tales of John Oliver Hobbes, 1894; Tales About Temperaments, 1902; Imperial India: Letters from the East, 1903; Letters From a Silent Study, 1903.

ABOUT: Craigie, P. M. T. The Life of John Oliver Hobbes Told in Her Correspondence With Numerous Friends (see Biographical Sketch by John Morgan Richards and Introduction by Bishop Welldon); Catholic World 84:73 October 1906; Dublin Review 180:266 April 1927; North American Review 183:1251 December 21, 1906.

CRAIK, DINAH MARIA MULOCK
(April 20, 1826-October 12, 1887), novelist, was born near Stoke-upon-Trent, Staffordshire, where her father, Thomas Mulock, was a Nonconformist clergyman.

Because of the eccentric and unreliable character of this father Mrs. Craik's youth was not entirely smooth or easy. She was a clever girl, wrote verses ("The Party of Cats") at the age of ten, and by the time she was thirteen had acquired enough education to assist her mother (Dinah Mellard Mulock) in the conduct of a small school, where the little girl taught elementary Latin. At this time the family was living in Newcastle-under-Lyme, where Dinah had attended Brampton House Academy.

Upon the death in 1839 of her mother, Mrs. Mulock inherited some property. Her husband, accordingly, who seems never to have been hesitant about using other people's money, removed with his family to London, where they moved about from place to place. Dinah studied Greek, Latin, French, and Italian, and learned Irish; she was given drawing-lessons and took great interest in music. In 1841 her first published poem, on the birth of the Princess Royal, appeared in the *Staffordshire Advertiser*.

At length, in 1844, the young girl decided to separate from her Micawber-like father, who, in the course of a varied life, drifted from business to preaching and to journalism. Her mother, whom she took back to Staffordshire, died in the next year. In 1847 Thomas, the elder of the two sons, was accidentally killed; and for the rest of their lives Dinah and Benjamin, her surviving brother, were left by their father to their own devices, and to such income as came to them from their grandmother's estate.

In 1849 Miss Mulock, who had written some children's stories, published *The Ogilvies,* a novel dedicated to her mother. She and her brother were living quietly and obscurely in London. With the beginning of her career, however, the literary and social world began to open to her; and she came to know such figures as Alexander Macmillan, of the publishing house, Charles Edward Mudie, the manager of a large and successful circulating library, John Westland Marston, the dramatist, and Margaret Oliphant, the novelist and historian. Miss Mulock proceeded to take a small house, where she became the center of a group of admiring and ambitious young ladies. She continued to write novels and short stories, in 1856 publishing her best-known work, *John Halifax: Gentleman,* which went through edition after edition.

Her new prosperity enabled her to remove, in 1859, with her brother, to a delightful old house in Hampstead, where she entertained her many friends, among them Sydney Dobell and W. J. Linton, the wood-engraver. To all appearances, she was settled for the rest of her life, but her brother's death by an accident in 1863 changed her plans, and in 1864 she sold her house.

In the next year she married a man eleven years younger than she, George Lillie Craik,

DINAH MARIA MULOCK CRAIK

a partner in the publishing company of Macmillan. They built a home, The Corner House, Shortlands, Bromley, where Mrs. Craik lived until her death, enjoying the society of her friends. She had no children, but in 1872 she adopted a little girl whom she named Dorothy. Her sudden death in 1887 from heart-failure occurred in the midst of plans for the wedding of this adopted daughter.

Of Mrs. Craik's character there seems to be nothing but praise. Her devotion to her mother and her brothers was matched by her loyalty to her trying father, whom, in his old age, she assisted with money. She was beloved by rich and poor, and was so generous that for a time she made a practice of placing loaves of bread on shelves outside her house, with a notice inviting the needy to help themselves. Her pension of £60, granted her in 1864, she used to help needy authors.

The nobility of her character is perhaps responsible for the moral and ethical emphasis of her writings, some of her essays, such as *Sermons Out of Church,* being definitely didactic. It is this Christian emphasis on virtue and a calm faith that true nobility is independent of social or economic situation, that gives the characteristic note to *John Halifax,* her best-known work (although Mrs. Craik preferred her *A Life for a Life*). Once she had written it, she had little more to say. Henry James summed up her faults by referring to her "kindly, somewhat dull, pious, and very sentimental." As a poet she was not important, although two lyrics, "Rothesay Bay" and "Philip My King" deserve mention. "She was not a genius, and she does not express the ideals and aspirations of women of exceptional genius," wrote Richard Garnett, "but the tender and philanthropic, and at the same time energetic and practical womanhood of ordinary life has never had a more sufficient representative." R. W. W.

PRINCIPAL WORKS: *Biography*—Fifty Golden Years: Incidents in the Queen's Reign, 1887. *Essays*—A Woman's Thoughts About Women, 1858; Sermons Out of Church, 1875; Plain Speaking, 1882; About Money and Other Things, 1886; Concerning Men and Other Papers, 1888. *Juvenile*—Michael the Miner, 1846; How to Win Love: or, Rhoda's Lesson, 1848; Cola Monti, 1849; Alice Learmont, 1852; Bread Upon the Waters, 1852; A Hero: Philip's Book, 1853; The Little Lychetts, 1855; Our Year, 1860; The Fairy Book, 1863; A New Year's Gift to Sick Children, 1865; Little Sunshine's Holiday, 1871; The Adventures of a Brownie As Told to My Child, 1872; The Little Lame Prince, 1874. *Novels*—The Ogilvies, 1849; Olive. 1850; The Head of the Family, 1852; Agatha's Husband, 1853; John Halifax: Gentleman, 1856; A Life for a Life, 1859; Mistress and Maid, 1863; Christian's Mistake, 1865; A Noble Life, 1866; Two Marriages, 1867; The Woman's Kingdom, 1869; A Brave Lady, 1870; Hannah, 1872; My Mother and I: A Girl's Love Story, 1874; The Laurel Bush; An Old-Fashioned Love Story, 1876; Young Mrs. Jardine, 1879; His Little Mother, 1881; Miss Tommy: A Mediaeval Romance, 1884; King Arthur; Not a Love Story, 1886. *Poetry*—Poems, 1859; Songs of Our Youth, 1875; Thirty Years, 1880; Children's Poetry, 1881. *Tales*—Avillion and Other Tales, 1853; Nothing New, 1857; Romantic Tales, 1859; Domestic Stories, 1860; Lord Erlestoun and Other Stories, 1864; The Unkind Word and Other Stories, 1870; Is It True? 1872. *Travel and Description*—Fair France: Impressions of a Traveller, 1871; An Unsentimental Journey Through Cornwall, 1884; An Unknown Country, 1887. *Miscellaneous*—Studies From Life, 1860; A Legacy: Being the Life and Remains of John Martin, 1878.

ABOUT: James, H. Notes and Reviews; Oliphant, M. O. W. Women Novelists of Victoria's Reign; Academy 32:269 October 22, 1867; Athenaeum October 22, 1887; Bookman 70:1 April 1926.

CRAIK, GEORGE LILLIE (1798-June 25, 1866),

Scottish historian and critic, was born in Fife, where his father was a minister and schoolmaster. He took the divinity course at St. Andrews University but was never licensed as a preacher. In 1816 he became editor of *The Star*, and also lectured on poetry. In 1826 he married Jeannette Dempster, by whom he had one son and three daughters; she died in 1856. In 1826 also he went to London to live. There he became a contributor to Charles Knight's publications for the Society for the Diffusion of Useful Knowledge. In 1849 he was made professor of English literature and history at Queen's College, Belfast. He suffered a stroke while lecturing to a class in February of 1866, and died four months later.

Craik's work is careful and accurate, though not very interesting. He was much interested in philology and made some valuable additions to the study of the English language.

PRINCIPAL WORKS: The Pursuit of Knowledge Under Difficulties, 1830; The Pictorial History of

England, 1837; Spenser and His Poetry, 1845; Bacon and His Writings, 1846-47; Outlines of the History of the English Language, 1851.

ABOUT: Gentleman's Magazine 2:265 1866.

CRAIK, SIR HENRY (October 18, 1846-March 16, 1927),

Scottish historian and biographer, was born in Glasgow. His father was moderator of the general assembly of the Church of Scotland. He was educated at the Glasgow High School, Glasgow University, and Balliol College, Oxford. He was an M.A. from Oxford, and received the honorary LL.D. degree from Glasgow and St. Andrews Universities.

In 1873 Craik married Fanny Duffield, who died in 1923. They had two sons. In 1870 he became an examiner of the Scotch Education Department, being senior examiner in 1878. He was secretary of the department from 1885 to 1904. From 1911 to 1914 he was principal of Queen's College, London. From 1906 to his death he was a member of Parliament, elected on the Conservative ticket.

In 1897 Craik was made a Knight Commander of the Bath, and in 1926 he was created a baronet. He died at eighty-one.

Craik's two chief interests were in the life and works of Swift, and in Scottish history. He wrote also on educational topics, and after a trip to India in 1907 produced a book on his journey. His work was sound but not markedly original, and his study of Swift uncovered no new sources and supplied no fresh critical views.

PRINCIPAL WORKS: Life of Jonathan Swift, 1882; The State and Education, 1883; Selections From Swift, 1893; English Prose Selections, 1892-96; A Century of Scottish History, 1901; Impressions of India, 1908; The Life of Edward, First Earl of Clarendon, 1911.

CRAWFORD, ISABELLA VALANCY (December 25, 1850-February 12, 1887),

Canadian poet, was born in Dublin, Ireland. She was the daughter of Dr. Stephen Crawford and of Sydney (Scott) Crawford, the latter of Scottish and the former of Irish descent.

The family migrated to Canada in 1858, first settling at Paisley, Ontario, whence they removed to a succession of towns in various parts of the country. Isabella and her sisters were educated at home and were taught Latin, French and English by their parents; Isabella, an eager reader, read such authors as Horace and Dante with great enjoyment, and was fired with the desire to write poetry. When Dr. Crawford died, she found it necessary, at an early age, to support her mother and invalid sister by her pen. The last remaining years of her life were filled with a desperate struggle for recognition and pay; and as she was a sufferer from impairment of the heart action, she did not manage to survive the strain. She died of cardiac disease at Peterborough, Ontario, at the age of thirty-seven.

Three years before her death she had published a small volume of poems. The edition was a complete failure, but the English journals recognized the talent of the poet and gave her warm praise, *The Spectator* saying that her work was full of promise and "her power of expression quite unusual."

Her best known poems "Old Spookses' Pass" and "Malcolm's Katie" are richly if unevenly written, skilful, and full of fire. Despite certain awkwardnesses and a bad taste in titles, they are worthy representatives of the cowboy life of western Canada and deserve a high place in the literature of that country. Their author may fairly be said to be the first Canadian poet of real distinction. Her collected poems were published in 1905.

PRINCIPAL WORKS: *Poetry*—Old Spookses' Pass and Other Poems, 1884; Poems, 1905.

ABOUT: Burpee, L. J. A Little Book of Canadian Essays; Garvin, J. W. Canadian Poets; Hale, K. (pseud.). Isabella Valancy Crawford; Logan, J. D. & French, D. G. Highways of Canadian Literature; Spectator 57:1381 October 18, 1884.

CREASY, SIR EDWARD SHEPHERD (1812-January 27, 1878), historian, was born in Kent, where his father was a land agent; the father then became an auctioneer in Brighton and published the *Brighton Gazette* mainly to carry his own advertisements. Creasy was educated at Eton and at King's College, Cambridge, where he was a fellow in 1834. He was called to the bar from Lincoln's Inn in 1837 and joined the home circuit, becoming assistant-judge of the Westminster sessions court. He abandoned the law temporarily for teaching in 1840 and became professor of modern and ancient history at London University; later he returned to the bar and was made chief justice of Ceylon. He was knighted in 1860. In 1870 he was invalided home, and retired in 1872.

Creasy's most popular work was *The Fifteen Decisive Battles of the World*, the attractive title of which must have had much to do with its success, for this, like all his work, is accurate but heavy and dull.

PRINCIPAL WORKS: The Fifteen Decisive Battles of the World, 1852; An Historical and Critical Account of the Several Invasions of England, 1852; History of England, 1869-70.

ABOUT: Athenaeum February 1878.

CREEVEY, THOMAS (March 1768-February 1838), diarist, was born in Liverpool, the son of a merchant. He was graduated from Queen's College, Cambridge, in 1789. He was called to the bar from the Inner Temple in 1794, and was a Whig member of Parliament from 1802.

Creevey married a widow, a Mrs. Ord, by whom he had sixteen children before she died in 1818. She was an heiress, but after her death Creevey was reduced to comparative poverty. In 1806 he was secretary of the Board of Control; in 1830 he became treasurer of the ordnance and later treasurer of Greenwich Hospital, these two latter posts improving his fortunes a little. Before 1830, however, he lost his seat in Parliament and never recovered it.

Thomas Creevey is in the peculiar position of being an author unknown until sixty-five years after his death. His journals and letters were willed by him to the woman who had been his mistress from 1814 to 1818, and who was his sole legatee and executrix. Strenuous efforts were made by his political associates, who feared his indiscreet remarks, to get hold of and suppress his papers, and it is probable that they did find and destroy a diary he had kept for thirty-six years. What was left of his literary remains was finally published in 1903, with a further selection in 1934.

Creevey was a racy and vigorous writer, almost of the caliber of the great diarist Pepys, and his correspondence and journals, written without thought of public reading, give an excellent picture of his period from the Whig point of view.

PRINCIPAL WORKS: The Creevey Papers (ed. Sir H. Maxwell) 1903; Creevey's Life and Times (ed. J. Gore) 1934.

CREIGHTON, MANDELL (July 5, 1843-January 14, 1901), historian, was born in Carlisle. He was educated at the Grammar School, Durham, and at Merton College, Oxford, where he received his B.A. in 1867. For three years he was a tutor, then was ordained deacon in 1870, and priest in 1873.

In 1872 he married Louise von Glehm, of Russian descent, who became a well known critical writer and her husband's biographer. They had three sons and four daughters.

At his own request, Creighton was given a college living on the coast of Northumberland, where he could gain experience and also have leisure for historical study. In 1883 he became honorary canon of Newcastle. The next year he was made a fellow of Emmanuel College, Cambridge, and professor of ecclesiastical history at the university. In 1885 he was canon of Worcester, and in 1890 was named canon of Windsor, but before he could be installed became Bishop of Peterborough. In 1897 he was named Bishop of London, and remained so until his death.

From 1886 to 1891 he was editor of the *English Historical Review*, and was president of the Church Historical Society from 1894 until he died. He represented Emmanuel

College at Harvard's 250th anniversary, and represented the English church at the coronation of Czar Nicholas II.

Tall, spare, with a long beard, Creighton was a striking figure. A moderate in religion and social views, he acted frequently as an arbitrator in labor disputes. He was noted for his wit, which not even the dignity of his office could vanquish.

Creighton's historical work has a practical and scientific bent. It is concise and sound, and unmarred by hollow rhetoric. Much of it is still useful to the student.

PRINCIPAL WORKS: A Primer of Roman History, 1875; The Age of Elizabeth, 1876; Simon de Montfort, 1876; History of England, 1879; History of the Papacy During the Reformation, 1882-94; Cardinal Wolsey, 1888; Persecution and Tolerance, 1895; The Early Renaissance in England, 1805; The English National Character, 1896; Queen Elizabeth, 1896; Church and State, 1897.

ABOUT: Creighton, L. von G. Life and Letters of Mandell Creighton; Paul, H. Stray Leaves; Church Quarterly Review October 1905; Quarterly Review April 1901.

CROCKETT, SAMUEL RUTHERFORD (September 24, 1860-April 21, 1914), Scottish novelist and poet, was born in Kirkcudbrightshire, the illegitimate son of a farmer's daughter, whose name he took. He was educated at the Free Church School in Edinburgh and at the University of Edinburgh, which he entered as a bursar. He worked his way through the university by writing for the press. In 1879 he went as a traveling tutor with a pupil to Germany, Switzerland, and Italy, a tour which provided him thereafter with romantic backgrounds for his stories.

Crockett then decided to study for the ministry, and, continuing his journalistic work, put himself through New College, Edinburgh, which he attended from 1882 to 1886. He was ordained and became a minister in Midlothian. At the same time he married Ruth Milner, by whom he had two sons and two daughters. In 1895 he resigned from the ministry to devote his entire time to writing. He produced about fifty books, nearly all of them novels. The best known was The Stickit Minister, which brought him much celebrity. In later years his popularity declined. His writing was vigorous, his humor gay though crude, his descriptions of natural scenery particularly good. He was a friend of Robert Louis Stevenson, who dedicated several poems to him.

PRINCIPAL WORKS: Dulce Cor (poems) 1886; The Stickit Minister, 1893; The Raiders, 1894; The Lilac Sunbonnet, 1894.

ABOUT: Harper, M. M. Rambles in Galloway.

CROKER, JOHN WILSON (December 20, 1780-August 10, 1857) Anglo-Irish statesman and man of letters, was born in Galway. His father, John Croker, was later surveyor-

JOHN WILSON CROKER

general of customs and excise in Ireland, and his mother, a former Miss Rathbone, was the daughter of a clergyman. As a boy, Croker had a tendency to stutter, and was sent, for the correction of this fault, to a school in Cork kept by a Mr. Knowles. His career as a political writer began very early, for his first attempt at composition was an election squib written when he was nine. He must have corrected his speech handicap early, for when, after preparation at various schools, he entered Trinity College in 1796, he made a name for himself as debater. Several medals were awarded to him for excellence in essay writing.

After he received his bachelor's degree in 1800, Croker began to study law and to write for The Times, and was successful in both legal and literary fields, being admitted to the Irish Bar and receiving considerable applause for his letters in verse, Familiar Epistles on the State of the Irish Stage (1804). In 1806, the year of his marriage to Rosamond Pennell, whose father was later consul to South Africa, he received a seat in Parliament representing Downpatrick—the first of many terms of service in the House.

Croker was now well on the way to success. His literary fame was growing. Songs of Trafalgar (1806) and the poem "The Battle of Talavera" had conspicuous success, the latter being singled out for praise by Wellington. A Sketch of Ireland Past and Present (1807), in which Croker appealed for Catholic emancipation, is said to have been the direct cause of his appointment to the post of assistant secretary for Ireland. In 1809 he had the good fortune to defend the Duke of York in the scandal over the supposed influence of the Duke's mistress, Mary Anne Clarke, in the granting of appointments. Croker's reward was the secretaryship of the admiralty.

He had scarcely taken office when he discovered an important defalcation involving a large sum and an official of high rank. His immediate refusal to issue further warrants for expenditure until the matter should be adjusted resulted in pressure being brought to bear for his dismissal; he then offered to resign, and an investigation was begun. This proved that he had been in the right and firmly entrenched him in the graces of the government. He had already impressed the minister Canning with his very first speech in the House, and with this fresh addition to his prestige soon became one of the leading lights of the Tory faction. It is fairly certain that it was he who finally persuaded Sir Robert Peel to join that party. Peel and Croker became close friends, and their unfortunate quarrel over Peel's refusal to support the Tories in their opposition to the Reform Bill was the only cause of their final break.

The *Quarterly Review,* of which he was part founder, was one of Croker's chief interests, and scarcely an issue in the years 1811-26 and 1831-45 appeared without an article by him. The drastic drubbing administered to Keats in the *Quarterly* was Croker's work—the review of an unsparing critic who honestly detested the new fashions in literature. Croker himself had bad treatment when his edition of Boswell's *Life of Johnson,* a fine piece of work which had occupied much of his time and thought, was published in 1831. Macaulay, possibly smarting under the memory of defeats in debate administered by Croker, unmercifully condemned the new edition and described it as stupid. When, twenty years later, Croker reviewed Macaulay's *History of England* and expressed doubts concerning its accuracy and authoritativeness, he laid himself open to charges of unfairness which have hurt his reputation to this day. Croker has been held up to posterity as an example of a malevolent politician—even to the extent of being the original of the contemptible Rigby in Disraeli's *Coningsby.* Yet he will be remembered as the befriender of such poets as Southey and Crabbe, and as a man whose death was mourned by a host of friends. Of course, Croker was a hard hitter and often laid about him with Celtic fervor and some bitterness, but it is likely that careful study of him will lead to a favorable opinion.

He was slender and rather small, but strongly built, with a quick wit, a pleasant manner, and a complete lack of fear. As an editor he produced, in his edition of Boswell, what John Forster, the biographer, called "the best-edited book in the English language"; a work whose accuracy was commended by Carlyle. Croker was also the founder of the Athenaeum Club, the distinguished literary society whose first membership committee included Thomas Moore and Walter Scott.

His various papers, diaries, and correspondence appeared in 1883 under the editorship of L. J. Jennings. R. M.

PRINCIPAL WORKS: *Miscellaneous Original Writings*—The Memoirs, Diaries, and Correspondence of John Wilson Croker, 1883. *Editor*—Boswell's *Life of Samuel Johnson,* 1831; Hervey's *Memoirs of the Reign of George II,* 1848; (in part) Pope's *Works,* 1871. *Translator*—Memoirs of the Embassy of the Maréchal de Bassompierre, 1819.
ABOUT: Croker, J. W. Memoirs, etc.; McCarthy, J. H. & others. Irish Literature; Walpole, S. Essays Political and Biographical; Annual Register 1857; National Review 82:414 November 1923; Quarterly Review 158:518 July-October 1884.

CROKER, THOMAS CROFTON (January 15, 1798-August 8, 1854), Irish story writer and antiquary, was born in Cork, the son of a major in the army. He had little formal education, but as a boy of fourteen to seventeen roamed all over southern Ireland collecting peasant songs and legends. His family were Quakers, and in 1816 apprenticed him to a family of Quaker merchants in Cork. His first interest was in painting, and he exhibited some of his pictures in Cork in 1817.

His father's death in 1818 offered him freedom from the mercantile career he hated, and he made his first literary venture by sending Thomas Moore, the poet, four songs to be included in his *Irish Melodies.* Moore became interested and invited the young man to London, where he remained permanently. He could not earn his way by writing, however, and became clerk of the Admiralty, a position he held until 1850. Thanks to his interest in art, he introduced the use of lithography into the Admiralty office. He continued to write, and with Sidney Taylor edited a magazine called *The Talisman* in 1820. In 1830 he married Marianne Nicholson, an artist; they had one son.

Croker's chief work, the *Fairy Legends,* first appeared anonymously, as he lost the only copy of his manuscript and others had to help him to rewrite the book. Enlarged and revised, later editions came out under his own name. He was extremely interested in antiquarian studies, and was one of the founders of the British Archaeological Association. From 1837 to 1854 he was registrar of the Royal Literary Fund.

Very small, Croker resembled a bright-eyed leprechaun. He was a witty and social creature, much liked by his friends. His stories and songs are quaint and racy, and he did genuine service in his antiquarian studies of his native island.

PRINCIPAL WORKS: Researches in the South of Ireland, 1824; The Fairy Legends and Traditions of the South of Ireland, 1825; Legends of the Lakes,

1829; Popular Songs of Ireland, 1839; The Adventures of Barney Mahoney, 1852; My Village Versus Our Village, 1852.

ABOUT: Croker, T. C. Fairy Legends and Traditions of the South of Ireland (see Memoir by T. F. D. Croker); Dublin University Magazine 34: 203 August 1849.

CROLY, GEORGE (August 17, 1780-November 24, 1860), Irish poet and novelist, was born in Dublin, the son of a physician. He was graduated from Trinity College, Dublin, and ordained in 1804. He became a curate in the north of Ireland, but his ambitious spirit rebelled, and, his father having died, he moved soon after with his mother and sisters to London. There, failing of preferment in the church, he depended mostly on literary work and journalism for a living. He became dramatic critic of the *New Times,* and contributed to *Blackwood's Magazine* and the *Literary Gazette.*

In 1819 he married Margaret Begbie, also a writer, who died in 1851. Lord Brougham, the famous liberal statesman, was a distant cousin of Mrs. Croly's, and in 1834 offered Croly a living near Dartmoor, but the place was so wild and solitary that he refused it. It is said that his rise in the church was slow because he became confused with a Roman Catholic priest of the same name. In 1835, however, he became rector of St. Stephen's Walbrook, in London. His incumbency was marked by a long controversy and litigation over church funds with his churchwarden.

As a preacher Croly was involved and ornate. In 1847 he was made lecturer to the Foundling Hospital, but his first sermon was so over the heads of his congregation that he resigned and published the series of sermons he had intended, with an offended preface. He was not popular with his parishioners, who accused him of rudeness; certainly he was contentious and supercilious, but he had the virtues of forthrightness and sturdy independence. He died very suddenly of heart failure at nearly eighty.

Croly's best known work, his novels, are a sort of combination imitation of Byron, De Quincey, and Moore. They are thoroughly meretricious and sensational, but colorful and bold, and *Salathiel* at least was very popular in its day.

PRINCIPAL WORKS: *Poetry*—Paris in 1815, 1817; The Angel of the World, 1820; Catiline (tragedy), 1822; The Modern Orlando, 1846. *Novels*—Salathiel, 1829; Marston, 1846.

ABOUT: Croly, F. W. Memoir of George Croly; Herring, R. Personal Recollections of George Croly.

CROMEK, ROBERT HARTLEY (1770-March 14, 1812), anthologist and biographer, was born in Hull. He was trained for the law but abandoned it almost at once, and for a time lived in Manchester as a book collector. He then went to London and studied engraving. He met the poet and painter William Blake, and, having set up as an engraver and bookseller, engaged Blake to make the drawings for Blair's *Grave,* only to give the work to the Italian Schiavonetti to engrave for publication. Later he treated Blake very shabbily again in practically stealing, for another artist to copy, the drawings for *The Canterbury Pilgrims.*

In his relations with another writer, Allan Cunningham, the Scottish poet, Cromek was more amiable but scarcely more honorable, for he published without credit or recompense many of Cunningham's songs. Cromek was altogether an unpleasant person, mean and shifty; he ruined nearly everyone who had dealings with him, and managed to ruin himself in the process as well. As someone has said, "he could not afford a conscience." Perhaps the kindest thing to say of him is that he was driven to his crooked dealing by ill health, for he died of tuberculosis at forty-two. He did have a sincere interest in Scottish folk-poetry, and did much to popularize it in England.

PRINCIPAL WORKS: Reliques of Burns, 1808; Remains of Nithsdale and Galloway Song, 1810.

CROMPTON, HENRY (August 27, 1836-March 15, 1904), Positivist and writer on social subjects, was born at Liverpool, the son of Sir Charles Crompton, judge of the Queen's bench. He was educated at Trinity College, Cambridge. For forty-three years he served as clerk of assize on the Chester and North Wales circuit (1858-1901). He was married in 1870 to Lucy Henrietta Romilly, daughter of Lord Romilly. They had two sons. He died at Churt near Farnham, in Surrey, at the age of sixty-seven.

Upon reading Comte's *Philosophie Positive* during a long illness in 1858-59, he became an ardent Positivist. He actively supported the trade unions in their fight to reform labor laws. While acting as referee to the board of arbitration for the Nottingham lace trade, he wrote *Industrial Conciliation,* which Sidney and Beatrice Webb have called "the classic work" on its subject.

PRINCIPAL WORKS: Letters on Social and Political Subjects, 1870; Industrial Conciliation, 1876; Our Criminal Justice, 1905; Selections of Prose and Poetry by Henry Crompton (ed. by his widow) 1910.

ABOUT: Crompton, H. Our Criminal Justice (see Introduction by Sir K. Digby); Positivist Review May 1904.

CROSS, MARY ANN. See "ELIOT, GEORGE"

CROWE, CATHERINE STEVENS (1800-1876), novelist, story-writer, and translator, was born at Borough Green, Kent. Nothing but the surname, Stevens, is known of the family. She married Lt.-Col. Crowe, and lived chiefly thereafter in Edinburgh. There she seems to have been associated with the Scottish phrenologist, George Combe, whose "disciple" she calls herself in her *Spiritualism and the Age We Live In.* Shortly after the publication of this book in 1859 she suffered an attack of insanity. After her recovery she wrote comparatively little.

Her first literary work, *Aristodemus,* was published anonymously. *Susan Hopley,* her most successful novel, was reviewed as a "creation worthy of Scott." This high praise no longer seems well founded. The nature of Mrs. Crowe's reputation in the 'forties is best indicated by the fact that she was one of those named as the possible author of Robert Chambers' anonymous treatise, *Vestiges of the Natural History of Creation.* Her interest in phrenology, physiology, spiritualism, and what we now know as psychology was well known to her reading public. The inspiration to study in these fields came chiefly from George Combe, and must have been well developed by 1844. She was undoubtedly influenced also by Justinus Kerner, German poet and scientist, whose *Seeress of Prevorst* she was translating about 1845. Probably her humanitarian interests also derive chiefly from Combe, who was active toward the betterment of public institutions. Mrs. Crowe's humanitarianism led her to publish an abridged *Uncle Tom's Cabin* for children.

Her pseudo-scientific interests and activities are all reflected in her writings which deal with ghosts, the supernatural, spiritualism, etc. She employs also the conventional terror of the eighteenth century—robberies, abductions, etc. But in the use of the supernatural and of scientific research as a basis for fiction she goes, as one critic remarks, far beyond Mary Shelley's *Frankenstein.* Her plots are ingenious and complicated affairs, loosely knit and extremely confusing. The supernatural stories, of which *The Night Side of Nature* is unsurpassed, show a morbidity in their weirdness and artistic naiveté. This volume is concerned with a psychic analysis of ghost appearances, etc. Of another work, *The Adventures of a Beauty,* the London *Athenaeum* said, it "shows that the whole doctrine of spirits is worthy of the most serious attention." In these fields Mrs. Crowe is something of a precursor of Marie Corelli. Their success is not dissimilar. Mrs. Crowe also pioneered in another field, that of the "novel of the domestic interior," working simultaneously with Mrs. Marsh-Caldwell.

D. F. A.

PRINCIPAL WORKS: *Drama*—Aristodemus, 1838; The Cruel Kindness, 1853. *Novels and Stories*—Susan Hopley, 1841; Men and Women, 1843; Night Side of Nature, 1848; Pippie's Warning, 1848; Story of Lilly Dawson, 1850; Light and Darkness, 1850; Adventures of a Beauty, 1852; Linny Lockwood, 1853; Juvenile Uncle Tom's Cabin, 1854; Ghosts and Family Legends, 1858; Story of Arthur Hunter, 1861; Adventures of a Monkey, 1861. *Miscellaneous*—Spiritualism and the Age We Live In, 1859.

ABOUT: Hale, S. J. Woman's Record; Littel's Living Age 17:289 May 13, 1848; 36:97 January 15, 1853.

CROWE, WILLIAM (1745-February 9, 1829), poet, was the son of a Winchester carpenter. As a child he sang in the Winchester College choir, and later was admitted as a "poor scholar." He went to New College, Oxford, where he received a B.C.L. in 1773. Having taken holy orders, he was presented with a college living at Dorsetshire in 1782, exchanged for one in Wiltshire in 1787; at the same time he held two other livings. In 1784 he became public orator at Oxford. Thomas Moore, the poet, who was his friend, says that he married "a fruitwoman's daughter at Oxford," and had several children by her, keeping his marriage secret for some time so as not to lose his college connections. Crowe was an ultra-Whig, simple, direct, and naively eccentric. His blank verse is harmonious and sonorous, and his occasional poems have much lyric sweetness. The chief characteristics of his poetry are amiability and scholarliness, attributes which relegate his work to an exceedingly minor category.

PRINCIPAL WORKS: Lewesdon Hill, 1788; A Treatise on English Versification, 1827.

ABOUT: Moore, T. Memoirs.

CUNNINGHAM, ALLAN (December 7, 1784-October 30, 1842), Scottish poet and biographer, was born in Dumfriesshire, the fourth son of a factor (or agent: he had some real estate dealings with Burns) and of a woman of rather more intellectual stature than was common to her station and time. He had a few years of reading and writing at a dames' school, but was only ten years old when he was apprenticed to his older brother James, a stonemason.

In his odd moments, which were few, the boy read every book he could find. His interests were literary and he was a worshipper of the few authors with whom he could come into any sort of contact. He walked in Burns' funeral procession; he made a pilgrimage with his brother to the home of James Hogg, the "Ettrick shepherd," to receive the older man's not over-cordial blessing; and once he walked all the way to Edinburgh and back merely to have a look at

Walter Scott. But he was no mere book-worm: he was a good mason, and he was noted for his keen sociability and his boisterous practical jokes.

The inspiration of Burns had set half the farmers' boys and workmen of Scotland to versifying. Cunningham wrote Scottish songs and poems like the rest, and Eugenius Roche, an editor who had become interested in him, published the earliest of them in his magazine, *Literary Recreations*. Then R. H. Cromek, a notorious literary pirate of the period, came to Scotland looking for folk-songs for a new collection. Cunningham disguised a number of his own original compositions and passed them off as anonymous songs of the people. Whether Cromek saw through the deception or not, he evidently recognized Cunningham's usefulness, for he induced the young man to come to London, ostensibly to help put the collection into shape. This was in 1810, when Cunningham was twenty-six; the book, *Remains of Nithsdale and Galloway Song*, appeared the same year, and all but two of the songs in it were Cunningham's own. By way of recompense he received one bound volume and joined the distinguished company (including William Blake and Thomas Stothard) of Cromek's literary and artistic victims.

However, Roche did what he could to introduce him and help him get a foothold in the literary world. Cunningham had secured work as an assistant to a poor and forgotten sculptor named Bubb (from masonry to stone-carving was an easy transition), but Roche, now editing *The Day*, gave him a guinea a week for any poetry he chose to write, and also made him his parliamentary reporter. With this supplement to the 25 to 32 shillings, which was all he earned from Bubb, Cunningham felt justified in sending for Jean Walker, a servant of his former employer in Scotland, with whom he had fallen in love at sight. She came to London in 1811 and they were married.

In 1814 Cunningham left Bubb, to the latter's permanent offense, and became secretary, assistant, and general factotum to a much more distinguished sculptor, Sir Francis Chantrey. He remained with Chantrey until the sculptor died. In the evenings, and in his spare hours he wrote—and it was necessary to do so, for five sons and a daughter came in quick succession. Every sort of journalism and hack writing was a means of increasing his livelihood. He contributed to *Blackwood's* and the *London Magazine*; edited Matthew Pilkington's *General Dictionary of Painters* and the poems of Allan Ramsay; and in 1829 and 1830 brought out *The Anniversary* (an "annual," of the sort then so popular) which was contributed to by his new literary friends, Hogg, Lockhart, and Southey. He became more or less of a minor figure in the literary world, and when in 1831 he went back to visit his old haunts in Dumfries, a public dinner was given to him (Carlyle came some distance to deliver a speech at it) and he was presented with the freedom of the town.

In 1842 he suffered a stroke, and a second one in October of that year killed him instantly. He had been at work to the last, getting ready his *Life of Sir David Wilkie* for the press. He was buried in Kensal Green Cemetery.

"Honest Allan Cunningham" was the phrase most frequently applied to him; Carlyle spoke of his "stalwart healthy figure and ways." He was a devoted son, husband, and father, a kindly, amiable man with always something of the rustic about him even in London.

His writing was of every sort, though none of it very distinguished. In verse he wrote ballads, Jacobite songs, and love lyrics in profusion, most of them imitative and sentimental—though his "A Wet Sheet and a Flowing Sea" is one of the best of sea songs. His style is "pleasant," and that is about the best that can be said of it. He had a genuine interest in art and artists, and probably summed up his own place in the world best when he wrote to Southey, in 1822: "The place which a love of poesie has filled in my heart might have been supplied by some more profitable thing, but I was bred in a lonely place, painting and sculpture seemed something like the work of sorcery and unattainable, and as my trade presented nothing to please my ambition I was fain in my twenty-first year to wooe the more accessible muse of homely country rhymes." M. A. deF.

PRINCIPAL WORKS: *Biography*—Lives of the Most Eminent British Painters, Sculptors, and

ALLAN CUNNINGHAM

Architects, 1829-33; Memoir of Burns, 1834; The Life of Sir David Wilkie, 1843. *Fiction*—Traditional Tales of the English and Scottish Peasantry, 1822; Paul Jones, 1826; Sir Michael Scott, 1828; Lord Roldan, 1836; The Magic Bridle. *Poetry*—Songs: Chiefly in the Rural Dialect of Scotland, 1813; The Songs of Scotland: Ancient and Modern, 1825; Maid of Elvar, 1833; Songs and Poems, 1847. *Miscellaneous*—Sir Marmaduke Maxwell (play) 1822; History of British Literature, 1834.

ABOUT: Cunningham, A. Songs and Poems (see Preface by P. Cunningham); Drinkwater, J. A Book for Bookmen; Gilfillan, G. Galleries of Literary Portraits (Vol. 1); Hogg, D. Life of Allan Cunningham.

CUNNINGHAM, THOMAS MOUNSEY

(June 25, 1776-October 28, 1834), Scottish poet, was the older brother of the more celebrated Allan Cunningham. He was born in Kirkcudbrightshire and educated at Dumfries Academy. He became first a clerk, then a millwright, moving successively to London, Lynn, Cambridge, and Dover, and at one time nearly emigrating to the West Indies. He ended his wandering career by becoming clerk and then chief clerk for the engineer Rennie, and died in London.

He had written dialect songs from childhood, but published very little; in 1806 some of his verses appeared in the *Scots Magazine*, and in 1817 in the *Edinburgh Magazine*. Toward the end of his life he became discouraged by his failure to reach his ideal standard as a writer, and destroyed most of his manuscripts. Yet his work has humor and tenderness, and his best known poem, "The Hills o' Gallowa'," was long attributed to Burns.

PRINCIPAL WORKS: The Har'st Kirn, 1797.

ABOUT: Rogers, C. Modern Scottish Minstrels: Vol 2.

CUNNINGHAM, WILLIAM

(December 29, 1849-June 10, 1919), Scottish economist, was born in Edinburgh, son of a writer to the signet. He was educated at the Universities of Edinburgh and Tübingen and at Caius and Trinity Colleges, Cambridge. He was ordained in 1873, and was a curate until 1887, then vicar of Great St. Mary's Church, Cambridge, until 1888. In 1878, when he was an examiner for the history tripos at Cambridge, he needed a text on economic history and found that none existed, so wrote one himself. He was the pioneer in this field, and remained a leader in it.

In 1891 Cunningham became Tooke professor of economics and statistics at King's College, London, and served until 1897. In 1899 he lectured on economic history at Harvard, and delivered the Lowell lectures there in 1914. He was one of the original fellows of the British Academy. He was a great traveler, touring the whole world several times. Perhaps because of this close acquaintance with the entire empire, he was an ardent Imperialist.

In 1876 he married his first cousin, Adéle Dunlop. They had one son and one daughter. He died in Cambridge, to which he had returned in his latest years.

Cunningham wrote on religious as well as economic topics. It is in the province of economic history, however, that his original thinking is most manifest. The subject can hardly be made entertaining, but his work on his special subject is far from dull, and is thoroughly scrupulous and scholarly.

PRINCIPAL WORKS: The Growth of English Industry and Commerce, 1880; Christian Opinion on Usury, 1884; An Alternative to Socialism, 1885; Modern Civilization in Some of Its Economic Aspects, 1896; Alien Immigrants to England, 1897; Western Civilization in Its Economic Aspect in Ancient Times, 1898; Western Civilization in Its Economic Aspect in Mediaeval and Modern Times, 1900; The Moral Witness of the Church on the Investment of Wealth, 1909; Christianity and Social Questions, 1910; Increase of True Religion, 1917.

CURRIE, LADY MARY MONTGOMERIE LAMB

("Violet Fane") (February 24, 1843-October 13, 1905), poet, novelist, story-writer, and essayist, was born at Beauport, Littlehampton, Sussex. She was the eldest daughter of Charles James Saville Montgomerie Lamb and Anna Charlotte Grey of Bersted, Sussex. The family was of distinguished lineage, and included many literary names on both the French and English sides.

She was educated privately at Beauport, where she early began to write, though she was discouraged by her family's disapproval. For this reason, when later she began seriously to publish, she adopted the pen-name of "Violet Fane," chosen from Disraeli's *Vivian Grey*. At twenty she did some etchings to accompany a reprint of Tennyson's *Mariana*. In 1864 she married an Irish land-owner, Henry Sydenham Singleton, of Counties Louth and Hampshire. Soon she became very popular in London society for her wit and originality. In 1877 W. H. Mallock dedicated his *New Republic* to her, describing her as "a sort of fashionable London Sappho."

Singleton died March 10, 1893, leaving her with four children. The following year, on January 24, she married Sir Philip Henry Wodehouse Currie, of Hawley, Hampshire. Currie had been appointed, on January 1, ambassador to Constantinople; on January 24 he was sworn Privy-Councillor. The bridal pair went to Constantinople, remaining until 1898 when Currie was transferred as ambassador to Rome. Here they lived until he retired in 1903. Meanwhile, in 1899, he was raised to the peerage. Upon returning to England they settled at Hawley, and Violet Fane devoted herself to gardening and the out of doors which she had always loved.

LADY CURRIE

Her death from heart failure occurred at Harrogate. She was buried at Mattingley Church, Hampshire.

She had great personal beauty and charm and easily dominated in social circles at home and abroad. Simple tastes and habits were characteristic of her entire life.

Wherever she went she was intensely interested in observing life in all its aspects. Her work shows a tendency to sentimental romance, but an intelligence both original and penetrating redeems her from over-sentimentality. Taking often an original attitude toward life, she portrays character brilliantly and carefully. Her poetry is delicate and melodious, somewhat minor in tone; it never achieves the level of the "true poets" of the period. Her position as poet was compared at her death to that of Letitia Elizabeth Landon. Some of her songs were set to music by Sir Paolo Tosti. She tried the drama (*Anthony Babington*) early in her career. She also translated from the French the *Memoirs of Marguerite de Valois* in eight volumes. Her later work was chiefly articles for the journals and essays. In some of these is perhaps to be found her best prose. These fugitive pieces were collected twice in her lifetime, but a great many essays and some poems appeared in the years 1902-05 and are uncollected. These are chiefly in the *Nineteenth Century*, *Blackwood's*, and *Littel's Living Age*. Her prose was "well considered," distinguished by real sympathy and genuine humanity, and varied widely in subject-matter, from travel to social problems.

D. F. A.

PRINCIPAL WORKS: *Poetry*—From Dawn to Noon, 1872; Great Peace-Maker, 1872; Denzil Place, 1875; Queen of the Fairies, 1876; Collected Verses, 1880; Autumn Songs, 1889; Under Cross and Cres-cent, 1895; Betwixt Two Seas, 1900; In Winter, 1904; From the Toll-bar of the Galata Bridge, 1905. *Novels and Stories*—Laura Dibalzo, 1880; Sophy, 1881-2; Through Love and War, 1886; Story of Helen Davenant, 1889; *Essays and Miscellaneous*—Edwin and Angelina Papers, 1878; Two Moods of Man, 1901; Collected Essays, 1902; Are Remarkable People Remarkable Looking? 1904; Enfants Trouvés of Literature, 1904; Feast of Kebobs, 1904; Way of Dreams, 1904. *Drama*—Anthony Babington, 1876.

ABOUT: Illustrated London News 127:563 October 21, 1905.

CURWEN, HENRY (1845-February 22, 1892), novelist, was born in Cumberland and educated at Rossall School. He came to London as a young man and worked for J. C. Hotten, the publisher, who also published Curwen's early translation from the French poets. In 1876 he went to India where he became assistant editor of the *Times of India*. By 1880 he was editor-in-chief, and in 1889, on the death of the owner, became co-proprietor. He raised the paper to a high standing and made it known far beyond India. His health failed and in 1892 he started back to England to receive medical treatment, but died on board ship and was buried at sea. He was never married.

His novels, most of which were published anonymously, are slight in plot, but marked by picturesque descriptions and good characterization. They are witty and satirical. He was much interested in Poe and other then neglected poets, and wrote an exceedingly interesting book on the subject, *Sorrow and Song: Studies of Literary Struggle* (1874).

PRINCIPAL WORKS: Within Bohemia: or, Love in London, 1876; Plodding On, 1879; Lady Bluebeard, 1888; Dr. Hermione, 1891.

ABOUT: Macmillan, M. A Globe Trotter in India and Other Essays.

CURZON, ROBERT (Lord De La Zouche) (March 16, 1810-August 2, 1873), travel writer, was born in London. His father was the son of Viscount Curzon, and his mother was the Baroness de la Zouche. He was educated at the Charterhouse and at Christ Church, Oxford, but left without a degree in 1831 to run for parliament. He was elected, but his borough was disenfranchised in 1832, and he never sat again.

In 1833 he began the travels which took up ten years of his life. In Egypt and Palestine he visited the monastery libraries and rescued many valuable manuscripts. He was one of the earliest foreign visitors to the famous monastery of Mount Athos. In 1841 he was made attaché of the British Embassy at Constantinople, and in 1843 was joint commissioner to define the boundaries between Turkey and Persia. Both shah and sultan were so pleased by his decision that they decorated him. He returned to England in 1843.

In 1850 Curzon married Emily Wilmot-Horton, by whom he had one son and one daughter. In 1870 he succeeded his mother in the barony, and became deputy lieutenant of Sussex and Staffordshire.

Besides being a collector of valuable ancient manuscripts, Curzon was a noted student of the history of handwriting. His travel books are as interesting as novels, entirely charming: they are well worth reading today.

PRINCIPAL WORKS: Visits to Monasteries in the Levant, 1849; Armenia, 1854; Account of the Most Celebrated Libraries of Italy, 1854.

ABOUT: London Times August 7, 1873.

DALBERG, JOHN EMERICH ED-WARD. See ACTON, LORD

DALLAS, ENEAS SWEETLAND (1828-January 17, 1879), journalist and philosopher, was born on the island of Jamaica, in the British West Indies, of Scottish parents. He was taken to Great Britain at the age of four and educated at Edinburgh University, where he studied philosophy under Sir William Hamilton. Making his home in London, he devoted himself to journalism as contributor to *The Times, Daily Mail, Saturday Review, Pall Mall Gazette,* and *The World.* His articles ranged in subject from politics to literary criticism. In his leisure time he wrote several books, notably *The Gay Science,* a philosophical analysis of poetic appreciation, which has been called one of the most remarkable books of its class, lucid and provocative, though limited in appeal. He completed only two volumes of the projected four. His wife, Isabella Glyn, a well-known actress, obtained a divorce from him in 1874, after a long separation. He died in London in his fifty-first year.

PRINCIPAL WORKS: Poetics: An Essay on Poetry, 1852; The Gay Science, 1866; Richardson's Clarissa Harlow (ed.) 1868; Kettner's Book of the Table: A Manual of Cookery (under pseud. of A. Kettner) 1877.

ABOUT: The Times, January 18, 1879.

DALTON, JOHN (September 6, 1766-July 24, 1844), scientist, was born in Cumberland, son of a poor Quaker weaver. After a very short period at a Quaker school, he became at ten the servant of a rich Friend named Elihu Robinson, who taught him mathematics at night. At only twelve Dalton became a schoolmaster, eking out the five shillings weekly in fees by selling stationery. In 1780 the school failed and he took to farm work. The next year he and his brother went to their cousin's school at Kendal, and from 1785 to 1793 they conducted it. During this time Dalton secured his real education by constant reading. He began a meteorological diary which he kept up until the day before his death. By 1793, thanks to the blind philosopher Gough, he was professor of mathematics and natural philosophy at New College, Manchester.

The next year he joined the Literary and Philosophical Society, and sent in his first paper, on color-blindness. (Both he and his brother were color-blind, and this condition used to be known as Daltonism.)

In 1801 his paper on the constitution of the atmosphere, establishing "Dalton's Law" (all elastic fluids expand to the same quantity under heat), made meteorology a science and established a European reputation for its author. Soon after came his atomic theory, including his first estimates of atomic weight— an epoch in chemistry. Dalton laid the foundations of chemical notation.

In 1799 New College moved to York, but Dalton stayed in Manchester, giving private lessons in mathematics and doing chemical analyses. His rates were very low, but he was so exceedingly thrifty that he managed to live. Abstemious in the extreme, he had a fixed routine of daily life. He "never had time to marry," though an early unrequited love gives perhaps a better explanation. In 1804 the vicar's wife, Mrs. Johns, met Dalton and asked why he never came to see them. He came that day—and stayed for twenty-six years! Honors poured in upon him, though he postponed fellowship in the Royal Society for years to avoid paying the fees. He was president of the Manchester Philosophical Society from 1817 to his death, and most of his writings were papers contributed to it. In 1830 the Johns family left Manchester, and he lived alone thereafter. The British Association for the Advancement of Science gave him a pension from 1833.

In 1837 he had a paralytic stroke which partially disabled him; he could not serve when elected president of the B.A.A.S. in 1842, because his speech had been affected. He suffered a second stroke in May, 1844, and died in July.

Narrow, rigid, egoistic, Dalton was one of the greatest of chemists, but never progressed beyond his first epochal discoveries. He was uncouth and rude, but inedependent, a loyal friend, and humane at heart and sometimes generous. His mind was slow, laborious, and tenacious, and his writing has the same qualities of doggedness and matter-of-factness.

PRINCIPAL WORKS: Meteorological Observations and Essays, 1793; A New System of Chemical Philosophy, 1808-10; second volume, 1827.

ABOUT: Henry, W. C. Memoirs of the Life and Scientific Researches of John Dalton; Millington, J. P. John Dalton; Neville-Polley, L. Q. John Dalton; Roscoe, H. E. John Dalton and the Rise of Modern Chemistry; Smith, A. Memoir of John Dalton and History of the Atomic Theory; Tilden, Sir W. A. Famous Chemists.

D'ARBLAY, MADAME. See BURNEY, FANNY

DARLEY, GEORGE (1795-November 23, 1846), poet and mathematician, was born in Dublin (the exact month and day are not known), his family being Anglo-Irish. They seem to have been a peculiar crew; when Darley was a mere infant, his father and mother left him with his paternal grandfather and went to America, remaining there for several years. Even after they returned, the boy lived with his grandfather until he was ten. He was fond of them, and interested all his life in the doings of his brothers, several of whom became eminent in various fields, but they never returned his affection or interest. In fact, after he left Dublin for London they seem to have had little more to do with him. It was only in his last years that he became acquainted with some young girl cousins in Ireland who did show some fondness for him and to whom he addressed a series of pathetically familiar letters.

Poor Darley was the weakling of the family, shy, sensitive, melancholy, and afflicted with so bad a stammer that he spoke as little as possible. He spoke of his exaggerated speech defect as "a hideous mask upon his mind, which not only disfigures but nearly suffocates it." He did, however, manage to attend Trinity College, Dublin, entering at the age of twenty and receiving his B.A. degree in 1820. Immediately afterwards he left for London. Unsuited for any other profession, he intended to force himself to success in a literary career.

He had a genuine, if sporadic, poetic gift, though he made the bad mistake of trying to become a dramatist, a kind of writing for which he was remarkably unfit. He was besides (rather unusually for a poet) a fine mathematician, and in his earlier years he earned his living by writing mathematical textbooks. Finally he became associated as critic (particularly of the drama) with the *London Magazine*, under the pseudonym of John Lacy, and later with the *Athenaeum*, for which he also did art criticisms. In the service of this magazine he made at least one trip to Italy, from which he sent letters from the art galleries.

Darley's crushing disappointments as a writer combined with his gloomy temperament to make him a cruel critic of other men's work. His reviews were slashing and caustic, and he made many enemies and few friends. He lived practically as a recluse, emerging occasionally to sit silent in the company of the few men (Allan Cunningham and Charles Lamb—another but a more cheerful stammerer—among them) who knew and liked him. Carlyle, who knew him well, spoke more kindly of him than most of his contemporaries: he called him "amiable, modest, veracious, and intelligent."

His earliest verse drama, *Sylvia*, had some success among its readers, but his two other plays were dismal failures. His two volumes of "tales" attracted little attention, though one of his stories, "Lilliam of the Vale," has real power and beauty. Besides his critical essays, never collected into a volume, he edited an edition of Beaumont and Fletcher, the Elizabethan dramatists, in 1840. He seems never to have given up his stubborn determination to be known as a playwright, and thought of himself in his magazine articles as an authorized mentor to all the dramatists of his day.

Darley, never very strong in health, aged prematurely. At fifty he was an old man, and a year later, unmarried and alone, he died in London of what was in those days called "a general decline."

His masterpiece as a poet is *Nepenthe*, which he had privately—and very wretchedly —printed in 1836, but which was not actually published until fifty years after his death. He spoke of it as "one half-finished work out of a hundred which indolence and hopelessness keep me from concluding." It and some parts of the unequal *Sylvia*, particularly the prologue, have melodiousness and fancy, and occasionally his verse as a whole displays "splendid bursts" of talent. But his other plays are strained and dull, his prose, with a few exceptions, artificial, and marred by bad taste and a fatal fluency. He was a poor critic of his own work, and had no idea of what was good in it and what was bad. In his criticisms, though he is harsh and censorious, he is often brilliant as well; his art criticisms have a strong personal flavor and still make good reading.

GEORGE DARLEY

Darley left a mass of unpublished and unfinished poems, many of which are still in manuscript. Any interest in his work today must be chiefly historical, since he was one of the most prominent figures in the great days of the foundation of the English monthly and weekly magazines. His works on mathematics, though of course outmoded now, were models of their kind when they were written. Had he not been afflicted in speech, he might have become one of the most celebrated professors of mathematics of his time.

M. A. deF.

PRINCIPAL WORKS: *Poetry*—The Errors of Ecstacie, 1822; Poems of the Late George Darley, 1890; Nepenthe, 1897 (privately printed, 1836). *Drama*—Sylvia: or, The May Queen, 1827; Thomas á Becket, 1840; Ethelstan, 1841. *Fiction*—The Labours of Idleness, 1826; The New Sketch Book, 1829. *Mathematics*—A System of Popular Geometry, 1826; A System of Popular Algebra, 1827; A System of Popular Trigonometry, 1827; The Geometrical Companion, 1828; Familiar Astronomy, 1830.

ABOUT: Abbott, C. C. Life and Letters of George Darley; Darley, G. Complete Poetical Works (see Introduction by R. Colles); Drinkwater, J. A Book for Bookmen.

DARWIN, CHARLES ROBERT (February 12, 1809-April 19, 1882), biologist and writer, was the grandson of the poet-naturalist Erasmus Darwin. He was the fifth of the six surviving children of a physician-father and a mother who was a daughter of the famous potter, Josiah Wedgwood. Darwin was born and received his earlier education in Shrewsbury. Nothing in his schooldays cast any shadow of his coming greatness, unless it be the passion for natural history which set him to collecting beetles and other insects. His father designed him for his own profession, and sent him—his mother had died when the boy was six—to Edinburgh University to study medicine. Again Darwin spent more time in desultory reading and naturalizing, and in the social activities of the university, than in any attention to his studies. "You care for nothing but horses and dogs," cried his despairing parent, "and you will never amount to anything." As a last resort he determined to send Charles to Cambridge to become a clergyman, and he matriculated in Christ's College in 1827. The choice was not so grotesque as it sounds now, for at the time Darwin's religious views were fully orthodox.

It cannot be said that Darwin got much more of formal training from Cambridge than he had received at Edinburgh. Here, however, he met the geologist Henslow, who fired and directed his natural tendency toward scientific inquiry, even though his influence was strongly conservative. Here also he read Humboldt's *Personal Narrative*, one of the great turning-points in his career. Soon, however, it became apparent that he was not

CHARLES DARWIN

going to be graduated with the honors necessary for a professional appointment in the church. It was at this time, in 1831, when Darwin was 22, that his great chance came to him: he was offered the post of naturalist on the ship *Beagle,* which was to be sent on a long exploring tour to South America and the Antipodes by the government.

For some time Dr. Darwin refused his son permission to join the expedition, principally because he thought such an experience would be upsetting to a future clergyman! Previously, he had almost missed the appointment because FitzRoy, the commander, an eccentric and an amateur physiognomist, did not like the shape of his nose! Fortunately for him and for the world, both authorities relented, and at the last minute Darwin sailed with the *Beagle.* He was with her from 1831 to her return to England in 1836.

The voyage, with its constant seasickness, ruined Darwin's formerly robust health and made him all his life a semi-invalid. But it made of him the Darwin known to fame. In a sense all his later work stemmed from that vitally important journey. When he reached England again, there was no question as to his future; he was already a biologist, and was to remain one.

In 1839 he married his first cousin, Emma Wedgwood. From this union of two fine strains, five sons and two daughters survived, of whom at least four achieved distinction. For three years they lived in London; then, as Darwin's health became increasingly frail, they moved to Down, in Sussex, where Darwin spent the remainder of his life. From this time on his history became the history of his work. The house at Down, now a national memorial, with its famous gravel walk which the great naturalist paced as he assembled and ordered his theories and their proofs, became the center of advanced scientific thought of the period. Because of his delicate health, his daily life had to be carefully regulated. He could work—since he worked intensively—only a very few hours at a time; then he had to rest for several hours more, lying on a couch, smoking cigarettes—a habit Huxley had too—and listening to music or reading novels indiscriminately, so long as they were cheerful. His children took it for granted that this was the normal existence of all mankind: "When does *your* father do his barnacles?" they asked a visiting child. So far as the outside world was concerned, Darwin had little contact with it except through a small group of scientific intimates, chiefly Lyell, Hooker, and later Huxley. From 1838 to 1841 he had served as secretary of the Geological Society, but after he moved to Down in 1842 he gave up all public office or associations.

Infinitely slow, laborious, and thorough, he built up gradually his theory of evolution through natural (including sexual) selection, a totally different viewpoint from the older evolutionary theories of Lamarck and others. In his eagerness to leave no point uncovered, he would probably have delayed still longer than till 1859 to announce his hypothesis; the strange chance, however, by which Alfred Russell Wallace hit fortuitously on the same idea caused him to yield to the insistence of his friends and make public the work he had already done. He was at once thrust into a maelstrom of controversy. But Darwin was a thinker and a worker, not a fighter; it was Huxley who went forth to battle, while Darwin, at home in Down, went on patiently piling up evidence.

The publication of *The Origin of Species*, in 1859—a crucial date in the history of science—was followed, after various supporting works, by that of *The Descent of Man*, in 1871. In this, of course, the revolutionary implications of the earlier book were brought home with devastating force as applied to the proud peak of creation himself. Linnaeus had already classified man as a member of the anthropoids; now Darwin gave the proof of the correctness of Linnaeus' classification. The storm that arose from these two books has not yet spent itself, and perhaps will not do so for a hundred years to come. In many minor points—chiefly in the frequency of mutations, or jumps in the process of evolution—later discoveries and research have made it necessary to modify some of Darwin's statements. The theory as a whole, however, is as valid today as it was in his lifetime, and is the prime cornerstone of modern scientific teaching. It is safe to say that there is not today one living biologist of competent standing who is not an evolutionist; not all are strict Darwinians, but without Darwin few of them could have made their contributions at all.

This, however, is an evaluation of Charles Darwin as a writer, not as a scientist. The reader who comes to either of the greatest of Darwin's books—most of the others are more highly technical—with the expectation of being confused or bored will have a happy surprise. Though Darwin did not possess the sharp picturesqueness, the aptness and conciseness, of Huxley, and though in writing as in speech sometimes he is betrayed by a tendency to verbosity which winds up rather far from the initial subject, he had a faculty of saying abstruse things in a simple manner, and on every page the nobility and kindliness of the man display themselves in characteristic form. Here is a plain man talking of things which he understands thoroughly, a born teacher pointing out the accumulated reasons for every assertion he makes. Occasionally a touch of reminiscence or a discursive anecdote lends color to the scientific expositions that are more often exciting than they are dry. The early volumes arising directly from the voyage of the *Beagle* make good reading simply as reading, as was evidenced when the complete diary of the voyage was published, the private record from which the scientific journal was compiled. And the autobiographical chapter incorporated in the *Life and Letters* of Darwin, by his son Francis, brief as it is, is one of the really fine autobiographies of the English language.

In person Darwin was tall, ruddy, with blue-grey eyes under heavy overhanging brows. In later life, like most men of his period, he wore a full beard, as in the better known pictures of him. By health and temperament he was obliged to live a life of retirement, but he was no dour recluse; he loved talking and was a good conversationalist, genial and courteous: only when some injustice met his eye did he explode in sudden anger. To his sorrow, his youthful esthetic sense faded in later life except as to music. He was frank and not overly diplomatic, and it is probably fortunate that circumstances compelled Huxley and others to be his spokesmen on the public platform. Gradually he became, as was Huxley, an agnostic, though never a dogmatic atheist. He was a devoted husband and father, and few men have led so utterly blameless and placid a life as this arch-fiend of anti-evolutionist mythology.

Indigestion and gout were Darwin's twin plagues from about 1837 on, but in 1882 his heart began to fail. He had for many years worked far beyond the strength of a lifelong invalid. In April, rather suddenly, he died.

The house at Down became a girls' school. Fifty years later, through the beneficence of an English Rationalist, it was bought and presented to the British Association for the Advancement of Science, under whose direction it has been restored to its condition in Darwin's day and made into a museum and an international shrine of science.

Darwin's writing is merely a by-product of his work and thought. But it is a worthy by-product, and two specimens of it at least are monuments, not only of the history of biology, but also of the history of English literature.   M. A. deF.

PRINCIPAL WORKS: Vol. III (Journal and Remarks) of the Narrative of the Surveying Voyages of H.M.S. *Adventure* and *Beagle*, 1842-46 (2nd edition as Journal of Researches into the Natural History and Geology of the Countries Visited During the Voyage of H.M.S. *Beagle*, 1845; 3rd edition as A Naturalist's Voyage, 1860); Zoology of the Voyage of H.M.S. *Beagle*, 1845; The Structure and Distribution of Coral Reefs (1st part of Geology of the Voyage of H.M.S. *Beagle*) 1842; Geological Observations of the Volcanic Islands Visited (2nd part) 1844; Geological Observations on South America (3rd part) 1846; A Monograph of the Fossil Lepapidae or Pedunculated Cirripedes of Great Britain, 1851; A Monograph of the Fossil Balanidae and Verricidae of Great Britain, 1854; On the Origin of Species by Means of Natural Selection, 1859; On the Various Contrivances by Which British and Foreign Orchids are Fertilized by Insects, 1862; On The Movements and Habits of Climbing Plants, 1864; The Variation of Animals and Plants Under Domestication, 1868; The Descent of Man and Selection in Relation to Sex, 1871; The Expression of the Emotions in Man and Animals, 1872; The Effects of Cross- and Self-Fertilization in the Vegetable Kingdom, 1876; The Different Forms of Flowers on Plants of the Same Species, 1877; The Power of Movement in Plants, 1880; The Formation of Vegetable Mould Through the Action of Worms, 1881.

ABOUT: Allen, G. Charles Darwin; Darwin, F. Life and Letters of Charles Darwin; Huxley, L. Charles Darwin; Judd, J. W. The Coming of Evolution; Poulton, E. B. Charles Darwin and the Theory of Natural Selection; Poulton, E. B. Charles Darwin and the Origin of Species; Romanes, G. J. Darwin and After Darwin; Seward, A. C. (ed.) Darwin and Modern Science; Ward, H. Charles Darwin; Contemporary Review 142:424 October 1932.

DASENT, SIR GEORGE WEBBE (May 22, 1817—June 11, 1896), scholar, whose translations aroused an interest in Icelandic literature, was born in the West Indies on the island of St. Vincent, where his father was attorney-general. He was educated in England at Westminster School and at Magdalen Hall, Oxford. After graduation he spent four years in Stockholm, Sweden, as secretary to the British envoy, and during this time he met Jacob Grimm, who encouraged him to begin the study of Scandinavian literature and mythology.

After his return to England, he served twenty-five years as assistant editor of *The*

Times under John Delane (whose sister he married) and subsequently twenty-two years as civil service commissioner. He visited Iceland in 1862 and was knighted in 1876. He retired from public service in 1892 and spent his remaining years at Tower Hill, Ascot, where he died at the age of seventy-nine. Surviving him were his wife, Fanny Delane, and their three children.

Particularly notable among his Icelandic translations were *The Story of Burnt Njal* and *The Story of Gisli the Outlaw*. His best original work, in his own opinion, was his introduction to Asbjörnsen's *Popular Tales From the Norse*.

PRINCIPAL WORKS: *Translations*—The Prose of Younger Edda, 1842; Popular Tales From the Norse, 1859; The Story of Burnt Njal: or, Life in Iceland at the End of the Tenth Century, 1861; The Story of Gisli the Outlaw, 1866; Tales From the Fjeld, 1874. *Original works*—Annals of an Eventful Life (autobiographical novel) 1870; Jest and Earnest: A Collection of Essays and Reviews, 1873.

ABOUT: Dasent, A. I. Life of Delane, 1908; Dasent, G. W. (tr.) Popular Tales from the Norse (see Biographical Preface by his son in 1903 ed).

DAVIDSON, ANDREW BRUCE (1831-January 20, 1902), Scottish Hebraist and theologian, was born in Aberdeenshire, the son of a small farmer. He was reared in a sternly evangelical household. He was educated at the Grammar School, Aberdeen, and Marischal University, in the same town, receiving his M.A. in 1849. Until 1852 he taught in the Free Church school in his native village of Ellon, where by himself he studied Hebrew and modern languages. From 1852 to 1856 he was a student at the New College, Edinburgh, and was then licensed to preach. He seldom served in a pulpit, however, but in 1858 became assistant professor of Hebrew at the New College, and in 1863 professor of Hebrew and Oriental Languages, a position he held until his death. He died unmarried.

Davidson was a born teacher, with the scientific attitude toward his subject. Although quiet and retiring, he had a keen sense of humor and much penetration. He was a real student of the Old Testament, a friend of the "higher criticism" of the Bible (W. R. Smith, one of the pioneers of Biblical criticism, was his pupil), and an exponent of the historical method of Biblical exegesis. His writing is as lucid as it is profound.

PRINCIPAL WORKS: Commentary on the Book of Job, 1862; Introductory Hebrew Grammar, 1874; Hebrew Syntax, 1894; Biblical and Literary Essays, 1902; Old Testament Prophecy, 1903; The Theology of the Old Testament, 1904.

ABOUT: British Weekly January 30, 1902; Expositor January 1888.

DAVIDSON, JOHN (April 11, 1857-March 23, 1909), Scottish poet, playwright, and novelist, was born at Barrhead, Renfrew-

shire, Scotland, the son of Alexander Davidson, a minister of the Evangelical Union. His
education was broken and peculiar. At the ag:
of thirteen, his family's poverty compelled his
father to take him out of the Highlanders'
Academy at Greenock, and put him to work
in the chemical laboratory of a sugar house
in the same town. His interest in science was
keen, and by 1871, when he was only sixteen,
he had become assistant to the town analyst
of Greenock. The next year, however—for
even in those days he thought of himself as a
poet rather than as a scientist—he abruptly
abandoned what had seemed to be a budding
career in chemistry to secure a further education in the humanities. It was only as a pupil-
teacher that he could return to the Academy.
The next year he was able to matriculate at
Edinburgh University, but he remained only
for one year, the school year of 1876-77, at
that famous seat of learning.

From then until the end of 1889 Davidson
acted as master in various private schools in
Glasgow, Perth, Paisley, and elsewhere in
Scotland, although in 1884 he deserted his
second profession to work for a year as clerk
for a Glasgow thread firm. The reason for
this unusual change of occupation is unknown,
but it is obvious that nature had never intended Davidson for a school-teacher, and he
was probably seeking vainly for a means of
escape from a hated bondage. Vainly, since
in 1885 he married Margaret McArthur, of
Perth, and the responsibility of a wife and
household sent him back to the classroom.
Two sons were born to the couple. Davidson
seemed tied forever to the teaching of small
boys.

Such emancipation as he achieved came
through misfortune. He was discharged because he asked for an increase in salary, and
in desperation he took his family to London,
and started, at 33, to seek his fortune as a
writer. He was penniless, and in true Grub
Street fashion he had to struggle to make the
barest living, by translations from the French
and "ghosting" for popular novelists. "Nine-
tenths of my time," he said once, "has been
wasted in endeavoring to earn a livelihood."
His health was poor, and an hour of intensive
work exhausted him. Although from the time
of publication of the first *Fleet Street
Eclogues,* in 1893, he acquired a fair amount
of celebrity and the acquaintance of well-
known writers, it was not until 1906 that he
was awarded a Civil List Pension of £100 a
year to take the bitterest edge off his poverty.

By then it was too late; Davidson was permanently disheartened and depressed. He felt
that he had received no acclaim commensurate
with his deserts, and he was worn out by the
mere struggle to keep alive. His "tragedies
and testaments," philosophical plays and poems

JOHN DAVIDSON

outlining his views of life, he considered to be
his most important message to posterity; but
they created little stir and found no disciples.

Then upon all this misery was piled a new
horror—the probability that the cause of his
ill health was the dreaded cancer. Davidson
with his wife and children had by this time
taken lodgings in Penzance. On a March day
in 1909 he left his rooms and was not seen
again. In September the sea cast up his body.
It was re-buried there, by his often expressed
wish.

A life such as this leaves its marks on the
man and on his work. Davidson remained
to the end a Scotch provincial, rough-
mannered, serious-minded, straight-speaking,
undiplomatic. Though like most men with a
melancholiac tendency he was capable of light-
hearted whimsicality and wit, he possessed no
personal charm and enjoyed no social popularity; and even this, as well as the subordi-
nation of his reputation to that of lesser men,
he resented. He seemed always older than his
age (for years he wore a wig to hide his bald-
ness), and he was actually older than the men
who were making the literary fame of the
decadent 'nineties.

All his life was a rebellion that never knew
quite against what it rebelled, or how to protest effectively. What he resented was the
present—his present; what he longed for was
a future never to be realized. He strove in
vain to fit himself into the hard age in which
he lived. From the urbanity of his "eclogues"
and earlier poems, and of his novels (*Earl
Lavender* was indeed an open burlesque of the
decadent school), he became more and more
thoroughly engrossed in his "gospel of philosophic science." Though he rejected both the
idea of the Superman and the theory of sexual

selection (substituting a "chemical selection" of his own devising as a factor in evolution), Nietzsche and Darwin formed his philosophy. He wished to de-rationalize science and infuse it with imagination; he thought of himself as a romantic, avoiding the "mystical abyss" and the "slough of realism" alike. His philosophy is confused and arrogant, too mechanistic for the conservatives, too reactionary for the radicals. In the end it became almost megalomaniac: he thought of himself as a herald of the future; "I begin," he proclaimed, "to destroy this unfit world and make it over again in my own image." His was, he said, "a new poetry, for the first time in a thousand years."

But partly this is only the self-assertion of a tragic spirit broken against circumstance. Davidson's work is rough and uneven, sometimes purposely vulgar in the effort to be true to life, frequently obscure and almost as frequently obvious. Yet it is illuminated by "splendid gleams," it has its moments of power and of felicity. In happier surroundings, with leisure, the companionship of like minds, the freedom from the crushing weight of penury and worry, his genuine and great talent could have come to fruition. The man himself, through lack of such good fortune, is now more interesting than is his writing. But poetic and dramatic power were truly his, and he ill deserves the desuetude into which his work has fallen.

M. A. deF.

PRINCIPAL WORKS: *Poetry*—The North Wall, 1885; In a Music Hall, 1891; Fleet Street Eclogues, 1893; Ballads and Songs, 1894; St. George's Day, 1895; Fleet Street Eclogues: Second Series, 1896; New Ballads, 1897; The Last Ballad, 1899; Ballad of a Nun, 1905; Holiday and Other Poems, 1906; Fleet Street and Other Poems, 1909. *Plays*—Bruce, 1886; Smith 1888; Plays (An Unhistorical Pastoral, A Romantic Farce, Scaramouch in Naxos) 1889; Godfrida, 1898; Self's the Man, 1901; The Knight of the Maypole, 1903. *Novels*—Perfervid, 1890; Laura Ruthven's Widowhood (with C. J. Wills) 1892; Baptist Lake, 1894; The Wonderful Mission of Earl Lavender, 1895; Miss Armstrong's and Other Circumstances, 1896. *Philosophy*—The Theatrocrat, 1905; God and Mammon, A Trilogy [unfinished]: The Triumph of Mammon, 1907; Mammon and His Message, 1909; Testaments: I. The Testament of a Vivisector, 1901; II. The Testament of a Man Forbid, 1901; III. The Testament of an Empire-Builder, 1902; IV. The Testament of a Prime Minister, 1904; V. The Testament of John Davidson, 1908. *Miscellaneous*—Sentences and Paragraphs, 1893; A Random Itinerary, 1894; A Rosary, 1903.

ABOUT: Burdett, O. The Beardsley Period; Jackson, H. The Eighteen Nineties; Rothenstein, W. Men and Memories; Yeats, W. B. Autobiographies.

DAVIDSON, THOMAS (October 25, 1840-September 14, 1900), Scottish philosopher and educator, was born in Aberdeenshire, his father a poor farmer, his mother a pious peasant. He attracted the attention of the parish schoolmaster, Robert Wilson, who took him into his home and prepared him for college, in return for his teaching of the younger pupils. In 1856 he entered King's College, Aberdeen, being graduated in 1860 with high classical honors. Until 1863 he was rector of Old Aberdeen Grammar School; then he taught Latin and Greek at Tunbridge Wells and Wimbledon. In 1866 he went to Canada, to teach in the Collegiate Institute at London, Ontario. The next year he went to Boston, then to St. Louis, where he became principal of a branch high school and edited the *Western Educational Review.*

Davidson had by this time lost his early piety and had become something of a Rationalist; in St. Louis, however, he came into contact with a mystical group that encouraged him to the study of philosophy. He returned to Boston in 1875, and for many years was a sort of wandering scholar, tutoring, lecturing, writing, and always on the move. From 1878 to 1884 he spent most of his time in Greece and Italy, living a hermit existence, and at one time almost joining the Roman Catholic Church. Back in London in 1883, he founded the Fellowship of the New Life, which later developed into the famous Fabian Society. He went to New York to establish a branch of this, and remained in America for the rest of his life. The great interest of his later years was the Bread Winners' College (for working men and women) which he founded in New York. He was never married.

Davidson was an exact scholar and a profound student, with a prodigious memory. Amiable yet strong-willed, a "born dissenter," with a vivid personality, his influence was enormous. His writing reflects the man—at once original and scholarly.

PRINCIPAL WORKS: The Parthenon Frieze and Other Essays, 1882; The Place of Art in Education, 1886; Aristotle and Ancient Educational Ideals, 1892; The Education of the Greek People and Its Influence on Civilization, 1894; Rousseau and Education According to Nature, 1898; A History of Education, 1900; The Education of the Wage-Earner, 1905.

ABOUT: James, W. Memories and Studies; Knight, W. Memorials of Thomas Davidson.

DAVIES, (SARAH) EMILY (April 24, 1830-July 13, 1921), educator, was born in Southampton, her father being a clergyman. She was educated entirely at home. Her father died in 1860 and she moved to London. Early in life she became a strong advocate of higher education for women, and was secretary of the first committee to obtain admission of women to university examinations. From this grew a committee to found a college for women, of which she was also secretary. The new college opened at Hitchin in 1869, with Miss Davies as honorary secretary. It moved to Cambridge in 1873, where as Girton College it became a constituent part of the university. Miss Davies lived at Girton as mistress until 1875.

She was also secretary of the London Schoolmistresses' Association, which she founded, from 1866 until its dissolution in 1888; was a member of the London School Board from 1870 to 1873; was a life-governor of University College, London, and a governor of the Grammar School at Hitchin. She was a pioneer suffragist, and helped to organize the first petition to Parliament, presented by John Stuart Mill in 1866.

Her writings were all on educational lines. Her work in print, like her activities outside of it, was logical, temperate, and tactful. She was one of the outstanding educators of her time.

PRINCIPAL WORKS: The Application of Funds to the Education of Girls, 1865; The Higher Education of Women, 1866; Thoughts on Some Questions Relating to Women, 1910.

ABOUT: Stephen, B. Emily Davies and Girton College.

DAVIS, FRANCIS (1810-1885), Irish poet, called "the Belfast man," was the son of a soldier of Ballincollig, County Cork. From his Scottish mother he inherited a love of poetry and music. He attended school in the village of Hillsborough until he was ten; thereafter he educated himself in odd moments snatched from his work as a muslin weaver in Belfast. His poems, he said, were "thrown up like hurried accounts during my hours of toil, amid the monotonous din of the workshop . . . and in very many cases the same hour which gave them birth also saw them away to push their fortunes in the columns of The Nation or some other journal." Later he left the loom to edit the Belfastman's Journal. It was his professed aim in poetry to help create "a true and universal feeling of national love" among his countrymen.

According to the Cambridge History of English Literature, "His political verse is pointed and spirited, but inferior to his countryside songs, which are simple and picturesque and full of unaffected feeling, though they often need the pruning hook."

PRINCIPAL WORKS: Lispings of the Lagan, 1844; Miscellaneous Poems and Songs, 1847; Earlier and Later Leaves: or, An Autumn Gathering, 1878.

ABOUT: Davis, F. Earlier and Later Leaves (see Introductory Essay by C. O'Grady).

DAVIS, THOMAS OSBORNE (October 14, 1814-September 16, 1845), Irish poet and political writer, was born in England, but of half-Irish parentage. His father, a surgeon, died before he was born. As a child he was shy, slow, and backward. He was educated at Trinity College, Dublin, receiving his B.A. in 1836. For the next two years he spent much time in London and on the Continent, studying modern languages and collecting books. He was called to the bar in 1838. He began contributing to the Dublin Morning Register, and became its co-editor in 1841. In 1842 with two other Irish Nationalists he founded The Nation, which became the most influential organ of the cause. He had never before written verse, but he contributed to the magazine a series of stirring ballads, among his best work. In 1843 he started to edit a series of speeches of Irish orators, and to write a biography of the nationalist leader, Wolfe Tone. Unfortunately his life was cut short at thirty, when he died of a fever.

A Protestant, Davis associated himself with Catholics and was an advocate of conciliation. His verse is sometimes fervent, sometimes tender and pathetic. It is better than his prose, which is apt to be involved and artificial.

PRINCIPAL WORKS: Poems, 1846; Literary and Historical Essays, 1846.

ABOUT: Duffy, C. G. Young Ireland.

DAVY, SIR HUMPHREY (December 17, 1778-May 29, 1829), scientist, was born at Penzance, Cornwall, grandson of a builder and son of a small farmer who did wood carving on the side. The father died when the boy was sixteen, and he passed to the guardianship of his mother's foster-father, John Tonkin, a surgeon. He had lived with Tonkin, owing to the poverty of the senior Davy, from the age of nine.

He was a precocious child, but learned little at either Penzance or Truro Grammar School, the latter of which he left just before he was fifteen. He had some instruction in French later, and at this time he read his first books on chemistry.

In 1795 Tonkin apprenticed young Davy to John Bingham Borlase, a surgeon and apothecary of Penzance. There the boy first began the experimental study of chemistry. In only a few months he had evolved revolutionary theories of light and heat, which led to his connection in 1798 with Dr. Beddoes, at Bristol, who was particularly interested in chemical problems. From his theoretical speculations Davy turned to experiments on nitrous oxide, anticipating by nearly 50 years its use as an anaesthetic. Though he was superintendent of Beddoes' research institution, he still hoped to become a regular physician, and did not abandon the hope for several years. At this time he also experimented in electricity.

In 1799 the Royal Institution, in London, invited him to become its lecturer in chemistry. His lectures were a sensational success, and by 1802 he was professor of chemistry, at only 24. From this time on his rise to fame was spectacular.

SIR HUMPHREY DAVY

Davy's contributions to applied chemistry are innumerable, including the isolation of potassium, sodium, and chlorine, and the invention of the miner's safety-lamp, the arc light, and the electric furnace. He withdrew from the Royal Institution in 1812, and after 1815 accomplished no great work in research. He lectured frequently, his lectures being published later, and in 1820 became president of the Royal Society. He was a founder of the British Museum of Natural History, the Zoological Gardens, and the Athenaeum Club. He made frequent triumphal speaking tours in Great Britain and on the Continent.

The primary cause of his change in occupation was his marriage, in 1812, to Jane (Kerr) Apreece, a widowed heiress and a relative of Sir Walter Scott, who, with Wordsworth and Coleridge, became one of Davy's close friends. He had been knighted the same year. The marriage was childless and far from happy; his wife turned Davy into a snob. (For example, he had given his first opportunity for research to the great chemist Michael Faraday, then a very young man; but when Faraday traveled with the Davys on the Continent, Lady Davy, with her husband's acquiescence, made him act as a personal servant!)

Davy's health failed in 1825 and he suffered a slight stroke. For four years he wandered, without his wife, in search of health, finally dying at Geneva at only 51.

Davy was a true genius, a great scientist, but he was also a social climber, commercially minded, and in his later years mercenary. He was typical of his period, the beginning of the great industrial expansion of England.

His first writing was verse, his poem, *The Sons of Genius*, being included in Southey's *Annual Anthology* of 1799. As late as 1805 he wrote a prologue to a comedy, *The Honey Moon*, played at Drury Lane. His verse, however, is uninspired and flatulent. His lectures shared in these deficiencies, though they were crowded with suggestive metaphors and occasionally had flashes of brilliance. On the whole his literary style is flat and pretentious. It is as a scientific discoverer that his name will live. M. A. deF.

PRINCIPAL WORKS: West Country Collections (includes the Essays on Light and Heat) 1799; Outlines of a Course of Lectures on Chemical Philosophy, 1804; Collected Works (ed. by J. Davy) 1839-40; Fragmentary Remains (ed. by J. Davy) 1858.

ABOUT: Crowther, J. G. British Scientists of the 19th Century; Gregory, J. C. The Scientific Achievements of Sir Humphrey Davy; Guye, P. A. Humphrey Davy; Paris, J. A. The Life of Sir Humphrey Davy; Thorpe, T. E. Humphrey Davy: Poet and Philosopher.

DE LA RAMÉE, LOUISE. See RAMÉE, LOUISE DE LA

DE LA ZOUCHE, LORD. See CURZON, ROBERT

DE MILLE, JAMES (August 2, 1837-January 28, 1880), Canadian novelist, was born in St. John, New Brunswick. He was educated at Brown University, Providence, Rhode Island, where the college songs he composed at that time are still sung. While yet very young he began contributing to Canadian newspapers. From 1860 to 1865 he was professor of classics at Acadia College, St. John, and from 1865 until his death was professor of history and rhetoric at Dalhousie College, Halifax, Nova Scotia. In addition to his novels, he published in 1878 a text-book on rhetoric.

De Mille's novels for adults were sensational, sentimental, and extravagant. He also wrote a long series of books for boys, including *The Boys of Grand Pré School, Among the Brigands, Picked up Adrift,* and *The Young Dodge Club.* His work was very popular at the period of its writing, but is little read now.

PRINCIPAL WORKS: Helena's Household, 1858; The Arkansas Ranger, 1865; The Lady of the Ice, 1870; The Cryptogram, 1871; The Living Link, 1874.

DE MORGAN, AUGUSTUS (1806-March 18, 1871), mathematician and logician, was born in Madras, India, where his father was a colonel in the army. His grandfather had been a mathematician before him. He was brought to England, to Worcester, as an infant. His parents were strict evangelists, and his childhood training was severe. He lost an eye in infancy, and suffered much from the teasing of other children in the various schools he attended. From his earliest years his mathematical genius was apparent.

In 1823 he entered Trinity College, Cambridge, where his mathematical ability did not interfere with his pleasure in flute-playing, drawing caricatures, and reading innumerable novels. He revolted from his parents' orthodoxy and became and remained a theist. He read law at Lincoln's Inn but could not endure a legal career and turned again to mathematics. In 1828, at only twenty-two, he became the first professor of mathematics at the new University of London (now University College).

In 1831 he resigned, in protest against the dismissal of the professor of anatomy. In 1836 his successor was drowned, and he returned temporarily. He was persuaded to stay, and acted as professor until 1866. He had been a fellow of the Astronomical Society from 1828, and served on its council. But he disliked and refused honorary degrees or any of the usual honors heaped on scientists. In 1837 he married Sophia Frend, and had by her one daughter and three sons. (William, the eldest, became the well known ceramist and novelist.) His salary was small, and he taught all day, worked as an actuary on the side, and wrote in the evenings. He contributed largely to the publications of the Society for the Diffusion of Useful Knowledge, and devoted much energy to advocacy of decimal coinage. In 1866 he resigned again from the university, this time in the controversy over the appointment of James Martineau, the Unitarian minister, to the chair of philosophy; he felt that Martineau's rejection was a violation of religious neutrality.

The shock of the rupture of this long and loved connection injured his health, and the next year his favorite son, a promising mathematician, died suddenly. Over-work and grief completed the ruin of his health; he had never taken a holiday, disliking the country extremely. In 1868 he suffered an attack of congestion of the brain. In 1870 his daughter died. From that time he sank until he followed her the next year.

DeMorgan was a man of the highest integrity and most idealistic standards. His writing is characterized by clear exposition and great learning, and outside of his logical works is as amusing as it is scholarly. His library of three thousand volumes was purchased after his death and presented to the University of London.

PRINCIPAL WORKS: An Essay on Probabilities, 1839; First Notions of Logic, 1839; Formal Logic, 1847; Arithmetical Books From the Invention of Printing to the Present Time, 1847; The Book of Almanacs, 1850; A Budget of Paradoxes, 1872.

ABOUT: DeMorgan, S. E. Memoir; Royal Astronomical Society Monthly Notices 211:112 February 9, 1872.

DE QUINCEY, THOMAS (August 15, 1785—December 8, 1859), essayist and miscellaneous writer, was born at Manchester, fifth child of Thomas Quincey, a man of business, and his wife, whose maiden name was Penson. The family was of Norman-French origin, and came to England at the Conquest, rising to the Earldom of Winchester in the thirteenth century but later becoming obscure. The "De" was restored by our subject. The Quinceys were in easy circumstances, and the child passed his early years first at "The Farm" and later (from about 1791) at "Greenhay," country houses of some opulence outside Manchester. The father died of tuberculosis in 1792; Mrs. Quincey, a refined and cultivated lady, remained at "Greenhay" till 1796, and seems to have allowed the boy the run of her library. In that year he was sent, with his elder brother, William, to take lessons from a clergyman known to us as Mr. S. H., who started him in Latin and Greek. William was a forceful and boisterous character, while Thomas was frail and diffident, and had to play second fiddle to his energetic and pugnacious brother.

Later in 1796 the family removed to Bath, and Thomas attended the Grammar School, where he quickly earned honors as a Latin scholar. His career there was cut short (in January 1799) by an accidental blow on the head from a cane, which laid him low for some time. On his recovery he went for about a year to a private school at Winkfield, Wiltshire, whence he was removed, in midsummer 1800, to make a tour in England and Ireland with Lord Westport, a boy of his own age whom he had met at Bath. Later in the same year he was entered at Manchester Grammar School with the idea of going on in due course with an exhibition to Brasenose College, Oxford. He was very unhappy there, however, and in July 1802, possessing two books and £10, he ran away.

He walked to Chester, where his mother was now living; and, on the intervention of his uncle, Colonel Thomas Penson, was allowed to wander off where he would, with a guinea a week. For some four months he led a vagrant life in North Wales; then, in November 1802, he borrowed twelve guineas and took coach to London. He was disappointed in the hope of raising funds from a money-lender, and led a life of great privation, roaming the streets and rubbing shoulders with many queer characters. One ineffaceable contact was that with the young street-walker, Ann, with whom his dealings were quite innocent and whose grace and pathos he never forgot.

In the autumn of 1803 De Quincey was found by his family and entered at Worcester College, Oxford, with an allowance of £100 a year. He made no mark at the University, though he was known to a few as a man of uncommon ability; but it was at this time that he began the study of German literature and philosophy which so profoundly influenced his thought. He read deeply in English literature; and, some time in 1804, began to take opium. His first experiment was to alleviate neuralgia, but later he used the drug to take away the pain of a gastric malady (probably the result of his London hardships) from which he suffered all his life.

Though he presented a brilliant paper for the B.A. degree, De Quincey neglected to attend the oral examination, and so left Oxford without a degree. He seems to have resided irregularly in 1808, and then he proposed to study for the Bar at the Middle Temple. From the attainment of his majority he came into money. Towards the end of 1807 he sought out Coleridge at Bridgewater, was kindly received by him, and anonymously furnished him with £300. He also escorted Mrs. Coleridge and her children to the Lakes, where he had the great joy of meeting Wordsworth, whom he had long revered and with whom he had been in correspondence.

In November 1809 De Quincey moved into a cottage at Townsend, Grasmere, near to Wordsworth, and became one of the famous "Lake District School." Southey was at Keswick; Coleridge moved between Southey's and Wordsworth's, and at Elleray, on Windermere, lived the Scotsman, John Wilson, robust, handsome, learned, wealthy—the future "Christopher North" of *Blackwood's*. In this congenial circle De Quincey walked the fells, took opium, surrounded himself with myriads of books, and read deeply in German metaphysics. By 1813 his daily allowance of opium had reached the enormous total of eight thousand drops. He visited Edinburgh in the winter of 1814-15. At the end of 1816 he married Margaret Simpson, a local farmer's daughter, his age being thirty-one and hers eighteen. The first two years of his married life were the darkest period of his opium-slavery; but in 1819 he was able to gain some control over the craving. The same year he was made editor of the *Westmoreland Gazette*, a local Tory paper; in 1820 he resigned, and in the following year he began that career of magazine journalism which thenceforward occupied most of his time.

It was the need of money that drove De Quincey to the periodical press, for a financial disaster had put an end to his hitherto comfortable situation. In September 1821 he published, in Taylor and Hessey's *London Magazine*, the first part of the *Confessions of an Opium-Eater*, the whole of which was separately published in 1822. He continued to write for this magazine through 1823 and 1824, on German literature, political economy

THOMAS DE QUINCEY

and history, one contribution being a severe attack on the young Carlyle's translation of *Wilhelm Meister*. At the age of thirty-five he stepped straight into considerable literary eminence.

Between 1821 and 1825, though his family were at Grasmere, he lived chiefly in London. He met Lamb, Hazlitt, Talfourd, Hood, and others of note, but avoided society as much as possible and spent many hours in solitary walks or in opium-dreams. By the discerning he was sought out, and, once enticed into a social circle, he was a richly-dowered conversationalist.

By the end of 1825 he was back at Grasmere, his financial troubles somewhat straightened out (probably by his mother), and in the following year his friend John Wilson accepted him as a contributor to *Blackwood's Magazine*. In this journal, in February 1827, appeared his celebrated essay "On Murder Considered as One of the Fine Arts." For several years he was alternately at Edinburgh and Grasmere; and in 1830 the whole family removed to the Scottish capital, then the domicile of many notable literary figures, including Wilson, Jeffrey, Sir William Hamilton, William Aytoun, and D. M. Moir. He wrote constantly for *Blackwood's* and other Edinburgh periodicals, including *Tait's Edinburgh Magazine*. During the ten years to 1840 he was thrice bereaved, losing two sons, and, in 1837, his wife.

Of his six children, the two eldest, Margaret and Horace, conceived the idea of taking a cottage at Lasswade, some seven miles from Edinburgh, and the family moved there in 1840. This was his permanent home for the rest of his life, but his work frequently took him to Edinburgh, where he occupied a series of lodgings and cluttered up each with books and papers, putting these into the care of the several landladies and being mulcted in fees for their custody. From March 1841 to June 1843 he was mainly in Glasgow, where he had formed friendships with Professors J. P. Nichol and E. L. Lushington. At this time his gastric illness was severe; he could eat only soft prepared foods; and he had periods of over-indulgence in opium. Yet he kept up a steady pressure of work, and among the notable products of the years 1840-49 were *The Logic of Political Economy* (1844), *Suspiria de Profundis* (1845), and *The English Mail-Coach* (1849). Always an indefatigable walker, he spent much time wandering in Edinburgh and its environs, preferably at night, and carrying a lantern. His eccentricities became a legend. They included an absolute indifference to what he wore and an unpracticality in the management of money that was more than childish.

Towards the end of the year 1849 began an important publishing connexion, with James Hogg, producer of *Hogg's Weekly Instructor*. De Quincey walked over from Lasswade with an article: Hogg not only accepted it, and others following, but undertook to produce a collective edition of his works. At the same time Messrs. Ticknor and Fields, of Boston, began a similar enterprise in America, and for the rest of his days De Quincey was busied in the task of collection, arrangement and supervision. In order to be near the press he returned, in 1852, to a former lodging at 42, Lothian Street, Edinburgh. But he was still a good deal at Lasswade, and received visitors there rather than in his Edinburgh rooms, which were his workshop. At so late an age as seventy he was planning a new history of England in twelve volumes. But the collective edition took up all his energies, and he did not live to see the publication of the fourteenth and final volume. In October 1859 he was compelled to seek his bed, more from the infirmity of age than from any specific illness; and on December 8 he died, at the age of seventy-four. Considering his lifelong devotion to opium this longevity may seem remarkable, though some authorities are of opinion that it was in fact the right drug for his gastric illness.

In person De Quincey was small and frail. Professor David Masson, who met him in later life, wrote: "In addition to the general impression of diminutiveness and fragility, one was struck with the peculiar beauty of his head and forehead, rising disproportionately high over his small wrinkly visage and gentle deep-set eyes."

Confronted by his literary production one is struck at once by its versatility. Essen-tially a scholar and a voracious reader, he was thirty-five before he published anything of note, and at that age he was able to draw on twenty years of hard reading and deep thinking. While he had a strong philosophic bias, he produced no formal essay or system of philosophy; and in history, too, he was a brilliant and enthusiastic amateur rather than an exact scholar. As a critic he was capable of amazing flashes of insight—like his exposition of the knocking at the gate in *Macbeth*—but again produced no long and solid study. His interests were very wide, ranging from the aridities of political economy to the esoteric mysteries of freemasonry and Rosicrucianism. He had a strong vein of humor (well shown in "On Murder Considered as One of the Fine Arts") which could be by turns rollicking and *macabre*. The *Opium-Eater* and the *English Mail-Coach* stand very high in descriptive imaginative literature and as monuments of the more ornate type of English prose. In politics he was a high Tory; in theology a faithful adherent of established opinions. He was profoundly intellectual, and in personal character modest, gentle, and generous.

De Quincey's style is the embodiment of his tortuous and overflowing mind. He was deeply sensitive to the music of words, and built up his paragraphs, clause on clause, sentence on sentence, with the elaboration and fineness of a Gothic cathedral. He stressed "continuity" as a virtue of style: he was not afraid of using "hard" classical words where they seemed to him best; and on occasion he resorted to a misplaced jocularity which jars. His greatest literary vices were a tendency to prolixity and a digressiveness that is sometimes almost intolerable.

"When De Quincey began to write," said Charles Whibley, "he had at his command the erudition of many years. He was ready to discourse upon all subjects with a freshness and learning that few of his contemporaries could surpass. His memory gave him the power of infinite and splendid illustration. Nothing perished from his well-stored mind that was worth remembering, though, as he said, 'rubbish died instantly.' The result is that he explored the remoter continents of knowledge, and travelled almost as far in the realms of thought as Coleridge himself."

H. B. G.

PRINCIPAL WORKS: Translation From Horace, Ode 22, Lib. 1, 1800; Close Comments Upon a Straggling Speech, 1818; Confessions of an English Opium Eater, 1822; Walladmor: A Novel [German forgery] 1825; Klosterheim: or, The Masque, 1832; The Logic of Political Economy, 1844; Writings (24 vols.) 1851-59; Selections, Grave and Gay, From Writings, Published and Unpublished, of Thomas De Quincey (revised and arranged by himself, 14 vols.) 1853-60; China, 1857; Works (17 vols.) 1862-63; Writings (11 vols.) 1877; The Collected Writings (14 vols., ed. by David Masson)

1889-90; The Uncollected Writings (2 vols., ed. by James Hogg) 1890; De Quincey Memorials (2 vols., ed. by A. H. Japp) 1891; The Posthumous Works (2 vols., ed. by A. H. Japp) 1891; A Diary of Thomas De Quincey: 1803 (ed. by H. A. Eaton) 1927.

ABOUT: Baudelaire, C. Les Paradis Artificiels: Opium et Hascisch; Clapton, G. T. Baudelaire et De Quincey; Dunn, W. A. Thomas De Quincey's Relation to German Literature and Philosophy; Findlay, J. R. Personal Recollections of Thomas De Quincey; Fowler, J. H. De Quincey as a Literary Critic; Gay, F. R. De Quincey as a Student of Greek; Gould, G. M. Biographic Clinics (Vol. 1); Green, J. A. Thomas De Quincey: A Bibliography; Guerrier, P. Etude Medico—Psychologique sur Thomas De Quincey; Hogg, J. De Quincey and His Friends; Hitchcock, R. Thomas De Quincey: A Study; Japp, A. H. De Quincey Memorial; Japp, A. H. Thomas De Quincey: His Life and Writings; Masson, D. De Quincey; Page, H. A. Thomas De Quincey.

DERBY, LORD (Edward George Geoffrey Smith Stanley, Fourteenth Earl of Derby) (March 29, 1799-October 23, 1869), statesman and poet, was born in Lancashire, eldest son of the thirteenth earl. His parents were cousins. He was educated at Eton and at Christ Church College, Oxford, where he won the Chancellor's prize for Latin verse but left without a degree. (In 1852 he received an honorary D.C.L. from Oxford). He entered Parliament in 1820 as a Whig, but even then was only a very moderate liberal in his views. In 1824 he traveled in Canada and the United States. The next year he married Emma Caroline Wilbraham, daughter of Lord Skelmersdale; they had two sons and a daughter.

After acting as home secretary for Ireland in 1831, Stanley was transferred to the Colonial Office. He resigned from office and from his party in 1834, becoming first an independent, then a Conservative. His grandfather's death the same year made him Lord Stanley, when his father succeeded to the earldom. In 1841 he was Colonial Secretary. In 1844 he was called to the House of Lords as Lord Stanley of Bickerstaffe, and in 1851 himself succeeded to the earldom on his father's death. He was prime minister in 1852, and again in 1858-59 and in 1866-67. He died two years after his last ministry, after a long illness from gout.

Under a superficial charm and a boisterous appearance of unconventionality, Lord Derby was aloof, autocratic, and arbitrary. He was a very good business man, a money-maker and money-saver, equally interested in sport and scholarship, a man of real brilliance and immense energy but lacking in intellectual depth and philosophy. His translations are really paraphrases, and are more poetic than most translations of poems. His prose was sinewy and masculine, but outside of his speeches in Parliament he wrote very little.

PRINCIPAL WORKS: Conversations on the Parables, 1837· A Translation of the Iliad, 1864.

ABOUT: Kebbel, T. E. Life of the Earl of Derby; Saintsbury, G. The Earl of Derby.

DE TABLEY, LORD (John Byrne Leicester Warren, Third Baron de Tabley) (April 26, 1835-November 22, 1895), poet, was born at Tabley Hall, Cheshire, eldest son of George Fleming Leicester (later Warren) and his wife, Catherina Barbara, daughter of Jerome, Count de Salis-Saglio. After spending several years as a child in Italy and Germany, with his mother, he went to Eton, and from there in 1852 to Christ Church, Oxford, where he took a second in Classics and history (1859). In the same year, in collaboration with an undergraduate friend, George Fortescue, he published a volume of *Poems* under the name of George F. Preston. Fortescue was shortly afterwards killed in a yachting accident.

After a short period as a diplomatic attaché in Constantinople, Warren read law, and was called to the Bar at Lincoln's Inn in 1860. He did not seek briefs, however, but went back to his native Cheshire, where he interested himself in local life (including the yeomanry, in which he attained high rank), in poetry, botany, and numismatics. His few months in the Near East had given opportunity for the collection of old coins, and in 1863 he published two books on the subject. Between 1860 and 1865 he brought out six volumes of poems, the first three as by "G. F. Preston" and the others as by "William Lancaster." They were in some degree derivative (especially from Tennyson), but showed close, sincere, and original power of natural description. The anonymous blank-verse poem, *Philoctetes* (1866) was the first of his works to attract attention, and is esteemed by John

LORD DE TABLEY

179

Drinkwater as "one of the most moving long poems of the century."

In 1868 Warren unsuccessfully stood for Parliament as a Liberal. Three years later he settled in London, where he lived thenceforward, with frequent long sojourns in the Isle of Wight or Dorsetshire. *Philoctetes* was followed in 1868 by *Orestes* (also anonymous), and he published further volumes in 1870, 1873, and 1876, still without winning much applause. Oddly enough it was a selection, with an appreciative commentary, by Alfred H. Miles in his *The Poets and the Poetry of the Century* (1891) that first attracted critical attention. In 1887 Warren had succeeded to the barony, and with it to a financial tangle which tried his patience and seriously strained his resources. In 1893 the critic, Theodore Watts-Dunton, and the publisher, John Lane, persuaded him to make a selection, which he called *Poems: Dramatic and Lyrical,* and with this for the first time he became well-known; so that he issued a second series in 1895. In this year he died somewhat suddenly of influenza.

Sir Edmund Gosse, meeting Warren in 1875, speaks of "his unobtrusive dress, with his timid, fluttering manner" and of "the noble modelling of his forehead" and "pale azure eyes." He was diffident and sensitive to a fault, high-minded and the pattern of courtesy. As a poet he was always sincere, observant, dignified, with many flashes of real power, but in technique his work suffered from being over-studied, and in thought from excess of gloom. Yet Richard Le Gallienne found that *Philoctetes* "has more of the statuesque severity of the antique than [Swinburne's] *Atalanta,*" while Robert Bridges and other good judges have drawn attention to the grave beauty of some of his lyrics. Besides his verse and volumes on coins, Warren wrote two novels, a treatise on book-plates, and a learned catalog of *The Flora of Cheshire,* which was published after his death.

H. B. G.

PRINCIPAL WORKS: *Poems—Poems* (with G. Fortescue) 1859; Ballads and Metrical Sketches, 1860; The Threshold of Atrides, 1861; Glimpses of Antiquity, 1862; Praeterita, 1863; Éclogues and Monodramas, 1864; Studies in Verse, 1865; Philoctetes: A Metrical Drama, 1866; Orestes: A Metrical Drama, 1867; Rehearsals: A Book of Verses, 1870; Searching the Net: A Book of Verses, 1873; The Soldier of Fortune: A Tragedy, 1876; Poems: Dramatic and Lyrical (2 ser.) 1893-5; Orpheus in Thrace and Other Poems, 1901; Collected Poems, 1903. *Novels—*A Screw Loose, 1868; Ropes of Sand, 1869. *Miscellaneous—*An Essay on Greek Federal Coinage, 1863; On Some Coins of Lycia, 1863; A Guide to the Study of Book Plates, 1880; The Flora of Cheshire, 1899.

ABOUT: Bridges, R. S. Collected Essays: VII; Drinkwater, J. The Muse in Council; Gosse, E. W. Critical Kit-Kats; Hearn, L. Life and Literature; Miles, A. H. The Poets and the Poetry of the Century (Vol. 6); Warren, J. B. L. The Flora of Cheshire (see Biographical Notice by Sir Mountstuart Grant Duff); Nineteenth Century 33:899 May 1893.

DE VERE, SIR AUBREY (August 28, 1788-July 5, 1846), Irish poet, was born Aubrey Thomas Hunt, son of Sir Vere Hunt, of County Limerick, of a family settled in Ireland since the days of Cromwell. He succeeded to the baronetcy in 1818, and in 1832 took by letters patent the family name of de Vere. He was educated in England, at Harrow, but never went to a university. In 1807 he married Mary Rice, the sister of Lord Monteagle. They had five sons and three daughters; one son, Aubrey de Vere, became a well known writer of light verse.

Modest, chivalrous, quietly patriotic, de Vere was averse to publication or public notice. His sonnets were highly praised by Wordsworth, who rated them even above his own.

PRINCIPAL WORKS: Julian the Apostate, 1822; The Duke of Mercia and Other Poems, 1823; The Song of Faith, Devout Exercises, and Sonnets, 1842; Mary Tudor, 1847.

ABOUT: De Vere, Sir A. Sonnets (see Memoir by Aubrey de Vere in 1875 ed.).

DE VERE, AUBREY THOMAS (January 10, 1814-January 21, 1902) poet, essayist, and critic, was born at Curragh Chase, Adare, County Limerick, Ireland. He was the third son of Sir Aubrey de Vere (see above).

De Vere spent 1821-24 traveling with his family in England, but his childhood was spent at the family estate in Ireland. Here he was privately educated, entering Trinity College, Dublin, in 1832. By his own account the curriculum was for the most part distasteful, so he devoted his time to metaphysics. An essay in theology brought him a university prize.

In 1838 he left Trinity. He had been intended for holy orders, but, while the idea persisted for years, nothing came of it. He now devoted himself to study and travel. A visit to Oxford in 1838 was productive of two life-long friendships with John Henry (Cardinal) Newman and Sir Henry Taylor. Newman was to be, after Wordsworth, de Vere's great idol; Taylor has left interesting memories of de Vere's friendship. Soon after this, de Vere was at Cambridge where he was introduced to his brother's circle, which included many future literary figures. Among them were Tennyson, Monckton Milnes, and Spedding. A brief trip to Rome was followed by a stay in London. Here, in 1841, he met Wordsworth with whom he soon became intimate. Two years later came "the greatest honor" of his life—an invitation to Rydal Mount. A year's travel in Italy with Taylor and his wife was followed in 1845 by a winter in London where he met Carlyle and fre-

AUBREY DE VERE

deeper, affecting his own spiritual development through the association with Newman. Wordsworth left a mark in his admirer's poetry, which uses the same simple language and achieves similar undramatic effects. To some critics his style is diffuse and even flat—faults which grow out of his striving for simplicity.

De Vere contributed to almost every poetic *genre*, his sacred verse (*May Carols*) being written at the suggestion of Pope Pius IX. His most successful poetry deals with Irish scenes and folklore. Although never regarded as notably Celtic, de Vere participated in the activity of the Celtic revival and employed its materials. His stately and austere effects are produced by the great dignity of his diction. In poetic drama he made three efforts, but none compares favorably with his father's *Julian the Apostate*.

In prose de Vere is a charming essayist and correspondent. The letters to Sir Henry Taylor are thought by many to contain his best literary criticism. Undoubtedly de Vere ranks higher as critic than as poet. He wrote also on economic, political, historical, and ecclesiastical subjects, bringing to each a great knowledge and fairness. He is loyal to England, but evinces a strong sympathy for Ireland in these writings. Landor, who enormously admired de Vere, says that *English Misrule and Irish Misdeeds* combines "the wisdom of Bacon and the eloquence of Burke."

De Vere was known for his charm and fascinating conversation. His appearance was imposing, his face kind and genial, the longish hair giving it a paternal quality.   D. F. A.

quently saw Tennyson. In 1846 he returned to Ireland.

The death of his father and the suffering from the famine seem to have stopped his poetic writing temporarily. His work on relief committees brought him into close touch with Irish conditions, a subject on which he was to write a great deal. In 1848 de Vere told some friends of his idea of joining the Roman church. Carlyle immediately warned him against such a move. Nevertheless, at Avignon on November 15, 1851, de Vere was formerly received into the Roman church. After the ceremony he continued to Italy with Henry Edward Manning. Newman had joined Rome in 1845, and probably his example to some degree influenced de Vere.

Returned to Ireland, he continued writing. Then in 1854 Newman was appointed head of the new Dublin University, and de Vere took the chair of social and political sciences. This was a subject in which he was well equipped, but he performed none of the duties associated with the professorship, although he held it until Newman's retirement in 1858. During the Irish residence de Vere entertained his English friends, Tennyson visiting at Curragh Chase in 1848 and 1854. De Vere returned these visits. He made another trip to Rome in 1870, and went to the Lake district in 1898. He died unmarried, and was buried in Askeaton Churchyard, County Limerick.

A voluminous man of letters, de Vere was closely associated with the intellectual leaders of his day, particularly with two groups—the Wordsworthians and the Oxford Movement. The influence of both is marked in his work, but the Oxford Movement was perhaps the

PRINCIPAL WORKS: *Poetry*—Waldenses, 1842; The Search After Proserpine, 1844; A Year of Sorrow, 1847; Poems Sacred and Miscellaneous, 1854; May Carols, 1857; Iniscail, 1862; The Infant Bridal, 1864; The Legends of St. Patrick, 1872; Alexander the Great, 1874; St. Thomas of Canterbury, 1876; Antar and Zara, 1877; Fall of Rora, 1877; The Foray of Queen Meave, 1882; Poetical Works (3 vols.) 1884-9; Legends and Records of the Church and Empire, 1887; St. Peter's Chains, 1888; Medieval Records and Sonnets, 1893; Poetical Works, 1897: *Prose*—English Misrule and Irish Misdeeds, 1848; Picturesque Sketches of Greece and Turkey, 1850; The Church Settlement of Ireland, 1866; Ireland's Church Property, 1867; Pleas for Secularization, 1867; Ireland's Church Question, 1868; Proteus and Amadeus, 1878; Legends of the Saxon Saints, 1879; Constitutional and Unconstitutional Political Action, 1882; Ireland and Representation, 1885; Critical Essays (3 vols.) 1887-9; Recollections, 1897.

ABOUT: Anderson, M. A Few Memories; de Vere, A. T. Recollections; Hallam, T. Alfred Lord Tennyson; *ibid.* Tennyson and His Friends; Landor, W. S. Letters; Taylor, H. Autobiography; Ward, W. Aubrey de Vere; Edinburgh Review 201:27-54 January, 1905; Illustrated London News 111:807 December 4, 1897.

DICKENS, CHARLES (February 7, 1812-June 9, 1870), novelist, was the son of a clerk in the Navy Pay Office, whose own mother had been a housekeeper famous for her story-telling ability. Charles Dickens' mother was of slightly higher social class, her father having been a naval lieutenant. Charles was the second of eight children, and in his early childhood was frail and given to mysterious "spasms," which ceased at adolescence. When it is said that the elder Dickens was the proto-type of Micawber, and that this was one of the acutest of his son's portraits, his nature will be understood immediately by all readers.

When the child was two, the father was transferred from Portsea, where Charles had been born, to London, and a few years later was transferred again to Chatham. At first the boy was taught his letters by his mother, and early lost himself in the classics of fiction that made up his father's library; from the beginning also he reveled in the theater, and his first writing was a very juvenile tragedy. When he was nine he was put to school with the son of a Baptist minister who was their next door neighbor, and when once more the family moved to London he was left behind for a while in this school. But soon he was dispatched to London, and to his darkest days. Micawber-Dickens was deep in debt, made futile compositions with his creditors, and finally found himself in Marshalsea Prison, familiar to all Dickens readers from *Little Dorrit*. His wife and younger children lodged with him there, but soon Charles found a room in a poor street by himself; for he was now a wage-earner, at barely twelve. The father never had much concern for his children's education, though his oldest child, Fanny, was given a musical training; when Charles came to London he was set to household tasks. Now, with the father in prison for debt, a step-cousin found a place for him in his blacking factory. In a window, with curious passers-by to see him, he and another boy spent long days labeling blacking-bottles for a few shillings a week. Charles had dreamed already of fame, he was intensely ambitious, eager for learning, and exaggeratedly sensitive; it is no wonder that he looked back with horror always on this experience—as witness *David Copperfield*.

But better days came. Just as in a Dickens novel, a legacy descended on the father, and he was free. He made no attempt to release his son, but Charles quarreled with his employer, and got himself discharged. He never forgave his mother for having gone and begged for his reinstatement; he gave to her the most unpleasant traits of Mrs. Nickleby. The father in some manner secured a small pension besides his legacy, and then a job as reporter. Gradually it came to his attention that his oldest son might do with a bit more schooling. (Before the Marshalsea episode, Mrs. Dickens had tried to open a private school of her own, but not one pupil appeared.) For three years Charles was sent to two small schools in succession. Then at fifteen he became a solicitor's clerk. He taught himself shorthand, and spent most of his leisure reading in the British Museum. He was graduated to court reporting, then to reporting in the House of Commons—for the *True Sun* (whose reporters he led in a successful strike), then for his uncle's *Mirror of Parliament,* and then for the *Morning Chronicle,* where his father was working. (It must be understood that in those days a reporter was merely a stenographer, not a writer.) During this period he tried unsuccessfully to get on the stage. And he fell violently in love, at eighteen, with Maria Beadnell, who was sent to Paris by her family and jilted him on her return.

His first published sketch appeared, without payment, in the *Monthly Magazine,* in 1833, and was signed "Boz," a brother's nickname. Later sketches appeared in the newly organized *Evening Chronicle,* which paid. These sketches, illustrated by Cruikshank, were issued as a book in 1836. In the same year Dickens was married to Catherine Hogarth. His real love among the Hogarth sisters (daughters of an editor) appears to have been Mary, who was the original of "Little Nell" and who died, to his lasting grief, in 1837. But she was too young to marry, and so by some strange transference he married her older sister Catherine—a most unfortunate decision for them both.

The *Pickwick Papers,* written merely to accompany some projected "cockney sporting prints" by an artist who killed himself before the series was finished, were Dickens' open sesame to fame and wealth. Before their publication he was the obscurest of men; after it he was made. An uninterrupted stream of novels followed in the thirty-odd years remaining to him. In 1841 he underwent a surgical operation, but not even that interrupted his work for long. Nor did his unhappy first trip to the United States, in 1842, a visit that resulted in *American Notes* and *Martin Chuzzlewit.* These turned the uncritical adulation of his reception into bitter resentment, all the more violent because much of his aspersion was deserved. Part of the antagonism was due to his righteous indignation over the absence of a copyright law and the pirating of his books.

Dickens by this time had a house in London, in Regent's Park, and a summer home at Broadstairs. In spite of ill-advised early contracts, and consequent quarrels with publishers, he was accumulating a fortune. But

CHARLES DICKENS

he had a large family—Georgina Hogarth, his wife's youngest sister, lived with them and helped care for the children from the end of 1842, when she herself was only fifteen—and he drove himself incessantly to provide for them generously, and to live in the comfort and luxury to which the little blacking-factory slave had aspired. At this time also he had, under the influence of Baroness Burdett-Coutts, become deeply interested in half a dozen expensive philanthropic enterprises.

It is to this period that belongs the Dickens best known by his portraits and by the memories of those who met him or heard him speak —a slight, rather undersized man with delicately aquiline features, fine florid skin, brown hair worn slightly too long, and thin, wiry beard and whiskers. To this portrait must unfortunately be added also a superfluity of gold chains and rings, and flamboyantly colored waistcoats, the pathetically naive vulgarities of a man who was a very poor boy and had become a rich man.

Though Dickens never paid attention to physical strain, he did realize that the calls upon his time—it was at this period that he began to act in private theatricals, a recreation which later absorbed enormous amounts of time and energy—were interfering with his work. The year of 1844-45 he spent with his family in Italy. He returned to England and engaged in his only financial failure—the editorship of the *Daily News*. At the end of two or three weeks he found that he was entirely incompetent to handle such a position on a political daily, and resigned, spending the next year in Lausanne and Paris. In 1849, however, he became editor of a magazine which was a huge success, largely because it contained much of his own writing. This was

the weekly *Household Words*. He remained as editor of this and its successor, *All the Year Round* (the change was due to a quarrel with the publishers of *Household Words* in the painful year 1858) until his death.

Even Dickens' unbounding energy was beginning to flag a little. But he was deep in private theatricals, benefits for Leigh Hunt and the widow of Douglas Jerrold, free readings of his Christmas stories—the predecessors of the highly paid public readings from his other works which finally killed him at fifty-eight. In 1856 he bought Gadshill Place, which he had dreamed of as a small boy in Chatham, and it became his permanent home. Two years later the English-speaking world was shocked by the news that Dickens had separated from his wife.

The marriage had been unhappy from the start. To modern eyes the shocking thing about it was, not that the couple parted amicably and with due financial settlement in 1858, but that for twenty-two years they had lived together, and produced ten children, when they had never really loved each other or been compatible at all. The oldest son went with his mother, the others stayed with their father and their Aunt Georgina. The rumor that connected Dickens' name with that of a young actress may have been pure libel; but his own public exhibition of his private affairs was a startling mixture of conceit and caddishness. It is true that the letter he wrote, explaining the separation and hinting at his wife's insanity, which was published in the *New York Tribune*, was probably meant to be circulated only among his friends; but he published another fulsome article on the subject in *Household Words*, and then quarreled with his publishers and his closest friend because they would not reprint it in *Punch*! Certainly the worst of Dickens appears in this affair.

Meanwhile he was undertaking more and more of the exhausting public readings, with the long, uncomfortable train journeys which they involved, and pouring out manuscript as copiously as ever. He was never slovenly in his writing, and put immense energy into it. His health broke, and in 1865 he had a slight stroke of paralysis which should have been a warning; he was lame thereafter. But in 1867 and 1868 he went to America again. This time he and the country, matured by Civil War, were both politer to each other, and he came back after a triumph, with £20,000 and permanently broken health. He was never well again. But he engaged himself for another long reading tour, which he was, to his distress, forced to leave uncompleted. He kept on writing, and was at work on *The Mystery of Edwin Drood* the day before he died. He came into the house from his writing (in a garden house called the "Chateau"), said a few incoherent words, and fell stricken with apoplexy. He died twenty-four hours later. Though his wish for a quiet funeral was observed, it was not in the country graveyard he had contemplated, but in Westminster Abbey.

To understand Dickens' nature, it must be remembered that he was the apotheosis of the English lower middle class. Because he was an authentic genius, he possessed all its attributes, good and bad, to a superlative degree. He was tender-hearted, courageous, generous, supremely industrious, social-minded, a hater of injustice and a champion of the oppressed —and he was also arrogant, obstinate, conceited, sentimental, and a bit of a bounder. His vulgar tastelessness in dress, which could not hide the fine distinction of his features, was no mere accident. He was entirely without self-criticism or self-discipline.

But he was also an inventive genius of the first order, with an enormous creative fertility. All the accusations leveled against the characters and the novels of Dickens are quite true: he is guilty often of mawkishness, of theatricality, of caricature, of artificiality. The world he created in thirty years is often quite unlike our world: the people in it are frequently unreal, the incidents strained, the drama stagy. But it is a coherent, vital, and immortal world in its own right. As one of his biographers has said, there is no other English author, not even Shakespeare, who is admired for so many different reasons by so many different kinds of people. His buoyancy, his charm, his tireless ebullience, attracted and held many friends for Charles Dickens the man. His imaginative freshness, his deep and sincere tenderness and pity, his whole-souled humor that is seldom sharpened into wit, his superabundance of creative energy, have built a deathless niche in the temple of fame for Charles Dickens the novelist.

M. A. deF.

PRINCIPAL WORKS: *Fiction*—Sketches by Boz, 1836; Posthumous Papers of the Pickwick Club, 1837; Oliver Twist, 1838; Sketches of Young Gentlemen, 1838; Life and Adventures of Nicholas Nickleby, 1839; Sketches of Young Couples, 1840; Master Humphrey's Clock (including the Old Curiosity Shop and Barnaby Rudge) 1840-41; A Christmas Carol in Prose, 1843; The Life and Adventures of Martin Chuzzlewit, 1844; The Chimes, 1844; The Cricket on the Hearth, 1845; The Battle of Life, 1846; Dealings With the Firm of Dombey and Son, 1848; The Haunted Man, and The Ghost's Bargain, 1848; The Personal History of David Copperfield, 1850; Bleak House, 1853; Hard Times for These Times, 1854; Little Dorrit, 1857; A Tale of Two Cities, 1859; Great Expectations, 1861; Our Mutual Friend, 1865; The Mystery of Edwin Drood (unfinished) 1870; A Child's Dream of a Star, 1871; Mudfrog Papers, 1880. *Plays*—The Village Coquettes, 1836; The Strange Gentleman, 1837; The Lamplighter (in The Pic-nic Papers) 1841; Mr. Nightingale's Diary (with Mark Lemon) 1851; No Thoroughfare (with Wilkie Collins) 1867; Is She His Wife? 1877. *Miscellaneous*—Sunday Under Three Heads (by Timothy Sparks) 1836; American Notes for General Circulation, 1842; Pictures From Italy, 1846; A Child's History of England, 1854; The Uncommercial Traveller, 1861; The Poems and Verses of Charles Dickens, 1903. *Edited*—Memoirs of Joseph Grimaldi, 1838; Religious Opinions of Dr. Townshend, 1869; The Dickens Bible, 1933.

ABOUT: Chancellor, E. B. Dickens and His Times; Chesterton, G. K. Charles Dickens: A Critical Study; Darwin, B. R. M. Dickens; Dickens, H. F. Memories of My Father; Forster, J. The Life of Charles Dickens; Gissing, G. R. The Immortal Dickens; Leacock, S. B. Charles Dickens: His Life and Work; Lunn, H. K. The Sentimental Journey: A Life of Charles Dickens; Mackenzie, R. S. Life of Charles Dickens; Marzials, F. T. Life of Charles Dickens; Sitwell, O. Dickens; Straus, R. Charles Dickens: A Biography From New Sources; Wagenknecht, E. C. The Man Charles Dickens; Zweig, S. Three Masters.

DIGBY, KENELM HENRY (1800-March 22, 1880), poet, novelist, and theological writer, was the youngest son of the Dean of Clonfert. In 1819 he entered Trinity College, Cambridge, where he became a convert to the Roman Catholic Church.

Most of his life was spent in London, in a career of literary leisure, and in the study of the history and customs of the Middle Ages and of scholasticism, the medieval theologic-philosophical system. He married Jane Dillon, by whom he had one son.

Digby's best known work, *The Broadstone of Honor*, was described as "rules for the gentlemen of England." Later he enlarged it to four volumes, each under a separate name —*Godefridus, Tancredus, Morus*, and *Orlandus*. It is very didactic, and is chiefly of interest for its description of medieval customs. He also wrote a number of volumes of poems, mostly of a religious nature, and several works of Catholic apology and exposition. He died in London at eighty.

PRINCIPAL WORKS: *Poetry*—Short Poems, 1866; Little Low Bushes, 1869; Halcyon Hours, 1870; The Temple of Memory, 1874. *Prose*—The Broadstone of Honor, 1822; Mores Catholici: or, Ages of Faith, 1831-40 (11 vol.); The Children's Bower, 1858.

ABOUT: Holland, B. Memoir of Kenelm Henry Digby.

DILKE, SIR CHARLES WENTWORTH (September 4, 1843-January 26, 1911), editor and economist, was born in London, eldest son of the first baronet Dilke. His grandfather, of the same name, was an antiquary and critic. His mother died when he was ten.

In 1862 he entered Trinity College, Cambridge, receiving the LL.B. degree in 1866 and the LL.M. in 1869, as head of the law tripos. He was also noted as an oarsman and fencer. He was called to the bar in 1866, but never practised.

In 1866 he made a world tour, beginning with the United States, and covering all the English-speaking countries. His first book. *Greater Britain,* was the outcome. In 1868 he was elected to Parliament. At once a republican and an imperialist, he gave rise to bitter controversies. In 1869 his father died and he succeeded to the baronetcy and also to the ownership of his father's magazine. *The Athenaeum.* He acted as editor only temporarily and occasionally, but contributed to it frequently. He also inherited *Notes and Queries.*

In 1872 Dilke married Katherine M. E. Sheil, who died two years later in giving birth to their son. In 1875 he made a second world tour. He bought a villa near Toulon and spent much of his time there when Parliament was not in session. He became under-secretary to the foreign office in 1880, and was a close friend of the Prince of Wales (Edward VII). In 1882 he was president of the local government board, an office carrying a cabinet seat. He was one of the earliest members of the Labor Party. He resigned his seat in 1885 in protest against Parliament's attitude on the Irish question.

At the next election he ran again and regained his seat, but the same year a public scandal lost him a great career. He was named by another Member of Parliament as corespondent in his divorce suit, the lady being sister of his own sister-in-law. A later trial trial failed legally to substantiate Dilke's claim of innocence. He had been engaged to Emilia (Strong) Pattison, widow of the art critic Mark Pattison and herself a critic. She married him at once to evidence her belief in him, and they were supremely happy until her death in 1804. Dilke was defeated for re-election in 1886, and made another trip to the Near East. In 1892 he returned to Parliament for the remainder of his life, but never again achieved a cabinet seat. His second wife's death crushed him, and he remained aloof from society until his sudden death from heart failure in 1911. His valuable art collection he willed to public use.

Dilke's writing is sound and forceful, and still worth reading. His satire, *Prince Florestan,* remains timely.

PRINCIPAL WORKS: Greater Britain, 1868; The Fall of Prince Florestan of Monaco, 1874; The Present Position of European Politics, 1887; The British Army, 1888; Problems of Greater Britain, 1890; Imperial Defense, 1898; Army Reform, 1898.

ABOUT: Gwynn, S. & Tuckwell, G. M. Life of the Right Honorable Sir Charles W. Dilke; Paul, H. History of Modern England.

DILKE, LADY (Emilia Frances Strong) (September 2, 1840-October 24, 1904), art historian and critic, was born at Ilfracombe. Her father, Major Henry Strong, left the army to become a bank manager. His father was deputy surveyor-general of Georgia before the American Revolution. Miss Strong spent her girlhood in Oxford, home-taught,

but in constant communication with the scholars of the university. She was talented in drawing, and in 1859 went to London to attend the South Kensington Art School. Two years later she married Mark Pattison, rector of Lincoln College, Oxford, and twenty-one years her senior. Her life with him was one long course of study under his tuition. The Pattisons established a sort of salon at Oxford, of which Browning, George Eliot, and other notables were intimates. From 1867 Mrs. Pattison was much abroad, and for the most part a nervous invalid. However, she wrote frequently on the history and criticism of art, and interested herself in social reform, woman's suffrage, and the welfare of working women, she was one of the founders of the Women's Trade Union League.

Her husband died in 1884, and she published his memoirs, leaving the next year for a visit to India. While there she announced her engagement to Sir Charles Wentworth Dilke, prominent as statesman and orator. Almost immediately afterwards he was involved in a scandal (a divorce suit naming him as corespondent) which ruined his career. Mrs. Pattison rushed to his defense, came back to England, married him at once, and devoted the remainder of her life to an unsuccessful effort to rehabilitate his name. They traveled constantly, and many of her books on art and all her fiction date from this period. She died at Woking at sixty-four. She had no children.

Lady Dilke's mystical stories show much individuality and originality. Her art books, however, though thorough and painstaking, reveal that she was not a good critic. They are conventional and laborious. She was much more important as a woman than as a writer.

PRINCIPAL WORKS: The Renaissance of Art in France, 1879; Art in the Modern State, 1884; The Shrine of Death and Other Stories, 1886; French Painters of the Eighteenth Century, 1889; The Shrine of Love and Other Stories, 1891; French Architects and Sculptors of the Eighteenth Century, 1900; French Engravers and Draughtsmen of the Eighteenth Century, 1902; The Book of the Spiritual Life, 1905.

ABOUT: Dilke, Lady. The Book of the Spiritual Life (see Memoir by Sir C. W. Dilke); Athenaeum October 3, 1904.

DISRAELI, BENJAMIN (First Earl of Beaconsfield) (December 21, 1804-April 19, 1881), statesman, novelist, poet, and miscellaneous writer, was born in London, the second child of Isaac D'Israeli and Mary Basevi. The family was wealthy and aristocratic, descended from Spanish and Venetian Jews. Isaac, never closely associated with the Jewish community in London, broke his connection early in the son's life, and Benjamin was baptized in the Anglican church in 1817.

His brief education was private. At seventeen he was articled to a firm of solicitors in

BENJAMIN DISRAELI

contemporary figures, their keen analysis of social maladjustments, and their hope of a national rebirth through recovery of the powers of sovereign and people. Believing that the Reform Bill of 1832 had stolen these powers, he aligned himself with the aristocracy and pled for a medieval paternalism as the salvation of the working-class. "It can hardly be disputed that the labouring classes are largely indebted to the sympathy inspired by Young England for their present improved condition." At this period came also the difference with Sir Robert Peel, whom Disraeli soon attacked bitterly in public.

In 1847 Disraeli became leader of the opposition in the House of Commons, a position he held for twenty-five years. He stood as an historical Tory, succeeding to the creed of Burke, and representing in politics very much what Newman stood for in religion. In 1853 he became Chancellor of the Exchequer, but his budget failed. Twice again he held this office, in 1857-58 and 1867. There were long years of quiet work against the great popularity of Palmerston, whom no weapon seemed to harm. The Tories even whispered in these years that "Dizzy" was no longer a suitable leader for them, but no break occurred between him and his party. Then, at the failure of Lord Derby's health, Disraeli in 1868 realized a boyhood dream and became Prime Minister. At the same time the title of viscountess was conferred upon his wife, though he refused a title. His first term as premier was brief, but he was again chosen to this office in 1874. Two years later he was forced by failing health to resign, but he entered the Lords as Earl of Beaconsfield and continued to lead the opposition. A final piece of brilliant statesmanship was the "peace with honor" achieved at the Congress of Berlin. For this he had great popularity and the Garter. But reverses soon came, and in 1880 he retired from public life.

His death was the occasion for a display of national grief similar to that for Wellington. The Queen, whom he had made Empress of India, had his Garter insignia transferred from Windsor to the grave at Hughenden. A public funeral was offered by Gladstone, but Disraeli had wished to lie beside his wife. A signal honor was the creation of "Primrose Day" (April 19), in the belief that this had been his favorite flower. Coningsby Disraeli, a nephew, was the heir.

Disraeli was handsome in a dark foreign manner, socially popular for his wit, tact, and shrewd cleverness. Among his friends are found the names of almost every one of repute in his day, and many obscure ones as well. A woman left him her estate, so great was her admiration for her fellow-Jew. She lies buried beside Disraeli and his wife.

the Old Jewry. Then in 1824 he entered Lincoln's Inn, only removing his name from there in 1831. But law did not engage his entire attention, and in 1826 he published *Vivian Grey*, which brought him immediate acclaim. Illness made travel desirable just then, and for three years Disraeli toured. *Home Letters* gives the best account of these years.

Upon his return he moved in the best literary and political circles, and was known throughout his wide acquaintance as a dandy. He affected eccentricities of dress and manner which greatly heightened his naturally exotic and foreign appearance. The latent interest in politics now first showed itself when, between 1832 and 1835, he repeatedly failed to win a Parliamentary seat. Standing for Maidstone, he won a seat in 1837, along with Wyndham Lewis, whose widow (Mary Anne Evans) he married two years later. Though she was fifteen years older than Disraeli, the marriage seems to have been remarkably happy, and, in the financial as well as the spiritual sense, enormously to Disraeli's advantage. Soon he established himself as a country gentleman at Hughenden, with a secure financial footing.

His elaborate maiden speech, ridiculed by the audience, gave little promise of the great career ahead. Not until 1847 was he assured of a permanent seat in Parliament. The intervening years Disraeli spent in developing the "Young England" party whose leadership and doctrines he supplied. The novels, *Coningsby, Sybil*, and *Tancred*, were written in this period in an effort to present to a wide public the theories of "Young England." They succeeded enormously, both as literature and as politics, thanks to their realistic portraits of

His literary work can scarcely be separated from his political. In achieving his high position he carved out a truly romantic career, raising himself in spite of the violent anti-Jewish prejudices of Victorian England. His place is unique in the modern history of his race. Proud of his Hebrew blood, he has set forth in the novels a vindication of the Jew. As a writer he showed the same sagacious insight, the same insolent and satiric cleverness associated with his political career. The novels, great powers for shaping public opinion in their day, combine romantic and realistic qualities, and recount much current episodical history. These topical allusions make the novels less intelligible to succeeding generations. Judged coolly, the novels now do not seem great artistic creations, but their place in the growth of nineteenth century thought was large. Perhaps Disraeli's unique contribution to literature is the biography designed as a vehicle for the study of ideas and their shaping force in the life of an individual (*The Life of Lord George Bentinck*).

D. F. A.

PRINCIPAL WORKS: *Novels and Tales*—Vivian Grey (5 vols.) 1826-27; The Voyage of Captain Popanilla, 1828; The Young Duke (3 vols.) 1831; Contarini Fleming (4 vols.) 1832; The Wondrous Tale of Alroy (3 vols.) 1833; The Rise of Iskander, 1833; Henrietta Temple (3 vols.) 1837; Venetia, 1837; Coningsby (3 vols.) 1844; Sybil (3 vols.) 1845; Tancred (3 vols.) 1847; Lothair (3 vols.) 1870; Endymion (3 vols.) 1880; Tales and Sketches (ed. by J. L. Robertson) 1891. *Verse and Dramatic Works*—The Modern Dunciad, 1826; The Revolutionary Epick, 1834; The Tragedy of Count Alarcos, 1839; *Miscellaneous*—An Enquiry Into Plans of American Mining Companies, 1825; Lawyers and Legislators, 1825; The Present State of Mexico, 1825; England and France, 1832; What Is He? 1833; The Crisis Examined, 1834; Vindication of the English Constitution, 1835; Letters of Runnymede, 1836; The Spirit of Whiggism, 1836; Lord George Bentinck, 1852; Home Letters (written in 1830-1) 1885; Correspondence (1852-3) 1886; Parliamentary Reform: Speeches in House of Commons (1848-66) 1867; Selected Speeches (2 vols., ed. by T. E. Kebbel) 1882; Letters of Disraeli to Lady Bradford and Lady Chesterfield (ed. by Marquis of Zetland) 1929.

ABOUT: Brandes, G. Beaconsfield: Ein Charakterbild; Cazamion, L. Le Roman Social en Angleterre; Cromer, E. B. Disraeli; Hitchman, F. The Public Life of Lord Beaconsfield; Hutcheon, W. Whigs and Whiggism; Lazaron, M. S. Seed of Abraham; Macknight, T. The Right Hon. Benjamin Disraeli; Monypenny, W. F. The Life of Benjamin Disraeli; Maurois, A. Disraeli; O'Connor, T. P. Lord Beaconsfield; Stephen, Sir L. Hours in a Library; Whibley, C. Disraeli the Younger; Contemporary Review 138:192 August 1930.

D'ISRAELI, ISAAC

(May 1766-January 19, 1848), critic and author, was born at Enfield, Middlesex, into a wealthy Jewish family. He was educated privately until 1780 when he was sent to Amsterdam. There under a free-thinking tutor he became a convert to the doctrines of Rousseau. He returned home in four or five years determined to embrace literature as his profession and armed with a long poem against commerce which was intended to confound his father's intention of placing him in a commercial house in Bordeaux. Left for a time to his own devices, he was then sent to travel in France. The youth cultivated his taste and became acquainted with numerous Parisian literary lights, but failed to acquire any liking for business.

At home in 1789 Isaac published a poem attacking the satirist Peter Pindar (Dr. John Wolcot). This brought him a valuable patron in the poetaster Henry James Pye, afterward (1790) laureate, who introduced him into London literary circles and persuaded the elder D'Israeli that his son had no commercial talent. D'Israeli's first book, *A Defence of Poetry*, 1790, was dedicated to Pye.

Now began the quiet, studious life for which D'Israeli had struggled. His *Curiosities of Literature* was widely read. A miscellany of literary and historical lore, anecdote, and curiosa, D'Israeli was constantly revising and adding to it. In 1797 he brought out three novels. *Vaurien* and *Flim Flams: or, The Life of My Uncle* were condemned as Voltairean. The third, *Mejnoun and Leila*, has the dubious distinction of being the first Oriental romance in English. Between 1799 and 1801 four more novels apeared and were forgotten.

D'Israeli married Maria Bassevi February 10, 1802. Benjamin, afterward Lord Beaconsfield, described his father as a small, nervous man of retiring disposition. At any rate Isaac never began a battle outside the bailiwick of literature. Without any particular convictions concerning the faith of his fathers, D'Israeli

ISAAC D'ISRAELI

until 1813 helped support the Portugese synagogue at Bevis Marks. Then the officials took the liberty of electing him deacon. Outraged, Isaac not only withdrew but had his children baptized *en masse* at St. Andrews, Holborn. Murray points out that this "indifferent decision of his sceptical father" made possible the political career from which Benjamin as a Jew would have been barred.

Between 1816 and 1828 D'Israeli's reputation as a writer of controversial articles increased and flourished. For his five-volume work on Charles I, which marked a distinct advance in methods of historical research, he was created a Doctor of Civil Law at Oxford. Blindness caused by paralysis in 1839 of the optic nerve did not prevent the completion of his three volume *Amenities of Literature*. He died at Bradenham House, Buckinghamshire.

Isaac D'Israeli was one of the most colorful personalities of his time. His talents, chiefly critical and added to a unique faculty for making others appreciate his enthusiasm, touched all and influenced many of his contemporaries. As a popularizer of literary research his importance cannot be overlooked.

P. B. S.

PRINCIPAL WORKS: *Novels*—Vaurien, 1797; Flim Flams: or, The Life of My Uncle, 1797; Mejnoun and Leila, 1797; Love and Humility, 1799; The Lovers, 1799; The Daughter, 1801. *Miscellaneous*—A Defence of Poetry, 1790; Curiosities of Literature, 1791; Miscellanies or Literary Recreations, 1796; Calamities of Authors, 1812-1813; Quarrels of Authors, 1814. *History*—Commentary on the Life and Reign of Charles I, 1828-1831; The Genius of Judaism, 1833; Amenities of Literature, 1840.

ABOUT: D'Israeli, I. Curiosities of Literature (see Memoir by Lord Beaconsfield to 1849 edition); Moneypenny, W. F. & Buckle, G. E. The Life of Benjamin D'Israeli (Vol. I); Murray, D. L. Disraeli.

DIXON, HENRY HALL (May 16, 1822-March 16, 1870), sporting and agricultural writer, was born in Cumberland, the son of a cotton manufacturer, his maternal grandfather being a general in the army. He was educated at Rugby, under the famous Dr. Thomas Arnold, and at Trinity College, Cambridge, where he secured his B.A. in 1846. He did well in classics, and would have done better had it not been for poor sight; but he was also writing on sports even at this time. Later, while he was clerk to an attorney in Doncaster, he became a regular sporting writer, and manager of the Doncaster *Gazette*. From 1850 he wrote regularly for Bell's *Life in London*, the editorship of which he refused in 1852. He was called to the bar in 1853, and for a while practised in the midland circuit, but soon he was back to his former occupation. In 1858 he wrote a book on *The Law of the Farm*, a standard work to this day, to please his father; and from then on he became increasingly interested in agri-

culture. He contributed articles on farming to the *Illustrated London News*, and won four prizes for essays from the Royal Agricultural Society. For a time he was on the staff of the *Daily News*. In 1847 he had married Caroline Lynes, and he was the father of a large family, a responsibility which kept him working to the last, though his health failed several years before his death.

Strange to say, Dixon seldom hunted and never bet on horse-races, though these were the chief subjects of his pen. He was a kindly man, though eccentric and solitary by nature, with no idea of the value of either money or time. There was a poetic streak in his writings, and his descriptions of the countryside are often very effective, but haste in writing made him sometimes obscure and caused a lack of finish in his work. His writing was all done under the pseudonym of "The Druid."

PRINCIPAL WORKS: The Post and the Paddock, 1856; Silk and Scarlet, 1858; Scott and Sebright, 1862; Field and Fern, 1865; Saddle and Sirloin, 1870.

ABOUT: Lawley, F. Life and Times of The Druid; The Field March 19, 1870; Sporting Times February 6, 1886.

DIXON, RICHARD WATSON (May 5, 1833-January 1900), poet and historian, was born in Islington, the son of a Methodist minister (who still remained within the Church of England) and of a mother unusually well educated for her times. He was sent to King Edward's School in Birmingham, and in 1851 entered Pembroke College, Oxford. There he became a close friend of Edward Jones (afterwards Burne-Jones, the painter) and of William Morris, and with them formed one of the group which helped D. G. Rossetti paint the murals on the Oxford Union—an enterprise from which grew his early connection with the Pre-Raphaelite painters, of whom Rossetti was the head. In after years Dixon painted very little (only one canvas of his survives), but he never lost his interest in the art. A better indication of his future career came from his founding, with Morris, of the *Oxford and Cambridge Magazine*.

Dixon secured his B.A. in 1857, later winning the Arnold historical prize and the Cramer prize for a poem on a Biblical subject. His early poetry resembles that of the other Pre-Raphaelites—full of color and imagery, and a little extravagant. After he went down from the university he lived with Morris and Jones in their famous house on Red Lion Square in London, but in 1859 he was ordained and became a curate at Lambeth (London). In 1861 he married Maria (Sturgeon) Thomson, a widow with two daughters, to whom he was an affectionate stepfather. (He never had any children of his own.) She died in 1876, and in 1882 he married Matilda Routledge.

From 1863 to 1868 Dixon was second master at the Carlisle Cathedral; until 1875 minor canon of Carlisle Cathedral; until 1883 a vicar in Cumberland; and from 1883 to his death vicar of Warkworth, Northumberland. In spite of the fact that from the mid-'70s he was engaged in writing a church history which is still the standard authority, he received no promotion or preferment that would give him leisure for this work; many offices were heaped upon him, but all of them meant more labor and responsibility without commensurate recompense. Modest and unambitious as he was, he felt this injustice keenly. It was not until the last year of his life that he received the slightest actual honor; then he was given an honorary D.D. by Oxford, and made honorary fellow of Pembroke.

In 1891 Dixon was extremely ill of influenza, and for a while his life was despaired of. A period of acute depression, almost amounting to derangement, followed, the result of his severe illness coupled with his naturally shy and melancholy temperament. Nevertheless, he continued through it all to labor on new volumes and revisions of his history, and to carry on the offices of his vicarage. He was left in a permanently susceptible condition physically, and a second attack of influenza at the beginning of 1900 caused his death.

Dixon's was a singularly lovable nature. He retained always some of the characteristics of his youth, and remained to the last a loyal member of the old Pre-Raphaelite group, long ago broken up as an entity, and the members of which had gone so far from the orbit of his ordinary life and interests. His most intimate friend in later years was Robert Bridges, the poet laureate, and with Bridges he helped to publicize the neglected work of that fine poet, Gerard Manley Hopkins. The Hopkins-Dixon correspondence has recently been published.

As a poet, Dixon was at his best in his later work, which grew in simplicity, intellectual vigor, and discipline. Unfortunately during his period of depression he destroyed many of his unpublished poems; how many of these may have been among his best, no one can say. His work is very unequal; his longest poem, *Mano,* though it has beautiful passages, also has long stretches of mere rhetoric and dullness. It is as a lyrist that he is greatest. He has that power of creating an atmosphere of strangeness, of transporting the reader into a private world of poetry, which is the mark of the genuine poet. It has been remarked that some of his finest lyrics— "Fallen Rain," "The Feathers of the Willow," "To Shadow, Ode on Advancing Age"—do not so much *resemble* Blake as they might, if

R. W. DIXON

offered anonymously, be taken for Blake's own. Higher praise than this no poet can receive.

As an historian, Dixon was not only sound, thorough, and scholarly, but he brought to his work keen critical powers. His history is a chronicle in form, not a philosophical review of the subject; it is his object simply to give an account of the origin, growth, and events of the Church of England from its beginning as a separate creed to his own day. This he presents not only with lucidity, but with what has been called "the prose style of a poet"—full of vivid imagery and incisive phrasing. It is good reading even for those with no special interest in ecclesiastical history.

It is strange that Dixon has so little reputation nowadays as a poet. His best lyrics are finer than most of the work of all but his greatest poetic contemporaries, and he has fallen into a neglect that is as undeserved as it is a deprivation to lovers of English poetry. Perhaps some day, like Hopkins, he will find a Bridges to urge his merits upon a too forgetful world. M. A. deF.

PRINCIPAL WORKS: *Poetry*—Christ's Company and Other Poems, 1861; St. John in Patmos, 1863; Historical Odes, 1864; Mano, 1883; Odes and Eclogues, 1884; Lyrical Poems, 1887; The Story of Eudocia and Her Brothers, 1888; Last Poems, (ed. by M. E. Coleridge) 1905; Poems (ed. by R. Bridges) 1909. *Prose*—Life of James Dixon, D.D., 1874; History of the Church of England From the Abolition of the Roman Jurisdiction, 1878-1902; The Monastic Comperta, 1879; Seven Sermons, 1888; A Sermon on the Diamond Jubilee, 1897.

ABOUT: Abbott, C. C. (ed.). The Correspondence of Gerard Manley Hopkins and Richard Watson Dixon; Bridges, R. Three Friends; Coleridge, M. E. Non Sequitur; Mackail, J. W. Life of William Morris.

DIXON, WILLIAM HEPWORTH (June 30, 1821-December 27, 1879), travel and miscellaneous writer, was born in Manchester. He was educated privately by his great uncle and became clerk of a merchant. Before he was twenty-one he had privately printed a tragedy, and was a contributor to the *North of England Magazine* and the *Illuminated Magazine*. In 1846 he edited the *Cheltenham Journal* for two months. The same year he went to London and was entered at the Inner Temple and called to the bar in 1854, but he never practised. He contributed to the *Daily News* and *The Athenaeum*, becoming editor of the latter in 1853. In 1861 he traveled in Portugal, Spain, and Morocco, and in 1862 in the Near East, on his return helping to found the Palestine Exploration Fund. In 1866 he toured the United States as far west as Salt Lake City. In the Philadelphia Public Library he discovered some valuable Irish state papers, which were returned to the British government.

In 1869 he resigned his editorship and for a year worked hard as a member of the London School Board. In 1871 he went to Switzerland. In 1874 he was again in the United States and Canada; in 1875 in Italy and Germany. Every trip was followed by a book.

His last years were a series of misfortunes. His house was blown up by an accidental explosion, he fell off his horse in Cyprus and received permanent injuries, his son and daughter died, and at the end of 1879 he himself died of apoplexy while he was revising the proofs of his last book.

Dixon's work was lively, open-minded, and interesting, but highly inaccurate, and more than once involved him in charges of libel.

PRINCIPAL WORKS: John Howard and Prison World of Europe, 1849; The London Prisons, 1850; Life of William Penn, 1851; Story of Lord Bacon's Life, 1862; The Holy Land, 1865; New America, 1867; History of Two Queens, 1873-4; Royal Windsor, 1878; British Cyprus, 1879.

ABOUT: Athenaeum February 1880.

DOBELL, SYDNEY THOMPSON (April 5, 1824-August 22, 1874), poet and critic, was born in Cranbrook, Kent, the son of a hide-merchant, John Dobell, and his wife, a daughter of a reformer and religious leader, Samuel Thompson.

The boy was educated at home, under strong religious influences, as the family was opposed to sending children to public schools or colleges. In 1835 John Dobell, now a London wine-merchant, removed to Cheltenham, where he remained until his death, carrying on his trade. His son assisted him, at the same time studying enthusiastically, more so than his strength well justified. His family regarded him as one destined to be the leader in his grandfather's sect of free-thinking Christians. This peculiar home influence and the absence of the discipline characteristic of schools and public education resulted in the somewhat visionary nature revealed in all his writings.

In 1839 he became engaged to Emily Fordham, whom he married in 1844, continuing to supervise his father's business. In 1848 he took charge of a branch establishment in Gloucester, living at Hucclecote, situated on an old Roman road. While he soon removed to a house near Cheltenham, much of *The Roman*, a poem showing the writer's enthuiastic support of Italian nationalism, was written at Hucclecote.

In the next year the publication of that poem brought him fame and new friends, among them Tennyson, Carlyle, and the foreign patriots Mazzini and Kossuth. He traveled in 1850 and 1851, first to North Wales, then to Switzerland, and was deeply moved by the mountain scenery of both countries, especially by that of the Alps.

The influence of these travels is seen clearly in *Balder*, which he finished in 1853. The poem was not so well received as *The Roman*; the subject, which failed to catch the popular enthusiasm as did that of the earlier work, being misunderstood. Then, because of the illness of his wife, Dobell, who had been making his home in Gloucestershire, went to Scotland, where he spent the winters in Edinburgh and the summers in the highlands. There he remained until 1857, issuing two books of verse on the general subject of the Crimean War.

His health, which had always been precarious, was further injured by the effort connected with the delivery before the Philosophical Institute of Edinburgh of a lecture on "The Nature of Poetry" (April 1857), and Dobell was obliged to seek a warmer climate, spending winters at Niton, Isle of Wight, and summers in the Cotswolds.

As he was forbidden by physicians to engage in literary work, he turned again to trade, organizing his wine business on modern and socially progressive principles. He became respected as a public-spirited and charitable citizen of Gloucester.

His declining health required travel in the winters from 1862 to 1866, which he spent in France, Spain, and Italy; but in 1866, when he suffered an injurious fall, not only this recreation but general mental activity of any considerable degree of effort was forbidden him by physicians.

While he continued to write for journals and to plan for continuing *Balder*, his condition, aggravated by an accident in which his horse fell over on him, made him an invalid. He lived for the rest of his life in Gloucestershire, at Noke Place, near Gloucester, from

SYDNEY DOBELL

1867 to 1871, and then at Barton-End House, near Nailsworth, where he cordially entertained his friends and continued his writing until the year of his death.

Despite his studious, guarded, and sanctimonious youth (and a marriage which merely reinforced the home influence) Dobell grew to be a man of charm and some knowledge of the world. It has been suggested that in his violent reaction to the reserve of his parental home he swung too far to the opposite extreme. Tennyson, offended by Dobell's effusive manner of compliment when they were introduced, said, "Don't talk such damned nonsense!" A corresponding change can be traced in Dobell's political views, which mellowed from their youthful radicalism to a rather conservative stand, although he continued to abhor tyranny of all kinds. His career was marked throughout by generosity and unselfishness toward men struggling for position. Robert Buchanan, the poet, said of himself and David Gray, the Scottish poet, that Dobell had helped them both "as no other living man could or would."

Dobell is perhaps the chief of the group of poets called by Aytoun the "spasmodic school," others being Philip James Bailey and Alexander Smith. The name refers to their chaotic passionate outpourings with little semblance of order or discipline. A further characteristic is strained figures and imagery, with consequent obscurity. Tennyson's *Maud* has not escaped the reproach of being called a typical "spasmodic" poem.

Dobell's poetry, accordingly, is not above criticism; indeed, much of it is beneath it. He neglected "the file," and believed in spontaneity rather than finish. His beauties, such as the descriptions of nature in *Balder*, are fragmentary. He managed often, by suggestions in his writings, to evoke comparisons, nearly always unfavorable to himself, with greater poets. "Dobell is a poet whom it is not easy to appraise," writes Hugh Walker. "On the one hand, there is none to whom more must be forgiven; and the reader who is irritated by his gross violations of taste, and his almost incredible lapses from poetry and even from sense, will be inclined to resent any praise whatsoever. . . And yet, on the other hand, whoever will bear with his faults must in the long run find the poetry of Dobell both attractive and stimulating. He is all compact of thought, and in his moments of true inspiration he handles the greatest themes with masterly ease. . . It is true he thought and wrote by spasms, but there is a magnificent energy in these spasms."   R. W. W.

PRINCIPAL WORKS: *Poetry*—The Roman, 1850; Balder, 1854; Sonnets on the War (with Alexander Smith) 1855; England in Time of War, 1856; To a Little Girl, 1863; Poetical Works, 1875. *Politics*—Parliamentary Reform, 1865. *Miscellaneous*—Thoughts on Art, Philosophy, and Religion, 1876.

ABOUT: Dobell, S. T. Life and Letters; Dobell, S. T. Poetical Works (see Memoir by J. Nichol to 1875 ed.); Gosse, E. W. Silhouettes; Meynell, A. C. T. The Second Person Singular and Other Essays; Walker, H. The Literature of the Victorian Era; Woodberry, G. E. Literary Memoirs of the Nineteenth Century; Argosy 2:313 September 1866; Temple Bar 56:80 May 1879.

DOBSON, (HENRY) AUSTIN (January 18, 1840-September 2, 1921), poet, essayist, and biographer, was born at Plymouth, the eldest son of George Clarisse Dobson and Augusta Harris.

George Dobson was a civil engineer, engaged upon work on the breakwater at Plymouth; and, when Austin was about eight or nine years of age, the family removed to Holyhead. The boy expected to be an engineer, following the traditions of his father's family.

His education was at the Beaumaris Grammar School, where he was not very happy, at a private school in Coventry, and at the Gymnase in Strasbourg. This French education and the fact that he had a French grandmother perhaps explain to some extent his familiarity with and affection for things French, qualities revealed in many of his poems and in the title of his *Four Frenchwomen*.

At sixteen he returned home. Although a good mechanical draughtsman (he became accomplished also in wood-engraving) Dobson decided against becoming an engineer, perhaps because of a dislike for mathematics; and he entered government service as a clerk in the Board of Trade. Receiving promotion, he remained in the Board until his retirement in 1901. In his work he was associated with William Cosmo Monkhouse, Samuel Wad-

AUSTIN DOBSON

dington, and Edmund Gosse, all literary men. His prolific pen may have interfered with the performance of his official duties, for an officer criticized the poor administrative work of the "indifferent poets" occupying positions in the Board of Trade.

Dobson's literary career may be said to fall into two divisions, to some extent overlapping. In the first he concerned himself mainly with poetry. His first poem, "A City Flower" (1864), appeared in *Temple Bar*; and he became a contributor to *St. Paul's*, edited by Anthony Trollope. *Vignettes in Rhyme* (1873), dedicated to Trollope, and *Proverbs in Porcelain* (1877) were Dobson's first two books of poetry.

The most important work of his later years was in prose. After the publication (1866) in the *Englishwoman's Domestic Magazine* of an essay on Mademoiselle de Corday (later republished in *Four Frenchwomen*), and the appearance, in 1874, of a pot-boiling *Handbook of English Literature,* Dobson began the series of biographical studies of the eighteenth century which made him famous. He became recognized as an authority on the period, editing texts and writing introductions to those edited by others.

During the twenty years of his life after his retirement he enjoyed a pension and engaged in eighteenth-century research. This work became increasingly difficult as his sight failed; he lost nearly all vision in one eye. An added affliction, which he bore patiently, was severe arthritis in the right leg. In June 1921 he suffered a heart attack, and died in his suburban home in the following September.

Although physically robust, Dobson was a shy, nervous man, described by William Dana Orcutt as "the most modest literary man I

ever met." He led an exceedingly conventional and circumscribed life, and avoided any elaborate social responsibilities. Gosse, a close friend, said of him that he "had no aptitude for fashionable converse, and in social respects was like a titmouse." In 1868 he married Frances Mary Beardmore, a writer of children's stories. They had five sons and five daughters, all, with their mother, surviving Dobson. Living in Ealing, a suburb of London, Dobson made regular trips to and from the city, with little change or variety except for church on Sunday. The single attempt of his friends to dislodge him from this drab routine resulted in a trip to Lucerne, which had so little effect that they despaired and made no further effort to disturb his methodical existence. "Ealing possessed no citizen more regular in his habits or more blameless in his conduct," wrote Gosse.

Something of the same inhibition is perhaps visible in Dobson's writings. Though a student of the eighteenth century and of such writers as Fielding, he carefully avoided any of the impurer aspects of the life of the period, and was repelled by anything coarse or low. In his prose studies he was particular and accurate, and it has been suggested that his writing is impeded by its very conscientiousness. Brander Matthew has described Dobson's ideal in prose as "a style exact and cool and straightforward."

His poetry is characterized by race, wit, lightness, point, and polish, qualities which he drew partly from his loving attention to eighteenth-century art. Of his own verse Dobson wrote:

Let others prate of problems and of powers;
I bring but fancies born of idle hours,
    That striving only after Art and Ease,
Have scarcely more of moral than the flowers
    And little else of mission than to please.

A careful workman, Dobson was attracted to old French forms, such as the rondeau, the ballade, the triolet, and the chant royal, with their rigid patterns; and he acquired great technical expertness in the composition of English verse in such moulds. Warned by Tennyson of the danger of facility, he studied, at the greater poet's suggestion, the Odes of Horace, translating them, catching some of their urbanity, and saving his own poetry from an excess of Victorian sentimentality. He has been called an "English Horace." "His art was of a neatness, a nicety," wrote Harriet Monroe at the time of his death.

The great defect in his verse is lack of vitality or strong originality. Stephen Lucius Gwynn, criticizing Dobson's poetry, observes: "In short, what Dobson lacked to be a great poet was personality: there is nowhere any strong vibration of his nature. Yet nobody can read the best of his verses . . . without delight in the exquisite finish, the witty invention, and the ease of movement." R. W. W.

PRINCIPAL WORKS: *Biography*—Hogarth, 1879; Fielding, 1883; Thomas Bewick and His Pupils, 1884; Richard Steele, 1886; Life of Oliver Goldsmith, 1888; Horace Walpole, 1890; Samuel Richardson, 1902; Fanny Burney, 1903. *Essays*—Four Frenchwomen, 1890; Eighteenth Century Vignettes, 1892, 1894, 1896; Miscellanies, 1898, 1901; A Paladin of Philanthropy and Other Papers, 1899; Side-Walk Studies, 1902; De Libris, 1908; Old Kensington Palace and Other Papers, 1910; At Prior Park and Other Papers, 1912; Rosalba's Journal and Other Papers, 1915; Later Essays, 1917-1920, 1921. *Poetry*—Vignettes in Rhyme, 1873; Proverbs in Porcelain, 1877; Old-World Idylls, 1883; At the Sign of the Lyre, 1885; The Sun Dial, 1890; Selected Poems, 1892; The Ballad of Beau Brocade, 1892; The Story of Rosina, 1895; Poems on Several Occasions, 1895; Collected Poems, 1897; Complete Poetical Works, 1923. *Miscellaneous*—The Civil Service Handbook of English Literature, 1874; A Bookman's Budget, 1917.

ABOUT: Dobson, A[lban]. Austin Dobson: Some Notes; Dobson, A[lban]. A Bibliography of the First Editions of Austin Dobson; Gosse, E. Silhouettes; Murray, F. E. A Bibliography of Austin Dobson; American Journal of Philology 50:1 1929; Century Magazine ns6:912 October 1884; Fortnightly Review 116:640 October 1921.

DODGSON, CHARLES LUTWIDGE. See "CARROLL, LEWIS"

DOLBEN, DIGBY MACKWORTH (February 8, 1848-June 28, 1867), poet, was born at Guernsey, the youngest of five children descended from two old English families. At Mr. Tabor's school in Cheam he was prepared for Eton, where he went in 1862. There he was put under the surveillance of Robert Bridges, later poet laureate of England, who was distantly related to him. The two became fast friends and remained such for the brief remainder of Dolben's life. This was despite circumstances which were, to say the least, trying to Bridges; for Dolben formed an indiscreet affection for one of his schoolfellows, and further perturbed masters and friends alike by his evident leanings to Catholicism. Bridges was afterward the close friend of the Catholic poet Gerard Manley Hopkins, but in his schooldays his sympathies were definitely not on the side of Dolben's religious yearnings. Dolben was finally asked to leave the school; however, upon the plea of his father, he was readmitted in 1864. Although he had not been formally received into the Church, he joined the Benedictine order. Indeed, as his father had refused to sanction his entrance into the Catholic church, he was never formally received into that communion.

In 1868 Dolben went to Lincolnshire for tutoring, and in 1866 went up to Oxford for his entrance examinations. However, he had recently been ill, and fainted from weakness, which prevented his taking the tests. The following June, while Dolben was swimming with a small boy on his back, he suddenly sank and was drowned.

For about three years Dolben had been writing verse of a mystical cast; some of it later found its way into magazines. In 1911 Robert Bridges collected, edited, and published his verse, which shows in general a strong poetic feeling, skill, and a profound religious exaltation. Like many youthful poets, such as Chatterton, Dolben really showed more promise than brilliant performance, although, as Louise Imogen Guiney has pointed out, his poems are by no means mediocre when viewed in their proper religious setting.

PRINCIPAL WORKS: Poems (ed. with Memoir by Robert Bridges) 1911.

ABOUT: Bridges, R. Three Friends; Catholic World 95:769 September 1912; Irish Monthly 61:603 October 1933.

DOMETT, ALFRED (May 20, 1811-November 2, 1887), poet, was born in Surrey. He attended St. John's College, Cambridge, but left without a degree. In 1833 he published his first volume of poems, and soon after became a contributor to *Blackwood's*. For several years he led a life of leisure, traveling frequently in America and on the Continent. He was an intimate friend of Robert Browning, who admired his work and lamented when Domett seemed to desert poetry for politics.

In 1841 he was called to the bar at the Middle Temple, and the next year emigrated to New Zealand. There he filled nearly all the chief administrative offices, being colonial secretary, commissioner of crown lands, legislative councillor, etc. After his marriage to an Englishwoman he returned to England in 1871 and settled in London. Besides his poetry (the later volumes being on New Zealand themes), he wrote several prose volumes on New Zealand politics.

PRINCIPAL WORKS: Ranolf and Amohia: A South Sea Day Dream, 1872; Flotsam and Jetsam, 1877.

ABOUT: Gilsborne, W. New Zealand Rulers and Statesmen; Kenyon, F. G. (ed.). Robert Browning and Alfred Domett.

DONALDSON, JOHN WILLIAM (June 7, 1811-February 10, 1861), classical and Biblical scholar, was born in London. His father had been a merchant in Australia and his brother later became a statesman there. He was educated privately, and at fourteen was articled to his uncle, a solicitor. However, in 1840 he won first prize in Greek in an examination conducted by University College, London, and by the advice of the examiner went to Trinity College, Cambridge. There, as fellow and tutor, he specialized in philology. In 1840 he married Letitia Matlock, and in 1841 became headmaster of King Edward's School at Bury St. Edmunds. This was un-

fortunate, for he was a bad teacher and the school declined under his charge. He resigned in 1855, in the midst of a controversy over his Latin work on the lost Biblical book of Jashar. Thereafter he lived at Cambridge as a private tutor. He edited Pindar and Sophocles, and completed K. O. Müller's unfinished *History of Greek Literature.* He was working on a Greek dictionary when he died, actually of overwork.

Donaldson's contribution to Greek and Latin comparative philology was brilliant—his work is never trite or dull—but it was highly speculative and he was rash and aggressive by nature. He was of more value in stirring up others than in what he himself produced. He was accused, not altogether unjustly, of plagiarism. *The New Cratylus,* however, marked an epoch in English scholarship.

PRINCIPAL WORKS: The New Cratylus, 1839; Varronianus, 1844; Jashar (in Latin) 1854; Christian Orthodoxy Reconciled to the Conclusions of Modern Biblical Learning, 1857.

ABOUT: Athenaeum February 16, 1861.

DONNE, WILLIAM BODHAM (July 29, 1807-June 20, 1882), essayist, was a descendant of the great poet John Donne and also related on both sides to the poet Cowper. He was educated at the Grammar School, Bury St. Edmunds, where he became a friend of Edward Fitzgerald, the translator of Omar Khayyam, and also of John M. Kemble, of the famous family of actors. He attended Caius College, Cambridge, but did not take a degree because of conscientious objections to the religious tests. (He was a lifelong liberal.)

In 1830 he married Catharine Hewitt; they had three sons and five daughters. He contributed to many magazines and lived by writing. In 1846 he returned to Bury St. Edmunds for the education of his sons. In 1852 he declined the editorship of the *Edinburgh Review* on the ground that his life was so retired he was not cognizant of social and political currents of thought. From 1852 to 1857 he was librarian of the London Library. From 1857 to his death he was examiner of plays, having previously been Kemble's deputy. He was a classical scholar, who contributed to classical dictionaries and edited Euripides and Tacitus. His work is marked by taste and delicate humor, but is not otherwise distinguished.

PRINCIPAL WORKS: Old Roads and New Roads, 1852; Essays Upon the Drama, 1858.

ABOUT: Johnson, C. B. Donne and His Friends; Kemble, F. Records of Later Life; Saturday Review July 4, 1882.

DORAN, JOHN (March 11, 1807-January 25, 1878), miscellaneous writer, was born in London of Irish parentage. His father had lived in France and from childhood Doran was familiar with the French language. He was educated at Matheson's Academy, but by seventeen was an orphan, and made his way by acting as tutor to the sons of several peers. In 1828 he traveled on the Continent with a pupil, and acted as correspondent to the *Literary Chronicle.* At only seventeen his melodrama, *Justice,* had been performed at the Surrey Theater. From 1830 he contributed verse translations from French, German, Latin, and Italian to the Bath *Journal.* In 1834 he married Emma Gilbert, by whom he had one son and one daughter. He retired from teaching and traveled for two or three years, gaining a Ph.D. from the University of Marburg, in Prussia. In 1841 he became literary editor of the *Church and State Gazette,* and in 1869 and 1870 he edited The *Athenaeum,* which had absorbed the *Literary Chronicle.* From 1871 to his death he was editor of *Notes and Queries.* He published an edition of Xenophon. In spite of his classical attainments, Doran was an indifferent writer, too voluminous, and most of his work, though entertaining, is perfunctory and superficial.

PRINCIPAL WORKS: History of Reading, 1835; Table Traits, 1854; Habits and Men, 1854; The Queens of the House of Hanover, 1855; Knights and Their Days, 1856; History of Court Fools, 1858; Book of the Prince of Wales, 1860; Their Majesties' Servants, 1860; Saints and Sinners, 1868; Memories of Our Great Towns, 1878.

ABOUT: Illustrated London News February 9, 1878.

DORSET, MRS. CATHERINE ANN (1750?-1817?), poet, was born in Sussex, her maiden name being Turner. Her mother died at her birth, and she was reared by an aunt. In 1770 she married Captain Michael Dorset, who died in 1805. She is believed to have had at least one son, but very little is known about her private life. Her first poems appeared anonymously in *Conversations,* by her sister, Mrs. Charlotte Smith. Not even the date of her death is known, though it is certain that she was still alive in 1816. Her best known poem, *The Peacock "at Home"* she later revised for adult reading (all her other work is for children) and published with the poems that originally appeared in her sister's book.

PRINCIPAL WORKS: The Lion's Masquerade, 1807; The Peacock "at Home," 1807; Think Before You Speak (adapted from the French) 1809.

"DOUGLAS, GEORGE." See BROWN, GEORGE DOUGLAS

DOUGHTY, CHARLES MONTAGU (August 19, 1843-January 30, 1926), explorer and poet, was the second of two sons of the Reverend C. M. Doughty, squire of Theberton Hall, Suffolk, and Frederica Beaumont Hotham of East Yorkshire nobility. Deprived of the naval career, for which he had prepared from childhood, by failure to pass the physical examination, Doughty turned to a secondary interest, geology. At Cambridge, where he was graduated in 1865, he took a second in his natural science tripos, because, his examiner said, he had "such a disheveled mind. If you asked him for a collar, he upset his whole wardrobe at your feet." A fellow student described him at the same period as "shy, nervous, and very polite. He had no sense of humor."

Living aloof from his fellows, but with idealistic ambitions of serving his country and his race, Doughty swung next to the study of early English literature. Particularly Chaucer and Spenser represented to his mind the language's golden age. He had already conceived a patriotic work of epic proportions to be written in what he deemed pure English.

Depressed finances did not deter him from leaving England in 1870 to pursue the long, wandering course of study through Europe, North Africa, Syria, and Palestine which led finally to his adventures in Arabia. After a year spent in learning Arabic, with fruitless efforts to enlist the support of the Royal Geographic Society and of his own consul, Doughty set out from Damascus in November 1876, following the Mecca pilgrims. His ambition was to trail the Haj, or caravan, to Medain Salih, where he had heard were ancient monuments never viewed by white man.

Dressed as a native, and with his tall figure and full red beard adequately resembling one, carrying a supply of simple remedies which would qualify him as a medicine-man, and conversant with the language, he nevertheless found his venture extremely hazardous. In the two years Doughty spent among the Bedouins he was almost constantly in danger of his life. Although an agnostic, he endured physical violence and frequent humiliation because he would not deny that he was a Christian. It may be suggested that Doughty knew his own limitations as a masquerader. Upon one occasion he betrayed himself by asking for food during Ramadan, when the Moslem fasts by day.

After an extensive exploration of the monuments and inscriptions at Al-Hijr, the ancient caravan city, making drawings and taking squeezes of the tomb-inscriptions, Doughty sent his records back to Damascus and in February 1877 attached himself to a tribe of Bedouins. Wandering with the natives, taking careful note of them and of the geological and hydrographical aspects of the country, he attained, in November 1877, the legendary oasis city of Keybar, forbidden to unbelievers. Here he inadvertently went shod into a mosque and from here after four months of inglorious detention he was expelled. He en-

CHARLES M. DOUGHTY

dured at the hands of his guides and from natives along the way a series of petty martyrdoms until he reached Taif, where the tolerant *sherif* Huseym made what amends he could.

October 1878 found Doughty ill in a hospital at Bombay. By December he was in England. Scientific reports of his explorations occupied him now, as well as the literary account of his travels. This latter secured a publisher only with difficulty. While admired as to content, its style was justly characterized as obscure. The author's involved, archaistic stiffness of phrasing and use of obsolete words and expressions were generally deplored. It was said that "some parts of it are not English at all." The work of publication of *Travels in Arabia Deserta* was finally commenced by the Cambridge University Press in 1885.

In 1886 Doughty married Caroline Amelia McMurdo. The Doughtys, after a sojourn in Palestine, lived chiefly on the Riviera until 1898, when they returned to England with their two daughters. During this period Doughty had been at work on his epic depicting the growth of Britain's national consciousness. Through the good offices of Edward Garnett this two-volume product of fourteen years' labor, consisting of thirty thousand unrhymed decasyllabic lines, was published (1906) as *The Dawn in Britain*. Doughty continued to work in the field of poetry and poetic drama, achieving some literary but no financial recognition.

The war brought Doughty, who had been prophesying these hostilities since 1908, considerable fame as a seer. There was a demand for a new edition of *Arabia Deserta* and a growing number of esthetes acclaimed his poetry. His last years discovered his physical but not his mental faculties weakened. He died at Sissinghurst, Kent.

Doughty conceived of *Arabia Deserta* as literature primarily. Those who, like his disciple Lawrence of Arabia, valued it sincerely did so by reason of its content, and what they considered its scientific merit enhanced for them its style. As Morris and Burne-Jones did before, professional litterateurs today exalt the book as an esoteric monument for the comprehension of the elect. The average student who hurdles its style may feel with Burton that the recorded "subjection of an Englishman to indignity and persecution over half Arabia" is "told with a nauseating insistence." But Hogarth refers significantly to Doughty as "a man of sorrows and acquainted with grief."

An enigma to his contemporaries, Doughty's unusual character and talents were slow in winning recognition. The few who knew him personally found his candor, honesty, and almost childlike simplicity lovable. His reserve was a life-long characteristic, and he held himself aloof from the life of his times. Once in his last years Thomas Hardy's name was mentioned in his presence. "Who is Hardy?" he asked in all innocence as his auditors gasped. Despite this remoteness from everyday affairs, he was called "the most patriotic of Englishmen" in his ideals and emotions.

Few have known the Arab so well. P. A. Sykes says that he understood the Bedouin mentality "better than any European of his generation," and T. E. Lawrence attested to the remarkable fact that after forty years he was still remembered in the desert, where "men are short-lived and their memories of strangers and events outside the family tree soon fail."

Doughty confessed in later years that style was more important to him than matter. This is particularly apparent in his work after 1912, but is recognizable in all his poetry, which "challenges the peace of eye and ear" and abounds with inversions, parentheses, archaisms, and even words which never existed in English. Generally speaking, Doughty, the patriot-reformer of his mother tongue, may be set down as a creator of literary curiosities. As an explorer he will always have a place among those who have opened new territory to scientific achievement.

P. B. S.

PRINCIPAL WORKS: *Travel*—Travels in Arabia Deserta, 1888; Wanderings in Arabia (excerpts from the larger work) 1908. *Poetry*—Under Arms, 1900; The Dawn in Britain, 1906; Adam Cast Forth, 1908; The Cliffs, 1909; The Clouds, 1912; The Titans, 1916; Mansoul, 1920. *Scientific*—On the Jöstedal-Brae Glaciers in Norway, 1866; Documents Epigraphiques Recueillis Dans le Nord de l'Arabie, 1884.

196

ABOUT: Doughty, C. M. Travels in Arabia Deserta (1921 ed., see Introduction by T. E. Lawrence); Fairley, B. Charles M. Doughty; Hogarth, D. G. The Life of Charles M. Doughty; Sykes, P. A History of Exploration.

DOWDEN, EDWARD (May 3, 1843-April 4, 1913), Irish essayist, critic, biographer, and poet, was the fourth son of John Wheeler Dowden and Alicia Bennett, and was born at Cork.

The boy early showed literary interests, for by the time he had reached the age of twelve he was writing essays. He was educated at Queen's College, Cork, and Trinity College, Dublin, from which he was graduated in 1863, with a scholastic record which, at the time of his death, had not been excelled.

When, in 1867, a new chair of English literature was established at Trinity, young Dowden was called to fill it; and he retained this post throughout the rest of his life, despite a distaste for the drudgery of papers and examinations. In 1889 he became the first Taylorian Lecturer at Oxford, from 1892 to 1896 he was Clark Lecturer at Trinity College, Cambridge, and in 1896 he delivered lectures in connection with the Sesquicentennial Celebration of Princeton University (*The French Revolution and English Literature*). He was made President (1888) of the English Goethe Society, a trustee of the (Irish) National Library, and Commissioner of Education.

Handsome and personally charming, Dowden attracted students and friends; and his home became an intellectual center. Quick to recognize Whitman's genius, he was a close friend of that poet. In 1866 he married Mary Clerke, by whom he had a son and two daughters; and, after her death in 1892, he married

EDWARD DOWDEN

(1895) Elizabeth Dickinson West, who, after his death in Dublin, 1913, published some of their correspondence. A "half-breed Irishman," Dowden opposed the nationalist movement, and was Secretary of the Irish Liberal Union and Vice-President of the Irish Unionist Alliance. This political attitude perhaps explains his lack of sympathy with the rising Irish literature, and his refusal to participate in the centenary observance of the birth of Thomas Moore.

With the publication of *Shakspere: A Critical Study of His Mind and Art* (1875) and *Poems* (1876), a long and fruitful literary career was opened. Though he considered himself a poet, it was his prose criticism and biography, and especially his first Shakespearian studies, that brought Dowden fame. His biography of Shelley (1886), which provoked Mark Twain's essay, "In Defence of Harriet Shelley," became the standard work on the subject, despite Matthew Arnold's strictures. Catholic in his interests and versatile in ability, Dowden as a critic was psychologically keen. In the words of Edward John Gwynn, he attempted "to find the dominant law of a writer's mind and to exhibit his work as the expression of a single character and temperament." In biography he tended to give facts without interpretative comment. Hugh Walker, in the *Cambridge History of English Literature*, describes Dowden's contribution to Shakespeare study as "a thoughtful interpretation of Shakespeare's work . . . expressed . . . in a style lucid and attractive." And of his essays Walker writes that they "are invariably scholarly, and they usually show that insight which a genial sympathy gives."

R. W. W.

PRINCIPAL WORKS: *Biography*—Southey, 1880; The Life of Percy Bysshe Shelley, 1886; Robert Browning, 1904: Michel de Montaigne, 1905. *Essays and Criticism*—Shakspere: A Critical Study of His Mind and Art, 1875; Shakespere: Scenes and Characters, 1876; A Shakespeare Primer, 1877; Studies in Literature: 1789-1877, 1878; Transcripts and Studies, 1888; Introduction to Shakespere, 1893; New Studies in Literature, 1805; The French Revolution and English Literature, 1895; A History of French Literature, 1897; Puritan and Anglican: Studies in Literature, 1900; Milton in the 18th Century: 1701-1750, 1908; Essays: Modern and Elizabethan, 1910. *Letters*—Fragments From Old Letters, E. D. to E. D. W.: 1869-1892, 1913-14; Letters of Edward Dowden and His Correspondents, 1914; Letters About Shelley, Interchanged by Three Friends—Edward Dowden, Richard Garnett, and Wm. Michael Rossetti, 1917. *Poetry*—Poems, 1876; A Woman's Reliquary, 1913; Poems, 1914; Goethe's West-Eastern Divan (trans.) 1914. *Editor*—The Correspondence of Robert Southey With Caroline Bowles, 1881; The Sonnets of William Shakspere, 1881; The Passionate Pilgrim, 1883; The Correspondence of Henry Taylor, 1888; Lyrical Ballads, 1890; The Poetical Works of Percy Bysshe Shelley, 1891; The Poetical Works of William Wordsworth, 1892-93; Poems of Robert Southey, 1895; Poems by William Wordsworth, 1897; The Tragedy of Hamlet, 1899: The Tragedy of Romeo and Juliet, 1900; Cymbeline, 1903; Robert Browning's The Ring and the Book, 1912.

ABOUT: Boyd, E. A. Appreciations and Depreciations; Fortnightly Review 101:1009 June 1914; Nation 96:413 April 24, 1913; Nation 96:520 May 22, 1913; Nation 100:324 March 25, 1915.

DOWSON, ERNEST (August 2, 1867-February 23, 1900), poet, was born in Kent, but spent most of his youth and much of his later life in France, where his father was obliged to live (principally on the Riviera) because of his delicate health. It is probable that the father suffered from the same disease, tuberculosis, which killed the son at 32. Dowson's early education was irregular, owing to his father's frequent changes of residence, but he matriculated at Queen's College, Oxford, leaving in 1887 without a degree and without any marked distinction.

His father's death left him, as part of his inheritance, a dock in the East End of London. There, in a tumbledown house, Dowson lived for several years, and in that malodorous neighborhood he met, loved, and lost the young girl whom he immortalized as "Cynara." She was rather stupid, and not even pretty, the daughter of a refugee Frenchman reduced to operating a third-class café. For two years Dowson ate there almost nightly, played a game of cards after dinner with the proprietor's daughter, and then for twenty-four hours more disappeared into his own special "city of dreadful night." It is doubtful if the girl ever knew, it is almost certain that she could never comprehend, the shy, passionate adoration of the young Englishman who spoke French like a native, whose manners were as exquisite as his appearance was tatterdemalion, and who when she saw him at least was infinitely her superior in both intellect and sensibility. At the end of the two years she married—her father's waiter. Dowson had lost her whom he had never possessed, but she gave birth to his most famous poem.

From London he went to live in Paris, near Les Halles, then in Dieppe, in waterfront dives. In all these places, his life was the same—days of translation from the French to earn his meager livelihood, of occasional poems wrung from him almost against his will, of rare meetings with the acquaintances and the few friends of his early youth—and nights of a wild drunkenness that approached true insanity. In Oxford, he had played with hashish; but he soon deserted drugs for the alcohol which was fatal to one of his mental and physical constitution. He became the archetype of the young poet of disordered life who sings from a dung-heap. But his degradation was an escape, not a rebellion; he was no more a conscious rebel against his time and place than was Poe or Baudelaire.

At the end of 1899, Dowson returned to London. He had relatives who would have

ERNEST DOWSON

brook Jackson calls "high-wrought intensity and indefinable glamor," but above all they are inimitably musical. There is in these slender volumes the unmistakable influence of Swinburne and the Pre-Raphaelites, but it is transmuted and made the poet's own. He is to the erotic versifiers of his day what Poe was to the jinglers of his. With Poe too he shares an innocent pedantry; the long Latin titles he gave to many of his poems was probably an expression of vague nostalgia for the world of culture which he had deserted.

Perhaps only one of his poems will live— "Non sum qualis eram bonae sub regno Cynarae," which, with its haunting refrain, "I have been faithful to thee, Cynara, in my fashion," will strike an answering chord in the hearts of new-come readers as long as youth is sentimental, melancholy, and self-dramatizing. Others, however, deserve to live—notably "Impoenitentia ultima," with the famous "viols in her voice" which illustrated Dowson's passion for the letter V.

A word should be said of Dowson's translations. They were done as hack work, but his profound familiarity with the French language and spirit raised them above the ordinary standard. Among the many French works which he translated were Balzac's *La Fille aux Yeux d'Or*, Choderlos de Laclos' once celebrated *Les Liaisons Dangereuses*, Voltaire's *La Pucelle*, and Zola's *La Terre*.

The "eternal and bitter anguish" of Dowson's poetry is authentic, the despairing cry of a man who did not want to live. Its beauty is as genuine as its pain. His contribution to English literature is slender, but it is real. From thirty years of weakness and agony he distilled a few drops of the true liquor of genius.   M. A. deF.

PRINCIPAL WORKS: *Poetry*—Verses, 1896; Poems, 1905. *Play*—The Pierrot of the Minute (in verse) 1897. *Novels*—A Comedy of Masks, 1893; Adrian Rome, 1899 (both with Arthur Moore). *Short Stories*—Dilemmas, 1895. *Miscellaneous*—Decorations in Verse and Prose, 1899.

ABOUT: Burdett, O. The Beardsley Period; Dowson, E. Poems (see Memoir by Arthur Symons); Jackson, H. The Eighteen Nineties; Plarr, V. G. Reminiscences, Unpublished Letters, and Marginalia; Rothenstein, W. Men and Memories; Virginia Quarterly Review 3:250 April 1927.

kept him from actual destitution, he was never wholly without resources, but his fierce pride kept him from appealing to anyone for help. A friend, almost as poor as he, found him, ill and starving, in a wine-cellar, and took him home to the room he had rented in a bricklayer's cottage. Dowson had no idea that he was dying; he was full of feverish gayety, eager to make plans for future work. But he never rose from his bed again. He died in surroundings almost as sordid as those he had known for thirteen years past. He was buried —though he had never been a faithful, and perhaps never a formal, member of that church—in the Roman Catholic portion of the Lewisham Cemetery.

To Arthur Symons, his friend and chief biographer, Dowson seemed to have "the face of a demoralized Keats." "Never," said Symons, was there "a simpler or more attaching charm." His was almost a dual personality: shy, delicate, and refined when he was sober, as gentle-mannered as he was "miserable and unkempt," when intoxicated he frequently became violent, obscene, easily aroused to reasonless anger, and sexually promiscuous, with an apparent preference for the most degraded women. He seems, indeed, to have been an arrested adolescent, and the fact that extreme immaturity attracted him in women is significant.

He was no judge of his own work. He preferred his forgotten prose, his fragmentary and impressionistic stories, to his poetry; and poetry to him meant simple music, without philosophic content. As a poet he was stationary; his earliest work was as finished as his latest, and toward the end he had begun to repeat himself, having said all that he had to say. His poems are marked by what Hol-

DOYLE, SIR FRANCIS HASTINGS CHARLES (August 21, 1810-June 8, 1888), poet, was born in Yorkshire, only son of the first baronet Doyle, a major general. Several of his cousins were high army officers and he always had military connections and interests.

In 1823 he went to Eton, where he was the classmate and friend of Gladstone and of Arthur Hallam, the friend of Tennyson. He proceeded to Christ Church College, Oxford, where he received the B.A. in 1832, B.C.L. 1843, and M.A. 1867. He was Fellow of All

Souls' College in 1835. In 1832 he read law and was called to the bar from the Inner Temple in 1837. He joined the northern circuit as revising barrister. He succeeded to the baronetcy in 1839.

In 1844 Doyle married Sidney Wynn, by whom he had a large family, of which two sons and one daughter survived. In 1845 he was assistant solicitor of excise, and in 1846 receiver-general of customs, a post he held for over twenty years.

After his early verses he published nothing for fourteen years; but in 1866, wishing to succeed Matthew Arnold as professor of poetry at Oxford, he issued a new volume "to bring himself before the younger members of the university." He was successful, and held the professorship from 1867 to 1877. At the same time he remained in his governmental post, but in 1869 was promoted to be commissioner of customs, remaining in this office until 1883.

Doyle was a sort of anticipatory Kipling (the Kipling of *Barrack Room Ballads*), without Kipling's genius. His poems are nearly all patriotic ballads in modern form. They are spirited, and a few, like "A Private of the Buffs," "The Loss of the Birkenhead," and "The Red Thread of Honour," became widely known, but for the most part his verses are mechanical and commonplace.

PRINCIPAL WORKS: Miscellaneous Verses, 1834 (revised and enlarged, 1840); The Two Destinies, 1844; The Duke's Funeral, 1852; The Return of the Guards and Other Poems, 1866; Lectures on Poetry, 1869-77; Reminiscences and Opinions, 1886.

ABOUT: Doyle, F. H. Reminiscences and Opinions; Miles. Poets and Poetry of the Century.

DOYLE, JOHN ANDREW (May 14, 1844-August 5, 1907),

historian, was born in London, his father, of Irish descent, being editor of the *Morning Chronicle*. The mother was an heiress, and her fortune made him independently wealthy. He was educated at Eton and at Balliol College, Oxford, where he received his B.A. in 1867 with a first class degree in *literae humaniores*. In 1869 he won the Arnold prize for an essay on the English colonies in America before 1776, and this event determined the main interest of his life. The same year he was made a fellow of All Souls College, and, as he never married, he spent the remainder of his years either at Oxford or with his parents, who had moved to Wales. From 1881 to 1888 he was librarian of Oxford.

Doyle was no recluse, however. From 1889 he was an alderman on the county council of Breconshire, Wales, and was high sheriff of Breconshire in 1892, interesting himself especially in agriculture and education. He was an expert rifle shot, and became an authority on the breeding of dogs and race-horses. He was a contributor to the *Cambridge Modern History* and the *Dictionary of National Biography*, but here as elsewhere his sole subject was the American colonies before the Revolution. His attitude was judicial, his work is detailed and accurate, and his writing is clear and vigorous. He is a reliable rather than a great historian.

PRINCIPAL WORKS: Summary History of America, 1875; A History of the American Colonies Down to the War of Independence, 1882-1907; Essays on Various Subjects, 1911.

ABOUT: Doyle, J. A. Essays on Various Subjects (see Introduction by Sir W. R. Anson).

DRENNAN, WILLIAM (May 23, 1754-February 5, 1820),

Irish political writer and poet, was born at Belfast, the son of William Drennan, a Presbyterian clergyman. He was sent to the University of Edinburgh to be educated for a career in medicine, and there distinguished himself both in that science and in philosophy. He was granted the degree of M.D. in 1778.

After some years of practice in Belfast and Newry, Drennan went to Dublin in 1879. Already imbued with the ideas animating the United Irishmen Movement, he became an active member of the group, one of its ablest writers and pamphleteers, and the author of its original manifesto. *The Wake of William Orr*, published in 1791, caused a furore all over Ireland, while Drennan's *Letters of Orellana, the Irish Helot* (1792) played a chief part in inducing Ulster to join the league. Drennan was intimate with the wits and men of letters of Dublin, "the Irish Athens," and he and his brilliant sister, Mrs. McTier, enjoyed a various and pleasant social life.

WILLIAM DRENNAN

In 1794 Drennan and an associate named Rowan were seized and brought to trial for having written the United Irishmen's manifesto, the *Address of the United Irishmen to the Volunteers of Ireland*. Rowan was fined £500 and sentenced to two years' imprisonment, while Drennan, the actual culprit, was acquitted and freed. The troubles incident to the rebellion of 1798, however, put an end to his political activities, and in 1800, after his marriage to a wealthy Englishwoman, he left Dublin and returned to Belfast. There he founded the *Belfast Magazine* and the Belfast Academical Institution, and found time in addition to bring out an edition of his poems and a translation of the *Electra* of Sophocles (1817). Most of his verse had been previously published in periodicals, and collected in great part in Joshua Edkins' *Collection of Poems* (1801).

Drennan's last twenty years were quiet. Two sons who survived him were both authors of acceptable verse. His own work consists of pleasing songs and ballads and hymns of worth above the average; as a poet, his reputation was eclipsed by that of his brilliant contemporary, Thomas Moore, who, incidentally, gave lavish praise to Drennan's poem "When Erin First Rose"—the lyric in which, for the first time, Ireland is referred to as "the Emerald Isle." Perhaps the invention of this seemingly inevitable epithet is the most distinguished of Drennan's accomplishments.

R. M.

PRINCIPAL WORKS: *Poetry*—Glendalough and Other Poems, 1815; Fugitive Pieces, 1815. *Miscellaneous*—Letters of Orellana, 1792.
ABOUT: Madden, J. A. Lives of the United Irishmen; McCarthy, J. A. & others. Irish Literature (v. 3); Studies 10:239 June 1921.

DRIVER, SAMUEL ROLLES (October 2, 1846-February 26, 1914), Hebraist and theologian, was born at Southampton, the only child of a Quaker family. He was educated at Winchester and at New College, Oxford, where he had a distinguished career, becoming a fellow in 1870 and a tutor in classics in 1875. From 1875 to 1884 he was one of the group engaged in revision of the Old Testament. He was ordained deacon in 1881 and priest in 1882, and succeeded the famous Dr. Pusey as regius professor and canon of Christ Church. In 1891 he married Mabel Burr; they had three sons and two daughters. He was a contributor to the Oxford Hebrew Lexicon from 1891 to 1905. In all he published commentaries on nearly half the Old Testament.

Driver was a good teacher, with a naturally philosophic and objective mind. He was an advocate of the higher criticism of the Bible, and welcomed the application of scientific methods to Biblical study, but he was always moderate, temperate, and diplomatic—a natural outgrowth of his retiring disposition. As a scholar and writer he was exact and sound, but seldom original.

PRINCIPAL WORKS: A Treatise on the Use of Tenses in Hebrew, 1874; An Introduction to the Literature of the Old Testament, 1891.
ABOUT: Sanday, W. The Life-Work of Samuel Rolles Driver.

"DRUID, THE." See DIXON, HENRY HALL

DRUMMOND, HENRY (August 17, 1851-March 11, 1897), Scottish theologian and naturalist, was born in Stirling, his father being a seed merchant and a pillar of the Free Church. He was educated at the University of Edinburgh, but left without taking a degree. In 1870 he went to New College, Edinburgh to study for the ministry, and in 1873 attended the University of Tübingen. He became connected with the American evangelists, Moody and Sankey, and assisted them in their first British tour in 1874 and 1875. They wanted him to go to America with them, but he returned to New College. In 1877 he was a lecturer on natural science at Free Church College, Glasgow. In 1879 he did go to the United States, but not as an evangelist; he accompanied the noted geologist, Sir Archibald Geikie, in a geological exploration of the Rocky Mountains. Returning to Scotland, Drummond did mission work in Glasgow until 1882, then joined Moody and Sankey in their second British tour. In 1883 he explored the Nyasa and Tanganyika districts in equatorial Africa for the African Lakes Corporation. He was finally ordained in 1884, and became a professor of theology, conducting students' missions in London, Oxford, Edinburgh, and Glasgow. In 1887 he made an evangelical tour of American colleges, and in 1890 of Australia. He died, unmarried, at Tunbridge Wells, at forty-five, of cancer of the bones.

Drummond's best known work is *Natural Law in the Spiritual World*, which enjoyed an immense vogue in its day. He was a "reconciler" between science and religion, and his attempt to reconcile the irreconcilable caused him to fall between two stools. His theory that the struggle for existence is really altruistic was torn to shreds by realistic biologists. His writing is brilliant, but specious and fallacious.

PRINCIPAL WORKS: Natural Law in the Spiritual World, 1883; Tropical Africa, 1888; The Ascent of Man, 1894; The Ideal Life, 1897.
ABOUT: Jones, P. L. Henry Drummond; Watson, R. A. Gospels of Yesterday.

"DUCHESS, THE." See HUNGERFORD, MRS. MARGARET WOLFE

DUFF, SIR M. E. See GRANT DUFF, M. E.

DUFF-GORDON, LADY LUCIE (June 24, 1821-July 14, 1869), travel writer, was born in London as Lucie (or Lucy) Austin, her father a well known jurist, her mother a translator. As a child she played with the great economist, John Stuart Mill, in his own childhood. In 1826 she went with her parents to Bonn, where she acquired a fine knowledge of German; aside from this she was educated at home. In 1840 she married Sir Alexander Cornewall Duff-Gordon, a Scotsman. They lived in a brilliant circle, of which Dickens, Tennyson, and Thackeray were intimates. She knew the German poet Heine well, and visited him in 1854 in Paris, just before his death. She translated widely from the German and the French, and in 1850, in Weybridge, established a library for working-men, but she did no original writing until after she went in 1860 to the Cape of Good Hope for her health. Her letters of 1860 to her mother were published posthumously (ten years after her later letters from Egypt). She was tubercular, and found it impossible to live in England; in 1862 she went to Egypt, and returned only twice for brief visits. There she was beloved by the natives, who called her Sitt el Kebeer, "the great lady." Sir Alexander died in 1861, leaving her with one daughter, afterwards Mrs. Ross.

Lady Duff-Gordon was a sympathetic person, very fond of animals, kindly and generous. Her writing shows independence and originality of thought, vivacity, and keen observation.

PRINCIPAL WORKS: Letters From Egypt, 1865; Last Letters From Egypt, With Letters From the Cape, 1875.

ABOUT: Duff-Gordon, L. Last Letters From Egypt (see Memoir by Janet Ross); Macmillan's Magazine September 1869, October 1874.

DUFFERIN, LADY (Helen Selina Sheridan) (1807-June 13, 1867), was the granddaughter of the dramatist Richard Brinsley Sheridan, the oldest of "the three beautiful Sheridan sisters." Her mother was a novelist, her father a colonial treasurer. When she was six the family went to the Cape of Good Hope, where the father died four years later. She was brought back to England, and the remainder of her girlhood was spent in Hampton Court Palace, by the hospitality of the Regent (later George IV). When she was only eighteen she married Commander Price Blackwood, the young heir to the Irish title of Baron Dufferin and Claudeboye. Since their families disapproved of the match, they lived for two years in Florence, where their son was born. In 1839 her husband succeeded to the title and estates, but two years later he died of an accidental overdose of morphia. Thenceforth she devoted herself to her son's education and for many years lived a retired life, in contrast to those of her sisters, the brilliant Mrs. Norton (made famous by her poetry and notorious by her husband's unsuccessful adultery charge against Lord Melbourne), and the Duchess of Somerset.

In 1862, on his deathbed, Lady Dufferin married George Hay, Earl of Gifford and son and heir of the Marquis of Tweedale. He died the next month: she had refused him (it was believed) until it was certain that his death was imminent.

From childhood she had written songs, but all that appeared were published anonymously. In 1863 her play, *Finesse,* was performed at the Haymarket, but she neither acknowledged her authorship of it nor saw it acted. A satirical book was brought out anonymously in 1863, but her poems did not appear under her name until long after her death. Her best known song is "The Irish Emigrant." Her work is tender and simple, with flashes of real talent.

PRINCIPAL WORKS: Lispings From Low Latitudes: or, Extracts From the Journal of the Hon. Impulsia Gushington, 1863; Songs, Poems, and Verses, 1894.

ABOUT: Dufferin, Lady. Songs, Poems, and Verses (see Memoir by her son, the Marquess of Dufferin and Ava).

DUFFERIN, LORD (Frederick Temple Hamilton-Temple Blackwood, First Marquess of Dufferin and Ava) (June 21, 1826-February 12, 1902), statesman, was born in Florence, where his parents were living because of the disapproval of their marriage by their families. His mother, later Lady Gifford, was the poet, Helen Sheridan, granddaughter of the famous dramatist, Richard Brinsley Sheridan.

Blackwood's father, by that time Baron Dufferin and Clandeboye, died in 1841, and his mother devoted herself to his education. He went to Eton, then from 1844 to 1846 to Christ Church, Oxford, following which he spent ten years in travel and in the care of his Irish estates (his title was Irish). A liberal, in 1850 he had entered the House of Lords (as Baron Clandeboye). For a time he was lord-in-waiting to Queen Victoria. He then entered the diplomatic service, being sent on missions to Austria and Turkey. In 1864 he was under-secretary for India, in 1868 chancellor of the Duchy of Lancaster. In 1871, by his grandfather's death, he became the Earl of Dufferin. From 1872 to 1878 he was governor-general of Canada, in 1879 ambassador to Russia; in 1881 he represented Great Britain in Turkey, in 1882 in Egypt. From 1884 to 1888 he was governor-general of India. He was created Marquess of Dufferin and Ava in 1888. In 1889 he was appointed ambassador to Italy, and in 1891 to France. He retired from the diplomatic service in 1896. He had been made lord rector of St. Andrews University in 1891.

In 1897 this distinguished career was ruined by his unfortunate connection with a mining finance corporation which swindled its stockholders; no dishonor attached to him but he had to bear the brunt of the attack, and was crippled financially. His oldest son was killed in the Boer War, and his last years were most unhappy. In 1862 he had married Harriot Hamilton, an Irish lady; they had four sons and three daughters.

Dufferin had great literary talent, but for the most part it was displayed only in brilliant official reports. The title of his only general book may have been suggested by his mother's early satirical volume, *Lispings From Low Latitudes*.

PRINCIPAL WORKS: Letters From High Latitudes, 1859; Mr. Mill's Plan for the Pacification of Ireland Examined, 1868.

ABOUT: Black, C. E. D. The Marquess of Dufferin and Ava; Lyell, A. Life of the Marquess of Dufferin and Ava.

DUFFY, SIR CHARLES GAVAN (April 12, 1816-February 9, 1903), Irish poet, journalist, and patriot, was born in Monaghan, the son of a shop-keeper, John Duffy.

His education was largely acquired with little aid, as, except for a short period of attendance at a Presbyterian academy, the boy had no formal schooling. He read voraciously, however, and before he reached eighteen he was writing for the *Northern Herald*, a Belfast journal standing for national Irish solidarity (regardless of religion).

In 1836 he proceeded to Dublin, where he continued his career, writing for various journals and becoming eventually sub-editor of the *Morning Register*. In 1839 he assumed

SIR CHARLES G. D. DUFFY

the editorship of The *Vindicator*, a Belfast Catholic paper, and in the same year he entered King's Inn, Dublin, as a law student.

Having met John Blake Dillon and Thomas Davis, Irish patriots, he suggested the establishment of a weekly journal to educate Irishmen politically by historical study. Accordingly *The Nation* was founded in 1842, and the brilliant group of contributors became known as "Young Irelanders," zealous for the re-establishment of a separate Irish parliament, which had not existed since 1801, when Ireland was united to England by representation in the English parliament. In accordance with their policy of popular education, they issued cheap histories and collections of Irish poetry and addresses, Duffy producing the "Library of Ireland" series.

Encouraged by the Paris revolution of 1848, the Irish Confederation, a radical organization formed by Duffy and others of the "Young Ireland" group, planned an uprising. The government, however, checked it by laying hands upon some of the leaders. Duffy was arrested in July 1848, and in the same month *The Nation* was suppressed. After considerable delay Duffy was discharged. He revived *The Nation*, and was elected to Parliament in 1852.

There he fought for the demands of the Irish Tenant League, which he had founded in 1850 to protect Irish tenants against their landlords, who could evict them with no compensation for improvements made by the tenants. By 1855, however, their cause seemed lost, and Duffy, unwell and discouraged, left for Australia, remarking that Ireland was "like a corpse on a dissecting table."

In his new home he rose rapidly to prominence in politics, entering the Victoria parliament, becoming chief minister of land and works in 1857 and 1862, and eventually becoming chief secretary of that colony. In 1877, after a second return trip to Europe, he was unanimously elected speaker of the House of Assembly. He resigned this office in 1880, returning to southern Europe, where he spent most of the rest of his life, writing, and keenly following events in Ireland. Among other efforts he edited the "New Irish Library" to supplement his earlier series. He died at Nice in 1903, and was buried in Dublin. He was thrice married, and left ten children.

A brilliant journalist, Duffy must be given commendation for the high quality of *The Nation*, which even conservatives were obliged to praise. The steady publication of Irish verse of fine standard (some of it reprinted in a brochure, *The Spirit of the Nation*) gave the journal part of its distinction. While some of this poetry was written by Duffy himself, the best came from such able contributors as Denis Florence MacCarthy and Thomas

D'Arcy McGee. Duffy was kind to men of genius, and in his later years became a generous patron to struggling young Australians. In 1891 he was made first president of the Irish Literary Society, and with the "New Irish Library" he helped to promote the revival of interest in Celtic literature.

"As a writer, for grace, power, and clearness of style, Gavan Duffy was always without a compeer among a galaxy of brilliant writers," wrote Thomas P. Gill. His historical writings, however, are marred, as one might expect they would be, by his obvious personal interest in the scenes and times he describes. His histories, nevertheless, have been praised for style, accuracy, proportion, and sentiment.

R. W. W.

PRINCIPAL WORKS: *Autobiography*—My Life in Two Hemispheres, 1898. *Biography*—Thomas Davis: The Memoirs of an Irish Patriot: 1840-1846; 1890; Short Life of Thomas Davis: 1840-1846, 1895. *Editor*—The Ballad Poetry of Ireland, 1845. *History*—Young Ireland: A Fragment of Irish History: 1840-1850, 1880-83; A Bird's-Eye View of Irish History, 1882; The League of North and South: An Episode in Irish History, 1886. *Poetry*—Lays of the Red Branch, 1901. *Miscellaneous*—Fair Constitution for Ireland, 1892 (2nd ed.); Conversations With Carlyle, 1892; The Revival of Irish Literature, 1894.

ABOUT: Duffy, C. G. The League of North and South; Duffy, C. G. My Life in Two Hemispheres; Duffy, C. G. Young Ireland; Catholic World 37:589 August 1883; English Illustrated Magazine 15:395 August 1896; The Times February 10, 1903.

DU MAURIER, GEORGE LOUIS PALMELLA BUSSON

(March 6, 1834-October 8, 1896), artist and novelist, was born in Paris March 6, 1834, the eldest son of Louis Mathurin, whose father, Robert Mathurin Busson du Maurier, had been a gentleman glass-blower. George's mother, formerly Miss Ellen Clarke, was an Englishwoman, and his father had been naturalized. So the children were brought up to speak English as well as French. And when their son was two the family moved to Belgium, only to move again three years later to London, where they lived in a house on Devonshire Terrace afterwards occupied by Dickens. Here George remembered waving his hat to the queen.

His father was an inventor, and not prospering in England he took his family to Boulogne, and finally back to Paris, where George received his first formal education at the Pension Froussard. But he was a "lazy lad," for when he went up to the Sorbonne for his *bachot* his small knowledge of Latin kept him from his degree. After this failure his father decided to make him a chemist. In spite of the fact that the son preferred a musical career he sent him to University College to study under Dr. Williamson. Here the son drew caricatures. In 1854, the father, still ambitious, provided his son with a chemical laboratory at Bard's Yard, Bucklersbury. As

GEORGE DU MAURIER

a result the young chemist spent most of his time drawing.

Upon his father's death in 1856, George returned to Paris, where he at last began to follow his artistic bent. During his Latin Quarter days at Gleyre's studio, he met Whistler, Armstrong, Poynter, and Lamont. But the time was short, for in 1857 he moved to Antwerp to study at the Academy under Van Lerius and De Keyser. Probably the greatest tragedy of his life occurred at Antwerp when he lost the sight of his left eye (1859).

A year later he set out to seek his fortune in London and to live in Newman Street with Whistler. In June 1860 his first drawing appeared in *Punch* and he began to send contributions to *Once a Week*. Indeed, from the first he seems to have been prosperous. For he says of his marriage to Emma, daughter of William Wightwick, in 1863, "My wife and I never once knew financial troubles." He not only continued to fill *Punch* with his caricatures for thirty-six years, but he went on to become one of its editors in 1864. He illustrated Mrs. Gaskell's *Sylvia's Lovers* (1863), Thackeray's *Henry Esmond* (1868), and George Meredith's *Harry Richmond* (1870). He even experimented with water colors from 1880 until 1889 although, because of his eyesight, he preferred the black and white medium.

His prose did not come until late in his life. In fact his success as a novelist surprised him almost as much as it did his public. For his writing had a rather casual beginning. Although he had always written jokes and captions for his drawings and a few parodies in verse he never had attempted fiction. But, coming in one evening, after offering Henry

James the plot of *Trilby,* he sat down and wrote the first two numbers of *Peter Ibbetson* (1891). *Trilby* followed in 1894.

Ill at Whitby in the fall of 1896, he was only just able to finish the proofs of *The Martian* before he died of heart trouble. Newspaper headlines proclaimed that he died on October 8 at Oxford Square, Hyde Park, of the same disease that carried off his villain Svengali.

To the end he had loved society, whether it consisted of the Bohemian life he described in *Trilby,* the more sophisticated existence in a London parlor with such celebrities as Arthur Sullivan and Kate Terry, or even the quieter life at home with his children, who called him "Kicky"—Trixie, Sylvia and May, Guy, who was to become a major, and Gerald, the actor. For he always enjoyed company, and for fifteen years he never missed a daily walk with Canon Ainger.

An optimist by nature, his drawings were those of a humorist and a poet. His province in art was to depict fads and fashions; to create types rather than individuals; to get at the surface of living. He is said to have put on *Punch* "the seal of gentility," and to have followed in the footsteps of Charles Keene and John Leech with his pen paintings.

The same skill was transferred to his writing, when at last he began to write. In *Trilby* there are the same daintiness, the same surface touches, the same love of the beautiful. Yet there was, too, as in his drawings, a vitality that caused a veritable "Trilby boom." A town was actually named Trilby, while the lake near it was called Little Billee. Today he is labeled Victorian and sentimental, but in his own period he was worshipped for his unconventional manner and the charm of his style. B. D. S.

PRINCIPAL WORKS: *Drawings, etc.*—English Society at Home, 1880; Society Pictures, 1891. *Novels*—Peter Ibbetson, 1892; Trilby, 1894; The Martian, 1897.
ABOUT: Du Maurier, D. Gerald: A Portrait; Gilder, J. B. & J. S. Trilbyana; James, H. Partial Portraits; Lamont, L. M. (ed.). Thomas Armstrong; Moscheles, F. In Bohemia With du Maurier; Wood, T. M. George du Maurier; McClure's Magazine 4:391 April 1895.

DUNDONALD, LORD (Thomas Cochrane, Tenth Earl of Dundonald) (December 14, 1775-October 31, 1860), Scottish biographer, was born in Lanarkshire. He went to sea in 1793, and three years later was commissioned lieutenant. After serving in the Napoleonic wars to 1802, he spent a year in the University of Edinburgh before returning to the navy. In 1807 he was elected a member of Parliament, but his attempts at naval reform brought him a recall to the service. His career was stormy from the start. After the exploits of his ship, the *Imperieuse,* had

brought him election to the Order of the Bath, he himself, as a member of Parliament, opposed a vote of thanks to himself and instead attacked his commander-in-chief. The latter was court-martialed and acquitted, and Cochrane's naval career was ruined in consequence. He refused his next command and was put on half pay; then he was falsely accused of a stock swindle and was given a year in prison and expelled from Parliament and the Order of the Bath. As soon as he left prison, paying his £1000 fine with a bank-note on the back of which he wrote his indignant protest, his constituents returned him to Parliament. He was re-arrested and fined £100 more, which he refused to pay. The amount of the two fines was raised for him by popular subscriptions of a penny each.

From 1818 to 1823 he organized and commanded the Chilean navy, then those of Peru and Brazil, helping to free these countries from the yokes of Spain and Portugal. In 1827 he took a similar office in the Grecian war for independence, but accomplished little and returned to England. In 1831 he succeeded to the title, and a year later won his fight for reinstatement to the British Navy. From that time he worked on naval inventions, some of much value. In 1848 he was made an admiral and until 1851 was commander-in-chief in the West Indian station; in 1847 he had been reinstated in the Order of the Bath. In 1854 he was made rear admiral of the United Kingdom. In 1812 he had married Katherine Barnes, by whom he had four sons, one of whom also became an admiral.

Dundonald was indiscreet, tactless, and hot-headed, but a true lover of justice and freedom. His autobiographical works are vainglorious, but full of vigor.

PRINCIPAL WORKS: Narrative of Service in the Liberation of Chile, Peru, and Brazil, 1859; Autobiography of a Seaman, 1860-61.
ABOUT: Dundonald, T. (11th Earl) & Fox Bourne, H. R. Life of Thomas, Tenth Earl of Dundonald.

DUNLOP, JOHN COLIN (c.1780-February 1842), Scottish miscellaneous writer, was the son of a well known writer of Scotch songs. He was born in Glasgow. Little is known of his personal life or education. He was admitted advocate in 1807, but never practised law. Nevertheless, in 1816 he was appointed deputy sheriff of Renfrew, and for several years undertook the duties of his office. For most of his life he led a very retired existence, making his living by his pen. He was a lovable personality with a wide circle of admiring friends; a gentle, amiable man whose health was frail and who seems never to have married. His work shows his studious and conscientious mind, but he has been accused of superficiality and of narrowness of views.

PRINCIPAL WORKS: The History of Fiction, 1814; The History of Roman Literature, 1823-28; Memoirs of Spain, 1834; Selections From the Latin Anthology Translated Into English Verse, 1838.

ABOUT: Cockburn, H. Journal; Gentleman's Magazine March 1842.

DUTT, ROMESH CHUNDER (August 13, 1848-November 30, 1909), Indian poet, novelist, and historian, was born in Calcutta. His father, deputy collector in Bengal, died when he was thirteen, and he was reared by his uncle, a writer and registrar of the Bengali secretariat. He was sent to Hare's School, and to the Presidency College, Calcutta. In 1868, with two friends who later also became distinguished officials, he ran away to study in England. They entered University College, London. In 1869 Dutt took third place in an examination for the Indian Civil Service. At the same time he read law at the Middle Temple, and was called to the bar in 1871. He returned to India, and in 1883 was collector at Backerganj. There (in 1886) he translated the *Rig Veda,* the sacred books of the Brahmans, from Sanskrit into Bengali. In 1894 he was acting commissioner of Burdwan, in 1895 a member of the Bengal legislative council and commissioner at Orissa. In 1897 he resigned from the civil service to interest himself in politics and literature, and went to London, visiting India in 1899 to preside at the National Congress at Lucknow. From 1898 to 1904 he was lecturer on Indian history at University College. He wrote widely on the relations of India and England, translated from the Sanskrit to Bengali and English, and wrote six historical and social novels in Bengali, three of which were translated into English. He did much to make modern Bengali a literary language. In 1904 he returned to India as revenue minister of Baroda, an independent state, an office he held until 1907. In 1909 he was named as prime minister of Baroda, but died very soon after of a heart attack. He was accorded a public funeral. In 1864 he had married a daughter of Nabo Gopal Bose, and had one son and five daughters.

PRINCIPAL WORKS: Three Years in Europe, 1872; The Peasantry of Bengal, 1874; History of Bengali Literature, 1877; History of Civilization in Ancient India, 1888-90; Lays of Ancient India, 1894; England and India, 1897; Famines in India, 1900; Economic History of British India, 1902; India in the Victorian Age, 1904.

ABOUT: Gupta, J. N. Life of Romesh Chunder Dutt; Times of India December 4, 1909.

DYCE, ALEXANDER (June 30, 1798-May 15, 1869), Scottish scholar and editor, was born in Edinburgh the eldest son of Lt. General Alexander Dyce, who was an official in the British East India Company. He was

ALEXANDER DYCE

educated at Edinburgh High School and Exeter College, Oxford, where he received his B.A. in 1819. His father desired him to enter the East India Company, but Dyce, having no inclination toward trade as a profession, accepted the alternative of taking orders. After 1825 he abandoned the clergy and devoted himself to the literary pursuits which had always been uppermost in his interest. While still an undergraduate he had edited Jarvis' *Dictionary of the Language of Shakespeare* and in 1821 he had published a volume of Quintus Smyrnaeus, translated into blank verse. In 1825 appeared his *Specimens of British Poetesses.* From 1831 to 1835, among other literary activities, he contributed biographies to Pickering's *Aldine Poets.* He limited the exhaustive study of Richard Bentley which he had projected to three volumes because, he said, "the indifference of general readers to classical literature prevented my carrying out the design."

Dyce was possessed of intense loyalties and capable of sincere friendship, but the ethical standards of his calling came before all else. Together with Halliwell-Phillips he was associated with John Payne Collier in the founding of the Percy Society for publishing old English Poetry, but when Collier proved to be a forger of Shakespeare manuscripts Dyce was among the first to denounce him. Dyce is himself best known today for his editions of Shakespeare. He set new standards in the field of textual criticism; his brief annotations are useful and to the point; and his glossaries cleared many difficulties hitherto unsolved.

Dyce led a serene existence, the incidents and associations of which were prescribed by the life of a scholar and bibliophile. The sedentary nature of his profession undoubtedly contributed to the liver complaint which troubled his last years. To his friend John Forster, the English biographer, he wrote in 1868: "I suspect I am very gradually dying and if such is the case, I certainly have no reason to make any childish lamentation, for I have lived a great deal longer than most . . . and I look back on my past life without much disapprobation." Until his death he continued work on the third revision of his edition of Shakespeare, which was completed by Forster. He left his valuable library to the South Kensington Museum.

Dyce represents that *rara avis,* the balanced critic. Possessed of no great originality of his own, he had nevertheless a nice appreciation of humanity. His collection of the anecdotes of Samuel Rogers (of whom it was said that an invitation to one of his breakfasts was a formal entry into literary society) is indication of this. His broad, impeccable scholarship, discriminating taste, and intellectual probity insure him a permanent position in the annals of English learning.   P. B. S.

PRINCIPAL WORKS: *Editions*—Jarvis' Dictionary of the Language of Shakespeare, 1818; Specimens of British Poetesses, 1825; Poems of Collins, 1827; Works of George Peele, 1828-1839; Richard Bentley, 1836-1838; Thomas Middleton, 1840; John Skelton, 1843; Beaumont and Fletcher, 1843-1846; William Shakespeare, 1857. *Criticism*—Remarks on Collier's and Knight's Editions of Shakespeare, 1844; A Few Notes on Shakespeare, 1853; Strictures on Collier's New Edition of Shakespeare, 1859. *Translations*—Select Translations From Quintus Smyrnaeus, 1821. *Miscellaneous*—Recollections of the Table Talk of Samuel Rogers, 1856.

ABOUT: Forster, J. Catalogue of Dyce Library (see biographical notice); Ingleby, V. C. M. Complete View of the Shakespeare Controversy.

EASTLAKE, LADY ELIZABETH (Rigby) (November 17, 1809-October 2, 1893), miscellaneous writer, was born in Norwich, the daughter and sister of well known surgeons. Her father died when she was twelve, and for two years she lived with her mother in Heidelberg, visiting Germany again in 1836. Her first article, a criticism of Goethe, appeared in the *Foreign Quarterly Review.* In 1838 she paid a long visit to a married sister in Reval, her letters being published as her first book. From 1842 she was a regular contributor to the *Quarterly Review,* to which she contributed a famous attack on *Jane Eyre* and the Brontës. In this same year she moved with her mother to Edinburgh, where she became an intimate of the circle of the critic John Wilson ("Christopher North"). In 1844 she revisited Russia, two volumes of fiction eventuating from the trip.

In 1849, when she was forty, she married Sir Charles Locke Eastlake, an eminent painter. Everybody of note visited her and was commented on in her diary, and she was close to Queen Victoria and her court. Her

chief interest was now in art, and she took to painting during her annual trips to Italy with her husband. Sir Charles died in Pisa in 1865. Lady Eastlake edited the literary remains of her husband and her father, and translated many works on art and other subjects. Very tall, strikingly handsome, she was the typical "grande dame" of high society, deeply conservative, very religious, and very arbitrary. Her writing, once very popular, is now without any except historical interest.

PRINCIPAL WORKS: A Residence on the Shores of Baltic (later called Letters From the Shores of the Baltic), 1841; The Jewess, 1846; Livonian Tales, 1846; Music and the Art of Dress, 1852; Fellowship: Letters Addressed to My Sister Mourners (anon.) 1868; Five Great Painters, 1883.

ABOUT: Eastlake, Lady. The Journals and Correspondence of Lady Eastlake (ed. by C. Eastlake Smith), 1895; Guardian October 7, 1893.

EDGEWORTH, MARIA (January 1, 1767-May 22, 1849), Irish novelist, was born at Black Bourton, Oxfordshire, second of the twenty-one children of Richard Lovell Edgeworth. Her mother was Anna Maria Elers of Black Bourton. Her father, of landed Irish descent, was something of a rake in his youth, but a man of evident charm and character and no mean practical and scientific talents. His first marriage at sixteen had been annulled. His second, a Gretna Green affair with Maria's mother, was not happy. Maria was a mischievous child of exuberant spirits, but she was a dutiful daughter to the stepmother which her father whom she adored had almost immediately provided her after Anna Edgeworth's death. This was the first of a series and Maria was never to be without one for more than a few months.

Her education was supplemented by her father, who early recognized and encouraged her writing ability. Female learning was generally discountenanced in that day, but Edgeworth was a disciple of Rousseau and a friend of Thomas Day, the eccentric educational theorist, and of Erasmus Darwin. When in 1782 Maria accompanied her father, her second stepmother, and her brothers and sisters to Ireland, she was mistress of more than the showy accomplishments which ordinarily constituted a young lady's education. Maria's home was henceforth to be the family estate, Edgeworthstown in Longford County.

Her father set about improving the condition of his land and tenants and made Maria his agent. His direct purpose was to "give her habits of business"; more importantly, she acquired an intimate knowledge of the habits, speech, and mental processes of the Irish peasant. The education, according to Mr. Edgeworth's Rousseauesque principles, of the ever-increasing family occupied her and at her father's behest she was also engaged on the translation of Madame de Genlis' *Adèle et*

Théodore. Society in Longford County was chiefly limited to that of the family of Lord Longford of Pakenham Hall, Lady Moira at Castle Forbes, and at Black Castle Maria's aunt and lifelong friend, Margaret Ruxton. Maria was somewhat shy in company at this time. She was short and upright, "elegantly" made, with minute hands and feet and a very characterful, intelligent countenance, but she was universally accounted plain. Apparently she sincerely regarded herself as ugly.

Publication of her translation of Madame de Genlis was prevented by the prior appearance of Holcroft's version. Mr. Day, who had a great antipathy to female authors, wrote to congratulate Maria on her escape from this odious category. It was partly her recollection of the correspondence which passed on the subject of this translation which inspired her *Letters to Literary Ladies,* a plea for education for women. Tales and novels were written and planned during this period, but nothing was published until after the death in 1789 of Mr. Day. Mr. Edgeworth had such reverence for this peculiar soul that Maria might never have published had he lived. Her stories for children were exposed to the unrepressed critical instincts of the juvenile Edgeworths. These, in *The Parent's Assistant,* which appeared in 1796, won immediate approval and additional volumes with illustrations were demanded. The daughter of a neighboring clergyman was given this work and Maria was quite well acquainted with her before (Mrs. Elizabeth Edgeworth having died in 1797) Mr. Edgeworth married her.

These activities, literary and matrimonial, were pursued in troublous times. The customary unrest of the population, coupled with the revolutionary influence of the Society of

MARIA EDGEWORTH

United Irishmen which was negotiating with France for aid against England, had more serious results than the casual insurrections of the past. Conflicts between Protestants and Catholics added fuel to the patriotic flames; the Rebellion of 1798 cost 150,000 Irish lives and before its course was run many gentry like the Edgeworths had incontinently been murdered in their beds. Maria's letters during this period are gay, witty, and genuinely courageous. "My father has made our little rooms so nice for us," she writes. "They are all fresh papered and painted. Oh rebels! Oh French! spare them." It reflects favorably upon Mr. Edgeworth's treatment of his tenants that, when in the autumn of 1798 the family had to decamp from Edgeworthstown for a few days, the house was untouched.

Maria collaborated with her father in the production of *Practical Education,* which delineated their experiences in rearing and teaching children. The book marks a definite step in the history of education. It was based on actual practise and for the first time cognizance was taken of the workings of a child's mind. In London in 1798 Maria was quiet and reserved, while Mr. Edgeworth was a literary lion taking all plaudits to himself. Mr. Edgeworth's influence upon his daughter has been universally deplored. Yet, although he revised and "corrected" her work, gave her style a stilted manner which her letters lack, provided inappropriate dénouements to her stories and otherwise played the arrogant literary vandal, he did encourage and stimulate her writing. He was considered cocky and offensive by some. For example, Thomas Moore suggested that, as a petition had been presented to recall Mrs. Siddons to the stage, so another should be *"subscribed* and *circumscribed"* for the recall of Mr. Edgeworth to Ireland. But Mr. Edgeworth was perfection of perfections to his daughter.

For some reason Maria's father did not tinker with *Castle Rackrent* and its lively spontaneity won immediate success. For the first time the Irish character was limned in its proper proportions and interpreted with the right mixture of sympathy and exasperation. Scott was influenced by the book and declared in the first edition of *Waverley* that his aim was "in some distant degree to emulate the admirable Irish portraits of Miss Edgeworth." The even tenor of Maria's life at Edgeworthstown, broken until now only by births, deaths and occasional trips to England, was not unduly disturbed by her sudden rise to fame. *Belinda,* a society novel, was successful in 1801 despite Mr. Edgeworth's unnatural ending. In 1802 Maria with her father and stepmother were abroad for a year. While in Paris Maria received an offer of marriage from a Swedish gentleman, the Chevalier

Edelcrantz. Her refusal of this proposal, according to her stepmother, had a prolonged effect upon her spirits. She wrote voluminously on her return to Edgeworthstown, working as always in the common sitting-room with the noise of children playing about her.

When Maria visited London in 1813 she was famous and sought after. Mr. Edgeworth, according to Byron, "bounced about and talked loud and long" and was cordially deplored. He died in 1817 and Maria's grief was such that she might never have written again had it not been to fulfill his desires. Her eyesight, which was never good, gave her much trouble at this time. She set herself to complete her father's memoirs, a labor of love justifiably abused by the reviewers, and in 1820 went abroad with her two young sisters. She compared the "jigging" of steamboats, which she first experienced on this journey, to the shaking made by a pig scratching himself on the back wheel of a carriage halted before an Irish inn. In 1813 in London Byron had said that Miss Edgeworth's "conversation was as quiet as herself. One would never have guessed she could write her name; whereas her father talked . . . as if nothing else [than his own] were worth writing." Now in Paris we find Maria set down a witty conversationalist who could collect a crowd five deep around her. She spent nearly a year in France and Switzerland and for the first time saw scenery that really impressed her. "Observe that . . . I prefer . . . good society to fine landscapes or even to volcanoes."

In 1823 Maria spent a fortnight with the Scotts at Abbotsford, and two years later Scott with Mr. and Mrs. Lockhart visited Edgeworthstown. Miss Edgeworth wrote much less after her father's death. Money had never been a consideration and, lacking his direction, she mistakenly lacked confidence. Her last novel, *Helen*, which was as enthusiastically received as her earlier work, shows marked advance in character delineation and an awareness of the Romantic movement which indicates that Miss Edgeworth when past sixty was still youthful in spirit. Her domestic activities were in no wise lessened, for nieces and nephews had appeared where formerly were brothers and sisters. Physically and mentally she continued with unimpaired faculties and at seventy set herself to learn Spanish. She was made an honorary member of the Royal Irish Academy and in 1844 went sightseeing in London, where she attended the opening of Parliament. During the Irish potato famine of 1847 she worked continually for the relief of the sufferers. This strain and the added blow of the loss of her favorite sister Fanny probably contributed to her death, which suddenly and without illness came to her at the age of eighty-two.

Miss Edgeworth to a lesser degree plays for Ireland the role Jane Austen filled for England. Perhaps the first sympathetic interpreter of national characteristics, her contribution to the Celtic revival is of paramount importance. Her novels are still of interest to modern readers and her letters utterly delightful.   P. B. S.

PRINCIPAL WORKS: *Tales*—The Parent's Assistant 1800; Moral Tales for Young People, 1801; Early Lessons, 1801; Popular Tales, 1804; Tales of Fashionable Life, 1809. *Novels*—Castle Rackrent, 1800; Belinda, 1801; The Modern Griselda, 1804; Leonora, 1806; Patronage, 1814; Harrington, 1817; Ormond, 1817; Helen, 1834. *Miscellaneous*—Letters to Literary Ladies, 1795; Practical Education, 1798; Essay on Irish Bulls, 1802; Memoirs of Richard Lovell Edgeworth, Esq., 1820 (the last three in collaboration with R. L. Edgeworth).

ABOUT: Hare, A. J. C. The Life and Letters of Maria Edgeworth; Lawless, E. Maria Edgeworth; Zimmern, H. Maria Edgeworth.

EDWARDS, AMELIA ANN BLANDFORD (June 7, 1831-April 15, 1892), novelist and Egyptologist, was born in London. Her father, formerly an officer under Wellington, had a post in the London and Westminster Bank. Miss Edwards was educated at home, chiefly by her mother. She exhibited an early precocity in art, music, and writing, and at the age of seven had a poem printed in a penny weekly. From 1846 to 1853 she studied music under Mrs. Mounsey Bartholemew. Her training and versatility were such that when straitened means compelled her to earn her own living she had pen, pencil, and voice from which to choose. Getting a check for a story from *Chambers Journal* decided her in favor of literature.

She worked for various magazines and served on the staff of the *Saturday Review* and the *Morning Post*, contributing leading articles, dramatic and art criticism, and stories. Eight novels, two histories, some poetry, and three books on travel appeared between 1865 and 1880. In the winter of 1873-74 Miss Edwards traveled in Egypt and was inspired with enthusiasm for the remainders of its ancient civilization. She threw herself into a study of Egyptian history and hieroglyphics. *A Thousand Miles up the Nile*, published in 1877, containing facsimiles of inscriptions, plans, maps, and more than eighty illustrations, was the best and most comprehensive book which had yet appeared on the subject. Horrified by the wanton destruction which she had witnessed of Egyptian antiquities by careless and unskilled handling, she drew up circulars, wrote innumerable letters, and published appeals in the press which resulted in the foundation of the Egypt Exploration Fund. Authorities from the British Museum, headed by Reginald Stuart Poole, supported her and

AMELIA B. EDWARDS

Sir William J. E. Wilson contributed generously. The Fund was founded formally in 1882 with Miss Edwards and Poole as joint honorary secretaries. The first expedition was sent in 1883 to excavate the treasure city of Pithom and determine the route of the Exodus.

Miss Edwards now abandoned her every other interest. For the remainder of her life she devoted herself to this cause, writing letters, lecturing, and contributing articles on Egyptology to the *Times* and the *Academy*. During an extremely successful lecture tour of the States in the winter of 1889 she had the misfortune to break an arm and never completely recovered her robust health. She continued her activities, however, until the spring of 1892 when she contracted influenza and died at Westbury-super-Mare. Her valuable Egyptological collection and library were bequeathed to University College of London with £2,415 to establish the first chair of Egyptology in England.

Miss Edwards' contribution to modern archaeology is far more important than the writing which she abandoned. Her thorough integrity of purpose and masculine grasp of essential detail, combined with an appropriate delicacy of feeling which made her a successful novelist, were equally significant in the pursuit of her later interests.   P. B. S.

PRINCIPAL WORKS: *Novels*—My Brother's Wife, 1855; The Ladder of Life, 1857; Hand and Glove, 1859; Barbara's History, 1864; Debenham's Vow, 1870; Lord Brackenbury, 1880. *History*—A Summary of English History, 1856; The History of France, 1858. *Travel*—Sights and Stories, 1862; Untrodden Peaks and Unfrequented Valleys, 1873; A Thousand Miles up the Nile, 1877; Pharaohs, Fellahs, and Explorers, 1891. *Poetry*—Ballads, 1865.

Miscellaneous—A Poetry Book of Elder Poets, 1879; A Poetry of Modern Poets, 1879.

ABOUT: Macquoid, K. S. Amelia Blandford Edwards.

EDWARDS, MATILDA BARBARA BETHAM-. See BETHAM-EDWARDS, MATILDA BARBARA

EGAN, PIERCE ("the Elder") (1772-August 3, 1849), sporting and humorous writer, was born in London and lived there or in its suburbs all his life, but traveled all over England to races, prize fights, and other sporting events. From 1812 to 1823 he was a regular sporting writer for the publisher E. Young. He was a wit, noted for his impromptu songs and epigrams. In 1821 he started a monthly serial, *Life in London*, with illustrations by Cruikshank, which was an enormous success, and was widely imitated, pirated, and dramatized. One dramatic version, *Tom and Jerry*, was popular for years in England and America, and may have been the origin of the name of the well known drink. *Life in London* was a sort of anticipation of the *Pickwick Papers*. Egan also wrote accounts of murder trials and executions, and guide books, for he knew all Great Britain well. In 1824 he edited a magazine called *Pierce Egan's Life in London and Sporting Guide* (later merged into *Bell's Life in London*). He was considered an authority on slang, and contributed to Grose's *Dictionary of the Vulgar Tongue*. He was married in 1812 and had a large family.

His eldest son, PIERCE EGAN ("the Younger") (1814-July 6, 1880), was trained as an artist, and started his career by illustrating his father's books. Later he became the author of innumerable sensational novels (the earliest ones historical tales of feudal life), some of which he himself illustrated. He edited the *Home Circle* from 1849 to 1851. One serial followed another, mostly in the *Weekly Times*. From unreal and bloody stories of the Middle Ages, he progressed to rural tales, predecessors of the dime novel. His powers degenerated toward the end, but at his best he had vigor and some dramatic ability. He was a liberal in politics. Little is known of his personal life.

PRINCIPAL WORKS: *Pierce Egan the Elder*—The Mistress of Royalty, 1814; Boxiana, 1818; Life in London, 1821; The Life of an Actor, 1824; The Finish to the Adventures of Tom, Jerry, and Logic, 1828; Pierce Egan's Book of Sports and Mirror of Life, 1832; Pilgrims of the Thames, 1838. *Pierce Egan the Younger*—Quintin Mastys, 1839; Wat Tyler, 1841; Robin Hood, 1842; The False Step, 1857; The Snake in the Grass, 1858; Love Me, Leave Me Not, 1860; Imogine: or, The Marble Heart, 1862; The Poor Girl, 1863; Eve, 1867; His Sworn Bride, 1878; A Shadow on the Future, 1880.

ABOUT: Egan, P. Life in London (see Introduction by J. C. Hatten to 1870 ed.).

"ELIA." See LAMB, CHARLES

"ELIOT, GEORGE" (Mary Ann Evans Cross) (November 22, 1819-December 22, 1880) was born Mary Ann (or Marian) Evans, at Arbury Farm in Warwickshire, on the edge of the Forest of Arden. Her father, Robert Evans, was estate agent for a large landholder, on whose property he moved when the child was still an infant. Her mother was the second wife, and Mary Ann was the last of Christiana Evans' three children. There are traces of Robert Evans in the character of "Adam Bede," and of Mrs. Evans in "Mrs. Poyser," but the characterizations are not photographic.

Mary Ann was first sent to school at five, and was a pupil in three schools, the last one in Coventry. The second school, at Nuneaton, was the one which chiefly influenced her later development; here she developed a passion for omnivorous reading, and became an intimate friend of the principal governess, a Miss Lewis, who was an evangelical, and fostered the girl's bent toward strict piety. Her chief gain at the Coventry school was training in music, for which she had unusual gifts, and which was always to her the most loved of the arts; her proficiency, however, was inhibited by an almost pathological shyness.

She left school finally at sixteen, and the following year her mother died. All her brothers and sisters had married and left home, and she became her father's household manager and companion, developing ability that in another period would have made her a successful executive. She did not, however, neglect her intellectual growth; she studied Italian and German with a teacher from the near-by town of Coventry, and read Latin and Greek with the headmaster of the town's grammar school. Apparently she had not thought of herself as destined to authorship or any other career; outwardly she was the typical dutiful daughter of her time—plain, rather awkward, given to household tasks and charitable works, and intensely devout. Her first published work was a religious poem.

When her brother took over their father's office as estate manager, the father and daughter moved to Coventry. There she met the friends, the Brays and their relatives the Hennells, who deflected and determined her future. They were skeptics and rationalists; she read the books they recommended and listened to their talk, and before long she found herself a prey to religious doubt. It was a bitter struggle, which left its mark on her, but with her immovable honesty, when once she was convinced, she threw overboard the entire load of her religious training. She broke openly with the church and announced that she would not again attend services. Her

father was outraged, and left her to live with another daughter. Deeply hurt, she made one of the few concessions of her life, and they became reconciled on her promise to reconsider her decision. But she did not change her mind; and the first signalizing of her new views was the translation of Strauss' famous *Leben Jesu,* which she started in 1844 and which was published anonymously in 1846. A relation that must have become a painful ordeal did not last much longer; her father's health began to fail, necessitating her constant attendance on him, and in 1849 he died, leaving her a small income for life.

For the first time she was free, and she had tasted the blood of authorship, if only at second hand. She went to the Continent, and spent several months in Geneva with the family of d'Albert, her future French translator. Then she returned to England, and for sixteen months lived with the Brays, while she worked on a translation of Spinoza that was never finished. Her great opportunity was at hand. In 1851 John Stuart Mill handed over the liberal *Westminster Review* to John Chapman, and Mary Ann Evans was offered an editorial position on it. For two years, though she retired from all public notice, she did most of the editorial drudgery, reading proofs, interviewing contributors, and writing constantly, mostly reviews of philosophical, religious, and political books. Meanwhile also she was translating Feuerbach, and her version of his *Essence of Christianity* appeared in 1854, the only book ever issued under her own name. Most of her present associates were Positivists, and she became and remained a sympathizer with the philosophy, though never a thorough-going Comtean.

She was now meeting the most eminent and brilliant of the serious English writers of her day. Herbert Spencer became her friend—and, if his own allusions and common gossip are to be trusted, rather more than a friend to the plain, lonely woman with deep if repressed emotional capacity. But the almost sexless Spencer shied away, and introduced her instead to George Henry Lewes, editor of *The Leader,* physiologist, biographer, essayist—a man almost too versatile, and greatly gifted.

Their affinity was instant and permanent. But Lewes was unhappily married, two years separated from an insane wife, and with three small sons. By English law he could never be freed from his wife except by death. And the year was 1854, the heart of the Victorian era. Mary Ann Evans did not hesitate. She was sensitive, shy, and the epitome of respectability, but she had courage above all things. She and Lewes sent out notices an-

"GEORGE ELIOT"

nouncing their union, and departed together for Germany. They remained together until his death, twenty-four years later, in what they always thought of as marriage, and what was certainly the most devoted of unions. On few women could the isolation and ostracism which such a step meant at that time have weighed so heavily; they had no social life except for a few devoted friends and the admirers—almost exclusively masculine—whom her later work brought to them, and they had to work terribly hard, both of them, to support not only themselves but also Lewes' wife and children. Even when she was rich and famous, Mary Ann Evans never lost her self-consciousness and pain at her anomalous position—a sufficient explanation of her strange marriage in her last year of life.

The world of literature owes a great debt to George Henry Lewes: he created "George Eliot." He was the first person to perceive his comrade's genius for fiction; he encouraged and persuaded her until she made her first tentative efforts in that direction, and he sold to *Blackwood's* her first story, *Amos Barton*, later one of the sketches in *Scenes of Clerical Life*. All her later writings were published under the pseudonym he chose for her.

The book was an immediate success; and the publication the next year of *Adam Bede* placed her securely in the first rank of English novelists. But she was still—and to some extent she remained all her life—diffident, self-distrustful, and subject to depression and melancholy. Probably she would never have persisted in her career had it not been for Lewes' self-forgetful, enthusiastic admiration and intellectual support.

After *The Mill on the Floss* and *Silas Marner*, "George Eliot" reached a transition point in her work as a novelist. Always a student, deeply erudite (someone has called her "a kind of Acton," so varied and profound was her learning), she longed to write an historical novel, and the personage of history who most attracted her was Savonarola. She went to Italy, and worked terrifically hard on the research which she felt to be necessary. The labor that finally eventuated in *Romola* exhausted her and made her ill, but soon she was in Spain, working as indefatigably on the background of a new kind of venture—the Positivist tract in verse (for it is that more than it is a genuine poem), *The Spanish Gypsy*.

With *Middlemarch*, in 1871, she returned to her earlier style, and the proceeds from this novel made her independently wealthy at last. (The other novel of this period, *Felix Holt*, was her only excursion into the political field made famous by Disraeli, and was among the least fortunate of her works.) In 1876 appeared her last novel, *Daniel Deronda*, a conscious effort to express her pro-Jewish sympathies, and definitely among her minor performances, though, like most of her books, it has a magnificent heroine.

During these years she and Lewes had been living in various places in London and its outskirts, with frequent travels in the country which was her childhood's environment and which she so loved. Now they bought a house near Godalming, and prepared to live permanently out of town. But suddenly disaster was upon them. In November of 1878, Lewes died, without warning, of a heart attack.

For months the woman who considered herself his true widow shut herself up and refused to see even her closest friends. She devoted herself to preparing for the press the unfinished writing he had left, and to establishing in his memory a scholarship in physiology which is still in existence. The friends who felt with her in her grief were shocked indeed—though most of them rallied loyally to her support—when in May, 1880, she announced her marriage to John Walter Cross.

She was sixty-one years old, Cross, an English-born banker who had spent most of his life in New York, at least twenty years her junior. They had met in 1867, when she and Lewes were on the Continent, and he was traveling with his mother. He had been her ardent and humble disciple, and he remained so. The marriage is difficult to understand, but when one considers how heavily her extra-legal position had weighed on Mary Ann Evans, how unused she was to a solitary life, how dependent on affection and companionship, perhaps it becomes more comprehensible. In any case it did not last long. The couple toured Europe for seven months, then returned to London and took a house on Cheyne

Walk, Chelsea—home of so many literary celebrities. Soon after, at a concert, Mrs. Cross, who had been very ill the year before with renal trouble, caught a chill which speedily developed into pneumonia. A few days later she was dead.

"George Eliot's" work has grave faults. The intellectual trend which led her to overvalue her essays and poetry and deprecate her novels emerged in the latter as didacticism, sometimes laid on with a heavy hand. On occasion she is long-winded and dull. Highly ethical, and inherently religious in spite of her skepticism, she gives us occasionally a stony sermon instead of the bread of fiction. But overwhelming all these defects are the glorious qualities which make her a supreme novelist in an age of great novelists: her penetrating sympathy, her deep knowledge of humanity, her dramatic and descriptive power, her lambent humor, the reflection of her extraordinary mind. Not until Meredith did English literature see again such women as were created in the novels of "George Eliot," and not until Hardy did the English countryside so come to life. She is one of the few to whom that overworked word "genius" can justly be applied.

M. A. deF.

PRINCIPAL WORKS: *Novels*—Scenes of Clerical Life, 1858; Adam Bede, 1859; The Mill on the Floss, 1860; Silas Marner, 1861; Romola, 1863; Felix Holt the Radical, 1866; Middlemarch, 1871; Daniel Deronda, 1876. *Poems*—The Spanish Gypsy, 1868; Jubal and Other Poems, 1874. *Essays*—Impressions of Theophrastus Such, 1879. *Translations*—Life of Jesus, Strauss, (anonymous) 1846; Essence of Christianity, Feuerbach (under own name) 1854. *Letters*—George Eliot's Life as Related in Her Letters and Journals (edited by J. W. Cross) 1885; Letters to Elena Stuart (edited by R. Stuart) 1909.

ABOUT: Browning, O. Life of George Eliot; Cross, J. W. (ed.). George Eliot's Life as Related in Her Letters and Journals; Fremantle, A. George Eliot; Haldane, E. S. George Eliot and Her Times; Kitchel, A. T. George Lewes and George Eliot; May, J. L. George Eliot; Paterson, A. H. George Eliot's Family Life and Letters; Romieu, E. & S. The Life of George Eliot (translated from the French); Stephen, L. George Eliot.

ELLIOTT, EBENEZER (March 17, 1781-December 1, 1849), "the corn-law rhymer," was born in Yorkshire of an unpromising ancestry, his direct progenitors being border raiders—in other words, horse and cattle thieves. His father was an ironmonger, a political radical, but a fanatical Calvinist in religion. His mother was a life-long invalid. Elliott was one of eleven children, brought up in poverty and ignorance; he was baptized by a wandering tinker who was of the Calvinist persuasion.

All the education he received, except for his own omnivorous reading, was in dame's schools and similar ill-equipped institutions. At five smallpox disfigured him badly and made him temporarily blind. In consequence

EBENEZER ELLIOTT

he became a shy and solitary child, who felt himself repulsive and kept away from his fellows.

From sixteen to twenty-three Elliott worked for his father for his board and lodging and pocket-money. His leisure was spent in reading, in rambling the country-side (for he was an intense lover of nature), and in writing poetry. He married young and had thirteen children. He invested all his wife's small fortune in a business in which her father was interested; his father died, the business failed, and Elliott became dependent on his wife's sisters. For all these misfortunes he blamed the iniquitous corn-laws, a heavy tax on grain which was starving the farmers of England and ruining the tradesmen supported by them. His indignation and resentment obsessed him; he abandoned his earlier poems of love and nature, and for the remainder of his life wrote on nothing but the evil effects of the corn-laws and the battle for their repeal. It is for this reason that he is known as "the corn-law rhymer."

In 1821 his wife's relatives came to his assistance again and set him up in the iron business in Sheffield. The business prospered until 1837, then began to decline, and he retired in 1842 with scarcely a competence. His interest in the corn-laws led him into other radical fields, and he became a Chartist. (The Chartists were the earliest English labor unionists.) By nature, however, he was really a conservative, made radical by injustice. He was quite willing that two of his sons should become clergymen.

In appearance Elliott was a small, meek man who would never have been suspected of harboring subversive ideas. He was good-natured and kindly almost to weakness; when aspiring poets sent him their efforts for criticism he always praised them, for he said writing gave them an outlet and means of expression, and he did not want to drive them into anti-social activities by suppression. He had the happiness before he died of seeing the corn-laws which he had fought for twenty-five years abolished, though too late to be of real benefit to English agriculture, already doomed by the advance of industrialism.

Elliott's early poems, dealing chiefly with natural beauty and with romantic love, are frequently turgid and bombastic, and show the defects of his education. They were extremely ambitious in scope. They do, however, display great natural talent, and have occasional gleams of lyric charm.

His corn-law rhymes, his best work, are in a different tradition altogether. They are vigorous, powerful, and direct. Few writers have excelled Elliott in power of invective and in the rhetoric of indignation. Some of them are reminiscent of Goldsmith's *The Deserted Village,* but with the superior advantage of being written from the viewpoint of a participant and sufferer, instead of from that of a sympathetic observer. He may be described in a phrase as a poet who lifted himself by his own boot-straps from an obscure versifier to the ranks of real poetry. Hatred of injustice gave him a voice. The corn-law rhymes were perhaps the greatest single factor in lifting from the English poor the unbearable burden of a cruel and brutal imposition.   M. A. deF.

PRINCIPAL WORKS: The Village Patriarch, 1829; Corn-Law Rhymes, 1831; Love, 1831; The Splendid Village, 1833-5; More Verse and Prose by the Corn-Law Rhymer, 1850.

ABOUT: "Searle, J." Memoirs of Ebenezer Elliott; Watkins, J. Life, Poetry, and Letters of Ebenezer Elliott.

ELLIS, ROBINSON (September 3, 1834-October 9, 1913), classicist, was born near Maidstone, his mother being the third wife of his father, a landowner. He was educated at Elizabeth College, Guernsey, then at Rugby, and in 1853 entered Balliol College, Oxford. Most of the remainder of his life was spent there. In 1858 he was made a fellow of Trinity. He became a lecturer on Latin, and began his long study and editing of the Latin poets, particularly Catullus, on whom he was the great authority. From 1870 to 1876 he was professor of Latin at University College, London, but he was by no means so successful there as in the more rarefied air of Oxford, and was glad to return. In 1893 he became professor of Latin at Oxford. His only real interests were in scholarship, literature, and music; he was a distinguished composer in his own right.

His sight became increasingly bad, and he died after an operation on his eyes.

Ellis was a "character," an eccentric, and a recluse, given to unconventional remarks, and the butt of many stories which he loved to tell on himself. He was the most erudite of scholars, though his preference as editor was for the more scabrous Latin poets. He never married.

PRINCIPAL WORKS: The Poems and Fragments of Catullus Translated, 1866; Commentary on Catullus, 1876.

ABOUT: British Academy Proceedings 1913-14; Times October 14, 1913.

ELPHINSTONE, MOUNTSTUART (October 6, 1779-November 20, 1859), historian, was the son of the eleventh Baron Elphinstone, his mother being the daughter of Lord Ruthven. As his father was governor of Edinburgh Castle, he was educated at the Edinburgh High School, and then at a school in Kensington. Through an uncle he was appointed to the Bengal Civil Service, and went to Calcutta in 1796. In 1801 he went to the College of Fort William, in India, established to train civil servants, where he studied Indian literature. He was then sent to Poona. When England declared war on the peshwa of Poona, Elphinstone was appointed to the general's staff. He was so well liked that at the conclusion of the war he was, in his mid-twenties, made resident at the court of Nagpur, ambassador to the Afghan court of Cabul, and in 1810 resident at Poona. By 1815 fresh revolts broke out. Elphinstone was superseded by an army officer, but without complaint stayed on as a subordinate. In 1817 he had to evacuate the residency, which was burned with all his books and property. His heroic but unassuming conduct restored him to authority. From 1827 to 1829 he was governor of Bombay, a college being founded in his name and honor on his departure. For the next two years he traveled in Greece, returning to London in 1829. He declined all honors offered him, and retired to Surrey. His last years were physically those of an invalid, but mentally his most creative. He died suddenly of a paralytic stroke.

In youth Elphinstone was energetic, sports-loving, liberal, and light-hearted; in his later years his most prominent characteristics were his modesty, conscientiousness, and impartiality. He was a Rationalist in religion, a real student, the very antithesis of the typical Indian civil servant. His *History of India* has become a classic.

PRINCIPAL WORKS: History of India, 1841; Rise of British Power in the East, 1887.

ABOUT: London Times November 21, 1859.

ELWIN, WHITWELL (February 26, 1816-January 1, 1900), editor and essayist, was born in Norfolk, and educated at North Walsham Grammar School and Caius College, Cambridge, where he took his B.A. in 1839. The year before he had married his cousin, Frances Elwin; they had four sons and a daughter. He was ordained deacon in 1839 and priest in 1840, and for a time served as a curate in Somerset. His connection with the *Quarterly Review* began in 1843 and lasted until 1885. From 1853 to 1860 he was editor of the magazine, coming from his rectory at Booton (where he served from 1849 until his death) to London four times a year to get out the quarterly numbers. He continued as contributor, but resigned as editor in order to edit the works of Pope. He published five volumes of the poet between 1860 and 1872, then handed the work over to another. Later he brought out an anonymous edition of Byron.

To forget his grief over the sudden death of a son and his daughter, he busied himself in rebuilding his church, an occupation which kept him from literature for years. His wife died in 1898, and he himself followed her the next year; he had conducted New Year's Eve services in his church, and dropped dead the next morning while dressing.

Elwin's best work is in his *Quarterly* articles, which have never been collected in a volume. At the time of his death he had begun a book of reminiscences of his friend Thackeray. He was a good critic, a brilliant conversationalist and letter writer, and he is at his best in writing which he has not polished with the elaboration he devoted to his more serious work.

PRINCIPAL WORKS: Life of John Forster, 1888; Some Seventeenth Century Men of Letters, 1875.

ABOUT: Elwin, W. Some Seventeenth Century Men of Letters (see Memoir by Warwick Elwin).

ERSKINE, THOMAS (1788-March 20, 1870), Scottish theologian, was left an orphan at two and reared by his maternal grandmother, a very religious woman who inspired him with a lifelong concern with theology. He was educated at the University of Edinburgh, and admitted advocate in 1810. In 1816 he succeeded to the family estate at Linlathen, Forfarshire, on the death of his brother, and retired from the bar to spend the rest of his life in the study of theology. He was kept from narrowness of mind by an income which permitted him to travel and by a deep interest in art. He became, indeed, so liberal in theory that, though he never left the official state church, his beliefs were undistinguishable from those of the Universalists. He was a close friend of Frederick Denison Maurice, the founder of Christian Socialism, and shared many of his views. He never

married, a sister to whom he was devoted being his housekeeper and constant companion. He outlived all his family, of whom he was the youngest. Surrounded by his friends, he died quietly, as he had wished, "with his door open."

Erskine's influence through conversation and correspondence greatly exceeded that exercised by his formal writings. His kindliness mixed with conservatism is evident in all his work. In general he displays stronger elements of sympathy than of logic or reasoning, and his appeal is emotional rather than intellectual.

PRINCIPAL WORKS: An Essay on Faith, 1822; The Brazen Serpent, 1831; The Doctrine of Election, 1837; The Spiritual Order, 1871.

ABOUT: Erskine, T. Letters.

EVANS, ANNE (1820-1870), poet, was born in Sandhurst, the oldest of six children of the Rev. Arthur Benoni Evans, a miscellaneous writer and headmaster of various schools. One of her brothers was a well known antiquary, another an editor and a poet. Practically nothing is known of her life, except that she died unmarried at fifty. None of her work was published during her lifetime. She was a friend of Thackeray's daughter, Mrs. Ritchie, who edited a posthumous volume ten years after Anne Evans' death. She was a talented musician, and many of her songs were set to music of her own composition, but both words and music are forgotten today.

PRINCIPAL WORK: Poems and Music, 1880.

ABOUT: Evans, A. Poems and Music (see Memorial Preface by Anne Thackeray Ritchie).

EVANS, MARY ANNE. See "ELIOT, GEORGE."

EVANS, SEBASTIAN (March 2, 1830-December 19, 1909), poet, was the son of the miscellaneous writer Arthur Benoni Evans, and brother of the song-writer Anne Evans. He was born in Leicestershire, and studied under his father, who was headmaster of the Free Grammar School at Market Bosworth. He then went to Emmanuel College, Cambridge, where he secured his B.A. in 1853 and his M.A. in 1857. His talent for both art and poetry found expression in early years, and he published a book of sonnets while at the university. He entered Lincoln's Inn to read law in 1855, but was appointed almost immediately secretary of the Indian Reform Association. In 1857 he resigned to become manager of the art department of a glass works near Birmingham, where he remained until 1867, designing glass windows for churches. An ardent Conservative, he left this position to edit the Birmingham *Daily Gazette,* and in 1868 was elected to Parliament. The same year he received an honorary LL.D. from Cambridge. In 1870 he returned to the study of law, and was called to the bar in 1873, joining the Oxford circuit. However, most of his time was given to literature, and he contributed articles and mystical stories to many magazines. In 1878 he helped to found a Conservative weekly, *The People,* and was its editor until 1881. At the same time he kept up his art, exhibited at the Royal Academy, and worked in wood carving, engraving, and book binding. He was an excellent translator from the French, Italian, Latin, and Greek. In 1857 he married Elizabeth Goldney, and they had two sons.

Evans' extreme versatility weakened his literary merit. However, his poetry, though lushly romantic, has much beauty and even a good deal of humor unusual in writers of his mystical, medieval school.

PRINCIPAL WORKS: Brother Fabian's Manuscripts and Other Poems, 1865; Songs and Etchings, 1871; In the Studio, 1875; In Quest of the Holy Graal, 1898.

ABOUT: Times December 20, 1909.

EWING, JULIANA HORATIA GATTY

(August 3, 1841-May 13, 1885) author of children's books, was born at Ecclesfield, Yorkshire, She was the eldest daughter of the Reverend Alfred Gatty, vicar of Ecclesfield, and of Margaret Gatty, author of children's stories. Her brother, Alfred Scott Gatty, became well known as a composer of songs.

Mrs. Gatty was ambitious for her children and made quite a scholar of herself in preparing to train and educate them. She knew various languages, sketched well, and was a capable musician. Juliana, in addition to her talent as a story-teller, which she developed in entertaining her younger sisters, had considerable ability as an illustrator and made drawings for one of her mother's books. Her first stories were published in *The Monthly Packet* in 1861, and her first volume appeared in 1862 under the title *Melchior's Dream and Other Tales.* Juliana and her sister, after the death of their mother, edited and published for seven years her magazine, *Aunt Judy's Magazine.*

In 1864 she married Major Alexander Ewing, who became known as a writer of hymns. His various appointments included a post in Canada, where the Ewings lived for two years after their marriage. Mrs. Ewing continued to write, although, upon their return to Europe, the ill-health that was to dog the rest of her life commenced to be manifest. When, in 1879, Major Ewing was ordered to Ceylon and Malta, she accompanied him part way and was then

JULIANA HORATIA EWING

obliged to turn back to England. Upon his return in 1883 the couple went to live in Devonshire, in a cottage they named Villa Ponente, where Juliana seemed to be very happy with books and gardening. However, she gradually became more ill, and they moved to Bath for her benefit. She failed to improve, and died there.

She was a prolific writer of children's stories, of which the best known are perhaps *Jackanapes* and *The Story of a Short Life.* Her books were immensely popular and still have their devoted readers. *The Athenaeum* said of her that she was "the best of English story-tellers for children, for she was one of themselves and yet something more." Her ideas often came to her while looking at illustrations, and she avowedly owed much inspiration to other writers of children's books.

R. M.

PRINCIPAL WORKS: Fiction—Lob-Lie-by-the-Fire and Other Tales, 1873; The Story of a Short Life, 1882; Jackanapes, 1883.

ABOUT: Ewing, J. H. Jackanapes and Other Tales (see Life prefixed by Horatia K. F. Gatty); Athenaeum 85:727 June 6, 1885.

FABER, FREDERICK WILLIAM (June

28, 1814-September 26, 1863), poet and theologian, was born in Yorkshire, of a family of clergymen. His parents died while he was in his minority. He was educated at Balliol and University Colleges, Oxford, gaining his B.A. in 1836, and in 1837 becoming a fellow. He won in 1836 the Newdigate prize for poetry. At about this time he became acquainted with Wordsworth, who thought highly of his poems.

In Oxford Faber was a disciple of the great Newman, and attached to his high church movement, which eventually led them both, with many others, to Roman Catholicism. However, he was ordained deacon and priest in the Church of England, and began to make his way as a tutor. In 1841 he made a continental tour with some pupils. In 1842 he was a rector in Huntingdonshire. But in 1845 he left the Anglican Church and became a Roman Catholic. He formed a community of converts at Birmingham, popularly known as the Wilfridians, and he, as "Brother Wilfrid," was its superior. They were given a manor house in Staffordshire, known as St. Wilfrid's, in 1846. In 1847 he was ordained a Catholic priest. The next year the entire community joined the Oratory of St. Philip Neri. After five months' novitiate Faber was made master of novices. The community, now Oratorians, went back to St. Wilfrid's, in 1846. In 1847 he was branch (later the Brompton Oratory), which Faber headed till his death. In 1851 he started to visit Palestine, but was turned back at Malta by illness. In 1854 Pope Pius IX conferred the degree of Ph.D. on him.

Faber was a pulpit orator, and the same eloquence appears in his prose treatises, which combine mysticism and theological learning with "a light and charming style." His lyrical poems have great beauty, and many of his hymns are in use in Protestant as well as in Catholic churches. He wrote also a long series of lives of the saints.

PRINCIPAL WORKS: The Cherwell Water Lily and Other Poems, 1840; The Styrian Lake and Other Poems, 1842; Sir Lancelot, 1844; The Rosary and Other Poems, 1845; Hymns, 1848.
ABOUT: Bowden, J. E. Life and Letters; Faber, F. A. Brief Sketch of the Early Life of F. W. Faber.

FAIRBAIRN, ANDREW MARTIN (November 4, 1838-February 9, 1912), Scottish theologian, was born in Fife. His father was a miller, the household was sternly religious, and he had little formal schooling, beginning to earn his living at ten. But he had a prodigious memory and was a voracious reader, and he prepared himself for the University of Edinburgh. He did not, however, take a degree. He then joined the Evangelical Union and entered its college in Edinburgh to study for the ministry. In 1860 he was put in charge of its church in Bathgate. A visit to Germany, where he studied at the University of Berlin, broadened his theological outlook. In 1872 he went to Aberdeen, and in 1877 became principal of the Airedale Theological Seminary Bradford. From this time on he was counted as Congregationalist, and was chairman of the Congregational Union in 1883. In 1886 he became principal of Mansfield College, Oxford, a newly founded Congregational theological seminary. He was keenly interested in education, and contributed to the Cambridge Modern History. He made several visits to the United States, and in 1898 visited India. He married Jane Shields in 1868 and had two sons and two daughters.

Fairbairn was learned, liberal in his views, an eloquent speaker. Personally he was kindly, but he loved controversy and was often accused of dogmatism. His writing is penetrating and original, with a gift for vivid analyses of men and movements.

PRINCIPAL WORKS: Studies in the Philosophy of Religion and History, 1876; Studies in the Life of Christ, 1881; The City of God, 1882; Religion in History and in Modern Life, 1884; Christ in Modern Theology, 1893; Christ in the Centuries, 1893; Catholicism: Roman and Anglican, 1899; The Philosophy of the Christian Religion, 1902.
ABOUT: Selbie, W. B. Life of Andrew Martin Fairbairn.

"FALCONER, LANCE." See HAWKER, MARY

"FANE, VIOLET." See CURRIE, LADY MARY MONTGOMERIE

FANSHAWE, CATHERINE MARIA (July 6, 1765-April 17, 1834), poet, was deformed and a semi-invalid all her life. She was born in Surrey, but after the deaths of her parents and her brothers she and her two sisters lived in London and Richmond, members of a circle of artistic and intellectually minded ladies. All the sisters, including Catherine, were gifted etchers and water color painters. They were noted for their coldness and formality, and were not very well liked; Catherine was the most agreeable of the three, but more or less affected by their manners. She frequently visited Italy for her health, and made many sketches of Italian scenes.

Her poems were all circulated in manuscript or published anonymously in the collections of others. Her best known verses are those on the letter "H" beginning, " 'Tis whispered in heaven, 'tis muttered in hell") which were once attributed to Byron.

PRINCIPAL WORKS: Memorials, 1865; Literary Remains (ed. by W. Harness) 1876.

FANU, JOSEPH SHERIDAN LE. See LE FANU, JOSEPH SHERIDAN

FARADAY, MICHAEL (September 22, 1791-August 25, 1867), physicist, was born in Surrey, the son of a blacksmith. In his childhood his father moved to London. There in 1804 Faraday, who had had very little formal education, was apprenticed to a bookbinder and stationer. While working as a bookbinder he was given tickets to hear the famous physicist Sir Humphrey Davy lecture at the Royal Institution. He took notes of the lectures, and on the strength of them asked Davy for a position in his laboratories.

Davy, much impressed by the young man's interest, took him on as laboratory assistant. In 1813 Faraday traveled with Davy and his wife on the Continent, a tour during which (though he was already beginning to show his scientific genius) he was obliged to act as Davy's valet and was treated by Lady Davy as a menial.

In 1815 he contributed his first original paper to the Royal Institution. 1821 was one of the great years in Faraday's life: he married Sarah Barnard (the marriage was childless but markedly happy); he joined the obscure apocalyptic sect of Sandemanians, to which he belonged for the remainder of his life; and he isolated chlorine. In 1829 he gave his first Bakerian lecture before the Royal Society, precursor of many years of highly popular lectures to adults and children. From 1831 most of his time was given to research in the field of electro-magnetism, in which his is one of the greatest names. From 1841 to 1844 Faraday was away from the Institution, his health, both mental and physical, having failed completely; much of this time he spent in Switzerland. He had stopped in 1838 doing commercial work on the side to eke out his small salary (even when he was acting head of the Institution); and this was now supplemented by a government pension. He declined the presidency both of the Royal Society and of the Royal Institution, since he knew his mind was again becoming clouded. He died in a house at Hampton Court lent him by Queen Victoria.

Small, with a remarkably large head and an animated countenance, Faraday was an emotional, tender-hearted, generous man, naive and lovable. He had no pretense to great literary ability, but his writing is clear and vigorous.

PRINCIPAL WORKS: History of the Progress of Electro-magnetism, 1821; Experimental Researches in Electricity, 1855; Researches in Chemistry and Physics, 1859.

ABOUT: Crowther, J. G. Men of Science; Jones, B. Life and Letters of Faraday; Tyndall, J. Faraday as a Discoverer.

FARGUS, FREDERICK JOHN (December 26, 1847-May 15, 1885), novelist, was born in Bristol, where his father was an auctioneer. His mother died while he was a child. He was eager to go to sea, though he was always a studious boy, and at thirteen his father sent him to the school frigate *Conway*. From the name of this ship, reminiscent of his happiest days, he took the pseudonym, "Hugh Conway," under which all his novels and stories were written. When he left the *Conway*, however, his father refused to allow him to enter the Royal Navy, and sent him to a private school in Bristol instead. He was then articled to a firm of public accountants, with whom he stayed until

1868, when his father died and he succeeded to the business. Even under these circumstances Fargus wrote a great deal, chiefly songs which were set to music. His first story was contributed to an "annual" in 1881.

His novel, *Called Back*, published in 1883, was a huge success. It was translated into half a dozen languages, and dramatized by himself. In the midst of this dual life of business and literature, Fargus developed symptoms of tuberculosis. He was ordered to the Riviera, but there unfortunately caught typhoid fever, from which he died at Monte Carlo at only thirty-seven. He was married in 1871 to Amy Spark, and left three sons and a daughter.

The epitaph written by Lord Houghton for Fargus' tombstone at Nice sums up his contribution to literature: "A British writer of fiction of great renown and greater promise, who died prematurely."

PRINCIPAL WORKS: A Life's Idyll and Other Poems, 1879; Called Back, 1883; Dark Days, 1884; A Family Affair, 1885; Living or Dead, 1886.

ABOUT: Fargus, F. J. Called Back (see Sketch of "Hugh Conway" in 1885 ed.); Athenaeum May 23, 1885; Illustrated London News May 30, 1885.

FARJEON, BENJAMIN LEOPOLD (May 12, 1838-July 23, 1903), novelist, was born in London of an orthodox Jewish family, his father being a merchant. He attended a private school for Jewish boys and at fourteen went to work on *The Nonconformist*. In 1855, at seventeen, he broke with his orthodox family and went to Australia. Publication of a ship's newspaper on board rescued him from the steerage. From the gold-fields of Victoria he went to those in New Zealand, but soon abandoned gold-seeking for journalism. He became joint-editor and part proprietor of the *Otago Daily Times*, of Dunedin, the first daily paper in New Zealand. At the same time he began to write novels and plays. Receiving some encouragement (actually only a polite letter from Dickens, who was his idol), he left New Zealand, and returned to London *via* New York to become a free lance writer. From 1868 he poured out novels, many of which were very popular. In 1877 he married Margaret Jefferson, daughter of the famous American actor, Joseph Jefferson. They had four sons and one daughter, Eleanor, a well known writer of the present day. He died at Hampstead, at fifty-five.

Farjeon's books may be classified as sentimental Christmas stories, conventional novels of humble life modeled on Dickens, and sensational mystery stories in the style of Wilkie Collins. *Grif*, the best known, was dramatized by himself with great success; he also produced, in 1876, a play called *Home, Sweet Home*.

PRINCIPAL WORKS: Grif: A Story of Australian Life, 1866; London's Heart, 1873; Blade o' Grass, 1874; Great Porter Square, 1884; Devlin the Barber, 1887.

ABOUT: Farjeon, E. Family History.

FARRAR, FREDERIC WILLIAM (August 7, 1831-March 22, 1903), novelist, historian, and theologian, was born at Bombay, where his father was a missionary. At three he was sent with his brother to his aunts in England. He attended the Latin School, Aylesbury, until his parents came home on furlough from 1839 to 1842. They settled in the Isle of Man, and sent him as a boarder to King William's College, where he became head of the school. He next attended London University, securing a B.A. degree in 1852, then went to Trinity College, Cambridge, where he became B.A. in 1854, M.A. in 1857, and D.D. in 1874. He became a master in Marlborough College, and was ordained as deacon in 1854 and priest in 1857. In 1860 he married Lucy Cardew; they had five sons and five daughters. From 1855 to 1870 Farrar was a master at Harrow, in 1869 also becoming chaplain to Queen Victoria, In 1871 he became headmaster of Marlborough, and in 1875 canon of Westminster. His sermons against eternal punishment in 1877 raised a theological storm, but he was nevertheless made archdeacon of Westminster in 1883 and dean of Canterbury in 1895. In 1885 he toured the United States and Canada, and his lectures on Browning started the vogue of that poet in America. In 1899 he began to suffer from progressive muscular atrophy, and was an invalid until his death.

Farrar was a real liberal, a close friend of Warwin, whose funeral service he preached, and an evolutionist. He was a keen and scientific student of philology. His book for boys, *Eric*, founded on his own days at King William's College, was immensely popular. In general his work is scholarly and broad-minded, but his style is too florid for modern taste.

PRINCIPAL WORKS: Eric: or, Little by Little, 1858; An Essay on the Origin of Language, 1860; St. Winifred's, 1862; Chapters on Language, 1865; Seekers After God, 1868; The Three Homes, 1873; Life of Christ, 1874; Eternal Hope, 1878; The Life and Works of St. Paul, 1879; Sermons and Addresses in America, 1886; Lives of the Fathers, 1889; Men I Have Known, 1897.

ABOUT: Farrar, R. F. Life of F. W. Farrar.

FAWCETT, HENRY (August 26, 1833-November 6, 1884), economist, was born in Salisbury. His father, a draper, had been mayor of the town. He was sent to Queenwood College, an agricultural school, and then to King's College School, in London, in 1849. From there he went to Peterhouse College, Cambridge, in 1852, changing to Trinity in 1853 and securing his B.A. in 1856.

From these days dated his keen interest in politics. He proceeded to study law at Lincoln's Inn, but was obliged to take a rest because of eye weakness. Ironically, while he was recuperating at his home, he was instantly and permanently blinded by his own father in a shooting accident.

Fawcett refused to sink into despair. He returned to Cambridge, where he was a fellow of Trinity, and by employing readers studied political economy. He was professor of political economy at Cambridge from 1863 to his death. In 1867 he married Millicent Garrett, his co-worker and helpmeet as well as his wife. She became later very prominent in the woman suffrage movement in England. They had one daughter.

Fawcett was a splendid speaker, and had never given up his political ambitions. After several defeats he was elected to Parliament in 1865 as a liberal. Gradually he grew away from his party, becoming more radical than they, though he served as postmaster general in 1880. (He was ineligible for a cabinet post because of his blindness.) He was a friend and disciple of such economists as Mill and Cairnes, and was showered with honors and honorary degrees. In 1882 he contracted diphtheria and typhoid fever, and never really recovered his health, though he lived for two years longer. A monument to him was erected in Westminster Abbey, and a scholarship for blind students was established at Cambridge in his memory.

Fawcett's writing shows a keen, powerful, but rather narrow and inflexible mind. Personally he was a man of sympathetic nature, devoted to his friends and affectionate. His work is solid if no longer of great value.

PRINCIPAL WORKS: Manual of Political Economy, 1863; The Economic Position of the British Labourer, 1865; Pauperism: Its Causes and Remedies, 1871; Speeches on Some Current Political Questions, 1873.

ABOUT: Stephen, L. Life of Henry Fawcett.

FELLOWS, SIR CHARLES (August 1799-November 8, 1860), archaeologist, was born in Nottingham, son of a wealthy banker. He was interested in archaeology from boyhood, an interest stimulated by his talent for drawing. In his youth he traveled throughout England and Scotland investigating archaeological remains. He had a taste for mountain climbing as well, and in 1827 mapped a new route to the summit of Mont Blanc which is still in use.

From 1832 to 1842 Fellows was in Italy, Greece, and Levant. He had concentrated now on classical archaeology, and headed four important expeditions in Asia Minor, at his own expense, though his finds were donated to the British Museum. He was the discoverer of the Xanthian marbles and explored three hitherto untouched ancient cities.

In 1845, returned to England, he was knighted. In the same year he married Eliza Hart, who died in 1847; in 1848 he married Harriet Knight, a widow, who died in 1874. He retired to the Isle of Wight, where he bought an estate and spent his last years chiefly in experimental agriculture. Though the archaeology of his books is outmoded, they are still readable because of the freshness of his enthusiasm and the vividness of his descriptions.

PRINCIPAL WORKS: A Journal Written During an Excursion in Asia Minor, 1839; An Account of Discoveries in Lycia, 1841: The Xanthian Marbles, 1843; Lycia, Carcia, Lydia, 1847; Travels and Researches in Asia Minor, 1852.

ABOUT: Brown, C. Lives of Nottinghamshire Worthies; Journal of the Royal Geographical Society 1861.

FENN, GEORGE MANVILLE (January 3, 1831-August 26, 1909), novelist, was born at Pimlico. After attending the Battersea Training College for Teachers from 1851 to 1854, he became master of a small national school in Lincolnshire, then a private tutor. In London he became a printer, then returned to Lincolnshire, bought a press, and started a small magazine of verse, *Modern Metre,* in 1862. In 1864 he became part owner of the *Hertfordshire and Essex Observer,* but both enterprises failed. Finally Dickens bought his first story for *All the Year Round,* and he began to succeed as a writer. He wrote in all more than 170 books—sketches, novels, and books for boys. In these last, which were heavily flavored with natural history, he was most successful. In 1870 he was editor of *Cassell's Magazine,* and from 1873 to 1879 published *Once a Week.* He was also dramatic critic of *The Echo,* and in 1887 and 1888 produced farces at the Comedy Theatre. He then moved to Essex, where he devoted himself to gardening, the making of telescopes, and the accumulation of a large library. In 1855 he had married Susanna Leake, and they had two sons and six daughters. In 1907 Fenn's health broke, and he died two years later.

His best work is in his juvenile stories, and he wrote little else of value after 1881. The boys' books were instructive as well as entertaining, and exerted an excellent influence on their young readers.

PRINCIPAL WORKS: Readings by Starlight, 1866; Hollowdell Grange, 1867; The Silver Salvers, 1898; The Canker Worm, 1901.

ABOUT: Sketch August 6, 1902.

FERGUSON, SIR SAMUEL (March 10, 1810-August 9, 1886), Irish poet and scholar, was born at Belfast, the third son of John Ferguson, a gentleman of Scottish descent.

He went for his first schooling to the Academical Institution in Belfast, and in 1822

SIR SAMUEL FERGUSON

to Trinity College, Dublin University, where he was graduated in 1826 with the degree of B.A., and where he was awarded the degree of M.A. six years later. After this he studied law and was called to the Irish Bar in 1838 and to the Inner Bar in 1859 as Queen's Counsel, combining a successful career as solicitor with thorough studies in the antiquities of Ireland; he had even spent a year (1845-46) on the continent, searching for Irish literary remains and evidences. This learning brought him in 1867 the honor of receiving the first appointment to the post of Deputy Keeper of the Records of Ireland, upon assuming which he abandoned his legal practice.

His literary career had begun early; "The Forging of the Anchor," a poem written in his twenty-first year, received a flattering notice from "Christopher North." He wrote much for the brilliant *Dublin University Magazine,* and many studies of everything that pertained to Irish life and history—annals, poetry, music, and Irish law. *Lays of the Westrn Gael* appeared in 1865 and the epic *Congal* in 1872, and *Deirdre* and his *Poems* in 1880. He rounded out fifty-one years of literary activity with *Shakespearian Brevities* (1882)—sound Shakespearian criticism which showed the author's versatility and keenness of judgment.

To Ferguson, more than to any other man, belongs the credit for the Irish Renaissance. It must be remembered that he had no public when he began to write and to translate Irish verse; his verse created that public. Alfred Perceval Graves, himself an Irish poet, says of him: "Ferguson was unquestionably the Irish poet of the past century who most powerfully influenced the literary history of his country. It was in his writings that the great work of restoring to Ireland the spiritual treasure it had lost in parting with the Gaelic tongue was begun."

Ferguson, however, must by no means be put aside with a mere appreciation of his significance in Irish literary history. He was in his own right a poet of nobility and sweep, and of effects that, although often harsh, were grand and stirring. Perhaps "Thomas Davis: An Elegy" gives as accurate an idea of Ferguson's virtues and defects as any other single work from his pen; it is considered one of the finest and most touching dirges in the English language. *Congal* was one of the rare poems which actually reach the epic tone for which they strive. Of the poems as a whole William Butler Yeats said in 1886: "The author of these poems is the greatest poet Ireland has produced."

A handsome man of great dignity and grace of appearance and manner, Ferguson was both popular and influential. He had founded the Protestant Repeal Association, a pro-Irish group, but he subsequently withdrew from politics and lived out his life quietly as scholar and poet. Many honors came to him: he received the honorary degree of LL.D. in 1865 from Dublin University and in 1884 from the University of Edinburgh; was made a member of the Society of Antiquaries of Scotland in 1874, was knighted in 1878, and was made president of the Royal Irish Academy in 1881. After his marriage to Miss Mary Catherine Guinness in 1848, his house became one of the centers of Dublin brilliance—it was said that he and his wife would entertain anyone who cared for art, literature, and music, and Ferguson's erudition, attainments, and charm made his company a delight. The excellence of his character made many friends for him too, and J. P. Mahaffy has characterized his kindness and sympathy in the simple statement: "Never did a poor author appeal to him in vain."

Ferguson died at Shand Lodge, Howth, after several months of illness; and his funeral was attended by half of Dublin, irrespective of class or faith. Lord Plunket, Archbishop of Ireland, delivered the funeral oration. Lady Ferguson, who survived her husband, wrote his biography.   R. M.

PRINCIPAL WORKS: *Poetry*—Lays of the Western Gael, 1864; Congal: An Epic Poem, 1872; Poems, 1880. *Miscellaneous*—Shakespearian Brevities, 1882; Hibernian Night's Entertainments, 1887; The Ogham Inscriptions in Ireland, Wales, and Scotland, 1887; Remains of St. Patrick (verse translations) 1888.

ABOUT: Brooke, S. A. & Rolleston, T. W. A Treasury of Irish Poetry; Ferguson. M. C. Sir Samuel Ferguson in the Ireland of His Day; McCarthy, J. H. & others. Irish Literature (v. 3); Athenaeum 88:205 August 14, 1886; Blackwood's Magazine 140:621 November 1886.

FERRIER, SUSAN EDMONDSTONE (September 17, 1782-November 5, 1854), Scottish novelist, was born at Edinburgh. She was the youngest of ten children of James Ferrier, a "writer to the signet" (as solicitors were then called in Scotland) and agent and friend of the Duke of Argyll.

Susan was a bright and promising child and was given an excellent education. Her father's connections made it easy for her to meet smart Edinburgh society, and she was often a visitor to Inverary, the castle of the Dukes of Argyll. Here, with the Duke's niece, Miss Clavering, she conceived the idea of writing a satirical novel of manners, and was encouraged in this by Lady Charlotte Campbell, afterwards Lady Bury, herself an author. The projected novel, with help in some details furnished by Miss Clavering, was written shortly after the turn of the century and was entitled *Marriage*; but it did not appear until 1818, when the publisher Blackwood urged Miss Ferrier to permit its publication. Its appearance was anonymous—Miss Ferrier had originally hesitated to publish it because of the real people portrayed, and this and her natural dislike of publicity led her to withhold her signature from it and from her two succeeding books.

In 1824 *The Inheritance*, the second and best of her novels, was published. In 1831 *Destiny*, the last, was bought by a publisher at an excellent price, owing to the influence of Sir Walter Scott, a friend of Miss Ferrier and the supposed author of her novels. Miss Ferrier was now in a position to continue the writer's career at a profit, but she intensely disliked professional writing and its accompanying notoriety and steadfastly refused to have anything further to do with professional

SUSAN FERRIER

authorship. Her eyesight, too, became very poor toward the end of her life and she was obliged to live in a very retired fashion. Moreover, a growing preoccupation with religious questions made novel writing seem even more distasteful to her. Her only further contributions to literature were narratives of visits to Ashestiel and to Abbotsford, where she visited Scott during his last illness. Her complete works were published in 1882 and her letters in 1898.

Miss Ferrier's three novels—satirical studies of English and Scottish society—are somewhat deficient as to plot, and it has been generally felt that her character drawing tends toward caricature and that her satire lacks the balance of such work as Jane Austen's. Nevertheless, the sharp wit and flavor of her writing long continued to attract readers. Stephen Gwynn said of her in 1899 that she had continued to amuse four generations, and George Saintsbury wrote that despite certain drawbacks she was "an admirable novelist, especially for those who enjoy unsparing social satire and a masterly faculty of caricature."

The conversation and social aptitude of Miss Ferrier were often praised during her life. She was perhaps rather terrifying, especially to those who remembered the merciless caricatures of her novels, but a passage in Lockhart's *Life of Scott* describes with considerable pathos her visit to Scott when the master was in the decline of his powers and gives a kinder idea of her character.

R. M.

WORKS: *Novels*—Marriage, 1818; The Inheritance, 1824; Destiny, 1831.

ABOUT: Douglas, G. The Blackwood Group; Ferrier, S. E. Memoir and Correspondence; Saintsbury, G. Essays in English Literature (2nd ser.); Academy 56-153 February 4, 1899; Contemporary Review 109:91 January 1916; Nineteenth Century 92:241 August 1922.

FERRIER, JAMES FREDERICK (June 16, 1808-June 11, 1864), Scottish philosopher, was born in Edinburgh. His father was writer to the signet; his aunt, Susan Edmondstone Ferrier, was a popular novelist, and his maternal uncle was the celebrated critic John Wilson ("Christopher North"). Ferrier was educated at the University of Edinburgh and at Magdalen College, Oxford, where he received his B.A. in 1831.

Throughout his life Ferrier was strongly influenced by his close friend and constant companion, Sir William Hamilton, the philosopher. He became an advocate in 1832 but never practised. Instead, he was made, in 1842, professor of civil history at the University of Edinburgh. In 1845 he became professor of moral philosophy and political economy at the University of St. Andrews, Aberdeen. Several times he tried to regain a position in Edinburgh, but was unsuccessful, and remained at St. Andrews until his death.

In 1837 he married his first cousin, Margaret Anne Wilson, John Wilson's daughter. They had two sons and three daughters. Ferrier lived the most retired of lives. His whole life was in his studies, and it was hard to persuade him to leave the university for even a short time. He was devoted to his pupils, and when he became too ill to go to his classes lectured in his own house. He suffered from angina pectoris from 1861, and died of it three years later.

Gentle and high-strung, Ferrier was marked by both dignity and charm of nature. His philosophy was essentially a theory of knowing and being; the only knowable, he held, was the object plus the subject. The only true existences are minds plus what they apprehend. He postulated a supreme, infinite, everlasting mind in synthesis with all things—the final subject plus object.

His style, in spite of the difficulty of his subject, was clear and direct. He was a frequent and well liked contributor of *Blackwood's Magazine,* but he published little in book form except his philosophical work, *The Institutes of Metaphysic.*

PRINCIPAL WORKS: The Institutes of Metaphysic, 1854; Lectures on Greek Philosophy and Other Philosophical Remains (ed. by A. Grant & E. L. Lushington) 1866.

ABOUT: Ferrier, J. F. Lectures on Greek Philosophy (see Life by A. Grant and E. L. Lushington); Haldane, E. S. J. F. Ferrier.

FIELD, BARRON (October 23, 1786-April 11, 1846), poet and essayist was born in London, where his father was treasurer of the Apothecaries' Company. He grew up an intimate of the circle of Lamb, Hunt, Coleridge, Wordsworth, and Hazlitt, but was never very popular with any of them. Wordsworth refused him permission to be his biographer.

He studied law in the Inner Temple from 1809, and was called to the bar in 1814. He practised little, however, and supported himself by writing, chiefly as theatrical critic of *The Times.* In 1816 he married Jane Carncroft; they had no children. The same year he secured an appointment as judge of the supreme court of New South Wales, where he lived until 1824. He had anything but a judicial mind, and left behind him little but controversy and dissatisfaction. Nevertheless in 1826 he became chief justice of Gibraltar, where his services were of no more value than they had been in Australia. He then returned to England and retired, spending his leisure in editing Elizabethan plays for the Shakespeare Society. He also published an analysis of Blackstone's *Commentaries.* His prose is described as "passing muster," but his verses were atrocious. His name gave an apt pun, and it was commonly said that in literature he was indeed a "barren field." He died at Torquay at fifty-nine.

PRINCIPAL WORKS: Hints to Witnesses in Courts of Justice, 1815; First Fruits of Australian Poetry, 1819; Geographical Memoirs of New South Wales, 1825.

ABOUT: Lamb, C. Life and Letters; Gentleman's Magazine 1846 Pt. 1:646.

"FIELD, MICHAEL," joint pseudonym of two women poets, KATHERINE HARRIS BRADLEY (October 27, 1848-September 26, 1914) and EDITH EMMA COOPER (January 12, 1862-December 13, 1913), aunt and niece. Katherine Harris Bradley was born in Birmingham, the daughter of a tobacco manufacturer. Edith Emma Cooper was born thirteen years later at Kenilworth, Warwickshire. Her mother was Miss Bradley's elder sister; her father was a merchant. When Edith's mother became a permanent invalid, upon the birth of a second child, her aunt Katherine joined the Cooper household to help look after the children. Aunt and niece were then sixteen and three, and thenceforth they lived together as devoted companions.

The elder, who had been privately tutored, educated the younger. And while her niece was growing up, she continued her own education briefly at Newnham College, Cambridge, and at the Collège de France in Paris. Here she fell in love with a Frenchman many years her senior, but he died not long after their meeting. She corresponded with Ruskin from 1875 to 1880.

In 1878 the family moved to Bristol, where the girls zestfully studied the classics and philosophy at University College and took active part in the college debating society. Ten years later they removed to Reigate, Surrey, and withdrew almost entirely from the world of affairs to devote themselves to their profession. After another ten years they removed in 1898 to Richmond, Surrey, and here they lived in an eighteenth century house, with a pair of doves and a chow for companions. Charles Shannon and Charles Ricketts, noted artists, were their close friends and neighbors.

They made numerous trips to the Continent, and in 1907 joined the Church of Rome. Both died of cancer, Miss Cooper at the age of fifty-one, Miss Bradley at sixty-five, less than a year apart. The elder nursed the younger through her fatal illness, never revealing that she herself was afflicted with the same disease.

Miss Bradley was known as "Michael"; Miss Cooper as "Field" or, more intimately, "Henry." They were both shy, imperious, gay, and witty. Sir William Rothenstein recalls them: "Michael stout, emphatic, splendid and adventurous in talk, rich in wit; Field wan and wistful, gentler in manner than Michael, but equally eminent in the quick give and take of ideas. . . Both were endowed with an ecstatic sense of beauty. . . They knew but few people, but from these few they expected—everything, all they had to give." Robert Browning, in his late years, was a close friend. Others included George Meredith, Herbert Spencer, Oscar Wilde, George Moore, and Gordon Bottomley. Both women were financially independent.

At nineteen and thirty-one they began their industrious collaboration in verse. Working in separate rooms, and seldom exchanging a word between 9 A.M. and 2 P.M., they produced twenty-seven tragedies, a masque, and eight volumes of lyrics, in which the hand of one was indistinguishable from that of the other. The tragedies were full of grandeur and dramatic emotion in the Elizabethan manner; some were based on classical themes, others on English and Scottish history. The lyrics, less ambitious than the dramas, were more charming and perfect in their kind.

The early writings of "Michael Field," before "his" identity was discovered, were highly praised by reviewers. Later critics, to quote George Saintsbury, "failed to discover much in the joint work which goes beyond the standard of nineteenth-century closet drama, or, in the lyrics, much more than the half machine-made verse which usually comes late in great periods of poetry."

From 1888 to 1914 the collaborators kept a journal which was left to T. Sturge Moore, their literary executor, with instructions to open it at the end of 1929 and "publish so much and whatever parts of it" he might think fit. The first selection from this material was published in 1933, together with some of their letters, as *Works and Days*.

W. C. H.

"MICHAEL FIELD"

PRINCIPAL WORKS: *Collected Lyrics*—Long Ago, 1889; Sight and Song, 1892; Underneath the Bough, 1893; Wild Honey, 1908; Poems of Adoration, 1912; Mystic Trees, 1913; A Selection From the Poems of Michael Field (ed. by M. Sturgeon and T. Sturge Moore) 1923. *Tragedies*—Callirrhoë, and Fair Rosamund, 1884; The Father's Tragedy, 1885; Canute the Great, 1887; The Tragic Mary, 1890; Anna Ruina, 1899; Noontide Branches (masque) 1899; Borgia, 1905; In the Name of Time, 1919. *Journal and Letters*—Works and Days From the Journal of Michael Field (ed. by T. & D. C. Sturge Moore) 1933.
ABOUT: Field, M. Works and Days; Marble, A. R. Pen Names and Personalities; Massingham, H. J. Letters to X; Maynard, T. Carven From the Laurel Tree; Sturgeon, M. Michael Field.

FINLAY, GEORGE (December 21, 1799-January 26, 1875), historian, was born in Kent of a Scottish family. His father, an inspector of the government powder mills, died in 1802. His mother's teaching first interested Finlay in history. He was sent to live with his uncle in Glasgow, where he was educated by private tutors, then studied law in Glasgow and Göttingen. In 1821, in Germany, he discovered that he had more vocation for historical study than for the law. On an impulse, in 1823, he went to Greece to help Byron in the Greek fight for independence of Turkey. He was with Byron at Missilonghi, but left before the poet died, and joined the chieftain Odysseus, Trelawny's friend. He soon left Odysseus, disgusted with the corruption and contentiousness of the Greek leaders, and ill with malaria. He returned to Glasgow and passed the examination in civil law.

Then, however, he returned to Greece and remained there the rest of his life. Occasionally he visited London, but not after 1854. From 1864 to 1870 he was correspondent of the London *Times*. He came to know Greece thoroughly, and sometimes wrote in modern Greek. Very little is known of his life there; most of it was devoted to his series of historical works, and he bought an estate in Attica and tried hard to introduce the Greeks to improvements in their primitive methods of agriculture. When they refused to take his advice he vituperated them, but essentially he was a public-spirited and public-minded man. He died in Athens at seventy-five.

Finlay was a competent historian, who dug beneath the surface, secured new facts and authenticated the old, and without rhetoric or bombast managed to make seemingly dull records interesting. He was an eccentric, but his mind and his work were both of genuinely high caliber.

PRINCIPAL WORKS: Greece Under the Romans, 1844; Greece to Its Conquest by the Turks, 1851; Greece Under Othoman and Venetian Domination, 1856; The Greek Revolution, 1861 (revised and enlarged as A History of Greece From Its Conquest by the Romans to the Present Time, 1877).
ABOUT: Finlay. G. A History of Greece, etc. (see Autobiography in Vol. 1).

FITCH, SIR JOSHUA GIRLING (February 13, 1824-July 14, 1903), educator, was born in London. His father was a clerk in Somerset House. His older brother later became a Roman Catholic priest. He was educated in a private school, and in 1838 became a pupil teacher in the Borough Road School, Southwark, advancing to the post of full assistant in 1842. In 1844 he was headmaster of the Kingsland Road School, Dalston. He studied by himself for the University of London examinations, and secured a B.A. in 1850 (in classics) and an M.A. in 1852. The same year he became vice-principal of the Borough Road Training College, and in 1856 its principal. He was a brilliant teacher, with a special enthusiasm for literature. In 1862 he became an inspector of schools in Yorkshire, and in 1883 chief inspector of the Eastern Division. From 1885 to 1889 he was inspector of all elementary training colleges for women. In 1888 he had leave of absence to study educational systems in the United States. He was not retired until 1894, five years after the usual age of retirement. He maintained all his life a close connection with the University of London, and was a member of its governing body. He was particularly interested in the education of women. After his retirement he continued to interest himself as a volunteer in numerous public enterprises. He was knighted in 1896. In 1856 he was married to Emma Wilkes. They had no children.

Fitch was advanced and liberal in his views, and his style has marked charm. Most of his writing is in reports, speeches, and articles.

PRINCIPAL WORKS: Lectures on Teaching, 1881; Thomas and Matthew Arnold and Their Influence on English Education, 1897; Educational Aims and Methods, 1900.
ABOUT: Lilley, A. L. Sir Joshua Fitch: An Account of His Life and Work.

FITZGERALD, EDWARD (March 31, 1809-June 14, 1883), famous as the translator of the *Rubaiyat of Omar Khayyám*, was born at Bredfield House near Woodbridge, Suffolk. His father, John Purcell, had married a cousin, Mary Frances Fitzgerald, and upon the death of her father in 1818 they took the name and arms of Fitzgerald. (This is common practice in England when a wife is the heiress of an important family.)

When Edward was seven his family took him to France where they lived for several years. In 1821 he was sent to King Edward the Sixth's School, at Bury St. Edmunds, where his two elder brothers were already enrolled. Here he began the accumulation of those life-long friendships for which he is so justly famous. Among these earliest friends were James Spedding, biographer and editor of Bacon, W. B. Donne, librarian and essayist, J. M. Kemble, philologist and historian, and William Airy.

He entered Trinity College, Cambridge, in 1826. There he added several new friends, three of whom, John Allen, Archdeacon of Sallop, W. M. Thackeray, and W. H. Thompson, Master of Trinity, became his greatest intimates in later life. Although he was a contemporary of the three Tennysons at Cambridge, he did not become acquainted with them until after graduating.

So much emphasis is laid upon Fitzgerald's friendships because they were directly responsible for one of his finest contributions to literature—his letters. Though not as widely known as his translation of the *Rubaiyat*, they are considered by many to be of equal literary merit. These letters are also important as being the chief source of biographical material about the man. As their editor (W. A. Wright, who was also Fitzgerald's choice as literary executor) says: "The mere narrative of the life of a man of leisure and literary tastes would have contained too few incidents to be of general interest, and it appeared to me best to let him be his own biographer, telling his own story and revealing his own character in his letters."

Fitzgerald was not ambitious for academic distinction in the University—in fact he was never ambitious for distinction of any sort. One of his friends described him as an eccentric man of genius, who took more pains to avoid fame than others do to seek it.

Graduated in 1830, after a period of suspense for fear he would not pass at all, he went to Paris to stay with a maiden aunt who lived there. He was joined by Thackeray for a short time, but by April of that year Fitzgerald was back in England. Writing to his friend Allen he announced his intentions of retiring from society: "You must know I am going to become a great bear: and have got all sorts of Utopian ideas into my head about society: these may all be very absurd, but I try the experiment on myself, so I can do no great hurt."

Gamaliel Bradford, in one of his soul-baring essays takes Edward Fitzgerald mildly to task for the indolent life which he led. After summarizing Fitzgerald's opportunities and abilities, quoting many excerpts from his letters which show that the man was fully aware of the indolence and purposelessness of his existence, Bradford says: "And no doubt a genuine modesty holds him back. He does not realize that he might do well if he tried, or that perhaps the best of the doing is in the trying."

From 1831 till his death, Fitzgerald spent practically all of his time in the country—first at Wherstead Lodge near Ipswich till 1835, then at a small cottage on the grounds of his family's estate, Boulge Hall; and later in various lodgings until he moved into his own

EDWARD FITZGERALD

house, Little Grange, in 1874. His favorite outdoor amusement was boating, and until he was 68 years old he spent much of his summer leisure in sailing along the coast of England. His other occupations were gardening, music, reading, the study of foreign languages, and tramping about the countryside.

Although he was something of a recluse from society in general, he was a cordial host to his intimates and a most delightful companion. He made occasional sallies out into the world, but as he wrote to his friend Donne, he had "no curiosity left for other places" and was "glad to get back to my own chair and bed after three or four days' absence." He was, in short, a confirmed bachelor with a great love of masculine comforts and the quiet pleasures of the garden and the fireside.

Fitzgerald did marry—the daughter of his friend and neighbor, Bernard Barton, the Quaker poet, but they separated after a brief period.

Except for a very few contributions to periodicals, Fitzgerald had nothing published until 1849 when he wrote a memoir to go with a collection of letters and poems of Bernard Barton. He next published, anonymously, *Euphranor: A Dialogue on Youth* in 1851 and *Polonius: A Collection of Wise Saws and Modern Instances* in 1852. In 1853 was published *Six Dramas of Calderon*, "freely translated by Edward Fitzgerald," the only book to which his name was attached during his lifetime.

Although contemporary reviewers gave these translations a poor reception, later critics have found them superior to the original works. Bradford says: "In these lines the substance of the thought is as much above the original as the solemn splendor of the iambics is above the agile ease of the Spanish verses." And Lafcadio Hearn, speaking of Fitzgerald's translations in general (Greek and Persian as well as Spanish) says: ". . .Fitzgerald was probably the best translator that ever lived. He did not make literal translations; he translated only the spirit, the ghost of things. But for that reason he did what no man had ever succeeded in doing before him, and what no one is likely to do again for hundreds of years. He had not only great scholarship, but exquisite taste."

In his translation of the *Rubaiyat*, Fitzgerald did even more than this. He invented a new verse form and he interpreted—or rather he crystalized the spirit of a new age which was just beginning to grope for an expression of its half formed thoughts and stifled emotions. John Bailey, on the occasion of Fitzgerald's centenary, wrote: "Fitzgerald had projected into the old Persian poet much that had never been his—projected himself, in fact, and more than himself, a great part of the mind of that generation of which he proved so intimate an interpreter, for all his air of standing aside from its goings altogether. It never struck Tennyson that the wistful agnosticism of Omar . . . was as exactly the voice of a very large part of England in the 'eighties and 'nineties as his own *In Memoriam. . .*" And again: "The books that are widely read outside the narrow literary world are always those in which people find themselves. It is a commonplace that the author who wins immediate success is the man who says to perfection what everybody around is wishing to say but cannot."

Fitzgerald did not win immediate success during his lifetime because he made no attempt to give his work wide circulation. Even his good friend Carlyle heard nothing about the *Rubaiyat* for a dozen years after its first appearance in print. It was not until his death that the world, outside his small circle of intimates, began to hear of Edward Fitzgerald. Tennyson wrote, upon hearing of his death, "I had no truer friend: he was the kindliest of men, and I have never known one of so fine and delicate a wit. I had written a poem to him the last week, a dedication which he will never see." This dedication to *Tiresias* with the epilogue added to the poem after Fitzgerald's death were probably the first that the general public ever heard of the man.

There are many ironical contrasts between Fitzgerald's character and his posthumous fame. Gamaliel Bradford chides him for not attempting greater accomplishments—yet, few poets and no translator ever accomplished more. Because of the sensual aspects of Omar's poetry, Fitzgerald's real preoccupation with the central theme—the greatest of all

questions—has been disregarded. Hailed by Bohemians as their patron-saint, Fitzgerald had nothing in common with such people. Although somewhat eccentric, he was essentially an English gentleman who, like his intimates, was a brilliant but orthodox product of the public schools and Cambridge University. To the charge that he was hedonistic and self-indulgent, the answer is that he lived very simply and applied much of his income to the welfare of others. No mere hedonist could have held the affections of so many friends. When Thackeray was asked which of his old friends he had loved most he replied: "Why dear old Fitz, to be sure." His housekeeper's verdict is probably as accurate as any: "So kind he was, not never one to make no obstacles. Such a joking gentleman he was, too!"

D. C.

PRINCIPAL WORKS: *Prose*—Euphranor, 1851; Polonius, 1852; *Translations*—Six Dramas of Calderon, 1853; Quatrains of Omar Khayyám, 1859; Agamemnon of Aeschylus, 1876; *General*—Collected Writings, 1889.

ABOUT: Bailey, J. C. Poets and Poetry; Bradford, G. Bare Souls; Campbell, A. Y. Great Victorians; Fitch, G. H. Comfort Found in Good Old Books; Hearn, L. Interpretations of Literature; More, P. E. Shelburne Essays (2d ser.); Platt, A. Nine Essays; Ralli, A. J. Critiques; Squire, J. C. Books in General (2nd ser.); Thomas, E. Literary Pilgrim in England; Torrey, B. Friends on the Shelf; Winterich, J. T. Books and the Man; Woodberry, G. E. Literary Memoirs of the 19th Century; Wright, W. A. (ed.). Letters of Edward Fitzgerald.

FLEMING, MARGARET (MARJORIE)
(November 15, 1803-December 19, 1811), is probably the youngest writer ever to have won a lasting reputation. She died when she was just a month over eight years of age. There can be little doubt that the world lost a vivacious, sprightly stylist and a keen critic when an attack of measles put an end so abruptly to the career of Sir Walter Scott's "Pet Marjorie." All these characteristics are already in the diary and verses she had written from the age of six. All her short life was spent in Kirkcaldy, Scotland. Besides Scott, other men of renown were her father's friends, and were delighted by her fascinating, precocious, yet thoroughly childlike personality. It is said that her death was such a blow to her father that he never could mention her name again. Her only sister lived until 1881, and if Marjorie could only have been vouchsafed half so long a life the world of literature would probably have been the richer for it.

PRINCIPAL WORKS: The Complete Marjorie Fleming.

ABOUT: Anon. Pet Margarie: A Story of Child Life Fifty Years Ago; Brown, J. Rab and His Friends.

FLINT, ROBERT (March 14, 1838-November 25, 1910), Scottish philosopher, was born near Dumfries, his father being a farm

225

overseer. After a distinguished career at Glasgow University (where, however, he left without a degree, he became a lay missionary, and was licensed to preach in 1858. Until 1864 he was a minster at Aberdeen and Fife, with several visits to Germany; then until 1876 he was professor of moral philosophy at St. Andrews. In 1876 he became professor of divinity at the University of Edinburgh, receiving also an LL.D. from Glasgow and a D.D. from Edinburgh. In 1880 he went to the United States to lecture at Princeton. He was a corresponding member of the Institute of France, a fellow of the Royal Society of Edinburgh, and a contributor to the *Encyclopaedia Britannica*. He was unmarried. He finally retired in order to devote himself to literary work, but his health failed, and he died at Edinburgh soon after.

Flint was a retired, studious man, whose only recreation was walking. He was a slow, deliberate worker, whose work was always planned on a vast scale. He was more or less of a liberal, eager to reconcile theology with science. His style is straightforward and clear.

PRINCIPAL WORKS: The Philosophy of History in France and Germany, 1874; Theism, 1877; Antitheistic Theories, 1879; Vico, 1884; Socialism, 1894; Agnosticism, 1903; Philosophy as Scientia Scientarum, 1904.
ABOUT: Hole, W. Quasi Cursores; Scott, H. Fasti Ecclesiae Scotticae; Times November 26, 1910.

FLOWER, SIR WILLIAM HENRY (November 30, 1831-July 1, 1899), scientific writer, was born at Stratford-on-Avon. After attending University College, London, he studied medicine and surgery at the Middlesex Hospital. He received his M.B. degree from London University in 1851. In 1854 he volunteered for the medical service in the Crimean War, but his health broke and he had to resign from the army. He then became lecturer on anatomy, assistant surgeon, and curator of the museum at Middlesex Hospital. From 1861 to 1884 he was curator of the Hunterian Museum of the Royal College of Surgeons; it was in this office that he began his real work as a zoologist. In 1870 he also became Hunterian professor of anatomy and physiology at the College, succeeding the great Thomas Henry Huxley. He became a member of the council of the Zoological Society in 1862, and advanced through various offices to become president from 1879 to his death. In 1864 he became a fellow of the Royal Society, and later was on its council and its vice-president. In 1858 he married Georgianna Rosetta Smythe, by whom he had three sons and three daughters.

In 1884 Flower succeeded Sir Richard Owen as director of the Natural History Museum. He did much to make the museum really educational to the public, and in museum work was rated as an "originator and inventor." In 1889 he was president of the British Association for the Advancement of Science. He became a Knight Commander of the Bath in 1892. In 1898 he retired because of ill health.

Flower was a convinced Darwinian, and a sound research worker in zoology. He was a cautious, tactful writer who did not stir up controversy or advance the philosophy of biology, but whose work was useful and frequently valuable. His special fields were the study of the monetremata and marsupials and the whales, and the classification of mammals.

PRINCIPAL WORKS: Diagrams of the Nerves of the Human Body, 1861; An Introduction to the Osteology of the Mammalia, 1870; Fashion in Deformity, 1881; The Horse: A Study in Natural History, 1890; An Introduction to the Study of Mammals, 1898; Essays on Museums and Other Subjects, 1898.
ABOUT: Nature July 13, 1899; Year Book of the Royal Society 1901.

FONBLANQUE, ALBANY (WILLIAM) (1793-October 13, 1872), journalist, was born in London, the grandson of a naturalized Huguenot Frenchman. He attended the military school at Woolwich, intending to enter the Royal Engineers, but a severe illness, lasting two years, forced him to give up and he studied law instead. However, before he was twenty he had become so successful a journalist that he decided to adapt this as his profession. Another serious illness delayed his progress, following which he was on the staff of the *Morning Chronicle* and *The Times*. He was married in 1820, very unhappily.

From 1826 Fonblanque was the principal leader (editorial) writer on Leigh Hunt's radical *Examiner*. In 1830 he became the editor and a few years later the owner. He contributed regularly also to the *Westminster Review*. His influence at one time was enormous but it declined with the decline of the liberal cause. In 1847 he resigned as editor of *The Examiner* (he remained as proprietor until 1865) and went into the statistical department of the Board of Trade, a post for which he was obviously badly unfitted. Only his domestic cares and responsibilities could have made him undertake it. He had been offered the governorship of Nova Scotia, but could not tear himself from London; nevertheless he voluntarily retired from society about 1862.

All Fonblanque's writing was done in newspapers and magazines. He was purely a journalist, but an extremely brilliant one, spirited, pungent, and caustically witty. He was a very slow writer, and his work is finely polished. Personally he was a shy, sensitive, melancholy man, a radical reformer, but not a revolutionary. His only book is made up of editorials from *The Examiner*.

PRINCIPAL WORK: England Under Seven Administrations, 1837.
ABOUT: deFonblanque, E. B. Life and Letters of Anthony Fonblanque; Fox Bourne, H. R. English Newspapers.

FORBES, ARCHIBALD (1838-March 30, 1900), Scottish miscellaneous writer, was born in Morayshire, his father being a clergyman. He attended the University of Aberdeen from 1854 to 1857, then enlisted as a trooper in the Royal Dragoons. He began to write at this time by contributing articles to the *Cornhill Magazine*. He left the army in 1867, and until 1871 published his own magazine, the *London Scotsman*. From 1870 he was a noted newspaper correspondent, first for the *Morning Advertiser*, then for the *Daily News*. He reported the Franco-Prussian war, the Carlist war in Spain, went with the Prince of Wales (Edward VII) to India, then covered the Russo-Turkish war (being decorated by Czar Alexander II), and disturbances in Serbia and Afghanistan. In 1880 he reported the Zulu War in Africa. He then returned to London and spent the rest of his life as a free-lance journalist and writer. His wife was Louisa Meigs, daughter of an American general.

Forbes's biographical works are superficial, but his war books are vivid and full of good stories, since he knew everyone of prominence in his day and had led the most adventurous of lives.

PRINCIPAL WORKS: Chinese Gordon, 1884; Barracks, Bivouacs, and Battles, 1891; Memories and Studies of War and Peace, 1895.
ABOUT: Forbes, A. Memories and Studies of War and Peace; Illustrated London News April 7, 1900.

FORBES, EDWARD (February 12, 1815-November 18, 1854), scientist, was born in the Isle of Man, where his father was a banker. His brother became a well known geologist and philologist. He was educated at home and in day schools, where his chief interests were in literature, drawing, and above all in natural history. At sixteen he went to London to study art, but he had overestimated his talent and found no encouragement. In 1831, at his mother's wish, he entered the University of Edinburgh to study medicine. His heart, however, was not in his proposed profession, but in pure science, and he spent his vacations in studying natural history in his home island. He began writing in 1831, with an article in the London *Mirror*. In 1836 his mother died, and he immediately abandoned his medical studies. He had already made tours of scientific exploration in Scandinavia, France, Germany, Switzerland, and Algeria, specializing in marine biology.

In 1837 he returned to Edinburgh, spending his time in research and lecturing, with grants from the British Association for the Advancement of Science. In 1841 he was appointed naturalist to *H.M.S. Beacon,* which was touring the Levant. A fever contracted on this trip impaired his health permanently. In 1842 he was professor of botany at King's College, London, and curator of the museum of the Geological Society. In 1844 he became palaeontologist of the Geological Survey. During 1845 and 1846 he had to retire because of illness, but continued to write and do research. He was a fellow of both the Royal Society and the Royal Geographical Society, and president of the latter in 1853.

In 1848 Forbes married Emily Ashworth; the marriage resulted in a son and a daughter. In 1851 he became lecturer of the School of Mines of the Geological Survey, and in 1854 professor of natural history at the University of Edinburgh. Shortly after this appointment he died of kidney disease.

Forbes was no dry-as-dust scientist, but a genial man, kindly and lovable, with a streak of melancholy hidden by his boisterous songs and verses and his broad caricatures. His writing is almost entirely technical, but his *Literary Papers* give a little of his private quality.

PRINCIPAL WORKS: History of British Star Fishes, 1841; History of British Molluscs (with Sylvanus Hanley), 1848; Literary Papers, 1858; Natural History of European Seas (completed by R. Godwin Austen), 1859.
ABOUT: Wilson, G. & Geikie, A. Life of Edward Forbes.

FORBES, JAMES DAVID (April 20, 1809-December 31, 1868), Scottish scientist, was the youngest child of the seventh Baronet of Pitsligo. His mother was the first love of Sir Walter Scott. He was educated at home until at sixteen he entered the University of Edinburgh. He had been intended for the law, but his strong interest in physics turned him to science as a profession. He was a member of the Royal Society of Edinburgh at only nineteen, and was one of the founders of the British Association for the Advancement of Science in 1831. The next year he was elected a Fellow of the Royal Society of London, and the year after he became professor of natural philosophy at the University of Edinburgh. He was then only twenty-four. Four years later he was made dean of the Faculty of Arts. His vacations he spent exploring and investigating the Alpine glaciers, on which he was an authority.

In 1843 Forbes married Alicia Wauchope, by whom he had two sons and three daughters. The next two years he spent in Italy for his health. In 1845 he was awarded a government pension of £200 in recognition of his scientific services. In 1850 he made a survey of the Mer de Glace—at that time the only correct Alpine map in existence. During this year and the next he headed a glacier study expedition in Norway. A hemorrhage warned him that he was affected with tuberculosis, and he moved to Clifton for its mild climate. In 1853 Oxford conferred an honorary D.C.L. upon him. The next year he was back at the University of Edinburgh, and remained there for five years, then in 1850 went as principal to the United Colleges of St. Andrews. But his health declined constantly, until in 1864 he was obliged to refuse the presidency of the British Association. In 1867 he went to the Riviera, but it was too late for a cure; he returned to Clifton for medical treatment and died soon after.

Forbes was cold and dignified, rather vain and contentious, but sensitive and upright, and a charming travel writer. Most of his work was done in scientific papers; he published only one book. Besides his glacial theories, he conducted important experiments on heat.

PRINCIPAL WORK: Travels Through the Alps, 1843.

ABOUT: Forbes, D. F. Life and Letters (ed. by Sharp, Tait, & Adams-Reilly); Tyndall, J. Principal Forbes and His Biographers.

FORD, RICHARD (1796-September 1, 1858), travel writer, was the eldest son of Sir Richard Forbes, under-secretary of state and chief police magistrate of London. He was educated at Winchester and at Trinity College, Oxford, where he secured his B.A. in 1817 and his M.A. in 1822. He was called to the bar from Lincoln's Inn, but never practised. In 1824 he married a daughter of the Earl of Essex, and for the next four years he and his wife lived in Spain. He became thoroughly conversant with the country (then little known in England), and particularly with its art. In 1834 he bought an estate near Exeter, where he lived for the remainder of his life. He was a regular contributor to the *Quarterly Review, Edinburgh Review, Westminster Review,* and other leading periodicals. His wife had died, and in 1838 he married the Hon. Eliza Cranstoun. She too died, and in 1851 he married Mary Molesworth.

Besides being a writer, Ford was a talented painter and an art collector. He was the first to make the work of Murillo and especially of Velazquez known to English readers. His one book (his *Gatherings from Spain* is made up of matter deleted from later editions of the *Handbook*) is practically an encyclopedia, a far more important work than its modest title indicates. It is not only thoroughly comprehensive, but also eminently readable, his style being brilliant, spirited, and full of enthusiasm.

PRINCIPAL WORK: Handbook for Travellers in Spain, 1845.

ABOUT: Fraser's Magazine, October 1858.

FORMAN, HARRY (HENRY) BUXTON (July 11, 1842-June 15, 1917), scholar, was the son of George Ellery Forman, a retired naval surgeon, and Maria Courthope. He was born and educated at Teignmouth.

At the age of eighteen he entered the postal service as a clerk, and rose, during his long career of forty-seven years, to high position in that department. He was delegate, also, to four Postal Union congresses—at Paris, Lisbon, Vienna, and Washington. He was one of the first supporters of the idea of a post-office library and was its secretary for several years.

His literary career had its beginning in 1869 when he wrote a series of articles for *Tinsley's Magazine* which was reprinted in 1871 as *Our Living Poets.* He met Rossetti at this time, and supported his productions and those of many other poets of the day—William Morris, Meredith, and Rossetti were among his chief interests. Forman contributed to the *London Quarterly Review,* and from 1876 and almost to the very end of his life collected, edited, and criticized verse and miscellanies.

Forman is chiefly important in English literature for his painstaking editions of Keats and Shelley, which have been criticized unfavorably only for their excessive exactness; but his interests included the Brownings, Horne, Wade, and Jeremiah Wells, and with his brother, Alfred William Forman, he collaborated in a series of articles on Dante's *Divine Comedy* and translations of the *terza rima.*

He was married in 1869 to Laura Selle, who bore two sons and a daughter.

Forman's library, which was extensive, was brought to the United States after his death to be sold at auction.

PRINCIPAL WORKS: Criticism—Our Living Poets, 1871; Elizabeth Barrett Browning and Her Scarcer Books, 1896; George Meredith: Some Early Appreciations, 1909. Biography—The Books of William Morris, 1907. Editor—The Poetical Works of Shelley, 1876; The Prose Works of Shelley, 1880; Letters of John Keats to Fanny Brawne, 1878; Poetical Works and Other Writings of John Keats, 1883; Three Essays by John Keats, 1889; Poetry and Prose of John Keats, 1890; Poetical Works of John Keats, 1906; The Note Books of Shelley, 1911; Hitherto Unpublished Poems and Stories of Elizabeth Barrett Browning, 1914. Miscellaneous—The Shelley Library and Essays in Bibliography, 1886.

FORSTER, JOHN (April 2, 1812-February 2, 1876), though known chiefly as the biographer of Dickens deserves recognition in a somewhat more extensive field of literary activity. He was born at Newcastle, the son of Robert and Mary Forster, a descendent of good Northumbrian yeoman stock in moderate circumstances. He was the favorite nephew of his father's elder brother, who financed his schooling.

At the Newcastle grammar school he distinguished himself. In fact he was something of an infant prodigy, having a story published "when he was fresh from the nursery," and a play produced at the age of fourteen. Such accomplishments encouraged his uncle to send John to Cambridge in 1828, but the boy chose to enter University College in London after only one month at Cambridge.

Shortly after his arrival in London, and while a law student of the Inner Temple, Forster began to contribute regularly to newspapers and magazines. And at this time too he became acquainted with Leigh Hunt—the first of his very large circle of literary friends. In 1833 Forster was a regular contributor to *True Sun, The Courier, The Athenaeum,* and *The Examiner.* For the last named he was appointed chief critic of both literature and drama.

In 1836 was published the first of his five volumes of *Lives of the Statesmen of the Commonwealth,* the final volume of which was published in 1839. For two years (1842-43) Forster edited the *Foreign Quarterly Review* and during the latter year he was called to the bar at the Inner Temple. Shortly after this he was contributing to the *Edinburgh Review* and to Douglas Jerrold's *Shilling Magazine,* in which was published his "History for Young England."

For a period of some ten years, beginning in 1845, Forster was associated with a group of literary celebrities, including Dickens and Bulwer-Lytton, in the production of amateur theatricals. He played such rôles as Ford in the *Merry Wives of Windsor* and the title rôle in Hugo's *Hernani.*

In 1846 Forster succeeded Dickens as editor of the *Daily News,* but resigned within nine months. The following year he became editor of *The Examiner.*

His *Life and Adventures of Oliver Goldsmith* was published in 1848 after having been rewritten no less than twelve times. It was a sumptuous volume, illustrated by his friends Leech, Maclise, Doyle, and others—and it was a popular success.

In 1855 Forster resigned his editorship of *The Examiner* to become secretary to the lunacy commission, a position paying £800 a year. The following year he married the widow of Henry Colburn, a well known publisher. In 1861 Forster was made a lunacy commissioner, with a salary of £1500 a year, which post he held until poor health forced his resignation in 1872. It is noteworthy to mention in passing that a man whose income had probably never exceeded $10,000 in any year, should upon his death have left a valuable library of some 18,000 volumes, which included first folios of Shakespeare and many valuable manuscripts and first editions.

JOHN FORSTER

Forster's last years were largely taken up with work as literary executor of such friends as Landor, Alexander Dyce, and Charles Dickens. Malcolm Elwin in his excellent sketch (in *Victorian Wallflowers*) says: ". . . after Dickens' death, as his literary executor, he wrote a surprisingly satisfactory biography, in spite of the handicap of discretion, laid down his pen, and died in his turn, as if he were a faithful old watchdog bereft of his master."

Bulwer-Lytton wrote: "John Forster, author of *The Statesmen of the Commonwealth, Life of Oliver Goldsmith,* etc. A most sterling man, with an intellect at once massive and delicate. Few indeed have his strong practical sense and sound judgment; fewer still unite with such qualities his exquisite appreciation of latent beauties in literary art. Hence, in ordinary life there is no safer adviser about literary work, especially poetry; no more refined critic. A large heart naturally accompanies so masculine an understanding. . . . Most of my literary contemporaries are his intimate companions, and their jealousies of each other do not diminish their trust in him. More than any living critic, he has served to establish reputations. Tennyson and Browning owed him much in their literary career. . . In more private matters I am greatly indebted to his counsels. His reading is extensive. What faults he has lie on the surface. He is sometimes bluff to rudeness. But all such faults of manner (and they are his only ones) are but trifling inequalities in a nature solid and valuable as a block of gold."   D. C.

PRINCIPAL WORKS: *History & Biography*—Lives of the Statesmen of the Commonwealth, 1836-39; The Life & Adventures of Oliver Goldsmith, 1848; Life and Times of Oliver Goldsmith, 1854; Historical and Biographical Essays, 1858; The Arrest of the Five Members by Charles I, 1860; The Debates on the Grand Remonstrance, 1860; Life of Sir John Eliot, 1864; Life of Landor, 1869; Life of Dickens (3 vols) 1872-74.

ABOUT: Renton, R. John Forster and His Friendships; Ellis, S. M. Mainly Victorian; Elwin, W. Catalogue of the Forster Collection (see Preface); Elwin M. Victorian Wallflowers.

FOSTER, JOHN (September 17, 1770-October 15, 1843), essayist, was born in Yorkshire, the son of a small farmer and weaver who was also a Baptist preacher. He had practically no schooling, but was set to work at spinning and weaving in early childhood. He grew up prematurely old, studious, introspective, and high-strung. At seventeen he was sent to a minister for instruction as a preacher, and in 1791 and 1792 was a student at the Baptist College in Bristol. He then began his ministerial career, but it could not be described as a success. Until 1804 he filled charges in various towns in England and also in Dublin, but his invariable experience was that the congregations declined after his arrival. A school in Dublin in 1795 also failed, and he came near to arrest for association with Irish nationalists. A thyroid condition finally made preaching impossible for a time, and he resigned in 1806, determined to make his way by writing. He was a regular contributor to the *Eclectic Review* from that date until 1839.

In 1808 Foster married Maria Snooke, to whom his *Essays* had first been addressed as letters—a rather strange form of courtship! They had one son, who died in 1826, and his wife died of tuberculosis in 1832. For several years they lived in Gloucestershire, where Foster used the attic of their house as a workshop from which he poured forth articles which brought hardly a bare livelihood. In 1817 he found himself able to preach again, and continued as a minister to 1821. From 1822 to 1825 he was a lecturer in Bristol. He never wrote very much after his son's death in 1826. Ten years later his health gave way completely, and in 1843 he was found dead in bed in the house where he lived alone.

Foster was an eccentric, very outspoken, a minister who never baptized anyone though he was a Baptist, and a lifelong republican. His *Essays* were popular in their day, but will hardly bear rereading now.

PRINCIPAL WORKS: Essays, 1805; On the Evils of Popular Ignorance, 1820.

ABOUT: Ryland, J. E. The Life and Correspondence of John Foster.

FOWLER, THOMAS (September 1, 1832-November 20, 1904), philosopher, was born in Lincolnshire. He was educated at the Hull Grammar School, King William's College (Isle of Man), and Merton College, Oxford, where he was graduated B.A. in 1854 with first class honors in classics and mathematics. His religious and political views, both very conservative originally, had by this time become much liberalized. In 1855 he was ordained. He remained in Oxford all the remainder of his life, first as fellow and tutor, then as sub-rector of Lincoln College, then as proctor, and as professor of logic from 1873 to 1889. In 1881 he was made president of Corpus Christi College, and from 1899 to his death was vice-chancellor of Oxford. He died directly as a result of over-work in this office. He was unmarried. Fowler edited Bacon and Locke in addition to his original writings. His style was exact and lucid, but formal.

PRINCIPAL WORKS: Elements of Deductive Logic, 1867; Elements of Inductive Logic. 1870; Principles of Morals (with J. M. Wilson) 1875-86; Locke, 1880; Bacon, 1881; Progressive Morality, 1884.

ABOUT: Foster, J. Alumni Oxonienses; Athenaeum November 26, 1904.

FRASER, ALEXANDER CAMPBELL (September 3, 1819-December 2, 1914), Scottish philosopher, was born in Argyllshire, the son of a minister. He entered the University of Glasow at fourteen, then went to the University of Edinburgh. He was ordained in 1844 as a Free Church minister. In 1846 he became professor of logic and metaphysics at the Free Church College, Edinburgh, and in 1856 professor of philosophy at the University of Edinburgh, being dean of the faculty of arts from 1859. From 1850 to 1857 he edited the *North British Review*. He married Jemima Gordon Dyce in 1850; they had three sons and two daughters. In 1891 he resigned his professorship, but from 1894 to 1896 was Gifford lecturer on natural theology. He edited the works of Berkeley besides writing many philosophical books. He died at ninety-five, having written and retained his mental faculties to the last. His was the type of mind which matures slowly but remains effective to old age. Fraser was a great teacher, better as teacher and editor than as writer. He held a point of view "midway between Agnosticism and Hegelianism, advocating both a wholesome skepticism and a strong moral faith."

PRINCIPAL WORKS: Essays in Philosophy, 1856; Life and Letters of Berkeley, 1871; Locke, 1890; The Philosophy of Theism, 1895-6; Biographia Philosophica, 1904; Berkeley and Spiritual Realism, 1908.

ABOUT: Fraser, A. C. Biographia Philosophica.

FOX, CAROLINE (May 24, 1819-January 12, 1871), diarist, was born at Falmouth, Cornwall. Her father was a scientist. She was a precocious girl, who started her notable journal in 1835. She met many of the most eminent men of her time, some as visitors to her father, others who came to Cornwall in search of health for themselves or for relatives. Thomas Carlyle and John Stuart Mill were among her close friends. With John Sterling, Carlyle's friend, and then known as a clergyman and author, she was probably in love, though without confessing it to him or even to herself, for he was married and she was a thoroughly conventional woman. After his death in 1844 the vivacity deserted her writing, and a gentle melancholy took its place.

Except for an occasional visit to the Continent, she never left Falmouth. With her sister, Anna Maria Fox, she translated into Italian several English religious works. Her main contribution to literature, however, is her journal, in which intimate pictures of the great and near-great of her day appear. At once spiritual and intellectual, she was uncritical; there are no dark pictures in her diary, but everything is couched in terms of affectionate admiration. This is saved from mawkishness by the sprightly humor of at least the earlier portions. The journal, published after her death, is a valuable source-book for its period.

PRINCIPAL WORK: Memories of Old Friends (ed. by H. N. Pym) 1882.

FOX, HENRY R. V. See HOLLAND, LORD

FRANKLIN, SIR JOHN (April 16, 1786-June 11, 1847), explorer, was born in Lincolnshire, the youngest of twelve sons. He was sent to St. Ives and Louth Grammar Schools, and was intended for the church, but from childhood his bent was for the sea. His father tried to cure him by sending him on a voyage to Lisbon, but as soon as he returned he entered the Royal Navy. He was on the *Polyphemus* at the Battle of Copenhagen, then on the *Investigator*, which went to Australia; there Franklin for a year was assistant in the astronomical observatory set up at Sydney. Another voyage was to China. He returned to Europe in time to be on the famous *Bellerophon* at the Battle of Trafalgar.

In 1808 he became a lieutenant. At first his rise was slow. In 1814 he was on the *Bedford*, which helped fight the War of 1812 against the United States, and was at the Battle of New Orleans. His Arctic career began in 1818, with Captain Buchan. In 1819 Franklin was appointed commander of an expedition to amend the coastal geography of upper North America, and to navigate and map out the Canadian rivers. The expedition did not return until 1822, after a terrible march through the Barren Grounds in northern Canada, and a journey in all of 5,550 miles. In 1821 Franklin had been given the rank of commander, and he was now advanced to post-captain and made a Fellow of the Royal Society.

In 1823 he married Eleanor Anne Porden, a poet. She died of tuberculosis in 1825, just six days after Franklin left on his second Canadian trip, leaving a year-old daughter. This second journey lasted to 1827, and added 1,200 more miles to the known coast. On Franklin's return, in 1828, he married Jane Griffin. He was knighted in 1829. From 1830 to 1833 he was with the *Rainbow* in the Mediterranean. In 1836 he was made lieutenant governor of Van Diemen's Land (Tasmania), and remained there until 1843. He was much loved by the inhabitants, and was a wise and kindly governor; he founded a college and a scientific society, and did a great deal for the transported convicts who then made up much of the population.

In 1845 he set out for his last expedition, an attempt—which finally succeeded, though at the cost of the lives of all the party—to discover the Northwest Passage. He had been promoted to rear admiral, his ships being the *Erebus* and the *Terror*. No word came back from the expedition, and search and relief ships, American and English, some financed by Lady Franklin, began going out from 1848. By 1854 there was evidence that the whole party had perished, and final proof came in 1859. A record found gave the date of Franklin's own death.

Courageous, upright, genial, and plainspoken, Franklin in his two *Narratives* displays the same characteristics as a writer as were his as a man. His death by exposure was a severe loss to the world of exploration, and deprived the world of literature of what would undoubtedly have been his masterpiece of unaffected narration.

PRINCIPAL WORKS: Narrative of a Journey to the Shores of the Polar Sea, 1823; Narrative of a Second Expedition to the Shores of the Polar Sea, 1828.

ABOUT: Browne, J. A. The Northwest Passage and the Fate of Sir John Franklin; Leacock, S. B. Adventurers of the Far North; Markham, A. H. Life of Sir John Franklin; Osborn, S. Career, Last Voyage, and Fate of Sir John Franklin; Petermann, A. Sir John Franklin; Smith, T. B. Sir John Franklin and the Romance of the Northwest Passage; Traill, H. D. Life of Sir John Franklin, R. N.

FREEMAN, EDWARD AUGUSTUS (August 2, 1823-March 16, 1892), historian, was born at Harborne, Staffordshire, the only son of John Freeman and Mary Anne Carless. While still a child he lost both parents, and was reared by his paternal grandmother at Northampton.

A precocious boy, reading Roman history before seven, and knowing Latin and Greek at eleven, Freeman went to a school at Northampton and thence (1837) to one in Surrey and in 1840 to the Reverend R. Gutch, Segrave, Leicestershire. He was much interested in religion and felt the influence of the

EDWARD A. FREEMAN

High-Church movement. In 1841 Freeman was elected to a scholarship in Trinity College, Oxford; and he was graduated in 1845 and made a probationary fellow of Trinity. He was an enthusiastic student of ancient history; and, when, in 1846 his essay on the effects of the Norman Conquest failed to win a prize, he was stirred to interest in that subject. Accordingly, he determined to be an historian, and gave up thoughts of taking orders or of following architecture as a profession.

In 1847 he married Eleanor Gutch, the daughter of his former tutor, and lived near Oxford until 1848, when they moved to Gloucestershire. Here he read extensively, wrote reviews, contributed to collections of ballads, and produced *A History of Architecture* and a work on Gothic window tracery. In 1855 he moved to Lanrumney Hall, near Cardiff.

Failing to receive an appointment at Oxford, Freeman took a house near Wells, in Somerset, in 1860. At this time he contribued generously to periodicals, as many as ninety-six of his articles appearing in the *Saturday Review* during one year. Many of his writings concerned the University.

During the years from 1860 to 1870 Freeman established his reputation as a historian. From 1860 onward he made frequent continental trips, and he was in Dalmatia when, in 1875, the revolt against the Turks broke out in Herzegovina. Freeman sympathized heartily with the cause of the oppressed peoples and emphatically opposed the Turks. He raised more than five thousand pounds for Eastern relief, and he attacked not only the Turks, but English Conservatives, in bitter speeches. Because of the journal's attitude on affairs in the East he ceased to write for the

Saturday Review, relinquishing a large income from that source. In 1877 he toured Greece, where he was warmly received, and was honored by the princes of Servia and Montenegro.

Although his health had begun to decline, Freeman continued to work regularly, making two short trips to France in 1879. The season of 1881-82 he spent in the United States. In 1884 he was appointed regius professor of modern history at Oxford. While he disapproved of much at the University and was annoyed at having to be away from his Somerset home, Freeman made himself an influence among history students.

Because of ill health he made several visits to Sicily, working on a history of that island. In 1891 he went for the last time to Normandy and in 1892 to Spain. He was taken ill at Valencia and died, of smallpox, at Alicante on March 16, leaving his wife, two sons, and four daughters.

Lytton Strachey has branded Freeman as "a man of considerable learning, and of an ill temper even more considerable," and Saintsbury has referred to his "hectoring and snarling habit." Warm-hearted and devoted to his friends, Freeman was tactless and undiplomatic in his speech; and he never obtained a seat in Parliament, although he sought election. He tended to project personal feeling into scholarly and public issues, and he was not always fair to his opponents, particularly Froude. Against these less attractive qualities must be placed his tenderness and kindness, revealed in his vigorous condemnation of the English sport of fox-hunting, and his generosity in his work for Eastern nations.

"Few historians have been subjected to such searching criticism, such pitiless analysis, as Freeman," writes Benjamin S. Terry. "For much of this Freeman's imperious cocksureness was quite as much to blame as his faulty methods and hasty judgment." Despite his stressing of the "unity of history" and his exposures of pseudo-historians, Freeman's own work was far from perfect. In his search for original authorities he went no farther than to the printed chronicles; and his conclusions are many of them correspondingly out of date. Besides his neglect of manuscripts, his emphasis upon the Germanic nature of English institutions and the persistence of the Anglo-Saxon influence on national character has lowered his reputation among present-day historians. His works, described by Strachey as "remarkable for their soporific qualities and for containing no words but those of Anglo-Saxon descent," have been both praised and condemned as to style; they confine themselves generally to political events. Their value has been indicated by Terry: "His account of the succession of events and his background of antiquarian information abound with suggestion and can generally be relied on."   R. W. W.

PRINCIPAL WORKS: *Architecture*—Principles of Church Restoration, 1846; A History of Architecture, 1849; Essay on the Origin and Development of Window Tracery in England, 1850; On the Architecture of Llandaff Cathedral, 1850. *History*—The History and Conquests of the Saracens, 1856; A History of Federal Government, 1863; History of the Norman Conquest of England, 1867-79; Old English History for Children, 1869; History of the Cathedral Church of Wells, 1870; Historical Essays, 1871, 1873, 1879, 1892; The Growth of the English Constitution From the Earliest Times, 1872; General Sketch of European History, 1872; History of Europe, 1875; The Ottoman Power in Europe, 1877; Short History of the Norman Conquest of England, 1880; The Historical Geography of Europe, 1881; The Reign of William Rufus and the Accession of Henry the First, 1882; Methods of Historical Study, 1886; Chief Periods of European History, 1886; William the Conqueror, 1888; History of Sicily From the Earliest Times, 1891-92, 1894. *Poetry*—Poems Legendary and Historical (with G. W. Cox) 1850. *Miscellaneous*—Historical and Architectural Sketches, 1876; Subject and Neighbour-Lands of Venice, 1881; Lectures to American Audiences, 1882; Some Impressions of the United States, 1883; Sketches From French Travel, 1891; The Story of Sicily, Phoenician, Greek, and Roman, 1892.

ABOUT: Fiske, J. A Century of Science and Other Essays; Harrison, F. Tennyson, Ruskin, Mill, and Other Literary Estimates; Stephens, W. R. W. The Life and Letters of Edward A. Freeman (includes complete bibliography).

FRERE, JOHN HOOKHAM (May 21, 1769-January 7, 1846), satirist, translator, and diplomatist, was born at Roydon Hall, Norfolk, the eldest son of John Frere, M.P., and Jane Hookham.

He attended school at Eton, where he had among his schoolfellows Canning, with whom he joined in the publication of the magazine *The Microcosm*. In 1788 he matriculated at Caius College, Cambridge, from which he was graduated in 1792 with the degree of B.A. and with the distinction of having won the Members' Prize for a Latin essay. In 1795 he was granted his M.A., and was elected a fellow.

A post in the foreign office next occupied him. He succeeded Canning as undersecretary for foreign affairs in 1799, having been his chief assistant in the publication of the short-lived but brilliant *Anti-Jacobin* (1797). In 1800 he was made envoy extraordinary to the Portuguese court, and in 1802 went to Madrid in a similar capacity, returning in 1804 to be made privy councillor. Three years later he served as ambassador to Prussia, and in 1808 returned to Madrid.

At this time the Spanish insurrection against France had broken out. Frere was an enthusiastic student of the past glories of Spain, and disliked the French, and he championed the Spanish cause with more warmth than wisdom. He induced the British government to take part in the War of the Peninsula, and was responsible for the death of Moore at

JOHN HOOKHAM FRERE

Coruna and for the subsequent defeat of his army. There was much unfavorable comment, and Frere was replaced by the Marquess of Wellesley. This marked the end of his diplomatic career. Although later offered the post of ambassador to St. Petersburg, he refused, and he later refused two offers of a peerage.

He married, in 1816, Elizabeth Jemima, dowager countess of Errol, and daughter of Joseph Blake. For the sake of her health, ne left England in 1820, and except for a visit in 1821, never returned. He lived at Malta until his death, which resulted from apoplexy.

Frere, with his erudition, wit, and brilliance, could have occupied a more commanding place in English letters, and his failure to do so may he said to have resulted from his own choice. He was completely unambitious for fame, and preferred the life of a country gentleman and the company of friends and books to any acquirement of distinction or popularity.

He is, despite his small production, a writer of great accomplishments in the fields of satire and translation. The humorous articles and poems written for the *Anti-Jacobin* are first-rate. His chief original work, the *Specimen of an Intended National Work . . . Intended to Comprise the Particulars Relating to King Arthur and His Round Table* (1817)—an imitation of the *Morgante Maggiore* of Luigi Pulci, a 15th century Italian mock-heroic poet—was the stylistic model of Byron's *Beppo* and *Don Juan*. By a strange turn of chance, Frere, who had thus introduced into English literature the Italian comic epos, was one of a group including Thomas Moore who, at Byron's request, read the first canto of *Don Juan* and censured it as unfit to print—for which they were scornfully referred to as the "damned puritanical committee" by the angry author.

Frere's translations of Aristophanes are ranked among the very finest renderings in the English language. His versions avoided with great skill the two pitfalls of translation from the ancient classics, too pedantic literalness or too modern translation of the idiomatic passages, and preserved the wit and freshness of the original in great measure.

Among the numerous friends of Frere, in addition to Canning, were the minister Pitt, Sir Walter Scott, Byron, and Thomas Moore. His nephew and biographer, Sir Bartle Frere, says that "no man was ever more beloved by his friends." He describes his uncle as having "a grand personal appearance. He was a very tall and altogether a very large man with bold commanding features, a good nose and brow, and a peculiar expression, perhaps of sarcasm, with perhaps a touch of hauteur. . ." Frere's wit was as well known as his generosity to the poor, and both were long remembered. R. M.

PRINCIPAL WORKS: *Satire*—The Monks and the Giants; Prospectus and Specimen of an Intended National Work. ., 1817, 1818. *Translations*—The Acharnians, Knights, and Birds of Aristophanes, 1839; The Frogs of Aristophanes, 1839; Theognis Restitutus, 1842. *Miscellaneous*—Fables for a Five-Year Old, 1830. *Collected Works*—Works, 1872.

ABOUT: Courthope, W. H. History of English Poetry (Vol. 6); Eichler, A. John Hookham Frere: Sein Leben und Seine Werke; Frere, J. H. Works (see Memoir by Sir B. Frere); Edinburgh Review 135:472 April 1872; Quarterly Review 132:28 January April 1872.

FROUDE, JAMES ANTHONY (April 23, 1818-October 20, 1894), historian and essayist, was born at Dartington, Devon, second son of the Venerable R. H. Froude, Archdeacon of Totnes, and Margaret Spedding.

After attending Westminster School from 1830 to 1833, he received two years of private tutoring at Merton, and matriculated at Oriel College, Oxford, in 1836, taking a second class in the final examinations in 1840. In 1842 he won the Chancellor's English Essay Prize and a fellowship at Exeter; in 1844 he took deacon's orders, which, despite the upheaval of his religious beliefs so soon to follow, he did not abjure until 1872.

One of Froude's fellow-students at Oriel was James Henry Newman, afterwards Cardinal Newman. The college was then the seat of the ecclesiastical revival, and Froude came strongly under its influence, all the more so since his elder brother, R. H. Froude, was a leader in the Oxford movement. The younger Froude, attracted to Newman, as were most people, collaborated with him in writing *The Lives of the English Saints*, and was himself the author of the *Life of St. Ninian*, published in 1844.

Despite the influence of Newman, Froude, who was strongminded then as later, underwent a change of heart in religious matters. He had been reading Lessing, Carlyle, Goethe, and other unorthodox authors, and when his *Shadows of the Clouds*, a work of fiction, appeared in 1847, under the pseudonym of "Zeta," to be followed in 1849 by *The Nemesis of Faith*, his loss of faith was obvious. The majority of the copies of the first work were bought up by his father, and the second book was publicly burned at Exeter by Dr. Sewell. Froude thereupon resigned his fellowship, surrendered the appointment he had just received as headmaster of the high school at Hobart Town, Tasmania, and decided to become a professional man of letters.

He began to write for *Fraser's Magazine* (of which he was editor from 1860 to 1874) and for the *Westminster Review*, and his fine style attracted almost immediate notice. Such essays as those on Job (1853) and Spinoza (1854) were highly commended, and those on "England's Forgotten Worthies," written in 1852, were a sort of advance guard for his *History of England*, of which the first two volumes appeared in 1856. This work, which embraced the period from the fall of Cardinal Wolsey to the Spanish Armada, was completed by the publication, in 1870, of the remaining two volumes. Despite the fact that the work was published while the popularity of Macaulay's history was at its height, it was successful, although there was much unfavorable criticism of Froude's inaccuracies and his treatment of Henry VIII and Elizabeth. Goldwin Smith and E. A. Freeman, in particular, singled out the work for harsh criticism, and Freeman continued to harp upon its defects for a quarter of a century.

Froude's career was made up of the controversies he aroused at every turn, though he seems to have occupied himself little with confutation. He was not a man to sidestep plain speaking; in 1869, upon being appointed Lord Rector of St. Andrews, he made pointed remarks about the duty of the clergy in his address of acceptance. His *History of the English in Ireland* (1872) was attacked on both sides, even Lecky writing a reply to it. In 1874 he made a trip to the Cape of Good Hope, at the invitation of Lord Carnarvon, to report upon conditions there, and his report had much to do with that minister's adoption of policy. Upon a subsequent visit, however, Froude, urging a South African confederation, unfortunately alienated the governor and the residents, and caused the complete downfall of Carnarvon's plans. Worst of all for him, he published, in his capacity of literary executor of Carlyle, all that author's minutiae of correspondence and business, as well as the diary and letters of his wife.

JAMES ANTHONY FROUDE

The Carlyle-Froude controversy still lives. Froude met Carlyle in 1849, and the famous author took an immediate interest in his young admirer, with whom he continued in close association all his life. It was understood that Froude was to act as Carlyle's literary executor; and although Carlyle opposed the idea of a biography, feeling that his *Reminiscences* would be sufficient, Froude persuaded him that since there were inevitably going to be biographies, an authorized one would be of advantage; and Carlyle, consenting, gave him *carte blanche* in the matter.

In 1881 Froude duly published the *Reminiscences,* and in 1882 the first two volumes of the biography appeared, to be succeeded by the last two in 1884. These, with the appearance of Mrs. Carlyle's correspondence in 1883, practically laid Carlyle bare to the world, and indignation was heaped upon Froude. He was even accused of having deliberately blackened Carlyle's reputation.

After the publication of the Carlyle biography, Froude turned his attention to contemporary politics, and wrote a brilliant sketch of Disraeli. He refused, however, to do the biography, saying that Disraeli "lived in and by the House of Commons," and that he was "no lover of Parliaments."

Froude's implacable critical opponent, Freeman, died in 1892, and Froude was asked to succeed him in the chair of modern history at Oxford. He accepted, and delivered lectures which were conspicuously successful, especially those on Erasmus, which appeared in book form just before his death. In the fall of 1894, after an illness and nervous prostration of several months duration, he died in his library at Woolcot, Salcombe.

Froude was twice married. His first wife was Charlotte Grenfell, sister-in-law of his friend Charles Kingsley. This marriage took place in 1849, and Mrs. Froude died in 1860. In 1861 Froude married a Miss Warre, whom he survived.

He is described as a man of fair height with a large head, black hair, and very dark eyes. Inclined to shyness, he had nevertheless many friends, and it was a common saying that he could win over any man or woman he chose. His conversation was considered delightful.

He was one of the supreme masters of English prose, ranking in modern times with Newman, Pater, Ruskin, and Macaulay, and perhaps less faulty than any of these. His style is perfectly transparent, flexible, eloquent, and smooth, and his employment of it was remarkably consistent. Even his harshest critics agree that he was one of the great stylists, however they may feel about his trustworthiness as historian or as thinker. For it cannot be denied that Froude was congenitally careless in his use of facts, and even in the simple mechanical matter of transcribing. Yet, although he was openly contemptuous of the expression "scientific history" and declared that facts could be used (like statistics) to show anything, he defended the accuracy of his history of England and stated positively that there were no more than twenty-five errors, great and small, in the entire work. His historical accuracy may be debated, but it cannot be denied that he actually sought the truth. There was perhaps more of the artist than of the thinker about him. His historical personages have a lifelike quality which is remarkable, and his narrative is striking in its vitality. Perhaps it was his weakness that he thought of history as the succession, not of social movements, but of great personages. Such works as his *Oceana* and *Short Studies of Great Subjects* were popular; his style charmed, and there was solid matter back of it. Of him Sir Leslie Stephen said "No man of his generation, I think, had a finer literary faculty." R. M.

PRINCIPAL WORKS: *History*—History of England From the Fall of Wolsey to the Spanish Armada, 1856, 1870; The English in Ireland in the Eighteenth Century, 1872-74; The English in the West Indies, 1888; The Divorce of Catherine of Aragon, 1891; The Spanish Story of the Armada, 1892; Lectures on the Council of Trent, 1896. *Biography*—Life of St. Ninian, 1844; Caesar, 1879; Bunyan, 1880; Carlyle: 1795-1855, 1882; Life of Carlyle: 1834-81, 1884; Luther, 1883; Life and Letters of Erasmus, 1894; English Seamen in the 16th Century, 1895. *Fiction*—Shadows of the Clouds, 1847; The Two Chiefs of Dunboy, 1889. *Miscellaneous*—The Nemesis of Faith, 1849; Suggestions on the Teaching of English History, (Oxford Essays, Vol 1) 1855; Short Studies on Great Subjects (4 series) 1867-83; Oceana, 1886; My Relations with Carlyle, 1903. *Editor*—The Letters of Jane Welsh Carlyle, 1883.

ABOUT: Birrell, A. Miscellanies; Harrison, F. The Choice of Books; Paul, H. The Life of J. A. Froude; Stephen, Sir L. Studies of a Biographer (Vol. 3); Bookman 54:8 April 1918; North American Review 157:676 December 1894.

FROUDE, RICHARD HURRELL (March 25, 1803-February 28, 1836), poet and essayist, was born in Devonshire. His father was an archdeacon; his younger brother the historian, James Froude. Richard Froude was educated at Ottery Free School (where he lived with Coleridge's brother), at Eton, and at Oriel College, Oxford, where he received his B.A. in 1824, and his M.A. in 1827. He was a tutor in the college to 1830, and was ordained deacon in 1828, and priest in 1829.

He was a close friend of Cardinal Newman (not yet, of course, either a Cardinal or a Roman Catholic), and they were almost constant companions. Like Newman, Froude was a high churchman and a Tory, a member of the high church "Oxford Movement," and had he lived might very well have followed his friend into the Roman Catholic church.

From 1831, however, it was apparent his life would be short, since he was advanced in tuberculosis. In 1832 he traveled in the south of Europe, first with his father and then with Newman, and in Rome wrote with Newman the religious poems afterwards published as *Lyra Apostolica,* many of which were published in the *British Magazine,* Froude's being distinguished by the signature β.

He returned to England in 1833, and in 1834 and 1835 was in the West Indies, but his health grew worse instead of better, and he returned to his father's home to die. He was never married.

James Froude wrote after his brother's death that his was one of the finest intellects he had ever known; but the work Richard Froude left behind him showed only the barest promise of what he might have been. His writings display his strong prejudices more than any other quality, though many of his poems have lyric beauty of a high order.

PRINCIPAL WORKS: Lyra Apostolica (with Newman) 1833; Tracts for the Times (with Newman, Keble, Pusey, etc.) 1833-38; Remains (ed. by J. B. Mozley) 1837-39.

ABOUT: Guiney, L. I. Memoranda and Comments; Mozley, J. B. Reminiscences.

FULLERTON, LADY GEORGIANA CHARLOTTE (September 23, 1812-January 19, 1885), novelist and philanthropist, was born at Tixall Hall, Staffordshire, the youngest daughter of Lord Granville Leveson-Gower and Lady Harriet Elizabeth Cavendish, daughter of the fifth Duke of Devonshire.

She began to read at the age of four, and it is said that at ten she had read Chateaubriand's *Génie du Christianisme* with understanding and enjoyment, her early knowledge

LADY GEORGIANA FULLERTON

of French being due to residence in Paris, where her father was ambassador. In 1833 she married a young Irish guardsman, Alexander Fullerton, and after a visit to England continued to live at the English Embassy in Paris, where she remained until 1841.

Her husband became a Roman Catholic in 1843, and three years later she was received into the Church. Meanwhile her literary career had begun. She had commenced to write at the age of thirteen, but it was not until 1844 that her first work, a novel entitled *Ellen Middleton,* was published. This tale of the promptings of conscience was well received, and was favorably reviewed by Gladstone.

This was followed by several other works, until in 1854 the great tragedy of her life occurred—the death of her only son, at the age of twenty-one. This sorrow, from which she never recovered, led to her resolution to devote her life exclusively to charity. She wore mourning for the rest of her life, and joined the third order of St. Francis of Rome, of whom she wrote a biography in 1855.

She continued to write, principally to earn the money for her numerous benevolences, and her last work, a life of Lady Falkland (1585-1639), published in 1883, brought the total of her works to over thirty. Hers was the first translation into English of the *Fioretti* of St. Francis of Assisi. Her novels, which enjoyed a considerable success, were moral in tone, Catholic in background, and directed toward furthering the understanding of Catholicism and inspiring its adherents. They were much praised for their spiritual character.

Lady Fullerton died at Bournemouth, where for the ten years before her death she had spent most of her time. She was celebrated for her charities, was instrumental in bringing the Sisters of St. Vincent de Paul to England, and was co-founder of a religious community known as "The Poor Servants of the Mother of God Incarnate." Cardinal Newman knew and admired her for her long career of self-sacrifice.   R. M.

PRINCIPAL WORKS: *Fiction*—Ellen Middleton, 1844; Grantley Manor, 1847; Lady Bird, 1852; La Comtesse de Bonneval (in French) 1857; Rose Leblanc (in French) 1861; Too Strange Not to be True, 1864; Constance Sherwood, 1865; A Stormy Life, 1867; Mrs. Geral's Niece, 1869; Seven Stories, 1873; A Will and a Way, 1881. *Biography*—Life of St. Francis of Rome, 1855; Life of Louisa de Carvajal, 1873; Life of Elizabeth, Lady Falkland, 1883. *Poetry*—The Old Highlander and Other Poems, 1849; The Gold Digger and Other Poems, 1872. *Translations*—The Little Flowers of St. Francis, 1864; Life of the Marchesa G. Faletti di Baroto, by Silvio Pellico, 1866.

ABOUT: Craven, P. M. A. A. Lady Georgiana Fullerton; Riesch, H. Frauengeist der Vergangenheit.

FURNIVALL, FREDERICK JAMES
(February 4, 1825-July 2, 1910), scholar, was born at Egham, Surrey, eldest son of Dr. George F. Furnivall and Sophia Barwell.

His early schooling was obtained at Englefield Green and at Turnham Green. He attended University College, London, and matriculated at Trinity College, Cambridge, taking the degree of B.A. in 1846 and that of M.A. in 1849. He practised law for a short time, but was soon diverted to work in philology and educational promotion.

A born organizer, Furnivall was associated with the founding of Working Men's College, and became assistant secretary of the Philological Society, a post he occupied for sixty years. In 1858 a supplement to the dictionaries of Richardson and Johnson was proposed, and Furnivall undertook part of the research; however, he soon concluded that what was needed was a new dictionary, and thus the *New English Dictionary* was begun. Furnivall did the research, and was for a short time editor. Out of the philological work done for this dictionary arose the idea of the Early English Text Society, founded by Furnivall in the early 'sixties to publish ancient English literature, and first of a series of such associations which he brought into being: The Chaucer Society, 1868; Ballad Society, 1868; New Shakespeare Society, 1873; Browning Society, 1881; Wyclif Society, 1882, and Shelley Society, 1885. All these were guided by Furnivall, who managed the Early English Text Society for fifty years. His other services to literature included the performances of Browning's plays which he brought about and his constant encouragement of worthy scholarship.

His pecuniary rewards for his lifetime of hard work were extremely poor. It is said that £500 would be a generous estimate of his earnings for a long career of earnest endeavor. Other rewards were not lacking, however; he was made Honorable Fellow of Trinity College, a member of the British Academy, and received the degrees of Ph.D. from Berlin in 1884 and of D.Litt. from Oxford in 1901.

Furnivall's service to English scholarship is incalculable. Over a hundred texts were edited by him or upon his recommendation. A poor writer and a crude critic, his importance lay in his care as editor and in his rescuing of valuable works from oblivion. The Six-Text Chaucer is his most important work; and he encouraged the publication of such treasures as Skeat's edition of *Piers Plowman* and of Chaucer's prose, and assisted Dr. Hales in editing the Percy Folio manuscripts.

His death, after a short illness, brought to an end one of the busiest and stormiest careers ever the lot of man of letters. For Furnivall was as tactless as he was energetic, and as fearless; he never hesitated to make an enemy and was constantly embroiled. His most famous controversy was that with Swinburne, who ridiculed the metrical studies of the New Shakespeare Society, whereupon Furnivall, in a violent and scurrilous squib, called him "Pigsbrooke"—a pun on his name —and dealt summarily with all who interfered.

Despite these fiery tendencies, Furnivall was charming and had many friends who respected and loved him. Possibly his stormy temperament caused his divorce in 1883 from Eleanor Dalziel, whom he had married in 1862. Of his two children, the son, Percy, a well known surgeon, survived him.

F. J. FURNIVALL

Furnivall's favorite recreation was sculling, and he founded a rowing club for young women. It is said that he confidently expected to live to be a hundred, and in view of his extraordinary vitality, his illness and death at eighty-five were a great shock to his circle.

R. M.

WORKS: Numerous scholarly editions; see body of sketch.
ABOUT: Anon. Frederick James Furnivall: A Volume of Personal Record; Library 3:1 January 1912.

GAIRDNER, JAMES (March 22, 1828-November 4, 1912), Scottish historian and biographer, was born in Edinburgh, his father being a physician. He was educated privately at home. From 1846 to 1893 he was a clerk in the Public Record Office. With John Sherren Brewer he prepared, from 1856, the *Calendar of Letters and Papers of the Reign of Henry VIII*, and himself edited many other ancient documents. In 1867 he married Annie Sayer, and they had one daughter. He died in his home in Middlesex at eighty-four. Gairdner's historical and biographical volumes are logical, vigorous, and clear. He was naturally conservative, and rather academic in his viewpoint and style, but markedly fair-minded.

PRINCIPAL WORKS: Life of Richard III, 1878; Studies in English History, 1881; Lollardy and the Reformation in England, 1908-13.
ABOUT: Gairdner, J. Lollardy and the Reformation in England (see Preface to Vol. 4 by W. Hunt).

GALL, SIR WILLIAM (1777-February 4, 1836), classical topographer and archaeologist, was born in Derbyshire. He was educated at Jesus College, Cambridge, and then became a fellow of Emmanuel College, receiving his B.A. in 1798 and his M.A. in 1804. He also studied in the school of the Royal Academy in London, but though he illustrated his own books, his drawings are distinguished more by exactness than by beauty. In 1803 he visited the Troiad and fixed the site of Troy. In recognition of his services to classical learning he was knighted the same year, following a further tour of the Ionian Islands. He spent from 1804 to 1806 also in Greece, his interest at that time being more in topography than in actual archaeology. In 1814 he went to Italy as chamberlain to Princess, later Queen, Caroline. From 1820 he lived in Italy entirely, having houses both in Rome and in Naples. There he became a kind of unofficial ambassador of England for all English visitors. He was very sociable, kindly, and courteous, but garrulous and something of a bore—all of which characteristics appear in his writing. For years he was a cripple from gout, being unable to walk without crutches, and he finally died in Naples from this disease at less than fifty. His books were once standard works, but are now completely outdated.

PRINCIPAL WORKS: Topography of Troy, 1804; Geography and Antiquities of Ithaca, 1807; Itinerary of Greece, 1810; Itinerary of the Morea, 1817; Pompeiana (with J. P. Gandy) 1817-19; Narrative of a Journey in the Morea, 1823; Topography of Rome and Its Vicinity, 1834.
ABOUT: Athenaeum May 19, 1836.

GALT, JOHN (May 2, 1779-April 11, 1839), novelist, was born in the quiet Scottish town of Irvine, in Ayrshire, the son of John Galt, captain of a West Indiaman, and his wife, who seems to have exercised more influence over the son than did her more easy-going husband. Young John himself, the oldest of three children, was always a sensitive lad, who preferred books to games, and whose interest in ballads and legends led him to associate with old women rather than with his own contemporaries. His first poem was written at the tender age of six when some one presented him with two larks, whose "birth, parentage, and intended education" he immediately celebrated in verse.

His schooling varied with the state of his health, for he studied under a private tutor as well as attending the grammar school. When he was about ten, however, his family moved to Greenock, where he went to two schools, the first in the Royal Close, the other kept by "one M'Gregor." At the latter his most intimate friends were William Spence, the mathematician, and the poet, James Park. With Spence, Galt carried on many scientific experiments.

On leaving school Galt took up his life as junior clerk in the Customs House, along with Park. The two spent their evenings in study and writing. Galt later was employed by the mercantile house of James Miller & Company. At this establishment he asserted his independence when he followed the writer of a letter of abuse to Edinburgh and made him apologize to the firm. Shortly afterwards, Galt decided to leave Greenock, and in 1804 he started for London, armed with letters of introduction and an epic poem, entitled *The Battle of Largs*, which he published in 1804 and then suppressed.

Life in London led to a partnership with a man named M'Lachlan. For the most part, however, Galt was left to his own devices and he spent his time in experiments and literary work. In 1808 the business collapsed. Thereafter Galt began the study of law at Lincoln's Inn. Within a year he departed for two years of travel abroad. Among his chance acquaintances on this tour was the poet, Lord Byron, whom he met on the boat going from Gibraltar to Malta. After a visit to Greece Galt finally went to Turkey, where he cooked up a scheme for smuggling English goods into European centers of trade. But the plan never materialized, and he returned to London in 1811.

JOHN GALT

For a time he edited the *Political Review* and in 1812 he published his experiences abroad in a volume entitled *Voyages and Travels in the Years 1809, 1810, and 1811.* At this period, too, he was the guest of Alexander Tilloch, editor of the *Philosophical Magazine,* and a year later he married Tilloch's daughter, Elizabeth. His *Life of Wolsey* also came out in 1812, and he tried his hand at a series of blank verse tragedies. In 1814 he edited a magazine called *The Rejected Theatre.* His own play, *The Witness,* was acted in Edinburgh in 1818. A son, John was born in 1814; Thomas followed in 1815; and Alexander in 1817. Meanwhile Galt supported his growing family by writing articles for *Lives of the British Admirals,* by contributing to the *Monthly Magazine,* and publishing a tale called *The Majolo.* For a time he lived in Chelsea, although by 1818 he was in the vicinity of Greenock, and finally in London.

His greatest literary activity began in 1820 with the publication in *Blackwood's Edinburgh Magazine* of his tale, *The Ayrshire Legatees.* His narrative, *Annals of the Parish,* followed. Other Scottish novels and sketches were equally popular. By 1823 he had moved to Eskgrove House near Musselburgh. That he did not spend all his time in writing is evidenced by the fact that in 1824 he was appointed secretary to a commission appointed to investigate land claims in Canada. In February 1825 he took up his new duties in Canada. Not always tactful, he often fell into political disputes, but for the most part he was surprisingly efficient. He returned to London in June to make his report, and was ordered back to Canada the next year. Before he set out again, however, he wrote two novels, *The Omen* and *The Last of the Lairds.*

His second mission to Canada was beset with political difficulties. As the Canada Company's superintendent he directed plans for settlement, only to meet with the opposition and criticism of Lieutenant Governor Maitland. Despite such setbacks, he made progress with his system of land disposal and enjoyed life with his family in a log cabin in the woods. The town of Guelph was founded by him, while another town was named Galt in his honor. His literary activities were suspended until 1828, when his contributions to Canadian emigration ceased with his forced resignation and subsequent return to England.

Back in London his health suffered and he was reduced to poverty. In fact he spent a year in King's Bench Prison for debts incurred in the education of his sons. While in prison he wrote a novel called *Lawrie Todd: or, The Settlers in the Woods,* based on his own experiences in Canada. His *Life of Lord Byron* also appeared in 1830, as did a second novel, *Southennan.* Indeed, his last years were spent in writing one novel after another, in order to "wrench life from famine." Attempts to secure money for his services to the Canada Company were in vain. His health grew steadily worse. In 1832 at his house at Old Brompton he suffered a stroke, which was followed by other attacks. All three of his sons had departed for Canada, and in 1834 Galt went back to Scotland, where he died in Greenock on April 11, 1839.

In middle life Galt was accounted "a man of herculean frame, over six feet in height, and inclining to corpulency, with jet-black hair as yet ungrizzled, nose almost straight, small but piercing eyes, and finely rounded chin." To Carlyle, who saw Galt bowed down by poverty and ill health, Galt looked, on the other hand, old and "lovable with pity." He was always fond of society and his friends often met him at the "evenings" of Lady Blessington, with whom he was an especial favorite.

Probably Galt's greatest fault as a writer was his prolixity. In thirty-five years he wrote sixty volumes, twelve plays, as well as fugitive articles. "It would have been better for his fame," it is said, "if he had written four or five of his Scotch novels and nothing else." Galt rated himself with Sir Walter Scott. In reality he never attained Scott's popularity, although his *Annals of the Parish* has often been consulted as a source book of Scottish history. As the "forerunner of the realistic movement in Scottish fiction," he has an acknowledged place in literary history.

B. D. S.

PRINCIPAL WORKS: *Poetry*—The Battle of Largs, 1804; The Crusade, 1816; Poems, 1833; A Contribution to the Greenock Calamity Fund, 1835; The Demon of Destiny and Other Poems, 1839. *Fiction* —The Majalo, 1816; The Earthquake, 1820; The Ayrshire Legatees, 1821; Annals of the Parish, 1821; The Steam-Boat, 1822; The Provost, 1822; Sir Andrew Wylie, 1822; The Entail, 1823; Ringan Gilhaize, 1823; The Gathering of the West, 1823; The Spaewife, 1823; Rothelan, 1824; The Omen, 1825; The Last of the Lairds, 1826; Lawrie Todd, 1830; Southennan, 1830; Bogle Corbet, 1831; The Member, 1832; The Radical, 1832; Stanley Buxton, 1832; Eben Erskine, 1833; The Stolen Child, 1833; The Ouranalogos, 1833; Stories of the Study, 1833; The Book of Life, 1841; The Fatal Whisper, 1841; Haddad-Ben-Ahab, 1841; The Unguarded Hour, 1841; The Painter, 1841; The Howdie and Other Tales, 1923; A Rich Man and Other Stories, 1925; Works (ed. by D. Storrar Meldrum) 1895. *Biography*—The Life and Administration of Cardinal Wolsey, 1812; The Life and Studies of Benjamin West: Part I, 1816; George the Third, 1820; The Life, Studies, and Works of Benjamin West: Part II, 1820; The Life of Lord Byron, 1830; The Lives of the Players, 1831; Autobiography, 1833; The Literary Life and Miscellanies, 1834. *Drama*—The Tragedies of Maddalen, Agamemnon. Lady Macbeth, Antonia, and Clytemnestra, 1812; Edward III, 1814; The Sorceress: The Prophetess; Hector; Orpheus; The Apostate; Love, Honour and Interest; The Word of Honour; The Mermaid; The Witness; The Masquerade; The Minstrel; The Watch House, *in* The New British Theatre, 1814-1815; The Appeal, 1818. *Miscellaneous*—Cursory Reflections on Political and Commercial Topics, 1812; Voyages and Travels, 1812; Letters From the Levant, 1813; All the Voyages Round the World, 1820; A Tour of Europe and Asia, 1820; The Wandering Jew: or, The Travels and Observations of Hareach the Prolonged, 1820; An Abridgement of the Most Popular Modern Voyages and Travels, 1820; Pictures: Historical and Biographical, 1821; Modern Geography and History, 1823; The Bachelor's Wife, 1824; The Universal Traveller, 1824.

ABOUT: Douglas, G. The "Blackwood" Group; Galt, J. Autobiography; Galt, J. The Literary Life and Miscellanies; Galt, J. Works (see Memoir by D. Storrar Meldrum); Gillies, R. P. Memoirs of a Literary Veteran; Gordon, R. K. John Galt; Hall, Mrs. S. C. A Book of Memories; Jerdan, W. Men I Have Known; Millar, J. H. A Literary History of Scotland; Scadding, H. Toronto of Old; Bentley's Miscellany 18:285 1845; Blackwood's Edinburgh Magazine 159:871 June 1896; The New Review 13:207 August 1895.

GALTON, SIR FRANCIS (February 16, 1822-January 17, 1911), scientist, was a first half-cousin of Charles Darwin, his mother being the half-sister of Darwin's father. His father, a banker, belonged to a Quaker family. Galton was the youngest of seven children.

Born in Birmingham, he was educated at first at home and then in King Edward's School in that city, from 1836 to 1838. In the latter year he went as an assistant to the General Hospital in Birmingham, a very valuable training for his future work. For a year following he took courses at King's College, London, and in 1840 went to Trinity College, Cambridge. Because of illness, he left without a degree.

The Galton family was wealthy, and Francis Galton had already had a taste of travel before his father died in 1844 and left him

independently rich. He went to Giessen, Germany, to study under the famous chemist Liebig, but feeling that he was receiving nothing he suddenly left for Egypt and the Soudan. The next five years were devoted entirely to sport and travel, though Galton's inquiring mind made it impossible for him merely to amuse himself. In fact after his return from West South Africa in 1859, he set to work at once on his first book, *Narrative of an Explorer in Tropical South Africa*, which gained him the medal of the Royal Geographical Society in 1853 and made him a fellow of the Royal Society in 1856.

From 1865 dated Galton's particular interest in heredity. (It is a coincidence that he was born in the same year as Mendel, the lost and refound originator of modern genetic theory.) But he was born to break down the barriers between specialties. It would be impossible to outline all of Galton's scientific contributions; to mention only a few, he introduced the use of finger printing (invented by the astronomer, Sir William Herschel), originated composite photographs, and was the first to draw up meteorological charts.

Above all, he was the founder of the science of eugenics, in support of which he established and endowed a laboratory at the University of London. Since this term is so frequently misunderstood, it might be well to quote Galton's own definition: "the study of agencies, under social control, that may improve or impair the racial qualities of future generations, either physically or mentally." To this branch of science, closely related to anthropometry (human measurements) and statistics, the remainder of Galton's long life was devoted. His great work was the application of exact quantitative methods, chiefly mathematical, to biology.

Very many honors came to him, including knighthood. From 1863 to 1867 he was secretary of the British Association for the Advancement of Science, and twice refused to be made its president. In 1853 he married Louisa Butler, daughter of the dean of Peterborough; they had no children. She died in 1897, and in his old age Galton lived with a grandniece. Though his body grew infirm, his mind was keen to the last; he kept closely in touch with the work of his laboratory through the chief of his disciples, Karl Pearson, and when he was nearly eighty revisited Egypt. As late as 1901 he delivered a Huxley lecture "On the Possible Improvement of the Human Breed Under Existing Conditions of Law and Sentiment"; and he wrote an autobiography in 1908.

From the publication of *The Origin of Species* in 1859, Galton was a convert to the theory of his illustrious cousin. Like Darwin, he was an agnostic in religion. His many-

SIR FRANCIS GALTON

sided mind continued to take in other branches of science, including experimental psychology, to which he contributed a profound study of visual memory. Very resourceful, with unusual mechanical ingenuity, he was given to lovable eccentricities. In a crowd, for example, he carried either a sort of periscope by which to see over others' heads, or a brick on a cord, on which he could stand for the same purpose.

He died of heart failure during an attack of bronchitis, at Haslemere, where he had gone for his health, when he was almost eighty-nine, and is buried in Warwick.

With the calm of his Quaker ancestors, Galton never engaged in controversy, though he was courageous and outspoken. He was notably gentle, modest, and generous, a wholly admirable human being. (The Darwin-Galton-Wedgwood family is itself one of the finest eugenic instances on record.) As a teacher he was regarded with reverence by his pupils, so inspiring was he in lecturing and so considerate in personal relations.

Considering the very involved and erudite nature of his subjects, Galton writes with remarkable clarity and simplicity. In his letters, his non-technical books, and his uncompleted and unpublished "Utopia" called *Kantsaywhere*—an ideal land where eugenics is king—his style is easy and persuasive. Whatever the extravagances of some of his followers, Galton's own conclusions were always moderate and based on the most exhaustive research. The correlation of statistics instead of the deductive search for causation was the foundation-stone of his work. Modern genetics owes him an enormous debt. He belongs to science rather than to literature, but he is one of the most readable of original scientific

thinkers—another point in which he resembles his kinsman Charles Darwin.   M. A. deF.

PRINCIPAL WORKS: Narrative of an Explorer in Tropical South Africa, 1853; The Art of Travel, 1855; Meteorigraphica: or, Methods of Mapping the Weather, 1863; Hereditary Genius, 1869; Experiments in Pangenesis, 1871; English Men of Science, 1874; Inquiries Into the Human Faculty and Its Development, 1883; The Life History Album, 1884; Natural Inheritance, 1889; Finger Prints, 1893; Blurred Finger Prints, 1893; Finger Print Directory, 1895; Noteworthy Families, 1906; Memories of My Life, 1908.

ABOUT: Darbishire, A. D. An Introduction to a Biology; Pearson, K. The Life, Letters, and Labours of Francis Galton (4 vol.); Saleeby, C. W. The Progress of Eugenics; Eugenic Review 23:7 April 1931; 25:255 January 1934; Nation 92:79 January 26, 1911; Nature 85:440 February 2, 1911; World Today 21:134 November 1911.

GARDINER, SAMUEL RAWSON (March 4, 1829-February 23, 1902), historian, was born in Hampshire; on his mother's side he was a lineal descendant of Oliver Cromwell. He entered Winchester in 1841 and Christ Church, Oxford, in 1847, receiving his B.A. in 1851. His M.A., however, was delayed until 1884; he was appointed to a studentship, but could not keep it because he was, like his parents, an Irvingite (followers of Edward Irving, Carlyle's friend, who founded a Pentecostal sect). In 1856 he married Irving's daughter Isabella; she died in 1878, and in 1882 he married Bertha Cordery, by whom he had six sons and two daughters.

From 1851 to 1866 Gardiner was a deacon in the Irvingite church, but his name was taken off the register in 1872. In 1856 he began to read history at the British Museum, and two years later at the Record Office, supporting himself by private teaching. He wanted to write the complete history of the Puritan Revolution, starting from the reign of James I. From 1862, as a side issue, he edited historical volumes for the Camden Society; and wrote many historical text-books.

The reception given the earliest volumes of his history was very discouraging, but he persevered. The work finally appeared in sixteen volumes, from 1863 to 1901. All this time Gardiner had to teach to keep alive; from 1872 to 1877 he lectured at King's College, London, and from 1877 was professor of modern history there. He taught at Bedford College from 1863 to 1881, and also in private schools, at Toynbee Hall (the first college settlement), and for the Society for the Extension of University Teaching. In 1882 he received a civil list pension, in 1884 a research fellowship from All Souls College, Oxford, and in 1892 one from Merton College. From 1891 he was editor of the *English Historical Review*. In 1896 he lectured on history at Oxford.

He had intended to continue his history to the Restoration, but in 1901 a stroke partially paralyzed him, and he was never able to work again, though he lived for another year.

Gardiner as an historian appeals to the intellect rather than to the emotions; he is elevated and impressive, yet simple and conversational in style, conscientious, impartial, and trustworthy.

PRINCIPAL WORKS: History of England: 1603-40, 1863-84; The Great Civil War, 1886-91; The History of the Commonwealth and Protectorate, 1895-1901; Oliver Cromwell, 1899.

ABOUT: Learned, J. H. Samuel Rawson Gardiner; Rhodes, J. H. Historical Essays; Usher, R. G. Some Critical Notes on the Works of Samuel Rawson Gardiner.

GARNETT, RICHARD (February 27, 1835-April 13, 1906), critic, librarian, and man of letters, was born at Lichfield. He was the eldest son of the Reverend Richard Garnett, later Keeper of the Printed Books at the British Museum, and of Rayne Wreaks.

His childhood was spent in London. He was educated chiefly at home, although he spent some time at the Reverend Marcus' private school, where his classmates included E. H. Plumptre, later a distinguished scholar, and John Millais, the painter. Garnett the elder had a remarkable gift for languages, and the son, at fourteen, had read many of the Italian, French, German, Latin, and Greek classics and had laid the foundation for his later reputation as a sort of human encyclopedia.

In 1850, when Richard was at the Whalley Grammar School, his father died. Generous and interested relatives offered to send him to Oxford or Cambridge, but Garnett refused, and secured a position as clerk at the British

RICHARD GARNETT

Library Museum through the influence of Anthony Panizzi, former associate and now successor of the older Garnett. It was soon evident that Richard had been born to be a librarian, and he steadily advanced in this field, despite a certain shyness in his manner which could not conceal his natural amiability, or lessen his interest in the researches of others. In 1875 he became Assistant Keeper of the Printed Books, and in 1881 was chosen to edit the museum's general catalog, printing of which was to be resumed after a lapse of several years. In the succeeding year he sustained a severe disappointment at not receiving the appointment as librarian at the Bodleian Library, Oxford; but he turned patiently to preparation of the catalog. After eight years of this work he was elevated to the Chief Keepership at the British Museum, which more than recompensed him for his earlier disappointment. His new duties, however, made it necessary for other hands to complete the editing of the catalog. Meanwhile, he had been granted the honorary degree of LL.D. at Edinburgh (1883) in recognition of his literary and bibliographical accomplishments. For Garnett, after 1858, when his first volume of verse made an anonymous appearance, had been a systematic and versatile author, publishing translations, verse, and criticism. His discovery of unprinted verses by Shelley, which he published in 1862, brought as an acknowledgement from the Shelley family the gift of the poet's notebooks. In belles lettres his further work included biography, a history of Italian literature, and essays. He was given a C.B. in 1895. Four years later he resigned his Keepership, anticipating his retirement by one year because of the ill health of his wife, who was obliged to leave London. Mrs. Garnett, the former Olivia Narnay, died in 1903, the year of their fortieth anniversary, and Garnett survived her by only three years, dying at Hampstead in 1906. Of their three sons and three daughters, one, Edward (1868-) became well known as dramatist and critic and as the friend and adviser of Joseph Conrad; Edward's son David (1892-) is a novelist.

Garnett's position in English letters is a worthy one. His verse is scholarly and tasteful, though not of great fire or depth; and he was a stimulating, if not very profound, critic, with a vast range of knowledge and a pleasant way of using it; great catholicity of taste, and good humor. His best original work is *The Twilight of the Gods,* a series of apologues, or fables, in the manner of the Greek satirist Lucian. The dry, shrewd, polished, and penetrating wit of these little ironic tales was a new sort of thing in nineteenth century English literature, and they are written in English which may well serve as a model of its kind, and with a faint hint of malice which lends spice to their delicate flavor.

Dr. Garnett was also the author of distinguished contributions to the *Encyclopaedia Britannica* and to the *Dictionary of National Biography*.

A pleasant-looking, quiet, and friendly gentleman, Dr. Garnett was widely liked and admired. Arthur Symons said of him: "The death of Dr. Garnett has taken away a friend from every serious worker at literary research in England"; and *The Library* thus described the range of his tastes: "Dr. Garnett is especially interested in the Popes of Rome, the Byzantine Empire, the poetry of Shelley and his contemporaries, South America, and cats .. and . . . no man has ever been known to tell him a story without hearing a better one in return." He was also attracted to astrology, and defended it as worthy of a place among the sciences.   R. M.

PRINCIPAL WORKS: *Poetry*—Primula, 1858; Io in Egypt, 1859; Iphigenia in Delphi, 1891; The Queen and Other Poems, 1904; W. Shakespeare: Pedagogue and Poacher, 1904. *Fiction*—The Twilight of the Gods, 1888. *Biography*—Milton, 1887; Carlyle, 1887; Emerson, 1888; Edward Gibbon Wakefield, 1898; William Johnson Fox, 1910. *Translator*—Poems From the German, 1862; Idylls and Epigrams, 1869; Sonnets From Dante, Petrarch, and Camoens, 1896. *Miscellaneous*—Shelley and Lord Beaconsfield, 1887; The Age of Dryden, 1895; William Blake, 1895; History of Italian Literature, 1897; Essays in Librarianship and Bibliography, 1898; Essays of an Ex-Librarian, 1901; De Flagello Myrteo: Poems in Prose, 1905. *Editor*—Relics of Shelley, 1862.

ABOUT: Library (2nd ser.) 1:1 December 1, 1899; Living Age 249:431 May 19, 1906.

GASKELL, ELIZABETH CLEGHORN STEVENSON (September 29, 1810-November 12, 1865), novelist, was born at 12 Lindsey Row, Chelsea, not far from Carlyle's home. The eighth child of William Stevenson and his first wife, Elizabeth Holland, she had a literary heritage. Her paternal grandmother was a cousin of James Thomson, the poet, while her father was himself a contributor to the *Edinburgh* and *Westminster* reviews, and editor of the *Scots Magazine* as well as Unitarian minister and farmer, finally becoming Keeper of the Records of the Treasury in London. Her mother was the daughter of Samuel Holland, who owned a farm at Sandlebridge in Cheshire.

When Elizabeth was thirteen months old, Mrs. Stevenson died, leaving her husband with the baby and his other surviving child, John. The father, therefore, entrusted Elizabeth to his sister-in-law, Mrs. Hannah Lumb, who was otherwise encumbered by an insane husband and a crippled daughter. But Elizabeth was very happy in her new home at Knutsford, not far from the Sandlebridge

MRS. E. C. GASKELL

home of her mother's people. Although she made occasional visits to her father and stepmother in Chelsea she was, she confessed, *"very, very* unhappy" there. For she preferred picking "marsh saxifrage" on the moor or trotting about the country in a pony cart at Knutsford, or making the rounds with her uncle Peter, who was a doctor.

Her first real schooling began in 1825 when she was sent to the Avonbank School at Stratford-on-Avon, where she was taught Italian, French and Latin, drawing, music, and deportment by the Misses Byerley. When two years were up, however, she returned to Knutsford, though very shortly she was called to be with her father, who was then ill. That same year (1827) her brother disappeared at sea, and only two years later Mr. Stevenson also died.

There followed successive visits to her uncle Swinton Holland in Park Lane, to Sir Henry Holland in Brook Street, and finally a longer stay at the home of the Reverend William Turner at Newcastle-on-Tyne. A cholera epidemic, however, drove Elizabeth and Mr. Turner's daughter Ann to take up their residence in Edinburgh, where she had her first taste of society. She went also at about this time to Manchester to see Ann's sister, Mrs. John Gooch Robberds, whose husband was a minister at the Cross Street Unitarian Chapel. It was there that she was introduced to Mr. Robberds' assistant, William Gaskell, who was to become her husband.

She married the young minister on August 30, 1832, and after a wedding trip to Ffestiniog, Wales, settled down in Manchester with her husband. A graduate of the University of Glasgow, Mr. Gaskell remained at the Cross Street chapel until his death in

1884, although in the meanwhile he also served as professor of English history and literature at Manchester New College and lecturer in English literature at Workingman's College. He edited the *Unitarian Herald,* too, and wrote hymns as well as religious pamphlets.

Indeed, it was probably through her husband that Mrs. Gaskell first interested herself in writing, for until she married him there are no evidences of literary talent. Even her early married life was decidedly domestic. Her first child was born dead in 1833 and her daughter Marianne was born the year following. Although she did take up Sunday school teaching and work among the factory girls it was not until January 1837 that she made her first appearance in print when she collaborated with her husband on a poem, "Sketches Among the Poor, No. I." which came out in *Blackwood's.* Another daughter, Margaret was born the next month, and Mrs. Gaskell did no more writing until 1838, when she sent to William Howitt a description of Clopton Hall, which he published in his *Visits to Remarkable Places* (1840). There followed a trip to the Rhine in 1841, the birth of a daughter, Florence, in 1842, and that of her first son, William, two years later.

The death of this son of scarlet fever in 1845 was, more than anything else, the motivating cause of her writing. Grief-stricken by his death, she sat down and wrote *Mary Barton,* her first novel, which came out anonymously October 14, 1848. Her literary success was at once assured. She was invited to Dickens' dinner party in 1849, along with Carlyle and Thackeray and Douglas Jerrold. The next summer she met Crabb Robinson and Wordsworth in Skelwith, and she began at once to contribute short stories to the *Sunday School Penny Magazine, Howitt's Journal,* and *Household Words.*

This new source of income plus a legacy from Mrs. Lumb in 1848 allowed the Gaskells to move to a larger house at 42 Plymouth Grove. In new and more comfortable surroundings she continued to write. *Cranford* began to appear in *Household Words* in 1851. She spent part of 1852 writing *Ruth.* Winters spent in work, however, were interspersed with trips to the continent and summers in the country. *North and South* occupied her through 1853 and 1854, while the most important event of 1855 was her decision to undertake the biography of Charlotte Brontë, whom she had met and visited some five years before.

The collection of material for this work took several years and entailed trips to Brussels and elsewhere. The volume finally appeared in 1857. Immediately Mrs. Gaskell went to Paris to visit Madame Mohl of salon fame, and Rome where she stayed with the Storys. During this trip she met Charles Eliot Norton and the Brownings. The next autumn she made an even longer stay abroad with her daughters, and a summer at Whitby in 1859 allowed her to collect material for *Sylvia's Lovers* (1863). Other visits abroad followed in 1860 and 1862, years which were also notable for the publication of various minor tales. *Cousin Phillis* appeared in the *Cornhill Magazine* (1863-64), the same periodical that accepted *Wives and Daughters* for publication (1864-66). When she was abroad in 1863 she enjoyed her conversations with Landor and Swinburne, while in the spring of 1865 she spent part of a month with Madame Mohl.

Home again by summer she bought a country house, The Lawn, in Hampshire, at Holybourne, which she planned as a Christmas surprise for her husband. To it she went in November with three of her daughters. There, one Sunday afternoon, November 12, 1865, in the midst of tea, she suddenly fell dead from heart disease. Her health had never been good but her various journeys had apparently given her the necessary rest. Her husband was absent at the time and was summoned from a Unitarian meeting so that he could arrive in time for her funeral and burial at Knutsford. Four daughters also survived her. Her last novel, *Wives and Daughters,* came out posthumously in 1866.

Mrs. Gaskell's life had been an uneventful one. There was nothing dramatic about it. She was called "a good mother," a dutiful wife, and a sympathetic friend to such women as Florence Nightingale and Charlotte Brontë. Writing was hardly her only occupation. Her trips abroad were interludes in a busy life spent in housekeeping, sewing, and pickle-making, interspersed with charity work and intellectual conversation with Francis Newman and the professors who attended the "literary evenings" for which Manchester was famous. In general so humdrum was her existence that she looked back to her days in Rome with the Storys as the happiest of her life.

She herself was probably not the least of the attractions at home as well as abroad, for when she was a young girl she had been so lovely that Thompson drew her portrait and David Dunbar asked leave to make a bust. Even "to the end she was a comely woman. She was of medium height with blue eyes, brown hair and excellent carriage."

Her novels exemplify even better than her life just what were her thoughts, because most of them are so-called "social novels." *Mary Barton,* for example, dealt with the employee; *North and South* shifted to the employer, while in *Ruth* Mrs. Gaskell "poked her finger in the pie of gossiping morality." In order to write *Sylvia's Lovers* she had to unearth facts about the press-gangs of the eighteenth century. But in each of these earlier novels the moral is all too obvious. Not until late in her career did Mrs. Gaskell relegate her purpose to the background. When she pays less attention to the moral of her tale in *Cranford* and *Wives and Daughters*, she ranks high as a novelist. Then her humor is at its best. She is writing of characters she knows with a realism which is akin to George Eliot's. In fact *Wives and Daughters* has been called "one of the most exquisite examples in English fiction of the pure novel of character." More than one book has been written attempting to identify Cranford with Knutsford and Cranford's people with persons actually living in the town at that period. She was successful in such works because she was thoroughly acquainted with her characters and her settings. So *Mary Barton* and *North and South*, on the other hand, were chiefly significant for the heated arguments they provoked, while her moving life of Charlotte Brontë was "a veritable hornets' nest." Although she had tried to portray Charlotte and her relatives accurately, critics contended that she had occasionally failed to present them in their true light. In spite of this contemporary dissatisfaction, Mrs. Gaskell has been placed "among the first of biographers" for this her only biography. B. D. S.

PRINCIPAL WORKS: *Short Stories and Sketches*—Life in Manchester, 1848; Libbie Marsh's Three Eras, 1850; The Sexton's Hero, 1850; Cranford, 1853; Lizzie Leigh and Other Tales, 1854; Husband and Heart, 1855; Round the Sofa, 1859; Right at Last, 1860; Lois the Witch and Other Tales, 1861; Cousin Phillis, 1864; The Grey Woman and Other Tales, 1865. *Novels*—Mary Barton, 1838; The Moorland Cottage, 1850; Ruth, 1853; North and South, 1855; My Lady Ludlow, 1858; A Dark Night's Work, 1863; Sylvia's Lovers, 1863; Wives and Daughters, 1866. *Biography*—The Life of Charlotte Brontë, 1857. *Miscellaneous*—Two Lectures on Lancashire Dialect, 1854.
ABOUT: Haldane, E. Mrs. Gaskell and Her Friends; Payne, G. A. Mrs. Gaskell and Knutsford; Sanders, G. DeW. Elizabeth Gaskell; Whitfield, A. S. Mrs. Gaskell: Her Life and Work.

"GAULTIER, BON." See MARTIN, SIR THEODORE

GEIKIE, SIR ARCHIBALD (December 28, 1835-November 10, 1924), Scottish geologist, was born in Edinburgh, and educated at the Edinburgh high school and university. His honorary degrees in later life, when he was one of the most distinguished of living geologists, included an honorary D.C.L. from Oxford, D.S.C. from Cambridge and Dublin, LL.D. from Edinburgh, Glasgow, Aberdeen, and others, and Ph.D. from Upsala, Leipzig, Strasbourg, and Prague. In 1855 he entered the Geological Survey, and in 1867 became director of the Geological Survey of Scotland. He was professor of geology and mineralogy at the University of Edinburgh from 1871 to 1882. In 1871 he married Alice Gabrielle Pignatel, of Lyons, France. She died in 1916, leaving two daughters.

From 1882 to 1901 Geikie was Director-General of the Geological Survey of the United Kingdom and director of the Museum of Practical Geology. He was knighted in 1891, became a Knight Commander of the Bath in 1907, and received the Order of Merit in 1914. He was foreign secretary of the Royal Society from 1890 to 1894 and secretary from 1906 to 1908; president of the Geological Society in 1891-92 and again from 1906 to 1908, and president of the British Association for the Advancement of Science in 1892. He was the recipient of innumerable medals and other honors.

Geikie lectured frequently, and his lectures, like his non-technical books, have charm as well as learning. He also wrote occasionally on history and literature. His brother James (1839-1915) was likewise a geologist and writer on science.

PRINCIPAL WORKS: The Story of a Boulder, 1858; Geological Sketches at Home and Abroad, 1882; Text Book of Geology, 1882; The Founders of Geology, 1897; Landscape in History, 1905; A Long Life's Work, 1924.
ABOUT: Geikie, A. A Long Life's Work.

GIFFORD, WILLIAM (April 1756-December 31, 1826), poet and critic, was born in Ashburton, Devonshire, the son of a somewhat eccentric glazier, Edward Gifford, and Elizabeth (Cain) Gifford.

The boy's childhood was extraordinarily unfortunate. After William had had but a small amount of education, his father died of drink, and his mother, after an unsuccessful attempt to support herself by carrying on her husband's business, died shortly afterward, leaving William and a small brother. The boys' godfather, a creditor, seized the property and sent the younger boy to be bound to a farmer. Despite the older brother's efforts to help him, the little boy died not long afterward, having been sent to sea.

William went for a while to school, but the godfather, who had sent him there mainly because of local public opinion, withdrew his support and sent the boy to work on a farm, where an injury he had received prevented him from being very useful. After trying vainly to send him to Newfoundland, the godfather put him to sea when he was about thirteen. In 1770 he was taken home and sent to school, again because of the opinions of the neighbors, and he learned rapidly. Little more than a year later, however, the luckless boy was apprenticed to a shoemaker

WILLIAM GIFFORD

of strict ideas, who, when he found his assistant secretly learning algebra and even writing verses for a little money for books, took away his books and stopped him from writing.

Through the kindness of a local surgeon, William Cooksley, who got friends to buy up the apprenticeship, Gifford went back to school; and the same man, through a friend, made it possible for him to go to Exeter College at Oxford, where he was graduated in 1782.

He had already begun his translation of Juvenal, but was dissatisfied with it and accepted an invitation to live with Lord Grosvenor, who had become interested in him, and who became a close friend. He tutored Grosvenor's son and made two Continental trips.

His name became known when, in the *Baviad* (1894) and the *Maeviad* (1895), he held up to scorn a ridiculous but unimportant group of English writers living in Florence. So successful was Gifford's satire that a libel suit against him failed because the jury, after hearing a passage from the works he was ridiculing, saw his truthfulness and acquitted him of the charge.

In 1797 he joined George Canning, Under-Secretary for Foreign Affairs, and the Tories, as editor of the *Anti-Jacobin*. This journal in 1798 ceased to appear, but, when the *Quarterly Review* began its prosperous career in 1809, Gifford was the editor, and he remained in charge of this Tory periodical until his resignation in 1824, his health having broken in 1822. In this time his salary rose from £200 to £900; and he held government posts which brought him more money. He died in London in 1826, and was buried in Westminster Abbey.

A small man, physically almost deformed, and afflicted with illness, Gifford seems to have been rather sour. Southey, one of the regular contributors to the *Review,* complained that he regarded writers with sympathy no greater than that which Izaak Walton wasted on the worms which he used for bait. It was his ungrateful task to correct, to alter, and to compress the writings of others, and he performed it relentlessly, once even mangling a favorite brain-child of Charles Lamb's. Rather parsimonious in his habits during his life, he left £25,000 to the son of the surgeon who had befriended him in early life, and £3,000 to the relatives of a maid-servant of whom he had been very fond.

It is as a literary critic that Gifford assumes greatest importance. Successful from the very nature of their absurd subjects, his satires are essentially mediocre. "Although their merit was not great, his ample quotations from his victims made his conquest easy," writes C. W. Previté-Orton. His editions of the old dramatists, on the other hand, are thorough and careful. But it is his critical attacks on the rising school of Romantic writers which have made Gifford famous. Under his leadership the *Quarterly Review* joined its political opponent, the *Edinburgh Review,* in censures upon the Lake School of poets, and Gifford warmly championed the classical ideals of English poetry. As editor of the *Quarterly,* he must share the responsibility for Croker's review of *Endymion* which was commonly regarded as responsible for the death of Keats, and which evoked so much vituperation from Romantic poets.

An "acrid and deformed pedant," Sir Sidney Colvin called him, and the judgment seems likely to stand.   R. W. W.

PRINCIPAL WORKS: *Editor*—The Plays of Philip Massinger, 1805; The Works of Ben Jonson, 1816; The Dramatic Works of John Ford, 1827; The Dramatic Works and Poems of James Shirley, 1833. *Translator*—The Satires of Juvenal, 1802; The Satires of Persius, 1821. *Verse Satire*—The Baviad, 1794; The Maeviad, 1795; Epistle to Peter Pindar, 1800. *Miscellaneous*—Autobiography, 1827.

ABOUT: Clark, R. B. William Gifford: Tory Satirist, Critic, and Editor; Gifford, W. Autobiography; Hazlitt, W. Spirit of the Age; Southey, C. C. Life and Correspondence of Robert Southey.

GILBERT, SIR JOHN THOMAS (January 23, 1829-May 23, 1898), Irish historian, was born in Dublin. His father was an English Protestant, a wine merchant and consul of Portugal. His mother was Irish and a Roman Catholic, and he was reared in that faith, being all his life very devout. He was educated at Bective College, Dublin, and Prior Park College, Bath. In 1851 he began his literary career by an article on *The Historical Literature of Ireland* for the *Irish Quarterly*

Review. In 1855 he became honorary joint-secretary of the Irish Celtic and Archaeological Society. In 1863, following representations he had made to Parliament, he was appointed to organize a new Public Record Office in Dublin, and on its establishment he became its secretary from 1867 to 1875, when it was abolished. From 1865 on he ceased to do any original writing, but devoted all his time and energies to research in Irish antiquities, in which his work was of immense value. For thirty-five years he was vice-president and librarian of the Royal Irish Academy. In 1891 he married Rosa Mulholland, being then a bachelor of sixty-two. In 1897 he was knighted in recognition of his services. He died suddenly of heart failure at nearly seventy.

PRINCIPAL WORKS: Historical Essays on Ireland, 1851; History of the City of Dublin, 1854-59; Ancient Historical Irish Manuscripts, 1861; History of the Viceroys of Ireland, 1865.

ABOUT: Gilbert, J. T. Crede Mihi; Gilbert, Lady. Life of Sir J. T. Gilbert.

GILBERT, SIR WILLIAM SCHWENCK

(November 18, 1836-May 29, 1911), dramatist and librettist of the Gilbert-and-Sullivan operettas, was born in London, the only son of a retired naval surgeon with an interest in writing and a choleric temper, both of which he inherited. He disliked his middle name, and always signed himself "W. S. Gilbert."

At the age of two, he was kidnapped by bandits in Naples and held for ransom. At Great Ealing School, at thirteen, he was lazy and tried unsuccessfully to run away and become an actor; later his emulative spirit set him to work until he became head of his class. He went to King's College, London, in 1855, and to the University of London in 1857. Then he took the army examinations for the Royal Artillery, but before he could receive a commission the Crimean War had ended and he returned to college, receiving his B.A. in 1857.

After college Gilbert became assistant clerk in the Education Department of the Privy Council Office, a post he hated. After four years an aunt left him £400; he resigned and spent the entire amount in qualifying for the bar. He practised as a barrister for four years and earned exactly £75. Meanwhile he was finding himself as a writer. For the magazine Fun he wrote and illustrated his famous Bab Ballads, clever verses which, in the name of good fun, discoursed amiably on violence and crime. By the time he was twenty-four he had written fifteen plays, the first produced being Dulcamara, in 1866. At this period he also acted frequently, though not with much success. In 1867 he married

Lucy Blois Turner, a marriage childless but singularly happy.

In 1877, already a noted playwright, he met the composer Sir Arthur Sullivan—with whom his name was ever afterwards to be linked. With the producer Richard D'Oyly Carte, who leased the Savoy Theater in London, they began the series of operettas with which their names are immortally identified, the first being Trial by Jury, in 1875. The plots were never anything much; the essence of Gilbert's librettos lay in the songs, which were frequently topical, nearly always satiric, and intensely witty. Pinafore, for example, poked fun at the navy; Patience at the aesthetes, of whom Oscar Wilde was the spokesman; Trial by Jury at the law. Even The Mikado had its fling at men in office nearer home than Japan. Gilbert, the born Tory, nevertheless delighted in satire that to the authorities seemed at times almost seditious. His are probably the only librettos in the world where the words are as well known as the tunes. He directed the operas as well as writing the librettos. He was a martinet and a tyrant, but he built up a splendid company of actors and singers.

A man of violent temper, always in litigation over libel-suits, ultra-sensitive, yet commercially minded and with great business acumen, it was natural that Gilbert should quarrel frequently with his dreamy, sentimental partner. In 1879 they toured America in an effort to secure redress from the pirating of their copyrights, but their personal friendship ended soon after. For a while each quarrel was followed by a reconciliation; their best joint works, The Mikado and The Gondoliers, both came after violent ruptures and subsequent peace-making. In 1890 they had their worst quarrel of all, Carte siding with

SIR W. S. GILBERT

Sullivan against Gilbert; Gilbert withdrew from the Savoy and engaged Alfred Cellier to write the music for *The Mountebanks,* and he brought suit against Carte and Sullivan over a financial dispute. At the end of 1891 they were reconciled again, and produced two more operettas together—*Utopia, Ltd.* in 1893 and *The Grand Duke* in 1896. The latter was a failure, and ended their precarious peace; Sullivan, utterly different in temperament, with very dissimilar artistic ambitions, and tortured by kidney disease, no longer had strength to conciliate his testy collaborator. They met in 1898 at a revival of *The Sorcerers,* but did not speak. However, when Sullivan lay dying in 1900, Gilbert wrote him a friendly letter, and would have called had he not himself been ill. It is only fair to Gilbert to add that all his life he was tormented first by gout and then by arthritis, which did not improve his temper.

From 1883 to 1890 Gilbert lived in West Kensington, with a country home at Uxbridge. In 1891 he bought Grim's Dyke, Harrow Weald, and made of the house a sort of combined museum and menagerie. He became Justice of the Peace and took his duties seriously, being the terror of early motorists. Toward children and animals, however—in spite of the streak of sadism evident in all his writings—he was extremely tender, and the poor and unfortunate could always rely on him for help—if they displayed proper gratitude and complete dependence.

A money-maker and money-saver, Gilbert became very prosperous. He traveled a good deal, visiting Egypt and the Crimea, which had been the dream of his boyhood. In 1901 he was in a bad railway accident, and his heart was never strong thereafter. In 1909 his last opera, *Fallen Fairies,* was produced, and in 1911 his last play, *The Hooligan,* a macabre piece which ended with the prophetic words, "Death from heart failure."

The most typical of Englishmen, innately conservative and easy-going, Gilbert nevertheless had, besides his irascibility (he once exclaimed, on entering a club, "What, twelve men here, and I'm on good terms with them all?"), a streak of cynical rebellion that, as has been said, made him unpopular with the great. There was too much outspoken criticism in all his writing, and he received one severe snub from Queen Victoria when his name was omitted at a Royal Performance of one of his operas. It was not until 1907 that he was knighted, and then he almost refused the honor.

On May 29, 1911, he went to London, by some presentiment made his peace with an old friend to whom he had not spoken for twenty years, and returned to Grim's Dyke, where he was teaching two girls who were his guests to swim in the lake on his estate. One got out of her depth, and Gilbert went to her rescue. He died in the effort, not of drowning but of heart failure.

Perhaps the most remarkable thing about the work of Gilbert and Sullivan is its vitality. In the sixty-odd years since *Trial by Jury,* a cult has grown up around the two men which, in the intensity of its devotion, concedes nothing to the worshippers of such idols as Dickens, Browning, Wagner, or Beethoven. Both England and America have formal and highly earnest societies of Gilbert-and-Sullivan lovers. The term "Savoyard," once applied only to natives of Savoy, France, has come to mean a performer or devotee of the operettas. Singers studiously perfect themselves in the various rôles, and their performances are compared and contrasted by the critics with all the seriousness accorded the interpreters of grand opera. Revivals of the works are annual occurrences in London and New York, with several stock companies competing for popular favor. Of these the best known and most widely acclaimed is the D'Oyly Carte troupe, which—with successive generations of performers—has been filling theatres on both sides of the water for more than half a century. "Savoy opera," as it is frequently called, is a permanent and international dramatic institution, rivaled in popularity only by Shakespeare.

Yet both Gilbert and Sullivan labored under the delusion that their independent work was of more value than what they did together. But Sullivan, except for a few songs like "The Lost Chord" and "Onward, Christian Soldiers," is remembered as the composer of *The Mikado* and *Pinafore.* And Gilbert, except for the *Bab Ballads,* will be known forever as the librettist of the Gilbert-and-Sullivan operas. His many plays, which he fondly regarded as his best work, are artificial and dead as the proverbial door-nail. But the brilliant songs which he wrote for the operas will live as long as the English language is spoken. They are Gilbert's passport to permanent fame. M. A. deF.

PRINCIPAL PUBLISHED WORKS: Bab Ballads, 1869; The Palace of Truth, 1874; Pygmalion and Galatea, 1875; Sweethearts, 1878; Gretchen, 1879; Broken Hearts, 1881; Dan'l Druce, 1881; Engaged, 1881; Original Comic Operas (The Sorcerer, H.M.S. Pinafore, Pirates of Penzance, Iolanthe, Patience, Princess Ida, The Mikado, Trial by Jury) 1890.

ABOUT: Browne, E. A. W. S. Gilbert; Cellier, F. A. & Bridgeman, C. Gilbert, Sullivan, and O'Oyly Carte; Dark S. W. S. Gilbert: His Life and Letters; Fitzgerald, P. H. The Savoy Opera and the Savoyards; FitzGerald, S. J. A. The Story of the Savoy Opera; Goldberg, I. Sir William Gilbert; Goldberg, I. The Story of Gilbert and Sullivan; Pearson, H. Gilbert and Sullivan: A Biography; Walsh, S. Gilbert and Sullivan Jottings.

GILFILLAN, GEORGE (January 30, 1813-August 13, 1878), Scottish biographer, was born in Perthshire, the eleventh of twelve children of a secession (dissenting Presbyterian) minister. The father died when he was thirteen. He was educated at Glasgow College and at the University of Edinburgh, where he became a friend of De Quincey and Carlyle. He was licensed to preach in 1835. He was minister of the School-Wund Church, Dundee, from shortly after this until his death. In 1844 he began contributing, free of charge, to the Dumfries *Herald* a series of articles which later became the brilliant and deservedly popular *Gallery of Literary Portraits*. He published in all more than a hundred volumes, mostly of a biographical nature. He was keenly interested also in free libraries and in popular lectures to workingmen; he himself lectured frequently and brought distinguished men, including Emerson, to lecture in his town. As an editor of the older English poets, he was not successful, being inexact and careless. In 1836 he married Margaret Valentine. Twice Gilfillan was tried for disagreements with church policy, but both times he was acquitted. He died suddenly at Brechin. His public funeral was two miles long, and a fund was raised in his memory which after his widow's death was applied to the establishment of university scholarships for men and women.

PRINCIPAL WORKS: A Gallery of Literary Portraits (three series) 1845, 1850. 1854; Bards of the Bible, 1851; Life of Robert Burns, 1856; Night: A Poem, 1867; Modern Christian Heroes, 1869; Life of Sir Walter Scott, 1870.
ABOUT: Gilfillan, G. History of a Man (fictional autobiography).

GILFILLAN, ROBERT (July 7, 1798-December 4, 1850), Scottish poet, was born in Dunfermline, his father being a master weaver. In 1811 the family moved to Leith, and he was apprenticed to a cooper there. He remained with the cooper until 1818, and then became a grocer's clerk in his native town of Dunfermline. This, he said, was the happiest time of his life; he won early recognition for his poems, which he contributed to various Scottish newspapers, and he was the center of a group of admiring friends. He succeeded Burns as grand bard to the Grand Lodge of Masons of Scotland. However, he left Dunfermline and returned to Leith. After two other jobs as a clerk, he became collector of police rates (or taxes) in 1837, and held this position until his death. He never married, and a niece kept house for him. His best known songs were "Peter M'Craw," "Fare Thee Well," and "O Why Left I My Hame?" all of which were immensely popular during his lifetime.

PRINCIPAL WORK: Works (ed. by W. Anderson) 1851.

ABOUT: Gilfillan, R. Works (see Prefatory Biography).

GINSBURG, CHRISTIAN DAVID (December 25, 1831-March 7, 1914), Old Testament scholar, was born in Warsaw, Poland, of a Jewish family with traditions of descent from the Spanish (Sephardic) Jews. His mother was English. He was educated in the Rabbinic School at Warsaw. At sixteen he was converted to Christianity, added "Christian" to his name of David, and, having been cut off by his orthodox family, went to England, where the remainder of his life was spent. He was naturalized in 1858, married Margaret Crossfield, of a Quaker family, and settled in Liverpool. Mrs. Ginsburg died in 1867, and the next year he married Emilie Hausburg. By his two marriages he had four daughters and a son. He received an honorary LL.D. from Glasgow University in 1863, and in 1870 was one of the original members of the Old Testament Revision Company which brought out the Revised Bible. He moved to Berkshire at this time to be nearer his work in the British Museum. In 1872 he organized an archaeological expedition to Trans-Jordania, which, however, accomplished little. He was a liberal in politics, a friend of Gladstone, and acted as Justice of the Peace for Surrey and Middlesex. Besides his great work as editor of the critical text of the Massorah, he translated the New Testament into Hebrew. Ginsburg was a man of profound erudition, a true scholar, though sometimes affected by his early rabbinical training. His work is not, of course, of interest to general readers.

PRINCIPAL WORK: Edition of The Massorah, 1880.
ABOUT: Times March 9 and 11, 1914.

GISSING, GEORGE ROBERT (November 22, 1857-December 28, 1903), novelist, was the oldest child of a Wakefield pharmacist who had some literary and scientific accomplishments: he was the author of a "Wakefield Flora," and corresponded with Bentham and Hooker. A younger son, Algernon, also became the author of some novels, now forgotten.

Gissing was sent to a Quaker boarding school, where he distinguished himself in writing and public speaking, but where his lack of gregariousness and his consciousness of his own potentialities served to make him unpopular. He was a brilliant student, particularly in the classics and in English, and he passed first in all England in the Oxford local examinations. Oxford was out of the question, with his father's means, but he obtained an exhibition in Owens College, then newly founded, in Manchester. Here again he made the start on a remarkable

GEORGE GISSING

career, winning prizes for English poetry and in Greek and Latin—and overworking himself to the point of exhaustion.

The painful episode that followed determined and conditioned all Gissing's future life. This poor, studious, diligent boy was also an extreme idealist, with all the touching enthusiasms and beliefs of a young Shelley. He fell in with a youthful prostitute, who told him her pathetic history. Gissing decided to marry her and reform her. Meanwhile she must be taken at once from her former life, and he had not even enough money for his own proper support. He began to abstract sums from wealthier fellow-students. In the midst of the term the pride of the college was caught as a thief, disgraced, and sent to prison.

His term was short, but when he emerged his college days were of course over. A group of sympathetic citizens of Manchester got him a place as clerk in Liverpool, and when this proved a failure, raised enough money to send him by steerage to the United States. He was there from 1876 to 1877, and the vicissitudes he underwent are printed in blood on the pages of *New Grub Street*. He wandered about, sometimes able to find a pupil or two in the classics, sometimes reduced to manual labor—in Boston he worked as a gas-fitter. At Niagara Falls he contemplated throwing himself over the cataract, but his nerve failed him. He drifted to Chicago, where he came very near to starving as he tried futilely to find a job on a newspaper. Obviously he was not going to fit into the raw, bustling American life of the 'seventies.

A little better fortune came to him: he saved and scraped together a few dollars,

and his twentieth birthday found him again in Europe. Somehow he found his way to Jena for a few precious months of study; the authors he read then remained the guiding influences of his later work—Goethe, Haeckel, Shelley, Comte, and above all Schopenhauer. They, with the incongruous addition of Dickens, are the sources from which his thinking and feeling were drawn.

But the Jena months were a rare interlude: Gissing as usual rushed upon his fate. He returned to England, looked up the girl who had been the cause of all his torments, and true to his promise, married her. From the beginning the marriage was a ghastly failure. His wife took to drink, and when he could not supply her with funds she went back to her old profession. A dozen times they separated and were reunited, until in 1880 she left permanently; but Gissing continued to contribute to her support until she died in 1888.

Meanwhile, in the same year in which they separated forever, Gissing had published his first novel, *Workers in the Dawn*. He paid for its publication—with every penny he possessed, thinking with his usual lack of worldly knowledge that it would bring him vast returns. Instead it was mentioned by only one or two critics, and that disparagingly, and had almost no sale at all. But it did him one good service—it brought him to the attention of John Morley and Frederic Harrison, who praised the book highly. Harrison did more; he made the half-starved author tutor to his two sons, and helped him to get other pupils, and to place articles occasionally in the *Pall Mall Gazette* and elsewhere.

Though it was four years before Gissing published another novel—after that they poured forth at the rate of one or more a year, many of them pot-boilers written under the spur of necessity—he gave as little time as possible to his teaching or journalism. He had the born scholar's compulsion to constant study, and suffered the extremes of privation to give his days to voracious reading in the British Museum. It was a period when, because he was destitute, he fancied himself a friend of the workers, and lectured at workingmen's clubs; actually he was an aristocrat in spirit, and his temporary radicalism arose from hatred of the rich rather than from love of the poor.

Demos, published in 1886 (and incidentally a violently anti-labor novel), was his first to bring him in any appreciable sum. With the £100 he received for it he sailed in a collier for Naples, and went thence to Rome and Athens. A worshipper of the classics, it was the profoundest emotional experience of his life. Soon after came the final release from his farce of a marriage. It is no wonder that *A Life's Morning,* which appeared in 1888, was the most light-hearted of his novels. Slowly he was beginning to make a way for himself; almost it seemed that the nightmare of his youth was over.

But Gissing's temperament forbade any such happy ending. Only two years later, in 1890, he repeated almost exactly his first fatal error in marriage. Gissing and his second wife lived together only a few years, but long enough for her to bear him two sons, and to burden him with the support of another family for the remainder of his ill-starred life.

As his literary reputation spread, and his poverty became less absolute, Gissing spent much of his time away from London, returning to Wakefield several times, and staying frequently in various parts of southern England. George Meredith and H. G. Wells became his close friends; the latter accompanied him on a second trip to Italy in 1897. But a long life could hardly have been predicted for one who had undergone such hardships. An early disposition to tuberculosis reasserted itself, and by 1903 it became necessary for him to move to the south of France. In St. Jean de Luz he caught cold, developed pneumonia, and a few days later was dead at forty-five. He left much unfinished work, including three novels which have never been printed.

A nature such as Gissing's is difficult to analyze; it was contradictory, probably perverted from its original path. He has been called arrogant and sensual—and idealistic, gentle, and suave. His nature determined his career, but his career altered his nature. One thing is sure—he was a deeply unhappy man. It is when his novels are most autobiographical—or when, as in *The Private Letters of Henry Ryecroft,* they depict the life he should have led—that they most nearly approach greatness.

For greatness is the word which must be applied to Gissing's more sincere and serious work. With all the faults of his novels—their stilted dialogue, their sentimentality, their didacticism, their melodrama—they are the foundation-stones of a great edifice. He is more nearly akin to Zola than is any other English writer, yet he has a psychological subtlety that Zola lacked. And his style at its best is graceful and varied. Bitter, pessimistic, and sordid, Gissing's best novels are nevertheless the work of a powerful creative talent.

These "best" novels, in the sense intended, may be named as *New Grub Street, The Nether World, The Odd Women, In the Year of Jubilee,* and perhaps *Sleeping Fires.* Today, however, Gissing is chiefly remembered by a book not a novel, not in any real meaning of the word an autobiography, and difficult to classify at all—*The Private Letters of Henry Ryecroft.* He is known for perhaps the best

critical analysis of Dickens—his lifelong idol —in existence. But his novels of the London slums and the petty bourgeoisie of the suburbs will still repay reading. They depict no life truly and in the round, for they are colored by Gissing's own thwarted and frustrated spirit, by his desolation and his hatred. He could find liberation in his writing, but it was not in these despairing portraits of life on its lowest economic level; it was in "the books he wrote for his own pleasure"—the work on Dickens, and the travel book of Greece. Strangely enough, his third source of liberation came in a series of depictions of women so idealized that they are no longer human, women who appear oddly in the most unrelievedly gloomy and sordid of his books.

The fact becomes apparent that Gissing was primarily a spoiled idealist and classicist, a man whom nature had intended to live out his life in a scholar's cloister, and whom fate had tossed instead into the slums. He should have been an Oxford don, and instead he was cast penniless and disgraced on to the city streets. He is a figure almost as pathetic as is Francis Thompson. But like Thompson, though in a different way, not even long disaster could stifle the voice of his genius.   M. A. deF.

PRINCIPAL WORKS: *Novels*—Workers in the Dawn, 1880; The Unclassed, 1884; Isabel Clarendon, 1886; Demos, 1886; Thyrza, 1887; A Life's Morning, 1888; The Nether World, 1889; The Emancipated, 1890; New Grub Street, 1891; Born in Exile, 1892; Denzil Quarrier, 1892; The Odd Women, 1893; In the Year of Jubilee, 1894; Sleeping Fires, 1895; The Paying Guest, 1895; Eve's Ransom, 1895; The Whirlpool, 1895; The Town Traveler, 1898; The Crown of Life, 1899; Our Friend the Charlatan, 1901; Veranilda (posthumous) 1904; Will Warburton (posthumous) 1905. *Short Stories*—Human Odds and Ends, 1898; The House of Cobwebs (posthumous) 1906. *Essays and Miscellany*—Critical Studies of the Works of Charles Dickens, 1898; By the Ionian Sea, 1901; Dickens in Memory, 1902; The Private Letters of Henry Ryecroft, 1903.

ABOUT: Bjorkman, E. Critical Studies of the New Spirit in Literature; Gissing, G. Critical Studies of the Works of Charles Dickens (see Introduction by Temple Scott); Swinnerton, F. George Gissing: A Critical Study; Yates, M. George Gissing: An Appreciation; American Review 5:459 September 1935; Bookman 18:600 February 1904; Living Age 240:714 March 19, 1904; Monthly Review 5:4:459 August 1904.

GLASCOCK, WILLIAM NUGENT (1787?-October 8, 1847), novelist, was a captain in the Royal Navy. Not much is known of his life. He became a commander in 1818 and attained post rank as captain in 1833. He served throughout the Napoleonic wars in European and American waters, and was commended for notable service. He was married and had a family. During his last year (apparently on leave from the navy) he was a poor-relief inspector in Ireland. The long intervals of half-pay which punctuated his naval career he spent in turning out a series of stories of the sea. He also wrote a manual for naval officers, once considered very useful, but now obsolete. His novels and stories are exceedingly dull, and their only value is as sketches of the ordinary life in the navy in his time.

PRINCIPAL WORKS: The Naval Sketch-Book, 1826; Sailors and Saints, 1829; Tales of a Tar, 1836; Land Sharks and Sea Gulls, 1838.

GLEIG, GEORGE ROBERT (April 20, 1796-July 9, 1888), Scottish novelist and historian, was born in Stirling, the son of the later Bishop of Brechin. He was exceedingly frail as a child and was not expected to live— and he died at ninety-two! He was most precocious, and went up from the Stirling Grammar School to Glasgow University at thirteen. In 1811 he entered Balliol College, Oxford, but left almost immediately to take a commission in the army. He was an ensign in Ireland for two years, then was sent to Spain, to the Peninsular War, as a lieutenant. He served through the latter part of the War of 1812 in America, being present at the battles of Baltimore and New Orleans and the burning of Washington, and being wounded three times. He then returned to Europe and served to the end of the Napoleonic wars, being put on half pay after the battle of Waterloo. In 1816 he returned to Oxford, and secured his B.A. at Magdalen College in 1818, and his M.A. in 1821. In 1819 he married a Miss Cameron, who was his father's ward. He spent the next year in Cumberland preparing to take holy orders, and was ordained in 1820. For two years he was curate and rector of three successive churches in Kent. In 1834 he was named as chaplain of the Chelsea Hospital, in 1844 as chaplain-general of the forces, and in 1846 as inspector-general of the military schools. He contributed frequently to the more serious reviews, and lived to be the last of the early contributors to *Blackwood's*—as well as the last officer of his regiment who had served under Wellington. He retained all his faculties until his death, although he had ceased to write much some years before. His writing was largely based on his personal experiences, and has today more historical than literary interest.

PRINCIPAL WORKS: Campaigns of the British Army at Washington and New Orleans, 1820; The Subaltern, 1826; The Chelsea Pensioners, 1829; The Country Curate, 1830; History of India, 1830-35; The Chronicles of Waltham, 1834; Life of Warren Hastings, 1841; Story of the Battle of Waterloo, 1847; Life of Lord Clive, 1848; Essays: Biographical, Historical, and Miscellaneous, 1857; Life of Wellington, 1862.

ABOUT: Times July 10, 1888.

GLEN, WILLIAM (November 14, 1789-December 1826), Scottish poet, was born in Glasgow, the son of a prosperous Russia

merchant. At seventeen he went to work with a firm with interests in the West Indies, and lived there for several years as its representative. Returning to Scotland, he set up in business for himself, but failed in 1814. From this time on he never supported himself; he became an inebriate and spent most of his time singing his own songs and playing the flute in public houses or wandering around the country as a sort of tipsy minstrel, while his income came from a generous uncle in Russia. In 1818 he married Catherine Macfarlane, who with her brother ran a farm in Perthshire; she cared for him like a child and looked after his welfare until he died of tuberculosis at thirty-seven. They had one daughter. Glen was a quiet, harmless, gentle, amiable man who was his own worst enemy. His songs are sweet and plaintive, and the best of them, "Wae's Me for Prince Charlie," is one of the finest of Jacobite poems.

PRINCIPAL WORKS: Poems: Chiefly Lyrical, 1815; Poetical Remains (ed. by C. Rogers) 1874.

ABOUT: Glen, W. Poetical Remains (see Memoir).

"GODOLPHIN, MARY." See AIKIN, LUCY

GODWIN, WILLIAM (March 3, 1756-April 7, 1836), novelist, biographer, and philosopher, was born in Cambridgeshire, the seventh of thirteen children of a dissenting minister. By the time the child was four, the family had moved twice, first to Suffolk and then to Norfolk. Godwin was reared in the most extreme tradition of Puritanism. His schooling, in various Nonconformist institutions, ended temporarily when he was eleven, and he was sent as private pupil to a strict and severe minister at Norwich. At this period he was piously orthodox and exceedingly bigoted; in fact, he contracted smallpox in 1768 because, for religious reasons, he refused to be vaccinated.

1771 found Godwin an usher in his old school at Hindolveston, Norfolk. The next year his father died, and his mother took him to London. There he was refused admission at Homerton Academy because he was suspected of leanings toward Sandemanianism— that tiny fanatical sect to which the great physicist Michael Faraday belonged—but was received in Horton Academy, where he remained until he was twenty-one. He rose at five in the morning and until midnight spent his time, not so much in study as in constant conversation on metaphysical subjects. He was noted at the school for his curious combination of Calvinist theology with materialistic philosophy.

Godwin was now considered prepared for his own career in his father's profession, but though he preached during the summer of

1777 in Yarmouth and Lowestoft, it was the next year before he secured a regular pulpit, in Ware, Hertforshire. He was not a popular minister, and changed charges often. In 1780 he was at Stowmarket, Suffolk, where his reading of the French philosophers first aroused his religious doubts. These increased, until finally in 1882 he fell out with his congregation entirely, and went to London to pursue a literary career. This was not successful, and once more, and for the last time, he served in a chapel at Beaconsfield. By the autumn of 1783 he knew that he could no longer serve as a minister, and that writing must be his only means of livelihood.

He earned a very precarious living by doing translations, writing pamphlets, and contributing to *The English Review,* occasionally eking out his slender income by taking a pupil to tutor. At this time he dropped the title of "reverend" and broke finally with his orthodox family. He sympathized ardently with the French Revolution, and became a Jacobin in politics (a sympathizer with the extremists and terrorists of France), as he had become an atheist in religion.

The publication of *Political Justice,* his most important book, in 1793, brought him wide public attention. In fact, the book and its author escaped prosecution only because the government felt that "no harm could be done by a three guinea book"! The keynote of Godwin's entire literary career was in this book, which was marked by "extreme principles advocated dispassionately."

In 1796 he met Mary Wollstonecraft, author of *A Vindication of the Rights of Women,* and true to their common principles they formed a connection without the sanction of legality. However, when she became pregnant they bowed to convention; though they had kept separate establishments, they were married in March 1797—thus earning for Godwin the enmity of several of his lady admirers, chiefly the popular writer, Mrs. Inchbald. In August their daughter Mary was born, and ten days later Mary Wollstonecraft Godwin died. So far as Godwin could love anyone but himself, he had loved this singularly attractive and heroic woman. But he was left with two small children—for he had adopted Mary's other daughter, Fanny Imlay (her illegitimate child by Gilbert Imlay, an American)—and he looked about for a stepmother for them. One woman after another refused him, and at last to his misfortune and the children's he married Mary Jane Clairmont, a widow with a son and daughter of her own. In 1803 a son, William, was born to them; he died in 1832, after a brief literary career.

Mrs. Godwin the second was a shrew and a virago. The beginning of Godwin's long de-

WILLIAM GODWIN

scent in life had begun. He was involved in literary quarrels; his first play, produced at Drury Lane, was a dismal failure; he became poorer and poorer and finally grew into an incessant borrower, a sponger on the young men who looked up to him as a philosophic oracle. Mrs. Godwin conducted a publishing business for children's books (the Lambs' *Tales from Shakespeare* appeared under her imprint, and Godwin himself wrote some juvenile books for her under a pseudonym), but this too gradually sank to failure. Twice he became bankrupt and was rescued by friends. For a while Shelley became a source of supply, but even he wearied of incessantly giving to a man who denounced him publicly and extorted money from him privately. In 1816 Fanny Imlay killed herself; at the end of that year Shelley was married to Godwin's daughter Mary and ultimately ceased to contribute to his support.

In 1818 Godwin suffered a slight paralytic stroke. He continued to write, however, up to two years before his death, but of all his books, only the early *Political Justice* and *Caleb Williams* had any great success. In 1833 his financial troubles ended; he was made a yeoman usher of the exchequer, a sinecure which he retained until he died, when the government abolished the office. By this time his political and religious views had both softened; the influence of Coleridge had seduced him to a sort of vague theism.

After his son's death, Godwin's health gradually failed, until the end came in 1836. He was buried next to Mary Wollstonecraft in St. Pancras cemetery, but when the railroad was put through that part of London his grandson, Sir Percy Shelley, had the bodies disinterred and reburied beside his own mother's grave at Bournemouth.

It is hard to be just to Godwin. He was a pompous, hollow person, a professional optimist, self-centered and overbearing. This most extreme of the British revolutionary philosophers was almost without genuine emotion or idealism, a pedantic system-maker, with what someone has called "a remarkable capacity for reasoning without regard to experience." Nevertheless, he had his virtues: he was genuinely kindly, especially to the young, when it cost him no effort; he was hard-working, and he had the excuse of extreme and undeserved poverty for his unpleasant habit of cadging on his friends. His books now have merely an historical interest, though his novels are still curious reading as *tours de force*; he had no gift for fiction and they are purely efforts of the intellect, not of the creative imagination. He did one great service, however, to English literature—he fired and directed the genius of the young Shelley. For that much may be forgiven him, and posterity owes him its gratitude.
M. A. deF.

PRINCIPAL WORKS: *Philosophy*—Political Justice, 1793; The Enquirer, 1797; Of Population, 1820; Thoughts on Man, 1831. *History and Biography*—Life of Chatham, 1783; Sketches of History, 1784; Memoirs of the Author of A Vindication of the Rights of Women, 1798; Life of Chaucer, 1803; Essay on Sepulchres, 1809; Lives of Edward and John Phillips, 1815; History of the Commonwealth of England, 1824-28; Lives of the Necromancers, 1834; Essays, 1873. *Novels*—Caleb Williams, 1794; St. Leon, 1799; Fleetwood, 1805; Mandeville, 1817; Cloudsley, 1830; Deloraine, 1833. *Plays*—Antonio, 1800; Faulkener, 1807.

ABOUT: Brailsford, H. N. Shelley, Godwin, and Their Circle; Brown, F. K. The Life of William Godwin; Paul, C. K. William Godwin: His Friends and Contemporaries.

GORDON, ADAM LINDSAY (October 19, 1833-June 24, 1870), Australian poet, was born in the Azores of an old Scottish family. His father was a retired army captain, later professor of Oriental languages in Cheltenham College, his mother a spoiled and extravagant heiress. In his childhood the family moved to Madeira, and then to Cheltenham, in 1840. Gordon spent a year in the newly founded college in 1841, but was taken out as too young, and from 1843 to 1847 was at school at Dumbleton. He was then sent to the Royal Military College at Woolwich from 1848 to 1851, but was either expelled or his father was asked to take him away (the college records have been burnt). He was a wild boy whose chief interests were in boxing and horses; in fact his trouble at Woolwich arose from his stealing a horse from the stables to ride it in a race. By his father's influence, Cheltenham College took him back again in 1851, but he spent most of his time in the racing stables and the boxers' training

ADAM LINDSAY GORDON

quarters. His father then sent him to an uncle in Worcester, where he attended the Worcester Grammar School and he seems to have kept a few terms also at Merton College, Oxford. He had already started to write verses about his beloved horses, and had experienced his only (and unrequited) love affair, with Jane Bridges.

Finally, in despair, his father shipped him to South Australia in 1853. Australia was the making of him; he was excellently adapted to a pioneer country. Instead of presenting his letters of introduction, he joined the mounted police as a trooper. After two years he became a traveling horse-breaker and trainer. At this time he met J. E. Tenison Woods, then a Roman Catholic missionary, later a naturalist, who recognized the qualities of the young man and encouraged his intellectual interests and his writing. In 1862 Gordon married Maggie Park (niece of a Scottish innkeeper in Australia), who had nursed him after an accident. He was a kind husband, but never really loved his wife; a good deal of a snob, who felt keenly his social downfall, he never forgot their inequality in caste.

In 1864 Gordon came into £7000 by his father's death, bought some race horses, and became a steeplechase rider. In time he became the best in Australia. He also entered the Australian Parliament from Victoria. The next year he resigned and in 1867 went to Mt. Gambier to live by writing and horse-training, opening a livery stable. In 1868 he won three steeplechases in one day. He made constant attempts to get away from the gambling and drinking incumbent upon his racing associations, and each venture ran him more deeply into debt. Finally he was persuaded to sue for recovery of some ancestral lands in Scotland, and borrowed heavily to finance the suit. He had moved to Brighton, a suburb of Melbourne, and in 1869 suffered two bad falls while racing. In June 1870 he found he had lost his suit. He saw his last book of verses through the press, and the next day went out in the bush and shot himself. There is a monument to him in the Poet's Corner of Westminster Abbey.

With all Gordon's faults, which are obvious and which manifestly would have made his life a tragedy wherever he lived, Australia did more for him than any other place could have done, and he is rightly regarded as its national poet. Tall, thin, pale, moody, shy and haughty at the same time, ashamed of his extreme near-sightedness, he was more at home with horses than with men, and is indeed "the laureate of the horse." Phrases from his poems have become Australian proverbs, and such poems as "The Sick Stockrider" are known to every child. His verse is a strange compound of Kipling and Swinburne, with a touch of Byron, very reminiscent of other pioneer poetry, such as that produced in the west of America in its early days. Little of it is actual poetry, but his stirring ballads have still the authentic ring.   M. A. deF.

PRINCIPAL WORKS: The Feud, 1864; Sea Spray and Smoke Drift, 1867; Ashtaroth: A Dramatic Lyric, 1867; Bush Ballads and Galloping Rhymes, 1870; Collected Poems (ed. by M. Clarke) 1880.

ABOUT: Ross, J. H. Laureate of the Centaurs; Sladen, D. B. W. Adam Lindsey Gordon.

GORE, CATHERINE GRACE FRANCES
(Mrs. Charles Arthur Gore) (1799-January 20, 1861), novelist and dramatist, was born Catherine Moody, daughter of a Nottinghamshire wine merchant. She was very precocious, and was known to her childhood playmates as "the poetess." She was educated chiefly at home.

In 1823 she married Captain Charles Arthur Gore. Although she had ten children, her career as novelist, playwright, and publisher dated from her marriage. She wrote innumerable novels, many anonymously, which were tremendously popular. (One, The Banker's Wife, was dedicated to her guardian, a banker; it depicted an absconding banker, and apparently stimulated her guardian to go and do likewise—soon after, he absconded with £20,000 of her fortune!)

As a playwright, her most popular work was The School for Coquettes, which had a long run at the Haymarket; Lords and Commons (produced at Drury Lane), The King's Seal, and King O'Neil were less successful. In 1843 she won a £500 prize for Quid pro Quo. She also composed music, many of her songs being contemporary favorites.

From 1832 Mrs. Gore lived in France. She came into a fortune that year, and from then on her writing was less voluminous. In later years she became blind, and ceased to write. She returned to England, and bought a home in Hampshire, where she died at sixty. In all she wrote about seventy novels, in some two hundred volumes.

Mrs. Gore's were novels of high life, showing shrewd observation and keen insight. She had a gift for satire and for clever description. Nowadays the novels are of interest chiefly as social documents, since they depict ably the "high society" of the early and middle eighteen hundreds.

PRINCIPAL WORKS: Theresa Marchmont, 1824; The Lettre de Cachet, 1827; The Manners of a Day, 1830; Mrs. Armytage: or, Female Domination, 1836; Cecil: or, The Adventures of a Coxcomb, 1841; The Banker's Wife, 1843.

ABOUT: Hale, S. J. Woman's Record; Horne, R. H. The New Spirit of the Age.

GRAHAME, JAMES (April 22, 1765-September 14, 1811), Scottish poet, was born in Glasgow, where his father was a lawyer. He was educated at the University of Glasgow. He wished to enter the church, but instead was apprenticed to his cousin, a writer to the signet in Edinburgh, and was himself admitted as a writer to the signet in 1791. In 1795 he became an advocate. In 1802 he married his cousin; they had two sons and one daughter. Grahame was not very successful as an advocate, and once more his mind dwelt on the church. Finally, in 1809, he was ordained in London, and became a curate in Gloucestershire. The next year he moved to Durham; his health failed rapidly and he died about a year later.

Grahame's poems are deeply religious, meditative, and moving, with vivid descriptions of nature. Scott admired his work greatly. His most successful poem, The Sabbath, was published anonymously, because his wife had been very scornful of his writing: he had the satisfaction of hearing her enthusiasm over the authorless book, which he then proudly acknowledged as his own.

PRINCIPAL WORKS: The Rural Calendar, 1797; The Sabbath, 1804; Birds of Scotland (prose) 1806.

ABOUT: Lockhart, J. G. Life of Scott.

GRANT, MRS. ANNE ("of Laggan")
(February 21, 1755-November 7, 1838), Scottish poet, essayist, and biographer, was born Anne Macvicar, the daughter of an army officer who was sent to service in America in 1758, followed by his wife and child. They settled in Albany, where Anne was practically reared by the wife of General Schuyler. In 1765 her father was retired on half pay and bought an estate in what is now Vermont, which was confiscated during the Revolution. In 1768 he suddenly decided to return with his family to Scotland. In 1779 Miss Macvicar married a minister named Grant, who

had a church in Laggan. There she learned Gaelic, studied the Highland folklore, and wrote voluminous letters which afterwards formed the backbone of her best known book. Her husband died in 1801, leaving her penniless, with eight small children. Friends raised the money to publish a book of poems by subscription, and she made enough to move to Stirling in 1803. The publication of *Letters From the Mountains,* though it did not help her much financially, made her name famous, and in 1810 she moved to Edinburgh, where she became one of the circle of which Scott was a member. Meanwhile she supported herself and her children by taking boarders. From 1820 she was lame because of a fall. Finally in 1826 a government pension of £100 was secured for her, and her children now being grown, her last years were passed in easier circumstances.

Mrs. Grant's letters, and the book made of them, are lively and sympathetic. She was a noted wit and a good critic. Her more formal writing (including her verse) is highly artificial. A certain interest attaches to her *Memoirs of an American Lady,* for it was a tribute to her old benefactor, Mrs. Schuyler, though their opposite political creeds might well have made them enemies.

PRINCIPAL WORKS: Poems, 1802; Letters From the Mountains, 1806; The Highlands and Other Poems, 1808; Memoirs of an American Lady, 1808; Memoirs and Correspondence, 1844.

ABOUT: Grant, Mrs. A. Memoirs of an American Lady (see Memoir in ed. of 1876); "Paston, G." Little Memoirs of the Eighteenth Century.

GRANT, JAMES (August 1, 1822-May 5, 1887), Scottish novelist, was born in Edinburgh, of an old family of Jacobite leanings. His father was an army captain, his grandfather a noted advocate. His mother died when he was a small child. In 1833 his father was stationed in Newfoundland, and took with him his three motherless sons. They returned to Scotland in 1839. In 1840 Grant was gazetted as an ensign in the army, but in 1843 resigned his commission and entered the office of an Edinburgh architect. It was here that he began to write his long series of novels. Most of them were historical or based on his army experiences; in one of them he incorporated material from a book of travels, and was accused of plagiarism, but absolved. He also wrote a number of historical works. He moved to London, and in 1852 became the founder and secretary of the National Association for the Vindication of Scottish Rights, an organization which brought much ridicule upon him. He was an authority on military matters, and was frequently consulted by the War Office. He was married, his wife's maiden name having been Browne, and had two sons. In 1875 he became a Roman Cath-

olic. In later years his novels lost the popularity which had once been theirs, and he died destitute.

Grant was a modest, genial man, whose novels were vivacious, picturesque, and written in vigorous prose, but for the most part superficial.

PRINCIPAL WORKS: The Romance of War, 1845; Adventures of an Aide-de-Camp, 1848; Playing With Fire, 1887; Love's Labour Won, 1888.

ABOUT: Athenaeum May 14, 1887; Saturday Review May 14, 1887.

GRANT DUFF, SIR MOUNTSTUART ELPHINSTONE (February 21, 1829-January 12, 1906), Scottish essayist, was born in Aberdeenshire and educated at Edinburgh Academy, the Grange School, and Balliol College, Oxford, where he secured his B.A. in 1850 and his M.A. in 1854. He then went to London, studied law at the University of London (being given his LL.B. in 1854), and was called to the bar by the Inner Temple, joining the Midland Circuit.

He started writing at the same time, being one of the earliest contributors to the *Saturday Review.* He was elected to Parliament in 1857. In 1859 he married Anna Julia Webster, by whom he had four sons and four daughters. From 1868 to 1874 he was Under-Secretary of State for India, and in 1880 became Under-Secretary of State for the Colonies. From 1881, in which year he was knighted, to 1886 he was governor of Madras. He returned to England in 1887, and devoted the remainder of his life to study, writing, and social intercourse. He was a prominent clubman, traveled much, and knew most of the eminent men of his time. From 1866 to 1872 he had been lord rector of Aberdeen University; from 1889 to 1893 he was president of the Royal Geographical Society; and from 1892 to 1899 he was president of the Royal Historical Society. Besides his own writings, he edited a *Victorian Anthology.*

Frail, slight, and gentle, with extremely poor sight, Grant Duff was essentially a scholar, ultra-fastidious and refined, with a love of learning and a cultivated and rather precious style.

PRINCIPAL WORKS: Studies in European Politics, 1866; Notes on an Indian Journey, 1876; Miscellanies: Political and Literary, 1878; Ernest Renan, 1893-98; Notes From a Dairy, 1897-05; Out of the Past, 1903.

ABOUT: Grant Duff, M. E. Notes From a Diary; Out of the Past.

GRATTAN, THOMAS COLLEY (1792-July 4, 1864), Irish novelist and travel writer, was born in Dublin, the son of a solicitor who later retired from his profession and settled in the country. He was educated at a private school in Athy, and went to Dublin to study law, but instead became an officer in the militia, serving in the north of England. After trying unsuccessfully for an army commission, he set sail for South America to participate in the wars of independence against Spain, but on the boat met and fell in love with Eliza O'Donnel, married her, settled in France near Bordeaux, and began writing for a living. They had three sons and a daughter.

Grattan remained on the Continent for many years. He moved to Paris, where he became the friend of Lamartine, Thiers, and Washington Irving, contributed to the English magazines, and translated the French poets into English. In 1822 and 1823 he published a magazine of his own, the *Paris Monthly Review of British and Continental Literature*. In 1828 he was living in Brussels when his house was destroyed and he was driven to Antwerp by the revolution. In 1831 he lived in Heidelberg. In 1832 he became a gentleman of the privy chamber of William IV, then spent several more years in Belgium, as correspondent for the London *Times* and a friend of Leopold I.

In 1839 he was made British consul to Massachusetts, and lived in Boston until 1846, then resigning in favor of his son. His great achievement was assistance in drawing up the treaty which fixed the boundary line between the United States and Canada. Grattan returned to London, and spent the last years of his life in writing. His later novels are cheaply sensational, but the earlier ones, which are historical, are excellent and still make good reading. His travel sketches are delightful.

PRINCIPAL WORKS: Highways and Byways (three series) 1823, 1825, 1827; Traits of Travel, 1829; The Heiress of Bruges, 1831; Legends of the Rhine, 1832; Civilised America, 1859; Beaten Paths, 1862.

ABOUT: Grattan, T. C. Beaten Paths; Dublin University Magazine December 1853.

GRAVES, ALFRED PERCIVAL (July 22, 1846-December 27, 1931), Irish poet and editor, was born in Dublin, his father being the Anglican Bishop of Limerick. He was educated at Windermere College and at Dublin University, where he was graduated with high honors. From 1869 to 1875 he was clerk and private secretary in the Home Office. In 1874 he married Jane Cooper, who died in 1886. In 1891 he married Amalie von Ranke, daughter of the professor of medicine at the University of Munich. By his two marriages he had six sons and four daughters. One of his sons is Robert Graves, contemporary poet and novelist. He was editor-in-chief of *Every Irishman's Library*, a founder of the London Educational Councils, one of the founders of the Folk Song/Society, and president of the Irish Literary Society. From 1875 to 1910 he was Inspector of Schools. During his later years he lived in Harlech, Wales, and was much

interested in Welsh as well as in Irish folklore and poetry. He was closely associated with the Celtic renaissance movement.

Graves was primarily an editor and anthologist, though he wrote some plays and pageants, and is celebrated as author of the ballad, "Father O'Flynn." His poems have not been collected into a volume.

PRINCIPAL WORK: To Return to All That, 1930.
ABOUT: Graves, A. P. To Return to All That; Times December 28, 1931.

GRAY, DAVID (January 29, 1838-December 3, 1861), Scottish poet, was born in Dumbartonshire, the oldest of eight children of a poor hand-loom weaver. After leaving the parish school, Gray became a pupil-teacher in Glasgow, and with great hardship worked his way through the University of Glasgow. His parents wanted him to become a Free Church minister, but his heart was set on a literary career.

His first verses appeared in the *Glasgow Citizen*. They attracted the attention of R. Monckton Milnes, the critic (later Lord Houghton), and his words of commendation inspired Gray to go post haste to London in 1860.

It was a disastrous move. His first night, since he was penniless, was spent in Hyde Park, and the exposure excited a latent tubercular tendency. He had no money at all, and lived in the utmost privation, without sufficient food or clothing. His friend Robert Buchanan, the poet, who shared those painful days with Gray, has written touchingly of them in his essay on Gray and in his poems, "Poet Andrew" and "To David in Heaven." Milnes tried in vain to persuade him to return to Scotland and teaching, and then, since

DAVID GRAY

Gray would not do so, exerted himself to find reviewing and other literary work for him.

The progress of the disease was rapid. Gray revisited Scotland once, but had to leave at once for a warmer climate, going first to Richmond, and then, by the kind offices of Milnes, his constant benefactor, to a hospital at Torquay. All this time he was working on his chief poem, "The Luggie," an idyl of the stream which flowed past his birthplace.

At Torquay, Gray, realizing that he was near death, became hysterical with despair and fear. His whole heart was set now on returning to Scotland to die. In January, 1861, Milnes arranged for his journey. During the few months left to him, he wrote his sonnet sequence, "In the Shadows," a beautiful and moving work, though (perhaps inevitably) highly reminiscent of another young poet in similar circumstances—John Keats. The day before he died, at not quite twenty-three, Buchanan put in his hands a page proof of "The Luggie," and he died happy with that assurance that his work would see the light of day.

It is impossible to say what Gray's future might have been had he lived longer. His poetry has great natural beauty and high descriptive power, and a genius may have perished when he died. He was an experimenter and innovator in metrics, a poet of very great promise who by his own rash ambition destroyed himself too young to express very much of his natural endowment. No one can read "In the Shadows" without a pang of sympathetic anguish, and "The Luggie" still holds its own (though it has manifest defects due to the awkwardness of youth) in the ranks of nature poetry.   M. A. deF.

WORKS: The Luggie and Other Poems. 1862; Poetical Works, 1874.
ABOUT: Buchanan. R. W. David Gray and Other Essays; Gray, D. The Luggie, and Other Poems (see Memoir by J. Hedderwick and Prefatory Notice by R. M. Milnes).

GREEN, GEORGE (1793-June 1, 1841), mathematician, was born near Nottingham. His father was a miller. From his first childhood he showed a genius for mathematics. His family was too poor, however, to give him any but an elementary education, and he was obliged to study by himself. His work became known to various scholars, and he was enabled to publish his first research by subscription. It was not until 1833, when he was forty, that he entered Caius College, Cambridge. He received his B.A. in 1837 as fourth wrangler, his lack of training in formal mathematical practice keeping him from attaining the still higher standing which would otherwise have been his. He was made a fellow of Caius in 1839 but his health had broken down completely, and he went home to die at forty-seven. Green never attempted regular teaching, being of too retiring a nature, and confined himself as a tutor to setting examinations. He was an original research worker in mathematics and a great mathematical innovator. Considering what he accomplished in the few years remaining after he was able to secure proper training, the loss of the first forty years of his life is one of the tragedies of the history of science.

PRINCIPAL WORK: Mathematical Papers, 1871.
ABOUT: Green, G. Mathematical Papers (see Memoir by N. M. Ferrers).

GREEN, JOHN RICHARD (December 12, 1837-March 7, 1883), historian, the elder son of Richard Green, was born at Oxford. Reared at home in Tory and High Church traditions, the boy went to Magdalen College School at a little over eight. When his father died (1852) he became the charge of his uncle until he should reach the age of sixteen.

A sensitive and emotional youth, Green absorbed eagerly the traditions of Oxford and Magdalen College. Because, however, of his increasingly independent and liberal views, which caused friction both with his uncle and with the school authorities, he was removed from school, where he had done brilliantly, and sent to tutors. One of these, Mr. Yonge, entered him in a competition for a scholarship to Jesus College, Oxford. Green secured the election, although too young to accept the scholarship immediately.

At Oxford Green worked quietly by himself; little understanding or sympathy was given him, and he was graduated without distinction in 1860, having refused to read for honors. His lack of interest in the classics made an unfavorable impression upon college authorities. He had, however, contributed some papers on Oxford history to the *Oxford Chronicle*.

On leaving the University, he entered orders. At this time he was considering writing church history. A faithful clergyman, he assumed his duties in the poor East End district of London, working hard to better the condition of the ill and the wretched, and writing articles in the *Saturday Review* to get money for their needs. Ill health, and increasingly liberal theological views, led him to resign his post in 1869, and he accepted a librarianship at Lambeth.

During these years Green had made the acquaintance of such historians as Freeman and Stubbs, and had been planning a work on the Angevin kings. After his breakdown, fear for his health, and the requests of his friends, caused him to gather together his material in English history in *A Short History of the English People,* which, published in 1874, brought him fame and an enormous

JOHN RICHARD GREEN

reading public. In popularity the book compared with Macaulay's history. Feeling that an expansion of it would allow for more details in support of his views and would readjust to some extent the emphases in the earlier work, Green produced *A History of the English People* (published 1877-80).

In somewhat better health (the state of his lungs had forced him generally to spend winters in the Riviera), he married, in 1877, ALICE STOPFORD GREEN (1848-1929), herself an historian of considerable powers. Aided and encouraged by her, he began work on a history of the period of the early invasions in England.

Although his physical condition was aggravated by a hard journey to Egypt in the winter of 1880-81, Green finished *The Making of England*, which was published in 1882. He proceeded to work on *The Conquest of England* almost until his last day. In the autumn of 1882 he went to Mentone, where he died in the next March. His wife was able to publish *The Conquest of England* in 1883.

"You're a jolly vivid man," Tennyson said to Green when the latter visited him in 1877; and it is true that, despite the retirement occasioned by his invalidism, Green possessed considerable social charm. So absent-minded that he is said to have come home from school, as a boy, so absorbed in a book as to knock his head against lamp-posts, Green was keenly sensitive to beauty and to the more human aspects of nature. He was a powerful speaker and a successful clergyman because of his vivid imagination and his deep sympathies. During the cholera epidemic of 1866 he worked untiringly among the stricken, on one occasion falling downstairs in a vain attempt to carry down, alone, a sufferer whom

others would not help. Vivacious and curious, he was a delightful companion. It is thought that he was the original of Robert Elsmere in Mrs. Humphry Ward's novel. Politically he became Liberal, supporting Home Rule for Ireland and opposing Beaconsfield's pro-Turkish policy.

Green's success as an historian is due to his ability to relate materials dealing with the social, as well as the political, developments of the English people, his books presenting vivid pictures of the everyday things of the past. The author was keenly sensitive to the geographical aspects of local history, and was a sharp observer of the local phenomena explaining historical events. Of his work the historian Gooch writes: "The publication of the *Short History* in 1874 forms an epoch in historiography. The English-speaking world received the first coherent and intelligible account of its own past." While the existence of inaccuracies in the book has been indicated by such historians as Gardiner, and Green's writings are no longer completely trustworthy as history because of his tendency to accept hypotheses as facts and because of the discovery, since his time, of new material, their broad social interests and the charm of presentation give them permanent literary value. R. W. W.

PRINCIPAL WORKS: *Editor*—Readings From English History, 1879; Addison's Select Papers From the *Spectator*, 1880: Essays of Joseph Addison, 1881. *Geography*—A Short Geography of the British Isles (with Alice Stopford Greene) 1879. *History*—Papers in Oxford Studies, 1859; A Short History of the English People, 1874; A History of the English People, 1877-80; The Making of England, 1882; The Conquest of England, 1883. *Letters*—Letters of John Richard Green, 1901. *Miscellaneous*—Stray Studies in England and Italy, 1876.

ABOUT: Bryce, J. Studies in Contemporary Biography; Gooch, G. P. History and Historians in the Nineteenth Century: Green, J. R. Letters of John Richard Green (see biographical material by Leslie Stephen).

GREEN, MRS. MARY ANN EVERETT (July 19, 1818-November 1, 1895), historian and antiquary, was born in Sheffield, her maiden name being Wood. Her father was a Methodist minister, and her childhood was spent at chapels of which he was minister in various parts of Lancashire and Yorkshire, though for nine years they were settled in Manchester. She was educated at home. In 1841 she went to London and began a course of study by herself in the British Museum reading room. She began writing her *Lives of the Princesses* in 1843, but deferred publication until 1849, because of the appearance of Agnes Strickland's *Lives of the Queens of England*. In 1846 she married George Pycock Green, a painter, and spent two years with him in Paris and Antwerp, where she studied history while he painted. They returned to London at the end of 1848. In 1853 she was made one of the editors of *Calendars of State Papers,* and continued the work for forty years, editing forty-one volumes. This valuable but arduous task kept her from doing much original work she had contemplated; she did, however, contribute frequently to the magazines. Her husband was disabled by an accident, and she learned perspective in order to help him in his work; he died in 1893. She also interested herself in the education of her children, and wrote a text-book on pedagogy. She had one son, who died in 1876, and three daughters, one of whom became a novelist.

Simple, sincere, and noted for her charities, Mrs. Green was a true scholar, accurate and exhaustive, and a keen and discriminating critic.

PRINCIPAL WORKS: Letters of Royal Ladies of Great Britain, 1846; Lives of the Princesses of England, 1849-55; Letters of Queen Henrietta Maria, 1857.

ABOUT: The Queen December 14, 1895.

GREEN, THOMAS HILL (April 7, 1836-March 26, 1882), philosopher, was born in Yorkshire, of a clerical family on both sides: his father was a rector, his mother a vicar's daughter, and his great-uncle an archdeacon. His mother died when he was only one year of age, and his father looked after his education until at the age of fourteen, a bashful, awkward boy, he was sent to Rugby. In 1855 he went to Balliol College, Oxford, where his career was not remarkably brilliant. He was a sufficiently good student, however, to receive a temporary appointment as substitute lecturer on ancient and modern history at Balliol in 1860.

The same year he was made a fellow of Balliol, taking private pupils on the side to eke out his livelihood. For a long time he hesitated between journalism and teaching; his moderate heterodoxy shrank from signing the Thirty-Nine Articles of the Church of England (though he finally did so when he received his M.A. degree), and he refused to take holy orders.

In fact, Green did not actually settle on a career until the end of 1884, when he was nearly twenty-nine; his natural indolence stood in his way, as well as lack of agreeable opportunities. Then he became assistant commissioner to the Royal Commission upon Middle Class Schools, on which he served for two years. In 1866 he was made a lecturer on philosophy at Balliol, and in 1870 master of the college. He conquered an early distaste for his pupils and became friendly enough to take two or three of them with him on his vacations.

THOMAS HILL GREEN

Green's specialties as a lecturer were, first, Aristotle and the early Greek philosophers, second, the English thinkers of the seventeenth and eighteenth centuries. He became the foremost exponent in England of the philosophies of the Germans, Kant and Hegel, and the greatest antagonist of the Scottish philosopher Hume and of the utilitarian (pragmatic) school of Mill and Spencer. He published nothing except articles in technical journals, though he edited an edition of Hume and made some German translations, and all his posthumously published works are reprints of articles and lectures, except for his unfinished (and most important) contribution, the *Prolegomena to Ethics.*

In 1871 Green married Charlotte Symonds, sister of his old friend, the critic and essayist John Addington Symonds. They had no children. He became increasingly active as a speaker on various measure of political reform (he was always a mild liberal politically), and in 1874 was made a member of the Oxford School Board. An ardent teetotaller and advocate of local option, he established a coffee tavern in St. Clement's as a counter-attraction to the public houses. In 1878 he was appointed Whyte Professor of Moral Philosophy at Oxford and retained the post until his death.

Always frail, by 1878 it was apparent that he was afflicted with a congenital and incurable type of heart disease. He continued his active life, however, and was just about to move into a new house when he died suddenly, shortly before his forty-sixth birthday. By his will he left money for scholarships, and for a prize essay on moral philosophy.

A man of sturdy character and of great simplicity, plain, reserved, and typically middle class in his tastes and convictions, Green was respected by all who knew him. He was rather indolent of mind, and not a wide reader, but obstinately persistent in everything he undertook. The crux of his philosophy is a vindication of "the spiritual nature of the world and of men": he believed that "the whole world of human experience is the self-communication . . . of one eternal and absolute being," and that the universe is a self-conscious energy, and he laid particular stress, in his ethical theory, on "the importance of right thinking." He did a real service by his introduction to English-speaking students of the work of Kant and especially of Hegel. His style as a writer was unassuming and as lucid as the nature of his subject would allow.   M. A. deF.

PRINCIPAL WORKS: Hume's Treatise (ed. with T. H. Grose) 1874; Prolegomena to Ethics (ed. by A. C. Bradley) 1883; Works (ed. by R. L. Nettleship) 1885-8.

ABOUT: Fairbrother, W. H. The Philosophy of T. H. Green; Green, T. H. Works (see Memoir. Vol. 3); Maccunn, J. Six Radical Thinkers; Sidgwick, H. Lectures on the Ethics of Green.

GREG, WILLIAM RATHBONE (1809-
November 15, 1881), essayist, was born near Maidstone, the son of a prosperous merchant. Two of his brothers became well known, one as an economist, the other as a philanthropist. He passed his childhood in Cheshire, and was educated at the University of Edinburgh. In 1828 he became manager of one of his father's factories. In 1832 he set up in business for himself. In 1835 he married Lucy Henry. He moved to Ambleside for his wife's health a few years later, and his business, neglected from long-distance management, failed. In 1842 he had won a prize for an essay for the Anti-Corn Law League, and now he turned to writing for a living, and made his way by articles for the quarterlies on economic and political subjects. Meanwhile his wife had died, and he remarried, his second wife being a daughter of the economist, James Wilson. In 1856 Greg was made commissioner of the Board of Customs, and from 1864 to 1867 he was comptroller of customs. He was a natural aristocrat who was yet imbued with sympathy for the poor. As a writer he was urbane, super-cautious, and a good deal of a compromiser. His style was clear and simple.

His oldest son, PERCY GREG (1836-December 24, 1899), was a journalist, novelist, historian, and poet. He was a man of strong but changing opinions, being a Free Thinker in youth, a Spiritualist in middle life, and in his later years a reactionary who longed for the days of feudalism and was chiefly noted for his violent hatred of everything American. His lyric poems were good, and his novels showed much imaginative power, but his extreme prejudices vitiated the value of his work.

PRINCIPAL WORKS: *William Rathbone Greg*— The Creed of Christendom, 1851; Essays on Political and Social Science, 1853; Literary and Social Judgments, 1869; The Enigmas of Life, 1872; Miscellaneous Essays, 1882. *Percy Greg*—The Verge of Night, 1875; The Devil's Advocate, 1878; Across the Zodiac, 1880; History of the United States, 1887.

ABOUT: *William Rathbone Greg*—Greg, W. R. The Enigmas of Life (see Memoir in 18th ed.); Morley, J. Miscellanies. *Percy Greg*—Manchester Guardian December 30, 1899.

GREVILLE, CHARLES CAVENDISH
FULKE (April 2, 1794-January 18, 1865), political diarist, was the eldest of the three sons of Charles Greville, who was a grandson of the fifth Lord Warwick. His mother was the eldest daughter of the third Duke of Portland. Young Greville's education was in accordance with his position. He was sent to Eton after a childhood spent partly at Bulstrode, the house of his maternal grandfather, and partly at court, where he was page to King George III. He matriculated at Christ Church, Oxford, in 1810, but left before taking his degree to become private secretary to Earl Bathurst, a position to which he was appointed before he was twenty.

Greville cannot be named as one who struggled against odds to win his way in the world. It was through the influence of his grandfather, the Duke of Portland, that he received the secretaryship of the island of Jamaica. The duties of this office were deputized and, although Greville interested himself in Jamaica business, he never visited the island. His activities were those of a sporting young gentleman of fashion and were never hampered by lack of funds. His

CHARLES GREVILLE

especial interest was in the turf, where his wagers were heavy and for the most part successful. He had, however, a profound sense of ultimate values, which was impartial and disinterested and at the same time intensely human. Through his grandfather he obtained the reversion of the clerkship of the privy council and took over his duties in 1821. This clerkship is a permanent office, to which officially no political or confidential functions are attached. But Greville's qualities and personal friendships with both Whigs and Tories were such that he was frequently employed as negotiator by both parties. This was particularly the case during ministerial changes. He was especially active at the time of the Palmerston resignation in 1853.

It was Greville's considered opinion that his situation offered a splendid opportunity to make "a *contemporary* record of facts and opinions, not altered or made up to square with subsequent expressions." Temperamentally Greville was perfectly fitted for this undertaking, although it is likewise apparent that in assuming the clerkship he renounced what might have been a brilliant career in public life. The diary extends through the reign of three successive sovereigns, George IV, William IV, and Victoria. Greville spared no pains in completing his information and not only succeeded in accomplishing his purpose, but left upon the pages of his journals the imprint of his own fearless and manly character.

In his personal relations Greville was exceedingly happy. An avowed epicurean and cynic, he was popular with both the bon vivants and the serious-minded among his friends. His interest in blooded horses, which he frequently deplored, never abated. In 1821 he assumed the management of the racing stables of his friend the Duke of York and after the latter's death (1827) he trained with the Duke of Portland. He had several race horses of his own and it was one of the major disappointments of his sporting career that he never won a Derby. He was one of the oldest members of the Jockey Club. Greville's appearance was rather in keeping with his birth and interests. With a face both "solid and refined," of noble proportions and finely chiseled, his figure was square, sturdy and athletic.

During his lifetime Greville published several pamphlets on current events, and in 1845 anonymously a book advocating government pay for Roman Catholic clergy. But his principal concern was the journal which he intended for posthumous release. His friend, Sir George Cornewall Lewis, was chosen as executor. But Lewis died in 1863 and the papers were intrusted to Henry Reeve with the injunction that they were to be published at not too long a time after the writer's death. It is characteristic of Greville that so closely did he identify this work with his office that he closed the diary when he had resigned from the clerkship. He died suddenly of heart disease in his rooms in Lord Granville's house on Bruton Street, London, and was buried at Hatchford.

In the realm of historical portraiture Greville's sketches are masterly. The divinity hedging a king was not apparent to him and Victoria did not approve of these journals, which are probably the most valuable contribution of their time to nineteenth century history.   P. B. S.

PRINCIPAL WORKS: The Policy of England to Ireland, 1845; The Greville Memoirs: 1817-1837, 1875; The Greville Memoirs: 1837-1860, 1885.

ABOUT: Greville, C. C. F. The Greville Memoirs; Johnson, A. H. The Letters of Charles Greville and Henry Reeve.

GRIFFIN, GERALD (December 12, 1803-June 12, 1840), Irish poet, dramatist, and novelist, was born in Limerick, the son of a brewer.

His education was rather scattered, picked up at a school in Limerick, from a tutor, at a seminary where he learned something of the classics, and at a school in Loughill. In the Thespian Society of Limerick, a group of young dramatic writers to which he belonged, he met John Banim, Irish novelist, dramatist, and poet, who later proved to be a friend in need.

In 1823, having already written lyrics and experimented with drama, he went to London to begin a literary career. There, through Banim's influence, he contributed to periodicals. During this period of his life he was in considerable pecuniary distress, and underwent actual hardship. Having produced an English opera consisting entirely of recitative, he turned, at Banim's suggestion, to fiction his first success being *Holland Tide*. *Tales of the Munster Festivals*, descriptions of traditional Irish ceremonies, were very popular; and, after the appearance, in 1829 of *The Collegians*, Griffin had a reputation. While he continued to write, the precariousness of a career as an author induced him at one time to enter the University of London as a law student.

Indeed, he seems either to have lost his high hopes or to have allowed his religious leanings (always strong) to master him completely. In 1838 he returned to Limerick, and not long after, burning most of his unpublished works, he entered a religious organization, the Society of the Christian Brothers, and he worked as a member of the order until his death in 1840, which occurred at the North Monastery, Cork. His play, *Gisippus*, rejected again and again during his life, was

GERALD GRIFFIN

successfully produced in 1842, when the author was unable to enjoy his triumph.

"He was . . . a delicate, or rather refined-looking young man, tall and handsome, but with mournful eyes, and that unmistakeable something which prognosticates a sad life and an early death," wrote Samuel Carter Hall, in description of Griffin as a youth. "Though little more than a boy, he seemed almost exhausted; way-worn, though so fresh on life's journey." Apparently almost morbidly sensitive, the poet wandered about London nearly friendless, often going without food; and he was extremely reluctant to accept aid from acquaintances. While his actual sufferings were not very long, or even very dreadful, by comparison with those of many other authors, his spirit seems to have been dashed by his early struggles.

Griffin's literary reputation may be said to rest largely upon *The Collegians, Gisippus,* and his poetry. Of *The Collegians* Margaret Oliphant wrote, "Not even Miss Edgeworth's account of the successive squires of *Castle Rackrent* sets forth the wild groups of Irish gentry with so trenchant a touch as that with which Griffin represents his Cregans and Creaghs in their noisy carouses; and his peasants of all descriptions are full of humour and life. . . ." In general Griffin wrote better in the smaller forms; the want of unity and simplicity noticeable in his longer works did not show itself in the shorter tales. In poetry his gifts were lyrical, and his feeling for metre and rhythm places him definitely among the greater lyrical poets. Of the *dénouement* of *Gisippus,* Mary Russell Mitford, essayist, said that it "would draw tears from the stoniest heart that ever sate in a theatre."   R. W. W.

PRINCIPAL WORKS: *Novels*—The Collegians, 1829; The Invasion, 1831; The Duke of Monmouth, 1836; The Beautiful Queen of Leix: or, The Self-Consumed, 1853; The Day of Trial, 1853; The Voluptuary Cured, 1853. The Young Milesian and the Selfish Crotarie, 1853; The Kelp-Gatherer, 1854; A Story of Psyche, 1854; *Opera*—The Noyades, 1826. *Plays*—Gisippus, 1842. *Tales*—Holland Tide, 1827; Tales of the Munster Festivals, 1827, 1829; The Rivals [and] Tracy's Ambition, 1829; The Christian Physiologist: Tales Illustrative of the Five Senses, 1830 [repub. as The Offering of Friendship, 1853]; Tales of My Neighborhood, 1835; Talis Qualis: or, Tales of the Jury-Room, 1842.

ABOUT: Griffin, D. The Life of Gerald Griffin; Hall, S. C. A Book of Memories of Great Men and Women of the Age; Mitford, M. R. Recollections of a Literary Life; Monahan, M. Nova Hibernia; Oliphant, M. O. The Literary History of England in the End of the Eighteenth and Beginning of the Nineteenth Century; Brownson's Quarterly Review 16:342 July 1859; Dublin Review 16: 281 June 1844.

GROOME, FRANCIS HINDES (August 30, 1851-January 24, 1902), miscellaneous writer, was born in Suffolk, of which county his father was Archdeacon. He was educated at the Ipswich Grammar School, and at Corpus Christi and Merton Colleges, Oxford, but left in 1871 without taking a degree. From his boyhood he was fascinated by the gypsies, and came to know them intimately during his Oxford days. He studied for a while at the University of Göttingen, then for several years lived and traveled with the Hungarian and Roumanian gypsies. He married an English gypsy named Esmeralda Locke in 1876, but was separated from her later, though they were never divorced.

Groome's life falls into two divisions; his earlier years of Bohemian wandering, and his later years of slavery to an editorial desk. In 1876 he went to Edinburgh and joined the staff of the *Globe Encyclopaedia.* The next year he became sub-editor on the Ipswich *Journal,* and from 1882 to 1885 he edited the *Ordnance Gazetteer of Scotland.* In 1885 he entered the employment of W. and R. Chambers, the publishers, and was very prominent in the editing of *Chambers's Encyclopaedia.* He was a contributor to *Blackwood's, The Bookman,* and *The Athenaeum,* and to the *Dictionary of National Biography.* In spite of the failure of his marriage, he never lost interest in the gypsies, was joint-editor of the *Journal of the Gypsy Folk-lore Society,* and edited the books on gypsies of George Borrow, who was his distant cousin. He was a real authority on this subject, with a great fund of knowledge which he employed precisely and carefully. As a man he was frank and fearless; as a writer, vivacious and eminently readable.

PRINCIPAL WORKS: In Gypsy Tents, 1880; A Short Border History, 1887; Kriegspiel (novel) 1896; Gypsy Folk Tales, 1899.

ABOUT: Athenaeum February 22, 1902; Scotsman January 25, 1902.

GROTE, GEORGE (November 17, 1794-June 18, 1871), historian and philosopher, was the oldest of eleven children of a wealthy banker. On his father's side he was remotely of German ancestry, on his mother's of French Huguenot descent.

His mother was his first teacher, but at five and a half he was sent to school at Sevenoaks. From ten to sixteen, when his formal education ended, he was a pupil at the Charterhouse. The training was exclusively classical, whereas his own bent of mind was toward political and historical studies.

The life of Grote shows a strange parallelism with that of another English historian, Henry Thomas Buckle. Both were the sons of rich business men, denied university training and obliged to spend long years in their fathers' business, emancipated and made wealthy by the fathers' death, and devoted henceforth to lives of study and writing. Grote served in his father's bank until 1843, and until 1830 was obliged to give to it practically all his daytime hours.

He was of a melancholy, sensitive, and affectionate nature, and his home life was very unhappy. In the evenings he studied the classics, German, and economics by himself, and practised the violoncello, but his father heartily disapproved of these activities which took his son's mind off banking, and his mother was a severe and rigid Puritan who tormented him with naggings about his spiritual welfare. In spite of this discouragement and his natural dependence on sympathy for success, Grote persevered in his studies, which under the influence of a friend gradually turned largely to various aspects of philosophy.

But a still greater sorrow was to seize him. At twenty he fell deeply in love with Harriet Lewin, who was then twenty-two. A jealous rival told him (falsely) that she was already affianced; in despair at the thought that he had been trifled with, Grote swore never to marry without his father's consent. The consequence was that when he found out the falsehood and that Miss Lewin was more than receptive to his advances, his father refused to allow his marriage, and even prevented the lovers' communicating with each other for several years. Finally in 1820 Grote broke his rash vow and they were married.

It was a fortunate union, though their only child, a son, died at the age of one week. Mrs. Grote cheered her husband's melancholy, provided him with rest and recreation, encouraged him in his studies and writings, and pushed her shy and modest husband for-

GEORGE GROTE

ward in the attention of the world. Because of her health, they lived for the most part in the country (finally settling in Buckinghamshire), but Grote had to travel daily to the bank in London—in those days of slow locomotion—even being obliged to be present when the building was unlocked every morning and locked up again at night.

In spite of this servitude (in his thirties he seems still to have been completely under his father's thumb), Grote's plans for a career in authorship and public service were already laid. As early as 1822 he had begun to contemplate writing a history of Greece, which, strangely enough, did not then exist in English. (Mrs. Grote's memory is at fault when she says she gave him the idea in 1823, for previous mention of it exists in his letters). He had become a close friend of John Stuart Mill, and through him had become acquainted with the work of the economist David Ricardo and with the economist-philosopher Jeremy Bentham. All of these men, with their doctrine of "philosophic radicalism," their advanced reform liberalism, and their utilitarian theory of practicability as a guide to ethics, influenced him greatly. He was one of the several who endeavored to deal with Bentham's enormous mass of confused and repetitious notes and manuscripts, and to make coherent works out of them. He was keenly interested also in parliamentary reform, and (doubtless with a thought for his own curtailed education) in the establishment of London University (later University College). Of this he was one of the founders, with Mill and Brougham; for a while, however, he resigned in anger because they allowed a clergyman to become professor of philosophy.

In 1830 his poor health permitted even his morbid sense of duty to allow him a trip abroad. He spent the time in Paris, establishing relations with the French liberals who were to bring about the minor revolution of that year, which Grote helped to subsidize. For while he was in France his father died, and though he was not free of the family responsibility of the bank, he did inherit a sizable fortune and could regulate his own time.

Grote's fervor for parliamentary reform induced him to stand for election as a liberal, and he served from 1832 to 1841. He was an advocate of voting by ballot, a reform which, however, did not come about until just before his death. In 1841 he refused to run again, and spent the next year with his wife in Italy. In 1843 he definitely severed connections with the bank, to which he had been tied for 33 years, and resolved to live thenceforth the life of a scholar. All that he had published up to that time, besides the book made from Bentham's notes, were two brief works on parliamentary reform. Now he set to work in earnest on his vast history of Greece, which began to appear in 1845, though it was eleven years later before the twelfth and concluding volume was published.

Nevertheless Grote found time also for other activities. He had been active in founding the Mechanics' Institute for the education of working-men, and in 1846 he renewed his old connection with London University, becoming first treasurer, then president, of its council, and when it received full university rank being named as its vice-chancellor. The old fight over the eligibility of the clergy to teach philosophy was renewed, this time over the appointment of the celebrated James Martineau. Grote was defeated, and swallowed his defeat; after all Martineau was a Unitarian, not an Anglican, and so less unacceptable to Grote's rationalist views. Another cause for which he labored valiantly was the admission of women to the university examinations; this he did not secure until 1868.

As his history of Greece appeared, followed by his work on Plato, Grote's name became widely known and honors were showered upon him. He became a trustee of the British Museum in 1859, received an honorary D.C.L. from Oxford and LL.D. from Cambridge, was a fellow of the Royal Society, was made honorary professor of ancient history at the Royal Academy, and foreign correspondent of the French Academy of Moral and Political Sciences. In 1869 Gladstone offered him a peerage, but he declined it.

From 1870, Grote's health declined rapidly. He continued to work on his posthumously published book on Aristotle, but the history of science of which it was to be part was never completed. He died the next year, of the complications of old age, and was buried in Westminster Abby. By his own direction an autopsy was performed on his brain, which was found to be of unusually small size—another proof that mental ability depends, not on the size and weight of the brain, but on the depth and complexity of its convolutions.

Grote was a markedly public-spirited man, single-minded and courageous, conscientious, scrupulous of others, and very considerate. His shyness and modesty he hid under a dignified courtesy, and his natural impulsiveness and passion were firmly controlled. He was methodical and punctual to a fault. In spite of his long experience in banking, he had little aptitude for finance, and his wife relieved him of all property as well as household cares.

As a writer, he is a teacher, not an artist. He is given to downright statement, and appeals to the reader's judgment, not to his imagination or emotions. His history of Greece suffers by being too exclusively political (his dominant interest), and neglecting the sociological and economic aspects. But though he is sometimes too explicit and heavily earnest, his writing is essentially sound and sympathetic, and much of it is still valid and useful. The year after his death his widow published privately the poems he had written in their years of separation; but all Grote's poetry proves is that it is natural for a young man in love to turn to verse.

M. A. deF.

PRINCIPAL WORKS: *History*—History of Greece, 1845-56. *Philosophy*—Analysis of the Influence of Natural Religion on the Temporal Happiness of Mankind (from Bentham's notes) 1822; Plato and the Other Companions of Sokrates. 1865; Review of the Work [by J. S. Mill] Entitled Examination of Sir W. Hamilton's Philosophy, 1868; Aristotle (ed. by A. Bain & G. C. Robertson) 1872; Fragments on Ethical Subjects, 1876. *Miscellaneous*—The Minor Works of George Grote (ed. by A. Bain) 1873. *Politics*—Statement of the Question of Parliamentary Reform, 1821; Essentials of Parliamentary Reform, 1831; Seven Letters on the Recent Politics of Switzerland, 1847.

ABOUT: Grote, G. Minor Works (see Introduction by A. Bain); Grote, H. L. The Personal Life of George Grote; Warner, C. D. Library of the World's Best Literature (Vol. 12).

GROTE, JOHN (May 5, 1813-August 21, 1886), philosopher, was born in Kent. His older brother was the famous historian George Grote. He was educated privately, then went to Trinity College, Cambridge, in 1831. He was made a fellow in 1837 and stayed in residence until 1845, being ordained deacon in 1842 and priest in 1844. In 1847 he was given a perpetual curacy near Ware, then a college living at Trumpington, near Cambridge, where he spent the remainder of his life. In 1855 he became professor of moral philosophy at Cambridge. He was working on the second part of his *Exploratio Philosophica* when he died. He was unmarried, but had adopted a niece who lived with him. Besides his philosophical work, he wrote on history and education. He was a frail, highly nervous man, a very quick worker but with too widely scattered interests for great concentration on any one line. He was an independent thinker, with a simple, direct, reflective style. His work is eminently clear; he had a fine feeling for words, and contributed much of value to the glossology of philosophy.

PRINCIPAL. WORKS: Exploratio Philosophica: Rough Notes on Modern Intellectual Science, 1865; An Examination of the Utilitarian Philosophy (ed. by J. B. Mayor) 1870; A Treatise on Moral Ideas (ed. by J. B. Mayor) 1876.
ABOUT: Grote, J. An Examination of the Utilitarian Philosophy; A Treatise on Moral Ideas.

GROVER, HENRY MONTAGUE (1791-August 20, 1866), dramatist, poet, and miscellaneous writer, was born in Hertfordshire, his father being a solicitor. He was educated at St. Albans Grammar School. In 1816 he became a solicitor in London. He retired in 1824 and entered Peterhouse College, Cambridge, receiving his LL.B. in 1830. He then took holy orders, and in 1833 became rector of Hitcham, Buckinghamshire. A semi-invalid and a recluse, his clerical duties and his writing consumed all his time and energy. Besides his plays, which are closet dramas unfit for the stage, he wrote on theology, geography, history, economics, and physics. His work is competent, but hardly distinguished. It is more the writing of a cultured man with an interest in intellectual matters than the expression of any marked talent.

PRINCIPAL WORKS: Anne Boleyn: A Tragedy, 1826; Socrates: A Dramatic Poem, 1828; A Voice from Stonehenge, 1847.
ABOUT: Times August 21, 1866.

GRUNDY, SYDNEY (March 23, 1848-July 4, 1914), playwright, was born in Manchester, where his father was an alderman. His entire life was spent in his native city. He was educated at Owens College, Manchester, and called to the bar in 1869. He practised law in Manchester until 1876, when his success as a dramatist enabled him to give all his time to writing. Grundy never wrote an original play; all of his dramas, some of which became exceedingly popular and enjoyed long runs and many revivals, were adaptations from the French. They were not, however, so much translations as actual rewritings, and he had a distinct gift, especially for comedy.

PRINCIPAL WORKS: The Snowball, 1879; In Honor Bound, 1880. A Pair of Spectacles, 1890.
ABOUT: Times July 5, 1914.

GUEST, LADY CHARLOTTE. See SCHREIBER, LADY CHARLOTTE GUEST

GUEST, EDWIN (1800-November 23, 1880), historian and philologist, was born in Worcestershire; his father was a merchant, his mother (who died when he was a child) came of an old Scottish family. He was educated at King Edward VI's Grammar School, Birmingham, and at Gonville and Caius College, Cambridge, which he entered in 1819, receiving his B.A. in 1824, M.A. 1827, LL.D. and D.C.L. 1854; he was a fellow of Caius in 1824.

Guest was ambitious for a military career, but his father forbade it; He remained interested in army affairs all his life. He entered Lincoln's Inn in 1822, and was called to the bar in 1828, joining the midland circuit. He spent 1824 and 1825 in Germany, principally at Weimar with Goethe.

Finally Guest was able to abandon the law for literature. His chief interest was in the earliest history of England, and he delighted in walking tours for the study of ancient remains. In writing of Caesar's invasion of Britain he surveyed both sides of the Channel coast, and Napoleon III consulted him when he was writing his own life of Caesar. He was practically the founder of the Philological Society, for which he served as secretary for many years. He became a Fellow of the Royal Society in 1839, master of Caius in 1852, and Vice-Chancellor in 1854. In 1859 he married Anne (Ferguson) Banner, widow of a major in the Highlanders. He died in Oxfordshire at eighty.

Guest in a sense "created" Roman British history. Most of his work appeared originally in the *Transactions of the Philological Society*, the papers being collected after his death. His *History of English Rhythms* was the beginning of the modern study of English prosody.

PRINCIPAL WORKS: A History of English Rhythms, 1838; Origines Celticae and Other Contributions to the History of Britain (ed. by W. Stubbs & C. Deedes) 1883.
ABOUT: Guest, E. Origines Celticae (see Memoir by W. Stubbs and C. Deedes).

GURNEY, EDMUND (March 23, 1847-June 23, 1888), psychologist, was born in Surrey, his father being a clergyman. His mother died when he was ten. He went to day schools in London and in 1861 to a boarding-school at Blackheath. His father died, and his uncle was appointed guardian of the orphan family. The passion of Gurney's youth was music. His mother had been a musician, and he hoped to become a professional performer. In 1866 he went to Trinity College, Cambridge, securing his B.A. in 1871 and becoming a fellow in 1872. He suffered, however, from a congenital melancholy, almost melancholia, which alternated with periods of extreme elation, and in an endeavor to find peace of mind he left Cambridge and spent nearly a year in Italy. Returning, he lived in Harrow from 1872 to 1875, connected with a music school of which he had been one of the founders; but eventually he realized that his love for music was far greater than his ability, and that he could never succeed in it professionally. His interest in it, however, led him into valued researches on the physics and psychology of sound, and he wrote for the journals on all these topics. In 1877 he married Kate Sibley; they had one daughter.

Since music had failed him, he next studied medicine, first at University College, London, then in 1880 at Cambridge and in 1881 at St. George's Hospital; but his sympathy for suffering was so acute that he could not continue. He then turned to the law, and read at Lincoln's Inn until 1883, but this was outside his range of interest and he gave it up. He was by this time a regular contributor to *Mind*, and he was led gradually by the fusion of his philosophical and psychological studies into the investigation of psychic phenomena. His aproach was always strictly scientific, and he never became an entirely convinced Spiritualist, though he was one of the pioneers of modern study of the subject. He helped in 1882 to found the Society for Psychic Research, and was until his death its most active officer. He died at forty-one whether accidentally or not is not known, from an overdose of a narcotic taken for insomnia.

PRINCIPAL WORKS: The Power of Sound, 1880; Hallucinations, 1885; Phantasms of the Living (with F. W. H. Myers and F. Podmore) 1886; Tertium Quid, 1887.

ABOUT: Proceedings Society for Psychic Research Volume 359.

GUTHRIE, THOMAS (July 12, 1803-February 24, 1873), Scottish theologian and philanthropist, was born in Brechin, his father being a merchant and banker. He studied at the University of Edinburgh from 1815 to 1825, taking courses first in arts, then in divinity, then in medicine and science. He was licensed to preach in 1825, but not being able to secure a living he went the next year to Paris, where he studied science at the Sorbonne and medicine at the Hotel Dieu. From 1827 to 1829 he was manager of his father's bank. Finally in 1830, the same year he was married, he was made minister of a church near Arbroath. In 1837 he went to Edinburgh, becoming an extremely popular preacher. In 1843 he was one of 474 ministers who seceded from the national church, and became minister of Free St.

John's Church. He raised single-handed an immense fund to build manses for his fellow-seceders. The enormous amount of work he did made him a victim of heart disease, and from 1847 his physicians warned him that he must either rest or die. However, he did not retire until 1864, and he lived to be nearly seventy. In 1844 he became a total abstainer, and from this time he was a leading advocate of abstention from liquor. His great work as a philanthropist was in the establishment of the so-called ragged schools for poor children; he was not their originator, but he was their most active sponsor.

In 1849 the University of Edinburgh conferred a D.D. degree on Guthrie. In 1862 he was moderator of the Free Church General Assembly. From 1864 to his death he edited the *Sunday Magazine*. In 1865 he was given a fund of £5000 raised by subscription, most of which went to support the ragged schools. In 1869 he became a fellow of the Royal Society of Edinburgh.

It is not as a writer that Guthrie is most distinguished, but his books, like his sermons, were vigorous, moving, and eloquent.

PRINCIPAL WORKS: Pleas for Ragged Schools, 1847; The City: Its Sins and Sorrows, 1857; The Way to Life, 1862; Our Father's Business, 1867; Autobiography, 1874.

ABOUT: Guthrie, T. Autobiography.

HACK, MARIA (November 10, 1777-January 4, 1844), author of children's books, was born Maria Barton at Carlisle, in Cumberland, of Quaker parents. Bernard Barton, the poet and friend of Charles Lamb, was her brother. Three days before her twenty-third birthday she was married to Stephen Hack, a Chichester merchant. They had several children. After her husband's death she went to live in Southampton, where she joined the Church of England and died at the age of sixty-six.

Her books for children, once popular but now forgotten, were highly moral and educational. Particularly successful were three series of *English Stories*, delineating historical vents and characters between the accession of Alfred and the Reformation under the Tudor princes.

PRINCIPAL WORKS: Winter Evenings: or, Tales of Travellers, 1818; Grecian Stories, 1819; English Stories, 1820-25; Harry Beaufoy: or, The Pupil of Nature, 1821; Lectures at Home, 1834.

ABOUT: The Friend February 1844.

HAKE, THOMAS GORDON (March 10, 1809—January 11, 1895), physician and poet, was born at Leeds of an old Devonshire family. His mother was the daughter of Captain William Augustus Gordon. His father, who was something of a musician, died when Hake was three years old.

THOMAS GORDON HAKE

When a child of eleven he was deeply stirred on reading Shakespeare, and throughout his life he was haunted by a literary ambition, but it was not until his fiftieth year that he devoted himself seriously to the writing of poetry. He is rare among poets in that his poetic talents increased rather than diminished with advancing years.

He was educated at Christ's Hospital and took his M.D. at Glasgow. He traveled in Italy, studied medicine for a year in Paris, practised at Brighton, Bury St. Edmunds, where he became intimate with George Borrow and T. W. Donaldson, and at Richmond and elsewhere.

In his thirty-first year his *Vates: or, The Philosophy of Madness,* a fantastic romance, appeared in four incomplete numbers with illustrations by Landseer. *Vates* was later republished in *Ainsworth's Magazine* under the title of "Valdarno: or, The Ordeal of Art Worship." Dante Rossetti was impressed by this work and wrote about it to the author, who did not reply for many years. The friendship that eventually grew up between the two men was one of the most profound events in Hake's life. Rossetti encouraged Hake to devote himself to literature; and Hake, in turn, when Rossetti's physical and mental health gave way, was of great assistance to his friend. During the most critical period he nursed him in his own home, attended him on a trip to Scotland, and permitted his son, George, to act as Rossetti's companion and secretary. W. M. Rossetti, referring to this time said, "Dr. Hake was the earthly providence of our family."

Dante Rossetti paid Hake the singular honor of reviewing him in *The Academy* and the *Fortnightly Review;* and a group of

literary people were interested in his writing; but most readers of his day were not attracted. In his poetry he risked obscurity for depth, too often sacrificed grace and charm to grotesque elements, employed diction and symbolism too difficult and strange, and produced a music too disconcerting to suit the public at large. His prose also won him little popularity, largely because when dealing with anything but the most ordinary matters it seems labored and unnecessarily involved.

Maiden Ecstacy and *New Symbols* are generally considered his two finest volumes of verse. His most widely known poem, "The Blind Boy," was inspired by the blind poet, Phillip Bourke Marston. Christina Rossetti said that Hake's "Ecce Homo" impressed her more than did any other poem of her own time. His volume of pantheistic sonnets in the Shakespearean form, *The New Day,* displays a remarkable development in his mastery of poetry. He wrote them when he was eighty years old.

Hake was a strange mixture of scientist and poet. He knew nature, not in the way that Wordsworth, for instance, did, but as a scientific observer; and for many years while he was engaged in writing poetry, he contributed a number of scientific papers to medical journals.

During the latter years of his life, an injury confined him to one room, but his faculties remained unimpaired. His autobiography, published in his eighty-third year, is remarkably "unpoetic" and simple, and concerned mainly with every-day matters.

One of his sons, Alfred Egmont Hake, is the biographer of General Charles Gordon.

"Never was an English poet more exotic than Dr. Hake," wrote Arthur Symons in *Studies in Two Literatures.* "But no doubt the interest of his poetry is too exclusively intellectual and concerned in too abstract a way with what Mr. Swinburne calls the 'soul of sense.' He goes straight to the essence of things, and the essential is always a little meagre and unsatisfactory to the broad general taste." And again: "Dealing by preference with morbid themes, he impresses one as being himself no more morbid than a surgeon whom we see entering a hospital."

Alice Meynell has written of him: "The exceeding solemnity of what we have called Dr. Hake's note—and it is as indescribable and peculiar as the note of a voice—suggests a further meaning, even an allegory, where in fact he had no intention of proposing anything beyond the text. . . He wrote movingly of dreams and sleep; and his study of these has added to all or almost all his verse something of the ecstasy of dreams."   P. G.

PRINCIPAL WORKS: *Poetry*—The World's Epitaph, 1866; Madeline and Other Poems, 1871; Parables and Tales, 1872; New Symbols, 1876;

Legends of Morrow, 1879; Maiden Ecstacy, 1880; The Serpent Play, 1883; The New Day, 1890; Selected Poems (selected by Alice Meynell) 1894. *Drama*—Piromides, 1839. *Biography*—Memoirs of Eighty Years, 1892. *Miscellaneous*—Vates: or, The Philosophy of Madness, 1840; The Powers of the Alphabet, 1863; On Vital Force: Its Pulmonic Origin, 1876.

ABOUT: Hake, T. G. Memoirs of Eighty Years; Selected Poems of T. G. Hake (see Preface by Alice Meynell); Rossetti, W. M. Life of Dante Gabriel Rossetti; Symons, A. Studies in Two Literatures; Watts-Dunton, T. Old Familiar Faces.

HALIBURTON, THOMAS CHANDLER

(December 17, 1796—August 27, 1865), Canadian humorist and satirist, only son of William Hersey Otis Haliburton, District Judge of the Superior Court of Common Pleas, and Lucy Grant, was born in Windsor, Nova Scotia. He was fond of saying that his father and he were born in the same house, twenty miles apart, and then explaining that the house, a settler's cottage, had been floated down the Avon river, after his father's birth, to a new location at Windsor.

He was educated at grammar school and at King's College in his home town. He married Louisa Neville in 1816. Four years later he was admitted to the bar. He built up a lucrative law practice at Annapolis Royal, the former capital of Nova Scotia, and played a prominent Tory part in the legislature. When his father died, he accepted the vacant position as judge, and at the age of fifty-five he went to the Supreme Court of the Province.

His first published work, *Historical and Statistical Account of Nova Scotia*, won him official honors at home; and although it is still a useful reference, he had one of his characters in a later work ridicule it as "next to Mr. Josiah Slick's History of Cattyhunk in five volumes, the most important account of unimportant things."

It is, however, as the creator of Sam Slick, the wandering Yankee clockmaker, that Haliburton is remembered. His conception of the character came from a case he judged of a peddler from the States who swindled farmers by selling them clocks that would not go; and he first employed him in a series of sketches, published in *The Novascotian* newspaper in 1835, in an attempt to awaken the people of the province from what he considered their improvidence and lethargy, and to turn their interests from politics to industry. Haliburton's passionate devotion to imperial unity also motivated many of the early sketches.

There are certain inconsistencies in the character of Sam Slick as viewed in many adventures written over a period of twenty years, but on the whole he was a slangy, under-bred, vulgar, energetic, shrewd, cunning rogue. Occasionally when he voices for the author a serious thought, he sounds more

THOMAS CHANDLER HALIBURTON

like a supreme court judge than a peddler, but usually his speech is epigrammatic, rich in picturesque slang, and brilliantly amusing.

The newspaper sketches were collected and other sketches added, to make up *The Clockmaker: or, Sayings and Doings of Samuel Slick of Slickville*, in three series, which won instant popularity in Canada, England, and the United States, and gave rise to a number of imitations and pirated editions. From satirizing local affairs, Haliburton then turned to a larger world, and in the next books Slick comments on conditions throughout Canada and abroad. He pokes fun at Colonial bishops, society in England, camp meetings in the States, Mormons, reformers, drunkards and professional prohibitionists, selfish politicians posing as patriots, a popular Cheltenham preacher who advertises the gaieties of the place by denouncing them, talkative travelers, and hypocrites of all sorts. Haliburton's *Attaché* was a burlesque and kindly reply to Dickens' *American Notes*.

In 1856 Haliburton retired from the Supreme Court and went to England. There he married Sarah Harriet Owen Williams, joined the Athenaeum Club, and was elected to the House of Commons where his fellow members were disappointed that his occasional speeches were grave rather than humorous and where he was unhappy to find the Tories did not share his own rather old-fashioned views.

Artemus Ward has called him the founder of the American school of humor. The *London Spectator* described him as "one of the shrewdest of humorists." F. B. Crofton wrote of him as "more to be admired as a humorist than as a stylist, and more than either, perhaps, as a thorough student and acute judge of human nature."

Topsy, Peck's Bad Boy, and other comic American characters are indebted to the wit of Sam Slick, and many of his remarks seem worn today, because of their adoption by other characters. It is generally considered that Haliburton's greatest contribution to literature was his uncovering a rich store of dramatic material in Canada and the United States and indicating its possibilities for fiction.   P. G.

PRINCIPAL WORKS: Humor—The Clockmaker: or, Sayings and Doings of Samuel Slick of Slickville (3 series) 1836-38-40; The Letter-bag of the Great Western: or, Life on a Steamer, 1839; The Old Judge: or, Life in a Colony, 1843; Sam Slick's Saws and Modern Instances, 1843; Traits of American Humour by Native Authors (ed.) 1843; The Attaché; or, Sam Slick in England (4 vols.) 1843-4; Nature and Human Nature, 1855. History—A Historical and Statistical Account of Nova Scotia, 1829; The Bubbles of Canada, 1839; Rules and Misrules of English in America, 1850.

ABOUT: Chittick, V. L. O. Thomas Chandler Haliburton: A Study in Provincial Toryism; Crofton, F. B. Haliburton: The Man and the Writer.

HALL, BASIL (December 31, 1788-September 11, 1844), Scottish naval captain and author of travel books, was born in Edinburgh, the son of Sir James Hall, founder of experimental geology. After attending the high school of Edinburgh he entered the British navy in his fourteenth year. He made voyages of exploration and scientific inquiry and wrote books about them. Deservedly popular were his journal of travels along the coast of South America and his nine-volume Fragments of Voyages and Travels.

He retired from naval service in 1823. In 1827-28 he made a fourteen-months tour of the United States, recording his critical observations in a book which, together with the outspoken letters of his wife, MARGARET HUNTER HALL (1799-1876), published in 1931 as The Aristocratic Journey, forms a valuable record of American life.

His last years were taken up with literary and scientific pursuits in England. It was Hall who obtained passage for Sir Walter Scott to Malta in 1831. He died insane in a Portsmouth hospital at the age of fifty-five. Besides his travel works, he is remembered for Schloss Hainfeld, a novel of the duchy of Styria in Austria-Hungary.

PRINCIPAL WORKS: Account of a Voyage of Discovery to the West Coast of Corea, 1818; Journal Written on the Coasts of Chili, Peru, and Mexico, 1824; Travels in North America, 1829; Fragments of Voyages and Travels, 1831-33; Schloss Hainfeld: or, A Winter in Lower Styria, 1836; Patchwork, 1841; The Midshipman (autobiographical sketches of his own early career, from Fragments of Voyages and Travels) 1862.

ABOUT: see Hall's own works.

HALL, ROBERT (May 2, 1764-February 21, 1831), Baptist preacher and author of sermons, was born at Arnesby, Leicestershire, the youngest of fourteen children of a Baptist minister. He was educated at the Baptist Academy in Bristol and at King's College, Aberdeen, Scotland. Following a theological apprenticeship, he served successively as pastor of churches in Cambridge (1791-1806), Leicester (1807-25), and Bristol (1825-31). Of delicate health, he was temporarily insane in 1804-05 and again in 1805-06. He died at the age of sixty-six, leaving four children.

Hall's fame rests chiefly on his pulpit oratory; he was rated the outstanding preacher of his time. He created a sensation with publication of his discourse on Modern Infidelity, and delivered his most celebrated sermon on the death of Princess Charlotte in 1817. Dugald Stewart found in his writings "the English language in its perfection."

PRINCIPAL WORKS: Christianity Consistent With a Love of Freedom, 1791; Apology for the Freedom of the Press, 1793; Modern Infidelity Considered With Respect to Its Influence on Society, 1800; Works, 1832; Miscellaneous Works and Remains (in Bohn's Standard Library) 1846.

ABOUT: Gilfillan, G. Galleries of Literary Portraits: Vol. 2; Hall, R. Works (see Memoir by O. Gregory and Essay by J. Foster).

HALL, MRS. S. C. (January 6, 1800-January 30, 1881), Irish author of sketches and novels, was born Anna Maria Fielding in Dublin. She lived in England from the age of fifteen. After her marriage at twenty-four she became well-known as the author of books on Irish life, based on recollections of people and places she had known intimately in girlhood. Besides sketches and novels, she wrote short stories, plays, and children's books. Her works, which were marked by a high moral tone and delicate humor, never found popularity in her native country because she refused to side with either political party. She was an active worker for temperance, women's rights, and hospitals. In old age she received a yearly pension of £100. She died at eighty-one.

Her husband, SAMUEL CARTER HALL (1800-1889), was a London journalist, founder of the Art Journal (1839) in which he exposed the trade in spurious "old masters." He wrote several books on art and A Book of Memoirs of Great Men and Women (1871).

The works written and edited by Mr. and Mrs. S. C. Hall, independently and jointly, numbered more than five hundred volumes.

PRINCIPAL WORKS OF MRS. S. C. HALL: Sketches of Irish Character, 1829-31; Lights and Shadows of Irish Life, 1838; Tales of the Irish Peasantry, 1840; Marian: or, A Young Maid's Fortunes, 1840; Ireland: Its Scenery, Characters, Etc. (with S. C. Hall) 1841-43; The White Boy, 1845.

ABOUT: Hall, S. C. Retrospect of a Long Life.

HALLAM, ARTHUR HENRY (February 1, 1811-September 15, 1833), poet and essayist, was the son of the celebrated historian Henry Hallam. His brief life of twenty-two years bore little of incident, and what he left behind him was little more than an unfulfilled promise and an immortal memory in the heart of his greatest friend.

Hallam was born in London, but at the age of seven, already a remarkably precocious child, he was taken abroad by his father for several years. Even at seven, it was said that on this tour he "learned French and unlearned Latin." At Eton, where he went at eleven, he became the close friend of Gladstone, the future prime minister, who was two years his senior. Gladstone records that Hallam was "the best scholar of the school." His first published writing was in the *Eton Miscellany* in 1827.

He left Eton in that year, and traveled on the Continent for eight months with his family before he went to Cambridge. There his scholastic record was not quite so brilliant, since the subjects then most emphasized were those in which Hallam was weakest; he disliked mathematics, and had had no rigorous training in the classics. On the other hand, he had already gained an easy familiarity with and fluency in Italian. It was at Cambridge that he and Tennyson met and formed their deathless friendship. There were other friends, too, in their intimate debating society, and Hallam was greatly beloved.

In the Long Vacation of 1830 he and the youthful Tennyson made a romantic trip to the Pyrenees, to deliver funds to a group of democratic rebels against the Spanish monarchy. They returned unharmed, though a similar English mission the next year resulted in the killing of two of the emissaries when the rebellion was crushed. Hallam and Tennyson went back unscathed to Cambridge, where in 1831 Hallam won the first college prize for declamation. He was already writing notably fine poems, some of which were published in the *Englishman's Magazine*.

In 1832 Hallam left Cambridge and went to London to read law in Lincoln's Inn. That year he became engaged to marry Emily Tennyson, Alfred's sister. The following spring he had a sharp attack of influenza, and though he recovered, his always frail health alarmed his father, who took him from his studies for a tour of Germany and Austria. In Vienna, a month after they left England, Arthur Hallam died suddenly of a cerebral hemorrhage.

The scattered manuscripts, mostly unpublished, which he left were collected and published by his father. His highly subjective poems were much influenced, first by Byron, then by Shelley, Keats, and Wordsworth, and

ARTHUR HENRY HALLAM

he had begun to fall under the spell of Coleridge. He was devoted to Dante as well, and had started a translation of the great Italian's *Vita Nuova*. Hallam's was a naturally religious spirit, and he was becoming more and more engrossed in metaphysical thought and feeling. His prose shows a surprising maturity of mind and a sound critical faculty. Dr. John Brown said of him: "He was on his way to God and could rest in nothing short of Him, otherwise he might have been a poet of genuine excellence." And Tennyson, who immortalized Hallam in *In Memoriam*, summed up his friend's nature by the simple words: "He was as near perfection as mortal man could be." M. A. deF.

PRINCIPAL WORKS: Remains in Verse and Prose (edited by H. Hallam) 1834; The Poems of Arthur Henry Hallam: Together With His Essay on the Lyrical Poems of Alfred Tennyson (ed. by R. Le-Gallienne) 1893.

ABOUT: Brown, J. Horae Subsecivae; Hallam, A. H. Remains in Verse and Prose (see Memoir by H. Hallam); Hallam, A. H. The Poems of Arthur Henry Hallam, etc. (see Introduction by R. Le-Gallienne); North American Review 193:221 February 1911; Publications of the Modern Language Association of America 50:568 June 1935; Queen's Quarterly 41:194 May 1934.

HALLAM, HENRY (July 9, 1777-January 21, 1859), historian, was the only son of the canon of Windsor, dean of Bristol. He was a very precocious child, having read many books by the time he was four and written a sonnet sequence at ten.

At Eton and later at Christ Church College, Oxford, he had a brilliant career. He received his B.A. in 1799 and was soon after called to the bar, traveling the Oxford circuit. His father's death in 1812 made him heir to considerable property in Lincolnshire, and at

HENRY HALLAM

about the same time he was appointed to the sinecure office of Commissioner of Stamps, which involved very light duties and carried a good salary. He felt, therefore, in a financial position to devote all his time to study and to the writing of history, the chief interest of his life. He thereupon resigned from the bar and ceased to practise. The same lack of acquisitiveness led him later to relinquish the large pension which should normally have been his on retirement from the Commissionership of Stamps.

In 1807 Hallam married Julia Elton, by whom he had eleven children. Only four of these grew up, however, and of them all, only one daughter survived him. The best known of his children was the poet Arthur Henry Hallam, Tennyson's friend, who inspired *In Memoriam*; his father was with him in Austria when he died with shocking suddenness. A man of deep domestic affections, warmly attached to his family, the successive deaths of his children cast a veil over Hallam's life, and the death of his last son, Henry Fitzmaurice Hallam, in 1837, made the writing of the older man's last work, the *Introduction to the Literature of Europe*, a sadly burdensome task.

Hallam never withdrew entirely from social life, though he was no conversationalist and seems to have had more respect from than popularity with his associates. He was treasurer of the Statistical Society, which he helped to found, and very active as vice-president of the Society of Antiquaries. He was also honorary professor of history of the Royal Society, and foreign associate of the Institute of France. In 1830 he received one of the two medals, valued at fifty guineas each, offered by George IV for eminence in histori-

cal writing, the other going to the American writer, Washington Irving.

Hallam wrote very little outside of his three books, being represented otherwise only by a few brief magazine articles and essays. He was essentially a recluse, a scholar of the library, dignified and rather severe except in the bosom of his family. He was not handsome, but people noticed his "noble and massive head."

Although he was a lifelong Whig, Hallam could not be described as a liberal. He was greatly opposed to Parliamentary reform or to the giving of greater electoral privileges to the people. Throughout his work his prejudices are obvious. His Whiggism belonged to what someone has called the "finality school"—his admiration of the British constitution was based on his feeling that it was finished, perfect, and unalterable, and his democratic principles stopped with what had already been accomplished. His most pleasing personal trait, outside of his domestic devotion, was his really excessive generosity; his wealth was to him truly a trust, and he dispensed it freely.

Hallam was no generalizer and was averse to abstract thought. His writing is unimaginative, but it is honest and accurate, two very desirable traits in an historian. It is raised above the merely pedestrian level by the sense he gives of great issues and stirring combats at work below the surface of the plodding narrative. His *Europe During the Middle Ages* was the first history in English entirely from original sources, neither a compilation or a contemporary chronicle: in other words, it was the first true history written in England, and is a landmark in historical method. His greatest difficulty, especially in the *Introduction to the Literature of Europe*, is that he took in too wide a field. It is impossible to cover in a single work the vast territory which it includes and at the same time to give due notice to all the persons and movements involved. Yet his *Constitutional History of England* suffers from the opposite defect of not covering ground enough—of starting too late and ending too early to be a reasonably complete account of its subject.

It is curious that up to the date of the present writing Henry Hallam has not had a single biography published concerning him, and has received only cursory mention in general surveys. His work was thorough and in some sort monumental, and he deserves better of posterity than he has received. He has been called "the magistrate of history." Possibly this is the explanation of the neglect to which he has been subjected.   M. A. deF.

PRINCIPAL WORKS: A View of the State of Europe During the Middle Ages, 1818; A Constitutional History of England From the Accession of Henry VII to the Death of George II, 1827;

Introduction to the Literature of Europe During the Fifteenth, Sixteenth, and Seventeenth Centuries, 1837-9.

ABOUT: Garnett, R. History of English Literature; Mignet, F. A. M. Éloges Historiques.

HAMERTON, PHILIP GILBERT (September 10, 1834-November 4, 1894), art critic and essayist, was born at Laneside, Lancashire. His mother died a few days after his birth and he was brought up by aunts at Burnley. He was educated at Burnley and Doncaster grammar schools. An independent income enabled him to marry a French girl, Eugénie Gindriez, in 1858, and spend a few years painting on the island of Innistrynich in Loch Awe, a Scottish lake. Then he settled in France near Autun and turned to writing.

Of his many successful books on art, two volumes on French painting were particularly notable and *Etching and Etchers* became a standard text. His most important literary work, according to Richard Garnett, "was performed as an essayist, and included five books of the highest merit in their respective departments." Of these, *The Intellectual Life* and *Human Intercourse* were best known. He founded (1869) and edited (as long as he lived) *The Portfolio,* one of the leading art periodicals in England.

Saddened by the tragic death of a son, he removed in 1891 to Boulogne-sur-Seine, where he died of hypertrophy of the heart at sixty. His autobiography was completed by his widow.

PRINCIPAL WORKS: *Books on Art*—A Painter's Camp in the Highlands, 1862; Contemporary French Painters, 1865; Painting in France After the Decline of Classicism, 1868; Etching and Etchers, 1868; The Graphic Arts, 1882; Landscape in Art, 1883; Life of Turner, 1879. *Essays*—The Intellectual Life, 1873; Round My House, 1876; Modern Frenchmen, 1878; Human Intercourse, 1882; French and English, 1890.

ABOUT: Hamerton, P. G. Autobiography (see Memoir by Mrs. Hamerton).

HAMILTON, ELIZABETH (July 21, 1758-July 23, 1816), Scottish poet and novelist, was born in Belfast, Ireland. (Her mother was Irish.) Left an orphan at the age of nine, she grew up in Stirlingshire, Scotland, on the farm of her father's sister. After the deaths of her aunt and uncle she lived for a time in London with her brother, Charles Hamilton, eighteenth-century Orientalist, remembered as the author of a history of the Rohilla Afghans in India. Thereafter she lived with her sister Katherine (a Mrs. Blake) in the English countryside and (after 1804) in Edinburgh. She died two days after her fifty-eighth birthday at Harrogate, England, whither she went for her health.

Mrs. Hamilton (as she preferred to be called though she was unmarried) is known for two notable works, written during her last years in Scotland: a homely Scottish song, "My Ain Fireside," and a Scottish tale, *The Cottagers of Glenburnie.* The latter was born of her philanthropic interest in improving the farmers of the country, and contained reminiscences of her girlhood in Stirlingshire.

PRINCIPAL WORKS: The Hindoo Rajah, 1796; Memoirs of Modern Philosophers, 1800; The Cottagers of Glenburnie, 1808.

ABOUT: Benger, Miss. Memoirs of Mrs. Eliz. Hamilton.

HAMILTON, THOMAS (1789-December 7, 1842), Scottish novelist, was the son of a Glasgow professor of anatomy, William Hamilton, and the younger brother of Sir William Hamilton the philosopher. He attended Glasgow University but did not take a degree. After trying a business career in Glasgow without success, he spent about eight years in the army as a captain and saw service in Spain (where he was wounded in 1811), Nova Scotia, and France.

About 1818 he retired on half pay, settled in Edinburgh, and became an important member of the *Blackwood* group of writers. John Wilson praised him in *Noctes Ambrosianae.* He was intimate with Scott at Chiefswood, where he spent several summers at Lockhart's cottage and with Wordsworth at Elleray. He died of paralysis in his fifty-third year at Pisa, Italy, during a Continental sojourn, and was buried beside his first wife at Florence. (He was twice married.)

Hamilton is remembered mainly for a popular novel, *Cyril Thornton,* containing vivid sketches (sometimes uncomplimentary) of university life and social life in Glasgow, and of military campaigns he had experienced. It is a valuable record of the early 1800's. A book recording the author's unfavorable impressions of America caused resentment in the United States.

PRINCIPAL WORKS: Cyril Thornton, 1827; Annals of the Peninsular Campaign, 1829; Men and Manners in America, 1833.

ABOUT: Veitch, J. Memoir of Sir William Hamilton; Wilson, J. Noctes Ambrosianae.

HAMILTON, SIR WILLIAM (March 8, 1788-May 6, 1856), Scottish philosopher, was born in the precincts of the College of Glasgow, where his father, a surgeon, was professor of anatomy and botany. The father died when the child was only two. After terms at the Glasgow Grammar School, at other schools in Chiswick and in Bromley, Kent, and at Glasgow University, he went in 1806 to study medicine at Edinburgh University. The next year found him at Balliol College, Oxford. Handsome, athletic, and of exuberant spirits, he was a well known figure there, known as "the most learned Aristotelian in Oxford." His scholarly career, however, was injured both by his being a Whig, in a time of Tory

SIR WILLIAM HAMILTON

dominance, and by the unpopularity of Scottish students. He received his B.A. degree in 1811 (and his M.A., *in absentia,* in 1814), and suddenly resolved after years of study of medicine to enter the legal profession instead. He went to Edinburgh, his home thenceforth, and became an advocate in 1813, soon after that date being called to the bar.

As an attorney Hamilton was not a great success; he was a poor speaker, was averse to court appearances or to political maneuverings, and never had a large practice. In fact, at this period as throughout his life, he was reduced to real poverty. His legal experience did, however, procure a title for him, in a very peculiar manner: he studied his own genealogy, established himself in court as the "heir male in general" to one Sir Robert Hamilton, baronet, and thereafter always styled himself "Sir William," and his wife, when he married, "Lady Hamilton."

In all his life two short visits to Germany were his only trips outside England and Scotland. In 1821 he was made professor of civil history in the University of Edinburgh; but when his pay (drawn from the local duty on beer) ceased, he stopped lecturing. In 1827 his mother, to whom he was much attached, died, and the next year he married his cousin, Janet Marshall, who had lived with Mrs. Hamilton for ten years. She became his helpmate in every sense, even to being his amanuensis.

Hamilton's reputation as a philosopher was established by his articles for the *Edinburgh Review,* beginning in 1829. The three most celebrated of these, "The Philosophy of the Conditioned," "The Philosophy of Perception," and "Logic," written between 1829 and 1833, were later included with others in his

Discussions on Philosophy and Literature, Education and University Reform. He was the first seriously to introduce the German philosophers to British readers. Of university reform he was a great advocate, contending among other changes that dissenters should be admitted to Oxford on the same terms as members of the Church of England. Unfortunately his extreme aggressiveness made trouble for him and vitiated his advocacy of liberal reforms; for example, he resigned in 1835 from the Royal Society of Edinburgh because the other members refused to agree with his views on its constitution. In 1836 he was elected professor of logic and metaphysics in the University of Edinburgh, though his income, at this most prosperous period of his life, was under £300 a year. In spite of his constant battles with the authorities, and his inability to compromise on any point, he was a success as a teacher. Extremely erudite, admired for his vast and unprecedented learning (though this frequently became pedantry), dignified, earnest, and authoritative, he gained a reputation during his lifetime which, however, did not outlive him.

In 1844, owing to overwork—he often read and wrote all day and all night without rest—he was suddenly stricken with paralysis. His mind was uninjured, but he never fully recovered the use of his limbs or clearness of speech. He was offered a pension of £100 a year, but refused it because of its smallness; however, in 1849 a similar sum was settled on his wife, which Lord Palmerston, the prime minister, refused to increase after Hamilton's death. After a few years he was able to superintend his classes, but in 1853 he fell and broke his arm, and the cerebral shock reduced him to invalidism until his death three years later.

At home the quarrelsome Hamilton was perfection, as son, brother, husband, and father (he had a son and a daughter). He played with his children and entertained them by the horror stories and fantasies he loved; he could concentrate so that he could work while they played about him. He had some mechanical talent, and used to bind his own books; he was an ardent book collector, and left 10,000 volumes, chiefly on metaphysics and logic.

Hamilton's theories have been called "not philosophy, but common sense." It was from him that Herbert Spencer derived the famous idea of the ultimate Unknowable. He was opposed both to Hegel's dialectical idealism and to Mill's empiricism. Like the early Christian apologist who said, "I believe *because* it is ridiculous," Hamilton said that we could believe in the inconceivable on ethical grounds. For example, though freedom of the will is easily disproved, we can believe in it because it is the basis of moral judgment. He gave great stimulus to the speculative thought of his time, especially to the so-called Scottish school, was of great service in acquainting British thinkers with the German philosophers, and made some contribution to psychology and logic, markedly in the psychological theory of associated ideas. Mill, however, demolished his system once for all in his celebrated *Examination of Sir W. Hamilton's Philosophy*. In any event his work would not have survived very long, for his attempt to reconcile two opposing views—the philosophy of perception and the philosophy of the conditioned —led him into inconsistency. Moreover, his very erudition caused him too often to cite authorities rather for their number than for their authority or weight. Interest in him to-day must be purely historical.   M. A. deF.

PRINCIPAL WORKS: Works of Thomas Reid (ed.) 1846; Discussions on Philosophy and Literature, Education and University Reform, 1852; Lectures on Metaphysics and Logic (ed. by H. L. Mansel & J. Veitch) 1858-60.
ABOUT: Bolton, M. P. W. The Scoto-Oxonian Philosophy; Mill, J. S. An Examination of Sir W. Hamilton's Philosophy; Monck, W. H. S. Sir W. Hamilton; Stirling, J. H. Sir W. Hamilton: Being the Philosophy of Perception; Veitch, J. Hamilton; Veitch, J. Sir W. Hamilton: The Man and His Philosophy.

HANNAY, JAMES (February 17, 1827-January 9, 1873), Scottish critic, novelist, and journalist, was born at Dumfries, the son of a business man. He joined the navy at thirteen and after five years was dismissed from the service for insubordination. Miscellaneous journalism in England and Scotland occupied the greater part of his career. He was an important contributor to *Punch* in 1850 and edited the Edinburgh *Evening Courant* from 1860 to 1864, attracting attention with his vigorous attacks upon persons he disliked. The last five years of his life were spent in Barcelona, Spain, as British consul. He died suddenly at Putchet, a suburb of Barcelona, in his forty-sixth year. Seven children (by two marriages) survived him.

In a youthful attempt to follow in the steps of Marryat, he produced two novels and a book of short stories based on his naval experiences. These works did not measure up to those of his predecessor and he turned to criticism, in which he earned a reputation for good taste and judgment. Outstanding were his critical essays contributed to the *Quarterly Review* (afterwards reprinted) and a volume of lectures on Satire and Satirists.

PRINCIPAL WORKS: Fiction—Singleton Fontenoy, 1850; Sketches in Ultramarine, 1853; Eustace Conyers, 1855. Criticism—Satire and Satirists, 1854; Essays From the Quarterly Review, 1861; Characters and Criticisms, 1865; Studies on Thackeray, 1869.
ABOUT: Epinasse, F. Literary Recollections and Sketches; The Bookman 1893.

HARDY, THOMAS (June 2, 1840-January 11, 1928), novelist and poet, was born almost on the Egdon Heath which he made immortal —in Dorset, near Dorchester. He was the oldest child of a prosperous stonemason or builder, a strong, handsome man of marked musical talent. His mother came of a long line of yeoman farmers, and had inherited bookish tastes from her own mother.

When the child was born, he was thought to be dead, and was rescued only by the keener perception of a nurse. Until he was six his parents did not expect him to live, and because of his delicacy his mother became his first teacher. He lived to be over eighty-seven, in full possession of his powers and faculties to the last!

Hardy was precocious, and could read before he could talk plainly. He was not sent to school until he was eight. In all he attended four schools from 1848 to 1856, the last the Dorchester Grammar School, founded by one of his own ancestors, and of which he himself was governor from 1909 to 1926. He also studied French at home with a private teacher, and later in London took a few French courses at King's College.

This was the extent of his formal education. At sixteen he was apprenticed to a local ecclesiastical architect, with whom his father had long done business. This man was something of a classical scholar, easy-going and lenient, and he allowed his young apprentice to spend more time in studying Greek than in studying architecture. Perhaps for this reason, Hardy's father sent him in 1862 to study with the eminent architect later Sir Arthur Bloomfield. Here again, however, he seems to have had plenty of time for lecturing his fellow-students on poetry! It is true that he won a prize in 1863 in a national competition for essays on the application of colored bricks and terracotta to modern architecture—but the award explicitly says that he is to receive the medal, but not the £10 also offered, since his essay, though splendidly written, does not go very deeply or expertly into the subject.

Hardy nevertheless stayed with Bloomfield until 1867, and afterwards for six years was a practising architect. The chief achievement of his profession was the winning of a wife. In 1870 he went to Cornwall to restore a church, and in 1874 he married the vicar's sister-in-law, Emma Lavinia Gifford.

Meanwhile, he was assiduously writing poetry, which was his first literary love and his last. No one would have his poems, and not one of them was published until 1898, when his career as a novelist was over. Actually, his first published work was an anonymous humorous sketch in *Chambers's Journal* which he wrote for the amusement of his associates in Bloomfield's office.

In 1867 he had already written his first novel, *The Poor Man and the Lady.* George Meredith, who was then reader for Chapman and Hall, rejected it on the ground that it "had not enough plot"; and Hardy, whose opinion of his own fiction was always absurdly deprecatory, promptly destroyed the manuscript—perhaps a real loss to English literature. Certainly the next novel, and his first to be published, *Desperate Remedies,* was quite inferior to the one he had burnt, for he took Meredith's advice so seriously that he crowded it with a melodramatic and artificial plot. It too was anonymous, and he had advanced £75 (out of £123 he had in the world) toward its publication, of which only £60 was returned. The only attention it received was a scathing review or two. It is no wonder that, against the wishes of his fiancée, he decided that writing was not his forte and that he must henceforth devote himself strictly to architecture.

Nevertheless he could not keep his itching pen quiet very long. The very next year *Under the Greenwood Tree* appeared, and this time, though he did not make much profit, there was no loss. *A Pair of Blue Eyes* (reminiscent of his courtship days in Cornwall) followed, and Hardy was at last convinced that authorship would enable him to marry and support a wife as well as or better than architecture would do. He became sure of it in 1874, for *Far From the Madding Crowd,* commissioned first as a serial by *Cornhill's Magazine,* was his first great financial and literary success. (Much to Hardy's annoyance, one reviewer guessed the book to be by George Eliot under a new pseudonym!)

On the strength of it the young couple were married and settled down on the outskirts of London. For the next nine years, except for a trip to Holland and Germany, they lived and Hardy worked in various London suburbs. During this time, in 1880, he was bedridden for six months with an alarming series of internal hemorrhages. It is significant of the future that at this very moment when his life hung in the balance, and he was dictating in desperate haste in order to leave some income to his wife should he die, he wrote in his diary that he wanted more and more to devote himself entirely to poetry. This persistent urge throws light on his decision in 1896.

In 1883 the Hardys, actuated by consideration for his health, moved to Dorchester. Two years later—probably his last architectural effort—they built near-by their famous house which they called Max Gate. Thereafter most of the year was spent at Max Gate, with a few months in London and occasional tours on the Continent. Hardy frequently regretted the move, but there is no doubt that it helped to prolong his life and efficiency.

The succession of annual or biennial novels, almost every one a masterpiece of its kind, culminated in 1891 in *Tess of the D'Urbervilles.* Hardy had realized that this was strong meat for the conventional tastes of that stodgy era; he had had to mutilate the story badly for magazine publication, before he could restore the shattered limbs for its appearance in book form. The storm of abuse, aimed equally at the "infidelity" and "obscenity" of that mighty tragedy, he took calmly and with humor. It was nothing, however, to the cyclone which burst over his head with the publication of *Jude the Obscure* in 1896. This too had been emasculated for the magazines and then restored—the American serial version made the children of Jude and Sue into Jude's little brothers and sisters, to spare the delicacy of the reader! There had been no such shrieks of horror over a book since Swinburne's *Poems and Ballads* had appeared thirty years before. This powerful, tender study of the frustration of an aspiring soul, alive with indignation at injustice and sombrely pitiful, this magnificent psychological analysis, was denounced as mere pornography: the favorite nickname of the critics for the book was "Jude the Obscene." Hardy received a flood of defamatory letters—one reader in Australia sent him the ashes to which she had reduced his "filthy" novel!

It is customary to say that it was because of this reception of his two greatest novels that Hardy announced in 1896 that he would never write fiction again, and kept his word. (*The Well Beloved* was issued as a book in 1897, but had appeared as a serial in 1892.) This is a falsification of a complex situation. Thomas Hardy was hardly to be "snuffed out by an article." Disgusted and depressed by the stupidity of his fellow-beings he undoubtedly was. But it has been seen how his heart clung to poetry; he never valued his novels as he did his poems, never took them with complete seriousness or considered them his most valuable achievement. He had now reached a point of prosperity and fame when he could afford to give way to his lifelong desire to be known as a poet. Novels, though he expressed through them his sincerest convictions, were to him primarily the way by which he had earned his living since he had ceased to practise architecture. There was one more reason—a ludicrous but an actual one. Hardy, by instinct a recluse and a countryman, dreaded the social life into which he thought he was forced by the accident of being a popular novelist. Thinking so little of his fiction, he was amenable to every suggestion of his publishers, and lived in horror of the day when they would order him to write

THOMAS HARDY

a society novel! It was with real relief that he abandoned fiction forever.

Not only a series of volumes of poetry—many of the poems written long years before—now followed from his pen, but also the three parts of that masterly poetic drama, *The Dynasts*. Honors fell thick upon him; his public was growing up, and the furore over *Tess* and *Jude* was forgotten, or remembered with shame. In 1910 he received the Order of Merit, and in the same year something that he valued still more—the freedom of the city of Dorchester. He was showered with honorary degrees, from Oxford and Cambridge, from Aberdeen, Bristol, and St. Andrew's. He received the gold medal of the Royal Society of Literature. He became an honorary fellow of the Royal Institute of British Architects—an honor, like his first architectural prize, probably more of a tribute to his literary than to his architectural renown. He was the third president of the Incorporated Society of Authors, the first two being Tennyson and Meredith. (Barrie—his intimate friend—succeeded him on his death.) During the war, as the only contribution he could make at his age, he served diligently as a local Justice of the Peace.

Before this, in 1912, the first Mrs. Hardy had died, rather suddenly, though she had long been weakening in health and apparently had had a premonition of her approaching end. Their marriage had been childless, but it had been a close and devoted union. In 1914, at 74, he married again; his second wife was his longtime secretary, a journalist and writer of children's books in her own right, Florence Dugdale, who later became his chief biographer. She was, of course, very much his junior, but she devoted herself to him rather

as Watts-Dunton devoted himself to Swinburne, acting as companion, nurse, secretary, and, toward the end, perhaps a little as keeper of the museum. There is no doubt, however, that Hardy was extremely fond of her and happy in the fourteen years of his second marriage.

At the beginning of 1928, in spite of the care with which he was surrounded, he caught cold, and at his age the slightest illness proved fatal. His mind was clear to the last; the day before he died, he signed a check for the Royal Literary Pension Fund—the last time his hand held a pen—and on his very deathday he asked that his wife read him that stanza of the *Rubaiyat* which begins, "O Thou who man of baser Earth didst make." The stanza is an almost too perfect epitome of Hardy's own philosophy and of his attitude toward humanity.

Hardy's heart was removed and buried in his first wife's grave, near Dorchester; the remainder of his body was cremated and buried in the Poet's Corner in Westminster Abbey. On January 16th, five days after his death, there was an impressive memorial service there, attended by the most eminent men in England, and by thousands who came to do honor to one they revered. Few authors have had such tribute paid them so soon after their death.

In appearance, Hardy was under medium size (five feet, six and a half inches), slender, sandy-haired in youth, with blue-grey eyes and Roman nose. For years he grew a beard, but after 1890 wore only a mustache.

It was as a poet that he wished to be remembered, and it is possible that in the end his poetry will be felt to outweigh his prose. It is intellectual poetry, cryptic, sometimes difficult and gnomic, full of distinction and personal idiom, yet often beautifully lyric. He made no mistake in knowing himself for a poet.

If he had written only his earlier novels—that is, the series from *Under the Greenwood Tree* to *The Woodlanders*—it might be granted that his poems were his more valid contribution to English literature. Yet these novels are so instinct with the very soil of England, so penetrating in their psychology, so fresh and colorful, that they alone would have made any writer's fame. But it is the two books which brought down on their author the foul abuse of every bigot and dullard of three continents that are Thomas Hardy's great and unique achievement. Nowhere else in English fiction are to be found the profundity, the unification of feeling, the perfect presentation of great tragedy, that make *Tess of the D'Urbervilles* and *Jude the Obscure* immortal.

It is easier to say what Hardy was not than what he was. He was not a pessimist, he was not a Naturalist in the Zolaesque sense. He declined Joseph McCabe's offer to include him in the *Dictionary of Rationalists,* because he said he was an "irrationalist," and he would not call himself an atheist. But he was a thorough monist, and a mechanist in the true meaning of that vilified word. His philosophic attitude was more Greek—or even Russian— than English. There is a nobility in the last pages of *Tess,* and in some of the passages of *Jude,* that is almost Lucretian. Of him more than of most men it can be said that he saw life steadily and saw it whole.   M. A. deF.

PRINCIPAL WORKS: *Novels*—Desperate Remedies, 1871; Under the Greenwood Tree, 1872; A Pair of Blue Eyes, 1873; Far From the Madding Crowd, 1874; The Hand of Ethelberta, 1876; The Return of the Native, 1878; The Trumpet-Major, 1880; A Laodicean, 1881; Two on a Tower, 1882; The Mayor of Casterbridge, 1886; The Woodlanders, 1887; Tess of the D'Urbervilles, 1891; Jude the Obscure, 1896; The Well Beloved, 1897. *Short Stories*—The Romantic Adventures of a Milkmaid, 1884; Wessex Tales, 1888; A Group of Noble Dames, 1891; Life's Little Ironies, 1894; A Changed Man, The Waiting Supper, and Other Tales, 1913. *Poems*—Wessex Poems, 1898; Poems of the Past and Present, 1902; Time's Laughing-Stocks, 1909; Satires of Circumstance, 1914; Moments of Vision, 1917; Collected Poems, 1919; Late Lyrics and Earlier, 1922; Collected Poems, 1923; Human Shows, 1925; Christmas in the Elgin Room, 1927; Winter Words in Various Moods and Metres (posthumous) 1928. *Dramas*—The Three Wayfarers, 1893; The Dynasts: A Drama of the Napolenoic Wars, Part I, 1903, Part II, 1906, Part III, 1908; The Famous Tragedy of the Queen in Cornwall at Tintagel in Lyonesse, 1923.

ABOUT: Brennecke, E. Thomas Hardy's Universe; Chew, S. C. Thomas Hardy: Poet and Novelist; Child, H. Thomas Hardy; Hardy, F. E. The Early Life of Thomas Hardy; Hardy, F. E. The Later Years of Thomas Hardy; Holland, C. Thomas Hardy: O. M.; Johnson, L. P. 	he Art of Thomas Hardy; McDowall, A. S. Thomas Hardy: A Critical Study; Bookman (London) 78:245 July 1930.

HARE, AUGUSTUS JOHN CUTHBERT

(March 13, 1834-January 22, 1903), biographer and compiler of books on travel, was born at the Villa Strozzi, Rome, the youngest son of a large family of boys. His father was Francis George Hare of Sussex; and his mother was Anne Francis, daughter of Sir John Dean Paul of Rodborough. Augustus and Julius Hare, co-authors of *Guesses at Truth,* were his uncles.

When he was a year and a half old, his godmother, Maria Hare, who was the widow of his uncle Augustus, adopted him. Commenting on the adoption in his autobiography, he wrote with considerable resentment that his parents renounced all claim to him and informed his foster-mother that it would be a kindness if she would tell her friends that they had other boys to dispose of.

He was educated at Harnish Rectory, at Harrow and by private tutors before going to Oxford. After being graduated in 1857, he

AUGUSTUS J. C. HARE

lived mainly abroad in Italy and Riviera with his foster-mother until she died in 1870.

On her death he set to work writing a three-volume, pleasantly deferential biography of her. This work, *Memorials to a Quiet Life,* was markedly successful and established him as a popular writer.

Most of his books are guide books, composed of his own writings, from first-hand observation, padded generously with writings appropriated from other published sources. Edward Augustus Freeman, the historian, called him "a barefaced robber" for using in the three-volume *Cities of Northern and Central Italy* too many of Freeman's articles from the *Saturday Review.* Another time Hare was sued in court for copying too copiously from *Murray's Handbook to Northern Italy.* But criticism and lawsuits did not prevent him from continuing his practise.

He frequented fashionable society and prided himself on his distinguished friends, including the King of Sweden from whom he received the Order of St. Olaf. Hare's six volume autobiography, which *The Athenaeum* called "a history of an uneventful life," gives some interesting character sketches of friends and relatives, discourses on his travels, and tells of his many visits to English country estates. " All his hostesses were "adorable" and his hosts were "cultured" and they all told amusing anecdotes and ghost stories, which he retold in the autobiography. One reviewer wrote that in it, "good stories were more evident than good taste"; the rebuke was for Hare's gossip about Swinburne, his ill temper towards Freeman, and other indiscretions. On the whole the six volumes show him as kindly and amiable, beneath his apparent conceit and affectation; and he wrote pleasantly of Tennyson, although the poet had once snubbed him very effectively.

The same reviewer of the memoirs wrote: "The great passions and the high speculations of mankind are not Mr. Hare's interests. He prefers the tea-table, and he likes his talkers to be all 'of the quality.'"

Hare illustrated several of his travel books with his own pen-and-ink and water color illustrations; and an exhibit of his water colors was politely received in London. Like his writing, his painting was adequate for its purpose, and uninspired.

He never married. During the last few years of his life he lived at his home in Holmhurst, St. Leonards-on-Sea, and collected books and pictures. Although his travel books are reliable and still of value, it is generally believed that he was more gifted as a collector than as a creator.   P. G.

PRINCIPAL WORKS: *Travel*—Berks, Bucks, and Oxfordshire, 1860; A Winter in Mentone, 1862; Handbook to Durham, 1863; Walks in Rome, 1871; Wanderings in Spain, 1873; Days Near Rome, 1875; Walks in London, 1878; Cities of Northern and Central Italy, 1876; Cities of Southern Italy and Sicily, 1883; Florence, 1884; Venice, 1884; Cities of Central Italy, 1884; Cities of Northern Italy, 1884; Sketches in Holland and Scandinavia, 1885; Studies in Russia, 1885; Days Near Paris, 1887; Paris, 1887; North Eastern France, 1890; South Eastern France, 1890; Sussex, 1894; North Western France, 1895; The Rivieras, 1896; Shropshire, 1898. *Biography*—Memorials to a Quiet Life, 1872-6; Life and Letters of Frances, Baroness Bunsen, 1878; The Story of Two Noble Lives: Charlotte, Countess Canning and Louisa, Marchioness of Waterford, 1893; Biographical Sketches, 1895; The Gurneys of Earlham, 1895; The Story of My Life (6 vols.) 1896-1900.

ABOUT: Hare, A. J. C. The Story of My Life; Athenaeum November 24, 1900 and January 31, 1903.

HARE, JULIUS CHARLES (September 13, 1795—January 23, 1855), religious author, was born at Valdagno near Vicenza, Italy, the son of English parents. His father, FRANCIS HARE-NAYLOR (1753-1815), was the author of a *History of Germany* (1816). Julius was educated in England at Charterhouse and at Trinity College, Cambridge, where he became a fellow in 1818. Ordained in 1826, he served as parish priest of Hurstmonceaux (his family home in Sussex) from 1832 to 1840, under the curacy of John Sterling. In 1840 he was appointed archdeacon of Lewes. He was married in 1844 to Esther Maurice, sister of his friend the theologian Frederick Maurice. He died at Hurstmonceaux at fifty-nine.

Hare is best known for *Guesses at Truth*, a volume of essays on art, religion, literature, and philosophy, written in collaboration with his brother Augustus. Also notable is his translation of Niebuhr's *History of Rome*, a joint work with his college friend Connop Thirlwall. His chief work, however, was

The Mission of the Comforter, dedicated "to the honored memory of Samuel Taylor Coleridge," to whom he acknowledged deep obligation. Carlyle's *Life of Sterling* was written out of dissatisfaction with Hare's "Memoir."

His elder brother AUGUSTUS WILLIAM HARE (1792-1834) wrote, in addition to their joint work, sermons which were delivered to his small country congregation at Alton in Wiltshire and widely read after his death.

PRINCIPAL WORKS OF JULIUS CHARLES HARE: Guesses at Truth by Two Brothers (with A. W. Hare) 1827; Niebuhr's History of Rome (tr. with C. Thirlwall) 1828-32; Vindication of Niebuhr, 1829; The Victory of Faith, 1840; Sermons Preacht in Hurstmonceaux Church, 1840-49; The Mission of the Comforter, 1846; John Sterling: Essays and Tales, With Memoir, 1848; Vindication of Luther, 1855.

ABOUT: Hare, A. J. C. Memorials of a Quiet Life; Hare, J. C. The Victory of Faith (see Prefaces by F. D. Maurice and A. P. Stanley in 1874 ed.).

HARRISON, FREDERIC (October 18, 1831-January 14, 1923), critic, historian, and essayist, was born in London. He went to King's College, London, and then, in 1849, to Wadham College, Oxford, where he obtained his B.A. (First Class) and M.A. in 1853. From 1854 to 1856 he was a fellow and tutor at Wadham. He then read law in Lincoln's Inn and became a barrister in 1858. From 1867 to 1869 he was a member of the Royal Commission of Trades Unions, from 1869 to 1870 secretary of the Royal Commission for Digesting the Law, from 1877 to 1889 professor of jurisprudence and international law at the Inns of Court, and from 1889 to 1893 alderman of the city of London. More important, he was president of the English

FREDERIC HARRISON

Positivist meeting place, from 1881 on. He was perhaps the most prominent of all English Positivists, whose pragmatic philosophy, based on science and non-theological ethics, was founded by August Comte, the French philosopher.

In 1900 Harrison lectured at Cambridge, in 1901 at the University of Chicago, and in 1905 at Oxford. He was vice-president of the Royal Historical Society and the London Library, and justice of the peace in Kent and Somerset. He received honorary degrees from Oxford, Cambridge, and Aberdeen.

In 1870 he married his cousin, Ethel Harrison, an heiress, who died in 1916. They had three sons and one daughter. Harrison died in his sleep, at Bath, from the infirmities of old age, being mentally active to the very end.

Harrison was a strange combination, a republican and free thinker who was also a classicist. He was a radical who welcomed and helped refugees from the French Commune in 1870, yet (perhaps influenced by his son, Austin Harrison, a strong anti-German), he wrote on *The German Peril* and was fiercely pro-war in 1914. He had immense energy, physical and intellectual, from the days when he was famous for his bright color and intense vigor to the days when his dark hair and beard turned white.

He was a painfully voluminous writer during most of his ninety-one years, and very little of his work is likely to survive. His writing was solid, heavy, coolly intellectual, and often very dull. Out of all his writing, perhaps only his *Autobiographic Memoirs* are worth reading today, for his full life was of much more importance than was all his massive literary output. He himself said, when some fatuous admirer announced that he had read all of his books, "That is impossible; I couldn't read all of them myself!"

M. A. deF.

PRINCIPAL WORKS: The Meaning of History, 1862; Order and Progress, 1875; The Choice of Books, 1886; Oliver Cromwell, 1888; The New Calendar of Great Men (in part) 1892; Annals of an Old Manor House, 1893; Dickens' Place in Literature, 1894; Victorian Literature, 1895; Kingsley's Place in Literature, 1895; Charlotte Brontë's Place in Literature, 1895; William the Silent, 1897; The Millenary of King Alfred, 1897; Tennyson, Ruskin, Mill, and Others, 1899; Byzantine History in the Early Middle Ages, 1900; American Addresses, 1901; Life of Ruskin, 1902; Theophano, 1904; Chatham, 1905; Nicephorus (tragedy) 1906; Memories and Thoughts, 1906; Carlyle and the London Library, 1907; The Creed of a Layman, 1907; The Philosophy of Common Sense, 1907; My Alpine Jubilee, 1908; National and Social Problems, 1908; Realities and Ideals, 1908; Autobiographical Memoirs, 1911; Among My Books, 1912; The Positive Evolution of Religion, 1912; The German Peril, 1915; On Society, 1918; Jurisprudence and the Conflict of Nations, 1919; Obiter Scripta, 1919; Novissima Verba, 1920.
ABOUT: Harrison, A. Frederic Harrison: Thoughts and Memories; Harrison, F. Autobiographic Memories; Fortnightly Review 119:374 March 1923; Independent 110:83 February 3, 1923; Living Age 316:521 March 3, 1923; Nineteenth Century 93:427 March 1923; North American Review 217:510 April 1923.

HARWOOD, ISABELLA (1840?-June, 1888), dramatist and novelist, was the daughter of PHILLIP HARWOOD (1809-1887), editor of the *Saturday Review* and author of religious works. Between 1864 and 1870 she wrote a number of successful novels. Subsequently she produced fourteen blank-verse dramas which, according to Richard Garnett, "are always elegent and often truly poetical, and merit a high rank as literary compositions, though too purely literary and too little substantial for the stage." The plays were published under the pseudonym of "Ross Neil," derived in part from her Scottish mother's family name of Neil. Many of the dramas were based on the lives of historical characters. Inez de Castro, who died in 1355, was the chief character in *Inez: or, The Bride of Portugal,* produced in London in 1887 under the title of *Loyal Love.* There is no record of any of the other plays having been produced. Miss Harwood was about forty-eight years old when she died at Hastings, England, only six months after her father.

PRINCIPAL WORKS: Novels—Abbot's Cleve; Carleton Grange; Raymond's Heroine. Plays—Lady Jane Grey, 1871; Inez: or, The Bride of Portugal, 1871; The Cid; The King and the Angel, 1874; Duke for a Day, 1874; Elfinella; Lord and Lady Russell, 1876; Arabella Stuart; The Heir of Linne; Tasso, 1879; Andrea the Painter; Claudia's Choice; Orestes; Pandora, 1883.

HATTON, JOSEPH (February 3, 1841-July 31, 1907), novelist, dramatist, and journalist, was born at Andover, Hampshire, the son of a printer and bookseller. Educated at Bowker's School in Chesterfield, he edited the *Bristol Mirror* (1863-68), the *Gentleman's Magazine* (1868-74), and for brief periods the *Sunday Times* and *The People*. He visited America in 1881 and again in 1883, the second time with Henry Irving the actor. His death occurred in London when he was sixty-six.

He wrote easily and voluminously. Besides popular novels, his works include travel, reminiscences, and biography. He made successful dramatizations of his novel *Clytie* and of Hawthorne's *The Scarlet Letter*.

His son FRANK HATTON (1861-1883), who was accidentally killed while exploring in British North Borneo, left interesting letters and diaries which were published with a biographical sketch by his father in 1886.

PRINCIPAL WORKS: Novels—Clytie, 1874; John Needham's Double, 1885; By Order of the Czar, 1890; When Rogues Fall Out, 1899. Miscellaneous—Today in America, 1881; The New Ceylon, 1882; Henry Irving's Impressions of America, 1884; Old

Lamps and New, 1889; Cigarette Papers for After-Dinner Smoking, 1892.
ABOUT: Hatton, J. Journalistic London; Hatton, J. Old Lamps and New; The Times August 1, 1907.

HAVERGAL, FRANCES RIDLEY (December 14, 1836-June 3, 1879), hymn-writer and author of religious poems, tracts, and children's books, was born at Astley, Worcestershire, the daughter of William Henry Havergal, writer of sacred music. She died at Caswell Bay, Swansea, South Wales, at the age of forty-two. Her frequently-reprinted devotional works, after fifty years, are still used in religious circles. "In her poetical work," according to Ronald Bayne, "there is a lack of concentration, and a tendency to meaningless repetition of phrase, but some of her hymns are excellent, and will permanently preserve her name." Familiar among these hymns are "True-Hearted, Whole-Hearted," "O Saviour, Precious Saviour," "I Gave My Life for Thee," and "Tell It Out Among the Heathen." They were set to music by some of the best composers of the nineteenth century, including Gounod. An autobiographical sketch, contained in her *Memorials,* "presents a striking picture of an unusually eager, if somewhat narrow, spiritual life."

PRINCIPAL WORKS: *Poetry*—The Ministry of Song, 1870; Under the Surface, 1874; Loyal Responses, 1878; Life Chords, 1880; Life Echoes, 1883; Poetical Works, 1884; Coming to the King, 1886. *Children's Books*—Bruey: A Little Worker for Christ, 1872; Little Pillows: or, Good Night Thoughts, 1874; Morning Bells: or, Waking Thoughts, 1874.
ABOUT: Darlow, T. H. Frances Ridley Havergal: A Saint of God; Davies, E. Life of F. R. Havergal; Foster, W. D. Heroines of Modern Religion; Havergal, M. V. G. Memorials of Frances Ridley Havergal; Havergal, M. V. G. (ed.). Letters of Frances Ridley Havergal.

HAWKER, MARY ELIZABETH (January 29, 1848-June 16, 1908), Scottish short story writer under the pseudonym of "Lanoe Falconer," was born at Inverary, Aberdeenshire, the daughter of a soldier. Her grandfather, PETER HAWKER (1786-1853), was the author of a military journal (1810) and *Instructions of Young Sportsmen* (1814). She had no systematic education, but read industriously and learned French and German during a prolonged residence abroad. At the age of forty-two she achieved widespread success with *Mademoiselle Ixe,* one of the best short stories of its day. Taine and Gladstone were among the admirers of this clever mystery tale, which was banned in Russia because its heroine, a governess in an English household, allied herself with Russian nihilists. Ill health curtailed Miss Hawker's later writing, and she died of consumption at Broxwood Court, Herefordshire, England, at the age of sixty.

PRINCIPAL WORKS: Mademoiselle Ixe, 1890; Cecilia de Noël, 1891; Hampshire Vignettes, 1907.
ABOUT: Cornhill Magazine February, 1912; The Times June 20, 1908.

HAWKER, ROBERT STEPHEN (December 3, 1803-August 15, 1875), poet, was born in Devonshire, the eldest son of a physician who later became a clergyman; his grandfather was a well known Calvinist divine. He was taken from Liskeard Grammar School to be articled to a Plymouth solicitor, but was so unfitted for the work that his father sent him after a few months to the Cheltenham Grammar School, and then, in 1823, to Pembroke College, Oxford.

The same year, when not yet twenty, Hawker married Charlotte Eliza Rawleigh, who was forty-one! She was a translator from the German, a woman of culture, and since Hawker was already an eccentric, their odd union seems to have been a happy one.

He changed to Magdalen College, where he received his B.A. in 1828, his M.A. in 1836. He was ordained deacon in 1829, priest in 1831, and became a curate in Cornwall. His father had by this time also taken orders, and the son was offered a vicarage over his own father as curate, but declined, giving the post to the older man.

In 1834 he became vicar of Morwenstow, Cornwall, where he remained until two years before his death. This was a wild village on the coast, and Hawker was the most peculiar of pastors. He dressed in an outré collection of garments, and was most unconventional in his way of living. But he was the sailors' friend, and buried at his own expense those who were shipwrecked on the Cornish coast. He was careless with money, and always very poor and in debt. He worked hard at restoring his church, but his establishment of harvest thanksgivings and a weekly offertory caused him to be suspected of heresy. In 1863 his wife died, aged eighty-one, and the next year he married Pauline Anne Kuczynski, a governess, daughter of a Polish exile, by whom he had three daughters. His health failed in 1873, and he retired to Plymouth, where he died in 1875. On his death-bed he was confirmed in the Roman Catholic faith, giving rise to a bitter newspaper controversy for months afterwards.

Hawker's poems, except for his religious verses, are mostly ballads, direct, simple, and with the flavor of antiquity. He is best known for the famous

> And shall Trelawny die,
> And must Trelawny die?
> A hundred thousand Cornishmen
> will know the reason why.

PRINCIPAL WORKS: Tendrils by Reuben, 1821; Records of the Western Shore, 1832-36; Ecclesia, 1840-41; Reeds Shaken With the Wind, 1843-44; Echoes from Old Cornwall, 1846; The Quest of the Sangrael, 1864; Cornish Ballads and Other

Poems, 1867-84; Footprints of Former Men in Far Cornwall (prose) 1870.

ABOUT: Baring-Gould, S. Memoir of R. S. Hawker; Byles, C. E. Life and Letters of R. S. Hawker; Drinkwater, J. A Book for Bookmen; Lee, F. G. Memorials of the Late R. S. Hawker; More, P. E. Shelburne Essays; Noble, J. A. The Sonnet in England and Other Essays.

HAYDON, BENJAMIN ROBERT (January 26, 1786-June 22, 1846), painter and writer on painting, was born in Plymouth, his father being a printer and publisher. His parents and his first teacher were all fond of painting, and encouraged his precocious interest in art, though his father endeavored in vain to interest the boy in his own business. He was sent to the Grammar School at Plymouth, where he was head boy, then for six months was apprenticed to an accountant in Exeter, after which he was put to work in his father's office. At this time he suffered a severe inflammation of the eyes, which for a time blinded him, and left him with exceedingly weak eyesight—perhaps an explanation of the vast scope and grandiose execution of all his paintings.

After three years of rebellion, the family gave way and in 1804 Haydon was allowed to go to London to become a painter. He gave himself exactly two years of study, in the Royal Academy and the art galleries, then began his series of large historical canvases. His pictures, "Dentatus," "Macbeth," "The Judgment of Solomon," "Christ's Entry into Jerusalem," etc., brought him wide reputation but small money; he was besides several times cheated in promised payments or disappointed in definite orders. Furthermore, he had now become an associate of the Leigh Hunt group, and in Hunt's radical *Examiner* published scathing articles about the Royal Academy and its directors which had the natural effect of turning the official pundits of British art into his bitter enemies. In spite of his fame he never received one vote for membership into the Academy.

In 1821 he married Mary Hymans, a beautiful widow, with whom he fell deeply in love at first sight. They had eight children, of whom five died. His wife lost her small fortune and Haydon became involved in increasing financial difficulties. Before their first child was born he was arrested for debt, his "Lazarus" was seized for payment, and from this time his career was ruined. He struggled on valiantly through three imprisonments. He took free pupils (one of them became the famous painter Landseer), tried to start a rival academy, conducted single-handed a successful fight for the purchase of the famous Elgin marbles by the British Government, and interested himself actively in art reform. In 1835 he lectured for the Mechanics' Institute, and from this time his lectures

BENJAMIN ROBERT HAYDON

on painting became his chief source of livelihood, though he painted as assiduously as ever. He lectured throughout England, including one gratifying lecture at Oxford, and these lectures, printed, are his chief literary contribution, besides the diary in 26 volumes, meant for publication, which is the basis of his autobiography.

Many famous writers were among his friends and admirers. Keats and Wordsworth both wrote sonnets to him. Lamb, Scott, Southey, and Hazlitt were of his circle. He had saved the Elgin marbles for the nation. His paintings were known all over the civilized world. But he could not make a living.

In 1846 he held an exhibit of his paintings in London. In the next hall the American dwarf, Tom Thumb, was also on exhibition. Tom Thumb (or Barnum, his manager) made a fortune; Haydon lost over £100. It was too much. He went to his studio, made a last entry in his diary, cut his throat, and sent a bullet through his brain. In order to secure him church burial, the inquest stated that he was of unsound mind, but no man was ever saner.

Courageous, industrious, energetic, public-spirited, Haydon's only defect was a not unjustifiable egotism. His writing shows natural talent; it is clear, vigorous, and picturesque, and well worth reading even today, both for its content and for its style.

M. A. deF.

PRINCIPAL WORKS: Lectures on Painting and Design, 1844-46; Autobiography, 1847.

ABOUT: Graham, H. Splendid Failures; Haydon, B. R. Autobiography; Haydon, F. W. Benjamin Robert Haydon; "Paston, G." (E. M. Symonds). B. R. Haydon and His Friends; Stoddard, R. H. Life, Letters, and Table Talk of Benjamin Robert Haydon; Taylor, T. The Life of Benjamin Robert Haydon; Harper's Magazine 53:651 October 1876.

HAYLEY, WILLIAM (October 29, 1745-November 12, 1820), poet and miscellaneous writer, was the second son of Thomas Hayley and Mary Yates, and was born at Chichester where his grandfather had been dean of the cathedral.

He was first sent to school at Kingston-upon-Thames and there he contracted what now appears to have been infantile paralysis. During the long illness he became extremely fond of reading, and decided on a career of letters for himself. In his twelfth year he went to Eton where his lameness made him the bewildered and miserable butt of endless schoolboy jokes and insults, which marked his character as much as the illness marked his body. His extreme kindliness throughout his life; his craving and never quite expecting fame, are generally traced to the boyhood unhappiness. At eighteen he entered Trinity College, Cambridge, and four years later he left with no degree.

His first published piece, "Ode on the Birth of the Prince of Wales," was reprinted from the *Cambridge Collection*, in the *Gentleman's Magazine* of 1763. For the next few years he wrote many poems to Frances Page, his fiancée. That engagement broken, he turned to Eliza, daughter of Dean Ball, his guardian. When Hayley's mother warned him that Eliza might inherit insanity from her mother, he replied, "In that case I should bless God for having given me courage sufficient to make myself the legal guardian of the most amiable and most pitiable woman on earth." They were married in 1769 and went to his estate of Eartham in Sussex where he wrote laboriously at poems and plays in verse, added to his library which at his death included the then rather large number of 1542 titles, and presented his wife with an illegitimate son whom she adopted and treated as her own.

His *Triumphs of Temper*, a poem designed "to promote good humor" and attempting to combine certain excellences of the Italian poet, Ariosto, with others of Dante and Pope, brought him his first popular success and won Lord Byron's ridicule in *English Bards and Scotch Reviewers*.

After seventeen years of marriage, he had to admit that his wife's "inscrutable source of suffering" was insanity, and in another three years he arranged a separation. Through his work on a *Life of Milton*, he became acquainted with William Cowper and a warm friendship, of which he was very proud, sprung up. It was largely through Hayley's persistent efforts with William Pitt, the statesman, that Cowper was given a much needed pension. Cowper, Hayley's wife, and his idolized son all died in 1800—Cowper and the youth only a week apart. Hayley, overcome by grief, fled to Felpham.

WILLIAM HAYLEY

He generously invited the fiery genius, William Blake, to live with him there under his patronage; and for three years, according to Blake, he pestered him "with his genteel ignorance and polite disapprobation." His *Ballads: Founded on Anecdotes Relating to Animals* are now valued for Blake's illustrations.

Hayley's *Life of Cowper* was his last work to receive popular acclaim. He considered that work so important that he had himself identified on the title page of his *Memoirs* as "The Friend and Biographer of Cowper."

At the age of 65, he married young Mary Welford, and separated from her three years later. The latter part of his life was spent in seclusion, writing his *Memoirs*, for which he received an annuity from the publishers, and entertaining distinguished friends to whom he had dedicated poems.

Although his works have worn badly, he once attained such popularity that he was given the chance of declining the laureateship. Robert Southey, reviewing the *Memoirs* after Hayley's death, praised his modesty, cheerfulness and generosity; suggested that he would have been better suited to a career in the church than a career of letters; and declared that "everything about that man is good except his poetry." Later critics generally except also his prose from goodness, and consider him a literary country gentleman rather than a poet or biographer. P. G.

PRINCIPAL WORKS: *Poetry*—An Elegy on the Ancient Greek Model, 1779; A Poetical Epistle to an Eminent Painter, 1779; An Essay on History, 1780; An Essay on Painting, 1781; The Triumphs of Temper, 1781; An Essay on Epic Poetry, 1782; The Happy Prescription: or, The Lady Relieved From Her Lovers, 1785; A Philosophical Essay on Old Maids, 1785; The Two Connoisseurs, 1785;

Poetical Works of William Hayley, 1785; Occasional Stanzas, 1788; The Young Widow: or, A History of Cornelia Sudley, 1789; The Eulogies of Howard, 1791; An Elegy on the Death of Sir William Jones, 1795; An Essay on Sculpture, 1800: The Triumphs of Music, 1804; Ballads: Founded on Anecdotes Relating to Animals, 1805; Poems on Serious and Sacred Subjects, 1818. *Biography*—Life of Milton, 1794; William Cowper: His Life and Works, 1803; The Life of George Romney, 1809; Memoirs of the Life and Writings of William Hayley, 1823. *Miscellaneous*—Three Plays With a Preface, 1811.

ABOUT: Gilchrist, A. Life of Blake; Hayley, W. Memoirs of William Hayley; Swinburne, A. C. Life of Blake; Quarterly Review 31:263.

HAYWARD, ABRAHAM (November 22, 1801-February 2, 1884), essayist, was born at Wilton near Salisbury, the eldest son of Joseph Hayward and Mary Abraham. He was educated at Bath and at Blundell's school at Tiverton. He had a private tutor for a time and in 1818 was articled to George Touson, a solicitor of Northover. He entered himself as a student in the Inner Temple in October 1824, and joined the London Debating Society, which considered him an excellent speaker for the Tory side.

In June 1828, with his friend W. T. Cornish, he issued the first number of the *Law Magazine or Quarterly Review of Jurisprudence*. By the following year Hayward was sole editor. The magazine was very successful and through it he made many valuable contacts. After his first visit to Germany in 1831 he printed for private distribution and in 1833 published his translation of Goethe's *Faust*. In the same year he was called to the bar. The book met with general approbation. Carlyle said it was the best English version of the classic. And thereafter Hayward moved in London's most brilliant society.

Although not himself a brilliant talker, Hayward's personality stimulated conversation. The dinners he gave in his chambers for such favored friends as Lockhart, Macaulay, Sidney Smith, Bulwer, Theodore Hook, and certain ladies of fashion were epicurean affairs in both senses of the word. He became a frequent contributor to reviews and journals and in political society rather succeeded to the place of Croker. Hayward cultivated the niceties of life, had many friends, and made numerous enemies. His book on the art of dining was received as an epicure's bible. At the same time his legal ambitions were such that, considering the diversity of his interests, disappointment was inevitable. Apparently those in power regarded him as primarily a bon vivant and litterateur. However, he wrote voluminously on jurisprudence and did not until his later years abandon hope for high appointment in public service. The vexed question "marriage with deceased wife's sister" (a custom widely favored by landowning families, but regarded by stricter ecclesiastics as incest) occupied him, as it did many.

Hayward was a self-made man of singularly independent cast of mind and with many amusing prejudices which he was never at a loss to defend. On the authorship of the famous Junius letters of 1769-1772, a question he regarded as preeminently his own, he wrote two books. From 1869 to 1883 Hayward was a regular contributor to the *Quarterly Review*. These articles, which seemed so unstudied and "flowing," were written with great care and scrupulous attention to accuracy of detail. He died in his rooms in Great James Street, London, at the age of eighty-three.

Hayward was a prominent figure in his day who gave his attention almost exclusively to matters of the moment. With the exception of his famous *Art of Dining* his works nowadays are mostly the concern of specialists. He is probably more interesting for what he was than for what he wrote.   P. B. S.

PRINCIPAL WORKS: 1833. *Legal*—Summary of Objections to the Doctrine That a Marriage With the Sister of a Deceased Wife is Contrary to Law Religion or Morality, 1839; Remarks on the Law Regarding Marriage With the Sister of a Deceased Wife, 1845. *Miscellaneous*—Some Account of a Journey Across the Alps, 1834; The Art of Dining: or, Gastronomy and Gastronomers, 1862. *Biographical and Critical*—Biographical and Critical Essays, 1858, 1873, 1874; The Autobiography, Letters, and Literary Remains of Mrs. Piozzi (ed.) 1861; Diaries of a Lady of Quality (Miss F. W. Wynn) From 1797 to 1844 (ed.) 1864; More About Junius, 1868; The Handwriting of Junius, 1874; Sketches of Eminent Statesmen and Writers, 1880.

ABOUT: Carlyle, H. E. Selections From Correspondence of Abraham Hayward; Yeats, E. Recollections.

ABRAHAM HAYWARD

HAZLITT, WILLIAM (April 10, 1778-September 18, 1830), essayist, was the youngest child of a Unitarian minister of Irish (probably originally of Netherlandish) descent. He was born in Maidstone, Kent, but from his infancy his father moved the family to various places in England, then to Cork, and, when the boy was six, to the new United States of America. There the older Hazlitt had churches in New York, Philadelphia, and Boston (the first Unitarian church in that city). In 1787, however, he returned to England, his wife and children following him a few months later, and settled down to a charge in Wem, Shropshire. Hazlitt narrowly missed being an American instead of a British writer—though conditions in this country were then most unpropitious for his becoming any sort of writer at all.

In Wem the Rev. Mr. Hazlitt, besides his church, took in pupils, and William was educated entirely by his scholarly father in his own home, reading hugely and beyond his years. At thirteen a newspaper published his first article, a protest against the burning of Joseph Priestley's house by a reactionary mob. The French Revolution had already made a little radical of him, and, though unattached to any faction or party, he remained of the same opinion all his life. (His championship of Napoleon was the exception.)

When he was fifteen, he was sent to Hackney Theological College to study for the Unitarian ministry. His older brother John was in London also, starting life as a miniature painter. But by 1795 Hazlitt had decided nature did not intend him for a preacher; he returned to Wem and for eight years, according to himself, he "did nothing." As a matter of fact, in those years he laid the foundation of all his future, prepared the background of erudition which lay behind his essays, and underwent the early formation of his mind and character by Wordsworth and particularly Coleridge, both of whom he met in 1798.

In 1802 he determined to become a painter, and set out for London to study with his brother. He had four months in Paris also, copying at the Louvre. Until 1811 he persisted in this profession, as an itinerant portrait painter, but his talent was mediocre and he himself came to realize the impossibility of his achieving the standards set by his ambition. Meanwhile, in 1808, he married Sarah Stoddart, sister of the literary editor of *The Times,* and an old friend of his friends Charles and Mary Lamb. The marriage was founded on no deep sentiment on either side except the bride's intention (she was three years older than Hazlitt) to marry someone before it was too late.

WILLIAM HAZLITT

It was a miserable failure. Of their three sons, only one lived, and the love of both parents for him was the only bond that united them. Mrs. Hazlitt was undomestic, eccentric, and unsympathetic; her husband, who from early youth had been given to sudden and briefly enduring passions, was no companion to her and was more than once unfaithful. Their union endured after a fashion, however, until 1822. For the first three years they lived on Mrs. Hazlitt's property at Winterslow, near Salisbury, and after their separation Hazlitt continued to go there for solitary work. An ardent pedestrian and a nature-lover, Winterslow became his nearest approach to a home.

By 1812 it was obvious that Hazlitt would never become a successful painter. The natural alternative was literature. He had already, by that date, published six books, though none of them had been widely read or brought him much money. He secured work as a Parliamentary reporter for the *Morning Chronicle,* and began connections also with the *Edinburgh Review,* Leigh Hunt's *Examiner,* and other periodicals, as a free lance journalist. Then, as now, this was an unremunerative calling, and Hazlitt was often hard put to it for a means of living: once, in later years, he was arrested for debt. At this period also he was a heavy drinker; but in 1815 he resolved to put a stop to the habit, and never touched alcohol thereafter, having recourse instead to innumerable cups of black tea. In 1806 he tried his hand as a dramatist, but his farce, *Mr. H.,* produced at Drury Lane, was a rank failure. It occured to him to try lecturing, and though at first he had small success, his lectures grew in popularity (they were really literary criticisms and essays read from manuscript), and for many years they were his chief method of support. His social life at the time fluctuated: he made acquaintances easily, and knew and was known by nearly every prominent London literary figure of the time, but he had few real friends, and with almost every one of these he quarreled at one time or another.

Finally, in 1822, came the events which cast a shadow of disrepute over his name among the respectable for the remainder of his life. Divorce was impossible in England; he resolved to make an end to the farce of his marriage (he and his wife had lived apart since 1819) by an action of highly questionable legality. This was to have Mrs. Hazlitt go to Scotland for forty days and then divorce him by Scottish law for adultery—the equivalent of pretending nowadays to be a resident of Nevada while actually staying there only for the six weeks to secure a divorce decree. The reason for this sudden decision was his infatuation for Sarah Walker, the daughter of a tailor with whom he had been lodging. Mrs. Hazlitt was willing to go through with the affair if he provided the money, though she shrank before having to take an oath that there was no collusion. At any rate the matter was concluded (though the divorce was never valid in England), and Hazlitt, who had followed her to Edinburgh, returned to London to find that the girl whom he had intended to marry had been playing fast and loose with him, accepting his adoration and his presents, and all the time entertaining another suitor whom she married soon after.

Hazlitt's shock, grief, and rage found vent in a curious book, *Liber Amoris*, which included his letters to her, his conversations about her, and some very unworthy and rather caddish invective. Though the book was published anonymously, everyone knew its authorship, and it created a scandal.

Yet in 1824 he married again, a young widow named Isabella Bridgwater, with an income of her own. They set out at once for France and Italy, and remained abroad for thirteen months. According to Hazlitt's son, who was by this time a boy of thirteen, at the end of this trip the second Mrs. Hazlitt left her husband, never to return. This, however, has been proved to be untrue: the couple lived together in London and went abroad again together in 1826, when Hazlitt was gathering material for his *Life of Napoleon*. It was at the end of this second tour, in 1827, that she went to her sister in Switzerland, and when Hazlitt, back in England, asked when he should come for her, replied "Never." The cause of this second marital failure was in all probability the boy whose memory was so inaccurate; he had accompanied them on this second tour (he had been

away at school previously) and his aggressive championship of his own mother gave his step-mother an unpleasant foretaste of what her life was likely to be. Besides, she may have been frightened off by the realization that in strict legality the marriage was probably bigamous.

Hazlitt returned to Winterslow, which seems to have been made free to him in return for a settlement on his first wife, and wrote his biography of Napoleon, which under the most auspicious circumstances would hardly have been a success, since, at that period, Napoleon was universally execrated in England and Hazlitt worshiped him. To add to his troubles, the publisher failed after the first two volumes were issued, and he not only lost a considerable sum of money which was due him, but had to see the last two volumes appear under another imprint in an un-uniform edition.

During these last two years of illness and poverty and failure Hazlitt lived in lodgings in Soho, the foreign quarter of London. He had long suffered from a chronic stomach complaint, and in this condition an attack which seems to have been dysentery proved easily fatal. In his distress he applied to the editor of the *Edinburgh Review* for funds, but the money did not arrive until after his death. However, he was not completely deserted; with him at his deathbed were his beloved son and his old friend Charles Lamb, returned after a long estrangement. Another with whom he had quarreled came forward after he died and paid for the erection of a tombstone over his grave in St. Anne's churchyard.

Hazlitt was short and stocky, with black, stiffly curling hair, pale skin and grey eyes. In spite of a too-long nose he was a beautiful child, and was not unhandsome in manhood: his smile was said to have been unusually sweet. He was careless and negligent in dress, and was accused, perhaps unjustly, of being neglectful of ordinary cleanliness. He was a man whom a few loved, but whom it was difficult to like. Thin-skinned, supersensitive, lonely and isolated in spirit, he was apt to respond to hurt by indiscriminate abuse, in and out of print. It is not surprising that sooner or later he was alienated from nearly every friend. He who never swerved from his early love of freedom, his championship of the under-dog, had small sympathy for such writers as Wordsworth and Southey, whom he considered to be well-fed renegades. He was most unjust and ill-considered—and later acknowledged it—in his strictures on Shelley and Leigh Hunt. To tell the truth, he himself did not understand how his aggressiveness reacted on others: "I think what I please and say what I think," he remarked proudly, only to write with real pathos, "I want to know why everybody has such a dislike to me." He had no tact whatever.

Yet he was a brilliant conversationalist, fond of games and proficient in them, eager for companionship in his less touchy moments. He hated injustice, and he had a passion for liberty. An extreme individualist, he must always be in a minority of one. His vitality was unquenchable. After all the wretchedness he had known, his last words were, "Well, I've had a happy life!"

Mentally his talent lacked discipline because of his informal early training. He boasted that he had never changed an opinion since he was sixteen, and is said never to have read a book through after he was thirty. He was primarily a journalist, but with no derogation attached to the word: the growth of the popular magazines made him a writer, for he never wrote except when in urgent need of money, but then rapidly and conscientiously. As a dramatic critic he was at his poorest, for his criticisms are more literary than dramatic. He "lacked unity of spirit," and that disunity was reflected in his writings: there is no single book of his which may be regarded as his credential to fame.

And yet, with all his faults, was there ever an essayist like Hazlitt? It is those scattered essays, collected, that have made his name immortal. Virile, trenchant, informal, enthusiastic, pointed, they are pure gems of literature. His literary criticisms now sound hackneyed, but in their day they were daring anticipations of modern judgments. His overuse of quotations (not always very accurate ones) is often annoying, but against this may be placed the beautifully balanced structure of his style, and his power as a phrase-maker. While Lamb and Stevenson are read—which is to say while essays are read—Hazlitt will be read with them, for he is of their company.

M. A. deF.

PRINCIPAL WORKS: Essay on the Principles of Human Action, 1805; Free Thoughts on Public Affairs, 1806; The Eloquence of the British Senate, 1807; Reply to the Essay on Population of Malthus, 1807; A New and Improved Grammar of the English Tongue, 1810; Memoirs of the Late Thomas Holcroft, 1816; The Characters of Shakespear's Plays, 1817; The Round Table, 1817; A View of the English Stage, 1818; Lectures on the English Poets, 1818; Lectures on the English Comic Writers, 1819; Letter to William Gifford, Esq., 1819; Political Essays, 1819; Lectures on the Dramatic Literature of the Age of Elizabeth, 1820; Table Talk, 1821-22; Characteristics, 1823; Liber Amoris, 1823; Select British Poets (anthology) 1824; Sketches of the Principal Picture Galleries in England, 1824; The Spirit of the Age, 1825; The Plain Speaker, 1826; Notes of a Journey Through France and Italy, 1826; The Life of Napoleon Buonaparte, 1828-30; Conversations of James Northcote, Esq., R.A., 1830; Literary Remains of the Late William Hazlitt (ed. by William Hazlitt, Jr.) 1836; Painting and the Fine Arts (with B. R. Haydon) 1838 (as Criticisms on Art, 1843); Sketches and Essays Now First Collected (ed. by William Hazlitt, Jr.) 1839 (as Men and Manners, 1852); Winterslow (ed. by William Hazlitt, Jr.) 1850; A Reply to Z, 1923; New Writings (ed. by P. P. Howe) 1925.

ABOUT: Birrell, A. William Hazlitt; Hazlitt, W. Liber Amoris; Hazlitt, W. C. Memoirs of William Hazlitt; Howe, P. P. The Life of William Hazlitt; Keynes, G. Bibliography; Pearson, H. The Fool of Love; Bookman (London) 78:319 September 20, 1930; Catholic World 58:489 January 1894; Nation (London) 47:760 September 20, 1930; Saturday Review of Literature 11:417 January 12, 1935; Spectator 145:373 September 1930.

HEAD, SIR EDMUND WALKER (1805-January, 28, 1868), colonial governor and writer on art, was born at Rayleigh, Essex, the son of the Rev. Sir John Head, baronet. After graduation from Oriel College, Oxford, he was successively a fellow at Merton College (1830-37), poor-law commissioner (1841-47), governor of New Brunswick (1847-54), and governor-general of Canada (1854-61). He retired in 1861 and died in London of heart disease in his sixty-third year. By his wife, Anna Maria Yorke, he had three children. The baronetcy became extinct at his death, since his only son had died before him.

An accomplished scholar and linguist, he made translations from the German and Icelandic, wrote a notable *Handbook of Painting*, and left poems which were collected after his death.

PRINCIPAL WORKS: Handbook of Painting of the German, Dutch, Spanish, and French Schools, 1848; F. T. Kugler's Handbook of Painting of the German, Dutch, Spanish, and French Schools (ed.) 1854; Sir G. L. Lewis's Essays on the Administration of Great Britain (ed.) 1864; The Story of Viga Glum (tr.) 1866; Ballads and Other Poems, 1868.

HEAD, SIR FRANCIS BOND (1793-July 20, 1875), author of travel works, was born in the parish of Higham, Kent, and educated at Rochester and Woolwich. He served fourteen years with the royal engineers (1811-25) and was present at Waterloo. Then he traveled in South America (1825-26) as manager of the unsuccessful Rio Plata Mining Association. During a brief lieutenant-governorship of Upper Canada (1835-37) he quelled an insurrection and was rewarded with a baronetcy (1836). Thenceforth he lived in England and contributed essays on varied topics to the *Quarterly Review.* He died at his Croydon residence at eighty-two. By his wife, Julia Valenza Somerville, who was his cousin, he had four children.

His writings were graphically descriptive, though sometimes inaccurate. Two volumes recounting his rapid horseback travels in South America brought him literary fame as "Galloping Head" and are notable for presenting a faithful picture of native life in the Pampas.

His elder brother, SIR GEORGE HEAD, (1782-1855), a veteran of the Peninsular War, won considerable attention with *Home Tours in England* (1840) and other books of travel.

PRINCIPAL WORKS OF SIR FRANCIS BOND HEAD: Rough Notes of Journeys in the Pampas and Andes, 1827; Life of Bruce the African Traveller, 1830; Bubbles From the Brunnens of Nassau, 1834; Stokers and Pokers, 1849; A Faggot of French Sticks, 1852; A Fortnight in Ireland, 1852; The Royal Engineer, 1869.

ABOUT: see Head's own books; The Times July 23, 1875.

HEBER, REGINALD (April 21, 1783-April 3, 1826), missionary bishop, prose-writer, hymnologist, was born at Malpas, Cheshire. He was the eldest son of the Rev. Reginald Heber and his second wife, Mary Allanson.

Reginald matriculated October 10, 1800, at Brasenose College, Oxford, where his father had been fellow and tutor. He had a distinguished career, taking prizes for his poems "Carmen Seculare" and "Palestine" and his essay "The Sense of Honor." He was elected fellow of All Souls' College in 1805 and then, with John Thornton, toured eastern and central Europe. In 1807 he took holy orders and received the family living of Hodnet, Shropshire. He married, in April 1809, Amelia Shipley, daughter of Dean William D. Shipley of St. Asaph's Cathedral. Soon he was appointed prebendary of St. Asaph's. In 1815 he was honored with the Bampton lectureship at Oxford and in 1822 he was appointed preacher at Lincoln's Inn. Through the kindness of his friend C. W. W. Wynn, Heber was elected to the great missionary bishopric of Calcutta, being consecrated at Lambeth on June 1, 1823.

His administration of his diocese (all of British India) was distinguished by the full establishment of Bishop's College in Calcutta, and excellent executive technique. Official travel proved a great tax upon his strength. In 1826 he was stricken with apoplexy at Trichinopoly, India, where he died. He was buried in St. John's Church, and a memorial bust by Chantrey was erected in Calcutta.

Of three daughters, two survived him. Emily married Algernon Percy, son of the bishop of Carlisle, who took the name of Heber; Mary married John Thornton.

Heber's literary interest developed early. At Oxford he talked with Scott of their literary ambitions. He had many literary friends and he was associated with Southey on the original staff of the *Quarterly Review*. Europe (written 1806) appeared in 1809 and 1811-16 he published specimens of his hymns in the *Christian Observer*. These early hymns had the approval of the church and were well received. His famous hymn "From Greenland's Icy Mountains" was written *ex tempore* April 1820. Other of his best known hymns still in constant use include: "Bread of the World";

REGINALD HEBER

"Holy, holy, holy! Lord God Almighty"; "Brightest and best of the sons of the morning"; "The Son of God goes forth to war." He left a considerable body of miscellaneous writing, including translations from the French, German, Italian, Hindoostani. His style is polished and elegant, but lucidity and simplicity mark the hymns which are deeply religious. He is often regarded as linking the Presbyterian Pollok and the high-churchman Keble. Heber's high-church tendencies, minimized by certain critics, should not be overlooked.

Heber was handsome and elegant, amiable and popular everywhere he went. He was talented beyond most, deeply interested in literature and music. The spontaneity of his fun-loving high spirits made him a charming companion to such men as Southey, Scott, and the two Lushingtons. The religious side of his character developed later, but was of the deepest sincerity and catholicity.   D. F. A.

PRINCIPAL WORKS: *Poetry*—Palestine, 1809; Europe, 1809; Poems, 1812; Hymns 1827; Poems and Translations, 1829; Claudian, 1836. *Sermons and Lectures*—Bampton Lectures on the Personality and Office of the Christian Comforter, 1816; The Omnipotence of God, 1821; A Life of Bishop Jeremy Taylor (2 vols.) 1824; A Journey Through India, 1828; Sermons Preached in England, 1829; Sermons Preached in India, 1829; Sermons on the Lessons, the Gospel, or the Epistles, 1837.

ABOUT: Anon. Some Account of the Life of Reginald Heber; Heber, A. Life of Reginald Heber (2 vols.) Smith, Dr. G. Memoir; Taylor, T. Life of Bishop Heber.

HELPS, SIR ARTHUR (July 10, 1813-March 7, 1875), historian, novelist, and essayist, was born at Streatham, Surrey, the youngest son of Thomas Helps and Ann (Plucknett) Helps.

He received his education at a preparatory school, at Eton, where he went in 1829, and at Trinity College, Cambridge, where he took the B.A. degree in 1835 and the M.A. in 1839. Oxford later (1864) conferred a D.C.L. degree upon him. In these early years Helps began his literary work. At Eton he founded (with others) a school magazine, and his *Thoughts in the Cloister and the Crowd,* a collection of aphorisms, appeared as early as 1835.

In the next year he married Miss Elizabeth Fuller, and soon after turned to politics, becoming private secretary to Thomas Spring-Rice, Chancellor of the Exchequer. In 1840, as private secretary to Lord Morpeth, Chief Secretary for Ireland, he went to that country, living in Dublin Castle in 1840 and 1841. Not long after his return he was appointed a Commisioner of French, Danish, and Spanish claims. After these duties ceased, he devoted himself to study and writing, publishing *Essays Written in the Intervals of Business* (the result of his official experience) and *The Claims of Labour,* a study of social distress and needs for reform, as well as *Friends in Council,* perhaps his most popular work, and a series of political pamphlets in which he collaborated with Kingsley. His anti-slavery sympathies led to the writing of his histories of Spanish America.

In 1860 he accepted the Clerkship of the Privy Council, offered to him by Lord Palmerston, the Prime Minister (who had previously offered him the Chair of Modern History at Oxford) ; and he kept this post until his death. In this work he was in close contact with Queen Victoria, who came to depend upon his clear head and his advice. For her he revised and edited Prince Albert's speeches, and he also prepared two of the Queen's own works, her *Leaves From the Journal of Our Life in the Highlands* (1868) and her *Mountain, Loch, and Glen* (1869). He was given rank in the Order of the Bath in 1871 as a "Companion" in the Civil Division, and in 1872 as a "Knight Commander." Not quite three years later he died of a severe attack of pleurisy in London, leaving his wife, two sons, and four daughters.

"By the death of Sir Arthur Helps the Queen has sustained a loss which has caused her Majesty great affliction," declared the notice of Help's death published in the *Court Circular.* "As a loyal subject and as a kind friend, he rendered to her Majesty many important services. He assisted with a delicacy of feeling and an amount of sympathy which her Majesty can never forget, in the publication of her records of the Prince Consort's speeches and of her *Life in the Highlands* to which he willingly devoted the powers of his enlightened and accomplished mind. The Queen feels that in him she has lost a true and devoted friend."

SIR ARTHUR HELPS

A country gentleman of some means and moderately Liberal sympathies, Helps, who was fond of Prince Albert, was possibly the most trusted friend and adviser of the Queen, and he lived in a house she had arranged for him at Kew Gardens, after disastrous speculations in unsuccessful pottery-works (which he had hoped to make a model industry in relations between capital and labor) had forced him to abandon his beautiful home at Vernon Hill, Hampshire. Perhaps somewhat unduly sensitive to criticism, Helps had, nevertheless, a gift of gentle humor. While rather inclined to easy optimism and perhaps too careless of his own business affairs, Helps took interest in the welfare of others, hated war, and was energetic in the cause of social reform and in that of preventing cruelty to animals.

Kindly geniality, however, is not enough by itself to ensure permanent literary fame, and Helps' work lacks many more valuable qualities, although Ruskin praised him for his sincerity and for his "beautiful quiet English." While his history of the Spanish Conquest is not without value, the sections of it which he converted into biographies proved to be more popular than the original work; and his political novel *Realmah* is flimsily allegorical without the historical significance of Disraeli's work. His plays are forgotten. Helps' most characteristic work is in the vein of *Friends in Council* and *Brevia,* imaginary dialogues, short essays, and collections of aphorisms which reveal a certain wit, a certain cleverness, and a certain urbanity which gained for their writer some renown, but which lacked any solid merits sufficient to sustain his reputation. *The Nation,* after praising Helps as a good historian of the second class, commented (1872) as follows upon his work: "Mr. Helps, and still more his disciples, have done the best they can to stimulate two of the worst tendencies of their readers. The first is the tendency . . . to turn the mind towards little, trivial interests. . . The second evil tendency is the tendency to vulgarity which more or less besets all societies."

R. W. W.

PRINCIPAL WORKS: *Biography*—The Life of Las Casas, 1867; The Life of Columbus, 1869; The Life of Pizarro, 1869; The Life of Hernando Cortes, 1871; The Life and Labours of Mr. Brassey, 1872. *Correspondence*—Correspondence of Sir Arthur Helps, 1917. *Editor*—Leaves From the Journal of Our Life in the Highlands: From 1848 to 1861 (by Queen Victoria; Preface by Sir Arthur Helps) 1868; The Principal Speeches and Addresses of His Royal Highness the Prince Consort (by Prince Albert; Introduction by Sir Arthur Helps) 1862; Mountain, Loch, and Glen (by Queen Victoria; Preface by Sir Arthur Helps) 1869; Work and Wages Practically Illustrated (by Sir Thomas Brassey, i. e., Thomas Brassey the younger) 1872. *Essays, Aphorisms, Imaginary Dialogues, etc.*—Thoughts in the Cloister and the Crowd, 1835; Essays Written in the Intervals of Business, 1841; The Claims of Labour, 1844; Friends in Council (four series) 1847-59; Companions of My Solitude, 1851; Organization in Daily Life, 1862; Brevia, 1870; Conversations on War and General Culture, 1871; Thoughts Upon Government, 1872; Some Talk About Animals and Their Masters, 1873; Social Pressure, 1874. *History*—The Conquerors of the New World and Their Bondsmen, 1848-52; The Spanish Conquest in America and Its Relation to the History of Slavery and to the Government of Colonies, 1855-61. *Novels and Fiction*— Realmah, 1868; Casimir Maremma, 1870; Ivan de Biron, 1873. *Plays*—Catharine Douglas, 1843; King Henry the Second, 1843; Oulita the Serf, 1858. *Miscellaneous*—A Letter From One of the Special Constables in London on the Late Occasion of Their Being Called Out to Keep the Peace, 1848; A Letter on *Uncle Tom's Cabin*, 1852.

ABOUT: Helps, A. Correspondence of Sir Arthur Helps (see Introduction by E. A. Helps); Blackwood's Edinburgh Magazine 148:44 July 1890; Macmillan's Magazine 31:550 April 1875; Nation 14: 323 May 16, 1872; Times (London) March 8, 1875; March 9, 1875; March 10, 1875.

HEMANS, MRS. FELICIA DOROTHEA

(September 25, 1793-May 16, 1835), poetess, was born at Liverpool, the daughter of George Browne, a merchant, and Felicity Wagner.

In 1800 commercial disaster forced her father to remove from Liverpool to Gwrych, in Wales, and it was there, amid surroundings which she could always remember with the greatest pleasure, that Felicia was reared. Her mother, a woman in everyway qualified for the task, educated the girl, who was quick and possessed a fine memory. She began at an early age to write verses, and her parents rather unwisely issued in 1808 a volume of her poems. They received harsh criticism, and the youthful authoress went to bed under the strain and shock; but she recovered her spirits sufficiently to publish another poem in the same year. Shelley, having read her writings and having heard of her beauty and personal charm, wrote to her, suggesting that they might correspond. She declined, and, when he continued to write to her, her mother persuaded his friends to stop him from doing so.

In 1812, after she had known him for three years, the young girl married Captain Alfred Hemans, an Irishman, who had served, as had two of her brothers, in the Peninsular War. After a short stay in Northamptonshire, they made their home with her parents. Five sons were born to them in the next few years, and then, for a reason which no one has ever revealed, Captain Hemans took leave of his wife forever. He made a journey to Italy, ostensibly for his health, and decided to remain there. They continued to correspond concerning the children, two of whom later joined him, but they never saw each other again, although Mrs. Hemans is said to have offered, after her mother's death, to join him, and to have been refused.

In the meantime she devoted herself to writing, as a means of earning money for the support and education of her children. She was fortunate enough to live in a time when there was a great popular demand for poetry, even from women writers. She was a prolific writer, but, even so, requests from editors flooded her, and by 1825 her reputation was such that Andrews Norton issued a separate American edition of her poems. She was even offered a position in Boston as editor of a periodical, but she did not accept. She took prizes in poetry-writing, and wrote magazine essays and even plays, only one of which, *The Vespers of Palermo*, was ever acted, and that without muh success, although Sir Walter Scott supplied an epilogue for it.

In 1825 she removed from her brother's house to another one near it, and lived there until 1827, when her mother died. Mrs. Hemans was devoted to her mother, and after this loss her health began to cause alarm. She moved to Wavertree, near Liverpool, in the same year, in order to secure better educational advantages for her sons.

During the ensuing years she traveled, going twice to Scotland, where she met Scott and Lord Jeffrey, and to the Lake Country, where she met and was fascinated by Wordsworth. In 1831 she removed to Dublin, to live with a brother, and there she spent the rest of her life, gradually sinking in health until her death in May 1835.

An atmosphere of pathos clings about any biography of Mrs. Hemans, and this is the stranger beause it is attended by nearly all the marks of success. Her poetry was in great demand and was widely read and admired by such critics as Lord Jeffrey, Lord Byron, the Countess of Blessington, and Christopher North; and of her personal brilliance and charm there are the most flattering testimonials. Maria Jewsbury described her (under a fictitious name) as "totally different from any

FELICIA HEMANS

other woman I had ever seen," and said of her: "She did not dazzle, she subdued me . . . I never saw one so exquisitely feminine . . . Her birth, her education, the genius with which she was gifted, combined to inspire a passion for the ethereal, the tender, the imaginative, the heroic—in one word, the beautiful." While, of course, much of the almost universal chorus of praise refers to her personal beauty—she was of medium height, well proportioned, with a beautifully formed head—there can be no doubt that her mental powers were of no common order. She early acquired a knowledge of French, Italian, Spanish, and Portuguese, and translated from all these languages. In addition she had some knowledge of Latin, and in 1825 she began the study of the German language and literature, for which she conceived such enthusiasm that she once remarked that when she found any similar-minded friend she could not refrain from discussing them. In her last years Mrs. Hemans was much troubled by notoriety-seekers and autograph-hunters, toward whom her attitude was humorously tolerant. Although she did not go much into society, she never lacked distinguished friends. The shadow which darkened her whole life was her unhappy marriage; and, while she never lost her sweetness and transparency of character, her existence was one of disappointment and frustration.

As a poet, Mrs. Hemans is not unlike Longfellow, and "Casabianca" and "The Landing of the Pilgrim Fathers in New England" have placed her on a similar plane of schoolroom familiarity. Like him she was very successful and much respected in her own time, and like him she has lost much of her reputation in the course of the years. Her pen was too active to produce nothing but gold, and in her later

life she herself regretted the prolificness which to some extent must be attributed to necessity. In some respects a follower of Cowper, she loved the pathetic; and there is a great enthusiasm for chivalry and heroism revealed in her work. She was also given to stressing moral and ethical considerations, and W. M. Rossetti called her poetry not merely "feminine" but "female." Her faults Saintsbury has described as "want of originality," "want of intensity," and "want of concentration." While many of her poems reveal deep and tender feeling, she does not show great subtlety of thought or polish of workmanship, and Scott complained of her work that it had "too many flowers" and "too little fruit." R. W. W

PRINCIPAL WORKS: *Poetry*—Juvenile Poems, 1808; England and Spain, 1808; The Domestic Affections, 1812; The Restoration of the Works of Art to Italy, 1816; Modern Greece, 1817; Translations from Camoens and Other Poets, 1818; Tales and Historic Scenes, 1819; The Sceptic, 1820; Superstition and Error, 1820; Stanzas on the Death of the Late King, 1820; Welsh Melodies, 1822; Lays of Many Lands, 1825; The Forest Sanctuary, 1825; Records of Woman, 1828; Songs of the Affections, 1830; Hymns on the Works of Nature, 1833; Hymns for Childhood, 1834; National Lyrics and Songs in Music, 1834; Scenes and Hymns of Life, 1834. *Drama*—The Vespers of Palermo, 1823; The Siege of Valencia, 1823.

ABOUT: Chorley, H. F. Memorial of Mrs. Hemans; Courtney, J. E. The Adventurous Thirties; Hemans, F. Works, (1839 ed., see Introductory Memoir by her sister).

HENLEY, WILLIAM ERNEST (August 23, 1849-June 11, 1903), poet, critic, and editor, was born at Gloucester, one of five sons of a bookseller. There seems to have been artistic talent diffused throughout the family: one of the brothers became a landscape painter, another a popular actor.

After a few weeks at a school kept by a Mr. Green, Henley was sent to the Crypt Grammar School in Gloucester, of which the poet, Thomas Edward Brown, was then headmaster. Teacher and pupil cemented an unusual friendship, which endured to the former's death. But Henley was often absent from school for long periods before he finally left about 1866 or 1867. From his twelfth year he was a victim of tuberculosis of the bone. In spite of this he persevered in his studies, and in 1867 successfully passed the Oxford local examinations as a senior student.

But a hospital was to be Henley's university. His diseased foot, treated by the crude methods of the day, had to be amputated directly below the knee. Worse, the surgeons announced that the only way to save his life was to amputate the other foot also. Henley rebelled with all the force of his spirit. The great Lister, founder of modern antisepsis, was then head of the Edinburgh Infirmary, ridiculed and looked at askance by his orthodox colleagues. To him Henley insisted on going. He went, and stayed for twenty months, and Lister saved his foot for him. (The poems, *In Hospital*, were written while he was a patient there.) He was discharged in 1875, and was able to lead an active life for nearly thirty years, though he was of course a cripple, with an artificial foot, and suffered horribly all his life from his disease, before it killed him at fifty-four.

By nature Henley was a robust, burly assertive man, full of vigor and high spirits, and he never gave the impression of invalidism. He got around his disease by ignoring it whenever he could, and by exaggerated interest in physical activity and sport, particularly prizefighting. (Perhaps his jingoism had the same source in over-compensation for his enforced weakness.) Moreover, he had no income, and he had to earn a living all the more urgently because he was already engaged to Ann Boyle —sister of a sea-captain who had been his room-mate in the hospital—whom he married in 1878. At first he stayed in Edinburgh, doing French biographies for the *Encyclopaedia Britannica*. But in a few months he left for London. Already he had started up the literary ladder. Some of his hospital verses had appeared in the *Cornhill Magazine*, and the editor, the famous Sir Leslie Stephen, had been so impressed that he had called on him in Edinburgh. He had made another renowned connection during those bedridden days—he had met Robert Louis Stevenson, who was to become his close friend and collaborator, from whom he was to be estranged, and whose memory he was to attack in an article in the *Pall Mall Magazine* in 1901 (Stevenson had died in 1894) for which the admirers of "R. L. S." never forgave him.

Henley became editor of a magazine named *London*, to which he contributed essays and poems, and to which for the first time gave scope to his editorial genius. Here as in his other magazines, he was a keen sniffer out of new talent; the contributors' list of any periodical Henley edited reads like a literary history of the period. But *London* lived only from 1877 to 1879, and Henley was once more a free lance, doing criticisms for *The Athenaeum, St. James's Gazette, Saturday Review,* and *Vanity Fair.* In 1882 he was in editorial harness again, with the *Magazine of Art,* in whose pages he championed Rodin and Whistler. (Art, with music, was his passion.) This chair he held until 1886; then, after three years more of free-lancing, he was called to Edinburgh again, this time to edit the weekly *Scots Observer,* under its two names the most celebrated of his magazines.

In 1891 the owners moved the weekly to London, and changed its name to the *National Observer.* Most of Henley's own best essays were published in it, and it carried the early work of Barrie, Hardy, Kipling, Andrew Lang,

W. E. HENLEY

Sir Gilbert Parker, Stevenson, Wells, and Shaw. It was an imperialist organ, staunchly Tory and hotly anti-Gladstone, but Henley's chief interest was in literature and art, and here this ultra-conservative periodical was made by him iconoclastic, rebellious, and heterodox. (Henley himself in his character displayed exactly the same contradiction.) Around him the editor gathered his group of young men, budding writers and editors, many of them to become famous. He was absolute arbiter, rewrote their work as he pleased, insisted on complete submission; but he defended them, encouraged them, helped them generously. He was a tyrant, but a benevolent one. The magazine had immense influence. Yet it never possessed as many as a thousand subscribers!

In 1894 he retired, overwhelmed by private grief and worn by illness. The only child of the Henleys was their daughter Margaret, born ten years after their marriage. She died in 1894, at the age of five and a half. She seems to have been a rare spirit, adored by her parents and their friends. (Barrie immortalized her as "Reddy" in *Sentimental Tommy,* and as "Wendy" in *Peter Pan.*) Her death was a shock from which her father never recovered.

But he could not remain long out of harness, and in 1898 he was editing the monthly *New Review.* This was a literary success but a financial failure. It was Henley's last editorial venture. As his health grew worse, he left London, living first at Worthing and then at Woking. He was indefatigably busy as editor of many of the English classics (including Shakespeare, Fielding, Smollett, Hazlitt, an unfinished Byron, and, with T. F. Henderson, the centenary edition of Burns, the introduction to which drove Scottish readers into an ecstasy of rage and resentment.) With Stevenson he had collaborated in the writing of four plays, the best of which was *Deacon Brodie*, acted in the United States by Henley's brother, Edward. (An operetta, *Mephisto*, was also produced with his brother in the title rôle.) But Henley's great contribution, besides his discovery and encouragement of new talent in his magazine editorships, was the editing of the Tudor Translations, begun in 1892 and completed by the Tudor Bible, the preface of which Henley had not yet finished when he died.

In 1893 he had been honored by an LL. D. degree from the University of St. Andrews, and in 1898 had been granted a civil list pension of £225, thus relieving him of financial anxiety. But the two honors he most coveted he lost, to his bitter disappointment. One was the chair of English literature at Edinburgh University, of which he was deprived because of his deflation of the private character of Burns; the other was the poet laureateship at Tennyson's death; though he spoke slightingly of his own poems, it was hard to be passed over for a voluminous rhymester like Alfred Austin.

Early in 1903, a train which he was boarding at Woking started suddenly, threw him off, and dragged him. Not only was the nervous shock extreme, but the accident reawoke his old tubercular disorder. He was bedridden in consequence, but in the end died suddenly and without warning. He was cremated, and his ashes buried by his beloved little daughter's grave, his wife surviving for several years before she joined them there.

Henley was a man to be worshiped or detested. Tall, broad-shouldered, with a mop of stiff yellow hair (white at his later period), a full reddish beard, and expressive but very nearsighted blue eyes, he was a striking figure, who might have been taken for a pirate or a Viking chief rather than an editor and a poet. He was masterful, autocratic, often violent in his language and eccentric in his actions, yet on the other hand he was loyal, devoted, prodigally generous and a lion for courage. Above all things he hated and abhorred sham and humbug, yet he was taken in completely by the worst humbug of all, that chauvinistic insularity called jingoism. Even those who differed from him most strongly granted him utter sincerity and fearlessness. Cant and hypocrisy were his arch enemies, though he was apt to find them where they were not as well as where they were. His disciples, his young men whom he licked into shape and pushed forward in the world, regarded him with something like religious ardor and awe.

Yet in his poetry, this aggressive battler could be delicate and tender, could lose himself in artificial conceits and fragile card-palaces of rhyme. Francis Thompson—whom Henley could not accept because he loved Shelley, hated by Henley—spoke of his "rich and lovely verbal music." He was perhaps the first to introduce into English literature the ultra-modern note of free verse in the mode used by the impressionists and imagists of the "poetry revival" of 1915 or so. To read his poems as a whole is to realize also his intense preoccupation with death—a preoccupation equal to Whitman's. In religion he was a pagan rather than a formal free thinker, with no belief in survival but with the eager acceptance of death as a release that is natural to a lifelong sufferer.

It is unfortunate that to most readers Henley is a poet of one poem "Invictus," with its meretricious bravado. The false defiance of its spirit may be forgiven him, since it was written from a hospital bed; but only those indomitably facing equal affliction have the right to admire it.

In prose, Henley was a great phrase-maker. He was a brilliant conversationalist, but his choicest epigrams are in his essays. As a critic he was often sound and penetrating, when his prejudices did not get in the way. He had no power of sustained effort, and his shortest offerings are his best. His technical skill was great, in both prose and verse. But above all he was one of the greatest editors of history. As Vernon Blackburn puts it, "he was, for a few years, the doorkeeper to fame in the literature of England."   M. A. deF.

PRINCIPAL WORKS: *Poetry*—A Book of Verses, 1888; The Song of the Sword, 1892; London Voluntaries, 1893; Poems, 1898; For England's Sake, 1900; Hawthorn and Lavender, 1901; A Song of Speed, 1903. *Plays* (with Robert Louis Stevenson)—Deacon Brodie, Beau Austin, Admiral Guinea, 1892. *Essays*—Views and Reviews, 1890; Essays, 1921. *Miscellany*—Lyra Heroica (anthology), 1892; Book of English Prose (anthology, with Charles Whibley) 1894; Dictionary of Slang and Colloquial English (with John S. Farmer) 1905.

ABOUT: Cornford, L. C. William Ernest Henley; Jackson, H. The Eighteen Nineties; Meynell, V. Alice Meynell; Rothenstein, W. Men and Memories; Tynan, K. Twenty-Five Years; Williamson, K. W. E. Henley: A Memoir; Fortnightly Review ns74:232 August 1903; Independent 55:2038 August 27, 1903; Living Age 239:150 October 17, 1903.

HENTY, GEORGE ALFRED (December 8, 1832-November 16, 1902), novelist, was born at Trumpington, near Cambridge. He was the eldest son of James Henty, a stockbroker, and Mary Bovill.

His education was secured at Westminster School and at Gonville and Caius College, Cambridge, where he matriculated in 1852, but which he left, without obtaining his degree, when the outbreak of the Crimean War impelled him and his brother to volunteer. They joined the hospital commissariat in 1855

GEORGE ALFRED HENTY

and went to the Crimea, where, later in the same year, Henty's brother developed cholera and died.

Henty's first literary use of his adventures, nearly all of which he sooner or later turned into books, was a series of letters describing the siege of Sebastopol. These were accepted by the *Morning Advertiser*, but Henty did not yet consider turning to writing as a profession. In the meanwhile, having contracted a fever, he was sent home, and upon his recovery was decorated for distinguished service and promoted to the rank of purveyor, a position in the commissary department. During the struggle of Italy and Austria he was selected to organize the Italian hospitals, and afterwards held posts in the commissariats at Belfast and Portsmouth. He wearied of this occupation, resigned his commission, and assisted his father in the management of a coal mine in Wales, the experience being the source of 'nis novel *Facing Death* which was published in 1883. After going to Sardinia to operate another mine, Henty discovered that he did not care for this occupation either; he now (1865) definitely decided to earn his living by writing, and produced various articles for *The Standard,* which next year sent to him to cover the Austro-Italian War. He had thus the opportunity to be present at the battle of Lissa in 1866; in 1867-68 he accompanied Napier to Abyssinia and published his articles in book form as *The March to Magdala.* He attended the inauguration of the Suez Canal service, saw some of the winter campaign in the Franco-Prussian War, and had the illuminating experience of near-starvation in Paris during the days of the commune. His adventures continued with his presence at the Russian conquest of Kiev

in 1873 and participation in Lord Wolseley's expedition to Ashanti in this and the next year, as described in *The March to Coomassie.* Henty then observed the guerilla warfare during the Carlist insurrection in Spain, 1874; he accompanied the Prince of Wales, later Edward VII, on his tour of India in 1875, and also saw fighting with the Turkish army in the war with Servia in 1876.

Henty had now written various novels for adults, with ordinary success. It was not until he had been invited to contribute to the magazine *Union Jack,* and had written stories of adventure which immediately sprang into popularity, that he may be said to have embarked on the flood tide of popular favor. *Out on the Pampas* (1868) was the first of his novels for boys; from this time on he was to write about eighty of them, ranging in time and scene from the early days of Egypt to all other lands and to modern times. As a whole, Henty's work in this field is distinguished for its comparative sobriety, its clear style, and that quality to which Henty proudly referred as "manly tone." His popularity among boys has declined, but he is still widely read and has by no means been forgotten by those adults who like a good adventure story and remember the books they enjoyed as children.

Henty was a large burly man, very English in appearance, with a long full beard and an apparently limitless store of energy. At the peak of his productive power he dictated, under contract, three or four novels a year, concerning himself meanwhile with two boys' magazines, both of which were inexplicably unsuccessful. His capacity for enduring hardship, however, naturally diminished, and he found such trips as that to the California gold fields a bit too strenuous for him. His last years were passed quietly, and he died aboard his yacht.

He was twice married—first to Elizabeth Finucane in 1858, and later to Elizabeth Keylock, who survived him. By his first marriage he had two sons and two daughters, the eldest son, Captain Charles G. Henty, surviving.

R. M.

PRINCIPAL WORKS: *Novels*—Out on the Pampas, 1868; The Young Franc-Tireurs, 1872; The Young Buglers, 1880; Facing Death, 1883; With Clive in India, 1884; The Bravest of the Brave, 1887; Orange and Green, 1888; The Cat of Bubastes, 1889; By Pike and Dyke, 1890; by Right of Conquest, 1891.

ABOUT: Downey, E. Twenty Years Ago; Fenn, G. M. Alfred Henty; Athenaeum 120:683 November 22, 1902.

HERAUD, JOHN ABRAHAM (July 5, 1799—April 20, 1887), poet, dramatist, and critic, was born in London, the son of a law stationer. After receiving a private education, he contributed to the *Quarterly* and other reviews, was assistant editor of *Fraser's Magazine* (1830-33), edited the *Monthly Magazine* (1839-42) and the *Christian Monthly Magazine*, was dramatic critic of *The Athenaeum* (1843-68) and of the *Illustrated London News* (1849-79). Eventually he received pensions from the last two papers. He died in London at eighty-seven. By his wife, Ann Elizabeth Baddams, he had two children, including Edith Heraud, an actress.

As a disciple of Coleridge, he wrote grandiose poems, "psychological curiosities, evincing much misplaced power" (in the words of G. C. Boase). Carlyle remarked that Heraud contrives "to appropriate an Idea or two (even in Coleridge's sense), and re-echoes them in long continuance,—I fear, as from *un*furnished chambers." He was an astute critic of the theatre and the author of a successful tragedy. Thackeray's "Jawbrahim Heraudee" was modeled after him.

PRINCIPAL WORKS: *Poetry*—Tottenham, 1820; The Descent Into Hell, 1830; The Judgment of the Flood, 1834; The War of Ideas, 1871. *Drama*—Videna: or, The Mother's Tragedy, 1854. *Criticism*—Shakespeare, 1865.

ABOUT: Heraud, E. Memoirs of J. A. Heraud.

HERSCHEL, SIR JOHN FREDERICK WILLIAM (March 7, 1792-May 11, 1871), scientist and scientific writer, was the only child of the celebrated astronomer, Sir William Herschel, and nephew of the almost equally celebrated Caroline Herschel. After school at Hitcham, Buckinghamshire, and a few months at Eton, from which he was withdrawn because he was being persecuted by a bully, he was tutored in the scientific atmosphere of his home at Slough by a Scottish mathematician, and at seventeen entered St. John's College, Cambridge. There his career was an unbroken triumph; he gained all the first prizes for which he was eligible, and in 1813 secured his B.A. as senior wrangler, being elected immediately to a fellowship, and given his M.A. in 1816. In 1813 he, with his lifelong friend the mathematician Charles Babbage, helped to found the Analytical Society of Cambridge; and between 1816 and 1820 he translated from the French and edited, with examples, three volumes of mathematics that became standard textbooks. His first communication to the Royal Society was in 1812, and he was elected a fellow the next year, at twenty-one.

His father wished him to enter the church, but he preferred the law, and entered Lincoln's Inn in 1814. It was soon apparent that science must be his career. His earliest interest was in optics. "Light," he said, "was my first love." He knew no astronomy until he began to study with his father in 1816. Although eventually he became the more famous astronomer of the two, his heart was

SIR JOHN F. W. HERSCHEL

not really in that science, and it is said he never looked through a telescope after 1838!

To list all Herschel's medals and honors would be wearisome. He was a founder of the Royal Astronomical Society and its first foreign secretary, later being its president for three terms; from 1824 to 1827 he was secretary of the Royal Society. He traveled much abroad, being on the continent at the time of his father's death in 1822. In 1829 he married Margaret Stewart, by whom he had three sons (two of whom became distinguished scientists) and nine daughters. He continued to live at Slough with his widowed mother until her death in 1833, when he carried out an old dream of surveying the southern heavens, as his father had done the northern. For five years he and his family lived near Capetown. He had refused the offer of government subsidy of this venture. There he did invaluable work, laying the foundation of the study of stellar magnitudes; discovering 1,202 double stars and 1,708 star clusters and nebulae (his former catalog had listed 2,307 nebulae, 525 discovered by him); counting 70,000 stars in gauging the density of the Milky Way; making meterorological observations; and observing Halley's Comet in its visit of 1835-36. All this work he did with one, untrained assistant.

On his return to England he was overwhelmed with honors, was given an honorary D.C.L. by Oxford, and against his will accepted a baronetcy (in 1831 he had, like his father, been knighted). He refused to run for parliament for Cambridge or to be president of the Royal Society, but in 1842 did accept the lord rectorship of Marischal College, Aberdeen, and in 1835 was president of the British Association for the Advancement of

Science, which he had helped to found. He was made a member of practically all the learned societies of Europe and America, yet remained as diffident and retiring as he had been all his life.

Although he made no further direct observations in astronomy, he continued to expand the work already done, and to carry further his father's special studies. He revised the nomenclature of stars, discovered the connection between sunspots and the sun's rotation, and studied star clusters and the Magellanic Clouds. In 1840 he moved to Collingswood, Kent, expecting to lead a life of quiet study; but in 1850 he was appointed Master of the Mint, and served for five years before he retired on account of poor heath. In 1863 he published a catalog of all known nebulae and clusters (5,079), and in 1866 a general and descriptive catalogue of 812 pairs of double stars. He died at Collingswood at seventy-nine, and was buried in Westminster Abbey next to Sir Isaac Newton.

Herschel was an affectionate, devout, simple man, who shrank from public life and loved his domestic existence with his children and his gardening. He had less genius than his father, but far wider knowledge. His style in his few general writings (outside of catalogs) was lucid and powerful, with a quiet charm, though sometimes too discursive. His *Outlines of Astronomy* has been called "perhaps the most completely satisfactory general exposition of a science ever penned."

M. A. deF.

PRINCIPAL WORKS: Preliminary Discourse on the Study of Natural Philosophy, 1830; Results of Astronomical Observations at the Cape of Good Hope, 1847; Outlines of Astronomy, 1849; Essays From the Edinburgh and Quarterly Reviews, 1857; Familiar Lectures on Scientific Subjects, 1867.

ABOUT: Ball, R. S. Great Astronomers; Clerke, A. M. The Herschels and Modern Astronomy; Macpherson, H. C. Makers of Astronomy; Williams, H S. The Great Astronomers.

HILL, GEORGE BIRKBECK NORMAN
(June 7, 1835-February 27, 1903), eighteenth-century scholar and editor of Boswell's *Life of Johnson,* was born in Bruce Castle, Tottenham, Middlesex, the second son and third child of Arthur Hill and Ellen Tilt (Maurice) Hill.

His father was a schoolmaster, coming of a family of schoolmasters, and the boy, who lost his mother when he was four years old, was educated in his father's school at Bruce Castle. Here the discipline and organization were fine, but the actual learning of the masters was not great, and a conservative literary tradition was so strong that the boy knew nothing of Keats, Shelley, or Browning, and little even of Tennyson. At Oxford, however, where he matriculated at Pembroke College in 1855, he met William Morris and Rossetti and Swinburne, and a new world

was opened for him. He was prevented by ill health from taking honors, and received a bachelor's degree in the "honorary fourth class" in "humane letters" in 1858, later taking the B.C.L. and D.C.L. degrees although, because of dislike of the necessary religious tests, he never took the M.A. degree.

Although he originally had planned to take orders, he joined his father in 1858 as an assistant in the school, marrying in December of that year Miss Annie Scott, to whom he had become engaged before he went to Oxford. Untill 1877, despite lack of natural enthusiasm for the work, which entailed severe strain upon both himself and his wife, he continued in this position, becoming head master, and raising the scholastic standards of the institution. His health finally necessitated his withdrawal, and he turned to other work.

For some time he had been contributing criticism to the *Saturday Review,* writing also for the *Cornhill Magazine, the Pall Mall Gazette,* and *The Times.* He had aready begun to collect information and material upon Boswell's *Life of Johnson,* thus beginning his work upon the subject which was to engross him for the rest of his life.. His first Johnson study, *Dr Johnson: His Friends and His Critics,* appeared in 1878, and his edition of Boswell's *Journal of a Tour to Corsica* followed in the next year. Ill health, the loss of a son, and the necessity for writing a life of his uncle, Sir Rowland Hill, and editing Charles G. Gordon's letters on the history of the Egyptian Sudan, combined to delay the edition of Boswell's *Life.* During this time (1877-86) Hill lived at Burghfield, near Reading, in the country.

He removed, in the year of the publication of his edition of Boswell, to Oxford, where he could enjoy the society of scholarly men. His health, however, gave out; he suffered from asthma and bronchitis, and was obliged to pass several winters abroad. His summers he spent chiefly at Hampstead with a daughter. In 1893 Mr. and Mrs. Hill spent some time in America, visiting a daughter whose husband was a professor at Harvard; and *Harvard College by an Oxonian* (1894), a friendly critical appraisal, was the result of this visit.

Hill continued to work on his editions and Johnsonian books to the last, and, when he died (about four months after the death of his wife) in 1903, little was left for his nephew to complete in the edition of Johnson's *Lives of the English Poets,* which appeared in 1905.

Hill's life does not make a dramatic or spectacular record, largely because of his singleness of aim and purpose. He was charming, very popular with children, and democratic in his general sympathies toward others.

GEORGE BIRKBECK NORMAN HILL

More significant, however, for his reputation in English letters were his personal habits of thoroughness and method, which made the edition of Boswell's *Johnson* his memorial. The adverse criticism of Percy Fitzgerald, another editor of the same work, who charged inaccuracy and incompleteness, fails to accord with the general verdict, one of almost unqualified praise. "The edition was accepted as a masterpiece of spacious editing," wrote Thomas Seccombe. "The index, forming the sixth volume, is a monument of industry and completeness." The copious annotations in this work are valuable, as they are in many of Hill's other books, for the light they throw upon Johnson, Boswell, and their time, and justify Seccombe's description of Hill as "the benevolent interpreter of Johnson's era to his own generation," infusing into his work "a zeal and abundant knowledge which gave charm to his discursiveness." R. W. W.

PRINCIPAL WORKS: *Biography*—The Life of Sir Rowland Hill . . . and the History of Penny Postage (by Sir Rowland Hill; revised by G. B. N. Hill) 1880: *Editor*—Boswell's Correspondence With the Honourable Andrew Erskine, and His Journal of a Tour to Corsica, 1879; Colonel Gordon in Central Africa, 1874-1879 (by C. G. Gordon) 1881; Boswell's Life of Johnson (including Boswell's Journal of a Tour to the Hebrides and Johnson's Diary of a Journey Into North Wales) 1887; History of Rasselas: Prince of Abyssinia (by Samuel Johnson) 1887; The Traveller (by Oliver Goldsmith) 1888; Letters of David Hume to William Strahan, 1888; Wit and Wisdom of Samuel Johnson, 1888; Select Essays of Dr. Johnson, 1889; Lord Chesterfield's Worldly Wisdom, 1890; Letters of Samuel Johnson, LL.D., 1892; Johnsonian Miscellanies, 1897; Letters of Dante Gabriel Rossetti to William Allingham, 1854-1870, 1897; Unpublished Letters of Dean Swift, 1899; The Memoirs of the Life of Edward Gibbon, 1900; Lives of the English Poets by Samuel Johnson, LL. D., 1905. *Education*—Supplementary Exercises

to Henry's First Latin Book, 1865; A Key to the Supplementary Exercises to Henry's First Latin Book, 1865. *Johnsonian Studies*—Dr Johnson: His Friends and His Critics, 1878; Footsteps of Dr. Johnson (Scotland) 1890. *Letters*—Letters Written by a Grandfather, 1903; Letters of George Birkbeck Hill, 1906. *Miscellaneous*—Writers and Readers, 1891; Harvard College by an Oxonian, 1894; Talks About Autographs, 1896.

ABOUT: Fitzgerald, P. H. A Critical Examination of Dr G. Birkbeck Hill's "Johnsonian" Editions; Fitzgerald, P. H. Editing à la Mode; Hill, G. B. N. Letters of George Birkbeck Hill; Hill, G. B. N. Letters Written by a Grandfather; Johnson, S. Lives of the English Poets (see Memoir by Harold Spencer Scott); Forum 37:540 April 1906.

HILTON, APTHUR CLEMENT (1851-1877) is remembered for his clever parodies of contemporary poets in the two issues of the *Light Green*, a magazine edited and largely written by himself just before and after his graduation from St. John's College, Cambridge, in 1872. These parodies, particularly "The Heathen Pass-ee" after Bret Harte's "Heathen Chinee," "The Vulture and the Husbandman" after Lewis Carroll, and "Octopus" after Swinburne, rank among the best in the language and place their youthful author next to James and Horace Smith and C. S. Calverley as a parodist in verse. The parodies, representative of the life and thought of Cambridge, are still reprinted and enjoyed at the University.

Following his graduation from Cambridge, Hilton, who was the son of a clergyman, studied at the Theological College at Wells and became curate of the joint parishes of St. Mary and St. Clement in the borough of Sandwich. Thereafter he wrote only serious verse, which is forgotten. Of delicate constitution, he died in his twenty-sixth year. His few writings were gathered into a posthumous volume.

WORK: The Works of Arthur Clement Hilton: Together With His Life and Letters (ed. by R. P. Edgcumbe) 1904.
ABOUT: Hilton, A. C. Works (see Life by R. P. Edgcumbe); Manchester Quarterly 1915.

HINTON, JAMES (1822-December 16, 1875), philosopher, was born in Reading, the son of a Baptist minister. He attended first the school of his grandfather, the Rev. James Hinton, near Oxford, and then a school for nonconformists at Harpenden. As a boy he was religious and meditative and noted chiefly for his remarkable memory.

In 1838, at sixteen, he came from the country to serve as cashier for a wholesale woolen draper in Whitechapel. The poverty, filth, and degradation he witnessed obsessed him and formed the foundation of his philosophy. A year later he became a clerk in an insurance office, studying German, Italian, Russian, mathematics, history, and metaphysics by himself at night. In 1841, only nineteen, he fell deeply in love with Margaret Haddon, but she refused him. A long nervous illness followed. Then he resolved to make something of his life, and became a student of medicine at St. Bartholomew's. A voyage to China as a ship's surgeon followed. Returned to England, he received his M.B. degree in 1847, and became an assistant surgeon in Newport, Essex. Study and reflection caused him, much to his own pain, to give up faith in Christianity; and when he proposed again to Miss Haddon, she refused him once more, on religious grounds. To forget his grief he became medical officer on a ship carrying free Negroes from Sierra Leone, in Africa, to Jamaica. In Jamaica he remained two years, placing the Negroes on farms and studying the social life of the island. Then, after a visit to relatives in New Orleans, he returned to England. On the long voyage home a "sense of sin" oppressed him, and "almost made him a Christian again." At least it made him acceptable to Miss Haddon, for she became engaged to him at last, though they were not married until 1852.

In London he entered into partnership with a friend named Fisher and specialized in aural surgery. Interest in homoeopathy and the study of Coleridge influenced him to concentrate on the relation between mind and body, with the result that once more he became "a Christian—of a sort." In 1853 he dissolved his partnership, and started practise alone, becoming a successful specialist in diseases of the ear. In 1854-5 he gave public lectures on the theory of sound.

All this while he was gradually evolving his philosophy, starting with a theory of interpreting science by moral reason, and reconciling science and religion: a complete theory of the universe, he said, must satisfy the emotions, including the religious emotions, as well as the reason. His first publication was in 1856, in the *Christian Spectator*, a series of papers on physiology and ethics. He wrote largely also on professional topics, being one of the editors of the *Year Book of Medicine* in 1863. (A list of his writings does not include his highly technical surgical and anatomical text books.) In 1870 he went to the Azores, and bought a small estate there. Once more a long sea voyage gave him time for philosophical meditation, eventuating in what he called a "moral revolution," which led him to substitute altruism for individualism as the basis of morals: by this, he held, man transcends himself and becomes one with God. Gradually his thought became more liberal and "advanced"; in his posthumous book *The Law Breaker and the Coming of the Law* he even leans toward advocacy of the abolition of marriage.

Hinton now determined to resign his practise and devote himself entirely to philosophi-

JAMES HINTON

cal writing. He had already published three volumes, including the most celebrated, *The Mystery of Pain*. In order to provide the financial means, he concentrated on the writing of numerous surgical and anatomical works, particularly on aural surgery. In 1874 he also edited a manual of physiology. But overwork frustrated its own aim: before the year was over he suffered a nervous breakdown which rapidly grew into a chronic cerebral disorder. He decided to go to his estate in the Azores, but it was too late: he had hardly landed when he died of inflammation of the brain. He was buried there, on the island of São Miguel.

Hinton's mission was to show the source of pain in man himself: deeply compassionate, he endeavored to reconcile the tragedy of life with a loving God. Sin, he said, is the cause of suffering; pain is only misinterpretation of an actual good, and inertia keeps us from realizing this. The more vital the mind of the experient, the less can pain affect him as evil. Volition he identified with spirit. Our existence is limited by consciousness, and both materialism and theism must yield to the universal spirit as the only actuality. He has brought consolation to many religiously minded readers, but his theory is too complicated and too loosely worked out and his style too verbose and confused, to be of much value to those who base their conclusions on reason and scientific evidence. **M. A. deF.**

PRINCIPAL WORKS: Man and His Dwelling-Place, 1859; Life in Nature, 1862; The Mystery of Pain, 1866; Thoughts on Health, 1871; The Place of the Physician and Other Essays, 1874; Chapters on the Art of Thinking and Other Essays (ed. by C. H. Hinton) 1879; The Philosophy of Religion (ed. by C. Haddon) 1881; The Law Breaker and the Coming of the Law (ed. by M. H. Hinton) 1884.

ABOUT: Haddon, C. The Larger Life: Studies in Hinton's Ethics; Hinton, J. Life in Nature (see Introduction by H. Ellis); Hopkins, E. Life and Letters of James Hinton; Hibbert Journal 19:53 October 1920.

"HISLOP, ANDREW." See CLARKE, MARCUS

"HOBBES, JOHN OLIVER." See CRAIGIE, PEARL MARY THERESA

HODGKIN, THOMAS (July 29, 1831-March 2, 1913), historian, was born in Tottenham, a suburb of London, the son of a barrister, and educated at University College, London. He was a partner in the banking firm of Hodgkin, Barnett, & Company at Newcastle-on-Tyne, from 1859 until its absorption by Lloyds Bank in 1902. In 1861 he was married to Lucy Anna Fox, by whom he had three sons and three daughters. He took active part in the public affairs and Quaker meetings of Newcastle, and died at Falmouth at eighty-one.

His historical works, the product of leisure hours, were erudite, accurate, and bright with imagination, but prolix and carelessly written. "From a literary point of view," wrote J. A. Hammerton of *Italy and Her Invaders*, "his book is quite undistinguished, from the historical it is a study of first importance." This, his major opus, the product of twenty years' labor, was a seven-volume history of Italy after the fall of the Roman Empire. Through it and subsequent works he was recognized as a leading authority on the history of the middle ages.

PRINCIPAL WORKS: Italy and Her Invaders, 1879-99; The Dynasty of Theodosius, 1889; Theodoric the Goth, 1891; History of England From the Earliest Times to the Norman Conquest, 1906.
ABOUT: Creighton, L. Life and Letters of Thomas Hodgkin; Hammerton, J. A. Memories of Books and Places.

HODGSON, SHADWORTH (December 25, 1832-June 13, 1912), philosopher, was born in Boston, Lincolnshire, and educated at Rugby and at Corpus Christi College, Oxford. After the untimely death of his wife Ann Everard and their only child in 1858, he devoted himself wholly to philosophical reflection and writing. He helped to found the Aristotelian Society "for the systematic study of philosophy" and was its first president (1880-94); many of his papers were contributed to its *Proceedings*. He died in London at the age of seventy-nine.

It was his aim to continue and correct the work of Kant and Hume. William David Ross describes his system as "a bold and able attempt to work out a complete metaphysic by a thoroughgoing analysis of experience. His precise point of view was, however, one which other philosophers found it difficult to share,

and he founded no school; the main value of his work probably resides in his detailed psychological ananlysis." His style is somewhat formal and obscure.

PRINCIPAL WORKS: Time and Space, 1865; The Theory of Practice, 1870; The Philosophy of Reflection, 1878; The Metaphysic of Experience, 1898.
ABOUT: The Times June 18, 1912.

HOFLAND, BARBARA (1770-November 9, 1844), novelist and author of children's stories, was born Barbara Wreaks at Sheffield, where her father was a manufacturer. Her first marriage, in 1796, to T. Bradshawe Hoole, a Sheffield merchant, was terminated by his death in two years. After ten years of widowhood she was married in 1808 to Thomas Christopher Hofland, a noted landscape painter, with whom she lived in London and the Lake District. She was a friend and correspondent of Mary Russell Mitford.

She wrote in all about seventy works (mostly instructive tales) of which nearly 300,000 copies were sold in Great Britain. Least didactic and most enduring of her works was *The Son of a Genius*, a vivid study of the artistic temperament as she had observed it in her husband. According to the *Cambridge History*, she "was more stagey and pompous, without the clearness of equally determined but less heavy moralists."

PRINCIPAL WORKS: The Clergyman's Widow, 1812; Matilda: or, The Barbadoes Girl, 1816; The Son of a Genius, 1816; The Daughter of a Genius, 1823; The Young Pilgrim, 1825; William and His Uncle Ben, 1826.
ABOUT: Ramsay, T. Life and Literary Remains of Barbara Hofland; L'Estrange, A. G. (ed.). The Friendships of Mary Russell Mitford; London Gentleman's Magazine January, 1845.

HOGG, JAMES ("the Ettrick Shepherd") (November 25?, 1770-November 21, 1835), Scottish poet and novelist, was born in Selkirkshire in a poor farmer's family. In all his life he had only six months' schooling, and when he started to write down his verses, he could do only four to six lines at a sitting because writing was so laborious a task. Before he was seven he was taking care of ewes, and at fifteen was a fully qualified shepherd. He was ambitious, with a longing for culture; he taught himself to play the violin, and he was always making up verses; but he had never in his life read anything except parts of the Bible and some of the songs of Allan Ramsay and "Blind Harry."

In 1790 Hogg went as shepherd to a farm in Yarrow, where he remained ten years. The farmer was better educated than was usual, and there were books in his house, which Hogg devoured. He made friends also with the farmer's sons, one of whom, William Laidlaw, later became the steward for Sir Walter Scott and gained for Hogg Scott's patronage. Gradually he became known

JAMES HOGG

herd"—a rustic, foolish, hard-drinking, boisterous person whom gentlemen of wealth and education might patronize and use as a butt for their wit. It was this relationship between Hogg and the Forum members that later suggested to William Maginn and "Christopher North" their famous "Noctes Ambrosianae" papers, which appeared for many years in *Blackwood's*, with "the Ettrick Shepherd" as the central figure. [See sketch of John Wilson in this volume.] After the first few installments, however, the "Noctes" dealt little with the real Hogg, and the "Shepherd" of the papers became almost entirely a fictional character. But Hogg's antics at the Forum brought their own reward. Byron introduced him to the publisher John Murray, who proved a real benefactor; and in 1816, by bequest of the Duchess of Buccleuch, he received the farm of Altrive Lake, in Yarrow, at a nominal rent.

From this time on Hogg prospered, though he continued to lose money in ill-advised farming schemes. He was one of the earliest contributors to *Blackwood's*, and had until his death a regular department in it known as the *Shepherd's Calendar*. In 1820 he married Margaret Phillips, and soon after lost most of his money in trying to enlarge his farm. He was ill-advised enough to trust a publisher who became bankrupt, and then to trust him again as far as a second bankruptcy. But his worst days were over forever; in 1832 he went to London and found himself lionized, and he wrote voluminously and found a ready market.

After his death, however, his widow and children were in straitened circumstances until a royal pension was granted in 1853, and it was not until 1860 that his native country erected a monument to him near the lake he had made famous.

Hogg is the best known poet of humble Scottish birth after Burns, but he is a very pale reflection of that genius. He had emotion rather than passion, and he was essentially superficial. He lacked the fierce pride and the extreme sensitiveness of Burns, and so he missed both the misery and the immortality of his great predecessor. "The Queen's Wake" is his best poem, the most imaginative, and it brought him his first celebrity. He had a good musical ear and a real sympathy with nature, and a buoyant and optimistic disposition which shines through his poems and stories, but he was hampered by a truly fatal fluency and an absolute inability to condense anything he wrote. A great deal of his work is actually what he called it in self-derision—"ranting rhymes." Though he wrote often in the Scottish vernacular, it was not native to him as it was to Burns, and the artificiality is often apparent; on the other hand, he wrote much

through the countryside as the "poeter," who "made songs for the lassies to sing in chorus." In 1796 he began to write these down. Hogg liked to romanticize his early life, and so the story may not be true that he never heard of Burns until 1797, and then determined to be his successor. His poem "Donald McDonald" was published in a Scottish journal in 1800.

His brother married that year in Ettrick, and Hogg had to leave his job with the Laidlaws and go back to help his aged parents, who had three years yet to run on the lease of their farm. In 1801, when he was in Edinburgh selling stock, he collected his poems from memory and·had them crudely printed. The next year he first met Scott. In 1803 he lost all his savings over a fraudulent lease of a sheep farm, and had to go again as a shepherd to Nithsdale. In 1807 he published two books, one of verse, one on the diseases of sheep, and lost the proceeds of both. He tried in vain to secure a commission in the militia or an excise (tax) post. He had to go back bankrupt to Ettrick, where the neighbors looked askance at him.

Suddenly in 1810 he decided to leave for Edinburgh and to make his way there as a writer. He brought out *The Forest Minstrel*, two-thirds of the poems in which were his own, and the Countess of Dalkeith, to whom it was dedicated, gave him a hundred pounds, but there were no other profits. Then he started a critical weekly called *The Spy*, most of which he wrote himself, but it deteriorated rapidly and was dead in a year.

He next determined on a more original course of personal advancement. He joined a sort of debating club known as the Forum, and proceeded deliberately to build up for himself his character of "the Ettrick Shep more fluently in ordinary English than did Burns, who is usually a little stiff in that unfamiliar medium. His tales and novels are extremely dead, but many of his poems and songs still survive, and he stands as a noted example of an entirely self-taught man who lifted himself into literary celebrity by his own boot-straps.   M. A. deF.

PRINCIPAL WORKS: *Poetry*—Scottish Pastorals, Poems, Songs, etc., 1801; The Mountain Bard, 1807; The Forest Minstrel, 1810; The Queen's Wake, 1813; The Ettrick Garland, 1813; The Pilgrims of the Sun, 1815; Mador of the Moor, 1816; The Poetic Mirror (parodies) 1816; Jacobite Relics of Scotland (in part) 1819-21; The Royal Jubilee, 1822; Queen Hynde, 1826; Select and Rare Scottish Melodies (music by Henry Bishop) 1829; Songs, 1831. *Prose*—Dramatic Tales, 1817; The Brownie of Bodsbeck and Other Tales, 1818; Winter Evening Tales, 1820; The Three Perils of Man, 1822; The Three Perils of Woman, 1823; The Private Memoirs and Confessions of a Justified Sinner (anon.) 1824 (as The Suicide's Grave, 1828; as Confessions of a Fanatic, 1831); Altrive Tales, 1832; A Queer Book, 1832; A Series of Lay Sermons, 1834; The Domestic Manners and Private Life of Sir Walter Scott, 1834; Tales of the Wars of Montrose, 1834; Tales and Sketches, 1837.

ABOUT: Batho, E. C. The Ettrick Shepherd; Carswell, D. Sir Walter; Douglas, G. B. S. James Hogg; Garden, M. Memorials of James Hogg; Lang, A. Life of Lockhart.

HOLLAND, LORD (Henry Richard Vassall Fox, Third Baron Holland) (November 21, 1773-October 22, 1840),

politician, author of political reminiscences, and patron of literature, was born in Wiltshire, a nephew of Ch.rles James Fox the statesman. He was educated at Eton and at Christ Church, Oxford. A prominent Whig, he took a leading part in debates in the House of Lords. He was lord privy seal (1806-07) and chancellor of the duchy of Lancaster (1830-34), 1835-40). Holland House, his London residence, was a gathering place for the celebrated politicians and writers of the time. His wife, Elizabeth, LADY HOLLAND (1770-1845), famous as a hostess, kept a *Journal* which was published in 1908 and is notable for its intimate portraits of herself and those who came to her salon.

Lord Holland is remembered as a patron of literature and the author of lucid, authentic contributions to social and political history. His posthumous *Memoirs* and *Reminiscences* were edited by his son the fourth baron, whose own *Journal* was published in 1923. He also performed minor services as a scholar, with translations from the Spanish and Italian, an edition of Horace Walpole's *George II*, and other works.

PRINCIPAL WORKS: Foreign Reminiscences (ed. by his son) 1850; Memoirs of the Whig Party During My Time (ed. by his son) 1852; Further Memoirs of the Whig Party (ed. by Lord Staverdale) 1905.

ABOUT: Bradford, G. Portraits of Women; Courtney, Mrs. J. E. H. The Adventurous Thirties;

Holland, Lady E. Journal; Holland, Lord. Journal; Sanders, L. The Holland House Circle; see also Lord Holland's Memoirs and Reminiscences.

HOLYOAKE, GEORGE JACOB (April 13, 1817-January 22, 1906),

social reformer and miscellaneous author, was born in Birmingham, the son of an engineer. In boyhood he worked in his father's foundry. With a London bookselling and publishing shop as his headquarters, he engaged in a great variety of propaganda through books, pamphlets, a series of short-lived journals (notably *The Reasoner*), copious contributions to the press, and public debates. He was the last to be imprisoned in England for blasphemy. The spread of the workers' cooperative movement was largely the result of his persistent agitation, and he was the chief exponent of "secularism," which he invented to define his religious views. His works included histories of cooperation and secularism, biographies of several distinguished radicals, an autobiography, and educational handbooks. He was twice married and had seven children by his first wife. His last years were spent at Brighton, where he died at eighty-eight.

PRINCIPAL WORKS: Richard Carlile, 1848; Rudiments of Public Speaking and Debate, 1849; Tom Paine, 1851; The Logic of Death, 1851; Self-Help by the People, 1855; Robert Owen, 1859; John Stuart Mill, 1873; A History of Co-operation in England, 1875-77; Joseph Rayner Stephens, 1881; Sixty Years of an Agitator's Life, 1892.

ABOUT: Holyoake, G. J. Bygones Worth Remembering; Holyoake, G. J. Sixty Years of an Agitator's Life.

HONE, WILLIAM (June 3, 1780-November 6, 1842),

political satirist, pamphleteer, and bookseller, was born at Bath. While managing a bookshop in London he wrote a series of highly successful tracts against the government, illustrated by George Cruikshank. For three of them he was tried and acquitted in 1817. The most popular was *The Political House That Jack Built*, which ran through fifty-four editions. Twelve of the pamphlets were gathered in book form as *Facetiae and Miscellanies*.

Hone is remembered chiefly, however, for the widely-read *Every Day Book, Table Book*, and *Year Book*, three entertaining collections of curious information on manners and men. Among the contributors were Charles Lamb and Edward Fitzgerald. But the books were not profitable and the compiler was lodged in debtor's prison, whence he was rescued by his friends. In his last years he became deeply religious and preached at Eastcheap. He died of paralysis at Tottenham at sixty-three, leaving his wife and nine children. He published popular reprints known as "Hone's Editions," and labored for the freedom of the press.

PRINCIPAL WORKS: *Political Satires*—The Political House That Jack Built, 1819; The Man in the

Moon, 1820; The Queen's Matrimonial Ladder, 1820; The Political Showman at Home, 1821; Facetiae and Miscellanies, 1827. *Compilations*—The Every Day Book, 1826-27; The Table Book, 1827-28; The Year Book, 1832.

ABOUT: Hackwood, F. W. William Hone; Hone, W. The Early Life and Conversion of William Hone.

HOOD, THOMAS (May 23, 1799-May 3, 1845), poet, humorist, and editor, was born in London, the second son of Thomas Hood, a Scotch bookseller. His mother was a sister of Sands, the engraver.

Hood's education was in private schools in London. At about thirteen he entered service in a counting-house, but upon the resultant breakdown of his health he was sent to Dundee, to stay with relatives of his father. Here he lived from 1815 to 1818, reading, sketching, and writing for newspapers. Upon his return to London he was apprenticed to Sands and then to Le Keux, but again his health gave out, and he was obliged to leave engraving.

In 1821 he became assistant sub-editor of the *London Magazine,* and contributed to it until 1823, writing verse, for the most part, and meeting his brilliant fellow-contributors, who included De Quincey, Hazlitt, and Lamb. On May 5, 1824, Hood married Jane Reynolds. Their first child died almost at birth, and this misfortune occasioned Lamb's "On an Infant Dying As Soon As Born." Later a daughter and a son (Tom Hood, the humorist) were born.

In 1825 *Odes and Addresses to Great People,* a collection of humorous verse, appeared, issued anonymously by Hood and his brother-in-law; and Coleridge ascribed the verses to Charles Lamb. Hood continued to write industriously, and in 1829, when he became editor of *The Gem,* an annual which

boasted Tennyson among its contributors and in which "The Dream of Eugene Aram," one of Hood's better-known poems, appeared, he moved from London to Winchmore Hill, then a pleasant country spot not far from the city. After the establishment (1830) of the *Comic Annual* he moved (1832) to Wanstead, where he collaborated with others in play-writing.

His fortunes declined markedly in 1834, the year of publication of *Tylney Hall.* He lost very heavily in a publisher's failure. Although he could have relieved himself of some of his burdens under the bankruptcy laws, he chose rather to assume complete responsibility for his obligations, accepting an advance payment from a publisher for future work.

Early in 1835 he left for the Continent. The voyage was a hard one and seriously upset his health, which never had been good. From 1835 to 1837 he lived in Coblenz, and from 1837 to 1840 in Ostend, continuing to write his annual and publishing (1838) a humorous miscellany, *Hood's Own. Up the Rhine,* on which he had worked since 1836, appeared in 1839; but, despite its speedy success, the author gathered small financial reward.

He returned in 1840 to England, making his home first at Camberwell and later at St. John's Wood, and writing for the *New Monthly Magazine,* of which he became editor in 1841. He left the *New Monthly* in 1843, the year in which "The Song of the Shirt" appeared in the Christmas number of *Punch.*

Hood's Magazine, a joint enterprise established in January 1844, proved too much for Hood's failing energies, and in the same year he became confined to his bed. The financial worries which had dogged his career from early days were to some extent relieved by the grant to Mrs. Hood, at the instance of Sir Robert Peel, of a pension amounting to £100 per annum. One of Hood's last expressions of opinion was a letter to Peel, on the subject of the class differences in society. He died in May 1845 at Devonshire Lodge, Finchley Road; and in 1854 a monument was erected to him in Kensal Green Cemetery, where he was buried.

Cazamian writes of Hood, "His life is one long story of suffering, fraught with troubles, and he appears to have been a creature singled out by Fate for affliction." If his biography is painful, all commentators unite in praising the peculiar beauty and bravery of Hood's character. A wasted, poverty-stricken invalid, burdened with heavy responsibilities and compelled, as he remarked, to be a "lively Hood" in order to secure a "livelihood," he spent a life of disease trying to help those about him; and he entertained his family and friends by a gift for practical joking which must at times have been wearying. On one occasion, after

THOMAS HOOD

cautioning his gullible and long-suffering wife never to buy plaice marked with red or orange spots, explaining that the spots indicated a stage of decomposition, he burst out laughing at her discomfiture when a fishwoman, from whom she had refused to take any plaice that had the spots, burst out: "Lord bless your eyes, Mum! who ever seed any without 'em?" Often accused of lack of religious feeling, Hood was naturally devout, but despised cant.

"The spectacle which his life presents of simple, natural, unpretentious enjoyment of such modest good things as fell to his lot, and of equally natural and unpretentious fortitude in bearing things not good (whereof he had plenty) is not more unbroken than the spectacle of native simplicity and strength presented by his work," writes Saintsbury; and there is a most definite connection between Hood's life and his writings, indicated in the epitaph which he himself suggested: "Here lies one who spat more blood and made more puns than any man living." It was Hood's tragedy that the poet in him was all but killed by the funny man. He produced not only a huge amount of humorous prose (with his own grotesque illustrations) but a large output of humorous verse.

Hood's broad human sympathies and fundamental pathos expressed themselves particularly forcefully in "The Song of the Shirt," probably his poem best known today and one which shows his keen sympathy for underprivileged classes of society. In his more conventional poetry Hood was graceful and delicate, with an occasional suggestion of Keats, but he lacked power, often allowing too many fancies and figures to spoil an otherwise spontaneous product. Most characteristic of the author are the poems combining humor and seriousness, of which the best example is perhaps "Miss Kilmansegg."

Saintsbury has described Hood's literary claim as two-fold, "the first part resting on the extraordinary excellence of his comic vein, and the second on its combination, in a way nowhere else paralleled except in the very greatest men of letters (among whom, of course, he does not rank) with a vein of perfectly serious and genuine poetry."

R. W. W.

PRINCIPAL WORKS: *Drama*—Lamia, 1852. *Humorous Verse*—Odes and Addresses to Great People, 1825. *Novels and Novelettes*—Tylney Hall, 1834; National Tales, 1827. *Serious Verse*—The Plea of the Midsummer Fairies, Hero and Leander, Lycus the Centaur, and Other Poems, 1827. *Miscellaneous*—Whims and Oddities, 1826, 1827; The Comic Annual, 1830-42; Hood's Own: or, Laughter From Year to Year, 1838, 1861; Up the Rhine, 1840; Hood's Magazine and Comic Miscellany, 1844-48; Whimsicalities, 1844.

ABOUT: Broderip, F. F. Memorials of Hood; Elliott, A. Hood in Scotland; Gilfillan, G. A Second Gallery of Literary Portraits; Hall, S. C. A Book of Memories of Great Men and Women of the Age; Jerrold, W. Thomas Hood: His Life and Times; Oswald, E. Thomas Hood und Die Soziale Tendenzdichtung Seiner Zeit; Saintsbury, G. Essays in English Literature (second series).

HOOD, TOM (January 19, 1835-November 20, 1874), humorist, was born in Wanstead, Essex, the son of Thomas Hood, the poet, and Jane (Reynolds) Hood. Soon after his birth the family went abroad, and the boy did not return to England until 1838.

His education was at a private school at St. John's Wood, the University College School, the Louth Grammar School in Lincolnshire, and finally at Pembroke College, Oxford, where he matriculated in 1853. He expected to read for a clerical career; but, while he passed the examinations for the bachelor's degree, he left the University without taking it, and began to write. His first poem had appeared in *Sharpe's Magazine* in 1853.

For a few years he was employed on the *Liskeard Gazette*, of which he was editor in 1858-59, and he lived at this time in Cornwall. Through the friendship of Lady Molesworth, however, he was given (1860) a position as "temporary clerk" in the Accountant-General's department of the War Office, and there he remained for five or six years, performing his duties with care, and making himself very popular by his good-natured humor and his skill in caricature. He wrote for the *Cornhill Magazine,* and he edited a successful periodical, *Saturday Night.* Prospering, he moved to Brompton, where he was host to a lively circle of friends at Friday-night gatherings.

He left the War Office in 1865 to become the editor of *Fun,* for which he not only wrote verse but did illustrations as well, and which he made a rival of *Punch.* In addition, he

TOM HOOD

collaborated with his sister in the production of illustrated children's books. Beginning in 1867 *Tom Hood's Comic Annual* made its appearance; and it was continued after his death.

The genial "Friday nights" were broken up when Hood, in 1866, moved to Penge. The rest of his life consisted of hard work and steady production. In his last year, in which he married a second time, he suffered from a liver complaint.

"In his personal disposition Tom Hood was the gentlest and most lovable of men," writes Henry W. Lucy; and he tells of the humorist's great affection for children and his kindness to animals, his house resembling a menagerie. Hood was skillful with his hands; he could paint, draw, model, and carve; and he was passionately fond of flowers.

His works are marred by the mechanical production. His practise of writing five or six columns of verse weekly for *Fun* necessitated the publication of much that, if not entirely commonplace, was trivial and ephemeral. While he wrote in various *genres*, his greatest gift was for light lyrical verse. In the words of H. W. Lucy, "It is as a versifier—not to use the sacred and much abused word 'poet'— that Tom Hood claims a place, and a high place, in literature." R. W. W.

PRINCIPAL WORKS: *Editor*—Tom Hood's Comic Annual, 1867-74; The Book of Modern English Anecdotes: Humour, Wit, and Wisdom, 1872; The Book of Modern Anecdotes: English—Irish—Scotch, 1873. *For Children*—Fairy-Land: For the Rising Generation (with F. F. Broderip) 1860; The Loves of Tom Tucker and Little Bo-Peep: A Rhyming Chronicle, 1862; Merry Songs for Little Voices (with F. F. Broderip) 1864; Jingles and Jokes for the Little Folks, 1865; Petsetilla's Posy: A Fairy-Tale, 1870; The Pleasant Tale of Puss and Robin and Their Friends Kitty and Bob, 1871; From Nowhere to the North Pole, 1874; Excursions into Puzzledom (with F. F. Broderip) 1879. *Novels*—A Disputed Inheritance: The Story of a Cornish Family, 1863; Vere Vereker's Vengeance: A Sensation in Several Paroxysms, 1864; Captain Masters' Children, 1865; A Golden Heart, 1867; The Lost Link, 1868; Money's Worth, 1870; Love and Valour, 1871. *Poetry*—The Daughters of King Daher and Other Poems, 1861; Favourite Poems, 1877. *Miscellaneous*—Pen and Pencil Pictures, 1856-57; Quips and Cranks, 1861; Rainbow's Rest, 1864; Great Fun Stories (with T. Archer) 1866; Comic Readings in Prose and Verse, 1869; The Rhymester: or, The Rules of Rhyme, 1869; Life in Lodgings, 1877.

ABOUT: Hood, T. Favourite Poems (see Memoir by his sister); Gentleman's Magazine ns14:77 January 1875; Illustrated London News 65:521 November 28, 1874.

HOOK, JAMES (1772-February 5, 1828), novelist, divine, miscellaneous man of letters, was born in London, the eldest son of James Hook and his wife, Miss Madden. He was an elder brother of Theodore Hook, the author.

James was educated at Westminster School, where he edited the paper *The Trifler.* Ad-

mission to Christ Church College, Oxford, was denied him because of his school record of "insubordination." He therefore entered St. Mary's Hall, from where he was graduated in 1796. The next year he took orders and married Anne, daughter of Sir Walter Farquhar. Hook's livings were in Leicestershire, and Hertfordshire. Then in 1814 he became archdeacon of Huntington, and, in 1817, rector of Whippingham, Isle of Wight. Through Farquhar's friendship with the Prince of Wales he became the Prince's private chaplain. In 1825 he was appointed dean of Worcester, where he served until his death. He is buried in Worcester Cathedral.

Like his brother, he inherited the paternal musical ability, and collaborated with his father. He wrote the librettos for two musical entertainments, *Jack of Newbery* and *Diamond Cut Diamond*. He inherited also his mother's skill in painting, and was so talented that Sir Joshua Reynolds thought he should be educated as an artist.

James' literary work is often ascribed to his brother, to whose writings it bears some resemblance. James published, besides sermons and other professional work, two novels "which would be readable at the present day but for the antiquated style of treatment." *Pen Owen* is considerably superior to *Percy Mallory*. James also tried satire in *Al Kalomeric*, directed at Napoleon.

PRINCIPAL WORKS: *Novels and Tales*—Al Kalomeric, n.d.; Pen Owen, 1822; Percy Mallory, 1824. *History*—The Good Old Times, n.d.; *Miscellaneous*—Anguis in Herba, 1802; A Sermon, 1812; A Charge to Clergy, 1816; A Sermon, 1818; A Sermon at St. Paul's, 1819.

ABOUT: Barham, R. H. S. Life of Theodore Hook; Stephens, W. R. W. Life of Walter Farquhar Hook.

HOOK, THEODORE EDWARD (September 22, 1788-August 24, 1841), novelist, playwright, biographer, and journalist, was born in London, the second son of the composer James Hook. From his father Hook inherited musical ability, and from his mother, literary.

His education included a year at Harrow. He matriculated at Oxford but was not in residence. He was early introduced to theatrical life, and at sixteen became a successful playwright, having collaborated with his father on *The Soldier's Return*. Its remarkable success was followed by a dozen more plays, whose vogue only partially resulted from the popularity of the actors.

Hook soon became a "lion" in the best society and in gay circles. His facile improvising of songs, his epigrams and witty conversation insured his social position. R. B. Sheridan, witnessing Hook's improvising of a song for sixty people, each stanza containing an epigram, was astounded at his skill. He had a

THEODORE HOOK

penchant for practical jokes which is best illustrated by the "Berners Street Hoax" of 1809, when, on one pretext or another, he annoyed a Mrs. Tottenham with some 4,000 callers in one day.

About 1812, through the Prince Regent, Hook was appointed accountant-general and treasurer of Mauritius, and held the post five years. Deficiencies were discovered in 1817, and Hook was brought to trial in England, as he said, "for a disorder in the chest." The matter has never been cleared up, but Hook was held responsible for £12,000 embezzled, apparently, by a minor official. He spent two years in the King's Bench Prison, and there wrote nine volumes of fiction. He was henceforth haunted by debt; at his death the crown, as preferred creditor, seized his effects.

In 1820 Hook founded the newspaper, *John Bull*, a Tory organ devoted to the political ruin of Queen Caroline, whose premature death forestalled the attempt. The paper became a political power and brought Hook £2000 annually. He persistently denied connection with it. In 1830 he founded *The Arcadian*, another journal. He was editor, 1836-37, of the *New Monthly Magazine*, contributing fiction. The publisher would often drive to Hook's house for belated copy, and, finding nothing written, would wait—sometimes all night—for it. Thus was *Gilbert Gurney* written.

Hook's death left penniless five illegitimate children whose mother was socially Hook's inferior. To her he remained loyal. A public subscription was raised for the children. Everyone knew Hook. Lamb called him "as true a genius as Dante," but the genius burned itself out in gay living. The dinners at the Athenaeum reputedly declined £300 annually

when death removed Hook from the club. He was buried in Fulham Churchyard.

In appearance he was tall, robust, and dark; his eyes were small and his features weak.

He was enormously popular in life, but his writing lacks the charm of his personality and seems faded. He himself said, "Give me a story to tell, and I can tell it, but I cannot create." Dickens owes to Hook's novels both incident and characters; Byron's satire of Hook's *Tekeli* is still pertinent.　　D. F. A.

PRINCIPAL WORKS: *Biography*—Life of General Sir David Baird, 1832. *Plays and Operas*—The Soldier's Return, 1805; Tekeli, 1806; Catch Him Who Catch Can, 1806; The Invisible Girl, 1806; Fortress, 1807; Siege of St. Quintin, 1807; Music Mad, 1808; Killing No Murder, 1809; Safe and Sound, 1809; Darkness Visible, 1811; Trial by Jury, 1811; Pigeons and Crows, 1819; Exchange No Robbery, 1819-20. *Novels and Stories*—Man of Sorrow, 1809; Tentamen, 1820; Peter and Paul, 1821; Sayings and Doings (9 vols.) 1824-8; Maxwell, 1830; Love and Pride, 1833; The Parson's Daughter, 1833; Gilbert Gurney, 1835; Jack Brag, 1837; Pascal Bruin, 1837; Gurney Married, 1838; Births, Deaths, and Marriages (3 vols.) 1839-40; Cousin Geoffrey, 1840; Precept and Practice, 1840; Fathers and Sons, 1841; Peregrine Bunce, 1842; The Widow and the Marquess, 1842; The Ramsbottom Letters, 1872; Choice Humorous Works, 1873; The Ramsbottom Papers, 1874. *Miscellaneous*—Facts Illustrative of the Treatment of Napoleon, 1819; Reminiscences of Michael Kelly, 1826.

ABOUT: Byron, G. G. N. English Bards and Scotch Reviewers; Daniel, G. Modern Dunciad; Hook, T. E. Life and Remains; Jerrold, W. Bon-Mots of Samuel Foote and Theodore Hook; Lockhart, J. G. Theodore Hook; Maclise, D. Portrait Gallery; Saintsbury, G. Essays in English Literature (2nd. ser.); Atlantic Monthly 158:210 August 1936; Harper's Weekly 15:465 May 20, 1871.

HOOK, WALTER FARQUHAR (March 13, 1798-October 20, 1875), churchman and ecclesiastical biographer, was born in London. His father was James Hook, and Theodore Edward Hook, the humorous novelist, was his uncle. Educated at Winchester and at Christ Church, Oxford, he served successively as curate at Whippingham in the Isle of Wight (1821-25), vicar of Holy Trinity, Coventry (1828-37), vicar of Leeds (1837-59), and dean of Chichester (1859-75). He was one of the leading theologians of his day.

Outstanding among his works was *Lives of the Archbishops of Canterbury*, in twelve volumes, covering the entire history of the English church, which occupied the leisure of his last fifteen years. Besides biographies and dictionaries, he published sermons, lectures, and treatises. In the opinion of the *Cambridge History*, his writings were "without sufficient research or originality to give them permanent value."

PRINCIPAL WORKS: Hear the Church: A Sermon, 1838; A Church Dictionary, 1482; Dictionary of Ecclesiastical Biography, 1845-52; Lives of the Archbishops of Canterbury, 1860-76; Parish Sermons (ed. by W. Hook) 1879.

ABOUT: Stephens, W. R. W. Life and Letters of Walter Farquhar Hook.

HOOKER, SIR JOSEPH DALTON

(June 30, 1817-December 10, 1911), botanist, traveler, and author of botanical works, was the son of Sir William Jackson Hooker, botanist. Born at Halesworth, Suffolk, he was educated at the University of Glasgow. He made botanical expeditions to foreign lands and recorded his findings in a long series of works which placed him among the leading taxonomists of the day. He assisted Darwin in his researches in the origin of species, and was responsible (with Sir William Lyell) for the publication of Darwin's theory of evolution. For twenty years (1865-85) he was director of Kew Gardens, London, succeeding his father. He was ninety-four when he died in his sleep and was buried at Kew. Twice married, he left eight children.

The most remarkable of his speculative writings was an essay on the flora of Tasmania, in which he adopted the yet unpublished Darwin-Wallace theory "that species are derivative and mutable." His *Student's Flora of the British Islands* became a standard text.

PRINCIPAL WORKS: Flora Antarctica, 1844-47; Himalayan Journals: or, Notes of a Naturalist, 1854; Flora of British India, 1855-97; Introductory Essay on the Flora of Tasmania, 1859; Genera Plantarum (with G. Bentham) 1862-83; Handbook of the New Zealand Flora, 1867; Student's Flora of the British Islands, 1870; Index Kewensis (with D. Jackson) 1892-95.

ABOUT: Huxley, L. Life and Letters of Sir J. D. Hooker.

HOOKER, SIR WILLIAM JACKSON

(July 6, 1785-August 12, 1865), botanist and author of botanial works, was born at Norwich and educated at the local grammar school. He was for twenty-one years regius professor of botany at Glasgow University (1820-41) and thenceforth director of London's Kew Gardens, which he developed greatly and made the site of the first museum of economic botany. He was the foremost authority on ferns in his time. His private herbarium, the richest ever accumulated by one man, was purchased by the nation after his death. He died of a throat disease at Kew at the age of eighty, leaving a widow and three children.

As a leisure-time author and editor, he produced about a hundred volumes accurately descriptive of thousands of botanical species, with many drawings by himself. He edited numerous botanical journals.

PRINCIPAL WORKS: British Jungermanniae, 1816; Flora Scotica, 1821; Exotic Flora, 1823-27; Icones Plantarum, 1827-54; Icones Filicum (with R. K. Greville) 1829-31; British Flora, 1830-31; Genera Filicum, 1842; Species Filicum, 1846-64; A Century of Ferns, 1854; A Second Century of Ferns, 1861; British Ferns, 1861-62; Synopsis Filicum (with J. G. Baker) 1868.

ABOUT: Hooker, J. D. Sir William Jackson Hooker.

HOPE, THOMAS

(1770-February 3, 1831), novelist and art collector, was born in Amsterdam, son of a merchant of English descent. He was trained in architecture, and spent eight years studying and sketching in Egypt, Greece, Turkey, Syria, Sicily, and Spain. In 1796, Holland being occupied by the French, the whole family came to live in London. Hope had a large fortune (his brother, who collected jewels, was the first owner of the famous Hope diamond), and bought two houses, one in London and one in Deepdene, Surrey, to house his collections of statues, vases, and Italian pictures. He was the patron of the sculptors Canova, Chantrey, and Thorwaldsen, and the painter Flaxman. (Dubost, a French artist, quarreled with him over the price of a picture, and in revenge exhibited a caricature of Hope and his wife as Beauty and the Beast; Mrs. Hope's brother mutilated the picture at an exhibition; Dubost sued him and was awarded five shillings damages!)

Hope was a Fellow of the Royal Society and of the Society of Antiquaries, and vice-president of the Society for the Encouragement of Arts. In 1806 he married Louisa Beresford, daughter of Lord Decies, Archbishop of Tuan; of their children three sons survived.

Anastasius, a brilliant satirical novel, was published anonymously, and was thought to be by Byron, who said he wept that he had not written it, and that Hope had. Hope's only other writing published before his death was on furniture design; he was the originator of the "English Empire" style.

PRINCIPAL WORKS: Household Furniture and Interior Decoration, 1807; Anastasius: or, The Memoirs of a Greek, 1819; An Essay on the Origin and Prospects of Man, 1831; An Historical Essay on Architecture, 1835; Costume of the Ancients, 1841.

ABOUT: Blackwood's Magazine 10:200 1821, 11: 312 1822; Edinburgh Review 35:92 1821; Quarterly Review 24:511 January 1821.

HOPKINS, GERARD MANLEY

(June 11, 1844-June 8, 1889), poet, was born at Stratford, Essex, now part of London. His father Manley Hopkins, was Consul General of Hawaii in Great Britain; his mother was the daughter of Samuel Smith, a London physician; both were cultivated people, and Gerard showed precocious talent in music and painting.

In 1852 the family moved to Oak Hill, Hampstead (to the north-west of London), and after attending a preparatory school in that neighborhood Gerard went, in 1854, to Sir Robert Cholmondeley's Grammar School, Highgate, two miles across the Heath. The poet R. W. Dixon was for some time on the teaching staff, but there seems to have been no contact until, in 1878, Hopkins initiated what was to become a voluminous correspondence. Always a reading boy and a dreamer by nature, Hopkins disliked games, and soon began to write verse. In 1859 he won a school prize with the poem, "The Escorial." He had two foreign trips with his father, to the Rhineland in 1857 and to South Germany in 1860. A second prize poem, "A Vision of the Mermaids," 1862, in the heroic couplet, was a very considerable achievement for a youth of eighteen, and is illustrated in the *Poems* by an amazing Blake-like headpiece which shows how far he might have gone in the graphic arts.

Hopkins matriculated at Balliol College, Oxford, with an exhibition in 1863. He was tutored by Walter Pater, and became the friend of Robert Bridges, later to be Poet Laureate and the sponsor and editor of Hopkins' poems. The Oxford of that time was still in the backwash of the Tractarian movement; and Hopkins, as a High Churchman of deep religious feeling, could hardly fail to be swept in. We find him friendly with H. P. Liddon, confessing to Dr. Pusey, submitting to stringent deprivations in Lent, and producing the beautiful and delicate lyric, "Heaven-Haven," on a nun taking the veil. A visit, with his friend W. E. Addis, to Canon Raynal, at Belmont Monastery, Heresford, in the early summer of 1865, seems to have turned his mind definitely to the Roman Catholic Church, and in October 1866 he was received into its faith by Dr. John Henry Newman, afterwards Cardinal Newman, at Birmingham. In 1867 he took his degree with first-class honors in Classics.

Leaving Oxford in September 1867, Hopkins went to work under Newman at the Oratory School, Birmingham. A year later he entered the Jesuit novitiate at Roehampton, London, and his subsequent history is that of a devout and devoted novice and priest. He took a course in philosophy at St. Mary's Hall, Stonyhurst, Lancashire, read theology at St. Beuno's College, North Wales, and, after ordination in 1874, became preacher successively at Farm Street Church, London, St. Mary's College, Chesterfield, St. Aloysius Church, Oxford, and St. Francis Xavier's, Liverpool. His devotion and assiduity were unquestioned, but his highly wrought nervous temperament made the rigid discipline of the priestly life irksome and onerous to him. His spiritual conflict was not due to the attraction of worldly pleasures, for no one could have been more withdrawn, but to his voluntary suppression of the creative urge and to his unfitness for the practical business which forms so large a part of a Jesuit's work. The sonnets numbered 40, 41, and 45 in the *Poems* bear eloquent witness to the deep, heartbreaking despair that often assailed him. The sestet of No. 41 is typical:

GERARD MANLEY HOPKINS

O the mind, mind has mountains; cliffs of fall
Frightful, sheer, no-man-fathomed. Hold them cheap
May who ne'er hung there. Nor does long our small
Durance deal with that steep or deep. Here! creep,
Wretch, under a comfort serves in a whirlwind: all
Life death does end and each day dies with sleep.

In 1881 Hopkins was back at Roehampton, in a third-year novitiate; the next year he was teaching classics at Stonyhurst, the Lancashire Catholic college; and in 1884 he was nominated to the chair of Greek at the Royal University of Ireland. He proved himself an able and acutely conscientious teacher. In Dublin, as in Liverpool before, he was deeply shocked by the terrible living conditions of the poor in the slums. A disease engendered by just such conditions laid hold of him in 1889: he died of typhoid fever on June 8.

Hopkins had burnt all his poems on becoming a Jesuit, and it was not until 1875 that he wrote verse again, the occasion being "The Wreck of the Deutschland," a calamity in which perished five German nuns going into exile. He published no volumes of verse, but kept up a correspondence with Bridges, who from time to time would insert a poem or two in an anthology, and who made a collective edition in 1918. To Dixon he wrote at great length, often discussing prosodic method and technique with much learned detail. With this evident preoccupation with the sheer mechanics of verse it may not be altogether fanciful to link up his keen interest in music, to the composition of which he frequently turned as a relief from poetic creation.

Another correspondent, Coventry Patmore, writing to him in 1884 expressed the puzzlement felt by many in the face of a system that eschews normal syntactical arrangement and makes havoc among the parts of speech. "System and learned theory are manifest in all these experiments," wrote Patmore, "but they seem to me to be *too* manifest. To me they often darken the thought and feeling which all arts and artifices of language should only illustrate: and I often find it as hard to follow you as I have found it to follow the darkest parts of Browning." Bridges found his defects to be "oddity" and "obscurity." Dixon, on the other hand, writing to him on October 26, 1881, spoke of finding in his work "something that I cannot describe, but know to myself by the inadequate word *terrible pathos*—something of what you call temper in poetry: a right temper which goes to the point of the terrible; the terrible crystal."

Historically the volume of 1918 was singularly apposite, for these poems, all written more than thirty-four years before, sorted well with the post-war experiments. Hopkins was undoubtedly a metrical and technical innovator whose influence has been considerable. He made very skilful use of alliteration and assonance (devices, of course, going back to the very beginnings of our poetry), and his important invention, "sprung rhythm," is itself in some sort a throwback to very early models. It is defined in his own statement prefixed to the *Poems*: "Sprung Rhythm, as used in this book, is measured by feet of from one to four syllables, regularly, and for particular effects **any** number of weak or slack syllables may be used. It has one stress, which falls on the only syllable, if there is only one, or, if there are more, then scanning as above, on the first, and so gives rise to four sorts of feet, a monosyllable and the so-called accentual Trochee, Dactyl, and the First Paeon."

The most lucid guide to this very difficult poet is one of the young writers who has felt his influence, Cecil Day Lewis, who, in *A Hope for Poetry*, numbers him with Wilfrid Owen and T. S. Eliot as one of the "ancestors" of modern poetry. "The search for methods of restoring freshness to words," writes Lewis, "contributes to the obscurity of post-war poetry. Poets have gone back to old grammatical usages and have taken new grammatical licenses." And again: "What obscurity we may find when first we read him is due, not to a clouded imagination or an unsettled intellect, but to his lightning dashes from image to image, so quick that we are unable at first to perceive the points of contact. He is a true revolutionary poet, for his imagination was always breaking up and melting down the inherited forms of language, fusing them into new possibilities, hammering them into new shapes." Hopkins himself, writing in 1879, gives further light: "But as air, melody, is what strikes me most of all in music and design in painting, so design, pattern, or what I am in the habit of calling *inscape* is what I above all aim at in poetry."

His verse is for incantation; and he often insisted that it was to be read aloud. Once enter sympathetically into this strange world, and it will be found to be a realm of singular and haunting beauty.   H. B. G.

PRINCIPAL WORKS: Poems (ed. by R. Bridges) 1918 (new ed., with Critical Introduction by C. Williams, 1930); Letters to Robert Bridges, 1935; Correspondence With R. W. Dixon, 1935.

ABOUT: Kelly, B. The Mind and Poetry of Gerard Manley Hopkins; Lahey, G. F. Gerard Manley Hopkins; Leavis, F. R. New Bearings in English Poetry; Lewis, C. D. A Hope for Poetry; Murry, J. M. Aspects of Literature; Phare, E. E. The Poetry of Gerard Manley Hopkins.

HORNE, RICHARD HENRY or **HENGIST** (January 1, 1803-March 13, 1884), poet, novelist, story-teller, essayist, and writer of children's stories, was born in London. He was educated at Sandhurst but failed to secure a commission. Disappointed, he left England and joined the Mexican navy. After great adventures with sharks, mutiny, fire, and war, he returned from his travels in America and settled down in England to journalism.

As editor of the *New Monthly Repository* (1836-37) and as a playwright, he soon gained a reputation. In 1839 he began a correspondence with Elizabeth Barrett. This association, continuing until 1846, was productive for both. In 1841 Horne was appointed to a commission to investigate conditions in mines and factories employing women and children. Miss Barrett read his report and wrote *The Cry of the Children*. Horne's *New Spirit of the Age* (1844) was done in collaboration with Miss Barrett and others. The published letters of the two poets indicate the reciprocal benefits of this friendship. In 1843 Horne published *Orion*, the so-called "farthing epic." It was an allegory, taking as subject the growth of a poet's mind, and was published at a farthing in brave protest against the low estate of epic poetry. Edgar Allan Poe thought it "one of the noblest, if not the very noblest, poetical work of the age. Its defects are trivial and conventional—its beauties intrinsic and *supreme*." Most present-day critics, however, considers Poe's enthusiasm for the work somewhat excessive.

Horne's marriage in 1849 to a Miss Foggo, daughter of one of the Foggo brothers, prominent artists of the day, seems to have been unhappy, and about 1852 he went with William Howitt, the writer, to Australia's gold fields. He remained there until 1869, making no provision for his wife, who returned to her family. In Australia Horne served as commander of the gold escort in Victoria, as commissioner for crown lands, as swimming instructor, as magistrate, and editor. In the bush he met adventure, and borrowed the name "Hengist" from a man

RICHARD HENRY HORNE

he found there. The *Australian Autobiography*, written at Melbourne, is full of adventure and interest.

On returning to England he was granted a civil list pension of £50, later increased to £100. He now wrote chiefly for journals. He died at Margate and is buried there.

Horne was an adventurer by temperament, a remarkable athlete, a good musician. Though small, he was strong and capable, almost to the end, of spectacular feats. He became almost blind when old.

As dramatist (of unproduced plays) he has excellent structure and great intensity. As poet he is philosophic, working chiefly in the English classic tradition, but also influenced by Wordsworth. He has been called Elizabethan in taste and temperament. His children's stories are classics. *Memoirs of a London Doll, King Penguin,* and *The Good-Natured Bear* are as popular today as when they were written. Horne's reputation as essayist suffers from a self-invited comparison with Hazlitt, whose *Spirit of the Age* is more penetrating and rich than Horne's *New Spirit of the Age.* Horne's was a talent that early wrote itself out. As critic his services include the early recognition of Keats and Tennyson and the encouragement of talented Australian poets.

D. F. A.

PRINCIPAL WORKS: *Poetry*—Hecatompylos, 1828; Poems of Geoffrey Chaucer Modernized (contributions to) 1841; Orion, 1843; Prometheus. 1864; Sol'loquium Fratres Rogeri Baconi, 1882; The Last Words of Cleanthes, 1883. *Plays*—Cosmo de Medici, 1837; The Death of Marlowe, 1838; Gregory VII, 1840; Judas Iscariot, 1848; The South-Sea Sisters, 1866. *Novels and Stories*—The Good-Natured Bear, 1846; Memoirs of a London Doll, 1846; Gottlieb Einhalter, 1846; King Penguin, 1848; Poor Artist, 1849; Dreamer and the Worker, 1851; The Tragic Story of Emilia Daròna, 1874; The Countess von

Labanoff, 1877; Laura Dibalzo, 1880; King Nihil's Round Table. 1881; Sithron, 1883. *Miscellaneous*—Exposition of the False Mediums and Barriers, 1833; Spirit of Peers and People, 1834; The Russian Catechism, 1837; Essay on Tragic Influence, 1840; History of Napoleon, 1841; A New Spirit of the Age, 1844; The Life of Van Amburgh, 1846; The Great Peace-Maker, 1851; Australian Autobiography, 1859; The Lady Jocelyn's Weekly Mail, 1869.

ABOUT: Browning, E. B. Letters to Richard Hengist Horne; Forman, H. B. The Poets and the Poetry of the Nineteenth Century; Horne, R. H. Australian Autobiography; Howitt, M. Autobiography; Nicoll, W. R. & Wise, T. J. Literary Anecdotes of the Nineteenth Century; Poe, E. A. Horne's *Orion;* Sharp, W. Sonnets of This Century.

HORT, FENTON JOHN ANTHONY
(April 23, 1828-November 30, 1892), Irish theological scholar, was born in Dublin, and educated at Rugby and at Trinity College, Cambridge. After fifteen years as pastor of St. Ippolyts and Great Wymondley, in Hertfordshire (1857-72), he spent the remainder of his life at Emmanuel College, Cambridge, first as lecturer in theology and then as Hulsean professor of divinity.

His chief work, which occupied him for more than twenty years, in collaboration with Brooke Foss Westcott, was a famous critical revision of the *New Testament* in Greek, accepted as a standard basis for translation. Hort's "Introduction" to the text, though difficult reading, marked a great advance in New Testament criticism. A passion for meticulous thoroughness prevented his producing a large body of work, and shyness hampered his influence as a teacher, but his posthumous Hulsean lectures, *The Way the Truth the Life,* showed him adept at pithy expression. With his colleagues Westcott and J. B. Lightfoot he played an important part in establishing an improved theological scholarship.

PRINCIPAL WORKS: Two Dissertations, 1876; The New Testament in the Original Greek (ed. with B. F. Westcott) 1881; The Way the Truth the Life, 1893; Judaistic Christianity, 1894; The Christian Ecclesia, 1897.

ABOUT: Hort, A. F. The Life and Letters of Fenton J. A. Hort.

HOUGHTON, LORD (Richard Monckton Milnes, First Baron Houghton) (June 19, 1809-August 11, 1885), was born in London, the son of Robert Pemberton Milnes and the Hon. Henrietta Monckton Milnes.

Milnes was privately educated at the family home in Yorkshire, and in Italy. In 1827 he entered Trinity College, Cambridge, where he took his M.A. in 1831. At Trinity he joined the "Apostles" club and knew Tennyson, Arthur Hallam, and Thackeray. Upon graduating he went abroad, studying at Bonn and touring Italy and Greece. His first volume of poems describes part of this tour.

Back in London he entered politics, representing Pontefract (1837-63), and ac-

LORD HOUGHTON

tively interested himself in such questions as slave fugitives, women's rights, the franchise, copyright, freedom of conscience, subject national groups, etc. At first a follower of Peel, he bitterly disagreed on the Corn Laws and henceforth sided with Lord Palmerston. About this time he began contributing to the journals. In 1851 he married the Hon. Annabel Crewe; in 1863 he was created Lord Houghton. He maintained interest in Cambridge, and in 1866 inaugurated the new Cambridge Union Clubhouse. He founded the Philobiblion Society, assisted Florence Nightingale, and traveled widely in the East and America. He died at Vichy and is buried at Fryton.

Houghton wrote for the journals on various subjects, including travel, literature, politics (*The Political State of Prussia*). His tastes were catholic; in fact the real man is not readily isolated, so impressionable was he. In 1841 his *One Tract More,* in defence of the Tractarian Movement, was praised by Newman; but in the East he fell equally under the spell of Mohamedanism. Some critics attribute to this very eclecticism his failure to achieve a highly distinguished place in creative literature. He was, however, keen in detecting literary ability in others and performed noble services as a patron, spending his wealth and strength generously. For Tennyson he secured a pension; Emerson he publicized in England; for David Gray he wrote a preface to *The Luggie*; Swinburne he was among the first to recognize and acclaim as a genius; for Keats he prepared a most timely and excellent life and edition. Thus Houghton's place as patron is demonstrated. The *Quarterly Review* attacked his

"worship of such baby idols as Mr. John Keats and Mr. Alfred Tennyson."

Houghton did achieve a place in literature. He became an "unrivaled after-dinner speaker" and almost attained the rank of popular poet. Had he concentrated upon one aspect of his interests he might have made a high name. Such was the promise of his deservedly popular *The Brookside* and *Strangers Yet,* which rank high in a minor class of verse. His consistently high performance in *vers de société* and the meditative delicacy of his poetry are his greatest achievements. His prose is elegant and beautiful, but unaffected.

Disraeli's *Tancred* portrays Houghton as Vavasour; Carlyle said of him, "There is only one post fit for you, and that is the office of perpetual president of the Heaven and Hell Amalgamation Society."

In appearance he was sturdy, cultivated, and kindly. D. F. A.

PRINCIPAL WORKS: *Poetry*—Memorials of a Tour in Some Parts of Greece, 1833; Memorials of Residence Upon the Continent, 1838; Poetry of the People, 1840; Memorials of Many Scenes, 1843; Poems of Many Years, 1844; Palm Leaves, 1844; Poems: Legendary and Historical, 1844; Good Night and Good Morning, 1859; Poetical Works, 1876; Stray Verses, 1891-3; Turk at Constantinople, 1912. *Prose*—A Speech on the Ballot, 1839; One Tract More, 1841; Thoughts on Purity of Election, 1842; Real Union of England and Ireland, 1845; The Political State of Prussia, 1846; The Events of 1848, 1849; Life of Keats, 1848; Answer to R. Baxter, 1852; On the Apologies for the Massacre of St. Bartholomew, 1856; A Discourse on Witchcraft, 1858; Address on Social Economy, 1862; Selections, 1867; Monographs, 1873.

ABOUT: Carlyle, T. The Correspondence of Carlyle and Emerson; Horne, R. H. New Spirit of the Age; Hutton, R. H. The Late Lord Houghton; Reid, T. W. The Life of Lord Houghton; Russell, G. W. E. Collections and Recollections; Taylor, H. Autobiography.

HOWARD, EDWARD (d. December 30, 1841), maritime novelist, was a lieutenant in the navy and shipmate of Captain Marryat, whose *Metropolitan Magazine* he sub-edited, beginning in 1832, after he had obtained a discharge. He wrote popular sea novels, notably *Rattlin the Reefer,* which, to insure a large sale, was published as "edited by the author of *Peter Simple*" and for this reason was wrongly attributed to Marryat and sometimes published with his works. Howard's stories, particularly *Outward Bound,* were stronger of plot than those of his rival, Captain Glascock, but lacked their broad humor.

He died suddenly while still a comparatively young man. Tom Hood, on whose staff of the *New Monthy Magazine* he served, reviewed his posthumous tale, *Sir Henry Morgan,* with the comment that the author had "just felt the true use of his powers when he was called upon to resign them."

PRINCIPAL WORKS: Rattlin the Reefer, 1836; The Old Commerce, 1837; Outward Bound: or, A Merchant's Adventures, 1838; Memoirs of Admiral Sir Sidney Smith, 1839; Jack Ashore, 1840; Sir Henry Morgan the Buccaneer, 1842.

ABOUT: New Monthly Magazine 1842.

HOWE, JOSEPH (December 13, 1804-June 1, 1873), Canadian political writer, was born in Halifax, Nova Scotia. His father was the king's printer and postmaster of the Lower Provinces; his mother was his father's second wife. Howe had no regular education. At fourteen he was apprenticed as a compositer to the Halifax *Gazette*, and educated himself by reading. In 1827 he bought the Halifax *Weekly Chronicle* with James Spike, changed its name to the *Acadian*, and became its non-political editor. The same year he sold out his share and bought the *Nova Scotian*, of which he was sole editor and proprietor. Two departments, "Western and Eastern Rambles," and "The Club," became immensely popular, and he also reported all court trials. At great loss to himself, he published a famous early Canadian work, a history of Nova Scotia by T. C. Haliburton ("Sam Slick").

From 1829 on Howe was an ardent free trader. From this viewpoint he published his "Legislative Reviews" in the paper from 1830. In 1835 he was sued for libel, and after six and a half hours' speech in his own defense secured a triumphant vindication which settled the question of freedom of the press in Nova Scotia.

In 1836 he became a member of the Provincial Assembly for Halifax, as an independent. His oratory forced the lieutenant governor, Lord Falkland, to resign. In 1838 he went with Haliburton to England and secured a contract for the mails between the British government and the Cunard Line, first of the trans-Atlantic steamships. In 1840 he became a member of the executive council and speaker of the House of Assembly. He was in England again in 1850 and 1851 as a delegate of the Intercolonial Railway. In 1854 he resigned from the cabinet and became chief commissioner of railways. He was opposed to Canadian confederation, and became head of the Anti-Confederation League; in 1867 he went to England in the League's interests, but after his mission failed he reluctantly accepted office in the new Dominion government.

In 1860 to 1863 Howe was premier of Nova Scotia; from 1863 to 1866, fishery commissioner (fishing being the chief industry of the province). In 1870 he became Secretary of State for the Lower Provinces, a Dominion office. In 1873 he was named as lieutenant governor of Nova Scotia, but died suddenly of heart failure a few weeks after his installation. In 1828 he had married Catharine MacNab, by whom he had ten children.

Known as "the Tribune of the People," Howe's influence was far greater than his literary output would indicate. Most of his writings appeared in his newspaper, or as political pamphlets or speeches. His is one of the great names of Canadian history.

PRINCIPAL WORKS: The Nova Scotian in England, 1838; The Speeches and Public Letters of the Honorable Joseph Howe, 1858; Poems and Essays, 1874.

ABOUT: Burpee, L. J. Joseph Howe and the Anti-Confederation League; Fenety, G. E. Life and Times of Joseph Howe; Grant, W. L. The Tribune of Nova Scotia; Longley, J. W. Joseph Howe.

HOWITT, MARY (March 12, 1799-January 30, 1888), miscellaneous writer, was born at Coleford, Gloucestershire, the daughter of Samuel Botham and Annie (Wood) Botham, both Quakers.

Educated at home and in Quaker Schools and reading widely, the girl wrote verses at an early age. Her literary career, however, was to be associated definitely with that of her husband, William Howitt, whom she married in 1821. Their first published volume, appearing in 1823, was a collection of poems, *The Forest Minstrel*. The Howitts settled in Nottingham, after a walking tour through Scotland; and Howitt became a chemist and druggist, engaging also in public life and becoming an alderman.

Upon his retirement from this position, the family removed to West End Cottage, Esher, and here Mrs. Howitt began writing her long and successful series of tales for children. Her interests were broadened by residence in Heidelberg, where the Howitts settled in 1840, in order to give their children superior educational advantages; and she became acquainted with Scandinavian literature. From 1842 to 1863 she translated from the Swedish the novels of Frederika Bremer, and in the same period she translated many of Hans Andersen's stories. After returning to England in 1843, she assisted her husband in the conduct of *Howitt's Journal*, which was unsuccessful; and, some years later, having abandoned the orthodox Quaker faith in which they had been reared, they took up belief in spiritualism.

With her husband she removed to Italy in 1870, spending the winters in Rome and the summers in the Tyrol. Her last years were saddened by the loss of her husband in 1879 and that of a daughter in 1884. In her old age Mrs. Howitt joined the Roman Catholic Church, being baptized in 1882. Her death, the result of bronchitis, came in 1868, in Rome. In the course of a long life she had, singly or in collaboration, written, edited, or translated more than one hundred and ten works. She was the recipient of a Civil List pension and had been honored by the Literary Academy of Stockholm.

MARY and WILLIAM HOWITT

Mrs. Howitt had from her early youth a love for beauty which led her to rebel against the stricter manifestations of the Quaker zeal of her home, where a stern silence was so definitely the rule that the children were backward about acquiring speech; Anna, Mary's elder sister, was sent, at the age of four, to a dame's school, to learn to talk! The two girls were obliged to do some of their reading in secret; they borrowed vases and jugs, reproducing the Wedgwood figures by paper moulds, and they attempted in various other ways to express themselves artistically. Possessed of the uprightness and the devoutness of the Quaker, Mrs. Howitt opened herself to new art and new influences, and with her husband's help she tried to reach a fuller knowledge through the avenues of poetry and nature. She and her husband were among the early supporters of the Pre-Raphaelite movement in art, and they served as leaders in many other causes, including that of the anti-slavery agitation and the movements for bettering conditions in industry for women and children and for the prevention of cruelty to animals. To the end Mrs. Howitt retained her modest nature, more at ease in the simpler society in which she had lived in Germany than in that of England, where her friends and acquaintances included Tennyson, Mrs. Hemans, and Mrs. Gaskell.

The tremendous success which the Howitts enjoyed in their time is balanced by the oblivion to which they have since been consigned. While Mary's was the more original and the more imaginative mind, her work, as her husband's, shows the limitations resulting from self-education and from a lack of a rich background of experience. Her translations were perhaps her most permanently suc-

cessful works. She was the first to introduce Frederika Bremer, the Swedish novelist, to the English public; and in vain Hans Christian Andersen besought her to translate all his tales. Her books, however, range from history to poetry and fiction, and, with those of her husband, have been described by Emily Morse Symonds as "careful, conscientious work, the work of honest craftsmen rather than artists, with the quality of a finished piece of cabinet-making, or a strip of fine embroidery." R. W. W.

PRINCIPAL WORKS: *Autobiography*—My Own Story, 1845; Mary Howitt: An Autobiography, 1889. *Children's Books and Miscellaneous Fiction*—Tales in Prose, 1836; Hope On, Hope Ever! 1840; Strive and Thrive, 1840; Sowing and Reaping, 1841; Work and Wages, 1842; Which Is the Wiser, 1842; Little Coin, Much Care, 1842; No Sense Like Common Sense, 1843; Love and Money, 1843; My Uncle the Clockmaker, 1844; The Two Apprentices, 1844; The Children's Year, 1847; The Childhood of Mary Leeson, 1848; Our Cousins in Ohio, 1849; Stories of English and Foreign Life (with W. Howitt) 1853; The Picture Book for the Young, 1855; M. Howitt's Illustrated Library for the Young, 1856; Lillieslea, 1860; Little Arthur's Letters to His Sister Mary, 1861; The Poet's Children, 1863; The Story of Little Cristal, 1863; Stories of Stapleford, 1864; Our Four-footed Friends, 1867; John Oriel's Start in Life, 1868; A Pleasant Life, 1871; Natural History Stories, 1875; Tales for All Seasons, 1881; Tales of English Life, 1881. *Description*—Ruined Abbeys and Castles of Great Britain (with W. Howitt) 1861, 1863. *Editor*—Biographical Sketches of the Queens of Great Britain, 1851; Pictorial Calendar of the Seasons, 1862. *History*—The Literature and Romance of Northern Europe (with W. Howitt) 1852; A Popular History of the United States of America, 1859; Vignettes of American History, 1869. *Nature*—Birds and Flowers, 1838; Pictures From Nature, 1869; Birds and Their Nests, 1872. *Novels*—Wood Leighton, 1836; The Heir of Wast-Waylan, 1851; The Cost of Caergwyn, 1864. *Poetry*—The Forest Ministrel (with W. Howitt) 1823; The Desolation of Eyam (with W. Howitt) 1827; The Seven Temptations, 1834; Sketches of Natural History, 1834; Tales in Verse, 1836; Hymns and Fire Side Verses, 1839; Fireside Verses, 1845; Ballads and Other Poems, 1847.

ABOUT: Howitt, M. Mary Howitt: An Autobiography; Howitt, M. My Own Story; Symonds, E. M. (*pseud.* "George Paston"). Little Memoirs of the Nineteenth Century; Watts, A. M. H. The Pioneers of the Spiritual Reformation.

HOWITT, WILLIAM (December 18, 1792-March 3, 1879), miscellaneous writer, was born at Heanor, Derbyshire, the son of Thomas Howitt and Phoebe (Tantum) Howitt.

As his parents were both members of the Society of Friends, William, a precocious boy, who, when he was but thirteen, contributed "An Address to Spring" to the *Monthly Magazine*, was sent to a Friends' public school at Ackworth in Yorkshire, which he attended from 1802 to 1806. Subsequently he went to another school at Tamworth, where he studied chemistry and natural philosophy, and for four years he was apprenticed to a carpenter. Apt at foreign languages, he taught himself

Latin, French, and Italian; and he obtained much information from private reading.

In 1821, a chemist and druggist at Hanley, he married Miss Mary Botham, with whom, in 1823, he issued a volume of poetry, *The Forest Minstrel*. After a walking journey through Scotland Mr. and Mrs. Howitt settled in Nottingham, where Mr. Howitt became a chemist and druggist, continuing his writing. His *Popular History of Priestcraft* (1833) caused his election as alderman of Nottingham, and he came to be identified with a radical group advocating disestablishment of the Church of England.

Having spent some years in West End Cottage, Esher, where he had retired in 1836 for leisure for writing, he removed in 1840 to Heidelberg, in order to secure educational advantages for his children. Here, in a simpler and more congenial society, he improved his acquaintance with German life and literature, publishing *The Student Life of Germany* (1841) and *Rural and Domestic Life of Germany* (1842). The last-mentioned work was praised by a German journal as more accurate than any simiar work written by a foreign visitor.

After returning to England in 1843, where he took up the study of mesmerism, continued his literary work, and launched *Howitt's Journal*, which was a failure, he proceeded in 1852 to Australia to visit a brother and to survey possibilities of new opportunities for his sons. There he spent two years in travel and exploration.

On his return to England in 1854 he utilized his experiences in several works on Australia and the colonies nearby. Besides continuing his never-ceasing writing (in this period he worked on an illustrated history of England) Howitt, with his wife, became interested in spiritualism, and he contributed more than one hundred articles on personal experiences to the *Spiritual Magazine*. In 1865 he was granted a pension on the Civil List of £140 a year.

His last years were spent on the Continent. In the summer he lived in the Tyrol; his winters he spent in Rome, where he settled in 1870. Active as always in new movements, he participated in the formation of a Society for the Protection of Animals and in a plan for planting Eucalyptus globulus (a destroyer of malaria) on the Campagna, the plain surrounding Rome. His death, which was caused by bronchitis and hemorrhage, occurred in Rome in 1879, and he was buried in the Protestant cemetery.

William Howitt seems to have been of an adventurous nature. This capacity for new enthusiasms and interests explains his leaving the orthodox circles of the Quakers and his experiments with other varieties of belief.

His trip to Australia, made when he was about sixty years old, is an excellent example. In the course of this period of two years Howitt marched weary miles under a hot sun, waded through rivers, slept in the out-door air, and did his own washing and cooking, and returned in excellent physical condition, with only renewed zeal for the new and untried. With his wife he championed many new causes, among them the removal of civil disabilities from the Roman Catholics of Great Britain and Ireland, the Pre-Raphaelite movement in art, and the anti-slavery agitation. He is said to have lacked the Quaker virtue of meekness, to have been rather backbiting in his remarks about other authors and somewhat conceited.

It is undeniably true that the great literary popularity which the Howitts had in their day has not lasted. Their work, embracing a wide range of types, is careful, wholesome, and pure; but it lacks sufficient merit to ensure permanency of favor. Of the two authors Mary had the more originality and the greater power of imagination. So close were husband and wife, however, in their writing, that friends referred to them as "William and Mary" in allusion to the joint reign of the English sovereigns of those names. "Nothing that either of them wrote will live," commented *The Times*, "but they were so industrious. so disinterested, so amiable, so devoted to the work of spreading good and innocent literature, that their names ought not to disappear unmourned."

R. W. W.

PRINCIPAL WORKS: *Children's Books and Miscellaneous Fiction*—The Boy's Country-Book, 1839; The Life and Adventures of Jack of the Mill, 1844; Stories of English and Foreign Life (with M. Howitt) 1853; A Boy's Adventures in the Wilds of Australia, 1854. *Description*—The Rural Life of England, 1838; Visits to Remarkable Places, 1840, 1842; The Student Life of Germany, 1841; The Rural and Domestic Life of Germany, 1842; German Experiences, 1844; The Hall and the Hamlet, 1847; Homes and Haunts of the Most Eminent British Poets, 1847; Land, Labour, and Gold, 1855; Tallangetta, 1857; Ruined Abbeys and Castles of Great Britain (with M. Howitt) 1861, 1863. *History*—A Popular History of Priestcraft in All Ages and Nations, 1833; Pantika, 1835; Colonization and Christianity, 1838; The Literature and Romance of Northern Europe (with M. Howitt) 1852; John Cassell's Illustrated History of England (with J. F. Smith) 1856-64; The History of the Supernatural, 1863; The History of Discovery in Australia, Tasmania, and New Zealand, 1865; The Northern Heights of London, 1869. *Nature*—The Book of the Seasons: or, The Calendar of Nature, 1831; The Year-Book of the Country, 1850. *Novels*—Madam Dorrington of the Dene, 1851; The Man of the People, 1860; Woodburn Grange, 1867. *Poetry*—The Forest Minstrel (with M. Howitt) 1823; The Desolation of Eyam (with M. Howitt) 1827; The Mad War-Planet, 1871.

ABOUT: Howitt, M. Mary Howitt: An Autobiography; Symonds, E. M. (*pseud.* "George Paston"). Little Memoirs of the Nineteenth Century; Watts, A. M. H. The Pioneers of the Spiritual Reformation.

HUGHES, THOMAS (October 29, 1822-March 21, 1896), novelist and miscellaneous writer, was born at Uffington, Berkshire, where his grandfather had been vicar. His father was an editor and occasional writer. Hughes was one of seven children; his brother, a year older, was a lasting influence on his life, though he died young. Their mother also died when they were children, and the household was ruled by a dominating grandmother. Both brother and grandmother appear, thinly disguised, in *Tom Brown's School Days*.

After attending a private school at Twyford with his brother, Hughes entered Rugby. The headmaster was the famous Dr. Thomas Arnold, father of Matthew Arnold and one of the foremost educators of all time in England. Hughes' school and college days were important, for on memories of them he founded all of his work of permanent value. From Rugby he went to Oriel College, Oxford, where he was chiefly conspicuous as a cricketeer. He received his B.A. in 1845 and then read law, first in Lincoln's Inn, then in the Inner Temple. He was called to the bar in 1848.

The same year he married Frances Ford. Of their children, three sons and three daughters survived. With his great friend, John Ludlow, also a barrister, Hughes took a joint house in Wimbledon in 1853. Ludlow was a Christian Socialist, and through him Hughes also became active in the movement, and the close friend of its chief proponents, Charles Kingsley and Frederick Denison Maurice. He helped to found the Working Men's College, and acted as its principal from 1872 to 1883, and for a while he edited the Christian Socialist organ, the *Journal of Association*.

THOMAS HUGHES

He had become Queen's Counselor in 1869, and was a Member of Parliament, as a liberal unionist, from 1865 to 1874. Not much of a speaker, he made little mark in Parliament, but was active in advocating many reform measures. He was strongly in sympathy with the north during the American Civil War, having already written against slavery. In 1870 he made his first of three visits and lecture tours to the United States, his primary purpose being to make the personal acquaintance of James Russell Lowell, whom he admired greatly. Whie in America he founded, in the mountains of Tennessee, a cooperative colony he called Rugby. Though the colony at one time had 300 members, it failed eventually, and Hughes lost much money by it. The colony no longer exists, but its library, founded by Hughes, is still there.

Hughes became County Court Judge in 1882, moving to Chester, but naming his new home Uffington, after his beloved birthplace. He remained a Christian Socialist throughout his life, though in 1870 and again on its revival in 1886 he was active in the Church Reform Union (together with Arnold Toynbee, "father of social settlements"), the object of which was to broaden the Church of England and emphasize its social function. He died at Brighton at 73. In the church where his grandfather was vicar is a memorial plaque to Hughes, and the organ there is also a memorial.

Hughes' best known work, *Tom Brown's School Days,* was written at Wimbledon, and sent by his friend Ludlow to Macmillan's, then a very new firm. It continues to be one of their best sellers, even today. Its publication was delayed by the death of the author's eldest daughter, and it was completed during the most distressing period of his life. No one, however, would guess this from its unfailing high spirits. Kingsley called it "the jolliest book ever written," but it is more than this; it is impregnated with Hughes' lofty ideals. It has done more than any other single thing to impress on the world the figure of the high-minded, sportsmanlike English boy of the upper classes. *Tom Brown at Oxford* was far inferior, and none of Hughes' other books, even his touching memoir of his beloved brother—and including his travel sketches, which he wrote originally for the *Spectator* to raise funds for the trips they described—is at all in its class.

Hughes always insisted that Tom Brown had no prototype, but undoubtedly he strongly resembled his creator. Hughes remained all his life the sincere, straightforward, un-self-seeking person foreshadowed in this picture of the ideal schoolboy living under the aegis of the ideal schoolmaster.   M. A. deF.

PRINCIPAL WORKS: Tom Brown's School Days, 1857; The Scouring of the White Horse, 1859; Religio Laici, 1861 (as A Layman's Faith, 1881); The Cause of Freedom, 1863; Young Heroes of the Civil War, 1866 (in Old South Leaflets, 1907); Tom Brown at Oxford, 1868; Alfred the Great, 1869; Memoir of a Brother, 1873; The Manliness of Christ, 1877; The Old Church, 1878; Rugby, Tennessee, 1881; Life of Daniel Macmillan, 1882; Gone to Texas, 1884; James Fraser: Second Bishop of Manchester, 1887; Life of Livingstone, 1889; Vacation Rambles (ed. by C. Cornish) 1895.

ABOUT: Warner's Library of the World's Best Literature, Vol. 13 (see Biographical Note); Outlook 133:275 February 7, 1923.

HUME, ALEXANDER (February 7, 1811-February 4, 1859), one of three Scottish poets of the same name, was born in Edinburgh. He received only an elementary education. At eighteen he was married to Margaret Leys, by whom he had seven children. In Edinburgh and later in Glasgow (where he settled in 1855) he worked as a cabinet-maker and gained a considerable reputation as composer of verse and music. A self-taught musician, tenor in St. Paul's Episcopal Church of Edinburgh and chorus-master in the Theatre Royal, he composed successful melodies for standard Scottish lyrics, including Burns' "Afton Water," and for his own verses, among them the pathetic "My Ain Dear Nell."

Three years before his death he edited *Lyric Gems of Scotland,* to which he contributed more than fifty poems of his own, with accompanying tunes arranged or written by himself. He died three days before his forty-eighth birthday, and was buried in the Glasgow necropolis. There was no collected edition of his poetry until fourteen years after his death.

His fame is not so great as that of the sixteenth century Alexander Hume, but greater than that of his contemporary, ALEXANDER HUME, (1809-1851), whose collected *Poems and Songs* appeared in 1845.

PRINCIPAL WORKS: Lyric Gems of Scotland (ed.) 1856; Green Leaves: Poems of Sylvan Life, 1873; The Christian Hour, 1875.

HUME, MARTIN ANDREW SHARP (December 8, 1843-July 1, 1910), author of books on Spain, was born in London. His father's name was Sharp; his mother's was Hume. He was educated at private school. Following repeated visits to his mother's kinsfolk in Spain, he inherited the estate of the last of the Spanish Humes and in 1877 assumed his mother's name. Subsequently he traveled extensively in Central and South America, stood four times for Parliament without success, and at fifty-two adopted a literary career. During the last twelve years of his life he was editor of the *Spanish State Papers* at the Public Record Office in London. Having overtaxed himself with work, he died of inflammation of the brain at his sister's house in Forest Gate, Essex, at the age of sixty-six. He was never married.

His authentic histories of Spain and Spanish politics did much to popularize these subjects. Miguel de Unamuno calls his *The Spanish People* "an excellent psychological study," offering "much food for reflection." His books on the love affairs of Queen Elizabeth, Mary Queen of Scots, and Henry the Eighth have been frequently reprinted. He had a gift of vivid narrative.

PRINCIPAL WORKS: Calendars of State Papers Relating to Negotiations Between England and Spain (ed.) 1892-1912; The Courtships of Queen Elizabeth, 1896; The Year After the Armada and Other Historical Studies, 1896; Sir Walter Raleigh, 1897; Philip II of Spain, 1897; Spain: Its Greatness and Decay, 1898; Modern Spain, 1899; The Spanish People: Their Origin, Growth and Influence, 1901; Love Affairs of Mary Queen of Scots, 1903; Spanish Influence on English Literature, 1905; The Wives of Henry the Eighth, 1905; The Court of Philip IV, 1907.

ABOUT: Unamuno, M. de. Essays and Soliloquies; The Times July 4, 1910.

HUNGERFORD, MRS. MARGARET WOLFE (1850-January 24, 1897), Irish novelist, was born Margaret Wolfe Hamilton, the daughter of Canon Fitzjohn Stannus Hamilton, vicar-choral of Ross Cathedral and rector of Ross, County Cork. She was educated in Ireland. Her first husband was Edward Argles, a Dublin solicitor, by whom she had three daughters. Subsequently she was married to Thomas H. Hungerford, to whom she bore two sons and a daughter. She died of typhoid fever at Bandon, Country Cork, in approximately her forty-second year.

Writing sometimes as "The Duchess" and more often anonymously, she produced more than thirty light novels which had a wide vogue in their time. Most successful of all was her second, *Molly Bawn.* Her works were appraised by *The Spectator* as follows: "There is no guile in the novels of the author of *Molly Bawn,* nor any consistency, nor analysis of character; but they exhibit a faculty truly remarkable for reproducing the vapid small-talk, the shallow but harmless 'chaff' of certain *strata* of modern fashionable society."

PRINCIPAL WORKS: Phyllis, 1877; Molly Bawn, 1878; Faith and Unfaith, 1881; Portia, 1883; Rossmoyne, 1883; In Durance Vile and Other Stories, 1885; Lady Valworth's Diamonds, 1886; The Duchess, 1887.

ABOUT: The Times January 25, 1897.

HUNT, (JAMES HENRY) LEIGH (October 19, 1784-August 28, 1859), poet and critic, was born in Middlesex of an interesting ancestry: his father was a native of Barbados who had been educated in Philadelphia and New York, and married a Quaker lady from the former city, daughter of a wealthy merchant. Since his sympathies were loyalist, he was persecuted and finally driven with his family from the newly born United States. In England he became a clergyman (he had formerly been an attorney), but his improvidence and unpracticality (qualities which his son inherited), kept him all his life a financial failure.

Leigh Hunt was a delicate, nervous child, who at six was sent to Christ's Hospital School (Lamb and Coleridge had left just before), where he suffered much because of his hatred of the current flogging system and sympathy with the flogged. He was considered too frail to send to the university, and had besides a hesitation in speech which he afterwards overcame. By the time he was thirteen (he was already writing verse, and involved in an ardent passion for a cousin of fifteen), he was released from school but trained to no occupation. In 1801 he had enough verses for a volume, and his father secured its publication by rounding up subscribers from his congregation. The boy found his way into literary circles in Oxford and London, where he contributed his first essays to *The Traveler,* under the grandiloquent pseudonym of "Mr. Town, Junior, Critic and Censor-General." In 1805 he was dramatic critic for his brother John's ephemeral paper, *The News.* Then he became a clerk in the office of his brother Stephen, an attorney, going from there to a clerkship in the War Office.

In 1808 he and his brother John founded the most famous and longest lived of all the periodicals of which Leigh Hunt was publisher. It was the liberal *Examiner,* a weekly which he edited for thirteen years. The next year he married Marianne Kent, by whom he had seven children.

The Examiner was a power in its day, a power for freedom of speech and tolerance, and it earned many and mighty enemies in consequence. Several times Leigh and John Hunt were prosecuted for offensive political remarks in the paper, and acquitted—one of these acquittals gaining for Leigh Hunt the acquaintance of Shelley, who became his closest and most generous friend. Finally, in December 1812, the paper published a scathing article on the Regent, afterwards George IV. This time both brothers were convicted and sentenced to two years each in separate prisons and £500 fine, after they had indignantly refused to recant for remission of their sentences. Leigh Hunt was given two rooms in the infirmary of the Surrey Gaol (his health was always frail), and Mrs. Hunt was allowed to spend most of her term there with him. He turned his cell into a bower of pictures and flowers, and received there visits from Thomas Moore, Byron, Lamb, Shelley, and Jeremy Bentham. All the time he edited *The Examiner* from prison, but it gradually failed in circulation and finally expired in 1821, following some litigation over its owner-

LEIGH HUNT

ship with John Hunt. (The brothers, however, were not estranged.)

In 1816, released from prison and living in Hampstead, he met Keats. Hunt was the steadfast champion of both Keats and Shelley, and his espousal of the latter, involving Shelley's heterodox religious and political views which Hunt personally did not altogether share, earned for him such a storm of abuse and calumny as few editors have had to bear. Hunt's second journalistic enterprise, *The Indicator,* belongs to this period: it lasted about a year and a half. In 1821 Byron, then in Italy, was induced by Shelley to invite Hunt to join him in publishing a magazine to be known as *The Liberal.* After over a year, a near shipwreck, and a financial stranding at Plymouth, from which he was rescued by Shelley, Hunt arrived at Leghorn with his invalid (and dipsomaniac) wife and his seven children. Byron received them most grudgingly. Shelley, then at Lerici, went to Leghorn to try to get the Hunts settled with their unwilling host, and on his return journey was drowned. *The Liberal* lived for only four numbers. In 1823 Byron went to Greece, abandoning the Hunts without funds in a strange country. They found their way back to England in 1825, after much suffering. There for half a year Hunt published another magazine, the *Literary Examiner.* In 1828 he published a very indiscreet book on Byron, who had died in 1824; everything he said in it was true and based on sad experience, but he received much abuse and lost friends because of his imprudence.

Other short-lived periodicals followed—*The Companion, The Tatler,* the *Chat of the Week.* Hunt was a persuasive writer and a highly talented editor, but he never had sufficient financial backing. *The Tatler* was a four-page daily on literature and the stage, which he wrote entirely alone. These were hard years for him, and he was often destitute. In London again, he became Carlyle's friend and next-door neighbor, and began to prosper a bit more, though his health was alarmingly poor. *Leigh Hunt's London Journal* was added to his journalistic projects. In 1840 his play, *A Legend of Florence,* was performed at Covent Garden, and was a real success, much admired by the young Queen Victoria. Twice in the next few years he received a royal grant of £200, and in 1844, when Shelley's son Percy came into his estate, he gave Hunt an annuity of £120 in memory of his friendship and services to Sir Percy's father. Finally in 1847 he was granted a royal pension of £200. From 1850 to his death he lived in Hammersmith, where he published the last of his magazines, a revival of *Leigh Hunt's London Journal.* The only salaried position he had ever held since his early days of clerkship was as editor of *The Repository,* in 1837 and 1838.

In 1852 his youngest son, Vincent, his father's assistant (as was also the oldest, Thornton), and his favorite, died, and the father's always delicate health never entirely recovered from this shock. He lingered on for seven years more, however, writing beyond his strength as usual, but not publishing so voluminously as in the past. In the summer of 1850 he went with a friend to Putney, and there died very quietly and suddenly, actually of exhaustion. He was buried at Kensal Green Cemetery.

Hunt was a striking figure, tall, straight, and slender, with dark hair and eyes that apparently showed his West Indian ancestry, though actually he inherited them from his mother. He lived with the utmost frugality, drinking nothing but water, and eating little besides bread and fruit. The man who was vilified by half the magazines of England and Scotland (though in later years he received handsome apologies from more than one of them) was beloved by a wide circle of friends, many of them among the most celebrated men of their time. His nature was simple, cheerful, effusive, and romantic. It is supposed that Dickens lampooned him as "Harold Skimpole" in *Bleak House,* but Dickens himself insisted that the unpleasant traits of this character were decidedly not Hunt's, and he certainly had the warmest affection for him; at one time he took part in an amateur theatrical venture for Hunt's benefit. Hunt was perhaps a bit of a prig, but he was genuinely social-minded, a sprightly conversationalist, and a devoted husband and father under sometimes very trying ciriumstances.

As a writer, Leigh Hunt may be summed up by saying that he was an inspired journalist (many of his best newspaper and magazine articles have never been reprinted), and a keen critic, especially of the drama, but he published too much and his work is very uneven. He is best in the familiar essay, which he and Lamb revived as a literary form after the fashion of Addison and Steele in the eighteenth century. His prose is often too facile, but at its best (his *Autobiography* is the prime example of this) it is limpid and charming. A few of his poems, such as "Abou ben Adhem"and the delightful "Jenny Kissed Me," written for Jane Carlyle, are permanent ornaments of English literature, and in straight verse narrative, as in a few portions of "The Story of Rimini," he has vividness and vigor. But his verse is apt to descend into mawkishness and rather silly affectation, and is often trivial in manner as well as in matter.

It is as the earliest champion of Keats, whose lasting fame he prophesied when it was the fashion to ignore or laugh at him, and of Shelley, whom he defended and acclaimed when Shelley's name was a synonym for obloquy, that Leigh Hunt did his greatest service. Often enough he was a harried literary hack (even his editions of Beaumont and Fletcher and of Sheridan come under this classification), a journalist writing against time, poor and ill and distraught by domestic sorrows but always unconsciously the courageous, high-minded gentleman. Although he had little taste or judgment where his own work was concerned, he had very much when it came to the work of others, and he would have been the first to consider it a compliment to have it said that his publicizing of the work of his great young friends was far more important than was any of his own meritorious but second-rate production as a writer.

M. A. deF.

PRINCIPAL WORKS: *Poetry*—Juvenilia, 1801; The Feast of the Poets, 1814; The Story of Rimini, 1816; Foliage: or, Poems Original and Translated, 1818; Hero and Leander, and Bacchus and Ariadne, 1819; The Poetical Works of Leigh Hunt, 1832 (with subsequent additions, 1844, 1857, 1859, 1880); Captain Sword and Captain Pen, 1835. *Stories*—Sir Ralph Esher, 1830; The Palfrey, 1842; A Hundred Romances of Real Life, 1843. *Plays*—The Descent of Liberty: A Masque, 1815; A Legend of Florence, 1840. *Biography*—Lord Byron and Some of His Contemporaries, 1828; Autobiography of Leigh Hunt, 1850. *Essays*—Critical Essays on the Performers of the London Theatres, 1807; An Attempt to Show the Folly and Danger of Methodism, 1809; The Round Table (with William Hazlitt) 1817; The Months, 1821; Ultra-Crepidarius, 1823; The Seer. 1840; Men, Women, and Books, 1847; A Jar of Honey from Mount Hybla, 1847; The Town, 1848; The Religion of the Heart, 1853 (privately printed as Christianism, 1832); The Old Court Suburb, 1855; A Saunter Through the West End, 1861. *Anthologies and Miscellany*—Classic Tales, 1806; Imagination and Fancy, 1844; Wit and Humour, 1846; Stories From the Italian Poets, 1846; A Book for a Corner, 1849; Readings for Railroads, 1849; Table Talk, 1851; The Correspondence of Leigh Hunt,

1862; The Book of the Sonnet (with S. A. Lee) 1867.

ABOUT: Blunden. E. Leigh Hunt; Hunt, L. Autobiography; Hunt, T. (ed). The Correspondence of Leigh Hunt; Monkhouse, W. C. Life of Leigh Hunt.

HUNTER, SIR WILLIAM WILSON
(July 15, 1840-February 6, 1900), Scottish historian and statistician of India, was born in Glasgow, the son of a manufacturer. Educated at Glasgow University, he entered the Indian civil service in 1861. He spent twelve years (1869-81) supervising and compiling a vast statistical survey of the Indian empire, filling 128 volumes which he compressed into the nine-volume *Imperial Gazetteer of India,* subsequently much enlarged and rewritten by other hands. Retiring from the service in 1887, he settled in England and devoted the remainder of his life to energetic literary activity dealing with India. He died at his Oxford home at the age of fifty-nine, leaving his wife, Jessie Murray, and their two sons.

His death at a time when he had completed only two volumes of his monumental *History of British India* has been called "the severest blow ever sustained by Indian historical studies." He wrote impartially, in picturesque style, revealing accuracy and insight.

PRINCIPAL WORKS: The Annals of Rural Bengal, 1868; A Comparative Dictionary of Non-Aryan Languages of India and High Asia, 1868; The Imperial Gazetteer of India, 1881; The Indian Empire: Its People, History, and Products, 1882; A Brief History of the Indian Peoples, 1882; The Marquis of Dalhousie, 1890; The Earl of Mayo, 1892; The Old Missionary, 1895; The Thackerays in India, 1897; A History of British India, 1899-1900; The India of the Queen and Other Essays (ed. by Lady Hunter) 1903.

ABOUT: Hunter, W. W. The India of the Queen (see Introduction by F. H. Skrine).

HUTTON, CATHERINE (February 11, 1756-March 13, 1846), novelist, biographer, and historian, was the only daughter of William Hutton, seventeenth century topographer, of Birmingham. She was the close companion of her father, whose biography she wrote after his death. Though her health was always delicate, she lived to the ripe age of ninety; she died of paralysis at the family residence at Bennett's Hill, near Birmingham. She was never married.

During her long life she published twelve miscellaneous volumes, contributed sixty papers to various periodicals, and provided Sir Walter Scott with a short memoir of Robert Bage, the eighteenth century novelist, for the ninth volume of Ballantyne's "Novelist's Library." Her works showed some literary talent. An assiduous autograph collector, she corresponded with many famous persons and accumulated more than two thousand valuable letters. A selection from these letters was published in 1891 by her cousin, Mrs. Catherine Hutton Beale.

PRINCIPAL WORKS: The Miser Married: A Novel, 1813; The Life of William Hutton, 1816; The History of Birmingham, 1819.

ABOUT: Beale, C. H. (ed). Reminiscences of a Gentlewoman of the Last Century; Jewitt, L. (ed.). The Life of William Hutton and the History of the Hutton Family.

HUTTON, RICHARD HOLT (June 2, 1826-September 9, 1897), critic, journalist, and theologian, was born at Leeds, the son of a Unitarian minister. He was educated at University College, London, and (in theology) at Manchester New College. Among many journalistic activities, he was for nine years joint editor (with Walter Bagehot) of the *National Review* (1855-64) and for more than thirty-five years joint editor and part proprietor of *The Spectator* (1861-97), well-known weekly liberal paper, through which he exerted wide influence as a literary critic. He was twice married; his wives were cousins, both granddaughters of the historian William Roscoe. He died at his Twickenham residence at the age of seventy-one, leaving no children.

Many of his books were selections of essays from *The Spectator.* A predominating interest in theology narrowed his range of criticism. In the words of the *Cambridge History of English Literature,* "To purely aesthetic considerations he was not highly sensitive, and his criticisms are not, intrinsically, of very great value."

PRINCIPAL WORKS: Studies in Parliament, 1866; Essays: Theological and Literary, 1871; Sir Walter Scott, 1878; Essays on Some of the Modern Guides of English Thought in Matters of Faith, 1887; Cardinal Newman, 1891; Criticisms on Contemporary Thought and Thinkers, 1894; Aspects of Religious and Scientific Thought (ed. by his niece E. M. Roscoe) 1899; Brief Literary Criticisms (ed. by E. M. Roscoe) 1906.

ABOUT: Hogben, J. Richard Holt Hutton of the Spectator; Nicoll, R. Study of Richard Holt Hutton as Critic and Theologian; Ward, W. P. Ten Personal Studies.

HUXLEY, THOMAS HENRY (May 4, 1825-June 29, 1895), biologist, teacher, and writer, was born at Ealing, where his father, the undistinguished descendant of an old family, was an assistant schoolmaster. Until he was ten, Huxley attended his father's school, which he detested and where he learned very little. The headmaster died and George Huxley found himself jobless; he moved back to his native town of Coventry and became manager of a savings bank. That ended the formal academic education of his seventh and youngest surviving child. Thereafter, until he studied medicine, Huxley's only education was given by himself to himself, in a long course of varied and intensive reading. Carlyle, and through Carlyle Goethe, had the profoundest influence on his thinking in early

THOMAS HENRY HUXLEY

youth, though he accepted them more as stimulation than as gospel.

His two sisters, much older than he, had both married physicians in 1839. Huxley had dreamed of being an engineer; now he decided on medicine as a career. One of his brothers-in-law took the boy to a post-mortem, the shock of which to a sensitive nature laid the foundation for a lifetime of ill health. Huxley himself believed that he was poisoned, and that in consequence he suffered thereafter from indigestion; it is more likely that the poisoning was psychological, and that his constant illness was three-quarters hypochondria —though no less painful for that.

In any event, in 1841 he was apprenticed to a medical man named Chandler, in the East End of London, after having received some elementary lessons from his brother-in-law, Dr. Cooke. From the sights and experiences of that apprenticeship among the very poor, Huxley dated his deep interest in the welfare of the workers (though he was an anti-Socialist and never called himself a liberal), which led in later years to his famous lectures to workingmen.

After a year with Mr. Chandler, Huxley was apprenticed to his other brother-in-law John Scott, and went to live with him and his favorite sister Elizabeth. He began to attend lectures at Sydenham College and the College of Surgeons, and received his first honor in the form of a silver medal in a public competition in botany. In 1842 both he and his older brother James received free scholarships at Charing Cross Hospital, where he remained for three years, under the great pioneer anatomist Thomas Wharton Jones. In 1845 he received the M.B. degree; he was then only twenty, and too young to enter the College of

Surgeons. Instead, being badly in need of money, he took the naval examination and was assigned to duty at Haslar Hospital.

But Huxley, like Darwin, Wallace, and Tyndall, was to have his chance at scientific investigation in far places. He was recommended as assistant surgeon to the S.S. *Rattlesnake*, sent to explore Australia and the Great Barrier Reef, and was with the ship throughout its journey, from 1846 to 1850. Not only did he during this voyage lay the foundations of his career as an original investigator, principally with respect to the morphology of jellyfish and other marine invertebrates (while still in Charing Cross Hospital he had shown his bent for research by a brilliant piece of work which has given the name of Huxley's Layer to a cell-layer in the root-sheath of hair), but he also found in Australia the woman, Henrietta Anne Heathorn, who was to be his devoted wife and the mother of his three sons (one of whom died in childhood) and four daughters. Aldous and Julian Huxley are his grandchildren, sons of his son Leonard. It was 1855, however, before he was financially able to marry.

In 1851 Huxley was made a Fellow of the Royal Society, and the next year received its medal. It is during this period also that he first formed the friendships with Tyndall, Hooker, and above all Darwin, and the enmity with Owen, which determined all the course of his middle and later years. In 1852 he began, too, his remarkable career as a lecturer —and before that august body, the Royal Institution. He was meanwhile on leave of absence from the navy, editing and publishing his scientific reports from the work done on the *Rattlesnake*. Vainly he applied for teaching positions in England, Scotland, and Canada; he was on half pay and could not possibly send for his fiancée. Finally in the beginning of 1854 further leave was denied him, and he sent in his resignation.

Soon after, his friend Edward Forbes was called to Aberdeen, and turned over to Huxley his lectureship at the Government School of Mines in London. It was the start of Huxley's great teaching career. He also received a grant from the Royal Society for publication of his monograph on *The Oceanic Hydrozoa*, and was appointed lecturer in comparative anatomy at St. Thomas's Hospital and given work with the Coast Survey. The Heathorn family came home from Sydney, and at last Huxley and his Henrietta could be married. But the year brought one great sorrow; the generous, kindly Forbes died suddenly in his youth.

It was in 1855 that Huxley began to lecture to workingmen in an auditorium on Jermyn Street, lectures which continued for many years, were of the greatest influence on hundreds of his listeners, and in published form are among the finest of his literary work.

In 1859, that epochal date for science, Darwin's *Origin of Species* was published. Huxley had not, with Lyell, Hooker, and Asa Gray, been a convert to Darwin's ideas from their first inception; but with the publication of this "Bible of biology," he surrendered completely. For the rest of his life Huxley was "Darwin's bulldog," the "under nurse of the Darwinian child," the man who carried the theories of the retiring, semi-invalid at Down into the arena, in lectures and debates and the printed word. Gradually—though he was one of the foremost anatomists of his time—he gave up his original work, and devoted himself more and more exclusively to the defense and exposition of Darwinian evolution. Some of his battles, particularly the controversies with Gladstone and the Duke of Argyll, and the famous set-to with Bishop Wilberforce at the Oxford meeting of the British Association for the Advancement of Science, are known to everyone in the least familiar with the history of science. Except for those who were involved in the struggle against the Fundamentalist anti-evolution campaign of the 1920's in America, it would be difficult to realize the terrific storm of attack, invective, and calumny which Huxley had to endure (though with his fighting spirit the endurance was no hardship) for the next twenty years or more.

In 1863 Huxley was appointed Hunterian professor of the Royal College of Surgeons, and served until 1869; from 1863 to 1867 he was also Fullerian professor of the Royal Institution. For a short time he was editor of the *Natural History Review*, which preceded *Nature*. From 1870 to 1872 he was a member of the London School Board; he was keenly interested in education, and advocated a curriculum which sounds strangely modern and was directly opposed to the narrow course of study of his day. He served also on numerous commissions, chiefly in the Fisheries Department (where he was inspector from 1881 to 1885), was rector of Aberdeen University from 1872 to 1875, and was first secretary and then president of the Royal Society. Not one of these positions was a sinecure or merely honorary in nature. Meanwhile he was still lecturing to the workingmen on Jermyn Street, engaging in innumerable debates, and pouring out articles and books, all of which, even though most of them were printed lectures, had to be edited and seen through the press. All this, for a man who never knew one day without pain or physical weakness, inevitably meant a breakdown. After several warnings, it came in 1885. Huxley retired from public life and from London, and built a house in Eastbourne; he continued his writing, however, being chiefly concerned in this last decade of his life with Biblical criticism. In 1881 he had received the degree of D.C.L. from Oxford, and he had honorary degrees also from numerous universities of Great Britain and the Continent.

An attack of influenza in 1894 was followed by cardiac and renal complications, and he died the following June. His mind was active and flexible to the last, and he wrote up to three days before his death.

"What great fun Huxley is!" Darwin once exclaimed. He was indeed—witty, high-spirited, indefatigable. He was quick-tempered, sometimes rash, occasionally opinionated, but one of the most lovable of great men. Like many men rich in humor, he was naturally melancholy, and suffered constantly from fits of depression, but he had a firm and fine reticence in personal matters that hid his darker side from his friends and his public. He was a latter-day Stoic, with a strong vein of Puritanism that made him hold views in social and economic matters seeming strangely at variance with his scientific radicalism. Essentially emotional, his intellect was nevertheless polished and controlled. He was the great Agnostic—the inventor, indeed, of that term. He himself was a living example of the high ethical standards of the true evolutionist and the true Rationalist.

He was not prepossessing in appearance, with his grim tight lips that yet broke into the sweetest of smiles, his beetling brows over "nut brown eyes," and what H. G. Wells called his "yellow leonine face." He was tall and ungainly, with a certain arrogance hiding his real modesty. But he had the heart of a poet, loved music and played the violin, and there was something boyish always in his zeal for a fight and his affection for his few chosen friends.

As a writer he is unsurpassed for clarity, unornamented eloquence, and persuasiveness. He had, as Houston Peterson puts it, "the gift for the apt and acid phrase." His letters are among his best writing, spontaneous and powerfully phrased. His "pure, rapid, athletic English" is a model for all scientific writers; none has outdone and few have equaled it. To say that the writer Huxley was of the same caliber as the teacher and investigator is to praise him highly but to do him no more than justice.　M. A. deF.

PRINCIPAL WORKS: The Oceanic Hydrozoa, 1859; On Our Knowledge of the Causes of the Phenomena of Organic Lecture, 1862; Evidence as to Man's Place in Nature, 1863; Lectures on the Elements of Comparative Anatomy, 1864; A Catalogue of the Collection of Fossils in the Museum of Practical Geology (with Robert Etheridge) 1865; Lessons in Elementary Physiology, 1866; An Introduction to the Classification of Animals, 1869; Lay Sermons, Addresses, and Reviews, 1870; Manual of the Anatomy of Vertebrated Animals, 1871; Critiques and Addresses, 1873; A Course of Practical Instruction in Elementary Biology (with H. N. Martin) 1875;

American Addresses, 1877; The Anatomy of Invertebrated Animals, 1877; Physiography, 1877; Hume, 1878; The Crayfish: An Introduction to the Study of Zoology, 1878; Introductory Science Primer, 1880; Science and Culture and Other Essays, 1881; Social Diseases and Worse Remedies, 1891; Essays on Some Controverted Questions, 1892; Collected Essays, 1893-4: I. Methods and Results; II. Darwiniana; III. Science and Education; IV. Science and Hebrew Tradition; V. Science and Christian Tradition; VI. Hume, With Helps to the Study of Berkeley; VII. Man's Place in Nature and Other Anthropological Essays (sometimes entitled Ethical and Philosophical Essays); VIII. Discourses, Biological and Geological; IX. Evolution and Ethics and Other Essays (tenth volume uncompleted); Scientific Memoirs (ed. by Michael Foster and E. Ray Lankester; 4 vols. and supplement) 1898-1903. Diary of the Voyage of H. M. S. *Rattlesnake* (ed. by Julian Huxley) 1936.

ABOUT: Ayres, C. E. Huxley; Clodd, E. Thomas Henry Huxley; Davis, J. R. A. Thomas H. Huxley. Huxley, L. Life and Letters of Thomas Henry Huxley; MacBride, E. W. Huxley; Mitchell, P. C. Thomas Henry Huxley: A Sketch of His Life and Work; Peterson, H. Huxley: Prophet of Science; Fortune 137:661 June 1935; Nature 115: Supplement May 9, 1925 (Centenary Number); New Republic 72:182 May 28, 1932.

HYSLOP, JAMES (July 23, 1798-November 4, 1827), Scottish shepherd poet, was born in the parish of Kirkconnel, Dumfriesshire. He began farm work at an early age, and taught himself English, Latin, French, and mathematics. He was a shepherd on Nether Wellwood farm, in the parish of Muirkirk, Ayrshire (1812-16) and at Corsebank (1816-18). He operated a day-school at Greenock, a seaport in County Renfrew (1818-21), and tutored aboard ship during a three-year voyage to South America (1821-24). Subsequently he was a reporter in London (where he knew the poet Allan Cunningham intimately) but the work proved too strenuous for him and he returned to teaching. He died of fever at the age of twenty-nine while cruising off the Cape Verde Islands as tutor on a battleship, and was buried at sea.

Most of his poetry appeared in the *Edinburgh Magazine* during the last eight years of his life. His eighty-two poems were collected sixty years after he died. Only one of these is well known outside of Scotland: "The Cameronian Dream," written at Nether Wellwood, near the scene of Richard Cameron's death, and made into a cantata by Hamish MacCunn in 1899.

WORK: Poems, 1887.

ABOUT: Hyslop, J. Poems (see Sketch by P. Mearns); Scottish Presbyterian Magazine, 1840, 1853.

INGELOW, JEAN (March 17, 1820-July 20, 1897), poet, writer of stories for children, and novelist, was the eldest child of William Ingelow, a banker, and his wife, Jean Kilgour, and was born in Boston, Lincolnshire, at the mouth of the Witham River.

JEAN INGELOW

The family house faced the water, and the rising tides, moving ships, and the play of sunlight on the waves were a source of daily delight during her early years; and later her memories of the river frequently entered her writings. She was educated by governesses and tutors at home under her mother's supervision. Hers was a "happy, bright, joyous childhood." When she was about fourteen, she moved with her family to Ipswich; and after 1863 she went to London where she spent most of her life.

Her first lines of which we have any record, are childishly romantic ones she wrote on the shutters of her room, and were supposed to be addressed by Catherine of Arragon to Henry VIII before he divorced her.

Her first published poetry, *A Rhyming Chronicle of Incidents and Feelings,* attracted little attention, although Tennyson, meeting her shortly after publication of the volume, generously said, "I declare, you do the trick better than I do." With the publication of her first series of *Poems* in 1863, she was hailed as a lyric poet of high importance; and it is as the author of "Divided" in this volume that she is best known. The English and American critics hailed her enthusiastically, and the volume, as subsequent ones did to a somewhat lesser degree, went through a large number of editions.

Both before and after the publication of the first *Poems,* she contributed children's stories to the *Youth's Magazine.* These, signed by the pen name, "Orris," were later reprinted under her own name and under the titles of *Studies for Stories, Stories Told to a Child,* and *A Sister's Bye House. Studies for Stories* attracted many adult readers, and *The Athenaeum* called them "prose poems carefully meditated and exquisitely touched in by a teacher ready to sympathize with every joy and sorrow." Her *Mopsa the Fairy*, still widely read by children, is unique among her works. It is a fanciful, well-constructed, fast-moving story, and owes much of its strange charm to *Alice's Adventures in Wonderland*, which preceded Miss Ingelow's story by four years. A dozen or so poems in *Mopsa*, pleasing in themselves, are generally considered too mature to be integral parts of the story.

Her several novels added to her popularity during her lifetime, but are little read now. The chief one, *Off the Skelligs*, gives many interesting accounts of her childhood and contains some fine writing, but is too long and moves too leisurely for most modern readers. Her "The High Tide on the Coast of Lincolnshire," ranks as one of the finest of modern ballads. The main poem in her *Story of Doom*, a rather ambitious piece in blank verse, tells of Noah's warning and makes use of other Biblical material, and reminds the reader in several places of both Tennyson and Milton. Wordsworth and Tennyson are generally believed to have been the greatest and most consistent influences on her writing and most sympathetic to her peculiar gift.

Her verse on the whole is remarkable for its intimate observation of nature, interest in common things of life, dignified pathos, introspection that is often religious, wealth and freshness of fancy, and sustained lyrical charm. She preferred clear and simple language and anapaestic measures. Many of her poems were set to music, for which they are particularly suited, and became popular to the point of tediousness.

She was acquainted with most of the better-known writers and painters of her time. In public she was reserved to the point of shyness and was afraid of being considered "literary" or affected. G. B. Stuart describes her as "a small woman with a gentle and nervous manner, a roughly-hewn, almost masculine face, an incisive voice, and the most delightful smile in the world! She was a trifle prim, but this was tempered by a keen sense of humor... She always wore a Quakerish cap tied under her chin, and a folded handkerchief of frilled book-muslin across her black dress."

George Saintsbury wrote of her: "If we had nothing of Jean Ingelow's but the most remarkable poem entitled 'Divided,' it would be permissible to suppose the loss, in fact or in might-have-been, of a poetess of almost the highest rank."

P. G.

PRINCIPAL WORKS: *Poetry*—A Rhyming Chronicle of Incidents and Feelings, 1850; Poems (1st ser.) 1863; A Story of Doom, 1867; Poems (2nd ser.) 1876; The High Tide on the Coast of Lincolnshire, 1883; Poems (3rd ser.) 1885; Poems of the Old Days and the New, 1885. *Stories for Children*—Studies for Stories, 1864; Stories Told to a Child, 1865; Mopsa the Fairy, 1869. *Novels*—Off the

Skelligs, 1872; Fated to be Free, 1875; Sarah de Berenger, 1879; Don John, 1881; John Jerome, 1886.

ABOUT: Anon. Some Recollections of Jean Ingelow; Papers of the Manchester Literary Club 57:145.

INGRAM, JOHN KELLS (July 7, 1823-May 1, 1907), Irish poet and economist, was born in County Donegal of a Scottish Presbyterian family; his father, however, was a curate in the Established Church. He received his B.A. at Trinity College, Dublin, in 1843, after displaying remarkable precocity in both mathematics and classics. In the same year he suddenly sprang into fame by the anonymous publication of his poem, "The Memory of the Dead" ("Who fears to speak of Ninety-Eight?"), which became the anthem of the Nationalist cause. In 1846 he became a fellow of Trinity, and was connected in one way or another with the university for fifty-three years. He read law both in King's Inn, Dublin, and Lincoln's Inn, but was never admitted to the bar. As evidence of his remarkable versatility, he contributed articles on mathematical research to the Royal Irish Society (of which he became a fellow in 1847, holding various offices until he was president from 1892 to 1896), and at the same time, following his first of many visits to England and the Continent, was in 1852 made professor of oratory at Trinity. There being at the time no chair of English literature, this branch fell to him also. In 1862 he married Madeline Clark, who died in 1889, leaving four sons and two daughters. In 1866 he was made regius professor of Greek, in 1879 senior fellow, in 1887 senior lecturer. In 1891 he received a D.Litt. degree, as well as an honorary LL.D. from Glasgow University. In 1898 he became vice-provost, but resigned and left Trinity the next year.

Then he entered an entirely new phase of thought, winning his real fame as an economist. He had been for many years an ardent follower of the French social philosopher Comte (founder of Positivism) but did not publish his Positivist beliefs until he had severed his connections with the university. He had, however, already shown his interest in political economy, being a founder of the Dublin Statistical Society in 1847, and its president from 1878 to 1880. Now he contributed on economics to the *Encyclopaedia Britannica* (ninth edition) and on Comtean philosophy to the *Positivist Review*. He was a pacifist, and strongly opposed the Boer War. He died in Dublin at nearly eighty-four.

Ingram's prose work was useful, but in spite of his versatility he was essentially a poet. His sonnets are especially fine, stirring and exalted. He has been called "the most perfectly educated of men."

PRINCIPAL WORKS: History of Political Economy, 1888; Outlines of the History of Religion, 1900;

Sonnets and Other Poems, 1900; Practical Morals, 1904; The Final Transition, 1905.

ABOUT: Falkiner, C. L. Memoir of John Kells Ingram; Positivist Review June 1907.

INNES, COSMO (September 9, 1798-July 31, 1874), Scottish antiquary, was born in a land-owning family on its estate on Deeside, the fifteenth of sixteen children. He was educated at the Universities of Aberdeen and Glasgow, and at Balliol College, Oxford, receiving his B.A. in 1820, his M.A. in 1824. In 1822 he was admitted advocate at the Scottish bar. His practice was not large, but he soon began to specialize in cases involving genealogy and antiquarianism, in which his authority was early recognized. In 1826 he married a Miss Rose, by whom he had nine children. From 1840 to 1852 he was sheriff of Moray. He edited the *Acts of the Scots Parliament,* preparing the *General Index* from 1865 to his death. From 1846 to the time he died he was professor of constitutional law and history at the University of Edinburgh. He died while on a trip to the Highlands.

A shy man, who covered his shyness by talkativeness, Innes was no recluse, but a keen sportsman and gardener. He was an "unrivaled" antiquary, and wrote entertainingly as well as accurately on the early history of Scotland.

PRINCIPAL WORKS: Scotland in the Middle Ages, 1860; Sketches of Early Scotch History, 1861.

ABOUT: Burton, Mrs. H. Memoir of Cosmo Innes; Academy August 15, 1874.

IRVING, EDWARD (August 4, 1792-December 7, 1834), Scottish theologian, was born (on the same day as Shelley) in Annan, the son of a tanner. He was graduated from Edinburgh University in 1809, and became master in a "mathematical school" at Haddington. There also he had a private pupil, a girl named Jane Welsh, who later became the wife of Thomas Carlyle. In 1812 he became master in an academy at Kirkcaldy, and here he met Carlyle, became his close friend, and introduced him to Jane Welsh. He was licensed to preach in 1815, but at first was an utter failure, and in 1818 went to Edinburgh to study to equip himself for the pulpit. By 1819 he had so improved that the famous Dr. Hugh Chalmers made him his assistant at Glasgow, and his eloquence made him a rival of that celebrated pulpit orator. In 1822 he went as preacher to the chapel of the Caledonian Asylum at London. There again he was an immense success—fiery, emotional, and markedly handsome (in spite of a squint). That year he was married to another former pupil, Isabella Martin; they had been engaged for nine years, during which time he had fallen out of love with her and into love with Jane Welsh, who at the time reciprocated his passion. But he tried in vain to break his engagement, and to his lasting grief he was obliged to marry a woman who adored him, while he continued to adore the woman who married Carlyle.

Irving's great success as a preacher paved the way for a new, rich church in Regent Square. He was becoming increasingly heretical, his views being apocalyptic and adventist in nature. His vanity made him the prey of both fanatics and flatterers, and his prolixity finally wore his congregation out. In 1830 members of his church began "speaking in unknown tongues," and he added faith-healing to his other beliefs. He was tried for heresy in 1831, removed from his church the next year, and founded his own Holy Catholic Apostolic Church (which still survives as a pentecostal sect). Finally the presbytery of the Church of Scotland dropped him from its rolls in 1833; and by his own theories he became a mere figure-head in his church, deposed by an "inspired voice." Heartbroken, his health failed, and he died in Glasgow at forty-two.

Irving's emotions over-rode his intellect. His writings, though frequently "strings of sonorous commonplaces," have dignity and sincerity, and though rhetorical are models of composition.

PRINCIPAL WORKS: Orations, 1823; Lectures on Baptism, 1828.

ABOUT: Carlyle, J. W. Letters; Publications Holy Catholic Apostolic (Irvingite) Church.

JACOBS, JOSEPH (August 29, 1854-January 30, 1916), Jewish historian and writer on many subjects, was born in Sydney, South Wales, Australia, the son of John and Sarah Jacobs.

His education he received at Sydney, where he attended the Grammar School and the University, and in England, where he attended the University of London and proceeded to King's College, Cambridge, when he was about eighteen. His interests were broad, and included history, literature, and anthropology, as well as mathematics and philosophy. In 1876 he took his bachelor's degree, taking senior rank in the honors examination in moral sciences.

His further studies resulted from a growing interest in problems connected with the Jewish people. George Eliot's novel, *Daniel Deronda,* appearing in the year of Jacobs' graduation, aroused interest in Zionism, and under the stimulus of this book and the discussion caused by it Jacobs went to Berlin, where he studied with noted Jewish scholars of the time. On his return to England, he devoted his attention to anthropology, and published in 1891 *Studies in Jewish Statistics: Social, Vital and Anthropometric.*

In the meantime he had made his influence felt as an English Jew. He called public attention to the persecutions of Jews in Russia, and served as honorary secretary of the committee formed to aid the Russian victims. and edited the first issues (1896-99) of *The Jewish Year Book*. In 1898 he was made President of the Jewish Historical Society of England, of which he had been a founder. His researches into source material in Spain resulted in his being elected to membership in the Royal Academy of History of Madrid.

His literary production was swelled considerably by the works which naturally grew out of his studies in anthropology. He edited (1890-93) *Folk Lore*, and, besides editing the *Arabian Nights* and Aesop's *Fables,* produced a series of fairy-tale books for children which placed him in a position much like that of his contemporary, Andrew Lang, editor of *The Blue Fairy Book* and *The Red Fairy Book*.

The more scholarly side of his nature was recognized in his being offered a position as revising editor of *The Jewish Encyclopaedia*. In this capacity he came to America in 1900, and lived here for the rest of his life. Besides the work connected with the *Encyclopaedia* he was engaged in writing articles for the *Encyclopaedia Britannica*, and served as Registrar and Professor of English at the Jewish Theological Seminary in New York City. Resigning from this position in 1913, he continued to conduct the *American Hebrew* (with which he had been associated since 1906) until his death in 1916, in Yonkers, New York.

"That fountain of fun frozen! Incredible!" is said to have been the obituary comment, of a man who had met him just once. Jacobs was described by Israel Zangwill as "a prince of good fellows." His pleasing personality and cheerfulness and humor seem all the more remarkable in view of his busy, active life and his heavy responsibilities, in spite of which he managed to charm other people's children by the tales he collected for his own.

His voluminous production (he is said to have spoken of himself as one of the greatest "contributors" to the British Museum Catalogue) was not an unmixed blessing, but it is fair to say that his work, even in books that were frankly pot-boilers, such as his translations and his editing, was sound and thorough.

R. W. W.

PRINCIPAL WORKS: *Bibliography of History*—Bibliotheca Anglo-Judaica: A Bibliographical Guide to Anglo-Jewish History (with Lucien Wolf) 1888; An Inquiry Into the Sources of the History of the Jews in Spain, 1894. *Editor*—The Fables of Aesop, 1889; Epistolae Ho-Elianae: The Familiar Letters of James Howell, 1890; The Palace of Pleasure (by William Painter) 1890; Barlaam and Josaphat: English Lives of Buddha, 1896. *Essays, Literary Studies, etc.*—Essays and Reviews, 1891; Tennyson and "In Memoriam": An Appreciation and a Study, 1892; Literary Studies, 1895; Jewish Ideals and Other Essays, 1896. *Fiction*—As Others Saw Him: A Retrospect, A. D. 54, 1895. *For Children*—English Fairy Tales, 1890; Celtic Fairy Tales, 1891; Indian Fairy Tales, 1892; More English Fairy Tales, 1893; More Celtic Fairy Tales, 1894; The Fables of Aesop, 1894; The Book of Wonder Voyages, 1896; The Story of Geographical Discovery: How the World Became Known, 1898; Europa's Fairy Book, 1915. *Sociological and Historical Studies*—Studies in Jewish Statistics: Social, Vital, and Anthropometric, 1891; The Jews of Angevin England: Documents and Records From Latin and Hebrew Sources, Printed and Manuscripts, 1893; Studies in Biblical Archaeology, 1894; Statistics of Jewish Populations in London, 1894; Jewish Contributions to Civilization: An Estimate, 1919.

ABOUT: Jewish Historical Society of England Transactions 8:129 1915-1917; Publications of the American Jewish Historical Society No. 25.

JAMES, GEORGE PAYNE RAINSFORD

(August 9, 1799-June 9, 1860), novelist and writer on history, was born in London, the son of a physician, Pinkston James.

His education was at a school in Putney, where he learned French and Italian. He traveled considerably and served in the Napoleonic wars, being held prisoner in France. During this enforced vacation he read French history, and on one occasion took part in a duel, fatally injuring his opponent, a French officer. This incident is said to have cast a shadow over his whole life.

Returned to England, as a Tory of fashionable pretensions, he entertained hopes of a political appointment; but these were dashed upon the death of Lord Liverpool, and he turned instead to literature. After writing anonymous pieces for magazines and some short stories for the amusement of himself and his friends, he was encouraged by Washington Irving, who had seen one of the tales, to try his hand at something larger. Accordingly, *Richelieu* was produced and shown to Sir Walter Scott, who heartily praised it.

Thus began an amazing career, in which, during a period of eighteen years, James pro-

JOSEPH JACOBS

G. P. R. JAMES

duced a novel for every nine months, and, still more wonderful, was almost uniformly successful. He is said to have written more than one hundred novels, and his collected edition occupies twenty-one volumes. He ventured also into historical writing, biography, and poetry, and was appointed Historiographer Royal by William IV.

Despite all these evidences of prosperity, James accepted, apparently after losing heavily in a publisher's failure, an appointment (about 1850) as consul to Massachusetts. About 1852 he removed to Virginia, in a similar capacity, where he remained until his appointment, about 1856, to the consul-generalship to the Austrian ports in the Adriatic. He died of apoplexy at Venice in 1860, leaving a widow, a daughter, and three sons.

As a man James was an affable Tory gentleman, popular and charming in society, but to all evidences very conventional. He was too proud to accept financial aid when he was in need. His personality does not seem to have impressed itself forcibly upon his contemporaries.

A very revealing story is told of a lady who took from a library two volumes of an edition of James' works. After reading with great pleasure what she supposed to be a two-volume novel, she discovered, to her surprise, that she had been reading the first volume of one of his novels and the second of another. Nothing could indicate more pointedly the shortcomings of the writer.

"Without a particle of Scott's genius, James was a quick, patient, indefatigable worker," writes Harold Child. "He poured forth historical novel after historical novel, all conscientiously accurate in historical fact, all

dressed in well-invented incident, all diffuse and pompous in style, and all lifeless, humorless, and characterless." R. W. W.

PRINCIPAL WORKS: *Biography*—The History of Charlemagne, 1832; Memoirs of Great Commanders, 1832; Life of Edward the Black Prince, 1836; Memoirs of Celebrated Women, 1837; Lives of the Most Eminent Foreign Statesmen (with E. E. Crowe) 1830-38; The Life and Times of Louis the Fourteenth, 1838; A History of the Life of Richard Coeur-de-Lion, 1842-49; Life of Henry IV, King of France and Navarre, 1847. *Editor*—Letters Illustrative of the Reign of William III, 1841; Rizzio (by W. H. Ireland) 1849; Means of Relief from Taxation (by R. Heathfield) 1849. *History*—A Brief History of the United States Boundary Question, 1839; A History of Chivalry, 1843; Dark Scenes of History, 1849; An Investigation Into the Murder of the Earl of Gowrie and Alexander Ruthven, 1849. *Novels*—Richelieu, 1829; Darnley, 1830; Philip Augustus, 1831; Henry Masterton, 1832; Mary of Burgundy, 1833; The Gypsey, 1835; Attila, 1837; The Man-at-Arms, 1840; The King's Highway, 1840; Corse de Léon, 1841; Agincourt, 1844; Arabella Stuart, 1844; The Smuggler, 1845; Henry Smeaton, 1851; Ticonderoga, 1854; The Cavalier, 1859. *Poetic Drama*—Blanche of Navarre, 1839; Caramalzaman, 1848. *Poetry*—The Ruined City, 1828. *Miscellaneous* —On the Educational Institutions of Germany, 1835; Some Remarks on the Corn Laws, 1841.

ABOUT: Field, M. B. Memories of Many Men; Hall, S. C. Book of Memories; Horne, R. H. A New Spirit of the Age; James, G. P. R. Works (see introductory preface); Joline, A. H. At the Library Table; Athenaeum 2:856 June 23, 1860; Edinburgh Review 65:180 April 1837.

JAMESON, ANNA BROWNELL MURPHY (May 17, 1794-March 17, 1860), was born in Dublin the eldest of five daughters of D. Brownell Murphy, a talented and patriotic Irish miniaturist. He was probably saved from disaster in the rebellion of 1798 by professional engagements which took him and his family to England in that year. Anna Murphy was an impetuous, independent, and gifted child who amused her sisters with stories of her own composition and led them in revolt against their governess. Her education was of the desultory variety common for girls in the period. She went when she was sixteen as governess in the family of the Marquis of Winchester.

In 1820 or 1821 Anna met Robert Jameson, a brilliant young lawyer with artistic leanings. Before June 1821 an engagement had been made and broken. To heal her bruised heart Anna went now as governess-companion with a wealthy family on a highly luxurious grand tour, but in 1825 she married Jameson. They were not settled a week in London before Mrs. Jameson was aware that she had made a mistake. Jameson, though he had no major faults, seems to have been quite incapable of the small, humane decencies of consideration and courtesy which make or mar a marriage.

A journal kept while she was abroad came to the attention of an eccentric bookseller named Thomas, who had taught Mrs. Jameson to play the guitar. She told him jestingly that

ANNA BROWNELL JAMESON

he might print it and, if there were any profits, give her a Spanish guitar. Thomas disposed of the copyright for fifty pounds. *The Diary of an Ennuyée* was an immediate success and Mrs. Jameson had a guitar and the beginnings of a literary career.

She commenced work on a book of essays and widened her circle of literary and artistic friendships. No better evidence for her considerable personal charm can be suggested than the host of great and near-great who loved her. Fanny Kemble wrote of her at this time as having a "skin of that dazzling whiteness which generally accompanies reddish hair." She was a "small, delicately featured woman. Her figure was extremely pretty." In 1829 Mr. Jameson was appointed Puisne judge in the island of Dominica. He went out alone and Mrs. Jameson accompanied her father and a friend on a jaunt to Germany. She was now well-known, if not famous, as an essayist. Mr. Jameson returned to England in 1833 and through the influence of his wife's powerful friends received a valuable legal appointment in Canada. He left immediately to take up his duties, and as before Mrs. Jameson went to Germany. Her warm friendships with Major Robert Noel and his wife and with Ottilie von Goethe commenced at this time. She made the acquaintance of the critic Tieck, of Retzsch the painter, of Schlegel, and other distinguished Germans.

In 1836, against her better judgment, Mrs. Jameson joined her husband in Canada. As before he proved himself devoted only from a distance. She returned to England in 1838 and wrote constantly from this time on. Translations, travel literature, guides to art galleries, and miscellaneous essays came from

her pen. She witnessed the crowning of Victoria and cultivated a friendship with Lady Byron, wife of the poet. Her literary and artistic relationships were numerous at this time. Carlyle, the Baillies, Miss Barrett (who made two translations from the *Odyssey* for Mrs. Jameson's essay on the Xanthian marbles), and Miss Mitford—these are but a few. It is a tribute to Mrs. Jameson's disposition that the only serious quarrel of her life was with Lady Byron. This took place after a trip to Italy in 1847, where for a time she had shepherded the honeymooning Brownings. She was occupied now with the work on *Sacred and Legendary Art,* to which she devoted the remainder of her life. Mr. Jameson died in 1854, leaving no provision for her in his will. Her friends raised an annuity of £100, which together with a royal pension for the same amount kept her in reasonably comfortable circumstances. In her later years she became interested in Sisters of Charity and spent much of her time abroad inquiring into methods of organization as yet unknown in England. She died at Ealing, London of bronchial pneumonia, resulting from a cold which she refused to consider serious.

Some of Mrs. Jameson's work still retains the charm of its creator. Her *Sacred and Legendary Art,* says Richard Garnett, "is a storehouse of delightful knowledge, as admirable for its accurate research as for poetic and artistic feeling." However, her travel books are today interesting only as historical documents. She wrote from the heart more than from the head and, although her analyses of Shakespearean heroines still make acceptable character-sketch cribs for preparatory-school students, her place is in the history of nineteenth-century literature rather than in the literature itself. P. B. S.

PRINCIPAL WORKS: *Diary*—The Diary of an Ennuyée, 1826. *Essays*—Loves of the Poets, 1829; Celebrated Female Sovereigns, 1831; Characteristics of Women, 1832; A Commonplace Book of Thoughts, Memories, and Fancies, 1854. *Travel*—Visits and Sketches, 1834; Winter Studies and Summer Rambles in Canada, 1838. *Art*—Companion to the Public Picture Galleries of London, 1842; Memoir of the Early Italian Painters, 1845; Sacred and Legendary Art, 1848-1860. *Translation*—Social Life in Germany (domestic dramas by Princess Amelia of Saxony) 1840.

ABOUT: Kemble, F. Records of a Girlhood; Macpherson, G. Memoirs of the Life of Anna Jameson; Martineau, H. Biographical Sketches; Parkes, B. Vignettes.

JEBB, SIR RICHARD CLAVERHOUSE

(August 27, 1841-December 9, 1905), classicist, was born at Dundee, while his mother was visiting her father, the Dean of Brechin, but his own father was an Irish barrister, and his youth was spent near Dublin. He was educated at St. Columbia's College, Rathfarnham; Charterhouse, and Trinity College, Cambridge, where he had a brilliant career, winning every classical prize seemingly without effort. From 1863 to 1875 he was fellow and classical lecturer of Trinity, and in 1869 public orator of Cambridge. He founded the Cambridge Philological Society, was examiner for London University, and wrote editorials and reviews for the London *Times*. His first published work consisted of editions of Sophocles and Theophrastus, and brilliant translations of English poets into Latin and Greek (1873 and 1878). In 1874 he married Caroline Lane (Reynolds) Slemmer, daughter of a Philadelphia clergyman, and widow of an American general. It was a markedly happy marriage.

In 1875 Jebb became professor of Greek at Glasgow University, lecturing one day a week in modern Greek. He visited Greece in 1878, and his archaeological researches caused him to be decorated by the Greek king. In 1884 he went to the United States to receive an honorary LL.D. from Harvard. From 1889 to his death he was regius professor of Greek at Cambridge. From 1898 he was also professor of ancient history at the Royal Academy, succeeding Gladstone. He was one of the founders of the Society for the Promotion of Hellenic Studies in 1879, and of the British School of Archaeology at Athens in 1887, and an original fellow of the British Academy in 1902. From 1891 to 1900 he served in Parliament as a Conservative, but took no active part in politics. He was knighted in 1900, and received the Order of Merit in 1905.

In that year he went to Capetown to a meeting of the British Association for the Advancement of Science, as vice-president of the section on education. The journey ruined his health, and he died at Cambridge before the year was out.

Jebb's great work was as editor of Sophocles from 1880 to 1896. He is the greatest of all editors of that immortal tragedian, and here, as in all his work, his writing is lucid and compact, with an exquisite feeling for words.

PRINCIPAL WORKS: The Attic Orators, 1876; Primer of Greek Literature, 1877; Modern Greece, 1880; Homer: An Introduction to the Iliad and Odyssey, 1887.

ABOUT: Jebb, R. C. Life and Letters; Athenaeum December 16, 1905.

JEFFERIES, (JOHN) RICHARD (November 6, 1848-August 14, 1887), essayist, novelist, and naturalist, was born at Coate Farm near Swindon, North Wiltshire, the eldest of four children of James Luckett Jefferies. Both of Richard's parents were from families which had by generations gravitated from city to country. His father, born in London, was an eccentric soul who had as a young man worked his passage to America, returning to settle on the farm, which he had freehold from his father, after

RICHARD JEFFERIES

marrying Elizabeth Gyde, daughter of a Fleet Street bookbinder. During Richard's early years the farm was quite prosperous. An ardent hunter and bird's-nester, the boy was friendly with gamekeepers and intimate with the life of field and coppice. His formal education was spasmodic and he did no regular farm work. Solitary, bookish, and generally unlike the common run of country lads he was regarded with suspicion by his neighbors.

In his sixteenth year Jefferies, with his cousin Jimmy Fox, ran away to France. They intended to walk to Moscow, but various circumstances stood in the way of this undertaking and the boys returned to England, where a trip to America was frustrated because they spent all their money for tickets and had none left to buy food during the voyage. These adventures, coupled with his unproductive habits, did not raise Richard in the local estimation. James Jefferies was not an energetic husbandman and the farm brought little ready cash. Richard, most frequently to be seen idling through field and wood with his gun on his arm, earned nothing but a few shillings for an occasional hare. A neighbor said, "That young Jefferies is not the sort of fellow you want hanging about in your covers." And the country people opined that Richard was "cut out for a gentleman if only there had been money." His aunt, Mrs. Harrild, whom he often visited at Sydenham was virtually his only friend and confidante during this period.

In 1866 Jefferies had a position reporting, reviewing, and writing stories for the *North Wilts Herald* at Swindon. The stories were trashy echoes of the worst kind of romantic fiction and are in no way prophetic of Jefferies' future work. By 1870 he had planned and partially written several novels and tragedies and had saved enough money for a trip to Belgium. After this indulgence he returned to England penniless, without position, and in disgrace with his family. Jefferies at this time is described as tall, thin and slightly stooping, with long hair and a beard, but no moustache. He had full, sensuous lips and his eyes were a bright, "noticeable" blue. Restless, dissatisfied, but always confident of ultimate success, his writing in the next years ranged from ordinary, reportorial hackwork and political pamphlets to a written-to-order family history and a book on how to be an author. He could not market his own novels about high life. Articles on agriculture and current events in *Fraser's, Fortnightly* and other magazines and several letters to *The Times* attracted some notice.

In 1874 Jefferies married Jessie Baden of Day House Farm and published *The Scarlet Shawl.* This and his following novels were failures. But their author, though still overmuch concerned with "people who always gave sovereigns to footmen," was gradually finding himself. In 1877 he moved with his family to London and commenced the articles in the *Pall Mall Gazette* which, reprinted as *The Gamekeeper at Home,* brought Jefferies his first recognition. Half a dozen volumes describing country life appeared in the next five years. These culminated in the novels *Wood Magic* and *Bevis.* In *Wood Magic* the boy Bevis is the only human character. The others are animals, birds, insects and the elements. Written from the point of view of a child, the book leans rather toward allegorizing bestiary types and attempts no particular insight into animal character. The dialogue of Bevis and the wind in the last chapter has been called one of the finest prose poems in the language.

Bevis is an idealization of Jefferies' childhood. He had two children of his own now. His treatment of the life of field and wood is essentially that of a countryman, albeit an exceptionally sentient and aware countryman. His love of nature was without sentimentality; his command of exquisite fancy and his mysticism flowered over a basis of solid, even · brutal common sense. Jefferies personally was a kind of domesticated Pan and he could, after watching an animal with loving patience from a hidden covert until he knew its ways, habits, and every aspect, kill it with elemental satisfaction "as the neck gave with a sudden looseness, and in a moment what had been a living, straining creature became limp." Something of this same quality of tenderness and cruelty is discernible in Jefferies' attitude toward women.

In 1882 Jefferies submitted to four operations for fistula. His health, never constant,

declined rapidly from this period. He wrote voluminously in an effort to meet increased expenses, but in September 1885 he broke down completely and was unable to sit or lie so as to write without pain. He refused the aid of the Royal Literary Fund. As his body wasted away in intense pain his mind was somehow stimulated and his sense impressions heightened. He wrote and dictated some of his best work during these last years. In 1886 a fund was privately raised to help him. He died at Goring near Worthing.

Jefferies in his mysticism and diffuse expression of cosmic unity has been compared to Whitman, whose works he knew and admired. His singular talent for close and accurate observation was limited in its expression by the very misanthropy which developed it. His intuition, according to the critic Louis Cazamian, "is in absolute control of his sensibility because his culture, being entirely self-made, does not oppose to it any negative social complex."

P. B. S.

PRINCIPAL WORKS: *Sketches*—The Gamekeeper at Home, 1878; Wild Life in a Southern County, 1879; The Amateur Poacher, 1879; Hodge and His Masters, 1880; Round About a Great Estate, 1880; Nature Near London, 1883; Red Deer, 1884; Life of the Fields, 1884; Field and Hedgerow, 1889. *Novels* —The Scarlet Shawl, 1874; Restless Human Hearts, 1875; World's End, 1877; Wood Magic, 1881; Bevis, 1882; The Dewy Morn, 1884; After London, 1885; Amaryllis at the Fair, 1887. *Miscellaneous*—A Memoir of the Goddards of North Wilts, 1873. *Autobiography*—The Story of My Heart, 1883.

ABOUT: Masseck, C. J. Richard Jefferies: Étude d'une Personalité; Salt, H. S. Richard Jefferies: His Life and His Ideas; Thomas, E. Richard Jefferies: His Life and Work.

JEFFREY, LORD FRANCIS (October 23, 1773-January 26, 1850), critic and editor of the *Edinburgh Review,* was born in Edinburgh, one of five children of George and Henrietta (Louden) Jeffrey. The father was a depute-clerk in the court of session, "not a high, but a very respectable position."

When Francis was eight he entered the famous old High School which has figured in the education of many other famous men such as Sir Walter Scott and George Borrow, the novelists, and Henry Brougham, one of the co-founders of the *Edinburgh Review.* From 1787 to 1789 Francis attended Glasgow College. His father, who was a high Tory, forbade his attendance at the classes of John Millar, the most famous and popular member of the faculty, because of his liberal Whig beliefs. In later years old Mr. Jeffrey bemoaned the fact that Francis had been permitted to attend the college at all, blaming his physical proximity to Millar for his son's objectionable liberal views; but it is not unlikely that these views were due, fully as much, to his son's contacts with himself. In 1791-92 Francis attended Queen's College, Oxford, for eleven months, but hated it.

LORD JEFFREY

Returning to Edinburgh, Francis studied law and was called to the bar in 1794. During this period the young man had also devoted considerable time to writing upon philosophy and politics, as well as lighter matters such as poetry and plays. He developed his critical faculty by writing criticisms of his own work. As a member of the Speculative Society and of the Academy of Physicks he became acquainted with many distinguished contemporaries. His prospects in the legal profession did not appear bright at this time because the Tories, who controlled all the patronage, did not approve of his ideas. In 1798 he went down to London for a try at a literary career, but soon returned home.

In 1801 he married his second cousin, Catherine Wilson, although neither his family nor hers was very well off, and the young lawyer's practice was bringing in less than £100 a year. About this time Jeffrey and his friends were developing their plans for the new *Edinburgh Review*, the first issue of which appeared October 10, 1802.

Greatly to Jeffrey's surprise, for he was a timid and pessimistic soul, the new venture was an immediate success. Although Sydney Smith had been the originator and nominal editor of the first number, the successful continuation of the *Review* was due to Jeffrey's energy and his skill—though inexperienced—as an editor. The first issue sold 2,500 copies and in a very few years the circulation had increased to 13,000. The reason for this success was the novelty of its style of reviewing. Until the appearance of "the yellow and blue," reviewing was a flabby art. Reviewers were either the underpaid hacks of the booksellers or nonentities who were glad to write reviews for nothing more than the glory of

being thought literary. In either case the review was usually worthless as criticism. But the young men of Edinburgh were "violently partisan, unhesitatingly personal, and more inclined to find fault, the more distinguished the subject was," according to Mr. Saintsbury.

Jeffrey became the official editor in 1803, a post which he continued to hold for twenty-seven years. From comparative idleness, Jeffrey was suddenly thrown into a whirl of activity. Not only did the duties of editor occupy a great deal of his time and attention, but with the success of the *Review* his law practice also began to increase. He also began to lead a much more active social life. Sir Walter Scott's Friday Club was formed and here the most distinguished men of Edinburgh gathered.

In this same year Jeffrey volunteered and was made an ensign in the army then being formed to repel the expected Napoleonic invasion. Jeffrey was probably the worst soldier Scotland ever produced, but his action was none-the-less heroic. Unlike most volunteers, he was absolutely certain that both he and his country were doomed.

Jeffrey was desolated by the death of his wife in 1805, and the following year, when a duel between himself and the poet Moore almost took place (it was prevented by the arrival of police) he wrote, ". . .I am really as little in love with life as I have been for some time in the habit of professing." The encounter with Moore, incidentally, was the beginning of a lifelong friendship between them. Moore had challenged his critic to a duel over a review of *Epistles, Odes, and Other Poems*. This incident is mentioned in *English Bards and Scotch Reviewers*, where Byron states erroneously that Moore's pistol was unloaded—it was Jeffrey's which was found by the police to contain no bullet.

In 1813 Jeffrey came to America to marry Charlotte Wilkes. While here he visited President Madison and James Monroe, defending, to them, the English claims leading to the war of 1812 which he had vigorously attacked in the *Review* at home.

Jeffrey's importance and reputation had been growing steadily, in the legal profession as well as in the literary. His long devotion to the Whig cause at length brought reward. He was appointed Lord Advocate in 1830. This entailed a parliamentary career, which was not highly successful nor congenial, and it was with relief that he became a judge of the court of session in 1834. This post he held until shortly before his death.

Jeffrey was a most kind and affectionate man, in spite of the opposite impression created by many of his critical reviews. His many acts of generosity to less affluent writers are well known. As a critic he was the most respected in the British Isles during his own lifetime. For the validity of that criticism in the eyes of a modern critic, we cannot do better than quote George Saintsbury: "And it must be again and again repeated that Jeffrey is by no means justly chargeable with the Dryasdust failings so often attributed to academic criticism. . . however much he may sometimes seem to carp and complain, however much we may sometimes wish for a little more equity and a little less law, it is astonishing how weighty Jeffrey's critical judgments are after three quarters of a century which has seen so many seeming heavy things grows light. There may be much that he does not see; there may be some things which he is physically unable to see; but what he does see, he sees with a clearness, and co-ordinates . . . with a precision, which are hardly to be matched among the fluctuating and diverse race of critics."

D. C.

PRINCIPAL WORKS: *Critical Essays*—Contributions to the *Edinburgh Review* (4 vols.) 1844.

ABOUT: Cockburn, H. Life of Lord Jeffrey; Gates, L. E. Three Studies in Literature; Saintsbury, G. Essays in English Literature; Wilson, D. A. Carlyle to *The French Revolution;* Winchester, C. T. A Group of English Essayists of the Early 19th Century.

JERROLD, DOUGLAS WILLIAM (January 3, 1803-June 8, 1857), dramatist and wit, was connected with the theatre from birth. Born in London on January 3, 1803, he was the youngest son of Samuel Jerrold and his second wife, Mary Reid. The father was a strolling player, as well as printer to his company and the "proprietor of many Theatres *Rural*," and his mother was an actress.

So the young Douglas was brought up by his Scotch grandmother Reid, first in Willsley in Kent and afterwards (1807) in Sheerness where Samuel Jerrold then had a theatre. The boy was taught by an actor, Wilkinson, until he went to Mr. Herbert's school in Sheerness and still later to a Mr. Glass at Southend.

Even before school age he was carried on the stage by Edmund Kean in "Rolla," and had a child's part in "The Stranger." But in 1813 he left the theatre far behind when he joined the Navy as a first-class volunteer on the *Namur.* Here he was allowed to indulge his passion for reading and to get up private theatricals with Clarkson Stanfield. At the tender age of twelve, however, Douglas had his fill of the Navy and the following year took up his apprenticeship with the printer Sidney in London.

He showed a continued interest in the stage by his authorship in 1818 of "The Duellist," which was staged at Sadler's Wells on April 30, 1821. Meanwhile the young dramatist worked as compositor on the *Sunday Monitor,* to which he occasionally contributed. In fact, his interests were decidedly varied. In 1823

he and his friend, Laman Blanchard, fired with enthusiasm for Byron, considered joining the Greek cause. He was also deep in the study of Latin and French and was writing plays as well as dramatic sketches for Duncombe's *Mirror of the Stage,* and prose and verse for *Arliss's Literary Collections.*

He married Thomas Swann's daughter, Mary Ann, of Wetherby in Yorkshire, in 1824. The next year he secured his first important literary engagement as dramatist for the Coburg Theatre, where he was dubbed "the little Shakespeare in a camlet cloak." His small salary here was eked out by contributions to the *Weekly Times, The Ballot* and the *Monthly Magazine.* A quarrel with Davidge in 1829, however, led him to offer his "Black-Eyed Susan" to Elliston of the Surrey Theatre. Produced there on June 8, 1829, this piece was probably his greatest success.

Although Jerrold continued to write plays until 1835, he began in 1832 to edit *Punch in London.* He also wrote for the *Freemason's Quarterly, Blackwood's,* and the *New Monthly Magazine,* while in 1841 he became definitely associated with the newly established *Punch* as the writer of political articles signed "Q." His only novel, *St. Giles and St. James* also appeared in the same magazine. At about this time, too, he began his editorial career, for he was connected in turn with the *Illuminated Magazine* (1843), *Douglas Jerrold's Shilling Magazine* (1845), the *Daily News* (1846), *Douglas Jerrold's Weekly Newspaper* (1846), and *Lloyd's Illustrated Weekly Newspaper,* which he edited from 1852 until his death.

Through most of these years he had suffered with rheumatism. At fifty-two his hair was white and his back bent. Trips to Malvern and the Continent did him no good. On

DOUGLAS JERROLD

June 8, 1857, at Greville Place, Kilburn Priory, he died from a combination of painter's cholera and heart trouble.

The same generosity that made him poor, gave Jerrold a place among the *littérateurs* of his time. He was called "a snarling critic" by those who did not know him, and Hawthorne termed his wit "acrid." In reality he was an enemy to meanness, and even Hawthorne was forced to admit that he liked Douglas Jerrold very much, for he was at heart gentle and affectionate. Like Johnson he was a man of clubs, and the founder of the Mulberries as well as the Whittington Club. A visitor at one of these clubs described him as having a "leonine head" and "finely chiseled features."

Jerrold himself wanted to be known as a writer of serious prose instead of a creator of a wit, that was "all steel points." But it was actually his humorous work, *Mrs. Caudle's Curtain Lectures*, that brought him most fame. He was one of the few writers in his day of genuine English comedy, but the plays, like the essays, are no longer popular. For he is but a minor figure in his century. B. D. S.

PRINCIPAL WORKS: *Plays*—More Frightened Than Hurt, 1821; The Gipsey of Derncleugh, 1821; The Smoked Miser, 1823; The Seven Ages, 1824; Bampfylde Moore Carew, 1824; The Statue Lover, 1828; The Tower of Lochlain, 1828; Descart the Buccaneer, 1828; Wives by Advertisement, 1828; Ambrose Gwinett, 1828; Two Eyes Between Two, 1828; Fifteen Years of a Drunkard's Life, 1828; Law and Lions, 1829; John Overy, 1829; Black-Eyed Susan, 1829; Vidocq, 1829; Thomas à Becket, 1829; Sally in Our Alley, 1830; The Mutiny at the Nore, 1830; The Devil's Ducat, 1830; Martha Willis, 1831; The Bride of Ludgate, 1831; The Rent Day, 1832; The Golden Calf, 1832; Nell Gwynne, 1833; The Housekeeper, 1833; The Wedding Gown, 1834; Beau Nash, 1834; The Schoolfellow, 1835; The Hazard of the Die, 1835; Doves in a Cage, 1835; The Painter of Ghent, 1836; The Man for the Ladies, 1836; The Perils of Pippin, 1836; The White Milliner, 1841; The Prisoner of War, 1842; Bubbles of the Day, 1842; Gertrude's Cherries, 1842; Time Works Wonders, 1845; The Catspaw, 1850; Retired From Business, 1851; St. Cupid, 1853; A Heart of Gold, 1854. *Miscellaneous*—Men of Character, 1838; The Handbook of Swindling, 1839; Heads of the People, 1840; Cakes and Ale, 1842; Punch's Letters to His Son, 1843; The Story of a Feather, 1844; Punch's Complete Letter Writer, 1845; The Chronicles of Clovernook, 1846; Mrs. Caudle's Curtain Lectures, 1846; St. Giles and St. James, 1846; A Man Made of Money, 1849; Collected Edition of the Writings of Douglas Jerrold, 1851-54; Other Times, 1852-54; The Brownrigg Papers, 1860; The Works of Douglas Jerrold, 1863-64; The Barber's Chair and The Hedgehog Letters, 1874; Tales by Douglas Jerrold, 1891; The Essays of Douglas Jerrold, 1903; Douglas Jerrold and "Punch," 1910

ABOUT: Jerrold, W. Douglas Jerrold; Jerrold, W. B. The Life of Douglas Jerrold; Mackay, C. Forty Years' Recollections of Life, Literature, and Public Affairs; Stirling, J. H. Jerrold, Tennyson and Macaulay; Atlantic Monthly, 1:1 November, 1857; New Review 7:358 September 1892.

JERROLD, WILLIAM BLANCHARD
(December 23, 1826-March 10, 1884), journalist and miscellaneous writer, was born in London, the eldest son of Douglas Jerrold, the humorist, editor, and playwright. He was educated at the Brompton Grammar School and at a private school in Boulogne-sur-Mer, then entered the schools of the Royal Academy; but his sight failed and he had to give up art as a profession. He began writing by contributing to his father's *Weekly Newspaper*, and to the recently founded *Daily News*. In 1849 he married Lillie Blanchard, daughter of his godfather. In 1853 he was Crystal Palace Commissioner, and traveled in this connection in Norway and Sweden. From 1855 he spent half of every year in Paris. There he acted as correspondent for English papers, and collaborated with his intimate friend, the famous artist Gustave Doré. He was on terms of close friendship with Napoleon III and Eugénie, and was his passionate partisan, though otherwise he was an ardent liberal and friend of labor. Between 1851 and 1871 he had four successful plays produced, the best known being *Beau Brummel*. His father died in 1857, and the son succeeded as editor of *Lloyd's Weekly London News* for the remainder of his life. He was so strong an advocate of the Union in the American Civil War that his editorials were ordered placarded in New York. He founded the English branch of the International Association for the Assimilation of Copyright Laws, of which he was president. For this work he was decorated by France and Portugal. At the time of his death he was engaged in writing a biography of Doré which was never finished. He was a noted gourmet, and published cookbooks under a pseudonym.

Jerrold's writing is hardly distinguished, but it is competent, and was deservedly popular in his time. His books on France are weakened by his intense prejudice in favor of Napoleon III.

PRINCIPAL WORKS: Imperial Paris, 1855; Life and Remains of Douglas Jerrold, 1859; The Brownrigg Papers, 1860; Up and Down in the World (novel) 1863; The Best of All Good Company, 1871; Life of George Cruikshank, 1871.

ABOUT: Illustrated Review March, 1873.

JESSOPP, AUGUSTUS
(December 20, 1823-February 12, 1914), educator and antiquarian, was born at Cheshunt, the youngest of ten children. His mother was a native of Bermuda. When he was a small child the family moved to Belgium, and he was educated at various Continental schools. Then for three years he was in a merchant's office in Liverpool. He was most unhappy, and finally in 1844 was able to enter St. John's College, Cambridge. He took holy orders, and in 1843 became a curate in Cambridgeshire. In 1855 he was made headmaster of a grammar school at Helston, Cornwall, which had run to seed, and restored it physically and

educationally. In 1859 he had a similar and harder task in the run-down King Edward VI's School at Norwich; this school he also built up into a first-class institution. But his tastes were for antiquarianism and ecclesiastical history, and in 1879 he retired to Scarning, Norfolk, as rector, to have leisure for study. In 1873, at fifty, he had married Mary Ann Cotesworth, daughter of a naval officer; they had no children. From Scarning he contributed to the *Nineteenth Century* and the *Dictionary of National Biography*. He received a D.D. degree from Oxford in 1870, and in 1895, on the same day, was made honorary fellow of Oxford and of Cambridge. In 1902 he was named chaplain-in-ordinary to the king, and he was honorary canon of Norwich Cathedral. His wife died in 1905; he lost his fortune, having to be rescued by a civil list pension; and finally his mind failed. He resigned his living in 1911, and died insane in 1914.

Jessopp regretted his move to Scarning, feeling he had put himself outside the current of life. He underestimated his ability, calling himself a "smatterer and fumbler." But he had real historic gifts within a narrow compass, he had genuine learning, and he was a truly great schoolmaster.

PRINCIPAL WORKS: One Generation of a Norfolk House, 1878; Arcady: For Better or for Worse, 1887; The Coming of the Friars, 1889; Trials of a Country Parson, 1890; Studies by a Recluse, 1893; Before the Great Pillage, 1901.

ABOUT: Cornhill Magazine November 1921.

JEVONS, WILLIAM STANLEY (September 1, 1835-August 13, 1882), economist and philosopher, was born in Liverpool. His father was an iron merchant and inventor, his mother a poet well known in Unitarian circles. He was the ninth of eleven children. His mother died when he was ten, and his elder sister took her place in the unusually devoted family. He was educated at University College School and then in University College, London. The father had failed in business in 1848 and it was necessary for him to earn his living. In 1853 he became assayer of the mint at Sydney, Australia, and remained there until 1859. He was also much interested in meteorology, and made weather reports, used by the government, from 1856 to 1858.

Jevons returned to University College to study mathematics, physics, and political economy. In 1862 he obtained his M.A. degree, and in 1863 became a tutor at Owens College, Manchester. He detested lecturing, and in later years spoke in public as little as possible. He remained at the college until 1876 (with a year's leave of absence in 1872 because of illness, when he traveled in Norway)—first as lecturer in logic and political economy, then as professor of these subjects and of mental and moral philosophy. In 1867 he married Harriet Ann Taylor, daughter of the founder of the *Manchester Guardian*. From 1876 to 1880 he was professor of political economy at University College. He retained his interest in natural science, and wrote on scientific subjects frequently. He died by accidental drowning while bathing near Hastings. His death at forty-seven was a severe loss to the world of learning, for he was an original thinker in several fields. He was one of the greatest of statistical economists. His was a singularly attractive nature, modest, simple, tender-hearted, high-minded. His writing is highly technical, but informed with a deep sympathy and humanity in spite of its necessary dryness.

PRINCIPAL WORKS: Remarks on the Australian Gold Fields, 1859; Pure Logic, 1864; Theory of Political Economy, 1871; Principles of Science, 1874; Primer of Logic, 1876; Primer of Political Economy, 1878; The State in Relation to Labour, 1882; Methods of Social Reform and Other Papers (ed. by H. T. Jevons) 1883.

ABOUT: Jevons, W. S. Letters and Journal (ed. by H. T. Jevons).

JEWSBURY, GERALDINE ENDSOR (1812-September 23, 1880), novelist, was born in Derbyshire. Her father was a merchant and insurance agent. The family moved to Norwich when she was six. Her mother died, and her older sister MARIA (afterwards Mrs. Fletcher), also well known in her time as a writer, reared her, educating her at home. In 1832 the sister married, and she took charge of the household. Her father died in 1840, and she then acted as housekeeper for her brother until he too married, in 1853.

In 1841 she met the Carlyles, and became the intimate friend of both, moving to London in 1854 to be near Mrs. Carlyle. There she became the center of a literary circle, having already published several novels, as well as stories for children. Her ambition was to be a journalist, but her health forbade. However, she contributed occasionally to the reviews. In 1866 she moved to Sevenoaks, Kent. In 1880, finding she had cancer, she went to a private hospital in London, where she died.

Brilliant, with keen humor and charming manners, Geraldine Jewsbury was the life of the group to which she belonged, and many of the most eminent persons of her period delighted in the society of this middle-aged spinster. Her novels, some historical, others realistic pictures of working-class life in the north of England, have not survived her own day; her personality was more compelling than her talent.

PRINCIPAL WORKS: Zoe: The History of Two Lives, 1845; The Half-Sisters, 1848; Marian Withers, 1851; The Sorrows of Gentility, 1856; Right or Wrong, 1859.

ABOUT: Athenaeum October 2, 1880; Manchester Examiner and Times September 24, 1880.

JOHNSON, EMILY PAULINE (1862-March 7, 1913), Canadian poet, was a half-breed Indian, her father being head chief of the Six Nation Indians, her mother an Englishwoman. She was born at the Six Nations Indian Reservation, Brant, Ontario, and educated at the Brantford Model School. She contributed to English, Canadian, and United States periodicals; and as an entertainer, reciting her own poems under her Indian name of Tekahionwake, made numerous tours of Canada and the United States from 1891 onward. In 1906 she appeared as a *diseuse* in London, with great success. Besides her poetry and recitations, she was noted as an expert canoeist. She died unmarried, at Vancouver, British Columbia.

Her best poems are those on Indian subjects, which are marked by deep passion, keen feeling for nature, and ardent sympathy.

PRINCIPAL WORKS: White Wampum, 1895; Canadian Born, 1903; Flint and Feathers, 1913.

ABOUT: Logan, J. D. & French, D. Highways of Canadian Literature.

JOHNSON, JAMES (d. February 26, 1811), Scottish editor and publisher, is supposed to have been born in Ettrick. Practically nothing is known about his life. He was an engraver and music seller in Edinburgh, and his best known publication was the *Scots Musical Museum*, in six volumes, which may have been edited by Burns. In any event, Burns contributed many poems to the collection, and was Johnson's friend, describing him as "a good, honest fellow." He is said to have been the first to try to engrave music on pewter. He died destitute, and in 1819 funds were raised publicly for the care of his widow.

PRINCIPAL WORKS: The Scots Musical Museum, 1787-1803.

ABOUT: Scots Magazine 1811.

JOHNSON, LIONEL PIGOT (March 15, 1867-October 4, 1902), poet and critic, was born at Broadstairs, the son of an infantry captain and the grandson of a baronet. His education followed the usual leisure-class pattern of his time; from lower school he progressed to Winchester and thence to New College, Oxford, where he specialized in English and was graduated with modest honors. He began to write while still an undergraduate, and in fact at both Winchester and Oxford he became something of a literary dictator. For a while he edited the school magazine at Winchester, and tried, without much success, to give it a flavor of literary distinction. At only twenty his first published work appeared, an essay on "The Fools of Shakespeare" in the *Noctes Shakespearianae*.

On leaving Oxford, Johnson settled in London, and except for numerous visits to Ireland, beginning in 1893, he spent there the

LIONEL JOHNSON

remainder of his outwardly uneventful life. From early youth he had been drawn to the Roman Catholic Church, and in 1891 he was received into it. Newman, though Johnson never met him, had an enormous influence on his life and thought. For a while he thought of taking orders, but his natural aloofness and need for seclusion determined him on a retired secular existence instead.

In his pleasant rooms, surrounded by books, he settled down to a life as nearly as possible like the comfortable, semi-monastic existence of an Oxford don. He became a contributor, chiefly of reviews and criticism, to *The Academy*, the *Pall Mall Gazette*, and other journals of the more conservative sort. He was not wealthy; for several years, though he was eager for wider publication, he was obliged to devote himself strictly to this journalistic labor, until he had paid off the rather large debts left behind him at Oxford through the purchase of books and prints beyond his financial means.

His interest in Ireland, and his espousal of the cause of Home Rule, became increasingly keen and active. He visited the island often, took a part in Home Rule agitation, and began to speak of himself as an Irishman, though as a matter of fact the Celtic strain in his ancestry was not Gaelic, but Cymric. He became accepted by many of the Irish as one of themselves. Perhaps this innocent deception was merely another manifestation of a queer quirk in Johnson's mind—his habitual quotations from and accounts of conversations with famous men, such as Newman and Gladstone, whom in fact he had never seen.

Except for the one great interest of the Irish question, he lived the life of a recluse in his bachelor apartments. He was a devoted and solicitous friend, and attached others to him strongly, but his friendship had no need of personal contact to keep it alive. Exceedingly fastidious and ultra-sensitive, he had besides a secret to keep. From his university days he had been an alcoholic, though few among his acquaintances suspected it. He never lost control of himself, however intoxicated he might be; the only sign of his drunkenness was his increased asceticism and his denunciation of sexual emotion. This attitude had a physical basis; in the autopsy performed after his death it was found that, except for his brain, his body had never developed after his fifteenth year.

This arrested development accounts also for Johnson's appearance of extreme youth. His whole physique was small and frail, though Yeats says that he had "the delicate strong features" of a Greek cast. His health was never very strong, and for several years his hands and feet were badly crippled. This affliction, especially distressing to a man whose greatest delight had been long, solitary walks at night (because of insomnia, he slept during the day), did not embitter him; it only deepened the vein of religious mysticism in his nature and retired him still further from the world of men. His intense devoutness and his inherent awareness of a natural aristocracy combined to make some of his judgments seem grotesque to a less fastidious ear. "I wish," he said for example, "those people who deny the eternity of punishment would realize their unspeakable vulgarity!"

In October, 1902, urging his crippled body to one more nocturnal ramble—and perhaps not entirely sober—he slipped on Fleet Street and was found unconscious. He died shortly after, of a fractured skull; the autopsy revealed that his skull was abnormally thin.

Johnson said that while still in Oxford he had consciously molded his prose style on that of his great namesake (but no relation), Samuel Johnson. It has the orotundity and labored periods of the eighteenth century, and the air of omniscience which he adopted as a critic went well with such style, but precluded any wide influence from his writing. "In my library," he remarked, "I have all the knowledge of the world that I need," and that bookish aura clings to all his work. His poetry is highly intellectualized—"marmorean," Yeats called it—but it is simple, austere, and not altogether unimpassioned. He was strongly influenced by Walter Pater; in fact, his very last writing was an elegy on Pater, which he had put into the mail just before his fatal accident.

At its best, Johnson's poetry is noble and profound. He belongs to the small but exquisite group of religious lyrists of the late nineteenth century, though without the mysti-

cal ardor of Francis Thompson or the grace of Alice Meynell.   M. A. deF.

PRINCIPAL WORKS: *Poetry*—Poems, 1895; Ireland and Other Poems, 1897; Selections, 1908. *Essays* —The Art of Thomas Hardy, 1894; Post Liminium (ed. by Thomas Whittemore) 1912.

ABOUT: Burdett, O. The Beardsley Period; Johnson, L. P. Selections (see Memoir by Clement K. Shorter); Jackson, H. The Eighteen Nineties; Yeats, W. B. Autobiographies; Atlantic Monthly 90:856 December 1902

JOHNSON, WILLIAM. See CORY, WILLIAM

JONES, EBENEZER (January 20, 1820-September 14, 1860), poet, was born at Islington, the third child of Robert Jones and Hannah (Sumner) Jones. His family was comfortably situated, but, as his parents were strict Calvinists, the boy's education was rather meagre. He was allowed only books which emphasized religion. Shakespeare and Milton were forbidden, and Byron was regarded as a kind of arch-fiend.

In such a family schools were selected because of their Calvinistic instructors, and the severe tenets of a grim creed were a terror to the young boy. He was obliged, however, to leave school when his father's long illness had impoverished the family. With the leap of reaction he plunged into the reading of once-forbidden books, and fairly devoured Carlyle.

In 1837 Jones was put to work twelve hours a day in a wholesale firm connected with the tea trade. As the company was dishonest, he was not happy in his work, and determined to leave as early as possible. At about this time he began writing verse. Carlyle and Shelley acted as stimulants upon him, and he became rapidly more radical in his thought. While he was never strictly a Chartist, he became a follower, for a short time, of Robert Owen.

During this period he fell in love with a young woman who failed to return his passion, and in despair Jones threw his poetry together into a volume, *Studies of Sensation and Event*, which appeared in 1843. The public was indifferent, and the few distinguished critics, such as Thomas Hood, to whom the poet submitted his volume, were, for the most part, extremely severe in their censures. Jones was in despair, and not long after destroyed his unpublished manuscripts.

To add to his tribulations came an unhappy marriage to Catherine Atherstone, niece of the writer Edwin Atherstone, which resulted in a separation. Jones determined to leave literature for politics, hoping to achieve some measure of social reform.

He supported himself by working as an accountant, and assisted W. J. Linton in political writing; he wrote for radical publishers and published a pamphlet on reform in landownership which, though it anticipated Henry

George, drew little notice. He became consumptive, and it was his fate to waste away, dying at Brentwood in 1860, with no recognition, by public or critics, of his genius. In fact, he was hardly noticed as a poet until Dante Gabriel Rossetti, in *Notes and Queries* (1870), praised him; by 1879 interest had grown sufficiently to justify the republication of *Studies of Sensation and Event,* with the addition of biographical material.

Admired by Rossetti as "full of vivid disorderly power" despite their "glaring defects" and "wilful 'newness,'" Jones' poems are full of a passion which often breaks through the limits of metrical form and produces jarring rhythms. He improved his work, however, and produced perhaps his finest writing in three poems written near the end of his life, "Winter Hymn to the Snow," "When the World Is Burning," and "To Death." He was admired by Browning and Swinburne. "When he writes a bad line he writes a bad one with a vengeance," wrote John Leicester Warren. "It is hardly possible to say how excruciatingly bad he is now and then. And yet at his best, in organic rightness, beauty, and, above all, spontaneity, one must go among the very highest poetic names to match him." R. W. W.

PRINCIPAL WORKS: *Poetry*—Studies of Sensation and Event, 1843; Studies of Resemblance and Consent (included in 1879 edition of Studies of Sensation and Event). *Politics*—The Land Monopoly, 1849; The Condition of England Question (date unknown).

ABOUT: Jones, E. Studies of Sensation and Event (see biographical material by Sumner Jones and W. J. Linton to 1879 ed.); Rees, T. M. Ebenezer Jones: The Neglected Poet; Athenaeum 1878:368, 401, 466; Gentleman's Magazine 297:143 August 1904; Notes and Queries 4th series 5:154, 264.

JONES, ERNEST CHARLES (January 25, 1819-January 26, 1868), poet, and novelist, was born in Berlin, where his father, a major, was equerry to the Duke of Cumberland, for whom Jones was named. He was educated principally at the College of St. Michael, Luneberg. Before he was ten he had poems published in Germany. At eleven he ran away to join the Polish rebels, but was brought back. In 1838 his father returned to England, and Jones was presented at court and married an aristocratic lady named Atherley, who stayed by him through all his vicissitudes. He became a journalist, and in 1844 was called to the bar from Middle Temple, but did not practise at this time.

In 1846 Jones joined the Chartists (the extreme radicals of the time), and his entire career took a new turn. He was a remarkable orator, but his open advocacy of violence caused a split in the movement and left him largely isolated. In 1848 he was sentenced to two years' imprisonment for sedition; one of his books of poems is said to have been written in prison in his own blood. In 1852 he became editor of the Chartist *People's Paper,* and he was a frequent but unsuccessful candidate for Parliament. By 1854 he was the only Chartist lecturer remaining; the party was nearly dead, and Jones joined the new Radical Party in its most extreme faction. He began the practice of law, joined the northern circuit, and had some criminal practice. He stood for Parliament again as a Radical, and was almost sure of election when he died suddenly at Manchester. He was given a public funeral.

Jones was a man of great magnetism, and sincere and disinterested; he is said to have given up a fortune rather than relinquish his principles. His prose is sensational and extravagant, but his poems, especially his songs of labor, display great talent and a remarkable lyric gift.

PRINCIPAL WORKS: The Wood Spirit (novel) 1841; The Lass and the Lady (novel) 1855; The Battle Day and Other Poems, 1885; Songs of Democracy, 1856-57; Corayda and Other Poems, 1859.

ABOUT: London Times January 27 and 29, March 31, 1868.

JONES, HENRY ARTHUR (September 20, 1851-January 7, 1929), dramatist, was born at Grandborough, Buckinghamshire, eldest son of Silvanus Jones, farmer, and Elizabeth (Stephens) Jones. His only formal education was at the village school, and at the age of twelve he went to work for an uncle who kept a drapery shop at Ramsgate. He remained in trade till 1879, first as a shopman, and from 1869 as a commercial traveler. An assiduous reader in his spare time, he began writing plays in 1869, but these early attempts found no producer. In December 1878 he had his first production, the comedy *It's Only Round the Corner,* at the Theatre Royal, Exeter. In the following October his work reached the boards in London, where the actor-manager Wilson Barrett put on the comedietta, *A Clerical Error.* On November 16, 1882 he blazed into fame with *The Silver King,* the most celebrated melodrama of the day, which was again produced by Barrett and provided him with his most successful part. The play ran at the Princess' Theatre for 289 nights, and put Jones on a firm financial footing. Barrett and one Henry Herman had had some small share in the composition; and in course of time Barrett was fatuous enough to claim sole authorship; but Jones indignantly repudiated this exaggeration, and was finally vindicated by an arbitration board in 1905.

There now began a period of some thirty years of almost unbroken success, in which Jones worked in association with many of the leading producers and actors in England and America. In 1887 Herbert Tree appeared in *Hard Hit* at the Haymarket Theater; *The Middleman* (Shaftesbury Theater, 1889) began a long connection with E. S. Willard;

Judah (1890) and *The Dancing Girl* (1891) brought Jones to the height of popular favor, the latter play running for 310 nights at the Haymarket Theater with Tree in the chief rôle. *The Bauble Shop* (Criterion Theater, January 1893) was his first play under the management of Charles Wyndham. In the same year he entered fresh fields in *The Tempter*, a blank verse tragedy, which was put on at the Haymarket by Tree with Julia Neilson, Fred Terry, and Irene Vanbrugh in the cast, and with incidental music by Edward German. Jones' own view of this as one of his five best plays has not been endorsed by critical opinion.

Odd as it may appear after forty years, when this dramatist's social criticism seems mild enough, his next two plays caused acrimonious discussion. *The Triumph of the Philistines* (St. James's, May 11, 1895) offended the unco' guid by ironical treatment of the prudery of the day; and *Michael and His Lost Angel* (Lyceum, January 15, 1896) not only contained a church scene but showed a clergyman guilty of adultery. Even its title was by many considered blasphemous. Johnstone Forbes-Robertson vainly urged him to change it, and Mrs. Patrick Campbell threw up her part after seven weeks' rehearsals because of the offending scene in church.

In *The Liars* (1897) and *Mrs. Dane's Defence* (1900) Jones may be said to have reached the summit of his power as a dramatist, both evincing not only consummate stagecraft but considerable power of limning character in the round, shrewd social commentary, and living dialogue. *The Hypocrites* (produced by Charles Frohman at the Hudson Theater, New York, in 1906) and *The Lie* (played in New York in 1914 and at the New Theater, London, in October 1923), crowned a brilliant career.

Jones wrote many articles in periodicals, chiefly on the drama, which he approached as a high vocation; and fought hard but unsuccessfully to abolish the censorship of plays. He was a pugnacious controversialist, and in his later years never tired of attacking advanced views (especially as personified by Mr. Bernard Shaw and Mr. H. G. Wells) with vitriolic pen. However, *Patriotism and Popular Education* (1919) and *My Dear Wells* (1921) are heavily shot with war-prejudice, ill-tempered, and rather incoherent. From early sympathy with socialism, swayed by his friend Emery Walker and by William Morris, Jones underwent the political transmutation often experienced by successful men, and became an uncompromising Conservative. In religion he passed from agnosticism to a vague pantheism, which he expounded in 1925 in a popular newspaper symposium on *My Religion*.

Jones married, in 1875, Jane Eliza Seeley, daughter of a manufacturer of artificial flowers, who died in 1924, leaving three sons and four daughters. Jones himself died of pneumonia at his house in Kidderpore Avenue, Hampstead, on January 7, 1929, his will being proved at only £15,000, though in his time he had drawn some ten times that amount in royalties.

Jones has indubitable rights as a pioneer in the revival of the English drama after a period of decay lasting nearly a century. With A. W. Pinero he shares the honor of bringing thought and reality back to the stage; his dramatic construction was expert, and at his best he had a command of flexible and convincing dialogue. His friend Percy Allen rightly said of him in an obituary article that he was "always a shrewd observer rather than a deep philosopher" (*Fortnightly Review*, 1929). He lacked the nimble wit of a Wilde and the profound social sense of a Shaw, but he blazed a trail for such men to follow later. Harvard honored him with a degree in 1907 and he refused the insignia of the Legion of Honor offered by the French government.

H. B. G.

PRINCIPAL WORKS: *Plays*—A Clerical Error, 1879; The Silver King, 1882; The Middleman, 1889; Judah, 1890; Saints and Sinners, 1891; The Dancing Girl, 1891; The Bauble Shop, 1893; Michael and His Lost Angel, 1896; The Case of Rebellious Susan, 1897; The Tempter, 1898; The Masqueraders, 1899; The Triumph of the Philistines, 1899; Carnac Sahib, 1899; The Liars, 1904; Mrs. Dane's Defence, 1905; The Hypocrites, 1906; Dolly Reforming Herself, 1908; The Divine Gift, 1913; The Lie, 1915. *Miscellaneous* —The Renascence of the English Drama, 1895; The Foundations of a National Drama, 1913; The Theatre of Ideas, 1915; Patriotism and Popular Education, 1919; My Dear Wells, 1921; What is the State? 1924.

HENRY ARTHUR JONES

ABOUT: Cordell, R. A. Henry Arthur Jones and the Modern Drama; Howe, P. P. Dramatic Portraits; Jones, J. D. The Life and Letters of Henry Arthur Jones; Fortnightly Review 1929.

JONES, RICHARD (1790-January 26, 1855), economist, was born at Tunbridge Wells, the son of a solicitor. He was intended for the bar, but his health being poor, it was decided to make a clergyman of him! He was educated at Caius College, Cambridge, receiving his B.A. and M.A. both in 1816. He served as curate in Sussex and Kent. In 1823 he married Charlotte Altree. In 1833 he was appointed professor of political economy at King's College, London, and in 1835 succeeded the great Malthus as professor of political economy and history at the East India College, Haileybury. From 1836 to 1851 he was commissioner of the Tithe Commutation Act. He had resigned his professorial chair shortly before his death.

As an economist he was noted as an aggressive critic of the deductive method in political economy, but sometimes he misinterprets the statements of those he criticizes. His greatest contribution was his insistence on the inductive, scientific method of economic thought, and his tentative approach to the historical attitude.

PRINCIPAL WORKS: An Essay on the Distribution of Wealth, 1831; Collected Works, 1850; Text Book of Lectures on the Political Economy of Nations, 1852.

ABOUT: Jones, R. Collected Works (see Preface by W. Whewell).

JOWETT, BENJAMIN (April 15, 1817-October 1, 1893), scholar and divine, was born in Camberwell, Surrey, eldest son of the nine children of Benjamin and Isabella Langhorne Jowett. Benjamin Senior was of Yorkshire yeoman descent and unsuccessfully followed a variety of professions. His wife was the grandniece of John Langhorne the poet and translator of Plutarch. Young Benjamin, who was supposed to have inherited the poet's good looks, was a lively, precocious, delicate-looking child. His youth, though not enlivened by the pietism of the family, was apparently quite happy.

In 1829 Benjamin was admitted to St. Paul's school. It was a lonely boyhood, but he was happy in his studies and his father would take him to dine at places like the Cheshire Cheese and discuss the progress of his education. In 1835 he won the open scholarship for Balliol, Oxford, a "slightly built, curly-headed lad who seemed the last candidate likely to gain what was then considered the blue ribbon of scholarship." Straitened means made his first year at Oxford quite difficult, and the Hertford Scholarship for Latin, which he took in 1837, was as much a convenience as an honor.

BENJAMIN JOWETT

Jowett acquired a few friends and was warmly regarded by them, but, being too poor to entertain, he felt he could not much indulge his liking for company. An almost unprecedented honor was his election in 1838, while still an undergraduate, to a fellowship in his college. "Little Jowett was carried in triumph around the quadrangle." The young scholar was actually rather of medium stature, but his delicate complexion, small hands and feet and high-pitched voice gave an illusion of juvenility. He took his B.A. in 1839. In 1842 Jowett received his M.A. and was appointed to a tutorship at Balliol. He took orders and settled to his chosen vocation of teaching and study. During the long vacations he traveled on the Continent, where he met and consulted with distinguished European scholars.

Jowett began the study of Plato and with his friend Arthur P. Stanley planned an edition of the Epistles of St. Paul. His devotion to his pupils was something unique at Oxford. He visited Paris in the days of the Revolution and was not unaffected by the implications of what he saw. He had already begun a work on university reform when the movement swept Oxford which culminated in the Act of 1850, providing for the admission of dissenters to the Universities.

Jowett's translation of Thessalonians, Galatians, and Romans appeared in 1855. For presenting a new and disputed view of the language of the New Testament and for his prefatory essays which implied disagreement with the usual conclusions, Jowett was accused of heresy. When his appointment as regius professor of Greek was made known in the same year, Jowett had to subscribe anew to the Articles of Faith. The ringleader in this petty business was the Rev.

Charles Pourtales Golightly, whom some New-manite wit had surnamed "Agag." As regius professor, Jowett did not conform to the traditional mould. He continued his tutorial work and, instead of editing *scholia,* began a series of lectures on the *Republic* of Plato. Jowett recognized no distinction between professorial and tutorial teaching. He even helped undergraduates from other colleges.

The years between 1860 and 1870 were very active ones. Remembering his own privation as an undergraduate, he was anxious to lessen the expense of a college career. Through his efforts the rule that undergraduates must live within college walls was removed. Elected Master of Balliol in 1870, he concerned himself with students' living-quarters, sports and health. From 1882 to 1886 he was Vice-Chancellor of the university. His various activities during his term of office were of lasting benefit to Oxford, but the strain brought on a heart ailment from which he never fully recovered. He died at Headley Park near Oxford and was buried there at St. Sepulchre.

Jowett, the kindly and courageous Master of Balliol, was a great scholar, so devoted to the path he had chosen that he gave his life to making that path easier for others to follow. Bagehot said that Jowett in his essays "exhausted impending controversies years before they arrived" and saw "the conclusion to which the disputants would arrive long before the public issue was joined." Though, from the standpoint of the modern scholar, Jowett's knowledge of Greek is sometimes at fault, yet his translations of Plato and of Thucydides combine to an unusual degree that accuracy and perfection of style which still make them unique introductions to the study of the classics.   P. B. S.

PRINCIPAL WORKS: *Translations*—St. Paul's Epistles to the Thessalonians, Galatians, and Romans, 1855; The Dialogues of Plato, 1871; Thucydides, 1881; Aristotle's Politics, 1885. *Editions*—Plato's Republic (with Lewis Campbell) 1894. *Sermons*—College Sermons, 1895; Sermons Biographical, 1899; Sermons on Faith and Doctrine, 1901.
ABOUT: Abbott, E. & Campbell, L. The Life and Letters of Benjamin Jowett, M. A.; Swinburne, A. Studies in Prose and Poetry; Tollenmache, L. Benjamin Jowett.

JOYCE, PATRICK WESTON (1827-1914), Irish historian, was born in County Limerick, and educated at Trinity College, Dublin, being graduated in 1861, at the age of thirty-five. He held several positions under the National Education Commission, being for a long time a professor in the training school for teachers. He received an LL.D. degree from Dublin and was a member of the Royal Irish Academy. His brother, a physician, was long professor of English literature at the Roman Catholic University, and later lived and died in Boston. Patrick Joyce had some

interest in education, but his main preoccupation was with Irish history and the Gaelic language, translations from which he published. He also wrote two books on Irish music. He approached Irish antiquities in the scientific spirit, and his work displays both "scholarship and good sense."

PRINCIPAL WORKS: The Origin and History of Irish Names of Places, 1869; Irish Local Names Explained, 1870; Grammar of Irish, 1879; Short History of Ireland, 1895; Reading Book in Irish History, 1901; Social History of Ireland, 1903; The Story of Ancient Irish Civilization, 1907.

KAVANAGH, JULIA (1824-October 28, 1877), novelist, was born at Thurles. She was the only child of a would-be poet, novelist, and philologist, who when ridiculed by the critics claimed her work as his, and implied through a long controversy that she was the author of his own worst productions. Julia was taken to London as a small child, then to Paris, and returned to London in 1844. She was educated at home, and though it was necessary for her to earn her living by writing, most of her time was given to the care of her mother, an invalid for years, and she had only spare hours for her books. She started by contributing stories to magazines, then wrote books for children. Her success came with a series of novels once very popular. She was also the author of two biographical books, on women of France and on Christian women. After her mother's death she moved to Nice, where she died suddenly, unmarried, at fifty-three.

Miss Kavanagh's books were for the most part domestic in scene and pious in mood. However, she had a graceful style and much poetic feeling. None of her novels has survived to the present day.

PRINCIPAL WORKS: Madeleine, 1848; Nathalie, 1850; Daisy Burns, 1853; Grace Lee, 1855; Adele, 1858; Queen Mab, 1863; Bessie, 1872.
ABOUT: Academy November 10, 1877; Athenaeum November 17, 1877.

KAYE, SIR JOHN WILLIAM (1814-July 24, 1876), historian, was the son of a solicitor to the Bank of England. He was educated at Eton and at the Royal Military College, Addiscombe. In 1832 he went to India as a cadet in the Bengal Artillery. In 1839 he married Mary Catherine Puckle. He resigned from the army in 1841, but remained in India and founded the *Calcutta Review* in 1844. The next year he returned to England. In 1856 he entered the home civil service of the East India Company, and later became secretary of the political and secret department of the India Office. He was made Knight Commander of the Star of India in 1871. He retired in 1874 because of poor health, and died two years later. Besides his own histories, he edited numerous works on India by others. His history of the Sepoy War contained a criticism of one of the regiments in the Delhi Rebellion which gave rise to a long controversy, with bitter pamphlets on both sides. His books are written purely from the military point of view, but have been praised as "well ordered and comprehensive."

PRINCIPAL WORKS: Long Engagements (novel) 1841; History of the War in Afghanistan, 1851; History of the Sepoy War in India, 1864-76; Lives of Indian Officers, 1867; Essays of an Optimist, 1870.

ABOUT: Academy August 5, 1876; Athenaeum July 29, 1876.

KEARY, ANNIE (March 3, 1825-March 3, 1879), novelist, was born in Yorkshire, the daughter of a rector of Irish birth. She was a precocious, imaginative child, who told stories before she could write them. Her education was private. She wrote her first book of children's stories to entertain her brother's motherless children, who were in her care. Her brother remarried and took the children from her, and at the same time her engagement to marry was broken. The double blow affected her health, and in 1858 she went to Egypt to recuperate. A period of religious disturbance followed, until she found in writing an outlet for her sensitive, emotional nature. She wrote first a series of children's books, of which *Sidney Grey* was the most popular, and followed this by numerous novels for adults. She also wrote two historical works, which are useful if not original compilations. Poor health made her spend much time on the Riviera, but she died in England, at Eastbourne, on her fifty-fourth birthday.

Miss Keary's best novel is *A Doubting Heart*, which her father left unfinished. It was completed by Mrs. K. Macquoid. Her greatest success was *Castle Daly*, which she herself disliked; it has an Irish background, and she never saw Ireland except through her father's eyes, so that the book is rather a *tour de force*. Her novels in general are domestic, "Victorian," and obviously feminine; she was noted, however, for her impartial delineation of character.

PRINCIPAL WORKS: The Heroes of Asgard (with Eliza Keary) 1857; Early Egyptian History (anon.) 1861; Janet's Home, 1863; Oldbury, 1869; The Nations Around (history) 1870; Castle Daly, 1875; A Doubting Heart, 1879.

ABOUT: Keary, E. Memoir of Annie Keary.

KEATS, JOHN (October 31, 1795-February 23, 1821), poet, eldest child of Thomas Keats, livery-stable keeper and Frances (Jennings) Keats, was born at the Swan and Hoop Stables, Finsbury Pavement, in the City of London. (The official register shows October 31 as the date, but Keats himself always observed the 29th.) He was educated at the Rev. John Clarke's school at Enfield, where he made enduring friendships with Edward

Holmes, afterwards author of a *Life of Mozart*, and with Charles Cowden Clarke, son of the headmaster, and where he was a popular boy, generous but extremely pugnacious. In April 1804 his father was killed by a fall from a horse. The widow quickly remarried one William Rawlings, but a separation soon took place and Mrs. Rawlings went to Edmonton, to live with her mother, taking her sons, John, George, and Tom, and her daughter, Frances Mary (Fanny). In February 1810 she died of tuberculosis, and the children's financial affairs were put in the hands of two guardians, Rowland Sandell and Richard Abbey.

In very early youth Keats was not bookish, but at the age of fourteen or thereabouts he began to read deeply, and was especially attracted by Spenser and by Lemprière's *Classical Dictionary* and other works which set forth the myths of Greece and Rome. He knew Latin, but no Greek, and drew all his knowledge of Hellenic myth from works of reference. At the end of 1810 he was removed from school and apprenticed to a surgeon, Thomas Hammond, of Edmonton. In 1814 the indentures were cancelled by mutual consent, and Keats went to London, pursuing his studies at the joint school of St. Thomas's and Guy's Hospitals. In March 1816 he became a dresser at Guy's; in July he passed his examination as licentiate at Apothecaries' Hall; and for another year or so seems to have practised efficiently as a surgeon.

But it was poetry, not medicine, that he had most truly at heart; and it was the *Faerie Queene* that first aroused his poetic ardor. Some early lines, "Imitation of Spenser," were written at the age of seventeen or eighteen. While still at Edmonton he was writing verse; and in the summer of 1815, when not quite twenty, he produced what is now admitted to be one of the finest sonnets in English, "On First Looking into Chapman's Homer," which is known wherever the English language is spoken. It was his good friend Cowden Clarke who introduced him to Chapman's translation of Homer; and it was Clarke, too, who brought him into contact with a man who exerted great influence on his career, Leigh Hunt. Hunt was a poet and pamphleteer of talent, and was regarded as a pillar of the Liberal movement, above all after he had served two years' imprisonment for an alleged libel on the Prince Regent in his paper, *The Examiner*. He had a house in the Vale of Health, at Hampstead (then a beautiful country village outside London), and here, from the spring of 1816 onwards, Keats became so frequent a visitor that there was always a bed for him when he wished to stay. The friendship was an inspiration to the young poet, and procured him the society of established writers who were of Hunt's acquaintance. On the debit side, Hunt's habit of importing jarring colloquialisms into verse left some traces on Keats' style, and his political views, obnoxious as they were in Tory circles, drew down the contumely of Tory critics on both alike. It was in *The Examiner* of May 5, 1816, that Keats first appeared in print, with the sonnet, "O Solitude! if I must with thee dwell," which has more than a trace of eighteenth-century diction but is of the Romantic school in feeling.

At Hunt's house Keats met a number of men more or less prominent in the worlds of art and letters, and it is good testimony to his charm and capacity for friendship that all became deeply attached to him. From Shelley he kept somewhat aloof, out of inverted pride in his humble birth, but the other poet never ceased to cultivate him. Others whom he met in 1816 were John Hamilton Reynolds, a wit and minor versifier, James Rice, solicitor, Cornelius Webb, a now forgotten poet, and Benjamin Robert Haydon, the painter. He was the friend of many of the outstanding men of the day, and with Keats he immediately struck up a strong friendship, which was only clouded later on by Haydon's slackness in repaying borrowed money. Another friend, not of this group, was the young artist, Joseph Severn, who became his closest intimate in the last few months of his life.

Sir Sidney Colvin (on p. 46 of his book) thus describes Keats at this time: " 'The character and expression of his features,' it is said, 'would arrest even the casual passenger in the street.' A small, handsome, ardent-looking youth—the stature little over five feet: the figure compact and well-turned, with the neck thrust eagerly forward, carrying a strong and shapely head set off by thickly clustering gold-brown hair: the features powerful, finished and mobile: the mouth rich and wide, with an expression at once combative and sensitive in the extreme: the forehead not high, but broad and strong: the eyebrows nobly arched, and eyes hazel-brown, liquid-flashing, visibly inspired—'an eye that had an inward look, perfectly divine, like a Delphian priestess who saw visions'. . ."

Early in 1817 the Ollier brothers published Keats first volume of *Poems,* in which the *pièce de résistance* was the magnificent "Chapman's Homer" sonnet aforementioned. For the rest, there were echoes of Spenser and Chapman, and, not unnaturally, of Leigh Hunt, in the diction; while in substance the volume showed a true poet, looking direct at nature with seeing eyes, bemused almost to enchantment by classic myths, and a forthright rebel against eighteenth-century conventions—expressing that rebellion with ardor in "Sleep and Poetry." The book fell quite flat.

On April 14 Keats gave up surgery and retired to the Isle of Wight to work in quiet and seclusion.

At Carisbrooke he began the long poem "Endymion," on the loves of the goddess Selene and the shepherd-lad. In May he moved to Margate; thence, with his brother Tom, to Canterbury; and in the summer to Well Walk, Hampstead, where he took lodgings with George and Tom. He was living at this time largely on advances from the publishers, Taylor and Hessey, since a good deal of the capital due to him had been eaten up during his final student years. He now met Charles Wentworth Dilke and Charles Armitage Brown, who lived side by side in John Street, Hampstead (now Keats Grove) in semi-detached houses named Wentworth Place (now the Keats Memorial house). Brown had a small private income and was interested in literature. "Endymion" progressed somewhat haltingly, with dampening criticism from Hunt, but it was finished at Burford Bridge, Surrey, in November 1817, and published in April 1818. It was a long poem, in four books, in the heroic couplet, not written in the eighteenth-century manner, but with the sense mainly running on from line to line and not ending with the couplet. His own preface warned the reader that he "must soon perceive great inexperience, immaturity, and every error denoting a feverish attempt, rather than a deed accomplished." This says the worst that later criticism has resumed; yet for all its frequent lusciousness and archaisms, its lack of form, and its mixture of other and irrelevant myths with the main story, it has a rich texture and contains beautiful lyric passages.

Meanwhile, in December 1817, Keats had met Wordsworth and Lamb, at a supper-party given by Haydon. The next March he joined George and Tom at Teignmouth. In June he and Brown, after seeing George off to America at Liverpool, made a walking-tour in the Lake District and Scotland; and over-exertion on this expedition seems to have first brought to light symptoms of the tuberculosis which was dormant in his blood. In August he was scurrilously attacked in *Blackwood's Magazine* and the *Quarterly Review* as a "Cockney." In December his brother Tom, after long ailing, at last died. At Brown's invitation Keats moved into his house and it was there, during the spring, that he produced three of his best odes, "To Psyche," "To a Nightingale," and "On a Grecian Urn" —the last being among the supremely great short poems in English. It was there, too, that he fell in love with Fanny Brawne, who, with her widowed mother, had occupied Dilke's house during the previous summer, and now lived in the adjacent Downshire disease, Keats was in misery. On September 18 he sailed for Naples with Joseph Severn, who was going to study in Rome. During a landing on the Dorset coast, made possible by contrary winds, he composed the last of his exquisite sonnets, "Bright star, would I were stedfast as thou art." Refusing two invitations from Shelley to go to Pisa, Keats took lodgings with Severn in Rome. Successive hemorrhages and fever soon followed; and on February 23, 1821, he died in the arms of Severn, who had nobly and assiduously nursed him. He was buried in the Protestant cemetery, Rome, and his own bitter epitaph on the tombstone that bears no name was: "Here lies one whose name was writ in water."

In the whole line of British poets none was so truly and utterly a dedicated spirit as Keats. His own words, "I have loved the principle of beauty in all things," strike the keynote; yet this preoccupation with aesthetic values by no means connoted any effeminacy. Keats was not killed (as Shelley's "Adonais" and a passage in Byron's "Don Juan" might lead one to believe) by the vile stabs of reviewers but by a more deadly enemy, tuberculosis. He was not a precious weakling, but a manly, noble, generous and sympathetic nature, as is attested by the number and variety of his friendships. His weaker side came out in his dealings with Fanny Brawne; yet here the full difficulty of the relationship will never be known, in the absence of more precise data as to Fanny's character.

In poetry he is the incarnation of the romantic spirit, bodying forth all its virtues and all its faults. His outlook on nature was fresh and untrammelled by convention; his observation was keen; despite his lack of Greek he got very near to the Greek spirit; and his language at its best attained to the very summit of nobility and fitness. Phrase after phrase lingers in the consciousness of the English-speaking races: "deep-brow'd Homer"; "a thing of beauty is a joy for ever"; "season of mists and mellow fruitfulness"; "heard melodies are sweet, but those unheard are sweeter"; and a hundred others. Keats could indulge in bad word-coinages, over-luxurious particularity, even long passages of boring irrelevance. But in lyrics like "La Belle Dame Sans Merci," and in the Odes and the Sonnets, he made a contribution to English poetry that is pure gold. H. B. G.

JOHN KEATS

Hill. Keats' love for this lady became a tormenting and devastating passion. Her personality does not clearly emerge, but it is plain that she was not sensitive or mature enough to appraise Keats at his true worth, and that all through their engagement (which shortly followed) she caused him great heartburning and jealousy.

Financial difficulties were now added to the cares of ill-health and the pangs of love. In July 1819 he went to Shanklin, on money borrowed from Brown. The two began the blank-verse tragedy, "Otho the Great" and Keats worked independently on "Lamia" and "Hyperion" (which last he had begun the previous winter). Moving to Winchester, he revised "The Eve of St. Agnes" (begun in January), finished "Lamia" and wrote another splendid ode, "To Autumn."

In October he went to London, determined to find journalistic work; but within a few days he was back at Wentworth Place. The Brawnes now lived in the next-door house and this propinquity naturally fed the flame. "Otho" failed to find a producer; Keats began a satirical fairy poem, "Cap and Bells," and set himself to remodel "Hyperion" as a vision. On February 3, 1820, he returned from London on the outside of the coach and came in feverish and very ill. As he got into bed he coughed up blood: his medical knowledge told him that it was arterial blood, and he said to Brown: "that drop of blood is my death-warrant; I must die." Nursed by Brown and visited by Fanny, he rallied sufficiently to get about in the spring, and to see through the press in July his third volume, *Lamia, Isabella, The Eve of St. Agnes, and Other Poems.* It had some measure of success; but between love and the rapid progress of

PRINCIPAL WORKS: *Important Collected Editions* —The Poetical Works (ed. with Memoir by Lord Houghton) 1854; The Poems (2 vols., ed. by Lord Houghton with Memoir by J. G. Speed) 1883; The Complete Works (5 vols., ed. with textual notes and bibliography by H. B. Forman) 1900-01; Poems (ed. by E. de Selincourt) 1905; The Poetical Works (ed. by H. B. Forman) 1906; Poems and Verses (2 vols., ed. by J. M. Murry.) 1930. *Poems*—Poems,

1817; Endymion: A Poetic Romance, 1818; Lamia, Isabella, The Eve of St. Agnes, and Other Poems, 1820. *Letters*—The Letters (ed. by M. B. Forman) 1931 (rev. and enl., 1935).

ABOUT: Arnold, M. Essays in Criticism; Blunden, E. Shelley and Keats as They Struck Their Contemporaries; Bridges, R. Collected Essays, Papers, etc. (Vol. 4); Colvin, S. Keats; Fausset, H. I'A. Keats: A Study in Development; Garrod, H. W. Keats; Hancock, A. E. John Keats: A Literary Biography; Haydon, B. R. Life; Hunt, J. H. L. Autobiography; Keats, J. Life, Letters and Literary Remains (ed. by Lord Houghton); The John Keats Memorial Volume (ed. by G. C. Williamson); Lowell, A. John Keats; Murry, J. M. Keats and Shakespeare; Murry, J. M. Studies in Keats; Owen, F. M. John Keats: A Study; Ridley, M. R. Keats's Craftsmanship: A Study in Poetic Development; Rossetti, W. M. Life of John Keats; Swinburne, A. C. Miscellanies.

KEBLE, JOHN (April 25, 1792-March 29, 1866), poet, divine, and essayist, was born at Fairford, the second child of the Rev. John and Sarah Maule Keble.

John and his brother Thomas were educated at home by their father, a former fellow of Corpus Christi. The thoroughness of their training is attested by their winning scholarships to Corpus Christi, Oxford, to which John was elected in December 1806. He took double first-class honors in 1811, a degree taken only once before (by Sir Robert Peel). Among his friends at Oxford were Thomas Arnold and Sir John Taylor Coleridge. He was elected fellow of Oriel and in 1812 took prizes for both English and Latin essays. The fellowship was significant, because Oriel was, in those years, the intellectual and spiritual heart of Oxford and Keble's associates there included John Henry Newman, Richard Whateley, Edward Copleston, and Edward Pusey. Keble was thrown into the center of the ferment. He served in several connections, was college tutor (1818) and public examiner (1821-23), all the while having private pupils. The younger men at Oxford already spoke of him in awed tones. Here he wrote the poems of *The Christian Year* (1819-23), intending to keep them for his lifetime. But Arnold and others urged publication, and to please his father, he consented, though the volumes were anonymous.

His mother's death in 1823 led him to resign and return to Fairford to his father. He had taken orders in 1816. Now he held three small livings and took pupils, among them Richard Hurrell Froude, Robert Wilberforce, and Isaac Williams.

Keble's quiet godliness and poetry had already established him in the high regard of Oxford men, and he was now sought repeatedly for various appointments, from curacies to an archdeaconate. He refused all to remain with his father, but served, 1826-27, at Hursley. In 1827 he withdrew his name from the contest for Oriel's provostship. In 1830-32 he served as examiner for the India

JOHN KEBLE

House examinations for civil service. 1831-41 was his term as Professor of Poetry at Oxford, a position of influence in which he greatly distinguished himself.

Following his father's death, Keble married (1835) Charlotte Clarke, whose sister had married his brother Thomas. He accepted the living of Hursley and there made his home to the end. Elizabeth, his invalid sister, shared the home part of each year, till her death in 1860. The failing health of his wife drove them to Cornwall and the south coast for a time and Keble had an attack of paralysis in 1864. His death was followed six weeks later by his wife's, and both are buried in Hursley churchyard.

Keble's significance as theologian and poet was appreciated by his contemporaries, and two memorials were set up. A bust by Thomas Woolner was placed in the Abbey, and in 1869 Keble College was opened at Oxford. This was dedicated to principles for which Keble had stood, and was established on the land which he had procured in 1854 for a "poor man's college."

Keble was shy, quiet, saintly, motivated by a strong sense of duty, personally unambitious, and yet the "primary author" of the great Oxford Movement. Unaffected, devout, and retiring, he was able to set in motion one of the century's most active forces. As preacher he was not so great as might be expected; his voice scarcely filled St. Mary's, Oxford, and yet his assize sermon, July 14, 1833, on "National Apostasy" was called by Newman the beginning of the Oxford Movement. High-church, sincere, able to work with all kinds of people, he was deeply grieved by Newman's conversion to the Roman Catholic church.

The Christian Year was immensely successful; Arnold said there was "nothing equal" to it in English, and Newman considered it "one of the classics of the language." Its simplicity of expression, its piety, its use of natural scenery, and its quiet faith were all conspicuous. Wordsworth is reputed to have volunteered to go over it for "bad English" with Keble! Some of the best known poems of the series are "New EveryMorning," "Sun of My Soul," and "Red o'er the forest peers the setting sun." None of his subsequent poetry achieves the same high level. The income from this and from *Lyra Innocentium* Keble gave toward the restoration of Hursley Church. Keble's literary work includes translations for Pusey's *Library of the Fathers*, seven *Tracts for the Times*, sermons, some controversial pamphlets, an edition of the *Remains* of R. Hurrell Froude, his former pupil, the Latin lectures on poetry, and some critical essays in English.

Keble's life and poetry resemble more closely those of George Herbert than of any one else; W. E. Gladstone's "sweet singer of Israel" was a fitting epithet for Keble. To religious poetry his relation corresponds to that of Wordsworth to poetry in general, for Keble "has shown what many were beginning to doubt, that poetry is a requirement, or at all events a high enjoyment of, the religious mind; . . .and that it is limited to no class of feelings, or language, or doctrines."

The poetry professorship produced some stimulating criticism, only recently translated, and shows Keble the inheritor of the Wordsworth tradition. "The indirect expression in words, most appropriately metrical words, of some overpowering emotion or ruling taste or feeling, the direct indulgence of which is somehow repressed," is poetry, said Keble.

Keble's prose is less important than his verse. His life of Thomas Wilson occupied him for years, but it is not a great monument. He is a more successful essayist and critic showing real fire and maintaining a high stylistic quality always.   D. F. A.

PRINCIPAL WORKS: *Poetry*—Christian Year, 1827; Psalter in English Verse, 1840; Lyra Innocentium, 1846; Child's Christian Year, 1857; Miscellaneous Poems, 1869. *Sermons and Miscellaneous*—Pamphlet in Defence of W. G. Ward, 1844; Sermons Academical and Occasional, 1848; Pastoral Tracts, 1850; An Argument Against Repealing the Laws Which Treat the Nuptial Bond as Indissoluble, 1857; On Eucharistical Adoration, 1857; The Life of Thomas Wilson, 1863; Pentecostal Year, 1864; A Litany of Our Lord's Warnings, 1864; Catholic Subscription to the XXXIX Articles, 1865; Sermons Occasional and Parochial, 1868; The State and Its Relations With the Church, 1869; Letters of Spiritual Counsel and Guidance (ed. by R. F. Wilson) 1870; Sermons for the Christian Year, 1875-80; Occasional Papers and Reviews, 1877; Studia Sacra, 1877; Sermons, 1880; Outlines of Instructions, 1880. *Essays on Literature*

—Sacred Poetry, 1825; De Poeticae vi Medicâ: Praelectiones Academicae Oxonii Habitæ, 1844.

ABOUT: Coleridge, J. T. Memoir of John Keble; Donaldson, A. B. Five Great Oxford Leaders; Gladstone, W. E. A. Chapter of Autobiography; Lock, W. John Keble; Mozley, T. Reminiscences of Oriel College and the Oxford Movement; Newman, J. H. Apologia Pro Vita Sua; Paul C. K. Biographical Sketches; Price, C. Leading Ideas of Keble's *Christian Year*; Shairp, J. C. Studies in Poetry and Philosophy; Wood, E. John Keble; Younge, J. Keble's Parishes.

KEBLE, THOMAS (October 25, 1793-September 5, 1875), theologian, was the younger brother of John Keble, the celebrated poet and one of the founders of the Oxford (Puseyite) Movement which rent the Church of England in the mid-nineteenth century. He was born in Fairford, where his father was vicar, and with his brother was educated entirely by his father until in 1808, at only fourteen, he won a scholarship to Corpus Christi College, Oxford. He received his B.A. in 1811, and was ordained deacon in 1816 and priest in 1817. After a curacy in Gloucestershire he was made college tutor of Corpus Christi in 1819. In 1820 he became probationary fellow of the college and also shared two curacies with his brother. In 1825 he married Elizabeth Jane Clarke; he had one son. By 1827 Keble was vicar of the poor, scattered parish of Bisley, Gloucestershire, which he built up by constant and devoted labor. He was one of the first clergymen in England to institute a daily service in his church. He threw himself into the Oxford Movement, and wrote four of its famous *Tracts for the Times* and forty-eight of its *Plain Sermons*. He also translated the writings of St. John Chrysostom from the Greek. His health, however, was too poor and he was too overworked by his clerical duties to have much strength or time for writing, although his brother and his brother's associates valued his judgment highly and frequently asked him for advice. When he died his son succeeded him as vicar.

PRINCIPAL WORKS: Considerations on the Athanasian Creed, 1872.
ABOUT: Coleridge. Memoir of John Keble.

KEIGHTLEY, THOMAS (October 1789-November 4, 1872), Irish miscellaneous writer, was born in County Kildare and educated at Trinity College, Dublin, but left college without a degree because of ill health, which compelled him to give up his intention of studying law. He went to London in 1824 and engaged in journalism and general literary work. He helped Thomas Crofton Croker to compile his *Fairy Legends of South Ireland,* he wrote historical manuals for popular education, he edited the Latin classics, and also essayed to edit Shakespeare and Milton, though in this last instance his emendations were rash and unscholarly. He spent much time in Italy, and during the last years of his life was the recipient of a pension in the civil service list.

Keightley's best known book is his history of England, which was openly based on that of Lingard, but was intended to counteract Lingard's Roman Catholic bias. His books on Milton and Shakespeare have been called "succinct and useful compilations," but they were not original. He was a good linguist, and something of a student, but absurdly and almost insanely conceited. He claimed, for example, that his history of Rome was the best ever written in any language!

PRINCIPAL WORKS: Fairy Mythology (anon.) 1928; Outlines of History, 1829; Mythology of Ancient Greece and Italy, 1831; Tales and Popular Fictions, 1834; History of Greece, 1835; History of Rome, 1836; History of England, 1837-39; Account of the Life, Opinions, and Writings of John Milton, 1855; Shakespeare Expositor, 1867.

ABOUT: London Times November 7, 1872.

KELVIN, LORD (William Thomson, First Baron Kelvin of Largs) (June 26, 1824-December 17, 1907), Irish scientist, was born at Belfast, where his father was a professor of mathematics. His mother died when he was six, and his father was his only teacher; he never went to a school. Incredible as it seems, he entered the University of Glasgow, where his father was now professor, before he was ten! In 1841, after a brilliant career, he left without a degree and entered Peterhouse College, Cambridge, where in 1845 he was graduated as second wrangler (second highest in mathematics). His heroes at the time were Michael Faraday, the great physicist, and Charles Fourier, the French Utopian Socialist; accordingly he first visited Faraday at the Royal Institution, and then went to the University of Paris. He returned to Peterhouse as fellow and junior mathematical lecturer, but in 1846 was made professor of natural philosophy at Glasgow, when he was only twenty-two. By 1850 he had published over fifty original mathematical papers, several in French.

Thomson remained at Glasgow until 1899, an inspiring teacher who gathered around him a group of budding physicists. His first work was in thermodynamics, from which he went to research in electricity. In the end, he was the most famous mathematician and physicist of his time. He was made a Fellow of the Royal Society in 1851, and was its president from 1890 to 1894. In 1852 he married his second cousin, Margaret Crum; the marriage was most happy, but she was always a semi-invalid, and they spent much time in the south of Europe for her health. In 1866, after his successful superintendence of laying the first Atlantic cable, he was knighted. In 1871 he was president of the British Association for the Advancement of Science, and from this time on honors flowed in upon him. He was an inventor as well as a pure scientist, and founded the firm of Kelvin and White to exploit his inventions. In 1884 he visited the United States and lectured at Johns Hopkins. In 1892 he was raised to the peerage as the first baron of Largs, and in 1902 was given the Order of Merit and made Privy Councillor. In 1904 he became chancellor of the University of Glasgow. In September, 1907, his wife suffered a paralytic stroke. The shock induced an illness which proved fatal, and he died in December at his home, Largs, Ayrshire. He was buried in Westminster Abbey.

Kelvin's writing, though technical and profound, is clear and able. It is all on physical and mathematical subjects.

PRINCIPAL WORKS: Electrostatics and Magnetism, 1874; Mathematical and Physical Papers, 1882-1911; Molecular Dynamics and the Wave Theory of Light, 1904.

ABOUT: Casson, H. N. Kelvin; Crowther, J. G. Men of Science; Thompson, S. P. Life of Lord Kelvin.

KEMBLE, FRANCES ANNE (FANNY) (November 27, 1809-January 15, 1893), actress, poet, dramatist, and memoir writer, was born in London of the famous Kemble family, nearly all of whom were distinguished actors and actresses. Her father was Charles Kemble, her aunt Mrs. Siddons. She was educated privately in France, and made her first appearance in 1829, at twenty, as Juliet, with a cast made up of her own relatives. She was an enormous success, and after a brilliant tour of England went in 1833 to America. There, the next year, she married Pierce Butler, a Georgia planter. They were divorced in 1848, and he died in 1867. In 1847 she returned to the stage in England, resuming her maiden name in 1849. She then returned to America, again retired from the stage, and lived in Lenox, Massachusetts. In 1868 she emerged from her retirement to appear as a reader, mostly of her own plays, in New York. In 1873 she went to live near Philadelphia. In 1877 she returned permanently to England, and died in London at eighty-three.

Fanny Kemble, as she was usually known, was the special favorite of many of the most eminent men of her day. She was sparkling, vivacious, a bit boisterous—all of which characteristics of the actress and the woman appear in the writer. Her plays were not very successful, and her verses were negligible; as an author she lives by reason of her autobiographical books. These are animated and vivid in style, and make absorbing reading; but as she was most indiscreet and never hesitated to say frankly what she thought of people and causes, she offended many and was constantly in hot water because of her entire lack of diplomacy.

PRINCIPAL WORKS: Poems, 1844; Plays, 1863; Record of Girlhood, 1878; Records of Later Life, 1882; Far Away and Long Ago, 1809; Further Records, 1891.

ABOUT: Autobiographical works.

KEMBLE, JOHN MITCHELL (April 2, 1807-March 26, 1857), historian and philologist, was the son of Charles Kemble, the actor, nephew of Mrs. Siddons, and brother of Fanny Kemble. He was almost the only member of his family who never went on the stage. From childhood he was interested in philology (and also in chemistry). After leaving Grammar School at Bury St. Edmunds, he went in 1826 to Trinity College, Cambridge, where Tennyson was a classmate. Because of his refusal to follow college rules he did not receive his B.A. until 1830, having meanwhile studied briefly at the Inner Temple, at Heidelberg, and at Munich. In 1833 he took his M.A. and contemplated taking holy orders; then suddenly he joined an expedition to assist the Spanish rebels, went to Gibraltar for that purpose, and on the failure of the expedition returned to London in 1831. The next year found him at Göttingen, still brilliant, still rebellious, and still disappointing to his hopeful family.

Finally, in 1833, his translation of the Anglo-Saxon epic *Beowulf* established his reputation. He lectured at Cambridge, on his own responsibility, on Anglo-Saxon, and from 1835 to 1844 edited the *British and Foreign Review*. In 1836 he married Nathalie Wendt, daughter of a Göttingen professor. The marriage proved unhappy, and for the last ten years of his life he lived away from his wife, two daughters, and son. In 1840 he succeeded his father as examiner of plays, but made nothing from his philological studies, and was obliged in 1847 to advertise for private pupils. Most of his time was spent in Hanover, while a friend carried on his duties as examiner. In 1854 he began to be interested in prehistoric archaeology, and he died suddenly in Dublin, of pneumonia, while he was on an archaeological trip.

Kemble had a good critical faculty, a fine memory, and a vigorous mind. His work was careful and detailed, but he was rather given to exaggerated claims. He was best in Teutonic philology.

PRINCIPAL WORKS: The Poems of Beowulf, 1833; The Saxons in England, 1849; Horae Ferales, 1857.

ABOUT: Kemble, F. A. Record of Girlhood; Records of Later Life; Fraser's Magazine May 1857.

KENDALL, HENRY CLARENCE (April 18, 1841-August 1, 1882), Australian poet, was born in New South Wales. His grandfather had been a missionary, his father was a ne'er-do-well who with his family led a roving life all over Australia. Kendall had very little formal education, but he read poetry omnivorously and he learned to love the Australian bush with passion. In 1860 he became clerk to a Sydney lawyer, J. L. Michael, who had literary interests and encouraged his writing. In 1862 he sent some verses to the *Athenaeum*, and their acceptance encouraged him to print a volume privately. However, he withdrew the book soon after, being convinced of its immaturity.

In 1863 he became clerk in the lands department of the New South Wales government, then was transferred to the colonial secretary's office. In 1867 he married Charlotte Rutter, daughter of a physician; they had five children. Two years later he suddenly resigned his post and went to Melbourne to engage in journalism. He managed to get by through correspondence and hack writing, but never escaped from actual poverty. In 1870 his name became known all over the colony through his words for a highly successful cantata, *Euterpe;* this success, however, was not repeated. By 1873 his health had become so poor that he could no longer keep up the support of his family by free-lance writing. Accordingly he returned to New South Wales, and after some effort secured work as a clerk for a business firm. Finally, only shortly before his death, influence was brought to bear and he was made inspector of forests. But it was too late; he died at only forty-two, leaving his family destitute. A subscription raised for his widow netted £1,200. Kendall died near Sydney, where a monument was erected to his memory later.

Kendall is known as the "poet of the bush." No Australian writer has a keener feeling for the beauties of nature in his native land or a more ardent patriotism. His poems are marked by aesthetic feeling and passionate sympathy. He wrote much light verse besides, which is not nearly so well done as his more serious poems.

PRINCIPAL WORKS: Leaves From an Australian Forest, 1869; Songs From the Mountains, 1880; Collected Poems, 1886.

ABOUT: Kendall, H. C. Collected Poems (see Prefatory Memoir); Sladen, D. B. W. Australian Poets.

KENNEDY, CHARLES RANN (1808-December 17, 1867), poet and classicist, was the son of a poet and schoolmaster. He was educated at Shrewsbury Grammar School, at King Edwards VI's School at Birmingham, and at Trinity College, Cambridge, where he won several scholarships and numerous prizes for poetry. He received his B.A. in 1831 as senior classic, was made a fellow, and secured his M.A. in 1834. Instead of devoting himself to literature, however, he read law at Lincoln's Inn and was called to the bar in 1835. In 1849 he became professor of law at Queen's College, Birmingham. His legal career was a series of controversies, including one over the circuit in which he might practise, and another with a client over a disputed fee. Though he wrote many legal works, he was happiest as translator of Demosthenes and Virgil, as a scholar, and as a linguist. The American dramatist, Charles Rann Kennedy, who was English-born, was his grandson.

PRINCIPAL WORKS: Poems: Original and Translated, 1843; Works of Demosthenes Translated, 1848; Specimens of Greek and Latin Verse, 1853; Hannibal: A Poem, 1866.

ABOUT: Gentleman's Magazine 681:255.

KENNEDY, PATRICK (January 1801-March 28, 1873), Irish story writer and antiquary, was born in Wexford of a peasant family. Through the charity of the wealthy Carews he received a fair education, and in 1823 was assistant in a training school in Dublin. Later he established a book store and circulating library in the same city, which remained his means of livelihood for the rest of his life. As a lifelong student of Irish mythology and antiquities, he contributed regularly to the *Dublin University Magazine* and the *Dublin Review*. Kennedy was an amiable, kindly man, but excessively and even morbidly shy. He never married. His stories have vigor and much humor, but are written with no fidelity to Irish speech, and are marred by their author's slavish imitation of "proper" English style.

PRINCIPAL WORKS: Legendary Fictions of the Irish Celts, 1866; Banks of the Boro, 1867; Evenings in the Duffrey, 1869; The Bardic Stories of Ireland, 1871.

ABOUT: Dublin University Magazine: Vol. 81.

KEPPEL, GEORGE THOMAS. See ALBERMARLE, LORD

KINGLAKE, ALEXANDER WILLIAM (August 5, 1809-January 2, 1891), traveler, historian, barrister, and member of Parliament, was the eldest son of Mary (Woodforde) and William Kinglake, a well-to-do banker and solicitor of Taunton in Somerset.

Educated at Eton and Trinity College, Cambridge, he did not distinguish himself scholastically but took the degrees of B.A. and M.A. in 1832 and 1836 respectively. At Cambridge Kinglake was the contemporary of Thackeray, Tennyson, and many other men of literary note. Richard B. Ince says: "Kinglake, who was the equal of the greatest of these in literary power should have shone in their society. But he did not. The mutual admiration by which literary coteries subsist chilled him." Kinglake was a wit, a cynic, and an agnostic.

Kinglake wanted a career in the army, but his weak eyes made that profession impossible. Consequently he entered Lincoln's Inn and was called to the bar in 1837.

About 1835 he had made a tour of the Near East. and in 1844 he published an account of his tour, *Eothen: or, Traces of Travel Brought Home From the East.* In the preface to this book the author says that he had written the book twice before but it had not satisfied him. *Eothen* is one of the great classics in the field of travel narratives. Some critics have called it the greatest in the English language. In its witty recording of personal impressions it somewhat resembles Sterne's *Sentimental Journey.*

Although a barrister, Kinglake did not devote a great deal of his life to the profession. In 1845 he accompanied the flying column of St. Arnaud in Algiers and later he went to the Crimea and witnessed the battle of the Alma (September 20, 1854). There he met Lord Raglan and dined with him on the evening after the battle. After Lord Raglan's death, Kinglake undertook to write the history of *The Invasion of the Crimea* at Lady Raglan's request.

This work was so much to his liking that he devoted the next thirty-one years to it, publishing eight volumes between 1863 and 1887. This monumental work, though somewhat prejudiced by personal likes and dislikes of certain important figures, was most carefully checked by inquiry into every detail possible by the author. Having always been fascinated by works of a military nature, Kinglake expended more time and care upon this history than the subject may seem to warrant to modern readers.

Kinglake's only other published works were a few articles published in periodicals of the day. He requested his executor to destroy any manuscripts which might be found among his papers. His passion for perfection gave

ALEXANDER WILLIAM KINGLAKE

the world of letters one masterpiece, but may have deprived it of considerable excellent entertainment.

In 1857 Kinglake was elected to Parliament on the liberal ticket and remained an M.P. until 1868. A weak voice prevented his becoming an important debater in the House, but he was active in defending those whom he felt to be oppressed.　　　　　D. C.

PRINCIPAL WORKS: *Travel*—Eothen: or, Traces of Travel Brought Home From the East, 1844. *History*—The Invasion of Crimea, 1863-87.

ABOUT: Abraham H. Mr. Kinglake and the Quarterleys; Ince, R. B. Calverley and Some Cambridge Wits of the 19th Century.

KINGSFORD, WILLIAM (December 23, 1819-September 28, 1898), Canadian historian, was born in London and educated at a private school in Camberwell. He was articled to an architect, but in 1836 left his employment and enlisted in the First Dragoon Guards. He came with his regiment to Canada the next year, and was made a sergeant. In spite of the offer of a commission he took his discharge, and in 1841 entered the office of the city surveyor of Montreal. There he qualified as a civil engineer, his profession for the next thirty-eight years, except for two years as publisher of the *Montreal Times*.

Kingsford worked as an engineer on the Hudson River Railroad in New York, on the Panama Isthmus Railroad, and particularly on the Grand Trunk Railroad, then building its trans-Canadian lines. In 1848 he married Margaret Lindsay, daughter of the clerk of the Legislative Assembly of Canada. In 1855 for a few months he was chief engineer of Toronto. From 1865 to 1867 he returned to England and worked as an engineer, but soon came back to Canada permanently. In 1873 he was the government's chief engineer in charge of harbors of the Great Lakes and St. Lawrence. In 1879 his office was suddenly and unfairly abolished, and he was able to secure no redress.

Kingsford was then sixty. Nothing daunted, he abandoned his profession and began a new career as historian of Canada. Previously he had published nothing. He labored indefatigably and completed his history just before his death. His work won recognition and he received an honorary LL.D. from two Canadian universities and in 1866 was made a Fellow of the Royal Society of Canada. He died in Toronto at nearly seventy-nine. His history, though dull, is full, fair, and painstaking, and still has merit and standing.

PRINCIPAL WORKS: Canadian Archaeology, 1886; History of Canada (10 vol.) 1887-98.

ABOUTS Canadian Magazine January 1899; Proceedings of the Royal Society of Canada

KINGSLEY, CHARLES (June 12, 1819-January 23, 1875), novelist and poet, was born at Holne Vicarage, Dartmoor, Devon, the eldest and most famous of three author sons of the Rev. Charles Kingsley, the others being George Henry and Henry. (His own daughter, MARY ST. LEGER KINGSLEY HARRISON, also became known later as a novelist under the pseudonym of "Lucas Malet.")

Charles was a precocious child, but never showed a great fondness for formal studies. He was sent to school first at Clifton and later to the grammar school at Helston, Cornwall. He entered King's College, London, at the age of seventeen, his father having become rector of a London church. But Charles disliked the city and two years later entered Magdalen College, Cambridge.

At Cambridge he was well liked by his fellow students but was not so popular with the faculty. He led a pleasant life with plenty of distraction in the form of boating, boxing, and fishing—particularly the last. He managed to secure a scholarship in his second year, but failed to receive a fellowship.

During the summer vacation of 1839 young Kingsley met Fanny Grenfell and fell in love with her. The affair was opposed by her family. Kingsley's life at Cambridge was considered rather dissipated and his prospects were not very brilliant. For a year the young couple were not permitted to correspond. But they were devoted to each other and eventually they were married. This emotional disturbance had, however, profoundly affected Kingsley. From moods of black despair he sought relief in wild dissipations after which he would suffer violent remorse and self-reproach. Thus at first hand Kingsley acquired knowledge of, and sympathy for, human frailty.

At about this time too, Kingsley became a disciple of the religious and social philosophies of Carlyle and Frederick D. Maurice. Maurice was the leader of the Christian Socialist movement which advocated the application of Christ's ethics to social and political action. While all Christendom pays lip service to these principles, any man who seriously advocates their application in fact is pretty certain to suffer denunciation as a dangerous radical. Thus Kingsley became known as a radical in spite of his deep respect for the established social order. He advocated improved living conditions for the laboring classes, both rural and industrial, but he sought to bring this about without political upheaval, by the simple process of getting all men to live by the Golden Rule.

He was not, however, the fatuous idealist which this may make him seem. In 1842 he was ordained to the curacy of Eversley in Hampshire. This was a parish on the outskirts of the old Windsor Forest. The coun-

CHARLES KINGSLEY

try was wild heathery moorland inhabited by a poor, uneducated population of poachers, gypsies, and "broom-squires." Among these people Kingsley's devotion to his parish duties, his sympathetic understanding and his generosity soon gained for him the loyal affection of everyone he encountered. Aside from his parishoners, Kingsley's chief associates were officers from Sandhurst, with whom he fished and rode to hounds with as much zest as any country squire.

After two years as curate, Kingsley married Fanny Grenfell and the same year succeeded to the living of his parish. But even this advancement failed to provide a very adequate income and to augment it he took pupils and lectured around the country.

In 1842 he had started to write *The Saint's Tragedy* which he changed from his original prose biography of St. Elizabeth of Hungary into a poetical drama. It was published in 1848 and created considerable interest both at home and in Germany.

Political events in 1848 led Kingsley into a more active part in the Christian Socialist movement where his literary ability was particularly welcome. He contributed papers to *Politics for the People* and other politico-social pamphlets. It was also under this influence that his first two novels were written, *Yeast* and *Alton Locke*. *Yeast* appeared serially in *Fraser's Magazine*, but was abbreviated at the request of the publishers who feared its radicalism. Of this work A. C. Benson says, "To myself the strange, formless, digressive, inconclusive, noble book, *Yeast*, is the most characteristic of all, because he here really bared his heart." This book was stupidly attacked as immoral when published in 1851.

In all his writing Kingsley was trying to teach a lesson or point a moral. W. J. Dawson says that ". . .Kingsley did not possess the highest kind of genius. His books were wrung out of him by an effort that told severely on his physical health. He is apt to become hysterical through excess of feeling." And again, "He became the intermediary of greater minds than his own. He gave currency to the religious views of Maurice and the social gospel of Carlyle. He lifted up his voice in noble anger, and took possession of the platform of fiction as a prophet of righteousness. His books were impassioned declarations of faith and principle."

But with all this emphasis upon the didacticism of his work it must not be overlooked that Kingsley wrote some of the most enthralling romances in the English language. *Westward Ho!*, *Hypatia*, and *The Water Babies* in their several fields are very near to being classics. Kingsley's deep interest in all aspects of natural history gives his descriptive passages a vivid truthfulness which, for brilliance of word-painting, is difficult to rival.

Hypatia, like most of Kingsley's books, was intended to teach a lesson. In this instance he drew a picture of early civilization undergoing a period of social and intellectual ferment comparable to that of England in his own day His next novel, *Westward Ho!*, was written while he and his wife were at Bideford on one of their frequent convalescent vacations. This novel was dedicated to Sir James Brooke, the Englishman who became the Rajah of Sarawak. He was a personal friend of Kingsley's and a hero after his own heart—a most appropriate man to receive the dedication of this romantic story of Elizabethan adventure.

The Water Babies was a modern fairy tale written as a gift for Kingsley's youngest child. It is one of the last of his imaginative works, and one of the happiest. But even in this story of and for children Kingsley's preoccupation with social problems shows through.

In the same year that his first book appeared, Kingsley was appointed professor of English Literature at Queen's College, London, but ill health forced him to abandon the post within a year. The work of his parish at Eversley was his primary concern at all times and he would never permit any other activities to interfere with it. As a result, he suffered frequent breakdowns caused by overexertion, his nervous intensity, and the damp climate of Eversley. His writing was frequently done at night after a day devoted to work in the parish. His wife also suffered from the climate and in consequence they were forced to make numerous trips for their health.

During the Crimean War Kingsley had published an anonymous tract, *Brave Words to*

Brave Soldiers, and thousands of copies were distributed to the army. When the authorship of the tract was made known it did much to overcome the prejudice of the more orthodox and conservative church element, and led to Kingsley's appointment as chaplain in ordinary to Queen Victoria.

In 1860 he was made professor of modern history at Cambridge, where he had as a student the Prince of Wales. He was an inspiring teacher, but not a very sound historian, and when his lectures appeared in print they were severely criticized by more authoritative writers. He was aware of his weakness and was glad to resign from the office in 1869 when he became canon of Chester.

His controversy with Cardinal Newman, which resulted in the latter's famous *Apologia,* occurred in 1864. It arose out of Kingsley's statement in a book review that, "Truth, for its own sake, had never been a virtue of the Roman Catholic clergy," which opinion he attributed to the Cardinal. One commentator has remarked that it was one of those unhappy arguments in which both opponents are right.

Following publication of *The Water Babies* in 1863, Kingsley's health became steadily worse. He made several journeys abroad, one to the West Indies, about which he published a book. In 1873 he went to America, travelling about Canada and the far west. An attack of pleurisy forced him to stop in Colorado Springs for some time. This same year Kingsley had become canon of Westminster. Here he suffered an attack shortly after his return from America. With his wife, who was also very ill, he returned to Eversley, where he remained until his death.

A. C. Benson, whose father was a near neighbor of Charles Kingsley, tells many interesting anecdotes—all illustrating some delightful trait of character—humor, kindliness, unconventionality . . ., but finds it difficult to sum up the man's character in a few words. "It is an almost impossible thing," says he, "to try to analyse and summarise the life of Charles Kingsley. It is like analysing a flame, a thing that glows and leaps and vanishes before you can fix your gaze upon it. He did not found a school of thought or dazzle his age with great, fruitful ideas, but he belonged to the party of those who, like Carlyle, dared to look facts in the face and say what they thought of them. . . He was a democrat in surplice and hood . . . he was a poet from head to heel, and all his work, verse or prose, sermon or scientific lecture, was done in the spirit of the poet. . . . He had that note of high greatness—the power of tormenting himself into a kind of frenzy at all patient and stupid acquiescence in remediable evil. . . ."

As for his appearance, G. W. E. Russell has described him as ". . .not above the middle height but his extreme attenuation made him look taller. There was not a superfluous ounce of flesh on his bones, and he seemed to be compact of wire and whipcord. His features were strongly marked, trenchant nose and prominent chin; his eyes bright and penetrating; his skin furrowed and weather-beaten; his abundant hair and bushy whiskers originally dark but tinged with grey. In all his movements, actions and gestures he was nervous and restless." Kingsley loved to talk but his stammer was a great hindrance. However, when he prayed, preached, or lectured, his stammer left him.   D. C.

PRINCIPAL WORKS: *Poetry*—The Saint's Tragedy, 1848; Andromeda, 1858; Poems, 1875. *Sermons*—Twenty-five Village Sermons, 1849; Sermons on National Subjects, 1852-54; Sermons for the Times, 1855; The Good News of God, 1859; Town and Country Sermons, 1861; Sermons on the Pentateuch, 1863; David, 1865; The Water of Life, 1867; Discipline, 1868; Westminster Sermons, 1874; All Saints Day, 1878. *Prose*—Alton Locke, 1850; Yeast, 1851; Phaeton: or, Loose Thoughts for Loose Thinkers, 1852; Hypatia, 1853; Alexandria and Her Schools, 1854; Westward Ho! 1855; Glaucus: or, The Wonders of the Shore, 1855; The Heroes: or, Greek Fairy Tales, 1856; Two Years Ago, 1857; Miscellanies, 1859; The Water Babies, 1863; Hereward the Wake, 1866; The Ancien Regime, 1867; The Hermits, 1868; Madam How and Lady Why, 1869; At Last: A Christmas in the West Indies, 1871; Town Geology, 1872; Prose Idylls, 1873; Plays and Puritans, 1873; Health and Education, 1874; Lectures Delivered in America, 1875.

ABOUT: Benson, A. C. Leaves of the Tree; Courtney, Mrs. J. E. H. Freethinkers of the 19th Century; Dawson, W. J. Makers of English Fiction; Hearn, L. Appreciations of Poetry; Kingsley, F. E. G. (ed.). Charles Kingsley: His Letters and Memories of His Life; Russell, G. W. E. Afterthoughts.

KINGSLEY, GEORGE HENRY (February 14, 1827-February 5, 1892), travel writer, came of a distinguished family: his older brother was Charles Kingsley, the celebrated novelist, clergyman, and one of the pioneers of Christian Socialism; his younger brother, Henry, was also a novelist popular in his day; and his daughter was a celebrated African traveler. Kingsley was born in Northampton shire, where his father was a vicar. He was educated at King's College School, London, and then went to the University of Edinburgh, where he received an M.D. degree in 1846. He proceeded to the University of Paris for further medical study, and during the Revolution of 1848 was slightly wounded in the fighting on the barricades. He next studied at the University of Heidelberg, and finally returned to England in 1850. He had not previously practised his profession, though during a visit home he had been active in combating a cholera epidemic.

He now started in practice as a peculiar kind of specialist, in a specialty invented by himself. He treated only individual patients, and his one method of cure was foreign travel, on which he accompanied the patient! In this manner he not only made some remarkable cures (apparently all of psychological or nervous disorders), but also saw the entire world. During his travels he had time for the study of natural history, and contributed articles as a naturalist to *The Field*, signing his contributions "The Doctor." He left behind him also a mass of unpublished manuscripts on the folklore and ethnology of the countries he had visited; none of this has ever appeared in print.

In 1860 he married Mary Bailey, and they had one son and one daughter. Mrs. Kingsley was an invalid from about 1888, and died only two months after her husband. His home when he was in England was in Cambridge, and it was there he died. He was a genial, companionable man, whose society probably helped his patients as much as their journeys did. He was a brilliant conversationalist, very witty, and extremely versatile in his interests.

Kingsley's one important book, *South Sea Bubbles*, written during his travels with the young Earl of Pembroke, his patient, was an immense success. It is frank, unconventional, highly humorous, and most vivid and graphic —one of the very best of English travel books.

PRINCIPAL WORKS: South Sea Bubbles: By the Earl and the Doctor, 1872; Notes on Sport and Travel, 1900.

ABOUT: Kingsley, G. H. Notes on Sport and Travel (see Memoir by M. H. Kingsley).

KINGSLEY, HENRY (January 2, 1830- May 24, 1876), novelist, was born at Barnack, Northamptonshire, the fifth son of the Reverend Charles Kingsley and Mary (Lucas) Kingsley. Charles Kingsley, the novelist, was an elder brother.

His youth was spent, for the most part, in London. A well-stocked home library and the privilege of browsing in secondhand bookstalls guided the boy's literary ramblings; his formal education, after some preliminary training, began at King's College School in 1844.

At Oxford, where he matriculated at Worcester College in 1850, Kingsley gave himself up to social pleasures and especially to violent athletic exercise, becoming conspicuous even in a day of "muscular Christianity" for his delight in physical prowess. On one occasion he won a wager by running a mile, rowing a mile, and trotting a mile, all within fifteen minutes. With his friend Edwin Arnold he founded the Fez Club, a society of fifty young men pledged to celibacy and misogyny, which caused some excitement because of reports that free love was the aim of the group. Kingsley's activities at Oxford not only wasted his time but ran him into debt.

After three years virtually thrown away at Oxford, where he had disappointed his family's hopes for him, Kingsley left England (without a degree) for Australia, having fallen heir to a legacy which more than paid his debts. There he managed for five years, in which time he never wrote to his family, to keep alive, but only by undergoing great hardship in the primitive society of the gold-seekers of the new land. It was during those years that *Geoffry Hamlyn*, a novel based upon his Australian experiences, was begun.

On his return to England he joined his parents at Eversley, Hampshire, where his brother Charles encouraged him in his literary work, recommending *Geoffry Hamlyn* to his own publisher, Alexander Macmillan. Henry Kingsley, in these years perhaps happier than in any others, became a contributor to the new *Macmillan's Magazine*, and a warm friend of Alexander Macmillan. So popular was *Geoffry Hamlyn* that Mudie's Lending Library ordered five hundred copies not long after publication, and *Ravenshoe* was likewise well received. At this time Kingsley was living with his mother, his father having died in 1862.

In 1864 he married a cousin, Miss Sarah Maria Kingsley Haselwood, and with his wife removed to Wargrave, Berkshire, where they took a delightful cottage called Hillside House. There they frequently entertained their literary friends; at this time Kingsley knew Huxley, Matthew Arnold, George Meredith, John Morley, A. C. Swinburne, and Lewis Carroll. Unfortunately hospitality proved a steady monetary drain, and there were other calls upon Kingsley's purse. Now that he no longer had his wants supplied by his mother, he could ill afford a lavish scale of expenditure. He told his publisher in 1866, "The fearful expenses of pulling a sick wife about the country, literally to save her life, and setting up a new house, have superinduced an alarming financial crisis, and left me without any money at all." Furthermore, his earning powers were dwindling with the declining quality of his novels, which suffered from the necessity under which he labored. The pressure finally was too much, and the Kingsleys left Wargrave in 1869 for Edinburgh, where he had secured the editorship of the *Daily Review*, an organ of the Free Church Party (a group which had seceded from the Church of Scotland on political and civil, rather than doctrinal, grounds).

For this task, his independent tastes, his inability to meet requirements of routine, and his ingrained affection for the Church of England made him unsuitable. With the outbreak of the Franco-Prussian War, however, a new field was opened for him, and in August 1870 he journeyed to the battlefields to write dis-

HENRY KINGSLEY

patches for his own paper. He was present at Sedan, the scene of the defeat of the French army and the surrender of Napoleon. His descriptions are noteworthy for vivid detail and for a sense of beauty which could find loveliness even in the dead. His editorial work as a whole, nevertheless, was so unsatisfactory that in 1871 he left the paper (which was no longer profitable) before the expiration of his contract, at the request of the proprietors.

More troubles were in store for him. *The Boy in Grey, Old Margaret,* and *Hetty* (all published in 1871) had failed to achieve the success of his earlier works; after his removal to London, where he made his home in Bloomsbury, Kingsley was unable to produce anything above the level of mediocrity. Unwilling to live in squalor, he applied to his brother Charles (for whom he had always had great affection) for aid. At first it came readily, but repeated demands (coming from Mrs. Kingsley, to whom her husband had turned over a painful task) wore out the patience of Mr. and Mrs. Charles Kingsley. Weakness and poverty operated to produce confusion and unreality in *Oakshott Castle,* which Kingsley blindly regarded as equal to his best work.

In 1873 an increase of fortune, apparently due to a legacy, enabled the novelist to remove from Bloomsbury to a semi-rural spot in Kentish Town. Not long after his mother died, and in 1875 his brother Charles followed her. The final blow came with the discovery that he himself was dying, a victim of cancer of the tongue and throat, said to have been caused by excessive smoking. Determined to spend his last days in the country, he removed to an old cottage in Cuckfield, Sussex, where he lived in comparative seclusion until his

death in May 1876, leaving a reputation which has been the subject of considerable discussion.

Both as a man and as a writer Henry Kingsley has suffered by comparison with his more serious brother, Charles. It is evident that, though lovable and attractive, he had less force of character and less steadiness of purpose than Charles, but there is no established basis for the widely circulated belief that his deficiencies are attributable to alcohol. Lack of discipline is perhaps the best explanation for his failure as an editor and his generally erratic career (which has caused suspicion of insanity); and S. M. Ellis, a modern student of his life and work, has attributed Kingsley's marked interest in youthful masculine beauty and physical perfection, his tendency to glorify the English gentleman in his more virile aspects, his "muscular Christianity," to a strain of homosexuality, which reveals itself at times in his writings.

The best of these, as *Geoffry Hamlyn, Ravenshoe, The Hillyars and the Burtons,* and *Mademoiselle Mathilde,* show considerable ability in description, powers of vivid narration, and a control of language; the later works indicate a marked deterioration, an evidence, in Saintsbury's opinion, that the author was working himself dry. R. W. W.

PRINCIPAL WORKS: *Novels*—The Recollections of Geoffrey Hamlyn, 1859; Ravenshoe, 1862; Austin Elliott, 1863; The Hillyars and the Burtons, 1865; Leighton Court, 1866; Silcotes of Silcote, 1867; Mademoiselle Mathilde, 1868; Stretton, 1869; Old Margaret, 1871; The Harveys, 1872; Oakshott Castle, 1873; Reginald Hetherege, 1874; Number Seventeen, 1875; The Grange Garden, 1876; The Mystery of the Island, 1877; The Novels of Henry Kingsley, 1894-95. *Stories*—Tales of Old Travel Re-narrated, 1869; Hetty and Other Stories, 1871; Hornby Mills and Other Stories, 1872. *Essays*—Fireside Studies, 1876. *Juvenile*—The Boy in Grey, 1871; Valentin: A French Boy's Story of Sedan, 1872.

ABOUT: Ellis, S. M. Henry Kingsley: Towards a Vindication; James, H. Notes and Reviews; Kingsley, H. The Novels of Henry Kingsley (see the Memoir by C. K. Shorter); Quiller-Couch, A. T. Adventures in Criticism; Saintsbury, G. E. B. Collected Essays and Papers; Edinburgh Review 240:330 October 1924; Nineteenth Century and After 55: 996 June 1904.

KINGSLEY, MARY HENRIETTA (October 13, 1862-June 3, 1900), travel writer, was the daughter of George Henry Kingsley, physician and travel writer, and the niece of Charles Kingsley the novelist. She was born at Islington, but spent her first sixteen years at Highgate. She was educated at home, chiefly by private reading, and grew up a shy, silent girl, fond of travel and natural history. In 1879, when the family moved to Kent, she studied chemistry and electricity, then became interested in ethnography and anthropology. In 1886 they moved to Cambridge, where the friendship of learned professors gave her confidence in herself. In 1888 she visited Paris,

but was called home to nurse her mother and then her father, both of whom died in 1892. She then went to London with her brother, determined to become a traveler in the interests of research in the history of law and religion. In 1893 she set out by herself for tropical West Africa, financing her trip by collecting scientific material for Cambridge. In 1894 and 1895 she made a second trip, amassing a valuable collection of shells and insects, and also trading in rubber and oil. For two years after her return she lectured all over England on tropical Africa. In 1899 she set out on a third journey, to South Africa, but the next year she died from overwork in nursing Boer prisoners. By her own wish, she was buried at sea. The Mary Kingsley West Africa Society was established in her memory.

Miss Kingsley was a remarkable woman, combining courage with modesty, humor with devotion. She was an ardent advocate of a better understanding between the black and white races. Her books have both scientific value and intense interest.

PRINCIPAL WORKS: Travels in West Africa, 1897; West African Studies, 1899.

ABOUT: T. P. O'Connor's M.A.P. May 20, 1899.

KINGSTON, WILLIAM HENRY GILES
(February 28, 1814-August 5, 1880), writer of boys' books and travel writer, was born in London. His father, however, was in business in Oporto, and he spent his boyhood between England and Portugal, without much formal education. On his father's death he inherited the business, but writing was always his chief concern. In 1844 he settled in England, and edited the *Colonial Magazine,* being keenly interested in emigration, on which he wrote numerous pamphlets. He also wrote several historical novels and many books on travel and adventure in Canada, Africa, India, Australia, etc., all of which he had visited; and he translated the works of Jules Verne; but his fame was gained chiefly as a writer of books for boys—nearly 150 of them—and as editor of boys' magazines. He never married. A few days before his death, he wrote a farewell letter to his boy readers, knowing that his end was near. His books are simple, vigorous, "manly," full of adventure and healthy in tone, but quite ephemeral, and unknown to the present generation of boys, though in his day he was perhaps the most popular of juvenile writers.

PRINCIPAL WORKS: The Circassian Chief, 1844; Peter the Whaler, 1851; The Cruise of the Frolic, 1860; Eldol the Druid, 1874; Jovinian, 1877; Kidnapping in the Pacific, 1879.

ABOUT: Athenaeum August 14, 1880; Boys' Own Paper September 11, 1880.

KNIGHT, CHARLES (March 15, 1791-March 9, 1873), editor, publisher, and writer of history, was the son of a bookseller of Windsor who was a friend of George III.

His formal education was short, and resulted in the small knowledge of the classics picked up at a school in Ealing. Removed from school in 1805, he became apprenticed to his father and learned the bookseller's trade, acquiring a store of information on books and bibliography. Given by his father an imperfect copy of Shakespeare's first folio, he restored the missing parts, producing a perfect copy by following a facsimile, using similar paper and type. In this way he gained an accurate acquaintance with the text.

Already possessed of his lifelong enthusiasm for the spreading of knowledge among the people, he founded a reading society at Windsor, and became a newspaper reporter. He turned, after a brief time in official position as parish overseer at Windsor, to the business of editing and publishing, and in 1820 began the *Plain Englishman,* containing original work by prominent men, and about the same time commenced to edit *The Guardian.* In 1822 he abandoned both these organs, selling the latter.

In the next year he started his own publishing business, issuing *Knight's Quarterly Magazine.* One of his most important early publications was Bishop Sumner's translations of Milton's *Christian Doctrine,* which Knight produced for the Cambridge University Press.

A panic shortly descended upon the booktrade; by 1827 Knight had lost his business, and for a while he wrote for papers and magazines. In 1828 he became connected with the Society for the Diffusion of Useful Knowledge, beginning in that year his association with the *British Almanack.* By 1829 he was again publishing for himself, and produced *The Menageries,* one of the volumes of the "Library of Entertaining Knowledge," issued under the superintendence of the Society.

Thus began a long and uneventful career as publisher (and, in many cases, writer) of popular books of knowledge, often bearing the name of the Society. Perhaps the dearest to his heart of any of Knight's publications was his edition of Shakespeare, which leans perhaps too heavily upon the first folio, but has merits which other editors cannot afford to overlook.

With the last number of the *Penny Magazine* and the dissolution of the Society of the Diffusion of Useful Knowledge (1846), Knight's publishing career began to ebb. He continued, however, to write, collaborating with Harriet Martineau in *A History of the Thirty Years' Peace.* His most important venture in this field was *The Popular History of England,* which he subsequently abridged to make a schoolbook.

"Good Knight" was the pun by which Douglas Jerrold once described him, and

CHARLES KNIGHT

land, 1856-62. *Politics*—The Rights of Industry, 1831; Results of Machinery, 1831; Capital and Labour, 1831; Trades Unions and Strikes, 1834; The Struggles of a Book Against Excessive Taxation, 1850; Knowledge Is Power, 1855. *Miscellaneous*—The Menageries, 1829; The Elephant, 1830; Old England (with others) c. 1845; Studies and Illustrations of the Writings of Shakspere, and of His Life and Times, 1850; Once Upon a Time, 1854; The Old Printer and the Modern Press, 1854; The Shadows of the Old Booksellers, 1865. *Editor*—The Pictorial History of England (by G. L. Craik and C. Macfarlane) 1837-41; The Pictorial Edition of the Works of Shakspere, 1838-41; Knight's Store of Knowledge for All Readers, 1841-44; London, 1841-44; Half Hours With the Best Authors, 1847-48; Pictorial Half Hours, 1850-51; Pictorial Half Hours of London Topography, 1851; Half Hours of English History, 1857; Half Hours With the Best Letter-Writers and Autobiographers, 1867, 1868.

ABOUT: Clowes, A. A. Knight: A Sketch; Curwen, H. A History of Booksellers: The Old and the New; Japp, A. H. Noble Workers; Knight, C. Passages of a Working Life During Half a Century; Nicoll, H. S. Great Movements; Smith, G. B. Leaders of Modern Industry; Smith, S. F. Noble Workers; Athenaeum March 15, 1873; Christian Remembrancer 50:87 July 1865.

others' pictures are amiable. He seems to have been an incurable optimist, not only as to popular education, but also as to social reform. Strictly honest in his business and a clever man (he invented improvements in a surface-printing process), Knight was not very prosperous. The *Penny Cyclopaedia*, considered tremendously successful, is said to have cost him more than £ 30,000. His losses apparently failed to affect his general good nature; he seems to have been without enemies. He married (1815) a Miss Vincombe, and had several children. In his last years his sight failed; he died in Addlestone, Surrey, in 1873.

"It cannot be said that he earned for himself a place amongst our great writers," commented *The Athenaeum* in its obituary notice, "nor was he, in the commercial sense of the term, a successful publisher; but he was in both capacities a highly useful man. His Shakespearian productions do not satisfy the requirements of critical students, and to readers of the higher and more scholarly kind his historical works have obvious defects; but, bearing his object in mind, 'the instruction of the people,' i. e. the comparatively unlettered portions of the people, and at the same time taking a right view of the intellectual conditions of those sections of society at the time when he began to provide them with the means of self-instruction, fair judges will not regard him lightly as a popular educator."

R. W. W.

PRINCIPAL WORKS: *Biography*—Shakspere's Biography, 1843; William Caxton, 1844; Passages of a Working Life During Half a Century, 1864-65. *Drama*—Arminius, 1814; The Bridal of the Isles, 1817. *Fiction*—Begged at Court, 1867. *History*—A History of the Thirty Years' Peace (with Harriet Martineau) 1846-51; The Popular History of Eng-

KNIGHT, JOSEPH (May 24, 1829-June 23, 1907), dramatic critic and biographer, was born in London, the son of a cloth merchant of Scottish birth. His mother was blind from his childhood. He was educated in a private school, of which he became the head student, and wrote poetry very early; one of his poems was printed by the schoolmaster as an example to the school. At nineteen he joined his father's business, but devoted his leisure to literature. With Alfred Austin, later poet laureate, he founded the Mechanics' Institute at Leeds, and lectured there on literature. In 1856 he married Rachel Wilkinson; they had one son and two daughters.

In 1860 Knight went to London to become a journalist. By a chance meeting with the famous John (later Lord) Morley, he became dramatic critic of Morley's *London Gazette*. From 1869 to his death he was dramatic critic of *The Athenaeum*, though he also contributed criticisms of plays to three newspapers. He wrote over 500 articles on dramatists and actors for the *Dictionary of National Biography*. He was no narrow specialist, however: he reviewed works of general literature also for *The Athenaeum*, contributed essays to the *Gentleman's Magazine*, and from 1883 to his death was editor of *Notes and Queries*.

Knight was a true Bohemian, a boon companion and witty conversationalist; but he was also a man of real knowledge, deep culture, and fine taste, characteristics which appear in his magazine articles and in his books.

PRINCIPAL WORKS: Life of D. G. Rossetti, 1887; Theatrical Notes, 1893; Memoir of David Garrick, 1894.

ABOUT: Francis, J. C. Notes by the Way; Athenaeum June 1907; Nineteenth Century December 1911.

KNOWLES, JAMES SHERIDAN (May 12, 1784-November 30, 1862), Irish dramatist and actor, was born in Cork, the son of James Knowles, the lexicographer, who was a first cousin of the dramatist Richard Brinsley Sheridan.

Upon the failure of his father's school at Cork the family went to London (1793), where Knowles met Hazlitt, Lamb, and Coleridge. The boy's taste ran early to drama, but he received little encouragement at home, and ran away because of a step-mother. For a time he was in the army; then he studied medicine with a Dr. Willan, whom, however, he left, after he had received an M.D. degree, deciding to turn to the stage. He began to act, and he met and married Maria Charteris, an actress.

Despite the success of *Leo*, Knowles found acting a precarious livelihood, and he turned to teaching, eventually starting his own school in Belfast. In 1816 he removed to Glasgow, where he continued his teaching.

With the success of *Virginius* (1820), *Caius Gracchus* (1823), and *William Tell* (1825), his career as a dramatist was launched, although the financial returns were so small that the author turned to the lecture platform. He moved to Edinburgh in 1830, and not long after returned to the stage as an actor in an effort to support his ten children. He made a successful tour in the United States, 1834-35, and continued play-writing until 1843. His first wife died in 1841, and in the next year he married Emma Elphinstone, an actress and a pupil of his.

At about this time he yielded to his naturally religious nature and embraced an evangelical belief. He became ordained as a Baptist minister and turned his back on his past

frivolities, although he never attacked the stage. His income, which was comfortable, was dissipated through his generosity, and in 1848 he accepted a civil-list pension of £200. Despite ill health he continued to preach and to lecture, and was actually selected by Lord Russell, with three others, as a candidate for the laureateship left vacant in 1850 by Wordsworth's death; Tennyson was chosen. In his last year Knowles was honored by a banquet in his native city, and died at Torquay in November 1862.

"The world is his friend," wrote James Grant of Knowles; "he finds a well-wisher in every face he encounters in the streets or the highways." He was rather hot-headed, quarreling with his father and with his friends, but so generous that he impoverished himself in his efforts to pay his father's debts. Rather peculiar in appearance, more like a sailor than an actor or a preacher, he might be said to combine feminine sensibility with manly courage. He lacked powers of self-appraisal, and was deficient in tact and judgment. He sought comfort for his losses and discouragements in his family, to which he was devotedly attached.

As an actor Knowles was little better than mediocre, and many of his contemporaries recognized his shortcomings. With his plays, however, he made a temporary success of considerable proportions, despite their unevennesses. Technically adept enough, he lacked natural riches or originality, and is said to have avoided reading for fear of plagiarism. ". . .The fatal thing about him is that he is content to dwell in decencies for ever," writes Saintsbury. "There is no inspiration in him; his style, his verse, his theme, his character, his treatment are all emphatically mediocre, and his technique as a dramatist deserves only a little, though a little, warmer praise." "On almost every page he promises to rise to a genuine literary level, often touches it with his finger tips, but seldom does he actually grasp it," writes Leslie Howard Meeks. "Skilled in stagecraft, he was almost a great dramatist; indeed, he might fully have merited that title had his time and environment been more favorable to the development of his talents."

R. W. W.

PRINCIPAL WORKS: *Drama and Dramatic Adaptations*—Leo: or, The Gipsy, 1810; Brian Bohroihme: or, The Maid of Erin, 1811; Caius Gracchus, 1815, 1823; Virginius, 1820; William Tell, 1825; The Beggar's Daughter of Bethnal Green, 1828, 1834; Alfred the Great: or, The Patriot King, 1831; The Hunchback, 1832; A Masque on the Death of Sir Walter Scott, 1832; The Wife: A Tale of Mantua, 1833; The Daughter, 1836; The Bridal, 1837; The Love Chase, 1837; Woman's Wit: or, Love's Disguises, 1838; The Maid of Mariendorpt, 1838; Love, 1839; John of Procida: or, The Bridals of Messina, 1840; Old Maids, 1841; The Rose of Arragon, 1842; The Secretary, 1843; Alexina: or, True Unto Death, 1866. *Education*—The Elocutionist, 1823 (3rd ed.); A Debate Upon the Character of Julius

JAMES SHERIDAN KNOWLES

Caesar, 1856; Lectures on Oratory, Gesture, and Poetry, 1873; Lectures on Dramatic Literature. . . Macbeth, 1875. *Novels and Tales*—The Magdalen and Other Tales, 1832; George Lovell, 1846; Fortexcue, 1847; Tales and Novelettes, 1874. *Poetry*—The Welch Harper, 1796; Fugitive Pieces, 1810; *Religion*—The Rock of Rome: or, The Arch Heresy, 1849; The Idol Demolished by Its Own Priest, 1851; The Gospel Attributed to Matthew Is the Record of the Whole Original Apostlehood, 1855. *Miscellaneous*—Sheridan Knowles' Conception and Mr. Irving's Performance of Macbeth, 1876.

ABOUT: Collier, W. F. A History of English Literature in a Series of Biographical Sketches; Grant, J. Portraits of Public Characters; Hodder, G. Memories of My Time; Horne, R. H. A New Spirit of the Age; Knowles, R. S. B. Life of J. S. Knowles; Maclise, D. The Maclise Portrait Gallery; Marston, J. W. Our Recent Actors; Meeks, L. H. Sheridan Knowles and the Theatre of His Time; Athenaeum 20:223 February 27, 1847; Blackwood's Edinburgh Magazine 94:429 October 1863; London Mercury 22:324 August 1930.

KNOX, ALEXANDER (March 17, 1757-June 17, 1831), Irish theologian, was born in Londonderry of a family of Scottish descent, a collateral descendant of the reformer John Knox. His parents were Methodists, and friends (as he was also) of John Wesley, founder of Methodism, but by the time he was twenty he had abandoned Methodism for the established church. His father died when he was twelve. He was thought too frail for school (he was an epileptic), and studied by himself. For a while he busied himself in politics in the interests of Irish reform, then became secretary to Lord Castlereagh; but he retired from active life before middle age and lived as a recluse in Dublin. He never married. In 1801 and 1802 he was in England, where he came under evangelical influence. Though most of his life was devoted to the study of theology, Knox does not seem ever to have been ordained. He was a friend of Bishop Jebb, and through him was a potent influence in the Oxford (Tractarian) Movement, Jebb in turn influencing Pusey and Newman, its chief exponents. Much of his time in later years he spent with a friend in Wicklow, but the friend died in 1827 and Knox returned to his secluded lodging in Dublin, where he died at seventy-four.

PRINCIPAL WORKS: Essays on the Political Circumstances of Ireland, 1799; Correspondence With Bishop Jebb, 1834; Literary Remains, 1834-37.

ABOUT: Knox, A. Correspondence With Bishop Jebb; Contemporary Review August 1887.

KNOX, ISA. See CRAIG, ISA

"L.E.L." See LANDON, LETITIA ELIZABETH

LAIDLAW, WILLIAM (November 19, 1780-May 18, 1845), Scottish poet, was born in Selkirkshire. His father was a prosperous sheep-farmer, and after a very elementary education the boy started work as his helper.

When he was in his teens a young man came to work on the farm who was later known to fame as "the Ettrick Shepherd"—the future poet, James Hogg. Hogg and young Laidlaw became fast friends, and through Hogg, Laidlaw met Sir Walter Scott. In 1801 they both helped him compile songs for *Border Minstrelsy.*

After two failures as an independent farmer, Laidlaw in 1817 became Scott's steward. He was more than a steward, however; he was a close friend, and he was also an amanuensis. Several of Scott's novels were dictated to Laidlaw. When Scott died in 1832, Laidlaw became factor to Sir Charles Lockhart Ross. In 1844 his health failed, and he went to his brother's farm in Ross-shire, where he died the following May.

Laidlaw compiled, under Scott's direction, parts of the *Edinburgh Annual Register* for the years following 1817. He is also supposed to have written on the geology of Selkirkshire, but if he did so the writing has not survived. He wrote many poems, of which only one has been remembered—the tender "Lucy's Flittin'," which Hogg published in 1810 in his *Forest Minstrel.*

PRINCIPAL WORKS: Poems: Chiefly on Jedburgh and Vicinity, 1845.

ABOUT: Laidlaw, W. Poems (see Biographical Sketch by Sir G. B. Douglas); Lockhart, J. G. Life of Scott.

LAING, DAVID (April 20, 1793-October 18, 1878), Scottish antiquary, was born in Edinburgh, where his father was a bookseller. He was educated at the Canongate Grammar School, and also studied Greek at Edinburgh University. At thirteen he was appenticed to his father, at that time the only bookseller in the city who handled foreign books. The boy showed a real aptitude for the business, and soon was being sent on trips abroad looking for literary finds. In 1821 he became his father's partner, and on the latter's death the son succeeded him. His first work as an editor was in the field of old Scottish ballads and metrical romances. When Sir Walter Scott started the Bannatyne Club for antiquarian study, Laing became its secretary, and served in this office for the entire life of the club, from 1823 to 1861. He edited altogether twenty-seven of its publications. In 1826 he became a Fellow of the Royal Society of Antiquaries of Scotland.

In 1836 Laing was elected librarian of the Society of Writers to the Signet, and gave up his bookselling business, devoting the remainder of his life to this post. From 1854 to his death he was honorary professor of antiquities to the Royal Scottish Academy. He died, unmarried, at Portobello, at eighty-four.

Laing had an unrivalled knowledge of books especially in the field of Scottish antiquities, and though he wrote no original works he was the keystone of Scottish literature of his period.

PRINCIPAL WORKS (edited): Select Remains of the Ancient Popular Poetry of Scotland, 1821; Fugitive Scottish Poetry, 1823-25; Early Metrical Tales, 1826; Baillie's Letters and Journals, 1835; Collected Works of John Knox, 1846-64.

ABOUT: Laing, D. Popular Poetry of Scotland (see Biographical Memoir by John Small); Stevenson, T. G. Notices of David Laing.

LAING, MALCOLM (1762-November 6, 1818), Scottish historian, was born on the island of Orkney, of a family long resident there. He was educated at Kirkwall Grammar School and at the University of Edinburgh, and called to the Scottish bar in 1785. A very poor speaker, Laing spent little time at his profession, but devoted himself to the study of history. In 1793 he completed Dr. Robert Henry's *History of Great Britain*, left unfinished at its author's death. He was a liberal, a close friend of Charles James Fox, the Whig leader, and from 1807 to 1812 was a member of Parliament. He was married, his wife having been a Miss Carnegie, but had no children. In 1808 he moved from Edinburgh back to his ancestral estate on Orkney, and soon after was seized by a nervous illness from which he never recovered, and which made it impossible for him to do any work or to leave his home.

Rather brusque in manner, he was yet a man of great humanity. Lord Cockburn speaks of his "depth, truth, and independence as a historian." His best known work, *A History of Scotland,* contained a complete exposure of the literary fraud of the Ossianic poems, supposed to be ancient Scottish discoveries but actually written by James Macpherson. The history as a whole was thorough and painstaking, but his style has been criticized as "awkward and ungainly."

PRINCIPAL WORK: A History of Scotland, 1802.

ABOUT: Cockburn, Lord. Memorials; Lockhart, J. G. Life of Scott.

LAMB, LADY CAROLINE PONSONBY (November 13, 1785-January 24, 1828), novelist, was born Caroline Ponsonby, daughter of the third Earl of Bessborough. At the age of three she was sent with a nurse to Italy, and remained there until she was nine. As a small child she was so high-strung that a doctor had told her parents it would be dangerous to her nervous system to teach her anything! In lieu of real schooling, therefore, she was next sent to her aunt, the beautiful Duchess of Devonshire, to be brought up with her own children.

Caro Ponsonby, an ethereal, golden-haired girl with dark eyes, whose slightness gave her the nickname of "Ariel" and "Squirrel," was only sixteen when she was married to William

CAROLINE LAMB

Lamb, later Lord Melbourne, Queen Victoria's prime minister and advisor. Lamb was ten years her senior. It was a marriage of love, but the bride was so unstrung nervously that she collapsed in hysterics—an anticipation of nearly twenty years of a troubled marriage. Few husbands have ever been so patient, tolerant, and tenderly long-suffering as William Lamb.

In 1812 Lady Caroline met Byron, and after writing that he was "mad, bad, and dangerous to know," fell violently in love with him. Byron amused himself by a brief affair with her, then wearied of her importunities and cast her off. Years of public and private scenes ensued, including one attempt at suicide and one runaway from which she was ignominiously brought back by her husband from Kensington to their country house at Brocket. In 1816 Lamb's family tried to have her declared insane and to secure the formal separation of the couple, but they were reconciled instead—if they ever were anything else, for Lamb always loved her and she, strange to say, in spite of her infatuation for Byron, loved and valued him. That was the year *Glenarvon,* her fictional exposure of Byron, appeared. Finally, in 1824, Byron's funeral accidentally passed her house on its way to Newstead. The shock was too much; she tried to find forgetfulness in a mad frenzy of drugs and lovers, and Lamb saw that they must part. Soon he allowed her to return to her beloved Brocket, but though he visited her occasionlly, they never lived together again. She died in Melbourne House, Lamb's London residence. Their only surviving child lived to twenty-nine, a complete imbecile.

It is probable that Caroline Lamb was never actually insane, though highly neurotic and utterly uncontrolled. She is in many ways a tragic and lovable figure, her own cruelest enemy. As a writer she is negligible. *Glenarvon,* that novel "unattractive in form and delirious in style," caused contemporary excitement because it was a *roman à clef,* with real and well known people concealed under the names of its characters. *Ada Reis,* her own favorite, is an incoherent Oriental tale. It is easy to love Caro Lamb (hard as it must have been to be in her company) and to be exceedingly sorry for her, but there is nothing in the "blend of acuteness and frenzy" which marked her writing as well as her personality to make her work of anything more than historical interest. All of it was published anonymously, though its authorship was no secret.   M. A. deF.

PRINCIPAL WORKS: *Novels*—Glenarvon, 1816; Graham Hamilton, 1820; Ada Reis, 1823. *Verse*—A New Canto, 1819.

ABOUT: Jenkins, E. Lady Caroline Lamb; Paul C. K. William Godwin: His Friends and Contemporaries; Sadleir, M. Life of Bulwer Lytton; Smiles, S. A Publisher and His Friends; Bookman (London) 77:228 January 1930; Cornhill Magazine 149:641, 150-1 June, July 1934.

LAMB, CHARLES (February 10, 1775-December 27, 1834), essayist and critic, was born at 2, Crown Office Row, in the Temple, London, youngest son of John and Elizabeth (Field) Lamb. The father was personal servant and clerk to one Samuel Salt, a bencher of the Inner Temple. The maternal grandmother, Mary Field, comes into Lamb's history, for at Blakesware, Hertfordshire, she served as housekeeper for fifty years, and the large old house there was often a place of wandering and exploration for Charles as a boy and familiarized him from infancy with the prints of Hogarth, on which he was later to write with so much insight. John Lamb's status in Salt's chambers was not menial; he was a man of parts and reading, and both Charles and his sister MARY ANN (1764-1847) were allowed to browse in the bencher's well-stocked library. There was a taint of insanity in the Lambs, and indeed their medical history seems to have been bad, for of seven children only three (Charles; Mary; and John, born 1763) survived infancy. Charles himself spent six weeks in an asylum in the winter of 1795-96, and of Mary's far more serious malady more will appear.

Charles and Mary both began their education at a day-school kept by William Bird in a court off Fetter Lane, Fleet Street. In October 1782 Charles was accepted as a pupil at Christ's Hospital ("the Bluecoat School"). A schoolmate, C. V. Le Grice, describes him as "an amiable, gentle boy, very sensible and keenly observing, indulged by his schoolfel-

CHARLES LAMB

lows and by his master on account of his infirmity of speech." This defect, a pronounced stammer, prevented his rising to the highest form, the "Grecians," since it forbade any aspiration to the Church, for which these boys were intended. The future poet and critic, S. T. Coleridge, was Lamb's contemporary at Christ's Hospital and their lifelong intimacy began there.

University education was ruled out by expense, and could not be had at reduced fees save by the "Grecians"; so in 1789, through Salt, Lamb was made a clerk at the South Sea House, passing from there in 1792 to India House, and continuing in the employ of the East India Company until his retirement on pension in 1825. Salt died in 1792, leaving some small provision for the Lambs but the family was poor, the mother became an invalid, the father lapsed into extreme dotage for some years before his death in 1799, and Charles's exiguous earnings had to be supplemented by what Mary could earn by needlework. A love-affair in 1795, with one Ann Simmons in Hertfordshire, came to nothing, and as the mainstay of an ailing and indigent family Lamb could not think of marriage. In common with Coleridge (who frequently came up from Oxford) he wrote poems, spurred to emulation by the sonnets of William Lisle Bowles; and in the spring of 1796 Coleridge's *Poems on Various Subjects* contained four of his sonnets. But on September 22 of that year occurred a tragedy which for a time filled his life and which was to overshadow it to the end. Mary, in an access of mania, wounded her father and stabbed her mother to the heart. Declared insane at the inquest, she remained for some time under restraint at Hoxton; but early the next year she was allowed to live with Charles at Pentonville. The brother John seems to have behaved badly, wishing to consign Mary to Bethlehem, the London public asylum. Charles bore all the burden, and it was a heavy one, for throughout her life Mary was subject to recurrent bouts of insanity and frequently had to spend periods in asylums. From Pentonville the pair moved in 1799 to Southampton Buildings, Holborn, in another part of London; then, at the end of that year, back to the Temple (King's Bench Walk).

A volume published in 1798, *Blank Verse by Charles Lloyd and Charles Lamb* (Lloyd being a Quaker friend) contained Lamb's best poem, "The Old Familiar Faces," but he was not destined to make good as a poet, lacking the sense of words in this kind. Nor had he any native dramatic talent, though as an interpreter of drama he ranked high. A farce, *Mr. H.*, got as far as the boards of Drury Lane on December 10, 1805, but was damned by the audience (Lamb hissing with the rest!) and was at once withdrawn. An inveterate joker, he contributed quips and anecdotes to the *Morning Post* and other papers. He kept office hours at India House, and his evenings were devoted to playgoing, to reading and writing, or to convivial gatherings with the flocks of friends which his keen mind and lovable disposition collected round him. Among these at various times were Coleridge and Southey, the mathematician, Thomas Manning, Talfourd (his future biographer), Bryan Waller Procter, Leigh Hunt, and those doughty recorders of their age, Crabb Robinson and B. R. Haydon, the painter. Wordsworth he knew and revered, but that great man was seldom in London, nor, it may be surmised, would he have felt much at home in these gatherings, for Lamb himself was more than a thought too fond of his glass and the company was not only intellectual but boisterous.

Lamb's literary interests centred above all in the Elizabethan dramatists, and William Godwin's excursion into the publishing trade first allowed them public expression, for, in January 1807, he issued *Tales From Shakespear*, which he had commissioned from Charles and Mary jointly. Charles did the tragedies and Mary the comedies, and the book skilfully guided the young through the stories of the plays while avoiding the canting humbug which mars so much of the work written for children in that age. "It is the first book," wrote A. Hamilton Thompson in the *Camridge History of English Literature*, "which, appealing to a general audience and to a rising generation, made Shakespeare a familiar and popular author. . ." *The Adventures of Ulysses* (1808), by Charles alone, did less successfully the same service for Homer; but in the same year his *Specimens of English*

Dramatic Poets, in the words of A. C. Ward, "opened the door to what was then, to all intents and purposes, a locked room"— the magnificently furnished room of the Elizabethan drama. He was now an established critic, and his alert and imaginative mind could apply itself not only to books but to pictures, as was shown in an essay "On the Character and Genius of Hogarth" which appeared in Leigh Hunt's *Reflector* in 1811. The two volumes of *Works* published in 1818 contained very little of the writing that has spread Lamb's fame to both ends of the earth. It is, of course, by his papers written as "Elia" that Lamb takes his place among the great essayists not only of England but of the world. The first, "Recollections of South Sea House," came out in the *London Magazine* for August 1820 and the series appeared in book form in 1823 and 1833. The only other book published after the *Works* was *Album Verses* (1830), which contains the delicate lyric, "On an Infant Dying as Soon as Born."

In 1819 Lamb had proposed marriage to an actress, Fanny Kelly, and had been gracefully rejected. He never married, but in 1823 he and Mary adopted an orphan girl, Emma Isola, daughter of an official at Cambridge University. She was much loved by them, and they educated and looked after her for ten years, until her marriage with Edward Moxon, the publisher. From August 1823 the household was at Islington; in March 1825 Lamb retired on a pension of £441 a year; in 1827 they moved out to Enfield and in 1833 to Edmonton (both suburbs of London now, but then country places). On December 22, 1834 Lamb fell when out for a walk, grazed his face, and contracted erysipelas, from which he died five days later. Mary survived him by more than twelve years, dying at St. John's Wood, London, on May 20, 1847.

There are good descriptions of Lamb by T. N. Talfourd, Thomas Hood, Philarète Chasles, Bryan Waller Procter and other contemporaries. Talfourd wrote: "A light frame, so fragile that it seemed as if a breath would overthrow it, clad in clerk-like black, was surmounted by a head of form and expression the most noble and sweet. His black hair curled crisply about an expanded forehead; his eyes, softly brown, twinkled with varying expression, though the prevalent feeling was sad; and the nose slightly curved, and delicately carved at the nostril, with the lower outline of the face regularly oval, completed a head which was finely placed on the shoulders, and gave importance and even dignity to a diminutive and shadowy stem."

All observers agree on his small stature. Chasles writes of his "impossible feet, encased in large shoes, which placed flatly on the ground advanced slowly in the manner of a web-footed creature." There is virtual unanimity in the estimates of his character as to the very exceptional charm and loveableness of his nature. The epithet "gentle" clings to him, and may be accepted if it be cleansed of all connotations of weakness, futility, and the being of all things to all men—imputations which must have been in Lamb's mind when he urged Coleridge to alter "gentle-hearted Charles" to "drunken dog, ragged-head, seldshaven, odd-eyed, stuttering." His all-pervading humor often expressed itself in life by way of puns, quips, and horseplay; but in literature it was delicate, subtle, allusive, poetic, and often verging on the borders of pathos. He served the East India Company faithfully and efficiently; his self-sacrificing and understanding devotion to Mary is beyond praise; and it would be a churl who should accord undue blame, in a life so full of sorrow, to his over-indulgence in alcohol and tobacco.

Considered as an avatar of the romantic movement Lamb differs radically from the generality of its leaders in that he was primarily a man of the town, a Londoner of the Londoners, savoring the rough, rapid life of the metropolis with gusto and remaining comparatively untouched by the love and solitude and natural grandeur which so strongly swayed the others. As an essayist he is supreme in his tender, humorous, semi-autobiographical reminiscent vein, his fantasy, his humanity, in "the wide sympathy, the blending of tears and laughter, the freakishness of Elia." His prose has a music deriving partly from his own unusual and resourceful intellect and partly from echoes of Browne and other elaborate writers of earlier days. In criticism he played a great rôle as the enlightened and penetrating interpreter of the Elizabethans; but when he disliked a work his judgment was less reliable than when it appealed to his heart. In Ainger's words: "He did more than recall attention to certain forgotten writers. He flashed a light from himself upon them, not only heightening every charm and deepening every truth, but making even their eccentricities beautiful and lovable. And in doing this he has linked his name for ever with theirs."   H. B. G.

PRINCIPAL WORKS: *Essays and Criticism*—Specimens of English Dramatic Poets, 1808; Elia: Essays, 1823; The Last Essays of Elia, 1833. *Writings for Children*—Tales From Shakespeare (with Mary Lamb) 1807; The Adventures of Ulysses, 1808; Poetry for Children (with Mary Lamb) 1808; *Poems*—Poems on Various Subjects by S. T. Coleridge (containing four sonnets by Lamb) 1796 (2nd ed. with additional poems, 1797); Blank Verse by Charles Lloyd and Charles Lamb, 1798; Album Verses, 1830. *Miscellaneous*—A Tale of Rosamund Gray and Old Blind Margaret, 1798; John Woodvil: A Tragedy, 1802; Prince Dorus, 1811; The Works of Charles Lamb, 1818; Satan in Search of a Wife, 1831; Eliana, 1866. *Important Collected Editions*

and Letters—The Letters of Charles Lamb (ed. with a Sketch of his Life by T. N. Talfourd) 1837; Final Memorials of Charles Lamb (ed. by T. N. Talfourd) 1848; The Works of Charles and Mary Lamb (ed. by E. V. Lucas) 1903-05; The Letters of Charles Lamb (ed. by H. H. Harper) 1907; Letters of Charles and Mary Lamb (ed. by E. V. Lucas) 1935.

ABOUT: Ainger, A. Charles Lamb; Blunden, E. Charles Lamb: His Life Recorded by His Contemporaries; Blunden, E. Charles Lamb and His Contemporaries; Cornwall, B. (B. W. Procter). Charles Lamb: A Memoir; Daniel G. Recollections of Charles Lamb; Dobell, B. Sidelights on Charles Lamb; Haydon, B. R. Life (ed. by T. Taylor); Hazlitt, W. C. The Lambs; Johnson, Edith C. Lamb Always Elia; Lamb, C. Letters (see Sketch by J. N. Talfourd); Lamb, C. Letters of Charles and Mary Lamb; Livingston, L. S. A Bibliography of the First Editions in Book Form of the Writings of Charles and Mary Lamb; Lucas, E. V. The Life of Charles Lamb; Martin, B. E. In the Footprints of Charles Lamb (with Bibliography by E. D. North); Morley, F. V. Lamb Before Elia; Robinson, H. C. Diary; Ward, A. C. The Frolic and the Gentle; Williams, O. C. Charles Lamb.

LAMB, MARY MONTGOMERIE. See CURRIE, LADY

LAMPMAN, ARCHIBALD (November 17, 1861-February 10, 1899), Canadian poet, was born at Marpeth, Ontario. He was the son of the Rev. Archibald Lampman and Susannah Gessner.

His first education was gained at home. When he was six years old the family moved to Gore's Landing, a community on Rice's Lake, and the seven years spent there greatly influenced the work of the mature poet. It was unfortunate that the rectory had to be situated in a damp house, however, for this caused Lampman to contract rheumatic fever in his eighth year, the disease laming him for four years and resulting in a permanent impairment of his health.

In 1869 he attended Mr. Barnes' school and was thoroughly grounded in classics; he spent the year 1879-80 at Coburg Collegiate Institute, and two years at Trinity School, where he won many prizes. He matriculated at Trinity College, Toronto, in 1879, and was graduated in 1882 with honors in classics; meanwhile he had gained writing experience as editor of the college paper. After a brief career as teacher at the Orangeville High School, where he showed himself a very poor disciplinarian, Lampman was glad to accept a postoffice appointment in Ottawa in 1883, and remained with that organization until his death. A camping trip, with overstrain of the heart from unusual exertions, was fatal to Lampman. He left his widow, the former Maud Playter, whom he had married in 1887, and several children.

The elder Lampman was an amateur poet whose model was Pope. He did not fail to recommend the excellencies of the great Eng-

ARCHIBALD LAMPMAN

lish master to his son, but also called his attention to the beauties of Keats, Tennyson, and Coleridge. Later Wordsworth and Swinburne were to influence Lampman, but never to the extent of supplanting Keats.

The poet's first appearance before the public occurred in 1884 when Charles G. D. Roberts, a distinguished Canadian fellow-poet, accepted "The Coming of Winter" and "Three Flower Petals" for *The Week*. Lampman's first book was published at his own expense in 1888, a slender volume entitled *Among the Millet*. His second volume appeared in 1893 and a third was being manufactured when he died.

Lampman has been called the greatest of Canadian poets. Such critics as William Dean Howells and Robert Louis Stevenson expressed their admiration for his verse, and he is generally ranked among the very first writers of his country. Much of his poetry is derivative, however, and he never succeeded in forming an individual style. Sweetness and polish and a genuine understanding of nature characterize his work, which was that of a genuine, if limited, artist.

R. M.

PRINCIPAL WORKS: Among the Millet, 1888; Lyrics of Earth, 1893; Alcyone, 1899; Poems, 1900.

ABOUT: Garvin, J. W. Canadian Poets; Lampman, A. Poems (see Memoir by D. C. Scott); Logan, J. D. & D. G. French Highways of Canadian Literature; North American Notes and Queries 1:84 August 1900 and 1:105 September 1900; Queen's Quarterly 9:63 July 1901.

LANCASTER, JOSEPH (1778-October 24, 1838), educator, was born in London. His father had been a British soldier in the American Revolution, then became a small shopkeeper. Intended for the Nonconformist ministry, the boy was very religious. At fourteen he left home with the intention of becoming a missionary in Jamaica; having no funds, however, he enlisted in the navy, but was released from his enlistment by friends after one voyage. At about this time he became a Quaker, and remained in that faith even after the Society of Friends had repudiated him. His interest in educating poor children was already lively, and he would bring them in from the streets to teach them to read.

In 1801 he rented a large room which he turned into a school, but since he could not pay teachers, he used the older pupils to teach the younger ones. The children were divided into small classes, each under a monitor. This military system (which the kind-hearted Lancaster never realized was cruel to the less aggressive children) was the foundation of the Lancastrian system. In 1801 the approbation of George III went to his head; he expanded beyond his means, got into money difficulties, and a committee of Friends took him and the school over as the Royal Lancastrian Society. In opposition there was the church-dominated National Society, which used the rival system of Andrew Bell. Lancaster was frequently in prison for debt, his wife had become hopelessly insane, and he chafed under the restrictions of the committee; finally, in 1818, he emigrated to the United States, and started a school in Baltimore. This failed, and so did a disastrous trip to Venezuela. It was at this time that he remarried, his wife having died; his second wife was the widow of John Robinson, of Philadelphia. Lancaster was devoted to his stepchildren, more so than to his daughter by his first marriage.

He had written so far nothing but controversial pamphlets, autobiographical in nature. Now he projected a larger book, outlining his whole system. A small annuity was raised for him in England, but just when his hopes were high he was killed in an accident on the streets of New York.

An unselfish, earnest, deadly sincere man, Lancaster was yet impulsive, extravagant, and uncontrolled in nature. His writing is of purely historical interest, being incoherent, disordered, and vehement almost to the point of lunacy.

PRINCIPAL WORKS: Report of Joseph Lancaster's Progress From 1798, 1810; The Lancastrian System of Education, 1821; Epitome of Some of the Chief Events and Transactions in the Life of Joseph Lancaster, 1833.

ABOUT: Corston, W. Life of Joseph Lancaster; Lancaster, J. Epitome, etc.

LANDON, LETITIA ELIZABETH (August 14, 1802-October 15, 1838), poet and novelist, was born on August 14, 1802, at 25, Hans Place, Chelsea, where she was to spend most of her life. Her ancestors included Sir William Landon of Crednall, Herfordshire, who lost his property in the South Sea bubble, and her great grandfather, Reverend John Landon, who achieved fame in his cause against dissenters. Her father, John Landon, on the other hand, was no celebrity. For he married Catharine Jane Bishop, of Welsh descent, and settled down in Chelsea as a poor army agent. Letitia was the eldest of three children. A younger sister died at thirteen, while her brother, Whittington, became a prominent clergyman.

Tradition says that Letitia was an infant prodigy. If so, she had a fitting instructor in Miss Rowden, herself a poetess and the teacher also of Miss Mitford and Lady Caroline Lamb. The pupil's memory was accounted prodigious, and although she was poor in music and writing, she was so fond of reading that as she rolled her hoop in the garden she held a copy of Scott or some other classic in her free hand.

In 1815 the family moved to Old Brompton. It was there that her cousin Elizabeth showed some of Letitia's verse to their neighbor, William Jerdan, the editor, who almost at once began publishing them in the *Literary Gazette* under the initials, "L.", and finally "L.E.L." Their popularity was almost immediate, and Letitia's reviews also came out in the same paper.

Nor were her books long in appearing. *The Fate of Adelaide* (1821) was followed by *The Improvisatrice* (1824), *The Troubadour* (1825), *The Golden Violet* (1827), *The Venetian Bracelet* (1829), besides scattered contributions to annuals and albums. A first novel, *Romance and Reality,* was published in 1831.

It is hard to believe, therefore, that such a busy person would have time to attend literary salons at Miss Spence's and make a pleasure trip to Paris in 1834. Although she had left home to live at 22, Hans Place with the Lance ladies and later with Mrs. Sheldon she still helped support her mother with the proceeds from her writing. Literary success, however, seems to have made her imprudent, or perhaps it was sheer malice that linked her name with that of Dr. Maginn as well as her friend Jerdan. Her engagement to an unnamed man, thought to be John Forster, the biographer, was duly broken, but she seemed to find quick solace in one George Maclean, who was then the governor at Cape Coast Castle, and much older than Letitia.

Secretly married to him on June 7, 1838, she sailed for a three years' stay in Africa. Cheerful letters reached her friends in England after her arrival on August 16, but when the next ship returned it brought news of her sudden death on October 15. She had been found dead in her room with a bottle of prussic acid in her hand. Rumor decided that she had either committed suicide, been

LETITIA E. LANDON

murdered by her husband or her husband's mistress; or that, always subject to spasms, she had accidently taken an overdose of the medicine she sometimes used for relief. The mystery has never been satisfactorily solved, and has added a glamour to her life which it would not otherwise have had.

Letitia's charm was undoubted as she flitted about, blue-turbaned, among her friends, the S. C. Halls and the Bulwer-Lyttons. She was not handsome, but, as James Hogg, "the Ettrick Shepherd," observed when he first saw her, "I did nae think ye had been sae bonny." Her conversation was sprightly and was not often so melancholy as her verse.

The works themselves were conventional products of their age, and were therefore overrated. For in reality she was "a gifted improvisatrice," but by no means a genius. Her sentiment always outweighed her true feelings; her imitation of Byron and Scott hid her own descriptive ability.   B. D. S.

PRINCIPAL WORKS: *Poetry*—The Fate of Adelaide, 1821; The Improvisatrice, 1824; The Troubadour, 1825; The Golden Violet, 1827; The Venetian Bracelet, 1829; The Vow of the Peacock, 1835; A Birthday Tribute, 1837; The Easter Gift, 1838; Flowers of Loveliness, 1838; The Zenana, 1839. *Prose*—Romance and Reality, 1831; Francesca Carrara, 1834; Traits and Trials of Early Life, 1836; Ethel Churchill, 1837; Castruccio Castracani, 1837; Duty and Inclination, 1838; Lady Anne Granard, 1842.

ABOUT: Berkeley, G. F. My Life and Recollections; Blanchard, L. Life and Literary Remains of L. E. L.; Cruickshank, B. Eighteen Years on the Gold Coast of Africa; Elwood, A. K. Memoirs of the Literary Ladies of England; Enfield, D. E. L. E. L.: A Mystery of the Thirties; Hall, S. C. A Book of Memories; Howitt, W. Homes and Haunts; Jerdan, W. Autobiography; Landon, L. E. Poetical Works (see Introductory Memoir by W. B. Scott); Madden, R. R. The Literary Life and Correspondence of the Countess

361

of Blessington; Thomson, K. Recollections of Literary Characters; Wharton, G. & P. The Queens of Society; London Mercury 26:326 August 1932.

LANDOR, ROBERT EYRES (1781-January 26, 1869), poet and novelist, was the youngest brother of the famous poet and essayist Walter Savage Landor, who was six years his senior. He was born in Warwick, his father a physician, his mother (the second wife) an heiress. He was educated at Worcester College, Oxford, where he was fellow and scholar, and from 1829 to his death was rector of Nafford-with-Birlingham, Worcestershire. In forty years he was never absent from his church a single Sunday, and he spent far more on the church than he received in salary. Extremely modest, he said that he came near to fame just twice—when his tragedy, *Count Arezzi*, was thought to be Byron's, and when his *Fawn of Sertorius* was thought to be his brother's. In each case he immediately corrected the mistake (they had been published anonymously), and the sales dropped immediately to nothing. Nevertheless, this retiring, unassuming man had an authentic talent, overshadowed by his brother's name and his greater aggressiveness. He died at nearly eighty-eight, leaving a legacy to the church which paid for its restoration.

PRINCIPAL WORKS: Count Arezzi, 1823; Three Tragedies, 1841; The Fawn of Sertorius, 1846; The Fountain of Arethusa, 1848.

ABOUT: Colville, F. L. Worthies of Warwickshire; Forster, J. Life of Walter Savage Landor; Swinburne, A. C. Studies; Edinburgh Review, 1850.

LANDOR, WALTER SAVAGE (January 30, 1775-September 17, 1864), poet and essayist, was born in Warwick on January 30, 1775, of an old Staffordshire family. He always relished the fact that his birthday came on the anniversary of the execution of Charles I. His father was Dr. Walter Landor, and his mother, formerly Elizabeth Savage of Warwickshire, was Dr. Landor's second wife. By his first marriage to a Miss Wright, also of Warwick, he had had six children, but only one daughter now survived. By this wife there were three sons and three daughters. Walter Savage, as the eldest son, was destined to inherit his wealthy mother's property.

Little is known of the boy's childhood except that at the age of four he went to school at Knowle where he remained for five years. At ten he was called one of the best Latin students at Rugby. In addition he was rated an omnivorous reader of English books. Nor was he backward at sports. Even thus early he was known for his irascible temper, and when a quarrel arose over a Latin quantity he was expelled from school and given into the charge of Dr. Langley of Ashbourne in Derbyshire. There he stayed for two years

preceding his entrance in 1793 to Trinity College, Oxford, where he found two Rugby friends, Walter Birch of Magdalen, who was to become a clergyman, and Henry Cary, later the translator of Dante. Landor again showed his rebellious nature when he appeared in college with his hair unpowdered. Soon, too, he was dubbed the "mad Jacobin." In due time he was rusticated from Oxford for firing a shot at a Tory undergraduate across the hall. He did not return to college, because, as he said, "Oxford could teach him nothing that he wanted to know." To his father this behavior seemed deplorable, so Landor left home and college at about the same time. Later his friend, the young and lovely Dorothea Lyttleton, tried, though without success, to intercede with Dr. Landor, who wanted his son to study law.

The youth departed for London, where he studied Italian and French at lodgings in Portland Place. In 1795 he published a first volume of verse, *The Poems of Walter Savage Landor*, which he suppressed. Granted an allowance by his family, he spent the next year on the lonely coast of South Wales. It was at Tenby that he met his friend, Rose Aylmer, and it was there, too, that he began work on his first important poem, entitled *Gebir*, and published in 1798. Through the influence of his friend, Dr. Parr, the author, he became a contributor to the Whig paper, *The Courier*, a connection that terminated in 1801. He visited Paris in 1802, and by this time his sympathies were with the revolutionists.

When at last his father died in 1805 Landor inherited his patrimony. But he continued to make Bath his headquarters. Deeply moved by the death of Rose Aylmer in India, he soon wrote the elegy named for her, which won him fame. He also inscribed verses to Sarah Jane Swift, whom he called "Ianthe." He set out for a tour of the lake district in 1807. Later, in Wales, he admired an estate known as Llanthony, which he longed to purchase. He met Robert Southey, the poet, for the first time in Bristol. A long correspondence ensued, and the two remained friends for thirty years. At this period, too, Landor translated his liberal ideas into action when he started for Spain to fight against Napoleon. For his services, which were brief, he was awarded an honorary commission as colonel in the Spanish Army. When he returned he bought the coveted property on the Welsh border and set about restoring the place to its original grandeur.

At Bath in 1811 he found the lady of his choice in golden-haired Julia Thuillier, daughter of a poor banker of Swiss descent. He married her at once. Almost immediately his troubles began. He had been taken in, he

WALTER SAVAGE LANDOR

admitted, "by a pretty face." At least that was his side of the story. In the midst of the storm and stress of his domestic life and his quarrels with the Welsh peasants on his estate, he published his verse tragedy, *Count Julian* (1812). Murray brought out the work for Landor, as well as his prose *Commentary on Memoirs of Mr. Fox*. Impending lawsuits, however, between Landor and his neighbors and tenants, caused him to leave Wales in May 1814 and withdraw to France. His wife refused to accompany him, so he left in a rage and set sail alone in an oyster-boat. Early in 1815 his wife joined him at Tours, where he was hard at work on a poem called *Ulysses in Argiripa*. But he soon grew restless. In September of the same year he and his wife joined his brother Robert on a visit to Italy. Indeed, it was there that his first child, Arnold, was born. Two more sons and a daughter were to follow. For a while Landor stayed quietly in Italy entertaining his friends and writing. But the next year he was charged with libel by an Italian poet and ordered to leave the country. He found refuge first in Genoa and finally in Pisa where he remained until 1821. While at Pisa he published a volume of Latin tales which he called *Idyllia Heroica* (1820). His next place of residence was Florence. There he settled down with his ménage in the Medici palace for five years, and busied himself with the composition of a series of prose dialogues. These came out in two volumes (1824) under the title, *Imaginary Conversations*. A third volume followed in 1828, while a second series of two volumes appeared the next year.

Meanwhile he found time to quarrel with his publishers, the police, and his landlord; to frolic with his children, who called him

"Babbo"; to become a collector of pictures, and to entertain such important visitors as William Hazlitt, the essayist, and Leigh Hunt, the poet. In 1830, however, his mother died, and in the summer of 1832, Landor was persuaded to leave his present home in Fiesole and return to London for the first time in eighteen years. From there he went to Cambridge to catch a glimpse of his sisters, to the lake country to see Southey and the poet Wordsworth. During a trip up the Rhine he met Schlegel, the German critic. And in England he supervised the publication of the work he had done in Italy. His *Citation and Examination of William Shakespeare*, in prose, came out in 1834. His dialogue, *Pericles and Aspasia*, and *The Pentameron*, also in prose, followed.

In the meantime, Landor left Italy to make his home in England. To quote his own story, "domestic life was rendered impossible to him." So he deserted his wife and his children. In England he lived now at Clifton, now in London, though he finally settled down at Bath. He enjoyed visiting Lady Blessington, and he made friends with the younger group in London, with men like John Forster, who was to become his biographer, and Charles Dickens, the novelist. His own writing at this period might be classed as miscellaneous. A book of plays appeared in 1839. A collected edition of his works came out in 1846 and a volume of his Latin verses, or *Poemata et Inscriptiones*, in 1847. His *Conversations of the Greeks and Romans* (1853) he dedicated to Dickens. One of his last volumes consisted of a collection of minor pieces, and he wanted to call it *Dry Sticks Fagoted by the Late W. S. Landor* (1858). But the publishers left out the "Late." Ironically enough, the author collapsed from a stroke just before one of his enemies sued him for a lampoon that had appeared in this very volume. But Landor did not die. When he recovered he sought safety in Genoa, and at length in Fiesole, where he found a cool welcome awaiting him. Nor by running away did he escape the verdict of £1000 damages against him. Furthermore, his troubles with his family were not over. He left home several times, and for the last five years of his life lived near the poet Browning's residence in Florence with his dog, Giallo, as his only companion. By the spring of 1864, however he had sunk into a stupor. Tended by his two youngest sons, he finally died on September 17, and was buried in the English cemetery in Florence.

Landor was always "a king and a lion among men," for his appearance was decidedly impressive. In youth he was termed "a solid, massive, energetic presence," while in age he was "beautifully venerable," with his "bold and keen grey eyes," and his "thick white

363

fringe of backward-flowing hair." His character was likewise unusual. He was called "proud and passionate." Moods of hilarity alternated with those of anger. In spite of his violence and his strange habits he did not live a life of solitude. He loved, said Browning, "a pretty girl to talk nonsense with, and he finds comfort in American visitors, who hold him in proper respect." Among the latter were William Story, the artist, Ralph Waldo Emerson, the author, and Miss Kate Field, who studied Latin under his tutelage. Shortly before Landor died, the poet Swinburne "came out from England for no other purpose than to see Landor without knowing him." Afterwards Swinburne dedicated his poem, *Atalanta in Calydon,* to Landor.

Landor himself claimed "no place in the world of letters," for, "I am," he announced, "and will be alone, as long as I live and after." So Landor judged himself, and to some extent he was right. His popularity was not great. He was little read in his own age. His meaning was occasionally obscure; he was not always sympathetic. But in general his work, though uneven, remains unique. His elegy, "Rose Aylmer," has become a classic. His dramatic scenes, *Imaginary Conversations,* have survived. Finally, his style, both in prose and verse, approaches perfection to such a degree that critics have charged the author with coldness. He seemed, they said, "to write in marble." But when they searched, these same critics found passages of great beauty and striking epigrams, that challenged censure. A portion of his work, both in prose and verse, defies oblivion.   B. D. S.

PRINCIPAL WORKS: *Poetry*—Poems, 1795; Moral Epistle, 1795; Gebir, 1798; Iambi, 1800; Poems From the Arabic and Persian, 1800; Poetry, 1802; Gebirus, 1803; Simonidea, 1806; The Dun Cow, 1808; Ode ad Gustavum Regem, 1810; Count Julian, 1812; Idyllia Nova Quinque, 1815; Idyllia Heroica Decem, 1820; Gebir, Count Julian, and Other Poems, 1831; Terry Hogan, 1836; A Satire on Satirists, 1836; Andrea of Hungary, and Giovanna of Naples, 1839; Fra Rupert, 1840; The Hellenics, 1847; Poemata et Inscriptiones, 1847; Italics, 1848; On Kossuth's Voyage to America, 1851; Tyrannicide, 1851; Carmen ad Heroinam, 1852; Antony and Octavius, 1856; Dry Sticks, 1858; Heroic Idylls, 1863. *Prose*—Letters Addressed to Lord Liverpool and the Parliament, 1814; Imaginary Conversations of Literary Men and Statesmen, 1824-29; Imaginary Conversation: Solon and Pisistratus, 1832; Citation and Examination of William Shakespeare, 1834; The Letters of a Conservative, 1836; Pericles and Aspasia, 1836; The Pentameron and Pentalogia, 1837; Imaginary Conversation of King Carlo-Alberto and the Duchess Belgioioso, 1848; Statement and Occurrences at Llanbedr, 1849; Popery: British and Foreign, 1851; Imaginary Conversations of Greeks and Romans, 1853; Letters of an American, 1854; Letter From W. S. Landor to R. W. Emerson, 1856; Walter Savage Landor and the Honourable Mrs. Yescombe, 1857; Mr. Landor Threatened, 1857; Mr. Landor's Remarks, 1859; Savonarola e il Priore di San Marco, 1860; Letters (ed. by S. Wheeler) 1899; Charles James Fox, 1907; Last Days, Letters, and Conversations (ed.

by H. C. Minchin) 1934. *Miscellaneous*—Works, 1846; The Last Fruit off an Old Tree, 1853; Works and Life (ed. by J. Forster) 1874-76; Letters and Other Unpublished Writings (ed. by S. Wheeler) 1897; Complete Works (ed. by T. E. Welby) 1927-.

ABOUT: Bradley, W. A. The Early Poems of Walter Savage Landor; Colvin, S. Landor; Elkin, F. Walter Savage Landor's Studies of Italian Life and Literature; Evans, E. W. Walter Savage Landor; Forster, J. Walter Savage Landor: A Biography; Henderson, W. B. D. Swinburne and Landor; Milnes, R. M. Monographs; Wheeler, S. & Wise, T. J. A Bibliography of the Writings in Prose and Verse of Walter Savage Landor; Whiting, L. The Florence of Landor; Wise, T. J. A Landor Library; The Atlantic Monthly 17: (385) April 1866; The Atlantic Monthly 17: 540 May 1866; The Atlantic Monthly 17: 684 June 1866; Fraser's Magazine ns2: 113 July 1870; Temple Bar 92: 191 June 1891.

LANE, EDWARD WILLIAM (September 17, 1801-August 10, 1876), Arabic scholar, was born at Hereford, the son of Theophilus Lane, prebendary of Withington Parva, and Sylvia (Gardiner) Lane, a niece of Gainsborough, the painter.

The boy was educated at Bath and Hereford, showing ability in mathematics and the classics. Instead, however, of proceeding to Cambridge (he had considered entering the Church), he went to London to study engraving. His health did not permit (in the London climate) the steady application required, and his condition made it advisable for him to go to a warmer region.

With the hope of a consulship he sailed in 1825 for Egypt. The voyage was a hard one, and during the incapacity of the master of the ship Lane took the helm and guided the vessel through a hurricane; the crew mutinied, and he barely escaped with his life.

He arrived to find himself in a country little known, with a group of brilliant men enthusiastic for research. He threw himself into exploration and discovery, becoming so thoroughly a part of his surroundings that in appearance and speech he could pose as a native. In 1826 and 1827 he ascended the Nile, studying the monuments at Thebes and making drawings of them; much of the time he lived in tombs.

In 1828 he returned to England, with a book of description of Egypt, including one hundred and one sepia illustrations. The book was too difficult to reproduce satisfactorily, and was not published. The Society for the Diffusion of Useful Knowledge, however, accepted for publication the chapters concerning the modern Egyptians.

To insure the greatest accuracy Lane returned to Egypt to make a study of the people of Cairo, living in the Mohammedan quarters, associating almost entirely with those of that faith, and attending their ceremonies. The results of his researches are embodied in his *Account of the Manners and Customs of the*

Modern Egyptians, which sold out an entire edition within two weeks. Lane, returned to England, produced next his translation of the *Arabian Nights,* the first version of a high degree of accuracy.

In 1842 he journeyed again to Egypt, this time with a view to the preparation of an exhaustive Arabic dictionary to be compiled from native books and lexicons. The amount of work demanded was tremendous, and kept Lane confined for whole months to his place of residence. The expenses connected with the dictionary were so huge that it was owing mainly to the generosity of Lord Prudhoe (and his widow) that the book was finally published.

By 1849 work had progressed sufficiently to allow Lane to return to England. Honors were showered upon him, at home and abroad, and in 1863, when the dictionary began to appear, he received the grant of a Civil List Pension. He continued to work almost to his last day, dying at Worthing in 1876.

Lane's life is the record of an extraordinarily complete devotion to scholarship. At Cairo he worked twelve to fourteen hours every day on the lexicon, taking only Friday (the Moslem sabbath) for rest. He denied himself rest, recreation, and society for the purposes of his work. He was, however, devoted to his family, and his Cairo household consisted of his wife (a Greek lady whom he married in England in 1840) and his sister and her two sons. Later, in England, upon the death of a nephew, he took in the three fatherless children, and he interested himself in the education of his nephews and grandnephews. A deeply religious man, he regularly observed Sunday, reading the Bible (he was a fine Hebrew scholar) and attending church; during all his years of life as a nominal Mohammedan he never lost his loyal devotion to the Church of England.

Of his works it is perhaps sufficient to say that they are unquestioningly accepted as standard. *Modern Egyptians* remains the accepted authority on its subject, thanks not only to its composition at a time when Cairo was still Saracenic, but to its exhaustive detail as well. The translation of the *Arabian Nights* was the first to convey an eastern manner, and, though too incomplete and too definitely purified for the specialist student, is the best version for the general reader. But perhaps his greatest contribution to scholarship is the *Arabic-English Lexicon,* published in eight parts (three, edited by Stephen Lane-Poole, after Lane's death), which is described in the *Encyclopaedia Britannica* as "an enduring monument, the completeness and finished scholarship with which it is executed making each article an exhaustive monograph."

R. W. W.

PRINCIPAL WORKS: *Description and Research*—An Account of the Manners and Customs of the Modern Egyptians, 1836; Arabian Society in the Middle Ages: Studies From the Thousand and One Nights (ed. by S. Lane-Poole) 1883; Cairo Fifty Years Ago, 1896. *Philology*—Über die Lexicographie der Arabischen Sprache (Zeitschrift der Deutschen Morgenländdschen Gesellschaft 3. 90 1849 Heft 1) 1849; Über die Aussprache der Arabische Vocale und die Betonung der Arabischen Wörter (Zeitschrift der Deutschen Morganländischen Gesellschaft 4:171 1850 Heft 2) 1850; An Arabic-English Lexicon, 1863-92. *Miscellaneous*—Arabian Tales and Anecdotes, 1845; Forty-one Eastern Tales and Anecdotes, 1854. *Translator*—The Thousand and One Nights, 1838-40; Selections From the Kur-án, 1843.

ABOUT: Lane-Poole, S. Life of Edward William Lane; Athenaeum 2:268 August 26,) 1876; Times August 15, 1876.

LANG, ANDREW (March 31, 1844-July 20, 1912), man of letters, poet, folk-lorist, editor, journalist, humorist, historian, and translator, was born at Selkirk, the eldest son of John Lang, sheriff-clerk, whose father was a business acquaintance of Sir Walter Scott, and Jane Plenderleath (Sellar) Lang, daughter of the Factor to the first Duke of Sutherland. It was a family tradition that the Langs came originally from Bohemia.

He was brought up at Clifton in the care of a Cameronian nurse and before he had put down his coral and bells, he was taking up the cudgels for the Jacobites. Like Sir Walter Scott whom he adored, his whole life was influenced by the ballads and folk-tales he heard as a child.

At thirteen, Lang was considered a bad careless little boy and "aye the stupid ane o' the fam'ly." After attending Selkirk Grammar School and Edinburgh Academy, he went to St. Andrews University where he developed lasting passions for cricket, golf, and the

E. W. LANE

gentle art of angling. Most important of all, he practised journalism in St. Leonard's Hall by the light of stolen candle-ends. He studied Greek under his uncle, Professor Sellars, and said that he "loathed" it, going on to add that it was "hissing and malignant." But when he came to Homer, a sea-change took place, as Shakespeare would say. Of Homer, Lang wrote, "the very sound of the hexameter, that long inimitable roll of the most various music, was enough to win the heart."

In 1861, he matriculated from St. Andrews and three years later was a candidate for the Snell Exhibition at the University of Glasgow. With the Snell Exhibition he went to Oxford in 1865 and there came under the influence of Matthew Arnold. Not only did Lang imitate Arnold's fastidious mode of dress, but his prose style was determined by Arnold's book, *Friendship's Garland,* published in 1871. Later on, however, Lang did not like to admit how much Arnold had influenced him.

Three years after his arrival at Oxford, Lang became a Merton don. Thomas Seccombe remarked that the British Museum was "a nest of singing birds," owing to the presence there [about 1870] of such writers as Gosse, Patmore, Dobson, Garnett, O'Shaughnessy, and Lang. In 1872, Lang's first book of verse was published, *Ballads and Lyrics of Old France.*

In 1875 Lang gave up the peace of Oxford cloisters for the hubbub of Fleet Street, a decision that Edmund Gosse evaluated as the most momentous of his life. In this same year he was working on a series of articles for the ninth edition of the *Encyclopaedia Britannica,* the subjects ranging from ghosts to crystal-gazing.

For almost forty years Lang was to pursue a distinguished journalistic career. He amazed the most hardened Fleet Street veterans by his brilliant wit, scholarship, encyclopedic memory, and ability to write, oblivious of interruption. He often wrote articles between the games of a cricket match. He contributed leaders to the *Daily News,* literary articles to the *Morning Post* and other papers, reviewed for *The Academy,* and wrote monthly topical paragraphs for *Longman's Magazine* under the title, "At the Sign of the Ship."

But journalism was for Lang with his hydra-headed mind merely one of his many careers. Lang wanted to be to England what the French poet, Ronsard, with his chansons and his lays, had been to France. His *XXII Ballades in Blue China* and *XXXII Ballades in Blue China* gave new life to English poetry. Unfortunately, Lang resembled Ronsard not only in his successes, but in his failures as well. Of his one attempt at a serious claim as a poet, *Helen of Troy,* a narrative poem in

six books, the critics said that it had beauty but it was the cold beauty of a still life. Gosse called the year 1882 the tomb of Lang's brightest ambitions. After the reception accorded *Helen of Troy,* Lang vowed that he would never write another poem he could not finish at a sitting.

Lang carried a lance in many a controversial tourney. His theory of totemism was to revolutionize the attitude of scholars towards the origin of folk-tales. At that time, it was commonly believed that folk-tales sprang from one language used by a primitive tribe. Lang believed that these stories, with their surprisingly similar plots, developed from the worship of an ancient tribe for one God. His two most important books on this subject were *Custom and Myth,* and *Myth, Ritual, and Religion.* Much of the credit belongs to Lang for establishing as a fact that which most of us take for granted nowadays—the unity of Homer. In Lang's day it was the minority that believed Homer to be an actual person and the author of all the books attributed to his name. Of the several books that Lang contributed to this controversy, the last one, *The World of Homer,* was the best.

Nothing appealed to Lang's romantic nature more than a good mystery. He is to history what Sherlock Holmes is to crime. Robert Louis Stevenson suggested to Lang that he ought to write something about the Jacobites. While doing research work on that subject, Lang stumbled upon the solution of a historical mystery—the identity of the Jacobite spy mentioned by Scott in his introduction to *Red Gauntlet.* The result of Lang's discoveries appeared in *Pickle the Spy.* He also wrote several detective monographs based on material found while he was doing historical research work. Another controversy he took part in was about the Maid of Orleans. In 1908 Anatole France wrote *Vie de Jeanne d'Arc.* Six months later, Lang's *Maid of France* appeared in answer to the charges that France made against Jeanne d'Arc.

Ironically enough, as Lang, himself, has pointed out, of all the many books he was to write (so many it is impossible to find a complete bibliography of them) the books to bring him the most fame were ones he edited but did not write. In 1889 was published the first of that enchanted rainbow-hued series of fairy books,

. . . .books Yellow, Red, Green and Blue,
   All true, or just as good as true.

To-day, the gilt-edged volumes of the first edition, small enough to slip into the pocket of a child's pinafore, are cherished collectors' items.

Lang was given many honors during his life, from being presented with the freedom of his native town in 1889, to being elected

ANDREW LANG

president of the Psychical Research Society in 1911. Of all these honors, his favorite was the St. Andrews Doctorate, 1888, and next to that, the Oxford Doctorate, 1904.

In 1875, Lang married Miss Leonora Blanche Alleyne, the youngest daughter of Mr. C. T. Alleyne, of Clifton and Barbadoes. There were no children.

He died of angina pectoris at Banchory, Aberdeenshire, July 20, 1912.

Lang's personality was essentially a romantic one. He delighted in the idea of his having gypsy blood. He worshipped the past and disdained the present. He had a merciless wit that made him many enemies and embarrassed even his devoted friends. Never of strong health, he had a languid manner exceedingly irritating to those who have too much thyroid. Pedants and bores of any description fled from his barbs. But among his friends were Sidney Colvin, Stevenson, and Gosse. For all his apparent mercilessness, he loved dogs. After his death it was discovered that he had supported many poor writers and their entire families. But Watts-Dunton, Swinburne's friend and benefactor, said, "I never knew a man of genius who didn't loathe Lang." Gosse compared Lang to an angora cat that quickly unsheathes its claws when too many liberties are taken with it, or too much asked of it. Writing of Lang after his death, Colvin speaks of his "intellectual energies so keen and varied, accomplishments so high, so insatiable a spirit of curiosity and research under a guise so airy and playful." Probably Sir James Barrie understood him the best of all when he said, "Mr. Lang puzzled the Sasserach [i.e. the English] a little. Perhaps this is the first duty of a Scot. He was so prodigal of his showers and so wayward.

There was a touch of the elf about him." Lang was a brilliant talker and improvisor. Mrs. Lang tells of how her husband would make up nonsense verse by the hour while on long walks. There is a certain mystery about Lang that is solved, perhaps, by his saying that his mind was gay, but his soul was melancholy. He was greatly averse to all publicity and refused to have any authorized biography of his life made, or to have his letters published after his death.

His looks were as romantic as his personality. He was one of those rare authors who look like their books. But which book? The fairy tales. He looked as if he might have been the prince who was turned into a bluebird. Max Beerbohm described him as an ornament in a drawing-room, "like a palm in a pot."

"Versatile" is the adjective most frequently applied to Lang's writing, but nothing could be more incorrect. To be versatile means to be able to write on any subject. Lang did write on many subjects, but on many others his mind was a blank. He could not pay any attention to a subject that bored him. As Gosse points out, he shunned reality and could only with the utmost difficulty have any traffic with it. Of Lang's poetry, J. H. Millar said, "His dexterity in grappling with critical schemes of versification is amazing. The ballade, the rondeau, even the mysterious pantoum, withheld no secrets from him." Salomon Reinach looked upon Lang's discovery of the sources of folk-tales as the work of a genius. As a translator from the classical poets, Sir George Douglas considered that Lang probably had no equal in English literature. Louis Cazamian believed that Lang's portrait of Jeanne d'Arc was the best one in the English language. J. P. Mackie, the historian, makes this comment: "While it is true to say that Lang was a romantic, it is quite false to suggest he was that and nothing more. He was in all subjects an investigator with an almost uncanny flair for finding things out, and though he entered the study of history through the portals of romance he soon became a serious historian." Lang was a master of parody. He wrote several novels, but they were the poorest of all his work, which, as a rule, maintained a uniform excellence. Two of his faults were that he wrote too much and when tracking down an idea was apt to ignore the trees for the underbrush. He is best described by the words of G. S. Gordan, who calls him "the greatest bookman of his age," the last great man of letters in the Scottish tradition.   D. H.

PRINCIPAL WORKS: *Poetry*—Ballads and Lyrics of Old France, 1872; XXII Ballades in Blue China, 1880; XXXII Ballades in Blue China, 1881; Helen of Troy, 1882; Rhymes à la Mode, 1884; Grass of Parnassus, 1888; The Poetical Works of Andrew

Lang, 1923. *Edited*—The Poems of E. A. Poe, 1881; Grimm's Household Tales, 1884; English Worthies (8 vols.) 1885-87; The Blue Fairy Book, 1889; The Red Fairy Book, 1890; The Green Fairy Book, 1892; Border Edition of the Waverly Novels, 1892; The Yellow Fairy Book, 1894; Poems and Songs of Robert Burns, 1896; The Complete Angler by Walton, 1896; The Pink Fairy Book, 1897; The Nursery Rhyme Book, 1897; The Gadshill Dickens, 1897; The Arabian Nights, 1898; The Poetical Works of Scott, 1899; The Gray Fairy Book, 1900; The Brown Fairy Book, 1904; The Olive Fairy Book, 1907; The Lilac Fairy Book, 1910; *Miscellaneous*—The Library, 1881; Letters to Dead Authors, 1886; Books and Bookmen, 1886; Pictures at Play, 1888; Letters on Literature, 1889; How to Fail in Literature, 1890; Old Friends: Essays in Epistolary Parody, 1890; Essays in Little, 1891; Homer and the Epic, 1893; Homer and His Age, 1908; The World of Homer, 1910. *Novels*—The Mark of Cain, 1884; A Monk of Fife, 1896; The Valet's Tragedy, 1903. *History*—Oxford: Brief Historical and Descriptive Notes, 1882; Pickle the Spy, 1897; The Companion of Pickle, 1898; A History of Scotland From the Roman Occupation to the Suppression of the Last Jacobite Uprising, 1900; Mystery of Mary Stuart, 1901; Historical Mysteries, 1904; The Portraits and Jewels of Mary Stuart, 1906; History of English Literature, 1912. *Biography*—Life, Letters, and Diaries of Sir Stopford Northcote: First Earl of Iddesligh, 1890; Life and Letters of J. G. Lockhart, 1896; Prince Charles Edward 1900; Tennyson, 1901; John Knox and the Reformation, 1906; Maid of France, 1908; The Life of Sir George Mackenzie, 1909; Sir Walter Scott and the Border Minstrelsy, 1910. *Mythology, Religion and Superstition*—Custom and Myth, 1884; Myth, Ritual, and Religion, 1887; Modern Mythology, 1887; The Making of Religion, 1891; Cock Lane and Common Sense, 1894; The Book of Dreams and Ghosts, 1897; Magic and Religion, 1901.

ABOUT: Lang, A. Poetical Works (see Preface by Mrs. Lang); Lucas, E. V. The Colvins and Their Friends; Blackwood's Magazine 92:425 September 1912; Bookman's Journal and Print Collector n.s. 5:75 1921; Life and Letters 1:1 June 1928; Literature 9:484 November 23, 1901; Quarterly Review 218:299 April 1913.

LANG, JOHN DUNMORE (August 25, 1799-August 8, 1878), Australian poet and miscellaneous writer, was born in Greenock, Scotland. He was educated at the University of Glasgow, received his M.A. in 1820, and was licensed to preach the same year. In 1822 he was ordained and sent to form a Scottish church in Sydney; this church, founded in 1823, was the first Presbyterian church in New South Wales. In 1825 he received a D.D. degree from Glasgow.

Besides his clerical duties, Lang, published and edited three newspapers—*The Colonist* from 1835 to 1840, the *Colonial Journal* in 1841, and *The Press* in 1851 and 1852. As he had very strong opinions on controversial subjects, being opposed to the economic and political success of transported ex-convicts, violently anti-Irish and anti-Roman Catholic, and Puritanical in sexual matters, his papers were frequently in hot water, and on one occasion he was fined for libel. An advocate of free immigration, he brought out colonists at his own expense, particularly ministers and teachers. He was the first to suggest the taking over of New Zealand by England. In all he made six visits to England on behalf of the various projects he advocated for his adopted country. In 1842, following a quarrel over matters of church discipline, he was deposed by the Presbyterian Synod of Sydney, but most of his congregation followed him, and in 1865 a reconciliation was effected. From 1843 to 1846, and again in 1850, 1854, 1859, 1860, and 1864, he was a very active member of the legislative council, his terms of office being interspersed by journeys to England. He died in Sydney, and was accorded a public funeral.

As a poet, Lang is negligible, and his work is of interest only because his subject is Australia over a hundred years ago. His books on Australian matters are still of historical if not of literary interest.

PRINCIPAL WORKS: Aurora Australia (poems) 1826; Emigration, 1833; An Historical and Statistical Account of New South Wales, 1834; Transportation and Colonisation, 1837; Religion and Education in America, 1840; Origin and Migration of the Polynesian Nation, 1876.

ABOUT: Lang, J. D. A Brief Sketch of my Parliamentary Life, 1870.

LA RAMÉE, LOUISE DE. See RAMÉE, LOUISE DE LA

LARDNER, DIONYSIUS (April 3, 1793-April 29, 1859), Irish scientist, was born in London. His father was a solicitor and he too was educated for the bar, but disliking the profession he entered Trinity College, Dublin. He received a B.A. degree in 1817, M.A. in 1819, and LL.B. and LL.D. in 1827. He took holy orders but never acted as a clergyman, his interest already being entirely in science, particularly mathematics and physics. In 1821 he became professor of natural philosophy and astronomy in London University (now University College, London). In 1829 he started publishing his *Cabinet Cyclopaedia*, securing such contributors as Scott, Moore, Sismondi, Herschel, and DeMorgan; he himself wrote the physical portions. He was an early advocate of trans-oceanic steamships. In the 'forties he engaged in a highly successful lecture tour throughout the United States. He was a Fellow of the Royal Society and a member of almost every learned society of his time.

So far, his was a normal career for a scientist; but his personal life was strangely at variance with his sober intellectual interests. In 1815 he married Cecilia Flood, and they had three children. They were separated in 1820, and legally divorced in 1849. Meanwhile he was conducting a long liaison with Mary Heaviside, the wife of Capt. Richard Heaviside. In 1840 they eloped. Captain Heaviside sued Lardner for seduction, and secured a verdict of £8000, then divorced his wife, in 1845. On Lardner's own divorce in 1849, the two were married, and they had two daughters. Living no longer being comfortable in England, they moved to Paris and lived there thenceforth. Lardner died in Naples soon after his sixty-fourth birthday.

Lardner was an excellent popularizer of science, versatile in interests and lucid in style, and the various collections he edited and published were of great merit. His own work, however, was highly superficial and not very reliable.

PRINCIPAL WORKS: *Edited*—The Cabinet Cyclopaedia (133 vols) 1829-49; Dr. Lardner's Cabinet Library (unfinished; 9 historical vols.) 1830-32; Edinburgh Cabinet Library (38 vols.) 1830-44; The Museum of Science and Art (12 vols.) 1853-56. *Original* (mostly from the Museum of Science and Art)—Handbook of Natural Philosophy and Astronomy, 1851-53; Common Things Explained, 1855-56; Popular Astronomy, 1851-53; Common Things Explained, 1855-56; Popular Astronomy, 1855-57; Popular Physics, 1856; The Bees and White Ants, 1856; Popular Geology, 1856; The Microscope, 1856; Steam and Its Uses, 1856; Animal Physics, 1857; Chemistry for Schools, 1859.

ABOUT: Dublin University Magazine Vol. 35.

LAUDER, SIR THOMAS DICK (1784-May 29, 1848), Scottish novelist, was the oldest son of the sixth baronet. He was an officer in the Cameron Highlanders, but resigned his commission on his marriage to Charlotte Cumin, an heiress, by whom he had two sons and ten daughters. He succeeded to the baronetcy on his father's death in 1820.

In 1815 he began to write on chemistry, natural history, and meteorology for the *Annals of Philosophy*. At the same time he began his series of historical stories, mostly of Scotland in the days of Bruce; one, in *Blackwood's*, was supposed to be by Scott. (All magazine entries in those days were anonymous.) In 1832 he moved near Edinburgh, where he lived for the remainder of his life. A liberal Whig, he was nevertheless in 1839 made secretary of the Board of Scottish Manufactures, and in that capacity founded several art and technical schools.

Lauder was extremely versatile; besides his stories and his scientific interests, he was an accomplished violinist, and an artist sufficiently talented to illustrate many of his own books. Dr. John Brown, the essayist, who was his close friend, praised his "descriptive power, humor, sympathy for suffering, and sense of the picturesque." His novels were, however, weak in characterization, and are chiefly to be read for their vivid descriptions of places and of the life of the time of which he treated.

PRINCIPAL WORKS: Lochindhu, 1825; The Wolf of Bodenoch, 1827; Account of the Great Moray Floods, 1830; Highland Rambles and Legends, 1837; Legends and Tales of the Highlands, 1841.

ABOUT: Constable, T. Archibald Constable and His Literary Correspondents; Lauder, T. D. Scottish Rivers (see Preface by John Brown to 1874 ed.).

LAUGHTON, SIR JOHN KNOX (April 23, 1830-September 14, 1915), historian, was born in Liverpool, the son of a sea captain. He was educated at the Royal Institute School in Liverpool, and at Caius College, Cambridge, where he was graduated B.A. in 1852 as a wrangler. The next year he entered the Royal Navy as a naval instructor, and served throughout the Crimean War. In 1856 he was transferred to the Far East where he served through the Chinese War. His status was that of a civilian, but his participation in actual fighting gained him two medals. In 1859 he was sent to the Mediteranean, and in 1866 was attached to the Royal Naval College at Portsmouth. In 1873 he was made a Fellow of the Royal Meteorological Society, becoming its president in 1882. In 1873 also, when the Naval University was established at Greenwich, he went to it as professor of meteorology and marine surveying. In 1876 he instituted the first lectures on naval history ever given. This was his specialty from this time on, and is the subject of most of his writing.

In 1885 Laughton reached the retirement age, but he continued to lecture, became a regular contributor to the *Edinburgh Review* and the *Dictionary of National Biography*, and from 1885 to 1914 was professor of history at King's College, London. He was the first secretary of the Navy Records Society, serving from 1893 to 1912. He was the recipient of numerous honorary degrees and other honors, and in 1907 was knighted. He was married twice, in 1866 to Isabella Carr, who died, leaving one son and three daughters, and in 1886 to Maria Josefa di Alberti, of Cadiz, Spain, by whom he had three sons and two daughters.

Laughton was the founder of naval history. His influence on others is more important than his own histories, though these were sound and reliable.

PRINCIPAL WORKS: Physical Geography, 1870; Studies in Naval History, 1887; Life of Nelson, 1895.

ABOUT: London Times September 15, 1915.

LAURIE, SIMON SOMERVILLE (November 13, 1829-March 2, 1909), Scottish educator and philosopher, was born in Edinburgh, the oldest of five sons of the chaplain of the Edinburgh Royal Infirmary. The family was poor, and it was necessary for him to pay for his own education; at eleven he was already teaching younger children besides conducting his own studies. From the High School at Edinburgh he went to the University of Edinburgh, where he acted as class

assistant throughout his course. He received his M.A. in 1849, and for five years was a private tutor, traveling with his pupils. From 1855 to 1905 he was secretary and visitor to schools of the Educational Committee of the Church of Scotland at Edinburgh, which at that time controlled all elementary and training schools in Scotland. He was a strong advocate of university training for teachers, and helped to raise teaching to the status of a real profession. He founded a high school for girls in Edinburgh, and helped to secure the admission of women to the universities. From 1876 to 1903 he was professor of education in the University of Edinburgh. In 1891 he was president of the Teachers' Guild of Great Britain and Ireland. He received honorary LL.D. degrees from the Universities of Edinburgh, St. Andrew's, and Aberdeen. He was married twice, in 1860 to Catherine Ann Hibburd, whose death left him with two sons and two daughters, and in 1901 to Lucy Struthers.

Laurie's educational interests led him into the philosophy of education, and thence into philosophy in general. He was, however, more of a philosophical commentator than an original thinker in this field.

PRINCIPAL WORKS: The Philosophy of Ethics, 1866; Notes on Certain British Theories of Morals, 1868; Metaphysica, 1884; Ethica, 1885; Synthetica, 1906.

ABOUT: Remacle, G. La Philosophie de S. S. Laurie.

LAWLESS, HON. EMILY (June 17, 1845-October 19, 1913) Irish poet and novelist, was born in County Kildare, the daughter of the third Baron Cloncurry. She led a very uneventful life, a society lady by birth, a secluded writer by preference. She was privately educated at home. Except for some Continental travel and occasional visits to Dublin and London, most of her life was spent on her ancestral estate in Ireland, though she died in Surrey, England. She never married.

Most of her novels are studies of the Irish peasantry, rather serious and heavy in mood. She has, however, a sensitive feeling for nature, reflected in her novels as well as in her poems, most of which also bear on Irish themes. Her one book of prose non-fiction, her history of Ireland, was called "clear and temperate" by The Spectator in a contemporary review.

PRINCIPAL WORKS: A Millionaire's Cousin, 1885; Hurrish, 1886; Ireland, 1887; With Essex in Ireland, 1890; Grania, 1892; With the Wild Geese (poems) 1902.

ABOUT: London Times October 23, 1913.

LAW, THOMAS GRAVES (December 14, 1836-March 12, 1904), historian, was born in Somersetshire. His great-grandfather was the Bishop of Carlisle, his grandfather the first Lord Ellenborough, his father a rector.

His mother died when he was eight. He was sent to Winchester School, but in 1851 his father became a Roman Catholic, and the son being automatically converted also, he had to leave the school. After a year at University College, London, he went in 1853 to the Catholic College at Stonyhurst. For a time he hesitated between an army career and the priesthood, and his father had already secured for him a cadetship in the East India Company when in 1855 he entered the Brompton Oratory, founded by Father Faber, another convert from the Church of England. He was ordained as a priest in 1860.

Law remained in the Brompton Oratory until 1878. Then he repudiated the faith and left the church. Two years later he signalized his desertion of the priesthood by marrying Wilhelmina Allen; they had one son and five daughters. In 1879 he had been made keeper of the Library of Writers to the Signet in Edinburgh, and he remained in this city and this position until his death. He had already spent years as a student of history, and now specialized in the history of Scotland, being one of the founders and the honorary secretary of the Scottish Historical Society. In 1898 he received an honorary LL.D. from the University of Edinburgh. He died at sixty-eight after a long illness.

Law's chief interest was in sixteenth century religious history, on which he was perhaps the greatest authority of his time. His work showed a remarkable lack of bias, considering his own religious history. He was a noted bibliographer, and edited numerous historical works, besides contributing to the Dictionary of National Biography and the Cambridge Modern History.

PRINCIPAL WORKS: The Conflicts Between Jesuits and Seculars in the Reign of Queen Elizabeth, 1889; Collected Essays and Reviews, 1904.

ABOUT: Law, T. G. Collected Essays and Reviews (see Memoir by P. Hume Brown).

LAWRENCE, GEORGE ALFRED (March 25, 1827-September 23, 1876), novelist, was born at Buxted, Sussex, the son of the Reverend Alfred Charnley Lawrence and Lady Emily Mary (Finch-Hatton) Lawrence.

He was educated at Rugby and at Oxford, entering the former institution in 1841, the last year of the headship of the famous Dr. Thomas Arnold (father of Matthew Arnold); and in Guy Livingstone he gave a picture of the school in its harder and more virile aspects. In 1845 he proceeded to Oxford, where he matriculated in Balliol College, although he received his B.A. (with second-class honors in classics) from New Inn Hall in 1850.

Called to the bar at the Inner Temple in 1852, he practised the law for a time, but soon turned to letters, publishing Guy Livingstone:

or, *Thorough,* his first and best known novel, in 1857. The book, by its frank glorification of brute strength, together with questionable standards of morality, amazed the public of the time, and provoked considerable criticism and also great applause. It enjoyed a tremendous sale, and the author issued a series of successors with great regularity, a new book appearing almost every other year.

Although by this time he had a wife and a son (he had married Miss Mary Kirwan in 1851), Lawrence's desire for adventure and his enthusiasm for the Confederate cause led him to journey to the United States to offer his services to the South. Before he reached the Confederate lines he was taken prisoner and kept in a guard-house. After correspondence with Lord Lyons, the British Minister at Washington, he succeeded in regaining his freedom, which was given to him only on condition that he return forthwith to England. This experience is related in *Border and Bastille.*

The rest of his life was spent in travel and in writing; he made his home at Gressenhall, near Old Buckingham, Norfolk, and in London. He died in a nursing home in Edinburgh, at the age of forty-nine.

Accounts of Lawrence's character are not consistent, possibly because of the natural tendency of critics to link him with his famous hero in *Guy Livingstone.* His enemies called him lawless and unprincipled; one of his publishers revealed that Lawrence was reckless, and such a confirmed gambler that he could squander £1,000 (the price paid for a novel) in less than a week, but he admitted that Lawrence was honorable about finishing his work according to agreement, even when it had already been paid for.

GEORGE LAWRENCE

The most brilliant example of "muscular blackguardism" (as opposed to "muscular Christianity," a term associated with Charles Kingsley), *Guy Livingston* set a fashion which influenced not only literatuure, but even dress and manner in the young men of the period. "Even the chubbiest of the Adonises of the time affected *'to set his face like a flint,'* and adopted to his sweetheart the tones of calm command, in place of the old ones of beseeching adoration," wrote a critic in *The Spectator.* The novel was parodied by Bret Harte in *Sensation Novels Condensed* (1871) as "Guy Heavystone, or Entire," the hero of which wears a snaffle-bit to keep his ferocity from manifesting itself too forcibly, lays out his schoolmates with a piston rod, and, in his death spasms, pulls down the house. Humor, it is evident, was not Lawrence's forte; and this lack appears also in his seriously writing an account of his comic-opera adventure in America. He was, however, a man of wide knowledge and a background of classical education, and these elements are represented in his works, most of which are distinctly in the manner described above, probably the most successful being *Sword and Gown* (1859). The use of archaisms and foreign phrases in his books often lends them an absurdity evidently not perceived by the author. His philosophical attitude is one of arrogant contempt for business or professional men, and admiration for aristocracy and the army. Despite the apparent faults and weaknesses suggested above, his novels are superior to those written to imitate them, and they have a narrative force and "go" which evoked comparison with Dumas and *The Three Musketeers.* With the "holier-than-thou" criticisms and those of shallow admirers discarded, the writer takes a place, in Saintsbury's words, as "really a novelist and a writer of great talent, which somehow came short, but not so very far short, of genius."   R. W. W.

PRINCIPAL WORKS: *Editor*—A Bundle of Ballads, 1863. *Novels*—Guy Livingstone: or, Thorough; 1857; Sword and Gown, 1859; Barren Honour, 1862; Maurice Dering: or, The Quadrilateral, 1864; Sans Merci: or, Kestrels and Falcons, 1866; Brakespeare: or, The Fortunes of a Free Lance, 1868; Breaking a Butterfly: or, Blanche Ellerslie's Ending, 1869; Anteros, 1871; Hagarene, 1874. *Poems*—Songs of Feast, Field, and Fray, 1852. *Travel*—Border and Bastille, 1863; Silverland, 1873.

ABOUT: Ellis, S. M. Wilkie Collins, Le Fanu, and Others; Lawrence, G. A. Guy Livingstone (see Introduction and Biographical Note by Sheila Kaye-Smith to 1928 ed.); Bookman (London) 72:10 April 1927; Edinburgh Review 108:532 October 1858; Spectator 49:1345 October 28, 1876.

LAYARD, SIR AUSTEN HENRY (March 5, 1817-July 5, 1894), travel writer and archaeologist, was born in Paris. His father, of a family of Huguenot descent, was in the Ceylon Civil Service. Most of his youth was passed in Italy, but at sixteen he was put into the office of his great-uncle, a London solicitor. He endured this life until 1839, when he made up his mind to go to Ceylon, where a position was offered him. He traveled overland through Asia, abandoned the thought of Ceylon, and traveled instead to Turkey and Persia, going on foot and living like the natives. Starting back to England, he was halted in Constantinople by the British ambassador, who employed him to wander through Turkey picking up information for the British government. The ambassador then raised funds to allow him to excavate what he thought was the site of Nineveh. Although he did not find the real site, he remained until 1847, during the latter part of this period working for the British Museum. Returned to England, he brought out his first book on Nineveh, which created a great sensation and won him an honorary D.D.L. from Oxford. In 1849 he was an attaché of the embassy at Constantinople. He returned to England again in 1851, and never revisited Mesopotamia. He received the freedom of the city of London in 1853, and was made lord rector of Aberdeen in 1855. He was a member of Parliament from 1852 to 1857, and was under-secretary for foreign affairs then and again in 1861, having been re-elected to Parliament in 1860. In the interval he revisited Turkey and visited India. In 1869 he was made ambassador to Spain, and in the same year he married Mary Evelyn Guest. They had no children. In 1880 his official career ended, and he spent the remainder of his life in Italy, writing extensively—and dully—on Italian art.

Layard did much to arouse British interest in Mesopotamia archaeology, but he was no real archaeologist. In evidence of this statement, he was in the habit of giving bits of stone he had excavated, covered with priceless inscriptions, to friends as souvenirs! In consequence, frequently the inscriptions were unreadable without these lost portions.

PRINCIPAL WORKS: Popular Account of Discoveries at Nineveh and Its Remains, 1848-49; Discoveries in the Ruins of Nineveh and Babylon, 1853; Early Adventures in Persia, Susiana, and Babylonia, 1887.

ABOUT: London Times July 12, 1894.

LEADBEATER, MARY (December 1758-June 27, 1826), Irish poet and story-writer, was born in County Kildare as Mary Shackleton. Her grandfather, a Quaker, had been Sir Edmund Burke's schoolmaster. She was educated at home, but by a good tutor, and on a visit to London with her father (also a Quaker schoolmaster) in 1784 she met Burke, Crabbe, Sir Joshua Reynolds, and other great men of the time. In 1791 she married William Leadbeater, a former pupil of her father's, who, though only a small farmer,

had literary interests and translated from the Latin. She went to live with him at Ballitore, and acted as the village postmistress. They had several children. In 1798 Ballitore was sacked by the French and the Irish insurgents, and she and her husband narrowly escaped with their lives. The shock affected her nerves for years thereafter. She had written poems from childhood, some of them published anonymously, and now began a series of moral tales, intended to convey sugar-coated lessons to the village poor. Her stories are highly didactic and moral. Her best work is what she called the *Annals of Ballitore,* containing valuable material relating to Irish life of the time, which was published in 1862 as the *Leadbeater Papers.*

PRINCIPAL WORKS: Extracts and Original Anecdotes for the Improvement of Youth, 1794; Poems, 1808; Cottage Dialogues, 1811; Tales for Cottages (with Elizabeth Shackleton) 1814; Cottage Biography, 1822; The Leadbeater Papers, 1862.

ABOUT: Leadbeater M. The Leadbeater Papers (see Memoir).

LEAKE, WILLIAM MARTIN (January 14, 1777-January 6, 1860), classical topographer, was born in London. His father and grandfather were both heralds, and his grandfather a numismatist as well. He was educated at the Royal Military Academy, Woolwich, and in 1794 entered the Royal Artillery as a second lieutenant, being sent to serve in the West Indies. In 1799, as a captain, he was sent to instruct the Turkish troops, allies of the British, in Egypt. He made his first explorations of Greece at this time, but his manuscript notes were lost in a shipwreck. From 1804 to 1807 he was again in Greece, and besides his topographical studies, he collected coins and ancient objects of art. He was promoted to major, and from 1808 to 1810 carried out various diplomatic errands in Greece. In 1813 he was promoted to lieutenant colonel. In 1815 he was sent by the government to Switzerland; he then retired, with the rank of colonel, and devoted the remainder of his life to writing the results of his surveys. In 1838 he married Elizabeth Wray (Wilkins) Marsden, widow of an Orientalist. Leake was a Fellow of the Royal Society and of the Royal Geographical Society, vice-president of the Royal Society of Literature, and a member of numerous learned associations. Although an extremely modest man, he was one of the foremost Greek topographers of his time, and was also a noted numismatist.

PRINCIPAL WORKS: Aegyptica: The Ancient and Modern State of Egypt, 1810; Researches in Greece, 1814; The Topography of Athens, 1821; Journal of a Tour in Asia Minor, 1824; Travels in the Morea, 1830; Travels in Northern Greece, 1835; On Some Disputed Questions of Ancient Geography, 1857.

ABOUT: Marsden, J. H. Memoir of Col. William Martin Leake.

LEAR, EDWARD (May 12, 1812-January 29, 1888), writer of nonsense verse and prose, landscape artist, draughtsman, and wanderer, was born in Halloway, London, the youngest son in a family of twelve children of Danish descent.

Left at an early age to be cared for by an elder sister, he tried to earn money by sketching birds on cardboard that he colored by a method then known as Oriental tinting. These sketches he sold for small sums.

At fifteen, he did artistic work for hospitals and medical men. Then through the offices of a friend he found employment as a draughtsman in the Gardens of the Zoological Society. In 1831, his first book, *The Family of the Psittacidae* was published, one of the earliest volumes of the colored plates of birds on a large scale. These brilliant-hued studies attracted the attention of the thirteenth Earl of Derby. One day while Lear was sketching in the Zoological Gardens, a stranger said to him, "You must come and draw my birds at Knowlsey." It was the Earl of Derby.

Lear accepted the invitation and from 1832-1836, made his home at Knowlsey, under the patronage of the Earl. There he met Lord Carlingford, Lord Northbrook, Lady Waldegrave, and her niece, Lady Strachie. Lear wanted to compose some nonsense verses to amuse the children at Knowsley. A friend suggested the line, "There was an old man of Tobago." Lear decided to make a limerick out of it. In those days limericks were only used in nursery rhymes but he thought they were "a form of verse lending itself to limitless variety of rhymes and pictures."

He took up landscape painting in 1836 and exhibited at the Suffolk Galeries. But English winters did not agree with him. Also, there was always a wolf at Lear's door, although as one biographer puts it, he was such a genteel wolf. A subscription was raised by the Earl of Derby to send Lear to Rome.

He went there in 1857 and stayed for ten years, supporting himself by giving drawing lessons. In the summer he wandered with a sketch book through Southern Europe and Palestine. In the winter, he would make occasional visits to England. In 1841, his *Views in Rome and Its Environs* was published.

Four years later, while on one of his visits to England, he gave Queen Victoria drawing lessons. Tennyson wrote a poem about him, "To E.L. On his Travels in Greece."

He had three books published in 1846, *Gleanings from the Menagerie at Knowlsey,* *Illustrated Excursions in Italy,* and *A Book of Nonsense,* the collection of verses he made up to amuse the Earl of Derby's young grandson. This last book was to sweep England like a delightful species of plague, equally virulent in nursery and drawing-room.

EDWARD LEAR

Lear was exhibiting in the Royal Academy in 1850. Then came more wanderings and a winter on the Nile in 1854-1855. Soon after this, he had a villa built for himself in San Remo that he called the Villa Emily after Lady Tennyson. Here he settled down and devoted the last twenty years of his life to his greatest ambition, a series of pen and ink sketches, water-colors, and oils to illustrate Tennyson's works. But two years before his death, he was compelled to give up this dream because of failing eyesight and health. All of the drawings but thirty he destroyed.

He died in San Remo, attended only by an old man servant. His doctor's wife wrote that "the great good heart simply ceased to beat. . . I have never forgotten it, it was all so sad and lonely." Lear, himself, chose the words that were inscribed on his gravestone: "A Landscape Painter in Many Lands."

Lear never married. In his youth, he was extremely sociable. At one time he became almost a professional diner-out. He could be charming if he liked a person, but the opposite if he did not. James T. Fields compared him to the Pied Piper of Hamelin and thought that he must have had an extremely magnetic nature to attract people as he did. As Lear grew older, he withdrew more and more into himself. Like Lewis Carroll, he was happiest and most at ease with children. Lear could be the most amusing of companions but there were times when overwhelmed by a fit of depression he would take a steamer and not even know where it was going. It was also this desire to escape from his own personality that made Lear drown himself in the "Jerry-down-Jerry" of the *Nonsense Books.*

Lear delighted in lingering around bookstalls to hear what the public thought about his books. Once in a railroad carriage he overheard a father tell his children, who were reading *A Nonsense Book,* that its author was the Earl of Derby. Lear was an anagram of Earl! Incidentally, the Earl's first name was Edward, too. It was too much for any author to stand. Lear introduced himself, offering his card as proof of his identity. But the gentleman refused to be convinced. "I have it on the best authority," he said.

Many of the sketches Lear made to illustrate his nonsense verses are pictures of himself. He was a short, thick-set, extremely near-sighted man with spectacles. He had an enormous black beard. In one of his drawings he sketches himself showing a doubting stranger his name in his hat. And he wrote this description of himself:

> He has many friends, laymen and clerical,
> Old Foss is the name of his cat;
> His body is perfectly spherical,
> He weareth a runcible hat.

In what direction Lear's real genius lay has become increasingly clear with the passage of time. It was not in those ornithological sketches, admirable as they were. (William Swainson, the naturalist, thought Lear's drawing of a red and yellow macaw that he made in 1831 "equal to any figures ever painted by Barraband or Audubon for grace and design.") Nor in his draughtsmanship, that severe critics in the art of design ranked as excellent. Nor yet in the "topographical landscapes" as he liked to call them. So remarkable was Lear's sense of perspective, particularly when drawing from a great height that Sir Roderick Murchison could understand the peculiarities of a country merely by studying Lear's sketches of it. His travel books, while interesting, have no real claim to literary distinction. When it came to writing pure nonsense, however, Lear's hat might be runcible, but his pen was enchanted, an inky Merlin's wand making young and old "dance by the light of the moon." It is in the hands of the courageous young lady from Norway who was squeezed in a doorway, the Jumblies that went to sea in a sieve, the adventuresome owl and pussy-cat, the cooperative cauliflower, and the "visibly vicious vulture who wrote some verses to a veal-cutlet in a volume bound in vellum," and all the rest of that mad and uproarious crew that Lear's genius rests.

Ruskin put Lear first on his list of the best hundred authors. Saintsbury declared that "the irresistible parody of sense and pathos that he contrived to instill into his rigamarole are unapproachable." Chesterton called him "The Father of Nonsense," while *The Spectator* hailed him as the laureate of nonsense writers, and, like Chesterton, ranked him above Lewis Carroll. Today, a first edition

of *A Nonsense Book* is as rare as an *Alice. Art-Work* said of the sketches that are an inseparable part of the text in the *Nonsense Books:* "His drawings are to him what mathematics were to Lewis Carroll, who insisted that mathematics were the true wonderland where nothing is impossible and the incredible must always be credited."   D. H.

PRINCIPAL WORKS: *Nonsense*—A Book of Nonsense, 1846; Nonsense Songs and Stories, 1871; More Nonsense Songs, Pictures, Etc., 1872; Laughable Lyrics, 1877; Nonsense Botany and Nonsense Alphabets, 1851. *Natural History*—Illustrations of the Family of the Psittacidae, 1832; Gleanings From the Menagerie at Knowsley Hall, 1846. *Travel*—Views in Rome and Its Environs, 1841; Illustrated Excursions in Italy, 1846; Journal of a Landscape Painter in Greece and Albania, 1852; Views in the Seven Ionian Islands, 1863; Journal of a Landscape Painter in Corsica, 1870. *Autobiography*—Letters of Edward Lear, 1907.

ABOUT: Cruse, A. The Victorians and Their Books; Chesterton, G. K. A Defense of Nonsense and Other Essays; Saintsbury, G. History of Nineteenth Century Literature; Strachie, Lady. Later Letters of Edward Lear; Colophon 9:49 February 1932; Landmark 14:538 November 1932.

LECKY, WILLIAM EDWARD HARTPOLE (March 26, 1838-October 22, 1903), Irish historian and essayist, was born at Newtown Park, near Dublin, the only son of John Hartpole Lecky and Mary Anne Tallents. The boy's mother died in 1839, and he was reared by a stepmother. His father died in 1852.

Lecky's early education was at various schools in England and, in Ireland, at a day-school at Kingstown, at Armagh School, and at Cheltenham, whither he went in 1852. As Lecky did not like the life at Cheltenham, he left in 1855, going first to a private tutor and then to Trinity College, Dublin, where he studied divinity. Here freedom, wide reading, and stimulating friends contributed much to his development; and in the year (1859) of his graduation he won the gold medal for oratory. In 1863 he received his M.A.

Although his early literary ventures, including a volume of poems issued in 1859 and religious essays published in 1860, were not successful, Lecky gave up thoughts of an ecclesiastical or a political career to continue his writing. His success came with the publication (1865) of his *History of Rationalism,* which made him famous at twenty-seven. The book traces the decay of superstition and theology and the corresponding rise of reason as a force in human history. Full to the point of discursiveness, the work carries the application of its theory over many fields of endeavor. The *History of Morals* (1869) examines more closely the beliefs and faiths of men, and brings out the notion of a moral progress made by humanity. It was attacked by utilitarians, and caused lively discussion.

Lecky's society became sought by men of the highest literary and political standing, and

W. E. H. LECKY

in 1867 he was elected to the Athenaeum. In 1870 he met Queen Sophia, of the Netherlands, whose maid-of-honor, Elisabeth van Dedem, he married in 1871. Their circle of friends included Tennyson, Browning, Huxley, and Herbert Spencer.

His work continued without interruption, and his *History of England in the Fifteenth Century* entailed considerable research in Ireland. The book, impartial, and particularly thorough in its treatment of Irish problems, was Lecky's greatest project, and occupied him for nineteen years. His later works were not so important as the three histories. *Democracy and Liberty* (1896) takes a conservative attitude unfavorable to democracy, and *The Map of Life* (1899) is a collection of rather commonplace reflections on life and conduct.

Actively interested in politics, Lecky was elected (1895) to Parliament, to represent Dublin University. While he made a good reputation, he was not so successful here as in other fields, perhaps because of his lack of strong partisan feeling. His delivery was not effective, and his tall, willowy figure and peculiar gestures made him a likely subject for cartoons. A Liberal, he took great interest in Ireland, although he opposed Home Rule, and became a Unionist as early as 1886.

Because of increasingly ill health he was obliged, in 1902, to resign his place in Parliament, having suffered in the previous year from influenza and consequent dilatation of the heart. From this time his condition grew worse, and he died quietly in his study on October 22, 1903. His wife endowed, with funds from her husband's properties, the Lecky Chair of History at Trinity College, Dublin.

A tall, striking man with fair hair, Lecky was refined in appearance and not physically very active. He was naturally shy and reserved, but, because of his reputation, enjoyed the friendship of such men as Trevelyan, Froude, Lord Russell, and Carlyle. His fluency and readiness of speech, charming in personal intercourse, were actual obstacles in Parliament. In his youth emotional and susceptible to religious influences, especially those of the Roman Catholic Church, he is said to have become later much graver and more settled, and indeed seems to have lacked great vigor of personality.

Except for the *History of England in the Eighteenth Century*, Lecky's important works do not, for the most part, deal with objective facts, but rather with ideas and influences. Cazamian writes of him: "He allows for the activity of ideas, and fits them in with the development of economic and social history. The belief in progress, the optimism of the age of Spencer, form . . . the very soul of his work, as lucid in thought as it is calm in outlook." Lecky's histories were written to expound a thesis, that of the downfall of superstition and the rise of reason; and the subject required a certain faculty of intuition. James Ford Rhodes wrote: "Lecky had the faculty of historic divination which compensated to some extent for the lack of a more thorough study of the sources. Genius stood in the place of painstaking engrossment in a single task." While the historical works are remarkable for fullness of research and clarity of style, the author's place, as John White Chadwick wrote, "is neither with the annalists nor with the political historians, but with those for whom the philosophy of history has had a perennial fascination." R. W. W.

PRINCIPAL WORKS: *History and Historical Philosophy*—The Declining Sense of the Miraculous, 1863; The History of the Rise and Influence of Rationalism in Europe, 1865; The History of European Morals From Augustus to Charlemagne, 1869; The History of England in the Eighteenth Century, 1878-90: *Poetry*—Friendship and Other Poems, 1859; Poems, 1891. *Miscellaneous*—The Religious Tendencies of the Age, 1860; The Leaders of Public Opinion in Ireland, 1861. 1871. 1903; Democracy and Liberty, 1896; The Map of Life; Conduct and Character, 1899; Historical and Political Essays, 1908.

ABOUT: British Academy: Proceedings for 1903-04; Gooch, G. P. History and Historians of the Nineteenth Century; Lecky, E. van D. A Memoir of the Right Hon. William Edward Hartpole Lecky; Rhodes, J. F. Historical Essays; Living Age 241: 38 April 1904.

LE FANU, JOSEPH SHERIDAN (August 28, 1814-February 7, 1873), Irish novelist of the supernatural, was born in Dublin, his father being the Dean of Emly. His paternal ancestry was Huguenot French; and his paternal great-uncle was the famous dramatist, Richard Brinsley Sheridan. He is one of several celebrated writers with Sheridan blood in their veins.

Le Fanu was precocious, writing verses as a small child, and producing a long Irish poem at fourteen. He was privately educated by his father, until in 1833 he entered Trinity College, Dublin. His career as a professional writer began while he was still in college, with his contributions to the *Dublin University Magazine* (not a college publication). In 1837 he joined its staff, contributed to it in 1869 the stories later collected as the pseudonymous *Purcell Papers,* and in 1872 became its editor and proprietor.

He was called to the bar in 1839, but he never practised law; he had a sufficient income to live by journalism, which he very much preferred. Already, in 1837, he had published two brilliant Irish ballads, "Phaudrig Croohore" and "Shaumus O'Brien," the latter of which, recited during lecture tours in England and the United States by the novelist Samuel Lover, was frequently attributed to Lover instead of to young Le Fanu.

In 1839, the year in which he became officially a barrister, Le Fanu bought two newspapers, *The Warden* and the *Evening Packet,* and became part owner of the Dublin *Evening Mail.* These he amalgamated as the *Evening Mail,* with a weekly as well as a daily edition, and continued as their owner and editor-in-chief throughout the remainder of his life. An ardent Conservative, he built the combined paper into a powerful organ of his party and one of the principal newspapers of Ireland.

In 1844 he married Susan Bennett, a childless marriage which was singularly happy. Le Fanu adored his wife, and never recovered from the shock of her death in 1858. Handsome, charming, and a brilliant conversationalist, he had been a noted figure in society; but after she died he withdrew from all social life and except for necessary business saw no one and went nowhere.

His career as a novelist dates from this personal tragedy. Hitherto, outside of his editorial work, his writing had been chiefly in verse, which was not collected into book form until thirteen years after his death. He had published two volumes of fiction, but was scarcely known as a story-writer. Now, from 1863 onwards, he began to pour out a series of powerful novels, most of them dealing with the supernatural with which his melancholy thoughts were so constantly engaged. Like Mark Twain, Le Fanu wrote his books in bed, in pencil, on scraps of paper. By a strange coincidence, worthy of his own novels, he finished his last book, *Willing to Die,* only a few days before his death in his home in Dublin.

Le Fanu is almost supreme in his field. He has been called the greatest Irish novelist, next to Lever, of the nineteenth century, but the analogy is inexact; Lever's—like his almost-namesake Lover's—novels are stories of Irish life; Le Fanu's are stories of Irish life plus the all enveloping air of another world. He is a master of the supernatural, as only a man obsessed by grief can be. His mind dwelt unweariedly on death, which had snatched from him all he loved, and he lived in a spectral atmosphere which he was able to communicate unerringly to his readers. The mysterious and the terrible are his dwelling-place, and the most materialistic reader can scarcely suppress an atavistic shudder on entering with him into that ghostly realm.

This man of much imaginative power, was, however, also a competent newspaper editor, with an observant eye and a strongly satirical bent; he did not live wholly with the dead, and interspersed with his horrors is a world of living beings, sharply depicted and acidly real. He wrote his novels in an era when novels had to have plots, instead of being merely pieces of consciousness or special pleadings, and in the construction of complicated and ingenious plots he is surpassed only by Wilkie Collins, with whom his name is often associated. There is in him a touch of Hawthorne, a good deal of Poe, but also considerable of Wilkie Collins or even of Rider Haggard. As a literary age passes, the greatest names survive, but those very near to their greatness fall into unmerited desuetude. Few persons read Le Fanu now, yet such a critic-in-chief of the mystery story as Dorothy Sayers has recommended him to connoisseurs in gooseflesh. *Uncle Silas* is perhaps his best known novel, but actually his masterpiece in the supernatural is *The House by the Churchyard.*

J. S. LE FANU

In Le Fanu's verse—in his poetic drama called Beatrice, in *The Legend of the Glaive*, and the tragic *Song of the Bottle*, as well as in his stirring Irish ballads—many of the characteristics of his fiction reappear. His poetry is delicate but strong, and though he was little of a lyrist his narrative verse often recaptures the thrilling atmosphere of his stories.

The *Purcell Papers* have a peculiar interest for all Brontë addicts, for it is probably from a subconscious memory of one story in them that Charlotte Brontë derived the main theme of *Jane Eyre*—the young woman in love with the older man who keeps hidden in his house, in the Brontë story an insane wife, in Le Fanu's a blind wife who is also maniacally vindictive. There is no question of plagiarism—Le Fanu's husband, who has attempted bigamy, finally cuts his throat, whereas Brontë's Rochester, his burdensome wife disposed of by arson, is united with his Jane—but there seems little doubt that it was from a forgotten reading of the Le Fanu story that the germ of *Jane Eyre* arose.   M. A. deF.

PRINCIPAL WORKS: The Cock and Anchor, 1845; Torlogh O'Brien 1847; The House by the Church-yard, 1863; Uncle Silas, 1864; Wylder's Hand, 1864; Guy Deverell, 1865; All in the Dark, 1866; The Tenants of Malory, 1867; A Lost Name, 1868; Haunted Lives, 1868; The Wyvern Mystery, 1869; Checkmate, 1870; The Rose and the Key, 1871; Chronicles of Golden Friars, 1871; In a Glass Darkly, 1872; Willing to Die, 1875; The Purcell Papers, 1880; The Watcher and Other Weird Stories, 1894; Poems, 1896.

ABOUT: Ellis, S. M. Wilkie Collins, Le Fanu, and Others; Le Fanu, J. S. Poems (see Biographical Preface by A. P. Graves); Le Fanu, J. S. Purcell Papers (see Memoir by A. P. Graves in 1880 ed.); Le Fanu, W. Seventy Years of Irish Life.

LEIGH, PERCIVAL (November 3, 1813-October 24, 1889), humorist, was born in Haddington and educated for the medical profession at St. Bartholomew's Hospital, London. He received his license to practise in 1834 and was made a Member of the Royal College of Surgeons in 1835, but soon abandoned his profession to become a writer. He joined the staff of *Punch* in 1841, and continued to contribute to it until his death. He was also an enthusiastic amateur actor, and belonged to the famous company of which Dickens was one. He was an intimate friend of Thackeray as well. His wife, born Letitia Morison, predeceased him. His last years were spent in seclusion at Hammersmith.

Most of Leigh's books were illustrated by the famous John Leech. He was an inimitable satirist, and his burlesque grammars and histories, some produced under the pseudonym of "Paul Prendergast," were highly popular.

PRINCIPAL WORKS: The Comic Latin Grammar, 1840: The Comic English Grammar, 1840; Ye Man-

ners and Customs of Ye Englyshe, 1849; Paul Prendergast: or, The Comic Schoolmaster, 1859.

ABOUT: Athenaeum November 2, 1889.

LEMON, MARK (November 30, 1809-May 23, 1870), dramatist and editor of *Punch*, was born in London, the eldest son of a hop-merchant, Martin Lemon, and Alice (Collis) Lemon.

He was reared, after the death of his father, by his grandfather, and went to school in Surrey. He then proceeded to Boston, Lincolnshire, where his uncle, a hop-merchant, initiated him into the mysteries of that business. Thence he returned to London, and was at one time manager of Verey's brewery. Before long, however, he turned to literature as a means of livelihood.

Having already contributed to magazines, Lemon bent his energies to the stage, and began a busy career as a dramatist in 1835, when *P. L.* was produced at the Strand Theatre. In the course of his career as a playwright he wrote sixty or more plays, and at the same time continued to contribute to magazines. At various times he was editor of the *London Journal*, the *Family Herald*, and *Once a Week;* and he was the founder and editor of *The Field*, and assisted with the *London Illustrated News*.

But his real literary fame rests upon his connection with *Punch*, the paper which he helped found in 1841. He tided the magazine over its early financial difficulties by the income from his plays. Under Lemon, *Punch* attained a position of influence, and included work by most of the noted humorists of his time.

In addition to his editorial duties Lemon took part in dramatic performances, having considerable histrionic power, especially in

MARK LEMON

humorous rôles. He played Falstaff in his own *The Story of Falstaff*, adapted from Shakespeare. And in 1863, having already written for children, he turned to the novel with *Wait for the End*. His work on *Punch* continued almost to his last day; he died at Crawley, Sussex, in 1870.

"He believed in one God, in one woman, in one publication," said his friend Joseph Hatton, and this remark gives an insight into the simple amiability of "Uncle Mark," who was very popular. A roly-poly figure, not unlike the Falstaff he represented, Lemon was extremely sensitive to pathos and easily moved to tears. He was, however, the picture of good cheer and cordiality. In 1839 he married Helen Romer, by whom he had ten children.

Hans Christian Andersen is said to have remarked, having watched him at a garden-party, "Mr. Lemon is most excellent full of comic." While his sense of humor was not always pointed enough for wit, it was scrupulously pure, and the tone of *Punch* never descended from that level. Lemon was a capable and efficient editor, patient under fire from his contributors and skilful in pulling them together to produce a magazine suited to the public that read it. The Wednesday-evening "*Punch* dinners" for contributors, given under his régime, were brilliant affairs.

"He was an excellent actor, as well as an artful and effective dramatist," commented *The Athenaeum* in its obituary notice. His plays, however, rather emotional in appeal, have not kept Lemon a place in literary history, much less his novels. His true significance is indicated rather by the fact that, in the words of *The Athenaeum*, "To his nice discrimination and his instinctive abhorrence of extremes in opinion and expression, the famous journal, of which he was editor from the beginning, owes the services of men much more brilliant than he ever pretended to be . . ." Under his powerful hands *Punch* became an effective vehicle for humor and social satire.   R. W. W.

PRINCIPAL WORKS: *Editor*—Legends of Number Nip (by J. C. A. Musaeus) 1864; The New Table Book (by F. Eltze) 1867. *For Children*—The Enchanted Doll, 1849; Fairy Tales, 1868; Tinykin's Transformations, 1869. *Novels*—Wait for the End, 1863; Loved at Last, 1864; Falkner Lyle, 1866; Leyton Hall, 1866; Golden Fetters, 1867. *Plays*—The P. L.: or, 30 Strand, 1835; Arnold Winkelried, 1835; The Chimes (with G. A. à Beckett) 1837; St. George and the Dragon, 1837; A Familiar Friend, 1840; What Will the World Say? 1841; The Turf, 1842; Hearts are Trumps, 1849; Slave Life: or, Uncle Tom's Cabin, 1852; Mind Your Own Business, 1852; Mrs. Webster at Home, 1853; A Moving Tale, 1854; Number Nip, 1854; Paula Lazzaro, 1854; The Railway Belle, 1854; Medea, 1856; The Story of Falstaff, c.1868. *Tales*—A Christmas Hamper, 1860; Leyton Hall and Other Tales, 1866; Tom Moody's Tales, 1869; The Small House Over the Water, 1888. *Miscellaneous*—Prose and Verse, 1852; The Jest Book, 1864; Up and Down the London Streets, 1867.

ABOUT: Beale, W. Light of Other Days; Forster, J. The Life of Charles Dickens; Friswell, J. H. Modern Men of Letters; Hatton, J. With a Show in the North; Hatton, J. True Story of "Punch" in London Society; Spielmann, M. H. The History of "Punch"; Appleton's Journal 8:493 November 2, 1872; Athenaeum 1870 1:708 May 28; Illustrated London News 56:573 June 4, 1870.

LENNOX, LORD WILLIAM PITT (September 20, 1799-February 18, 1881), novelist and miscellaneous writer, was born in Yorkshire, the fourth son of the fourth Duke of Richmond. He was a godson of William Pitt and a cousin of Charles James Fox. He was educated at Westminster School, and while still a schoolboy, in 1813, was gazetted cornet of the Royal Horse Guards. It was his mother who gave the ball on the eve of Waterloo (celebrated in Byron's famous poem) and he was present. He was aide-de-camp to Wellington until 1818, and to his father, then governor-general of Canada, in the following year, and was a page at the coronation of George IV in 1821. He was made a captain in 1822, but sold his commission in 1829. He served as a Whig member of Parliament, as a moderate reformer, from 1832 to 1834, but his real interests were in horse-racing, private theatricals, "society," and writing. He contributed to many of the then popular "annuals," and to Dickens' magazine, *Once a Week*, his subjects usually being sport or the army. In 1858 he acted for a while as editor of the *Edinburgh Review*. In his later years he lost his fortune, and made his living by lecturing and contributing to the *Court Journal*. He was married three times: in 1824 to Mary Anne Paton, a singer, from whom he was separated by a Scotch divorce in 1831; in 1854 to Ellen Smith, who died in 1859; and in 1869 to Maria Jane Molyneaux, who in 1888 wrote a novel, *Castle Heather*.

Lennox's novels are imitative and feeble, and he was accused of plagiarism by Thomas Hood and Douglas Jerrold. He was caricatured as "Lord Prima Donna" in Disraeli's *Vivian Grey*. His personal reminiscences, however, are highly entertaining, since he knew most people of importance in his day and loved to talk about himself.

PRINCIPAL WORKS: Compton Audley, 1841; The Tuft Hunter, 1843; The Story of My Life, 1857; Pictures of Sporting Life and Character, 1860; Fifty Years' Biographical Reminiscence, 1863; The Adventures of a Man of Family, 1864; Drafts on My Memory, 1866; My Recollections From 1806 to 1873; Lord of Himself, 1880.

ABOUT: Lennox, Lord W. P. The Story of My Life; Fifty Years' Biographical Reminiscence; Drafts on My Memory; My Recollections; Illustrated London News February 26, 1881.

LESLIE, THOMAS EDWARD CLIFFE (1827?-January 27, 1882), Irish economist, was born in County Wexford, his father being an Anglican rector. He was educated at King

William's College, Isle of Man, and at Trinity College, Dublin, where he received a B.A. degree in 1847, LL.B. in 1851, and later an honorary LL.D. He read law at Lincoln's Inn in 1848, and was called to the bar in 1857, also to the Irish bar, but never practised. In 1853 he was made professor of jurisprudence and political economy at Queen's College, Belfast, He contributed frequently to *Fraser's Magazine, Macmillan's Magazine,* and other reviews. He never married, and for much of his life was a semi-invalid, which, together with the accidental loss of much of his manuscript, accounts for the fragmentary nature of his work. He was an advocate of the historical and comparative method in economic study, and was in fact one of the earliest teachers of sociology. A student of the French philosopher Comte, he did not follow Comte into his system of Positivism, but nevertheless was strongly influenced by him. On the whole, however, he was a better critic than he was a constructive thinker.

PRINCIPAL WORKS: The Military Systems of Europe Economically Considered, 1856; Land Systems and Industrial Economy, 1870; Essays on Political and Moral Philosophy, 1879.
ABOUT: London Times January 30, 1882.

LEVER, CHARLES JAMES (August 31, 1806-June 3, 1872), Irish novelist, was born in Dublin the second son of a prosperous and well known architect and builder of that city. His mother was Julia Candler from a landed Irish Protestant family of County Kilkenny. Lever attended a variety of schools from the age of four. A handsome, bright lad, he early displayed the high spirits and taste for mischief and practical jokes which remained with him through life.

He entered Trinity College, Dublin, in 1822. There his serious study of medicine and surgery was considerably enlivened by omnivorous reading and wild pranks of a relatively harmless nature. His first literary efforts were ballads and on one occasion; disguised as a wandering minstrel, singing timely snatches of his own composition, he collected thirty shillings before his political sentiments provoked a street fight. In 1827 he took his B.A. and matriculated at the University of Göttingen, where he found German student life much to his taste. After a short period at Heidelberg he went to Vienna, walking through Germany as he "walked the hospitals."

In 1829 Lever obtained an appointment as medical officer on an emigrant ship bound for Quebec. Conjecture alone can draw the line between fact and fiction in the account which the wild young Irishman gave of his adventures among the Indians, his adoption into a tribe, and his hair-raising escape from it. In

CHARLES LEVER

1830 he first broke into print in *Bolster's Cork Quarterly Magazine* with "Recollections of Dreamland," purporting to be the author's experiences as a user of opium. His German diary was serialized in the *Dublin Literary Gazette* and Lever contributed stories and articles to other equally short-lived magazines.

In 1831 he took his medical degree and in 1832, concurrent with the cholera epidemic, he obtained a dispensary at Portstewart near Coleraine and took charge of the cholera hospital in the latter town. The epidemic ceased during 1833 and Lever found his duties as a simple country doctor increasingly onerous. About this time (there still exists considerable confusion as to dates in the early part of Lever's life, some authorities claiming that the American trip was made before his European tour) he acknowledged his marriage to a childhood sweetheart. His father's objection to Miss Kate Barker was her dowerless condition and Lever married her secretly some time in 1832 or 1833. Mrs. Lever was the author's lifelong companion, amanuensis, proof reader, and editor, and Lever further credits her with curing him of not only the use of snuff but opium as well!

The first of his *Confessions of Harry Lorriquer* appeared anonymously in 1836. The character and his adventures won instant favor. Lever had for some time been anxious to get away from Portstewart. The little watering place was not lively enough for him and his own amusements won the disapprobation of more conservative local magnates. The city of Brussels, where he established himself in 1837, was more to his liking, for as a fashionable physician he found company to his taste and characters galore for his future novels. He continued his contributions to the

Dublin University Magazine, writing at night after his professional and social obligations were completed. Authorship eventually proving more attractive than medicine, he returned to Dublin in 1842 to assume the editorship of the *Dublin University Magazine.*

In Dublin his literary output was as lavish as the establishment he set up at "Templogue," a storied mansion where he lived at the rate of three thousand pounds a year. Here Thackeray visited and wrote his *Irish Sketch Book.* Lever, between 1842 and 1845, wrote five novels and many short papers, entertained and gambled with visiting big wigs, and traveled to London for an abortive duel arising from a temperance article which had appeared in his magazine. The strain was eventually more than even Lever's Hibernian energy could support, so in 1845 he relinquished his editorship and with his family embarked on a tour of central Europe. With gaudy opulence Lever traveled in a family coach—"ten souls and five (later seven) quadrupeds," driving where fancy led them, pausing when Mrs. Lever gave evidence of making an addition to the family or Lever himself felt the urge to rent a castle and entertain whatever celebrities (such as Dickens) came to hand.

During this tour Lever wrote with journalistic copiosity and quarreled with his publishers by every mail. His works were immensely popular, but the rewards were never more than he found convenient for his mode of life. He met the Brownings in 1849, and Mrs. Browning was hurt that the famous novelist, though residing at Florence where they were, made no effort to improve his acquaintance. The reason obviously was Lever's acute terror of lady intellectuals.

In 1865 Lever obtained a post as vice-consul at Spezzia. The office was a sinecure, as was the consulship at Trieste which he acquired in 1867. At sixty Lever had lost some of his ebullience while still retaining the habit—or necessity—of constant literary composition. He detested the thought of growing old and successfully resisted the encroachments of gout and incipient heart disease so long as his wife lived. After her death in 1870 he became more reconciled to his years and in 1872, exercising his Gaelic prerogative to prophesy, he declared the novel (*Lord Kilgobbin*), published in the spring of that year, would be his last. He died at Trieste and was buried in the British cemetery beside his wife.

No notice of Lever's work can be made without consideration of its enormous bulk. The 1897 library edition of the novels runs to thirty-seven volumes. In general the novels may be divided into the Irish and military extravaganzas of his earlier vein and, beginning about 1860, the more sober and careful studies of ordinary life and manners. Some of his later writings appeared under the pseudonym of "Cornelius O'Dowd." In his own time Lever was regarded in England as a brilliant and amusing novelist. His own easily offended countrymen were divided in their estimate. An important member of the Irish school, he is known today chiefly for such modern-picaresque creations as Lorriquer and O'Malley.

P. B. S.

PRINCIPAL WORKS: *Novels*—The Confessions of Harry Lorriquer, 1839; Charles O'Malley, 1841; Jack Hinton, 1843; Tom Burke of Ours, 1843; The O'Donoghue, 1845; Arthur O'Leary, 1845; The Knight of Gwynne, 1847; The Confessions of Con Creagan: The Irish Gil Blas, 1849; Roland Cashel, 1850; Maurice Tiernay: Soldier of Fortune, 1852; The Martins of Cro-Martin, 1855; The Fortunes of Glencore, 1857; Tony Butler, 1865; Luttrell of Arran, 1865; Sir Brook Fosbrooke, 1866; Lord Kilgobbin, 1872. *Miscellaneous*—Cornelius O'Dowd Upon Men and Women, 1874.

ABOUT: Downey, E. Charles Lever: His Life in His Letters (2 vols.); Fitzpatrick, W. J. The Life of Charles James Lever (2 vols.); Walker, H. Literature of the Victorian Era.

LEVY, AMY (November 10, 1861-September 10, 1889), poet and novelist, was born in Clapham on November 10, 1861, the second daughter of Jewish parents, Lewis Levy, an editor, and his wife, Isabelle Levin. She has been called a forgotten poetess and certainly there has been little written about her. The few facts available are vague and sometimes inaccurate.

Her education began with school at Brighton where her family moved in 1876, and continued with four terms of fitful study at Newnham College, Cambridge. Although apparently not of a studious nature she seems always to have been poetically inclined. In fact she showed signs of talent before she was eight. By the time she reached her teens she had long been writing prose as well as verse. One poem had already been printed in a quarterly called *The Pelican,* and during her first term at college she published a story in *Temple Bar,* while in 1881 her first book of poems appeared as *Xantippe.*

Her later life is uncertain. One critic puts her to work at a loom in a factory, has her live in a garret; another is silent; a third makes her a teacher in London, with a winter spent in Florence as well as a visit to Dresden. At any rate she seems to have read a great deal and written much. *A Minor Poet* came out in 1884, and was quickly followed by such prose works as *The Romance of a Shop* and her novel called *Reuben Sachs.*

Her poems were considered melancholy, even bitter, and to some extent they must have been her actual reactions to life, for on September 10, 1889, hardly a week after correcting the proofs for *A London Plane-Tree,* she committed suicide by suffocating herself with charcoal fumes at the Levy house at 7, Endsleigh Gardens. The coroner pronounced it "self destruction . . . cause unknown." Richard Garnett, however, thinks it more likely that her death was the result of a combination of causes. Inherently melancholy, she probably brooded over her growing deafness; worried over the possibility of insanity; and grieved over losses in her family.

Although her verse was imitative of Browning and Heine, and suffused with sadness, it contained, critics thought, "prophetic notes" of future power. The versification was often at fault, but there was in her poetry a delicacy and a beauty, "a matured simplicity," which made it worthy of praise. Of her prose works *Reuben Sachs* was the most remarkable for a "bold delineation of Jewish life" that was destined to cause more than one controversy in London.

Such were the qualities which made Oscar Wilde call the slight dark writer "a girl of genius," and which caused Thomas Bailey Aldrich to write a poem in her honor, and Richard Garnett to accord her sympathetic appreciation. With all her faults she has been unjustly forgotten.   B. D. S.

PRINCIPAL WORKS: *Poetry*—Xantippe, 1881; A Minor Poet, 1884; A London Plane-Tree, 1889. *Prose*—The Romance of a Shop, 1888; Reuben Sachs, 1888; Miss Meredith, 1889; The Unhappy Princess, 1888. *Translation*—Historic and Other Doubts: or, The Non-Existence of Napoleon Proved (from the French of M. J. B. Pérès) 1885.

ABOUT: Dictionary of National Biography; The Jewish Encyclopaedia; The Academy 362:185 September 21, 1883; The Academy 37:76 February 1, 1890; The Academy 57:162 August, 12, 1899; Athenaeum 62:457 October 5, 1889; The Critic (New York) 15:192 October 19, 1899; The Forum 47:361 March 1912; The Literary World 20:123 April 13, 1889.

LEWES, GEORGE HENRY

(April 18, 1817-November 28, 1878), biographer, physiologist, and journalist, was born in London, the youngest of three sons of an actor and theatrical manager. His paternal grandfather was Charles Lee Lewes, a well known comedian. George Henry Lewes' father died in the early 1820's, and his mother took for a second husband a retired sea captain named William.

The boy went to school in London, Jersey, Brittany (his French was fluent throughout his life), and Dulwich, but his education was at an end by 1833. For a while he was a notary's clerk, then clerk to a Russia merchant, and then became a medical student, but gave up the course because of his sensitive shrinking from pain. He never lost, however, his deep interest in physiology. Somehow (the financial means are not clear) he was able to go to Germany in 1838; he may have earned his way by tutoring. In 1840 he returned to London, thoroughly conversant with German, and with a lasting interest in Goethe. He began the hard-working journalistic career

GEORGE HENRY LEWES

from which he was not entirely free until 1866. Also, he made sundry attempts to secure a footing for himself on the stage, but though he did not give up for ten years, he was never a real success. His stage associations did make him valuable, though, as a dramatic critic.

In 1840, his first year in London after the German visit, Lewes married Agnes Jervis, daughter of a member of Parliament. Lewes had been for years a free-thinker and a radical, and he was closely connected with the group of which the center was Thornton Hunt, son of the poet Leigh Hunt, the friend of Shelley and Byron. Into this group, which among other doctrines believed in "free love," Lewes introduced his young wife, and when the fact became known to him that she and Hunt had become lovers, it was against his principles for him not to condone the step. He continued his friendship and association with Hunt; in fact, in 1850 the two became editors of a new radical weekly, *The Leader,* of which the manager was the famous free-thinker Jacob George Holyoake. When, however, Lewes discovered that the youngest of his wife's four sons was not his, but Hunt's (she had another son later by Hunt), he ceased to live with her—though they remained on the best of terms until his death, and their own children lived with her, supported by Lewes, until they were grown.

Under all these circumstances, it is easy to understand why, when in 1851 Herbert Spencer introduced to Lewes an earnest young essayist and translator named Marian Evans, and the two gradually fell in love, there were not the usual conventional barriers to their irregular union. Lewes could not by English law secure a divorce, and he did not believe in marriage as an institution. In 1854 the couple went to Germany together, informing their friends of their intention. At that time Lewes was far better known than was the woman who was later to be famous as "George Eliot." In fact, in one sense George Eliot was Lewes' creation—he discovered her genius for fiction, encouraged her, went over her manuscripts with her, shielded her from business worries over her books, and surrounded her with an atmosphere of tender solicitude, admiration, and even reverence. He was especially eager that the world should realize that their relation was in every sense but the legal one a true and enduring marriage; "their whole life together," someone has said, "was one long defense." Certainly no woman could have had a more devoted, faithful, and congenial husband.

In 1855 Lewes began serious work in the field of marine biology. Eventually this brought him the respectful attention of the most prominent scientists of his day. Contrary to the usual opinion of him, he was no slapdash journalist; his work was always thorough, painstaking, and careful. From anatomy and physiology he gradually turned to the nervous systems of the lower animals, and from that study to physiological psychology, emerging in the end into a renewal of his earliest concern with philosophy. For several years he continued his regular connection with *The Leader*, the *Cornhill Magazine*, and the *Pall Mall Gazette*, and in 1865 and 1866 was the first editor of the *Fortnightly Review*, the first English magazine to publish signed articles. By this date, however, the income from his books, added to the really large sums earned by George Eliot's novels, enabled him to give up journalism. His three sons also were educated and established—though the second and third both died in early youth of diseases caught in Natal, Africa, where they were gentlemen farmers.

In 1863 Lewes and George Eliot bought the Priory, St. John's Wood, where their famous Sunday afternoon causeries were held. Nearly always they spent two summer months on the Continent, usually in Germany and Austria. In 1876 they bought a country home in Surrey, and it was there that Lewes died two years later. The immediate cause of his death seems to have been pneumonia, but he was a lifelong semi-invalid, suffering constantly from gout, migraine, and other disabilities which suggest a damaged heart. In his memory George Eliot, who was prostrated by his death, founded a Physiological Studentship—he had been one of the founders of the Physiological Society, and on its council.

Small, thin, with sunken cheeks, straggling mustache and chin-whiskers, and burning eyes, Lewes was far from handsome, and

Jane Welsh Carlyle used to call him "the ape." But under his unprepossessing exterior were a fine mind and a nature with many virtues—generosity, kindliness, sympathy, unpretentiousness, the love of justice and the devotion to truth. He had a talent for the tactful social graces, and was bubbling over always with vivacity and good spirits. His style was sprightly, sparkling, and eminently clear—he had a horror of the allegorical or mystical. As a critic he was sympathetic, fair, and objective.

Lewes has been called "a literary man among the scientists," but his work was taken seriously by the most eminent biologists of a great age in biology. He was an early Darwinian, and his psychology is strangely modern in tone: for example, he considered mind a unit, and thought psychology must have its physiological and social aspects. He discovered proof of the functional indifference of nerves (all nerves are of the same structure, and differ only because of the organs they serve), later one of the acclaimed statements of the great psychologist Wundt. His *Problems of Life and Mind* was his most ambitious work, but it is "dated," and of all his books probably only the *Life of Goethe* and the *Biographical History of Philosophy* (a sort of forerunner of Will Durant's *Story of Philosophy*) are worth reading today. His novels were mere pot-boilers, and his only original play a rank failure. Lewes' greatest contribution to English literature is indirect—it is his fostering of the genius of George Eliot.

M. A. deF.

PRINCIPAL WORKS: *Biography*—The Life of Maximilien Robespierre, 1849; The Life and Works of Goethe, 1855. *Philosophy*—The Biographical History of Philosophy, 1845-46 (new edition with Prolegomina, 1867); Comte's Philosophy of the Sciences, 1853; Aristotle: A Chapter From the History of Sciences, 1864; Introductory Essay to the Ethics of Aristotle, 1886. *Science*—Seaside Studies at Ilfracombe, Tenby, the Scilly Isles, and Jersey, 1858; The Physiology of Common Life, 1859-60; Studies in Animal Life, 1862; Problems of Life and Mind: 1st ser., The Foundations of a Creed, 1874-75; 2nd ser., The Physical Basis of Mind, 1877; 3rd ser., A Study of Psychology, 1879. *Literature*—The Spanish Drama: Lope de Vega and Calderon, 1847; Introduction and Biographical Notes to Selections From the Modern British Dramatists, 1867; Female Characters of Goethe, 1874. *Novels*—Ranthorpe, 1847; Rose, Blanche, and Violet, 1848. *Plays*—The Noble Heart, 1850; Adaptations From the French (as "Slingsby Lawrence") 1896. *Miscellaneous*—On Actors and the Art of Acting, 1875; The Principles of Success in Literature, 1896.

ABOUT: Cross, J. W. George Eliot's Life as Related in Her Letters and Journals; Espinasse, F. Literary Recollections; Haldane, E. S. George Eliot and Her Times; Kitchell, A. T. George Lewes and George Eliot; May, I. L. George Eliot.

LEWIS, SIR GEORGE CORNEWALL

(April 21, 1806-April 13, 1863), historian, was born in London, the son of Sir Thomas Frankland Lewis, a prominent politician. He was educated at Eton, where he was noted for his Latin verses, and at Christ Church, Oxford, where he received his B.A. in 1829, M.A. in 1831, and D.C.L. in 1857. He read law at the Middle Temple, and was called to the bar in 1831, joining the Oxford circuit. Ill health soon compelled him to give up the law in favor of literature. He was a celebrated linguist, and a profound student of classical archaeology. In 1833 he was made assistant commissioner to inquire into the condition of the Irish poor in Ireland, England, and Scotland, and in 1834 was a member of the commission to inquire into religious instruction in Ireland. In 1836, and until 1838, he was joint commissioner to inquire into conditions in Malta. In 1839 he succeeded his father as poor law commissioner for England and Wales, a post he held until 1847, when, attacked from both the right and the left, he resigned. He sued some of his opponents for libel, but the cases never came to trial.

In 1844 Lewis married Maria Theresa (Villiers) Lister, widow of the novelist Thomas Henry Lister, and herself an editor and biographer. In 1847 he entered Parliament, and the next year was under-secretary for the home department. From 1850 to 1852 he was financial secretary to the treasury, but then lost his Parliamentary seat. For the next three years he acted as editor of the *Edinburgh Review*. His father died in 1855, and he succeeded not only to the title but also to his father's seat in Parliament, which he held until his death. Being made Chancellor of the Exchequer in 1855, he resigned his editorship; but in 1859 he refused the office in favor of Gladstone, and served as his secretary. In 1861, against his will, he was made secretary for war, and died while in that office.

Lewis was a quiet, industrious plodder, but shrewd and a good critic, with a real knowledge of his subject. His writing is sound and thorough, but makes no pretension to style.

PRINCIPAL WORKS: An Essay on the Origin and Formation of the Romance Languages, 1835; An Essay on the Influence of Authority in Matters of Opinion, 1849; Enquiry Into the Credibility of Early Roman History, 1855; An Historical Survey of the Astronomy of the Ancients, 1862.

ABOUT: Lewis, Sir G. C. Letters to Various Friends (ed. by Sir Gilbert F. Lewis) 1870.

LEWIS, MATTHEW GREGORY ("Monk Lewis") (July 9, 1775-May 14, 1818), novelist, dramatist, and poet, was born in London into a family of wealth and position. His father was Deputy-Secretary of War and owner of extensive West Indian property. His mother, a celebrated beauty, was Frances Maria Sewell, daughter of the Right Honorable Sir Thomas Sewell, bart., Master of the Rolls of George III.

Eldest and favorite of his mother's four children, the precocious Matthew shared her taste, which ran heavily to the florid romantic novels of the time and directed the bent he early exhibited toward the "terrible" in his writing. Matthew was educated at Westminster and at Christ Church, Oxford. While he was still at Westminster his parents separated, and Matthew's letters from this period show a maturity far exceeding his years. Mrs. Lewis was unable to live within the generous income provided her and Matthew shared his own allowance with her. There is scarcely a letter in their lifelong correspondence which does not in some way mention Mrs. Lewis' lack of funds.

Lewis' education was directed toward the diplomatic service and summers abroad were part of his training. At seventeen his literary activities had already commenced, and besides numerous poems he had written a drama, *The East Indian* (successfully produced in 1799), translated another from the French, and written two volumes of a novel and two of a romance. His appointment in 1794 as attaché to the British embassy at the Hague was marked by the composition in ten weeks, and before its author was twenty, of *Ambrosio: or, The Monk*. Its publication in 1795 cast Lewis into a furor of fame and notoriety comparable to that which was later experienced by Byron.

The Monk was universally read and universally condemned. A follower of Mrs. Radcliffe, influenced by the more forthright German Gothic tradition, Lewis had with youthful and almost Elizabethan enthusiasm multiplied the murder, demons, and ghosts and expanded in detail situations and ideas heretofore skirted in the English "horror" genre. The charge of immorality was based on the irreligion which critics discovered in such sen-

M. G. LEWIS

timents as one recommending that certain passages of the Bible be kept from the young. Lewis was himself as bewildered that his book could be considered vicious as is the modern undergraduate whom an obscure reference to the "immoral Monk Lewis" inspires with misdirected zeal to plough through the book.

His next venture, following a brief parliamentary career, was a musical drama, *The Castle Spectre*. Produced by Sheridan, properly expurgated by Lewis' sister, Lady Lushington, and replete with ghosts in blood-stained cerements, thunder, lightning, and horror, it pleased the public taste and was very successful. Several plays and translations of plays in much the same vein came next and the old accusation of immorality was not raised again until 1799 when, in *Adelmorn the Outlaw*, Lewis' first opera, a spirit ascending to heaven with a choir of cherubim was deemed irreverent.

In 1801 Lewis transferred his allegiance from Sheridan at Drury Lane to Harris at Covent Garden. Free from Sheridan's restraint, Lewis indulged his extravagant fancy to the utmost, sending his delighted audiences into fits of hysteria and fainting. Besides numerous dramas, Lewis produced in the years following two romances—*The Bravo of Venice* and *Feudal Tyrants*; also *Tales of Terror* and *Romantic Tales*, taken from German and Spanish sources; and, in collaboration with Scott, a collection of ballads, *Tales of Wonder*.

When he inherited his father's Jamaica property, Lewis, a man of genuinely humane instincts in a period artificially sensitive and essentially brutal, sailed (1815) to investigate the condition of his five hundred slaves. This action was regarded as mad by his family and friends. *The Journal of a West India Proprietor*, which he began now, attests a philanthropy unique in its time.

During the return voyage from a second trip to Jamaica Lewis was seized with yellow fever and died May 14, 1817. A truly "Gothic" atmosphere surrounded his burial at sea, for the coffin escaped its weights and floated away on the current in the direction of Jamaica.

The considerable literary output of Lewis is neglected today, but his influence upon contemporary romanticism and the catharsis which his extravagance effected upon its morbid elements cannot be overlooked by students of the period.

P. B. S.

PRINCIPAL WORKS: *Novels*—Ambrosio: or, The Monk, 1795; The Bravo of Venice, 1804; Feudal Tyrants, 1806. *Drama*—The Castle Spectre, 1796: Village Virtues, 1796; The Minister (translation of Schiller's Cabale und Liebe) 1797; Rolla (translation of Kotzebue) 1799; The East Indian, 1799; Adelmorn the Outlaw, 1800; Alphonso King of Castile, 1801; Rugantino, 1805; Adelgitha, 1806;

Wood Demon, 1807; Venoni, 1809; Timour the Tartar, 1812; Rich and Poor, 1812. *Poetry*—The Love of Cain, 1799; Tales of Wonder, 1801; Tales of Terror, 1807; Romantic Tales, 1809; Poems, 1812. *Journal*—The Journal of a West India Proprietor, 1834. *Letters*—Life and Correspondence of Matthew Gregory Lewis (includes unpublished work and *juvenalia*) 1839.

ABOUT: Lewis, M. G. Life and Correspondence of Matthew Gregory Lewis; Birkhead, E. The Tale of Terror; Killen, A. M. Le Roman Terrifiant; Scarborough, D. The Supernatural in Modern English Fiction.

LEYDEN, JOHN (September 8, 1775-August 28, 1811), Scottish poet and philologist, was born in Roxburghshire, and educated from 1790 to 1797 at the University of Edinburgh. From 1796 to 1798 he acted as a tutor, and then was licensed to preach, but was a failure in the pulpit. He contributed to the *Edinburgh Literary Magazine* and assisted Scott with his *Border Minstrelsy*. For six months of 1802 he edited the *Scots Magazine*. Having been promised a position as assistant surgeon in Madras, and having already studied considerable medicine, he received a nominal M.D. from St. Andrews in 1803 and early in the next year reported at Mysore Province. He fell ill with fever, and nearly died, but the next year made a tour in the Indian Ocean, when he narrowly escaped from a privateer. In 1806 he was in India again, at work on grammars and dictionaries of the Indian and Malayan languages. In 1809 he was commissioner of the Court of Requests at Calcutta, but gave a great deal of his time to his philological writings and translations. In 1810 he was assay-master of the Calcutta mint. The next year he went to Java with the British governor, and met his death from fever incurred in a native library which he had visited for study of its manuscripts. His death at less than thirty-six was a severe loss, not only because he was a master of Asiatic tongues, with a brilliant future as a philologist, but also because his lyrical poems showed great promise and a fine, delicate talent.

PRINCIPAL WORKS: Scenes of Infancy, 1803; Poetical Remains, 1819; Poems and Ballads, 1838.

ABOUT: Leyden, J. Scenes of Infancy (see Memoir by W. W. Tulloch in 1875 ed.); Poetical Remains (see Memoir by J. Morton); Poems and Ballads (see Memoirs by Sir Walter Scott and R. White).

LIDDELL, HENRY GEORGE (February 6, 1811-January 18, 1898), Greek lexicographer, was the son of a rector, and nephew of Lord Ravensworth, while his mother was the niece of an earl. His younger brother became a well-known engraver. He was educated at the Charterhouse and at Christ Church, Oxford, where he took his B.A. degree in 1833, M.A. 1835, B.D. and D.D. 1855. He was a tutor of his college in 1836, and a censor in 1845, in the latter year becoming professor of moral philosophy. In 1846 he became domestic chaplain to Prince Albert and headmaster of Westminster School. The same year he married Lorina Reeve; they had three sons and five daughters. (It was for Alice Liddell, 1852-1934, afterwards Mrs. Ralph Hargreaves, that Lewis Carroll wrote *Alice in Wonderland.*) Liddell was dean of Christ Church from 1855 to 1891, then the longest tenure in its history, and was vice-chancellor of Oxford from 1870 to 1874. He retired in 1891 at the age of eighty. He received an honorary LL.D. from Edinburgh in 1884 and an honorary D.C.L. from Oxford in 1893.

A stern, austere man who mellowed with the years, Liddell was a good teacher, but his great work is the famous *Greek-English Lexicon,* compiled with Robert Scott (1811-1887). This was nine years in the making, and new editions under Liddell's editorship continued to come out until 1897. There was also a condensed version for less advanced students. It is still a standard in its field.

PRINCIPAL WORKS: A Greek-English Lexicon (with R. Scott) 1843; A History of Ancient Rome, 1855.
ABOUT: Thompson, H. L. Memoir of H. G. Liddell, D.D.

LIDDON, HENRY PARRY (August 20, 1829-September 9, 1890), theologian, was born in Hampshire, son of a naval captain who had been an Arctic explorer. The family moved to Devonshire when Liddon was three. He was educated at King's College School, where his natural piety made him known as "the little priest," and at Christ Church, Oxford, where he received his B.A. in 1850. He was ordained deacon in 1852, priest in 1853, and from this time on his whole heart and soul were in the Christian ministry. As a curate at Wantage he first displayed his extraordinary genius as a preacher. Nevertheless, he abandoned the ministry for a while to become in 1854 the first vice-president of Bishop Wilberforce's Theological College, at Cuddesdown. Here he stayed until 1859, when he resigned because of attacks on his theological views which were strongly Puseyite (Tractarian). Returning to Oxford, he became vice-president of St. Edmunds Hall, and his lectures on the New Testament were extremely popular; he gave these until 1869, then resumed them in 1883. In 1864 he was made chaplain to the Bishop of Salisbury; in 1870 he received the B.D. and D.D. degrees, besides an honorary D.C.L. Until 1882 Liddon was professor of exegesis at Oxford; and a canon of St. Paul's Cathedral, London, from 1870 to his death. In 1886 he became chancellor of St. Paul's. His health failed during a trip to Egypt and Palestine, and on his return a cold caught at a funeral caused his death two months later.

Although a liberal in politics, Liddon was an extreme conservative, almost a reactionary, in religion and education. Especially did he hate any changes whatever in his beloved Oxford. His other great hatred was of indefiniteness and mysticism; his mind was clearcut and sharp. He was universally considered the greatest preacher of his time.

PRINCIPAL WORKS: Some Words for God (later, Sermons Preached Before the University of Oxford) 1865-79; Some Elements of Religion, 1872; Essays and Addresses, 1892.
ABOUT: Donaldson, A. B. Five Great Oxford Leaders; Holland, H. S. Personal Studies; Johnston, J. O. Life and Letters of Henry Parry Liddon; Russell, G. W. E. Dr. Liddon.

LIGHTFOOT, JOSEPH BARBER (April 13, 1828-December 21, 1889), theologian, was born in Liverpool, where his father was an accountant. He was a frail and sickly child. He was educated at the Liverpool Royal Institution, then, on his father's death in 1843 and removal of the family to Birmingham, at King Edward's School. He received his B.A. from Trinity College, Cambridge, in 1852, remained there as a fellow until 1855, and was ordained deacon in 1854 and priest in 1858. He was known then as a shy, serious, studious young man, whose chief interest was Biblical exegesis. He was a founder and editor of the *Journal of Classical and Sacred Philology,* which lasted from 1854 to 1859. In 1861 he became Hulsean professor of divinity at Cambridge, specializing in the New Testament, particularly the Epistles. He was a member of the council of the university from 1860 to 1878 and was active in its affairs. In 1862 he was appointed chaplain to Prince Albert, and in 1862 to Queen Victoria. In 1875 he was named as deputy clerk of the closet in the royal household. He received a D.D. degree from Cambridge in 1864; later he had honorary doctorates from five universities. In 1862 he was examining chaplain to the Bishop of London, and in 1871 a canon of St. Paul's Cathedral. In 1875 he became Lady Margaret's professor of divinity at Cambridge. He was one of the original members of the New Testament Company of Revisers, which issued the Revised Version of the New Testament from 1870 to 1880. In 1877 he was commissioner for Cambridge. In 1879 he became Bishop of Durham. From 1888 he was an invalid, dying a year later of heart disease.

Lightfoot's commentaries were intended to be part of a complete edition of all the Epistles, which he never finished. In addition to his original writing, he edited a number of patristic writers.

PRINCIPAL WORKS: Commentary on St. Paul's Epistle to the Galatians, 1865; A Fresh Revision of the New Testament, 1871; Commentary on St. Paul's Epistle to the Colossians, 1875; Commentary on St. Paul's Epistle to the Philippians, 1886; Leaders in the Northern Church, 1890.
ABOUT: Cambridge Review January 23, 1890.

LINGARD, JOHN (February 5, 1771-July 17, 1851), historian, was born in Winchester, but of a long-settled Lincolnshire family. His father, a carpenter, was a convert to the Roman Catholic Church; his mother belonged to it by birth, and her father had been imprisoned and fined for his adherence to it. Through the influence of a bishop, John was sent in 1782 to the English (Catholic) College at Douay, France. It was a good place to train a priest, but not an historian, for no history was taught there.

The French Revolution of course meant the dissolution of the college, and danger to the lives of its pupils and teachers. Lingard had a narrow escape, finally reaching England with some fellow-students in 1793. One of these fellow-refugees was the son and heir of Lord Stourton, who engaged Lingard to act as his son's tutor. An effort was made to found a new college in England, and when one was established at Crookhall, near Durham, Lingard became its vice-president. He was ordained as a priest in 1795. He acted as prefect of studies and professor of natural and moral philosophy there until 1808, when the school was finally moved to and consolidated with St. Cuthbert's College, Ushaw. At Ushaw Lingard remained until 1811, declining offers of appointment as its president, of a professorship at Maynooth, and of the presidency of a seminary.

What he wanted was leisure from teaching for his studies and his growing interest in historical writing, and he finally achieved this in 1811. He retired and spent the rest of his long life at Hornby, near Lancaster, where he built a little chapel, in which he officiated, next to the small house where he lived and worked alone. He had already published

JOHN LINGARD

articles in the *Newcastle Courant*. Outside a number of controversial and propaganda volumes, and one or two of Catholic doctrine, the remainder of Lingard's life was strictly devoted to his historical researches and writing. His modest home became a sort of literary center for northern England, and after the publication of his *History of England* many distinguished men sought him out. He made two trips to Rome, in 1817 and in 1821, and on the second of these was presented by the pope with a gold medal and a hint of a cardinal's hat, which, however, never materialized; the pope himself might be an admirer of this tolerant historian but the very orthodox circle around him was not, and he had enemies both there and in the ultra-Protestant camp. He did, however, receive a gift of three hundred pounds from Queen Victoria's privy purse in 1839, most of the profits of his history having gone to help poor theological students at Ushaw. In 1821 he was made Doctor of Divinity and of Canon and Civil Law. He lived in the utmost simplicity, like a poor village priest, kindly and obliging, a favorite in the village where there were few adherents of his church. In old age he suffered greatly from a complication of diseases, from which he was not released until he was over eighty. He died and was buried at Hornby.

The object of Lingard's history was to show non-Catholics their errors of judgment concerning the Church and its followers. His viewpoint was invariably temperate and candid, and he was exceedingly discreet, since he wished to produce a book which Protestants would read. He was, as said, attacked from both sides—by the ultramontane papal circle in Rome as being pro-French, timid, and apologetic; by the *Edinburgh Review* and its group as being disingenuous and prejudiced. Nevertheless his book was exceedingly popular, and each new volume as it came out enhanced his reputation. In this as in the earlier *Antiquities of the Anglo-Saxon Church*, Lingard carefully consulted original sources. His history is purely political, not social or literary; it was intended originally as a mere abridgment for students, but grew far beyond its intention. It is marred in part by haste in writing to meet a publisher's date-demands, and Lingard paid little attention to style in any case. But his writing is unostentatious and straightforward just as he himself was. It is now superseded for the Anglo-Saxon and Norman periods, but still worth consulting for the fourteenth. and fifteenth centuries.   M. A. deF.

PRINCIPAL WORKS: Catholic Loyalty Vindicated, 1805; The Antiquities of the Anglo-Saxon Church, 1806 (as The History and Antiquities of the Anglo-Saxon Church, with additional material, 1845); Documents to Ascertain the Sentiments of British Catholics, 1812; A Review of Certain Anti-Catholic

Publications, 1813; A Collection of Tracts on the Civil and Religious Principles of Catholics, 1813; Observations on . . . Laws and Ordinances [of] Foreign States [as to] Roman Catholic Subjects, 1817; History of England (8 vols.) 1819-30; A New Version of the Four Gospels, 1836; Catechetical Instructions, 1840.

ABOUT: Haile, M. & Binney, E. Life and Letters of John Lingard; Lingard, J. History of England (see Memoir in 6th ed., 1855, by Canon Tierney); London Times July 21, 1851.

LINTON, ELIZA LYNN (February 10, 1822—July 14, 1898), novelist and essayist,

was born Eliza Lynn, daughter of the vicar of Keswick. Her mother died when she was an infant. Rebelling early against her family, in 1845 she went to London with a year's allowance from her father, to make her way as a journalist—a most unusual procedure in her day. Her only preparation was a rather undigested mass of reading in the classics. From 1848 to 1851 she was on the staff of the *Morning Chronicle*. Then, discouraged by the failure of her first three novels, she went to Paris, and until 1854 lived there as a correspondent for the London newspapers. In 1858 at the request of his dying wife, she married William James Linton, the engraver, but their complete incompatibility was apparent from the beginning. They separated in a few years, but remained friends; she kept one of his daughters with her for years, received occasional visits from him until 1866, when he emigrated to America; and corresponded with him until his death, only six months before her own. From 1866 Mrs. Linton, who used her husband's name thereafter in her writings, was on the staff of the *Saturday Review*.

Mrs. Linton's first novels are glaringly unreal and emotional. Her marriage seemed to galvanize her into a new phase; her later novels are clear, vigorous, but entirely without feeling, as practical as the earlier ones are sentimental. She was a kind-hearted, generous woman, but extremely sharp-spoken and impulsive, rather a meddler and gossip, and a blind partisan. In consequence she collected probably the largest and most distinguished set of enemies of anyone of her period. Although her own life was a vindication of the economic freedom of women, she was a bitter anti-feminist.

PRINCIPAL WORKS: Azeth the Egyptian, 1846; Realities, 1851; Witch Stories, 1861; Grasp Your Nettle, 1865; Joshua Davidson, 1872; Under Which Lord? 1879; The Girl of the Period and Other Essays, 1883; The Autobiography of Christopher Kirkland, 1885; My Literary Life, 1899.

ABOUT: Layard, G. S. Eliza Lynn Linton: Her Life, Letters, and Opinions; Linton, E. L. My Literary Life (see Prefatory Notice by Beatrice Harraden).

LINTON, WILLIAM JAMES (December 7, 1812-January 1, 1898), poet and engraver,

was born in London of a family of Scottish descent. His younger brother, like himself, became an engraver. After attending a private school at Stratford, he was apprenticed from 1828 to 1834 to two noted wood-engravers. In 1836 he married a sister of the poet Thomas Wade; she died soon after, and he married her sister. This latter marriage, which resulted in several children, must have been illegal, since the British law until very recently forbade marrying a deceased wife's sister. Such unconventionalities, however, would not have troubled Linton, since he was a disciple of Shelley, a free-thinker, and a radical republican. For several years he gravitated between art and literature; in 1839 he founded a short-lived magazine called *The National*, in 1842 became a partner to his former employer, as an engraver, and in 1845 succeeded Douglas Jerrold as editor of the *Illuminated Magazine*. Meanwhile he contributed political verse to the Dublin *Nation* under the pseudonym of "Spartacus." In 1858 he founded *The Leader*, with Thornton Hunt and G. H. Lewes, but becoming dissatisfied with their conduct of it he left them and founded the *English Republic*, which he edited and printed himself until 1855. In 1858, at the request of his second wife before her death, he married the novelist Eliza Lynn; however, the marriage proved impossible and was soon ended by an amicable separation. During this period Linton's chief source of livelihood was his engraving; he engraved the covers of the *Cornhill Magazine* and *Macmillan's Magazine*.

In 1866 he emigrated to the United States of America, and established, near New Haven, a school and colony for the study and practice of wood-engraving. He also had a private press, from which he published anthologies and books of his own original verse. The rise of process engraving, which filled him with impotent anger, brought an end to his venture. He nevertheless remained one of the finest engravers of his day. As a poet he is undeservingly forgotten. In their clear-cut, artless grace and charm, his lyrics have almost a seventeenth century air. He merits rescue from obscurity.

PRINCIPAL WORKS: The Plaint of Freedom (poems) 1852; Claribel and Other Poems, 1865; A History of Wood Engraving in America, 1882; Poems and Translations, 1884; The Masters of Wood Engraving, 1890; Life of John Greenleaf Whittier, 1893; Memories, 1895.

ABOUT: Linton, W. J. Memories; Athenaeum January 8 and 15, 1898.

LISTER, THOMAS HENRY (1800-June 5, 1842), novelist, was born at Lichfield and ed-

ucated at Westminster and at Trinity College, Cambridge, which he left without a degree. He was never able to devote his entire time to writing, but served in various governmental capacities—in 1834 as a commissioner for inquiring into religious and other instruction in Ireland, in 1835 in the same office for Scotland, and in 1836 as the first registrar-general of England and Wales. In 1830 he married Maria Theresa Villiers, herself an editor and writer of biographies, who after his death married Sir George Cornewall Lewis. The Listers had one son and two daughters.

· In addition to his novels, Lister wrote a tragedy, *Epicharis,* produced at Drury Lane with some success in 1829, and a biography of the first Earl of Clarendon. He was a contributor to the *Edinburgh Review* and the *Encyclopaedia Britannica,* and edited a novel, *Anne Grey,* written by his sister Harriet, later Mrs. Craddock. *Granby* is Lister's best-known work; it is a clever, satirical society novel, which brought upon him unjust accusations of plagiarism. His death at only forty-two left his talents undeveloped.

PRINCIPAL WORKS: Granby, 1826; Herbert Lacy, 1828; Arlington, 1832; Hulse House, 1860.
ABOUT: Gentleman's Magazine 1842, part 2, page 323.

LIVINGSTONE, DAVID (March 19, 1813-May 1, 1873), Scottish explorer and travel writer, was born in Lanarkshire. His father was a small tea dealer, and a deacon in the Independent Church. At ten David was sent to work in a cotton factory, as a piecer; although he had to work from six in the morning till dark, he spent his first earnings for a Latin grammar, and studied Latin and science until late at night. Finally he decided to learn medicine so as to be a medical missionary to China. At nineteen he became a cotton spinner, and in his scant leisure hours studied medicine at Anderson College and Greek and divinity at Glasgow University. He offered his services to the London Missionary Society, because it was non-sectarian, and being accepted went to London in 1839 and "walked the hospitals." In 1840 he was admitted licentiate to the Faculty of Physicians and Surgeons in Glasgow University, and was also ordained as a missionary.

The China War changing his objective from China to Africa, he arrived in South Africa in 1841. From the first he undertook long journeys into the interior to become acquainted with native life. In 1843 he was wounded by a lion, causing a permanent injury to his left arm. In 1844 he married Mary Moffet, who shared all his adventures and hardships, helped him build his mission stations, made her own soap and candles and wove her clothes, and bore his children, until the hardships of their life killed her in 1862. Livingstone continued his long exploratory tours, on one of which he discovered the Zambesi River. In 1856 he led an expedition from Capetown across all of West Central Africa.

Returning to England in that year, he published an account of his journeys, and received a D.C.L. degree from Oxford and became a Fellow of the Royal Society. In 1857 he resigned from the Missionary Society. From 1858 to 1864 he was consul at Quilmane, and conducted explorations of Eastern and Central Africa. He was in England again in 1864, explored the Nile Basin in 1864, and in 1871 led a trip to the cannibal country from which he was rescued by H. M. Stanley, sent to find him by the New York *Herald.* A new tour in search of the source of the Nile, in 1873, caused his death from exhaustion and fever. His body was brought home and buried in Westminster Abbey.

Livingstone was not only a great explorer, but a great travel writer as well. His books are classics of their genre.

PRINCIPAL WORKS: Missionary Travels in South Africa, 1857; The Zambesi and Its Tributaries, 1865.
ABOUT: Blaikie, W. G. The Personal Life of David Livingstone; Hughes, T. David Livingstone; Marrat, J. David Livingstone: Missionary and Discoverer; Mossman, S. Heroes of Discovery.

LLOYD, CHARLES (February 12, 1775-January 16, 1839), poet and story-teller, was born at Birmingham, the eldest son of Charles and Mary Farmer Lloyd.

He was educated privately for entrance into his father's bank, but at twenty he was already publishing poems and choosing a literary career. In 1796 he met Coleridge and was so fascinated that he proposed that they live together. Coleridge was to tutor Lloyd three hours daily in return for a generous payment. Thus Lloyd was with Coleridge at Kingsdown, Bristol, and Nether Stowey until the summer of 1796. In January 1797 Lloyd met Charles Lamb who at once liked the young Quaker. In October both men were represented by poems added to Coleridge's *Poems,* and in 1798 they published jointly *Blank Verse.* About this time the friendship with Coleridge was broken, and in time the Lamb friendship cooled, though Lamb had been an ardent admirer at first.

In 1797 Lloyd married Sophia Pemberton of Birmingham, following an elopement in which Robert Southey acted as his proxy. Lloyd's father gave him a generous allowance, and they lived at Bardwell. After August 1800 they were near Ambleside where Southey visited them. Thomas DeQuincey, between 1809 and 1814, used regularly to sit with Lloyd from nine until one in the morning, talking. In these years Lloyd was no longer a professing Quaker, having found himself too sensitive to bear the publicity which the Quaker costume gave him in the Lake district.

Six years (1805-11) were spent in translating Ovid's *Metamorphoses,* which has not

CHARLES LLOYD

ABOUT: Bates, E. Miscellaneous Repository; DeQuincey, T. Literary Reminiscenses; ibid., Conversations With Wodehouse: Hunt, L. Correspondence; Lucas, E. V. Charles Lamb and the Lloyds; Southey, R. Letters; Talfourd, T. N. Critical and Miscellaneous Writings.

LOCKER-LAMPSON, FREDERICK

(May 29, 1821-May 30, 1895), poet, bibliophile and collector, was the second son of Edward Hawke and Eleanor Mary Elizabeth (Boucher) Locker. He was born in Greenwich Naval Hospital, of which his father was civil commissioner and his grandfather had been Lieutenant Governor.

Frederick Locker, as he is generally known, is one of a considerable number of minor English writers of the 19th century whose names are today more familiar than their works. One reason for this familiarity with names is to be found in the comparatively small number of people who constituted the fashionable, political, and literary society of 19th century England. The same persons will be encountered over and over again in almost any memoirs, criticisms, or histories of the period. Locker is a particularly notable example of this—his contacts and connections, and those of his family, reading like a combination of social register and Who's Who. His first wife, a great favorite with Queen Victoria, was Lady Charlotte Bruce, daughter of Lord Elgin of Elgin Marbles fame.

Unlike that of most of the men who mingled in this society, Locker's education was very sketchy and did not include a period at one of the great public schools. This was because he was a remarkably unpromising pupil. He spent seven years in six schools and at the end of that time "he spelt abominably and couldn't construe a line of Latin." His parents gave up all hope of a profession for him and found him a place as clerk (without pay) in a colonial broker's counting house, where he was to learn the business. But he showed no more aptness as a pupil here than he had in school and his father was "advised to remove him."

At this point (1841) a friend of his father's, Lord Haddington, got Frederick appointed a junior in his office at the Admiralty. Here his wit and rhyming ability first began to come to the fore. As a deputy reader and *précis* writer he amused his superior with rhymed versions of official papers.

In 1849 Locker's health, never rugged, necessitated a long leave of absence. He went to Paris where he first met Lady Charlotte Bruce, and in 1850 they were married. This marriage was very happy. Shortly after this he retired from the Admiralty. Although Locker recorded that "I have never felt much at my ease with royalty, and never shall," he moved in the most brilliant society of England, Paris, and Rome.

yet been published in full. He also translated Alfieri's tragedies. Auditory illusions, which finally overthrew his reason, began about 1811 to cause Lloyd much suffering. DeQuincey has described these attacks. Lloyd's mind was so affected that he was placed in an asylum near York. In 1818 he escaped and made his way to DeQuincey, who took him in, found him increasingly rational, and allowed him to leave with Sophia for London. The next year he seemed much improved and wrote a good deal of verse. But his illness recurred seriously in 1831, and he died in a sanitarium at Chaillot, near Versailles, where his wife died at almost the same time.

Lloyd was tall, clumsy, polished in manner, "not intellectual so much as benign and conciliatory in his expression of face." He used an excess of exercise, ether, and opium to blot out his auditory illusions, and the effect is visible in his worn countenance.

DeQuincey notes the "mournful merit" of Lloyd's poems in relation to his life, calling them "true solitary sighs, wrung from his own meditative heart by excess of suffering." In his sensibility DeQuincey found Lloyd "Rousseauish." Lamb "valued rarely" Lloyd's poetry. Its descriptive accuracy and subjective intensity are best seen in *Desultory Thoughts in London*. T. N. Talfourd says, "His mind was chiefly remarkable for a fine power of analysis."   D. F. A.

PRINCIPAL WORKS: *Poetry*—Poems, 1796; Poem, 1796; Blank Verse, 1798; Lines, 1799; Nugae Canorae, 1819; Desultory Thoughts in London, 1821; Beritola, 1823; Poems, 1823. *Drama*—The Duke D'Ormond, 1822. *Novels*—Edmund Oliver, 1798; Isabel, 1820. *Miscellaneous and Translations*—Letter to the Anti-Jacobin Review, 1799; The Tragedies of Vittorio Alfieri (13 vols.) 1815; Poetical Essays on the Character of Pope, 1821; Speech at Bible Society, 1828; Speech, 1828.

For some time he had contributed both prose and verse to *Blackwood's*, the *Cornhill*, and *The Times*. In 1857 Chapman & Hall published his first collection of verse, *London Lyrics*. With rearrangements and additions this volume was republished many times under the same title, and with a supplemental volume privately printed in 1882 entitled *London Rhymes* constitutes almost the whole of his published verse. In 1879 he published *Patchwork*, a miscellany of prose "extracts of unrivalled merit." These, with his autobiographical *My Confidences*, published posthumously by his son-in-law, Augustine Birrell, constitute his original works. In addition to these he published the anthology of *vers de société*, *Lyra Elegantiarum*.

In 1872 Lady Charlotte Locker died and in 1874 he married Hannah Jane Lampson, whose name he took in 1885. It was at her home, Rowfant, Sussex, that they chiefly resided. Here Locker-Lampson assembled his famous Rowfant Library of Shakespeare quartos, priceless manuscripts and first editions; and here he died in 1895.

A writer of light verse and *vers de société*, Locker belonged to the school of Prior, Praed, and Hood. Austin Dobson, his friend for over twenty years, says of Locker, ". . . easily bored himself, the dread of boring others that kept his poems brief was invaluable to him as a raconteur. . . . Modest by nature, and with a real reverence for learning, Mr. Locker would have shrunk from calling himself a scholar . . . or even a student; and in truth his . . . researches lay more among men than books. . ." In closing his sketch Dobson says that he can find nothing more suitable than the following quotation from Augustine Birrell: "Frederick Locker was essentially a man of the world; he devoted his leisure hours to studying the various sides of human nature, and drawing the good that he could out of all sorts and conditions of men. His delicate health prevented him from taking any very active share in stirring events; but he was content, unembittered, to look on, and his energies were continually directed towards gathering about him those friends and acquaintances who, with their intellectual acquirements, combined the charms of good manners, culture and refinement."   -D. C.

PRINCIPAL WORKS: *Poetry*—London Rhymes, 1857. *Miscellaneous*—Patchwork, 1879. *Autobiography*—My Confidences, 1896.

ABOUT: Birrell, A. Frederick Locker-Lampson; Locker-Lampson, F. London Rhymes (1904 ed., see Introduction by Austin Dobson).

LOCKHART, JOHN GIBSON

LOCKHART, JOHN GIBSON (July 14, 1794-November 25, 1854), Scottish biographer and historian, was born at Cambusnethan, Lanarkshire, the eldest son of the second marriage of the Reverend John Lockhart. His mother was Elizabeth Gibson, daughter of the Reverend John Gibson of St. Cuthbert's, Edinburgh, and granddaughter of Henry Erskine, Lord Cardross. Lockhart Senior was a son of the Laird of Berkhill, Lanarkshire. Young John was delicate as a lad, but lively and full of fun. Before he was twelve he entered the University of Glasgow. He was popular with his fellow students, despite his indifference to games and his humane attitude toward sport. In later life he wrote that, "Of all the world's wonders none is to us more incomprehensible than the fact that there have been deep philosophers, solemn divines, nay, tender, thoughtful, meditative poets, who could wander from morn to dewy eve torturing fish and massacring birds."

Lockhart's humanitarianism did not extend to his fellow men. His satiric turn of mind revealed itself at an early age and doubtless contributed to his popularity with his contemporaries in school. One of his cruelest japes was perpetrated at Balliol College, Oxford, where he entered in 1809, upon a tutor who was overfond of pointing out Hebraisms in the Greek New Testament. This worthy was delighted when Lockhart turned in what was apparently an exercise written in Hebrew. The master of the college, to whom he showed the manuscript, recognized it as a lampoon on the teacher written in English with Hebrew characters. Lockhart was a good classical scholar, wrote excellent Latin, and was conversant with French, Spanish, Italian and German. He was interested in antiquities and studied heraldic and genealogical lore. He took a first in classics in 1813.

Upon leaving Oxford he went to Edinburgh to study law. He was called to the bar in 1816, but he never took his profession

FREDERICK LOCKER-LAMPSON

seriously and was at this time chiefly interested in German literature. In exchange for a promised translation of F. Schlegel's *Lectures on the History of Literature* the publisher William Blackwood financed Lockhart's tour of the Continent in 1817. Like all literary neophytes who traveled in the period he paid a visit to Goethe at Weimar.

In this fashion Lockhart came to be associated with the modern British periodical. The *Edinburgh Review*, founded in 1802 and devoted to liberal politics, attracted wide attention and roused Tory spirits to defend their reactionary doctrines in the *Quarterly Review*. In April 1817 Blackwood launched his *Edinburgh Monthly Magazine*. Lockhart's first contribution appeared in the seventh number, when the journal first came out with the now familiar name of *Blackwood's Magazine*. Like the *Quarterly*, *Blackwood's* was Tory and opposed to the *Edinburgh Review*. Though generally sympathetic on literary matters and equally suspicious of innovations in *belles lettres*, their political views were strongly, even murderously opposed. In 1821 the editor of the *London Magazine* was killed in a duel by *Blackwood's* representative, Christie. Lockhart soon had made a name and many enemies for himself as a controversial writer.

In May 1818 Lockhart met Sir Walter Scott and in April 1820 married his daughter Sophia. Although they were very unlike in temperament, there was genuine affection and understanding between Scott and his son-in-law. Strikingly handsome in appearance, tall, slender and dark, Lockhart's hauteur and reserve disconcerted strangers. "To be one of the best," Scott wrote of him, "and one of the kindest, as well of the cleverest of men I know, John's taste and talents for making enemies and powerful enemies is something quite extraordinary."

In 1825, as a result of editorial connections with the *Quarterly Review* and a newspaper, *The Representative*, Lockhart moved to London. He continued to write for Blackwood, produced his delightful life of Burns for *Constable's Miscellany* of 1828, and wrote a life of Napoleon for *Murray's Family Library* in the following year.

Lockhart's eldest son (the "Hugh Littlejohn" of Scott's *Tales of a Grandfather*) died in 1831 and Scott himself in 1832. Lockhart had the letters, journals, and private papers of the great man in his possession. His talents were entirely worthy of the material and equal to the huge task to which he now set himself. The *Life of Sir Walter Scott* which appeared in 1837-38 in eight volumes, and in a second edition of ten volumes in 1839, had a mixed reception. By modern standards Lockhart's treatment of Sir Walter seems eulogistic, but biography at this time was still

JOHN GIBSON LOCKHART

overshadowed by the gilded traditions of the memoir. Lockhart's methods are, by present day notions, unorthodox, particularly in the telescoping (what he termed "manipulation") of the letters, but he does give a true picture of the author of *Waverley*. This is precisely what Lockhart was accused of not doing by none other than Carlyle, whose own biographer Froude was to be attacked even in his grave for attempting to present his subject as a human being. Lockhart turned the profits of the book over to Scott's creditors.

Mrs. Lockhart died in 1837 and Lockhart's last years were saddened and lonely. His son was estranged from him by his own conduct, but his relations with his daughter Charlotte (Mrs. James Robert Hope-Scott) were always most affectionate. He isolated himself from society and seriously injured his health by excessive abstinence. In 1853 he gave up the *Quarterly Review* and went to Italy for the winter. Returning in the following year, he died at Abbottsford in the room next to the one in which Sir Walter had breathed his last.

By his method of selection, arrangement, and descriptive digression Lockhart is considered to have achieved almost as vivid a picture of Scott as Boswell did of Johnson. Lockhart's novels are not without merit and his verse is competent, but his importance lies in biography and the history of controversial journalism.   P. B. S.

PRINCIPAL WORKS: *Fiction*—Valerius: A Roman Story, 1821; Reginald Dalton: A Story of English University Life, 1823; Matthew Wald, 1824. *Translations*—Ancient Spanish Ballads: Historical and Romantic, 1823; F. Schlegel's *Lectures on the History of Literature*, 1838. *Biography*—The Life of Robert Burns, 1828; History of Napoleon Buonaparte, 1829; History of the Late War: With Sketches of Nelson, Wellington, and Napoleon, 1832; Memoirs of the Life of Sir Walter Scott,

1837-1838. *Miscellaneous*—Peter's Letters to his Kinsfolk: By Peter Morris the Odontist, 1819; Motteux's translation of *Don Quixote* (ed. with notes) 1822; The Ballantyne Humbug Handled, 1839.

ABOUT: Grierson, H. J. C. Lang, Lockhart, and Biography; Lang, A. The Life of John Gibson Lockhart.

LONG, GEORGE (November 4, 1800-August 10, 1879), classicist, was born in Lancashire, the son of a merchant. He was educated at Macclesfield Grammar School, and at Trinity College, Cambridge, where he received his B.A. degree in 1822. In 1824 he became professor of ancient languages in Jefferson's newly founded University of Virginia. He left in 1828 to become professor of Greek in the young University of London (later University College), where he remained until 1831. He edited the *Quarterly Journal of Education,* as well as other publications of the Society for the Diffusion of Useful Knowledge, of whose committee he was a member. He was a founder of the Royal Geographical Society, and honorary secretary from 1846 to 1848; geography was always his second greatest interest. He was called to the bar in 1837, and for a time was lecturer on jurisprudence and civil law at the Inner Temple, but he never practised as a barrister. From 1842 to 1846 he was professor of Latin at University College, and from 1849 to 1871, when he retired for age, classical lecturer at Brighton College. He received a civil list pension in 1873. Long was married three times, his first wife, by whom he had four sons and one daughter, being Harriet Selden, widow of a lieutenant-colonel in the United States Army.

Long's best known work was as editor of the *Penny Cyclopaedia,* issued by the Society for the Diffusion of Useful Knowledge from 1833 to 1846. He was also a prominent contributor to Smith's dictionaries of Greek and Roman antiquities and Greek and Roman biography. He was a true scholar, an accomplished translator, profoundly learned, and a disciple of the great stoic, Marcus Aurelius. His mind was clear and judicial; he is an excellent teacher in print, as he was by word of mouth.

PRINCIPAL WORKS: Two Discourses on Roman Law, 1847; The Geography of Great Britain (with G. R. Porter) 1850; An Old Man's Thoughts About Many Things, 1862; Decline of the Roman Republic, 1864-74.

ABOUT: Mathews, H. J. In Memoriam George Long; Athenaeum August 23, 1879.

LOUDON, JOHN CLAUDIUS (April 8, 1783-December 14, 1843), Scottish horticultural writer, was born in Lanarkshire, son of a farmer. From childhood he was fond of gardening. He was sent to live with an uncle at Edinburgh for his schooling, and at fourteen was apprenticed to a nurseryman and landscape gardener. At night he studied academic subjects, and paid his teachers by translations from the French and Italian. In 1803 he went to London. In 1806 he became a member of the Linnaean Society. For two years he was disabled by rheumatic fever, which left him lame and with a crippled left arm. Undaunted, he got his father to join him in a lease on a farm near Pinner, and in 1809 on a larger farm in Oxfordshire, where he took pupils. He made enough money to give up his farm in 1812 and travel on the Continent, but he returned to find his fortune lost and himself heavily in debt. In 1820 his right arm was broken and badly set, and in 1825 it was amputated. He contracted the opium habit from the constant agony he endured, but conquered it unaided.

In 1826 he began publishing the *Gardener's Magazine,* and by 1834 was editing and publishing five separate periodicals on gardening, natural history, and architecture. In 1830 he had married Jane Webb, who herself became a botanical writer and was his greatest help. They had one daughter. By 1838 he was in the hands of his creditors, and the crippled man went to work again as a landscape gardener, laying out arboreta and cemeteries. In 1840 he edited the *Gardener's Gazette,* his last magazine. He died literally on his feet, worn out by over-work.

PRINCIPAL WORKS: Encyclopaedia of Gardening, 1822; Encyclopaedia of Agriculture, 1825; Encyclopaedia of Plants, 1829; Encyclopaedia of Cottage, Farm, and Villa Architecture, 1833; Arboretum et Fruticetum Britannicum, 1838; Encyclopaedia of Trees and Shrubs, 1842: Self Instruction for Gardeners, 1844.

ABOUT: Loudon, J. C. Self Instruction for Gardeners (see Preface by J. W. Loudon); Proceedings of Linnaean Society 1:204.

LOVER, SAMUEL (February 24, 1797-July 6, 1868), Irish novelist, song-writer, and painter, was born in Dublin, of a Protestant family, eldest son of John Lover, a stockbroker, and Abigail Maher. Samuel was a delicate child whose propensity for all the arts evidenced itself at an early age. Sent in his twelfth year to the country for his health, he learned to know and love the Irish peasantry, which he was afterwards to defend.

At fifteen he was introduced to the uncongenial trade of stockbroker. Heretofore his father's idol, the boy and his artistic pursuits were now held up to ridicule. On one occasion Mr. Lover took a poker and demolished Samuel's miniature theatre. The complete break with his father came when the boy was seventeen. He returned from London, whither he had been sent to further his business career, and without formal training in art prepared to earn his living as a painter.

For a banquet in honor of Thomas Moore, Lover sang a song of his own composition

SAMUEL LOVER

and thus began his lifelong friendship with the Irish bard. Moore's influence might be considered a prevailing motif in Lover's career. It was Moore's song, "Will you come to the bower?" which the infant Lover, barely able to stand and reach the keyboard, picked out on the piano and Lover's first success as a painter was won with a portrait of Moore's son Russell.

Lover continued to write and publish songs, ballads, and stories, but his major occupation was painting. In 1827, well established in life, he married Lucy, daughter of John Berrel, a Dutch architect. The same year his first play, *Grania Vaile*, a fairy spectacle, was produced. No manuscript of it survives. Elected secretary of the Royal Hibernian Society in 1828, he still had time and inclination to exert himself in behalf of the downtrodden Irish peasantry. His anonymous contributions to the *Parson's Hornbook* of 1831 were widely discussed. In 1832 he published a collection of tales and legends which had previously appeared in various periodicals.

Lover's portrait of Paganini, which was exhibited by the Royal Academy at London, led to his removal there in 1835. In London he moved in literary and artistic circles and was associated with Dickens in the founding of *Bentley's Magazine*. In addition to painting he amused himself with writing songs and theatrical trifles, of which he did not always trouble to preserve the manuscripts, as well as some more enduring works. In 1837 appeared his first novel, *Rory o'More*, the title of which he had previously used for a ballad. This sympathetic portrayal of the Irish peasant was immediately cast in dramatic form and ran for 109 nights at the Adelphi.

Lover's weakening eyesight, which forced him to relinquish his etching tools and the painting of miniatures, was advantageous to his pen. In 1849 appeared his second and best-known novel, *Handy Andy*. He commenced (1844) a series of public entertainments consisting of readings from his own works and selections from Irish songs and ballads, known as "Irish Nights." He made a literally triumphal progress through the British Isles and America. This type of diversion was novel at the time and Lover himself, whose name and personality were commonly punned upon, was deservedly popular. While he was in America his wife died and his return to London was saddened by the loss from consumption of the elder of his two daughters.

In January 1852 Lover married again. Mary Jane Wandby was the daughter of William Wandby, squire of Coldham Hall, Cambridgeshire. Of the five children of this marriage only one daughter, Fannie, survived. She married a Dublin barrister, Edward Herbert, and became the mother of Victor Herbert, the composer.

Never robust, Lover suffered a hemorrhage of the lungs in 1864. Four years later he died at St. Helier on the island of Jersey.

Among interpreters of and apologists for Ireland's awakening national consciousness Lover is an important figure. Like others of the Irish school the characters of his novels are objectively interpreted rather than subjectively expressed. Lover did much to change the popular conception of the Irish peasant from an apelike buffoon to a genuine human being. His poems, as he himself said, must be considered in conjunction with the music for which they are written. Certain of his songs, like "The Low Backed Car," are to this day stock in trade for tenors.   P. B. S.

PRINCIPAL WORKS: *Novels*—Rory o'More, 1837; Handy Andy, 1842. *Stories*—Legends and Stories of Ireland, 1831. *Poetry*—Songs and Ballads, 1839; Rival Rhymes, 1859; Volunteer Songs, 1859. *Miscellaneous*—Selected Irish Lyrics, 1858.

ABOUT: Bernard, B. Life of Samuel Lover; Boyd, E. A. Ireland's Literary Renaissance; Symington, A. J. Samuel Lover.

LUBBOCK, SIR JOHN. See AVEBURY, LORD

LUGARD, LADY. See SHAW, FLORA L.

LYALL, SIR ALFRED COMYN (January 4, 1835-April 10, 1911), poet and historian, was born in Surrey, the son of a clergyman and the nephew of the dean of Canterbury. He was educated at Eton from 1845 to 1852, and then had three years at Haileybury, from which in 1856 he was appointed to the Indian civil service. He was caught in the great mutiny, and participated in the siege of Delhi. In 1863 he married Cora Cloete, of a Boer family; they had two sons and two daughters.

In 1865 Lyall was commissioner of Nagpur, and in 1867 of West Berar, where he wrote a gazetteer of the district, one of the first to be produced. In 1873 he was home secretary to the Indian government, and in 1874 the governor-general's agent in Rajputana. In 1878, as foreign secretary to the Indian government, he participated in the Afghan War. In 1882 he became lieutenant governor of the Northwest Provinces and Oudha, now known as the United Provinces. He retired from the civil service in 1887 and returned to London, where he was a member of the India Council until 1902—an unusual length of service, the regular term being ten years. In 1887 he became a Knight Commander of the Indian Empire and in 1906 Grand Commander; in 1902 Edward VII made him a privy councillor. He contributed to the *Edinburgh Review* and the *Fortnightly*, received honorary degrees from Oxford and Cambridge, and was the recipient of many other honors, including a trusteeship of the British Museum. Though a liberal in politics, he was an outstanding opponent of woman's suffrage.

Lyall's histories of India are really primarily studies of comparative religion, done in masterly style. His poems showed much imaginative sympathy, and were mostly meditative and philosophical in nature, strongly tinged with melancholy. He died suddenly of heart disease while on a visit to Tennyson's son.

PRINCIPAL WORKS: Asiatic Studies, 1882 and 1899; Verse Written in India, 1889; Rise and Expansion of the British Dominion in India, 1893.

ABOUT: Durand, Sir M. Life of Sir Alfred Lyall.

LYELL, SIR CHARLES (November 14, 1797-February 22, 1875), geologist, was born in Forfarshire, the eldest son of a well-known botanist and student of Dante. When the boy was a year old the family moved to the New Forest, where he was brought up—an environment that early awakened his interest in nature. Lyell's first passion was for entomology, but he was also an ardent collector of quartz and other geological specimens even in childhood.

After school years at Ringwood, Salisbury, and Midhurst, he entered Exeter College, Oxford, in 1816, receiving his B.A. three years later, with second class honors in classics. His weakness in Latin and Greek was a lifelong cause of chagrin to him. In spite of his aptitude for science, he was destined for the law. Two happenings made it impossible for him to devote his life to a legal career—extreme near-sightedness, which physicians of that day were powerless to correct, and a series of

SIR CHARLES LYELL

tours on the Continent, and particularly in the Alps, which kept his appetite whetted for geology, and laid the foundation for his best known work. William Smith's famous book on fossils, published in 1816, had revolutionized that science, linking it with biology instead of, as hitherto, with engineering; and Lyell was from the first receptive to the evolutionary implications of Smith's work.

As if to signalize his true bent, in the same year, 1819, he entered Lincoln's Inn, and joined the Geological and Linnaean Societies. He received his M.A. from Oxford in 1821, but most of his attention was given to geology, and from 1823 to 1826 he acted as secretary of the Geological Society. In the latter year he was made a Fellow of the Royal Society. In 1825 he had resumed the practice of law, and even went on circuit in 1827; but he was already contributing articles on geology to the *Quarterly Review*. His *Principles of Geology*, published in 1830, gave the death-blow to the anti-evolutionary "catastrophic theory," which said that fossils were the remains of various separately created animals killed by successive catastrophes.

In 1831 he was appointed professor of geology at King's College, London, but gave only two lecture courses. It is interesting to note that ladies were excluded from these, since they were too "advanced" and irreligious! In 1832 he married Mary Horner, who acted as his amanuensis as his sight continued to fail.

In 1834 Lyell received the medal of the Royal Society, but with reservations because of his unorthodox opinions, and in 1835 and 1836, and again in 1849 and 1850, he acted as president of the Geological Society. He was knighted in 1848, and made a baronet in 1864 —probably fruits not so much of his scientific eminence, for it was not a period when scientists were so honored, but of his friendship with Prince Albert. Lyell always felt that travel was the foundation of real education, and was himself a constant traveler. He visited the United States in 1841, 1845, 1852, and 1853, and spent the following year in the Canary Islands. In 1854 Oxford made him a doctor of civil law.

He was one of the earliest converts to Darwin's theory after the publication of *The Origin of Species* in 1859—an unpopular stand which, as Darwin said, in view of his age, his distinction, and his strong religious bias, was truly heroic. By this time Lyell was easily the greatest geologist in England; not even his evolutionary views could keep him from being elected president of the British Association for the Advancement of Science in 1864.

In 1873 Lady Lyell died, and her aged husband never recovered his health after the shock and misery of his bereavement. He failed gradually until early in 1875 he died. He was buried in Westminster Abbey.

Lyell was a fascinating lecturer, and much of his inimitable style is in his lucid and fluent writing. He was a constant student, a great teacher, and a kindly, retiring, methodically minded, tolerant man. His chief fame is as an investigator, but his books are readable today and much of their content is still valid.

M. A. deF.

PRINCIPAL WORKS: Principles of Geology, 1830; Elements of Geology, 1838; Travels in North America, 1845; A Second Visit to the United States of North America, 1849; The Geological Evidences of the Antiquity of Man, 1863; The Student's Elements of Geology 1871; Life, Letters and Journal (ed. by his sister-in-law) 1881.
ABOUT: Bonney, T. G. Charles Lyell and Modern Geology; Darwin, C. Life and Letters; Lyell, C. Life, Letters, and Journal; Nature 12:325 August 26, 1875.

LYNN, ELIZABETH. See LINTON, ELIZABETH LYNN

LYTE, HENRY FRANCIS (June 1, 1793-November 20, 1847), hymn writer, was born in Roxburghshire, his father being an army captain. He was educated at Portora School and at Trinity College, Dublin, where in three successive years he won prizes for poems. Having taken holy orders, he became a curate near Wexford, but was obliged to resign because of ill health. During this period he married Anne Maxwell. He was then for a while curate in Hampshire and Devonshire, and finally settled down for twenty-five years in a church at Lower Brixham. He was always a semi-invalid, however, and spent much time in the south of France seeking health; he died in Nice during one of these journeys.

Although Lyte also wrote secular poetry, he is remembered only for his hymns. These have remained popular, and one—"Abide With Me"—bids fair to be immortal.

PRINCIPAL WORKS: Tales in Verse, 1826; Poems Chiefly Religious, 1833; The Spirit of the Psalms, 1834; Remains, 1850.
ABOUT: Lyte, H. F. Remains (see Memoir).

LYTTON, EDWARD G.E.L. BULWER-. See BULWER-LYTTON, EDWARD G.E.L.

LYTTON, LORD (Edward Robert Bulwer, First Earl of Lytton) (November 18, 1831-November 24, 1891), statesman and poet, who wrote as "Owen Meredith," was born in London, the only son of the novelist Edward G.E.L. Bulwer-Lytton, the first baron, and the brilliant Rosina Wheeler. He did not live long in England, however, for, after the separation of his parents in 1836 "Teddy," as he was called, and his sister Emily, four years older, were taken by their mother to live in St. Douloughs, Ireland, with their guardian, Miss Greene, who afterwards took them to Coventry and Cheltenham.

At nine Edward left for school at Twickenham, while his sister was sent to Germany. At a second school in Brighton Lytton composed his first poetry. He was then twelve. His greatest pleasures at this period were holiday visits to the theatre with his father's friend, John Forster, the biographer. In 1845 he left Brighton to go to Harrow for three years, where he was, he confesses, "an idle boy." He dallied with his Latin and Greek, and spent long hours reading English works of his own choice. Even when he was studying under an English tutor at Bonn his father was compelled to rebuke him for his lack of interest in his studies. As a result, perhaps, he was sent, not to Oxford or Cambridge, but to Washington (1850) to serve as an unpaid attaché to his uncle, Sir Henry Bulwer, who was then minister to the United States, and when the uncle was called to Florence in 1852 the nephew also went along.

In Italy he continued his literary activities and had the pleasure of close association with the Brownings. Soon his prose began to appear in the magazines and in 1855 his first volume of poems, *Clytemnestra*, was published under the *nom de plume* "Owen Meredith," a name suggested by the fact that a relative called Ann Meredith was connected with the historical Owen Tudor. He continued to write under this pseudonym until 1866 when George Meredith, the novelist, began to make serious objections.

In 1854 he was ordered to Paris, this time as unpaid attaché to the ambassador, Lord Cowley, whence he was transferred to a similar position at the Hague in 1856. His second volume, a collection of lyrics called *The Wanderer*, appeared in 1858, and the follow-

LORD LYTTON

ing year he was appointed to the embassy at Vienna as second secretary. There he was able to finish *Lucile,* a novel in verse, which came out in 1860, the same year in which he went on a mission to Belgrade. Back in Vienna he met Wilfred Blunt and Julian Fane, who like him, were authors as well as diplomats. With the latter he wrote *Tannhäuser* (1861), a poem based on Wagner's opera of the same name.

He left Vienna, however, in 1863 to accept the post of first secretary of legation at Copenhagen. Before he took up his next post at Athens he fell in love and was married on October 4, 1864, to Edith Villiers, the charming niece of his friend, Lady Bloomfield, and the niece also of the Earl of Clarendon. He was transferred to Lisbon the next spring.

Meanwhile he was contributing to such magazines as *All the Year Round* and *Blackwood's,* and *Chronicles and Characters,* another volume of poems, appeared in 1868, the year after Lytton's daughter Elizabeth was born, his first son having been born in 1865. He went to Madrid in 1868 and positions at Vienna (1869-72) and Paris (1873-4) followed. But probably the climax of his career came in November 1875, when Disraeli offered him the Viceroyalty of India, which he finally accepted. On March 1, 1876, he left for Bombay. His Viceroyalty was significant for his management of the Afghan war, the famine relief, the proclamation of the Queen as Empress of India, the new native civil service system, the salt duties, and the vernacular press laws, though at the same time his career was marred by a miscalculated estimate of the war costs.

After four years in India Lord Lytton returned to England in 1880 and settled down

with his family at Knebworth. He busied himself there with his writing and his interests in the House of Lords. He wrote his father's biography (1883) as well as the long narrative poem, *Glenaveril* (1885). At this period, too, he refurbished a fantastic poem called *King Poppy* (1892), and rewrote some of the verses which he afterwards published in *After Paradise* (1887).

These few years in England, interspersed with several trips abroad in search of health, were ended, however, in December 1887, when Lord Lytton accepted the post of British Ambassador to Paris, where he died on November 24, 1891, at the age of sixty, after a long period of ill health.

Although Lord Lytton had the "beautiful dreamy face and curly hair" of a typical romantic poet, he was extremely successful as a diplomat. Perhaps a rival school of "Imperial politics" did find fault with his Indian policies, but even such critics were forced to admit that his official dispatches were little short of brilliant. Moreover, he was one of the most popular ambassadors Paris had ever had. He was not primarily an executive, and from that point of view his Indian administration failed, but his wit and his personal charm made him a general favorite at home as well as abroad. And, although he was an ultra-Conservative, his politics were nothing if not original.

Probably his diplomatic career prevented him from being more than a second or third rate poet, who never equaled his father as a writer. His friend, Wilfred Blunt, gave him a place above Browning, Arnold, and William Morris. Swinburne, on the other hand, satirized him as a plagiarist. His lyrics were certainly his best work, but even they are criticized for their imitation of Byron. As a poet Lytton was "an ambitious failure." B. D. S.

PRINCIPAL WORKS: *Poetry*—Clytemnestra, 1855; The Wanderer, 1857; Lucile, 1860; Serbski Pesme, 1861; Tannhäuser, 1861; The Ring of Amasis, 1863; The Apple of Life, 1865; Chronicles and Characters, 1868; Orval, 1863; Fables in Song, 1874; Glenaveril, 1885; The Earl's Return, 1886; After Paradise, 1887; King Poppy, 1892; Marah, 1892. *Prose*—Julian Fane, 1871. *Editor*—The Life, Letters, and Literary Remains of Edward Bulwer, 1883.

ABOUT: Balfour, B. The History of Lord Lytton's Indian Administration; Betham-Edwards, M. Friendly Faces; Eminent Persons; Farrar, F. W. Men I Have Known; Forbes, A. The Afghan Wars; Lytton, E. R. B. Personal & Literary Letters (ed. by B. Balfour); Lytton, E. R. B. Poems (see Introduction by M. Betham-Edwards); Strachey, J. & R. The Finances and Public Works of India; Strachey, J. India; The Critic 1: 254 September 24, 1881; The Nineteenth Century 31: 566 April 1892; The Saturday Review 72:600 November 28, 1891.

MACAULAY, LORD THOMAS BABINGTON (First Baron) (October 25, 1800-December 28, 1859), historian, essayist, and statesman, was born at Rothley Temple,

Leicestershire, eldest son of Zachary Macaulay, the abolitionist, and Selina Mills.

He was a child of extraordinary precocity, reading with entire ease at the age of three, and possessing from the earliest a remarkable vocabulary. At four he became a favorite of Hannah More, who had been his mother's teacher. At seven, when he was put under the tutorship of a Mr. Greaves, he had begun a "compendium of universal history," and before he was twelve had commenced various ambitious works.

In 1812 he entered Mr. Preston's school near Cambridge, later (1814) moved to Aspenden Hall in Hertfordshire. Macaulay was not a student of the closest application, possibly because his amazing memory—he knew by heart, at twelve, *Paradise Lost* and *The Pilgrim's Progress*—made the systematic acquirement of knowledge distasteful. He entered Trinity College, Cambridge, in 1818. Here his lack of really systematic training in Latin and Greek composition and his weakness in mathematics prevented his receiving honors when he was graduated, although he passed the tripos. He won a prize for Latin declamation in 1821, composed the English prize poems *Pompeii* in 1819 and *Evening* in 1821, and wrote the college prize essay on William III. He was elected a fellow in 1824, after three trials.

Among Macaulay's friends at college was Charles Austin, who is believed to have converted him to radicalism for a time; but he left college imbued with Whig principles from which he never deviated all the rest of his life.

The elder Macaulay had been wealthy, but before his son had won his fellowship, the need of money had led him to accept pupils. Yet, though admitted to the bar in 1826, he did not solicit clients, and it was jokingly said that his only case had been the prosecution of a boy for stealing some poultry.

Macaulay had grown up under the influence of the Clapham sect; he had joined the anti-slavery movement, and in 1824 had made a speech which was praised in the *Edinburgh Review,* for which he was now asked to write. He complied with an essay on Milton (1825) of which Jeffrey thought highly, and this was the first of a long and brilliant series of essays written for that periodical. Upon Jeffrey's retirement, Macaulay might have had the post of editor, but declined because of the location of the headquarters. He continued to write for Napier the new editor, until 1844, when the importance of his work on the *History* prevented the use of time for shorter works.

In 1826 he definitely abandoned the law, and began to frequent the House of Commons. In 1828 Lord Lyndhurst, though opposed to him politically, appointed him petitioner in

bankruptcy; in 1830 he was offered a seat for Calne by Lord Lansdowne, and in April of that year made his first speech in the house, supporting the bill to abolish Jewish disabilities. After the recess, he traveled in France, then recovering from the July Revolution of 1830. Upon his return, he spoke in favor of the Reform Bill, and this speech attracted considerable notice; was praised even by his adversary Peel, and led to friendship with Rogers and acquaintance with Sydney Smith, Moore, and other celebrities.

At this time, the petitionership ended and the fellowship was about to expire, so that Macaulay was for a time in financial straits. He was elected for Leeds in 1831, appointed to the board of control for India in 1832, and made a secretary the year after that. He made an excellent speech in favor of the bill for renewing the charter of the East India Company, and then, because his father and the latter's adherents opposed the slavery provision in the bill, offered his resignation. A compromise was effected and the resignation was not accepted.

Macaulay was now offered a seat on the supreme council, at an excellent salary, and went to India. Here he did a great deal of work, composing a new criminal code and code of procedure almost unaided, owing to the ill health and unfavorable circumstances affecting his associates. Considered a fine piece of work, the code, slightly revised, became a law in 1860, a year after his death.

His fortune made, Macaulay was now ready to return to England, with the Trevelyans, his sister's family. After a trip to Italy, which led to the composition of the *Lays of Ancient Rome,* he settled down to the writing of his *History of England*; was elected for Edin-

LORD MACAULAY

burgh in 1839, but was hampered by the weakness of the government, which fell in 1841. In this year he wrote his famous essay on Warren Hastings, published the *Lays* in 1842, and his first collection, the *Essays,* in 1843. Offered a post in a possible coalition cabinet, he refused, accepted an appointment to the position of paymaster general, and was re-elected for Edinburgh. He received an appointment to the secretaryship of the war ministry, stood for Edinburgh in 1847, and for the first time was defeated because his forthrightness on the Maynooth question had offended his constituents.

The first two volumes of the *History* appeared in 1848, and the work leaped into immediate success, bringing Macaulay one of the largest fortunes ever paid to a writer at that time. He was honored with the post of Lord Rector of Glasgow University, and might have had the chair of modern history at Cambridge, which he declined.

In 1852 he was asked to stand for Edinburgh, but refused on the ground of ill-health. He was nevertheless elected, and managed to make a speech to his constituents. He delivered a fine oration in 1853 against a bill for excluding the master of the rolls from the House, supported the India Bill, and was instrumental in promoting civil service, reform. His last speech was made in the House in July of 1853, and in that year his collected speeches were published to combat the piracy of American publishers.

The third and fourth volumes of the *History* appeared in 1855, and although they did not excite the same intense admiration as the first two, were nevertheless gratifyingly received. In 1857 Palmerston offered him a peerage, and he assumed the title of Baron Macaulay of Rothley. He was made High Steward of the borough of Cambridge in 1858, and his last public appearance on the platform was in acknowledgment of the honor.

He contributed some articles to the *Encyclopaedia Brittannica,* and though his health was now quite poor, visited the lake country and Scotland. Upon his return he was noticeably worse, suffered occasional fainting fits as the result of his heart condition, and died in his library, with a magazine in his lap, December 28, 1859. He was buried in Westminster Abbey, close to the Addison monument.

A just estimate of Macaulay as a writer has always given difficulty to critics. His formal and imposing style was more admired in his time than it now is, although a wave of reaction against him at the end of the last century has been succeeded by a fairer view of his numerous excellencies. The essays are full of faults of fact and judgment, but Mac-

aulay himself regarded them as periodical contributions and was diffident about publishing them in a permanent form. Those with sensitive ears for prose rhythm are offended by the somewhat monotonous periods of Macaulay, which were the result of his oratorical bent; he was a critic of rather narrow sympathies, made no pretense of aesthetic exquisiteness, and undoubtedly lacked depth and fineness of perception. Nevertheless, it must be remembered that he was one of the first English critics to appreciate the genius of Jane Austen and to judge accurately of Shelley's importance. Moreover, if prejudiced, he was fearless and honest; he is practically the creator of his form of essay, and the essays themselves, however untrustworthy, have been found stimulating by several generations of students and critics.

As poet, Macaulay had definite limitations, which he seems to have realized. The *Lays of Ancient Rome,* immensely popular when published and since, are not great poetry, but they have a far from mediocre swing and rhetorical power, and Arnold's characterization of them as "pinchbeck" has been justly censured by Saintsbury. As an introduction to the study of poetry they offer few difficulties and are of considerable value.

The *History* is of course a fragment, the five volumes covering a period of only sixteen years. Here, as elsewhere, Macaulay was a Whig, inclined to view all periods with the distortion inevitable in a man of his characteristics. On the other hand, the history is a magnificent piece of writing, brilliant, kaleidoscopic, impressive in its narrative power and wealth of detail, the work of a man of prodigious erudition if not of faultless judgment. Of the clarity of the writing there is no question; it popularized the reading of history, and Saintsbury says: ". . . of no other period of English history does an idea so clear, vivid, and on the whole accurate, exist in so large a number of people, and . . . . this is due to Macaulay." It must be remembered that historical research was attended with many difficulties in Macaulay's time; and if his wide reading and rhetorical tendencies often led him into disproportion and overstatement, it is easy now to find his errors by reading his critics.

As statesman, Macaulay was first and foremost a partisan; he had enormous knowledge, but his memory, as some one has said, was often better than his reasoning. He was a practical man, with no patience for theorizing and abstractions, weak in logic, and given to citing a number of precedents in a given case rather than to propounding logical arguments to support his standpoint. He lacked the traditional forensic graces of voice and gesture, but even his opponents were forced to admit that he was convincing in prepared discussion, and he was always listened to with respect and attention. He was obviously sincere—"I believe Macaulay to be incorruptible," said Sydney Smith. "You might lay ribbons, stars, garters, titles, wealth, before him in vain. He has an honest, genuine love of his country, and the world would not bribe him to neglect her interests."

His memory is legendary, and he read with amazing speed and complete retention. He knew Latin, Greek, French, Italian, Spanish, German, and Portuguese, was forever reading, sometimes even while walking, and always made marginal notes.

Macaulay was short of stature and rather plump, with somewhat plain features, good eyes, and a capacious forehead. He was forthright and masculine in manner, somewhat lengthy in conversation when once started upon an interesting topic, but good company and a good host. Though a shrewd business man, he was generous with money. He was a sincere friend, if sometimes an unjust and implacable enemy, and an excellent master. He was never married, and indeed there is no record of any romantic attachment on his part, but he was devoted to his family, particularly to his sisters, his nephews and nieces, the Trevelyans; and his devotion has been repaid by his nephew, Sir George Trevelyan, who in his biography of Macaulay has produced one of the best works of its kind in the English language.   R. M.

PRINCIPAL WORKS: *History*—The History of England from the Accession of James II (5 vols.) 1849-1861. *Essays*—Critical and Historical Essays, 1843. *Poetry*—Lays of Ancient Rome, 1842. *Speeches*—Glasgow Inaugural Address, 1849; Speeches, 1854. *Miscellaneous*—Miscellaneous Writings, 1860.

ABOUT: Arnold, F. Public Life of Lord Macaulay; Bagehot, W. Literary Studies; Bryant, A. Macaulay; Napier, M. Correspondence; Paget, J. The New Examen; Saintsbury, G. Corrected Impressions; Trevelyan, G. O. The Life and Letters of Lord Macaulay; Criterion 12:593 July 1933; Fortnightly Review ns124:441 October 1, 1928.

MacCARTHY, DENIS FLORENCE

(May 26, 1817-April 7, 1882), Irish poet, was born in Dublin of a Roman Catholic family. He was educated at Maynooth, the Catholic college, where he showed a particular interest in Spanish language and literature. From 1834 to 1836 he was a contributor to the Dublin *Satirist*, and from 1843 published in the Dublin *Nation*, organ of the Nationalists, political poems signed "Desmond." In spite of this, and also of his active work in the Young Ireland Party in 1845, his primary interests were not in politics, but in literature. Much of his magazine work, including both poems and humorous prose, has never been collected into a volume. In addition to his original work, he edited two anthologies, *Poets and Dramatists of Ireland* and the *Book of*

Irish Ballads. Between 1848 and 1873 he translated all the works of the great Spanish dramatist, Calderon, and in 1881 he received a medal from the Royal Academy of Spain in recognition of his services to Spanish literature.

In 1853 MacCarthy was appointed lecturer on literature at the Catholic University, Dublin, but he shrank from public speaking, and suffered so greatly that he resigned after giving only three lectures. In 1864, after a Continental tour, he went to live in London. In 1871 he was awarded a pension from the civil list. He was married and had nine children, of whom only three survived him.

MacCarthy's poems have real lyric beauty, and his earlier political verses are stirring and vigorous.

PRINCIPAL WORKS: Ballads, Poems, and Lyrics, 1850; Poems (ed. by J. MacCarthy) 1884.

ABOUT: MacCarthy, D. F. Poems (see Introduction by J. MacCarthy); Dublin Review April 1883.

McCARTHY, JUSTIN

(November 22, 1830-April 24, 1912), Irish novelist and statesman, was born near Cork, his father being clerk to the Cork city magistrates. He was intended for the bar but from seventeen had to support his family. Accordingly he became a reporter on the Cork *Examiner*. At first an adherent of the Young Ireland movement, he became in time an advocate of conciliation of England. In 1854 he joined the staff of the *Northern Daily Times*, Liverpool. In 1855 he married Charlotte Allman, who died in 1879, leaving one son and one daughter. In 1859 McCarthy went to London as foreign editor of the *Morning Star*, becoming its editor in 1864. He resigned in 1868 and visited his brother in the United States, almost deciding to remain there. However, he returned to London and in 1871 was a leader writer on the *Daily News*. In 1879 he entered Parliament as a Parnellite; but after Parnell's downfall he became the leader of the anti-Parnell party, while still retaining Parnell's personal friendship. In 1896 he resigned the leadership of the party, but remained in Parliament until 1900: From 1897 on, however, he was in bad health, almost blind, and weakened mentally, though retaining his gayety and his kindly nature. In 1903 he was awarded a civil list pension.

McCarthy practically gave up literature to serve his country. Nevertheless, his novels are in almost the first rank. They have not much originality but display charm of style, simplicity of manner, and the deceptive ease which means hard work. His son, Justin Huntley McCarthy, became a well-known playwright, novelist, and historian.

PRINCIPAL WORKS: Dear Lady Disdain, 1875; History of Our Own Times, 1877; Miss Misanthrope, 1878; Reminiscences, 1899; Monomia, 1901; Story of an Irishman, 1904; Irish Recollections, 1911.

ABOUT: McCarthy, J. Reminiscences; Story of an Irishman; Irish Recollections; O'Connor, T. P. The Parnell Movement.

McCLINTOCK, SIR FRANCIS LEOPOLD

(July 8, 1819-November 17, 1907), Scottish naval officer and travel writer, was born in Dundalk, and entered the Royal Navy in 1831 as a mate. In 1845 he became a lieutenant and was in service in the Pacific; In 1848 he went to the Arctic with Capt. Sir James Clark Ross, and in 1850 was first lieutenant in the Arctic expedition of Sir Erasmus Ommanney. In 1851 he made a remarkable sledge journey of 760 miles in eighty days. In the same year he was promoted to commander, and in 1852 was in the Arctic again with Capt. Sir Edward Belcher. At this time he made a sledge journey of 1210 miles in 105 days.

By 1854 he was a captain, and when Lady Franklin fitted out a ship to try to find her husband, who had been long unheard from in the Arctic wastes, McClintock volunteered to command the search expedition. He found indubitable evidence that Franklin and his companions had perished. In 1860 he was knighted in recognition of this service. In 1861 and 1862 he was in service in the Mediterranean, in 1864 in the North Sea, and from 1865 to 1868 he was commodore in charge at Jamaica. In 1870 he married Annette Dunlap. The next year he was promoted to flag rank, and from 1872 to 1877 he was taken from active service to be admiral superintendent of the Portsmouth Dockyard. In 1877 he was made vice-admiral, and from 1879 to 1882 commander-in-chief of the North American and West Indian stations. He retired from the navy in 1884 with the rank of admiral. In 1891 he became a Knight Commander of the Bath.

McClintock's one book, his description of his discovery of the fate of Franklin, was highly popular, and is clearly and ably written, though he had no literary ambitions.

PRINCIPAL WORK: Voyage of the Fox in the Arctic Seas: A Narrative of the Fate of Sir John Franklin, 1859.

ABOUT: Markham, Sir C. R. Life of Sir Francis McClintock.

McCOSH, JAMES

(April 1, 1811-November 16, 1894), Scottish theologian, was born in Ayrshire, a farmer's son. He was early devoted to the Presbyterian ministry, and educated at the University of Glasgow and the University of Edinburgh, where he received an M.A. degree in 1834. Licensed to preach by the presbytery, he was minister at Arbroath and Brechin until 1850. In 1845 he married a Miss Guthrie. He was a member of the Free Church, and joined in its secession. His book, *The Method of the Divine Government,* led to his appointment as professor of logic and metaphysics in Queen's College, Belfast, in 1851. In 1868 he went to America to become president and professor of philosophy at Princeton. He resigned the presidency in 1888, but remained as professor until his death. He received LL.D. degrees from Aberdeen and Harvard, a D.Litt. from Queen's College, and a D.D. from Princeton.

McCosh's books are really polemics, rather obtuse advocacies of his anti-empiricist philosophy. His style, however, is simple and unpretentious.

PRINCIPAL WORKS: The Method of the Divine Government, 1850; Intuitions of the Mind Inductively Investigated, 1860; Philosophical Papers, 1868.

McCRIE, THOMAS

(November 1772-August 8, 1835), Scottish ecclesiastical historian, was born in Berwickshire, where his father was a prosperous linen weaver. After leaving the parish school, he became an elementary teacher, then in 1788 entered the University of Edinburgh, but left without a degree. In 1791, as a teacher in Brechin, he studied divinity, and was licensed to preach in 1795, ordained in 1796, and became a minister at Edinburgh. In 1806 he was deposed by the presbytery, as one of the group later known as "original seceders," precursors of the Free Church. His congregation promptly built him a new church and followed him to it. In 1813 he received a D.D. degree from the University of Edinburgh, the first Scottish dissenter to do so. From 1816 to 1818 he was professor of divinity at the university. He was married twice, to Janet Dickson in 1796, and to Mary Chalmers in 1827. By his first marriage he had four sons and one daughter; one of his sons, his namesake, also wrote ecclesiastical histories.

McCrie was a biographical historian, or an historical biographer; his works were actually histories of principle and policy, rather than of individuals and events.

PRINCIPAL WORKS: The Life of John Knox, 1812; The Life of Andrew Melville, 1819; History of the Progress and Suppression of the Reformation in Italy; 1827; History of the Progress and Suppression of the Reformation in Spain, 1829; Miscellaneous Writings, 1841.

ABOUT: McCrie, T. Life of Thomas McCrie, D.D.

MACDONALD, GEORGE

(December 10, 1824-September 18, 1905), Scotch novelist, poet, clergyman, and author of children's stories, was born at Huntley, West Aberdeenshire, the son of George Macdonald and Helen MacKay. He attended the country schools, and went to Aberdeen University in 1840-41 and 1844-45, taking prizes in chemistry and natural philosophy. Three years of tutoring in London followed; he then studied for the Congregationalist ministry at Independent College, Highbury. He was made pastor at Arun-

GEORGE MACDONALD

del in 1850, displeased his congregation by the lack of dogmatic material in his sermons, and after three unsatisfactory years, found it necessary to resign. He went to Manchester; was obliged to go to Algiers for the sake of his health, and returned to England resolved to be a professional author. Macdonald was converted to the church of England, becoming a lay member in 1860; but he continued to preach independently at intervals.

His poem *Within and Without* appeared in 1855; *Poems* in 1857; and *Phantastes* in 1858. However, his first real success came with his novels of Scotch country life, *David Elginbrod* (1862), *Alec Forbes* (1865), and *Robert Falconer* (1868). In this year he received the degree of LL.D.; he attracted the notice of Lady Byron, who befriended him and later left him a legacy; and met Ruskin, Arnold, Carlyle, Tennyson, and others. An American lecture tour in 1872 won many friends, including Emerson. Macdonald lectured chiefly on Burns, and a subscription was made up to reimburse him for losses he had suffered through the pirating of his works in this country.

Although his Scottish novels and his charming children's books such as *At the Back of the North Wind*, *The Princess and the Goblin*, and *The Princess and Curdie* were successful, Macdonald's financial returns from his works had not been sufficient to provide for the needs of his wife and family, and in 1877 he was pensioned at the request of Queen Victoria. He had never been strong, and indeed was obliged to care for his health during all his long life. When his daughter had to be taken to Italy for her health in 1877—a trip which ended in her death—Macdonald found the climate so beneficial to himself that he spent the greater part of each year from 1881

to 1902 at Bordighera, in the house he had built with the aid of friends, Casa Coraggio. His wife became organist of the Catholic church there, and organ concerts were often held at the Macdonald home for the benefit of the parish. Here the Macdonald family led a merry life, for although Macdonald had a vein of Celtic melancholy in him, he was merry and amiable, and readings and amateur theatricals were frequent in his house. (The praise of the Macdonald children for his manuscripts was what induced Lewis Carroll to publish his work.)

Mrs. Macdonald, the former Louisa Powell, died the year after their golden wedding anniversary, in 1902. Macdonald, after a long illness, died at Ashstead in England in 1905. His remains were cremated and taken for burial to Bordighera, where his wife had been interred.

The Macdonalds had six sons and five daughters. One of the sons, Greville Macdonald, later became a writer. He is the author of the biography of his father.

George Macdonald published over fifty volumes of fiction, verse, children's stories, sermons, etc. His verse is delicate, graceful, and tender in feeling, with a pervading spiritual quality. *The Diary of an Old Soul* strikes a deeper note of thoughtfulness. In his prose Macdonald too often yielded to the suggestion of fantasy, and much of his work is disfigured by this trait. His stories for children rank among the classics of juvenile literature.

R. M.

PRINCIPAL WORKS: *Fiction*—David Elginbrod, 1862; Alec Forbes, 1865; Robert Falconer, 1868; Malcolm, 1875; The Marquis of Lossie, 1877; Sir Gibbie, 1879; Castle Warlock, 1882; Lilith, 1895. *Juvenile*—At the Back of the North Wind, 1871; The Princess and the Goblin, 1872; The Princess and Curdie, 1873. *Poetry*—Within and Without, 1855; Poems, 1857; Phantastes, 1858; The Diary of an Old Soul, 1880; Poetical Works, 1893.

ABOUT: Colvile, K. N. Fame's Twilight; Macdonald, G[reville]. George Macdonald; Bookman 29:59 November 1905.

McGEE, THOMAS D'ARCY (April 13, 1825-April 7, 1868), Irish-Canadian poet and politician, was born in Louth, his father being a coastguard. When he was eight they moved to Wexford, and he went to school there. In 1842 he emigrated to the United States, becoming first a clerk and then editor of the Boston *Pilot*. He then went to England as Parliamentary correspondent of the *Freeman's Journal*, and London correspondent of the Dublin *Nation*, to which he also contributed many poems. In 1847 he was in Ireland as secretary of the Irish Confederation, and was arrested but released. He was soon after engaged in a secret mission to stir up the Irish in Glasgow, which failed, and he was obliged to escape to America disguised as a priest. He landed in Philadelphia in 1848 and went to

New York, where he started a magazine called *The Nation,* which failed when he attacked the priests for their pro-English activities. He then went to Boston and edited the *American Celt,* but gradually lost his revolutionary fervor, and was even connected with the anti-Papal "Know Nothing" party. Accused of treachery by his Irish compatriots, he moved his paper first to Buffalo, then to New York, but finally had to sell it and go to Montreal in 1857. There he started the *New Era.* He was soon elected to the Legislative Assembly, and was president of the council in 1862 and 1864. He was active in the movement for Canadian federation, and when the Dominion was established in 1867 he was made minister of agriculture and emigration and a member of the Dominion Parliament. He was shot in the streets of Montreal by a political enemy, one P. J. Whalen, who was hanged for the crime. McGee was accorded a great state funeral.

McGee's poems are strong, condensed, and eloquent, his prose picturesque and vigorous. Besides his poetry, he wrote several books on Irish history and literature.

PRINCIPAL WORKS: Irish Writers of the Seventeenth Century, 1846; Irish Settlers in America, 1851; Irish Letters, 1852; Catholic History of North America, 1854; Popular History of Ireland, 1862; Poems, 1869.

ABOUT: McGee, T. D'A. Poems (see Introductory Memoir by Mrs. M. A. Sadlier).

MacGREGOR, JOHN (January 24, 1825-July 16, 1892), travel writer, was the son of a general, a K.C.B. He nearly died in a fire at sea while an infant. He was an athlete as a boy, but also a pious lad who wanted to be a missionary. He attended seven different schools as his father's commands were changed, and in 1839 entered Trinity College, Dublin. In 1844 he went to Trinity College, Cambridge, where he secured his B.A. in 1847 and his M.A. in 1850. He was called to the bar from the Inner Temple in 1851, and for a while was a patent attorney, but having a large private income he abandoned his practice and devoted his life to travel, writing, philanthropy, and mechanical studies. He was in Paris during the Revolution of 1848, the next year in Egypt and Palestine, and in 1851 in Russia, North Africa, and the United States From 1853 to 1863 he made a special study of marine mechanics, and wrote on this subject for the *Mechanics' Magazine.*

In 1865 he built his canoe "Rob Roy," the first of a series, and toured the rivers of the Continent. He really started the sport of canoeing in Europe. He finally went all the way to and through Palestine in a canoe. He was also a noted philanthropist, being prominent in the work of the Shoeblack Brigade, the Ragged Schools, the Open Air Mission, the British and Foreign Bible Society, the Protestant Alliance, the Pure Literature Society, and the Reformatory and Refuge Union. All the profits from his books and lectures went to these charities. He was also a member of the London School Board. In 1873 he married a Miss Coffin, by whom he had two daughters.

MacGregor was a talented artist, and illustrated his own books. These are facilely written, bright, and entertaining even today.

PRINCIPAL WORKS: Three Days in the East, 1850; Our Brothers and Cousins: A Tour in Canada, 1859; A Thousand Miles in the "Rob Roy" Canoe, 1866; The "Rob Roy" on the Baltic, 1867; The "Rob Roy" on the Jordan, Red Sea, and Gennesareth, 1869.

ABOUT: London Times July 20 and 22, 1892.

MACKAY, CHARLES (March 27, 1814-December 24, 1889), Scottish song writer, was born in Perth, the son of a half-pay lieutenant. His mother died while he was an infant, and he lived with his nurse in a lonely cottage in the country. In 1822 he moved with her and her husband to Woolwich. In 1825 he attended the Caledonian Asylum (really a school), and in 1828 was put to school in Brussels. In 1830 he became private secretary to an ironmaster in Belgium, all his leisure being given to verse, which he wrote and published both in English and in French. In 1832 he came to London, where he supported himself by teaching Italian. From 1838 to 1844 he was assistant sub-editor of the *Morning Chronicle,* and then became editor of the Glasgow *Argus.* Nearly all his verses were set to music, and became very popular; it is said that 400,000 copies were sold of "A Good Time Coming." In 1846 he received an honorary LL.D. from Glasgow University, an unusual honor for a song-writer.

In 1848 Mackay joined the staff of the *Illustrated London News,* and was its editor from 1852 to 1858. From 1851 to 1855 the magazine issued one of his songs weekly as a supplement. In 1857 he lectured in the United States and Canada. In 1860 he established the *London Review,* and in 1861 *Robin Goodfellow,* but both magazines failed. During the American Civil War he was in New York as correspondent of the London *Times.* He was married in 1845 to Rosa Henrietta Vale, who died in 1859, leaving three sons and one daughter. His second wife was a widow, Ellen (Kirtland) Mills, but she too predeceased him, dying in 1875.

Besides his extremely popular songs, some of which still live, Mackay wrote books of travel, history, and biography, and was a good all-round journalist.

PRINCIPAL WORKS: Songs and Poems, 1834; The Hope of the World, 1840; Voices From the Crowd, 1846; Voices From the Mountain, 1847; Town Lyrics, 1848; Under Green Leaves, 1857; Forty Years' Recollections, 1877; Interludes and Overtones, 1884; Through the Long Day, 1887; Gossamer and Snowdrift, 1890.

ABOUT: Mackay, C. Forty Years' Recollections; Through the Long Day.

MACKAY, G. R. ABERIGH-. See ABERIGH-MACKAY, G. R.

MACKENZIE, SIR ALEXANDER (1755?-March 11, 1820), Scottish explorer and travel writer, was born in Inverness. Nothing is known of his life until 1779, when he was in a counting-house in Toronto, with a firm which was a rival of the Hudson's Bay Company and its fur monopoly. His employers sent him in 1784 to Detroit, to trade and explore. Several times he came near to death at the hands of hostile Indians. In 1789 he was sent to explore the northwest, and discovered the Mackenzie River, which was named for him. In 1792 he was the first white man to cross the Rockies to the Pacific Coast. He was knighted in 1802, and became a member of the provincial parliament of Ontario. In 1812 he married a distant cousin of his own name. Soon after this he returned to Scotland, and bought an estate in Ross-shire. He died suddenly while on a journey with his family to Edinburgh.

Mackenzie's books on his explorations had a wide circulation, and are ably written, though he was far from a literary man. They have today a purely historical interest.

PRINCIPAL WORKS: Voyages From Montreal Through the Continent of North America, 1801; Voyages on the River St. Lawrence and Through the Continent of North America to the Frozen and Pacific Oceans, 1801.

MACKINTOSH, SIR JAMES (October 24, 1765-May 30, 1832), Scottish historian, was born on Loch Ness, near Inverness, the only child of an army captain. His father followed his regiment to Dublin and left the mother in poverty with her mother and sisters. The boy went to school in Ross-shire, where he was noted for his precocity. Finally his mother joined her husband in Gibraltar in 1779, and died there.

In 1780 Mackintosh entered King's College. Aberdeen, where he was known as "the poet," a melancholy youth in the throes of an unhappy love affair. He studied medicine at Edinburgh from 1784, and received his M.D. in 1787. He then went to London, but his thriftlessness and laziness soon dragged him into debt. In 1789 he married Catherine Stuart, a sensible woman who tried in vain to arouse some ambition in her dreamy husband. She died in 1797, leaving three daughters. Meanwhile Mackintosh had become a contributor to The Oracle, on a regular salary, dabbled in politics, and studied law. He was called to the bar from Lincoln's Inn in 1795 and joined the home circuit. Gradually he

lost the radical sympathies which had caused him to espouse the cause of the French Revolution, and became a Tory. In 1798 he married Catherine Allen, whose sisters married Josiah and John Wedgwood, one of them becoming the ancestress of Charles Darwin. She died in 1830, leaving two daughters.

In 1799 and 1800 Mackintosh lectured on The Law of Nature and Nations at Lincoln's Inn. Much to his subsequent regret, he then applied for a post in India, and in 1804 was made recorder in Bombay. He had been knighted the year before. In 1806 he was judge in the court of vice-admiralty at Bombay, but his health was ruined, and he grew lazier than ever. He returned to England in 1811, and was a Member of Parliament from 1813 to 1818. In 1824 he became professor of "law and general politics" at Haileybury. He died in consequence of accidentally swallowing a chicken-bone.

Mackintosh's histories are entirely superseded, and were never so much actual histories as illustrations of his unoriginal eclectic philosophy.

PRINCIPAL WORKS: A History of England, 1830; A Dissertation on the Progress of Ethical Philosophy, 1830; History of the Revolution in England, 1834; Miscellaneous Works, 1846.

ABOUT: Mackintosh, Sir J. History of the Revolution in England (see Biographical Notice); Mackintosh, R. J. Memoirs of Sir James Mackintosh.

"MACLAREN, IAN." See WATSON, JOHN

McLENNAN, JOHN FERGUSON (October 14, 1827-June 16, 1881), Scottish sociologist, was born in Inverness, where his father was an insurance agent. He was educated at King's College, Aberdeen, where he received his M.A. in 1849, and at Trinity College, Cambridge, where he left without a degree but was distinguished as a mathematician. He went to London and worked as a contributor to The Leader and other periodicals, until he was called to the Scottish bar in 1857. He served for a long time as secretary of the Scottish Law Amendment Society. In 1871 he became parliamentary draughtsman for Scotland. His contributions on the history of law to the Encyclopaedia Britannica led him to researches in the history of marriage. His stimulating and original but confused and shaky theory of the progress of marriage from promiscuity through exogamy, polygamy, polyandry, and patriarchal monandry to monogamy, gave a great impetus to further and better-founded research on the subject. He wrote on marriage and totemism for Chambers's Encyclopaedia, the Fortnightly Review, and elsewhere, but never lived to finish a projected full-length work on the subject closest to him. He had long been a sufferer from tuberculosis, and the complication of malaria caused his death at fifty-three. He was married twice, in 1862 to Mary Bell Mc-Culloch, by whom he had one daughter, and in 1875 to Eleanora Brandram.

PRINCIPAL WORKS: An Inquiry Into the Origin of the Form of Capture in Marriage Ceremonies, 1865 (revised as Studies in Ancient History, 1876); The Patriarchal Theory (ed. by Donald McLennan) 1885.

ABOUT: Athenaeum June 25, 1881, May 30, 1885; Scotsman June 20, 1881.

"MACLEOD, FIONA." See SHARP, WILLIAM

MACLEOD, HENRY DUNNING (March 31, 1821-July 16, 1902), Scottish economist, was born in Edinburgh. His father, a member of Parliament, was Lord Lieutenant of Cromarty. He was educated at Edinburgh Academy, Eton, and Trinity College, Cambridge, where he received his B.A. in 1843, and his M.A. in 1863. He was called to the bar from the Inner Temple in 1849 and joined the midland circuit. However, he devoted more attention to economics than to law, though from 1868 to 1870 he prepared for the government a digest of the law on bills of exchange. He also acted as commisioner of poor law relief for Easter Ross, where his father had large holdings. In 1853 he married Elizabeth Mackenzie. They had three sons and four daughters, one of whom became a writer of books for children.

The year of his marriage he moved to London and remained there thenceforth. Most of his fortune had been lost in a series of bank failures. Curiously enough, from this time on, banking was his special subject. Macleod was much disliked by the orthodox economists against whom he railed constantly, and he applied in vain for chairs in three universities. He was an independent, overconfident, aggressive man, always engaged in controversies. Nevertheless, his work had much value. He was the first to formulate the famous "Gresham's Law," that bad money drives out good.

PRINCIPAL WORKS: The Theory and Practice of Banking, 1856; Dictionary of Political Economy, 1858; Elements of Banking, 1876; History of Economics, 1896; History of Banking of All Nations, 1896.

ABOUT: London Times July 18, 1902.

MACLEOD, NORMAN (June 3, 1812-June 16, 1872), Scottish theologian and juvenile writer, was born in Argyllshire, the son of a well-known Presbyterian minister. He attended Glasgow College, and in 1831 went to Edinburgh to study divinity. After three years as a private tutor he returned to Glasgow College, in 1837 was licensed to preach, and in 1838 was ordained. He became a parish minister in Ayrshire, taking a middle ground in the Free Church controversy but refusing to secede when the break came. In 1843 he was made minister of a church in Dalkeith, near Edinburgh, where he was particularly active in foreign mission work. In 1849 he edited the Christian Instructor. In 1851 he married Catherine Ann Mackintosh: the same year he became a minister in Glasgow, where he was equally noted for his eloquence and for his labor for the poor of the parish. In 1857 he became chaplain to Queen Victoria, who thought highly of him. The next year Glasgow University bestowed an honorary D.D. upon him.

In 1860 Macleod became editor of another religious magazine, Good Words. In these two periodicals which he edited, many of his moral stories for children originally appeared. In 1864 he visited Egypt and Palestine, and in 1867 made a tour of the mission stations in India. From the strain of this latter journey he never recovered, and he was a semi-invalid until his death.

PRINCIPAL WORKS: Deborah, 1857; The Gold Thread, 1861; Wee Davie, 1864; Eastward, 1866; The Starling, 1867; Peeps at the Far East, 1871.

ABOUT: Macleod, D. Memoir of Norman Macleod.

MacNEILL, HECTOR (October 22, 1746-March 15, 1818), Scottish poet, was born in Midlothian, the son of a retired army captain. After leaving the Stirling Grammar School, he was sent at thirteen to Bristol, to a cousin in the West Indian trade, who shipped him as a sailor on a ship bound for St. Christopher's. As he disliked the sailor's life, he stayed a year in St. Christopher's, then for three years worked for a merchant in Guadalupe, and in 1763 went to Antigua. Following this he was for three years assistant to the provost marshal of Granada. He returned to England about 1776. For six years after 1780 he was assistant secretary in the navy, for the last three years in Indian waters. Then he returned to Scotland, where he tried in vain to make a living by his pen. In 1786 he went to Jamaica, but could find no prospects there, so he went back to Scotland, where for ten years he lived with various friends, spending most of his time writing poetry, and contributing to the Scots Magazine, which for a short time he edited. In 1796 he tried Jamaica again, once more without luck. Finally a friend raised an annuity for him of £100 a year, and on this he lived in Edinburgh for the rest of his life, a praiser of old times who warned boys to go into business and never to nourish literary ambitions. He was married and had two sons. Besides his poems, he was the author of a novel, The Memoirs of Charles Macpherson, which was a thinly veiled autobiography.

PRINCIPAL WORKS: The Harp, 1789; Scotland's Scaith, 1795; The Waes o' War, 1796; Poetic Works, 1801; The Pastoral or Lyric Muse of Scotland, 1809; Bygone Times and Late-Come Changes, 1812.

ABOUT: Scots Magazine 1818, 1:396.

MACNISH, ROBERT (February 15, 1802-January 16, 1837), Scottish miscellaneous writer, was born in Glasgow of a long line of physicians. He received his M.Ch. degree from the University of Glasgow when he was only sixteen, and for a year and a half practiced under a doctor in Caithness. Then he studied in Paris for a year, and returned to assist his father, also a physician, while he studied again at the university. He became an M.D. in 1825. *The Anatomy of Drunkenness,* an interesting and penetrating book, was his doctor's thesis. His chief medical interest was in psychiatry; he was also a convert to phrenology, on which he wrote. Macnish was a congenital melancholiac, with a marked talent for the fantastic and grotesque. He wrote verses weakly imitative of Byron and Moore, medical works more curious than sound, and numerous stories. His masterpiece was a story call "The Metempsychosis," published in *Blackwood's* in 1826. After that the columns of all the better magazines were open to him, but he never wrote anything so good again. He died of influenza at not quite thirty-five.

PRINCIPAL WORKS: The Anatomy of Drunkenness. 1827; The Philosophy of Sleep, 1830; The Modern Pythagorean, 1838.

ABOUT: Macnish, R. The Modern Pythagorean (see Life by D. M. Moir).

MAGINN, WILLIAM (July 10, 1793-August 21, 1842), Anglo-Irish satirist, was born at Cork, where his father, Dr. William Maginn, conducted an academy for boys. He entered Trinity College, Dublin University, at the age of ten, according to various biographical witnesses, and was graduated at fourteen with a knowledge of Greek and Latin, Hebrew, Sanskrit, Syriac, Gaelic, and varous languages of modern Europe. At twenty, upon the death of his father, he took charge of the academy, and in 1817 received the degree of LL.D. from Trinity.

Maginn had begun to write in 1818, and in 1819 contributed to the *Literary Gazette* under the pseudonym of P. J. Crossman. In 1824 he went to London, met Blackwood, to whose magazine he had regularly contributed under an assumed name, and being well known as a brilliant author, was offered the editorship of Hook's *John Bull* In 1827 his satire on Scott's novels had a great success; he became assistant editor of the *Evening Standard* in 1828 and in 1830 began the publication of *Fraser's Magazine* in competition with *Blackwood's.* An attack upon the novel Berkeley

Hall resulted in a duel with its author, the Honorable Grantly Berkeley, but Maginn was no adventurer and except for the bad habit of drinking seems to have been a quiet citizen. His last days were clouded by the suicide of his friend Letitia E. Landon, the poet, of whom his wife was extremely jealous; and his intemperance had brought him to debtor's prison a year before his death. He died of consumption shortly after being released, penniless except for the personal gift of Sir Robert Peel, leader of the Tory party which Maginn had always supported. He left his widow, the former Miss Bullen, whom he had married in 1817, a son and two daughters.

Maginn was essentially a journalist, and the value of nearly all his work is ephemeral. Nevertheless, the *Maxims of Sir Morgan O'-Doherty,* a parody of La Rochefoucauld's *Maxims,* shows him to be a humorist who could mingle common sense, erudition, humor, and brilliance. "Bob Burke's Duel With Ensign Brady" is considered one of the funniest of all Irish short stories, and Saintsbury ranks "The Story Without a Tail" among the masterpieces of fiction, a genre little cultivated by Maginn. The parodies of Coleridge and Moore are clever, the *Shakespearian Papers* are excellent criticism, and nearly all Maginn's contributions to the "Noctes Ambrosianae" (the famous series of humorous papers which he instigated in *Blackwood's*) and to *Punch,* are amusing to read. It is true that Maginn wasted his genius, but it is equally certain that he had it to waste. Even before his death, he was sometimes called "the modern Rabelais," for, as Saintsbury said, "many of the greatest wits have had nothing like his learning, and hardly any man of very great learning has had anything like his wit."

WILLIAM MAGINN

Maginn, in society, was an amiable eccentric Irishman, completely innocent in wordly affairs, however shrewd he could be as a wit.

R. M.

PRINCIPAL WORKS: (5 vols.) 1845. *Fiction*—John Manesty, 1844; Whitehall, 1827; Ten Tales, 1833. *Translations*—The Homeric Ballads, 1850. *Criticism* —Shakespearean Papers, 1859.

ABOUT: Maginn, W. Miscellanies (see Life by R. W. Montagu); Works (see Memoir by S. Mackenzie); Saintsbury, G. Essays in English Literature (2nd Ser.); Dublin University Magazine 23:73 January 1844.

MAHONY, FRANCIS SYLVESTER

("Father Prout") (December 31, 1804-May 18, 1866), Irish humorist, was born in Cork, the second son of Martin Mahony, a woolen manufacturer, and Mary (Reynolds) Mahony.

His youth was notable chiefly for his foreign education. After attending a Jesuit college at Clongoweswood in Kildare, he went to a similar institution in France, at Amiens, and then proceeded to a Parisian seminary. He was anxious to be a Jesuit and a priest. His education was sound and thorough in the classics, and his knowledge of Latin was almost like that of his native tongue.

Admitted at length to the order, although even at this time evidences of his wit and independence caused distrust of him, he accepted a school position in Clongoweswood in 1830, becoming a teacher of rhetoric. This career was but short-lived. Returning from an outing with a group of boys under his charge, he allowed the whole party (including himself) to indulge excessively in liquor. The group was caught in a thunderstorm, and it was only owing to the kind (though not unrewarded) offices of some men hauling loads

F. S. MAHONY

of peat, who conducted the boys back to their school, strapped to the loads of turf, that the party arrived very late at night safely at its destination. Naturally this escapade ended Mahony's connection with the institution. He was dismissed from the Jesuit order in November 1830.

He returned to his studies, going to Italy, where he attended theological lectures at Rome, and after two years was ordained priest in 1832. His first charge was in Cork, where, during an epidemic of cholera, he is said to have performed fine service. A conflict with authority, however, ended this work, and with his removal to London about 1833, his life became essentially that of a man of letters.

Befriended by his fellow Irishman William Maginn, be became a contributor to *Fraser's Magazine*, for which he wrote (1834-36) the "Prout Papers," purporting to be the autobiographical remains and reflections of an actual Irish parish priest. The cleverness of these papers and the mastery of languages and styles shown by their author came as a revelation to the public. He was one of the first writers in *Bentley's Miscellany*, founded in 1837 under Charles Dickens, with a poem on the first page of the first issue.

In the same year Mahony left for the Continent, traveling for some years in Italy, Hungary, Greece, and Asia Minor. He sent contributions to *Bentley's Miscellany*, and, after a brief stay in London, returned (1846) to Italy as correspondent for the *Daily News*. This function he ceased to perform in 1847 publishing his collected contributions as *Facts and Figures From Italy*, by "Don Jeremy Savonarola." These papers are interesting as showing his sympathy with the Italian patriots of the time, for his sympathies in Great Britain had been strongly conservative.

The following year was marked by his removal to Paris, where he spent most of the rest of his life, coming to be in many ways as much a Frenchman as an Irishman. He lived in rather poor lodgings, and seems to have led a life that was a strange combination of solitude and Bohemian sensuality. From 1858 until 1866 he contributed daily to *The Globe*, a newspaper of which he was part owner. In 1863 he was released from some of his priestly duties because of his failing health; and he died of bronchitis and diabetes in 1866, with the last rites administered to him by a clerical friend. He was buried in Cork.

Endowed with Irish gifts of humor and lightness, Mahony was less noteworthy for good nature. At times friendly, he could on other occasions ignore friends or even, as in the case of the novelist William Harrison Ainsworth, turn on them and attack them

In appearance he was short and shabbily dressed in a half-clerical garb, with sharp little eyes which indicated the owner's cleverness. Inspired with nothing but contempt by radicals or even Whigs—he had small respect for the Irish statesman Daniel O'Connell—as well as the unlearned, he had marvelous erudition in the classics and an amazing control of other foreign languages. His translations of Horace and other poets, Latin, French, and Greek, have, unfortunately a doggerelish stamp, as does his masterpiece in poetry, "The Bells of Shandon," with its short line-lengths and abrupt rhythms. Humor was Mahony's forte, and his charming, witty, and learned essays in the "Prout Papers" ensure him a minor but individual place in English literary history. R. W. W.

PRINCIPAL WORKS: *Humorous Miscellany*—Reliques of Father Prout, Late P. P. of Watergrasshill in the County of Cork, 1836; The Final Reliques of Father Prout, 1875. *Newspaper Correspondence*—Facts and Figures From Italy, 1847. *Miscellaneous*—The Works of Father Prout, 1880.

ABOUT: Maclise, D. The Maclise Portrait-Gallery of Illustrious Literary Characters; Mahony, F. S. The Final Reliques of Father Prout; Mahony, F. S. The Works of Father Prout (see Biographical Introduction by Charles Kent); Monahan, M. Nova Hibernia.

MAINE, SIR HENRY JAMES SUMNER

(August 15, 1822-February 3, 1888), jurist and legal historian, was born near Leighton, the son of Dr. James Maine and Eliza (Fell) Maine.

His childhood was spent in Jersey and at Henley-on-Thames, where he lived with his mother, who had separated from her husband. His formal education, begun at a school at Henley, was continued in Christ's Hospital, where he showed unusual ability; and he won a scholarship (1840) to Pembroke College, Cambridge.

Maine's career at Cambridge was brilliant and marked by scholarships and prizes; he took medals in Greek and Latin composition and for English verse, and in 1844, the year of his graduation, he won the chancellor's senior classical medal, a distinction which required him previously to have taken honors in mathematics. Although he was hampered by ill health, and was unable to pursue all the normal activities of students, he became known to the most intellectually distinguished of his fellows.

In 1845 he accepted the junior tutorship at Trinity Hall, the income from which he supplemented by taking private pupils. Two years later, at the remarkably early age of twenty-five, he was made regius professor of civil law, filling this post until 1854, and in the same year (1847) he married a cousin, Miss Jane Maine. In 1850 he was called to the bar, and, although he continued his work

SIR HENRY J. S. MAINE

at Cambridge, he spent most of his time in or near London.

He began to contribute to various papers, writing on foreign and American questions for the *Morning Chronicle* and later for the *Saturday Review*, with which he was associated from its very beginning. His activities were further extended by his appointment as reader on Roman law and jurisprudence (1852) at the Inns of Court. He never had a large practice, and his precarious health gave him much trouble.

Maine's reputation as a jurist was established by a paper on "Roman Law and Legal Education" contributed to *Cambridge Essays* (1856) and especially by his epoch-making *Ancient Law* (1861), based upon his lectures at the Inns of Court. In 1861 he was offered an appointment as legal member of the Governor-General's Council in India, which he at first refused upon medical advice but, when it was offered a second time (1862), accepted. There he spent seven years, performing valuable service in lending his influence to the passing of numerous acts; and he was appointed vice-chancellor of the University of Calcutta. Fortunately his health, thought to be in jeopardy in India, was not injured by his stay, and he returned to England in 1869 apparently stronger than when he had left.

There he assumed the duties of the new corpus professorship of jurisprudence at Oxford, virtually created for him, and his first lectures were published in 1871 as *Village-Communities in the East and West,* a work which combined the results of German researches (by von Maurer and Nasse) with information acquired by Maine in his experience in India. In the same year he was gazetted Knight Commander of the Star of India, and appointed to a seat on the Council of the Secretary of State for India. He resigned his professorship at Oxford in 1878, having previously accepted a position as master of Trinity Hall, Cambridge; and in 1883 the last of his Oxford lectures were published as *Dissertations on Early Law and Custom.*

Honors came thick and fast, and Maine was offered many governmental posts which he declined. In 1887 he became Whewell professor of international law at Cambridge, and the lectures delivered in connection with this position were published (as *International Law*) after the author's death. In the winter of 1887-88 Maine went to the Riviera under medical advice, and in February he died at Cannes, of apoplexy, leaving his wife and two sons.

Often appearing rather cold or reserved, Maine was prevented by his health from enjoying many things of life; actually he was a charming companion and a man of sweetness and gentleness. He made a striking appearance as a lecturer, with his tall well-proportioned figure, his powerful voice, and his delicate face illuminated by nervous energy. He was particularly gifted in extracting from books the material which he found valuable, and in presenting this material with all the force of a lucid style and unusual powers of exposition. Naturally conservative, he offended many believers in democracy by his *Popular Government*, essays which pointed out some weaknesses in democratic societies. This is the only one of his works which can be considered in any real sense partisan, or directly concerned with contemporary politics. Maine's attitude throughout his life was that of the observer, the recorder, and the interpreter.

This interpretive, rather than original, interest of his work is to be attributed partly, at least, to his health. The drudgery of scholarship was beyond Maine's powers, the result being that his books lack references to authorities, and are not entirely trustworthy. *Ancient Law,* his greatest work, is not a piece of original research; it is an interpretation of the facts set forth by the work of others. Maine's singular ability was his power to acquire information and to shape it in such a way as to bring out theories of great significance. By his studies of ancient law he applied to the study of jurisprudence the same historical method that Darwin had brought to bear upon natural philosophy and that was applied with such fruitfulness to philology; and by emphasizing the historical, as opposed to the analytical, approach to legal problems he indicated a whole area for investigation which subsequent students have with profit studied more minutely. "Later speculation and research have, on the whole," said Sir

Frederick Pollock, "confirmed Maine's leading ideas in the most striking manner, partly by actual verification of consequences indicated by him as probable, partly by new examples and applications in regions which he had not himself explored." If some of his conclusions have become outdated, his fundamental attitude toward the study of law remains vital and has exerted an enormous influence.

R. W. W.

PRINCIPAL WORKS: *Biography*—Memoir of Henry Fitzmaurice Hallam (with Franklin Lushington) 1851. *Essays, Lectures, and Studies on Law*—Roman Law and Legal Education, 1856; Ancient Law: Its Connection With the Early History of Society, etc., 1861; Village-Communities in the East and West, 1871; Lectures on the Early History of Institutions, 1875; Dissertations on Early Law and Custom, 1883; Popular Government, 1885; International Law, 1888.

ABOUT: Grant Duff, M. E. Sir Henry Maine: A Brief Memoir of His Life; Holdsworth, W. S. The Historians of Anglo-American Law; Maine, H. J. S. Ancient Law (see Introduction and Notes to 1906 ed.); Morley, J. M. Oracles on Man and Government; Pollock, F. Oxford Lectures; Vinogradoff, P. The Teaching of Sir Henry Maine; Atlantic Monthly 82:363 September 1898; Edinburgh Review 178:100 July 1893; Times (London) February 6, 1888.

MAITLAND, EDWARD (October 27, 1824-October 2, 1897), novelist and mystical writer, was born in Ipswich, son of an evangelical clergyman, his childhood having been spent in an atmosphere of extreme piety. After private school at Brighton, he went to Caius College, Cambridge, receiving his B.A. in 1847. He wanted to enter the church, but religious doubts kept him from signing the Thirty-Nine Articles. To make up his mind, he took "a year's leave of absence" and went to California as one of the "forty-niners" in the Gold Rush. He stayed in California and Australia (where he was commissioner of crown lands) until 1857, marrying in Australia and after a year losing his wife, who left him with one son. He then returned to England and began his series of mystical novels, while at the same time engaging in journalism. Through *By and By* he met Anna Kingsford, wife of a Shropshire vicar, whose views coincided with Maitland's. In 1874 the two went together to Paris. From there the strange pair directed a stream of polemics against materialism, vivisection, and meat-eating. In 1876 Maitland announced he had seen his father's ghost and discovered he was a mystic; he could remember past lives, when he was Daniel, St. John, and Marcus Aurelius. In 1883 he and Anna Kingsford became Theosophists, but soon seceded and founded the Hermetic Society. Anna Kingsford died in 1888 and Maitland returned to England. He died at a friend's house in Tonbridge after having been speechless from paralysis for several months.

Maitland was undoubtedly insane, but his was a great natural talent gone to waste. His style, no matter what his aberrations of thought, remained flexible and pure.

PRINCIPAL WORKS: The Pilgrim and the Shrine, 1867; The Higher Law, 1869; By and By, 1873; The Keys of the Creeds (with Anna Kingsford) 1875; The Perfect Way (with Anna Kingsford) 1882; Clothed With the Sun: Being the Illuminations of Anna, 1889; Anna Kingsford: Her Life, Letters, and Journal, 1896.

ABOUT: Maitland, E. Anna Kingsford; Athenaeum October 16, 1897; Light October 16, 1897.

MAITLAND, FREDERIC WILLIAM (May 28, 1850-December 19, 1906), legal historian, was born in London, the only son of John Gorham Maitland, civil servant and linguist and scholar, and Emma (Daniell) Maitland, daughter of the chemist and physicist John Frederick Daniell. As his mother died not long after Frederic's birth and his father died in 1863, the boy's youth was passed, for the most part, in the care of his aunt, Charlotte Louisa Daniell.

His preliminary education began at home under the tutelage of German governesses, who gave him a good background in their language, and at a Brighton preparatory school. In 1863 he proceeded to Eton, and in 1869 entered Trinity College, Cambridge.

Although at first he gave his attention to mathematics, he turned in 1870 to moral and mental science, studying under the philosopher Henry Sidgwick to such good advantage that he won distinction and secured the Whewell international law scholarship (1873). He was secretary and later president of the Cambridge Union Society, and attracted notice also in athletics. He graduated in 1873, taking his master's degree in 1876 (he was given an

F. W. MAITLAND

honorary LL.D. in 1891), and proceeded to study law at Lincoln's Inn.

In 1876 he was called to the bar, and practised for a time. While his education in practical law had been thorough, Maitland was interested more especially in legal theory and history, and formed a plan for organizing a scientific history of English law. In 1884 he was elected reader in English law at Cambridge, where he made his home for most of the rest of his life, and in 1888, two years after his marriage to Florence Henrietta Fisher, he became Downing professor of English law. The story of his life from this time forward is one of scholarly activity; lecturing, correspondence, reviewing, and essay-writing.

Feeling the need of cooperation in his work, Maitland founded (1887) the Selden Society for the advancement of legal knowledge by the publication of basic legal materials; and the twenty-one volumes on detailed points of legal history issued in the next twenty years were directly or indirectly under his charge. His *History of English Law Before the Time of Edward I*, planned with Sir Frederick Pollock, although most of the work was Maitland's, appeared in 1895, the year when Maitland was made literary director of the Selden Society, and the book immediately became the accepted textbook for its period.

Applying himself next to the relation of Roman and English law, he published *Bracton and Azo* (1895), and with *Roman Canon Law in the Church of England* (1898) successfully confuted the theories of Stubbs and Anglican writers that there existed in England before the Reformation a system of Anglican (independent of Roman) canon law. His views concerning the Reformation have been praised for their impartiality.

The main preoccupation of his later years was with the editing of source material for the Selden Society. He translated and edited *Year Books* of the period of Edward II, working out also a grammar of the original legal Anglo-French. The fourth of these volumes was finished after his death by G. J. Turner.

Weakened in health by pleurisy in 1898, Maitland had spent the ensuing winters abroad in the Grand Canary, where he had continued his work. On the last of these voyages to the Islands (1906) he fell a victim to pneumonia and died at Quiney's Hotel, Las Palmas.

Tall and gaunt, and in his later years, at least, not free of physical weakness, Maitland, by the force of learning, humor, and charm, succeeded in holding the interest of his students; his lectures were so interesting that little note-taking was done. Himself thoroughly and completely immersed in his studies, although he had other interests, notably musical ones, and was a gifted conversationalist, he resolutely denied himself indulgence in pleasures which threatened to interfere with his work. It is said that in 1902 he refused the regius professorship of modern history (at Cambridge) because of the state of his health, and his high professional and intellectual standards. These same rigorous standards explain his welcome of criticism (if it seemed well-founded) of his own work.

As an historian of law he combined a practical knowledge of his subject with broad historical scholarship. Thus he brought the law under the microscope of sound historical knowledge and criticism, and he showed how legal history is a vital part of history as a whole, and forms a solid ground for real advance in knowledge of social and economic developments. The thoroughness of his work can be seen in his grammar of legal Anglo-French, a reconstruction of an old language which placed him on an enviable plane as a philologist but which was undertaken as an aid to more perfect historical knowledge. The French linguistic authority Paul Meyer recommended it as a textbook for students of mediaeval French. If occasionally Maitland, like most historians, was led to read ideas or theories into the past without real justification, it may very safely be said that his errors of this kind are not sufficient to undo his work, which, with the merit of scientific completeness, is marked by the further excellence of a literary charm which made it almost impossible for the author to be dull or dry. It is this peculiar combination in Maitland of the scholar and the artist that explains the chorus of praise voiced at home and abroad at the time of his death, which was described by the historian G. P. Gooch as "an irreparable blow to scholarship." "If all his theories could be overthrown, all his positive results peptonized into textbooks," said A. L. Smith, "he would still live as a model of critical method, a model of style, and a model of intellectual temper."

R. W. W.

PRINCIPAL WORKS: *Biography*—The Life and Letters of Leslie Stephen, 1906. *Editor*—Pleas of the Crown for the County of Gloucester Before the Abbot of Reading: 1221, 1884; Bracton's Note-Book, 1887; Select Pleas of the Crown: . . . 1200-1225, 1888; Select Pleas in Manorial and Other Seignorial Courts: . . . . . Reigns of Henry III and Edward I, 1889; Three Rolls of the King's Court in the Reign of King Richard I, 1891; The Court Baron (with W. P. Baildon) 1891; Records of the Parliament Holden at Westminster: . . . in the . . . Reign of King Edward I, 1893; Select Passages From the Works of Bracton and Azo, 1895; The Charters of the Borough of Cambridge (with M. Bateson) 1901; Year Books of Edward II, 1903-05, 1907 (Vol. 4 completed by G. J. Turner); Hobbes (by L. Stephen) 1904. *Essays, Lectures, and Other Works on Law and Legal History*—Justice and Police, 1885; Why the History of English Law Is Not Written,

1888; The History of English Law Before the Time of Edward I (with Sir F. Pollock) 1895; Domesday Book and Beyond, 1897; Township and Borough, 1898; Roman Canon Law in the Church of England, 1898; English Law and the Renaissance, 1901; The Constitutional History of England, 1908; Equity: Also, the Forms of Action at Common Law, 1909. *Translator*—Political Theories of the Middle Age (by O. F. von Gierke) 1900. *Miscellaneous*—The Mirror of Justices (attributed to Andrew Horn; ed. by W. J. Whittaker; introduction by F. W. Maitland) 1895; Essays on the Teaching of History (with H. M. Gwatkin & others) 1901; The Collected Papers of Frederic William Maitland, 1911.

ABOUT: Fisher, H. A. L. Frederick William Maitland; Gooch, G. P. History and Historians in the Nineteenth Century; Holdsworth, W. S. The Historians of Anglo-American Law; Smith, A. L. Frederic William Maitland; English Historical Reviews 22:280 April 1907; Quarterly Review 206:401 April 1907.

MAITLAND, SAMUEL ROFFEY (January 7, 1792-January 19, 1866), historian, was born in London, the son of a merchant of Scottish descent and Presbyterian faith. He was sent to various very bad schools until 1807, when by good luck a real scholar became his tutor and he began to lay the foundations of his education. In 1809 he entered St. John's College, Cambridge, and the Inner Temple simultaneously. The next year he transferred to Trinity College, but left without a degree. In 1815, finding he had not sufficiently fulfilled the requirements, he returned to St. John's for further study for the bar, to which he was called in 1816. He was always, however, more of a scholar than a barrister.

In 1816 he married Selina Stephenson; they had one son, F. W. Maitland, also an ecclesiastical writer. Maitland's Presbyterian views finally changed and in 1821 he was ordained deacon and became a curate in Norwich; the next year he was ordained priest and made perpetual curate of Christ Church, Gloucester. As a Hebrew scholar, he was keenly interested in the Society for the Conversion of Jews, and in 1828 made a Continental tour to observe its work; a brilliant linguist, he easily learned the language of every country he visited. He was a contributor to the *British Magazine*, and its editor from 1839 to its decease in 1849. From 1838 to 1848 he was librarian at Lambeth, but the only recognition he received was a D.D. degree. Although one of the most renowned scholars of the Church, he was never given any preferment. He became a Fellow of the Royal Society in 1839.

Maitland was a very versatile and brilliant man, with a sparkling, stimulating style. But he was cross-grained and truculent and consequently never had the recognition due his labors.

PRINCIPAL WORKS: Documents Illustrative of the History, Doctrine, and Rites of the Ancient Albigenses and Waldenses, 1832; The Dark Ages, 1844; Essays on Subjects Connected With the Reforma-

tion in England, 1849; Eight Essays on Various Subjects, 1852.
ABOUT: Gentleman's Magazine April 1866; Proceedings of the Royal Society 16:21.

MALCOLM, SIR JOHN (May 2, 1769-May 30, 1833), Scottish military historian, was born in Dumfriesshire of a good family. He left school at twelve, a strong-willed, obstinate boy, and at thirteen actually entered the army of the East India Company as an ensign. He arrived in India in 1783, and for several years led a wild, adventurous life. His first intellectual stirrings came when he studied Persian in 1791 in order to enter the diplomatic service. His attempt was unsuccessful at that time, but the next year he was promoted to lieutenant and appointed Persian interpreter. In 1794 he went on furlough to England, but returned to India the next year. From 1795 to 1798 he was assistant to the resident of Hyderabad. From 1799 to 1801 he was at last envoy to Persia, appointed by Lord Wellesley (later the Duke of Wellington), whose private secretary he was for the year following. Other governmental missions took him to Persia in 1808, 1809, 1810, and 1823.

In 1807 Malcolm married Charlotte Campbell. They had one son and several daughters, but for most of the time he left his family in England while he served in India. From 1812 to 1817 he lived with them in England, becoming a Knight Commander of the Bath in 1815 and receiving an honorary D.C.L. from Oxford in 1816, in recognition of his books on India and Persia, but he could not stand a settled life, and left to serve in the second Mahratta War as a brigadier. In 1822 he tried England and literature again, but India drew him back once more. He was governor of Bombay from 1826 to 1830. Then he came home for good. In 1831 and 1832 he was a member of Parliament, an extreme Tory, and arch-enemy of the Reform Bills. He died the next year of a stroke of paralysis following influenza.

PRINCIPAL WORKS: Political History of India, 1811; History of Persia, 1815; Administration of India, 1833; Life of Clive, 1836.
ABOUT: Kaye, Sir J. Life of Malcolm.

MALLESON, GEORGE BRUCE (May 18, 1825-March 1, 1898), historian, was born in London and educated at Wimbledon and Winchester. In 1842 he went to Bengal as an ensign of the East India Company. He became a lieutenant in 1847. In 1856 he was assistant military auditor-general. He was promoted to captain in 1861 and rose rapidly through other ranks until in 1873 he was a colonel and a Commander of the Star of India. He held various civil offices in India and was guardian of the young Maharajah of Mysore from 1869 to 1877. In that year he retired on full pay. In 1856 Malleson married Marian Battye,

whose five officer brothers had all been killed in the Indian service. Throughout his career he was interested in writing, was a contributor to the *Calcutta Review* from 1857 onward, and acted as correspondent for the London *Times*. His work shows great industry, vigor, and breadth of view, but he was an extreme partisan and was incapable of writing a really impartial history.

PRINCIPAL WORKS: Mutiny of the Bengal Army (anon.) 1857; History of the French in India, 1868; Recreations of an Indian Official, 1872; Historical Sketch of the Native States of India, 1875; History of Afghanistan, 1879; Wellesley, 1889; Warren Hastings, 1894.
ABOUT: London Times March 2, 1898.

MALLOCK, WILLIAM HURRELL (1849-April 2, 1923), miscellaneous writer, was born in Devonshire. His maternal uncle was the famous historian, J. A. Froude. After private tuition he entered Balliol College, Oxford, but left without a degree, though he won the Newdigate prize for a poem in 1872. He had been intended for the diplomatic service but abandoned the plan and never adopted any profession. A man of means, he devoted his life to writing and travel. He lived for long periods in France and Italy, and traveled much in Cyprus and the Near East.

Mallock deliberately aimed in all his prose writing at two things—the exposition of his dogmatic religious views and his life-long battle with Socialism. His religion is difficult to describe: it was a sort of half-Rationalism, at odds with the Rationalist movement. Some of his books were once very popular, particularly the satirical *New Paul and Virginia* and *Is Life Worth Living?*, but if he is to be remembered at all it will be for his fine metrical translation of Lucretius.

PRINCIPAL WORKS: A Human Document (novel) 1872; The New Republic, 1877; The New Paul and Virginia, 1878; Is Life Worth Living?, 1879; The Old Order Changes, 1886; Labour and the Popular Welfare, 1893; Classes and Masses, 1896; Lucretius on Life and Death, 1900; The Veil of the Temple (novel) 1904; Social Reform, 1914; The Limits of Pure Democracy, 1918; Memoirs of Life and Literature, 1920.
ABOUT: Mallock, W. H. Memoirs of Life and Literature.

MALTHUS, THOMAS ROBERT (February 17, 1766-December 23, 1834), economist, was born near Guilford, the son of a devout Rousseauist (in fact, Rousseau's executor), who educated him strictly according to the recommendations of *Émile*. The boy emerged from a series of rather surprising tutors without harm, noted only for his belligerency, his keen sense of humor, and his athletic prowess. At eighteen he entered Jesus College, Cambridge, and four years later received his B.A., with prizes in Latin and Greek declamation, but less eminence in mathematics. In 1793 he was appointed to a fellow-

T. R. MALTHUS

ship in Jesus, which he held until his marriage in 1804 to Harriet Eckersall; he had become an M.A. in 1791, and in 1798 entered holy orders.

Malthus became a curate at Albury, Surrey, but he was very different from the ordinary country clergyman. In the very year of his ordainment, he published the first version of his famous *Essay on the Principle of Population,* containing the celebrated central thesis that population increases in geometrical ratio, subsistence in arithmetical ratio. In this rather unfinished early form he considered the inevitable result of this conflict between population growth and subsistence to be the eventual extinction of man, except by the kindly intervention of war and disease; later, influenced by Godwin, he regarded extinction as a possibility, but not necessarily as a certainty. It was to this later view that he converted Pitt and Paley. The remedy of birth control, today often called neo-Malthusianism, probably never occurred to him, or at least never met with his approval.

Feeling the need of securing more information to support his theory, in 1799 Malthus traveled in Germany, Sweden, Norway, Finland, and Russia, and later in France and Switzerland. His father died during this absence. In 1803, on the basis of his new observations and conclusions, he published what was practically a new book under the same title as the old. The following year he married, and a year later found him professor of history and political economy in the new college at Haileybury. In this small town, with the exception of one trip to Ireland and one more to the Continent, he lived for the remainder of his life. In 1819 he was made a fellow of the Royal Society. His membership

in the Political Economy Club brought him into association with such men as Tooke, James Mill, Grote, and Ricardo. He was a member also of the Royal Society of Literature, and one of the first fellows of the Statistical Society.

Malthus died suddenly of heart disease while on a Christmas visit to his father-in-law near Bath, and was buried in that city. He was survived by a son and a daughter.

Although he never formally left the clergy, and was buried with Anglican rites, Malthus was really a utilitarian, though a follower of Paley rather than of Bentham. He was a devout lover of concrete facts, and distrusted abstract conclusions. His style as a writer was not distinguished, but he was noted for his ability to make the "dismal science" of political economy not only clear but "not even dull." Personally, he was the most amiable, serene, and cheerful of men, calm under long abuse from both radicals and conservatives. He was modest and self-effacing. He suffered from a speech defect arising from a cleft palate, but in spite of this he served with success both as a clergyman and as a teacher. Like Mendel, Malthus had been neglected and almost forgotten until in recent years his theory was revived and in modified form incorporated into the body of modern science.

M. A. deF.

PRINCIPAL WORKS: An Essay on the Principle of Population, 1798 (practically new version 1803); On the High Price of Provisions, 1800; Letter to Whitbread on . . . . Amendment of the Poor Laws, 1807; Observations on the Effects of the Corn Laws, 1814; Letter to Lord Granville, 1815; Grounds of an Opinion on the Policy of Restricting the Importation of Foreign Corn, 1815; Principles of Political Economy, 1820; The Measure of Value, 1823; Definitions in Political Economy, 1827; Summary View of the Principle of Population, 1830.

ABOUT: Bonar, J. Malthus and His Work; Finch, A. E. Malthusiana; Martineau, H. Autobiography; Ricardo, D. Notes on Malthus's Principles of Political Economy (see Introduction and Notes by J. H. Hollander and T. E. Gregory); Contemporary Review 146:691 December 1934; Economic Journal 45:221 June 1935.

MANGAN, JAMES CLARENCE (May 1, 1803-June 20, 1849), Irish poet, was born in Dublin. He was the son of James Mangan, a grocer, and Catherine Smith. He was not given the name Clarence, but assumed it after using it as a pseudonym.

He went to school in Saul's Court, Dublin, and when he left had acquired a good knowledge of Latin, Italian, French, and Spanish. (He never learned the Gaelic tongue, and his versions of the old Celtic poems were made from literal translations supplied by others.) From his thirteenth to his twentieth year he worked as a copyist and for three more years as clerk in a lawyer's office, where his peculiar appearance and eccentricity of manner made him a butt for the other clerks. The unbearable tedium of the work led Mangan to contract the habit of drinking, which, with the use of opium, was later to be his ruin. A position was made for him in the library of Trinity College by those who appreciated his talents, and he had occasional verses published in Dublin almanacs and papers. Then a clerk's position was found for him in the office of the Irish Ordnance Survey, and Charles Gavan Duffy, the editor, offered him some work for the *Belfast Vindicator*. Mangan, however, was a man of difficult temperament, and his habits made any regular industry impossible. He drifted gradually downhill, and died, possibly of the cholera then raging in Dublin, but more likely of starvation.

Mangan published no volumes during his life, and nothing outside Ireland. He contributed to such periodicals as the *Dublin Penny Journal* from 1832 to 1837, to the *Irish Penny Journal*, *The Nation*, the *Dublin University Magazine*, and many others. All his work has never been collected, which is doubtless best for him, as much that he wrote was poor. At his best, however, he is a poet of fiery genius. "'The Dark Rosaleen,'" says Lionel Johnson of Mangan's English version of the old Irish poem "Roisin Dubh," "ranks with the great lyrics of the world; it is one of the fairest and fiercest in its perfection of imagery and rhythm." "The Nameless One" and "Cáhál Mór of the Wine-Red Hand" are lyrics which have won enthusiastic praise. It was natural that this "genius-cursed Irishman," as Michael Monahan called him, should have done much hasty and unworthy work, but many critics consider him the greatest of Irish poets who wrote in English. He was a remarkably convincing, though very free translator, and the first to make really good versions of Goethe. He was influenced by Byron and Coleridge, and there has been some question of his debt to Poe, or the reverse. However, Poe was much the greater master of verse, being strong in Mangan's chief weakness, which was rhyming; and though the two men were contemporaries and of similar descent, and used the device of a refrain somewhat similarly, the attempt to couple their names seems far-fetched.

Mangan was a small, thin man, with a well-shaped head, clear blue eyes, and delicate features. According to James Mitchel, his face was worn and pale and his light-colored hair had a bleached look. He was never married, supposedly because of a blighted romance which he described in a fictionized autobiography first printed in the *Irish Monthly* in 1882 and now included in his *Essays in Prose and Verse*.   R. M.

PRINCIPAL WORKS: *Poetry*—Poems, 1859. *Translations*—German Anthology, 1845; Poets and Poetry of Munster, 1849; The Tribes of Ireland, by Aengus O'Daly, 1852. *Miscellaneous*—Essays in Prose and Verse, 1884; Prose Writings, 1904.

ABOUT: Brooks & Rolleston. A Treasury of Irish Poetry; Cain, H. E. The Poe-Mangan Question; Graves, A. P. Irish Literary and Musical Studies; McCarthy. & others. Irish Literature; Mangan, J. C. Selected Poems (see Study by L. I. Guiney); O'Donoghue, D. J. Life of James Clarence Mangan; Dublin Review 142:288 April 1908; Forum 48:565 November 1912.

MANNING, ANNE (February 17, 1807-September 14, 1879), novelist, was born in London. Her father was an insurance broker, her grandfather a Unitarian minister. She was educated entirely by her mother, an unusually well-read woman, who taught her languages, history, and science. She was talented in painting, and received a gold medal from the Royal Academy for a copy of Murillo. As she grew older she taught her younger brothers and sisters, and wrote for them her first book, *A Sister's Gift* (1826). Her life was very uneventful, marked only by a move to Mickleham and another, after her parents' death, to Reigate Hill. She died in her sister's house at Tunbridge Wells, unmarried, at seventy-four.

Miss Manning's best work is in her numerous historical novels, which were accurate in detail, well-constructed, but occasionally rather pedantic.

PRINCIPAL WORKS: The Village Belle, 1838; The Maiden and Married Life of Mary Powell, 1849; Cherry and Violet, 1853; The Household of Sir Thomas More, 1860; Family Pictures, 1861.

ABOUT: Manning, A. Family Pictures; Yonge, C. M. Women Novelists of Queen Victoria's Reign; Golden Hours January to May 1872 (containing Miss Manning's Passages in an Authoress's Life).

J. C. MANGAN

MANNING, HENRY EDWARD (CARDINAL)

MANNING, HENRY EDWARD (CARDINAL) (July 15, 1808-January 14, 1892), theologian, was born in Hertfordshire, son of a West Indian merchant and of his second wife, who was of partly Italian descent. He was educated at Harrow, where he was a noted athlete, and at Balliol College, Oxford, receiving his B.A. in 1830. His father's straitened circumstances preventing the political career he desired, he took a subordinate post in the Colonial Office, until he returned to Oxford as a fellow of Merton in 1832. He was ordained and became a curate in Sussex. The next year he received his M.A. degree and became rector of the same charge, the rector having died meanwhile. He married the deceased rector's daughter, Caroline Sargent. The marriage was childless but very happy, and even when he was a Roman Catholic cardinal, Manning kept the anniversary of his wife's death (from tuberculosis) in 1837. The year she died he became rural dean of Midhurst. His views became increasingly high church, and he was also influenced by the Tractarians (Puseyites) but was not one of them. In 1840 he became archdeacon of Chichester, and in 1842 select preacher at Oxford. As late as 1843 he preached an anti-papal sermon, and though he traveled on the Continent in 1847 and 1848 and had an audience with Pope Pius IX, in 1850 he presided at a "No Popery" meeting.

Yet immediately after, he resigned from the church and the next year became a Roman Catholic. He was ordained by Cardinal Wiseman and for several years spent most of his time in Rome, where a D.D. degree was conferred on him by the pope. In 1857 he became superior of a community of secular priests in London, in 1865 Archbishop of Westminster, and in 1875 a cardinal. As cardinal he was ultramontane (strongly papal) and Italianizing, and was an inflexible autocrat. Yet personally he was a kindly and philanthropic man. He was the arch-enemy of Rationalism and what he called "a-Catholic science," and was an ardent teetotaler. As a writer he was eloquent, subtle, but essentially uncritical.

PRINCIPAL WORKS: The English Church, 1835; The Rule of Faith, 1838; The Unity of the Church, 1842; The Grounds of Faith, 1852; Sermons on Ecclesiastical Subjects, 1863-73; England and Christendom, 1867; Miscellanies, 1877-88.

ABOUT: Hutton, A. W. Cardinal Manning; Purcell, E. S. Life of Cardinal Manning.

MANSEL, HENRY LONGUEVILLE

MANSEL, HENRY LONGUEVILLE (October 6, 1820-July 30, 1871), philosopher, was born in Northamptonshire, the son of a clergyman. Early in boyhood he was noted for his interest in religion and metaphysics. He was educated at the Merchant Taylors' School, where he won many prizes, and laid the foundations of his career as both scholar and deep-dyed Tory; and at St. John's College, Oxford, where he was called "the model student." He received his B.A. in 1843 with a "double first" in classics and mathematics. He then became a private tutor. In 1844 he was ordained deacon, and in 1845 ordained priest. Except for his keen wit and turn for satire, he was the typical conservative, absent-minded, unworldly Oxford don. In 1854 he became a member of the university council. The next year he married Charlotte Augusta Taylor, and became reader in moral and metaphysical theology at Magdalen College. In 1864 he was made "professor fellow" at his old college, St. John's.

As might be expected from his philosophical and social views, Mansel engaged in long and heated controversies with Herbert Spencer, F. D. Maurice, and Goldwin Smith, who were by no means in agreement with one another. He was more or less of a disciple of Sir William Hamilton, and edited his works. In 1865 he was in Rome. From 1864 to 1868 he was examining chaplain to the Bishop of Peterborough, and in 1866 he became professor of ecclesiastical history at Oxford and Dean of St. Paul's Cathedral. He died in his sleep, of a cerebral hemorrhage.

Besides his metaphysical works, Mansel wrote poems and a tragedy. His celebrated wit is not in evidence, naturally, in his philosophical writings. These, though they aroused much interest in his own time, are now completely out-dated.

PRINCIPAL WORKS: The Limits of Demonstrative Science, 1853; Metaphysics, 1860; Letters, Lectures, and Reviews, 1873; The Gnostic Heresies of the First and Second Centuries (ed. by J. B. Lightfoot) 1875.

ABOUT: Mansel, H. L. The Gnostic Heresies (see Sketch by Lord Carnarvon).

MARKHAM, SIR CLEMENTS ROBERT

MARKHAM, SIR CLEMENTS ROBERT (July 20, 1830-January 30, 1916), geographer and historian, was born in Yorkshire, son of the canon of Windsor and grandson of the Archbishop of York. He spent two years at Westminster, and then, in 1844, entered the Royal Navy. Until 1848 he was stationed mostly at South American ports, and laid the foundation of his interest in South America and in geography alike. In 1850 and 1851 he was in the Arctic with Captain Austin on one of the search expeditions sent to look for Sir John Franklin. He then resigned from the navy, and after a visit to the American historian of Peru, W. H. Prescott, he spent a year among the Inca ruins. In 1853 he returned to England and entered the civil service, in the India Office. In 1857 he married Minna Chichester, a linguist who was of great help to him in his work. They had one daughter. In 1860 Markham was sent to collect cinchona trees and seeds (source of quinine) in the Andes, and acclimate them in India. From 1867 to 1877 he was in charge of geographical works in the India Office, and in 1868 accompanied Baron Napier as geographer of the Abyssinian (Ethiopian) campaign. In 1875 he accompanied the Nares Arctic expedition as far as Greenland. He retired in 1877, and gave the rest of his life to geography. He was honorary secretary of the Royal Geographical Society from 1863 to 1888, president from 1893 to 1905; he was also secretary of the Hakluyt Society (made up of explorers) from 1858 to 1886, and its president from 1889 to 1909. He was a promotor of Antarctic exploration, and chose the ill-fated Capt. R. F. Scott to head his first expedition. The leading British geographer of his time, Markham became Commander of the Bath in 1871 (K.C.B. 1896), and a Fellow of the Royal Society in 1873. He died as the result of an accident.

Markham was a hero-worshiper, obstinate and vehement, uncritical and fond of paradox. His work, while showing signs of haste, is eminently readable. He wrote numerous biographies and books of travel.

PRINCIPAL WORKS: History of Peru, 1853; The Incas of Peru, 1910; History of Arctic and Antarctic Exploration, 1921.

ABOUT: Markham, Sir A. H. Life of Sir Clements Markham; Geographical Journal 1916.

"MARKHAM, MRS." See PENROSE, ELIZABETH

MARRIOTT, CHARLES (August 24, 1811-September 15, 1858), theologian, was born near Rugby. His father was a clergyman and most of Marriott's childhood was spent at his charge in Devonshire. Both his parents died while he was a boy, and he was reared by two aunts. He had one term at Rugby, but was considered too delicate for school and was educated by tutors. He entered Exeter College, Oxford, then transferred as a scholar of Balliol, receiving his B.A. in 1832. In 1833 he was named fellow of Oriel, took holy orders, and became mathematical lecturer and tutor of the college. He was a disciple of Newman, and when Newman became a Roman Catholic in 1845, Marriott practically took his place in the university. His only period away from Oxford was from 1839 to 1841, when he was principal of the Diocesan College, Chichester. In 1841 he returned as sub-dean of Oriel. In 1850 he was made vicar of St. Mary the Virgin, the university church. Marriott wore himself out in his college duties; fought epidemics of cholera and smallpox, contracting the latter disease; ran a printing press for religious works; and even, without business experience, managed a cooperative enterprise. Overwork brought on total paralysis in 1855, and he died three years later at his brother's house in Berkshire. With Pusey and Keble, he edited many of the Church Fathers. He wrote very little, and his influence on others was far more powerful than was anything done by himself.

PRINCIPAL WORKS: Sermons, 1843 and 1850; Hints to Devotion, 1848.

ABOUT: Burgon, Dean. Lives of Twelve Good Men.

MARRYAT, FREDERICK (July 10, 1792-August 9, 1848), naval officer and novelist, was born at Westminster, the second son of Joseph Marryat, who was colonial agent for Granada, member of Parliament for Sandwich, and chairman of the committee of Lloyds. His grandfather, Dr. Thomas Marryat, was a poet of sorts and Joseph wrote pamphlets in defense of the slave trade. The boy was not so well educated as his father's means should have warranted and Frederick's life at home and at school at Ponders End does not seem to have been particularly happy. Before he was fourteen he tried three times to run away to sea, "but the end of the adventure was always capture, return to school and more cane." The elder Marryat finally capitulated and in September 1806 the boy was placed aboard the crack frigate *Impérieuse* under Capt. Lord Cochrane, Earl of Dundonald. Frederick was a sturdy, venturesome lad and his naval life, begun under very favorable conditions, shaped the course of his career as an author. Marryat would have been a writer in any case. But, as his private log shows, he took an early pleasure in the use of his pen and had boundless enthusiasm for the life he had chosen.

Marryat saw various service in the North Sea, the Channel, the Mediterranean, and the eastern coast of America from Nova Scotia

FREDERICK MARRYAT

to Surinam. He won rapid promotion and the peace of 1815 left him a Commander at the age of twenty-three. He made his first visit to the Continent, which had been virtually closed to the peaceful traveler for twenty-two years, at this time and in 1819 married a Miss Shairp, daughter of a former consul-general to Russia. He was at sea again in eighteen months. In 1823 a gig upset in Falmouth harbor, containing a midshipman, Marryat, and a bumboat woman. The latter, so the story goes, eager for the profit and distinction of rescuing a Commander, fastened herself upon Marryat and nearly prevented his saving the life of the sailor, who could not swim.

Marryat published his first novel, *Frank Mildmay*, in 1829. Written with that particular verve which characterizes all his work, it caught the public fancy. The success of this book, boredom with peacetime navy routine, a growing family, and pique because of real or fancied discrimination on the part of King William IV or the Admiralty or both actuated Marryat's rather sudden resignation of his command in November 1830.

From now on Marryat led the life of a working man of letters. *The King's Own* was published in 1830. He worked rapidly and always, it seems, under a press of financial urgency. Marryat fancied good living and like many authors and many men used to the paternalistic economy of Army or Navy had a talent for disastrous speculation. From 1832 to 1835 he edited the *Metropolitan Magazine* and during that period contributed to it no less than five of his best novels. In 1833 he stood unsuccessfully and expensively for Parliament.

Marryat then took his family to the Continent, an economic expediency to which Lever and Thackerary likewise resorted, and in 1837 set off alone for the United States. Author of ten novels and numerous sketches, short stories, and articles, he felt the need for new material and a literary breathing spell. His entrance into the field of letters had been at a time favorable to one of his vigor and originality. He was exceptionally competent at realizing the market value of his goods. Twenty guineas a sheet was his price in 1837 exactly what Carlyle was getting from Fraser. A kind of amiable hostility hovered over Marryat's dealings with his publishers. He informed one that his temper warranted a double fire-insurance premium on his quarters and regarding proposed terms exhorted the fellow to read his Bible. "We all have our own ideas of Paradise . . . and the more pleasurable portion of anticipated bliss is that there will be no publishers there."

Marryat was among the first of a long line of British authors to visit the States and write a book which, to say the least, annoyed his hosts. He remained in America two years and before he left sold the American copyright for his *Diary in America* for about $3000.

Marryat's output continued to be enormous and the erratic way in which he worked began to tell upon his strength. He was volatile by nature, easily offended, and had few friendships of long standing. He could never bear to settle long in one spot. His own minute handwriting put a great strain on his eyes and a tendency to break blood vessels which he had shown in youth made itself felt more frequently now.

Marryat's *Masterman Ready* (1841), the first of his childrens' books, shows indirectly a knowledge of the child mind that is startling when one considers the mawkish sentimentality of juveniles of the period. In 1843 Marryat removed himself and his younger children to Langham Manor in Norfolk. This property was an unprofitable estate of some seven hundred acres. But like many sailors and non-agriculturalists Marryat believed himself capable of managing a farm. There were additional reasons for financial retrenchment. The West India property inherited from his father had become almost valueless and tradesmen were now beginning to bring action for goods supplied to Marryat's sons. There seem to have been domestic upheavals too, for no mention is made of Mrs. Marryat being at Langham. Marryat's "agricultural vagaries," his daughter writes, " appeared almost like insanity to those steady, plodding minds that could not understand that a man may have genius and no common sense."

However, Marryat's last years at Langham were quite happy. Unfortunately his haemoptysis had become aggravated beyond control. He died at Langham, his death hastened, it is said, by news of the loss at sea of his eldest son.

Marryat, says G. E. B. Saintsbury, "played, but much more thoroughly, the same part toward the navy that Lever occupied toward the army." He is "perhaps the most remarkable instance of a man working his professional knowledge with effect in literature." Though not a first-rank novelist, Marryat's robust humor has amused generations of readers and, while his juveniles may not abide by all the tenets of modern pediatrics, they are still among the best of their kind.

Marryat's daughter FLORENCE (1838-1899) (afterwards Church and Lean), was her father's biographer and also wrote numerous novels popular in their time.   P. B. S

PRINCIPAL WORKS: *Novels*—The Adventures of a Naval Officer: or, Frank Mildmay, 1829; The King's Own, 1830; Newton Foster, 1832; Peter Simple, 1834; Jacob Faithful, 1834; Mr. Midshipman Easy, 1836; Japhet in Search of a Father, 1836; The Pirate and the Three Cutters, 1836; Snarley-Yow:

or, the Dog Fiend, 1837; The Phantom Ship, 1839. *Juveniles*—Masterman Ready, 1841; Percival Keene, 1842; Monsieur Violet, 1842; The Settlers in Canada, 1844; The Children of the New Forest, 1847. *Miscellaneous*—A Diary in America, 1839; Olla Podrida, 1840; The Mission or Scenes in Africa, 1845.

ABOUT: Hannay, D. Life of Frederick Marryat; Löwe, D. Marryat als Jugendschriftsteller; Marryat, F. Life and Letters of Captain Marryat.

MARSH-CALDWELL, MRS. ANNE. See CALDWELL, MRS. ANNE MARSH-

MARSHMAN, JOHN CLARK (August 1794-July 8, 1877), historian, was the son of a missionary to India who was a noted Orientalist. He went with his father to his post at Serampur, Bengal, in 1800, and was educated by him. From 1812 he directed all religious activities for his father. For twenty years he acted as a secular bishop, then surrendered this mission to the Baptists. He started the only paper mill in India, and with his father founded the first paper in the Bengali language, and (in 1821) the first English weekly in India, the *Friend of India.* He published a series of law books, and his *Guide to the Civil Law,* which was for years the civil code of India, is said to be the most profitable law book ever issued—though Blackstone's *Commentaries* would seem to be much more widely circulated. He also established a Christian colony in the Sunderbunds, and contributed large sums to native education. Against his will he became the official Bengali translator to the government, and though he gave all his salary to educational institutions, he was so abused as a "government tool" that he resigned and returned to England in 1852. There his immense services received no recognition; he was refused a seat on the India Council, and having given most of his money away had to become chairman of the committee of audit for the East India Railway. Three times he stood for Parliament, but without success. In 1868, in tardy recognition, he received the order of the Star of India.

PRINCIPAL WORKS: The History of India, 1842, 1863, 1867; The History of Bengal, 1844.

ABOUT: Illustrated London News July 28, 1877; London Times July 10, 1877.

MARSTON, JOHN WESTLAND (January 30, 1819-January 5, 1890), poetic dramatist, was born in Boston, Lincolnshire, the son of a Baptist minister. In 1834 he was articled to his uncle, a London solicitor, but he had no taste for the law, and was fascinated by the theatre and everything pertaining to it. He fell in with a mystical group, something on the style of the American Transcendentalists of the same era, and securing a release from his articles, he devoted himself to writing for and editing their organ, the *Psyche.*

In 1840 he married Eleanor Jane Potts, against the snobbish objections of her family, and worked an idealized version of his love-story into his first play, *The Patrician's Daughter,* produced by Macready in 1842. He became a member of the Dickens circle, sharing the novelist's passion for amateur acting. He himself tried to write novels, but soon found that though he had dramatic ability it could be expressed only in plays. In 1837 he was editor of the *National Magazine,* and from 1863 he was critic of poetry for *The Athenaeum.*

Marston's last years were tragic ones. His wife died in 1870, his two daughters in 1878 and 1879, and in 1887 he lost his only son, the celebrated blind poet, Philip Bourke Marston. His fortune disappeared, and he was rescued by Sir Henry Irving, who gave a benefit for him which netted nearly £1000.

Marston's best play was *Donna Diana;* his worst, and also his last, was *Under Fire.* He had the high aim of elevating ordinary life of his own time to the level where blank verse would be appropriate for its expression; but his talents were unequal to his ambitions; his characterization was weak, and his plays were unreal and exaggerated. He was a far better critic than he was a poet or a dramatist. Yet for years his were almost the only acted plays which had any literary aspirations at all.

PRINCIPAL WORKS (dates of production): The Patrician's Daughter, 1842; Strathmore, 1849; Anne Blake, 1852; A Life's Ransom, 1857; A Hard Struggle, 1858; Donna Diana, 1863; The Favourite of Fortune, 1866; Life for Life, 1869; Broken Spells, 1873; Under Fire, 1885.

ABOUT: Athenaeum January 1890.

MARSTON, PHILIP BOURKE (August 13, 1850-February 14, 1887), poet, was born in London, August 13, 1850, the son of Dr. John Westland Marston and his wife, Eleanor Jane Potts. It has been said that the boy, Philip, was "born to poetry," for he was descended from John Marston, the Elizabethan dramatist. His own father was a well known playwright and poet, and his mother was the daughter of the proprietor of *Saunders' News Letter.* Indeed, he was brought up in a literary atmosphere. Furthermore, Philip James Bailey, the author, was his godfather, while Dinah Mulock, who wrote a poem calling him "Philip the King," was his godmother.

He was hampered, however, by a partial loss of his eyesight at the age of three. Most of his life he was almost virtually blind. For this reason he never learned to read, and was forced to dictate a youthful novel of three volumes to his mother. Nor did bad eyesight prevent him from composing a book of verse before he was fourteen. His love of poetry was further stimulated by his association with his father's guests. By the time he was twenty-one he had met Dickens,

PHILIP BOURKE MARSTON

Browning, and Tennyson, as well as Rossetti, William Morris, and Swinburne.

When he was twenty, however, not long after his mother's death, he fell in love with a beautiful girl named Mary Nesbit. His first book, *Song-Tide and Other Poems*, is decidedly reminiscent of his devotion to his fiancée. But the very year it was published the girl died of consumption, and henceforth Marston's life seems to consist of a series of calamities.

His friend, Oliver Madox Brown, the author, died in 1874. Meanwhile Philip moved to London with his sister Cicely, who served as his amanuensis and companion. When they were not at Notting Hill or Euston Road, they were traveling together in France and in Italy. But Cicely died in 1878 and her death was followed the next year by that of his other sister, Eleanor, who was married to Arthur O'Shaughnessy, the poet. The brother-in-law died in 1881, and Rossetti and his friend James Thomson, the poet, in 1882.

These tragedies undoubtedly had their effects upon Marston, although *All in All* came out in 1874 and *Wind Voices* in 1883. By the autumn of this last year, however, the poet's health was decidedly impaired. In 1886 he came down with brain fever while he was in Brighton with his father. The next January he suffered a paralytic stroke and died on February 14, 1887.

Melancholia, however, was only one aspect of his character. He loved society. He was the founder of a club called "The Vagabonds," and was often "the life of the party." "Close upon five feet eleven in height, his erect carriage and alert attitude afforded him a buoyant and youthful aspect" which made him popular in London circles. In fact it was

at one of these literary gatherings that he met his friend, Louise Chandler Moulton, the American poet, who was largely responsible for his success in the United States.

Sadness, on the other hand, was the dominant note in his works. He was such a sceptic that on his deathbed he requested a burial without religious services and in unconsecrated ground. This philosophy of life crept into his writing. Most of his love sonnets are tinged with melancholy. He dubbed his own short stories "Prose Bitters." His ballads, it is true, contained an "Elizabethan lilt," but, for the most part, he was too much indebted to Rossetti to win lasting fame as a poet.   B. D. S.

PRINCIPAL WORKS: *Poetry*—Song-Tide and Other Poems, 1871; All in All, 1875; Wind Voices, 1883; Garden Secrets, 1887; A Last Harvest, 1891; Collected Poems, 1892. *Prose*—For a Song's Sake and Other Stories, 1887.

ABOUT: McCabe, J. (comp.). A Biographical Dictionary of Modern Rationalists; Marston, P. B. Collected Poems (see Biographical Sketch by L. C. Moulton); Marston, P. B. For a Song's Sake (see Memoir by W. Sharp); Marston, P. B. Garden Secrets (see Philip Bourke Marston: A Sketch, by L. C. Moulton); Osborne, C. C. Philip Bourke Marston; The Academy 24:374 December 8, 1883; The Fortnightly Review 57:81 January 1, 1892; Lippincott's Monthly Magazine 39:971 June 1887; The Literary World 15:133 April 19, 1884; The Saturday Review 63:259 February 19, 1887.

MARTIN, SIR THEODORE (September 16, 1816-September 18, 1909), Scottish poet and biographer, was born in Edinburgh, the son of a solicitor. He was educated at the Edinburgh High School, and at the University of Edinburgh from 1830 to 1833. He received an honorary LL.D. degree from his alma mater in 1873. He was admitted to the Scottish bar, and practised in his native city until 1846. Then he went to London and set up as a Parliamentary solicitor and agent, alone and with various partners, building up a very successful business which he did not give up until 1907, when he was ninety-one.

He began writing humorous verse and prose for the magazines, under the pseudonym of "Bon Gaultier." His verse came to the attention of W. E. Aytoun, whom he had known slightly at the university, and until Aytoun's death in 1865 they collaborated. In 1840 Martin met Helena Faucit, one of the most distinguished actresses of the time, and fell romantically in love with her. They were married in 1851. She remained on the stage until 1871, and died in 1898. Martin translated and adapted plays for her, and wrote her biography after her death. The marriage was childless, but supremely happy. In 1862 they bought a country house in Wales, where Martin finally died.

His connection with the stage led him to write many articles on theatrical subjects for the magazines. He also translated widely from the Danish, German, and Latin (chiefly Horace and Catullus), but as a translator he was fluent rather than accurate. He became a personal confidant and correspondent of Queen Victoria, and was chosen by her to write the life of Prince Albert. He was made C.B. in 1878 and K.C.B. in 1880. The next year he was lord rector of St. Andrews University. He held various offices on the Royal Literary Fund, and was a trustee of Shakespeare's birthplace. He died at the great age of ninety-three, with all his faculties intact.

Martin may be described as industrious and versatile rather than highly gifted. He made the very most of a rather meager talent.

PRINCIPLE WORKS: Bon Gaultier's Ballads (with W. E. Aytoun) 1845; Memoir of W. E. Aytoun, 1867; Life of the Prince Consort, 1875-80; Helena Faucit, 1900.

ABOUT: Dunckley, H. The Crown and the Cabinet; Martin, Sir T. Helena Faucit; Scotsman August 19, 1909.

MARTIN, WILLIAM (1801-October 22, 1867), writer of didactic juvenile literature, principal English user of the pseudonym "Peter Parley," was born at Woodbridge, Suffolk. He was the illegitimate son of a laundress, Jane Martin, who was employed by the officers of the garrison stationed at Woodbridge during the Napoleonic wars. His father was believed to be Sir Benjamin Blomfield, one of the officers.

Martin was educated at a dame school in Woodbridge and later informally by a Mrs. Thomas Howe (wife of a woolen-draper at Battersea, to whom he was for a time assistant) and her friend, Elizabeth Gurney Fry, the Quaker preacher and reformer. Thanks to the learning acquired in this way, he became master of a school at Uxbridge, remaining there until 1836, when he returned to Woodbridge.

The rest of his life was devoted to literary hackwork of various sorts. He wrote numberless cheap didactic books for children under the Parley pseudonym; still others under his own name; and a series ("Household Tracts for the People") as "Old Chatty Cheerful." From 1840 to the year of his death he was editor of *Peter Parley's Annual.*

Little more is known of Martin except that he died at his home, Holly Lodge, Woodbridge, at the age of sixty-six and was buried in the cemetery there. He was married three times and was survived by his third wife and two sons. In his later years he was reputedly given to habits of dissipation and loose morality.

The only interest attaching to Martin today is his association with the historic Parley pseudonym, which was shared by a number of English and American writers of indifferent talent in the second quarter of the nineteenth century. The original Parley was an American, Samuel Griswold Goodrich, whose prissy books of juvenile "instruction," thinly disguised as fiction, had in their time a vogue that now seems incredible. In England they became so popular that unscrupulous publishers soon found it profitable not only to "pirate" them (international copyrights were not to be perfected for another half-century) but also to issue Parley books of their own. In addition to Martin a lesser hack (GEORGE MOGRIDGE, 1787-1854) and four editor-publishers of sorts are definitely known to have used the name in England. There were also several American rivals. The combined output of the Parley books, original and imitative, was enormous: the number of titles ran literally into the hundreds and the sale of individual copies into millions.

Of the British imitators of Goodrich, Martin was the most prolific and (according to Goodrich's autobiography, *Recollections of a Lifetime*) the most annoying to the American. F. J. Harvey Darton, the noted authority on early juvenile literature, says of Martin: "He produced more and better Parley than any other rival; he was livelier than Goodrich." Despite this dubious distinction, Martin's writings are today without significance or interest, save as *curiosa.*   H. H.

WORKS: See above.

ABOUT: Darton, F. J. H. Children's Books in England; Goodrich, S. G. Recollections of a Lifetime; Cornhill Magazine ns73:542 November 1932.

MARTINEAU, HARRIET (June 12, 1802-June 27, 1876), novelist, political economist, and writer for children, was born in Norwich, the sixth of eight children of a woolen manufacturer of Huguenot descent, whose ancestors for generations had been surgeons. The family were Unitarians but not of the liberal variety; Harriet's childhood was wretched from over-discipline and Puritanical suppression, and she even tried once to kill herself to reach that heaven which seemed her only chance of happiness! She was besides born without the senses of smell and taste, suffered from nervous dyspepsia from childhood, and from the age of twelve became increasingly deaf. The mother, though as severe as the father, was intellectual, and insisted on her daughters being educated as well as her sons. With this object the boys were set to teach the girls. At eleven Harriet was sent to school for a year or two, but soon returned, already quite deaf, to her home, where she was so miserable that in 1819 she was sent for a fifteen months' visit to her very studious aunt and cousins, who kept a school in Bristol.

From this visit she emerged with a religiosity that bordered on the morbid. Her first writing was an article on "Female Writers in Practical Divinity" for the Unitarian *Monthly*

HARRIET MARTINEAU

Depository (edited by Charles Fox), to which she became a regular contributor. Then her brother Thomas, who had encouraged her, died; her father lost his fortune and grieved to death in 1826, and the young man, named Worthington, to whom against the opposition of his family she was engaged, became insane and then died. To add to all these troubles the last of the family's money was lost, and 1829 found Harriet in extreme poverty, helping to keep her mother and sisters alive by needlework.

In 1831 the *Monthly Depository* offered three prizes for essays on converting Roman Catholics, Jews, and Mohammedans to Unitarianism. Miss Martineau won all three. With the prize money she visited her brother James in Dublin, where she conceived the idea of fictitious stories to illustrate principles of political economy. At the end of the year she set out for London to find a publisher. Turned down everywhere, she accepted at last a very poor offer from Charles Fox's brother, and her "Political Economy Series" began publication by subscription.

It was an enormous and immediate success. Miss Martineau became a social lioness, courted by the great and solicited for stories and articles by editors and statesmen. She took a house in Conduit Street, but a year or so later joined her mother and aunt in a larger house in Westminster. Her days of poverty and failure were over.

In 1834 she visited the United States. Discretion and tact were never her characteristics; she insisted, though a foreign visitor, on attending and speaking at Abolitionist meetings, and her visit was attended by snubs and some threats of violence. The two censorious books she wrote on America on her return did not serve to endear her further to the Americans. She had already had a taste of censorship, her "Political Economy Series" being forbidden in Russia, Austria, and Italy. During this period she also wrote her best known children's tales: *The Peasant and the Prince, Feats on the Fjord, The Crofton Boys,* and *Settlers at Home,* which were published jointly in 1841 under the general title *The Playfellow.*

In 1845, after being told that she was the victim of incurable disease (though of what nature is not revealed), she became interested in mesmerism, of which she was ever after an advocate, even practising it herself on others. She decided to move to Westmoreland, and lived for the rest of her life in the Lake Country, where she became a familiar acquaintance of the Wordsworth ménage. She began also at this time her regular connection with the London *Daily News,* to which she contributed two articles weekly. For this paper she wrote sixty articles against the establishment of licensed brothels in India. Education for women also interested her, and in 1849 she became secretary of Bedford College for Women, affiliated with University College. This was after her return from an extended trip to Egypt and Palestine, her last journey abroad. Her later years, though she continued her voluminous —too voluminous—writing almost to the end, were spent largely in supervising her "two-acre farm" and in "good works" in the village, including lectures on sanitation and the evils of drink.

Her religious views had long passed from Unitarianism to a sort of Rationalism which she called "Necessarianism." In 1851 her joint writing of a book with H. G. Atkinson, a noted Free-Thinker, led to a final alienation from her brother James, the well known Unitarian divine, from whom she had been partly estranged for some time. In 1854 she was again told that she was hopelessly ill and could live only a short while—this time on the diagnosis of heart disease. She set to work to write her autobiography, expecting a near demise; she lived, however, for twenty-two years more, the autobiography not being published until after her death. She was buried, by her own wishes, without religious rites.

It must be frankly confessed that Harriet Martineau was something of a busybody, a universal mentor, and a prig. Probably no more utterly self-complacent person ever lived. But she had her virtues. She was intensely sincere and most courageous in her expression of her unpopular religious views; she really meant well by humanity, and her scrupulous ethical standard made her twice refuse offers of government pensions. As a writer she boasted that she wrote fast and never revised, and her work is evidence that she need not have confessed it. Just why her exceedingly dull and dreary stories should have aroused such enthusiasm it is hard to discern; army officers wept over them, Queen Victoria adored them, and the rich and great, who could never make her like or approve of them, flocked to her doors. Her one really readable book today is her autobiography, a magnificent piece of self-revelation. She was primarily a journalist, and a good one; historically she is of importance in the history of women and work. She was the perfect expression of her age—a fortunate thing for her in life, but ruinous to any posthumous reputation.   M. A. deF.

PRINCIPAL WORKS: *Fiction and Semi-Fiction*—Five Years of Youth (juvenile) 1831; Illustrations of Political Economy (9 vols.) 1832-34; Poor Laws and Paupers Illustrated, 1833; Illustrations of Taxation, 1834; Deerbrook, 1839; The Playfellow (juvenile) 1841; The Hour and the Man, 1841; Forest and Game Law Tales, 1845; Dawn Island, 1845; The Billow and the Rock, 1846; Merdhen; The Manor and the Eyrie; and Old Landmarks and Old Laws, 1852. *Religious Essays*—Devotional Exercises, 1823; Traditions of Palestine, 1830; Essential Faith of the Universal Church, 1831; The Faith as Unfolded by Many Prophets, 1832; Providence Manifested Through Israel, 1832; Addresses: With Prayers and Original Hymns, 1838; Letters on the Laws of Man's Nature and Development (with H. G. Atkinson) 1851. *History and Biography*—History of England During the Thirty Years' Peace (with Charles Knight) 1849; Introduction to the History of the Peace, 1851; Biographical Sketches, 1869; Autobiography, 1877. *Political Economy and Sociology*—Society in America, 1837; Retrospect of Western Travel, 1838; Eastern Life: Past and Present, 1848; The Philosophy of Comte, 1853; The Factory Controversy, 1855; Corporate Traditions and National Rights, 1857; British Rule in India, 1857; Suggestions Toward the Future Good of East India, 1858; England and Her Soldiers, 1859; Health, Husbandry, and Handicraft, 1861. *Miscellaneous*—How to Observe: Morals and Manners, 1838; Life in the Sick Room, 1843; Letters on Mesmerism, 1845; Household Education, 1849; A Complete Guide to the English Lakes, 1855.

ABOUT: Bosanquet, T. Harriet Martineau: An Essay in Comprehension; Colson, P. Victorian Portraits; Martineau, H. Autobiography; Pope-Hennessy, U. Three English Women in America.

MARTINEAU, JAMES (April 21, 1805-January 11, 1900), theologian, was the younger brother of Harriet Martineau, the essayist and novelist. Like her, he suffered from the rigors of a tyrannical household, but his was a sweet and gentle nature, and he escaped also by being sent away to school from the age of ten. From the Norwich Grammar School, he went to the school kept by the Unitarian minister, Lant Carpenter, at Bristol. The original intention was to have him trained for science and in 1821 he was apprenticed to a civil engineer at Derby; but the next year he decided to enter the Unitarian ministry, and enrolled at Manchester College, then in York, as a divinity student.

In 1827 he came back to Carpenter's school as an assistant, and in 1828 was ordained and became a co-pastor in Dublin, where he married Helen Higginson, daughter of a Unitarian minister in Derby. By her he had three sons and five daughters, and eked out his small pay to support this large family by tutoring.

In 1831 he became full minister, but resigned from scruples about accepting a government subsidy and went to Liverpool. There he took private pupils and held public classes in chemistry and other sciences, while he served again as co-pastor until 1835, when he was put in sole charge of the chapel. In 1840 he became professor of mental and moral philosophy and political economy at his alma mater, since moved to Manchester and called Manchester New College. With his family he spent 1848-49 in Germany, studying, while the Manchester chapel he served was being rebuilt. He began to write for various journals, and from 1845 to 1864 was co-editor of the *Prospective Review* and its successor the *National Review*. Manchester New College moved in 1853 to London, and in 1857 Martineau followed, to become professor of mental, moral and religious philosophy. In 1859 he was made co-pastor of Little Portland Street Chapel, and full pastor in 1860.

In 1869 he became principal of Manchester New College, and in 1872, on his physician's advice, gave up preaching permanently. He had been suggested as professor of philosophy for the new University College (London University), but was kept out by the opposition of the historian George Grote, who was one of its founders. A controversy with the scientist Tyndall also marked this period. As

JAMES MARTINEAU

his books found successive publication, and he was recognized as one of the two real theological philosophers of the time (F. D. Maurice was the other), honors poured in upon him: he received honorary degrees from Harvard, Leyden, Edinburgh, Oxford, and Dublin. In 1885, at the age of eighty, he resigned his principalship, but acted as president of the college for two years more. He retained his faculties until the last, though he began to show some confusion and failure of memory. As late as 1898 he indulged in mountain climbing near his country home in Invernessshire! Finally he sank quietly into death within three months of having attained the age of ninety-five.

Martineau was a man of great charm, courtly and aristocratic in manner, markedly handsome, a witty conversationalist. His lectures were dry, but his sermons were eloquently rendered: he said "a sermon should be a lyric utterance." In politics he was an old-fashioned Whig, against home rule, opposed to free education, and a sympathizer with the Confederate States in the American Civil War. His religious views broadened from their original orthodox Unitarianism, but in the direction not of free thought but of belief in free will. He was truly modest and deeply devout.

Strangely his best books were written when he was nearly eighty. His work is faulty in arrangement, often diffuse—which is odd when one considers the scholarly precision of his mind—but penetrating. His chief value is not as an original thinker, but as a critic of other men's thought. M. A. deF.

PRINCIPAL WORKS: The Rationale of Religious Enquiry, 1836; Unitarianism Defended, 1839; Hymns for the Christian Church and Home, 1840; Endeavours After the Christian Life: 1st series, 1843, 2nd series, 1847; Miscellanies, 1852; Studies of Christianity, 1858; Essays: Philosophical and Theological, 1868; Hymns of Praise and Prayer, 1873; Religion as Affected by Modern Materialism, 1874; Modern Materialism: Its Attitude Towards Theology, 1876; Hours of Thought on Sacred Things: 1st series, 1876, 2nd series, 1879; Ideal Substitutes for God Considered, 1879; The Relation Between Ethics and Religion, 1881; A Study of Spinoza, 1882; Types of Ethical Theory, 1885; A Study of Religion, 1888; The Seat of Authority in Religion, 1890; Essays, Reviews, and Addresses, 1890-91; Home Prayers, 1891; Faith and Self Surrender, 1897.

ABOUT: Carpenter, J. E. James Martineau: Theologian and Teacher; Drummond, J. & Upton, C. B. Life and Letters of James Martineau; Jackson, A. W. James Martineau: A Biography and a Study; Outlook 64:259 February 3, 1900.

MASSEY, GERALD (May 29, 1828-October 29, 1907), poet, was born in a hut at Gamble Wharf, on the canal near Tring. His father was a poor canal boatman who reared a large family on ten shillings a week. No wonder Massey said he had "no childhood." After a very few terms in the national school, he went to work at eight in a silk mill at

Tring, his hours being from 5 a.m. to 6 p.m. Then he worked at straw plaiting, and at fifteen became an errand boy in London. All this time, in what leisure he had, he read, studied French, and wrote poetry. Reading of Paine and Volney made him a Free-Thinker and a Chartist, and in 1849 he edited the Chartist paper, the Spirit of Freedom. F. D. Maurice converted him to Christian Socialism. After 1860 he abandoned the writing of poetry altogether for journalism. He had already worked a while for the publisher, John Chapman, and in 1854 had moved to Edinburgh with his family, where he supported himself by writing and lecturing. After moving from place to place, Earl Brownlow gave him a house on his estate near Little Gaddesden, where Massey lived from 1862 to 1877. He became an ardent Spiritualist, and finally a bit "cracked" on the subject; he was quite convinced that his last works, his "psychic" compilations of Egyptian history, were far better than his poems. As a matter of fact, they were rubbish. In 1863 he received a civil list pension. He made three lecture tours in the United States and Canada, and one in Australasia. He was twice married: in 1850 to Rosina Knowles, who died in 1866, leaving three daughters and one son, and in 1868 to Eva Byron, by whom he had one son and four daughters.

Massey's poems show the defects of his education, but he is a fine lyrist, powerful and imaginative. His greatest recognition came from American readers.

PRINCIPAL WORKS: Poems and Chansons, 1848; Voices of Freedom and Lyrics of Love, 1850; The Ballad of Babe Christabel and Other Poems, 1854; Poetical Works, 1857; A Tale of Eternity and Other Poems, 1869; My Lyrical Life, 1899.

ABOUT: Collins, J. C. Studies in Poetry and Criticism; Massey, G. Poetical Works (see Biographical Sketch); Miles, A. H. Poets and Poetry of the Century; Book Monthly July 1905 and September 1907.

MASSEY, WILLIAM NATHANAEL (1809-October 25, 1881), historian, was primarily a politician. Nothing is known of his birth and education. He was called to the bar in 1844, and was recorder of Portsmouth in 1852 and of Plymouth in 1855. He was a member of Parliament, as a liberal, from 1855 to 1863, served as under-secretary for the home department, and in 1853 was chairman of committees. From 1863 to 1868 he was financial member of the government of India. He returned to England in 1868, and was made a privy councillor. He was again elected to Parliament in 1872, and served until his death.

Massey was a very able and well informed man, but notoriously lazy and ambitionless. His writing is lucid, but without distinction.

The only thing he wrote besides his history was an essay on legal reform.

PRINCIPAL WORK: A History of England During the Reign of George III (unfinished) 1855-63.

MASSON, DAVID (December 2, 1822-October 6, 1907), Scottish biographer and miscellaneous writer, was born in Aberdeen, the son of a stonecutter. He was educated at the Aberdeen Grammar School and at Marischal College (Aberdeen University), where he took his M.A. degree in 1839, with first honors. Until 1842 he studied divinity at Edinburgh, but decided not to enter the church, and for two years served as editor of an Aberdeen weekly, *The Banner*. During this time he went to London and met Thomas and Jane Carlyle, through whose influence his first article was published, in *Fraser's Magazine*. From 1844 to 1847 he was on the staff of W. and R. Chambers, the Edinburgh publishers, issuing a series of text books on history. Then he went to London to live as a contributor to the magazines and the *Encyclopaedia Brittannica*. There he was a member of the circle of the Carlyles, Thackeray, and other notables.

In 1853 Masson married Emily Orme; they had one son and three daughters. In the year of his marriage he became professor of English literature at University College, London. From 1859 to 1867 he served as the first editor of *Macmillan's Magazine*, and in 1863 also edited another magazine called *The Reader*. In 1865 he became professor of rhetoric and English literature at the University of Edinburgh. He was very popular with his pupils, and remained in the post until 1895. He was particularly interested in the higher education of women, and lectured in its behalf; Masson Hall, the women's dormitory at Edinburgh, was named for him in 1897. From 1880 to 1899 he edited the Privy Council Register of Scotland. In 1893 he was appointed historiographer royal for Scotland, and in 1896 professor of ancient history at the Royal Scottish Academy.

Besides his original writing, Masson edited the works of Milton, Goldsmith, and DeQuincey. He remains a standard authority on these authors, a writer of good judgment and sound sense. The only defect of his writing is that it is almost too painstaking and thorough, so that the amount of detail given is often overwhelming.

PRINCIPAL WORKS: Ancient History, 1848; Essays: Biographical and Critical, 1856; British Novelists and Their Styles, 1859; Life of Milton, 1859-80; Recent British Philosophy, 1865; Edinburgh Sketches and Memories, 1892; Memories of London in the Forties (ed. by F. Masson) 1908.

ABOUT: Masson, D. Edinburgh Sketches and Memories; Memories of London in the Forties; Scotsman November 24, 1897 and October 8, 1907.

MATHERS, HELEN BUCKINGHAM (Mrs. Henry Reeves) (August 26, 1853-March 11, 1920), novelist, was born in Somerset, the eldest daughter of a well-to-do father. She was educated at the Chantry School in Frome. In 1876 she married Henry Albert Reeves, a well known orthopedic surgeon, and author of several surgical works, who died in 1914. Her life was completely uneventful. She was a prolific novelist, producing almost a book a year from 1875 to her last years. Her novels were very popular, especially in her earlier period, but they are highly sentimental and sugared, and are quite outdated today.

PRINCIPAL WORKS: Comin' Thro' the Rye, 1875; Cherry Ripe, 1877; My Lady Greensleeves, 1879; Jock o'Hazeldean, 1884; The Fashion of this World, 1886; The Sin of Hagar; Blind Justice.

MATHEWS, CHARLES JAMES (December 26, 1803-June 24, 1878), playwright, was born in Liverpool, son of the celebrated actor Charles Mathews. He was educated at the Merchant Taylors' School and at a private school kept by the lexicographer Richardson. In 1819 he was apprenticed to an architect. He made his first appearance as an actor in an amateur performance in 1822. In 1823 he went to Ireland to design a house, but instead accompanied the prospective owner to Italy. For two years thereafter he was in Wales as architect to a coal and iron company. He set up in London as an architect, but spent most of his time writing songs and light plays. From 1827 to 1830 he was in Italy, where he nearly died of smallpox and malaria. This life of dilettante leisure lasted until 1835, when his father became bankrupt, and the son had to go on the stage professionally. He became one of the best known comedians of his time, the only English actor who also played in French in Paris.

In 1838 he married Lucia Elizabeth Bartolozzi, better known as Madame Vestris, and with her leased Covent Garden Theater. He had to give it up in 1842, overwhelmed by debt, and from this time on his life was a hopeless struggle to escape from bankruptcy, interspersed with imprisonments for debt, giving him an entirely undeserved reputation as a shiftless Bohemian. His wife died in 1856, a month after he had been released from prison. The next year, in New York, he married another actress, Lizzie (Mrs. A. H.) Davenport, and in 1870 he started with her a two years' world tour. In 1875 they toured India. He died on tour in Manchester, having acted up to two weeks before his death.

Mathews adapted and translated many plays, and it is hard to say which of the numerous titles ascribed to him are original. They were nearly all light farces. None of his plays survived his acting of them; a few have been published in play collections.

PRINCIPAL WORKS: The Humpbacked Lover, 1835; Patter vs. Clatter, 1838; Black Domino, 1838; The White Milliner, 1840; The Savannah, 1860; The Chain of Events (with Slingsby Lawrence); Married for Money; Cool as a Cucumber.

ABOUT: Colman, J. Plays and Playwrights I Have Known; Dickens, C. Jr. The Life of Charles James Mathews: Chiefly Autobiographical; Mathews, A. Memoirs of Charles Mathews.

MATHIAS, THOMAS JAMES (1754?-August 1835), poet and scholar, was born in a family connected with the court, his father being sub-treasurer of the queen's household. He probably attended Eton, and certainly entered Trinity College, Cambridge, in 1770, taking his M.A. in 1777 and becoming a fellow. In 1782 he inherited his father's office, and later became the queen's treasurer. In 1812 he was librarian of Buckingham Palace. He was an ardent devotee of the poet Thomas Gray, and issued an edition of his works so vastly expensive that it bankrupted him. Worry over this brought on a paralytic stroke, and in 1814 he went to Italy for his health and remained there the rest of his life, the recipient of a pension from the Royal Society of Literature. *The Pursuits of Literature,* a satirical poem which created a sensation and called forth many rejoinders from the authors attacked, was published anonymously and its author not known until long after his death. He wrote numerous other satirical epistles in prose and verse, all anonymous, most of them savage and all of them very dull. Mathias' other claim to fame is better grounded; he was the greatest English scholar in Italian after the days of Milton, and wrote many Italian poems and translated Milton, Spenser, and other English poets into Italian. He died in Naples, where he had lived for many years.

PRINCIPAL WORKS: The Pursuits of Literature, 1794-97; Prose on Various Occasions, 1801; Lyrics From Italian Poets, 1802, 1808, 1819.

ABOUT: Gentleman's Magazine 1835:1-524; 2:550.

MATURIN, CHARLES ROBERT (1780-October 30, 1824), Irish novelist and dramatist, was born in Dublin the son of an official in the Irish post office. The youngest of six sons, he showed as a child the interest in the theatre which was later to scandalize relatives and parishioners. His early taste for the fiction of Radcliffe, Lewis, and their ilk was enhanced by a romantic family legend concerning the mysterious origin of his French Huguenot ancestor, Gabriel Maturin.

Clerical traditions of the family made the profession to which young Maturin's histrionic talent pointed out of the question and he entered Trinity College at the age of fifteen (1785) to prepare for the church. Having distinguished himself in oratory and composition-writing, he took Holy Orders and in 1803 married Miss Henrietta Kingsbury. He was curate first at Loughrea and in 1804-05 at-

C. R. MATURIN

tained the curacy of St. Peter's in Dublin, which he held until his death.

Spiritual concerns, tutoring, and domestic affairs (Maturin was called "the most uxorious man breathing") did not prevent his writing his first novel, *Fatal Revenge: or, The Family of Montorio.* Published under the pseudonym of Dennis Jasper Murphy, it was of the Gothic or "terror" order, owing much to Mrs. Radcliffe's *Italian* and Lewis' *Monk.* Scott's review termed it "a remarkable instance of genius degraded by the labor in which it was engaged." Maturin's bent toward the Gothic shows itself in everything he attempted. Scott's influence brought Maturin's tragedy, *Bertram,* to Drury Lane May 9, 1816. The terror element was paramount; the play abounded with mysterious strangers, forced marriages, shipwreck, and murder; Edmund Kean played the title-rôle; and the play was successful. Maturin, after being fêted in London, returned to Dublin and embarked on a lavish mode of existence which later failures proved unwarranted. Conspiring against the efforts of his numerous friends, his typically Irish improvidence kept him in continual financial straits.

Maturin's novel, *Women,* is an early specimen of the psychological novel. In *Melmoth,* his greatest success, he indulged his Gothic forte and achieved genuine power with a satanic-Faustian theme based on an unusual framework of interlacing episodes. *The Albigenses,* patterned on Scott's novels, was published the year Maturin died. He never met the author of *Waverley* and the letters recording their epistolary friendship were burned by Maturin's son who, a better clergyman than his father, deplored his sire's literary propensities.

Maturin holds a disputed position among the writers of Gothic fiction. He was more highly regarded on the continent than in England, where it was felt that he overloaded his horrors and defeated his purpose by saturation. Had he lived longer, he might have controlled the exuberance of his literary flow and produced in his vein a work placing him beside, instead of below, Radcliffe and Lewis in the Gothic hierarchy. P. B. S.

PRINCIPAL WORKS: *Novels*—Fatal Revenge: or, The Family of Montorio, 1807; The Wild Irish Boy, 1808; The Milesian Chief, 1812; Women: or, Pour et Contre, 1818; Melmoth: The Wanderer, 1820; The Albigenses, 1824. *Drama*—Bertram: or, The Castle of St. Aldabrand, 1816; Manuel, 1817; Fredolfo, 1819. *Sermons*—Sermons, 1819; Five Sermons on the Errors of the Roman Catholic Clergy, 1824. *Verse*—The Universe, 1821.

ABOUT: Idman, N. Charles Robert Maturin; Scholten, W. Charles Robert Maturin.

MAURICE, (JOHN) FREDERICK DENISON (August 29, 1805-April 1, 1872), theologian and founder of the "Christian Socialist" movement, was born near Lowestoft, the son of a Unitarian minister. It was the father's sorrow to see his wife and every one of his children successively abandon his religion and become members of either the Baptist Church or the Church of England.

Maurice was sent to Trinity College, Cambridge, in 1823 to study law. He left in 1827, unable to secure a degree because he was not a member of the Established Church, and went to London—not, however, to enter the bar, but to become editor of the *Athenaeum*. The influence of Coleridge, whom he never met, changed his religious views, and he entered the Anglican Church in 1831. The year before he had enrolled at Exeter College, Oxford—one of the very rare Englishmen to attend both major universities. He received his B.A. in 1832, and soon after was ordained. In 1834 he was a curate in Warwickshire, from where he went to London as chaplain of Guy's Hospital. From 1839 to 1841 he also edited the *Educational Magazine*. In 1840 he became professor of modern history and English literature at King's College, and in 1846 chaplain of Lincoln's Inn, resigning his hospital appointment. He also added to his professorial duties the chair of ecclesiastical history at King's College.

Maurice's keen social feeling, culminating in his connection with the Christian Socialist movement, made him one of the founders, with Ruskin and others, of Queen's College for Women (where he taught also) in 1848, and principal of the Working Men's College in 1854. He also edited *Politics for the People*, the Christian Socialist organ, and was active in the early Cooperatives.

This affiliation with the workers (including his close friendship with Charles Kingsley, the poet and clergyman, who was suspect to the orthodox), combined with the publication of his *Theological Essays* in 1853—adjudged heretical because he claimed that "eternal punishment" did not mean "everlasting in duration"—led to a scandal, and Dr. Jelf, principal of King's College, ordered him to resign. He was warmly defended by his friends, by none more warmly than Tennyson. Queen's College, which he had helped to establish, took similar action, but Lincoln's Inn refused to discharge him as chaplain.

However, he resigned from this position in 1860 to become minister of St. Peter's Chapel, in Cavendish Square. In 1866 he was appointed professor of casuistry, moral theology, and moral philosophy at Cambridge, where the remainder of his life was spent.

In 1837 he had married Anna Barton, who died in 1845, leaving him two sons. In 1849 he remarried, his second wife being Georgiana Hare-Naylor. These ladies were sister-in-law and half-sister, respectively, of his two greatest friends, John Sterling and Julius Hare.

Maurice's health broke in 1870, though he continued to teach up to the end of 1871. In the following spring he died. The King's College episode had long been forgotten, and he was universally accepted and admired.

"The most beautiful human soul I have ever known," Kingsley called him. He was small, but fine of feature, with an ascetic, spiritual face. As a teacher he was over the boys' heads, and was too mild to keep discipline, but the rarer souls among them loved him. Scrupulous, unworldly, almost exaggeratedly diffident, it took real courage for him to force himself into the arena of social movement and theological dispute. His passion was the unity of the Christian Church, and he disliked to be

FREDERICK DENISON MAURICE

425

called a leader of the "Broad Church" or of any faction of Anglicanism.

He was perhaps the greatest spiritual influence of the Victorian era, restoring the Platonic outlook to Anglican theology. But he belongs to divinity rather than to literature. Most of his many books were published sermons and lectures, too numerous and too utterly dead to be worth listing. His style was exceedingly obscure, and it is safe to say that only an impassioned theologian would or could read him today. It is as a man, and as "the father of Christian Socialism," that Maurice may lay claim to contemporary note.

M. A. deF.

PRINCIPAL WORKS: Eustace Conway (novel) 1834; The Kingdom of Christ, 1838; Christmas Day, 1843; The Epistle to the Hebrews, 1846; The Religions of the World, 1847; The Lord's Prayer, 1848; The Prayer Book, 1849; The Church a Family, 1850; The Old Testament, 1851; Theological Essays, 1853; The Prophets and Kings; 1853; Ecclesiastical History, 1854; The Unity of the New Testament, 1854; Learning and Working, 1855; What Is Revelation? 1859; The Claims of the Bible and Science, 1863; The Gospel of the Kingdom of Heaven, 1864; The Workman and the Franchise, 1866; The Commandments as Instruments of National Reformation, 1866; The Ground and Object of Hope for Mankind, 1867; The Conscience, 1868; Social Morality, 1869; Moral and Metaphysical Philosophy, 1872; The Friendship of Books, 1874.

ABOUT: Hutton, R. H. Essays on Some of the Modern Guides of English Thought in Matters of Faith; Masterman, C. G. F. Life of Frederick Denison Maurice; Maurice, F. The Life of Frederick Denison Maurice: Chiefly Told in His Letters; Contemporary Review 135:584 May 1929; Hibbert Journal 28:311 January 1930; Illustrated London News 60:358 April 13, 1872; Outlook 80:967 August 19, 1905; Spectator 142:609 April 20, 1929; 150:330 March 10, 1933.

MAURICE, THOMAS (1754-March 30, 1824), poet and historian, was born in Hertford, the son of a schoolmaster who died in 1763. His mother remarried unhappily, and his step-father was unkind to him. He was educated at Christ's Hospital and at Kingswood School, Bath. He entered the Inner Temple, but instead of reading law devoted himself to study of the classics. In 1774 he entered St. John's College, Oxford, the next year transferred to University College, and secured his B.A. in 1778 and his M.A. in 1808. He was ordained and became a curate in Essex. In 1785 he bought a chaplaincy of a regiment about to be disbanded, and thereby received half-pay the remainder of his life. In 1798 he was a vicar in Warwickshire. The same year he became assistant keeper of manuscripts of the British Museum, and in 1804 was given another living in Kent. All three of these posts he held for life, but he lived and wrote in the British Museum, and died in his apartments there. In 1786 he had married a Miss Pearce, but she died in 1790.

Maurice was the first to popularize Oriental history and especially the history of Oriental religions for English readers. He was painstaking and industrious, but appallingly dull. His poetry is so boresome that it almost becomes a burlesque.

PRINCIPAL WORKS: Poems and Miscellaneous Pieces, 1779; Westminster Abbey, 1784; Indian Antiquities, 1793-1800; Poems: Epistolary, Lyric, and Elegiacal, 1800; Richmond Hill, 1807; Memoirs, 1819-22.

ABOUT: Maurice, T. Memoirs.

MAURIER, GEORGE DU. See DU MAURIER, GEORGE

MAXWELL, LADY CAROLINE STIRLING. See NORTON, CAROLINE E. S.

MAXWELL, JAMES CLERK (November 13, 1831-November 5, 1879), Scottish physicist, was born in Edinburgh. His father, originally James Clerk, had added the name of Maxwell to inherit an estate. His mother died in 1839. He was educated at Edinburgh Academy and the University of Edinburgh. At fifteen he had already sent mathematical papers to the Royal Society of Edinburgh. In 1850 he entered Trinity College, Cambridge, receiving his B.A. in 1854 as second wrangler (mathematician). The next year he became fellow and lecturer, and in 1856 professor of natural philosophy at Marischal College, Aberdeen. In 1858 he married the principal's daughter, Katherine Mary Dewar; they had no children.

In 1860 Marischal College became the University of Aberdeen, and Maxwell resigned his chair. He was immediately appointed professor of natural history at King's College, London. He resigned in 1865 and retired for private study, but in 1871 was persuaded to become the first professor of experimental physics at Cambridge, establishing the laboratory there. He died at only forty-eight, to the great loss of science.

Maxwell did important work in the theory of color, the investigation of the rings of Saturn, and the kinetic theory of gases; but his greatest fame comes from his immensely valuable researches in electricity and magnetism. His more elementary books are clear and simple as well as scholarly, for he was an unusually good teacher.

PRINCIPAL WORKS: The Theory of Heat, 1871; Treatise on Electricity and Magnetism, 1873; Matter and Motion, 1876; Collected Papers (ed. by W. D. Niven) 1890.

ABOUT: Campbell, L. and Garnett, W. Life of J. Clerk Maxwell; Crowther, J. G. Men of Science.

MAXWELL, MARY ELIZABETH. See BRADDON, MARY ELIZABETH

MAXWELL, WILLIAM HAMILTON

(1792-December 29, 1850), Irish novelist, was born in County Down. His father was a merchant, of Scottish descent. He was educated at Trinity College, Dublin, where he wasted a good deal of his time, but nevertheless took his B.A. with distinction in 1812. He then entered the army and was a captain of infantry at the battle of Waterloo. For several years after leaving the army he lived at home, reading, hunting, and shooting, able to lead this leisurely life because he had married an heiress. Suddenly he decided to take holy orders, and in 1820 was made rector of a living at Ballagh, Connemara. Here he had few parishioners, but there was plenty of game, which suited him better. He was a typical sporting clergyman of a type commoner in the eighteenth than the nineteenth century. The Marquis of Sligo gave him a house rent free, and he lived without much concern for his clerical duties, writing for the *Dublin University Magazine* and *Bentley's Miscellany*, editing the *Military and Naval Almanack*, and composing his novels. This delightful existence came to an abrupt end when in 1844 he was deprived of his living for non-residence.

By this time his wife's money was spent and she was dead, and since Maxwell was utterly thriftless, he spent his last years in poverty and ill-health. He went to Scotland and with the occasional assistance of friends who enjoyed his amiable company managed to eke out some sort of existence until he died, near Edinburgh, at fifty-eight.

Maxwell wrote very rapidly, and often carelessly. His novels are of interest chiefly because he originated a school of Irish fiction, rollicking and adventurous and devil-may-care, that culminated in the far better work of Charles Lever and Samuel Lover. Besides his novels, he wrote frequently on sport and military topics.

PRINCIPAL WORKS: O'Hara, 1825; Wild Sports of the West [of Ireland] 1832; Stories of Waterloo, 1834; My Life (novel) 1835; The Bivouac, 1837; Rambling Recollections of a Soldier of Fortune, 1842; Captain O'Sullivan, 1846; Barry O'Lynn, 1848; Erin-Go-Bragh, 1859.

ABOUT: Maxwell, W. H. Rambling Recollections of a Soldier of Fortune; Erin-Go-Bragh (see Biographical Sketch by Dr. Maginn).

MAXWELL, SIR WILLIAM STIRL-

ING-. See STIRLING-MAXWELL, SIR WILLIAM

MAY, SIR THOMAS ERSKINE (Lord

Farnborough) (February 8, 1815-May 17, 1886), historian, was born in London. He attended the Bedford Grammar School, and in 1831 was made assistant librarian of the House of Commons. He was called to the bar from the Middle Temple in 1838. The next year he married Louisa Laughton; they had no children. From 1847 to 1856 he was examiner of petitions for private bills for both houses of Parliament, and from 1856 to 1871 he was clerk assistant. From 1871 up to a month before his death he was clerk of the House of Commons. He was made C.B. in 1860 and K.C.B. in 1866, in 1874 received an honorary D.C.L. from Oxford, and in 1885 was made a privy councillor. He resigned his clerkship in April 1886; in May was raised to the peerage as Baron Farnborough; and a week later died suddenly in Westminster Palace.

May was essentially a constitutional lawyer, whose history is written purely from the constitutional point of view.

PRINCIPAL WORKS: A Practical Treatise on the Law, Privileges, Proceedings, and Usages of Parliament, 1844; The Constitutional History of England, 1861-63; Democracy in Europe, 1877.

ABOUT: Biography January 1882; London Times May 18, 25, 27, 1886.

MAYHEW, HENRY (1812-July 25, 1887),

miscellaneous writer, was born in London, the son of an attorney. He was sent to Westminster School, but ran away to sea and made a voyage to Calcutta. He was then articled to his father, but soon abandoned the law for literature. From 1831 to 1839, with Gilbert Abbott à Beckett, he published and edited *Figaro in London*, a humorous magazine. In 1832 he edited *The Thief*, the first of the magazines made up of clippings and reprints. His first farce, *The Wandering Minstrel*, was produced in 1834. In 1841 he became one of the founders, and for a while a joint-editor, of *Punch*. For several years he spent much of his time in Germany, spending all of 1862 there. In 1870 he edited a short-lived magazine, *Only Once a Year*. Another phase of his work, very different from his humorous writing, was sociological research, with particular reference to the conditions of the poor and of criminals; in 1871 he prepared a report on workingmen's clubs. His two brothers, with one of whom he collaborated, were also humorous writers.

PRINCIPAL WORKS: The Greatest Plague of Life (with A. S. Mayhew) 1847; Adventures of the Sandboys Family, 1851; London Labour and the London Poor (with J. Binny) 1851; The Mormons, 1852; The Wonders of Science, 1855; The Rhine, 1856; The Criminal Prisons of London, 1862; The Boyhood of Martin Luther, 1865; Ephemerides: or, The Comic Almanack, 1870; London Characters, 1874.

ABOUT: Athenaeum August 6, 1887; London Times July 27, 1887.

MAYNE, JOHN (March 26, 1759-March

14, 1836), Scottish poet, was born in Dumfries of a working-class family and educated at the local Grammar School. He learned printing and became a printer on the Dumfries *Journal*. In 1782 his family moved to

Glasgow and he accompanied them, working as printer for a firm of publishers in that city for five years. In 1787 he moved to London, where he lived thenceforth. He secured a position on *The Star*, first as printer, finally as proprietor and joint editor. Many of his poems first appeared in his newspaper. Occasionally also he contributed poems to the *Gentleman's Magazine*, the *Glasgow Magazine*, and *Ruddiman's Weekly Magazine* (Edinburgh). He thought of himself as British rather than Scottish, and his *English, Scots, and Irishmen* is a patriotic attempt to express this viewpoint. Nevertheless, he spent nearly fifty years in a state of homesickness, constantly writing and talking about revisiting Dumfries, but never finding an opportunity to do so. He died in London without seeing Scotland again.

Mayne's best known poem was *The Siller Gun*. Scott thought very highly of this vivacious work, considering Mayne nearly on a level with Burns. And Burns himself, seeing some of Mayne's poems in *Ruddiman's Weekly Magazine*, paid him the compliment of borrowing some of his lines and incorporating them in poems of his own, thinking them not original compositions but adaptations of authentic folk poetry.

PRINCIPAL WORKS: The Siller Gun, 1777-1836; Glasgow, 1783; Logan Braes, 1789; English, Scots, and Irishmen, 1803.

ABOUT: Wilson, G. Poets and Poetry of Scotland; Gentleman's Magazine May 1836.

MAYOR, JOHN EYTON BICKERSTETH (January 28, 1825-December 1, 1910), classical scholar, was the third son of a missionary, formerly a surgeon, and was born at his father's mission in Ceylon. He was a very precocious child, reveling in books from the age of four. Taken back to England in early childhood, he was a student at Christ's Hospital from 1833 to 1836, at Shrewsbury from 1838 to 1844, and at St. John's College, Cambridge (where he and his two brothers were all fellows) from 1844 to 1849. Until 1853 he was classical master at Marlborough College; then he returned to St. John's and lived there the remainder of his life.

As a lecturer he was not a success, since his vast learning made it impossible for him to condense. He brought with him his immense library, the growth of which made it necessary for him to rent a house for it. In 1855 he took holy orders, but remained at the university, where he was respected for his almost unwieldy erudition. He was well acquainted not only with Latin and Greek, his own subjects, but with French, Italian, Spanish, and particularly German and Dutch; in 1907, at eighty-two, he learned Esperanto with ease.

In 1864 Mayor, who among his antiquarian interests placed first the history of his own

J. E. B. MAYOR

college, was made university librarian. During this incumbency he cataloged all the manuscripts in the library. He resigned in three years, however, so as to have more leisure for his studies and for the making of his unique collection of biographical notes. (Many of these were put at the service of the *Dictionary of National Biography*.) In 1872 he was appointed professor of Latin, but seems not to have conducted classes. In 1875 he made his only visit to Rome, though he traveled occasionally elsewhere on the Continent. In 1902 he was made president of St. John's College.

Though Mayor wrote very few original books, the list of those he edited (either Latin classics or English antiquarian works) is almost endless. Outside of his work, his chief interests were in mission work and in vegetarianism; he was for many years president of the Vegetarian Society. He received many honorary degrees, and was a member of the first council of the British Academy. He never married.

At eighty-five Mayor was still active both physically and mentally, and in fact was dressing to go to read prayers in the university chapel when he died of sudden heart failure.

In appearance, he was rather unprepossessing, but he was respected for his dignity and his old-fashioned courtesy. He left a great amount of work unfinished, even at an advanced age planning as if he still had many years in which to labor.

As a writer it is scarcely possible to judge him at all, since his few original volumes are either propaganda for vegetarianism or outdated missionary arguments. It was as an editor of the Latin classics, particularly of Juvenal, Quintillian, and Pliny, that he was chiefly noted, and even this work has now been superseded by later scholars. In his own time, however, he was one of the foremost classicists of the day.　　　　　M. A. deF.

PRINCIPAL WORKS: *Edited*—Thirteen Satires of Juvenal, 1853; Two Lives of Nicholas Ferrar, 1855; Autobiography of Matthew Robinson, 1856; Cicero's Second Philippic, 1861: Life of Ambrose Bonwicke, 1870; Life of William Bedell, 1871; Homer's Odyssey, 1872-82; Quintillian, 1872; Pliny's Letters, 1880; Cambridge Under Queen Anne, 1911. *Miscellaneous* —First Greek Reader, 1868; Modicus Cibi Medicus Sibi, 1880; Spain, Portugal, the Bible, 1895; The Spanish Reformed Church, 1895; Plain Living and High Thinking, 1897; Jacula Prudentium: A First German Reader, 1910; Twelve Cambridge Sermons (ed. by H. F. Stewart) 1911; Twelve Parochial Sermons (ed. by H. F. Stewart) 1913.

ABOUT: Mayor, J. E. B. Twelve Cambridge Sermons (see Memoir by H. F. Stewart); London Times December 2, 1910.

MEEKE, MRS. MARY (d. 1816?), novelist, is almost unknown except for her books. She is probably the Mrs. Meeke, wife of the Rev. Francis Meeke, who died in Staffordshire in October 1816. She may also have written a number of novels under the name of Gabrielli, which may perhaps have been her maiden name (in which case she was probably of Italian descent), and it is also probable that several of her novels were published posthumously. Her work is pure trash of the commercial variety; in fact, she advised budding novelists always to consult their publishers before starting a book, so as to be sure of writing what readers would like! But she was a great favorite of Macaulay's, though he was forced to agree that she was his "favorite among bad novelists." Miss Mitford also confessed that she was addicted to these novels, all built on a pattern in which the supposedly poor and humble hero turns out to be a wealthy duke. Besides her novels, Mrs. Meeke also translated from the French and German.

PRINCIPAL WORKS: Poems, 1782; Count St. Blancard, 1795; Ellesmere, 1799; Midnight Weddings, 1802; Ellen, Heiress of the Castle, 1807; Matrimony the Height of Bliss or Extreme of Misery, 1811; Conscience, 1814.

MEREDITH, GEORGE (February 12, 1828-May 18, 1909), novelist and poet, was born at 73 High Street, Portsmouth. He was the only son of Augustus Meredith and Jane Eliza Macnamara, daughter of a prosperous innkeeper. The Merediths were a lively, intelligent, handsome family who were successful in looking "above" their well-known ancestral tailoring-establishment. Meredith's grandfather (the 'Old Mel' of *Evan Harrington*) is said to have posed as a marquis at Bath and he was accepted in county society around Portsmouth. One of his granddaughters became a marquise. His death interrupted the medical training of Augustus, who had

to take over the tailoring business. Augustus' wife was a beautiful, talented woman who died when George was five.

This family history is significant because it was not until after Meredith's death that anything concerning his birthplace or forebears became known to the world at large. Meredith's silence about his origin was caused by British prejudice against tailors. The Ruskins' family closet concealed a tailor-skeleton and Meredith in maturity allowed it to be understood that he was of high-born, illegitimate parentage.

Meredith as a boy was petted and cared for and the unhappy childhood he later obliquely referred to must have been due to temperamental maladjustment. He was a reserved and sensitive lad who disliked other children and was afraid of ghosts and the dark. He was handsome, aristocratic-looking, better dressed, and more genteelly educated than his Portsmouth contemporaries, who called him "gentleman Georgy." In 1841 Augustus Meredith moved his establishment to London. George was sent to the Moravian school at Neuwied on the Rhine. The romantic Coblentz-Cologne country, German literature, music and thought had a strong influence on his mental growth. He probably spent the years of 1844-1845 in his father's shop in London.

In 1846 he was articled as clerk to W. R. S. Charnock, a solicitor. Meredith said of his employer that he "had neither business nor morals." But Charnock was a cultured man, a member of the Arundel Club to which Dickens belonged, and apparently released George from his articles when he decided to abandon law for literature. Through Charnock he met Edward Gryffydh Peacock and Mary Ellen Peacock Nicolls, the son and daughter of Thomas Love Peacock, the novelist and former friend of Shelley. In Charnock's manuscript magazine, the *Monthly Observer*, appeared Meredith's earliest published poem, "Chillian Wallah," which attained actual print in *Chambers's Journal* in 1849. That year Meredith's father emigrated to Capetown, South Africa, leaving Meredith to take lodgings. He had little money at this time, but the story that he lived on uncooked oatmeal and water is ridiculous.

On April 9, 1849, Meredith married Mrs. Nicolls, widow of a naval lieutenant drowned at sea four months after marriage. A beautiful, brilliant woman with a temperament much like Meredith's own, she was nine years his senior. They lived mostly at Peacock's several homes and the first few years of their life together were fairly happy. They had many literary friends and similar literary pursuits. They collaborated on some poetry and together compiled a treatise on cookery, a science in which both—Mrs. Meredith as the

GEORGE MEREDITH

daughter of a famous epicure, Meredith as grandson of an innkeeper—took a creative as well as an appreciative interest. Although in after years Meredith never mentioned his relationship with Peacock and is said to have destroyed three hundred copies of his first book of poems (1851) in order to conceal its dedication to Peacock, the influence of this fantastical and fascinating man of letters was a "rock in the foundation of his philosophy."

Meredith was not easy to live with. He had nervous, restless habits, hummed to himself, and fidgeted with the furniture. These characteristics of his handsome son-in-law probably inspired the quiet-loving Peacock to give him a cottage near his own residence at Lower Halliford. Here Meredith finished *The Shaving of Shagpat,* an oriental romance bearing some resemblance to Beckford's *Vathek.* It was at Seaford near Newhaven that Meredith wrote *Farina* and *Richard Feverel* and here in 1858 his wife deserted him. Definitely soured on the sex, he settled in London, eschewing feminine companionship to the extent of having a boy nurse for his son. Of several children born to the Merediths, Arthur Gryffydh Meredith (1853) was the first to survive. The boy was very like his father and Meredith in rearing him repeated many of the mistakes of his own upbringing and got in return much of the heartache that George gave his own father.

Although he had contributed to various papers, Meredith did not become a professional journalist until 1860 when he took a position with the *Ipswich Journal.* With this and his connection as reader for the publishers Chapman and Hall he had an income of about £400 a year. At this period he dressed quite fastidiously and was remembered in later years for his courtly bearing and his lavender kid gloves. A tall, strong, distinguished-looking man, he had tremendous vitality and delighted in long country walks. Francis Burnand says, "George Meredith never merely walked, never lounged; he strode, he took giant strides . . . His laughter was something to hear; it was of short duration, but it was a roar; it set you off. . ."

His literary opinions were amusingly iconoclastic. He referred to Gray's "Elegy" as "the Undertaker's Waltz," said Dickens was "the incarnation of Cockneydom," and with Chapman and Hall his personal tastes were occasionally ruinous. He disliked sensational books and twice refused *East Lynne,* which later sold over a million copies. More difficult to comprehend is his rejection of Samuel Butler's *Erewhon* and his opinion that the public would "shun" the collected letters of Jane and Thomas Carlyle. But Hardy declared that, but for Meredith's encouragement, he would never have devoted himself to literature.

For a time (1862-1864) Meredith shared a house with the Rossettis and Swinburne in Chelsea, but eventually found their quaint attempts at housekeeping too bohemian for his taste. Mary Peacock Meredith died in 1861 and in 1864 George married Miss Marie Vulliamy in the same church at Mickleham where Fanny Burney wedded D'Arblay. A son was born the following year, and Arthur Meredith so resented the division in his father's affection that he eventually became estranged. (Arthur died, unrelenting, at the house of his stepsister, Edith Nicolls Clarke, in 1890.)

From 1867 until his death Meredith lived at Flint Cottage, Box Hill, Surrey. Here his daughter was born in 1871. The second Mrs. Meredith was a tactful Frenchwoman and made him a good wife. When for a time he insisted on turning vegetarian, she did not directly oppose him, but as she saw him getting more gaunt connived with the baker to put shredded meat into his bread.

Meredith once said, "Thank God I have never written a word to please the public," but he was nevertheless furious with the public because it would not be pleased with his novels. They were caviar to the general, and after the failure of *Vittoria,* for which, in order to study types, he had taken a position as correspondent during the Austro-Italian war of 1866, he feared he would have to give up novel-writing and depend for a living on journalism, which he always disliked. But he continued to write, producing *Harry Richmond, Beauchamp's Career, The Egoist,* and *The Tragic Comedians* between 1871 and 1880. *Diana of the Crossways* (1885) was the first of his books to strike the general public and from this time Meredith deliberately set himself to win revenge upon the critics who had called him obscure by, as he said, serving "these critics a strong dose of my most indigestible productions ... Nothing drove them so crazy as *One of Our Conquerors.*" Box Hill became a shrine for literary pilgrims. In 1892 St. Andrews University conferred the degree LL.D. on Meredith. In 1894, a grandfather, he was working on his last novel, *The Amazing Marriage.*

Meredith's declining years were mentally active, although he became deaf and a partial invalid. He received the Order of Merit from Edward VII in 1905 and developed a taste for motoring. On his eighty-first birthday he said he was "going quickly down, no belief in future existence." He died at Box Hill and his ashes were interred at Dorking.

As in his character there is in the poetry and prose of George Meredith a certain duality of elements. Retaining traces of the earlier romanticism, his analyses are both poetic and scientific. His heroines are "new" women and the series of these is "a chivalrous profession of faith." His style, complex and impressionistic, runs to stream-of-consciousness and is, as LeGallienne says, "at once a pillar of cloud and a pillar of fire."   P. B. S

PRINCIPAL WORKS: *Poetry*—Poems, 1851; Modern Love, 1862; Poems and Lyrics of the Joy of Earth, 1883; Ballads and Poems of Tragic Life, 1887; A Reading of Earth, 1888; A Reading of Life, 1901; Last Poems, 1909. *Prose*—The Shaving of Shagpat, 1856; Farina, 1857; The Ordeal of Richard Feverel, 1859; Evan Harrington, 1861; Amelia in England, 1864 (reprinted in 1887 as Sandra Belloni); Rhoda Fleming, 1865; Vittoria, 1867; The Adventures of Harry Richmond, 1871; Beauchamp's Career, 1876; The House on the Beach, 1877; The Egoist, 1879; The Tragic Comedians, 1880; Diana of the Crossways, 1885; One of our Conquerors, 1891; Lord Ormont and His Aminta, 1894; The Amazing Marriage, 1895; Celt and Saxon (fragment) 1910.

ABOUT: Abel, A. H. George Meredith and Thomas Love Peacock: A Study in Literary Influence; Burnand, F. Records and Reminiscences; Ellis, S. M. George Meredith: His Life and Friends in Relation to His Work; Hammerton, J. A. George Meredith in Anecdote and Criticism; LeGallienne, R. George Meredith: Some Characteristics; Meredith, G. The Ordeal of Richard Feverel (see Introduction by David Lambuth to Modern Reader's Series edition); Wolff, L. George Meredith: Poète et Romancier.

"MEREDITH, OWEN." See LYTTON, LORD

MERIVALE, CHARLES (March 8, 1808-December 27, 1893), historian, was the son of a Unitarian father and an Anglican mother (John Herman and Louisa Drury Merivale), and so grew up outside the church in which most of his long life was spent. He was sent to Harrow, but withdrawn and transferred to Haileybury on the offer of an official post in India if he would study economics. This, however, did not appeal to young Merivale, so

finally his father was persuaded to send him to St. John's College, Cambridge. There he received his B.A. in 1830, his M.A. in 1833, and his B.D. in 1840.

Until 1833, when he was appointed to a fellowship and took holy orders, Merivale, though he had subscribed to the Church of England to receive his degree, was a liberal, a Free Mason, and even something of a Socialist. Thereafter he may be ranked as a conservative, though never an extreme Tory. In fact, he disliked the very reactionary atmosphere of St. John's, where by his fellowship he was obliged to live and teach, and tried in vain to secure a professorship of the classics at King's College and elsewhere.

Primarily, Merivale's interest was in Latin rather than in Greek, and it is natural that he turned more and more to the study of Roman history. He did, it is true, help to bring science teaching into Cambridge, but afterwards he regretted it. His increased dissastisfaction with St. John's, his love of seclusion and his growing desire for leisure to write, led him to accept an appointment as rector of Lawford, Essex, in 1848, and to remain there until he was made Dean of Ely in 1869. From 1863 to 1869 he acted also as chaplain to the Speaker of the House of Commons. In 1866 he received an honorary D.C.L. from Oxford.

As dean, Merivale, who disliked polemics and church politics, took little part in convocations, but devoted himself to enlarging the cathedral school and partially restoring the cathedral itself. In 1873 he organized the twelve-hundredth anniversary of the founding of Ely Minster in 673 A.D.

In 1850 Merivale married Judith Frere, by whom he had a daughter. He found time in

CHARLES MERIVALE

431

a busy life to edit the Latin historian Sallust, to translate from the German Abeken's *Life of Cicero*, to form an editorial connection with the *Saturday Review*, and to lecture frequently. In 1892, at eighty-four, he suffered a paralytic stroke, and a second one the following November caused his death before the end of the year.

In his youth Merivale was an ardent oarsman, having rowed in the first university race at Cambridge and helped to found the Oxford-Cambridge races. He was also during his university days the author of a number of prize poems in Latin, but never wrote verse in any language in later years, except a rather unfortunate rhymed translation of Homer. He was a thoroughly orthodox clergyman, and his Roman histories were compilations rather than history in the modern sense. In fact, Merivale was a good deal of a recluse, and so shrank from travel that he, who wrote at least six books on the history of Rome, visited that city only once, in 1845. It is natural that he was criticized for the absence of first-hand study from monuments and inscriptions evident in his work. His histories were popular in their day, but for the most part they are no longer of interest.

M. A. deF.

PRINCIPAL WORKS: The Church of England a Faithful Witness, 1839; Sermons Preached in the Chapel Royal, 1841; History of the Romans Under the Empire (7 vol.) 1850-64; The Fall of the Roman Republic, 1853; The Conversion of the Roman Empire, 1864; The Conversion of the Northern Nations, 1866; Homer's Iliad in English Rhymed Verse, 1869; The Contrast Between Pagan and Christian Society, 1872; General History of Rome, 1875; The Roman Triumvirates, 1876; St. Paul at Rome, 1877; The Conversion of the Continental Teutons, 1878; Four Lectures on Some Epochs of Early Church History, 1879; Autobiography (ed. by Judith A. Merivale) 1899.

ABOUT: Merivale, C. Autobiography; Illustrated London News 104:5 January 6, 1894; London Times December 28, 1893.

MERIVALE, HERMAN (November 8, 1806-February 8, 1874), historian, was born in Devonshire, the eldest son of John Herman Merivale, the poet and scholar, and brother of the historian Charles Merivale, Dean of Ely. He was a remarkably precocious child, who read Latin at four. At Harrow he captured every available prize, then proceeded to Oriel College, Oxford, in 1823, transferring in 1825, as a scholar, to Trinity. He received his B.A. in 1828 in the first class, and became a fellow at Balliol. He was called to the bar from the Inner Temple in 1832 and joined the western circuit. In 1834 he married Caroline Penelope Robinson. They had one son, the poet and playwright Herman Charles Merivale, and two daughters.

In 1837 Merivale became professor of political economy at Oxford, for the usual term

of five years. In 1841 he was recorder of Falmouth, Helston, and Penzance. Through the influence of his father, who was commissioner in bankruptcy, he was in 1847 made assistant under-secretary of state for colonies, the next year became permanent under-secretary of state, and from 1859 to his death was permanent under-secretary for India. Grief at his daughter's death broke his health, and he died after a short illness.

A man of high intellect and liberal sympathies, Merivale's writing was a mere by-product of his leisure, and gives no evidence of his mental powers. His only important work is his lectures on colonization, which are now quite outdated.

PRINCIPAL WORKS: Introduction to the Course Upon Colonisation, 1839; Lectures on Colonisation and Colonies, 1841; Historical Studies, 1865.

ABOUT: Merivale, C. Memoir.

MERIVALE, HERMAN CHARLES (January 27, 1839-January 14, 1906), poet and dramatist, was born in London, the only son of Herman Merivale, the historian. He received his B.A. at Balliol College, Oxford, in 1861. While there he had tried in vain to establish a dramatic club. He was called to the bar from the Inner Temple in 1864, and joined the western circuit, and also the Norfolk circuit, which he traveled with Matthew Arnold. He became junior counsel for the government on Indian appeals, in 1867 boundary commissioner for North Wales, and from 1870 to 1880 edited the *Annual Register*. But when his father died, in 1874, he immediately gave up the law for literature and the theatre. He had already written several farces under a pseudonym.

In 1878 Merivale married Elizabeth Pitman, an Irishwoman. They had no children. Mrs. Merivale collaborated with him in several of his plays. An ardent liberal, Merivale was a hard worker for his party, but his health did not permit his standing for Parliament. In 1891 he was ordered to Australia by his physician, and was shipwrecked at Pernambuco. He returned to England, his health recovered, but the power of attorney he had left with a defaulting solicitor cost him his entire fortune. In 1900 he was given a pension from the civil list. A few years before his death he became a Roman Catholic.

Merivale's best work is in poetic drama, where he displays both wit and imaginative sympathy. His only novel gives a good picture of Oxford in the nineteenth century.

PRINCIPAL WORKS: All for Her, 1875; Faucit of Balliol (novel), 1882; The White Pilgrim, 1883; Florien, 1884; Bar, Stage, and Platform, 1902.

ABOUT: Merivale, H. C. Bar, Stage, and Platform.

MERIVALE, JOHN HERMAN (August 5, 1779-April 25, 1844), poet, was born in Exeter. His mother was of German descent. He was reared as a Presbyterian, and hence had to leave St. John's College, Cambridge, without a degree; in later life he conformed to the Church of England, in which his son Charles became distinguished. He was called to the bar from Lincoln's Inn in 1804. The next year he married Louisa Heath Drury; they had six sons and six daughters. Two of the sons, Charles and Herman, became known as historians.

Merivale published numerous legal works, and practiced in chancery until 1831, when he was appointed commissioner in bankruptcy, a post he held until his death. His deepest interest was always in literature; he was a friend of Byron, who admired his verse; he translated well from Greek, Italian, and German; and he was a steady contributor to the reviews. His poems, though slight, are felicitous in style; his translations are accurate and what in his time was known as "elegant."

PRINCIPAL WORK: Poems: Original and Translated, 1838.

ABOUT: Quarterly Review October 1839.

"MERRIAM, HENRY SETON." See SCOTT, HUGH STOWELL

MILL, JAMES (April 6, 1773-June 23, 1836), historian and economist, was the oldest son of a country shoemaker in Forfarshire, Scotland. His mother, of a slightly higher social grade, determined to make her oldest boy a gentleman, and he was excused from the work of the other children and sent by great sacrifice to Montrose Academy. Undoubtedly his obvious intelligence determined

JAMES MILL

this decision, though his brothers and sisters naturally resented it greatly.

Mill became a tutor in the household of Sir James Stuart, who was his lifelong benefactor, and saw to it that he entered the University of Edinburgh as a divinity student in 1790. He remained there for eight years, and was then licensed to preach. As a preacher, however, he was not a success. For the most part he lived at home, supporting himself by what tutoring he could find. In 1802 he went to London, and gradually found his way into literary and journalistic work; the next year he became editor of the *Literary Journal*, and in 1805 took on at the same time the editorship of *St. James's Chronicle*. In this same year he married Harriet Burrow, daughter of the matron of a private insane asylum, who bore him four sons and five daughters.

The family was desperately poor, and Mill worked night and day for their support. His editorial work brought him very little. In 1808 he met Jeremy Bentham, the famous political economist and leader of the "philosophical radicals," whose complete disciple he became. He espoused Bentham's rationalist views at once and abandoned Christianity forever. At times he lived with Bentham and assisted in arranging and editing his master's voluminous and terribly confused notes and manuscripts. He was associated also with Francis Place, the radical writer, and with him helped to found London University.

The publication of Mill's *History of British India*, in 1817, brought the turn in his fortunes. The book was not a tremendous financial success, but in spite of his severe strictures on British rule in India, the India House officials in 1819 appointed him to a place in the examiner's office, and he remained there the rest of his life, finally becoming head of the office. His position allowed him much leisure for writing, and he contributed extensively to the *Encyclopaedia Britannica*, and helped to found the *Westminster Review*. In 1822 he bought a house at Dorking where his family lived for half the year and he spent vacations and week-ends. Up to this time he had undertaken the entire charge of his children's education at home. In 1830 he bought a city home in Kensington, where six years later he died of tuberculosis. His last writing was a series of articles in the *London Review*.

Mill was a most unprepossessing person, physically and socially. His eyes bulged from his massive forehead, and he was short and thick-set. He was a dour Scot of the most severe type, unable to show the slightest affection for anyone, irritable (gout had something to do with this) and unamiable. He despised his wife, and said so, and though devoted to his children showed it only by overworking them mentally to express his pride in their intelligence. He quarreled even with Bentham (though not permanently), and his family lived in awe and terror of him. Yet he had great virtues—frugality, industry, sincerity, and devotion to the good of humanity, however much he disliked individuals. His intellect was powerful, but rigid and narrow. He was at once a stoic and a cynic.

His chief contribution to thought is in the realm of psychology, which he founded on the "law of contiguity," now usually spoken of as the doctrine of association. He was a completely orthodox Benthamite, and carried out Bentham's pragmatic philosophy to the letter. His style is harsh and dull at the same time. His greatest claim to celebrity is that he was the father of John Stuart Mill.   M. A. deF.

PRINCIPAL WORKS: Essay on the Impolicy of a Bounty on the Exportation of Grain, 1804; Commerce Defended, 1808; History of British India, 1817; Elements of Political Economy, 1821; Analysis of the Phenomena of the Human Mind, 1829; Fragment on Mackintosh, 1835; The Principles of Toleration, 1837.

ABOUT: Bain, A. James Mill: A Biography; Bower, G. S. Hartley and James Mill; Stephen, L. The English Utilitarians.

MILL, JOHN STUART (May 20, 1806-May 8, 1873), political economist and philosopher, was the first of the nine children of James Mill, the Scottish economist. He was an infant prodigy, thanks partly to an innate capacity for learning, and partly to an inhumanly rigorous training by his father. He could read Greek at three, and by twelve was the master of several languages and of mathematics and had already begun authorship. The little Millses, entirely educated by their father, were kept hard at it all day, learning lessons even on their walks, and having absolutely no play-time. Their only relaxation was to hear their father read, in the evenings, selections from classical English authors. Later on, but still in early childhood, the older ones were supposed to assist in the education of their juniors.

J. S. Mill's only other education was a year in France, at fourteen, when he studied French nine hours daily, and otherwise kept up his education by himself. He returned to read for the bar, but instead was appointed clerk in the examiner's office of India House, under his father. He remained there from 1823 to 1856, when India House was abolished, and he was retired on a pension.

This position, as in his father's case, gave him plenty of leisure for study and writing. He had not at first been particularly interested in political economy, but now he came into touch with the work of Jeremy Bentham, the utilitarian philosopher who was his father's master, and he too applied himself ardently to economic thought. His first published work was an article on economics in The Traveller

in 1823, when he was seventeen. At about the same time he founded the Utilitarians, a short-lived, somewhat radical and agnostic group, devoted to the philosophy of pragmatism.

The relentless zeal with which his childhood and boyhood had been regulated had permanently ruined his health, and at twenty-one he had what he called a "spiritual crisis," which was probably a sort of nervous breakdown. In 1836 he suffered another severe nervous illness, a sort of brain exhaustion which left him with a constant twitching over one eye. In 1839 and again in 1854 he endured long sieges of sickness and was obliged to ask for leave of absence for considerable periods. But he kept indefatigably at work up to the time of his death at sixty-seven.

Under the influence, first of Wordsworth and Coleridge, then of Auguste Comte, the French philosopher, founder of the school of Positivism, Mill gradually diverged from his father's orthodox Benthamism. He humanized and widened the utilitarian system, his being a much more flexible nature than his father's. He never entirely deserted the agnosticism in which he had been reared, but came at length to believe in a sort of modified free will, though he retained his basic belief in determinism. In Paris in 1830 he became associated with the followers of St. Simon, one of the early Communist thinkers, and politically he was always what in those days was called a "philosophic radical."

In that same year he met the woman who was the one love of his life. Mrs. Taylor was an invalid, probably tubercular. She and Mill apparently fell in love at sight, and her worthy husband, a drysalter who recognized his intellectual incompatability with his wife, scrupulously retired in Mill's favor. It was his custom, for example, to dine out on the evenings when Mill was to call on his wife, and though divorce was impossible under the English law, he did everything he could to obliterate himself. In 1849 he died, but for some reason the lovers were not married until 1851.

There was, of course, a terrific scandal. It did not affect Mill's public career, but it made him a permanent recluse, socially, even after his wife's death. They had few friends and practically no social life. Mill adored his wife, and never tired of telling of her intellect, her nobility, and her invaluable services to him. (It was she, incidentally, who by her carelessness or possibly something worse—jealousy because Mill had contemplated working on the same theme—allowed a servant to burn the only manuscript of Carlyle's French Revolution.) She did undoubtedly influence him in one direction, and that was in his advocacy of the rights and political and economic claims of women. The only writing of her own she ever did was on this subject. She

JOHN STUART MILL

a fall, according to another. Only three days before his death he had taken a walk of fourteen miles.

Mill was tall and slight, with florid complexion and fair hair (most of which he lost in old age). He dressed always in black. He was extremely abstemious, and the only pleasure he allowed himself was long walks in the country, for he was a great lover of natural scenery. Though his lungs were weak, he had originally a good constitution, weakened by constant over-strain.

Carlyle called him a "logic-chopping machine," and he had perhaps one of the finest thinking-organs the world has ever known; but he had also a personal warmth not usually associated with logicians. As a man he was highly emotional, sensitive, and tender-hearted, though his passions were deep rather than ardent. He hated oppression and injustice, was affectionate, truly public-spirited, and warmly generous. Calm in his writing, in later years he was often nervously irritable in speech, but he had none of his father's cold moroseness. He has well been called "the saint of Rationalism."

As Lord Morley put it, Mill in his time set the problems and defined the channels for all people with a taste for thinking. Taine, the French historian, remarked that he excelled in giving precision to an idea. He was the standard-bearer of liberalism for his period. In economics he stood about half way between the individualistic, *laissez faire* theories of David Ricardo and what today is known as Socialism. He was a radical, but at the same time a genuine democrat, with an uncompromising belief in the worth of the individual and no love for any sort of dictatorship. His religious views softened with age, and in his last writings he approached near to a sort of modified deism.

His style was grave and unassuming and lucid. Though his subjects make him far from light or easy reading, he is never dull, pompous, or obscure. Mill's works which are most likely to survive are the essays *On Liberty* and *On the Subjection of Women*, and his masterly autobiography. He was a really great and original thinker.   M. A. deF.

loved him deeply in turn, and their marriage was without a flaw except the delicate health of both. Her daughter by her first marriage lived with them, and stayed with Mill after her mother's death.

From 1835 to 1840 Mill was closely connected with the *London Review*, as part owner and virtual editor, though his official position in India House prevented him from assuming technical editorship. After his release from India House he spent six months of the year in Avignon, in southern France, where Mrs. Mill died, in 1859. Mill was heartbroken; he bought a house as near as possible to the cemetery where she was buried, and spent most of his time by her grave. Gradually it was necessary for him to force himself back into life, and—as he acknowledged with gratitude—both emotionally and intellectually his grown step-daughter was of the greatest help to him in this process of readjustment which made up his remaining years.

He had often been solicited to run for Parliament, where liberal influence was badly needed, and finally in 1865 he agreed and was elected. He served until 1868, being one of the moving spirits in the passage of the great Reform Bill of 1867. Though he was a poor speaker, the liberal and radical group in Parliament to some extent centered about him, and his Parliamentary career was a notable one. In 1866 he became Rector of St. Andrews University, his inaugural address being a landmark in educational history. He still spent half the year at Avignon, and the other half in a house he had bought at Blackheath, England. Just before his sixty-seventh birthday he died (as he would have wished) at Avignon—of "a local endemic disease," according to one report; of erysipelas following

PRINCIPAL WORKS: Essays on Some Unsettled Questions of Political Economy, 1831-44; A System of Logic, 1843; Principles of Political Economy, 1848; On Liberty, 1859; Thoughts on Parliamentary Reform, 1859; Dissertations and Discussions, 1859-75; Considerations on Representative Government, 1861; Utilitarianism, 1863; Examination of Sir W. Hamilton's Philosophy, 1865; Auguste Comte and Positivism, 1865; Inaugural Address, St. Andrew's University, 1867; England and Ireland, 1868; On the Subjection of Women, 1869; Chapters and Speeches on the Irish Land Question, 1870; Autobiography, 1873; Three Essays on Religion, 1874; Letters (ed. by H. S. R. Elliot) 1910.

ABOUT: Bain, A. J. S. Mill: A Criticism; Courtney, W. L. Life of John Stuart Mill; Douglas, C.

John Stuart Mill: A Study of His Philosophy; Maccunn, J. Six Radical Thinkers; Mill, J. S. Autobiography; Mill, J. S. Letters; Stephen, L. The English Utilitarians; Current Literature 41:74 July 1906; Harper's Magazine 47:528 September 1873; Living Age 250:3 July 7, 1906; London Mercury 19: 395 February 1929.

MILLER, HUGH (October 10, 1802-December 23, 1856), Scottish geologist and miscellaneous writer, was born in Cromarty, the son of Hugh Miller, a sailor, and his wife, Harriet (Ross) Miller. When the boy was about five, his father was lost at sea, and the child was left to the care of his mother and his two uncles.

Having made some progress at a dame's school, and learned the joy that could come to him from reading, young Miller was sent to a local school, to proceed in his studies. Although he enjoyed reading, and fascinated his classmates by his tales and anecdotes, he was marked as the dunce of his group, and showed no aptitude for study. His scholastic career was terminated abruptly by a physical encounter with the schoolmaster, who proved too much for his doughty pupil. Miller revenged himself by a piece of satirical verse which he called "The Pedagogue," and for a time distinguished himself by leading a band of lawless ruffians, at the same time, strangely, conducting a small paper.

About 1819 he became apprenticed to a stone-mason; and this occupation, distasteful as it appears to have been at first, proved to be of great benefit to him, for it drew his attention to geology. When, about 1822, he became a journeyman mason in his own right, he spent much time observing stones in various parts of Scotland where he worked. In the same period the steady work, with its sobering influence, seems to have disciplined his na-

HUGH MILLER

ture; during this time his strong religious sentiments were developed, and in 1829 he issued a volume of *Poems Written in the Leisure Hours of a Journeyman Mason.*

He was not destined to engage in his humble activity as mason and tombstone-cutter very long, for so respectable a citizen had he become that, upon the establishment at Cromarty of a branch of the Commercial Bank, he was selected, despite his slight training, for the position of accountant. In definitely improved status, Miller married Lydia Falconer Fraser, a young woman of a background somewhat more exalted than his own, who later became known as a writer of children's stories. His literary work continued, *Scenes and Legends of the North of England* appearing in 1835; and Miller began to devote his attention to the problem of the Scottish Church. His *Letter to Lord Brougham,* protesting against the insistence of the British government upon the right of certain laymen to place clergymen in charge of congregations that did not want them, brought him to the attention of the Non-Intrusionist group, as the adherents of this attitude came to be known. The result was that he was offered the editorship of *The Witness,* the semi-weekly paper serving as the organ of this ecclesiastical party. Accepting his new responsibilities (1840) with some diffidence, Miller removed to Edinburgh, where he proved to be an excellent editor.

Meanwhile Miller had published his geological study, *The Old Red Sandstone,* which immediately drew attention to his work in this field, and pointed out the importance of fossil remains in this particular formation. His later works, *Footprints of the Creator* and *The Testimony of the Rocks* dealt with the problem of reconciling science and religion. Opposing the evolutionary view advanced by Robert Chambers in *Vestiges of Creation* (1844), and the idea of a progressive transmutation of species, Miller defended the Biblical account of the Creation, identifying the "days" of Genesis with geological periods, and regarding the Biblical narrative as one of a series of prophetic visions.

The Testimony of the Rocks was the last work to receive Miller's attention; he finished it on the day of his death. His frame weakened by the lung trouble caused by his early occupation as stone-mason, and his mind broken by work and illness, he became a victim of frights and delusions; and on the night of December 23, 1856, after writing an affectionate note to his wife, he committed suicide by shooting himself. He was widely mourned, and his funeral was one of the largest ever held in Scotland.

For this popularity Miller's personality was at least partly responsible. He was possessed of the qualities which appeal to men. Self-made, he prided himself on his former situation as a stone-mason, and all his life his tall, strong, though hardly very athletic, body, with his large head and reddish hair, and his clothes and his manner suggested his humble origin. His charming autobiography, *My Schools and Schoolmasters,* was written to encourage Scottish workers. Despite his democratic attitude and his sincerely felt religion he was, however, a powerful and unsparing controversialist. "I know no instance," wrote David Masson, "in which he did not leave his adversary not only slain, but battered, bruised, and beaten out of shape."

His own theories are more notable for their form than their substance (now out of date); and the merit of his books lies in their charms of style and imaginative power (the latter quality more noticeable in his prose than in his rather unsuccessful verse). His scientific work, although praised by such men as Thomas Henry Huxley and Louis Agassiz, could not rank with that of trained research workers.   R. W. W.

PRINCIPAL WORKS: *Autobiography*—My Schools and Schoolmasters, 1854. *Church Government, etc.* —Letter From One of the Scotch People to the Right Hon. Lord Brougham and Vaux, 1839; The Whiggism of the Old School, 1839; The Two Parties in the Church of Scotland, 1841; The Headship of Christ, 1861. *Geology*—The Old Red Sandstone, (1841); The Fossiliferous Deposits of Scotland, 1854; The Cruise of the Betsy, 1858; Sketch-Book of Popular Geology, 1859; Edinburgh and Its Neighbourhood, 1864. *Philosophy and Metaphysics*— Footprints of the Creator, 1849; Geology Versus Astronomy, 1855. The Testimony of the Rocks, 1857. *Poetry*—Poems Written in the Leisure Hours of a Journeyman Mason, 1829. *Miscellaneous Essays, Travel, etc.*—Scenes and Legends of the North of Scotland, 1835; First Impressions of England and Its People, 1847; Essays, 1862; Tales and Sketches, 1863.

ABOUT: Bayne, P. The Life and Letters of Hugh Miller; Brown, T. N. The Life and Times of Hugh Miller; Leask, W. K. Hugh Miller; Mackenzie, W. M. Hugh Miller: A Critical Study; Miller, H. My Schools and Schoolmasters; Chambers's Journal 6th ser. 5:305 April 19, 1902; 369 May 17, 1902; 461 June 21, 1902; 513 July 19, 1902.

MILLER, THOMAS (August 31, 1807-October 24, 1874), poet, novelist, and miscellaneous writer, was born in Gainsborough, the son of a wharfinger who disappeared the day of the Burnett Riots in 1810 and was never seen again. Thomas was aprenticed to a basket maker in early childhood, after the most cursory schooling. He wrote poems from his earliest years, and the success of his first volume, in 1832, enabled him to set up in business for himself. In 1835 he went to London to work at his trade; some fine baskets sent with original verses to the Countess of Blessington secured him her patronage and he was taken up by society. In 1841, through Samuel Rogers, he was enabled to give up his trade and open a book shop. He remained in this business the rest of his life, though he became the intimate of the rich and great. He contributed many stories to the *London Journal,* and also published his own writings in book form. He wrote about fifty books in all, including many juvenile stories. In 1874, through Disraeli, he was awarded £100 from the Royal Bounty Fund. He was married and had one son and two daughters.

Miller's verses are cheerful and simple, with a pleasant feeling for nature. His novels are for the most part vivid and accurate renderings of humble life.

PRINCIPAL WORKS: Songs of the Sea Nymphs, 1832; A Day in the Woods: Tales and Poems, 1836; Beauties of the Country, 1837; Royston Gower, 1838; Gideon Giles the Roper, 1849; A History of the Anglo-Saxons, 1848; Birds, Bees, and Blossoms, 1858; My Father's Garden, 1867.

ABOUT: Illustrated London News 64:425, 1874; Pall Mall Gazette October 27, 1874.

MILMAN, HENRY HART (February 10, 1791-September 24, 1868), poet and historian, was born in London. His father was Sir Francis Milman, physician to George III. He was educated at Eton and at Brasenose College, Oxford, where he had a brilliant career, receiving his B.A. and M.A. in 1816, his B.D. and D.D in 1849. He won the Newdigate prize for poetry and the chancellor's prize for an English essay while at Oxford, was made a fellow of Brasenose, and took orders the year of his graduation. In 1818 he was a vicar at Reading. In 1821 he was made professor of poetry at Oxford.

Milman was at first best known as a poet, or more particularly as an author of poetic dramas. He also wrote many hymns for Reginald Heber's hymnal. His play, *Fazio,* was performed by Charles Kemble, without his knowledge (there being no copyright in those days) but not, in spite of his clerical position, against his will. In 1824 he married Mary Ann Cockell, by whom he had four sons and two daughters.

Milman translated from the Greek and edited Horace. His most important work as a translator, however, is his translations from the Sanskrit sacred poems, the first which had been adequately done in English. He abandoned the writing of poetry by 1830 and turned to history. His *History of the Jews* created a sensation, for it was the first to treat the people of the Bible as an Oriental desert tribe. It earned him the enmity of the clergy and deferred his preferment in the church. He had friends among the statesmen, however, who finally saw to his promotion. In 1835 he was made canon of Westminster, and in 1849 dean of St. Paul's Cathedral, his history of the cathedral being published posthumously, edited by his son.

Milman raised the standard of ecclesiastical history tremendously. His work is sound, sympathetic, and informed throughout by a liberal spirit. It is dry, however; he lacked creative imagination and was incapable of vivid characterization. The same defect permeates his poetic plays, which are, besides, florid, often in poor taste, and full of "fine writing" in the opprobrious sense of the term. But his realistic attitude toward religious history and his services as a translator from the Sanskrit outweigh these faults of his youthful work.

PRINCIPAL WORKS: Fazio, 1815; Samor, the Lord of the Bright City, 1818; The Fall of Jerusalem, 1820; Belshazzar, 1822; History of the Jews, 1830; Life of Gibbon, 1839; History of Christianity Under the Empire, 1840; History of Latin Christianity, 1855.

ABOUT: Milman, A. Henry Hart Milman. Dean of St. Paul's.

MILNES, (RICHARD) MONCKTON. See HOUGHTON, LORD

MILTON, VISCOUNT (William Wentworth Fitzwilliam) (1839-1877), travel writer, was the eldest son of the sixth Earl Fitzwilliam. He was born in the ancestral estate, Milton Manor, Northamptonshire. He was a member of Parliament from 1865 to 1872. In the year he entered Parliament he also published the work by which he is chiefly known, an account of his "expedition from the Atlantic to the Pacific," across Canada, written in conjunction with Walter Butler Cheadle. In 1868 he was a member of the commission which settled one of the boundary disputes between the United States and Canada, and he later published a history of these negotiations. He died at only forty-four. He was not primarily a writer, and his principal book is a rather pedestrian work.

PRINCIPAL WORKS: The North-West Passage by Land (with W. B. Cheadle) 1865; A History of the San Juan Water Boundary Question, 1869.

MINTO, WILLIAM (October 10, 1845-March 1, 1893), Scottish critic and novelist, was born near Alford in Aberdeenshire, the son of James Minto and Barbara (Copland) Minto.

His youth is noteworthy for his brilliant career at Aberdeen University, which, after attendance at various schools, he entered on a bursary (scholarship) in 1861. In 1865, the year of his graduation, he made an all-time record by taking not only the most important prizes but first honors in classics and second honors in mathematics and mental philosophy as well. For a time he studied divinity, then proceeded in 1866 to Merton College, Oxford, where he stayed but a short while, leaving in 1867 without a degree.

He returned to Aberdeen, and assumed a position as assistant to David Thomson, professor of natural philosophy at the Univer-

WILLIAM MINTO

sity. Unfortunately one of the duties he was expected to perform was to act as the subject of an experiment with electricity, in which the assistant, before the eyes of the class, was to be given a shock. This demand was too much for Minto's sense of dignity, and he left his post, later becoming assistant to Dr. Alexander Bain, professor of logic and English literature. His resultant preoccupation with the subject led to A Manual of English Prose Literature, published in 1872. Minto was at this time a powerful influence in the University community, especially in the election in 1869 of Mountstuart Grant Duff as Rector.

In 1873 he removed to London, where he became a journalist and writer on literary subjects, editing The Examiner from 1874 to 1878, and writing reviews and articles for The Encyclopaedia Britannica, as well as his works on Defoe and on English poets.

Returning to Aberdeen in 1880, the year of his marriage to Cornelia Griffiths, he took the professorship left vacant by Dr. Bain's retirement. During the remainder of his life he wrote novels and edited various works, including autobiographical material of the poet and painter William Bell Scott, which, because of its frankness and its statements about important literary and artistic figures of the day, caused considerable criticism and hard feeling. His declining health induced him to undertake a Mediterranean voyage in 1891. He died in March 1893.

While Minto's activities extended over a wider range of types than those of most professors, he was at his best as a teacher of English literature. Indeed, he thoroughly disliked the drudgery connected with editing. His success as a teacher was due not only to his thorough scholarship but also to his painstaking efforts to present his material in such a way as to make it comprehensible to his students. His personality was attractive and winning, and he was able to be fair and even charitable toward those who disagreed with him. He was interested in young writers of promise. Edmund Gosse and Theodore Watts-Dunton were among his protégés. So popular and influential was he in Aberdeen that after his death the students issued in his honor an "In Memoriam" supplement to their magazine, *Alma Mater*. It included many warm tributes from professors as well as pupils. It was regretted by some that he did not live to see the separation of instruction in logic from that in English literature, an innovation which would have freed him for his most characteristic interests.

As a writer he is not of first importance. His novels, if not negligible, lack permanent value. His criticism is somewhat better remembered. By exactness and sanity of judgment he was often able to hit upon a new truth or a new way of regarding something old. Thus he brought forth the idea that Burns was not merely an untutored genius but a student; and in the study of Shakespeare he made a contribution in the identification of the "rival poet" of Shakespeare's sonnets as the poet Chapman. For all his critical astuteness, however, his reputation as a writer probably never will equal his importance in his own time as a personal force.

R. W. W.

PRINCIPAL WORKS: *Biography*—Daniel Defoe, 1879. *History and Criticism of English Literature* —A Manual of English Prose Literature, 1872; Characteristics of English Poets From Chaucer to Shirley, 1874; The Literature of the Georgian Era, 1894. *Novels*—The Crack of Doom, 1886; The Mediation of Ralph Hardelot, 1888; Was She Good or Bad? 1889. *Play*—The Colorado Beetle, 1887. *Textbooks on Miscellaneous Subjects*—Plain Principles of Prose Composition, 1893; Logic, Inductive and Deductive, 1893.

ABOUT: Knight, W. A. Some Nineteenth Century Scotsmen; Minto, W. The Literature of the Georgian Era (see Biographical Introduction by W. A. Knight); Academy 43:221 March 11, 1893; Bookman (London) 4:11 April 1893.

MITCHEL, JOHN (November 3, 1815-March 20, 1875), Irish nationalist and miscellaneous writer, was born in County Londonderry, the son of a Presbyterian minister. He was educated at Trinity College, Dublin, and worked as a bank clerk in London, and in a solicitor's office in Newry. In 1836 he eloped with Jane Verner, a girl of sixteen; they were overtaken and he was jailed for a few days; but the next year they succeeded in marrying. They had three daughters and three sons, two of whom were later killed, and one wounded, as Confederate soldiers in the American Civil War. In 1840 Mitchel was admitted solicitor, and practised at Bainbridge. Soon after, he met T. O. Davis, the

nationalist leader, and in 1845 he abandoned his profession, and joined the staff of *The Nation*. He left two years later, and joined the Young Ireland party. In 1848 he established a weekly, the *United Irishman*, in Dublin, was twice arrested for sedition, and finally sentenced to fourteen years' transportation. He was sent to Bermuda, then to the Cape of Good Hope, and finally to Van Diemen's Land (Tasmania), where he lived as a ticket-of-leave man, his family joining him in 1851. In 1853 he escaped and came to America. In 1854 he founded in New York an anti-abolitionist paper, *The Citizen*. From 1857 to 1859 he edited the *Southern Citizen*, in Knoxville and Washington. He then went to live in Paris, but in 1862 returned to New York and got through the Federal lines to Richmond. There, until a quarrel with Jefferson Davis, he edited *The Enquirer*. For five months he was a prisoner of war in Fortress Monroe. After the war he edited the *Daily News* in New York, and from 1867 to 1872 edited the *Irish Citizen*, once visiting Ireland, where he was not molested. He was elected to Parliament in 1875, *in absentia;* his election was contested on the ground that he was an ex-convict and an alien, and he died in the midst of the fight concerning it, in Dromalone, Ireland.

Mitchel edited the poems of Davis and Mangan. His writing was a mere side-line, and his personality was far more interesting than his books, but he had a forcible and vigorous style.

PRINCIPAL WORKS: Life of Aodh O'Neill, 1846; Jail Journal, 1854; History of Ireland, 1869.

ABOUT: Dillon, W. John Mitchel; Mitchel, J. Jail Journal.

MITCHELL, THOMAS (May 30, 1783-May 4, 1845), poet and classicist, was born in London, the son of a prosperous riding-master. He was educated at Christ's Hospital and at Pembroke College, Cambridge, where he took his B.A. in 1806 and his M.A. in 1809. He was elected a fellow but had to vacate his fellowship in 1812 because he would not be ordained. He acted as a private tutor from 1806 to 1816, refusing an offer of a chair in a Scottish university because he would have had to conform to the church. In association with various publishers he edited numerous Greek authors, and contributed thirteen articles on Aristophanes to the *Quarterly Review*. From 1825 he lived with relatives in Oxfordshire. In 1842 he received £150 from the Royal Bounty Fund. He was never married. He died suddenly of apoplexy.

Mitchell was a fine classical scholar, but a very minor and derivative poet. He was one of the leading Hellenists of his day.

MITFORD

PRINCIPAL WORK: The Comedies of Aristophanes Translated, 1822.

ABOUT: Kennedy, G. J. Remarks on Mr. Mitchell's Edition of the Comedies of Aristophanes.

MITFORD, JOHN (August 31, 1781-April 27, 1859), poet, was born in Richmond, the son of a sea captain, and educated by private tutors at Richmond, Tunbridge, and Winchester. For a while he was clerk in the army pay office, then entered Oriel College, Oxford, where he secured his B.A. in 1804. He was ordained in 1809 and became a curate in Suffolk, but never paid much attention to his clerical duties. Through his distant cousin, Lord Redesdale, Mitford added to his curacy a vicarage in Benhall, Suffolk, a rectory, also in Suffolk, and the post of domestic chaplain to Lord Redesdale himself. All of these benefices he retained to his death, though without much devotion to any of them. He lived for the most part in Benhall, where his chief concern was the building of a house and the laying out of a garden; but he also had lodgings in London and spent much time there. An ardent lover of natural beauty, he traveled all over England and the Continent merely to behold the scenery. In 1814 he had married Augusta Boodle, and they had one son, but the marriage was unhappy and they lived together as little as possible. From 1833 to 1850 he contributed regularly to the *Gentleman's Magazine*. He also edited, for the Aldine Edition, the works of Gray, Cowper, Goldsmith, Milton, Dryden, and other poets. He was a collector of paintings and books and miscellaneous antiquities, and in general much more of a connoisseur and dilettante than he was of a clergyman. In 1858 he suffered a stroke, while in London, and soon after died at Benhall.

PRINCIPAL WORKS: Agnes, the Indian Captive, 1811; Lines Suggested by a Fatal Shipwreck, 1855; Miscellaneous Poems, 1858.

ABOUT: Houston, M. Sylvanus Redivivus (the Rev. John Mitford).

MITFORD, JOHN ("Alfred Burton") January, 1782-December 24, 1831), poet, was a third cousin of the Rev. John Mitford and a distant cousin of Lord Redesdale. Through Lord Redesdale's influence he entered the Royal Navy as a midshipman. He was present at the Battle of the Nile, and said that he deserted in 1801, but as he was most untrustworthy and told many incredible tales the exact history of his naval experience is uncertain. From 1804 to 1806 he is known to have commanded a revenue cutter off the coast of Ireland, and from 1809 to 1811 to have been acting master of a brig in the Mediterranean. In 1808 he married Emily Street, of New Brunswick, Canada, and they had several children. In 1811 he was in London, trying to get a civil service appointment, and

writing for *The News* and *The Star*, when he was certified as insane, and for two years was an inmate of a private asylum. On his release he was discharged from the navy, and lapsed into drunkenness. Lord Redesdale took care of his family, but Mitford himself lived apart from them in destitution and filth. Until 1815 he may have edited, and certainly wrote for, *The Scourge: or, Monthly Expositor of Imposture and Folly*. The only way his publisher could compel him to write his narrative poems of the sea was to limit him to a shilling a day—twopence for bread, cheese, and an onion, the rest for gin. His later work was written anonymously, for the most part in a cellar, with a ragged quilt and a candle its only furnishing. Finally he went to the workhouse and died there, but he was still a literary man, for from the workhouse he edited the *Quizzical Gazette*. Mitford was utterly untruthful, dissipated, and half-crazy, but his earlier poems at least are racy tales in verse written with flowing ease.

PRINCIPAL WORKS: The Adventures of Johnny Newcome in the Navy, 1818; The Poems of a British Sailor, 1818.

ABOUT: Gentleman's Magazine Part 2:647 (1831).

MITFORD, MARY RUSSELL (December 16, 1786-January 10, 1855), poet, playwright, novelist, and essayist, was born at Alresford, Hampshire, the only child of Dr. George and Mary Russell Mitford.

In 1797 Mary drew a lottery prize in London of £20,000, and until 1802 she was able to attend a very good school in London. The family built a house at Reading with the money, and Dr. Mitford "went through" the fortune as he done previously with about £50,000. He ended entirely dependent on Mary's earnings.

After 1802 she was at home, reading voraciously in Greek drama and European literature, watching the approach of poverty. Financial necessity drove her to publish, in 1810, some poems written earlier. These, echoing Scott and Coleridge, grew out of her ambition to become the supreme English poetess. She sent the manuscript of *Blanche of Castile* to Coleridge, and was encouraged to believe she had talent for writing tragic drama; but when published in 1813 it only drew a bitter attack from the *Quarterly Review*. Need increased, and the family moved to a mean cottage at Three Mile Cross. Mary anticipated a larger income from the stage, and from 1820 to 1835 she wrote some successful plays. *Julian* played at Covent Garden eight times, with Charles Macready in the title rôle. She realized £200 from this. Three years later *Foscari*, played by Charles Kemble, ran fifteen nights at Covent Garden. But *Rienzi*, her best play, had thirty-four performances at Drury Lane and brought Miss Mitford £400. It had a certain vogue in

MARY RUSSELL MITFORD

She maintained a huge correspondence with Macready, Mrs. Hemans, Harriet Martineau, and others. Her talk and letters were "stronger and wider" than her novels, thought Elizabeth Barrett Browning. She added, "The heat of human sympathy seemed to bring out her powerful vitality."

In drama Miss Mitford's achievement is creditable, and not merely "for a woman" as Macready said. To her omission of prologue and epilogue must be attributed some of the credit for the new convention of allowing plays to speak for themselves. This was a realistic move on her part. Her poetry has not lasted well, nor is her single real novel a great success, though Ruskin admired it. As essayist she achieved real distinction and is unsurpassed. Continuing the tradition of Goldsmith, she wrote sketches of local color and provincial life. She has been called the Claude of English village life and her resemblance to the work of the Dutch painters has been noted. Realism, humor, a perennial freshness, and a delight in all kinds of incongruity combine to produce a delightfully truthful portrait of life. Christopher North commented, "Miss Mitford has not, in my opinion, either the pathos or humor of Washington Irving; but she excells him in vigorous conception of character, and in the truth of her picture of English life and manners."

D. F. A.

America as well. *Charles the First* was suppressed by the Lord Chamberlain's office, but in 1834 when poverty had made her desperate, Miss Mitford sold this to the Victoria Theatre on the south bank of the Thames, outside of the Chamberlain's province. Some dramatic scenes in the *London Magazine* and *Sadak* complete the drama-writing period.

Meanwhile, she had been pioneering in a new branch of literature, the sketches called *Our Village*. Rejected by Thomas Campbell, these appeared serially in the *Ladies' Magazine* and proved extremely popular. Her reputation grew fabulously; she soon knew Lamb, Amelia Opie, Elizabeth Barrett Browning, John Wilson, and others. Her cottage was thronged with callers and her London excursions became gala events. Though she had contributed, 1826-36, to S. C. Hall's *Amulet* and to other periodicals, only now did she become a high-priced contributor to *Chambers's Edinburgh Journal*, etc. For three years she edited *Finden's Tableaux*. Her father died in 1842, and a public subscription was raised to pay his debts. Still the struggle was great, and she continued writing "when very few people could even have held a pen." In 1842 she wrote that for four years she had "not bought a bonnet, a cloak, a gown, hardly a pair of gloves." The strain weakened her, and her last years were sickly. She died at Swallowfield, her last home, and was buried there.

"A Sancho Panza in petticoats" was Letitia Landon's terse description of Miss Mitford. Remarkably bright eyes, a sweet soft voice, keen perception, and great enthusiasm did much to make listeners forget the shabbiness and unbecoming stoutness of the lady in her garden or drawing-room at Three Mile Cross.

PRINCIPAL WORKS: *Poetry*—Miscellaneous Poems, 1810; Christina, 1811; Narrative Poems on the Female Character, 1813; Blanche of Castile, 1813; Dramatic Scenes, Sonnets, 1827; Mary Queen of Scots, 1831. *Drama*—Julian, 1823; Foscari, 1826; Rinezi, 1828; Sadak and Kalasrade, 1835; Dramatic Works (2 vols.) 1854. *Novels and Sketches*—Our Village, 1819-32; Stories of American Life by American Authors, 1820; Stories of American Life for Little Boys and Girls, 1821; Lights and Shadows of American Life, 1832; Stories for Young People, 1835; Tales for Young People, 1835; Country Stories, 1835; Atherton, 1854. *Miscellaneous*—Recollections of a Literary Life (3 vols.) 1852.

ABOUT: Belhune, G. W. The British Female Poets; Fields, J. T. Yesterdays With Authors; Hall, S. C. Memories; Harness, W. The Life of Mary Russell Mitford; Landor, W. S. To Miss Mitford; L'Estrange, A. G. K. The Friendships of Mary Russell Mitford; Maclise, D. Gallery of Portraits; Mitford, M. R. Correspondence With Charles Boner and John Ruskin.

MIVART, ST. GEORGE JACKSON (November 20, 1827-April 1, 1900), zoologist, was born in London, the son of a hotelkeeper. He was educated at Harrow and entered King's College, London, but having in 1844 become a Roman Catholic, he finished his education at St. Mary's College, Oscott. He was called to the bar in 1851 from Lincoln's Inn, but never practised, his whole interest being in science. From 1849 he was a member of the Royal Institution, and a Fellow of the Zoological Society from 1858. In 1862 he was appointed lecturer of comparative anatomy at St. Mary's Hospital, London. The same year he was made a fellow of the Linnaean Society, of which he was secretary from 1874 to 1880, and vice-president in 1892. In 1869 he became a Fellow of the Royal Society. He claimed to be an evolutionist "up to the creation of man," but though strongly influenced by Darwin, he became estranged from him and Huxley. He wrote innumerable zoological papers, and lectured at the Zoological Gardens and the London Institution. In 1874 he was professor of biology at the University College, Kensington (Roman Catholic), but the college did not have a very long existence. In 1878 he received a Ph.D. degree from the pope, and from 1890 to 1893 he was professor of the philosophy of natural history at Louvain, which had given him an M.D. degree in 1884. Mivart was one of the greatest comparative anatomists of his time; unfortunately he was also deeply interested in metaphysics, wasted a great deal of energy on philosophical questions, tried in vain to reconcile science and religion, and ended by getting himself excommunicated. He was married and had one son. He died at sixty-two of diabetes.

Most of Mivart's writings are technical papers for learned societies. His more extended works in zoology are marked by fullness, accuracy, and lucidity. He was a poor metaphysician, and his philosophical disquisitions are best forgotten.

PRINCIPAL WORKS: Man and Apes, 1873; Lessons From Nature, 1876; The Cat, 1881; The Origin of Human Reason, 1889; Essays and Criticisms, 1892; Introduction to the Elements of Science, 1894.

ABOUT: Nature April 12, 1900; London Times April 2, 3, 4, 1900.

MOGRIDGE, GEORGE. See MARTIN, WILLIAM

MOIR, DAVID MACBETH (January 5, 1798-July 6, 1851), Scottish physician and author, was born at Musselburgh, son of Robert Moir and Elizabeth (Macbeth) Moir.

He went to school at Musselburgh until 1811, when he was apprenticed to Dr. Stewart, whom he served four years; he was able, during the last two years of his apprenticeship, to study medicine at Edinburgh, and in 1816 he received his diploma. The next year, when he was but nineteen, he became the partner of Dr. Brown at Musselburgh, sharing an intensely busy practise.

Most of Mivart's writings are technical small journals had published his work when in 1816 he brought out a small volume of verse, The Bombardment of Algiers and Other Poems. After becoming a practicing physician he wrote for Constable's Edinburgh Magazine and for Blackwood's, achieving a reputation as poet with the signature "Delta," and contributing humorous pieces which some

D. M. MOIR

critics flatteringly attributed to Maginn. In 1823 he met the novelist Galt and won his confidence to such a degree that the older man persuaded Moir to finish The Last of the Lairds for him. The editorship of the Quarterly Journal of Agriculture was offered him, but, as he always averred, he was a physician by profession, and he refused the post. His most lasting work, the humorous sketches collected as The Autobiography of Mansie Wauch: Tailor in Dalkeith, appeared in 1828; he felt that it was one of his least worthy efforts.

About this time Moir conceived the idea of a history of medical science, and published the first volume, Outlines of the Ancient History of Medicine, in 1831. In the next year the cholera broke out in Musselburgh, and Moir played a heroic part, attending to his double duties as physician and a secretary to the Board of Health at Musselburgh. Whether this upset his plans for the History is not known, but he never published any more of it.

In 1844 he became ill through exposure and from sitting all night in wet clothing at the bedside of a patient. In 1846 a carriage accident injured him seriously, but by 1849 he had recovered sufficiently to make a tour of the highlands with John Wilson ("Christopher North"). In June, two years later, he fell from his horse and died from the effects of this second accident.

Moir was married in 1828 to Catherine Bell, by whom he had eleven children. Much of his verse was written about his home and family, and one volume was actually entitled Domestic Verses. As a poet, he was content with a casual output and did not achieve genuine distinction, although he won high praise during his lifetime. As with so many men of letters, he goes down to fame with work he despised—the previously mentioned *genre* sketches, *The Autobiography of Mansie Wauch*—good broad humor with many a telling little touch of character description.

Moir also wrote concerning the cholera, and his lectures on *The Roman Antiquities of Inveresk* were published in 1860.

He is described as a tall erect man with sandy hair, of ruddy complexion, and of a jolly expression. "A better man and a lovelier specimen of the literary character did not exist," said his friend Gilfillan; and his townsmen erected a monument to his memory.

R. M.

PRINCIPAL WORKS: *Poetry*—The Bombardment of Algiers, 1816; Domestic Verses, by "Delta," 1832. *Fiction*—The Autobiography of Mansie Wauch, 1828. *Medical*—Outlines of the Ancient History of Medicine, 1831; Practical Observations on Malignant Cholera, 1832; Proofs of the Contagion of Malignant Cholera, 1832. *Miscellaneous*—Poetical Literature of the Last Half Century, 1852; The Roman Antiquities of Inveresk, 1860. *Complete Works*—Works, 1852.

ABOUT: Douglas, G. B. The Blackwood Group; Gilfillan, G. A Third Gallery of Portraits; Moir, D. M. Works (see Memoir by T. Aird); Blackwood's Magazine 70:249 August 1851; Fraser's Magazine 8:290 September 1833.

MOLESWORTH, MRS. MARY LOUISA STEWART

(May 29, 1839-July 20, 1921), novelist and juvenile writer, was born in Rotterdam, Holland, of a family of Scottish descent on both sides. Her grandfather had been a major in the army, stationed in New Brunswick, Canada.

She was privately educated at home, and also attended a school in Switzerland. Most of her girlhood was spent in the north of England, but in later years she lived for some time in both France and Germany. In 1861 she married Major R. Molesworth, a nephew of Viscount Molesworth, who died in 1900. They had one son and three daughters.

Mrs. Molesworth, who in her later works used her married name as a writer, began writing novels in 1869. All her earlier books, up to 1874, were written under the pseudonym of "Ennis Graham." They were for the most part rather sentimental and melodramatic romances, which enjoyed a fair popularity in their time but are unread now, and which had no great literary merit. It was not until 1876 that she discovered her real forte, as a writer for children. Even after her children's books went into edition after edition, she continued occasionally to write novels for adults.

If her name is to live at all, however, it will be as that of one of the most charming of juvenile writers. The tender humor and easy warmth of her children's stories, particularly *Carrots, The Cuckoo Clock,* and *The Tap-*

estry Room, have seldom been excelled. As a novelist her writing was rather high-flown and artificial; but when she wrote for children she became a realist, with a wealth of detail even in her adventures into the realm of fantasy.

After her husband's death, Mrs. Molesworth's life was uneventful. She settled in London with her children and continued to write up to 1910 or later. She died in London at the age of eighty-three..

PRINCIPAL WORKS: Lover and Husband, 1869; She Was Young and He Was Old, 1872; Cicely, 1874; Carrots, 1876; The Cuckoo Clock, 1877; The Tapestry Room, 1879; Miss Bouverie, 1880; A Charge Fulfilled, 1886; Marrying and Giving in Marriage, 1887; The Third Miss St. Quentin, 1888; Meg Langholme, 1897; The Laurel Walk, 1898; The Grim House, 1899; The Story of a Year, 1910.

ABOUT: London Times July 21, 1921.

MOLESWORTH, WILLIAM NASSAU

(November 8, 1816-December 19, 1890), historian, was born near Southampton, the son of a clergyman. He was educated at King's School, Canterbury, and at St. John's and Pembroke Colleges, Cambridge, receiving his B.A. in 1837 and his M.A. in 1842. He was ordained in 1839, and became curate to his father at Rochdale, Lancashire. In 1841 he was a vicar in Manchester, but in 1844 his father presented him to a living near Rochdale, which he held until in 1889 he was obliged to resign because of poor health. In 1842 and 1843 he and his father edited *Common Sense.* In 1844 he married Margaret Murray; they had six sons and one daughter. Although Molesworth was a poor preacher, he was a faithful clergyman. In 1881 he was made honorary canon of Manchester Cathedral. In 1883 Glasgow University gave him an honorary LL.D.

A high churchman in religion, Molesworth was a radical in politics, a friend of John Bright and Richard Cobden. He was one of the first of the "Rochdale Pioneers" who founded the cooperative movement in England. For several years before he died at Rochdale he had been a semi-invalid. His histories are copious and accurate, but have been described as "rather annals than history" in any real sense.

PRINCIPAL WORKS: Plain Lectures on Astronomy, 1862; The History of England From 1830, 1871-73; History of the Church of England From 1660, 1882.

ABOUT: Manchester Guardian December 20, 1890.

MONCRIEFF, WILLIAM THOMAS

(August 24, 1794-December 3, 1857), playwright, was born in London, the son of a tradesman. In 1804 he was articled as clerk in a solicitor's office, and he continued as a solicitor's clerk for ten years thereafter, but meanwhile he had written songs which had become popular. He became manager of the Regency Theater, then wrote theatrical criticisms for *The Satirist* and *The Scourge*. For a while he worked as a law stationer, but the stage drew him back. He was at various times lessee or manager of numerous London theaters, and wrote 170 plays in all, produced by himself and by other managers. From 1818 he published Pierce Egan's *Boxiana,* and he dramatized Egan's *Tom and Jerry: or, Life in London,* which had as enormous a success as a play as it had had in magazine and book form. His sight began to fail about 1830, and by 1843 he was totally blind, but he continued to write until 1851. In 1844, through Queen Victoria, he was admitted as a brother of the Charterhouse, and died there. Most of his plays were ephemeral, but he had a real dramatic gift and much robust humor.

PRINCIPAL WORKS: Tom and Jerry: or, Life in London, 1821; Poems, 1829; Selections From Dramatic Works (24 plays) 1850.
ABOUT: Era December 13, 1857.

MONKHOUSE, WILLIAM COSMO
(March 18, 1840-July 2, 1901), poet and critic, was born in London of Huguenot descent on the maternal side. His father was a solicitor. He was educated at St. Paul's School from 1848 to 1856, and then became a clerk for the Board of Trade. He remained with the Board for all the rest of his life, rising finally to be assistant secretary of the finance department. In 1870 and 1871 he was in South America for the Board, in the interest of Seamen's Hospitals.

From his schooldays Monkhouse had written verse, and in his leisure hours from the office he contributed poems to the *Temple Bar, Argosy, Englishwoman's Magazine,* and other periodicals. Between 1868 and 1890, he wrote little except literary and art criticism, which he contributed to *The Academy,* the *Magazine of Art,* and finally to the *Saturday Review,* whose regular art critic he became. In later years he returned to the writing of poetry, but was primarily known as a critic and historian of art. He contributed many of the lives of painters to the *Dictionary of National Biography.*

Monkhouse was married twice, in 1865 to Laura Keymer, who died soon after, and in 1873 to Leonora Blount. By his second marriage he had two sons and six daughters. He died at Skegness at sixty-one.

As a poet Monkhouse was a disciple of Wordsworth and Tennyson. He was unassuming and made no great claims for his verse, but it has much quiet beauty. His best known poem was the stately "Dead March." His work is thoughtful and meditative, of a philosophic cast now out of favor, but well worth the reading. He was an acute and gracious critic, making no pretension to omniscience but remarkably accomplished, with a thoroughly sound background of knowledge, particularly in the field of art.

PRINCIPAL WORKS: A Dream of Idleness and Other Poems, 1865; A Question of Honour (novel) 1868; Masterpieces of English Art, 1869; Life of Turner, 1879; The Earlier English Water Colour Painters, 1890; Corn and Poppies (poems) 1890; Memoir of Leigh Hunt, 1893; British Contemporary Artists, 1899; Pasiteles the Elder and Other Poems, 1901; Life of Sir John Tenniel, 1901.
ABOUT: Art Journal March 1902.

"MONTGOMERY, GERARD." See MOULTRIE, JOHN.

MONTGOMERY, JAMES (November 4, 1771-April 30, 1854), Scottish poet, was born in Ayrshire. His father, of a Scottish family living for several generations in Ireland, was the only Moravian (Mennonite) minister in Scotland. He returned to Ireland in 1775, while James was educated from 1777 at the Moravian school near Leeds. His parents both went to the Barbadoes as missionaries and died there. The boy was apprenticed to a baker by the school authorities, to punish him for writing poetry, but in 1787 he ran away. He worked in a general store at Wath, and in 1792 became clerk and bookkeeper for the Sheffield *Register.* Finally he became its working editor, the name of the paper having been changed to the *Iris.* In 1795 the proprietor resigned and he became owner, in addition conducting a printing business. Twice he was imprisoned for libel because of the paper's radical politics. He lost his ownership of it in 1825, and helped to found the *Eclectic Review,* to which he also contributed. In 1830 and 1831 he was lecturer on poetry to the Royal Institution. In 1835 he received a civil list pension. He was a contributor to the *Cabinet Cyclopaedia,* and was widely known as a poet and critic. He died unmarried. His many philanthropies earned him a public funeral.

As a critic, Montgomery was so extremely impartial that he had hardly any opinions at all. His poems were highly praised in his lifetime, but they are rhetorical and frequently dull. Over a hundred of his hymns are still in use in various churches.

PRINCIPAL WORKS: Prison Amusements, 1796; The Ocean, 1805; The Wanderer of Switzerland, 1806; The West Indies, 1810; The World Before the Flood, 1812; Greenland, 1819; The Pelican Island, 1827; Collected Poems, 1841; Hymns, 1853.
ABOUT: Holland, J. & Everett, J. Life of James Montgomery; King, J. W. James Montgomery.

MONTGOMERY, JEMIMA. See TAUTPHOEUS, BARONESS VON

MONTGOMERY, ROBERT (1807-December 1855), poet, was the illegitimate son of a school-mistress by a well-known clown named Robert Gomery. He was reared by his father in Bath, where he was born, and took his father's name, adding the prefix "Mont" to make it sound more aristocratic. At vari-

ous private schools he indulged himself in versifying. The foolish adulation he received from his father's theatrical friends turned his head, and he conceived of himself as a great poet. His verses being largely religious, the praise of the pious continued to feed his vanity. He imitated Byron sedulously, and even dressed and arranged his hair to look like his idol. At seventeen he was for a time publisher of a weekly called *The Inspector,* but it failed. His name is perpetuated because of Macaulay's cruel castigation of his work in the *Edinburgh Review.* Montgomery, however, was proof against any attacks. He made enough money from his books to enter Lincoln College, Oxford, in 1830. He received his B.A. in 1833 and his M.A. in 1838, was ordained in 1835, and became a curate in Shropshire. In 1836 he assumed charge of a church in Glasgow. There he became popular as a preacher and a writer on theology. It should be said for him that he had ceased to write his abominable verses. In 1843 he married Rachel Mackenzie; they had one child. The same year he became minister of the Percy Chapel, in London, and remained there until his death, which occurred at Brighton when he was only forty-eight.

Montgomery had no talent whatever, only a fatal fluency in florid versification. He was a worthy man, however, who conquered apparently insuperable obstacles in the way of a respectable career, and he did not deserve the excessive violence he received at the hands of Macaulay.

PRINCIPAL WORKS: The Stage Coach, 1827; The Omnipresence of the Deity, 1828; Satan, 1830; Oxford, 1831; The Messiah, 1832; Woman, The Angel of Life, and Other Poems, 1833.

ABOUT: Fraser's Magazine 1:95, 721; 4:672.

MOODIE, MRS. SUSANNAH (December 6, 1803-April 8, 1885), novelist, was born a Strickland, the youngest sister of Agnes Strickland, the biographer. In 1831 she married Lt. JOHN WEDDERBURN DUNBAR MOODIE (1797-1869), who had led an adventurous life in South Africa, and with him emigrated to Canada the following year. They lived in various parts of Ontario, then very wild country. Twenty years later her husband was involved in difficulties arising from his activities as sheriff, and though her only writing hitherto had been a volume of innocuous verse, she began publishing very minor novels to help support the family. After his death she lived in Toronto, where she died at eighty-two.

Mrs. Moodie's novels have been described as "innocent and negative." Her books describing the experiences of Canadian pioneers are much more effective, and are valuable pictures of pioneer life in Canada. There seems, however, to be some doubt as to

whether these are hers or her husband's; he wrote other books dealing with his former experiences in Africa, and they are not at all in the style of her other writing.

PRINCIPAL WORKS: Enthusiasm and Other Poems, 1831; Roughing It in the Bush, 1852; Life in the Clearing vs. the Bush, 1853; Mark Huddlestone, 1853; Flora Lindsay, 1854; Matrimonial Speculations, 1854; Geoffrey Moncton, 1856.

ABOUT: Baker, R. P. History of English-Canadian Literature to the Confederation.

MOORE, DUGALD (August 12, 1805-January 2, 1841), Scottish poet, was born in Glasgow. His father was a private soldier, who died while Moore was a child. His mother taught him to read and write, but at the earliest possible age he was apprenticed to a tobacco manufacturer. He was next sent to work for a firm of Glasgow booksellers, who encouraged his writing of verses and helped him to publish his first volume by subscription. This brought in sufficient money to enable him, in 1831, to start his own business, which was most successful. Unfortunately he died at thirty-five, after a short illness, with his best work perhaps undone. He was unmarried.

Moore had a genuine lyrical gift, and his writing showed real power. He never used the Scottish dialect, all his poems being in orthodox English.

PRINCIPAL WORKS: The African, 1829; Scenes From the Flood and Other Poems, 1830; The Bridal Night and Other Poems, 1831; The Bard of the North, 1833; The Hour of Retribution and Other Poems, 1835; The Devoted One and Other Poems, 1839.

ABOUT: Wilson, G. Poets and Poetry of Scotland.

MOORE, EDWARD (February 28, 1835-September 2, 1916), Dante scholar, was born at Cardiff, where his father was a physician. He was educated at Bromsgrove and at Pembroke College, Oxford. In 1858 he was made a fellow of Queen's College. He was ordained in 1861. In 1864 he became principal of St. Edmund Hall, Oxford, and remained in this post for nearly fifty years, resigning in 1913. He was a staunch champion of the independence of the Hall, and several times saved it from being merged with other foundations. In 1803 he became a canon of Canterbury Cathedral. He is best known, however, as a leading English authority on Dante. In 1876 he founded the Oxford Dante Society, from 1886 to 1903 he was Barlow lecturer on Dante at University College, London, and in 1895 the Taylorian Institution at Oxford created for him a Dante lectureship. He was twice married: in 1868 to Katherine Stogdon, who died in 1873; and in 1878 to Annie Mackenzie, who died in 1906. By each marriage he had one son and two daughters.

PRINCIPAL WORKS: The Time References in the *Divina Comedia*, 1887; Contributions to the Textual Criticism of the *Divina Comedia*, 1889; Dante and His Early Biographers, 1890; The Oxford Dante, 1894; Studies in Dante (four series) 1896-1914.

ABOUT: Moore, E. Studies in Dante (see Preface to 4th series by P. J. Toynbee); London Times September 5, 1916.

MOORE, THOMAS (May 28, 1779-February 25, 1852), Irish poet, was born in Dublin, the son of John Moore, a grocer, and Anastasia (Codd) Moore, both Catholics.

His early education was, for the most part, at the school of Samuel Whyte, considered the best in Dublin. With special preparation in Latin, Moore, who was precocious, was admitted (1794) to Trinity College, Dublin having already published poems in an Irish periodical. While he obtained but few university honors, he became known for his literary ability, and produced a verse translation of Anacreon which brought him considerable praise At the same time he became an enthusiastic Irish patriot.

Moore's personal charm and his musical ability won his way in society, and he was a friend of Lord Moira, and accepted by English aristocrats. In 1803 he was appointed admiralty registrar at Bermuda. He journeyed thither, but remained only a short time, leaving his duties to a deputy, and making a tour of the United States and Canada. He returned to England in 1804.

The publication of the *Epistles, Odes, and Other Poems* provoked an attack by Jeffrey which led to a near-duel (the two later became fast friends). *Irish Melodies,* however (the music by Sir John Stevenson), found a ready audience, and Moore earned a good income together with a reputation as Ireland's national singer.

His patriotism, as well as his disappointment on finding the Prince Regent (once his friend) indifferent to the cause of Catholic Emancipation, led Moore to write lampoons in verse, from 1813 on, beginning with *The Two-Penny Post-Bag*. They were highly successful, and gained the author fame and fortune.

Meanwhile he had been acquiring new friends and a family. In 1811 he married Bessie Dyke, an actress of lowly birth, and took up his abode in the country, in Leicestershire and then Ashbourne. Also in 1811 he met Lord Byron, with whom he formed a friendship which was of great importance.

In order to get more money Moore contracted with a publisher, at the highest current rate, to write a poem. In emulation of Bryon he choose an Eastern subject, and at length completed the highly successful *Lalla Rookh*, which made him known over Europe. He followed his success with a series of humorous skits in the manner of *The Two-Penny Post-Bag*.

His financial condition seemed secure, and in 1817 he settled in Wiltshire near Lord Lansdowne's home. Almost at once word came of an embezzlement by his Bermuda deputy. Moore was liable for £6000 and fled to Paris. Thence he went to Italy, returning not before 1822, when the debt, reduced to £1000, was paid by Lord Lansdowne's help. Characteristically proud, Moore reimbursed Lord Lansdowne almost at once.

In 1824 Byron died, having given Moore his memoirs several years earlier. Moore sold them to a publisher, then bought them back and burned them. This action caused criticism, but it seems to have been the result of disinterested deliberation. To pay for the expenses involved by this transaction, Moore wrote his *Life of Byron*, which was very successful.

The History of Ireland, Moore's last work, was too much for his failing energies and too unsuited to his peculiar genius. The effort of writing it broke the author's strength. At the same time he lost several children. Almost no members of his father's family were left, and the affectionate poet felt these losses deeply. His mind gave way, and he died, after some years of virtual imbecility, in 1852. His last years had been eased by two pensions from the government.

Nothing could be more delightfully characteristic of Moore's character than his telling an Irish joke to Jeffrey on the occasion of their first meeting, while the seconds were preparing the guns for the duel. His amiability could not be suppressed, and various of his contemporaries have drawn appealing pictures

THOMAS MOORE

of a nature almost childlike in its simple charm. Moore had a host of friends, was worshipped by women, and was a trifle vain. His singing of his songs is said to have been ineffably sweet and touching. He was somewhat high-strung, and on one occasion burst into a fit of hysterics in the middle of a song. Like a child he apparently failed to notice or to mind his own petty vanities, his frequent ostrich-like disregard of adverse criticism, and the somewhat undue respect for rank and title that caused Saintsbury to mention his "cat-like disposition to curl himself up near something or somebody comfortable." But, whatever his superficialities, he was a tender husband and father; and he was pathetically scrupulous in the discharge of financial obligations.

Exceedingly popular in his own day, almost as much as Scott or Byron, Moore's poetry has since been harshly condemned as mediocre, shallow, and insincere. It is unquestionably true that his poetry lacks "divine fire" and that he is not one of the great poets, even of his generation. There is a certain artificiality that marks Moore as of the drawing-room variety of poet, and there is an ornateness which overweights *Lalla Rookh*. He had, however, a troubadour's ability to combine words and music happily. While his Irish quality seems rather faint to a generation that has known the Irish Revival, his songs have lived. And in satire and epigram he was extremely successful.

"With the passing of a century, the talent of Moore has had its deficiencies shown up, but it has not lost its charm," writes Louis Cazamian. "Literary history will probably leave him one of the first ranks among the Romanticists of the second order; for his poetry, however nerveless it may be, yet possesses an element of inspired originality in its musical flow and the felicity of its language."

R. W. W.

PRINCIPAL WORKS: *Biography*—Memoirs of the Life of the Rt. Hon. R. B. Sheridan, 1825; The Life and Death of Lord Edward Fitzgerald, 1831. *Editor* —The World of Westminster, 1816; Letters and Journals of Lord Byron, 1830; The Works of Lord Byron, 1832-35; The Works of R. B. Sheridan, 1833. *History*—History of Ireland, 1835-46. *Letters and Journals*—Memoirs, Journals, and Correspondence, 1853-56. *Novel*—The Epicurean, 1827. *Poetical Works*—The Poetical Works of the Late Thomas Little, Esq., 1801; Epistles, Odes, and Other Poems, 1806; A Selection of Irish Melodies, 1807-34; Corruption and Intolerance, 1808; The Sceptic, 1809; M. P.: or The Blue Stocking, 1811; Intercepted Letters: or, The Two-Penny Post-Bag, 1813; A Selection of Popular National Airs, 1815; Sacred Songs, 1816; Lines on the Death of [R. B. Sheridan] 1816; Lalla Rookh, 1817; The Fudge Family in Paris, 1818; Tom Crib's Memorial to Congress, 1819; Fables for the Holy Alliance, 1823; The Loves of the Angels, 1823; Evenings in Greece, 1825; Odes Upon Cash, Corn, Catholics, and Other Matters, 1928; Legendary Ballads, 1830; The Summer Fête, 1831; The Fudges in England, 1835; Alciphron, 1839. *Translator*—Odes of Anacreon. 1800; *Miscellaneous* —A Candidate Appeal to Public Confidence, 1803; A Letter to the Roman Catholics of Dublin, 1810; Memoirs of Captain Rock, 1824; Prose and Verse, 1878.

ABOUT: Burke, J. The Life of Thomas Moore; Gwynn, S. Thomas Moore; Hazlitt, W. Spirit of the Age; Montgomery, H. R. Thomas Moore: His Life, Writings, and Contemporaries; Saintsbury, G. Essays in English Literature: 1780-1860; Symington, A. J. Thomas Moore: His Life and Works.

MORE, HANNAH (February 2, 1745-September 7, 1835), poet, playwright, and religious writer, the "laureate of the bluestockings," was born at Fishponds, Stapleton Parish, in Gloucestershire near Bristol, the fourth of five daughters of Jacob More, headmaster of a boys' school. Her mother was a sensible woman who scouted her husband's alarm at Hannah's precocity and insisted that the child's instructions match her abilities. When about twelve, Hannah entered the school for young ladies which her elder sisters were conducting at Bristol. She was fluent in French, competent in Latin, and already better educated than most women of her day.

Until she was twenty-two Hannah taught in the Misses More's academy. Then she became involved in a singular romantic entanglement. Her fiancé, a Mr. Turner was an elderly gentleman of considerable fortune. But he proved himself an inveterate postponer. The concrete fact emerging from the diffident accounts of Hannah's biographers is that, after six years' engagement, Mr. Turner settled £200 *per annum* on Hannah to "compensate for the robbery he had committed on her time."

Accompanied by a sister, Hannah went to London. Sprightly, witty and handsome, she was soon established in blue-stocking circles. Her friendship with David Garrick and his wife apparently overcame what scruples she may have had against the stage and she was for a time regarded as the most successful tragedy-writer in London. Her poetry received the accolade of Dr. Johnson and Hannah's letters record a bewildering round of festivity of every description.

Though a strict Sabbatarian, Hannah does not appear at this time to have had any qualms about associating with interesting infidels. For thirty years after Garrick's death she lived with Mrs. Garrick, who was a Roman Catholic and a former ballet-dancer. Miss More's biographers are particularly concerned to explain away her friendship with Horace Walpole. It is asseverated that in his correspondence with her he considerably avoided a "too worldly tone." Until 1802, however, she spent at least a part of every year in London.

Hannah's withdrawal from London society was very gradual and probably due mostly to deaths and changes in the ranks of her coterie.

HANNAH MORE

Her *Sacred Dramas* (1782) and the poems *Florio* (1786) and *Bas Bleu* (1786) indicated the change in her attitude which *Thoughts on the Importance of Manners of the Great* (1788) and *An Estimate on the Religion of the Fashionable World* (1790) fully exemplify. Her individual philanthropies were of the unorganized, dramatic, sentimental, and frequently disastrous variety which make good reading in tracts.

It was at the instigation of her friend William Wilberforce that she and her sisters began their schools in the Mendip Hills. The ignorance and depravity of this mining region near Cowslip Green where Hannah had a cottage were such that is was almost dangerous to visit the Cheddar Caves. The eighteenth-century conception of education for the poor does not seem revolutionary today. Humility, sobriety, industry, sewing and reading, reverence for the British constitution, the Established Church and the gentry were taught. The pupils, Hannah said, learned "such coarse works as may fit them to be servants. I allow of no writing for the poor." Nevertheless the schools met with bitter opposition from both land-owners and clergy.

The success of some pamphlets written against French atheism inspired Hannah's *Cheap Repository Tracts.* Designed for the lowest classes, they inculcated the customary virtues. Miss More was herself horrified in later years at the lengths to which her educational schemes had been carried. She had had no intention, she said, of making philosophers out of the poor.

At the turn of the century Miss More again turned her attention to the morals of the fashionable and in December 1809 she published her nearest approach to a novel, *Coelebs in Search of a Wife.* The odiously pious hero anticipates Richard Feverel on the spiritual side. The book went into eleven editions in nine months, showing as Sidney Smith remarked in the *Edinburgh Review,* the "advantage from a worldly point of view of writing orthodox, didactic works." Hannah More continued busy and active until her death. She died in her eighty-ninth year at Clifton near Bristol, leaving an estate of £30,000.

The pious effusions of Miss More are likely to amuse rather than repel the rising generation. Her forceful, spirited style and telling character sketches are grounds for regret that she chose the evangelical road to self-expression. In the development of workaday ethics and philanthropy she played an important rôle. Students of private life will find her invaluable on account of the minutely described customs which she excoriates.

P. B. S.

PRINCIPAL WORKS: *Plays*—A Search After Happiness, 1762; The Inflexible Captive, 1774; Percy, 1775; The Fatal Falsehood, 1779; Sacred Dramas, 1782. *Poetry*—Sir Eldred of the Bower, 1776; Bas Bleu, 1786; Florio, 1786; Slavery, 1788. *Prose*—An Estimate of the Religion of the Fashionable World, 1790; Cheap Repository Tracts, 1795-1798; Strictures on the Modern System of Female Education, 1799; Hints Toward Forming the Character of a Young Princess, 1805; Coelebs in Search of a Wife, 1809; Essay on the Character and Practical Writing of St. Paul, 1815; Moral Sketches, 1819; The Spirit of Prayer, 1824.

ABOUT: Meakin, A. M. Hannah More; Shaw, W. Life of Hannah More; Roberts, A. Mendip Annals.

MORGAN, AUGUSTUS DE. See DE MORGAN, AUGUSTUS

MORGAN, LADY SYDNEY OWENSON (December 25, 1783?-April 14, 1859), Irish novelist, was born in Dublin, her father a well-known actor, her mother an English tradesman's daughter. The date of her birth (though it seems to have occured on Christmas Day), is in doubt, since from vanity she pushed it forward to 1795, whereas envious friends put it back as far as 1775. She attended various schools near Dublin, but actually was brought up back-stage, the pet of her father's theatrical company. From 1798 to 1800 she was a governess, and she may have appeared as an actress, but this is not certain. In 1801 she published a volume of verses, and later some Irish songs, with words by herself to fit the old tunes. Her first novels, which have been called "trashy imitations of the *Sorrows of Werther,*" were deliberately written in the hope of making as much money as Fanny Burney was reputed to receive.

However, Miss Owenson, as she then was, had real talent, and when she dealt with Irish peasants or the Irish Nationalist cause, she gave proof of it. *The Wild Irish Girl,* her best work, caused a sensation, and she was thereafter known as "Glorvina," after its heroine. In 1807 she wrote an opera, *The First Attempt,* which was performed in Dublin but was also the Last Attempt. The Marquis of Abercorn became her patron and took her into his household; in 1812 she married his surgeon, Sir Thomas Charles Morgan. He died in 1843. The marriage was childless, and none too happy, since she had married to oblige the Marchioness.

Lady Morgan was the object of attacks by the *Quarterly Review* and other Tory organs, but her popularity both in society and in the literary world remained unabated. After a book on France, she lived for a year, from 1818, in Italy, to write a book on that country. In 1837 she received a pension of £300, the first ever granted to a woman. In 1839 she moved to London, and devoted her time to social activities, no longer writing except to revise her earlier work.

Her novels are sentimental and florid, often slipshod and inflated, but she had a fund of humor almost as rich as Samuel Lever's, and a touch of real genius.

PRINCIPAL WORKS: St. Clair: or, The Heiress of Desmond, 1804; The Novice of· St. Dominick, 1805; The Wild Irish Girl, 1806; Woman: or, Ida of Athens, 1809; The Missionary, 1811 (rewritten as Luximia the Prophetess, 1859); O'Donnel: A National Tale, 1814; Florence McCarthy, 1816; France, 1817; Italy, 1821; Absenteeism, 1825; The O'Briens and the O'Flaherties, 1827; The Princess, 1835.

ABOUT: Dixon, W. H. (ed.) Lady Morgan's Memoirs: Autobiography, Diaries, and Correspondence; Fitzpatrick, W. J. Lady Morgan: Her Career, Literary and Personal; Paston, G. Little Memoirs of the Nineteenth Century.

MORIER, JAMES JUSTINIAN (1780?-March 19, 1849), satirist, diplomat, and traveler, was born in Smyrna, the second son of Isaac Morier who was to become the consul-general of the Levant Company at Constantinople. The Moriers were a Huguenot family that on the revocation of the Edict of Nantes, migrated to Switzerland.

Young Morier was educated at Harrow. In 1807, he entered the diplomatic service, there to remain ten years. In 1809, he was made secretary to the legation at Teheran. The following year he became secretary of the embassy to Sir Gore Ouseley. During 1810-1816, he was the British representative to the Persian court. In connection with his diplomatic work he traveled a great deal. The material collected on these journeys he used in his first book that was published in 1812, *A Journey Through Persia, Armenia, and Asia Minor to Constantinople in the Years 1808 and 1809.*

In 1817 the government granted him a retiring pension and he returned to England to live. There he had a residence in London, "in very good style in Charles Street, Berkeley Square." He now devoted his time to literature. In 1824 *The Adventures of Hajji Baba of Ispahan* appeared, that immortal satire about a Persian barber who with quotations from the poets soothed his patrons while he trimmed their beards, and, if Allah were good, the patrons themselves were trimmed, too.

Morier's literary work was interrupted by the government's sending him to Mexico. He was special commissioner to that country during 1824-1826. He was one of the plenipotentiaries who signed a treaty with Mexico on December 26, 1826.

He married Harriet, daughter of William Fulke Greville. They had one son, Greville. The latter part of his life was spent at Brighton where he died in 1849.

Morier was said to resemble in several ways his own creation of Hajji Baba. He liked adventure, enjoyed life thoroughly, and was not at all averse to a glass of port. It was said of this handsome, good-natured Tory that he was never at home except when he was abroad.

The travel books Morier wrote were among the first about Persia to be ranked of any importance. His romances with scenes laid in the Far East have little value. It was his satires about Hajji Baba, witty rogue, knave, and charlatan that made him famous. Sir Walter Scott called Hajji Baba "the Oriental *Gil Blas.*" . . Richard Ferrar Patterson labelled *The Adventures of Hajji Baba of Ispahan* "the best picaresque novel in the English language." While the second book about Hajji in England is delightful, it was bound to be, in a certain sense, a repetition of the first. It has been said that you would know

JAMES J. MORIER

449

more about Persia after reading *Hajji Baba* than if you lived in Persia twenty years.

In the preface to *Hajji Baba*, George N. Curzon wrote ". . . the book is an invaluable contribution to sociology and conveys a more truthful and instructive impression of Persian habits, methods, points of view, and courses of action, than any disquisition of which I am aware in the more serious volumes of states-men, travelers, and men of affairs."   D. H.

PRINCIPAL WORKS: *Satires*—The Adventures of Hajji Baba of Ispahan, 1824; The Adventures of Hajji Baba of Ispahan in England, 1828. *Travel*— A Journey Through Persia, Armenia, and Asia Minor to Constantinople in the Years 1808 and 1809, 1812; A Second Journey Through Persia, 1818. *Romances*—Zohrab the Hostage, 1832; Ayesha: The Maid of Kais, 1834.

ABOUT: Morier, J. J. The Adventures of Hajji Baba of Ispahan (see Preface by G. N. Curzon); Fraser's Magazine 7:159 February 1833; Quarterly 39:73 January 1829.

MORISON, JAMES AUGUSTUS COT-TER (April 20, 1832-February 26, 1888), biographer and miscellaneous writer, was born in London, but reared in Paris until his father died in 1840, his residence giving him a fluent knowledge of French and a life-long interest in French history. He also traveled in Germany, but his health was too delicate for him to have very regular schooling. In 1850 he entered Lincoln College, Oxford, but because of his own and his mother's invalid-ism, it was 1859 before he received the B.A. and M.A. degrees. He was for a long time on the staff of the *Saturday Review,* where most of his essays appeared. In 1878 he married Frances Virtue, who died in 1878, leaving one son and one daughter. After leaving the *Saturday Review* he devoted himself to philosophical writing, being one of Comte's chief Positivist disciples. His great work, which he projected for years, a history of France under Louis XIV, was never fin-ished. Morison was a man of very wide sympathies and admired by a large and emi-nent circle of friends. However, his health was too frail to permit him to produce a body of work worthy of his extensive knowledge and good critical and historical judgment.

PRINCIPAL WORK: Life of St. Bernard, 1863; Life of Gibbon, 1878; Life of Macaulay, 1822; The Service of Man, 1887.

ABOUT: London Times February 28, 1888.

MORLEY, HENRY (September 15, 1822-May 14, 1894), essayist, biographer, and ed-itor, was born in London, the son of Henry Morley, apothecary, of Midhurst, Sussex.

His unhappiness in English schools was the cause of his being sent while quite young to a Moravian school at Neuwied on the Rhine. Destined for medicine, he entered King's Col-lege, London, in 1838. At graduation in 1843, he became assistant to a Somersetshire physician, but soon bought a partnership at Madeley, Shropshire. This venture ended in 1848 in the loss of everything through his partner's dishonesty.

He gave up practise and established a school at Liscard, near Liverpool, employing many of the Neuwied principles. Difficulties were great, but in two years he had achieved success. Meanwhile, he was employing his literary talent upon medical subjects, writing for the periodicals. One of these, *How to Make Home Unhealthy*, interested Charles Dickens, who asked Morley to contribute to *Household Words*. Morley sent *Adventures in Skitzland*, written during university years. The amazing result was a request from Dick-ens to close the school and come to assist in managing *Household Words*. The offer led to fifteen years of editorial experience with *Household Words, All the Year Round*, and *The Examiner* (1861-67).

In 1852 Morley married Miss Sayer of Newport, Isle of Wight. His first academic appointment (1857) was that of English lec-turer for evening classes at King's College, London. In 1865 he succeeded David Mas-son as professor of English language and literature at University College, and in 1878 won a similar appointment at Queen's Col-lege. Four years later he became principal of University Hall. Craving leisure for editing, he resigned in 1890 and settled at Carisbrooke, Isle of Wight. Here he died two years after his wife.

Morley was known for his teaching ability, his fluency as a speaker, and his retentiveness of memory. Urbane, widely read, genial, he was one of the most popular lecturers of his day. His appearance was charming and ge-nial, and he revealed a warm personality.

HENRY MORLEY

His literary career began in university years when he edited a college magazine and contributed to the *Foreign Quarterly Review*. In 1848, stimulated by the revolutions, he published a poem, *Sunrise in Italy*. But his best creative work was done in 1850-65. *Palissy the Potter*, a biography, was also a portrait of medieval French life. This biography was followed by two others, all well received.

As editor Morley did an enormous quantity of work. Intending to write a great history of English literature, he published ten volumes of *English Writers*, but never completed the task. During his last ten years he edited, and personally wrote introductions for, over three hundred volumes of English and French literature (in translation). The greatest concentration of his powers alone made this bulk possible. Morley performed a high service in stimulating an interest in good books. But his zeal in gathering information was yoked with a less penetrating critical ability which weakens the permanent value of his work.   D. F. A.

PRINCIPAL WORKS: Poetry—Dream of the Lily Bell, 1845; Sunrise in Italy, 1848; *Biography*—Life of Palissy the Potter, 1852; Jerome Cardan, 1854; Cornelius Agrippa, 1856; Clement Marot, 1870. *Essays*—How to Make Home Unhealthy, 1849; Adventures in Skitzland, 1850; Defence of Ignorance, 1851; Memories of Bartholomew Fair, 1857; English Writers, 1864-89; Journal of a London Playgoer, 1866; A First Sketch of English Literature, 1873; Library of English Literature (5 vols.) 1875-81; Morley's Universal Library (63 vols.) 1883-8; Cassell's National Library (214 vols.) 1886-90; Carisbrooke Library (14 vols.) 1889-91; Early Papers and Some Memories, 1891; Companion Poets (9 vols.) 1891-2. *Stories*—Fairy Tales, 1859-1860.

ABOUT: Solly, H. S. Life of Henry Morley; Illustrated London News 104:611 May 19, 1894; Public Opinion 17:173 May 24, 1894.

MORLEY, JOHN (Viscount Morley of Blackburn) (December 24, 1838-September 23, 1923), statesman and man of letters, was born at Blackburn, the son of Jonathan Morley, a surgeon. He was educated at Cheltenham and at Lincoln College, Oxford (1856-59) from which he was graduated with the degree of B.A.

Immediately after his graduation, Morley embarked upon a career of journalism in London. His unusual literary ability was not long in attracting attention, and after experience on various journals he became editor of the *Fortnightly Review* in 1867, in which position he remained for fifteen years. In 1867 his study of Burke was published, and by 1871 he had contributed so many excellent articles to his magazine that the first book of his *Critical Miscellanies* was brought out.

During his fifteen years' editorship of the *Fortnightly Review*, Morley gathered around him many of the most brilliant liberal leaders

JOHN MORLEY

and writers, and himself wrote many articles upon history, biography, and questions of the day, all notable for their vividness, insight, and style. Morley later edited the *Pall Mall Gazette* (1880-83) and, for a time, *Macmillan's Magazine*. Meanwhile he had published his brilliant study *On Compromise* (1874) and among other works biographies of Rousseau, Voltaire, and Richard Cobden, the English statesman and advocate of Free Trade. In these works, as in most of his thinking, he showed the influence of the French Positivist philosopher Auguste Comte, and of his friend and master John Stuart Mill, the liberalist philosopher. He was known as an agnostic, and has been good-humoredly laughed at for having written the name of the deity with a small "g" in some of his earlier works.

In 1882 Morley commenced an active career in politics when he was returned as Liberal member for Newcastle. He became chief assistant to Gladstone, and when the latter regained the prime ministry in 1885 he appointed Morley chief secretary for Ireland. An advocate, naturally, of Home Rule, of which Gladstone was the arch-agitator, Morley retained his office even after his chief's resignation in 1894, and filled it justly and efficiently despite much opposition and lack of cooperation. Although he lost his seat for Newcastle in 1895 because of his views on the Eight Hour Labor Bill and his anti-imperialism, another constituency was found for him and he continued to be active in the House of Commons until 1908, the year of his elevation to the peerage and consequent transference to the House of Lords. Here he remained until his voluntary retirement in 1914 upon the outbreak of the war (which he, a known pacifist, preferred to observe as a layman)

As secretary for India from 1905 to 1910, he brought about the passage of important legislation.

Gladstone's death had occured in 1898, and his family had asked Morley to be his official biographer. After sorting and selecting a vast store of papers, Morley completed the work, one of exemplary thoroughness, which was published in 1903. Perhaps because of this experience, he did not feel that he himself wished to have a biographer; after his retirement he brought out his *Recollections* (1917) and forbade, in his will, the use of his papers and journals to anyone desirous of writing his life. He characterized such an undertaking as "unnecessary."

As a liberal, Morley belonged to the old, intellectual tradition—a man who dissociated theory from action and who could remark that "the chief business of a government was to govern," which practical belief, as secretary for India, he put into unwavering practise.

His literary output, while lacking any profound or lasting significance, was of a high level both for the character of his thought and for the smooth and accomplished style of his writing. In it he revealed himself as a man of high ideals and quiet tolerance—"the most famous of the philosophical liberals of the 19th century," said H. W. Massingham. In addition to his critical works, Morley's *English Men of Letters Series* (1878-) should be mentioned for the brilliant contributions of so many English authorities.

Morley was a man of small stature, somewhat frail in appearance, with keen eyes and with the large head of the typical intellectual. In private life as well as in politics his learning and sincerity were impressive, and his manner was amiable and easy.   R. M.

PRINCIPAL WORKS: *Criticism*—Critical Miscellanies, 1871, 1877, 1886, 1908; Studies in Literature, 1891. *Philosophy*—On Compromise, 1874. *Biography* —Burke, 1867; Voltaire, 1872; Richard Cobden, 1881; Walpole, 1889; William Ewart Gladstone, 1903. *Editor*—English Men of Letters Series, 1878-. *Autobiography*—Recollections, 1917. *Complete Works*—Works, 1921.

ABOUT: Hirst, F. W. Early Life and Letters of John Morley; Morley, J. Recollections; Morgan, H. W. John Morley; Contemporary Review 124: 545 November 1, 1923; Current History 19:209 November 1923; Fortnightly Review ns114:695 November 1, 1923.

MORRIS, SIR LEWIS

MORRIS, SIR LEWIS (January 23, 1833-November 12, 1907), Welsh poet and educator, was born at Carmarthen. His father, Lewis E. W. Morris, a solicitor and official, was the grandson of the earlier Welsh poet, Lewis Morris; his mother was the former Sophia Hughes.

He was educated at Queen Elizabeth's Grammar School in Carmarthen, at Cowbridge, and at Sherburne for one year, after

LEWIS MORRIS

which preparation he matriculated at Jesus College, Oxford, 1851. His scholastic distinctions included a first place in classical moderations and in litterae humaniores, and, after he had been graduated with the degree of B.A. in 1856, the chancellor's prize for his essay on "The Greatness and Decline of Venice." He received his M.A. in 1858 and then enrolled as a law student at Lincoln's Inn, being called to the bar in 1861. His practice, largely in conveyancing, continued until about 1880.

In 1871 he published the first volume of *Songs of Two Worlds,* inspired by Tennyson's verse and immediately popular. In 1874 and 1875 a second and third volume appeared, followed in 1876-77 by his best known work, *The Epic of Hades.* It was at this time that he began to be active in the interests of Welsh education, but he continued to publish lyric and dramatic verse with great financial success. As the friend and follower of Tennyson, he was held one of the logical candidates for the post of Poet Laureate when Tennyson died in 1892. Morris was bitterly disappointed at his failure to receive this appointment, but was partially recompensed by being knighted in 1895 in recognition of his odes on the marriage of the Duke of York (afterwards George V).

In 1878 Morris became one of the joint honorary secretaries to the University College of Wales, and in 1880 was appointed to the committee for Welsh education; he served for a time as joint treasurer and joint vice-president of the University College, aided in the founding of the University of Wales in 1893, was chancellor from 1901 to 1903, and received the degree of D.Litt. in 1906. His activities also included much active political campaigning, though he was a generally unsuccessful candidate, being returned only once. He was an advocate of the higher education of women and of Welsh Home Rule, and for twenty-seven years (1880-1907) was chairman of the committee for Eisteddfod, the great Welsh festival.

Sir Lewis died at Penbryn, leaving his widow, the former Mrs. Florence Julia Pollard, whom he had married in 1868, although the marriage was not announced until 1902. They had two daughters and one son.

Morris was a poet of facility and skill and certainly not without power; but it is not unfair to say that he owed his popularity to the fact that his verse was exactly attuned to the middle class taste and similar to that of Tennyson. The vogue of his work ended by arousing a reaction against Tennysonian verse in general. Most critics would agree with George Saintsbury, who described it as smooth, respectable poetry, excellently calculated for the public taste, or with *The Athenaeum*, which said that his work "lacked personality" and that "it had no manner of its own." R. M.

PRINCIPAL WORKS: *Poetry*—Songs of Two Worlds (3 vols.) 1871, 1874, 1875; The Epic of Hades (2 vols.) 1876, 1877. *Essays*—The New Rambler, 1905.

ABOUT: Miles, A. H. Poets and Poetry of the Century; Athenaeum November 16, 1907; Times November 13 and December 24, 1907.

MORRIS, WILLIAM

MORRIS, WILLIAM (March 24, 1834-October 3, 1896), poet, romance-writer, craftsman, printer, and socialist, was born at Walthamstow, near Epping, to the north of London, eldest son and third child of William Morris, bill-broker, and Emma (Shelton) Morris. Morris *père* (who was of Welsh origin) prospered extremely in his business, and made one fantastically lucky investment, in a Devon copper-mine, which appreciated to the extent of 800 per cent. William was thus brought up in easy circumstances. In 1840 a move was made to a big estate at Woodford, also on the borders of Epping Forest, and much of the boy's childhood was passed in wandering and riding in that beautiful tract of country. He went first to a private school; and in February 1848 (his father having died the year before) he was entered at Marlborough College, then the newest of the public schools; and during his four years there he was able to indulge in private reading and develop his interest in archaeology, without the more severe discipline with which he would have been restrained at one of the older schools. During 1852 he was reading for matriculation with the Rev. F. B. Guy, a master at the Forest School, Walthamstow, and in January 1853 he went into residence at Exeter College, Oxford. At the same time Edward Burne-Jones came up from Birmingham. The two undergraduates at once found common ground in love of mediaeval chivalry, of old Gothic churches, of memorial brasses, and the like. With R. W. Dixon, C. J. Faulkner (later a partner in the Morris firm of decorators), and others, Morris and Burne-Jones shared an enthusiasm for poetry and fine art, especially as exemplified and interpreted in the writings of Tennyson and Ruskin. Morris's high Anglicanism at one point almost led him to Rome, but there he stopped short. When he came of age in 1855 he drew an income of £900 a year, and he spent money lavishly in the subsidizing of the *Oxford and Cambridge Magazine*—a periodical which ran for only twelve issues, but which published three of Rossetti's best poems and some of Morris' early work in verse and prose. In the vacations he visited Northern France and made firsthand acquaintance with its cathedrals. He took a pass degree in the winter of 1855, and, giving up his original intention of taking orders, became articled the following January to G. E. Street, an architect then practising in Oxford.

A little later Street transferred his business to London, and in 1857 Morris was in occupation of a studio at Red Lion Square, Holborn, with Burne-Jones. Philip Webb, Street's assistant, was a firm friend at this time; but the great mentor was Rossetti, who formed a high opinion of the talent of both men from his first acquaintance with them—which did not prevent his often making game of Morris' notoriously violent temper. These men, with Holman Hunt and Millais, were the chief figures in the group known as the Pre-Raphaelite Brotherhood.

WILLIAM MORRIS

Morris' energies were now mainly devoted to the arts of design—to painting, drawing, modeling, illuminating, and designing. He still wrote poetry, as he had done at college, but as an occupation it was secondary to his craftwork. The summer of 1857 saw an ill-starred venture, the painting of the walls of the Oxford Union Society, in which task he worked alongside Burne-Jones, Rossetti, Val Prinsep, and others—ill-starred because technical ignorance failed to take into account the unsuitability of the surface, and the decorations began to fade out in six months. It was during these weeks spent at Oxford that Morris met Jane Burden, a beautiful, dark, queenly woman, whose lineaments are familiar to the public from a number of Rossetti's paintings. He was not long in winning her to an engagement, and on April 26, 1859, they were married.

Meanwhile, the year before, he had published his first volume of poems, *The Defence of Guenevere*, which, despite almost inevitable Tennysonian echoes, gave evidence of a personal outlook and an individual music and which drew new values out of the Arthurian theme. After his marriage Morris' creative urge found practical expression in designing (with Webb) his own house, at Bexleyheath, Upton, Kent. The difficulty of obtaining the right appurtenances for this Red House, and Morris' consequent determination to make them himself, led naturally enough to the foundation, in April 1861, of the firm of Morris, Marshall, Faulkner & Company, which undertook all kinds of decoration, from murals to the smallest objects of applied art. Rossetti and Ford Madox Brown were the prime movers in the scheme; Morris was the chief financial prop; a great deal of church work and general decoration was carried out; and in the thirteen years of its existence the firm exercised a profound influence on all the crafts, playing a large part in the resuscitation of original and truly-felt design. In November 1865 the Morrisses came in from Kent to live at Queen Square, Bloomsbury, in the upper part of a building which housed the firm in its lower story.

The phenomenal copper-mine had now begun to yield much less; two daughters had arrived; the daily journey from Upton consumed much time: all these were reasons for coming to London. Once settled at Queen Square, Morris took up poetry again, embarking on a grandiose project of a cycle of verse tales, *The Earthly Paradise*, deriving from Greek, Scandinavian, and mediaeval sources. One epic story, *The Life and Death of Jason*, outran the scale of the whole and came out first, as a separate poem, in June 1867. *The Earthly Paradise* appeared in three volumes between 1868 and 1870. Both these works of great length well display Morris' poetic quality at its highest. The point of view is essentially romantic; the fundamental aestheticism of the man is everywhere revealed—his delight in rich colors, jewels, and brocades—mythology ceases to be a text-book affair and comes to life; yet there is a certain emotional lack, and the heroic couplets often fringe the borders of commonplace. But by and large these epics struck the note of great poetry and put Morris in the first rank.

In 1870 Morris' work as a craftsman was mainly on illuminated manuscripts. His literary side was occupied with Icelandic studies, aided by Eirikr Magnússon, who collaborated with him in that year in a translation of the Völsunga-saga. At midsummer 1871 he bought his beautiful country home, Kelmscott Manor, near Lechlade, on the upper Thames; and soon after he made a memorable journey to Iceland. On his return he began *Love is Enough*, a poem in which he harked back to Middle English alliterative verse. Of his remaining poetical works there is room here only for a word on *Sigurd the Volsung*, which came out in November 1876. An immense epic, in six-foot anapestic rhyming couplets, it catches the stark, grim heroism of the ancient Northern mythology, moves forward with majestic rhythm, and was considered by Morris himself to mark his highest achievement.

At the end of 1874 the business partnership was dissolved, and the firm formerly directed by seven men came under Morris' sole control. In the next year he took up dyeing with enthusiasm; and for some time he worked principally at this and at carpet-weaving. Meanwhile his philosophic attitude was moving him to take an increasing interest in public affairs. In 1877 he founded the Society for the Protection of Ancient Buildings; his approach to social questions was by way of aesthetics, and he gradually came to feel that only in socialism could be found conditions suitable for the leading of seemly, free, and beautiful lives. At the beginning of 1883 he joined the Democratic Federation. Internecine quarrels led to its dissolution the next year; and on its ruins was founded the Socialist League, into the work of which Morris threw much of his abounding energy. Two very notable prose works came out of his socialist phase, *The Dream of John Ball* and *News From Nowhere*, the latter a protest against the "regimentation" of Edward Bellamy's *Looking Backward*. The atmosphere of these books is as different as could be from the hard-fact social and statistical works of the early Socialist period: it is an atmosphere of poetry, good-fellowship, and mediaevalism; it shows a world in which the ugliness and slavery of the machine have been replaced by beauty created by the loving hands of free craftsmen, and in which money grubbing has been forgotten. His last writings were a series of prose romances, beginning with *The House of the Wolfings* (1889), which develop a fairy-tale arcadian optimism in a prose that is consciously archaic.

One last great work remained. So great a bibliophile as Morris could never be indifferent to the material form of books; and in 1890, spurred to enthusiasm by his friend Emery Walker, he set up the Kelmscott Press at Hammersmith (where he now lived), and with characteristic thoroughness began to design his own types and decorations and to seek out the best possible ink and paper. The Press published fifty-three books before it was wound up in March 1898; the *Chaucer* (1896) is one of the marvels of modern typography; and in general Morris' influence on the craft of printing has been profound and enduring. He insisted on the unity of the double-page spread, with type, type-area, margins and decoration all designed as a whole: his only fault was over-elaborateness.

His health failing early in 1896, Morris took a journey to Norway in the hope of recuperation, but on his return in August he became worse, and steadily sank towards death, which took place on October 3.

"Morris," writes R. B. Cunninghame Graham, "was of middle height and very strongly built . . . His face was ruddy, and his hair inclined to red and grew in waves like water just before it breaks over a fall. His beard was of the same color as his hair. His eyes were blue and fiery. His teeth small and irregular . . . When he walked he swayed a little, not like a sailor sways, but as a man who lives a sedentary life, toddles a little in his gait. His ears were small, his nose high and well made, his hands and feet small for a man of his considerable bulk. His speech and his address were fitting to the man: bold, bluff and hearty . . . He was quick-tempered and irritable, swift to anger and swift to reconciliation, and I should think never bore malice in his life."

Morris had a logical, far-seeing and poetic mind, and his whole career, so diverse in its activities, was presided over by a single-hearted quest after beauty. In the phrase of the old epitaph, "he touched nothing that he did not adorn"; yet, as Montague Weekley puts it, he was "as matter-of-fact in referring to his work as though he were talking about plumbing." This attitude was not accidental, but arose naturally from his philosophy of art and life. He devoted time, care, study, money and boundless enthusiasm to demonstrating in a practical way the kind of existence he envisaged for an artist-craftsman or poet in a remade world. This world was too much a sentimentalizing of the past. The flaw in his scheme was that it deplored modern developments wholeheartedly instead of aiming to evolve a new technique which would refine out the grosser elements and make use of what was good. Morris achieved greatly as a poet and as a printer, and his influence on the arts of design, on social philosophy, and on taste, has been wide and deep.   H. B. G.

PRINCIPAL WORKS: *Poetry*—The Defence of Guenevere, 1858; The Life and Death of Jason, 1867; The Earthly Paradise (3 vols.) 1868-70; Love Is Enough, 1872; The Æneids of Virgil, 1875; Sigurd the Volsung, 1876; The Odyssey of Homer, 1887; Poems by the Way, 1891. *Prose*—Völsunga Saga (trans. with E. Magnússon) 1870; Hopes and Fears for Art, 1882; The Dream of John Ball, 1888; The House of the Wolfings, 1888; The Roots of the Mountains, 1889; News From Nowhere, 1890; The Story of the Glittering Plain, 1891; The Wood Beyond the World, 1895; The Well at the World's End, 1896; The Water of the Wondrous Isles, 1898; The Sundering Flood, 1898. Collected Works (ed. by May Morris, 24 vols.) 1910-15.

ABOUT: Cockerell, S. C. A Description of the Kelmscott Press; Clutton-Brock, A. William Morris; Compton-Rickett, A. William Morris: A Study in Personality; Drinkwater, J. William Morris: A Critical Study; Jackson, H. William Morris; Mackail, J. W. Life of William Morris; Noyes, A. William Morris; Vallance, A. William Morris; Weekley, M. William Morris.

MORTON, JOHN MADDISON (January 3, 1811-December 19, 1891), playwright, was the son of the dramatist, Thomas Morton. He was educated in France and Germany from 1817 to 1820, then sent to the school of Charles Richardson, the lexicographer, which seems to have been a favorite among theatrical persons. From 1832 to 1840 he was a clerk in the Chelsea Hospital. His first farce was produced in 1835. Morton was essentially a writer of farces, nearly all adapted from the French. *Box and Cox*, the best known, was made up of two French farces combined. He was extremely prolific, but conditions changed in the English theatre and by the time he reached middle age his work was no longer in demand. The soured old man began in 1867 to keep himself alive by giving public readings. This too failed him, and in 1881, through Queen Victoria, he was named a brother of the Charterhouse. In 1889 his stage friends of former days gave a great benefit for him. He continued to write almost to the last, and died in the Charterhouse at nearly eighty-two. At least one of Morton's plays was written in collaboration with his father. His work was highly humorous, but frequently coarse, and without literary merit, being intended only for ephemeral stage production.

PRINCIPAL WORKS: Box and Cox, 1847; Done on Both Sides, 1847; From Village to Court, 1850; Maggie's Situation, 1875; The Garden Party, 1877; The Miser's Treasure, 1878; Going It, 1885.

ABOUT: Era December 26, 1891; London Times December 21 and 24, 1891.

MORTON, THOMAS (1764?-March 28, 1838), dramatist, was born in Durham. His father died early and he was reared by his uncle, a London stockbroker. He was sent to Soho Square School, where he became an ardent amateur actor. He entered Lincoln's Inn, but was not called to the bar. His first plays met with success, and from 1792 he devoted all his time to play-writing. He was married, and had two sons and one daughter; one of the sons, John Maddison Morton, became a well-known writer of farces. In 1837 Morton was made an honorary member of the Garrick Club, a rare proceeding. He was a cricket enthusiast, and was senior member of Lord's. His plays, mostly comedies or farces, were popular in their day, but have not survived.

PRINCIPAL WORKS: Columbus, 1792; The Way to Get Married, 1796; Speed the Plough, 1798; The Blind Girl, 1801; The School of Reform, 1805; Town and Country, 1807; Education, 1813; The Slave, 1816; School for Grown Children, 1827.

ABOUT: Gentleman's Magazine Part 1, 1838.

MOTHERWELL, WILLIAM (October 13, 1797-November 1, 1835), Scottish poet, was born at Glasgow. His earliest education was obtained there, but after his eleventh year he was reared by his uncle in Paisley. At fifteen he began the study of law in the office of the sheriff-clerk of Paisley, and had later the benefit of one session at Glasgow University. He has been described as a dreamy sort of boy, with little taste for either science or the classics; but at the age of twenty-one he began the entirely practical career of deputy sheriff-clerk of Renfrewshire, and was later promoted to the chief clerkship.

As early as 1819 he had edited a miscellany, *The Harp of Renfrewshire*, and had gained some experience as a contributor to newspapers and periodicals. He gradually drifted into journalism, changing, over a period of years from radical to Tory, and remained in this profession until his death. It was of course unsuited to one of his temperament, and handicapped him as a poet; but he was able enough to hold the position of editor of the *Glasgow Gazette*, which he secured in 1832.

In 1827 Motherwell published a collection of songs entitled *Minstrelsy Ancient and Modern*, with an introduction so well planned and executed that it aroused the interest and admiration of Scott. He became an authority on the subject of the ancient ballads. A volume of his poems which appeared in 1832 received high praise from "Christopher North," although today they do not seem impressive. He continued his literary endeavors by collaboration with James Hogg on an edition of Burns' poems, and planned a life of Tannahill, another Scottish poet, which he was never to finish.

His death was a sudden one. Motherwell had joined the Society of Orangemen, a political organization, without a very clear comprehension of what its objects were; and when he was called to London to testify concerning the society, he broke down completely on the stand and was sent home in an exhausted condition. This precipitated the apoplectic stroke which shortly afterward killed him.

Motherwell's Scottish poems have a certain sweet and tender quality which accounts for their earlier popularity. One of them, "Jeanie Morison," written about a boyhood sweetheart, has been much quoted and admired. Motherwell was also considered successful in his imitations of Scandinavian war songs and ballads, as in "The Battle Flag of Sigurd" and "The Sword Chant of Thorstein Raudi." However, it is doubtful if these will outlast his lyrics, which were a more natural representation of his spirit.

He was a small man, vigorous, of good physique, with large head, curly brown hair, and deep-set eyes—a man who looked like the poet he was and who might have amounted to more as a lyrist had he not been obliged to engage in other and more lucrative work.

R. M.

PRINCIPAL WORKS: *Poetry*—Poems, 1832. *Editor* —The Harp of Renfrewshire, 1819; Minstrelsy Ancient and Modern, 1827.

ABOUT: Motherwell, W. Poems, 1846 (see Life by McConechy); Blackwood's Magazine 33:670 April 1833.

MOULTRIE, JOHN (December 30, 1799-December 26, 1874), poet, was born in London, the son of a clergyman of Scottish descent. His paternal grandfather left South Carolina for England on the outbreak of the American Revolution; his great-uncle, for whom Fort Moultrie was named, was a well

WILLIAM MOTHERWELL

known American Revolutionary officer. He was educated at Eton, where Shelley was a fellow-pupil, but seven years his senior. He began writing poems for *The Etonian* and for the *Quarterly Magazine,* using the pseudonym of "Gerard Montgomery." He then entered Trinity College, Cambridge, receiving his M.A. in 1822. He read law at the Middle Temple, acting meanwhile as a private tutor, but abandoned this profession and was ordained in 1825 on promise of a living at Rugby. In the same year he married Harriet Fergusson, who died in 1864, leaving three sons and four daughters. Moultrie went to Rugby the same year the famous Dr. Thomas Arnold became headmaster of Rugby School, and the two were close friends and co-workers for many years.

Moultrie wrote many hymns besides his secular poems. His earliest work is by far the best, with mingled humor and pathos and real lyric beauty. His later poems were labored, and were obviously imitative of Wordsworth.

PRINCIPAL WORKS: My Brother's Grave, 1820; Godiva, 1821; Poems, 1837; The Dream of Life, 1843; The Black Fence, 1850; Altars, Hearths, and Graves, 1854.

ABOUT: Moultrie, J. Poems (see Memoir by D. Coleridge in 1876 ed.).

MOXON, EDWARD (December 1801-June 3, 1858), poet, was born at Wakefield, and educated at the Green Coat School. At nine he was apprenticed to a bookseller, and in 1817 went to London to work at his trade. On Sundays after midnight he studied, gaining a good knowledge of English literature. From 1821 to 1827 he was connected with Longman & Company, the publishers, soon becoming a department head, and leaving them to become literary advisor to another publisher named Hurst. In 1830, with help of his friend Samuel Rogers, the writer, he was enabled to establish his own publishing business. He became a close friend of Charles Lamb, and in 1833 married Lamb's adopted daughter, Emma Isola. They had one son and five daughters. When Lamb died in 1834 he left his library to Moxon, and it was not dispersed until after Moxon's death. In 1831 Moxon started the *Englishman's Magazine,* which died within a year. He was Wordsworth's publisher until the poet's death, and was especially encouraging to young poets, among whom Tennyson and Browning were numbered. His publication of the first complete edition of Shelley's poems caused him to be prosecuted and convicted, but the sentence was never carried out. The business outlived him, but finally expired in 1878.

Moxon was personally a pleasant, modest man, a true lover of poetry, but his own writing shows more literary appreciation than it does original talent.

PRINCIPAL WORKS: The Prospect and Other Poems, 1826; Christmas, 1829; Sonnets, 1830 and 1835.

ABOUT: Illustrated London News June 12, 1858.

MOZLEY, JAMES BOWLING (September 15, 1813-January 4, 1878), theologian, was the brother of Thomas and ANNE MOZLEY, both writers. He was born in Gainsborough, the son of a bookseller, who moved to Derby when Thomas was two. He was educated at Grantham Grammar School and at Oriel College, Oxford, where he won an English essay prize, and received his M.A. in 1838, B.D. in 1846, and D.D. 1877. In 1840 he was named a fellow of Magdalen College. He was a close friend of Pusey and Newman, an ardent member of the Oxford High Church Movement, and at one time almost followed Newman into the Roman Catholic Church. He was from 1845 to 1855 joint editor of the high church *Christian Remembrancer,* resigning when his views became more evangelical. From 1856 to his death he was a vicar of Old Shoreham, Sussex. In 1856 also he married Amelia Ogle, daughter of the regius professor of medicine at Oxford. She died in 1872. The marriage was childless.

A Liberal and a friend of Gladstone, the prime minister made him a canon of Worcester in 1869. In 1871 he became regius professor of divinity. He was a dull and lifeless lecturer, but the fulness and solidity of his subject matter made him respected. In 1875 he suffered a stroke; he recovered partially and lectured again in 1876, but the effort brought on a relapse, and he died at Shoreham two years later. Unpleasing as he was as a lecturer, his writing was forceful and impressive, and he had a great influence on theological thought in Great Britain.

PRINCIPAL WORKS: On Miracles, 1865; University and Other Sermons, 1876; Ruling Ideas in Early Ages, 1877; Essays: Historical and Theological, 1878.

ABOUT: Mozley, A. (ed.). Letters of the Rev. J. B. Mozley, D.D.; Mozley, J. B. Essays: Historical and Theological (see Biographical Introduction by A. Mozley).

MOZLEY, THOMAS (1806-June 17, 1893), theologian and editor, was born in Gainsborough, son of a bookseller, brother of ANNE and James Bowling Mozley, both writers. He was educated at the Charterhouse and at Oriel College, Oxford, where he was an intimate friend of John Henry (later Cardinal) Newman. He received his B.A. in 1828, became a tutor, and a fellow of Oriel. In 1831 he was ordained deacon, in 1832 priest. He overworked in the two college parishes to which he was presented, and was obliged to relinquish them and become a curate at Buckland near Oxford, finally becoming perpetual curate in Northamptonshire.

In 1835 he was made junior treasurer of Oriel. The next year he married Harriet Elizabeth Newman, Newman's sister, and became rector of a college living at Wiltshire. MRS. MOZLEY, who died in 1852, leaving a daughter, was a novelist, author of *Louisa: or, The Bride* (1842), *Family Adventures* (1852), and other novels.

Mozley had been a contributor to the *British Critic,* the organ of the Tractarians (Puseyites), and in 1844 joined the staff of *The Times,* becoming one of their principal leader writers. In 1857 he retired to Berkshire, and in 1861 married again, a Miss Bradshaw. He was called back to the church in 1868, to a college living in Plymtree, Devon. In 1869 he reported the Ecumenical Conference at Rome for *The Times.* In 1874 he was made rural dean of Plymtree. In 1880 failing sight forced his final retirement to Cheltenham, where he lived for thirteen years more, almost entirely blind.

Mozley was unusually versatile, an acute writer with a vast fund of information, and in his non-theological works possessed a persuasive style.

PRINCIPAL WRITINGS: Reminiscences: Chiefly of Oriel and the Oxford Movement, 1882; Reminiscences of Towns, Villages, and Schools, 1889; The Word, 1889; The Son, 1891; The Creed: or, A Philosophy, 1893.
ABOUT: Mozley, T. Reminiscences; The Creed (see Autobiographical Preface).

MUIR, SIR WILLIAM (April 27, 1819-July 11, 1905), Scottish Arabic scholar and historian of Islam, was born in Glasgow, the son of a merchant, and educated at Glasgow University. During thirty-nine years' service with the East India Company (1837-76) he served notably as foreign secretary to the Indian government, lieutenant-governor of the North-West Provinces, and financial member of Lord Northbrook's council. He received knighthood in 1867. Muir College and the University at Allahabad were founded by him. After his retirement from India he was for nine years a member of the Council of India in London, and spent the last twenty years of his life in Scotland as principal of Edinburgh University. He died in Edinburgh at the age of eighty-six. By his wife, Elizabeth Huntly Wemyss, he had fifteen children.

During his busy administrative career he earned a widespread reputation as an Arabic scholar. In recognition of "the great value, importance, and volume" of his work on Islamic history and literature, he was awarded the triennial jubilee gold medal in 1903. The best known of his works is his standard four-volume *Life of Mahomet.*

His eldest brother, JOHN MUIR (1810-1822), Orientalist, edited *Original Sanskrit Texts* (1858-70), of importance in the study of the Vedic era.

PRINCIPAL WORKS OF SIR WILLIAM MUIR: Life of Mahomet: History of Islam to the Era of the Hegira, 1858-61; The Corân: Its Composition and Teaching, 1878; Annals of the Early Caliphate, 1883; The Caliphate: Its Rise, Decline and Fall, 1891; The Mameluke or Slave Dynasty of Egypt, 1896.
ABOUT: Royal Asiatic Society's Journal, 1905; The Times July 12, 1905.

MÜLLER, (FRIEDRICH) MAX (December 6, 1823-October 28, 1900), philologist, essayist, philosopher, and miscellaneous writer, though born at Dessau, Germany, comes within our purview because fifty-two years of his life were spent in Oxford and nearly all his writing was done in English. He was the son of Wilhelm Müller, the poet, and Adelheid, eldest daughter of Präsident von Basedow, Prime Minister of the Duchy of Anhalt-Dessau. He was educated first at the local grammar school; then from 1836 to 1841, at Leipzig, and finally at the University of Leipzig, which he entered in the spring of 1841. He had already shown considerable talent in music, but at the University his feet were set on the road that he was to follow to the end—that of philology. Herman Brockhaus, first occupant of the chair of Sanskrit, persuaded him to take up that language, and so rapidly did he progress that at the age of twenty (1844) he published a translation of the *Hitopadeśa* into German. He had graduated Ph.D. in September 1843. Early in 1844 he went to Berlin, where he studied philology under Bopp and philosophy under Schelling. The next year he was in Paris, working with the noted Sanskrit and Zend scholar, Eugène Burnouf. He earned a thin livelihood by copying manuscripts and kindred work, and set about the collection of materials for an edition of the *Rigveda,* the most important sacred book of the Brahmans.

Coming to England in June 1846, he obtained support for this big project from the East India Company. In 1848 he was again in Paris, at work on manuscripts, but left on the outbreak of the Revolution. In May of that year he settled in Oxford. In 1850 he was made deputy Taylorian professor of modern European languages, and in 1854 full professor and M.A. by decree. In 1859 he married Georgiana Adelaide, daughter of Riversdale Grenfell.

Max Müller's defeat in 1860 (largely owing to his foreign origin and liberal theological views) by Sir Monier Monier-Williams in the election to the chair of Sanskrit turned his energies to the more general subject of comparative philology, which he

MAX MÜLLER

illuminated with philosophy and humor. His Royal Institution lectures *On the Science of Language* (1861 and 1863) provoked great public interest and opened up new fields of speculation. Though much of their argument has been superseded by later research, they have never been surpassed for nimble and agile thought and charm and grace of style. Philology was never a water-tight compartment to Müller. It led him to comparative mythology and comparative religion, in both of which he was a pioneer. He lectured on religion at the Royal Institution in 1870 and delivered the Hibbert Lectures in 1878 and the Gifford Lectures in 1888 and 1892.

His retirement from active teaching work in 1875 left him free for his great task as general editor of the *Sacred Books of the East*, forty-eight volumes of which he issued for the Oxford University Press. Quite apart from his immense services to Sanskrit study and comparative philology, he wrote much general matter and a romantic book, *Deutsche Liebe*, which was pirated in America as *Memories* and ran into many editions. He even found time for politics, and stood up for Germany in the Franco-Prussian war and for England in the fight with the Boers. He was a Privy Councillor of England, and won very numerous academic and public honors in many countries. His humane and friendly temperament, so evident in all he wrote, found social expression in a courteous and abundant hospitality, and he was *persona grata* not only to Indians and Oxford colleagues but to many men of mark throughout Europe. Müller died at Oxford in 1900. He left three daughters and one son.   H. B. G.

PRINCIPAL WORKS: *Comparative Philology*—A History of Ancient Sanskrit Literature, 1859; Lectures on the Science of Language (2 vols.) 1861-4; On the Stratification of Language, 1868; Biographies of Words and the Home of the Aryas, 1888. *Religion and Mythology*—Introduction to the Science of Religion, 1873; Lectures on the Origin and Growth of Religion, 1878; Natural Religion, 1889; Physical Religion, 1891; Anthropological Religion, 1892; Theosophy: or, Psychological Religion, 1893; Contributions to the Science of Mythology, 1897. *Oriental Translations and Editions*—Hitopadeśa (in German) 1844; Meghadūta (in German) 1847; Rigveda (6 vols.) 1849-73; Dhammapada 1870; Upanishads, 1879; Sacred Books of the East (49 vols.) 1879-94. *Philosophy*—Kant's Critique of Pure Reason (trans.) 1881; The Science of Thought, 1887; Three Lectures on the Vedānta Philosophy, 1894; The Six Systems of Indian Philosophy, 1899. *Biography*—Biographical Essays 1884; Ramakrsna: His Life and Sayings, 1898; Auld Lang Syne (2 vols.) 1898-99; My Autobiography: A Fragment, 1901. *Miscellaneous*—The German Classics From the Fourth to the Nineteenth Century, 1858; Deutsche Liebe, 1857; Chips From a German Workshop (4 vols.) 1867-75; India: What Can It Teach Us? 1883.
ABOUT: Müller, G. A. The Life and Letters of the Right Honorable Friedrich Max Müller; Müller, F. M. My Autobiography: A Fragment; North American Review 171:884 December 1900; Forum 30:620 January 1901.

MULOCK, DINAH MARIA. See CRAIK. DINAH MARIA MULOCK

MUNBY, ARTHUR JOSEPH (1828-January 29, 1910), poet, was born at Clifton Holme, Yorkshire, the son of a solicitor, and educated at Trinity College, Cambridge. Called to the bar at Lincoln's Inn in 1855, he held a position in the ecclesiastical commissioners' office for thirty years (1858-88) and retired at the age of sixty. He died at his cottage at Pyrford, Surrey, in his eighty-second year. His will disclosed the fact that he had been secretly married in 1873 to his servant, Hannah Cullwick, who retained her menial position until her death in 1909. He left no children.

According to Austin Dobson, "Munby's poetry is characterized by its absolute sincerity, its scholarship, its technical skill, its descriptive power, and its keen feeling for and close observation of nature and rural life." His country elegy, *Dorothy*, dedicated to his lifelong friend the novelist Richard Doddridge Blackmore, was warmly praised by Robert Browning. George Saintsbury calls Munby "an eccentric poet of rather wasted talent" whom some would rank (not without reason) above several of his more celebrated contemporaries.

PRINCIPAL WORKS: Benoni, 1852; Verses New and Old, 1865; Dorothy: A Country Story in Elegaic Verse, 1880; Vulgar Verses by "Jones Brown," 1890; Vestigia Retrorsum, 1891; Susan, 1893; Poems: Chiefly Lyric and Elegaic, 1901; Relicta, 1909.
ABOUT: The Times February 5, 1910.

MUNRO, HUGH ANDREW JOHN-STONE (October 19, 1819-March 30, 1885), classical scholar, was an illegitimate child, his father being a wealthy collector of paintings whose name was given to the child. He seems, in spite of his illegitimacy, to have had every advantage of education. Born at Elgin, he was sent in 1833 to Shrewsbury Grammar School, and in 1838 he entered Trinity College, Cambridge, as a pensioner, becoming a scholar in 1840. In 1842 he was graduated second in classics, and in 1843 was made a fellow.

After traveling in Paris, Florence, and Berlin, Munro returned to Cambridge and took holy orders. The rest of his life was spent at Trinity. At first he lectured on the classics, but as a lecturer he was a rank failure: he was an extremely slow and deliberate speaker, and besides was so very absent-minded that any diversion was likely to send him off on another subject. All his life he was the typical—though seldom seen—"absent-minded professor." From 1869 to 1872, in spite of this handicap, he was professor of Latin, but resigned at the first opportunity and thereafter devoted himself to his studies and translations of Latin authors, his specialty being the study of the great Roman poet, Lucretius.

Though Munro's permanent residence was at Trinity, he traveled a good deal on the continent and spent almost every summer in Scotland. His chief recreation was the writing of original Greek and Latin verses, in which he excelled, and the classical correctness of which he defended against all attacks. He was never married.

Unusually strong in body, he was attacked in his middle sixties by an inflammation of the mucous membranes; going to Italy for its warmer climate he was seized by a malignant abscess which caused his death in Rome in March 1885. He is buried in the English Protestant Cemetery in that city.

Munro was handsome, with a remarkably broad forehead, and thick dark brown hair. He had few intimates, but those he loved devotedly. A man of quiet, reserved manners, he yet hated outspokenly anything false or mean. He was dignified and courteous, though his extreme deliberation of manner and speech caused him to be regarded by his associates as something of a bore.

There was nothing narrow or exclusive in Munro's devotion to the classics; he knew and loved also the best in French, German, and Italian poetry, and was particularly devoted to Dante. No one has excelled him as an authority on Lucretius, of whom so little is actually known. His translations have a nobility and felicity which exalts them into works of literature in their own right. In a very limited field his work still stands supreme.   M. A. deF.

PRINCIPAL WORKS: *Translations and Editions*—Lucretius, 1860-64; Aetna, 1867; Horace, 1869. *Miscellaneous*—Pronunciation of Latin, 1871; Palmer and Munro's Syllabus, 1872; Criticisms and Elucidations of Catullus, 1878; Translations Into Latin and Greek Verse, 1906.

ABOUT: Athenaeum April 4, 1885; London Times March 31, 1885.

MURCHISON, SIR RODERICK IMPEY (February 19, 1792-October 22, 1871), Scottish geologist, was born at Tarradale, Ross-shire, and educated at the military college at Great Marlow, England. He fought in Portugal and Spain, devoted himself for several years to fox-hunting, and took up geology at thirty-two. Between 1831 and 1838 he made pioneer researches in the underlying rock strata of the west of England; his findings resulted in the establishment of the Silurian System, and later (with Adam Sedgwick) of the Devonian System. In the early 1840's he and two others made a geological survey of Russia. These activities resulted in his two principal books, of which *The Silurian System* was later revised as *Siluria*. He was president of the Royal Geographical Society from 1843 onwards, and in 1855 became director-general of the Geological Survey of the United Kingdom and director of the Royal School of Mines. He was knighted in 1863. Shortly before his death he endowed a chair of geology and mineralogy at the University of Edinburgh. He died

H. A. J. MUNRO

in London of bronchitis at the age of seventy-nine.

In the words of his biographer, "He was not a profound thinker, but his contemporaries could hardly find a clearer, more keen-eyed and careful observer."

PRINCIPAL WORKS: The Silurian System, 1838; The Geology of Russia and the Ural Mountains (with A. von Keyserling and E. de Verneuil) 1845.

ABOUT: Geike, Sir A. Life of Sir Roderick I. Murchison.

MURE, WILLIAM (July 9, 1799-April 1, 1860), Scottish classical scholar, was born at Caldwell, Ayrshire, the grandson of William Mure, baron of the Scots exchequer. He was educated at the University of Edinburgh and the University of Bonn in Germany. On his father's death in 1831, he succeeded to the Caldwell estates. Like his father, he was for many years a colonel in the Renfrewshire militia and was lord rector of Glasgow University (1847-1848). From 1846 to 1855 he sat in Parliament for Renfrewshire as a conservative, seldom taking part in debate. He died in London at the age of sixty. By his wife, Laura Markham, he had three sons and three daughters.

He was an able scholar, devoted to Greek literature for twenty years. In his interesting *Journal* of the visit to Greece in 1838 he engaged in Homeric controversy, particularly as to the localities of the *Odyssey*. His chief work, *A Critical History of the Language and Literature of Ancient Greece*, dealt specially with Xenophon and argued for the originality and authenticity of Homer's creations. This work filled five volumes but was unfinished; it stopped at 380 B.C.

PRINCIPAL WORKS: Journal of a Tour in Greece and the Ionian Islands, 1842; A Critical History of the Language and Literature of Ancient Greece, 1850-57.

ABOUT: Mure, W. (ed.). Selections From the Family Papers Preserved at Caldwell.

MURRAY, ALEXANDER STUART (January 8, 1841-March 5, 1904), Scottish classical archaeologist, was born at Arbirlot, Forfarshire, the son of a tradesman. He was educated at the universities of Edinburgh and Berlin. From 1867 onwards he was associated with the British Museum, first as assistant and after 1886 as keeper of the department of Greek and Roman antiquities. In this capacity he reorganized the galleries, made frequent visits to classical sites on the Continent, and supervised the excavations at Enkomi (Salamis) in Cyprus in 1896. Twice married he died of pneumonia at his London house near the Museum at the age of sixty-three, leaving his second wife and no children.

According to A. H. Smith, "His writings showed the width of his knowledge, and were full of curious observations on points of detail; but his power of broad elementary exposition was limited, and though he was always interesting and suggestive, it was by no means easy to follow the general drift of his thought."

PRINCIPAL WORKS: A Manual of Mythology, 1873; A History of Greek Sculpture, 1880-83; Handbook of Archaeology, 1892; Greek Bronzes, 1898; Terracotta Sarcophagi in the British Museum, 1898; Excavations in Cyprus, 1900; The Sculptures of the Parthenon, 1903.

MURRAY, DAVID CHRISTIE (April 13, 1847-August 1, 1907), novelist, was born in West Bromwich, Staffordshire, and privately schooled. At twelve he was set to work in his father's printing establishment; early in his teens, as a police court reporter for the *Birmingham Morning News*, he began an active journalistic career which took him soon to London and thence periodically to many parts of the world. During the Russo-Turkish War of 1877-78 he was special correspondent for *The Times* and *The Scotsman*. He lived mainly in Belgium and France from 1881 to 1886. As a popular lecturer, he toured Australia and New Zealand in 1889-91, and America in 1894-95. From 1898 onwards much of his writing and lecturing was done in behalf of Captain Dreyfus, the famous French accused. He died in London at the age of sixty, after a long illness. By two marriages he had two children.

He produced some thirty loosely plotted novels, in journalistic style, with many incidents drawn from his reportorial experiences. These works were notable chiefly for their faithful representation of the country life of Staffordshire.

PRINCIPAL WORKS: Novels—A Life's Atonement, 1879; Joseph's Coat, 1881; Val Strange, 1882; By the Gate of the Sea, 1883; Rainbow Gold, 1885; Aunt Rachel, 1886. Autobiography—A Novelist's Notebook, 1887; The Making of a Novelist, 1894; Recollections, 1908. Essays—Guesses at Truth, 1908.

ABOUT: See Murray's autobiographical works; The Times August 2, 1907.

MURRAY, SIR JAMES AUGUSTUS HENRY (February 7, 1837-July 26, 1915), Scottish lexicographer and philologist, was born at Denholm, near Harwick, Scotland. He was educated at Cavers and Minto Schools, where he was noted for his studiousness. At seventeen he was assistant master of the Harwick Grammar School, at twenty headmaster of the Subscription Academy. While he taught, he studied as well—languages, natural science, archaeology, but above all, philology. In 1862 he married Maggie I. S. Scott, of Belfast. For the sake of his wife's health he went to

London, and secured a position with the Chartered Bank of India. She died in childbirth in 1864, and in 1867 he married Ada Agnes Ruthven, by whom he had six sons and five daughters.

From 1870 to 1885 Murray was master of Mill Hill School. He secured a B.A. from London University in 1873. His work on Scottish dialects appeared the same year, and gave him a reputation as a philologist which led in 1879 to his appointment by the Philological Society as editor of the New English Dictionary, commonly known as the Oxford Dictionary, which is his great monument. Until 1885 he combined his editorial and teaching duties, then moved to Oxford to give the dictionary all his time. At first only ten years had been alloted to the task, and Murray died unhappy because he had not been able to complete it by 1915; as a matter of fact it took twenty years after that. From 1885 he had no opportunity for any other work, his last contribution aside from the dictionary being an important article on the English language in the 1878 edition of the *Encyclopaedia Britannica*.

Murray's indefatigable labors were recognized by various honors: he received honorary degrees from nine universities, was three times president of the London Philological Society; was Romanes lecturer at Oxford in 1900, was an original fellow of the British Academy, and was knighted in 1908. The first volume of the dictionary was published in 1884; he edited the volumes A-D, H-K, O, P, and T. He was a formal, aloof man, a devout Congregationalist, and a strong advocate of abstinence from liquor. He died after a year's illness, struggling vainly to be able to go on with what had become his lifework.

PRINCIPAL WORK: Dialect of the Southern Counties of Scotland, 1873; see also above.

ABOUT: Proceedings of the British Academy Vol. VIII, 1917-18.

MURRAY, JOHN (November 27, 1778-June 27, 1843), and **MURRAY, JOHN** (April 16, 1808-April 2, 1892), publishers, were father and son. The father was born in London of a Scottish family, his father being a half-pay lieutenant of marines turned bookseller. He was educated at private schools. He lost the sight of his right eye in childhood from an accident. His father died in 1793, and he inherited the business, which he took over at twenty-one. For a while he was London agent for the Edinburgh publisher, Archibald Constable. In 1807 he married Anne Elliott, a Scotswoman. With Scott and Southey as editorial contributors, in 1809 he started the Tory *Quarterly Review*. The magazine had

hard sledding at first, but by 1817 was a great success, and is still published. Murray built up the greatest publishing business of his time; he brought out the works of Jane Austen, Crabbe, Disraeli (between quarrels), and Byron, until a breach because of what Murray considered the radical sentiments of *Don Juan*. He edited the *Quarterly Review* himself until 1824, when because of ill health he was succeeded by J. G. Lockhart, Scott's son-in-law and biographer. Murray was known as a generous friend to his authors, and did much to dignify the profession of bookselling. Nearly all the great writers of his day were members of his personal circle.

His eldest son and namesake was brought up to inherit the business and the famous house which contained it and the Murray family, at 50 Albermarle Street. He was educated at the Charterhouse and at Edinburgh University, where he was graduated in 1827. Then for three years he traveled on the Continent. From this journey grew the celebrated handbooks of travel, of which he himself wrote those on Holland, Belgium, and the Rhine, France, Southern Germany, and Switzerland. After his father's death he continued the high standards and expansion of the business, publishing such authors as Borrow, Grote, Livingstone, Milman, and Darwin. The *Origin of Species* first appeared under the Murray imprint. *Murray's British Classics* were among the first of the moderately priced reprints of the classics. From 1887 to 1891 he published *Murray's Magazine*. He specialized in books of travel, and being himself an ardent geologist, published anonymously in 1877 a book of his own, *Scepticism in Geology*. In 1847 he married Marion Smith, daughter of an Edinburgh banker; they had two sons and two daughters, and the sons continued the firm.

The younger Murray was the last of the patriarchal publishers who were also literary patrons, and who became close friends and advisors of all the famous authors of their day.

ABOUT: (John Murray, Sr.)—Constable, T. Memoir of Archibald Constable; Moore, T. Life of Byron; Smiles, S. A Publisher and His Friends. (John Murray, Jr.)—Academy April 9, 1892; Athenaeum April 9, 1892; Saturday Review April 9, 1892.

MURRAY, SIR JOHN (March 3, 1841-March 16, 1914), marine naturalist and oceanographer, was born at Cobourg, Ontario, of Scottish parents. He lived in Canada until he was seventeen, and completed his education in Scotland at the University of Edinburgh. A naturalist with the famous round-the-world "Challenger" expedition of 1872-75, he spent twenty years thereafter in editing its fifty-volume *Report*, in caring for its scientific collections on display in London, and in writing the results of his own observations during the voyage. Subsequently he devoted himself mainly to explorations and surveys in Scottish waters and in the North Atlantic. He was responsible for Britain's annexation of Christmas Island, in the Indian Ocean, and himself financed two expeditions to it. He was knighted in 1898. A motor accident at Kirkliston, near Edinburgh, ended his life at seventy-three. By his wife, Isabel Henderson, he had two sons and three daughters.

Of his several works resulting from the "Challenger" expedition, the report on *Deep Sea Deposits*, with A. F. Renard, became a standard reference. Through his scientific writings, which included important papers on oceanography and marine biology, he is remembered as a pioneer in deep sea exploration.

PRINCIPAL WORKS: Report on the Scientific Results of the Voyage of H.M.S. "Challenger" (ed.) 1880-95; Narrative of the Cruise of H.M.S. "Challenger" (with others) 1885; Deep Sea Deposits (with A. F. Renard) 1891; The Depths of the Sea (with J. Hjort) 1912.

MYERS, ERNEST JAMES (October 13, 1844-November 25, 1921), poet and translator, was born at Keswick, the second son of FREDERIC MYERS (1811-1851), perpetual curate of St. John's, Keswick, and author of *Catholic Thoughts* (1834-41). His elder brother was Frederic William Henry Myers, poet and essayist. Educated at Balliol College, Oxford, he was for three years a lecturer and fellow of Wadham College. From 1871 to 1891 he lived in London, devoting himself to literature, teaching, and charity. Thereafter his home was in the village of Chislehurst, Kent. He died at Fontridge, Etchingham, Sussex, at the age of seventy-seven. His wife and three children survived him.

Myers' writings reflected an interest in Greece stimulated by frequent travel. His essay on Aeschylus (in Evelyn Abbott's *Hellenica*) was widely noticed, and critics praised the scholarship, diction and rhythm of his prose translations of Homer and Pindar. The poems on Greek subjects (as well as those dealing with King Alfred, Milton, Garibaldi, and other men of later times) showed his liking for the heroic.

PRINCIPAL WORKS: *Poetry*—The Puritans, 1869; Poems, 1877; The Defence of Rome, 1880; The Judgment of Prometheus, 1886; Gathered Poems, 1904. *Prose*—The Odes of Pindar (tr.) 1874; The Iliad (last eight books, ed. with A. Lang and W. Leaf) 1882; Selected Prose Writings of John Milton (ed.) 1884; Biography of Viscount Althorp, 1890.

MYERS, FREDERIC WILLIAM HENRY (February 6, 1843-January 17, 1901), essayist and poet, was born at Keswick in Cumberland, the elder and more celebrated of the two sons of FREDERIC MYERS, clergyman and author. After taking honors at Trinity College, Cambridge, he lectured at his college for a few years, and from 1871 onwards was an inspector of schools, with residence in Cambridge. He died at fifty-seven in Rome, and was buried at Keswick. His wife Eveleen Tennant, survived him.

With a fervent and highly original poem, *St. Paul*, written in his twenty-fourth year, he won a considerable poetic reputation which did not endure, though there was sufficient interest in his verse to warrant a reprinting as late as 1916. Of more permanent value are his penetrating essays on Virgil, Wordsworth, Shelley, and George Eliot (whom he knew personally). Edmund Gosse has rated him "a delicate, if slightly over-subtle, critic," and a skilful translator of classical poetry. He is best known, however, for his investigations of psychic phenomena, conducted through the Society for Psychical Research (which he helped to found in 1882) and summed up in a posthumous volume. William James acknowledged his services to psychology.

PRINCIPAL WORKS: *Poetry*—St. Paul, 1867; The Renewal of Youth, 1882. *Prose*—Wordsworth, 1881; Essays: Classical and Modern, 1883; Science and a Future Life, 1893; Human Personality and Its Survival of Bodily Death, 1903.
ABOUT: Benson, A. C. Leaves of the Tree; Gosse, E. W. More Books on the Table; James, W. Memories and Studies.

NADEN, CONSTANCE CAROLINE WOODHILL (January 24, 1858-December 23, 1889), poet and philosopher, was born in Birmingham, where her father was an architect. Her mother died at her birth and she was reared by her grandparents. Until sixteen she was educated at a Unitarian day school at Edgbaston. She wanted to be a painter, but gave up her ambition when her paintings were rejected by the Birmingham Society of Artists. She turned then to the study of languages and philosophy. In 1881 she attended Mason College, where she studied science intensively, becoming a disciple of Herbert Spencer. She contributed regularly to the *Journal of Science, Knowledge,* and similar magazines. On the death of her grandparents she inherited a fortune. In 1887 she toured Turkey, Palestine, Egypt, and India. On her return she became a public speaker and expositor of a philosophic system she called "monistic positivism." A serious illness required a major operation from which she did not recover. Both as poet and as writer on philosophy she displayed evidences of great ability, but she died before her powers had come to full fruition.

PRINCIPAL WORKS: Songs and Sonnets of Springtime, 1881; A Modern Apostle and Other Poems, 1887; Induction and Deduction and Other Essays, 1890.

ABOUT: Hughes, W. R. Constance Naden; Contemporary Review April 1891.

NAIRNE, LADY CAROLINA (August 16, 1776-October 26, 1845), Scottish poet, was born at Gask in Perthshire, the third child of Laurence Oliphant and Margaret Robertson. Both parents were descended from Jacobite families, the Oliphants being known to history as "The Lairds of Gask," and the daughter was named Carolina in honor of Prince Charles Stuart.

She was a promising student, and at an early age sang, played, and danced so well as to receive the praise of Neil Gow, the prince of Scotch fiddlers; while her appearance was so striking that she was constantly referred to as "the Flower of Strathearn." Her early interest in Scotch songs was supplemented by reading Burns and she imitated the great poet with her first lyric, "The Pleuchman" (plowman) which appeared in 1792 and immediately became popular. Six years later, while in North England with her brother, a member of the Perthshire Light Dragoons, she wrote what is perhaps her most famous poem—"The Land o' the Leal," a song of homesickness which is sometimes referred to as "I'm Wearin' Awa'."

In 1806 after she had refused to marry a man of high rank, she married her cousin, Major William Murray Nairne, and went with him to Edinburgh, where he was stationed. Her shyness prevented her from taking an active part in Edinburgh Society. It was also the cause of Lady Nairne's lifelong literary anonymity, which was so complete that even her own family was ignorant of her work. Major Nairne (later Baron Nairne, when Scottish titles were restored in 1824 by George IV) died in 1829, wholly ignorant of the fact that his wife had written distinguished lyric verse. Her editors, too, were ignorant of her identity.

Lady Nairne's chief interest was in the education of her son, born in 1808, the sixth and last Baron Nairne, whose health was delicate. She took care of his instruction until 1823, when he was put under the guidance of the best tutors she could find, and later accompanied him to various European resorts for the sake of his health. He died at Brussels in 1837, and Lady Nairne spent the next three or four years solacing herself with travel, residing for a while in Paris. A paralytic stroke overcame her in 1843, but she was able to busy herself with her church work and charities, which were as anonymous as her verse. Shortly before her death, which occurred in 1845, she had consented to the anonymous publication of her poems, which appeared posthumously in 1846 as *Lays From Strathearn*, with accompaniments by Finlay Dun. A later edition was brought out in 1869, with a memoir by Charles Rogers.

She was an excellent balladist. Although her Jacobitism was of a sentimental sort and did not prevent her from being a loyal British subject, she wrote excellent Jacobite songs, often compared with those of James Hogg. Her humorous songs, although occasionally mere Bowdlerized versions of folk poems, were excellent, and one, "The Laird of Cockpen," has few equals in English. "The Hundred Pipers," "Charlie Is My Darling," and "Will Ye No Come Back Again?" are among her still remembered lyrics.   R. M.

PRINCIPAL WORKS: *Poetry*—Lays From Strathearn, 1846; Life and Songs, 1869.

ABOUT: Nairne, C. O. Life and Songs (see Life by Charles Rogers); Simpson, M. S. The Scottish Songstress; Tytler, S. & Watson, J. L. Songstresses of Scotland.

NAPIER, MARK (July 24, 1798-November 23, 1879), Scottish biographer, was born in Edinburgh, the son of a writer to the signet. He was educated at the Edinburgh High School and the University of Edinburgh, and admitted to the Scottish bar in 1820. From 1844 to his death he was sheriff depute of Dumfriesshire and Galloway. His reputation was mostly in the field of historical biography, but he also

BARONESS NAIRNE

wrote several legal works, and some verse described as "touching and spirited." He married his cousin, Charlotte (Ogilvie) Macfarlane, a widow, and had one son and one daughter. At his death he was the oldest member of the Faculty of Advocates still in active practice. In addition to his own books he edited a number of works relating to Scottish history. His biographical researches were valuable, though marred by his rather out-dated and excessive devotion to the Jacobite (Stuart) cause.

PRINCIPAL WORKS: The Life and Times of Montrose, 1840; Memoirs of the Marquis of Montrose, 1856; Memorials of Graham of Claverhouse, Viscount Dundee, 1859-62.
ABOUT: Scotsman November 24, 1879.

NAPIER, SIR WILLIAM FRANCIS PATRICK (December 17, 1785-February 10, 1860), historian and soldier, was born at Celbridge, County Kildare, Ireland. He was descended from an old and distinguished Scottish family which included the inventor of logarithms, John Napier (1550-1617). His father was Colonel George Napier, and his mother, the latter's second wife, was Lady Sarah Bunbury, daughter of the Duke of Richmond and Lennox, and a famous beauty, to whom, in her youth, George III had been romantically attracted.

With his brothers, George and Charles, who were also to be distinguished as soldiers and who later were also knighted, William Napier began a short and inglorious scholastic career. There seems to have been little or no restraint placed upon the three boys, and William was more often absent from school than present. As he began his military career at the age of fourteen, it is perhaps not to be wondered at that the chronicler of the Peninsular War could neither write nor speak grammatically until special study, when he was in his early thirties, enabled him to remedy the defects of his schooling.

After preliminary service in two regiments, the youthful soldier received a cornetcy in the "Blues," a famous regiment, from his uncle, the Duke of Richmond. General Moore, the hero of Corunna, then became interested in William and his warlike brothers; he offered William a place in his 52d regiment and later a captaincy in his 43d. This was at the time an ill-trained and ill-organized body, and Napier received a complete grounding in military discipline through his association with it. He was too poor to purchase the more rapid advancement he might have had, and from this time on his own efforts were responsible for all his promotions, despite the fact that he enjoyed the friendship of such a power as the minister William Pitt.

Napier's experience of warfare was concentrated in the years 1807-14, when he saw service in Denmark and in Spain, taking a leading part in the Peninsular War, in which he was three times wounded in thirty engagements. Finally sent home by Wellington to recover, he married Carolina Amelia Fox, niece of the statesman, Charles James Fox; and although he might have remained with his bride, the call of war was too strong, and he returned to action when he heard that Badajoz was being besieged. He commanded there and at Salamanca and received a decoration for valor, the rank of lieutenant-colonel, and the newly adopted Order of the Bath (C.B.). He remained in France as commander of the 43d until 1819 and greatly improved his education during his stay.

Upon his return to England he decided to earn his living as an artist, for he had genuine talents as draughtsman and sculptor, and it was only upon the suggestion of Henry Bickersteth, afterward Lord Lansdale, that he considered writing an account of the Peninsular War. (His only indication of ability as writer had been a review written in 1821.) Napier set about collecting the necessary documents, furnished him by Wellington and others; decoded, with the aid of his wife, the journals of Joseph Bonaparte; and set to work upon a sixteen years' task. The first of the six volumes of his history appeared in 1828, the last in 1840, and the consensus of opinion was and still is that the work has every title to the designation of masterpiece of its kind.

Napier's further career was one of regular promotion. He had become a colonel in 1830; in 1842 he was made Lieutenant-Governor of Guernsey, remaining there until 1847, when he resigned. The rank of lieutenant-general was conferred upon him in

SIR WILLIAM NAPIER

1851 and in 1859 he received the full rank of general.

His literary activities during this time consisted of an abridgment of his history, and participation in the violent controversy aroused by the appearance of his brother, Sir Charles James Napier's, account of his conquest of the rebellious princes of Sind (in India) and his subsequent administration of the province. Sir C. J. Napier's recital of the events in which he had a part was greeted by fiery criticism, and William Napier came to his rescue; he wrote *The Conquest of Scinde* (Sind) and later the *History of Sir C. J. Napier's Administration of Scinde*, in which he defended his brother's actions and scored his detractors. He was also engaged in considerable political controversy, although he never stood for office, and wrote innumerable letters to *The Times* in which he heaped coals of fire upon the heads of all who opposed or annoyed him. He had inherited a violent temper and an absurd sensitiveness, and warfare, whether of the pen or the sword, seems to have been a distinct source of pleasure for him. This activity was the more remarkable in view of the fact that Napier had never thoroughly recovered from his wounds and was crippled during the last years of his life from the effects of these injuries. His death followed a long period of partial paralysis. Lady Napier survived him by only six weeks, leaving several of their ten children (of whom the only son was congenitally deaf and dumb, though otherwise normal). One of his daughters, Norah, married H. A. Bruce, afterwards Lord Kildare, and author of Napier's biography.

Aside from his great talents, Napier would have been a remarkable man for his appearance alone. He was over six feet tall, and of great strength and grace, with a classical profile and clustering curls in youth and a patriarchal and commanding appearance in age. To these attractions of appearance he added a charitable and generous, if somewhat volcanic disposition, and a hatred of cruelty and injustice.

This last quality is strikingly revealed in his history, in which he gave full credit to the skill of his opponents—the very proofs were read by the arch-opponent of the English forces, Marshal Soult—and in which he propounded the unorthodox theory that the common soldier should receive his share of glory as well as of danger.

Controversy raged over the history, of course, and those who opposed the author's liberalism, or who felt slighted or injured by criticism, attacked the work and its author in no uncertain terms. Time, however, has vindicated Napier, and his history ranks with those of Caesar, Thucydides, and Davila. Abounding in technical details, it is neverthe-

less a work of tremendous brilliance, verve, and spontaneity, and the outstanding authority on its subject. Macaulay said immediately that it seemed fated to supersede all other histories of the Peninsular War; "Christopher North" pronounced it "an immortal work"; and in our own day C. Grant Robertson has called it "Napier's immortal epic." R. M.

PRINCIPAL WORKS: *History*—The History of the War in the Peninsula and South of France (6 vols.) 1828-40; The Conquest of Scinde, 1845; History of Sir C. Napier's Administration of Scinde and Campaign in the Cutchee Hills, 1851; English Battles and Sieges in the Peninsula (author's abridgment) 1852. *Biography*—The Life and Opinions of General Sir C. J. Napier, 1857.

ABOUT: Aberdare, Lord (H. A. Bruce). Life of Sir William F. P. Napier; Holmes, T. R. E. Four Famous Soldiers; Blackwood's Magazine 95:667 June 1864; Edinburgh Review 121:74 January 1865; Quarterly Review 61:51 January 1838.

NEALE, JOHN MASON (January 24, 1818-August 6, 1866), poet, historian, novelist, essayist, and priest, was born in London, the only son of the Rev. Cornelius Neale and his wife, Susanna Good. Both parents were decidedly evangelical. The father was a fellow of St. John's College and the author of numerous allegories, sermons, essays, and poems, published posthumously.

When the boy was five years old, his father died, and he was taken to Shepperton and placed for training under the rector there. At eighteen he won a scholarship at Trinity College, Cambridge. After winning several honors and prizes for classical study, he graduated in 1840, and acted for a time as chaplain and assistant tutor at Downing College. He was not elected a fellow.

The high-church movement was beginning to attract many new adherents while Neale was at Cambridge, and he enthusiastically joined them. During his undergraduate days he helped found and was active in the Cambridge Camden Society, later known as the Ecclesiological Society. He began his parochial work as an assistant curate at Guilford, Surrey, but the bishop of the diocese, on learning that he was a "Camdenian," would not license him.

In 1842 he married Sarah Webster, was ordained a priest by Bishop Monk, and accepted a small living in Sussex. Shortly afterwards, ill health made it necessary for him to go to Madeira, where he occupied himself writing verses and essays and making translations. Throughout his life he read omnivorously; and he knew more or less of twenty languages.

In 1846 he was made warden of Sackville College, East Grinstead, a charitable institution for the thrifty poor and aged householders; and there he remained until his death, writing with amazing erudition on innumerable theological and historical subjects,

JOHN MASON NEALE

restoring the college buildings, quarreling with his bishop over the ornamentation of his church, winning adherents to high-church doctrines and practices, encountering much opposition and occasional mob violence because of these same doctrines and practices, and establishing a nursing sisterhood and several benevolent institutions. One of his institutions, a reformatory for fallen women, he was forced to abandon because of public indignation.

His various writings made a deep mark on the generation following his death, in Scotland, America, Russia, and other countries, as well as in England. Since then, his theological and historical works have been read less widely, and he is now best known as the author of *Theodora Phranza*, a novel dealing with the fall of Christian Constantinople, and as the translator of Latin and Greek hymns: "Jerusalem the Golden," "The Day Is Past and Over," and "Art Thou Weary, Art Thou Languid" are three of the most successful.

George Saintsbury has written: "His original verse has, perhaps, been sometimes too contemptuously spoken of; but at best, it is second rate. Some of his translations are really marvelous—not merely as compositions, but when taken in close connection with their originals."

Eleanor A. Towle, his biographer, wrote of him:

"His mind was a reliquary where stones of little value lay mingled with pearls of great price. They had been gathered rather than assorted."   P. G.

PRINCIPAL WORKS: *Theology and Ecclesiology*—A History of Pews, 1841; A Translation of Durandus on Symbolism, 1843; History of the Holy Eastern Church, 1847; The Patriarchate of Alexandria, 1848; Ecclesiological Notes on the Isle of Man, 1848; The Liturgies of St. Mark, St. James, St. Clement, St. Chrysostom, and St. Basil, 1859; Essays on Liturgiology, 1863; Sermons for the Black-Letter Days, 1868; Thirty-three Sermons for Children, 1869; Commentary on the Psalms From Primitive and Mediaeval Writers, 1874. *Hymns*—Hymns for the Sick, 1843; Hymni Ecclesiae Breviariis Quibusdam et Missalibus Gallicanis, Germanis, Hispanis, Lustianis Desumpti, 1851; Hymns Chiefly Mediaeval on the Joys and Glories of Paradise, 1865; Hymns for Use During the Cattle Plague, 1866; Hymnal Noted, 1851 and 1854; Carols for Christmastide, 1853; Carols for Eastertide, 1854. *Fiction and Books for the Young*—Herbert Tresham, 1842; A Mirror of Faith, 1845: Annals of Virgin Saints, 1845; A Pilgrim's Progress, 1853; The Egyptian Wanderers, 1854; Lent Legends, 1855; Theodora Phranza, 1857. *Miscellaneous*—Songs and Ballads for Manufacturers, 1850; Handbook for Travelers in Portugal, 1855; Seatonian Poems, 1864.

ABOUT: Neale, J. M. Letters; Towle, E. A. Memoir of J. M. Neale.

NEAVES, CHARLES (October 14, 1800-December 23, 1876), Scottish poet and essayist, was born in Edinburgh. His father had added an "s" to the family name of Neave. He was educated at the high school and university in his native city, and called to the Scottish bar in 1822. From 1841-1845 he was advocate depute, from 1845 to 1852 sheriff of Orkney and Shetland, the next year solicitor-general for Scotland, from 1853 to 1858 judge in the court of session, and from 1858 to his death lord of justiciary. He was married, his wife's maiden name having been Macdonald, and had several children. Neaves was one of the most distinguished lawyers of his time. For forty years he contributed prose and verse, ranging in subject from humor to philology, to *Blackwood's Magazine*, but only a small part of his work was republished. He was an honorary LL.D. of the University of Edinburgh, and in 1872 was lord rector of St. Andrews.

PRINCIPAL WORKS: Songs and Verses: Social and Scientific, 1868; On Fiction as a Means of Popular Teaching, 1869; The Greek Anthology, 1870; Lecture on Cheap and Accessible Pleasures, 1872.

ABOUT: Smith, C. Writings by the Way.

"NEIL, ROSS." See HARWOOD, ISABELLA

NEWMAN, FRANCIS WILLIAM (June 27, 1805-October 4, 1897), miscellaneous writer, was the younger brother of John Henry (Cardinal) Newman. He was born in London, his father a banker of Holland Dutch descent and rationalist sympathies, his mother of Huguenot French family. He was educated at a private school at Ealing and at Worcester College, Oxford, receiving his B.A. with a "double first" (in classics and mathematics) in 1826. He served as a tutor in Dublin, then returned to Oxford as a fellow in 1828, but resigned his fellowship because his religious views were unorthodox.

From the first, though he and his brother were good friends, he resisted the latter's religious influence. Francis Newman became a Baptist, and after a missionary journey to Bagdad became, in 1834, class tutor in Bristol College. In 1836 he married a Miss Kennaway; after her death he was remarried, but he had no children by either union. In 1840 he became professor of classical literature at Manchester New College, now an affiliate of Oxford. From 1846 to 1869 he was professor of Latin at University College London (and also for a short time after 1848 principal of University Hall). He introduced the "Roman" pronunciation of Latin into England, and translated into Latin many English classics, from *Hiawatha* to *Robinson Crusoe*. In 1878 he formally declared himself a Unitarian. He was a radical in politics, and a bit of a crank, writing and speaking against vaccination and vivisection and in favor of vegetarianism. He was a voluminous writer on mathematics, history, languages, social questions, and theology. His works on the last-named subject were the most influential, but none of his writing is of much interest today.

PRINCIPAL WORKS: Lectures, 1838; Catholic Union, 1844; The Soul, 1849; Phases of Faith, 1850; Miscellaneous, 1869-80; Discourses, 1875; Life After Death? 1887.

ABOUT: Sieveking, I. G. Memoirs and Letters of Francis W. Newman.

NEWMAN, JOHN HENRY (CARDINAL) (February 21, 1801-August 11, 1890), theologian, poet, and ecclesiastic, was born in the City of London, the eldest son of John Newman, banker, and Jemima (Fourdrinier) Newman, daughter of a London draper of Huguenot ancestry.

He was educated at Great Ealing School and Trinity College, Oxford, having preferred to omit Winchester in order to remain longer at Ealing. Going up in June 1817, he was, says Henry Tristram, "somewhat solitary and apart, as always at school, but feeling intensely the pangs of loneliness amid new scenes and with strange companions, a good classic and a competent mathematician, anxious not to lose a moment of time before settling down to further studies, more eager to obtain information than his tutors were to impart it, and inclined to be scandalised at the social side of University life." Elected a scholar of Trinity a year later, he concentrated so intensely on getting a first class that he was overcome by a confusion of mind when he went up for his examinations, and barely received his degree.

Abandoning a half-formed plan to study law, he tried for and won a fellowship at Oriel where he came into close association with a brilliant set of young men including Keble, Pusey, and Hurrell Froude. In 1824 he was ordained in the Church of England and became curate of St. Clement's, Oxford. In 1828 he became vicar of St. Mary's, and for the next fifteen years his remarkable sermons were one of the principal features of University life, and his fascinating personality "alone in Oxford of his generation, alone of many generations," as Matthew Arnold declared, seemed to embody the genius of the place itself.

But the seeds of controversy and change had already begun to sprout. Having experienced a strong conversion at sixteen, Newman had arrived at Oxford permeated with an intense Evangelicalism, which later, under the influence of Whately in his early Oriel days, broadened into a more apostolic view of the Church, and from the year in which he assumed the charge of St. Mary's, he was convinced that his mission in life was to oppose intellectual and religious "liberalism." Having begun by opposing it in the person of Hawkins, the provost of Oriel, he was forced fairly soon to resign his tutorship. A preliminary doubt as to the validity of the Anglican "via media" crossed his mind while preparing his work on *The Arians of the Fourth Century* in 1831.

In the following year he went on a long voyage in the Mediterranean with Hurrell Froude, in the course of which he wrote many of the poems later to be published in the collection called *Lyra Apostolica*, as well as the celebrated "Lead, Kindly Light." He had also a serious illness, but recovered completely and hastened with a renewed feeling of important work to do, to Oxford, where he arrived in time to hear on July 14, 1833, Keble's epoch-making sermon on "National Apostasy," which launched the "Oxford Movement" to restore the doctrine of the apostolic succession and the sacerdotal view of the Church of England, which had largely fallen into abeyance.

A few months later appeared the first of the "Tracts for the Times," a series edited and largely written by Newman, culminating in 1841 with the famous Tract XC in which he attempted to prove that a Catholic view of theology was not incompatible with the Thirty-Nine Articles, and finally called down the official ban of the University of Oxford and the Church of England on the Tractarian Movement.

More honest with himself than some of his followers who remained to found the Anglo-Catholic party, Newman saw what this implied. "He had asserted and believed," writes Sidney Dark, "that the English Church was the Catholic Church in England. When that Church authoritatively said that it was nothing of the sort, he was persuaded that he was wrong." He began to perceive that if he believed what he did, he belonged in the Church of Rome.

Accordingly he retired to the village of Littlemore, near Oxford, and in 1843 resigned the living of St. Mary's. In 1845 he was received into the Roman Catholic Church, and in the following year set out for France and Italy with his henceforth inseparable friend Ambrose St. John. Arriving in Rome at the end of the year, he was ordained priest and became an Oratorian.

In 1847 he returned to England to found the Oratory at Birmingham where he was to pass most of the second half of his life in comparative retirement. In 1851, however, several sermons detailing charges of immorality against a renegade priest named Achilli who was then being lionized by a group of extreme Protestants, involved Newman in a libel suit which he lost. Though he was fined a hundred pounds and refused a new trial, the costs of twelve thousand pounds were paid by a popular subscription from admirers all over the world.

In 1852 he went to Dublin where, after a series of lectures afterward embodied in *The Idea of a University*, he was installed in 1854 as rector of the new Catholic University: but after several years of finding it impossible to induce the Irish clergy to carry out his ideas, he resigned the post and returned, in 1858, to Birmingham and, as he fancied obscurity. In fact, his real fame was still to come.

Newman had always been inclined to brood over the general misunderstanding of his motives, and hoped for an opportunity of vindication. A chance aspersion by Kingsley, reviewing Froude's *History of England* in the 1863 Christmas number of *Macmillan's Magazine*, woke Newman to life. It led first to an exchange of letters; then to an exchange of pamphlets; and then to what many have called the most beautiful piece of prose in the English language, the greatest confession since Rousseau and St. Augustine, the *Apologia pro Vita Sua*. Written under great pressure and published in parts as they were completed from April to June 1864, it aroused an instantaneous response among Catholics and Protestants alike. From that moment its author, who had not scrupled to display his inmost emotions to the world, remained secure in the world's sympathy and admiration, confirmed by *The Dream of Gerontius and Other Poems* published a year or two later.

Especially welcome was a tribute from Oxford, which, though he had declared it was "of all human things" perhaps nearest his heart, he had not visited for thirty-one years. In 1877 he was elected honorary fellow of Trinity, the first in the history of the college.

The slight suspicion with which he had been regarded within the Catholic Church having been dissipated by the *Apologia*, and

CARDINAL NEWMAN

the accession of a new pope removing reluctance in higher quarters, the long-awaited recognition came, and in 1879 Newman was created Cardinal of St. George in Velabro. Dispensed on account of his years from living in Rome, Newman, after receiving the purple, retired again to Birmingham, serene at last, to spend a happy old age at the Oratory at Edgbaston, where on August 11, 1890, he died. On his gravestone at Rednal, in Warwickshire, was written the phrase he had chosen to epitomize his life—*Ex umbris et imaginibus in veritatem*—"Out of shadows and pictures into truth."

Although it is often difficult, in following Newman's reasoning, not to feel that he is perhaps going deeper into the shadows, the phrase contains in concentrated form his central doctrine as applied both to the individual's life and to that of the Church—"development." "Old principles," in his own words, "reappear under new forms."

Similarly, the motto which he took on becoming a Cardinal—*Cor ad cor loquitur*—gives the key to his personality. "Heart speaks to heart." Newman's most striking characteristic was his unusual emotional sensitiveness. He is said to have written much of his *Apologia* with the tears streaming down his face; and his biographer Wilfrid Ward records that walking from Oxford to Littlemore with Albany Christie just before leaving the Church of England, "Newman never spoke a word all the way, and "Christie's hand when they arrived was wet with Newman's tears. When he made his confession in Littlemore Chapel his exhaustion was such that he could not walk without help ... When Ambrose St. John died Newman threw himself on the bed by the corpse and spent the night there." Through this ready outpouring of his emotions Newman aroused the extreme devotion of his followers (the creed of his Oxford disciples was said to be: *Credo in Newmannum*) and formed a very large number of intimate friendships. For the same reason, however, he was often involved in bitter controversy and was estranged from many of his early friends, though never losing his affection for them. As Ward says: "Deep natures are not the most equable. . . . When there is intense love and gratitude, there will be at times deep anger, deep resentment." Nevertheless he had a natural brightness which "made him at times the most charming of companions." Ward says of the Oriel days, "His senses were exceptionally keen. He chose the wines for his college cellars, though he himself drank very sparingly. He played the violin with considerable proficiency. . . . He took extraordinary delight in the beauties of nature."

"His appearance was striking," writes J. A. Froude. "He was above the middle height, slight and spare. His head was large, his face remarkably like that of Julius Caesar. The forehead, the shape of the ears and nose were almost the same. The lines of the mouth were very peculiar, and I should say exactly the same. I have often thought of the resemblance, and believed that it extended to the temperament. In both there was an original force of character which refused to be moulded by circumstances, which was to make its own way and become a power in the world; a clearness of intellectual perception, a disdain for conventionalities, a temper imperious and wilful, but along with it a most attaching gentleness, sweetness, singleness of heart and purpose. Both were formed by nature to command others, both had the faculty of attracting to themselves the passionate devotion of their friends and followers."

Aubrey de Vere recollects: "The slight form and gracious address might have belonged either to a youthful ascetic of the middle ages or to a graceful high-bred lady of our own days. He was pale and thin almost to emaciation, swift of pace, but when not walking intensely still, with a voice sweet and pathetic, and so distinct that you could count each vowel and consonant in every word. When touching on subjects that interested him much, he used gestures rapid and decisive, though not vehement."

Many have recorded what Sir Rowland Blennerhassett calls "the inexplicable fascination which all men, high and low, rich and poor, intellectual or otherwise, felt in his presence. It is hard to define the secret of his spell. It consisted partly in the bright, original, startling way in which he touched into life old truths, moral, religious, or politi-

cal. Then there was the extraordinary attraction of his voice and manner."

It is to be feared that the verdict of a large part of posterity coincides with that of James Russell Lowell at the time of Newman's death: ". . . a beautiful old man, as I remember him, but surely a futile life if there ever was one, trying to make a past unreality supply the place of a present one that was becoming past. . . . He will be remembered chiefly by his 'Lead Kindly Light.' "

For lovers of literature, however, Newman in his *Apologia,* is perhaps the writer of the most beautiful prose in English. Though much influenced by Gibbon according to his own account, his style is more subtle, varied, and emotionally colored, as would be expected from his talent as a violinist and his great love of music. For students of education and for the general reader, *The Idea of a University* remains a stimulating and suggestive book. Although his theological works and his sermons are now little read, in the Church of England his fame endures in connection with the Oxford Movement, and among Catholics in English-speaking countries his position is outstanding. His personality still fascinates, though it is difficult to rely on his mental processes.

J. B. O.

PRINCIPAL WORKS: *Verse*—St. Bartholomew's Eve, 1821; Lyra Apostolica, 1836; Verses on Religious Subjects, 1853; The Dream of Gerontius, 1866. *Novels*—Loss and Gain: The Story of a Convert, 1848; Callista: A Sketch of the Third Century, 1856. *Autobiography*—Apologia pro Vita Sua, 1864 (second version, History of My Religious Opinions, 1865). *Theology*—The Arians of the Fourth Century, 1833; Tracts for the Times, 1834-41; Lectures on the Prophetical Office of the Church, 1837; Lectures on the Doctrine of Justification, 1838; Select Treatises of St. Athanasius (tr.) 1842-4; Sermons Preached Before the University of Oxford, 1843; Sermons Bearing on Subjects of the Day, 1843; Lives of the English Saints, 1844-5; An Essay on the Development of Christian Doctrine, 1845; Lectures on Certain Difficulties Felt by Anglicans in Submitting to the Catholic Church, 1850; The Present Position of Catholics in England, 1851; Sermons Preached on Various Occasions, 1854; Parochial and Plain Sermons, 1868; An Essay in Aid of a Grammar of Assent, 1870; Two Essays on Miracles, 1870; The "Via Media" of the Anglican Church, 1877. *Miscellaneous*—University Subjects Discussed in Occasional Lectures and Essays, 1858; The Scope and Nature of a University Education, 1852 (new ed., The Idea of a University, 1903); Discussions and Arguments on Various Subjects, 1872; Essays Critical and Historical, 1872; Historical Sketches, 1872-3.

ABOUT: Atkins, G. G. Life of Cardinal Newman; Barry, W. Newman; Bellasis, E. Coram Cardinali; Birrell, A. Res Judicatae; Bloss, W. E. 'Twixt the Old and the New: A Study in the Life and Times of John Henry Cardinal Newman; Church, R. W. Occasional Papers: Vol. II; Cross, F. L. John Henry Newman; Dark, S. Newman; Faber, G. Oxford Apostles; Flood, J. M. Cardinal Newman and Oxford; Harper, G. H. Cardinal Newman and William Froude: A Correspondence; Hutton, R. H. Cardinal Newman; Jennings, H. J. Cardinal Newman: The Story of His Life; May, J. L. Cardinal Newman: A Study; Mozley, A. Letters and Correspondence of John Henry Newman During His Life in the English Church; Newman, B. Cardinal Newman: A Biographical and Literary Study; Reilly, J. J. Newman as a Man of Letters; Rickaby, J. Index to the Works of John Henry Cardinal Newman; Ross, J. E. John Henry Newman; Stockley, W. E. Newman, Education, and Ireland; Ward, W. The Life of John Henry Cardinal Newman: Based on his Private Journals and Correspondence; Ward, W. Men and Letters; Ward, W. Ten Personal Studies; Ward, W. Last Lectures; Cornhill Magazine 3ns11:84 November 1901; Cornhill Magazine 3ns58:131 June 1925; Downside Review January, May, October, 1931; Downside Review July 1933; Dublin Review July 1933; Fortnightly Review July 1900; Revue Anglo-Américaine August 1934.

NEWTON, SIR CHARLES THOMAS (1816-November 28, 1894), classical archaeologist, was the son of a clergyman. He was educated at Shrewsbury School and at Christ's College, Oxford, taking his B.A. in 1837 and his M.A. in 1840. Classical archaeology fascinated him from early youth, and against his family's wishes he entered the British Museum as an assistant in the department of archaeology. In 1852 he was vice-consul at Mytilene, the next year consul at Rhodes, and the year following directed excavations at Calymnos, securing many valuable antiquities for the museum. In 1860 he became consul at Rome, but was recalled the following year to become the first keeper of Greek and Roman antiquities at the British Museum. The same year he married the distinguished painter, Ann Mary Severn, daughter of Keats' artist-friend, Joseph Severn. She died in 1866. In 1880 Newton became the first Yates professor of classical archaeology at University College, London, being permitted to retain his museum post by special ruling. He was also antiquary to the Royal Academy. He was the recipient of many degrees and other honors, including knighthood. In 1885 he resigned everything except his university post; his health became worse and he finally retired completely in 1888.

PRINCIPAL WORKS: Method of the Study of Ancient Art, 1850; History of Discoveries at Halicarnassus, Cnidus, and Branchidae, 1862-63; Travels and Discoveries in the Levant, 1865; Essays in Art and Archaeology, 1880.

ABOUT: National Review January 1895.

NICHOL, JOHN (September 8, 1833-October 11, 1894), Scottish poet and biographer, was born in Montrose, son of a distinguished astronomer. From 1836 he was reared in Glasgow, where he attended the Western Academy. After extensive travel, he entered the University of Glasgow in 1848, and in 1855 went to Balliol College, Oxford, where he received his B.A. in 1860 with first honors in the classical school; he did not take his M.A. until 1874, after the religious tests were abolished. At Oxford he became an intimate friend of the young Swinburne. In 1859 he entered Gray's Inn, but was never called to the bar. He returned to Oxford as a coach, and occasionally continued to coach in philosophy up to 1873. In 1861 he married Jane Stewart Bell, a markedly happy marriage which resulted in the birth of one son and two daughters. From 1862 to 1889 he was professor of English language and literature at the University of Glasgow, a brilliant but restless and discontented teacher. By request, he re-delivered two of his courses at Oxford. He was one of the pioneers of university extension. In 1865 he visited the United States, and became personally acquainted with Emerson and Longfellow. He contributed the article on American Literature to the *Encyclopaedia Britannica* in 1882. In 1890 he resigned his professorship, and lived thereafter in London. His wife died in January 1894 and he never recovered from the blow, dying nine months later.

Nichol was immensely ambitious for literary fame, and felt that he had been defrauded of it by inimical critics. He was a fiery, original, independent thinker; his verse is thoughtful and has much beauty.

PRINCIPAL WORKS: Fragments of Criticism, 1860; Hannibal: A Historical Drama, 1873; Byron, 1880; The Death of Themistocles and Other Poems, 1881; Robert Burns, 1881; Francis Bacon, 1888-9; Carlyle, 1892.

ABOUT: Knight, W. A. Memoir of John Nichol.

NICHOLSON, JOHN (November 29, 1790-April 13, 1843), poet, was born in Yorkshire. His father owned a small wool factory. He was educated at the Bingley Grammar School, but became a wool sorter in early boyhood and remained in this trade, first with his father, and then in mills in various parts of Yorkshire, all his life, except when he traveled about hawking his poems. From youth he had periods of extreme dissipation. In 1810 he married a Miss Driver, reformed, and became a Methodist local preacher, but she died soon after their marriage, and with his second marriage, in 1813, he relapsed into habitual drunkenness. He spent most of his time in alehouses, while his friends helped to support him and his large family, with assistance from the Royal Literary Fund. He died as a result of a cold caught by falling into the Aire River while intoxicated. Nicholson had much local fame; his poetry shows originality, grace, and sincere emotion, but it also shows very obviously the defects of his education.

PRINCIPAL WORKS: The Siege of Bradford, 1821; Airedale in Ancient Times, 1825; Poems, 1844.

ABOUT: Nicholson, J. Poems (see Life by W. J. Hird in 1876 ed.).

NICHOLSON, WILLIAM (August 15, 1782 or 1783-May 16, 1849), Scottish poet, was born in Kirkcudbrightshire, the son of a carrier between Dumfries and Galloway. Owing to poverty, lack of studiousness, and poor sight, he had very little education, but his mother interested him in the native songs and ballads. At fourteen he became a peddler, but made little money, since his mind was more on the girls than on his trade, and what profits he made went for adventure and romance. Encouraged by James Hogg, the shepherd-poet, who admired his verses, and with Hogg's help, he secured publication of his only volume by subscription, earning £100 by selling it himself. Unfortunately his succes made of him a wandering drunkard. Always thriftless, he spent his time in piping and singing, ceasing to sell his wares or to write. He became a little insane on religion, and conceived it his mission to preach the doctrine of universal redemption; in 1826 he went to London and tried to see George IV in order to convert him! The next year he was in London again, but as a drover. From this time to his death, little is known of his life. He was probably unmarried.

Nicholson's ballads, especially "The Brownie of Blednoch," are his best work, vivid and weird, with the atmosphere of authentic folk-ballads. His songs are tender and graceful, and he had a lively fancy. He was a genuine poet, with character unequal to his talents.

PRINCIPAL WORK: Tales in Verse, 1814.

ABOUT: Harper, M. McL. Bards of Galloway; Nicholson, W. Tales in Verse (see Memoir by J. McDiarmid).

NICOLL, ROBERT (January 17, 1814-December 7, 1837), Scottish poet, was born in Perthshire, son of a farmer who had been defrauded of his land and became a day laborer. After a very slender education, he apprenticed himself at sixteen to a grocer in Perth, saving his wages to establish his mother in a shop. He wrote poems from early youth, but destroyed them because he could not write correct English. His first story was contributed to *Johnstone's Magazine*, in 1883, and Mr. and Mrs. Johnstone became his fast friends. Already tubercular, his poor health ended his indentures; after a few months at home he went to Edinburgh, where, on the verge of emigration to America he was persuaded to open a circulating library at Dundee. It was a failure, and in 1836, encouraged by the reception given his only volume of poems, he went to Leeds, where the Johnstones got him an ill-paying job as editor of the Leeds *Times*. At the same time he

married Alice Suter. An ardent radical, he made his paper an influence, but the overwork ruined his health, and he returned to Scotland to die at not quite twenty-four.

Nicoll's poems in the Scottish dialect are far superior to those he wrote in literary English—melodious, simple, humorous, and pathetic. At the same age Burns had written no better verses. His powers were increasing, and his early death was a literary tragedy.

PRINCIPAL WORK: Poems and Lyrics, 1835.

ABOUT: Nicoll, R. Poems and Lyrics (see Memoir by Mrs. C. I. Johnstone in 1844 ed.).

"NIMROD." See APPERLEY, CHARLES JAMES

NOEL, RODEN BERKELEY WRIOTH-ESLEY (August 27, 1834-May 26, 1894), poet, was a son of Charles Noel, Lord Barham (in 1841 created Earl of Gainsborough), and Frances (Jocelyn) Noel.

His education was at Harrow, with a tutor, and at Trinity College, Cambridge, where he took the master's degree in 1858, having spent some time abroad with his parents in France, Germany, and Italy. He had expected to enter the church, and there was a family living intended for him, but he gave up this plan after traveling in Egypt and Palestine. He entered business in London, but, not suited by training or gifts to this work, he was, in the words of a friend, "ludicrously incapable." In 1863 he married Alice de Broë.

Thanks to the influence of his mother, who was lady-in-waiting to Queen Victoria, he was given office as groom of the Privy Chamber, and held this post from 1867 to 1871. Despite his personal loyalty to the Queen, Noel felt obliged to resign as his ideas became more equalitarian and leaned toward socialism. His poetry and his whole thought began to reflect this interest and concern in the sufferings of the oppressed, and his art became definitely subordinated to a moral code. His later years were marked by efforts, literary and otherwise, to combat smugness and indifference to wretchedness. His life was darkened by the loss of a five-year-old son, and his intense grief found its expression in *A Little Child's Monument*. He died suddenly at Mainz in 1894, leaving a son and a daughter.

Personally Noel was shy and sensitive, yet possessed of charm. He loved the out-of-doors, inheriting this taste from a boyhood spent at Exton Park, Rutlandshire, and his early experiences in Ireland, where the wild loveliness of the scenery had impressed him greatly. He was especially fond of the sea, enjoyed climbing, and was a member of the English Alpine Club. His

RODEN NOEL

philosophical interests and his sympatny for the suffering made him become often indiscriminately bitter in his fight for greater social justice, particularly for children. "Aristocrat by birth and breeding, he was democrat by principle, based on strong conviction and spiritual sympathy, however the clash of the dual strain might make itself felt," wrote Emily Hickey.

His writings are characterized by social protest, love of nature, and a philosophical mysticism (perhaps the result of his emancipation from Calvinism) which John Addington Symonds described as "more a religion, an enthusiasm, than an organized scheme of speculation." He was decidedly a poet of matter, rather than manner; in a time when both were plentiful in the works of others, his poetry lacked polish and refinement of technique, and it suffered accordingly. "An eminently thoughtful writer, he lacked singing power, his versification was was frequently harsh, and, except in *A Little Child's Monument*, his poetry gave his readers the idea of being rather the work of deliberation and reflection than of inspiration," commented *The Athenaeum*. He steadily improved, however, in artistry and finish in his poems. In other forms he was not entirely successful. In satire he lost effectiveness through his vehemence, in prose he failed to mould his materials into a satisfactory and effective structure, and he lacked power as a dramatist. "His real strength," wrote Symonds, "consists in the combination of full sensuous feeling for the material world with an ever-present sense of the spirit informing it and bringing all its products into vital harmony." R. W. W.

PRINCIPAL WORKS: *Biography*—Life of Lord Byron, 1890. *Drama*—The House of Ravensburg, 1877. *Essays*—Essays Upon Poetry and Poets, 1886. *Philosophy*—A Philosophy of Immortality, 1882. *Poetry*—Behind the Veil, 1863; Beatrice, 1868; The Red Flag, 1872; Livingstone in Africa, 1874; A Little Child's Monument, 1881; Songs of the Heights and Deeps, 1885; A Modern Faust, 1888; The People's Christmas, 1890; My Sea, 1896; Collected Poems, 1902. *Editor*—The Poems of Edmund Spenser (selected) 1887; The Plays of Thomas Otway, 1888.

ABOUT: Ellis, S. M. Mainly Victorian; Miles, A. H. Poets and Poetry of the Century; Noel, R. B. W. Collected Poems (see Notice by J. A. Symonds); Noel, R. B. W. Selected Poems (see Preface by Percy Addleshaw); Athenaeum June 2, 1894; Nineteenth Century and After 91:264 April 1922.

"NORTH, CHRISTOPHER." See WILSON, JOHN

NORTHCOTE, JAMES (October 22, 1746-July 13, 1831), painter and miscellaneous writer, was born at Plymouth. His father was a watchmaker, his mother a haberdasher; the family were Unitarians. He had very little education, and was apprenticed very young to his father, who refused to allow him to study art, as he longed to do. Accordingly in 1771 he ran away to London and was taken in by the great painter Sir Joshua Reynolds, living in his home and working for him, at the same time studying at the Royal Academy. He set up for himself as a painter in 1776, then went to Italy until 1780. On his return he became well known as an historical and portrait painter, becoming an Academician in 1787. From 1807, having literary ambitions also, he contributed articles to *The Artist*. His life of Reynolds is very sketchy, and his life of Titian quite incompetent, but he had much originality and wit, displayed principally in his stories. He was a friend of William Hazlitt, who incorporated Northcote's conversation in the *New Monthly Magazine* as *Boswell Redivivus*. Later, in 1830, though they had ceased to be friends long before Northcote's death, Hazlitt published his *Conversations With James Northcote*.

Northcote was unmarried and lived with a sister. He and she were both misers, living in filth and abject poverty, though he spent a fortune trying to prove that his poor watchmaker father was really of noble descent.

PRINCIPAL WORKS: Memoirs of Sir Joshua Reynolds, 1813; One Hundred Fables, 1828; The Life of Titian, 1830.

ABOUT: Gentleman's Magazine 2:102, 1831.

NORTON, MRS. CAROLINE ELIZABETH SARAH (afterwards Lady Stirling-Maxwell) (March 22, 1808-June 15, 1877), poet, was born to fame. She was the granddaughter of Richard Brinsley Sher-

MRS. CAROLINE NORTON

idan, the dramatist, and daughter of Thomas Sheridan and his wife, formerly the beautiful Caroline Henrietta Callander of Craigforth, Scotland, who was herself a writer. Young Caroline, the second daughter, was born in London, March 22, 1808. When Tom Sheridan accepted a colonial secretaryship at the Cape of Good Hope in 1813 his wife was forced to leave all but one of her children in Scotland with her two sisters. So Caroline's first teacher was a Scotchman named Wilson.

Sheridan died in 1817, leaving his widow with seven young children to care for and not much money with which to do it. But the children were all clever and all gifted. They used to amuse themselves by giving private theatricals. Indeed, Caroline was only eleven when she and her sister Helen drew and wrote *The Dandies' Rout*, which was actually published. Later Caroline was sent to school at Wonersh in Surrey, and it was at Wonersh Park at the home of Lord Grantley that she met her future husband, George Chapple Norton, brother of her host. Although Norton proposed to the lady almost as soon as he met her the marriage did not take place until 1827, and then the bride was only nineteen.

Her husband was a barrister and the couple lived first in Garden Court in the Temple, although they later moved to their own house at Storey's Gate where they spent most of their time quarreling over money matters. Caroline was forced to support the family by her writing. She published a book of verse called *The Sorrows of Rosalie* in 1829 before the birth of her son, Spencer. Almost at once she began a new poem, entitled *The Undying One*, which ap-

peared the next year. When Norton lost his Tory seat for Guilford it was his wife whose influence secured him an appointment in the Metropolitan Police Courts through her good friend, Lord Melbourne.

In 1831 her son Brinsley was born and the next year his mother became the editor of *La Belle Assemblée*, a court magazine, as well as the *English Annual* for 1834-38. She gave birth to a third son, William, in 1833. The year following the Nortons went abroad. Mrs Norton's first novel, *The Wife and Woman's Reward*, came out in 1835. Meanwhile affairs at home had been going from bad to worse, and came to a climax in June 1836 when George Norton brought court action against Lord Melbourne for alienating his wife's affections. The suit was a failure, although Mrs. Norton left her husband and finally went to live with her mother at Hampton Court.

Her poem, *A Voice From the Factories*, was published in 1836. She also began a long fight for the custody of her children by writing prose pamphlets on the subject Her interest in such matters led to several attacks on her character in the journals of the day.

She left gossip behind, however, when she accompanied her sister, Lady Dufferin, on a trip to Italy. Back in England by 1840 she renewed her struggles to regain her children. But her youngest son died (1842) before she could reach him. In 1845 she went to Chesterfield Street, Mayfair, to live by herself. She worked on a new novel, *Stuart of Dunleath*, through 1850, and not long afterwards she went to Italy to be with her son, Fletcher, although she was soon (1853) compelled to return to England to face an unpleasant suit brought against her for debt by her husband, who, after her mother's death, had cut short her allowance, and taken possession of her copyright interests. So once more she took to writing pamphlets, this time in behalf of the Divorce Bill. Her famous *Letter to the Queen* was published in 1855. In 1854 she attended Brinsley's marriage in Italy and spent some time in Paris.

Fletcher's death in 1859 was a great blow to her. Her last long poem, *The Lady of La Garaye*, came out in 1861, while her last novel, *Old Sir Douglas*, was published in 1867. Her husband died in 1875. She fell ill, and spent most of the rest of her days in her room as an invalid, although in the spring of 1877 she married her old friend Sir William Stirling-Maxwell. But her happiness was short-lived, for on June 15, 1877, as she was about to set out for Scotland, she died very suddenly, only a few days before the death of her son Brinsley.

Probably many of Mrs. Norton's matrimonial difficulties were the result of her quick Irish temper, which met an equal match in the brutal violence of her husband. She showed another side of her character in the ballroom where her wit and her beauty were the admiration of all who beheld her. Tom Moore, the poet, dedicated a poem to her. Macready, the actor, remarked that "her face was one to think of," while George Meredith, the novelist, is said to have had her in mind when he wrote *Diana of the Crossways*. To the end she never lost her beauty, which was Grecian in type.

In her own age Mrs. Norton was termed "the Byron of her sex." But her verse, though graceful, was too saturated with her own personal and domestic affairs to achieve a lasting success. Her prose is likewise mostly autobiographical. B. D. S.

PRINCIPAL WORKS: *Poetry*—Dandies' Rout 1820; The Sorrows of Rosalie, 1829; The Undying One, 1830; A Voice From the Factories, 1836; The Centenary Festival, 1840; The Dream, 1840; Lines, 1840; The Child of the Islands, 1845; Aunt Carry's Ballads for Children, 1847; The Lady of La Garaye, 1861; Bingen on the Rhine, 1883. *Prose*—Kate Bouverie and Other Tales and Sketches, 1835; The Wife and Woman's Reward, 1835; The Natural Claim of a Mother to the Custody of Her Child, 1837; Separation of the Mother and Child by the Law of Custody, 1837; A Plain Letter to the Lord Chancellor on the Infant Custody Bill, 1839; Letters to the Mob, 1848; Stuart of Dunleath, 1851; English Laws for Women in the Nineteenth Century, 1854; A Letter to the Queen on Lord Chancellor Cranworth's Marriage and Divorce Bill, 1855; Lost and Saved, 1863; Old Sir Douglas, 1867; Taxation 1874; Some Unrecorded Letters, 1934. *Drama*—The Martyr, 1849.

ABOUT: Bethune, G. W. The British Female Poets; Horne, R. H. (ed.). A New Spirit of the Age; Perkins, J. G. The Life of the Honourable Mrs. Norton; Robertson, E. S. English Poetesses; Strachey, R. The Cause; Dublin University Magazine 16:637 December 1840; Edinburgh Review 53:361 June 1831; Fraser's Magazine 3:222 March 1831; Living Age 290:694 September 9, 1916; Longman's Magazine 45:70 November 1904; Temple Bar 52:101 January 1878.

O'DONNELL, JOHN FRANCIS (1837-May 7, 1874), Irish poet, was born in Limerick, the son of a poor shop-keeper. He was educated at the primary school of the Christian Brothers, and at sixteen became a short-hand reporter for the *Munster News*. From this time, throughout his lifetime, he contributed verse and prose to *The Nation*, organ of the Irish Nationalist movement. In 1855 he became sub-editor of the Tipperary *Examiner*. In 1860 he went to London and worked on the *Universal News*, at the same time publishing poems in *Chambers's Journal* and Dickens' *All the Year Round*. He returned to Ireland in 1862, joining the staff of *The Nation* in Dublin, and also editing *Duffy's Hibernian Magazine*. 1864 found him once more in London (he was always restless and on the move), as editor of the *Universal News*. The next year he became editor of *The Tablet*, organ of the Roman Catholic Church in England, at the same time writing Nationalist poems under the pseudonyms of "Caviare" and "Monkton West," and also acting as London correspondent of the Fenian *Irish People* until it was suppressed. In 1873 he deserted journalism, to enter the London office of the agent-general of New Zealand. He died at thirty-seven, a year after he had started this new and not very congenial work.

PRINCIPAL WORKS: The Emerald Wreath, 1865; Memories of the Irish Franciscans, 1871; Poems, 1891.
ABOUT: O'Donnell, J. F. Poems (see Introduction by Richard Dowling).

"O'DOWD, CORNELIUS." See LEVER, CHARLES JAMES

O'KEEFFE, JOHN (June 24, 1747-February 4, 1833), Irish dramatist, was born in Dublin, and educated at a private school run by the Jesuits and at the Dublin School of Design. He wrote his first comedy at fifteen. In his boyhood he became an actor, being obliged to leave the stage about 1780, because of failing eyesight. By 1797 he was totally blind, but continued to dictate his plays to an amanuensis. He was a prolific writer, mostly of farces and comic operas, and a facile rhymester. In 1780 he went to London, and wrote for the Haymarket and Covent Garden Theatres. He moved to Acton in 1798. In 1800 he was given a benefit, and from 1803 received a small annuity from Covent Garden. In 1802 he was granted a royal pension of a hundred guineas a year. In 1815 he moved to Chichester, and in 1830 to Southampton, where he died. He was married, and had two sons and a daughter, Adelaide, who became a novelist and miscellaneous writer, and edited her father's works. His best known play, *Wild Oats*, remained on the stage for many years after his death.

PRINCIPAL WORKS: Tony Lumpkin, 1778; Oatlands: or, The Transfer of the Laurel (poems) 1795; Plays, 1798; Recollections, 1826; A Father's Legacy to his Daughter (poems, ed. by A. O'Keeffe) 1834.
ABOUT: Stoddard, R. H. Personal Recollections of O'Keeffe, Kelly, and Taylor.

O'LEARY, JOHN (July 23, 1830-March 16, 1907), Irish journalist and historian, was born in Tipperary, his father a shopkeeper. A sister later became known as a poet. He was educated at Erasmus High School, Carlow School, and Trinity College, Dublin. He had intended to practise law, but in 1848 joined the Nationalist movement, and turned to medicine as a career rather than take the

475

oath of allegiance to the British Government. In 1850 he entered Queen's College, Cork, and the next year transferred to Queen's College, Galway, but left without passing his final examinations. He spent 1855 and 1856 in Dublin and Paris, contributing to *The Nation*. Though he was never actually a member of the Irish Republican Brotherhood (Fenians), in 1859 he went to the United States on Fenian business, and contributed to *The Phoenix* (New York), the first avowed Fenian organ. In 1861 he was in London, and in 1863 returned to Dublin to edit the *Irish People*. The paper was seized by the government in 1865, and he was sentenced to twenty years' imprisonment. After serving nine years he was released, under order of banishment. This period he spent in Paris, where he was a friend of the painter Whistler and a member of his circle. In 1885, on passage of the Amnesty Act, he returned to Dublin, where he died unmarried. His only full-length book caused much disappointment among his colleagues; it was too long and prolix, and full of rather ill-natured criticism and belittling judgments.

PRINCIPAL WORKS: Young Ireland: The Old and the New, 1885; What Irishmen Should Read, What Irishmen Should Feel, 1886; Recollections of Fenians and Fenianism, 1896.
ABOUT: O'Leary, J. Recollections of Fenians and Fenianism; London Daily Telegraph March 18, 1907.

OLIPHANT, LAURENCE (1829 December 23, 1888), novelist and travel writer, was born at Cape Town in South Africa. His father, one of the Oliphants of Gask, a distinguished Scottish family, was Anthony Oliphant, attorney-general of Cape of Good Hope. His mother was Maria Campbell, daughter of Colonel Campbell of the 72d Highlanders.

Young Oliphant was over-indulged from the first, and only the intense religious zeal of his parents kept him from utter ruin at their hands. His education was extremely irregular, which doubtless accounts for the eccentric course of his ideas in later life. Sent to England to study, he returned to his family, now in Ceylon, where his father was chief justice; and having persuaded his family that experience would be more valuable to him than formal education at a university, he became his father's secretary. At the age of nineteen, however, he commenced that wandering, restless life which was to be his course until he died. A hunting trip with the Indian minister, Jung Bahador, he described in a successful novel, *Khatmandu* (1852), and this fired him with the desire to write more. He journeyed through Russia to the Crimea and the Black Sea; accompanied Lord Elgin on a special mission to the United States and went with him to Canada and the Far West;

LAURENCE OLIPHANT

then to India, where the Mutiny was at its height. Of important wars and revolutions of his time there were few in which he did not play the part of participant or observer; he was associated with Garibaldi, was in Nicaragua, where he narrowly escaped hanging, scaled the walls of Tientsin, was nearly killed in the Japanese attempt to exterminate foreigners at Yedo, where he was a member of the British Legation, was concerned in the Polish insurrection of 1863, and saw the war in Schleswig-Holstein in 1864.

Upon his return to England in the next year Oliphant received a seat in Parliament, but was dissatisfied with his progress there and resigned, determined now to make a living as a writer. This he might easily have done, with his fine talent and a excellent newspaper appointment plus the prestige of a well-received and brightly written satirical novel, *Piccadilly*. Unfortunately Oliphant had been won over to the absurd teachings of the American "prophet," Thomas Lake Harris, and went to America to live in his colony. Otherwise a clear-headed business man—he had been associated with Jay Gould —Oliphant had not been fortified by an education which might have made him more of a skeptic, and he became a complete slave to Harris, to whom he made over his property and that of his first wife, Alice Le Strange, when he married her in 1872. His mother joined the sect too and became a more ardent and lasting devotee than her son, who finally threw off the yoke in 1881, recovering lands which were his by going to law. Lady Oliphant, however, remained a member of the sect until her death in 1887.

Oliphant later became interested in the colonization of Palestine by Jews, and developed into a sort of unofficial overlord there. Rosamond Owen, granddaughter of the great industrialist and social reformer, Robert Owen—his second wife, whom he married in 1887, shortly after the death of his first wife —was associated with him in this enterprise and wrote of it later in *My Perilous Life in Palestine.*

Oliphant returned to England in 1888 and was a guest of Sir Mountstuart Grant Duff at Twickenham when he was stricken and died.

As a writer he had a bright pen and the ability to write with entertaining liveliness and vividness about his adventures. His satirical talent, called into play by the absurdities of others, was well evidenced by his novel *Piccadilly.* *Altiora Peto* was considered an excellent piece of serious fiction. It seems, however, that Oliphant in later life considered himself no more than a medium, for he had become interested in spiritualism. All his work points to a talent that might have developed into an important one had its possessor not been carried away by a lust for adventure and a predilection for eccentric and extravagant religious doctrine.

He was a man of almost boyish simplicity and warmth of heart and had many friends. His life is treated with sympathetic care, if not with complete understanding, by his cousin Margaret Oliphant, in her biography of him.   R. M.

PRINCIPAL WORKS: *Fiction*—Piccadilly, 1866; The Land of Gilead, 1880; Altiora Peto, 1883. *Travel and Adventure*—Khatmandu, 1852; Narrative of the Earl of Elgin's Mission to China and Japan, 1859. *Autobiography*—Episodes in a Life of Adventure.

ABOUT: Leesching, L. F. Personal Reminiscences of Laurence Oliphant; Oliphant, L. Episodes in a Life of Adventure; Oliphant, M. O. W. Memoir of the Life of Laurence Oliphant and of Alice Oliphant His Wife; Owen, R. D. My Perilous Life in Palestine.

OLIPHANT, MARGARET OLIPHANT

(April 4, 1828-June 25, 1897), Scottish novelist, was born at Musselburgh in Midlothian. She was the daughter of Francis and Margaret (Oliphant) Wilson, her mother being a cousin to Lady Caroline Nairne.

Her first memories were of Lasswade, near Edinburgh, where her father was employed as a customs official. Before she was out of her teens, she had begun to write, although, according to her, this ability and inclination aroused more amusement than admiration in her family. It was her real intention to earn her living as an artist, but she gravitated toward writing, and at twenty-one had published her first novel, *Some Passages in the Life of Mrs. Margaret Maitland of Sunnyside.* The book had a fair success and won for her the reward

of a letter of commendation from the critic Francis Jeffrey. Three more novels followed, and then David Macbeth Moir, the Musselburgh physician-poet, became interested in the young author and introduced her to the Blackwoods, the publishers, for whom, after 1852, she was to write all her life.

In 1852 she married her cousin Francis Oliphant, a designer of stained glass, and went to London, where a son and daughter were born to them. The young couple were soon responsible for the support of Mrs. Oliphant's brother and his family. Mrs. Oliphant wrote busily in order to assist them and also because she could not help writing. Her husband, who had not been strong for years, was obliged to leave England in 1859 for the sake of his health. Mrs. Oliphant accompanied him to Rome, where he died that year, leaving her burdened with debt and with another child soon to be born. She was now the entire support of her children, and such she remained, although the sons lived into early middle age. The daughter, to her mother's bitter grief, died in 1864.

Mrs. Oliphant was thereafter to live with a pen in her hand, turning out her better and poorer books at the same even astonishing rate. Her best extended work, a series known as The Chronicles of Carlingford and consisting of five volumes, began with two excellent novels, *The Rector and the Doctor's Family* and *Salem Chapel,* both published in 1863. *The Perpetual Curate* (1864) and *Miss Marjoriebanks* (1866) were followed by a dozen or so miscellaneous novels before *Phoebe Junior* completed the group in 1876. This study of the religious life of a

MRS. MARGARET OLIPHANT

small town was sometimes compared to George Eliot's *Scenes of Clerical Life,* to which, in justice, it does not now seem equal in quality. *Salem Chapel* was disfigured by sensational elements, possibly imitated from Wilkie Collin's novels. *Miss Marjoriebanks,* with its delicate irony, is in all likelihood the best of these works, and indeed, of all Mrs. Oliphant's writings.

Determined to give her sons the best possible education, Mrs. Oliphant went to live near Eton in 1866 and placed the boys at the famous school. The rest of her life is really no more than the account of her endless struggle to support them and to make something of them, which latter she failed to do. She survived them—the elder died in 1890 and the younger in 1894—and was still writing, this time *The Annals of the House of Blackwood,* when her last illness overtook her two weeks before her death.

Mrs. Oliphant's output was amazing in its variety and amount. Her published books, consisting of fiction, criticism, guide-books to Italian cities, translations, biographies—of such widely differing people as the Brontës, St. Francis, Cervantes, her cousin Laurence Oliphant—number over one hundred, and her contributions to *Blackwood's,* the *Cornhill Magazine,* and others, would fill an equal number of volumes. However, she was never able to rest on a single outstanding success. Artistic accomplishment of the higher sort was denied her. Yet she had a good style, a command of humor and pathos, and the ability to create characters so real that her analyses of them give the effect of unnecessary repetition; a fine imagination, and a gift of circumstantial invention shown at its best in such a fantastic novel as *The Beleaguered City.* Perhaps her failure is due to the fact that she did not think highly of her work and was obliged to turn it out at such a great rate.

Henry James pronounced her "a great improvisatrice"; Stephen Gwynn, the Irish critic, felt that "Old Lady Mary" was one of the finest short stories in the language; and Lewis Melville predicted that for some half-dozen works she would have "a place not far below Mrs. Gaskell and George Eliot."

Mrs. Oliphant was a short, rather plump little woman, with a fair smooth skin, bright eyes, and a generally pleasant expression. She had a kind heart and manner and a cheerful air which is belied by the intense melancholy of her *Days of My Life* and *Autobiography.*   R. M.

PRINCIPAL WORKS: *Novels*—Passages in the Life of Mrs. Margaret Maitland, 1849; Salem Chapel, 1863; Miss Marjoriebanks, 1866; The Beleaguered City, 1880; The Ladies Lindores, 1883. *Autobiog-*

478

raphy—Days of My Life, 1868; Autobiography, 1899.

ABOUT: Gwynn, S. Saints and Scholars; James, H. Notes on Novelists; Melville, L. Victorian Novelists; Oliphant, M. O. W. Autobiography; Temple Bar 118:233 October 1899.

OPIE, AMELIA (November 12, 1769-December 2, 1853), novelist and poet, was born at Norwich, the only child of Dr. James and Amelia Briggs Alderson. Her formal education was devoted chiefly to French, music, and dancing.

At her mother's death in 1784 Amelia assumed charge of her father's house and entered Norwich society where she was instantly very popular for the ballads which she composed and sang, and for her love of fun. She made annual trips to London, after 1794, becoming well known there. Several promising men courted her, among them being Thomas Holcroft, to whom she sat for a portrait. She knew theatrical people also—including Mrs. Siddons and the Henry Kembles. In London in 1797 she met John Opie, the painter, who fell in love with her at first sight. They were married May 8, 1798, at Marylebone Church and lived chiefly in London.

Opie was not fond of society and urged his wife to write in order to keep her at home. By 1801 she was known as the author of *Father and Daughter,* a popular tale. She had written plays and tales before, but she now became a professional writer.

She continued, until Opie's death in April 1807, to summer in Norwich lingering with her father until she was summoned home. The Opies were abroad in 1802, and Amelia was extremely popular in distinguished circles. Her account of the trip appeared in *Tait's Magazine.*

In 1807 she returned to Norwich to tend her ailing father, and here she made her home. Excursions to attend the May meetings of Friends in London each year brought her opportunities to know Scott, Wordsworth, Tom Moore, Sheridan, Lady Caroline Lamb, etc. Her literary work continued in eight- and ten-hour days. A memoir of her husband was a disappointment to Opie's professional associates. About 1814 she became interested, through J. J. Gurney, in Quakerism and attended the meetings. In 1825 (August 11), shortly before her father's death, she joined the Society of Friends and donned their grey habit. To do so cost her vanity a pang, as Robert Southey, Crabb Robinson, and others noticed. Amelia Opie was fond of fine clothes and contrived to make her silk or satin grey flattering. Parisian drawing-rooms mistook her for a *soeur de charité* and noted her simple purity.

MRS. AMELIA OPIE

Her life which had been filled with writing, was suddenly emptied. Her new religious views prevented her from writing stories and novels. A novel *The Painter and His Wife*, which was contracted for, was dropped and she announced in 1823 that it would never appear. She gave much time to charity, being associated with Southey in the reform of hospitals, etc. She attended the assizes, traveled widely, maintained a large correspondence, wrote for the periodicals, sketched portraits of her callers. In 1829 she sat, in Paris, for David d'Angers and met Lafayette, Baron Cuvier, and Queen Marie Amélie. She was active in anti-slavery circles, going as Norwich delegate, in 1840, to the London convention. She also sat to Benjamin Haydon on this visit. She died in Norwich and is buried beside her father in Gildencroft, the Friends' cemetery.

Mrs. Opie's vivacity and charm were remarkable and enhanced the beauty of her brown hair and grey eyes. She loved society, fun, and fine clothes. She was frank and sincere, intensely interested in many things.

Mrs. Opie's literary name has greatly declined. As a novelist she belonged to the revolutionary group associated with the name of William Godwin. She "excelled, like Godwin, in developing the morbid anatomy of the human heart, and possesses in some respects a kindred talent." *Father and Daughter* the *Edinburgh Review* considered "an appalling domestic tragedy" and *Adeline Mowbray* was openly unconventional. She found life "a very serious concern, and so she has represented it," realistically. Intellectually inferior to Maria Edgworth and Joanna Baillie, she still has power to tell a story well and to move her readers. Scott wept over *Father and Daughter*. Pathos also characterizes her poetry, both ballads and lyrics. The Dutch poet, Katherine Bilderdijk, translated some of her more delicate and poignant lyrics and ballads. Mary Mitford disapproved of Mrs. Opie's "bad English," but her work has sincerity, moral strength, and human sympathy, which lift it above such superficial criticism.

D. F. A.

PRINCIPAL WORKS: *Novels and Stories*—Dangers of Coquetry, n.d.; Father and Daughter, 1801; Adeline Mowbray, 1805; Simple Tales, 1806; Temper, 1812; First Chapter of Accidents, 1813; Tales of Real Life, 1813; Valentine's Eve, 1816; New Tales, 1818; Tales of the Heart, 1820; Madeline, 1822: Illustrations of Lying, 1824; Tales of the Pemberton Family for Children, 1825; The Last Voyage, 1828; Detraction Displayed, 1828; Miscellaneous Tales (12 vols.) 1845-7. *Biography*—Memoir of John Opie, 1809; Sketch of Mrs. Roberts, 1814. *Poetry*—Maid of Corinth, 1801; Elegy to the Memory of the Duke of Bedford, 1802; Poems, 1803; Lines to General Kosciusko, 1803; Song to Stella, 1803; The Warrior's Return, 1808; The Black Man's Lament, 1826; Lays for the Dead, 1834. *Miscellaneous*—Recollections of Days in Belgium, 1840.

ABOUT: Brightwell, C. L. Memorials; Earland, A. John Opie and His Circle; Fox, C. Memories of Old Friends; Jones, R. M. Later Periods of Quakerism; Julian, J. Dictionary of Hymnology; L'Estrange, A. G. K. The Friendships of Mary Russell Mitford; Ritchie, Mrs. T. Book of Sibyls; Southey, R. Colloquies: II; Harper's Weekly 15:513 June 3, 1871; Littel's Living Age 42:467 September 2, 1854; *ibid.* 74:103 July 1802; Norwich Cabinet or Monthly Report of Publication 1:217 (1807).

O'REILLY, JOHN BOYLE (June 28, 1844-August 10, 1890), Irish journalist and poet, was born near Drogheda. His father was a schoolmaster. At eleven he was sent to take his brother's place as apprentice compositor on *The Argus,* his brother having become ill. In 1858 his employer's death ended his apprenticeship. The next year he moved to Preston, England, where his aunt was living, and became a compositor on *The Guardian,* soon rising to be a reporter. In 1863 he enlisted in the Tenth Hussars as a secret agent of the Fenians. He was extremely reckless, teaching Fenian songs to the soldiers and otherwise hardly hiding his opinions. He was arrested in 1866 and sentenced to be shot. The sentence was commuted to twenty years, and in 1867 he was transported to West Australia. Two years later he escaped, and after numerous adventures reached America. He settled in Boston, where he became editor and part proprietor of *The Pilot.* In 1876 he engineered a successful rescue of all the military political prisoners in West Australia. He lived in Boston the rest of his life, becoming a well-known poet and speechmaker, who in 1885 received an honorary LL.D. from Notre Dame University. In 1889 he edited an anthology of *Poetry and Songs of Ireland*. He died from an overdose of chloral taken for insomnia. He was married, and his daughter, Mary Boyle O'Reilly, became well known as a writer.

O'Reilly's poems, though stirring and vigorous, are no longer much read. His one novel is a powerful story of convict life in West Australia.

PRINCIPAL WORKS: Songs From Southern Seas, 1873; Songs, Legends, and Ballads, 1878; Moondyne (novel) 1880; The Statues in the Block, 1881; In Bohemia, 1886; Poems and Speeches, 1891.

ABOUT: O'Reilly, J. B. Poems and Speeches (see Life by J. J. Roche).

O'SHAUGHNESSY, ARTHUR WIL-LIAM EDGAR (March 14, 1844-January 30, 1881), poet and scientist, was born at London and privately educated there. In June 1861 he received an appointment to the position of junior assistant in the library of the British Museum, and in August 1863 was transferred and made an assistant in the zoological department. As he was untrained, this appointment nettled the professional zoologists, and was condemned at a meeting of the society. However, during his lifetime of service, O'Shaughnessy must have applied himself zealously to his specialty, for his papers in the field of herpetology were well received.

O'Shaughnessy's life was short and very sad. Although he lived to be only thirty-seven, he survived his wife, the former Eleanor Marston, sister of Philip Bourke Marston, another poet, and also experienced the loss of his two children. He had published three volumes of verse and was preparing a third for the press when he died of a neglected cold and its effects, ending a career which had really no more than begun, for O'Shaughnessy was then finding a place for himself in literary life and had just been appointed English correspondent of *Le Livre*.

His works, in addition to a volume of children's stories which he wrote in collaboration with his wife, consist of four volumes, chiefly short lyrics, in which some exquisite verse is to be found. Many readers are familiar with his "Ode," better known perhaps as "The Music Makers," and with such lyrics as "I made another garden" and "Has Summer Come Without the Rose?" These and other characteristic works show him an exquisite poet of a very delicate touch, influenced by such poets as Baudelaire and Swinburne. There is some disagreement among critics as to his ranking. Many have felt that his verse is overloaded with imagery and that his material was unimportant. Yet such a critic as Edmund Gosse said that after his verse was sifted there would be "a small

ARTHUR O'SHAUGHNESSY

residue of exquisite poetry full of odour and melody, all in one key, and essentially unlike the verse of anyone else," and George Saintsbury found in him the one great essential of a poet, the gift of song.

O'Shaughnessy was a master in rendering French into English, and it was felt that he had a brilliant future as a critic. He enjoyed the friendship and respect of such men as Rossetti, Ford Madox Brown, François Coppée, and Victor Hugo. R. M.

PRINCIPAL WORKS: *Poetry*—An Epic of Women and Other Poems, 1870; Lays of France, 1872; Music and Moonlight, 1874; Songs of a Worker, 1881. *Fiction (juvenile)*—Toyland (with Eleanor W. O'Shaughnessy) 1875.

ABOUT: Moulton, L. C. Arthur O'Shaughnessy: His Life and Work; Stedman, E. C. Victorian Poets; Turquet-Milnes, G. The Influence of Baudelaire; Athenaeum February 5, 1881

OTWAY, CAESAR (1780-March 16, 1842), Irish miscellaneous writer, was born in County Tipperary of a family of English descent. He received his B.A. at Trinity College, Dublin, in 1801, and was ordained in the Established Church, being for seventeen years a country curate. In 1818 he was made assistant chaplain of a Dublin church, and became well known as a popular preacher. In 1825 he was one of the founders of the *Christian Examiner*, the first magazine of the Established Church in Ireland. At the same time he contributed frequently to the *Dublin Penny Journal* (under the name of "Terence O'Toole") and the *Dublin University Magazine*. He had prepared for years to write a history of Ireland, but his poor health prevented its ever coming to fruition. His travel books are valuable as giving authentic pictures of Ireland in his time.

PRINCIPAL WORKS: Sketches in Ireland, 1827; A Tour in Connaught, 1839; Sketches in Erris and Tyrawly, 1841; The Intellectuality of Domestic Animals, 1847.

ABOUT: Athenaeum 42:294.

"OUIDA." See RAMÉE, LOUISE DE LA

OUTRAM, GEORGE (March 25, 1805-September 15, 1856), Scottish poet, was born at the ironworks at Clydeside, near Glasgow, where his father was manager. He was educated at the Leith High School and at the University of Edinburgh, which he left without a degree. He was called to the Scottish bar in 1827, but failed completely as a lawyer, and turned to journalism. In 1837 he became editor of the Glasgow *Herald,* and later acquired a part-ownership, changing its policy from its former opposition to the corn laws, since he was an extreme conservative. He remained as editor to his death. In 1837 he married Frances McRobbie, of Jamaica, and they had four sons and six daughters. His verses are, for the most part, humorous songs in the Scottish dialect, bearing either on the law or on fishing, his favorite diversion.

PRINCIPAL WORK: Lyrics: Legal and Miscellaneous, 1874 (previously privately printed).

ABOUT: Outram, G. Lyrics: Legal and Miscellaneous (see Biographical Sketch by H. G. Bell).

OVERTON, JOHN HENRY (January 4, 1835-September 17, 1903), ecclesiastical historian, was born at Louth, Lincolnshire, only son of a surgeon. He was educated at Rugby and at Lincoln College, Oxford, receiving his B.A. in 1858 and his M.A. in 1860. In 1858 he was ordained, and became a curate in Gloucestershire. In 1860 he was made vicar of Legbourne, Lincolnshire. In 1862 he married Marianne Ludlam; they had one daughter. In 1883 he became rector of Epworth, Lincolnshire and rural dean of Axholme. Epworth was John Wesley's home, and Overton became much interested in the founder of Methodism. In 1898 he was named as rector of Gumley, Lincolnshire. From 1902 he was Burbeck lecturer at Trinity College, Cambridge. In 1903 he was made a canon of Peterborough, but as no income attached to the office he retained his charge at Gumley, where he died the following autumn. He was a contributor to the *Dictionary of National Biography* and to the *Church Quarterly Review.* He left at his death an enormous amount of unfinished historical writing.

Overton ranks high among church historians. He is fair and careful, with a pleasing style.

PRINCIPAL WORKS: The English Church in the Eighteenth Century (with C. J. Abbey) 1878; William Law: Nonjuror and Mystic, 1881; Life in the English Church, 1660-1714, 1885; John Wesley, 1891; The English Church in the Nineteenth Century, 1894; The Anglican Revival, 1897; The Nonjurors, 1902.

ABOUT: Guardian September 23, 1903.

OWEN, SIR RICHARD (July 20, 1804-December 18, 1892), scientist, was born in Lancaster, son of a West Indian merchant. He was educated at the Grammar School, Lancaster, and from 1820 to 1824 apprenticed to three different surgeons and apothecaries, the beginning of his deep interest in comparative anatomy. In 1824 he went to the University of Edinburgh to study medicine, and in 1825 to St. Bartholomew's Hospital, London. He became a member of the Royal College of Surgeons in 1826, and began private practice. In 1829 he became assistant conservator of the Hunterian Museum of the Royal College of Surgeons. In 1829 he lectured on comparative anatomy at St. Bartholomew's . He met the great biologist Cuvier, and visited him in Paris in 1831 for further scientific study. For a few months in 1833 he edited the *Zoological Magazine.* In 1834 he became a Fellow of the Royal Society.

In 1835, after seven years' engagement, he married Caroline Clift, daughter of the conservator of the Hunterian Museum. She died in 1873; they had one son. In 1842 he became joint-conservator, and on Clift's retirement full conservator. From 1836 to 1856 he was first Hunterian professor of comparative anatomy and physiology at the Royal College of Surgeons. His reputation grew until he was conceded to be the greatest comparative anatomist of his time. He received numerous public offices, honors, and degrees, and became acquainted with all the most eminent men in literary and political circles. In 1852 the queen presented him with Sheen Lodge, Richmond, which was his home thenceforth.

In 1866 Owen began a new career as the first superintendent of the natural history departments of the British Museum, resigning his professorship. From 1859 to 1861 he lectured on fossils at the Royal Institution. In 1860 he came out as an opponent of Darwinism, clinging to the non-evolutionary opinions of his youth. He traveled to Egypt with the Prince of Wales (Edward VII) in 1869. In 1881 he helped move the British Museum department to its present home in South Kensington. He helped Livingstone write his *Missionary Travels.* In 1883 he resigned from the museum. The next year he was knighted as a K.C.B. He died of old age at Sheen at nearly eighty-eight.

In spite of his scientific achievements, Owen was a hard, malicious fighter, and his engrossment in controversy on the losing side not only made him many enemies but has also injured his reputation.

PRINCIPAL WORKS: Memoir on the Pearly Nautilus, 1832; Descriptive and Illustrative Catalogue of the Physiological Series of Comparative Anatomy 1833-1840; Odontography, 1840-45; History of British Fossil Mammals and Birds, 1846; On the Anatomy of Invertebrates, 1866-68; Researches on Fossil Remains of Extinct Mammals of Australia, 1877-78.

ABOUT: Owen, Rev. R. Life of Sir Richard Owen; Royal Society Proceedings 1893.

OWEN, ROBERT (May 14, 1771-November 7, 1858), social philosopher, was born in Newtown, Montgomeryshire, Wales; in his early twenties he still "spoke more Welsh than English." His father was a saddler, ironmonger, and postmaster of the little town. Robert, the sixth of seven children, was noted as the best runner, jumper, and dancer of his associates. He was sent to day school almost in infancy, but to so poor a school that at seven he had learned all the teacher knew and was made an usher! At about the same age he injured his digestion for life by swallowing some scalding pap and burning his alimentary tract.

The child was mad about reading, and borrowed books indiscriminately. He believed implicitly in the truth of all he read, including the fiction. In later life he ceased reading anything except newspapers and statistical works; but as a boy he ranged far. Some Methodist tracts which came into his hands had the curious effect of persuading him before he was ten that "there was something wrong with all religions," a position from which he never receded.

He acted as usher for two years, then at nine went to work in a grocery and haberdashery. The next year he joined his oldest brother, William, a saddler, in London. Soon after, he was apprenticed to a draper in Stamford, from whom he learned his unusual knowledge of textiles. At fourteen he was in a haberdasher's shop on London Bridge, with work hours so long that he had only five hours for sleep. His last such position was in Manchester. There he met a mechanic named Jones, and with £100 borrowed from his brother, he and Jones commenced the manufacture of cotton-spinning machinery. The business was so successful that a capitalist bought them out, and Owen with two other young men spun yarn which they sold indepently to manufacturers. Before he was twenty he was manager of a mill in Manchester, where his talents for business soon made him a partner. It was there that he first became interested in the welfare of the workers. There too he made friends with

John Dalton and Robert Fulton, and joined the Literary and Philosophical Society. Soon he left the mill to become owner of the Chorlton Twist Company.

Visiting Glasgow on business, he met and fell in love with Anne Caroline Dale, daughter of the owner of the great New Lanark Mills. She reciprocated, but his free-thinking principles were an obstacle with her father. By way of persuasion, Owen sold his company and bought Dale's mills! It was thus that he acquired the property at New Lanark which he was to make famous.

Owen was married in 1799 and at once began to improve conditions at New Lanark—at first against the resentment of the workers at this "foreigner." He won them over when during the closing of the mills by the American embargo in 1806, he paid full wages for seven months. He established a commissary, abolished the practice of hiring pauper children from the foundling homes, and invented a quaint system of inspiring his workers to sobriety and virtue by a series of colored labels at each man's post. Finally, becoming interested in Lancaster's theory of undenominational, self-governing education, he wished to start a school at the mill. His partners objected, so he bought them out and secured new ones, who were to receive 5 per cent interest on their capital, the surplus to go for education and improvement of working conditions.

The new school emphasized dancing, music, drilling, and teaching through kindness. He believed that "men should be molded into goodness." He was the prime mover behind the Factory Act of 1819. But his

ROBERT OWEN

opposition to child labor as well as his outspoken antagonism to religion made him anathema to many who might otherwise have been his followers.

The remainder of Owen's life from about 1820 was devoted to advocacy of his theories. He withdrew gradually from his business connections, and gave himself over to writing, speaking, and editing short-lived magazines, and to organization of his "communities" and "village units." He was never a Socialist in any true sense, but believed in a return to handicraft, a sort of primitive Communism. The most famous of the Owenite communities was New Harmony, in Indiana, founded in 1825. Then and again twenty years later he spent several years at a time in America.

As Owen grew older, his mentality began to fail. Perhaps he had matured too early and worked too hard in childhood. He lost all his business acumen, and in New Harmony was the dupe of any cheat. His schemes grew more rash, his theories vaguer. In 1854 he was converted to Spiritualism, and became an extreme and gullible accepter of every supernatural wonder. His last public appearance was in the autumn of 1858; he was then practically in his second childhood. At his urgent plea he was taken back to his birthplace, where he died. He left three sons, one of whom, Robert Dale Owen, followed in his footsteps; the other two became college professors; all three were American citizens and residents.

Owen was a true philanthropist, a commercial genius, a man of the most virtuous life and the kindest impulses. It must also be added that he was vain, somewhat of a monomaniac, and one of the worst bores who ever lived. He has the honor of being a pioneer in Rationalism and in a sort of half-Socialism, and in the years of his mental power he was a selfless seeker for the good of humanity. As a writer in his earlier works, he was shrewd, succinct, and forthright; his later books became diffuse and sometimes incoherent. And yet his last work, his autobiography, is the most readable today of them all.   M. A. deF.

PRINCIPAL WORKS: A New View of Human Society, 1813; Report to the Committee on the Poor Law, 1817; Observations on the Effect of the Manufacturing System, 1818; The Book of the New Moral World (7 parts) 1836-44; The Revolution in the Mind and Practice of the Human Race, 1849; Letters to the Human Race, 1850; The New Existence of Man Upon Earth (8 parts) 1854-; The Life of Robert Owen, 1857; The Evidences of Christianity (debate with Alexander Campbell, 1829) 1906.

ABOUT: Cole, G. D. H. The Life of Robert Owen; Dolleans, E. Robert Owen; Holyoake, G. J. History of Co-operation in England; McCabe, J. Robert Owen; Podmore, F. Life of Robert Owen; Snedeker, C. D. The Town of the Fearless.

OXENFORD, JOHN (August 12, 1813-February 21, 1877), playwright and critic, was born in Camberwell. He was almost entirely self-educated, and in boyhood was articled to a London solicitor. His first writing was on finance, but his interest was in language and literature, and he translated well from French, German, Italian, and Spanish, and edited a German-English dictionary and a volume of French songs. He was the first to introduce Schopenhauer to English readers. His chief concern, however, was with the stage, and he produced about seventy plays and operas. From 1850 to shortly before his death he was dramatic critic of The Times. In 1867 he visited the United States, and later made a trip to Spain, on both occasions sending home articles to The Times about his travels. In 1875 he became a Roman Catholic.

Oxenford was so amiable and friendly a man that his criticisms are worthless—mere kindly blurbs. As a playwright his work was facile, but hardly any of his plays were published and none has survived him. The great bulk of his work still remains uncollected in the columns of The Times and in magazines.

PRINCIPAL WORKS: My Fellow Clerk, 1835; The Hemlock Draught, 1848.

ABOUT: Academy 2:194, 1877.

PAGET, FRANCIS EDWARD (May 24, 1806-August 4, 1882), cleric and writer of stories and novels, was the eldest son of the general Sir Edward Paget. Educated at Westminster School and Christ Church College, Oxford, he received his bachelor's degree in 1828. He sympathized with the Oxford (High Church) Movement, and became rector of Elford, near Lichfield, in 1835, holding this post for the rest of his life. In 1840 he married Fanny Chester, daughter of a clergyman. It was under his supervision that, in 1848, Elford Church was restored. Most of his works deal with religion; he gently satirized the Low Church group, and pointed to the Anglican Church as a middle way between Catholicism and dissent. Despite the failing health and ultimate blindness of his last years he retained his wit and humor. His tales are noteworthy for their descriptions of rural life and character.

PRINCIPAL WORKS: Caleb Kniveton, the Incendiary, 1833; Tales of the Village, 1841; St. Antholin's: or, Old Churches and New, 1841; The Warden of Berkingholt, 1843; The Owlet of Owlstone Edge, 1855; A Student Penitent of 1695, 1875.

ABOUT: Christian Observer 43:100 February 1843; Christian Remembrancer 5:222 February 1843; Guardian, 37:1124 August 16, 1882.

483

PALGRAVE, SIR FRANCIS (July 1788-July 6, 1861)

PALGRAVE, SIR FRANCIS (July 1788-July 6, 1861), antiquarian, was born in London, the son of Meyer Cohen, a stockbroker. He was known by his father's surname until in his forty-fourth year he embraced the Christian faith and adopted his mother-in-law's name.

An unusually precocious child, he was educated at home by tutors. He was always brilliantly quick at acquiring knowledge and skill. When only eight years old he translated the *Battle of the Frogs and Mice* from a Latin version into French. His father published the piece with something of a flourish.

When he was fifteen his father failed in business, and the youth was thus forced to become a solicitor's clerk. In 1821 he was employed under the Record Commission in the publication of original documents, and a few years later he was called to the bar. He made a mark for himself in his profession with pedigree cases before the House of Lords.

From childhood he had applied himself to literary and antiquarian studies. In 1814 he began contributing papers to the *Edinburgh* and *Quarterly* reviews, and he remained an important contributor for many years. One of his most original and noteworthy papers was "Fine Arts in Florence" in the *Quarterly Review* of June 1840; and from this paper a forger of Shelley's letters palmed off extracts as authentic correspondence of the poet.

Palgrave's position as an historian was established with the publication of *The Rise and Progress of the English Commonwealth* in 1832, described by the *Edinburgh Review* as "the most luminous work that has been produced on the early institutions of England."

The same year he changed his name from Cohen to Palgrave, became a Christian, married Elizabeth Turner of Yarmouth, and was knighted. The next year he became a commissioner of the Municipal Corporation; and in 1838 he was appointed deputy-keeper of Her Majesty's Records.

Palgrave's greatest work is *The History of Normandy and England* which opened new historical vistas for readers of his day. It still remains a valid and important work in its field.

He brought to his historical writings an erudition surpassed by only a few scholars, a fearless and independent spirit of inquiry, and a singularly brilliant imagination. Contemporary reviewers criticized him for being "careless of the dignity of history," and they resented his lack of Anglo-Saxon restraint in writing; but almost without exception they respected his findings and admired the zeal which led him to study exhaustively, to explore bravely, and then, at times, to exhibit his discoveries a bit too insistently.

He was attracted especially to mediaeval Europe. It is generally agreed that one of his most valuable discoveries was the importance of the enduring imperial power of the Roman Empire for centuries after the fifth century.

Sir A. W. Ward in the *Cambridge History of English Literature* has judiciously written: "Sir Francis Palgrave, who besides first strongly impressing upon Englishmen the value of study, by his own example pointed the way to a free original use of the national records by historians of imagination and constructive power, was a writer to whom the attributes of genius can hardly be denied . . . The inspiring and stimulating effect of his historical labors has of late, been under-valued rather than overrated."

Palgrave had four sons who won distinction in various fields. A friend who knew the father in his family circle, said that he was of such a bright and playful character and so excessively indulgent and kind, that with his sons he appeared almost as a boy among boys. He joined in their talk and in their childish punning matches, told them stories, and drew fabulous pictures for their amusement.

For many years Palgrave was a member of the Royal Society. He died at the age of seventy-two at his residence in Hampstead Green.

P. G.

PRINCIPAL WORKS: *History*—The Parliamentary Writs (ed.) 1827; History of England, 1832; The Rise and Progress of the English Commonwealth, 1832; Observations on the Establishment of the New Municipal Corporation, 1832; An Essay on

SIR FRANCIS PALGRAVE

the Original Authority of the King's Council, 1834; Rotuli Curiae Regis (ed.) 1835; The Ancient Kalendars and Inventories of the Treasury of His Majesty's Exchequer (ed.) 1836: Documents and Records Illustrating the History of Scotland, 1837; Truths and Fictions of the Middle Ages, 1837; Annual Report of the Deputy-Keeper of the Public Records, 1840-61; The Lord and Vassal, 1844: The History of Normandy and England, 1851-64.

ABOUT: Edinburgh Review April 1859; Gentleman's Magazine, 1861; Twenty-Third Report of the Deputy-Keeper of the Public Records.

PALGRAVE, FRANCIS TURNER (September 28, 1824-October 24, 1897), poet and anthologist, was the oldest son of Sir Francis Palgrave, the antiquarian. The father's name was originally Cohen, and Francis Turner Palgrave was of one-quarter Jewish blood. He was born at Yarmouth, in the home of his maternal grandfather, and his childhood was spent there and at the family home at Hampstead—both atmospheres of the greatest culture. He was a day pupil at the Charterhouse from 1838, and in 1843 went to Oxford, where he was a scholar of Balliol and a fellow of Exeter, being graduated with a first class in classics. He received both the B.A. and the M.A. in 1856.

In 1846 Palgrave was assistant private secretary to Gladstone, then prime minister, and from 1850 to 1855 taught at the government training school for teachers at Kneller Hall. From 1855 to 1884 he held various positions in the Education Department. From 1885 to 1895 he was Professor of Poetry at Oxford.

In 1862 he married Cecil Gaskell, daughter of a member of Parliament; his wife died in 1890, leaving four daughters. (A son had predeceased her.)

Palgrave was the art critic of the *Saturday Review*, and also wrote regularly for the *Quarterly Review*. In 1878 he received an honorary LL.D. from the University of Edinburgh. He continued to write almost to the day of his death, which occurred in consequence of a paralytic stroke.

In addition to his work as critic, poet, and anthologist, Palgrave edited many volumes of other men's work, particularly in poetry. He was essentially an appreciator rather than a creator. Affectionate and sympathetic in nature, his simplicity sometimes approached the naive. His poetic imagination was higher than his power of expression, though his verse is by no means negligible. The shorter lyrics are perhaps too Wordsworthian in Wordsworth's worst manner of exaggerated plainness, but his longer poems—particularly the *Visions of England,* an attempt to illustrate English history in stirring ballad form—have distinct merit. His hymns are pleasing, and many of them are well known; he was unobtrusively devout and an orthodox churchman, one of his closest friends being the Arch-

F. T. PALGRAVE

bishop of Canterbury, who pronounced his funeral sermon.

It is as an anthologist, however, that Palgrave's name is immortal. No anthology, in all probability, will ever wholly supersede the first *Golden Treasury.* The second series was not so happy—perhaps because it did not have, as the first did, the inestimable benefit of guidance by Palgrave's intimate friend, Tennyson. Besides, at seventy one's poetic judgment is not usually so acute as in earlier life.

Palgrave's interests were eclectic; he wrote on subjects as diverse as art criticism and stories for children. But his great achievement was that forerunner of all poetry anthologies, the indispensable *Golden Treasury of English Verse.* M. A. deF.

PRINCIPAL WORKS: *Poetry*—Idyls and Songs, 1854; Hymns, 1867; Lyrical Poems, 1871; The Visions of England, 1881; Amenophis, 1892. *Anthologies*—Golden Treasury of English Verse, 1861; second series, 1896; The Children's Treasury of English Song, 1875; The Treasury of Sacred Song, 1889. *Miscellaneous*—The Passionate Pilgrim (autobiography) 1858; Essays on Art, 1866; Gems of English Art, 1869; The Five Days' Entertainments at Wentworth Grange (juvenile) 1869; Landscape in Poetry, 1897.

ABOUT: Palgrave, F. T. The Passionate Pilgrim; Palgrave, G. F. Francis Turner Palgrave: His Journals and Memoirs of His Life; Illustrated London News 111:601 October 30, 1897.

PALGRAVE, WILLIAM GIFFORD (January 24, 1826-September 30, 1888), traveler and diplomatist, was born in Westminster, the second son of the historian Sir Francis Palgrave. After a brilliant career as a student at Charterhouse and Trinity College, Oxford, he joined the army in India. He decided, however, to become a missionary among the Arabian peoples, and was converted to Catholicism, becoming a Jesuit. In his missionary work, first in India and then in Syria, he was successful, and became acquainted with Arabian customs. In 1862-63 he traveled across central Arabia (then closed to Europeans), appearing as a Syrian Christian doctor and trader, studying the practicability of mission work among the Arabs. Finding the outlook dark, he left the Jesuit order and entered diplomatic work, holding various posts. The last was in Uruguay, where he died at Montevideo. His *Narrative of a Year's Journey* is an absorbing account of his dangerous travels.

PRINCIPAL WORKS: Narrative of a Year's Journey Through Central and Eastern Arabia, 1865; Essays on Eastern Questions; 1872; Hermann Agha, 1872; Dutch Guiana, 1876; Ulysses: or, Scenes and Studies in Many Lands, 1887; A Vision of Life: Semblance and Reality (poem) 1891.

ABOUT: Palgrave, W. G. A Vision of Life (see Preface); Royal Geographical Society Proceedings November 1888.

PALMER, ROUNDELL. See SELBORNE, LORD

PARDOE, JULIA (1806-November 26, 1862), novelist and historical writer, was born in Beverley, Yorkshire, the daughter of an army officer. A precocious child, she early wrote verse which, published when she was not yet fourteen, reached a second edition. She later followed up her success with a travel book on Portugal, occasioned by her residence there as a young woman; and in 1835 she went to Turkey, obtaining the intimate acquaintance with that country reflected in *The City of the Sultan*. Meanwhile she had issued her first novel; and she devoted herself to the writing of popular historical works. In 1860 she was granted a civil list pension, and in 1862 she died in London. Her narrative gift and grace of style secured popularity for her writings in her day.

PRINCIPAL WORKS: The City of the Sultan and Domestic Manners of the Turks, 1837; The Confessions of a Pretty Woman, 1846; Louis XIV and the Court of France in the Seventeenth Century, 1847; The Jealous Wife, 1847; The Court and Reign of Francis the First, King of France, 1849; Flies in Amber, 1850; The Life and Memoirs of Marie de Medicis, Queen and Regent of France, 1852.

ABOUT: Pardoe, J. The Court and Reign of Francis the First, King of France (see Memoir in Vol. I of 1887 ed.).

"PARLEY, PETER." See MARTIN, WILLIAM

PARRY, SIR WILLIAM EDWARD (December 19, 1790-July 8, 1855), Arctic explorer and rear-admiral, was born at Bath, the son of a physician. As a mere boy he joined the navy, and in 1810 he was made a lieutenant. In the course of his service near Spitzbergen he made a study of nautical astronomy, and produced a useful manual on the subject. After taking part in an Arctic expedition in 1818, he set out in 1819 on a voyage to find the Northwest Passage. He reached Melville Island, having gone farther than any known predecessor, and returned in 1820. Subsequent expeditions (1821-23 and 1824-25) and an unsuccessful attempt (1827) to reach the North Pole from Spitzbergen (establishing a new latitude record) brought him honor and fame, and he held various posts of responsibility. His journals are the interesting record of his travels.

PRINCIPAL WORKS: Journal of a Voyage for the Discovery of a North-west Passage from the Atlantic to the Pacific, 1821; Journal of a Second Voyage . . . ., 1824; Journal of a Third Voyage . . . ., 1826; Narrative of an Attempt to Reach the North Pole, 1828.

ABOUT: Marshall, J. Royal Naval Biography; Parry, E. Memoirs of Rear-Admiral Sir W. E. Parry; Yonge, C. D. Our Great Naval Commanders; see also own works, listed above.

PATER, WALTER HORATIO (August 4, 1839-July 30, 1894), essayist and critic, was born at Shadwell, East London, son of Richard Glode Pater, a physician, and Maria (Hill) Pater. It had been usual in the family to bring any sons up as Roman Catholics and daughters as Anglicans; but Dr. Pater had abandoned Catholicism and Walter was taught the precepts of the Church of England. The doctor died while Walter was an infant, and the family then removed to Chase Side, Enfield, a place not at that time absorbed in Greater London. The boy went to a local school until he was fourteen, when he passed on to the King's School, Canterbury. There he showed the future scholar's usual indifference to games, but evinced none of the precocious desire to write so common in the histories of men of letters. He was shy, sensitive, meditative, fond of pomps and ceremonies. He gave no special intellectual promise until he reached the sixth form. In June 1858 he went, with an exhibition, to Queen's College, Oxford; and though he took only a second-class in classics (1862) it is on record that Jowett once said to him: "I think you have a mind that will come to great eminence."

His original plan had been to take orders, but he abandoned it, and for two years after graduation lived in the High Street, Oxford, reading with private pupils. In 1864 he was elected to a fellowship at Brasenose College and went into residence there, living in a small set of rooms which he furnished simply and austerely. As a don he lectured to the passmen, and lived a quiet, regular, abstemious and studious life. One of his former pupils, C. L. Shadwell (later provost of Oriel) became his closest friend; and it was a journey with Shadwell, in 1865, to Ravenna,

WALTER PATER

Pisa, and Florence, that brought to a head Pater's interest in the arts of design and made them thenceforward his chief object of study and appreciation.

Pater's first publication was an essay on Coleridge in the *Westminster Review*, in 1866, treating of the philosophic side of that writer. In the same year his reading of Otto Jahn's *Life of Winckelmann* had a decisive effect in the orientation of his mind, leading him away from the more abstract idealism of his early master, Ruskin, to a position where he could devote his attention to the contemplation of beauty in the concrete. In January 1867 he published an essay on Winckelmann in the *Westminster Review*, and he now became an occasional contributor to the serious press, especially the *Fortnightly*. He had been elected in 1863 to an essay society called "Old Mortality," and there he met such men of mark as T. H. Green, H. Nettleship, Edward Caird, and Swinburne. Another early friend was Ingram Bywater; and somewhat later his circle included Mark Pattison, Mandell Creighton, Humphry Ward, Edmund Gosse, and Dr. F. W. Bussell. Between 1869 and 1871 there appeared in the *Fortnightly Review* his essays on Leonardo, Botticelli, Pico della Mirandola, and "The Poetry of Michelangelo." All these were included in his first book, *Studies in the History of the Renaissance*, which came out in 1873. These essays, finely wrought and deeply pondered, plough a new furrow in the field of art-criticism, eschewing any attempt at definitions of abstract beauty and closely examining individual works of art with unusual sympathy and penetration. The description of "La Gioconda," intensely subtle

and poetic, is one of the finest passages of prose that Pater ever produced.

From 1869 onwards, besides his Brasenose rooms, Pater had a house at Bradmore Road, Oxford, where his two sisters lived. His placid career as a teacher and scholar presents few external "events." His vacations were usually spent in France or Germany with his sisters; his only form of exercise was strenuous walking; his Continental tours never led him to acquire a colloquial knowledge of either French or German (though he read both easily). He got to know several members of the Pre-Raphaelite group; and though he never became an outstanding man in academic circles his prestige as a prophet of the aesthetic school did quietly make itself felt among the connoisseurs. One result of this, in 1877, was a cruel parody of his style and personality in W. H. Mallock's *New Republic*, which gave him some unsought notoriety and caused him no little pain by identifying him with the more extravagant manifestations of the school.

Pater's history is, in the main, that of his literary interests and of his publications. During the 'seventies he produced essays on Wordsworth, Charles Lamb, and romanticism. He delivered three of the lectures which appeared posthumously as *Greek Studies*; he wrote a brief study of "Love's Labour's Lost," and a semi-autobiographical piece, of singular charm and pathos, called *The Child in the House*. From 1878 onwards his energies were mainly engaged in the composition of *Marius the Epicurean*, the book which perhaps best displays the essential Pater, and by which he is now best known. In 1880 he resigned his tutorship at Brasenose (though continuing in his fellowship), thus setting himself free from a good deal of niggling college business which had interrupted his more significant work as a writer.

Marius appeared in 1885, the fruit of some six years' labor. It is the history of the intellectual and spiritual development of a Latin mind in the time of Marcus Aurelius—the mind of a meditative, eclectic, subtly literary young man—and of its gradual approach to the Christian point of view. The archaeological detail is closely studied, though not obtruded; a dreamy, reminiscent flavor hangs about the book; characters are not sharply realized in the round; and the whole is slow in movement, learned, and well-nigh devoid of all but intellectual action. But the landscape is exquisitely done, the language is highly finished, refined, and quietly colored, and the study is, in A. C. Benson's words, "a revelation of the possibilities of poetical prose which the English language contains."

In this same year, 1885, Pater took a house at Earl's Terrace, Kensington, London, and lived there during vacations, occupying his rooms at Brasenose during term time. *Marius* had won him some reputation; he made new social contacts, began to review for *The Guardian, The Athenaeum*, and *Pall Mall Gazette*, and embarked on a series of *Imaginary Portraits*—essays in philosophic description of characters that attracted him, closely studied in relation to their environment. A large historical task, *Gaston de Latour*, was projected, and five chapters appeared in *Macmillan's Magazine* during 1888, but the book was never finished. The chief occupation of his last years was *Plato and Platonism*, designed as an educational work for young students, aiming to illustrate the personality of Plato and his historical position.

Early in 1894 Pater was invested with the honorary degree of LL.D. by the University of Glasgow, and while in the North made visits to various cathedrals thereabouts. The year before he had given up his London house and taken one in St. Giles's, Oxford. Here, in June 1894, he was taken ill with rheumatic fever, and then, during convalescence, with pleurisy. Again he seemed in a fair way to recovery, but on the morning of July 30 he was suddenly attacked by heart-failure and died.

Humphry Ward, who entered Brasenose in October 1864, speaks of Pater's "high, rather receding forehead; his bright eyes, placed near together, his face clean-shaven except for a short moustache (this was rare in those days), his slight stoop, and his quick walk with a curious swing of the shoulders." In tastes he was simple to the point of austerity; in dress punctilious; in manner retiring and courteous. He disliked responsibility and business, and, though he had many friends and could shine in conversation, he was reticent and reserved, and not a "good mixer." He had a quiet irony of expression, was capable, on occasion, of stating a case with force and vigor, and had withal a genuine and natural sense of fun. His religious position was almost certainly far from orthodox, though he was a regular and very reverent attendant at college chapel.

As a literary artist Pater can be classified with no special group, though his emphasis on aesthetic, as distinguished from ethical or metaphysical values, gave a creed and a justification to such later and very different thinkers as Oscar Wilde. His works are all of a contemplative cast, philosophic without any exact metaphysic, and not related to current social trends, nor critical of existing conditions—as were, for example, the novels of his contemporary, Hardy, which were appearing at the same time. His method in art-criticism went beyond the appraisal of formal merits, and attempted an imaginative reconstruction of the artist's mood and mind. As a prose-writer, "he exhausted himself," wrote Gosse, "in the research after absolute perfection of expression, noting with extreme refinement fine shades of feeling and delicate distinctions of thought and sentiment. His fault was to overburden his sentences, to annex to them too many parenthetical clauses and adjectival glosses. . . He wrote with labor, incessantly revising his expression and adding to it, wearying himself in the pursuit of a vain perfection.. He possessed all the qualities of a humanist." A. C. Bensor wrote: "It may be said, then, that Pater really struck out a new line in English prose. . . The essence of his attempt was to produce prose that had never before been contemplated in English, full of color and melody, serious, exquisite, ornate." His own finely considered essay on "Style" (in *Appreciations*) states strikingly the paramount importance of sincerity: "Truth! there can be no merit, no craft at all without that. And further, all beauty is in the long run only *fineness* of truth, or what we call expression, the finer accommodation of speech to that vision within." H. B. G.

PRINCIPAL WORKS: Studies in the History of the Renaissance, 1873 (reissued, revised, as The Renaissance, 1877); Marius the Epicurean, 1885; Imaginary Portraits, 1887; Appreciations: With an Essay on Style, 1889; Plato and Platonism, 1893; The Child in the House, 1894; Greek Studies, 1895; Miscellaneous Studies, 1895; Gaston de Latour, 1896; Emerald Uthwart, 1905.

ABOUT: Benson, A. C. Walter Pater; Eaker, J. G. Walter Pater: A Study in Methods and Effects; Eliot, T. S. Selected Essays; Kennedy, J. M. English Literature, 1880-1905; More, P. E. The Drift of Romanticism; Symons, A. A Study of Walter Pater; Thomas, P. E. Walter Pater: A Critical Study; Wright, T. The Life of Walter Pater.

PATMORE, COVENTRY KERSEY DIGHTON (July 23, 1823-November 26, 1896), poet and essayist, was born at Woodford, Essex, the eldest son of Peter George Patmore, writer, and Eliza (Robertson) Patmore. He had no formal schooling in England, but was sent for six months in 1839 to a school at Saint Germains with a view to the improvement of his French. While there he paid many visits to the (probably third-rate) *salon* of the minor novelist, Mrs. Catherine Gore. His boyhood was dominated by a severe mother and an improvident and not very admirable father; and his cloistered upbringing helped to nurture the priggishness which became so strong an element in his character. Returned from France, he applied himself energetically to the study of chemistry for two years. Later he thought of the church as a profession, but abandoned the idea partly through doubts as to the status of the Church of England and partly because his father did not feel able to bear the expense of his university education. He began writing in 1840, and in 1844 published a volume of *Poems*, thin and weak in subject-matter, and owing some debt to Tennyson and Elizabeth Barrett. His father's *Chatsworth* contains a sentimental description of him at the age of twenty: "The pale face is resting on the clasped hand, over which, and all round the small, exquisitely modeled head, fall heavy waves of auburn hair, concealing all but one pale cheek—pale and cold as marble, but smooth and soft as a girl's."

Towards the end of 1845 Peter George Patmore, having lost heavily in railway speculations, suddenly went off to the Continent, leaving his son without a regular profession, to support himself as best he might. After an uneasy year of literary hack-work Coventry was made an assistant in the department of printed books at the British Museum, on the recommendation of Richard Monckton Milnes (later Lord Houghton). In September 1847, being now financially secure, he married Emily Augusta Andrews, daughter of a Congregationalist minister.

Patmore's safe and quiet post in the Museum left him plenty of leisure to pursue the study of poetry. He knew and admired Tennyson; Ruskin was also of his acquaintance; and in 1849 he met the young Pre-Raphaelite group of artists and contributed to their magazine, *The Germ*. More important periodicals for which he wrote were the *Edinburgh Review* and the *North British Review*. His criticism could rise on occasion to genuine insight, but in the mass it lacked sympathy and due appreciation of points of view far removed from his own.

His next published book of verse, *Tamerton Church Tower and Other Poems*, showed no advance in selection and grasp of vital subject-matter, though it had descriptive passages of merit. In 1854 he issued anonymously *The Betrothal*, which was the first part of the long poem known as *The Angel in the House*, the whole of which was designed to praise and illustrate happy marriage as the supreme expression of love between man and woman. The metre chosen was alternate rhyming eight-syllabled lines, and the work became the most popular poem of the day. It had some true poetic qualities, but a good deal of bathos, and for most people it is almost unreadable today. Its admirers, however, included Browning, Carlyle, Ruskin, and Tennyson. The later parts were *The Espousals, Faithful for Ever,* and *The Victories of Love.* The object of this devotion, Emily Patmore, died on

COVENTRY PATMORE

July 5, 1862, leaving three sons and three daughters.

Patmore's mystical leanings had for some time been bringing him nearer to Roman Catholicism, and in the spring of 1864, after instruction in Rome, he was received into that communion. On his visit to Rome he also met Marianne Caroline Byles, whom he married the same summer, not without some scruples because of her considerable fortune, of which he had not been aware on first acquaintance. This wealth, none the less, enabled him to retire from the British Museum at the end of 1865, and purchase an estate, Heron's Ghyll, near Uckfield, Sussex. In 1874 he sold this place to the Duke of Norfolk, and settled at The Mansion, Hastings, until 1891, when he went to his last home at Lymington.

The first nine *Odes*, privately printed in 1868, were in lines of irregular length, and reached greater heights of thought and diction than he had so far attained. A collected edition, called *The Unknown Eros, and Other Odes*, came out in 1877, and in the following year the idyll, *Amelia*. Religious preoccupations were now paramount, and he projected a long poem on the Virgin; but the idea was never pursued. A bolder scheme was actually carried out—namely a prose work, *Sponsa Dei*, an "interpretation of the love between the soul and God by an analogy of the love between a woman and a man." The dangers of such a theme are evident enough, and they were perceived by Father Gerard Manley Hopkins, at whose suggestion Patmore destroyed the manuscript. Sir Edmund Gosse, the critic, had seen *Sponsa Dei*, and felt that its destruction was a literary disaster. The same writer describes the poet as first seen by him in 1879: "Three things were in those days particularly noticeable in the head of Coventry Patmore: the vast convex brows, arched with vision; the bright, shrewd, bluish-grey eyes, the outer fold of one eyelid permanently and humorously drooping; and the wilful, sensuous mouth . . . When at rest, standing or sitting, he was remarkably graceful, falling easily into languid, undulating poses. No sooner did he begin to walk than he became grotesque at once, the long, thin neck thrust out, the angularity of the limbs emphasized in every rapid, inelegant movement."

The early 'eighties brought Patmore triple bereavement—of his second wife in 1880, his daughter Emily in 1882, and his son Henry in 1883. He was married for a third time in 1881, to Harriet Robson.

After 1877 Patmore published no more poetry. In that year he edited an autobiographical fragment by his friend, Bryan Waller Procter ("Barry Cornwall"); the middle years of the next decade saw frequent contributions to the *St. James's Gazette* (some of which were collected in 1889 as *Principle in Art* and others in 1893 as *Religio Poetae*); and in 1895 he issued *The Rod, the Root, and the Flower,* mainly concerned with religious subjects. He died on November 26, 1896, of angina pectoris.

The tameness of Patmore's work in general, and his position as amiable laureate of the Victorian home have given rise to a misconception as to his character. Observers who knew him well are agreed that he was far from being the insipid and namby-pamby figure of popular imagination. His nature, on the contrary, was haughty, combative, forthright, and plain-spoken to the point of churlishness; and some idea of this can be got from his political odes, which are reactionary and violent to a degree now almost incredible. His friends also agree as to the duality of his character: he is described as, on the one hand, imperious, sardonic, and a keen man of business, and on the other, sensitive, tender, and humorous.

Like many Roman Catholics he was capable of making game of his own religion, and invented "legends" which, to his delight, became actually incorporated in works of Catholic tradition. He was none the less a sincere and ardent convert to that faith, though he hated priests in general and Cardinal H. E. Manning in particular.

His poetry in general suffers from flatness and insipidity, but he was a keen observer of nature and had bursts of genuine song. Certain short pieces like "The Azalea" and "The Toys" have a pathos and delicacy of feeling that are exquisite. No writer has had a higher conception of the poetic function: what he lacked was the genius to fulfill it. "Like Gray," writes Gosse, "like Alfred de Vigny, like Leopardi (with whom he has several points in common), he knew the confines of his strength; he strove not to be copious but to be uniformly exquisite. He did not quite reach his aim, but even Catullus has scarcely done that. The peculiar beauty of his verse is not to everyone's taste; if it were he would have that universal attractiveness which we have admitted that he lacks. But he wrote, with extreme and conscientious care and with impassioned joy, a comparatively small body of poetry, the least successful portions of which are yet curiously his own, while the most successful fill those who are attuned to them with an exquisite and durable pleasure." H. B. G.

PRINCIPAL WORKS: *Poems*—Poems, 1844; Tamerton Church Tower, 1853; The Betrothal (Pt. 1 of The Angel in the House) 1854; The Espousals (Pt. 2 of The Angel in the House) 1856; The Angel in the House (the preceding, in 2 vols.) 1858; Faithful for Ever (Pt. 3 of The Angel in the House) 1860; The Victories of Love (Pt. 4 of The Angel in the House) 1863; Odes, 1868; The Unknown Eros and Other Odes, 1877; Amelia, Tamerton Church Tower, etc.: With Prefatory Study on English Metrical Law, 1878; Seven Unpublished Poems to Alice Meynell, 1922. *Prose*—Saint Bernard on the Love of God (trans. by W. C. and Coventry Patmore) 1881; How I Managed and Improved My Estate, 1886; Hastings, Lewes, Rye, and the Sussex Marshes, 1887; Principle in Art, 1889; Religio Poetæ, 1893; The Rod, the Root, and the Flower, 1895; Courage in Politics and Other Essays: 1885-1896, 1921.

ABOUT: Burdett, O. The Idea of Coventry Patmore; Champneys, B. Memories and Correspondence of Coventry Patmore; Evans, B. I. English Poetry in the Later Nineteenth Century; Gosse, E. Coventry Patmore; Page, F. Patmore: A Study in Poetry; Read, H. Coventry Patmore.

PATMORE, PETER GEORGE (1786-December 19, 1855), critic and essayist, was born in London, the son of a jeweler. The grandson (by his mother) of a German painter, the youth preferred literature to his father's profession, and took to journalism. His friends included Charles Lamb and William Hazlitt, both of whom addressed letters to him which can be found in their published correspondence. He edited the *New Monthly Magazine* from 1841 until 1853, and contributed frequently to other periodicals. His most discussed work was his *My Friends and Acquaintance,* in which he indulged in reminiscences concerning important figures in nineteenth-century literature. His gossiping provoked criticism, and his critical judgments were also taken to task. His work is of less permanent interest and value than that of his son, Coventry Patmore.

PRINCIPAL WORKS: Imitations of Celebrated Authors: or, Imaginary Rejected Articles, 1826; Chatsworth: or, The Romance of a Week, 1844; My Friends and Acquaintance, 1854.

ABOUT: Meynell, A. C. T. The Second Person Singular; Gentleman's Magazine February 1856 1:206.

PATTISON, MARK (October 10, 1813-July 30, 1844), rector of Lincoln College, biographer, and editor, was born at Hornby, North Riding, the eldest of the twelve children of Mark James Pattison, then curate in charge of Hornby, and Jane (Winn) Pattison. His youth was spent mainly in Hauxwell, Yorkshire, where his father for many years was rector.

Educated at home by his Evangelical (Low-Church) father, he gained a solid grounding in Latin, Greek, and mathematics, but on the whole his early studies were too unsystematic to prepare him adequately for what was to come. His social interests, moreover, included only such outdoor country sports as fishing and riding, and he was shy and awkward at the time he went to Oxford.

At Oriel College, where he matriculated in 1832, the diffidence resulting from his feeling of social inferiority was not relieved by the discovery that others could excel him in formal studies. While his random system of learning undoubtedly enriched his mind, he failed to secure first-class honors, and was obliged to content himself with a second-class degree (classical honors) in 1836.

The next few years were marked by his intense interest in the Oxford, or the Aldgate High-Church, Movement, also known as Puseyism, and for a while he lived in

MARK PATTISON

the Aldgate house of John Henry Newman, whom he assisted in the translation of St. Thomas Aquinas' *Catena Aurea.* After some difficulty, he secured a fellowship at Lincoln College, but a feeling of being a pariah among anti-Puseyites seem to have produced for a time a defensive and rather morbid High-Church religious fervor in his mind. At one period he wrote considerably upon theological subjects. He was ordained deacon in 1841 and priest in 1843.

In the last-mentioned year, however, he was appointed to a college tutorship, and for many years his thoughts were turned toward education. He was a stimulating and inspiring teacher, although he was never able "to talk down" to mediocrity; and he generously shared his vacations with students whom he helped in their work without charge. From 1848 to 1851 Lincoln College, almost exclusively under his care, was one of the best-managed colleges in Oxford.

Notwithstanding this record of achievement, when a vacancy in the rectorship occurred in 1851, Pattison failed of election through a rather disgusting intrigue, reflecting small credit on anyone. The consequent disappointment was undoubtedly keen, although it is difficult to believe Pattison's exaggerated account in his *Memoirs.* His academic work continued much as before, and by recreation and travel he managed to some extent to recover himself.

From this time forth he gave much attention to scholarship, becoming especially interested in the mediaeval scholars, Isaac Casaubon and Joseph Justus Scaliger. His projected life of Scaliger never was completely written, but he never lost interest in or enthusiasm for his subject. Although he gave up his tutorship in 1855 because of disagreement with the rector, he took private students, and spent some time studying at German universities. In 1859 he was made one of the assistant commissioners studying Continental education. His ideas on educational reform, reflected in his essays, hold up the ideal of a university as a center of education with genuine devotion to research, not a cramming-school for overgrown boys.

His own educational activity decreased, although in 1861, the year of his marriage to Emilia Frances Strong (later Lady Dilke), a writer on art, he was finally given his rectorship; and literary work took up an increasing share of his time. He wrote numerous articles on religious, educational, and literary subjects, and edited works of Pope and Milton, writing a biography of the latter for the "English Men of Letters" series. His most important work, his life of Isaac Casaubon, undertaken after Bernays' *Joseph Justus Scaliger* had anticipated his writing on that subject, appeared in 1875.

His health gave way in 1883, and, he died at Harrogate in July of the following year.

Pattison's warmest admirers were obliged to admit that he lacked many of the elements making for personal popularity. His disappointments not only warped his critical judgment but soured his disposition. He has been identified with the pedant (Mr. Casaubon) in George Eliot's *Middlemarch,* and with the elderly husband in Rhoda Broughton's *Belinda.* He worked his wife so hard as his secretary that she fell a victim to arthritis. He himself was so given to predicting his almost immediate death that his friends found it hard to recognize the real danger when it came. In spite of tempermental handicaps, Pattison was a sound scholar and a fine teacher.

Reflecting his caution and high standards, his published work is small in bulk, but high in quality.   R. W. W.

PRINCIPAL WORKS: *Autobiography*—Memoirs, 1885. *Biography*—Stephen Langton: Archbishop of Canterbury, 1845; St. Ninian, 1845; S. Edmund: Archbishop of Canterbury (with J. B. Dalgairns) 1845; Isaac Casaubon, 1875; Milton, 1879. *Editor*—Essay on Man (Pope) 1869; Satires and Epistles (Pope) 1872; The Sonnets of John Milton, 1883. *Miscellaneous*—Suggestions on Academical Organisation: With Especial Reference to Oxford, 1867; Sermons, 1885; Essays, 1889.

ABOUT: Althaus, T. F. Recollections of Mark Pattison; Church, R. W. Occasional Papers; Morley, J. M. Critical Miscellanies; Pattison, M. Memoirs; Cornhill Magazine ns62:539 May 1927.

PAYN, JAMES (February 28, 1830- March 25, 1898), novelist, was born at Cheltenham, the son of a government official. Rather unhappy in his early education, he left school to study with a tutor; and he contributed an article to *Household Words,* then edited by Dickens, as well as bits of verse to various periodicals. After being graduated from Oxford and marrying, Payn supported himself by writing for magazines, becoming editor of *Chambers's Journal.* From 1859 he wrote a great number of novels, establishing himself as one of the popular writers of the day. He was a friend and great admirer of Dickens. His last years were marked by failing health, and in 1898 he died in London. Payn's novels, which have not held their popularity, show technical skill and some humor and observation, but are conventional in subject and lack depth.

PRINCIPAL WORKS: Lost Sir Massingberd, 1864; A Woman's Vengeance, 1872; By Party, 1878; For Cash Only, 1882; Some Literary Recollections, 1884; A Prince of the Blood, 1888; The Modern Dick Whittington, 1892; The Backwater of Life, 1899.

ABOUT: Essays of the Year, 1929-1930; Payn, J. The Backwater of Life (see Introduction by Leslie Stephen); Payn, J. Gleams of Memory (see auto-biographical notices); Payn, J. Some Literary Recollections (see autobiographical notices); Russell, G. W. E. Afterthoughts.

PAYNE, EDWARD JOHN (July 22, 1844-December 26, 1904), historian, was born in Buckinghamshire. As his parents were poor, the boy was obliged to secure his schooling himself. After receiving a grammar-school education he worked for an architect and served as parish organist. He managed to support himself at Oxford and took his bachelor's degree in 1871 with brilliant standing. Although he became a lawyer, his time was devoted for the most part to writing. A student of exploration and colonial expansion, he planned a history of America which at his death was still incomplete. His musical tastes reflected themselves in his articles in *Grove's Dictionary.* A victim of heart trouble and vertigo, he was found drowned in a canal at Wendover, in 1904. His useful, if prosaic, study of European colonies was a pioneer in its field.

PRINCIPAL WORKS: History of European Colonies, 1875; Voyages of the Elizabethan Seamen to America (from Hakluyt) 1880; History of the New World Called America (Vols. I and II) 1892-99; Colonies and Colonial Federation, 1904.

ABOUT: Musical Times 46:114 February 1905; Oxford Magazine January 25, 1905; London Times December 28, 1904.

PEACOCK, THOMAS LOVE (October 18, 1785-January 23, 1866), novelist and poet, was born at Weymouth in Dorsetshire on October 18, 1785, the son of Samuel Peacock and his wife, who was formerly Sarah Love. The father was engaged in the glass business in London, so not long after his birth young Thomas was brought to the city. But he was not to remain there long. In 1788 his father died and Mrs. Peacock took her son to spend the next twelve years with his "old sea-dog of a grandfather," Thomas Love, in a cottage in Chertsey. From this grandfather Thomas probably learned many of his crotchets; from his mother he derived his love of books and his talent for verse.

The boy's only formal schooling was received at Englefield Green where he was famed for his precocity. It was while he was at this school that Queen Charlotte noticed his handsome face and his golden hair and stopped her carriage to kiss him. He remained there for six and a half years. By 1800, however, Peacock had left school forever, and was employed as a clerk by Messrs. Ludlow, Fraser & Co., London merchants. At about this time, too, he distinguished himself by winning a prize offered by a periodical called the *Monthly Preceptor,* for an essay entitled "Is History or Biography the More Improving Study?"

THOMAS LOVE PEACOCK

He was then fourteen, and though all formal education was over, he educated himself. After he gave up his job he spent long hours in the British Museum reading Latin and Greek for pleasure.

His first poetry probably came out in 1804 under the title, *The Monks of St. Mark*, although no trace of the pamphlet has been found, by his bibliographer. His first known book, *Palymyra*, was also a volume of verse, and was published two years later, shortly after Peacock had gone back to Chertsey following the death of his grandfather. He took a trip to Scotland in 1806, and in the summer of 1807 fell in love with Fanny Falker, to whom he became engaged, only to have the affair broken off by interfering relatives. Fanny married someone else and died the next year. According to legend, Peacock remembered her all his days.

In 1808 Peacock took up his new duties as secretary to Sir Home Riggs Popham of the Navy, and he spent a winter at sea in what he called "this floating Inferno." He managed, however, to write there a part of a long poem, *The Genius of the Thames*. Finished in 1810 the poem came out that summer. Meanwhile Peacock left his job and went rambling through Berkshire and Oxfordshire. He ended up in Wales, where he met "the local parson" of Maentwrog in Merionethshire, Dr. Gryffydh, and his daughter, Jane. Back in England he resumed his walking tour and mused on melancholy, which was the subject of his next poem. This work, *The Philosophy of Melancholy*, was published in 1812, the year he met the poet Shelley. In 1813 he made a tour of the North with this new friend and took another trip to Wales. Toward the end of the year, however, he settled down in Chertsey, and probably spent the winter working on two plays, *The Dilettanti* and *The Three Doctors*.

In 1814 Peacock went back to London with his mother only to return to the country in the summer of 1815. At Marlow he again enjoyed the companionship of the Shelleys. But he did not allow his social life to interfere with his writing. He published his first novel, *Headlong Hall*, in 1816, following it with the more satirical *Melincourt* (1817), as well as *Nightmare Abbey* (1818). His poem, *Rhododaphne*, appeared in 1818.

With the beginning of 1819, however, Peacock's life of leisure came to a sudden close when he accepted a post in the examiner's department of the East India Company along with James Mill, the philosopher and his son, John Stuart Mill. So he and his mother moved back to London. By autumn he decided he needed a wife, and although he had not seen Jane Gryffydh for eight years he wrote her a proposal of marriage, which, strangely enough, she accepted. On March 22, 1820, the wedding took place in Cardiganshire. His wife was, it is said, a "prettyish Welsh girl," and "a tolerable scholar." A daughter, Mary Ellen, who was to grow up to marry George Meredith, the novelist, was born to them in July 1821. Margaret arrived in two years, followed by a son, Edward Gryffydh, and still another daughter, Rosa Jane. Margaret died early, and the Peacocks adopted a little girl named Mary Rosewell, who resembled the dead child. In 1823 the author moved his family to a cottage in Halliford where he used to spend his weekends.

His writings did not altogether cease with the new work. An essay, "The Four Ages of Poetry," came out in *Ollier's Literary Miscellany* in 1820, while his most popular novel, *Maid Marian*, appeared two years later. His next tale was *The Misfortunes of Elphin* (1829), which was followed by *Crotchet Castle* in 1831. But promotions in the India House soon curtailed his authorship, for when James Mill died in 1836 Peacock succeeded him as examiner. According to Thackeray, he now held "one of the most comfortable posts in a very comfortable age." He interested himself particularly in steam navigation and investigated new routes to India. To him the ships were his "iron chickens." So he wrote practically nothing for twelve years. But in 1851, in collaboration with Mrs. Meredith, he wrote an article called "Gastronomy and Civilization," which appeared in *Fraser's Magazine*. The next year he did a series of articles entitled "Horæ Dramaticæ" for the same periodical, following it with his "Memoirs of Percy Bysshe Shelley" (1858-62). His last novel, *Gryll Grange,* came out as a serial in 1860. With his translation of Curzio Gonzago's play, *Gl' Ingannati,* however, his long literary career came to an end.

In 1852 Peacock had been shocked by the unexpected death of his invalid wife. Henceforth his life became more and more that of a recluse. After his retirement from India House in 1856 he rarely left his cottage in Lower Halliford. Usually he was found either in his library there or in his garden on the bank of the Thames. In fact when a fire broke out in his bedroom in 1865 he refused to leave the house. He seems never to have recovered from this shock, for after the fire he kept to his bedroom, and a few weeks later, on January 23, 1866, he died quite peacefully at the advanced age of eighty-one.

Even in old age Peacock was handsome. His face was "framed in thick white hair." His eyes were "shrewd and kindly," and there was "infinite humor" in his mouth. According to Thackeray he was a "jolly old worldling, full of information about India and everything else in the world." Indeed, among his most intimate friends he was known as the "Laughing Philosopher."

It was probably his gift of laughter that won him his place in literature, for he was always ready to satirize, whether the target was politics or education, people or books. But his audience was limited because his thought and style were unique. He was too much of an individualist to meet with the approval of his age. His novels were termed "eccentric" and "unreal." His poems lacked sentiment. When he died "he was probably as little known as any man of equal rank" in England. But now it is his very individuality that has given him a position in English literature which is stronger today than it was in his own century.   B. D. S.

PRINCIPAL WORKS: *Poetry*—The Monks of St. Mark, 1804 [?]; Palmyra and Other Poems, 1806; The Genius of the Thames, 1810; The Philosophy of Melancholy, 1812; Sir Proteus: A Satirical Ballad, 1814; Rhododaphne, 1818. *Novels*—Headlong Hall, 1816; Melincourt, 1817; Nightmare Abbey, 1818; Maid Marian, 1822; The Misfortunes of Elphin, 1829; Crotchet Castle, 1831; Gryll Grange, 1861. *Drama*—Plays, 1910. *Miscellaneous*—Works (ed. by H. Cole) 1875; Calidore & Miscellanea, 1891; Memoirs of Shelley (ed. by H. F. B. Brett-Smith) 1909; Letters to Edward Hookham and Percy B. Shelley (ed. by R. Garnett) 1910; Works (ed. by H. F. B. Brett-Smith and C. E. Jones) 1924-34.

ABOUT: Freeman, A. M. Thomas Love Peacock: A Critical Study; Peacock, T. L. Headlong Hall (see Introduction by R. Garnett to 1891 ed.); Peacock, T. L. Works (see Biographical Notice by E. Nicolls in 1875 ed.); Peacock, T. L. Works (see Biographical Introduction by H. F. B. Brett-

Smith to 1924-34 ed.); Priestley, J. B. Thomas Love Peacock; Van Doren, C. The Life of Thomas Love Peacock.

PEARSON, CHARLES HENRY (September 7, 1830-May 29, 1894), historian and colonial minister, was born at Islington, the son of an evangelical minister. After a promising career in Rugby, King's College, London, and Oxford he began to study medicine. The state of his health made a career as a physician inadvisable, and he became a lecturer in English literature at Oxford and then professor of modern history at King's College. In an effort to preserve his eyesight he removed to Australia, where he held educational posts and conducted an investigation of education in Victoria; as minister of education he introduced several reforms. His health caused him to return to England in 1892, and he died in London two years later. A graceful writer, Pearson was not a great historian. His *National Life and Character* expresses his fear of a coming state absolutism and the growing influence of the black and yellow races.

PRINCIPAL WORKS: History of England During the Early and Middle Ages, 1867; Historical Maps of England During the First Thirteen Centuries, 1870; English History in the Fourteenth Century, 1873; National Life and Character: A Forecast, 1893; Reviews and Critical Essays, 1896.

ABOUT: Pearson, C. H. & others. Charles Henry Pearson: Memorials by Himself, His Wife, and His Friends; Pearson, C. H. Reviews and Critical Essays (see Memoir by H. A. Strong); Athenaeum 1:677 June 2, 1900; Nation 71:331 October 25, 1900.

PELHAM, HENRY FRANCIS (September 19, 1846-February 12, 1907), historical scholar, was born at Bergh Apton, his father's parish. His scholastic career was brilliant at Harrow and Oxford, and he took his bachelor's degree in 1869. From 1870 until 1889 he was classical tutor and lecturer in Exeter College, Oxford, and in 1889 he became Camden Professor of Ancient History, his lectures drawing large audiences. Unfortunately trouble with his eyes forced him to give up historical research, and his projected history of the Roman Empire was never finished. He threw himself into administrative work, in which his personality made him successful, and was active in broadening education at Oxford. In 1897 he was made president of Trinity College, retaining this position until his death. Pelham was an able scholar, and his *Outlines of Roman History*, though it neglects certain aspects of the subject, is well written, and based upon sources.

PRINCIPAL WORKS: Outlines of Roman History, 1893; Essays, 1911.

ABOUT: Pelham, H. F. Essays (see Biographical Note by F. J. Haverfield); British Academy Proceedings 1907-08; London Times February 13, 1907.

PENROSE, ELIZABETH ("Mrs. Markham") (August 3, 1780-January 24, 1837), writer for children, was born at Goadby-Marwood. Her father was Edmund Cartwright, the inventor of the power loom. Educated at a boarding-school at York, the girl came to delight in reading, particularly in history. Some time after her marriage to the Reverend John Penrose she began to issue school histories, using "Mrs. Markham" as her pen name. Her history of England, although almost unnoticed at first, became, in a short while, a standard textbook, reaching in thirty-three years, a sale of eighty-eight thousand. The author issued a history of France on a similar plan, omitting scenes too cruel and questions too complex for her childish readers; and she wrote other children's books. Her death, the result of cancer, occurred in Lincoln. Her productions, though long popular, have passed into oblivion.

PRINCIPAL WORKS: A History of England From the First Invasion by the Romans to the End of the Reign of George III, 1823; A History of France, 1828; Sermons for Children, 1837.

ABOUT: Fletcher, Mrs. E. Autobiography; Hale, Mrs S. J. Biography of Distinguished Women; Smiles, S. A Publisher and His Friends.

PERCEVAL, ARTHUR PHILIP (November 22, 1799-June 11, 1853), author of religious works, was the son of Charles George Perceval, second Baron Arden. His education he received at Oxford, where he took the bachelor's degree in 1820 and that of B.C.L. in 1824. In the latter year he became rector of East Horsley, in Surrey, and two years later he was made chaplain to George IV. He remained royal chaplain for the rest of his life, serving William IV and Victoria. He was a sympathizer with the High-Church movement, and on one occasion preached a High-Church sermon before the Queen, seizing his chance when the Bishop of London, said to have filled the pulpit for several Sundays in an effort to keep Perceval from preaching, was disabled by a timely broken collarbone. Perceval's works, almost entirely theological, are marked by a great conservatism of belief; what small significance they hold is religious rather than literary.

PRINCIPAL WORKS: The Roman Schism Illustrated From the Records of the Catholic Church, 1836; An Apology for the Doctrine of Apostolical Succession, 1839; A Vindication of the Authors of the Tracts for the Times, 1841; A Collection of Papers Connected With the Theological Movement of 1833, 1842; Results of an Ecclesiastical Tour in Holland and Northern Germany, 1846; Origines Hibernicae, 1849.

ABOUT: Guardian 1853, p. 414.

PETRIE, GEORGE (January 1, 1790-January 17, 1866), Irish antiquary and painter, was born in Dublin, the son of a painter. Educated at Samuel White's school in Dublin and at the Dublin Society's art school, he early began to paint, combining this taste with his interest in Irish antiquities. In his travels about Ireland he collected information on music, art, and remains of ancient civilization, and his illustrations for various books on Ireland are not only artistic but scrupulously faithful to detail. His paintings of Irish landscapes won him recognition. He wrote antiquarian articles and assisted in a government survey of Ireland, in which he made a careful study of the topography of Tara, the seat of ancient Irish kings. This and his report on ancient ecclesiastical towers in Ireland constitute his most striking achievement. He continued his travels almost until his death.

PRINCIPAL WORKS: Essay on the Origin and Uses of the Round Towers of Ireland, 1833; On the History and Antiquities of Tara Hill, 1839; The Ecclesiastical Architecture of Ireland, Anterior to the Anglo-Norman Invasion, 1845; Ancient Music of Ireland, 1855.

ABOUT: Graves, A. P. Irish Literary and Musical Studies; Stokes, W. Life and Labours in Art and Archaeology of George Petrie; Fraser's Magazine 74:94 July 1866; Dublin University Magazine 73:363 April 1869.

PFEIFFER, EMILY JANE (November 26, 1827-January, 1890), Welsh poetess, was born Emily Jane Davis, the daughter of an army officer. Because of heavy financial losses sustained by her father the girl was unable to secure much formal education, and her youth was made unhappy by her poverty. With the encouragement of her father, who was artistic in his tastes, she began early to paint and write poetry. After some early poetic efforts she abandoned publication for a period of study and self-education; and not until twenty years after her marriage to J. E. Pfeiffer, a German-English merchant, did she begin frequent publication. She devoted her energy also to problems connected with the social position of women. Her husband's death in 1889 was a serious blow, and she died a year later. Her poetry, somewhat suggestive of Mrs. Browning's, has small value for all its moral integrity; her sonnets are her best work.

PRINCIPAL WORKS: Gerard's Monument, 1873; Quarterman's Grace, 1879; Sonnets and Songs, 1880; Flying Leaves From East and West, 1885; Women and Work, 1888.

ABOUT: Miles, A. H. (ed.). The Poets and the Poetry of the Century; Robertson, E. S. English Poetesses; Academy 37:80 February 1, 1890.

PHILLIPS, SAMUEL (December 28, 1814-October 14, 1854), novelist and journalist, was born in London, son of a Jewish tradesman. Precocious as a child (at fourteen he played in *Richard III*), he was forced by his father's death to discontinue his education (Universities of London, Göttingen, and Cambridge). After an unsuccessful attempt, with a brother, to carry on the business, Phillips, in great need and already married, began *Caleb Stukeley*. After working for a time as secretary and as tutor, he entered journalism; and he wrote literary reviews for the London *Times* from about 1845 until his death. For a while he owned and edited a rather unsuccessful newspaper; and he was literary director of the Crystal Palace. His conservative taste and his lively, biting style appear to best advantage in his critical articles for *The Times*. As a novelist he was too minor a figure to deserve more than passing comment.

PRINCIPAL WORKS: Caleb Stukeley (novel) 1844; Essays From *The Times*, 1851; A Second Series of Essays From *The Times*, 1854; We're All Low People There, 1854; Guide to the Crystal Palace and Park, 1854.

ABOUT: Bentley's Miscellany 38:129 1855; Gentleman's Magazine 1854 2:635 December; Living Age 44:126 January 13, 1855; Tait's Magazine ns22:41 January 1855.

PHILLIPS, WATTS (November, 1825-December 3, 1874), dramatist and illustrator, was the son of a business man. Although ambitious to be an actor, he studied under the artist George Cruikshank, and continued this work in Paris, where he tried to sell sketches. Upon his return to London he drew cartoons and wrote satirical sketches and began playwriting. His earliest true success was *The Dead Heart* (the plot resembling Dickens' *Tale of Two Cities*, and from this time on his work as a dramatist and a novelist overshadowed his drawing, although he continued the latter. Apparently because of financial embarrassments (he was hospitable and not very thrifty) he made frequent stays in Paris. His hastily written plays, examples of the melodrama of the period, show technical ability, ideas, and an understanding of human nature, but they are not unusual enough to keep their interest.

PRINCIPAL WORKS: The Dead Heart, 1859; Amos Clarke (novel) 1862 (presented in dramatic form 1872); Camilla's Husband, 1862; The Woman in Mauve, 1864; Lost in London, 1867; Nobody's Child, 1867; Maud's Peril, 1867; The Golden Fetter, 1869.

ABOUT: Phillips, E. W. Watts Phillips: Artist and Playwright; Academy 41:343 April 9, 1892; Saturday Review 72:728 December 26, 1891.

PICKEN, ANDREW (1788-November 23, 1833), Scottish novelist and man of letters, was born at Paisley, the son of a clothier. After an elementary school education, he became clerk successively in a Paisley factory, a Dublin brewery, and a Glasgow dye-works. Then he represented a Glasgow firm in the West Indies, and on his return married Janet Caxton, daughter of an Edinburgh bookseller. They moved to Glasgow, where in 1824 he brought out his first book of stories under the pseudonym of "Christopher Keelvine." This volume contained his best-known story, "Mary Ogilvie," which as a separate tale was several times reprinted. Unfortunately his satirical pictures of his neighbors made Picken so unpopular that he was obliged to move from Glasgow. He went to Liverpool, where, at his father-in-law's suggestion, he too set up as a bookseller, but the business failed, and he went on to London. There he became a member of the circle of William Godwin, the philosopher, and continued to write. His next book, *The Sectarian*, was a powerful study of a mind ruined by religious fanaticism, but if anything it increased his unpopularity. He did not receive any sort of recognition until publication of *The Dominie's Legacy* in 1830. One of his stories, "The Deerstalker," was dramatized, but without much success. In 1831 he edited an annual, *The Club Book*, which besides his own work contained contributions from James Hogg, "the Ettrick shepherd," and from the Scottish poet Allan Cunningham. He had four sons, one of whom became a well-known lithographer. At his death, which was hastened by over-work and directly caused by a stroke of apoplexy, he left behind him an unfinished life of John Wesley.

Picken's best work was in his studies of life and character among the lower classes in his native town of Paisley. He had traveled much in Ireland, and wrote stories of that country as well as of his own Scotland.

PRINCIPAL WORKS: Tales and Sketches of the West of Scotland, 1824; The Sectarian, 1829; The Dominie's Legacy, 1830; The Canadas, 1832; Waltham, 1833; The Black Watch, 1834.

ABOUT: Brown, R. Memoirs of Ebenezer Picken . . . . and Andrew Picken . . . .; Gentlemen's Magazine 1:111, 1834.

PICKEN, EBENEZER (1769-1816), Scottish poet, was born in Paisley, the son of a silk weaver. Educated at Paisley and at the University of Glasgow, he soon showed literary tastes, writing poetry as a student. Deciding not to be a clergyman, as his father wished, he began teaching school at Falkirk in 1791. The rest of his life was spent in teaching, at Carron, in Stirlingshire, and then in Edinburgh, except for a short time (about 1796) when he tried his luck in business in that city. Picken was poor all his life, and died of consumption in 1816, leaving a widow with five children. His poems, characteristically in Scottish dialect, include satires, descriptive verse, and some songs that were popular long after his death. In many ways more significant are the useful Scottish glossaries which accompany them, and the dictionary of the Scottish dialect.

PRINCIPAL WORKS: Poems and Epistles, 1788; Miscellaneous Poems, Songs, 1813; Pocket Dictionary of the Scottish Dialect, 1818.
ABOUT: Brown, R. Memoirs of Ebenezer Picken, Poet, and Andrew Picken, Novelist, Natives of Paisley; Brown, R. Paisley Poets.

PILKINGTON, MRS. MARY (born Hopkins) (1766-1839), miscellaneous writer, was born in Cambridge. Upon the death of her father, a surgeon, the young girl (then fifteen) made her home with her grandfather, a clergyman. In 1786 she married the surgeon who had succeeded her father. When he was appointed to a surgical position in the navy, she spent eight years as a governess in a private family. After the publication of her first book she became a most prolific author, turning out novels as well as educational and morally uplifting works for the young. Some were translated into French. The writer seems to have lived in retirement in her later years; and little more of her is known except that, having recovered from a serious and disabling illness (about 1810), she died in 1839. Her books helped to support her, but have no great value for succeeding generations.

PRINCIPAL WORKS: Obedience Rewarded and Prejudice Conquered, 1797; Edward Barnard, 1797; Scripture Histories, 1798; A Mirror for the Female Sex, 1798; Historical Beauties for Young Ladies, 1798; Marmontel's Tales (tr.) 1799; Biography for Boys, 1799; Biography for Girls, 1799; Marvellous Adventures, 1802; The Disgraceful Effects of Falsehood, 1807; Sinclair, 1809; Original Poems, 1811; Celebrity, 1825.
ABOUT: Biographie Universelle Ancienne et Moderne (Brussels, 1851); Lady's Monthly Museum ns13:61 August 1812.

PINERO, SIR ARTHUR WING (May 24, 1855-November 3, 1934), dramatist, was born in London, the son of a solicitor. On his father's side he was partly of Portuguese Jewish descent; the family name was originally Pinheiro.

Pinero was educated at private schools, and later attended evening classes at Birkbeck Institute (now Birkbeck College). He then became a minor clerk, first in his father's office, then in that of another solicitor. But he hated his job, and at nineteen, in 1874, he managed to escape and went on the stage. He was an actor until 1881, but never a good one. One of his rôles was described by a

critic as "the worst played in history." Realizing that he would never succeed as an actor, and already beginning to make his way as a playwright, Pinero retired from the stage and only once again, at a benefit, ever appeared on it. In fact, in later years, wealthy and famous, he seldom appeared in public at all—it is said that nothing but a cricket match could bring him out into a crowd. He particularly disliked making speeches, though in his early years he had lectured frequently on Browning, Stevenson, and other writers.

Between 1891 and 1912 Pinero wrote more than thirty-five plays, and before and after this, his chief productive period, almost as many more. *The Squire* (1881) was his first really mature, full length play. His earliest plays were farces; then he turned to sentimental comedy. *Sweet Lavender* (1888) made his fortune, and from that time on, beginning with *The Profligate,* his dramas nearly all had their basis in social problems. It is as a writer of "problem plays" that he became most widely known, though *Sweet Lavender* and *Trelawny of the "Wells"* still hold the stage. He frequently directed his own performances, and (like W. S. Gilbert) he was a dictator and an autocrat, but he got results.

In 1883 Pinero married Myra Emily (Moore) Hamilton, a widow, who died in 1919. They had no children. He was knighted in 1909. He died in London at nearly eighty, following an emergency operation which came too late to save his life.

A striking figure, short and stout, with black eyes, a high bald forehead, and very thick eyebrows, he was an apt subject for cartoons, and his face was far better known

ARTHUR WING PINERO

to the public in his later years than was his actual presence in the flesh.

Pinero was strictly a figure of his own best times—the end of the nineteenth and the beginning of the twentieth century. In those years he was regarded as a sort of English Ibsen, who, as one critic put it, "liberated the English theater from the doldrums of Puritan restraint and returned a modernized English drama to the middle class." Clayton Hamilton said that with *The Second Mrs. Tanqueray* "modern English drama was ushered into being." This is entirely too high praise. As a matter of fact, Pinero was far more a clever and opportunistic playwright than he was a dramatist in a literary sense. Contrary to expressed opinion, his plays act far better than they read; many, indeed, have never been published and probably never will be. On the other hand, technically they are very finely constructed; *The Second Mrs. Tanqueray* is a model of conciseness and compactness.

His treatment of the "problem play" is distinctly squeamish and Victorian; a critic of 1898 spoke more truly when he knew when he said of one of Pinero's *déclassée* heroines, "he treated her with so much cleverness that we almost forgot her shady past." Unlike Ibsen, with his crusading, reforming spirit; unlike Shaw, with his satire of revolt, Pinero takes an entirely conventional view of the social problems he presents. He does, however, deserve credit for having been one of the first to dare to put on the English-speaking stage "the kind of women one does not know socially." *The Second Mrs. Tanqueray* and *The Notorious Mrs. Ebbsmith* were produced at a period when Shaw and Ibsen were being denounced by the press as vile and obscene. Modern playgoers cannot become excited, however, over ladies whose lives are ruined by one false step, like the heroine of *Mid-Channel*, who confesses to her philandering husband that she, too, has philandered—just once—and is cast off forever.

What *is* likely to survive of Pinero is precisely the perennially charming sentimental comedy which he left behind him in his progress toward social documentation; there will probably be revivals for many years of that delightful play of stage-folk, *Trelawny of the "Wells."* In a sense, indeed, Pinero scarcely belongs to literature at all; but his work is an inherent part of the history of the English stage.   M. A. deF.

PRINCIPAL WORKS: (dates are of productions, not publication): £200 a Year, 1877; The Squire, 1881; The Magistrate, 1885; The Schoolmistress, 1886; Dandy Dick, 1887; The Hobby Horse, 1888; Sweet Lavender, 1888; The Profligate, 1889; The Weaker Sex, 1889; The Cabinet Minister, 1890; The Times, 1891; Lady Bountiful, 1891; The Amazons, 1893; The Second Mrs. Tanqueray, 1893; The Notorious Mrs. Ebbsmith, 1895; The Benefit of the Doubt, 1895; The Princess and the Butterfly, 1897; Trelawny of the "Wells," 1898; The Gay Lord Quex, 1899; Iris, 1901; Letty, 1903; A Wife Without a Smile, 1904; His House in Order, 1906; The Thunderbolt, 1908; Mid-Channel, 1909; Preserving Mr. Panmure, 1911; The "Mind-the-Paint" Girl, 1912; The Widow of Wasdale Head, 1912; Playgoers, 1913; The Big Drum, 1915; Mr. Livermore's Dream, 1917; The Freaks, 1918; A Seat in the Back, 1920; The Enchanted Cottage, 1922; A Private Room, 1928; A Cold June, 1932.

ABOUT: Archer, W. English Dramatists of Today; Armstrong, C. F. Shakespeare to Shaw; Fyfe, H. Arthur Wing Pinero: Playwright; Hale, E. E. Dramatists of Today; Literary Digest 118:12:8 December 1, 1934; Nation 139:664 December 12, 1934; Publishers' Weekly 126:2004 December 1, 1934; Theater Arts Monthly 19:86 February 1935.

PLACE, FRANCIS (November 3, 1771-January 1, 1854), political reformer, was almost entirely self-taught. He was a Londoner all his life, the son of a drunken father who had been a baker, then a bailiff at Marshalsea Prison, then a public house keeper. At thirteen Place was apprenticed to a leather breeches maker, and at sixteen was a journeyman. In 1791, before he was nineteen, he married Elizabeth Chadd, who was sixteen. Their marriage resulted in fifteen children, of whom ten survived.

Until this time Place had lived the haphazard life of any poor young workingman. Now he became serious, industrious, and thrifty. But his trade was a dying one, the times were hard, and when he organized a strike in 1793 he was blacklisted. He was jobless for eight months, during which he studied intensively—law, history, mathematics, and political economy. He became secretary of his own and several other "trade clubs" (labor unions were then illegal) and joined the Socialistic London Corresponding Society. His views were too moderate for the extremists of the society, and he resigned; but when the society in 1798 was declared seditious and all its committee was thrown into jail, Place raised money to care for the families of the prisoners.

In 1799, with a partner, he opened a tailor's shop, and a year later he went into business for himself in Charing Cross Road. He became extremely successful and acquired a modest fortune; for nearly ten years he abandoned all political activities. So far this is the history of many business men who have been radical workers in their youth. But Place was studying constantly in all his leisure hours, and merely preparing himself for greater service. He met and learned from such men as Godwin, Owen, Bentham, James Mill, and became a disciple of the educator Joseph Lancaster.

In 1817 Place turned his business over to his oldest son, and transformed himself into a sort of information bureau of economics. Behind his shop he had accumulated a splen-

FRANCIS PLACE

did reference library, and this became headquarters for all the reformers of his day From it inumerable tracts were issued, while Place worked from early morning to late at night gathering information and pouring out manuscript, the vast bulk of which has never been published. In spite of his known and openly expressed "infidelity," and his pioneer work as an advocate of birth control, his political influence became enormous; he was the power behind the throne in most of the reform measures of the time, including the great Reform Bill of 1832. He was the friend of Bentham and Mill, practically wrote Bentham's *Not Paul but Jesus,* from Bentham's scattered notes, and revised Robert Owen's *New View of Human Society.* His great triumph was the final legalization of labor unions in Great Britain.

After 1832, with the changes in the House of Commons, Place's influence declined. His wife died in 1827, and his second marriage in 1830 to an inferior woman—an unhappy union which ended in separation in 1851—alienated many of his friends for several years. In 1833 a solicitor's error lost him most of his fortune, and he had to give up the house and library that had been the meetingplace of the reformers. In the early days of the Chartist movement he was actively associated with the work, and wrote the People's Charter in 1838; but his anti-religious views and his birth control propaganda estranged the Chartists, who were radicals only in economics. In 1844 he suffered from a brain tumor, and remained an invalid thenceforth. He died ten years later, in his daughter's house in Hammersmith.

Place was no speaker, and he shrank from public notice. He was most valuable as an organizer and agitator, and as a practical politician. His *Principle of Population,* an answer to Godwin, contains his most forceful writing; most of what he wrote was diffuse and deadly dull—the mechanical output of an overworked, exhausted man. He left in manuscript a long history of the Reform Bill, now in the British Museum, and a manuscript autobiography as well as a mass of other unpublished material. The mainspring of his life was his passionate sympathy with the oppressed, which he expressed by incredible and indefatigable labor in their behalf. M. A. deF.

PRINCIPAL WORKS (published): Illustrations and Proofs of the Principle of Population, 1822; Improvement of the Working People, 1834.

ABOUT: Holyoake, G. Life and Last Days; Owen, R. Life of Robert Owen; Wallas, G. Life of Francis Place.

PLANCHÉ, JAMES ROBINSON (February 27, 1796-May 30, 1880), dramatist and antiquary, was born in London, the son of a watchmaker. Educated in Chelsea, he was apprenticed to a bookseller. When he was twenty-two he produced a successful burlesque. For most of his life he wrote or translated farces and other plays, libretti for operas, and songs for vaudeville, and served at times as producer and manager and costume designer. In the last capacity his investigations brought about important reforms, and he was noted as an authority on heraldry. His *History of British Costumes* is of perhaps more permanent value than his plays, although the latter (often burlesques compounded of mythological characters and fairies) had a strong influence on other writers, notably W. S. Gilbert.

PRINCIPAL WORKS: Kenilworth Castle, 1821; Oberon (opera by C. M. von Weber; libretto by J. R. Planché) 1826; Descent of the Danube From Ratisbon to Vienna (travel) 1828; Olympic Revels, 1831; The History of British Costumes, 1834; Island of Jewels, 1849; The Day of Reckoning, 1850; My Lord and My Lady, 1861; Orpheus in the Haymarket (adapted from J. Offenbach) 1866; Recollections and Reflections, 1872; A Cyclopaedia of Costume, 1876-79; Extravaganzas, 1879; Songs and Poems, 1881.

ABOUT: Miles, A. H. (ed.). The Poets and Poetry of the Century; Planché, J. R. Recollections and Reflections; Stoddart, R. H. (ed.). Personal Reminiscences by Chorley, Planché, and Young; Athenaeum I:727 June 5, 1880; London Mercury 25:457, 558 March-April 1932; Theatre s3v2:95 August 1880.

POCOCK, ISAAC (March 2, 1782-August 23, 1835), dramatist and painter, was born in Bristol, the son of a painter. He studied art with George Romney and Sir William Beechey, acquiring characteristics suggestive of each; and he exhibited his portraits and other works at the Royal Academy. In 1807 he was awarded a prize for his "Murder of St. Thomas à Becket." After 1818, when he inherited some property, he turned his attention more exclusively to his dramatic activities, writing plays, musical and otherwise; and for a time he was a magistrate for Berkshire. His plays lean toward the melodramatic, deriving their plots from foreign plays and English novels. Although they were successful in their time, they were not unusual enough to remain prominent.

PRINCIPAL WORKS: Hit or Miss, 1810; The Miller and His Men, 1813; John of Paris (opera from the French) 1814; The Magpie or the Maid, 1815; Robinson Crusoe, 1817; Rob Roy Macgregor, 1818; The Antiquary, 1820; Montrose, 1822; Woodstock, 1826; Peveril of the Peak, 1826; The Robber's Wife, 1829.

ABOUT: Bryan, M. Bryan's Dictionary of Painters and Engravers; Gentleman's Magazine 1835, 2:657 December.

POLLEN, JOHN HUNGERFORD (November 19, 1820-December 2, 1902), artist, was born in London. He was educated at Eton and Christ Church College, Oxford, from which he was graduated in 1842. He held university offices and entered the Church. His High Church principles, however, eventually led him to join (1852) the Roman Catholic Church. The rest of his life was devoted to art. He was a professor of fine arts in the Catholic University, Dublin; and he wrote criticisms and designed or decorated many public and private buildings. He was close to the Pre-Raphaelite group. In addition to his painting and designing he took an active interest in politics, supporting Liberal policies. As an artist he was skilful, even without complete training; and his historical working on furniture and woodwork, if not completely in accord with the findings of later scholars, is generally sound. The valuable *Universal Catalogue* and the autobiographical *Narrative* are of some importance.

PRINCIPAL WORKS: Letter to the Parishioners of St. Saviour's, Leeds, 1851; Narrative of Five Years at St. Saviour's, Leeds, 1851; First Proofs of the Universal Catalogue of Books on Art, 1870 (supplement 1877); Ancient and Modern Furniture and Woodwork, 1873; Description of the Trajan Column, 1874; Ancient and Modern Gold and Silversmith's Work in the South Kensington Museum, 1878.

ABOUT: Pollen, A. John Hungerford Pollen; Pollen, J. Narrative of Five Years at St. Saviour's, Leeds; Bryan, M. Bryan's Dictionary of Painters and Engravers; Athenaeum 2:795, 801 December 13, 1902.

POLLOK, ROBERT (October 19, 1798-September 18, 1827), Scottish poet, was born in Renfrewshire, the seventh of eight children of a poor farmer. He was educated at the parish schools, where he injured his health permanently by over-indulgence in athletics. At fifteen he was apprenticed to a cabinet-maker, but disliked the work so much that he left in a few weeks and returned to the farm. He and his brother determined to

become Secession (Presbyterian) ministers; and prepared at home for the university. At the same time he began writing poetry. In 1817 he entered the University of Glasgow, receiving his M.A. in 1822. While at college he founded a literary society. From 1822 to 1827 he studied theology, both at the university and at the United Secession Hall. His one book of poems, *The Course of Time*, was avowedly inspired by Byron's poem, "Darkness." The year of its publication, 1827, he was made a probationer preacher, but symptoms of tuberculosis displayed themselves, and he was never able to take charge of a church. Ordered to Italy, he started south, but at Southhampton he became so ill that he was unable to journey farther, and he died there at not quite twenty-nine.

Pollok's one poem was planned on a grand philosophical scale. It is prolix and discursive, but contains many brilliant passages showing great promise. He was also the author of three historical novels, published anonymously, which were mere pot-boilers designed to raise money for his livelihood while he studied.

PRINCIPAL WORK: The Course of Time, 1827.

ABOUT: Masson, R. Pollok and Aytoun; Pollok, D. Life of Robert Pollok; Blackwood's Magazine July, 1827.

POOLE, JOHN (1786?-February 5, 1872), was a successful dramatist whose farces and comedies were produced in London between 1813 and 1829. In his plays appeared such popular actors as Charles Kemble, John Liston, and William Farren. The most notable of his works was *Paul Pry*, a three-act comedy, produced at the Haymarket Theatre in 1825 with Liston in the leading rôle, and often revived. *'Twixt the Cup and the Lip* and *Lodgings for Single Gentlemen*, both farces, were other favorite vehicles for comic actors. The plays are not very good reading; they were dependent for their success largely upon the actors' personalities. In the opinion of John Genest, the dramatic historian, most of the plays were more successful than they deserved. Some of the plays are included in the collections of Lacy, Duncombe, and Dick; others were never printed. He also wrote miscellaneous works.

Poole, in his heyday, moved in fashionable society. The last twenty years of his life were spent in obscurity. Through the influence of Charles Dickens, he was given a yearly pension of £100. He died at his London residence in his late eighties.

PRINCIPAL PLAYS: Hamlet Travestie, 1810; Turning the Tables, 1821; Simpson & Co., 1823; Deaf as a Post, 1823; Married and Single, 1824; The Scape-Goat, 1825; Tribulation: or, Unwelcome Visitors, 1825; Paul Pry, 1825; 'Twixt the Cup and the Lip, 1826; The Wealthy Widow: or, They're Both to Blame, 1827; Lodgings for Single Gentlemen, 1829.

ABOUT: Poole, J. Sketches and Recollections; Daily Telegraph February 10, 1872.

POOLE, REGINALD STUART (February 27, 1832-February 8, 1895), numismatist and archaeologist, was born in London, the son of Edward Richard Poole, a well-known bibliophile. His mother was SOPHIA POOLE (1804-1891), author of *The English Woman in Egypt* (1844-46); his uncle was Edward William Lane, the noted Arabic scholar; and his elder brother, EDWARD STANLEY POOLE (1830-1867), was also an Arabic scholar. With these three he spent seven years of his youth (1842-49) in Cairo, devoting himself to a study of Egyptian antiquities.

For forty-one years he was on the staff of the British Museum, successively as assistant in the department of antiquities (1852-66), assistant keeper of the new department of coins and medals (1866-70), and keeper of this department (1870-93). In the last capacity he edited thirty-five catalogues, of which four were written by himself. In addition to his official work, he lectured and wrote numerous articles on Egyptology. He was joint founder of the Egypt Exploration Fund (1882) and the Society of English Medallists (1884). Two years after his retirement he died in London at sixty-two.

His two sons, Stanley Lane-Poole (1854-1931), and Reginald Lane Poole (b. 1857) carried on the family tradition of scholarship and authorship.

PRINCIPAL WORKS OF REGINALD STUART POOLE: Horae Ægyptiacae: or, The Chronology of Ancient Egypt, 1851; Coins of Italy, 1873; Cities of Egypt, 1882; Coins of the Ptolemaic Kings of Egypt, 1883; Coins of the Shahs of Persia, 1887; Coins of Alexandria, 1892.
ABOUT: The Times February 9, 1895; The Athenaeum February 16, 1895.

"PORCUPINE, PETER." See COBBETT, WILLIAM

PORTER, ANNA MARIA (1780-September 21, 1832), novelist, was born at Durham, the younger sister of the novelist Jane Porter and of Sir Robert Ker Porter, the painter and traveler. Educated with her sister at Edinburgh, she began to write at thirteen. In her early twenties she settled with her family in London, where she made an unsuccessful attempt at the drama. Later she lived for some time with her mother and sister in a cottage at Esher, Surrey. Here, in 1807, she completed her most popular work, *The Hungarian Brothers*, a novel dealing with the French Revolution. This was the first work to which she signed her name. On the death of her mother in 1831 she and her sister returned to London. Shortly thereafter, while visiting a brother at Bristol, she died of typhus fever in her fifty-second year.

She produced altogether about fifty volumes. Most of them were translated into French; some appeared in America. According to the critic George Saintsbury, there was not much in her books but "amiable incompetence."

PRINCIPAL WORKS: Artless Tales, 1793-95; Walsh Colville, 1797; Octavia, 1798; The Lake of Killarney, 1804; A Sailor's Friendship, 1805; A Soldier's Love, 1805; The Hungarian Brothers, 1807; Don Sebastian: or, The House of Braganza, 1809; Ballads and Romances and Other Poems, 1811; The Recluse of Norway, 1814; The Knight of St. John, 1817; The Fast of St. Magdalen, 1818; The Village of Mariendorpt, 1821; Roche Blanche: or, The Hunter of the Pyrenees, 1822; Honor O'Hara, 1826; Coming Out, 1828; The Barony, 1830.
ABOUT: Elwood, A. K. Memoirs of the Literary Ladies of England; Jerdan, W. National Portrait Gallery.

PORTER, JANE (1776-May 24, 1850), novelist, was born at Durham, the daughter of William Porter, an army officer, and Jane (Blenkinsop) Porter. Her father died in 1779, and her mother, a poor widow, removed with her family to Edinburgh in the next year.

The child's education was in a school in Edinburgh, and she advanced rapidly. One of her friends was Walter Scott, at that time but a boy. Jane was an enthusiastic student of literature and legend, and absorbed the old Scottish tales told by a poor woman living near by.

Except for a short-lived periodical, *The Quiz*, begun in 1797, in which she cooperated with several others, including her brother Robert, later famous as a painter and a traveler, and her younger sister Anna Maria, also an author, Jane Porter's literary achievements belong to the time after she had removed to London. There her family lived in a house once occupied by the painter Sir Joshua Reynolds, and there the young people met army friends of their father's and, more important, artists and other figures of note, among them Hannah More, playwright and religious writer.

In 1803 Miss Porter showed to Owen Rees, a friend in the publishing firm of Longman and Company, her romance of a Polish exile, *Thaddeus of Warsaw*. Rees was sufficiently impressed to offer to publish it, and it appeared in that year, soon achieving success, and reaching a ninth edition by 1810. Kosciusko, the Polish patriot leader, having seen a German translation of the book, sent to the author word of his pleasure and approbation, and one of his relatives gave her a ring with Kosciusko's portrait. Miss Porter was honored also by the King of Württemberg.

She followed up her success with *The Scottish Chiefs*, probably her best-known work, which, written within a year, involved careful study of accounts of the Scotch patriot, William Wallace, her hero. The novel met with an international success.

JANE PORTER

Her dramatic attempts were less fortunate. Having written a play, *Egmont: or, The Eve of St. Alyne,* which, apparently, was not sufficiently admired ever to be produced or even printed, she succeeded in having two others performed, and both were lamentable failures. She then returned to the historical novel, writing, at the suggestion of George IV, *Duke Christian of Luneburg. Sir Edward Seaward's Narrative of His Shipwreck* she claimed to have taken from an actual account found in a diary, which she had "edited." It is generally assumed that this assertion, which caused considerable argument, was false, and that the book was written by the "editor" herself.

Upon the death, in 1831, of their mother, with whom they had been living at Thames Ditton and Esher, Miss Porter and her sister removed to London. There they went considerably into society, and were acquainted with most of the people of their time who were famous in literature or in art. William Maginn, the Irish journalist, remarked of Jane Porter that she generally managed, at evening parties, "to be seen patronizing some sucking lion or lioness."

Aside from trips to Bristol to visit a brother, William Ogilvie Porter, and a journey in 1842 to St. Petersburg to visit her brother Robert, who died very suddenly in that year, Miss Porter lived a quiet and uneventful life until her death at her brother's house in Bristol, in 1850. Although her books were popular and widely read—American authors, publishers, and booksellers sent her, in 1844, as an expression of admiration and respect, a rosewood armchair—she was in financial embarrassment in these years, and

in 1842 she received £50 from the Literary Fund.

Tall and handsome, Jane Porter was described by Mary Russell Mitford, essayist, as the one literary woman of her acquaintance not fit "for a scarecrow." Her beauty was termed "statuesque" by Mrs. Samuel Carter Hall, her "deportment" "serious though cheerful." Unlike her sister she labored hard over her writing, and said of herself, ". . . I, from my childhood upwards, 'toiled up the hill' of knowledge half my days . . . ." Both she and her sister felt a religious sense of duty to employ their gifts rightly. ". . . When we began to write for publication," observed Jane Porter, "we regarded our works not as a pastime for ourselves, or as a mere amusement for others, but as the use to be made of an entrusted talent 'given to us for a purpose': and for every word we set down in our pages, we believed we must be accountable to Heaven, and our country. This sense of responsibility certainly deepened the constitutional concentration of my thoughts, *gravitating* them perhaps a little too heavily when employed with my pen." Her seriousness, however, cannot be said to have robbed her of charm. When she went to call upon Scott in London, after years had elapsed since their childhood friendship, she sent in word that, if he remembered the Porter family, Jane would like to see him. He rushed to the door, exclaiming, *"Remember you, Miss Porter!",* embraced her, and burst into tears. That her sense of responsibility extended to other matters than authorship is shown by a letter in which Miss Porter urges her publisher to proceed with some work she had sent him, explaining her need by telling him of a very poor friend whom she was trying to aid from her own slender purse.

Her place in literature rests upon her historical novels, which, unlike most of those preceding Scott's Waverley series, have managed to survive, at least as names. Great literary value, however, they have not, despite the picturesque narrative of the author; they lack historical accuracy, and the character of her hero, the Scotch William Wallace, is stilted and artificial. Saintsbury condemns Miss Porter's works as "almost utter, though virtuous and well-intentioned, rubbish," and declares, "Only to a taste as crude as their own can they give any direct pleasure now . . ."

R. W. W.

PRINCIPAL WORKS: *Novels*—Thaddeus of Warsaw, 1803; The Scottish Chiefs, 1810; The Pastor's Fireside, 1815; Duke Christian of Luneberg, 1824; The Field of the Forty Footsteps, 1828. *Plays*—Switzerland, 1819; Owen: Prince of Powys, 1822. *Tales*—Tales Round a Winter Hearth (with A. M. Porter) 1826. *Miscellaneous*—A Defence of the Profession of an Actor, 1800; Sketch of the Campaign of Count A. Suwarrow Ryminski, 1804; Aphorisms of Sir Philip Sidney [remarks by J.

Porter] 1807; Sir Edward Seaward's Narrative of His Shipwreck, 1831.

ABOUT: Elwood, A. K. Memoirs of the Literary Ladies of England; Hall, A. M. Pilgrimages to English Shrines (2nd ser.); Hall, S. C. A Book of Memories of Great Men and Women of the Age; Maclise, D. The Maclise Portrait Gallery; Vaughan, H. M. From Anne to Victoria; Scottish Review 29:321 April 1897.

PORTER, SIR ROBERT KER (1777-May 4, 1842), travel author and painter of battle-scenes, was born at Durham, a brother of Jane and Anna Porter the novelists. After serving for two years as historical painter to the Czar of Russia (1804-06), he traveled in Sweden and accompanied Sir John Moore throughout the Coruña campaign in Spain. These adventures were described in his first two books. During a visit to Russia in 1811-12 he was married to a Russian princess, Mary von Scherbatoff, by whom he had one daughter, and upon his return to England he published a vivid narrative of the 1812 campaign in Russia. He was knighted in 1813. Between 1817 and 1820 he visited Georgia, Persia, Armenia, and Babylonia; these travels formed his best and most interesting volume. His earlier works were more remarkable for their elaborate illustrations by the author than for their literary quality.

Following the death of his wife in 1826, he was for fourteen years British consul in Venezuela. He died suddenly of apoplexy in his sixty-fifth year during a visit to St. Petersburg, where he was buried. Several of his drawings are in the British Museum.

PRINCIPAL WORKS: Travelling Sketches in Russia and Sweden, 1809; Letters From Portugal and Spain: Written During the March of the Troops Under Sir John Moore, 1809; Narrative of the Campaign in Russia During 1812, 1813; Travels in Georgia, Persia, Armenia, Ancient Babylonia, 1821.

ABOUT: The Times May 28, 1842.

POWELL, BADEN (August 22, 1796-June 11, 1860), theological controversialist, was born in Stamford Hill, a borough of London, and educated at Oriel College, Oxford. His researches on optics and radiation, conducted during a six-year curacy at Plumstead, Kent, brought him a lifetime appointment as Savilian professor of geometry at Oxford in 1827. He was active in university reform. Much of his time was devoted to the writing of essays on religion and science which marked him as an extreme liberal and a foe of the tractarians. His works, particularly a final essay "On the Study of the Evidences of Christianity" contributed to *Essays and Reviews,* provoked much controversy. "But for his opportune death," says the *Cambridge History of English Literature,* "he could hardly have escaped prosecution. His generation would never have tolerated his attempt to free Christian theism from a dependence on miracles." He died in London at fifty-three.

Twice married, he had ten children, of whom SIR GEORGE SMYTH BADEN-POWELL (1847-1897) was an author of works on political and economic questions.

PRINCIPAL WORKS OF BADEN POWELL: Rational Religion Examined, 1826; Revelation and Science, 1833; The History of Natural Philosophy, 1834; The Connexion of Natural and Divine Truth, 1838; Tradition Unveiled, 1839; The Unity of Worlds and of Nature, 1855; The Study of Natural Theology, 1856; Christianity Without Judaism, 1857; The Order of Nature, 1859.

ABOUT: Morning Chronicle June 14, 1860.

POWELL, FREDERICK YORK (January 14, 1850-May 8, 1904), historian and scholar, was born in London, the son of a merchant. Educated at Rugby and at Christ Church, Oxford, he was called to the bar and lectured and tutored in law at his college from 1874 to 1894. In 1894 he succeeded James Anthony Froude as regius professor of modern history at Oxford, a position which he retained until his death in Oxford at the age of fifty-four. He helped to establish the *English Historical Review* in 1885 and took an active part in the founding of Ruskin College, Oxford, in 1899. A connoisseur of French poetry, he brought Verlaine and Mallarmé to Oxford as lecturers.

Through his works, most of which were published before his fortieth year, he earned a reputation as one of England's most penetrating scholars in medieval history and literature. His painstaking researches were of considerable value to other historians. Several of his outstanding works were translations from the Icelandic done in collaboration with the noted Scandinavian scholar Gudbrandr Vigfusson.

PRINCIPAL WORKS: Early England to the Norman Conquest, 1876; An Icelandic Prose Reader (tr. and ed. with G. Vigfusson) 1879; Poeticum Boreale (tr. and ed. with G. Vigfusson) 1881; Old Stories From British History, 1882; England From the Earliest Times to the Death of Henry VII, 1885; Origines Islandicae (tr. and ed. with G. Vigfusson) 1905.

ABOUT: Elton, O. Frederick York Powell: A Life and a Selection of His Letters and Occasional Writings; The Times May 10, 1904.

"POWER, CECIL." See ALLEN, GRANT

PRAED, WINTHROP MACKWORTH (July 26, 1802-July 15, 1839), is chiefly known today as a poet, by those who know of him at all. He was born in London, the third son of William Mackworth Praed, serjeant-at-law. His mother, who died a year after his birth, was a Winthrop of the same family which gave Massachusetts and Connecticut their famous governors. Young Praed was soon taken to the family seat, Britton House, Teignmouth, Devonshire.

At the age of eight he began his career as an English public schoolboy and it is largely upon his brilliant school career that his reputation was established. At this early age he began to write poems and dramas which he sent home to his father, who carefully read and criticized them. Sickly all his life, Praed was unable to achieve much in school sports, though he did play tennis and fives well, but he constantly walked off with all manner of scholastic prizes and scholarships.

When he was eighteen and a student at Eton, he began a manuscript journal called *Apis Matina* and from this evolved *The Etonian*, which he and Walter Blount co-edited. Although this magazine published only ten issues it remains today the most famous of all English school journals. In it appeared for the first time some of Praed's best poems and it resulted in Praed going "up to Cambridge with a higher reputation than any Etonian since the days of George Canning."

At Trinity College, Cambridge, he attracted much attention by his brilliance in prize-winning, debate and oratory, repartee, and writing. Contemporary with Macaulay, they were almost equally rated by their fellow members of the Union Debating Society. Edward Bulwer-Lytton, another member of the club wrote:

And every week that club-room, famous then,
Where striplings settled questions spoilt by men,
When grand Macaulay sat triumphant down
Heard Praed reply and longed to halve the crown.

During his second year at Trinity, Praed became associated with Charles Knight (who had also been the publisher of *The Etonian*) in his *Quarterly Magazine*, Praed being the chief contributor to the first four issues, after which he dropped out of the venture. The next year Knight published Praed's *Lillian: A Fairy Tale*.

After being graduated from Trinity in 1825, Praed returned to Eton for two years as private tutor to Lord Ernest Bruce, younger son of the Marquis of Ailesbury. During this period he assisted Charles Knight with the publication of a new weekly paper called the *Brazen Head*, which survived only four issues.

Following the two years at Eton as private tutor, Praed was elected to a fellowship at Trinity in 1827, and in 1829 he was called to the bar at the Middle Temple. However, he was more interested in a political than in a legal career and in 1830 he entered the House of Commons. Although he had regularly taken the liberal side in political discussions during his college days, and as late as 1829 had been a member of a Whig committee, he entered the House as a Tory and remained a thoroughgoing reactionary throughout his career. It is amusing to note that in college debates Praed's chief opponent was Macaulay on the conservative side and Praed the liberal or radical. When Praed first considered entering parliament, he was urged to accept a seat in the House of Commons with the special object of taking the conservative side in opposition to Macaulay's liberal support of the Reform Bill. Praed, however, refused to accept the seat offered on these terms because he did not wish "personal collision with any man."

Praed's maiden speech in the House was very successful but he never fully realized the expectations of his friends. He appears to have remained "a promising young man" to the end. It is probable that his sickly constitution was partially to blame for this failure to live up to expectations. But it is also likely that his gifts were better suited to the gentlemanly discussions of the Union Debating Society than to the rougher politics of the nation. In 1833 he was defeated at the polls, but at the general election of 1834 he was returned for Great Yarmouth and remained an M.P. until his death in 1839.

During all this period from his first appearance in *The Etonian*, Praed had been contributing both prose and verse to magazines and newspapers. His contributions to the *Morning Post* were largely credited with making that the leading conservative paper. But for readers of today his most interesting work will probably be in the field of *vers de société*. One of the greatest handicaps to modern appreciation of Praed's poems is the lack of a well annotated edition. So much of the wit is dependent upon subtle allusions to people and events unknown to modern readers that it is lost. George Saintsbury, who professed to be a great admirer of his poetry, said that Praed did not feel seriously enough

WINTHROP PRAED

for political satire. But he admits that Praed was admirable at political patter songs. Saintsbury continues: "But the chief merit of Praed's political verse as a whole seems to me to be that it kept his hand in, and enabled him to develop and refine the trick . . . of playing on words so as to give a graceful turn to verse composed in his true vocation. . . . Of the verse so composed there are more kinds than one . . . . But we find the perfect Praed, and we find him only, in verses of society proper . . . . "

As to Praed's character, Edward Bulwer-Lytton wrote: "Yet gossip, ever busy in collecting anecdotes of his sayings and doings, never accused him of the looser follies to which youth is the most prone. And yet, with all my genuine admiration of Praed (and no one, I think, esteemed him more highly than I did), there were touches in his character, tones in his mind, which, whenever I came into contact with them, chilled the sympathy, checked the affection, and sometimes even lowered the estimation, with which I regarded him from the first hour of our acquaintance with each other."

The first collection of Praed's poems was edited by an American, R. W. Griswold, and published in New York five years after the poet's death. In 1859 another American collection edited by W. A. Whitmore contained, mistakenly, some poems by Edward Fitzgerald.   D. C.

PRINCIPAL WORKS: *Poetry*—Poems (ed. by Derwent Coleridge) 1864; Selections (ed. by Sir George Young) 1866; Political and Occasional Poems (ed. by Sir George Young) 1888; *Prose*—Essays (ed. by Sir George Young) 1887.

ABOUT: Knight, C. Passages of a Working Life; Praed, W. M. Poems (see Life by Derwent Coleridge); Praed, W. M. Political and Occasional Poems (see Preface by Sir George Young); Saintsbury, G. Literary Essays: First Series.

PRENDERGAST, JOHN PATRICK (March 7, 1808-February 6, 1893), Irish historian, was born in Dublin and educated at Trinity College, of that city. Called to the bar in 1830, he succeeded his father as administrator of Lord Clifden's estates in 1836 and held this position for many years. The publication of his best known work, *The History of the Cromwellian Settlement in Ireland*, brought him an appointment in 1864 as one of two commissioners to select official papers dealing with Ireland from Carte manuscripts in the Bodleian Library at Oxford. He worked on these manuscripts until 1880, and died in Dublin at the age of eighty-four, leaving one son. His own manuscript collections, relating to the settlement of Ireland at the restoration of Charles II and to the Cromwellian settlement, were bequeathed to the King's Inn, Dublin. In addition to his valuable chronicles of Irish political history, he wrote authoritatively on Irish pedigrees and archaeology.

PRINCIPAL WORKS: The History of the Cromwellian Settlement, 1863; The Tory War in Ulster, 1868; Report of the Carte MSS. Commission (with Rev. Dr. Russell) 1871; Ireland From the Restoration to the Revolution, 1887.

PRINGLE, THOMAS (January 5, 1789-December 5, 1834), Scottish-South African poet, reformer, and anti-slavery crusader, was born at Blaiklaw, Teviotdale, Roxburghshire, the third son of William Pringle, a farmer, and Catherine (Haitlie) Pringle.

In childhood Pringle suffered an accident (concealed by his nurse) which caused him permanent lameness, and this affliction prevented him from enjoying the more active outdoor sports. His education he received at a parish school, at the grammar school at Kelso, and at Edinburgh University, where he proceeded in 1805 with his friend Robert Story. His college career was not brilliant, nor was it crowned by a degree; but he managed to secure a broad acquaintance with English literature.

He secured employment as a copyist of old records in the General Register House in Edinburgh, not, however, giving up his literary interests. With Robert Story he wrote an early satire directed at the Edinburgh Philomathic Society, a literary group. Through a poem contributed to James Hogg's *Poetic Mirror*, in which he parodied the introductions to Scott's *Marmion*, he won the attention and friendship of Sir Walter Scott in 1816.

This proved to be of substantial assistance when, in the next year (the year of his marriage to Margaret Brown, daughter of an East Lothian farmer), Pringle and his friend James Cleghorn started the *Edinburgh*

THOMAS PRINGLE

505

Monthly Magazine for William Blackwood, the Edinburgh publisher. In the first number Pringle used material given him by Scott. Upon a disagreement with the publisher the editors resigned, and *Blackwood's Edinburgh Magazine*, founded in 1817 by Blackwood himself, was the successor to the earlier journal. After a financially unsuccessful career, as editor of the *Edinburgh Star* (a newspaper) and of the *Edinburgh Magazine*, published by Constable, Pringle resumed work at the Register House in 1819.

Hoping to improve his unfortunate circumstances, he removed in 1820 with a party of Scots to South Africa, where the British government was encouraging by financial aid colonies designed to protect existing settlements from annoyance by unruly natives. He assumed control of a grant of land given to his father and brothers in Glen Lynden in the upper valley of the Baavians River.

After the establishment of the settlement, Pringle—who had served as gardener, mechanic, teacher, physician, and even, on occasion, chaplain—proceeded in 1822 to Cape Town, where he took a position in the Public Library. He worked also in the interests of the colony, and assisted in raising a fund for the relief of settlers in distress in Albany, South Africa. With a friend, John Fairbairn, he started an academy and published a newspaper, the *South African Journal*, and a magazine, the *South African Commercial Advertiser*. Because of Pringle's stand for reform, both publications were suppressed; and Pringle, his school a failure because of official persecution, and his social position ruined, journeyed to London in 1826 to seek compensation for his loss.

This he did not secure, and the rest of his life he spent mostly in London, taking active part in the anti-slavery movement, in which his African experiences had interested him. He was appointed (1827) secretary of the Anti-Slavery Society. In this work he was associated with and highly regarded by William Wilberforce and Thomas Clarkson, leaders of the movement, and in 1831 he successfully used his influence to prevent Coleridge's losing his government annuity.

He was not destined long to rejoice in the abolition of slavery in 1833, however, for in the summer of the following year he was taken ill, and, before he was able to return as he planned to South Africa, he died in London in the ensuing December.

"In vanity, in lameness, and in his absorbing passion for freedom, Pringle's temperament was almost Byronic," wrote J. F. Leishman. "He is a worthy creature, but conceited withal . . . . ," wrote Sir Walter Scott. If Pringle was unyielding and difficult, it should be remembered to his credit that his personal unselfishness can hardly be questioned.

As "the father of South African poetry" Pringle is in possession of a small literary niche which few are disposed to deny him. His verses, unequal in merit, are perhaps rather sweet than strong, and often show signs of hurry and lack of finish. "Often in Pringle," declared a writer in the *Academy and Literature*, "one comes across lines which are fine, and which haunt the imagination; but still oftener we meet the uncompleted line, the line which a sensitive ear rejects and which anyone with a feeling for verse could turn to something different and, indeed, better." The author himself, for all his reputed conceit, declared himself "not such a goose as to think myself an Aonian swan." Yet some of his verse shows a considerable mastery of diction; and of "Afar in the Desert," generally considered his masterpiece, Coleridge made the statement: "I do not hesitate to declare it, among the two or three most perfect lyric poems in our language." R. W. W.

PRINCIPAL WORKS: *Autobiography*—Narrative of a Residence in South Africa, 1835. *Pamphlet*—Some Account of the Present State of the English Settlers in Albany, South Africa, 1824. *Poetry*—The Institute (with R. Story) 1811; The Autumnal Excursion, 1819; Ephemerides, 1828; African Sketches, 1834; The Poetical Works of Thomas Pringle, 1838; Afar in the Desert, 1881.

ABOUT: Chambers, R. Biographical Dictionary of Eminent Scotsmen; Conder, J. A Biographical Sketch of the Late T. Pringle; Pringle, T. The Poetical Works of Thomas Pringle (see Sketch by L. Ritchie); London Quarterly Review 136:175 October 1921; Papers of the Bibliographical Society of America 17:21 1923; South African Quarterly March 1921, June 1921.

PROCTER, ADELAIDE ANN (October 30, 1825-February 2, 1864), poet—or poetess, as she would have been called in her own century—was born on October 30, 1825, at 25 Bedford Square, London, in the house of Basil Montagu, where her parents were then staying. She was the eldest daughter of Bryan Waller Procter, himself an author. Perhaps it was because of this fact that she looked, according to Frances Ann Kemble, "like a poet's child, and a poet." Even her father called her his "golden-tressed Adelaide," and wrote her a sonnet in November 1825.

The story of her life reads like a legend. Her childish accomplishments made her the center of attraction in the literary gatherings at her father's house in St. John's Wood. Wordsworth is said to have encouraged her, and Dickens wrote that she carried about a notepaper album of favorite poems as another child would have toted a doll. But her precocity extended beyond poetry to the intricacies of Euclid, French, Italian, German, and art as well as music.

Although she had published a poem in the *Book of Beauty* as early as 1843 her family did not discover her poetic talent until Dec-

ADELAIDE PROCTER

ember 1854, when they learned from her that she was the "Miss Mary Berwick," whom Dickens had just been praising. Unknown to them she had been publishing poetry under that name in his *Household Words* for over a year.

In 1849 or 1851, the date is uncertain, she became a Roman Catholic, and in 1853 she went to Turin to visit her aunt, Emily de Viry, where she interested herself in the Piedmontese dialect and the life of the peasant there.

This latter interest was but one of the many activities which engrossed her. In 1859, the year after the publication of her *Legends and Lyrics*, the Council of the National Association for the Promotion of Social Science made her a member of a committee to consider the possibilities "of providing new channels for the remunerative employment of women." In this capacity she edited *Victoria Regia* (1861), an anthology of prose and verse, that was actually set in type and printed by women at the Victoria Press. This project was followed in 1862 by her *A Chaplet of Verse*, published for the benefit of "The Providence Row Night Refuge for Homeless Women and Children."

Fanny Kemble had early noticed that there was something "doomed" in her appearance, and it is true that she was never strong. Her writing and her charities took their toll. In 1862 she journeyed to the water cure at Malvern in search of health. On the second of February 1864, however, after fifteen months in bed, she died.

Brought up in a literary household she had talked to Hawthorne, was admired by N. P. Willis, and was a friend of Mary Howitt's. Her poetry was once more in demand than

the work of any other living poet except Tennyson. She was compared to Keats, and Henry Chorley termed her lyrics more "complete, more delicate" than those of her predecessors. The *Victoria Magazine* praised her legends as "living." Her reviewers admitted, however, that her poems were often faulty in metre, and Dickens wrote that Adelaide herself never thought "that she was among the greatest of human beings." Today she is best known for "A Lost Chord," though certain of her hymns, like "One by One," "Strive, Wait, and Pray" and "The Pilgrims," continue to be sung in churches. Otherwise she has become a legend of the past and the daughter of a more famous father.   B. D. S.

PRINCIPAL WORKS: *Poetry*—Legends and Lyrics, 1858; Legends and Lyrics: Second Series, 1860; A Chaplet of Verses, 1862; Legends and Lyrics: Enlarged 1865. *Editor*—The Victoria Regia, 1861.

ABOUT: Armour, R. W. Barry Cornwall; Belloc, B. In a Walled Garden; Fields, J. T. Yesterdays with Authors; Hall, S. C. A Book of Memories; Howitt, M. An Autobiography; Janku, F. Adelaide Ann Procter; Julian, J. A Dictionary of Hymnology; Kemble, F. A. Records of a Girlhood; Kemble, F. A. Records of Later Life; Procter, A. A. Legends and Lyrics: Enlarged (see Introduction by Charles Dickens); Procter, B. W. Bryan Waller Procter: An Autobiographical Fragment.

PROCTER, BRYAN WALLER ("Barry Cornwall") (November 21, 1787-October 4, 1874), poet and barrister, had, as he said, no ancestors whom he had "any right to boast of," for they were all small farmers in Cumberland or Yorkshire for many generations. His birthplace has never been definitely established as Leeds or London. It is only certain that he was the son of Nicholas Procter, merchant, and Amelia Procter, who "may have been a Waller."

Before entering Harrow in 1801, where he was the schoolmate of Peel and Byron, Procter went to a small boarding school not far from his home in London. At neither place did he show any noticeable signs of genius other than "a passion for reading." Upon his leaving Harrow in 1803 or 1804 Bryan's father decided not to send him to Cambridge or Oxford. Instead he had his son articled to a solicitor, Nathaniel Atherton, at Calne in Wiltshire. Even here he showed no particular literary bent.

Indeed, it was not until he went up to London in 1807 that he began to take any serious interest in literature and a poetic career. He had, it is true, found William Lisle Bowles a pleasant companion in Wiltshire. But in London, where he began to practise law in 1812, his interests broadened. His father's death (1816) had left him with a small legacy. He bought a hunter; he took up pugilism under the tutelage of Tom Cribb; he went to the theatre as a man about town. By 1817

BRYAN WALLER PROCTER

popular than his earlier life of Kean. In fact it was considered one of his best works. Although his last years were spent in "a Bath chair in Regent's Park," so to speak, he lived to the ripe old age of 87, and died quietly on October 4, 1874. The deaths of two of his six children, Adelaide Ann (1825-1864), the poet, and Edward (1828-1835), had their effect upon him, but otherwise his life had been a peculiarly happy one.

In his own time he was acclaimed as a genius. Even if his merits as a poet were not so great as his friends believed, his ready sympathy and acute critical sense made him a favorite in literary circles and entitled him to a place in the "Literary Peerage Roll" of his time. For Browning inscribed to him his "Colombe's Birthday"; Thackeray dedicated to him his *Vanity Fair* as Hunt did his edition of Beaumont and Fletcher. Even Swinburne wrote a poem in his honor. Charles Lamb called him his "dear boy," and Carlyle dubbed him a "pretty little fellow." All of them agreed with Coventry Patmore that he was a "simple, sincere, shy, and delicate soul," with "his small figure, his head, not remarkable for much besides its expression of intelligent and warm good-will, and its singular likeness to that of Sir Walter Scott." Today he is known rather as a friend of poets than as a poet himself. Most of his imitative narrative poems have perished. A few of his more spontaneous lyrics, however, like "Touch us gently, Time," "King Death," and "The Sea," have lost none of their original music and charm.

B. D. S.

he had met not only Leigh Hunt, but also Charles Lamb and Hazlitt, Coleridge and Peacock, Wordsworth and Southey, Scott and Tom Moore. At about the same time, too, poems by Procter began to appear under various pseudonyms in the *Literary Gazette*, followed by the publication in 1819 of his *Dramatic Scenes* under the well-known *nom de plume* of "Barry Cornwall," which was actually an anagram of his own name.

In 1820 he became associated with the *London Magazine,* and henceforth his published works appeared in quick succession. His only drama, *Mirandola*, was staged at Covent Garden on January 9, 1821.

But in 1824, after his marriage to Anne Benson Skepper, stepdaughter of Basil Montagu, he devoted more and more time to his profession and less and less to his muse. Among his many pupils in conveyancing were Eliot Warburton and William Kinglake. As a member of the Montagu "menagerie," however, and as the husband of the witty Anne Skepper, familiarly called "Our Lady of Bitterness," he was in constant association with the literary men of his day. At the same time he continued to contribute scattered poems to annuals and albums. His most popular work, *English Songs*, was published in 1832, the same year he accepted the appointment of Commissioner of Lunacy, an office which he held until 1861 when he retired on a pension. During these years he became the friend of Dickens, Thackeray, Browning, and Swinburne; and many an American author, Hawthorne and Bayard Taylor and Willis among them, stopped at St. John's Wood for a visit with Barry Cornwall.

Not long before his death he wrote *Charles Lamb: A Memoir* (1866), which was more

PRINCIPAL WORKS: *Poetry*—Dramatic Scenes, 1819; A Sicilian Story, 1820; Marcian Colonna, 1820; Mirandola, 1821; Poetical Works, 1822; The Flood of Thessaly, 1823; The Poetical Works of Milman, Bowles, Wilson, and Barry Cornwall, 1829; English Songs, 1832. *Biography*—The Life of Edmund Kean, 1835; Charles Lamb: A Memoir, 1866; Bryan Waller Procter: An Autobiographical Fragment, 1877. *Miscellaneous*—Effigies Poeticae, 1824; Essays and Tales in Prose, 1853. *Editor*—Melanie and Other Poems, by N. P. Willis, 1835; The Works of Ben Jonson: With a Memoir, 1838; The Works of Shakespeare: With a Memoir and Essay on His Genius, 1843; Selections From the Poetical Works of Robert Browning (with John Forster) 1863.

ABOUT: Armour, R. W. Barry Cornwall; Becker, F. Bryan Waller Procter; Belloc, B. In a Walled Garden; Fields, J. T. Yesterdays With Authors; Martineau, H. Biographical Sketches; Procter, B. W. Bryan Waller Procter: An Autobiographical Fragment.

"PROUT, FATHER." See MAHONY, FRANCIS, SYLVESTER

PROWSE, WILLIAM JEFFERY (May 6, 1836-April 1870), poet and sports writer, was born in Torquay. His mother who had published a book of poems, was a friend of Keats. His father died when he was eight, and he was reared by his uncle, a notary public and shipbroker at Greenwich. From his schooldays at Greenwich he was devoted to sport and to the sea, and he turned naturally to journalism dealing with these topics. In 1856 he was on the Aylesbury *News*, and also started contributing to the magazines. By 1861, he was a leader (editorial) writer on the *Daily Telegraph*, most of his work appearing in the sporting columns. From 1856 onward he wrote regular articles for *Fun*, edited by his friend, Thomas Hood, Jr., his subject being horse-racing and his pseudonym "Nicholas." A year or two later, symptoms of tuberculosis appeared, and for three years he spent his winters in the south of France. Finally he died on one of these visits, near Nice, at thirty-three.

Prowse was a facile, witty versifier, especially good in parodies. His take-off on "The Ancient Mariner" was famous. "The City of Prague" is a clever defense of Bohemianism. His later poems, when he knew himself to be doomed, have much pathos mingled with their humor. Besides his one collected volume, he contributed frequently to the "annuals" then so popular.

PRINCIPAL WORKS: Nicholas's Notes and Sporting Prophecies: With Some Miscellaneous Poems, Serious and Humorous, 1870.
ABOUT: Prowse, W. J. Nicholas's Notes (see Memoir by T. Hood, Jr.).

PULLEN, HENRY WILLIAM (February 29, 1836-December 15, 1903), pamphleteer, was born at Little Gidding, Huntingdonshire, the son of a rector. Educated at Clare College, Cambridge, he was successively vicar-choral of Salisbury Cathedral (1863-75), chaplain with Sir George Nare's arctic expedition (1875-76), a Continental traveler with headquarters in Perugia, Italy (1876-98), and curate of Rockbeare in Devonshire (1898-99). He died unmarried in a Birmingham nursing home at the age of sixty-seven.

Towards the close of 1870, a month after the Germans had besieged Paris, he gained sudden fame with an allegorical pamphlet, *The Fight at Dame Europa's School*, accusing England of cowardice in remaining neutral in the Franco-Prussian War. This pamphlet sold 193,000 copies in four years, bringing the author £3,000 and provoking many replies. None of his other works approached its success; they included belligerent pamphlets urging reform in cathedral organizations and stories of school life criticizing the English educational system. Many of his works were published at his own expense, and at great loss.

PRINCIPAL WORKS: The Fight at Dame Europa's School, 1870; Tom Pippin's Wedding, 1871; The Radical Member, 1872; The Ground Ash, 1874; Clerical Errors, 1874; Dr. Bull's Academy, 1886; Pueris Reverentia, 1892.

ABOUT: Madan, F. The Fight at Dame Europa's School and the Literature Connected With It; Nares, Sir G. Narrative of a Voyage to the Polar Sea; Pullen, H. W. Affection's Offering (see Preface by his father Rev. W. Pullen); The Times December 18, 1903.

PUSEY, EDWARD BOUVERIE (August 22, 1800-September 14, 1882), English divine and ecclesiastical writer, "champion of orthodoxy," was the second son of Philip Pusey and Lucy, daughter of Robert Sherwood, fourth earl of Harborough. His father was the youngest son of Edward Bouverie, Viscount Folkestone, whose sister married the last male representative of the Pusey family. The estates at Pusey, a small village in Berkshire, where Edward Pusey was born, had been bequeathed to Philip Bouverie on condition that he assume this name, which would otherwise have become extinct.

Pusey went to Eton in 1812 and matriculated at Christ Church, Oxford, in 1819. He took a first in classics in 1822 and the following year won a fellowship at Oriel. It was here that he came under the influence of Dr. Charles Lloyd, regius professor of divinity, and developed the intimacy with John Henry Newman and John Keble which shaped the entire course of his life.

Lloyd was deeply apprehensive concerning the progress of rationalism in Germany and the danger to Anglican orthodoxy should the Biblical criticism and exegesis which characterized it be introduced into England. At his instigation Pusey spent about two years at various German universities studying the language and theological literature of the country. To "complete his equipment as a champion of or-

EDWARD BOUVERIE PUSEY

thodoxy," we are told, he also learned Syriac and Arabic. Overstudy seriously affected his health.

Pusey's first book, *An Historical Enquiry Into the Probable Causes of the Rationalist Character Lately Predominant in the Theology of Germany*, published after his return to England in June, 1827, had an unfortunate reception, which probably bore out Pusey's conviction that Anglican clergymen were quite unprepared to resist the threatened attack against revealed religion. The author was himself accused of being in sympathy with pietism and rationalism—than which nothing could have been more remote from the truth.

In June 1828, when he was only twenty-eight, Pusey was ordained deacon and married Maria Catherine, daughter of Raymond Barker of Gloucestershire. Five months later the Duke of Wellington, who was Prime Minister, gave him the chair of regius professor of Hebrew at Oxford. A canonry of Christ Church attached to this office necessitated his ordination into the Anglican priesthood. Pusey regarded the duties of his position as predominantly ecclesiastic. He treated Hebrew as a religious subject and addressed large classes on exalted themes of inspiration and prophecy.

On July 14, 1833, Keble preached the sermon on *National Apostasy*, which Newman afterward regarded as the inauguration of the Oxford Movement. Pusey had no part in the early stages of this work, which Keble, Froude, and Newman instituted. His association with the Tractarians, as (in reference to Newman's *Tracts for the Times*) they were popularly called, began in 1835. Pusey's office, social prestige, and reputation for philanthropy lent great weight. For the stirring appeals which the Tractarians had heretofore published, he substituted solid doctrinal treatises, stressing particularly the divinely inspired origin of the English Church.

"Puseyism" or "Newmania," as the Oxford Movement was now called, was regarded with suspicion by Low-Church Anglicans and with bewilderment by Roman Catholics. Unable to grasp the fine distinctions, many High-Church Anglicans reverted to Rome. From St. Saviour's, the church which Pusey himself built at Leeds, two sets of clergymen turned Roman Catholic in five years. But even the defection of Newman did not cloud Pusey's vision. He continued along what was to him a broad and well-marked path: established Anglican nunneries; instituted the confessional; and was in his preaching and writing so sincere and impervious to obloquy as to win the respect of even his bitterest critics.

510

Nevertheless, it must be admitted that the violence with which he attempted to enforce his beliefs on others sometimes approached fanaticism. He was in the forefront of every academic and theological controversy of the times, and was a particularly zealous prosecutor of heresy cases. He was a prime mover in the trial of Benjamin Jowett, afterwards Master of Balliol.

This extremism made him numerous enemies and in time inevitably lessened his influence. His last controversial work, the *Eirenicon*, in which he urged Roman Catholics to enter the Anglican fold, was coldly received by all parties. But Pusey continued preaching and writing indomitably until his death, which occured at Ascot Priory, Berkshire. He was buried in the Cathedral at Oxford. A bitter antagonist in public, he was kindly and benevolent in his personal relationships.

The Oxford Movement and its controversies seem remote and somewhat musty today, but Pusey's importance in the history of the Anglican Church through the critical events of the nineteenth century is not to be underestimated. Students of the period, though they may ignore him as a writer, cannot but be aware of his personality as it focused on the age in which he lived.   P. B. S.

PRINCIPAL WORKS: An Historical Enquiry Into the Probable Causes of the Rationalist Character Lately Predominant in the Theology of Germany, 1827; Scriptural Views on Holy Baptism, 1835; The Holy Eucharist, 1843; Sermons During the Season From Advent to Whitsuntide, 1848-1853; Parochial Sermons, 1848-1869; Marriage With a Deceased Wife's Sister Prohibited by Holy Scripture, 1854; The Doctrine of the Real Presence, 1855; The Real Presence. . . The Doctrine of the English Church, 1857; Lectures on Daniel the Prophet, 1864; Eirenicon, 1865-1869; University Sermons, 1872; Lenten Sermons, 1874; What Is Faith as to Everlasting Punishment, 1880; Parochial and Cathedral Sermons, 1883.

ABOUT: Liddon, H. P. Life of Edward Bouverie Pusey; Newman, J. H. Apologia; Savile, M. Dr. Pusey: An Historic Sketch, With Some Account of the Oxford Movement.

QUILLINAN, EDWARD (August 12. 1791-July 8, 1851), poet, was born of Irish parents at Oporto, Portugal, where his father was a wine merchant. Educated in England, he worked in his father's counting house in Portugal until the French invasion of 1807 forced the family to remove to England. For several years thereafter he was in the army. In 1821 he settled at Ambleside, near the poet Wordsworth, who was godfather to the younger of his two daughters. In 1841, nineteen years after the tragic death of his first wife, Jemima Brydges, he was married to Wordsworth's daughter Dorothy. He died at Ambleside at fifty-nine.

His original poems are negligible and probably would not have been collected but for the personal friendship of Wordsworth, Southey, Matthew Arnold, and others. Alone noteworthy, though incomplete, was his translation of Camoens' *Lusiad* from the Portuguese.

His wife, DOROTHY QUILLINAN (1804-1847), wrote a charming *Journal* of a visit to Spain and Portugal in company with her husband. Several of Wordsworth's later poems, particularly "The Triad," contain allusions to "Dora."

PRINCIPAL WORKS OF EDWARD QUILLINAN: Poems, 1853; The Lusiad of Camoens Translated (books I-IV, ed. by J. Adamson) 1853.

ABOUT: Quillinan, E. Poems (see Memoir by W. Johnston).

QUINCEY, THOMAS DE. See DE QUINCEY, THOMAS

RADCLIFFE, MRS. ANN (July 9, 1764-February 27, 1823), novelist and poet, was born in London, the daughter of Ann and William Ward. We know concerning her education that she received such instruction in music, drawing, and literature as was customary for elegant females of the period, and it has been assumed that she attended the school of Harriet and Sophia Lee at Bath. She was. at any rate, acquainted with the Misses Lee, and Sophia Lee's *The Recess* (1785) may have inspired *The Castles of Athlin and Dunbayne*.

William Radcliffe, whom Ann Ward married at Bath when she was twenty-three, was a graduate of Oxford. He abandoned a legal career to become editor of a weekly newspaper, the *English Chronicle*. But marriage did not lift the mantle of stubborn reserve with which Mrs. Radcliffe shrouded her private life. (In 1883 Christina Rossetti, an enthusiastic admirer of Mrs. Radcliffe, had to abandon a projected biography because of insufficient material.) Mrs. Radcliffe's novels were primarily time-fillers for a literarily-inclined young woman who had no children and did not care for society. Dorothy Scarborough puts it amusingly: "Her journalist husband was away until late at night, so while sitting up for him she wrote frightful stories to keep herself from being scared."

The Gothic tradition which Horace Walpole had made fashionable with *The Castle of Otranto* was now firmly established in the consciousness of the late eighteenth century. The cult of the horrible had, generally speaking, so transcended the efforts of its originator with "a surfeit of . . . pungent horrors" as to presage its ruin. Mrs. Radcliffe, her feet firmly planted in the Age of Reason, gave the genre a new twist and

geared it to the burgeoning spirit of Romanticism. Her first effort, *The Castles of Athlin and Dunbayne*, appeared anonymously. Here, with the exception of the supernatural, most of the elements of her later novels, the long-lost heir, distressed maid, underground vaults, secret panels, and unburied corpse, are faintly shadowed forth. In *A Sicilian Romance* of the following year Mrs. Radcliffe struck the vein which was soon recognized as peculiarly her own. This may be characterized in brief as consisting of greater emphasis on background and an explained supernatural.

The Romance of the Forest (1791) and *The Mysteries of Udolpho* (1794) caused an immense stir and brought Mrs. Radcliffe a literally world-wide fame. Abroad and in America her novels were admired and imitated. Not alone sensation-seekers but men like Sheridan and Fox praised her work. Her skilful handling of scenery and natural phenomena was recognized as coming from one who possessed an artist's eye for light and shade. The fact that she invariably, sometimes at once, sometimes not until several volumes later, revealed the natural origins of her phantoms, was criticized in some quarters. But the terror connoisseurs found a plethora of real horrors pursuing the supremely sensitive, strangely durable heroines. Mrs. Radcliffe's heroes are pale romantic youths of melancholy aspect. Her heroines, although they likewise love melancholy, weep easily, and delight in solitary rambles amid ruins, have an endearing core of practicality.

When *Udolpho* was going through the presses Mrs. Radcliffe went with her husband to visit some of the scenes which she had already described so vividly in her novels. Her impressions of this trip were presented as *A Journey Made in the Summer of 1794 Through Holland and The Western Frontier of Germany, With a Return Down the Rhine* . . . It has been pointed out that a visit to the continent during these troublous times would indicate that Mrs. Radcliffe's retiring disposition was not due to timidity. She was like her own heroines in that she was handsome, accomplished, and sensitive, but she possessed a pleasant malice of her own.

The Italian (1796) was the last novel to appear during Mrs. Radcliffe's lifetime. It leans almost wholly upon the physical aspects of terror and brings to perfection the author's original creation, the romantic villain, who repels by the enormity of his crime, yet fascinates by the tragic loneliness of his fate. He fathered the villains of Lewis and Maturin and is the direct antecedent of Scott's and Byron's heroes. Sir Walter Raleigh says, "The man that Byron tried to be was the invention of Mrs. Radcliffe." Critics were divided as to whether she had or could have surpassed *Udolpho*, and at the height of her popularity Mrs. Radcliffe withdrew completely and, save for a volume of collected poems in 1815, gave the public no more of her work.

Mrs. Radcliffe did not deign to refute the reports which were soon circulating to account for her retirement. It was said that she was dead and rumored that, obsessed by her own creations, she had gone mad. Nor did she trouble to deny authorship of the multitude (Wieten enumerates twenty) of pseudo-Radcliffean novels which arose. But she did disclaim Joanna Baillie's *Plays of the Passions* when these were ascribed to her.

By the turn of the century both Mrs. Radcliffe's parents were dead, and she had inherited a comfortable fortune and lands near Leicester. She lived here with her husband, traveling in England during the summer, occasionally attending the theatre in London, but remaining essentially a recluse. She died in 1823 of inflammation of the lungs. In 1826 *Gaston de Blondeville*, an historical novel, was released. The book, though itself tedious, is interesting in that, written in 1802 before Scott's first novel, it attempts to paint an accurate historical picture. It also contains the (for Mrs. Radcliffe) signal departure of an authentic ghost. Mrs. Radcliffe is of minor significance as an early romantic poet. She was, as LeFèvre-Deumier says, a much greater poet in her prose than in her poetry. The influence of Mrs. Radcliffe and her school of horror-mongers upon later Romanticism can scarcely be over-estimated. Although her individual popularity was short-lived, she set her mark in one way or another upon all the enduring great who followed.

P. B. S.

PRINCIPAL WORKS: *Novels*—The Castles of Athlin and Dunbayne, 1789; A Sicilian Romance, 1790; The Romance of the Forest, 1791; The Mysteries of Udolpho, 1794; The Italian, 1796; Gaston de Blondeville, 1826. *Poetry*—Poems, 1815-1816. *Travel*—A Journey . . . Through Holland and the Western Frontier of Germany . . ., 1795.

ABOUT: Birkhead, E. The Tale of Terror; Fèvre-Deumier, J. Le Célébrités Anglaises; MacIntyre, C. Ann Radcliffe in Relation to Her Time; Radcliffe, A. Works (1826 ed., see Memoir by Noon Talfourd); Scarborough, D. The Supernatural in Modern English Fiction; Wieten, A. A. S. Mrs. Radcliffe: Her Relation to Romanticism.

RAIKES, THOMAS (October 3, 1777-July 3, 1848), dandy and diarist, was the son of a London merchant and a nephew of Robert Raikes, the promoter of Sunday Schools. Educated at Eton, he became a partner in his father's business, but spent most of his time in the fashionable clubs of London's West End. He made frequent visits to Paris,

spent the winter of 1829-30 in Russia, and was compelled by financial difficulties to live abroad for eight years beginning in 1833. A large, tall man, heavily pockmarked, he was a popular guest of nobility. Between 1840 and 1844 he corresponded with the Duke of Wellington on French politics. By his wife, Sophia Bayly, he had one son and three daughters. He died at Brighton at the age of seventy.

His posthumous diary contained personal reminiscences of noted English and French politicians and dandies of the early nineteenth century, including the Duke of York, George Brummell, Alvanley, and Talleyrand.

PRINCIPAL WORKS: A Visit to St. Petersburg in the Winter of 1929-30, 1838; A Portion of the Journal Kept by Thomas Raikes From 1831 to 1847, 1856-57; Private Correspondence With the Duke of Wellington and Other Distinguished Contemporaries (ed. by his daughter Harriet Raikes) 1861.

ABOUT: See his own works.

RAMÉE, LOUISE DE LA ("Ouida") (January 1, 1839-January 25, 1908) novelist, was born at Bury St. Edmunds. Her mother was Susan Sutton, an Englishwoman, and her father, Louis Ramé, was an instructor in French. "Ouida" was a child's distortion of "Louise," and "de la Ramée" a fancification of plain "Ramé."

Louise Ramé was a precocious girl, who early formed the habit of reading and writing. She was sent at first to the local schools, but part of her childhood was spent in Paris. After the disappearance of her father, whose means of existence was shrouded in mystery, Louise and her mother returned to England. The girl soon developed the unfortunate tendency to fall in love with any man who was ordinarily polite to her, and this is doubtless the explanation of her later misanthropy and was the cause of many heartaches.

She began to contribute to *Bentley's Miscellany* in 1860, writing glamorous and completely unreal novels of a life she had never seen, but which, as she described it, began to exert a great fascination upon the English reading public. Her first real successes were *Held in Bondage* (1863) and *Chandos* (1866) and these were followed by *Under Two Flags* (1867) her most popular and one of her very best novels. At this time the attention of the German publisher Tauchnitz was drawn to the young author, and he entered into contract with her for her works.

Ouida, as she preferred to be called even in private life, was now on the high road of success, and moved to Florence, where she rented a large villa and began to live *en grande dame*. At the height of her popularity she received her guests while she stood

LOUISE DE LA RAMÉE

on a large white bearskin rug, draped in an expensive Worth gown, and surrounded by ill-trained dogs, of which she was inordinately fond. She wore her hair hanging down her back to enhance her looks, which contemporaries did not consider particularly appealing, and wrote all her novels with quill pens, in a huge round hand; after the sheets had gathered on the floor in sufficient quantities, they were picked up and sorted.

Always an egomaniac, Ouida bedeviled her publishers and insulted her friends and acquaintances. She moved to Lucca in 1894, living on a still grander scale, and of course making no provision for a possible loss of popularity. It is not surprising that she spent her declining years in something like neglect, her money gone and a civil list pension the only thing between her and absolute want—for she proudly refused any other help, doubtless preferring to indulge her belief that people were as despicable as she had always considered them. W. H. Huntington, who knew her well, says of her: "She despised humanity and attributed sordid and unworthy motives to innocent actions, and scoffed at virtue, domestic life, and fidelity." He found that "her conversation was disappointing, her opinions prejudiced, and her temperament intensely cynical." She died at Viareggio, after having lost the sight of one eye as the result of glaucoma, and after an exhausting illness. She was buried at Lucca. Bury St. Edmunds erected a monument to her memory.

Her much read and much admired novels were the product of a vivid and fertile imagination, highly colored in her earlier years and tending to sentimentality later. The style was flamboyant, and lent itself rather too easily to parody, of which there has been much. Nevertheless, there is something vital and arresting about Ouida's tales which makes children read *The Nürnberg Stove* and *A Dog of Flanders,* and which prompted G. K. Chesterton to remark: "It is impossible not to laugh at Ouida; and equally impossible not to read her."

R. M.

PRINCIPAL WORKS: *Novels*—Held in Bondage, 1863; Chandos, 1866; Under Two Flags, 1867; In A Winter City, 1876. *Tales*—A Dog of Flanders, etc., 1872. *Children's Stories*—Bimbi, 1882.
ABOUT: Huntington, H. G. Memories; Lee, E. Ouida: A Memoir; Van Vechten, C. Excavations.

RAMSAY, EDWARD BANNERMAN (January 31, 1793-December 27, 1872), Scottish clergyman and recorder of Scottish life, was born Edward Bannerman Burnett, the son of a sheriff. When he was thirteen years old his father, Alexander Burnett, inherited the estate of an uncle, changed the family name to Ramsay and was created baronet. Educated at St. John's College, Cambridge, Ramsay, held two curacies in Somerset, and then settled in Edinburgh, where he was pastor of St. John's Church from 1830 and dean of Edinburgh from 1841 until his death at seventy-nine. He was a patriotic Scot and a friend of Gladstone.

He is best known for his *Reminiscences of Scottish Life and Character,* a popular collection of humorous anecdotes, woven together in a personal narrative. Twenty-one editions appeared during his lifetime. Rated one of the best collections of Scottish stories, this work did much to spread a knowledge of the peculiarities of Scottish traits and customs. Ramsay also published sermons and lectures.

PRINCIPAL WORKS: A Catechism, 1835; Reminiscences of Scottish Life and Character, 1858; Two Lectures on the Genius of Handel, 1862.
ABOUT: Ramsay, E. B. Reminiscences of Scottish Life and Character (see Memoir by Cosmo Innes in posthumous editions).

RANDS, WILLIAM BRIGHTY (December 24, 1823-April 23, 1882), juvenile and miscellaneous writer, known as "the laureate of the nursery," was born in Chelsea, the son of a small shopkeeper. He wrote, besides using his own name, under the pseudonyms of Henry Holbeach, Matthew Brown, and T. Talker. He had little formal schooling, educating himself by reading at second-hand bookstalls. He worked from early youth in a warehouse, on the stage, and as an attorney's clerk. Then he taught himself shorthand and finally secured a position with a stenography office as reporter of the committee rooms of the

House of Commons. He held this job until 1875, when he retired because of failing health. At the same time he had an arrangement with his employers that when Parliament was not sitting he might do writing and editorial work. He was on the staff of the *Illustrated Times* from 1855 to 1871, and also wrote for the *Contemporary Review*, the *Saturday Journal*, the *Pall Mall Gazette*, *The Spectator*, and all the juvenile magazines, and helped to found *The Citizen*.

Rands was an eccentric. He does not seem to have been married but he acknowledged his parentage of four children. At the same time he wrote hymns, and was a frequent preacher in a Brixton chapel. Much of his work was mere hack writing under contract, but his verse is musical, and his fairy-tales, for which he is best known, display a delicate fancy and a real understanding of the child-mind.

PRINCIPAL WORKS: The Frost Upon the Pane, 1854; Chain of Lilies and Other Poems, 1857; Lilliput Levee, 1864; Verses and Opinions, 1866; Chaucer's England, 1869; Lilliput Lectures, 1871.

ABOUT: London Daily News April 26, 1882; Pictorial World June 7, 1882.

RATHBONE, HANNAH MARY (July 5, 1798-March 26, 1878), novelist, was born Hannah Mary Reynolds near Wellington in Shropshire. At nineteen she was married to her half-cousin, Richard Rathbone, by whom she had six children. She is notable for having initiated the autobiographic type of historical novel (as a variant of Scott's established form) in her *Diary of Lady Willoughby*. This work, dealing with the period of Charles the First's reign, appeared in two parts which were combined in 1848. The first part, published anonymously, was ascribed to Southey and various others until she acknowledged its authorship in the third edition, thereby winning fame.

Her other literary works included two anthologies of poetry, a volume of her own poems, and an edition of the letters of her paternal grandfather, Richard Reynolds, Quaker philanthropist. Though delicate in health, she supplemented her writing with painting and drawing, notably a series of charming designs for a bird book and a volume of pen-and-ink drawings from Pinelli's etchings of Italian peasantry. She died in Liverpool at the age of seventy-nine.

PRINCIPAL WORKS: Diary of Lady Willoughby: Part 1, 1844; Diary of Lady Willoughby: Part 2, 1847.

RAWLINSON, GEORGE (November 23, 1812-October 6, 1902), historian and Orientalist, was born at Chadlington, Oxfordshire. Following his graduation from Trinity College, Oxford, he was made a fellow of Exeter College, where he served as tutor for a few years. He was Camden professor of ancient history at Oxford from 1861 to 1889, and from 1872 onwards was canon of Canterbury. By his wife, Louisa Chermside, he had four sons and five daughters. He died of syncope at the age of eighty-nine.

He made a standard translation of Herodotus, with copious notes embodying the results of the cuneiform and hieroglyphic discoveries of his brother Sir Henry Rawlinson and Sir J. G. Wilkinson. This was followed by a series of authoritative works on the history, geography, and antiquities of the seven great Oriental monarchies, notably *The Five Great Monarchies of the Ancient Eastern World*. These works are still in use. Rawlinson took part in religious controversies (as a conservative) and contributed to Sir W. Smith's *History of the Bible*.

His brother SIR HENRY CRESWICKE RAWLINSON (1810-1895), Assyriologist, deciphered the cuneiform inscriptions of Persia, Assyria, and Babylonia between 1837 and 1851, and published valuable papers recording his findings.

PRINCIPAL WORKS: The History of Herodotus (with Sir H. Rawlinson and Sir J. G. Wilkinson) 1858-60; The Five Great Monarchies of the Ancient Eastern World: Chaldaea, Assyria, Babylonia, Media, and Persia, 1862-67; The Sixth Great Oriental Monarchy: Parthia, 1873; The Seventh Great Oriental Monarchy: The Sassanian or New Persian Empire, 1876; The History of Ancient Egypt, 1881; The History of Phoenicia, 1889; A Memoir of Major-General Sir H. C. Rawlinson, 1898.

ABOUT: The Times October 7, 1902; Athenaeum, October 11, 1902.

REACH, ANGUS BETHUNE (January 23, 1821-November 25, 1856), Scottish miscellaneous writer, was born in Inverness, son of a solicitor. He was educated at Inverness Academy and the University of Edinburgh. While still a student he contributed to the Inverness *Courier*. In 1842 the family moved to London, and through influence he secured at once a position as reporter of crime and Parliamentary news for the *Morning Chronicle*, in which he published his fine series on "Labour and the Poor." At the same time he wrote articles for many magazines, principally humorous series for *Punch*. In 1849 he was sent to France by the *Chronicle* and later became its music and art critic. He also acted as London correspondent for the Glasgow *Citizen* and the Inverness *Courier*. His health failed in 1854, and he was no longer able to work. The Fielding Club gave him a benefit and he received £100 from the Royal Bounty Fund. For a year before his death at less than thirty-five, his friend Shirley Brooks wrote his column in the paper under his name and gave Reach all the pay. He was deeply interested in sociological subjects, and his keen wit turned naturally to social satire.

PRINCIPAL WORKS: The Natural History of Bores, 1847; The Comic Bradshaw, 1848; Leonard Lindsay, 1850; Claret and Olives, 1852; Sketches of London Life and Character, 1858.

ABOUT: London Morning Chronicle November 26, 1856.

READE, CHARLES (June 8, 1814-April 11, 1884), novelist and dramatist, was born at Ipsden House in Oxfordshire, the youngest of eleven children. His father, John Reade, was "a high Tory (of tall and noble presence)"; his mother, née Anna Maria Scott-Waring, was the daughter of a prominent M.P.

Charles' six brothers, all older than he, were sent to public schools; but his mother chose to subject her youngest darling to private tuition. He was sent first to the Rev. Mr. Slatter of Rose Hill where he endured five years of instruction—administered chiefly by the cane. He was removed in 1827 to a more humane school at Staines under the Rev. Mr. Hearn, where he remained until 1829. The next two years were spent at home preparing to try for a demyship at Magdalen. (A "demyship" gives the holder half the income of a fellowship.) He won, out of a field of eight, not by brilliance but by pure luck. And four years later when he took an examination for a fellowship, on very brief notice, his good luck held once more. Out of the thirty-nine articles of religious doctrine, complete memorization of which was an absolute requirement, Reade knew but three. The article picked at random by the examiner was one of these three—and so Reade got the fellowship.

Reade's early schooling was, to a great extent, the cause of much unhappiness throughout life. With all their faults, the public schools usually served the purpose of teaching boys how to get on with their fellows. When Charles reached Oxford he had not learned this valuable lesson, with the result that he was unpopular and suffered unduly from every injury, real or fancied.

When the Vinerian scholarship was to be awarded there was a tacit conspiracy among the fellows of Magdalen to give Reade no assistance. The scholarship is awarded by the votes of Oxford masters of art. Ordinarily only those in residence vote, but Reade—Oxford being his home county—got his family to canvass the clergy and give them free trips to Oxford to cast votes. To the chagrin of his ill-wishers, Reade was elected Vinerian scholar and served a term as dean of arts.

Though he retained his fellowship and rooms at Oxford till death, he spent very little time there. He kept chambers in Leicester Square, London; moving later to a house opposite Hyde Park. He had entered his name at Lincoln's Inn and in 1843 was

CHARLES READE

called to the bar, but never practised. From 1837 to 1848 he traveled a great deal, staying much in Paris and Geneva, and visiting Scotland frequently. He played the violin well and became a collector of Cremonas. In Paris, during the Revolution of 1848, he was an object of hatred—being an Englishman—and was forced to make his escape from the city hidden in a truss of straw. When his parents exclaimed that he had had a narrow escape he replied calmly, "I have. They put me into a damp bed at Boulogne."

In 1849 Reade began writing plays, and in 1851 a comedy, *The Ladies' Battle*, was produced at the Olympic Theater. This was followed by five more within the next twenty-one months and at least two of them, *Gold* and *Masks and Faces* (written with Tom Taylor), were great successes.

Reade found the people of the theater—actors, managers and writers—far more congenial than his former associates at Oxford. One actress in particular, Laura Seymour, became his intimate friend and companion until her death in 1879.

It was she who prompted him to write his first novel, *Peg Woffington*, adapted from his comedy *Masks and Faces*. While her influence was an unquestioned factor in Reade's career as a novelist, it is doubtful if it was wholly beneficial. Sir Arthur Quiller-Couch says: "Now Mrs. Seymour, a woman of little cultivation, was quite incapable of correcting, because incapable of perceiving, those defects of taste and temper to which Reade was prone . . . she was an actress, and not a first-class actress, of a very bad period. She saw everything 'literary' in the light of the stage, and her stage was of the stagiest. By ill-luck Reade, too, suffered from this false

515

stage-eye." It is true. Many of his earlier novels were adapted from plays he had already written and he always seemed to visualize novels first as plays. Even in the printing of his books this tendency toward over-emphasis and melodrama may be seen: his striking lines are set in capitals.

In 1856 the first of his long novels, *It Is Never Too Late to Mend*, was published and from this time he concentrated most of his efforts upon his career as a novelist. Like Dickens, whom he greatly admired, Reade was a propagandist against social abuses of the age. *It Is Never Too Late to Mend* exposed the cruelties to which criminals were subjected. Later novels dealt with such problems as the care of the insane, unionization of labor, and illegitimacy.

This novel, like most of its successors, met with a poor reception at the hands of reviewers because, in the heat of his crusading passion, he exaggerated and thus failed to be convincing to people of literary taste. It might be remarked, in passing, that such people were, at that time, drawn almost exclusively from the upper classes—the people who, for their own peace of mind, were not anxious to be convinced. But the general public gave it an enthusiastic reception.

It Is Never Too Late to Mend was followed by a number of plays and novels, none of which added greatly to his fame, except a dramatization of the novel named above. This was successful and brought the author £2000 on its first run.

Reade's old fault of taking injuries too seriously had manifested itself, almost from the start of his literary career, by resort to the courts. A series of lawsuits against publishers and producers had brought him little satisfaction, but had run him considerably into debt.

In 1856-57 the *London Journal* published the first of his serial novels, *White Lies*. This was followed by his greatest work, *The Cloister and the Hearth*. Part of this had appeared serially in *Once a Week* with the title "A Good Fight" and the circulation was increased 20,000 copies while it was running. Expanded to about five times its original length, it was published in four volumes and has never ceased to be widely read. It may safely be called one of the greatest historical novels in the English language—some say *the* greatest.

Reade's next novel ran serially in *All the Year Round*, which Dickens edited, and was later published in book form under the title *Hard Cash*. With the publication of *Griffith Gaunt*, which followed *Hard Cash*, and appeared serially in *Argosy*, Reade paid off his debts and achieved financial security.

The preoccupation with social problems, so conspicuous in Reade's novels, was based upon a very genuine and passionate philanthropy. One of Reade's biographers states that Reade could never have been a successful lawyer because of his inability to separate the heart from the brain. The same difficulty hampered his art as a novelist, and complicated his private life. Although not a wealthy man, he is known to have given generously to many people; and since his giving was done without ostentation, there is no telling the extent of his private philanthropies. But it was not money alone which he gave to those who aroused his sympathies. He was always the champion of the under-dog and was ready to devote all his time and energies to fighting for his conception of the right. Unfortunately he lacked the tact, judgment and skill that might have made his fights more effective. He had the knack of putting himself in the wrong, shaming his friends and sympathizers, and laying himself open to ridicule. But even so, his pamphlets, letters, novels and plays were second only to those of Dickens in accomplishing the desired reforms.

Reade kept voluminous files of clippings and notebooks in which were recorded all manner of information which seemed interesting to him. In writing his novels he made use of this material. In his own words, "He was writing a novel based on facts—facts, incidents, living dialogues, pictures, reflections, situations, were all on these cards to choose from. . ." And this method brought to his books artistic truth in the handling of detail, setting and episodes; but his characters were usually unreal personifications of good or evil.

Sir Arthur Quiller-Couch sums up the man and his work thus: "He had other great merits too; but with them a fatal talent for murdering his own reputation, for capping every triumph with an instant folly, either in the books themselves or in his public behavior; and these follies were none the less disastrous for being prompted by a nature at once large, manly, generous, tender, incapable of self-control, constitutionally passionate, and in passion as blind as a bat. . . . [He] detested all writing that was nebulous, high-faluting, gushing. His style is ever lively and nervous. It may irritate even the moderately fastidious; it abounds in errors of taste; but is always vigorous, compelling—the style of a man."   D. C.

PRINCIPAL WORKS: *Novels*—Peg Woffington, 1853; Christie Johnstone, 1853; It Is Never Too Late to Mend, 1856; The Course of True Love Never Did Run Smooth, 1857; White Lies, 1857; The Box Tunnel; Cream, 1858; Love Me Little, Love Me Long, 1859; The Eighth Commandment, 1860; The Cloister and the Hearth, 1861; Hard Cash, 1863; Griffith Gaunt, 1867; Foul Play, 1868; Put Yourself in His Place, 1870; A Hero and a Martyr, 1874; Trade Malice & The Wandering Heir, 1875; A Woman Hater, 1877; Golden Crowns, 1883; Singleheart and Double Face, 1884;

Good Stories of Man and Other Animals, 1884; The Jilt, 1884; A Perilous Secret, 1884; Bible Characters, 1888; *Plays*—Peregrine Pickle, 1851; The Ladies' Battle; Angelo; The Lost Husband; Gold; The Courier of Lyons; Masks and Faces, 1854; Two Loves and a Life, 1854; The King's Rival, 1854; Poverty and Pride, 1856; The Hypochondriac, 1857; Le Faubourg Saint-Germain, 1859; Dora; The Double Marriage; Kate Peyton; It Is Never Too Late to Mend; The Well-Born Workman; Love and Money, 1883, The Countess and the Dancer, 1883.

ABOUT: Coleman, J. Charles Reade as I Knew Him; Collins, N. Facts of Fiction; Dawson, W. J. Makers of English Fiction; Elwin, M. Charles Reade; Phillips, W. C. Dickens, Reade, and Collins; Quiller-Couch, A. Studies in Literature (Ser. 1); Reade, C. L. & C. Charles Reade: Dramatist, Novelist, Journalist.

READE, JOHN EDMUND (1800-September 17, 1870), poetaster and novelist, was born in Gloucestershire and educated at a school near Shepton Mallet. He was really a phenomenal plagiarist; Byron was his chief victim, but he also borrowed from Scott, Wordsworth, and Ben Jonson. *Cain, the Wanderer,* his ablest work, though it was an obvious steal from Byron's *Cain,* drew an introduction by Coleridge and was praised by Goethe. He spent most of his life at Bath, where he died, but made many long visits to the Continent. He married his cousin, Maria Louisa Reade, and they had one daughter.

PRINCIPAL WORKS: The Broken Heart and Other Poems, 1825; Sybil Leaves, 1827; Cain, the Wanderer, 1830; Cataline, 1839; The Light of Other Days (novel) 1858; Saturday Sterne (novel) 1862.

READE (WILLIAM) WINWOOD (January 30, 1838-April 24, 1875), historian and miscellaneous writer, was a nephew of Charles Reade, the novelist. He was educated at Winchester and at Magdalen College, Oxford, but left without taking a degree. By this time he was already a pronounced Free Thinker and keenly interested in science. His curiosity aroused by Paul Du Chaillu's depicting of the gorilla as a savage beast, he raised money on his inheritance and went to Africa, revealing the fact that the gorilla is really a timid and almost inaccessible animal. He realized his lack of scientific knowledge, and on his return to England entered St. Mary's Hospital to study medicine. In 1866 he volunteered for service in the cholera hospital at Southampton. He went to Africa twice more, in 1869 for the Royal Geographical Society, and in 1873 as correspondent of the London *Times* in the Ashantee War, in which he actually participated as a soldier. The experience broke his health, and he came home to die at thirty-seven.

Reade's best work is *The Martyrdom of Man,* one of the most striking books in English. It is a running history of mankind in the light of the maleficent effects of religion. His novels were unconsciously imitative of his uncle, and his books of travel are no more than competent notebooks for the historico-philosophical work he had in mind.

PRINCIPAL WORKS: Liberty Hall, 1860; The Veil of Isis, 1861; Savage Africa, 1863; See-Saw (under the name of Francesco Abati) 1865; The Martyrdom of Man, 1872; African Sketch-Book, 1873; The Outcast, 1875.

ABOUT: Reade, W. The Martyrdom of Man (see Memoir in all modern reprints).

REDESDALE, LORD. See MITFORD, JOHN

REEVE, HENRY (September 9, 1813-October 21, 1895), miscellaneous writer, was born in Norwich, his father being a physician. At seven he was taken abroad, then sent to school in Norwich. From there he was sent to a school in Geneva, then to Italy and Munich; in these years he became a good deal of a linguist and met innumerable celebrities. At twenty-one he was contributing to the *British and Foreign Quarterly Review.* He lived for the next few years in Prague and Cracow, then returned to England in 1837, when he became clerk of the appeal judicial committee of the Privy Council. From 1840 to 1855 he was on the staff of *The Times,* and from 1843 to 1887 was registrar of the Privy Council. In 1841 he married Hope Richardson, who died the next year in giving birth to their one daughter. Later he married Christina G. J. Gallup. He was made editor of the *Edinburgh Review,* and while in that position edited the Greville *Memoirs,* volumes appearing in 1875, 1885, and 1887. In 1853 he went to Constantinople, and was frequently on the Continent. He was a constant correspondent of various foreign notables. He received an honorary D.C.L. from Oxford in 1869, and was the recipient of many other honors. He translated many French works and edited numerous memoirs and diaries besides Greville's. He died at eighty-two at his country home, Foxholes, Hampshire.

PRINCIPAL WORKS: Graphidae (poems) 1842; Royal and Republican France, 1872; Petrarch, 1878.

ABOUT: Academy October 26, 1895; Athenaeum October 26, 1895; Edinburgh Review January 1896.

REEVES, MRS. HENRY. See MATHERS, HELEN B.

REID, (THOMAS) MAYNE (April 4, 1818-October 22, 1883) Anglo-Irish novelist, was born at Ballyroney, County Down, Ireland, the eldest son of the Rev. Thomas Mayne Reid, a Presbyterian clergyman.

Reid was educated for the ministry but seems to have had no real vocation. In his college days he won prizes in mathematics, the classics, elocution, and athletics, but did

517

MAYNE REID

not distinguish himself in theology. He left home in 1840, taking ship for the United States, and upon his arrival at New Orleans promptly set out on an expedition into the interior. For several years he was trader, trapper, storekeeper, actor, poet, newspaper correspondent, and editor. Among his works of this period were a long poem, *La Cubana*, and a five-act tragedy, *Love's Martyr*. Drifting from place to place, he spent enough time in Philadelphia to become well acquainted with Poe, whom he considered a greatly overrated poet, but whose character he afterward was prompt to defend.

These early adventures laid the foundation for many of his novels. His greatest adventure, however, was his participation in the war with Mexico. He accepted a commission in 1845 and after winning the respect of his colleagues and men, played a distinguished part in the storming of Chapultepec, was wounded, and was reported dead, receiving high commendation of a supposedly posthumous character. While recuperating, he began work on his first novel, *The Rifle Rangers*, which, however, was not published until 1850. His period of convalescence at an end, he left for Europe, intending to raise volunteers to aid in the Hungarian insurrection, which, however, failed before he was able to participate.

Reid then went to London, where his stories began to find publishers and public favor. (It is said that both Alphonse Lamartine, the exquisite French poet, and Alexandre Dumas were fascinated by the French translation of *The Rifle Rangers*.) He then thought once more of joining the Hungarian patriot, Kossuth, in revolutionary activities, but the plan failed.

In 1853 Reid met Elizabeth Hyde, then a mere child of thirteen, whom he married two years later, and who wrote his biography. She was the inspiration of his novel *The Child Wife*.

He continued to be successful as an author until after 1866, when he had several financial reverses. A trip to the United States in 1867 was attended by an infection due to his old wound, which left him crippled. Under these difficulties, he lost his power of invention and his spirited style, and his popularity waned. He died in London in 1883, and was survived for many years by his widow.

The novels of adventure that came from his pen were highly colored and sensational accounts of derring-do, with a certain reality of atmosphere which overcame the poor plots and awkward characterization. "No better books for boys were ever written," said Rufus Wilson in *The Bookman*, and the *Daily News* commented: "He wrote with vigor and impetuosity as if under fire."

He was also the author of an autobiography written for boys, entitled *Ran Away to Sea*, and of a book on croquet.   R. M.

PRINCIPAL WORKS: *Fiction*—The Rifle Rangers, 1850; The Scalp Hunters, 1851; The Boy Hunters, 1852; The Quadroon, 1856; The Boy Slaves, 1865; The Headless Horseman, 1866; The Free Lances, 1881. *Autobiography*—Ran Away to Sea, 1859. *Miscellaneous*—Croquet, 1863.

ABOUT: Reid, E. H. Mayne Reid; Bookman 13:58 March 1901; Strand 2:93 July 1891.

REID, SIR THOMAS WEMYSS (March 29, 1842-February 26, 1905), biographer and novelist, was born at Newcastle-on-Tyne, son of a Congregational minister. He was educated at the Percy Street Academy and at St. Andrews. At fourteen he was a clerk, but already contributing papers to the *Northern Daily Express*. In 1861 he became chief reporter on the Newcastle *Journal*, and two years later was leader writer and dramatic critic. In 1864 he became editor of the Preston *Guardian*, and from 1866 to his death was on the staff of the Leeds *Mercury*. From 1867 to 1870 as London correspondent, and thereafter as "working editor." He made many journeys abroad, including one to Tunis in 1881. He resigned as editor in 1887, but continued to be a regular contributor, his viewpoint being that of a moderate liberal. As manager of Cassell & Company, the publishers, he moved to London in 1890 and until 1899 edited *The Speaker* there. Through the influence of his friend Lord Roseberry, he was knighted in 1894. From 1899 he contributed weekly political articles to the *Nineteenth Century*. In 1893 St. Andrews gave him an honorary LL.D., and he was president of the Institute of Journalists in 1898 and 1899. He was married twice: in 1867 to his cousin, Kate Thornton, who died in 1870, leaving one son, and in 1873 to Louisa Berry, who had one son and one daughter. As both biographer and novelist he may be described as competent rather than distinguished.

PRINCIPAL WORKS: Cabinet Portraits, 1872; Charlotte Brontë, 1877; Land of the Bey, 1882; Gladys Fane (novel) 1884; Mauleverer's Millions (novel) 1886; Life of William Edward Forster, 1888; Lord Houghton, 1890; William Black, 1902; Memoirs (ed. by Dr. Stuart Reid) 1905.

ABOUT: Reid, Sir. T. W. Memoirs; Leeds Mercury February 27, 1905; London Times February 27, March 3 and 4, 1905.

REYNOLDS, FREDERIC (November 1, 1764-April 16, 1841), playwright, was born in London, son of an attorney. His grandfathers were both very wealthy, and he had no need to earn his living. He was educated at Westminster, and in 1782 entered the Middle Temple, but soon discovered that the law was not his forte and that his interest was entirely in the stage. From 1814 to 1822 he was permanently attached to Covent Garden Theater, and from 1823 was on the staff of Drury Lane, officially labeled as "thinker." In 1799 he married a Miss Mansel, an actress, and they had one son. He composed in all nearly a hundred tragedies and comedies, the best known of which were *The Exile* and *The Renegade,* and some of his earlier plays were published, but whatever his capacities as a "thinker," as a dramatist they were very slight, and his plays are now quite forgotten.

PRINCIPAL WORKS: Werter, 1785; Eloise, 1786; The Dramatist, 1789; Life and Times of Frederick Reynolds: Written by Himself, 1826; A Playwright's Adventures (novel) 1831.

ABOUT: Reynolds, F. Life and Times of Frederick Reynolds; Athenaeum April 24, 1841.

REYNOLDS, GEORGE WILLIAM MCARTHUR (July 23, 1814-June 17, 1879), novelist, was born in Sandwich, the son of a naval captain. He was educated privately and by travel on the Continent. In 1846 he became editor of the London *Journal,* and, from the end of the same year until 1870, of *Reynolds's Miscellany*; to the latter he contributed many of his stories. From 1840 he had charge of the foreign intelligence department of the London *Despatch.* His sympathies were frankly revolutionary, and because of this he was obliged to resign in the troubled year of 1848. He became a leader of the Chartists, the working-class radicals of the time, and even in this group was an extremist. In 1849 and 1850 he edited *Reynolds's Political Instructor,* and from 1850 to his death, *Reynolds's Weekly Newspaper.* His novels were extremely sensational, and most of them were mere pot-boilers, not intended to be literature.

PRINCIPAL WORKS: The Youthful Impostor, 1835; Modern Literature of France, 1839; The Drunkard's Progress, 1841; Mysteries of London, 1846-55; Mary Price, 1850 (as play; as novel, 1852); The Soldier's Wife, 1853; The Loves of the Harem, 1855.

ABOUT: London Times June 18, 1879.

REYNOLDS, JOHN HAMILTON (September 9, 1796-November 15, 1852), poet, was born in Shrewsbury. His father was head writing-master at Christ's Hospital. He was educated at St. Paul's School and then became a clerk with an insurance company but spent most of his time on literature. He was a friend of Hunt and Byron, but above all of Keats, who admired his work and considered him his equal as a poet. He was even bracketed in some reviews with Shelley, though he showed so little understanding of the great poet's work that he even parodied Shelley's *Peter Bell,* which is of course itself a parody of Wordsworth's poem. Indeed poetry intrinsically meant so little to him that an attractive offer from a solicitor in 1818 diverted him from writing for a long time, and he wrote little of consequence after 1825. He traveled on the Continent in 1820, the year before his marriage, and then for a while contributed to the *Edinburgh Review,* the *London Magazine,* and other periodicals, but this phase ended with a quarrel with Hood, who had been his friend and collaborator, especially in his humorous verses. Until 1831 he was a part-owner of *The Athenaeum.* In 1838 his literary life came to a complete end when he moved to the Isle of Wight and became clerk of the County Court. There he died at fifty-six, a brilliant, witty writer, an authentic poet of great promise, especially as a sonneteer, but a man old before his time, soured and embittered by the failure of both his literary and legal careers—a failure largely due to some inherent defect in his own character.

PRINCIPAL WORKS: Safie, 1814; The Eden of Imagination, 1814; The Naiad, 1816; 1, 2, 3, 4, 5 (farce) 1819; The Fancy, 1820; The Garden of Florence and Other Poems (as John Hamilton) 1821; Odes and Addresses (with Thomas Hood) 1825.

ABOUT: Athenaeum November 27 1852.

RHODES, WILLIAM BARNES (December 25, 1772-April 1, 1826), was born at Leeds. Little is known of his early life, or indeed of his life in general. He was a "writer" (clerk) in an attorney's office, then in 1799 became a clerk in the Bank of England. He remained in its employ all his life long, and from 1823 to his death was its chief teller. He was married, and had one daughter, born posthumously. In 1801 he published a translation of Juvenal, and seems therefore to have had at least the rudiments of a classical education. He was a collector of published and manuscript plays, and had a large and valuable collection. His burlesque, *Bombastes Furioso,* by which his name lives, was performed in 1810, and published three years later, but it was anonymous, and its authorship was not known until 1822.

PRINCIPAL WORKS: Epigrams, 1803; Bombastes Furioso, 1813.

ABOUT: Gentleman's Magazine 2:471, 1826.

RHŶS, SIR JOHN (June 21, 1840-December 17, 1915), Welsh scholar, was born in Cardiganshire, son of a yeoman farmer. He was educated at the local schools and at Bangor Normal College, and became master of a school in Anglesey. In 1865 he entered Jesus College, Oxford, and later was made a fellow of Merton College. In 1870 and 1871 he was at Leipzig University, where his interest in linguistics was first aroused. From 1871 to 1877 he was inspector of schools in the counties of Flint and Denbigh, Wales, but at the same time wrote articles on Celtic grammar for the Revue Celtique. In 1872 he married Elspeth Hughes-Davies, who died in 1911, leaving two daughters. In 1877 he became the first professor of Celtic at Jesus College. From 1881 to 1895 he was fellow and bursar of Jesus, becoming its principal thereafter. He received an honorary LL.D. from Edinburgh University in 1893, and a Litt.D. from the University of Wales in 1902. He was knighted in 1907, and in 1911 became a privy councillor.

Rhŷs was an authority and a prolific writer on Celtic grammar, philology, phonology, history, religion, ethnology, and folklore. United with great industry and profound learning, he had a constructive imagination which enabled him to invest the dead bones of Celtic (particularly Welsh) language and literature with the flesh and blood of life.

PRINCIPAL WORKS: Lectures on Welsh Philology, 1877; Celtic Britain, 1879; The Origin and Growth of Religion, 1880; The Welsh People (with D. Brynmor-Jones) 1900.

ABOUT: Jesus College Magazine June 1919; Proceedings of the British Academy 1915.

RICARDO, DAVID (April 19, 1772-September 11, 1823), economist, was of a Sephardic (Spanish Jewish) family, resident in Holland since 1492. His father, however, had emigrated to England in his youth and had become very rich as a stockbroker. The boy was educated partly in England and partly with an uncle in Holland. From the age of fourteen he was associated with his father in business. In 1793, when he was twenty-one, he married Priscilla Anne Wilkinson; they had three sons and four daughters. This marriage to a Gentile caused a permanent breach with his pious father, especially since it involved the abandonment of his childhood's faith.

He was obliged, therefore, to set up in business for himself, and was very successful. His chief interest at this time was in science;

he had his own laboratory, and was an original member of the Geological Society. He first became interested in economics in 1799, from a reading of Adam Smith's famous Wealth of Nations. From 1809 he wrote articles on currency for the magazines; these attracted the attention of Malthus and of James Mill, who became his close friends, associated themselves with him in the working out of his theory of rent, and encouraged his production of his best known work, Principles of Political Economy and Taxation, which, though faulty in style (for he was never a skilled writer) marked an era in economics. In ,1814 he retired from business, and lived as a country gentleman in Gloucestershire. In 1818 he served as sheriff of Gloucestershire, and from 1819 to his death was a Member of Parliament. His Irish constituency had just thirty voters, and he was supposed to have bought the seat; nevertheless he was a valuable member of the House of Commons, a reformer, a member of the Radical Party, and a friend of the Utilitarians, whose leader was John Stuart Mill, the son of his old friend. He contributed articles on economics to the 1820 edition of the Encyclopaedia Britannica. In 1822 he traveled with his family, first to Holland to visit his relatives, then to Italy. He died of mastoiditis, from which he had long been a sufferer.

Ricardo was a kindly, attractive man, a born philanthropist. Though he was considered the head of the classical school of political economy, Karl Marx adopted in great part Ricardo's "iron law of wages" and his theory of labor value.

PRINCIPAL WORKS: The High Price of Bullion, 1810; Principals of Political Economy and Taxation, 1817; On Protection to Agriculture, 1821.

ABOUT: Ricardo, D. Collected Works (see Life by McCulloch in 1846 ed.).

RICHARDSON, JOHN (October 4, 1796-May 12, 1852), Canadian novelist and miscellaneous writer, was born in Queenstown, Upper Canada. His father was a physician, his mother a native of Detroit, Michigan, then a frontier outpost. Nothing is known of his education, and in fact, such elementary dates as those of his birth and death are more or less in dispute. It is known that he was a soldier in the War of 1812, and a prisoner of war for all of 1813, and that after the war he went to England and joined the British army. He was married in 1830, but all that is known of his wife is that her given names were Maria Caroline, and that she died in 1845. In 1818 Richardson was put on half pay, and devoted his leisure to writing. But the military life called him back, and from 1834 to 1837 he was with the British Auxiliary Legion in Spain; in 1836 he was promoted to major. He then quarreled violently with his commander, attacked him in a book, and caused an inquiry in the House of Commons. Since the result was the general's acquittal, the army was no longer a comfortable place for Major Richardson, and he returned to Canada in 1838. He acted at this time as Canadian correspondent for the London *Times*.

From 1840 to 1842 he lived at Brockville, Upper Canada, where in 1840 he established the *New Era*. In 1843 and 1844 he owned and edited the *Canadian Loyalist*, also recorded as the *Native Canadian*. In 1845 he was superintendent of police on the Welland Canal, but the post was abolished the next year. He was then for a time a resident of Montreal, and about 1850 moved to New York City. There, two years later, he died alone, in wretched poverty.

Richardson's historical and autobiographical works are more important than his novels. The early Canadian novels have some local interest, (*Wacousta* marks the beginning of Canadian fiction); but those written for a pittance in his last years in New York are mere cheap, sensational pot-boilers.

PRINCIPAL WORKS: Tecumseh (poem) 1828; Écarté: or, The Salons of Paris, 1829; Wacousta, 1832; Personal Memoirs, 1838; The Canadian Brothers, 1840 (as Matilda Montgomerie, 1851); The War of 1812, 1842; Eight Years in Canada, 1847; Hardscrabble, 1850; Wau-Nan-Gee: or, The Massacre of Chicago, 1850.
ABOUT: MacMechan, A. Headwaters of Canadian Literature; Richardson, J. Personal Memoirs; Riddell, W. R. John Richardson.

RIDDELL, HENRY SCOTT (September 23, 1798-July 30, 1870). Scottish poet, was born in Dumfriesshire, where his father was a farmer and later a shepherd. In summer in his childhood he herded the sheep, in winter he went to school or was taught at home. His father died in 1817, and for two years he attended the parish school, then entered Edinburgh University. In 1830 he was licensed to preach by the Church of Scotland, and in 1833 became incumbent of Caerlaning Chapel, Teviothead, Roxburghshire. The same year he married Eliza Clark; they had two sons. In 1841 he became insane, and for three years was an inmate of an asylum. By kindness of his patron, the Duke of Buccleuch, though he had to resign his living, he was allowed to retain for all his life the cottage in which he had lived. He interested himself in local archaeology, wrote songs for various miscellanies, wrote on agriculture, and translated St. Matthew and the Psalms into the Lowland Scottish dialect. His short lyrics have much beauty, but in his longer poems he is apt to be dull and heavy. His song, "Scotland Yet," is still sung in his native land.

PRINCIPAL WORKS: Songs of the Ark, 1831; The Christian Politician, 1844; Poems, Songs, and Miscellaneous Pieces, 1847; Poetical Works, 1871.

ABOUT: Riddell, H. F. Poetical Works (see Memoir by Dr. Brydon).

RIGBY, ELIZABETH. See EASTLAKE, LADY

RITCHIE, LEITCH (1800?-January 16, 1865), Scottish novelist, was born in Greenock. After leaving school he was apprenticed to a banker. In his early youth he went to London, but was called home again by his father, and placed in a mercantile establishment in Glasgow. Already interested in writing, in 1818 and 1819 he helped to found a fortnightly called *The Wanderers*. His firm failed, and he decided to make literature his profession. He wrote articles for the *Foreign Quarterly Review* and the *Westminster Review;* was on the staff of the London Weekly Review until its ownership changed; and from 1831 was editor of the *Englishman's Magazine*. He turned out books as a regular hack writer working on commission for various publishers, then edited *The Era*. and was the first editor, in 1840, of the *Indian News*. Then he went back to Scotland to edit *Chambers's Journal*. In 1862 he received a civil list pension of £100. He was married and had one daughter. His novels were purely hack jobs and have no literary merit.

PRINCIPAL WORKS: Tales and Confessions, 1829; The Game of Speculation, 1830; The Romance of History: France, 1831; The Magician, 1836; Wearyfoot Common, 1855; Winter Evenings, 1859.
ABOUT: Gentleman's Magazine March 1865; London Times January 21, 1865; Scotsman January 20, 1865.

RITCHIE, LADY ANNE ISABELLA (June 9, 1837-February 20, 1919), novelist and biographer, was the eldest daughter of William Makepeace Thackeray. She was educated privately, partly at Paris. In 1877 she married Richmond T. W. Ritchie (1854-1912), after a long courtship beginning when he was an Eton schoolboy. In spite of the disparity of their ages, the marriage was very happy, for she was young for her age, and he old for his. Her husband was knighted in 1907, making her Lady Ritchie. They had one son and one daughter. Lady Ritchie was one of the last links with the great of the Victorian age, for there was no celebrity of her youth whom she did not know. Not unnaturally, her biographical writings are her best work. She contributed many articles to the *Dictionary of National Biography*, and edited her father's works in 1908.

PRINCIPAL WORKS: The Story of Elizabeth, 1863; The Village on the Cliff, 1865; Old Kensington, 1873; Madame de Sevigné, 1881; Lord Tennyson and His Friends, 1893; Chapters From Some Memoirs, 1894; The Blackstick Papers, 1908.
ABOUT: Ritchie, A. E. Chapters From Some Memoirs; Letters of Anne Thackeray Ritchie; London Times February 28, 1919.

ROBERTSON, FREDERICK WILLIAM

(February 3, 1816-August 1, 1853), theologian, was born in London of a long line of army officers, including his father. He was educated at the Beverly Grammar School, in a school in Tours, France, at the New Edinburgh Academy, and at the University of Edinburgh. All his three brothers having become military officers, his father wished him to enter the church, but though he was very devout he considered himself unworthy, and found work in a solicitor's office. It was not long before his dislike of the law broke his health, and he was obliged to leave. In 1837 he finally agreed to enter Brasenose College, Oxford, and to consider a career in the church. Meanwhile, since he would not previously consent to become a clergyman, his father had secured an army commission for him, which arrived five days after he matriculated in Oxford, but by this time he declined it.

He eceived his B.A. in 1841 and M.A. in 1844, having been ordained in 1840. He became curate in a slum district of Winchester, where overwork, extreme asceticism, and passionate sympathy with the poor almost cost him his life. He was forced to leave and to spend some time in Switzerland. There he met Helen Denys, whom he married in 1841; they had one son and one daughter. From 1843 to 1845 he was a curate at Cheltenham, but by this time he had outgrown many of his old ideas, and found himself obliged to break with his former friends and associations. In 1846 he was in charge of the English Church at Heidelberg, then had a charge at Oxford, finally taking a church at Brighton, where he remained until his death. His sermons were especially popular with workingmen, and his influence was far wider than his writings would indicate, for he was too sensitive, excitable, and vehement for the rough-and-tumble of controversy. His letters show, however, how great was his actual literary ability.

PRINCIPAL WORKS: Sermons Preached at Trinity Chapel, Brighton (4 series) 1855-90; Literary Remains, 1876.

ABOUT: Arnold, Rev. T. Life of Frederick William Robertson; Brooke, S. A. Life and Letters of F. W. Robertson.

ROBERTSON, GEORGE CROOM

(March 10, 1842-September 20, 1892), Scottish philosopher, was born in Aberdeen and educated at Marischal College, Aberdeen. He was professor of mental philosophy and logic in University College, London, for twenty-six years (1866-92). During the first sixteen years of the existence of Mind, the influential English journal devoted to psychology and philosophy, he was its editor (1876-92). Under his skilful guidance it attained an important place in the history of British philosophy.

The title of the periodical was suggested by Robertson himself.

Failing health during the last twelve years of his life (he died at fifty) prevented his producing much literary work. He is remembered, however, for a praiseworthy monograph on Thomas Hobbes; a posthumous collection of his articles from Mind, the Encyclopaedia Britannica, and the Dictionary of National Biography; and two posthumous volumes of lectures on philosophy and psychology.

PRINCIPAL WORKS: Hobbes, 1886; Philosophical Remains (ed. by A. Bain and T. Whittaker) 1894; Elements of General Philosophy (ed. by C. A. F. R. Davids) 1896; Elements of the Psychology (ed. by C. A. F. R. Davids) 1896.

ABOUT: Robertson, G. C. Philosophical Remains (see Memoir by A. Bain).

ROBERTSON, JOSEPH

(May 17, 1810-December 13, 1866), Scottish historian and scholar, was born in Aberdeen and educated at Marischal College, Aberdeen. In 1839 he helped to found the Spalding Club for the publication of historical records of the north of Scotland; eight of its thirty-eight volumes were edited by him. He also edited two of the best publications of the Ballantyne Club; of these, Concilia Ecclesiae Scoticanae was his outstanding work. His editions earned him a reputation as one of the most learned and accurate of Scottish antiquaries. His lifelong friend, the historian John Hill Burton, credited him with "subtle powers of investigation and critical acumen, peculiarly his own, which have had a perceptible and substantial effect in raising archaeology out of that quackish repute which it had long to endure under the name of antiquarianism."

Robertson was successively editor of the Glasgow Constitutional. (1843-49), editor of the Edinburgh Courant (1849-53), and curator of the historical records in the Edinburgh Register House from 1853 until his death at the age of fifty-six. His wife and four children survived him. In recognition of his services to literature, Queen Victoria gave his widow a yearly pension of £100.

PRINCIPAL WORKS: Gordon of Rothiemay; History of Scots Affairs From 1637 to 1641 (ed. with G. Grub) 1841; Illustrations of the Topography and Antiquities of Aberdeen and Banff (ed. with G. Grub) 1842-69; Diary of General Patrick Gordon (ed.) 1862; Concilia Ecclesiae Scoticanae (ed.) 1866.

ROBERTSON, THOMAS WILLIAM

(January 9, 1829-February 3, 1871), actor and dramatist, was born in Newark-on-Trent, the eldest child of William Robertson (an actor, of an old theatrical family) and Margaretta Elizabetha (Margaret Elizabeth) Marinus (an actress).

Educated by his great-uncle's widow, the manager of the Lincoln Circuit, Robertson

T. W. ROBERTSON

played child rôles as early as 1834. In 1836 he was sent to Henry Young's school at Spalding, and in 1841 to a school at Whittlesea. Occasionally he acted during holiday periods.

In 1843 he left school, becoming scene-painter, prompter, and man-of-all-work for the Lincoln company, his father being manager. He acted various rôles, including Charles Surface and Hamlet, until the circuit broke up in 1848, when he went to London.

There he acted at the less-known theatres and taught himself French. For a few months he was an assistant in a school in Utrecht. Although, in 1851, his *A Night's Adventure* was produced, and in 1855 *Castles in the Air*, Robertson's success was small. He acted in provincial companies, wrote for newspapers, was prompter at the Olympic, and sold work to Lacy, the theatrical bookseller and publisher. He tried to enlist in the army and was rejected; and he played Macbeth in the Wallack company's unsuccessful Paris production (1855).

In 1856 he married an actress, Elizabeth Burton (real name Taylor), with whom he journeyed to Dublin, where she became a leading lady and he an assistant stage-manager and comedian. They toured England and Ireland with slight success. In 1857 a son was born.

Upon the death of a baby daughter (born 1858) Robertson, in despair of a theatrical career, repaired to London, where he wrote for magazines, edited a mining journal, and translated French plays for Lacy. Even the production (1861) of *The Cantab*, though it brought Robertson the friendship of a Bohemian group of literary men, did little to help his situation, and he considered leaving journalism to become a tobacconist.

His fortune changed when *David Garrick* was successfully produced by Sothern (1864). With the production of *Society* (1865) at the Prince of Wales Theatre, Robertson's career was begun. *Ours, Caste* (his masterpiece), *Play, School,* and *M. P.* all were given under the Bancrofts at the Prince of Wales, and, though Robertson continued to write for other theatres, these were his most successful plays.

His wife having died of illness and overwork in 1865, leaving a son and a daughter, Robertson married (1867) Rosetta Feist, a young German girl, who bore him a daughter. By 1870 his health had broken, and he was a sufferer from heart disease. In December he made a journey to Torquay, returning shortly with no improvement, and on February 3, 1871, he died in his chair.

While, as he himself recognized, he was not a great actor, and while his plays, intimate, satirical, and thinly clever, are no longer well-known or important, Robertson is a significant figure of his time because of his success with a peculiar combination of sentiment and shallow wordliness which inspired the epithet "cup-and-saucer." Though critics sneered, the public applauded Robertson's comedies. Of him A. E. Morgan writes: "Robertson stands out distinctly in the mid-Victorian period as one who made a very real attempt to bring the stage into closer touch with life. In the light of later developments his colors may appear faded; but in his own day he was undoubtedly a pioneer."

R. W. W.

PRINCIPAL WORKS: *Plays*—A Night's Adventure, 1851; Castles in the Air, 1854; The Cantab, 1861; David Garrick, 1864; Society, 1865; Ours, 1866; Caste, 1867; Play, 1868; Home, 1869; School, 1869; Dreams, 1869; A Breach of Promise, 1869; Progress, 1869; The Nightingale, 1870; M. P., 1870; War, 1871. *Collected Plays*—The Principal Dramatic Works of Thomas William Robertson. *Novel*—David Garrick, 1865.

ABOUT: Morgan, A. E. Tendencies of Modern English Drama; Pemberton, T. E. The Life and Writings of T. W. Robertson; Robertson, T. W. The Principal Dramatic Works of Thomas William Robertson (see Memoir by T. W. S. Robertson).

ROBINSON, HENRY CRABB (March 13, 1775-February 5, 1867), diarist, was born at Bury St. Edmunds, the youngest son of middle-class and dissenting parents.

After a schooling at Bury and Devizes, four years as an articled clerk to an attorney, and two years in the office of a Chancery Lane solicitor, he inherited a small income and went to Germany for travel and study. In 1801 he met Goethe and Schiller, the first of the many prominent men of letters he was to know. The next year he settled at Jena and entered the university there.

HENRY CRABB ROBINSON

During 1807-09 he reported for *The Times* in Holstein and Spain; and was the first English journalist to act as war correspondent. Next he studied law at the Middle Temple and was admitted to the bar in 1813. After rising to the leadership of the Norfolk circuit, he retired in 1828 with a comfortable income. He used to say that the wisest acts of his life were going to the bar and leaving the bar.

After his retirement and until his death at the age of ninety-one, he cultivated the society of literary men, entertained extensively, read all the important books of his day, and wrote in a diary.

"I early found," he wrote, "that I had not the literary ability to give me a place among English authors as I should have desired; but I thought that I had an opportunity of gaining knowledge of many of the most distinguished men of the age, and that I might do some good by keeping a record of my interviews with them. True, I want in an eminent degree the Boswell faculty; still the names recorded in *his* great work are not so important as Goethe, Schiller, Herder, Wieland, . . . Louisa of Weimar, Tieck; as Madame de Staël, La Fayette, . . . Benjamin Constant; as Wordsworth, Southey, Coleridge, Lamb, Rogers, Hazlitt, Mrs. Barbauld, Clarkson, &c., &c., &c., for I could add a great number of minor stars. And yet what has come of all this? Nothing. What will come of it? Perhaps nothing."

The answer to his first question might be, in part, that during his lifetime he gave intelligent encouragement and stimulus to men of genius, that he championed Wordsworth's verse when such support was greatly needed, that he made valuable contributions to Mrs. Hustin's *Characteristics of Goethe*, to Gil-

christ's *Memoirs of Blake,* and to similiar books, and that he brought to his age a literary sanity which was more of an influence than he knew.

At his death he left a hundred and two manuscript volumes of diary and letters that give accurate and vivid accounts of the social and the literary life of his time, in England and abroad. The original volumes, preserved by Dr. Williams' Library in Garden Square, London, have furnished material for several published volumes; and much material of value remains unprinted.

Wordsworth dedicated to Robinson the *Memorials* of a tour the two made in Scotland, Wales, Switzerland, and Italy. Robinson was a founder of the London University and an early member of the Athenaeum Club. He never married. The inscription on his tomb describes him as the friend and associate of Goethe, Wordsworth, Coleridge, Flaxman, Blake, Clarkson, and Charles Lamb.

Edith J. Morley, a recent editor of his diary, characterizes him as "a lovable personality—no Boswell certainly, but one who possessed a genuine gift for characterization, an instinct for friendship and the power to stamp himself and his experiences with extraordinary vividness on his papers."

Of a portrait of himself, painted for Goethe, he wrote, "It is frightfully ugly and very like."
P. G.

PRINCIPAL WORKS: *Biography*—Diary, Reminiscences, and Correspondence of H. Crabb Robinson, 1869; Selections from the Remains of Henry Crabb Robinson, 1922; Crabb Robinson in Germany, 1929; *Letters*—The Correspondence of Henry Crabb Robinson with the Wordsworth Circle, 1927.

ABOUT: Vincent, L. H. Dandies and Men of Letters; Modern Language Association of America Publications 1:395 1916. See also works above.

ROBY, HENRY JOHN (August 12, 1830-January 2, 1915), classical scholar and educational reformer, was born at Tamworth in Staffordshire, the son of a solicitor. Graduated from St. John's College, Cambridge, he became a fellow of his college and lectured there from 1855 to 1861. During the following four years he was second master at Dulwich College. As secretary of the Schools Inquiry Commission (1864-72) he rendered a valuable service by securing legislation for the improvement of school management. From 1874 to 1894 he was a partner in the Manchester business firm of Ermen & Roby, sewing-cotton manufacturers. He served the Eccles division of Lancaster as a liberal member of Parliament from 1890 to 1895. The last twenty years of his life were spent in retirement at Easedale, near Grasmere, where he died at the age of eighty-four.

He is best remembered for his epoch-making *Grammar of the Latin Language*

From *Plautus to Suetonius*, which became the basis for the compilation of future grammars. His useful volumes on Roman law were the outgrowth of a brief experience as professor of jurisprudence at University College, London (1866-68).

PRINCIPAL WORKS: Elementary Latin Grammar, 1862; Report of the Schools Inquiry Commission (chapters II and IV) 1868-69; Grammar of the Latin Language From Plautus to Suetonius, 1871-74; Latin Grammar for Schools, 1880; An Introduction to the Study of Justinian's Digest, 1884; Roman Private Law in the Times of Cicero and the Antonines, 1902; Essays on the Law in Cicero's Orations, 1902.

ROCHE, MRS. REGINA MARIA (1764?-May 17, 1845), Irish novelist, was born Regina Maria Dalton in the South of Ireland. Soon after the appearance of her first novel, *The Vicar of Lansdowne*, in 1793, she was married to a gentleman named Roche. In 1798, her thirty-fourth year, she achieved sudden fame with her third novel, *Children of the Abbey*, a luridly sentimental tale which enjoyed great popularity for many years, rivaling the success of Ann Radcliffe's *Mysteries of Udolpho*, published a year earlier. She continued to write in the same vein the rest of her life, producing in all sixteen novels, of which eleven appeared after 1800. She died at the age of eighty-one at her home in the Irish seaport of Waterford.

WORKS: The Vicar of Lansdowne, 1793; The Maid of the Hamlet 1793; The Children of the Abbey, 1798; Clermont, 1798; The Nocturnal Visit, 1800; The Discarded Son: or, The Haunt of the Banditti, 1807; The Houses of Osma and Almeria: or, The Convent of St. Ildefonso, 1810; The Monastery of St. Colomba, 1812; Trecothiek Bower, 1813; London Tales, 1814; The Munster Cottage Boy, 1819; The Bridal of Dunamore, and Lost and Won: Two Tales, 1823; The Castle Chapel, 1825; Contrast, 1828; The Nun's Picture, 1834; The Tradition of the Castle: or, Scenes in the Emerald Isle, 1824.

ABOUT: London Gentleman's Magazine July, 1845.

ROGERS, CHARLES (April 18, 1825-September 18, 1890), Scottish literary antiquary, was born at Denino in Fifeshire, the only son of a minister. Educated at the University of St. Andrews, he was for eight years chaplain of the garrison at Stirling Castle before he went to London in 1863 and began to devote himself to literature. In 1868 he founded the Grampian Club for the publication of Scottish antiquarian works; he was its secretary and chief editor until his death at sixty-five. He also claimed to be the founder of the Royal Historical Society, of which he was secretary and historiographer from its origin in 1868 to 1880. Eight of this society's *Transactions* were edited by him.

Best known of his works was *The Modern Scottish Minstrel*, a collection of the songs of Scotland since Burns. This compilation met with both praise and condemnation; the London *Athenaeum* called it "as bad in proportion as the promises made for it were arrogant and high-sounding." In addition to his editions, Rogers produced numerous original works in the varied fields of history, biography, topography, genealogy, theology, social life, religion, poetry, and autobiography.

PRINCIPAL WORKS: The Modern Scottish Minstrel: or, The Songs of Scotland of the Past Half Century (ed.) 1855-57; Sacred Songs of Scotland (ed.) 1860; Familiar Illustrations of Scottish Life, 1861; A Century of Scottish Life, 1871; Robert Burns and the Scottish House of Burnes, 1877; Social Life in Scotland, 1884-86.

ABOUT: Rogers, C. Leaves From My Autobiography, 1876; Rogers, C. The Serpent's Track: A Narrative of Twenty-two Years' Persecution, 1880; The Athenaeum September, 1890.

ROGERS, HENRY (October 18, 1806-August 20, 1877), essayist, and Christian apologist, was born at St. Albans. His father was a surgeon and a devout Congregationalist. At sixteen he was aprenticed to his father's profession, but a sermon he read turned him toward theology as a career, and he entered Highbury College. In 1829 he was licensed as a Congregationalist minister, and became assistant pastor at Poole, Dorset. In 1830 he married Sarah Frances Bentham, a relative of Jeremy Bentham the economist; she died in her third annual childbirth; and in 1834 he married her sister Elizabeth, who died a year later in giving birth to her first child. The legality of this second marriage is doubtful, though at that time marriage to a deceased wife's sister was merely voidable, not void *ab initio*.

In 1832 Rogers became lecturer on rhetoric and logic at Highbury College, in 1836 professor of English language and literature at University College, London, and from 1839 to 1858 he was professor of English language and literature, mathematics, and mental philosophy at Spring Hill Academy, Birmingham. An incurable throat disease made it impossible for him to lecture or preach, and he found it necessary to express himself entirely in writing. He edited many sermons and theological works of nonconformist ministers, and from 1839 was a contributor to the *Edinburgh Review*. From 1854 to 1860 he wrote many articles for the *Encyclopaedia Britannica*, including those on Gibbon, Hume, and Voltaire, though he was a pronounced anti-Rationalist. From 1858 to 1871 he was president and professor of theology at the Lancashire Independent College, then retired because of failing health, and spent his last years in retirement in Wales.

Rogers was by no means a learned theologian, and relied more on emotion than on logic in his self-constituted position of premier Christian apologist in England. In fact, one of his theses was that "reason rests on faith."

PRINCIPAL WORKS: Poems: Miscellaneous and Sacred, 1826; The Life and Character of John Howe, 1836; Essays From the Edinburgh Review (5 series) 1850-1874; The Eclipse of Faith, 1852; The Superhuman Origin of the Bible, 1873.

ABOUT: Rogers, H. The Superhuman Origin of the Bible (see memoir by Dr. R. W. Dale in 1893 ed.).

ROGERS, JAMES EDWIN THOROLD

(1823-October 12, 1890), political economist, was born at West Meon, Hampshire, and educated at Magdalen Hall, Oxford. After ten years as curate of St. Paul's, Oxford, he was from 1859 onwards (a period of thirty-one years) the first Tooke professor of statistics and economic science at King's College, London. He was also Drummond professor of political economy at Oxford from 1862 to 1876. A close friend and follower of Richard Cobden, he engaged effectively in political agitation and sat in Parliament for the borough of Southwark (1880-85) and for Bermondsey (1885-86). He died at Oxford in his sixty-seventh year. Twice married, he had six children by his second wife.

His reputation rests on his *History of Agriculture and Prices*, to which subsequent historians have been deeply indebted. The work appeared in eight volumes over a period of thirty-six years; the last two volumes were prepared for posthumous publication by his fourth son A. G. L. Rogers. Though the records contained in the work are of permanent value, some of the author's conclusions have been criticized as inaccurate. Several of his other publications are valuable.

PRINCIPAL WORKS: Education in Oxford: Its Method, Its Aids, Its Rewards, 1861; A History of Agriculture and Prices in England, 1866-1902; Manual of Political Economy, 1868; Adam Smith's Wealth of Nations (ed.) 1869; Cobden and Modern Political Opinion, 1873; The Protests of the Lords (ed.) 1875; Six Centuries of Work and Wages, 1884; First Nine Years of the Bank of England, 1887; The Economic Interpretation of History, 1888; The Industrial and Commercial History of England (ed. by A. G. L. Rogers) 1892.

ABOUT: Rogers, J. Reminiscences (ed. by J. E. T. Rogers); McCarthy, J. Portraits of the Sixties; The Times April 10, 1889, and October 14, 1890; Political Science Quarterly, 1889.

ROGERS, SAMUEL

(July 30, 1763-December 18, 1855), poet, banker, and patron of the arts was born at Stoke Newington, a village which now forms part of London, the son of Thomas and Mary (Radford) Rogers, one of eight children. Educated in private schools in Hackney and by private tutors, his original intention was to become a Presbyterian minister. At his father's request, however, he entered the family bank at an early age.

Poor health necessitated long vacations during which he read extensively, coming particularly under the influence of Johnson, Goldsmith, and Gray. The death of an elder brother in 1788 gave him a considerable share in the profits of the bank and five years later the death of his father left Samuel a controlling interest and an annual income of £5,000. After this a younger brother took over the active management of the business.

Rogers' literary career began with the publication of some short essays in the *Gentleman's Magazine* in 1781. His first volume of poems, *An Ode to Superstition*, was published anonymously in 1786, and in 1792, at the age of twenty-nine, he published his most successful work, *The Pleasures of Memory*, which had gone through fifteen editions by 1808. He was not a prolific writer, and although he enjoyed a considerable reputation as a poet among his contemporaries, he is remembered today for his associations far more than for his poems.

In 1803 he built a house in St. James Street, Westminster, which was furnished with fine antiques and housed his valuable art collection. When sold at Christie's after his death, this collection brought the sum of £50,000.

An excellent host, he entertained practically all the literary, social, and political lights of the first half of the nineteenth century. "Breakfast at Samuel Rogers'" was an institution of this period. Here gathered such men as Charles James Fox, Sheridan, Moore, Jeffrey, Byron, Lamb, Wordsworth, Lord Holland, and many more.

Alexander Dyce kept a detailed record of the anecdotes which he heard at these gatherings and published them in 1856. Rogers also kept notes on conversations which were published by his nephew in 1859. These valuable records give interesting and intimate sidelights on the social history of the period from 1790 to 1850, and in them lies the chief claim of Samuel Rogers to the attention of modern readers.

Perhaps among his greatest contributions to English literature should be listed the indirect ones of encouragement and assistance to men of talent. His generosity has been attested by many writers. Through his efforts a pension was obtained for Cary (translator of Dante); Wordsworth's sinecure as distributor of stamps was his doing; he aided Sheridan in his last days; many quarrels between literary men of the day were reconciled through his efforts. When someone complained to Campbell of Roger's caustic tongue, the former replied: "Borrow £500 of him and he will never say a word against you till you try to repay him."

His biting sarcasm was his greatest fault and at the same time one of his chief claims to conversational brilliance. Fanny Kemble said: " . . . he certainly had the kindest heart and unkindest tongue of anyone I ever knew." He excused this fault by saying that he had such a small voice that no one listened if he said pleasant things. That his actions spoke louder than his words is evidenced by the comparatively few unflattering judgments of his character recorded by his contemporaries. Henry Luttrell, contrasting the poetry and character of Rogers remarked that while his poetry was so pure and free from indelicacy, Rogers was the greatest sensualist he had ever known. Greville's obituary notice seems a fair judgment of Roger's character: "The poet Rogers died two days ago . . . I had known him all my life . . . but for some years past he had so great an aversion to me that I kept away from him . . . He was . . . very agreeable, though peculiar and eccentric; he was devoured by a morbid vanity, and could not endure any appearance of indifference or slight in society. . . . I was not a patient listener to him and that was what affronted him . . . He was undoubtedly a very clever man, with a great deal of taste and knowledge of the world . . . He was hospitable, generous, and charitable, with some weaknesses, many merits, and large abilities, and he was the last survivor of the generation to which he belonged."

While admitting that Rogers must be included among the poets of his time, practically all modern critics agree in placing him well toward the bottom of the list. Even in his own lifetime his popularity was not evenly sustained. When his poem *Italy* was first published anonymously in 1822 it failed to sell on its own merits. But a later edition, lavishly illustrated by Turner and Stothard, sold well enough to repay the £7,000 invested in the book.

SAMUEL ROGERS

Though living into the second half of the nineteenth century, Rogers was, literally speaking, of the eighteenth century. He never fully appreciated the romantic movement through which he lived, but remained subservient to the critical standards of classicism with its "good taste," elegance, and "improving sentiment." R. Ellis Roberts in *Samuel Rogers and His Circle* says: " . . . Rogers' own poetry, while it is careful, regular, smooth, finished, full of the most unexceptionable sentiment, is almost entirely devoid of life and personal truth. And it is in this last that we find the distinction between accomplished verse and real poetry."

The *Cambridge History of English Literature* remarks, "At the present time, it is probably a very exceptional thing to find anyone who, save in a vague traditional way, thinks of the author of *The Pleasures of Memory* as a poet at all; and even where that tradition survives, it is extremely questionable whether it is often supported by actual reading . . . He had tastes of various kinds: he might have been a greater poet if he had had less."

Perhaps one of the best examples of Rogers' good taste was his refusal of the laureateship when it was offered to him in 1850 on the death of Wordsworth.   D. C.

PRINCIPAL WORKS: *Poetry*—An Ode to Superstition, 1786; The Pleasures of Memory, 1792; An Epistle to a Friend, 1798; The Voyage of Columbus, 1810; Poems, 1812, 1814; Jacqueline, 1814; Human Life, 1819; Italy: Part I, 1822, Part II, 1828.

ABOUT: Clayden, P. W. The Early Life of Samuel Rogers; Clayden, P. W. Samuel Rogers and His Contemporaries (2 vols.); Dyce, A. Recollections of the Table Talk of Samuel Rogers; Powell, G. H. Reminiscences and Table Talk of Samuel Rogers; Roberts, R. E. Samuel Rogers and His Circle; Sharpe, W. (ed.). Recollections of Samuel Rogers; Edinburgh Review 104:73 July 1856; National Review 2:387 April 1856; Quarterly Review 167:504 October 1888.

ROMANES, GEORGE JOHN (May 20, 1848-May 23, 1894), Scottish biologist, was born in Canada at Kingston, Ontario, where his father was professor of Greek in the University. He was taken to England in the year of his birth and educated at Gonville and Caius College, Cambridge. An intimate friend and disciple of Charles Darwin, he did much to popularize Darwin's theories, which profoundly influenced his own work. He applied Darwin's theory to the evolution of the mind, and conducted researches comparing the mental faculties of animals and man; his results filled several volumes, of which *Animal Intelligence* is the best known. The lectures he delivered as special professor at Edinburgh (1886-90) and as Fullerian professor of physiology at the Royal Institution (1886-91) formed the substance of a treatise,

Darwin and After Darwin, which provoked much controversy.

In 1891 he founded the Romanes lecture at Oxford. He died in Oxford three days after his forty-sixth birthday. His widow survived him, together with their six children. A posthumous collection of his verse included a memorial poem to Darwin.

PRINCIPAL WORKS: A Candid Examination of Theism, 1878; Animal Intelligence, 1881; Mental Evolution in Animals, 1883; Jelly-Fish, Star-Fish, and Sea-Urchins, 1885; Mental Evolution in Man, 1888; Darwin and After Darwin, 1892-95; Mind and Motion: An Essay on Monism, 1895; Thoughts on Religion, 1895; Essays (ed. by C. L. Morgan) 1896. Poems, 1896.

ABOUT: Romanes, Mrs. G. J. (ed.). Life and Letters of George John Romanes; Nature May 31, 1894; The Times June 19, 1894.

ROMILLY, SIR SAMUEL (March 1, 1757-November 2, 1818), law reformer, was born in London, the son of a jeweler. Educated privately, he was called to the bar at Gray's Inn in 1783 and became king's counsel in 1800. In 1806 he became solicitor-general, was knighted, and took a seat in Parliament. An effective orator, he rendered valuable service by sponsoring a series of measures abolishing the death penalty for minor offenses. He committed suicide at sixty-one following the death of his wife. One daughter and six sons survived him. He was a friend of Jeremy Bentham.

To help bring about his reforms in the code of punishment, he wrote pamphlets. In his anonymous *Observations on a Late Publication Entitled "Thoughts on Executive Justice"* he exposed numerous irregularities in criminal law. Lord Brougham called his subsequent *Observations on the Criminal Law of England* a "beautiful and interesting tract." The grandson of a Frenchman, he spent much time in France and drafted for the use of the States-General a summary of the procedure in the House of Commons, which was translated by Mirabeau.

PRINCIPAL WORKS: A Fragment on the Constitutional Power and Duty of Juries Upon Trials for Libels, 1784; Observations on a Late Publication Entitled "Thoughts on Executive Justice" 1786; Thoughts on the Probable Influence of the French Revolution on Great Britain, 1790; H. F. Groenvelt's Letters Containing an Account of the Late Revolution in France (tr.) 1792; Observations on the Criminal Law of England, 1810; Speeches- in the House of Commons, 1820; Memoirs (ed. by his sons) 1840.

ABOUT: Romilly, Sir S. Memoirs; Romilly, Sir S. Speeches in the House of Commons (see Memoir by W. Peter); Transactions of the Huguenot Society, 1908.

ROSCOE, WILLIAM (March 8, 1753-June 30, 1831), biographer, poet, and essayist, was born at Old Bowling Green House, Mount Pleasant Liverpool, the only son of William Roscoe, market gardener and tavern keeper, and his wife Elizabeth.

WILLIAM ROSCOE

During his youth he went to school at Liverpool, worked at carpentry and painting on china, and helped in his father's garden. His mother encouraged his interest in books. When he was sixteen he was articled to a Liverpool attorney. While studying law he also studied French, Italian, and Latin. At twenty he was one of the founders of a Liverpool society for the encouragement of arts of painting and design. In 1774 he went into partnership with another Liverpool attorney.

His literary career began three years later with the publication of *Mount Pleasant,* a conventional and uninspired poem denouncing the slave trade. In the same volume, which won the praise of Sir Joshua Reynolds, was included an "Ode on the Institution of a Society of Art in Liverpool." For many years afterwards Roscoe continued to persevere at writing verse, and if he never rose to any poetic heights, he at least achieved a certain distinction with *The Butterfly's Ball and Grasshopper's Feast,* a poem written for the amusement of his youngest son, which so caught the fancy of the king and queen that they had it set to music for the young princesses, Elizabeth, Augusta, and Mary.

Roscoe's great work was a *Life of Lorenzo de' Medici,* written from material collected by his friend William Clarke in libraries of Florence. This biography was enthusiastically received in England and abroad and placed Roscoe among the most popular authors of the time.

In 1796, the year of the publication of *Lorenzo,* he gave up his practice as attorney, began adding more extensively to his large library, and resumed his studies of the classics; shortly afterwards he became a banker, studied botany, lectured on art, and started work on a biography of Leo X. This latter work met with less success than his *Lorenzo.* The Roman Church placed it on the *Index Expurgatorius,* Protestant reviewers complained that it was unfair to Luther, and nonsectarian critics found it verbose and pretentious. But both the *Lorenzo* and the *Leo X* did much to renew European interest in Italian literature and history and led to many similar works by later historians.

Throughout his life Roscoe was interested in social and political reforms, and when in 1806 he was elected a member of Parliament in the Whig interests, he spoke in favor of a bill to end slave trade and worked to support the claims of the Catholics. Thomas De Quincey wrote that in spite of Roscoe's boldness as a politician, there was "the feebleness of a mere belles-lettrist" in his views on many subjects.

In 1816 a bank of which he was a partner and manager suspended payments, and he sold his library, prints, and paintings to reimburse the creditors. Four years later, after some difficulty, he was declared bankrupt.

In 1824 he published a new edition of Pope's works which showed less than his usual penetration and research and led to a controversy with W. L. Bowles, who forcefully ended the argument with *Lessons in Criticism to William Roscoe.*

Roscoe married Jane Griffies, daughter of a Liverpool tradesman in 1781 and raised a family of seven sons and three daughters. Three of the children became poets and two others made names for themselves as authors.

In his seventy-first year he was elected an honorary associate of the Royal Society of Literature and later received the Society's gold medal. On March 8, 1853, his centenary festival was celebrated in Liverpool. P. G.

PRINCIPAL WORKS: *Poetry*—Mount Pleasant, 1777; The Wrongs of Africa, 1787; The Butterfly's Ball and the Grasshopper's Feast, 1807. *Biography*—The Life of Lorenzo de' Medici, 1795; The Life and Pontificate of Leo the Tenth, 1805; Illustrations Historical and Critical of the Life of Lorenzo de' Medici, 1822; *Miscellaneous*—A General View of the African Slave Trade, 1788; On the Origin and Vicissitudes of Literature, Science and Art, 1817; Observations on Penal Jurisprudence, 1819-25; The History of Liverpool, 1822; The Works of Alexander Pope, 1824; Monandrian Plants of the Order of Scitamineae, 1828.

ABOUT: Roscoe, H. Life of William Roscoe; Traill, J. S. Memoir of William Roscoe.

ROSCOE, WILLIAM CALDWELL (September 20, 1823-July 30, 1859), poet and essayist, was born in Liverpool, the son of WILLIAM STANLEY ROSCOE (1782-1843), a minor poet. He was a grandson of the historian William Roscoe. His mother was a sister of Mrs. Anne Marsh-Caldwell the novelist. Graduated from University College, London, he practised law for a time and in 1855 went into the business of slate-quarrying in Wales. He died of typhoid fever at Richmond in Surrey at the age of thirty-five.

During his short lifetime he published two tragedies, a number of minor poems, and numerous essays contributed mainly to the *National Review,* edited by his brother-in-law, Richard Holt Hutton, the critic. These works were collected after his death. Hutton enthusiastically sponsored his work, but in the opinion of George Saintsbury "it has no 'inevitableness' whatever and no very special poetic qualities of any kind." He was rated a discriminating if not profoundly penetrating critic.

PRINCIPAL WORKS: Eliduc, 1846; Violenzia, 1851; Poems and Essays (ed. by R. H. Hutton) 1860; Poems and Dramas (ed. by his daughter E. M. Roscoe) 1891.

ABOUT: Roscoe, W. C. Poems and Essays (see Memoir by R. H. Hutton)

ROSE, HUGH JAMES (June 9, 1795-December 22, 1838), leader and writer in the Oxford Movement, was born in the parsonage of Little Horsted in Sussex. Educated at Trinity College, Cambridge, he held two Sussex curacies and subsequently was rector of Hadleigh, Suffolk, from 1830 to 1833. He became rector of Fairsted, Essex, in 1834; perpetual curate of St. Thomas's, Southwark, in 1835, and principal of King's College, London, in 1836. But his career was brief; a chronic sufferer from asthma, he died at the age of forty-three in Florence, Italy, where he sought health.

He is remembered chiefly for having initiated the Catholic Revival at a meeting in his Hadleigh rectory in July 1833. The *British Magazine of Ecclesiastical Information* was founded by him in 1832, and he was its editor until 1836. His literary activities were not many; he made some contributions to Christian apologetics (mostly sermons and lectures), and earned a slight reputation as a Greek scholar. His *Discourses on the State of the Protestant Religion in Germany* provoked severe criticism from the tractarian E. B. Pusey, and is his best known work.

PRINCIPAL WORKS: Discourses on the State of the Protestant Religion in Germany, 1825; A New General Biographical Dictionary, Projected and Partly Arranged by the Late Hugh James Rose (Vol. I ed. by Henry John Rose, vols II-XII ed. by T. Wright) 1850.

ABOUT: Burgon, J. W. Lives of Twelve Good Men; Morse-Boycott, D. Lead, Kindly Light; London Gentleman's Magazine, 1839.

ROSE, WILLIAM STEWART (1775-April 30, 1843), translator and poet, was a son of the noted statesman George Rose. Through his father's influence, he entered Parliament after leaving Eton and was from 1800 to 1824 reading clerk of the House of Lords and clerk of the private committees. He traveled extensively on the Continent, lived a year in Venice, and was married to a Venetian lady. In his forty-ninth year, failing in health, he retired from his parliamentary post with an annual pension of £1,000. He died in his sixty-eighth year.

It was at the suggestion of Sir Walter Scott that he undertook his major work, a verse translation of *The Orlando Furioso* of Ariosto. Of this work *Blackwood's Magazine* said: "Never was such close, scrupulous fidelity of rendering associated with such light, dancing elegance of language." This became the standard translation of Ariosto and was reprinted in Bohn's Library. A translation of *Partenopex* was in the opinion of Samuel Rogers his best work, but in it the author was accused of plagiarizing Scott's *Marmion*.

PRINCIPAL WORKS: Amadis de Gaul (tr. from the French version of N. de Herberay) 1803; Partenopex of Blois (tr. from the French of M. Le Grand) 1807; Letters From the North of Italy: Addressed to Henry Hallam, 1819; The Orlando Innamorato (tr. into prose from the Italian of F. Berni) 1823; The Orlando Furioso (tr. into English verse from the Italian of L. Ariosto) 1823-31; Rhymes, 1837.

ABOUT: Rose, W. S. The Orlando Furioso (see Memoir by C. Townsend in 1858 Bohn reprint); Blackwood's Magazine June, 1824.

ROSS, SIR JAMES CLARK (April 15, 1800-April 3, 1862), Scottish polar explorer, rear admiral, and writer, was born at Balsarroch, Wigtonshire. He sailed with his uncle, Rear-Admiral Sir John Ross, on two voyages in search of a Northwest passage, in 1818 and in 1829-33, and during the second voyage himself discovered the north magnetic pole (1831). In between these two expeditions he made four Arctic voyages with W. E. Parry (1819-27). His greatest achievement was as commander of a notable expedition to the Antarctic in 1838-43, when he discovered Ross Sea, Ross Island, the Ross Ice Shelf, Weddell's Island, and Victoria Land. He penetrated to latitude 78° 9′ which was not again reached for sixty years. In recognition of his discoveries he was given many honors, including knighthood. His final voyage was in search of Sir John Franklin in 1848. He died at Aylesbury shortly before his sixty-second birthday. By his wife, Anne Coulman, he had four children.

He contributed to the literature of maritime discovery and travel with an account of his four-year voyage to the Antarctic.

WORK: A Voyage of Discovery and Research in the Southern and Antarctic Regions, 1847.

ROSS, SIR JOHN (June 24, 1877-August 30, 1856), Scottish Arctic navigator, rear admiral, and narrator of his own explorations, was born at Balsarroch in Wigtonshire. Between 1812 and 1817 he commanded vessels mainly in the Baltic and North Seas. In

1818 he sailed in search of a Northwest passage through Davis's Strait, but accomplished little more than a re-exploration of Baffin's Bay. On a second voyage to the Arctic in 1829-33, however, he discovered and surveyed Boothia Peninsula, surveyed a large part of King William Land and the Gulf of Boothia, and determined that the desired passage did not lie in that direction. The important geographical and scientific discoveries of this voyage brought him knighthood. From 1839 to 1846 he was consul at Stockholm, Sweden. In 1851 he commanded one of the vessels sent to rescue Sir John Franklin. He died in London at the age of seventy-nine. Twice married, he had one son.

He contributed to the annals of voyage and discovery with accounts of his two expeditions to the Arctic. Other works included controversial pamphlets (one of them in answer to an attack by Sir John Barrow) and a few minor treatises on navigation.

PRINCIPAL WORKS: A Voyage of Discovery for the Purpose of Exploring Baffin's Bay and a Northwest Passage, 1819; Narrative of a Second Voyage in Search of a Northwest Passage, 1835; Memoirs and Correspondence of Admiral Lord de Saumarez, 1838.

ROSSETTI, CHRISTINA GEORGINA (December 5, 1830-December 29, 1894), poet, was the youngest of the remarkable Rossetti brothers and sisters, born, like them all, in Charlotte (now Hallam) Street, London, in a dreary and only semi-respectable neighborhood mostly inhabited by foreigners. Her father was a political refugee from Naples and author of numerous works in Italian on "the inner—Masonic—meaning" of Dante, who earned his living by teaching Italian; her mother, who was a governess before her marriage, was half-English, being the sister of Byron's physician, Dr. John Polidori.

Christina was taught entirely at home, by her mother, and never attended a school. She was slow in learning to read, but precocious as a writer, and like all the family was bilingual from infancy. They all wrote as easily in Italian as in English. She was the prettiest of the children, with hazel eyes and light brown hair, and as a child was high-spirited and playful. In later life her constant invalidism and her extreme piety gave a melancholy tinge to her entire existence.

Her earliest volume of poems was privately printed by her maternal grandfather when she was only twelve, as was another volume when she was seventeen. When the little group of young artists calling themselves the Pre-Raphaelites, of which her brother Dante Gabriel was the leading spirit, started in 1849 a magazine called *The Germ*, which lived for four numbers, several of Christina's poems appeared in it, her first actual publication.

CHRISTINA ROSSETTI

From 1850 the older Rossetti's health failed badly and he was threatened with blindness and unable to teach. The family had always lived in straitened circumstances, but now they were faced with actual poverty. The only wage-earner was the younger brother, William Michael, who was a civil clerk on a small salary. Christina gave Italian lessons, and on one occasion at least was resident for weeks at a time with the family of one of her pupils, though she was never actually a governess as was her older sister Maria. (Maria, to sum her up succinctly, was Christina without the beauty and the genius; she too was a religious devotee, and ended her years as an Anglican nun.) Later Christina and her mother twice established day-schools, one in London, one in Somersetshire, but neither was very successful.

With the exception of this brief sojourn in Somersetshire in 1853, undertaken partly for the father's health just before his death, practically all of Christina Rossetti's life was passed in north London. In later years she made one short trip to Italy with her mother and her brother William Michael, and another in the same company to France. Her life might have been prolonged could she have lived in Italy, but she shrank from the uprooting of her lifetime habits. In childhood she sometimes visited her Polidori grandparents when they lived in the country, but nearly all her life was purely urban, in curious contrast to the fresh, keen feeling for nature in her poems.

Christina, like her mother and her sister, was an overwhelmingly devout member of the Church of England, attached to the so-called "High Church" faction. Religion made up most of her existence, as it did a good part of her writings. Though she could hardly be described as a bigot, her religious bent kept her mental and emotional life in a very narrow channel. She refused, for example, to read "impious" books, and even went so far as to paste strips of paper over passages that she considered irreligious in Swinburne's poetry—though she continued to be friendly to Swinburne himself. Her devoutness must also take the blame for the wreckage of her two love-affairs. In early youth she was attracted to, and finally became engaged to, James Collinson, a minor member of the Pre-Raphaelite group. He had been a convert to Roman Catholicism, but had returned to the Anglican Church in order to win Christina's consent to their marriage. After a few years he reverted to the Roman Catholic persuasion and Christina promptly broke the engagement.

In this case, though she was fond of Collinson and sufficiently affected by him to faint when later she met him unexpectedly on the street, her innermost feelings were not seriously involved. It was different with her later love for Charles Bagot Cayley, the translator and scholar. There is no doubt that she loved Cayley deeply, and all her life long. But here again religion intervened. Cayley had no theological affiliations at all, and Christina refused to marry a man who could not share with her her profoundest preconceptions. (A modern psychologist might go farther than this, and point out Christina's excessive devotion to her mother, and her obvious terror of sexual love and of the responsibilities of adult life.) They remained friends, and his death in 1883 was a severe blow to her. Her whole body of poetry shows how permanently and extensively he occupied her thoughts. But she was adamant in the face of their religious differences.

This turning upon itself of her inner life led in the end to an existence of actual seclusion, when she saw few people outside her family and "took the veil in every way except in outward act." Had she not felt herself unworthy, she would probably have followed her sister in the outward act as well. Another reason, of course, for this recluse's life was her continued ill health. Never strong and frequently ill, in 1873 she became afflicted with the rare Graves' Disease, and never was really well again. She died finally of cancer, soon after her sixty-fourth birthday.

Christina Rossetti, however, was no gentle nun by temperament. She had a caustic tongue on occasion, and showed plenty of that variety of courage which is expressed in steadfastness rather than in daring. The thought of death obsessed her; she wrote of it, spoke of it, dwelt on it always in her thoughts. How much of her other-worldliness was suppression of a naturally passionate spirit was evidenced by her long delirium in her last illness, which at times approached mania. Like Cowper, she became possessed of the horrible thought that she was damned —and such thoughts do not come to those, however pious, who do not know what fiery impulses they have felt and controlled. The outward woman was shy, introspective, patient, and humble. The inner personality escapes only in her poems.

Virginia Moore has justification for saying that "from Sappho to Christina Rossetti no woman wrote poetry of the first water." If she has poetic affiliations, they are more with the American Emily Dickinson than with any other. Edmund Gosse was inept in comparing her with the metaphysical poets of the seventeenth century; she has neither their crabbedness nor their chill. She is mystical and visionary, and yet at the same moment she is realistic and sensuous. Her images have all the bright solidity of her brother Dante's, though with an overtone which Dante Gabriel Rossetti, for all his anti-science and superstition, never attained.

Christina Rossetti's mind was fixed and set early in maturity; in forty years her art grew very little, remained unchanged, neither progressing nor declining. It is impossible to tell from the context whether a given poem was written in first youth or in late middle age. Throughout, her preoccupations in poetry were love, religion, children, and nature, and above all, death. Her work is prevailingly melancholy, though she herself was capable of moments of lightness and joy in pure beauty. She was associated in some small measure with the Pre-Raphaelite group, but she was no satellite and her poetry does not belong to it. She was supremely a lyrist, with a special vocation for the sonnet: some of her sonnet sequences are among the finest in English, finer than her brother's, finer than Elizabeth Barrett Browning's *Sonnets From the Portuguese,* worthy of comparison with that greatest master of the English sonnet, Shakespeare.

Her prose, mostly Anglican tracts and books of devotion, is gravely lovely; she can make even didacticism take on a beautiful garment. Her work is uneven, but never mediocre; her bad things are completely bad, never commonplace. Her best work is melodious, strong, and simple, with a flavor that marks it as peculiarly her own.

One is either enamored forever with Christina Rossetti's poetry, or one can find nothing in it at all; she is not an acquired taste in poetry. What she said of her first sight of the Alps applies very well to the affect of her poems on many readers: "their sublimity impressed me like want of sympathy, because my eyes were unaccustomed." It is unfortunate that, thanks to anthologies, she is best known by a handful of poems—particularly "When I Am Dead, My Dearest" and "Goblin Market," while some of her most splendid lyrics, such as "From House to Home" and "Monna Innominata," tend to be neglected. There was, rather incongruously, a vein of sprightliness in her genius that enabled her to write a book of poems for children, and even, in her girlhood, to join her brothers in the game called *bouts rimés,* where all the rhymes are given and one must make up verses using them in the same order.

Fruitful though Christina Rossetti's literary life was, in the sense that she continued to write almost to the time of her death, very much of this output was consumed by devotional prose. Her poetic legacy therefore is rather slender. There will probably be no discoveries of unpublished works of hers; her brother William Michael collected and edited every remaining manuscript he could find after her death. But she left enough to establish her reputation as one of the finest lyrists and one of the supreme sonneteers in the English language. She is not to be rated as a "woman poet": her genius, like all authentic genius, was irrespective of sex. She was a woman, of a type not unusual in her time. But above all, she was a poet.

M. A. deF.

PRINCIPAL WORKS: *Poetry*—Goblin Market and Other Poems, 1862; The Prince's Progress and Other Poems, 1866; Sing Song (juvenile) 1872; A Pageant and Other Poems, 1881; Verses, 1893; New Poems (ed. by W. M. Rossetti) 1896. *Fiction* —Commonplace, 1870; Maude: A Story for Girls, 1897. *Devotional Prose*—Speaking Likenesses, 1874; Annus Domini, 1874; Seek and Find, 1879; Called to Be Saints, 1881; Letter and Spirit, 1882; Time Flies, 1885; The Face of the Deep, 1892; Angels, 1910.

ABOUT: Bell, M. Christina Rossetti: A Biographical and Critical Study; Benson, A. C. Essays; Ford (Hueffer), F. M. Memories and Impressions; Rossetti, C. G. Family Letters (ed. W. M. Rossetti); Rossetti, W. M. Some Reminiscences; Sandars, M. F. The Life of Christina Rossetti; Shove, F. Christina Rossetti: A Study; Stuart, D. M. Christina Rossetti; Thomas, E. W. Christina Georgina Rossetti; Bookman (London) 79:179 December 1930; Contemporary Review 138:759 December 1930; Cornhill Magazine 69:662 December 1930; Yale Review 20:428 Winter 1931.

ROSSETTI, DANTE GABRIEL (May 12, 1828-April 10, 1882), poet and painter, was christened Gabriel Charles Dante, his godfather being his father's patron Charles Lyell, father of the famous geologist. He was the second child and older son of Gabriele Rossetti, the Neapolitan exile and writer of esoteric verse, and of the half-English Frances Lavinia (Polidori) Rossetti.

Gabriel, as he was called by his family, was a precocious child, writing his first verses at five or six. Taught in the beginning by his mother, who had been a governess, and early fluent in his father's tongue(the older Rossetti was professor of Italian at King's

College and gave private lessons as well), he was sent to preparatory school at eight, and then to the King's College School. He could not be said to have been an exceptional student; from the beginning his imagination outran his reason, and when he was barely fourteen he left school and began to prepare for a professional career as a painter. His grandfather Polidori privately printed his first juvenile volume, the ballad of *Sir Hugh the Heron,* when he was only fifteen. He had also begun his translation of Dante as early as 1845, though it did not appear until 1861. But throughout his life he was pre-eminently a painter, and his poetry was made subservient to his primary art. He published only two volumes of poems in his lifetime, and comparatively few appeared even in magazines.

For four years Rossetti was a student in F. S. Cary's Drawing Academy, known as Sass's. In 1846 he enrolled at the Royal Academy, but his impatience with what he considered outworn methods kept him from obtaining any particular distinction. His uncle paid for him to take lessons with Ford Madox Brown, but when this young but already distinguished artist set him to painting still life he quit in disgust and set up his own studio, first with Holman Hunt, then alone.

From this early association with Hunt, John Millais, Thomas Woolner, and a few other very young men just beginning careers as painters and sculptors, grew the famous Pre-Raphaelite Brotherhood, a loosely formed group whose fundamental purpose was to restore to art the naturalism and attention to realistic detail which they felt had been the characteristics of painters before Raphael. In essence it was a healthy revolt from the stiff prettiness of the official art of their day. The group spread to include others in its fringes, and had an immense effect on the history of British painting, which is outside the province of consideration of Rossetti as a writer. It may be mentioned, however, that an assignment to paint a mural in the Oxford Union, an enterprise which enlisted Burne-Jones and William Morris as well as Rossetti, led to the acquaintance of Swinburne, then a university student. Ruskin also was early attracted to the movement, and with practical benefits to Rossetti, for he undertook to buy at current prices all of Rossetti's paintings, as they were produced, that appealed to him—an arrangement that guaranteed the artist a sure if not a steady income.

In 1850 Rossetti's friend Walter Deverell, ranging the streets for acceptable models, reported the presence of a beautiful assistant in a millinery shop. This was Elizabeth Eleanor Siddall, who became model for many of Rossetti's most famous paintings, including every one of his presentations of Dante's Beatrice. Elizabeth Siddall ("Lizzie") had talents of her own as both painter and poet, and she was very lovely, with the auburn hair, languorous eyes, and swanlike neck which have become known as the "Rossetti type." The young couple fell in love and became engaged in 1851, though there was no possibility of their marriage on Rossetti's income at that time. They were not married, in fact, until 1860.

The story of Dante Gabriel Rossetti and Elizabeth Siddall is a painful one. She was tubercular, and she was afflicted with what approached real melancholia. She was also fiercely chaste, and their relations were strictly what in those days was called "proper." The consequence is that by the time they were financially able to marry, time had worn Rossetti's passion out. He had acquired a mistress, the lovely Fanny Hughes, and Lizzie had become for him simply an object of aching pity. In those times there was no one to warn the victim of tuberculosis against motherhood, and their two years of marriage were a succession of miscarriages, with their only child who came to full term dead at birth. It is true they were old and familiar friends; she was "Guggums" and he was "Gug," and they played together sometimes like pathetic children. But there is evidence in some of the unpublished poems she left behind her that her frustrated and embittered love had turned to hate. In any event, in February 1862 she was found dead, after a quarrel, from an overdose of laudanum, to which she had long been addicted; and whatever the arguments at the time, there is no doubt that her death was suicide.

DANTE GABRIEL ROSSETTI

In an agony of remorse, Rossetti buried with her, wrapped in her beautiful hair, the manuscript volume of his poems. Seven years later, though he himself could not face the ordeal, he had her body exhumed and recovered the book. It was published the following year.

After Lizzie died Rossetti could no longer endure the dank studio they had shared on the bank of the Thames. He bought a large house in Cheyne Walk which at first he shared with Swinburne and George Meredith —a combination doomed to brief concord— and intermittently with his brother William Michael until the latter's marriage. Here, with prosperity coming too late, he collected old furniture, blue china, and Japanese prints. His fame as a painter had been growing, and now it was doubled by his sudden reputation as a poet.

But his slow decline had begun. From the beginning Dante Gabriel Rossetti had been moody, self-centered, given to bursts of passion. He began taking chloral, and soon advanced to the deadlier combination of chloral and whiskey. In his youth he had been perforce and also by temperament highly abstemious; part of the Pre-Raphaelite creed was opposition to loose Bohemianism. In 1871 Robert Buchanan, under a pseudonym, published that calculated piece of critical calumny, *The Fleshly School of Poetry*. Rossetti answered it at first in a dignified manner, but soon he was involved in a bitter quarrel, and this rapidly developed into a real persecution mania. He had squabbled before with picture dealers and customers and fellow-artists (though no one was ever less jealous, professionally, or quicker to lend a helping hand to a young aspirant). Now he saw enmity in the most absurd quarters: Charles Dodgson ("Lewis Carroll") had caricatured him (he fancied) in *The Hunting of the Snark*, and Browning, his old hero, in *Fifine at the Fair*. Only one person he could not quarrel with: his brother, probably the most devoted and patient brother of literary history.

Finally, this same brother had to conclude that Gabriel was insane. He was removed to the home of his friend Dr. Hake and there attempted suicide with laudanum. Not so successful as Lizzie, he was saved by his old friend Ford Madox Brown, who when summoned had thoughtfully brought a surgeon with him. Rossetti was for a time partially paralyzed from this experience. For a while he went from friend to friend on extended visits, but his morbid suspicion, irritability, and egotism wore out even the most sympathetic. New friends came to take their places —Watts-Dunton, William Sharp, and Hall Caine, who lived with him on Cheyne Walk in his last year. He continued to take chloral,

and his delusions of persecution (a tendency inherited, perhaps from his father, who had a touch of it) became settled. His life was a series of recriminations and estrangements; he grew increasingly eccentric and unfit for social contracts.

Yet all this time, not only did he continue to paint with perfect competence (though his best painting was all before 1871), but suddenly he experienced a renascence of poetic ability, a great rekindling of genius after a silence of almost twenty years. It eventuated in his second volume of poems in 1881.

In December of that year, by heroic effort, he gave up the chloral habit at last. But it was too late for his exhausted body. By the kindness of a friend, a country house was put at his disposal at Birchington, near Margate, and he died and was buried there the following April.

The strange beetling brow and deep-set grey eyes of Dante Gabriel Rossetti are familiar from his self-portraits. His hair, dark in later life, was originally auburn. From earliest manhood he wore a full beard, as was the fashion of the time.

Strange to say, in view of the enameled beauty of his poetic descriptions, Rossetti detested travel and had no taste for natural scenery. He was a true Cockney, born like all the younger members of his family on Charlotte Street, and seldom leaving London. Only twice, and years apart, did he visit Belgium, and he never saw Italy, though Italian was as much his language as English was.

His was a personality based on instinct, congenitally anti-scientific and anti-rational, superstitious, and impulsive. He was equally removed from the devout orthodoxy of his sisters and the skepticism of his brother; though he was formally a Christian, religion was to him a thing of dark magic and thrilling ancient legend. He is probably greater as a poet than as a painter (and this is saying much), but his poetry is peculiarly that of a painter, made up of sumptuous color and static form. His memory was phenomenal, and his critical judgment sound and full of common sense. Though he was often rude and selfish, he was capable of self-denial and disinterested kindness, and he must not be judged by the sad wreck that life made of him in his later years.

All his life he was an extremist, and in the end he became something not far removed from a maniac. But he was also, in a very limited field, a superb poet. The strongest influence on his work was that of Keats, but to the imagery and richness of Keats he added a note of mystery all his own. From his earliest contributions to *The Germ*, the short-lived magazine published by the Pre-Raphaelite Brotherhood, to the last unpublished poems collected by his brother, his strange genius is evident. The best of his ballads have the authentic ring of actual folksong, and many of his sonnets, particularly in *The House of Life,* are magnificent. There is a note of mediaevalism in almost all he wrote, but it is never quaint or ornamental; it springs from his preoccupation with mediaeval literature and from his affinity with the mediaeval spirit. The man who wrote "The Blessed Damozel" and "Sister Helen" would be famous if he had never touched a brush or a palette. **M. A. deF.**

PRINCIPAL WORKS: Early Italian Poets (translations) 1861 (republished as Dante and His Circle, 1874); Poems, 1870; Ballads and Sonnets, 1881; Collected Works (ed. by W. M. Rossetti) 1886.

ABOUT: Benson, A. C. Rossetti; Bickley, F. L. The Pre-Raphaelite Comedy; Burdett, O. The Beardsley Period; Caine, H. My Story; Caine, H. Recollections of Rossetti; Ford (Hueffer), F. M. Rossetti: A Critical Essay on His Art; Hunt, V. The Wife of Rossetti; Mégroz, R. L. Dante Gabriel Rossetti: Painter Poet of Heaven in Earth; Rossetti, D. G. Family Letters (ed. with Memoir by W. M. Rossetti); Rossetti, W. M. Dante Gabriel Rossetti As Designer and Writer; Sharp, W. Dante Gabriel Rossetti: A Record and a Study; Symons, A. Studies in Strange Souls; Waugh, E. Rossetti: His Life and Works; Winwar, F. V. Poor Splendid Wings; Quarterly Review 260:84 January 1933; Saturday Review 152:144, 177, 208, 232, 261 August 1 to 29, 1931.

ROSSETTI, WILLIAM MICHAEL (September 25, 1829-February 5, 1919), biographer and editor, was the younger brother of Dante Gabriel and the older brother of Christina Rossetti, born like them in north London, of an exiled Italian father and a half-Italian mother. He went to a private school with his brother, to whom he was all his life devoted, and again with him to King's College day school. He remained there until 1845, when through the influence of Sir Isaac Goldsmid, a member of the council of King's College, where Rossetti's father was professor of Italian, he became a clerk in the Excise Office, later known as the Inland Revenue Board. He remained in the civil service until 1894, from 1869 on being senior assistant secretary, and from 1888 to 1905 acted for them also as referee of pictures.

For more than twenty years he was the chief support of his family, and maintained a home for them all. His closeness to his brother, however, kept him always on the fringes of the artistic and literary world. He was made the secretary of the young group of artists who called themselves the Pre-Raphaelite Brotherhood, and editor of their magazine *The Germ.* He became, later on, art critic for two magazines in succession, and contributed articles on art to many others. He wrote articles on art also for the *Encyclopaedia Britannica,* and was connected with the *Oxford English Dictionary* and the Early English Text Society. He assisted his brother in editing Anne Gilchrist's *Life of*

WILLIAM MICHAEL ROSSETTI

Blake, and in his own capacity became an outstanding editor of Shelley (issuing the first critical edition), of Walt Whitman, and of his brother and sister. A friendly and peaceable man, he was the acquaintance of nearly every painter and writer of his time in England.

In 1874 he married Lucy, the daughter of Ford Madox Brown the painter. She also painted and wrote a life of Mary Shelley. They had three daughters and two sons, the younger of whom died in infancy. From 1885 onward Mrs. Rossetti was an invalid, and she died in 1894. Her husband never remarried, but became the devoted companion of his daughters, as he had been of his brother and sisters. He traveled much, chiefly in Italy, once as far as Australia for his daughter's health. He was a republican and a Free Thinker; his *Democratic Sonnets,* written in 1881, were not published until 1907 because Dante Gabriel Rossetti feared they would imperil his brother's government position.

There is a myth that William Michael Rossetti was a great poet suppressed by his sacrifices for his brother and younger sister. Nothing could be less true. He was a cultured, high-minded man, methodical, patient, amiable, and industrious, with great ability but very little original talent. He outlived all his immediate family, dying at almost ninety. Competent, dull, and loyal, he was "the last of the Rossettis," and in his steady normality in many ways the strangest of that highly gifted family. **M. A. deF.**

PRINCIPAL WORKS: Fine Art: Chiefly Contemporary, 1867; Swinburne's Poems and Ballads: A Criticism, 1867; Notes on the Royal Academy Exhibition (with A. C. Swinburne) 1868; Lives of Some Famous Poets, 1878; Life of Keats, 1887;

Dante Gabriel Rossetti As Designer and Writer, 1889; Memoir of Dante Gabriel Rossetti (in Family Letters) 1895; Pre-Raphaelite Diaries and Letters, 1900 (in part); Some Reminiscences. 1906; Democratic Sonnets, 1907; Memoir of Christina Rossetti (in Family Letters) 1908; Dante and His Convito, 1910.

ABOUT: Burdett, O. The Beardsley Period; Ford (Hueffer), F. M. Memories and Impressions; Rossetti, W. M. Some Reminiscences; Living Age 300:637 March 8, 1919; Publications of the Modern Language Association 48:312 March 1933.

ROUTH, MARTIN JOSEPH (September 18, 1755-December 22, 1854), ecclesiastical scholar, was born at South Elmham, Suffolk, the son of a clergyman. For sixty-three years —from 1791 until his death at the age of ninety-nine—he was president of his alma mater, Magdalen College, Oxford. By careful research in his leisure time he produced a number of works which marked him as a scholar of remarkable learning and taste. He edited, notably, *Reliquiae Sacrae*, a collection of the writings of ecclesiastical authors of the second and third centuries. Through this work he served, in the words of Cardinal Newman, "to report to a forgetful generation what was the theology of their fathers." The *Cambridge History of English Literature* says that "he set the tone for the Oxford writers." It was his famous maxim "always to verify your references."

PRINCIPAL WORKS: Plato's Euthydemus and Gorgias (ed.) 1784; Reliquiae Sacrae (ed.) 1814-48; Scriptorum Ecclesiasticorum (ed.) 1832; Tres Breves Tractatus, 1853.

ABOUT: Burgon, J. W. The Lives of Twelve Good Men; The Times December 25, 1854; The Times January 1, 1855.

RUSKIN, JOHN (February 8, 1819-January 20, 1900), art critic and sociological and miscellaneous writer, was born at 54 Hunter Street, Bloomsbury, London, only child of John James Ruskin, wine merchant, and Margaret (Cox) Ruskin, both of Scottish descent. The parents were strict evangelicals; the child was from the first intended for the Church; and his early upbringing, with few toys and many whippings, was cloistered and gloomy. The chief feature in his mother's instruction of him consisted in long and assiduous reading of the Bible (large portions of which he had to commit to memory), with Scott's novels and Pope's Homer as light relief. In 1823 the increasing prosperity of the wine merchant, as partner in the firm of Ruskin, Telford and Domecq, enabled him to move into a larger house at Herne Hill. It was his practise to make extensive posting-tours every summer to solicit orders, taking the boy with him; so that the young John soon knew England and southern Scotland from end to end and had viewed the castles and mansions of the gentry everywhere. From the age of ten onwards he had

tutors for classics, French, mathematics, and drawing; at fifteen he attended a day-school at Camberwell, and, somewhat later, went to lectures at King's College, London. A tour to the Rhineland and Switzerland in 1833 gave him his ever-memorable first sight of the Alps. From early infancy he had begun to draw and write verse, diaries, and stories; and his receipt (in 1832) of a copy of Rogers' *Italy* with Turner's vignettes, was the foundation of his lifelong interest in that artist.

The year 1836 brought a visit from M. Domecq and four daughters, with one of whom, Adèle, Ruskin fell deeply in love; but his avowals caused only amusement. That autumn he was entered as a gentleman-commoner at Christ Church, Oxford. His university career included the winning of the Newdigate Prize for poetry in 1839; but the next year his always delicate frame showed menacing signs of consumption, and he was taken away to Switzerland, Italy, and Leamington, returning cured to graduate with an honorary double-fourth in 1842.

As early as 1836 Ruskin had been aroused to "black anger" by adverse comment on Turner in *Blackwood's Magazine*; the next year his father bought him his first example of Turner's work; he had had as long as he could remember the run of Mr. Windus' Turner collection at Tottenham; and on June 12, 1840, he met the great painter in the flesh. Now, under the stimulus of his huge admiration for Turner, he set about writing a book to be called "Turner and the Ancients," designed chiefly to prove the superiority of modern landscapists to such masters as Salvator Rosa, Poussin, and Claude, and to refer the attention of painters to a close and direct study of nature. The book appeared in May 1843 as *Modern Painters,* "by a Graduate of Oxford," Ruskin's father advising the suppression of the author's name on the score of his extreme youth. *Modern Painters,* Vol. I created something like a revolution in taste. It was approved by men like Wordsworth, Rogers, Tennyson, Sydney Smith, and Sir Henry Taylor; the authorship was an open secret, and the young writer was cultivated and sought after by the *cognoscenti*. Volume II appeared in 1846, Volumes III and IV in 1856, and Volume V in 1860. The whole work, written in gorgeous and often impassioned prose, is an encyclopedic conspectus (with notable gaps) of the whole art of painting, and develops an elaborate (if often inconsistent) aesthetic philosophy, founded on study not only of pictures but of natural forms. Among its main theses (baldly stated, for brevity) are that art is far more than a mere matter of line and color, and that the highest art is that which conveys the most and best ideas; that natural forms must be recognized "as the work and the

JOHN RUSKIN

gift of a Living Spirit greater than our own"; and that good art is only produced by true and pious men.

In 1843 the family moved into a big country house at Denmark Hill, to the south of London, and, except during the brief period of his marriage, this remained Ruskin's home until the death of his mother in 1871. In 1844 he went to Switzerland and Paris; and in 1845 to Pisa, Lucca, and Venice—where he was much impressed by the then neglected Tintorettos at the Scuola di San Rocco. Always strongly swayed by the opinion of his parents, he allowed a bride to be chosen by them. On April 10, 1848, he married Euphemia Chalmers Gray, daughter of a Perth lawyer, and settled at Park Street, Mayfair, in the heart of fashionable London. He had an ample allowance from his father; his wife was a notable beauty and loved society; and at this period the two joined a good deal in the social round. But there was some deep-seated maladjustment; apparently the marriage was never consummated, and in 1854 it was annulled, on the petition of the wife, Ruskin offering no opposition. In July 1855 Mrs. Ruskin married the painter, J. E. Millais.

From the appearance of the second volume of *Modern Painters* Ruskin had become a recognized power in the world of culture. In 1848 he turned his attention to architecture, producing the next year *The Seven Lamps of Architecture*, an elaborate work illustrated with engravings after his own drawings, the leading idea of which was the reliance of architecture on moral and spiritual values. In 1851 he defended Millais and Holman Hunt against strictures in *The Times*, and wrote the pamphlet, *Pre-Raphaelitism*, in defence of their principles. *The Stones of Venice* came out in three volumes between 1851 and 1853, its central thesis being "the dependence of all human work or edifice for its beauty on the happy life of the workman." From 1855 to 1859 he issued annual notes on the Royal Academy exhibitions; he was almost a dictator in art opinion, and his views quickly raised or lowered prices in the sale-rooms. He carried out the colossal labor of arranging 19,000 Turner drawings for the National Gallery; he lectured up and down the country; he took an active part in the courses at the Working Men's College, Great Ormond Street; and withal found time for frequent foreign travel.

Ruskin's meeting with Carlyle in 1846 was the beginning of a warm friendship, and it may well have been the force of Carlyle's personality, superimposed on his own strongly marked moralistic nature, that turned him from art to economics. *Unto This Last* (1860) and *Munera Pulveris* (1872) set out to demolish the current *laissez-faire* economics of the Manchester school. The first began in the *Cornhill Magazine* and the second in *Fraser's Magazine*, but in each case the editor was forced by indignant subscribers to stop the series. Yet Ruskin did not preach revolutionary socialism: he remained a Tory. The things which caused the outcry were his emphasis on "the dignity and moral destiny of man" and his advocacy of such measures as national education, old-age pensions, and better housing for the working classes. Social amelioration became the passion of his life, and he worked to further it not only by his pen but by princely charity and the organization of a community called the Guild of St. George. His father died in 1864, leaving him £157,000, and in course of time he gave away the whole of this great fortune, living comfortably enough in his later years on book-royalties amounting to some £4,000 a year. He had hundreds of pensioners; he started Octavia Hill on working-class house management; he wrote, from 1871 to 1884, a series of monthly letters to "the workmen and laborers of Great Britain," called *Fors Clavigera*. The Guild, started in 1871, was an elaborate community-system founded on a belief in "the nobleness of human nature, the majesty of its faculties, the fulness of its mercy, and the joy of its love." Members were to give a tithe of their possessions and to subscribe to an eight-point creed. Machines were to be banished except where utterly necessary; classes were to be distinguished by dress; and so on. The organization was to be hierarchical, not socialistic. It was a dream which had no practical outcome, save in a few offshoots like the Sheffield Art Museum.

After the death of his mother in 1871 Ruskin bought Brantwood, a beautifully situated house at Coniston, looking over the lake of that name to the fell known as the Old Man. From 1870 to 1884 he was for long periods holder of the Slade professorship of fine arts in the University of Oxford. He had rooms in Corpus Christi College (of which he was made honorary fellow); his lectures were thronged; he established a drawing-school, made munificent gifts, and poured out book after book of vigorous criticism. His labors were several times interrupted by periods of mental illness, one of which (in 1872) followed on the refusal of an offer of marriage by Rosa La Touche, a girl of twenty-four whom he had known from her childhood. In November 1878 the American painter, Whistler, sued him for libel, having been accused of "throwing a pot of paint in the face of the public" and was awarded damages of one farthing (half a cent).

Ruskin's final resignation of the Slade chair in 1884 was brought about by his indignation at the establishment in Oxford of a physiological laboratory in which vivisection was to be permitted. He lived thenceforward quietly at Brantwood, cared for devotedly by his cousin Joan, Mrs. Arthur Severn. In *Praeterita* (1885-89) he wrote a clear, easy, humorous account of his early days. His eightieth birthday brought him sheaves of congratulations, including addresses from Oxford and from a group of distinguished persons headed by the Prince of Wales. On January 18, 1900, he became a victim to an epidemic of influenza, and died two days later.

"In his central or later-central years," wrote Alice Meynell, "John Ruskin was a thin and rather tall man . . . active and light, with sloping shoulders; he had a small face with large features, the eyebrows, nose, and under-lip prominent; his eyes were blue, and the blue tie . . . made them look the bluest of all blue eyes. He had the *r* in the throat, the *r* of the Parisians, which gives a certain weakness to English speech; and in lecturing he had a rather clerical inflection."

Ruskin, like Carlyle, takes rank among the major prophets of the Victorian era. In this period he was, in the words of Frederic Harrison, "the writer who poured forth the greatest mass of literature upon the greatest variety of subjects, . . . who in the English-speaking world left the most direct and visible imprint of his tastes and thoughts." Many societies were founded to further his teachings, and an Oxford college bears his name. His strict evangelical upbringing could not but play a large part in the shaping of his thought; and though from his middle thirties onwards he was free of exact doctrinal theology, religion in the broad sense never ceased to be the moving impulse of his being. From this fact derives much of the burning, and often intolerant, zeal with which he advocated his opinions; and from it also the occasional absurdities into which his art-criticism fell, as when he educed his theory of the connection between moral worth and artistic excellence. He was over-fond of founding a philosophic or aesthetic theory on flimsy premises; he rushed into judgment on deep questions with inadequate learning; his dicta are highly inconsistent one with another. Yet in the whole history of art-criticism he stands out as a giant. In this field fashion rules more than elsewhere, and in our time of "pure aesthetic" his theories are temporarily out of favor. But they are theories founded on great imaginative penetration, on true analytical power, on considerable executive ability in draughtsmanship, and on a close study of nature that extended to such things as cloud forms and mineralogy; and, pruned of their extravagances, they must take their place in the canon. On the economic side he was shocked and appalled by the uglification brought about by the industrial revolution and by the tyranny of machinery over the souls of men. He did not see that if the machine was temporarily a bad master it might be made into a good servant; but on the moral side his conclusions were sound, and most of the social reforms he advocated are now commonplaces of political thought in free countries like Britain and America. His style was highly-colored, poetic and eloquent, inclined to sin through over-elaboration, but in his last works he saw this vice and corrected it.   H. B. G.

PRINCIPAL WORKS: *Art Criticism*—Modern Painters (5 vols.) 1843-60; The Seven Lamps of Architecture, 1849; Pre-Raphaelitism, 1851; The Stones of Venice (3 vols.) 1851-53; The Elements of Drawing, 1857; The Political Economy of Art, 1857; The Two Paths, 1859; Lectures on Art, 1870; Aratra Pentelici, 1872; The Eagle's Nest, 1872; Ariadne Florentina (7 pts.) 1873-76; Val d'Arno, 1874; The Art of England, 1884. *Sociological and Miscellaneous*—Unto This Last, 1862; Sesame and Lilies, 1865; The Ethics of the Dust, 1866; The Crown of Wild Olive, 1866; Time and Tide by Weare and Tyne, 1867; The Queen of the Air, 1869; Fors Clavigera (96 letters) 1871-84; Munera Pulveris, 1872. Praeterita (28 pts.) 1885-89.

ABOUT: Benson, A. C. Ruskin: A Study in Personality; Collingwood, W. G. The Life and Work of John Ruskin; Harrison, F. John Ruskin; Meynell, A. John Ruskin; Ruskin, J. Fors Clavigera, and Praeterita; Wilenski, R. H. John Ruskin; Williams-Ellis, A. The Tragedy of John Ruskin; Wise, T. J. and Smart, J. P. A Complete Bibliography of John Ruskin.

RUSSELL, LORD JOHN (August 18, 1792-May 28, 1878), statesman and author of political writings, was born in London, the third son of John Russell, sixth Duke of Bedford. Educated at Edinburgh University, he became a Whig leader in Parliament and successfully sponsored, among other measures, the Reform Bill of 1832. He served as colonial secretary in Lord Melbourne's administration, foreign secretary under Palmerston, and prime minister from 1846 to 1851 and again from 1865 to 1866. He was created Earl Russell in 1861.

During his busy political career and after his retirement in 1866 he devoted much time to literary work. His political biographies, correspondence, speeches, and histories form an important contribution to the chronicle of Whig politics. He also wrote tragedies, essays, and tales which are forgotten. According to Thomas Seccombe, "His literary skill is most marked in his epistolary writing, and his speeches and writings abound in happy and telling phrases."

PRINCIPAL WORKS: Life of Lord William Russell, 1819; Essays on the English Constitution, 1821; Memoirs of the Affairs of Europe, 1824; Letters of the Fourth Duke of Bedford (ed.) 1842-45; Memoirs, Journal, and Correspondence of Thomas Moore (ed.) 1853-56; Memorials and Letters of C. J. Fox (ed.) 1853-57; Selections From the Speeches of Russell and From His Despatches, 1870; The Latter Correspondence of Lord John Russell (ed. by J. Russell) 1925.

ABOUT: Reid, S. J. Lord John Russell; Russell, Lord J. Recollections and Suggestions; Russell, J. (ed.). The Latter Correspondence of Lord John Russell; Walpole, Sir S. Life of Lord John Russell.

RUSSELL, WILLIAM CLARK (February 24, 1844-November 8, 1911), novelist of sea life, was born in New York, of English parents. His father was Henry Russell, well-known singer and composer of "Cheer, Boys, Cheer" and other popular songs. The author's mother, Isabella Lloyd, was a relative of the poet Wordsworth and herself a verse-writer. Educated at private schools, Russell spent eight years of hardship and privation in the British merchant service, retiring at twenty-two. He worked at journalism for a while and from the age of thirty onward devoted himself to the writing of popular novels of maritime adventure based on his youthful experiences. The most successful of his books was *The Wreck of the Grosvenor*, ranked among famous sea novels. He produced in all fifty-seven volumes, including biographies of three noted seamen and a book of naval ballads. Partially as a result of his works, conditions were improved in the merchant service. His only son, Sir Herbert Russell (b. 1869), became a writer on naval subjects.

PRINCIPAL WORKS OF W. CLARK RUSSELL: *Novels*—John Holdsworth: Chief Mate, 1875; The Wreck of the Grosvenor, 1877; Round the Galley Fire, 1883; The Frozen Pirate, 1887; The Romance of a Midshipman, 1898. *Biographies*—Dampier, 1889; Nelson, 1890; Collingwood, 1891. *Verses*—The Turnpike Sailor: or, Rhymes on the Road, 1907 (reprinted in 1911 as The Father of the Sea).

ABOUT: Russell, W. C. The Father of the Sea (see Memoir by W. J. Ward); The Times November 9, 1911.

RUSSELL, SIR WILLIAM HOWARD (March 28, 1820-February 10, 1907), the first and one of the most famous of war correspondents, was born in Ireland in the parish of Tallaght, County Dublin, and educated at Trinity College, Dublin. He made his great reputation in the Crimean War of 1854-55. His outspoken, uncensored despatches to *The Times*, describing mismanagement and privation in the British Army, inspired the work of Florence Nightingale in organizing hospital service and contributed to the fall of the Aberdeen ministry. Subsequent assignments covered by Russell for *The Times* included the Indian Mutiny of 1858, the American Civil War (1861-62), and the Franco-German war of 1870. He founded the *Army and Navy Gazette* in 1860 and was its editor until his death at eighty-six.

The literary works of Russell were largely collections of his journalistic letters from various parts of the world. In addition to his war diaries, they included accounts of tours with the Prince of Wales through the Near East in 1869 and through India in 1875-76, as well as his own travels in the United States and Canada.

PRINCIPAL WORKS: The War From the Landing at Gallipoli to the Death of Lord Raglan, 1855-56; My Diary in India, 1860; My Diary North and South During the Civil War in America, 1862; My Diary in the East During the Tour of the Prince and Princess of Wales, 1869; Hesperothen: Being a Record of a Ramble in the United States and Canada, 1882; My Diary During the Last Great War, 1873; The Great War With Russia, 1895.

ABOUT: Atkins, J. B. The Life of Sir William Howard Russell; see also Russell's own works.

"RUTHERFORD, MARK." See WHITE, WILLIAM HALE

ST. JOHN, CHARLES GEORGE WILLIAM (December 3, 1809-July 12, 1856), naturalist, was a grandson of the famous Viscount Bolingbroke of the reign of Queen Anne. His father, a younger son, was a general, his mother a daughter of the Earl of Craven. He was educated at Midhurst School, where he showed very early his overwhelming interest in nature. In 1828 he became a clerk in the treasury, but nothing could have been more irksome to one of his temperament. His uncle, Lord Bolingbroke, took pity on him and lent him a shooting-box in Sutherland. There St. John buried himself, and devoted his entire time to a study of the animals and birds of the region. In 1834 he married Ann Gibson, who sympathized with and assisted him in his pursuits. They had three sons and one daughter. In 1844 it first occurred to St. John that his notes on Scottish wild life might be publishable, and he began sending them to the *Quarterly Review.* His books followed the line of these articles. In December 1853 he suffered a sudden stroke of paralysis, and never rallied from it, though he did not die until a year and a half later at Woolston. He was a born field naturalist, and natural history was his primary concern, his interest in sport being entirely subsidiary to it.

PRINCIPAL WORKS: Short Sketches of Wild Sports and Natural History of the Highlands, 1846; A Tour in Sutherlandshire, 1849; Natural History and Sport in Moray, 1863.

ABOUT: St. John, C. G. W. Wild Sport and Natural History of the Highlands (see Life by M. G. Watkins); A Tour in Sutherlandshire (see Recollections by his son); Natural History and Sport in Moray (see Memoir by C. Innes).

SALA, GEORGE AUGUSTUS (November 24, 1828-December 8, 1895), journalist, was born in Manchester Square, London, the youngest son of Augustus John James Sala and his wife, Henrietta Catherine Florentina Simon. His paternal grandfather left Rome, his native city, and went to England about 1776 to assist in the productions of ballets. His mother was an actress and opera singer. His father died in 1828.

Through some mistreatment by a nurse when he was seven years old, Sala lost both his sight and hearing, and did not regain them until a year and a half later. At an early age and even during the affliction, he evidenced a remarkable precocity. He attended school in Paris when he was eleven, and was later apprenticed to a miniature painter.

At fifteen he began making his own way in the world, as clerk, draughtsman, and scene painter. At nineteen he was doing book and commercial illustrations, with promising success. He taught himself to etch, worked at engraving, and hoped to emulate George Cruikshank.

Casting around for other means to fortune, he became editor of a small weekly paper called *Chat.* In 1851 he sold a humorous article, "The Key to the Street," to Charles Dickens for *Household Words;* and from then on, for the next five years, he contributed a weekly article or story to that magazine. Many of these early writings were at first attributed to Dickens, and they show Sala as an avid reader and a facile writer, a man who saw with the eyes of a painter, a good "mixer" who was equally at home with Bohemians, disreputable people, and members of Society.

In the spring of 1856, following the Crimean war, Dickens sent Sala to Russia for a series of articles for *Household Words.* Sala collected his Russian articles into book form under the title of *A Journey Due North.* Most of his subsequent books were made up of contributions to magazines and newspapers.

During the next few years he sold sketches and stories to *All the Year Round, Household*

GEORGE AUGUSTUS SALA

Words, Cornhill, and the *Illustrated Times,* and wrote a column, "Echoes of the Week," for the *Illustrated London News* and then for the Sunday *Times.* With Edmund Yates he managed and edited *The Train,* which had but a short run; and he edited, for a time, *The Welcome Guest,* in which appeared his most popular sketches of London, "Twice Round the Clock." In 1860 he established and edited *Temple Bar,* and it was in this periodical that his best novel, *The Strange Adventures of Captain Dangerous,* appeared.

For nearly twenty-five years, beginning in 1857, Sala was engaged in writing two articles a day for the *Daily Telegraph;* and except when traveling, he maintained this difficult schedule. The *Saturday Review* repeatedly ridiculed Sala for his bombast, his vague liberalism, his assortment of half-understood information, his excessive egotism, his careless reasoning, and his "earnest turgidity"; but he pleased a wide public and earned a magnificent salary. In 1867 James Hain Friswell, in *Modern Men of Letters,* described Sala as "a Bohemian writer of a bad school, but yet a brave man; one that has done very little good, and yet one full of capabilities for good; a writer of sound English and a scholar, and yet a driveler of tipsy, high-flown, and high-falutin' nonsense . . . utterly careless of his own reputation, of the dignity of letters, and of what is due himself."

This and more caused Sala to bring suit for libel. The court ordered Friswell to pay £500 damages; but that did not stop criticism and Matthew Arnold and others repeated Friswell's attack in better humored tones.

Sala's first commission as a special foreign correspondent for the *Daily Telegraph* took him to the United States in 1863 to do a series of articles on the Civil war. These articles, collected in book form under the title of *My Diary in the Midst of War,* shows him as increasingly egotistic and inaccurate. Next he traveled in Algiers in the train of Napoleon III, was with Garibaldi's army in north Italy, in Venice during the Austrian evacuation, in Paris for the exhibition, in Rome when the Italian troops ended Papal rule there, at the opening of the German parliament in 1871, in Spain for the close of the Carlist war, and in St. Petersburg after the murder of Alexander II. He traveled in Australia and India and America and, wherever he went, wrote endless articles for the *Daily Telegraph.*

During the last years of his life, creditors so pressed him that he had to sell his large library and many of his choice pieces of porcelain bric-a-brac. He was twice married. Before his death—from nervous exhaustion—he was received into the Roman Catholic Church.   P. G.

PRINCIPAL WORKS: *Travel*—A Journey Due North, 1858; Barbary by a Round-About Route, 1866; From Waterloo to the Peninsula, 1867; Rome and Venice, 1869; A Journey Due South, 1885; Right Round the World, 1888. *Essays*—Gaslight and Daylight, 1859; Twice Round the Clock, 1859; My Diary in the Midst of War, 1865; Living London, 1883; London Up-to-Date, 1895. *Humor*—Lady Chesterfield's Letters to Her Daughter, 1860; Breakfast in Bed, 1863; Yankee Drolleries, 1870. *Novels*—The Baddington Peerage, 1860; The Seven Sons of Mammon, 1862; Quite Alone, 1863; The Strange Adventures of Captain Dangerous, 1863. *Biography*—Robson: A Sketch, 1864; William Hogarth, 1866; Things I Have Seen and People I Have Known, 1894; Life and Adventure, 1895. *Miscellaneous*—Works of Charles Lamb, 1868; Wat Tyler, M. P.: An Operatic Extravaganza, 1869; The Thorough Good Cook, 1895.

ABOUT: Sala, G. A. H. Things I Have Seen and People I Have Known; Sala, G. A. H. Life and Adventure; Friswell, J. H. Men of Letters; Arnold, M. Friendship's Garland.

SANDAY, WILLIAM (August 1, 1843-September 16, 1920), theologian, was born in Nottingham, his father being a wealthy breeder of sheep and cattle. He was educated at Repton School, and at Balliol and Corpus Christi Colleges, Oxford. He became a fellow of Trinity College in 1866, and lectured there until 1869, when he was ordained priest. Until 1876 he held successively three college livings, then became principal of Hatfield Hall, Durham. In 1877 he married Marian Hastings, who died in 1904; they had no children.

Sanday in 1882 became professor of exegesis at Oxford, and, since the emolument was small, the next year he became also a fellow and tutor of Exeter. From 1895 to 1919, when he resigned, he was Lady Margaret professor of divinity. He was a modernist whose life was devoted to a "scientific study" of the Gospels. All his later volumes were part of a projected but never completed life of Christ.

PRINCIPAL WORKS: The Authorship and Historical Character of the Fourth Gospel, 1872; The Gospels in the Second Century, 1876; The Oracles of God, 1891; Outlines of the Life of Christ, 1905; The Life of Christ in Recent Research, 1907; Christologies Ancient and Modern, 1910; Spirit, Matter, and Miracle, 1916; The New Testament Background, 1918.

ABOUT: Church Times September 24, 1920; Oxford Magazine October 1920.

SANGSTER, CHARLES (July 16, 1822-December 19, 1893), Canadian poet, was born at Kingston, Ontario (then called Upper Canada). His father was a working shipwright in the Navy Yard, and the family was poor. The boy had very little formal education, receiving only a common school training. When he left school he went to work as a clerk in the Ordnance Office, also connected with the Navy Yard at Kingston. He held this position from 1838 to 1849. He had begun to write poems, however, which appeared in the Canadian papers and magazines, and he was eager to make his living by writing. Finally he secured a position, first as reporter and then as sub-editor, on the Kingston *Whig,* and was with this paper for another eleven years, from 1850 to 1861.

For a few years thereafter he tried to make his way as a free-lance writer, but though his two volumes of poems were widely read in Canada his writing brought him little financial return. In 1867 he secured a civil service post in a government office in Ottawa, the capital, and remained in this position, which gave him some leisure for writing, until just before his death. He resigned because of ill health and returned to his native town, Kingston, dying there at seventy-one.

Sangster's reputation in his native land is greater than the intrinsic merit of his poems would seem to justify. At the time of his first publication he was one of very few poets writing in Canada on Canadian themes. He had a deep feeling for his country and for its natural beauty, and though his work now seems stilted and old-fashioned, it had much felicity of phrase and simple love of nature. The manuscripts of his poems are preserved today in the library of McGill University as a part of Canadian literary history.

PRINCIPAL WORKS: The St. Lawrence and the Saguenay and Other Poems, 1856; Hesperus and Other Poems and Lyrics, 1860.

SAVAGE, MARMION W. (1803-May 1, 1872), Irish novelist, was the son of a clergyman of the Established Church in Ireland. He was educated at Trinity College, Dublin, receiving his B.A. in 1824. For several years he earned his living as a government official. In 1856 he went to London to edit *The Examiner,* and never returned to Ireland, dying at Torquay. He was twice married, and had one son by his first wife, but no children by the second, who was a Miss Hutton.

Savage's novels were light, but full of wit and vivacity, and well written. His first work, *The Falcon Family,* was a caustic satire on the extremists among the Irish Nationalists. *The Bachelor of the Albany* was his best work. His novelette, *Clover Cottage,* was dramatized by Tom Taylor, and performed in 1859.

PRINCIPAL WORKS: The Falcon Family, 1845; The Bachelor of the Albany, 1847; My Uncle the Curate, 1849; Reuben Medlicott, 1852; The Woman of Business, 1870.

ABOUT: Athenaeum May 11, 1872; London Times May 6, 1872.

SCHREIBER, LADY CHARLOTTE GUEST (May 19, 1812-January 15, 1895), Welsh scholar, was born at Uffington House, Lincolnshire, the daughter of Albermarle Bertie, the ninth Earl of Lindsey, and Charlotte (Layard) Bertie. In 1818 her father died, and three years later her mother married a cousin, the Reverend Peter Pegus.

The girl's education was acquired largely through her own efforts, as her mother was indulgent and not much interested, and her stepfather was uncongenial. An eager reader, she obtained a good knowledge of French, German, and Italian, and she studied, under her brother's tutor, Latin, Greek, Hebrew, and Persian. In addition she learned copperplate etching.

In 1833, at the age of 21, she married Sir John Guest, a widower of 49, the owner of one of the greatest iron-works in the country. It was situated in South Wales, and soon after her marriage Lady Guest mastered Welsh, and edited and translated *The Mabinogion,*

Celtic tales and legends taken from old Welsh manuscripts. She also took interest in the eisteddfods, festival congresses of Welsh bards.

Upon the death in 1852 of Sir John, Lady Guest, the mother of ten children, assumed control of the ironworks, for which she had previously kept elaborate accounts, and managed the business until her personal responsibilities, two or three years later, interfered.

In 1855 she married Charles Schreiber, a fellow of Trinity College, Cambridge. From this time her life was uneventful except for her enthusiasm for collecting. Possibly her fondness for fine and rare china, porcelain, and ceramics came originally from her husband, but, once established, it became an all-absorbing passion, and she spent years ransacking shops in Holland, France, Germany, Italy, Spain, and Turkey. When her husband died in 1884, she presented a large collection of some two thousand of her finest pieces to the South Kensington Museum.

Her interests extended to the collecting of other objects. She presented a collection of fans and fan-leaves to the British Museum in 1891, and offered prizes for fan-painting. In the same year she was presented with the freedom of the Fanmaker's Company. Shortly after the publication of her beautiful book on fans she began to issue a lavish book on playing-cards, of which she had made a collection. She died before the book had been completely published, and provided in her will that the British Museum be given from her collection such specimens as it did not already own. In 1892 she was presented with the freedom of the Company of Makers of Playing Cards.

Lady Schreiber was a woman of great energy and ability, and delighted in turning her powers to various applications. Naturally a good business-woman, she wrote of herself as a young lady, "I have so schooled myself into habits of business that it is more congenial to me to calculate the advantage of half per cent commission on a cargo of iron than to go to the finest ball in the world." And she speaks of her varied interests with enthusiasm: " . . . I delight in the contrast of the musty antiquarian researches, and the brilliant fêtes and plodding counting house, from all of which I seem to derive almost equal amusement." Her son describes her as extremely controlled and calm, "with a deep sense of moral duty," which, however, evidently did not restrain her from making a good bargain when she could use ignorance or need to do so. In 1877-1880 she assisted in the Turkish Compassionate Fund to aid Turkish women and children, and she was noted for her kindnesses to London cabmen, for whom she erected a shelter at Portland Place

LADY CHARLOTTE SCHREIBER

and for whom she knitted after she had become blind.

Her literary importance rests upon *The Mabinogion*, a valuable collection to Celtic tales and legends, taken largely from *The Red Book of Hergest*, a Welsh manuscript. The material from which she edited and translated her collection includes the most valuable mass of Welsh tradition, and is a mine for the student of Celtic folk-lore. Her translation, described by W. Lewis Jones as "singularly graceful," while it is not the most exact as to detail, has remained standard for nearly a century.   R. W. W.

PRINCIPAL WORKS: *Curiosities*—Fans and Fan Leaves, 1888-90; Playing Cards of Various Ages and Countries, 1892-95. *Editor*—(South Kensington Museum) Schreiber Collection of English Porcelain, etc. [a catalogue]; *Memoirs*—Lady Charlotte Schreiber's Journals, 1911. *Translator (and editor)*—The Mabinogion, 1838-49, 1877; The Boy's Mabinogion, 1881.

ABOUT: Schreiber, Lady C. Journals (see Introduction by Montague Guest); Athenaeum May 6, 1911; Nation 93:27 September 7, 1911; The Times January 16, 1895.

SCORESBY, WILLIAM (October 5, 1789-March 21, 1857), travel writer, was born near Whitby. His father before him was an Arctic navigator, and at eleven the boy accompanied him on a whale-fishing trip—being sent back to school, however, until 1803. He then worked regularly with his father, and by 1806 was chief officer of the ship. For a few months in that year he studied natural philosophy and chemistry at Edinburgh University. In 1807 he enlisted as a common seaman to fight the Danes, but was discharged the same year. Always interested in science, he kept observations of the natural history of the polar regions, collected plants, and drew snowflakes seen through the microscope. In 1809 he returned for a while to Edinburgh, and in 1811 married a Miss Lockwood, who died in 1822, leaving two sons. Rather surprisingly, in 1823 he decided to become a clergyman. He entered Queen's College, Cambridge, and received his B.A. and was ordained in 1825. He continued his scientific studies, and in 1824 became a Fellow of the Royal Society. In 1827, he was curate. Soon after he became a chaplain of the Mariners' Church in Liverpool, and remarried; his second wife died in 1848. In 1832 he was at Bedford Chapel Exeter; in 1834 he received his B.D. degree and in 1839 his D.D.; and the same year he became vicar of Bradford. A six months' trip to the United States having failed to restore his injured health, he resigned, and revisited the United States and Canada. He was married for the third time in 1849. In 1857 he went to Australia to make magnetic observations for the government, but the trip finally ruined his health, and he died at Torquay soon after his return.

His book on the Arctic was for many years a standard authority on its subject.

PRINCIPAL WORKS: The Arctic Regions, 1820; Memorials of the Sea, 1833; Magnetical Investigations, 1839-52; My Father, 1851; The Franklin Expedition, 1856.
ABOUT: Scoresby-Jackson, R. E. Life of William Scoresby.

SCOTT, HUGH STOWELL ("Henry Seton Merriman") (May 9, 1862-November 19, 1903), novelist, was born at Newcastle-on-Tyne. He was educated at the Loretto School, Musselburgh, and abroad at Vevey and Weisbaden. In 1880 he became a clerk in the insurance offices of Lloyd's of London. He longed to get away from the commercial life and to write and travel, and his novels were written in this ultimately successful hope. However, his family strongly disapproved of his artistic ambitions (although his maternal grandfather had been a marine painter), and therefore, after his first anonymous novel, all his books were written under the pseudonym of "Henry Seton Merriman." Even when he was a popular novelist, many persons never knew his right name, and imposters often claimed his books as theirs.

In 1889 he married Ethel Frances Hall; they had no children. By 1892 he was earning enough to leave Lloyd's and live by writing, and from 1894 on, he was one of the most popular of the current romanticists and romancers. His best book is *The Sowers;* and he is generally good in works of history and adventure; but his later novels tended to become unpleasantly sentential, stereotyped, and artificial.

PRINCIPAL WORKS: Young Mistley, 1888; The Phantom Future, 1889; Prisoners and Captives, 1891; From One Generation to Another, 1892; With Edged Tools, 1894; The Grey Lady, 1895; The Sowers, 1896; Raden's Corner, 1898; The Isle of Unrest, 1900; The Velvet Glove, 1901; Barlasch of the Guard, 1902; The Last Hope, 1904.
ABOUT: Scott, H. S. Memorial Edition (see Preface by E. F. Scott and "S. G. Tallentyre").

SCOTT, LADY JOHN (1810-1900), Scottish poet, born Alicia Ann Spottiswoode, was the author of both words and music of many popular Scotch songs, the best known of which is "Annie Laurie." Others of her compositions include "Douglas Tender and True," "Durisdeer," "The Comin' o' the Spring" and "Ettrick." The dates of her life are uncertain, sometimes being given as 1801-1890; at any rate she lived nearly the entire span of the nineteenth century, dying at the age of ninety or ninety-one. Her works are no longer seen except in anthologies of verse or song.

SCOTT, MICHAEL (October 30, 1789-November 7, 1835), Scotch novelist, was born at Cowlairs near Glasgow, the fifth and youngest son of Alan Scott, a merchant of Glasgow.

Between 1801 and 1805 he studied at the university in Glasgow, and a year later tried his fortunes in Jamaica. He acted as manager for some plantations there, and met a Mr. Hamilton who is the Aaron Bang of Scott's *Tom Cringle's Log.* In 1810 a Kingstown business firm employed Scott, and his subsequent traveling through the West Indies produced a wealth of experience for his first book. On a visit to Scotland in 1818 he married Margaret Bogle, daughter of a Scotch merchant; and soon afterwards returned to Jamaica as a partner in his father-in-law's firm.

Without revealing his identity as the author, he began contributing to *Blackwood's* magazine (1829) installments of the brilliant story of West Indian life that was later republished under the title of *Tom Cringle's Log.* The intermittent papers met with immediate success. Their stamp of authenticity, the author's keen observation, his zest and his humor, caught and held the popular imagination. Samuel Taylor Coleridge declared they were "most excellent," and planned to write a poem with Tom Cringle as the hero, in the manner of Goethe's *Faust.* The *London Quarterly* reviewer called the *Log* "the most brilliant series of magazine papers of the time," and John Wilson wrote that "Cringle is indeed a giant."

Scott's second story, *The Cruise of the Midge,* also appeared serially in *Blackwood's* and without his name. Like the first story, this one offers a wealth of incident and spirited writing; but it was not quite so popular as the *Log,* and that was doubtless due in part to the author's rather consistently forced humor.

The two novels were published in book form anonymously in Paris in 1836, and have been reprinted many times since. Scott preserved his incognito so successfully that no one, not even Mr. Blackwood, knew his identity until after his death. There was much speculation as to the authorship of the novels, and they were ascribed to John Wilson, Captains Chamier and Marryat, and others.

Scott died in Glasgow at the age of sixty-six, leaving a large family. Although he was no recluse, little is now known of him personally. A friend, some years after his death, described him as a "quiet, easy-going man"; and for further knowledge of him one must turn to his books.

Sir George Douglas, in *The Blackwood Group,* wrote: "If he possessed much genius, Michael Scott had little art. The effect of his fine pictures is not cumulative; each is alike revealed, as it were, by a powerful flash, and the result is that they obliterate one another . . . Quite towards the close, both books display some light tendency to 'drag,' but in this respect the *Cruise* is the worse transgressor . . . On the whole such fine books are they both that to criticize either is deserv-

edly to incur the imputation of being spoiled with good things."

Hugh Walker, in *The Age of Tennyson,* declared: "[Scott] would be not unworthy to be bracketed with Marryat if a man could be judged by parts of his book without regard to the whole; but unfortunately *Tom Cringle's Log* and *The Cruise of the Midge* are little more than scenes and incidents loosely strung together. Perhaps Scott was influenced by the *genius loci;* at any rate his books resemble the *Noctes Ambrosianae* in so far as they are the outlet to every riotous fancy and every lawless freak of the writer's humor." P. G.

WORKS: *Novels*—Tom Cringle's Log, 1836; The Cruise of the Midge, 1836.

ABOUT: Douglas, G. The Blackwood Group; Walker, H. The Age of Tennyson.

SCOTT, ROBERT (January 26, 1811-December 2, 1887), lexicographer, was born in Devonshire, the son of a clergyman. In his early childhood the family moved to Cumberland. He was educated at Shrewsbury and at Christ Church, Oxford, receiving his B.A. in 1833. In 1835 he was made fellow of Balliol, and was a tutor there until 1840, though he was ordained in 1835. He held a college living in Cornwall from 1845 to 1856, was prebendary of Exeter from 1845 to 1866, and rector of Rutland from 1850 to 1854. In 1854 he was made master of Balloil with the avowed object of opposing the unorthodoxy of Benjamin Jowett, the great Hellenist. He was professor of exegesis at Oxford from 1861 to 1870, and then dean of Rochester from 1870 to his death. He was twice married, in 1840 to Mary Harriet Bough, daughter of a rear-admiral, who died in 1845, and in 1849 to Mary J. A. Scott, daughter of a major, and his cousin.

Although Scott published two volumes of sermons, his name is remembered for his collaboration with H. C. Liddell in the preparation of the great Greek-English Lexicon which is still the standard in its field.

PRINCIPAL WORKS: A Greek-English Lexicon (with H. C. Liddell) 1843; Twelve Sermons, 1851; University Sermons, 1860.

ABOUT: Guardian December 14, 1887.

SCOTT, SIR WALTER (August 15, 1771-September 21, 1832), Scottish poet, novelist, historian, antiquarian, editor and biographer, was born in Edinburgh, son of Walter Scott, writer to the signet, Calvinist, lover of antiquities, and the original of the elder Fairford in *Redgauntlet;* and Anne (Rutherford) Scott, descended on her mother's side from a long line of warriors.

His childhood was what Polonius would have called "tragical-comical-historical-pastoral." The fourth surviving child in a family of twelve children, the first six of whom had died, Scott was the victim of a mysterious illness resulting in a life-long lameness that doctors now think was infantile paralysis. He was sent to recuperate at Sandy Knowe in the heart of the Border country, and his earliest memories are of that time and his lying wrapped in the skin of a freshly killed sheep (to give him strength) on the floor of his grandfather's primitive farmhouse. A symbolic start in life for one who was to be both lawyer and writer: two professions in which sheepskin has played an important rôle. There were days like poems of the Greek pastoral poets when Scott was put out on the hillside with the sheep and the shepherd would summon the nurse by blowing a loud whistle. His grandfather told Scott stirring legends of the old moss troopers, stories of his own Border ancestry, and "many a tale of . . . merry men all of the persuasion and calling of Robin Hood and Little John."

Scott's career at Edinburgh High School was distinguished, not for scholarship, but for his skill in climbing the steep "Kittle Nine Stanes" of the castle rocks despite his lameness, and for his already incomparable story-telling. To James Ballantyne he would say, "Come and slink over beside me, Jamie, and I'll tell you a story." In bad weather he kept students about the fire listening to his tales. Blacklock, the blind poet introduced him to the *Faerie Queen*. But Percy's *Reliques* influenced him the most. Before he was ten, he had begun collecting ballads and bound them into several volumes.

Five years later, after attending classes at the College for awhile, and spending holidays climbing to Arthur's Seat and Salisbury Crags with John Irving, where the two friends would recite "such wild adventures as we were able to devise," a severe illness resulted in Scott's leaving the College and spending much time by himself. Taine says "he continued to limp and became a reader." But so complete was his recovery that, although still lame, he walked from 20 to 30 miles a day.

While studying for the bar, 1788-1792, Scott joined several clubs in Edinburgh, "heard the chimes at midnight," "was the first to enter a row and the last to leave it," and had his heart broken. In 1792, the same year in which he was called to the bar, he began "raids" into Liddesdale, exploring ruins of old castles and peels, collecting "ancient riding ballads," and generally studying the lay of the land.

In 1796 Scott made his. first appearance in print with a thin quarto of verse, translations of Burger's "Leonore" and "Der Wilde Jäger." His appointment as sheriff-deputy in 1799 gave him more time for collecting ballads. A year later he met Richard Heber, the great book collector who helped him in medieval studies. In 1802, the first two volumes of *Border Minstrelsy* were published,

SIR WALTER SCOTT

Scott's first serious claim for the laurels of poetry. The third volume followed in 1803.

Scott's literary career was determined in 1805 by the success of *The Lay of the Last Minstrel*. Using the goblin pranks of Gilpin Horner in a ballad was suggested to him by the Countess of Dalkeith. A recital of Coleridge's then unpublished *Christabel* gave him the idea of using irregular octosyllabic verse, a "mescolanza of measures" that saved *The Lay* from being monotonous. This same year, he became a secret partner in the Border Press. His partners were two brothers, James Ballantyne, an excellent proof-reader and literary advisor but a careless business man, and John, shifty and fond of intrigue. The Ballantynes amused and flattered Scott and for this weakness he was to pay dearly.

During the next eight years, Scott wrote enough poetry to make three or four poetic reputations, besides contributing huge quantities to the *Edinburgh Review*, helping start, and then writing for, its rival, the *Quarterly*, finishing a brilliant and monumental edition of Dryden (1808) and an edition of Swift (1814), together with an enormous amount of other miscellaneous writings.

Marmion, for which Constable offered one thousand guineas before seeing it, was published in 1808. Of the battle-scene that Scott composed while galloping on horseback along the sands of Portobelle, Lang said: "I verily believe [it] is the battle-piece of all time, better even than the stand of Aias by the ships in the Iliad."

Two years later, *The Lady of the Lake* was to put money in the pockets of half of Scotland because the rush of visitors to Loch Katrine sent up the price of post chaises. Earls and commoners called their daughters "Margaret" in tribute to the Lady. Twenty thousand copies of the poem were sold in one year.

In 1812 Scott's popularity as a poet suffered an eclipse when Byron's *Childe Harold* appeared. Also a host of imitators took away the novelty of his work. Scott wanted more money. He planned to make an estate he had bought this same year, Abbotsford on the Tweed, into "a romance of stone and lime." He decided now that the way he could do it was by making more romances in paper and ink to give him money for his dreams. While hunting for fishing tackle in a "lumber garret," he came upon the unfinished manuscript of *Waverley* that he had put aside at the advice of William Erskine, who was to prove a better friend than he was critic. Scott completed the story, which, he said was partly inspired by Miss Edgeworth's studies of Irish life and partly by an unfinished romance, *Queenhoo Hall* by Joseph Strutt, from whose mistakes Scott learned much.

Waverley, published anonymously in July 1814, was an instant success. An edition of 1000 copies was sold out in five weeks. Scott wrote in a preface, "It must remain uncertain whether *Waverley* be the work of a poet, a lawyer, or a clergyman, or whether the writer, to use Mrs. Malaprop's phrase, be, "like Cerberus, three gentlemen at once." By using double sets of proofs (Ballantyne always transferring Scott's corrections at his home so that Scott's handwriting was never seen at the publishers), the identity of "the Great Unknown" was kept secret until 1826. Many guessed Scott wrote the *Waverley Novels*, among them the Prince Regent, but only about twenty actually knew. Scott's reasons for this literary masquerade were his fear of hurting his literary reputation by being classed as a novel writer, and his love of the mysterious.

Scott cruised around the Hebrides in 1814 and in 1815 visited France. In 1816, Abbotsford had been increased from 150 acres to 1000. To see this gothic castle with its stained glass windows and suits of armor in the paneled entrance hall, visitors came from all over the world; among them Washington Irving, Prince Leopold of Belgium, Miss Edgeworth, Moore, and Wordsworth, who was to write a poem about Abbotsford. When Scott was not busy writing or dispensing hospitality, he was hunting with Maida at his heels, a gigantic stag hound, "the noblest dog ever seen on the Border since Johnnie Armstrong's day." Then there were his servants and peasants to be looked after and struggling writers with their families to be supported.

In the spring of 1819 Scott became dangerously ill and was thought to be dying. The Duke of Buchan planned a splendid funeral for "the Shirra," and tried to push his way into the sick room to tell Scott the details and cheer him up. Unfortunately for the Duke's plans, Scott managed to recover and during this period, although often in the greatest pain, dictated the greater part of *The Bride of Lammermoor*, *The Legend of Montrose*, and *Ivanhoe*. By 1822, his health was improved enough for him to take part in the ceremonies of welcoming George IV to Edinburgh. With the greatest enthusiasm Scott flung himself into plans for banquets and pageants. But so much "pomp and circumstance" must have gone to the great romantic's head. His Majesty had toasted Scott, who begged for the glass to keep as a relic. In his excitement Scott broke it, not, alas, after the romantic fashion of the Cavaliers, by throwing the glass into the fireplace, but by sitting on it.

Scott, when he toured Ireland in the spring of 1825, received the ovation of a king. Crowds followed him wherever he went. The leading lady was compelled to leave the stage of a theatre when Scott entered, so great was the uproar. Perhaps no man has been more loved, either by humans or animals. Even a "judicious pig" was so attached to Scott that he never left him of his own free will, as Lockhart puts it.

1825-1826 was a period of wild speculation. Banks stopped making loans and firms began to fail. If ever there was a man who lived in a world of his own, it was Scott. Had there been a Greek chorus to warn him of the doom to come it is doubtful he would have heard it. Late in 1825, Scott was at a dinner with his friend, James Skene. The next morning Scott sent for Skene at seven o'clock and said, "Skene, this is the hand of a beggar. Constable has failed and I am a ruined man."

When Scott first heard the news of Constable's failure, he refused to believe it. He said Constable was as firm as Ben Lomand and rode all night to ask Constable himself for the truth. Hurst and Robinson, literary agents, whose business was deeply involved with Constable's, were supposed to have speculated heavily in hops. Scott's firm, Ballantyne and Company, were as deeply involved with Constable as he was with Hurst and Robinson. When Constable failed, Ballantyne and Company failed. It was like a pack of cards. One card knocked out and the rest come tumbling down. Ballantyne & Company's liabilities amounted to £117,000.

Scott could have made a compromise, declared himself bankrupt, and given Abbotsford (worth £76,000) in 1825 to the creditors. But he took the manly way out. At fifty-five, broken in health, he began writing more books to pay off a debt amounting to more than half a million dollars that had not been incurred by his personal expenditure. He went to live in narrow bug-ridden lodgings in Edinburgh, attended by his faithful butler, Dalgleish, who had wept and refused to leave Scott no matter how much his wages might be cut. From 1825-30 Scott wrote thirty pages daily. At the end of eighteen months, he had written the *Life of Napoleon* in nine volumes. By 1830 he paid to his creditors £40,000. On December 17, 1830, his creditors moved that Scott be given his library and other furniture for his "unparalleled exertions." At the beginning a stranger offered Scott £30,000 that he refused.

But his Herculean labors were too much for him. He resigned from his legal offices and stopped writing. A royal vessel took Scott on a voyage to the Mediterranean. But Scott pined for Abbotsford and was not content until he returned there in the autumn of 1832. On September 21, 1832, Scott died. Lockhart wrote in the biography, "It was so quiet a day that the sound he best loved, the gentle ripple of the Tweed over its pebbles, was distinctly audible as we knelt around the bed and his eldest son kissed and closed his eyes."

Only £50,000 remained of the debt when Scott died. In 1847, all his debts were cleared by the selling of copyrights of his books.

He had married Charlotte Mary Carpenter, daughter of a French refugee, December 24, 1797. They had four children, Walter, at whose death in 1847 the baronetcy became extinct, Charlotte Sophia, who was to marry Lockhart, Anne, and Charles.

Scott, "the father of the historical novel," was the first to attempt what Woodberry calls "the vivification of history." He showed that the past is not cut off completely from the present but influences it. He was a matchless improvisator. Balzac called him "the Homer of the novel." Palgrave says, "It may be a just estimate which places Scott second in our creative and imaginative literature to Shakespeare." Taine, that Scott gave to Scotland "a citizenship of literature." Lang wrote of Scott's poetry, "he was the Last Minstrel, the latest, greatest, the noblest of natural poets concerned with natural things."

Of his faults, R. H. Gordon remarked that Scott hated re-writing as much as Falstaff did paying back. Stevenson said, "Here we have a man of the finest creative instinct. . . . utterly careless, almost, it would seem, incapable, in the technical matter of style." Scott could be tedious for pages at a time. He would wander from the main story. His passion for the picturesque often got the better of him. But he had no knowledge of the passion of love and his women were puppets. He has often been accused of writing "with an eye to the main chance but not much of an eye for the eternities."

Scott deeply influenced Balzac, Flaubert, Dumas, Dickens, Stevenson, and Thackeray.

But was he merely a passing fashion, notwithstanding? Sir Leslie Stephens says, "If ever the *Waverley* novels should lose their interest, the last journals of Scott . . . can never lose their interest as the record of one of the noblest struggles ever carried on by a great man to redeem a lamentable error." And Chesterton, "It is said that Scott is neglected by modern readers; if so, the matter could be more appropriately described by saying that modern readers are neglected by Providence."

D. H.

PRINCIPAL WORKS: *Poetry*—The Chase and William and Helen: Two Ballads From the German of Gottfried A. Burger, 1796; Minstrelsy of the Scottish Border: Vols. I and II, 1802, Vol. III, 1803; The Lay of the Last Minstrel, 1805; Marmion, 1808; The Lady of the Lake, 1810; The Poetry Contained in the Novels, Tales and Romances of the Author of Waverley, 1822; Poetical Works: Complete Edition, 1904. *Novels*—Waverley, 1814; Guy Mannering, 1815; The Antiquary, 1816; Tales of My Landlord, Collected and Arranged by Jedidiah Cleishbotham (The Black Dwarf and Old Mortality) 1816; Tales of My Landlord: Second Series (The Heart of Midlothian) 1818; Rob Roy, 1818; Tales of My Landlord: Third Series (The Bride of Lammermoor and The Legend of Montrose) 1819; Ivanhoe, 1820; The Monastery, 1820; The Abbot, 1820; Kenilworth, 1821; The Pirate, 1822; The Fortunes of Nigel, 1822; Peveril of the Peak, 1822; Quentin Durward, 1823; Saint Ronan's Well, 1824; Redgauntlet, 1824; Tales of the Crusade (Vols. I & II, The Betrothed; Vols. III & IV, The Talisman) 1825; Woodstock: or, The Cavalier, 1826; Chronicles of the Canongate (The Highland Widow, The Two Drovers, The Surgeon's Daughter) 1827; Chronicles of the Canongate: Second Series (St. Valentine's Day: or, The Fair Maid of Perth) 1828; Anne of Geierstein, 1829; Tales of My Landlord: Fourth Series (Count Robert of Paris and Castle Dangerous) 1832; The Waverley Novels: Author's Favorite Edition, 1830-4; Abbotsford Edition, 1842-7; Centenary Edition, 1870-1; Border Illustrated Edition, 1892-4; Oxford Edition, 1912. *Biography*—The Works of John Dryden, 1808; The Works of Jonathan Swift, 1814; Lives of the Novelists, 1821-4; The Life of Napoleon Buonaparte: Emperor of the French, 1827. *Miscellaneous*—The Border Antiquities of England and Scotland, 1814-17; Provincial Antiquities of Scotland, 1819-26; Letters on Demonology and Witchcraft, 1830; The Miscellaneous Prose Works of Sir Walter Scott (30 Vols.) 1834-71. *Correspondence and Journals*—Scott's Last Journal: 1825-32, 1890; Familiar Letters, 1894.

ABOUT: Buchan, J. Sir Walter Scott; Carlyle, T. Critical and Miscellaneous Essays; Caw, J. L. The Scott Gallery: Chesterton, G. K. Varied Types; Crockett, W. S. Sir Walter Scott; The Scott Country; Gillies, R. P. Recollections of Sir Walter Scott; Grierson, H. J. C. Sir Walter Scott To-day; Irving, W. Abbotsford and Newstead Abbey; Lang, A. Letters to Dead Authors; Lockhart, J. G. Memoirs of the Life of Sir Walter Scott; Palgrave, T. Life of Sir Walter Scott; Saintsbury, G. Sir Walter Scott; Skene, J. Memories of Sir Walter Scott; Stephen, L. Hours In a Library; Studies of a Biographer; Scott and the Border Minstrelsy; Stevenson, R. L. A Gossip on Romance in Memories and Portraits; Woodberry, G. E. Great Writers; Cornhill Magazine 70:738, 71:75, 71:213 June-August 1931.

SCOTT, WILLIAM BELL (September 12, 1811-November 22, 1890), Scottish poet and painter, was born in Edinburgh, the son of an engraver. Robert Scott, and Ross (Bell) Scott. David Scott, the painter, was an elder brother.

Educated at the High School in Edinburgh, he received artistic training from his father and at the Trustees' Academy; later he helped in his invalid father's business. In this early period also he began to write poetry (his first work is said to have been an "Address to P. B. Shelley"), and met such literary men as "Christopher North" and Sir Walter Scott.

About 1837 he undertook an artist's career in London, painting, engraving, and etching. Several of his pictures were exibited in London, and in 1843 he submitted a cartoon in a competition for a design for frescoes for the new Houses of Parliament. While he was unsuccessful in the competition, he was offered a government appointment, a mastership in the Schools of Design (Newcastle-on-Tyne). Since he had married Letitia Margery Norquoy and was desirous of steady means of support, he accepted, spending twenty years in the work of organizing and conducting instruction in art in the government schools. In this same Newcastle period Scott executed a series of large pictures at Wallington Hall, for Sir George Trevelyan, illustrating border history and the Ballad of Chevy Chase. In addition to this work he painted a series of designs in encaustic at Penkill Castle, Ayrshire, where lived his close friend Miss Alice Boyd. These were illustrations of *The Kingis Quair*.

His return to London in 1864 followed the completion of his work at Wallington and the reorganization of the Government Schools of Art, which were placed under instructors especially trained, the previous teachers being retired on pensions. Scott remained in government service as an artist employed in decoration and an examiner in art schools until 1885.

His time for the most part he divided between London, where he had a home in Chelsea, and Ayrshire. His death, caused by angina pectoris, occurred at Penkill Castle in 1890.

Scott's life had been spent in the society of leading literary men and artists of his time; and these varied interests and acquaintances are reflected in the spicy autobiography which was edited, after Scott's death, by William Minto. The editor seems to have been surprised at the sensation created by the publication of these posthumous memoirs. The poet Swinburne, who had written memorial verses for Scott, was stung to such fury by the picture of him given by the memoirs that he rushed into print with remarks about Scott's "virulent senility," and wrote: "Here . . . is a man whose name would never have

WILLIAM BELL SCOTT

been heard, whose verse would never have been read, whose daubs would never have been seen, outside some aesthetic Lilliput of the North, but for his casual and parasitical association with the Trevelyans, the Rossettis, and myself." This personal estimate is, of course, too prejudiced to be trustworthy, and Scott has been described as a loyal, generous friend, as well as a writer of charming letters; but the lively discussion caused by the book and the pointed, if unfair, descriptions given in it of the characters of such men as Ruskin are unmistakable evidences of Scott's individuality.

While his paintings are said to have possessed unconventional qualities which gave them a certain vigor and freedom, the Reverend Ronald Bayne wrote of him: "It is probably upon his poetry that Scott's reputation will ultimately rest. Blake and Shelley were his chief models, and Rossetti's friendship was a continual stimulus to him. But he lacked Rossetti's intensity and artistic genius."   R. W. W.

PRINCIPAL WORKS: *Autobiography*—Autobiographical Notes of the Life of William Bell Scott, 1892. *Biography*—Memoir of David Scott, 1850; Albert Dürer: His Life and Works, 1869; The Little Masters, 1879. *Poetry*—Hades: or, The Transit, 1838; The Year of the World, 1846; Poems, 1854; Poems, 1875; A Poet's Harvest Home, 1882, 1893. *Works on Art*—Antiquarian Gleanings in the North of England, 1851; Half-Hour Lectures on the History and Practice of the Fine and Ornamental Arts, 1861; Gems of French Art, 1870; Gems of Modern Belgian Art, 1871; Gems of Modern German Art, 1872; The British School of Sculpture, 1872; Our British Landscape Painters From Samuel Scott to David Cox, 1872; Murillo and the Spanish School of Painting, 1872; William Blake: Etchings from His Works, 1878.

ABOUT: Scott, W. B. Autobiographical Notes of the Life of William Bell Scott; Academy 42:499 December 13, 1892; Athenaeum 1:113 January 28, 1893; Dial (Chicago) 13:382 December 16, 1892.

SCROPE, WILLIAM (1772-July 20, 1852), sporting writer, was the son of a clergyman. He was a direct descendant of the first Lord Scrope, of the time of Edward III, and on his father's death in 1787 succeeded to the ancestral Castle Comb, Wiltshire; in 1795 he also inherited large family estates in Lincolnshire. Although Scrope's main interest was in sport, he was also a good classical scholar, an able artist who illustrated his own works and exhibited at the Royal Academy and the British Institution (of which he was a director), and a Fellow of the Linnaean Society. He was an intimate friend of Sir Walter Scott. In 1794 Scrope married Emma Long, and they had one daughter.

PRINCIPAL WORKS: The Art of Deer-stalking, 1838; Days and Nights of Salmon-fishing in the Tweed, 1843.

SEDGWICK, ADAM (March 22, 1785-January 27, 1873), geologist, was born in Yorkshire, the son of a clergyman. He was educated at the Dent Grammar School (of which his father had become headmaster), at the Sedbergh School, and at Trinity College, Cambridge, where he received his B.A. in 1808. During his university years he nearly died of typhoid fever, and though, after two years of private tutoring, he was made a fellow of Trinity in 1810, he was actually an invalid until 1815. The next year he was ordained. In 1818 he was made Woodwardian professor of geology. Sedgwick knew nothing of geology, and the post had always been a mere sinecure. He determined to make it a real department. He helped to found the Cambridge Philosophical Society and built up the geological collection of the university, now one of the best in the world. He studied his new subject to such purpose that before the end of the year he was a fellow of the Geological Society (he was its president in 1831), and though he never wrote a complete book or made any important discovery, he was made a Fellow of the Royal Society in 1830, was president of the British Association for the Advancement of Science in 1833, and received honorary doctorates from Oxford and Cambridge. His specialty was the geology of Wales, in his work on which he was assisted by Charles Darwin, then a young man. In later years, however, he was one of the foremost opponents of Darwinism. He died unmarried at eighty-eight.

PRINCIPAL WORKS: Discourse on the Studies at the University of Cambridge, 1833; British Palaeozoic Fossils, 1854.

ABOUT: Clark, J. W. & Hughes, T. McK. Life and Letters of the Rev. Adam Sedgwick.

SEEBOHM, FREDERIC (November 23, 1833-February 6, 1912), historian, was born in Bradford. His father was a wool merchant, a native of Germany. The family were Quakers, and the home was very pious. After attending Bortham School, York, Seebohm read law and was called to the bar in 1856. In 1857 he married Mary Ann Exton, daughter of a banker; they had one son and five daughters. He moved to Hitchin, and lived there as partner in his father-in-law's bank to his death. All his history, like Grote's, was written in the leisure of a business career. He was besides very active in social work, being a Justice of the Peace, a poor law guardian, and a member of the Hertfordshire County Council. His writings brought him honorary degrees from Oxford, Cambridge, and Edinburgh. Seebohm wrote with ease, sympathy, and lucidity; his work is still readable because he understood the influence of economic conditions on history.

PRINCIPAL WORKS: The Oxford Reformers, 1867; The Era of the Protestant Revolution, 1872; The English Village Community, 1883; The Tribal System in Wales, 1895; Tribal Custom in Anglo-Saxon Law, 1902.

ABOUT: London Times February 7, 1912.

SEELEY, SIR JOHN ROBERT (September 10, 1834-January 13, 1895), philosopher, essayist, and historian, was born in London, the son of a publisher. He attended the City of London School, but being obliged to leave because of bad health, he read far more widely than the average student, and gained an unusual knowledge of English literature. He then entered Christ's College, Cambridge, securing his B.A. in 1857, and winning the senior chancellor's medal. He was fellow and classical lecturer at the college until 1859. Then he became chief classical assistant at his old school, the City of London, leaving it in 1863 to become professor of Latin at University College, London, until 1869. In the latter year he married Mary Phillott; they had one daughter. In this same memorable year he succeeded Charles Kingsley as professor of modern history at Cambridge, and there he remained until his death from cancer at sixty-one. He was knighted the year before he died.

From the beginning Seeley's twin interests were history and religion. In history his approach was political, and in politics he was an imperialist. His salary being small, he was obliged to supplement it by public lectures, and some of these have been published. He also edited Livy.

But he is best known by his religio-philosophical works, particularly *Ecce Homo*, which was published anonymously but soon discovered to be by Seeley. His object was to humanize Christianity, and to present religion free of supernaturalism—a sort of liberal Unitarianism or deism. Though he tried to avoid all difficulties, his books on religion roused a storm of criticism. His style in all his work is at once lucid and vigorous.

PRINCIPAL WORKS: Ecce Homo, 1865; Lectures and Essays, 1870; Life and Times of Stein, 1878; Natural Religion, 1882; Life of Napoleon, 1886; The Growth of British Policy, 1895.

ABOUT: Seeley, Sir J. R. The Growth of British Policy (see Memoir by G. W. Prothero).

SELLAR, WILLIAM YOUNG (February 22, 1825-October 1890), Scottish Latinist, was born in Sutherlandshire. He was educated at Edinburgh Academy (where he was head boy), Glasgow University, and Balliol College, Oxford, receiving his B.A. in 1847 and his M.A. in 1850. In 1848 he was fellow of Oriel. From 1851 to 1853 he was assistant professor of Latin at Glasgow University, then from 1853 to 1859 assistant professor of Greek at St. Andrews, and from 1859 to 1863 full professor. In 1863 he became professor of Latin at Edinburgh University, and remained so until his death. Sellar was a good teacher, and has been called a "sound and sensitive" literary critic, but he himself remarked that he was not brilliant, and he was right.

PRINCIPAL WORKS: Roman Poets of the Republic, 1863; Roman Poets of the Augustan Age: Virgil, 1877; Horace and the Elegiac Poets, 1892.

ABOUT: Sellar, W. Y. Horace and the Elegiac Poets (see Memoir by his nephew, Andrew Lang).

SELBORNE, LORD (Roundell Palmer, First Earl of Selbourne) (November 27, 1812-May 4, 1895), jurist and theological writer, was born in Oxfordshire, the son of a clergyman. He was educated at Rugby, Winchester, and Christ Church and Trinity Colleges, Oxford, receiving his M.A. in 1836 (D.C.L. 1862). He was called to the bar from Lincoln's Inn in 1837. In 1848 he married Lady Laura Waldegrave, daughter of the Earl of Waldegrave; she died in 1885, leaving one son and four daughters.

Palmer (as he then was) became a Queen's Councillor in 1849. From 1847 he was a member of Parliament, at first as a conservative, but gradually becoming a liberal. He was solicitor-general in 1861, and was knighted the same year. He was attorney-general from 1861 to 1866, and Lord Chancellor in 1872, being raised to the peerage of Baron Selborne. He retired in 1874, but was Lord Chancellor again from 1880 to 1885. In 1882 he became the Earl of Selborne. As a jurist Selborne was a reformer; in religion he was a high churchman, and all his writing, in prose or verse, bears on ecclesiastical questions.

PRINCIPAL WORKS: The Book of Praise, 1863; Ancient Facts and Fictions Concerning Churches and Titles, 1888; Hymns: Their History and Development, 1892.

ABOUT: Solicitors' Journal May 11, 1895; London Times May 6, 1895.

SENIOR, NASSAU WILLIAM (September 26, 1790-June 4, 1864), economist, was born in Berkshire, the son of a clergyman. His great grandfather had been a native of Spain, originally named Señor. He was educated at Eton and at Magdalen College, Oxford, receiving his B.A. in 1812, his M.A. in 1815. He was called to the bar from Lincoln's Inn in 1819. He was a certified conveyancer, and since his voice was weak he was obliged to continue exclusively in this line of practice. In 1821 he married Mary Charlotte Mair; they had one son and one daughter. Senior was attracted to the study of economics by observation of the unsatisfactory workings of the poor law in his father's parish. His first published work appeared in the *Quarterly Review* in 1821. From 1825 to 1830, and again from 1847 to 1852, he was professor of political economy at Oxford, being the first to hold the post. In 1833, as a member of the poor law Commission, he wrote the report on which the poor law of 1834 was based. He refused all rewards or honors offered him for this great service. From 1836 to the abolition of the office in 1855, he was Master in Chancery. He was a frequent contributor to the *Edinburgh Review*, and among his most valuable works are diaries and records of conversations he kept, especially those from the Revolution of 1848 in France. Greatly influenced by Malthus, Senior's economic views are chiefly characterized by practicality and sound common sense.

PRINCIPAL WORKS: An Outline of the Science of Political Economy, 1836; Journals, 1851 and 1871; Biographical Sketches, 1863; Historical and Philosophical Essays, 1865; Conversations, 1871-78.

ABOUT: Cornhill Magazine August 1864.

SERGEANT (EMILY FRANCES) ADELINE (July 4, 1851-December 4, 1904), novelist, was born in Derbyshire. Her father was a Methodist missionary and preacher, her mother a writer of devout verses and stories. She was educated at a school in Weston-Super-Mare and at Laleham School in Clapham, and at Queen's College, London. Her father died in 1870, and she immediately joined the Church of England. Her religious career was varied—in the '80's she was an agnostic and a member of the Fabian (Socialist) Society. In 1893 she affiliated herself with the High Church faction of the Church of England, and finally in 1899 she became a Roman Catholic. For ten years she was a governess in the family of a canon. In 1882 she visited Egypt, and while there wrote *Jacobi's Wife*, which won a prize offered by the Dundee *People's Friend*. Thereafter she became a regular contributor, under contract, to this paper, going to live in Dundee from 1885 to 1887, when she moved to London. She was much interested in humanitarian and reform projects.

Miss Sergeant was an extremely rapid writer; she produced over ninety novels, writing six a year from 1901 to 1903 and eight in the year following, and when she died in 1904 she left fourteen still unpublished, but completed. Her work has little value, but she is good in the depiction of provincial middle-class domestic life.

PRINCIPAL WORKS: Poems, 1866; Dicky and His Friends, 1879; Una's Crusade, 1880; Beyond Recall, 1883; An Open Foe, 1884; No Saint, 1886; Seventy Times Seven, 1888; Esther Denison, 1889; The Story of a Penitent Soul, 1892; The Idol Maker, 1897; This Body of Death, 1901; Roads to Rome (non-fiction) 1901.

ABOUT: Stephens, W. The Life of Adeline Sergeant; Athenaeum December 10, 1904.

SEWELL, ANNA (March 30, 1820-April 25, 1878), author of the classic animal story, *Black Beauty*, was born in Yarmouth, the daughter of Isaac Sewell and Mary (Wright) Sewell.

The home in which she was reared was a strict Quaker one; and, although its pious atmosphere might seem overpowering to many people today, there can be no doubt of the beauty and purity of the child's environment. Financial reverses compelled the family to spend about ten years in modest circumstances in a small house at Dalston, where they settled not long after Anna's birth. Mrs. Sewell, a woman of high principle and noble character, wrote the first of her long series of juvenile works (chiefly in words of one syllable), *Walks With Mamma*, in order to secure money for books with which to educate her own children.

Held to the highest standards of behavior, Anna Sewell showed the results of her training even when she was a small girl, on one occasion berating a man for shooting a blackbird and on another, when telling an aunt of a recent accident in which the little girl had dislocated her elbow, saying, "I bored it well!"

This childish expression of heroism might almost serve as an epitaph for the unfortunate girl, who not long after was called upon to bear much more suffering. Her family, after an attempt to increase its income by selling milk, was reduced to poverty by the dishonesty of a hired man, who stole the money paid by the customers. The major catastrophe, however, was yet to come. Returning from school, Anna, in an effort to escape a rainstorm, ran down a carriage road, fell, and sprained her ankle.

The consequences of this accident were so serious that the girl was crippled for the rest of her life, in spite of treatments (some of them painful) administered in the hope of improving her condition. She improved enough so that she could walk a little better, and, when the family moved from Brighton to Lancing (1845), she could drive her father to the station every day. In the next year she accompanied her mother, her brother, and her aunt to Germany; and in 1856, after considerable moving from place to place in England, Anna and her mother went to Marienberg, in Germany, where the daughter remained a year for treatment.

On her return her health was so much better that she could do some walking; and she and her mother took a holiday together at Dorking, reading, walking, and enjoying the beauties about them. In 1857 they made a trip to Spain to visit Anna's brother Philip and his family. The improvement, however, was but temporary, and not long after the Sewells' last removal, to Old Catton, near Norwich, Anna began to show signs of illness. Her last seven years or so were spent indoors, under her devoted mother's care.

In this period she devoted her attention to writing a book that might bring about kind treatment of horses. The idea is said to have been inspired by Horace Bushnell's *Essay on Animals*, as well as the author's own personal experience. *Black Beauty* was finished in 1877. While the manuscript had been sold to the publishers for but a few pounds, the book was tremendously successful; so great was its popularity that the writer was affected seriously by the joy it caused her. She never lived to see the true proportions of its success, for she died in the spring of the following year.

An extraordinary pathos and appeal cling to the memory of this gentle woman, who devoted much of a life of suffering to convincing people of the iniquity of inflicting pain on animals. Her relations with her family were of the most beautiful, and her mother, who relied upon her for criticism of her own writings, devoted her life to the care of this unfortunate daughter, to whom she referred as "an unclouded blessing, for fifty-eight years the perennial joy of my life." Mother and daughter worked together in the amelioration

ANNA SEWELL

of the lot of the poor; in their childhood Anna and Philip had given up a precious trip to the seaside to send money to famine victims in Ireland. Anna Sewell's feeling for animals, especially horses, explains her treatment of the family pony; it is said that when driving she guided the animal mainly by using her voice and her speech, talking to it as if it were human. When at her funeral the hearse appeared, drawn by horses with bearing-reins (to make the horses hold up their heads), her mother ordered the bearing-reins to be removed from all horses in the funeral train, knowing what her daughter's wish would have been.

The single work by which Anna Sewell made herself immortal is simply written in the form of an autobiography of a horse that, once an animal of beauty and value, descends in the scale of usefulness until he becomes a mere drudge; and it tells of the cruelties and hardships suffered by animals put to hard work under inconsiderate masters. Not used at first as propaganda, *Black Beauty* was recognized by George T. Angell, the founder of the Massachusetts Society for the Prevention of Cruelty to Animals, as having a value apart from its intrinsic merit; and the book was soon dispersed far and wide. "In the history of humane literature the book holds a place unique; in the history of all literature it maintains its position as an authentic classic, not alone for children but for their parents," declared Vincent Starrett; and he added, "It is unquestionably the most successful animal story ever written . . . ." R. W. W.

PRINCIPAL WORK: Black Beauty, 1877.

ABOUT: Ewart, H. C. True and Noble Women; Starrett, V. Buried Caesars.

SHACKLETON, MARY. See LEAD-BEATER, MARY

SHAIRP, JOHN CAMPBELL (July 30, 1819-September 18, 1885), Scottish poet and essayist, was born in West Lothian. His father was an army major who had served in India. He was educated in Edinburgh Academy, Glasgow University (where first he became interested in poetry, and where he started the long country rambles that were his lifelong habit), and at Balliol College, Oxford, where he won the Newdigate (poetry) Prize in 1842. In 1846 he became assistant master at Rugby, having been disappointed of an expected fellowship.

In 1853 Shairp married Eliza Douglas; they had one son. In 1856 he was substitute professor of the Greek classics at Glasgow University, from 1857 to 1861 assistant professor of Latin at St. Andrews, and from 1861 professor. In 1868 he became principal of the United Colleges of St. Andrews, remaining as Latin professor also until 1872.

From this position he was generally known thereafter as "Principal Laird."

In 1877 he became professor of poetry at Oxford, and remained so until his death. In 1844, soon after receiving an honorary LL.D. from Edinburgh, his health failed badly, he was found to be suffering from tuberculosis, and went to northern Italy. He grew worse, however, and returned to England. He died while on a visit in Argyllshire.

Literature owes Shairp a debt for his editing of Dorothy Wordsworth's *Journal*, unpublished for so many years after her death. As a critic he did not stand particularly high, but he was an interesting poet, with a strong feeling for nature and much originality, though his work was considered highly irregular and faulty in a formal and polished poetic age.

PRINCIPAL WORKS: Kilmahoe and Other Poems, 1864; Studies in Poetry and Philosophy, 1868; Culture and Religion, 1870; The Poetic Interpretation of Nature, 1877; Burns, 1879; Sketches in History and Poetry, 1887; Glen Desseray and Other Poems, 1888.

ABOUT: Rodger, M. John Campbell Shairp.

SHARP, WILLIAM (September 12, 1856-December 12, 1905), Scottish poet, biographer, and editor, was born in Paisley, Scotland, and spent all his early life in the Scotch Highlands. From the very beginning a vein of mystic pantheism, born of these mountains and his Gaelic blood, showed itself in the boy's nature. Three times he ran away from home to live in the mountain solitude, once spending an entire unforgettable summer in a gypsy encampment.

Such a boy fitted ill in the confines of formal education. For two years, from 1871 to 1873, he was a student at Glasgow University, but he left to become an attorney's clerk in Glasgow, an even more irksome environment for a burgeoning poet. After four years his health became affected, perhaps as a consequence of his mental discomfort. His family sent him to Australia, in the hope that the sea voyage would be beneficial to him, and that once there he might find an opening which would lead to permanent residence. It is doubtful if Sharp looked very hard for what would inevitably have been another uncongenial post, for in a few months, after a prolonged Pacific cruise, he was back again. This time he settled in London, and, of all unpromising positions, set to work as a bank clerk. It is noteworthy that one of his close friendships in later life was with the American, Edmund Clarence Stedman, who was also a banker-poet.

Gradually he became acquainted with the literary groups of the capital, notably with the Rossetti circle. His friendship with D. G. Rossetti made him, a few years later, the painter-poet's biographer. Another strong in-

WILLIAM SHARP

fluence was that of Walter Pater, who was the patron saint of so many young writers of the period. These two disparate associations were salutary; they saved Sharp from becoming a mere imitator of the style of either. His work began to appear regularly in the *Pall Mall Gazette,* so receptive to youthful talent, and in 1885 he was appointed art critic of the *Glasgow Herald.* His banking days were over forever. In the same year he married his first cousin, Elizabeth Amelia Sharp, daughter of his father's older brother. This childless marriage seems to have been more of a deep, affectionate friendship than an actual love-match; his cousin and wife became his collaborator and co-worker. Her chief contribution to his bibliography is her joint work with him in the anthology called *Lyra Celtica,* which appeared in 1896. She outlived him, and became his chief biographer.

Sharp's delicate health failed to improve, and it became apparent that he could no longer endure Scottish or even English winters. For a while he traveled sporadically, in France, Italy, Germany, Greece, North Africa, and in the United States (making one famous visit to Walt Whitman in Camden); but after a few years it became necessary for him to spend most of the year in the south, usually in Italy. Scotland, however, remained the home of his heart; he returned to the Highlands whenever possible, and left them always with sorrow. The Celtic background of his thought and feeling remained its most important constituent, and led directly to the strange dichotomy which marked his literary life.

Had it not been for one thing, William Sharp's career would have been that of a routine critic, anthologist, editor (*The Can-terbury Poets*), minor poet, and pedestrian biographer. That one thing was the creation of Fiona Macleod.

Until Sharp's death, only his wife and very few of his nearest friends knew the secret of Fiona's identity with her creator. It was widely suspected, of course, but Sharp went to unusual lengths in trying to force Fiona's actuality on a skeptical world. In her name, and by his sister's hand, he carried on her voluminous correspondence, and he wrote her biography for *Who's Who.* She was supposed to be a distant cousin of his, and to have brought out her Celtic tales and poems merely under his aegis and through his encouragement.

As a matter of fact, it is a question whether in the end Sharp did not himself almost believe that Fiona lived, though he must have realized that he himself wrote every book accredited to her. His susceptibility to autosuggestion and his mystical trend made it difficult for him to differentiate always between actuality and fancy. Yeats says of him, rather unkindly, that "he never told one anything that was true; the facts of life disturbed him and were forgotten." He relates an occasion when Sharp, habitually a most temperate man, became intoxicated and attributed his remorse to his infidelity to Fiona Macleod—he, the devoted husband of a devoted wife!

Certainly Fiona was the better writer of the two. Though even in her writings there is often something a bit too soft and vague, they are alive with the mystery of the mountains and forests of Scotland; they have the supernal thrill that goes to the bone, and carry us to a land where it is always autumn. In them, Sharp expressed not only his Celtic heritage, but also the feminine aspect of his being; he himself said that sometimes when he wrote in her name he felt half-woman.

In 1905, Sharp made one last visit to Scotland. "Goodbye, beloved trees," he whispered as he left them; he knew that he would never see them again. In December, visiting a friend in his palace in Sicily, he caught cold on a drive; a few days later he was dead.

An honest appraisal of William Sharp's work leads one to believe that only when he was hiding behind his pseudonymous self could he be free of self-consciousness and express the fulness of his gifts. He had prophesied for English literature "a great creative period," of "new complexity, new subtlety"; but in his own person he could contribute nothing to enrich this modern flowering. As William Sharp, his prose is thorough, balanced, and earnest, his poetry instinct with love of nature but undistinguished and "dated." Occasionally a sort of prankishness peeps through his serious style, akin to the impulse which led him to publish, edit, and write one number of a magazine, the *Pagan Review*, "to promote the New Paganism," completely by himself under various *noms de plume*.

But as Fiona Macleod his writing, in spite of sentimentality and occasional pose, acquires that haunting quality which raises it above mundane competence and gives it permanent value. In it the Celtic soul speaks in authentic and memorable cadences.

M. A. deF.

PRINCIPAL WORKS: (As William Sharp)—*Poetry* —Human Inheritance, 1882; Earth's Voices, 1884; Romantic Ballads and Poems of Fantasy, 1886; Sospiri di Roma, 1891; Flower o' the Vine, 1894; Sospiri d'Italia, 1906. *Biography*—D. G. Rossetti, 1882; Shelley, 1887; Heine, 1888; Browning, 1890; Life and Letters of Joseph Severn, 1892. *Novels*— Fellowe and His Wife (with Blanche Willis Howard) 1892; Wives in Exile, 1896; Silence Farm, 1899. *Short Stories*—The Gypsy Christ, 1895; Ecce Puella, 1896. *Criticism*—Progress of Art in the Century, 1902; Literary Geography, 1904. WORKS: (As Fiona Macleod)—Pharais, 1894; The Mountain Lovers, 1895; The Sin-Eater, 1895; The Washer of the Ford, 1896; Green Fire, 1896; The Dominion of Dreams, 1899; The Divine Adventure, 1900; Winged Destiny, 1904; The Immortal Hour, 1908.

ABOUT: Sharp, E. A. Memoir; Yeats, W. B. Autobiographies.

SHAW, FLORA LOUISE (Lady Lugard) (1851-January 25, 1929), Irish novelist, was born in Dublin, her father being a general in the British Army. She was privately educated, but from the beginning she rebelled against the aristocracy and snobbery of her family. In the early '80's she finally escaped from the life of leisure she detested, and by aid of a letter from George Meredith secured a staff position under W. T. Stead on the *Pall Mall Gazette*. When Stead left the magazine she left also, and became a member of the staff of *The Times*, rising to head of the colonial department—a most unusual position for a woman in those days. She was a good journalist, traveling for *The Times* on special commissions to South America, Australia, Canada and to the Klondike gold rush in 1898. In 1902, when she was fifty-one, she married Sir Frederick Lugard (later Baron Lugard of Abinger) a colonial administrator. Her strenuous life heretofore had injured her health, and she soon found herself unable to live in tropical climates with him. When the World War began, she interested herself in the Belgian Refugees, being joint founder of the War Refugees' Commission, and founder of the Lady Lugard Hospitality Commission. She was made a Dame of the British Empire, in recognition of her war services, in 1918. She died at Abinger Common, Surrey, her country residence, at seventy-nine.

Most of Flora Shaw's books (she always wrote under this name) were written for children. *Castle Blair*, the first, was especially successful, and was highly praised by Ruskin. It was based on memories of her own Irish childhood.

PRINCIPAL WORKS: Castle Blair, 1878; Hector, 1883; A Sea Change, 1885; Colonel Chiswick's Campaign, 1886; A Tropical Dependency, 1905. ABOUT: London Times January 28 and 30, 1929.

SHEIL, RICHARD LALOR (August 17, 1791-May 25, 1851), Irish dramatist and politician, was born in Kilkenny. His father was a country gentleman of a Roman Catholic family. He was at first tutored by an old French abbé, then sent to a school in Kensington kept by another émigré from the Revolution. He then attended Stonyhurst College and Trinity College, Dublin. In 1808, while he was still studying law at Trinity, his father became bankrupt, but a cousin of his mother's made it possible for him to remain until he secured his B.A. in 1811. He was called to the bar from Lincoln's Inn in 1814. Although he had a defect of speech, his ambition was to become an orator, and he turned naturally to politics. His tragedies were all written merely to make money for a young briefless attorney, and after he became prosperous he wrote no more. Another reason for his abandonment of literature may have been the fact that most of his later plays were unsuccessful. *Adelaide*, his first, was performed in 1814.

At this same time he married a Miss O'Halloran, who died in 1822. He began writing *Sketches of the Irish Bar*, with W. H. Curran, for the *New Monthly Magazine;* later these were published in book form. Sheil now became increasingly involved in the Catholic Emancipation movement, as a follower of O'Connell, and in 1827 was indicted for seditious libel, in consequence of an article in the *Morning Register*, but the case was dismissed. In 1830 he married a widow, Anastasia (Lalor) Power, an heiress, and was thenceforth independently wealthy. Catholic emancipation having been granted, he stood for Parliament and was elected in 1831, but he was a negligible figure in the House of Commons, partly because of his speech defect. In 1838 he was vice-president of the Board of Trade. In 1845 he went to Madeira for his son's health; the son died, but he remained for another year. On his return he was appointed Master of the Mint, a good deal to his disappointment. However, in 1851 he was named British Minister to the Court of Tuscany. He arrived in Florence in January, and by May he was dead of a sudden attack of gout, which killed him in an hour.

Sheil's plays are stilted and bombastic, without much merit, but were popular at the time. *Evadne* is the best written.

PRINCIPAL WORKS: The Apostate, 1817; Bellamira: or, The Fall of Tnis, 1818; Evadne: or, The Statue, 1819. ABOUT: McCullagh, T. Memoirs of Richard Lalor Sheil.

SHELLEY, MARY WOLLSTONE-
CRAFT GODWIN (August 30, 1797-Feb-
ruary 1, 1851), novelist, caused by her birth
the death of a mother far more illustrious
than she ever became. She was the daughter
and only child of the radical philosopher
William Godwin and the early feminist Mary
Wollstonecraft, who legitimized her by their
marriage five months before her nativity.

The younger Mary grew up in a strange
household—a hollow, pompous philosopher of
a father, always poor and in debt and pouring
forth unreadable books; a shrill termagant of
a stepmother who hated her for her mother's
sake; a negligible stepbrother and half-broth-
er; a stepsister who was a difficult companion
because of her hysterical flightiness, and a
melancholy illegitimate half-sister doomed to
suicide. If Mary Godwin ever had any formal
schooling, it does not appear in the record of
her life. But she lived for her first twenty-
five years in an atmosphere of learning and
scholarship, even when she was making long
visits to relatives in Scotland, and her good,
clear mind absorbed that atmosphere and fixed
her in habits of study. She was an eager
though not completely understanding disciple
of her father's religious and political radicalism. The other great influence on her youth
was her dead mother; convinced that she was
Mary Wollstonecraft's innocent murderer, she
spent much time reading by the tomb in St.
Pancras Cemetery, communing in thought with
the woman who lay there.

When this girl at sixteen met the twenty-
one-year-old Shelley, already an unhappy husband and father, incandescent with his genius
and his young passion for perfection, it was
inevitable that they should strike fire on flint.
They ran away together—with Mary's step-

MARY WOLLSTONECRAFT SHELLEY

sister (the second Mrs. Godwin's daughter
by her first marriage), Claire Clairmont, for
company—a month before Mary's seventeenth
birthday. Godwin was furious, disowned
them both—and continued to bleed Shelley
for money. Their first child died in infancy.
Harriet Shelley killed herself, a few months
after the suicide of poor Fanny Imlay, Mary
Wollstonecraft's other daughter, her illegitimate child by the American Gilbert Imlay.
At the end of 1816 Mary Godwin and Shelley
were finally able to marry. Early in 1817
they settled at Marlow, with their surviving
children, the year-old William, always his
mother's darling, and the new baby Clara,
who was to live hardly more than a year. A
life of anxiety, poverty, and wandering was
not good for the health of babies.

After Shelley was refused custody of his
two children by Harriet, he feared to lose
those by Mary also, and decided to leave England permanently. This they did in March
1818. Claire Clairmont went with them, and
stayed till 1821. After moving about for a
time from city to city, they settled for the most
part at Pisa, until in the spring of 1822 they
took the house near Lerici which was to be
Shelley's last home. It was in their first Italian
days, in company with Byron, that *Frankenstein*, immeasurably the best of Mary Shelley's
novels, was written.

Clara died in the autumn of 1818. In the
following June came a far worse blow; their
best-beloved child, little William, who could
walk and talk, died suddenly after an illness
of only a few days. Mary was desolated; her
grief combined with worry over her father's
misfortunes to plunge her into actual melancholy. The birth of their last and only surviving child, Percy Florence, at the end of
1819 did little to alleviate her sorrow. Nor did
it make things easier that the next year witnessed Shelley's idealizing but disturbing
passion for Emilia Viviani; Mary indulged in
a burst of quite ordinary jealousy which was
as futile as it was harrowing.

On July 8, 1822, Shelley was drowned in
the Gulf of Spezzia. In a sense, though Mary
lived for nearly thirty years after, and did
the bulk of her literary work, her life was
over. Their union had not been entirely
happy: Mary was cold and often impatient;
she was an intellectual but otherwise not extraordinary woman, married to a man unlike
any other on earth. She had loved him to
the depths of her being, and mingled with her
grief was that worst of all remorse, remorse
for failure in relations with the dead. She was
dedicated thenceforth to his memory and to
the care of their son. Trelawny, John Howard
Payne, and perhaps Washington Irving,
wanted to marry her, but she refused them
all. "I want to be Mary Shelley on my tombstone," she said.

SHELLEY

Trelawny took her back to London in 1823. Shelley's father offered to care for the child, but only on condition of her giving him up; she refused and slaved at hack writing jobs to supplement the miserly allowance he granted her, and to rear Percy as a gentleman's son. (That is all he became—a strange fate for the child of Shelley.) In 1826 Charles Shelley, Harriet's son, died, and Percy became the direct heir to the baronetcy, to which he succeeded on his grandfather's death. Mary sent him to Harrow and Cambridge—a sufficient commentary on her memories of Shelley's accounts of his bitter days at Eton and Oxford. When young Percy was twenty-one, and had been graduated from Cambridge, Sir Timothy Shelley increased his allowance to £400 a year; the old man did not die until 1844. William Godwin had died in 1836.

In 1838 the restrictions on editing Shelley's literary remains had been lifted, and Mary toiled at them for two years. Her health had been ruined by long and exhausting labor. With finances a little easier, she and her son traveled frequently on the continent between 1840 and 1843. After her father-in-law's death she was free at last to fulfill her great ambition of writing her husband's biography. But she no longer had the physical strength for such a task; only a fragment was completed. She grew increasingly an invalid until at the beginning of 1851, an old woman at fifty-three, she died. Her son had her buried at Bournemouth, and later removed the bodies of her parents from St. Pancras, to lie beside hers.

There was too much of her father in Mary Shelley to make her completely a sympathetic character. She looked like him, with pale skin, high forehead, and penetrating grey eyes; and she had his positive nature, his lack of sensibility. But she also had her mother's incisive mind, her high standard of duty and responsibility. What was deep in her emotionally was burnt away on the funeral pyre on the sands of Viareggio, except for what survived in her devotion to her son. Hers was the most quietly tragic of all existences—the life that outlasts its reason for being.

Frankenstein is Mary Shelley's only permanent contribution to literature. (The rest of her novels were written for bread, though there is a certain reminiscent strength in *Lodore*.) The production of that masterpiece of horror by a girl of twenty-one seems so incredible that someone has suggested that association with Shelley and Byron temporarily possessed her with their power! As a matter of fact, it is youth which revels in horror, and *Frankenstein* is therefore essentially a youthful book. In its genre it has never been surpassed.   M. A. deF.

PRINCIPAL WORKS: *Novels*—Frankenstein, 1818; Valperga, 1823; The Last Man, 1826; Lodore, 1835; Falkner, 1837. *Miscellaneous*—The Fortunes of Perkin Warbeck, 1830; Rambles in Germany and Italy, 1844; Proserpine and Midas: Two Unpublished Mythological Dramas, 1922.

ABOUT: Church, R. Mary Shelley; Gilfillan, G. Galleries of Literary Portraits; Marshall, F. A. The Life and Letters of Mary Wollstonecraft Shelley.

SHELLEY, PERCY BYSSHE (August 4, 1792-July 8, 1822), poet, was the oldest of seven children of a country squire both hard-and empty-headed, and his beautiful but narrow-minded wife. His earliest years were passed in his birthplace, Field Place, Horsham, Sussex, in the companionship of his adoring little sisters and his baby brother. They were probably the only happy years of his life. Already he was imaginative, "odd," given to strange wild flights of fancy; but he loved and was loved—a lifelong demand of his nature—as an engaging and innocent child.

From six to ten he learned Latin and Greek from a Welsh parson. Then, at ten, he was sent to Sion House Academy, near Brentford, and "the prison shades closed down." Probably no boy ever lived less fitted to the traditional education of the upper-class Englishman. Sion House was only a foretaste of Eton two years later—constant persecution by those savage conformists, adolescent boys, complete lack of sympathetic understanding from the hidebound masters. Uninterested in sports, living a deep imaginative life of his own, introspective and sensitive, he naturally became "Mad Shelley," and his existence a little hell. The only alleviation was the formation of the earliest of his many ardent friendships, and his ability to lose himself in cheap melodramatic romances and in scarcely less romantic scientific experiments. *Zastrozzi*, his first published work, was an imitation of these precursors of the dime novel.

Before Shelley went up to University College, Oxford, in the autumn of 1810, he had privately published also his first poems, "by Victor and Cazire" ("Cazire" being his sister Elizabeth, who had written a few of these juvenilia). It is said that his grandfather furnished the means of publication, but since Sir Bysshe was a notorious miser, it seems unlikely. Oxford at first was a great improvement on Eton; there was freedom from overt persecution, room to expand his eager, voracious intelligence. It was there he formed his close friendship with Thomas Jefferson Hogg (his name evidences a radical family background), a worldly, common-sense fellow in whose life Shelley was the one spark of idealism. There too he matured the economic, political, and religious principles which remained his throughout his brief life. The culmination of these was the publication of *The Necessity of Atheism* in 1811.

556

The result that might have been expected came quickly. Both Shelley and Hogg, who had had some hand in the production though not in the writing of the tract, were expelled from Oxford.

Shocked but defiant, the two boys went to London and took lodgings together. There Timothy Shelley visited his son and demanded that he disown his beliefs and his friend, on pain of complete abandonment. It is hardly surprising that Shelley firmly refused. Hogg, more compliant, became reconciled with his family and left him. Until a compromise was reached a few weeks later, by which Shelley received a small income, his sisters kept him alive by sending him their pocket-money. A school friend of theirs joined in this romantic sacrifice, a girl of sixteen named Harriet Westbrook, the daughter of a retired tavern-keeper.

To understand Shelley's love-relations it must always be kept in mind that the keynote of his nature was intellectual conviction, extreme idealism, and the missionary spirit in its most excessive form. He spread his gospel with fervor, and he loved those who, he convinced himself, accepted it. It was thus—aided by his belief that she had been ostracised for her association with him—that he entered into his unfortunate attachment to Harriet Westbrook. Eliza, her sister, schemed cannily to get the girl married to the heir to a wealthy baronetcy. Finally, when Shelley refused to accept the bait offered him, Harriet confessed her hopeless love for him. It was a shrewd move; nothing could so have appealed to Shelley's tender heart. They ran away to Edinburgh and were married there in August 1811, when he was just nineteen.

At first Harriet, her shallow character still unformed, entered enthusiastically into her husband's dreams and missions. For half a year, until both fathers grudgingly relented, they were desperately poor. The marriage cost him for a while his friendship with Hogg, who took advantage of his absence to try to seduce his wife. Early in 1812, all afire with ardor for the cause of Irish freedom, he and Harriet went to Dublin, in the naive belief that all the Irish needed to rebel against their tyrants was a scattering of inflammatory tracts. In a few months he was disabused and disgusted by the practical situation, and returned, discouraged, to England. But his pro-Irish activities caused him to come under surveillance of the government, and for comfort's sake he moved to Wales. It was during a visit to London during this period that he first met William Godwin, the radical philosopher, whose eager disciple he became.

A perhaps apocryphal attack upon his life sent them back to England, in the spring of 1814. He was living chiefly on post-obit loans on his father's estate; he would soon be

PERCY BYSSHE SHELLEY

of age; and some permanent financial arrangement had to be made. In June his first child, Ianthe, was born. Shelley was always a most affectionate father, and he delighted in the little girl. But her coming meant the end of any happiness with Harriet, for from that time on her sister Eliza became a part of the household. Under Eliza's vulgar and grasping influence, all Harriet's incipient extravagance, indolence, and frivolity bloomed lustily. She ceased to be in any sense a companion to her husband; she would not even nurse her own child, she demanded carriages and plate. Shelley acquiesced in everything, but his marriage had become a tragic farce, with Eliza as its evil demon. Nevertheless, in March 1814, he remarried Harriet in London, to insure the validity of the Scotch marriage and their children's legitimacy; she was then again two months pregnant.

But the end was at hand. It was at just about this time that he had first met Godwin's daughter Mary. Here was one who from heredity and early training was indeed receptive to his dreams and aspirations and beliefs. Their love was inevitable and immediate. In July they eloped to the continent—that grotesque elopement which included a sister in its train. Harriet's son Charles was born in November, soon after their return to England. It must not be forgotten that Shelley was a fervent opponent of orthodox marriage, and that Harriet from the beginning had known and apparently shared his views.

A period of desperate harassment followed. Shelley was hounded by creditors, and had to become practically a fugitive. Godwin thundered against him, but continued to dun him for money promised when he had had money to give. At the beginning of 1815 Shelley's grandfather, the old scoundrel Sir

Bysshe (an American by birth), died, and he became direct heir to his father's wealth and title. His family refused to see him, but after eighteen months financial settlements were made which put him out of the reach of penury thereafter, paid his debts, and provided for an allowance for Harriet and her children. The same year his first child by Mary was born and died.

Most of the next year was spent at Windsor, where his son William was born. Soon after, they went to Geneva for the summer, where Shelley first met Byron. *Alastor*, the first of Shelley's major poems, belongs to this period. They returned to England, to Bath, and were there in September when Fanny Imlay (Mary's half-sister) poisoned herself at Swansea. Two months later Harriet, who had disappeared from her father's house, was found drowned in the Serpentine, in which she found escape from the imminent prospect of bearing a child to another man than Shelley.

Shelley and Mary could now be married, and the marriage took place on the 30th of December. Shelley immediately took steps to secure custody of his two children by Harriet. The Westbrooks fought hard, and won. In the Chancery suit heard before Lord Eldon, decision was finally made that the children be placed under the guardianship of a Dr. Hume; their father was allowed to visit them monthly, but only in the presence of the Humes, and there was no such restriction on visits from the Westbrooks.

From early in 1817 to March 1818, Shelley, with his wife and her two children, and with Claire Clairmont (Mary's stepsister) and Claire's daughter, Allegra, by Byron, settled at Great Marlow. His activity as a political pamphleteer was nearly over; his serious poetic career was beginning. It is curious to reflect that this fragile-appearing young man of twenty-five, who lived on bread and vegetables and water, who spent most of his days writing great poetry or avidly reading the Greek classics, who wore himself out in kindness to acquaintances and benefactions to the poor, whose only relaxation was playing games with children, was the same monster of immorality and atheism, who, so far as he was noticed at all, was denounced and execrated by every respectable person in England.

This situation, combined with fear that his children by Mary might also be taken from him, and with a physician's warning of pulmonary trouble that demanded a warmer climate (actually, Shelley's long indisposition seems to have arisen chiefly from undernourishment!), finally determined him to leave England forever and to live in Italy. The little party—Claire and the baby as usual accompanying them, not without wear and tear on

Mary's patience—went first to Milan, where Allegra was turned over to her father's care. (She died early in 1822.) They made brief stays in and around Leghorn and Venice. There little Clara died in August. It was a period of intense melancholy for Shelley; the conflict between dream and reality was becoming too much for even a spirit naturally so buoyant and trustful. The next March, in Rome, the most beloved of their children, William, died suddenly, and plunged both his parents into the deepest distress.

In Florence, in November, their last and only surviving child, Percy, was born. It was here that Shelley finished *Prometheus Unbound*. Two months later they moved to Pisa, the neighborhood of which remained their home until the spring before Shelley's death. It was there, in the autumn of 1820, that he met Emilia Viviani, who became the inspiration of *Epipsychidion*—and a source of conflict between Mary and himself. There were other annoyances also; Godwin was still demanding money to fill a bottomless pit into which Shelley had already poured a small fortune, and Mary and Claire bickered until at last Claire left them. Scornful as he might be of the animosity felt toward him in England, he could not help feeling keenly the continued neglect of what he must have known were great and immortal poems. The words he wrote a little later were already true of him forever—"less oft is peace in Shelley's mind, than calm in waters seen."

Such were the conditions of Shelley's inner life when in May 1822 he settled with his family at Casa Magni, near Lerici, on the Gulf of Spezzia. A few days later the boat which he named the "Ariel"—one of his own nicknames—was bought. The nearest neighbors were those close friends, Edward and Jane Williams. Shelley was happier than for years past, though he had the hard task of breaking to Claire, who was with them for a while, the news of Allegra's death.

Early in July, Leigh Hunt with his dipsomaniac wife and all his squalling children arrived in Leghorn, in answer to an old and half-hearted invitation from Byron. It was a situation which only Shelley could smooth over. Against Mary's premonition of disaster, he and Williams, with a sailor boy, went to Leghorn in the "Ariel." On July 8, a few days later, having adjusted affairs between Byron and the Hunts, they set sail to return to Lerici. There was a sudden squall, and the boat disappeared from sight.

Ten days later, Trelawny and Hunt found Shelley's body washed up on the beach at Viareggio. It was recognizable only from its tall, slender form and the volumes of Aeschylus and Keats in the pockets. Trelawny secured permission to burn the three mutilated corpses on the shore. He, Hunt, and Byron were the only witnesses of that tragic rite. Trelawny snatched Shelley's heart from the flames, and it lies buried now in the English Protestant Cemetery at Rome.

To evaluate Shelley's poetical legacy is to deal necessarily in superlatives. Some of the loveliest lyrics in English, together with longer poems unsurpassed in beauty and grandeur, came from the pen of this visionary, half-unearthly man whose outward life was a long pilgrimage of frustration and pain. To those who knew him best Shelley appeared a creature apart from mundane humanity; there was in him always the strangeness of those who have aspired toward an impossible perfection. There was perhaps a vein of shrillness in his youthful propagandist writings, but the long discipline he served in Greek literature preserved his poetry from partaking of that defect. The dominant impression of his work is that of pure and ineffable beauty—not the lush earthly beauty of Keats, but the high-keyed beauty of the super-terrestrial. It is useless to speculate on the potential future that was drowned in the Gulf of Spezzia. It may be that it is well that Shelley died before he was thirty. Dreams like his seldom survive the hope and courage of youth. It is better, in any event, to think so, than to regret futilely the premature asphyxiation of unwritten poems as exalted and exquisite as those he lived to write.   M. A. deF.

PRINCIPAL WORKS: *Poetry*—Original Poems by Victor and Cazire, 1810; Posthumous Fragments of Margaret Nicholson, 1810; A Poetical Essay on the Existing State of Things by a Gentleman of Oxford, 1811; Queen Mab, 1813; Alastor, 1816; Laon and Cythna (The Revolt of Islam) 1818; Rosalind and Helen, 1819; The Cenci, 1819; Prometheus Unbound, 1820; Oedipus Tyrannus, 1820; Epipsychidion, 1821; Adonais, 1821; Hellas, 1822; Poetical Pieces, 1823; Posthumous Poems, 1824; Miscellaneous and Posthumous Poems, 1826; The Masque of Anarchy, 1832; The Daemon of the World, 1876; The Wandering Jew, 1876. *Prose*—Zastrozzi, 1810; St. Irvyne, 1811; The Necessity of Atheism, 1811; Address to the Irish People, 1812; Letter to Lord Ellenborough, 1812; A Vindication of a Natural Diet, 1813; A Refutation of Deism, 1814; Essays, Letters, Translations, and Fragments, 1852.

ABOUT: Bailey, R. Shelley; Brailsford, H. N. Shelley, Godwin, and Their Circle; Brock, A. C. Shelley: The Man and the Poet; Clarke, I. C. Shelley and Byron; Dowden, E. The Life of Percy Bysshe Shelley; Hogg, T. J. The Life of Shelley (including Trelawny, E. J. Recollections of Shelley, and Peacock, T. L. Memoirs of Shelley); Kurtz, B. P. The Pursuit of Death; Medwin, T. The Life of Percy Bysshe Shelley; Peck, W. E. Shelley: His Life and Work; Sharp, W. Life of Percy Bysshe Shelley; Shelley, P. Shelley Memorials; Winwar, F. The Romantic Rebels.

SHERIDAN, CAROLINE E. S. See NORTON, CAROLINE E. S.

SHERIDAN, HELEN S. See DUFFERIN, LADY

SHERWOOD, MARTHA MARY (May 6, 1775-September 22, 1851), children's writer, was born in Worcester. Her maiden name was Butt, and her father was a clergyman. She was educated at home, very rigorously and strictly, until 1790, when she was sent to a French school at Reading which soon moved to London. There she was a classmate of Mary Russell Mitford and Letitia Elizabeth Landon, both later well-known writers. Her father died in 1795, and the family moved to Bridgnorth. A pretty and pious girl, she taught in Sunday School and occupied herself in charitable work. The object of her first writing was "to teach religion to the poor."

In 1803 she married her cousin, Captain Henry Sherwood, and the next year she went to India with him. They had five children and adopted three orphans; Mrs. Sherwood founded the first orphan asylum in India. Returning to England, to Worcester, the whole family set about studying Hebrew, and at Mrs. Sherwood's death she left a dictionary of the prophetic books of the Bible which was never published. From 1830 to 1832 the family spent on the Continent. Captain Sherwood died in 1849, and two years later his wife followed him, all but two of their eight real and adopted children having predeceased them.

It is hard to believe that Mrs. Sherwood's *Little Henry and His Bearer* went through a hundred editions up to 1884, and was translated into a dozen languages. Practically every middle-class Victorian child was brought up on *The History of the Fairchild Family*. Her work is trite, prosy, heavily pious, mere sugar-coated didacticism, but she did have a sympathetic insight into the child mind.

PRINCIPAL WORKS: The Traditions, 1794; Susan Gray, 1802; Little Henry and His Bearer, 1815; The Indian Pilgrim, 1815; The History of the Fairchild Family, 1818-47.

ABOUT: Kelly, S. [daughter]. Life of Martha Mary Sherwood; Illustrated London News October 1851; Living Age November 1854.

SHORE, LOUISA CATHERINE (February 1824-May 1895), poet, was born in Bedfordshire. Her father was a clergyman and private tutor. Her sister Margaret Emily, who died at nineteen, left much unpublished prose and verse, and her other sister, Arabella, collaborated with Louisa in several books, though Louisa wrote most of the poems in these volumes. Louisa was the most talented of the family. She wrote plays as well as poems, and was a contributor to the *Westminster Review*. Both surviving sisters were early and militant feminists. They lived together in London, after the deaths of their parents and brother and sister, until Louisa died. Louisa's poems were lofty in subject and vigorous in style; she was especially good in elegiac poems written in memory of deceased relatives and friends.

PRINCIPAL WORKS: War Lyrics (with Arabella Shore) 1855; Gemma of the Isles, 1859; Hannibal, 1861; Fra Dolcino and Other Poems, 1871; Elegies and Memorials (with Arabella Shore) 1890; Poems, 1896.

ABOUT: Shore, L. Poems (see Memoir by A. Shore and Appreciation by F. Harrison).

SHORTHOUSE, J(OSEPH) HENRY (September 9, 1834-March 4, 1903), novelist, was born in Great Charles Street, Birmingham, the eldest son of Joseph Shorthouse and Mary Ann Hawker. His parents were Quakers, descended cn both sides from well-to-do manufacturing families. Shorthouse was a delicate and sensitive child. Sent to school at four, he developed a painful stammer, which afflicted him all his life. Except for a short stay at Tottenham College in his fifteenth year, he was subsequently educated at home. He entered his father's business at sixteen and proved himself a competent man of affairs, despite his handicap. This nervous disorder, while a great trial to one who was by temperament an eager conversationalist, was nevertheless, Shorthouse felt, a blessing, because it kept him from public life and activities, which would have shortened his existence and prevented his literary career.

The inactivity and leisure which his weak constitution enforced from childhood resulted in his being widely read in a variety of subjects. His reflective, even mystical, mentality and deep appreciation of beauty made him an enigma to the world of business with which he was associated. He belonged to an "Essay Meeting," a kind of literary society, and probably did his first serious writing for it. Although born a Quaker, Shorthouse in maturity never assumed the characteristic garb of the Friends. Indeed his love of fine apparel was such that he was known to his intimates as "the Marquis." His feeling for the past combined with his sense for beauty to turn him toward modes of worship which carried more appeal to his emotional and aesthetic nature. After his marriage to Sara, daughter of John and Elizabeth Scott, in 1857, he was baptized into the Church of England. He was also interested in spiritualism.

An epileptic attack (1862) intensified for him the importance of a quiet existence. He remained active in business and was for nine years churchwarden of St. John's parish, but literature and study were his most constant employments. For the space of ten years he worked on the novel John Inglesant. Three years after it was finished and laid away his wife persuaded him to have it printed privately for distribution among his friends. One hundred copies appeared and were given away. Shorthouse was apparently contented that one hundred people had admired the book and did

J. HENRY SHORTHOUSE

not particularly desire its general publication. One copy, however, fell into the hands of Mrs. Humphry Ward. She showed it to the publisher Alexander Macmillan, who wrote Shorthouse, asking permission to publish. The result was that the Birmingham manufacturer of vitriol found himself famous.

Shorthouse wrote several other novels after John Inglesant, but they never achieved its popularity. Though he enjoyed the literary associations and friendships which he now gained, he disliked being lionized and as for money his business had always supplied sufficient of that. He died at Edgbaston Park, Birmingham, after a long illness and was buried in the parish church. The Victorian aesthetics of Shorthouse's work are outmoded today, but John Inglesant's stained-glass atmosphere is not without appeal. P. B. S.

PRINCIPAL WORKS: Novels—John Inglesant, 1880; The Little Schoolmaster Mark, 1883; Sir Percival, 1886; The Countess Eve, 1888; Blanche Lady Falaise, 1891. Essays—The Platonism of Wordsworth, 1882; The Royal Supremacy, 1899. Stories—A Teacher of the Violin and other Tales, 1888.

ABOUT: Gosse, E. Portraits and Sketches; Shorthouse, S. The Life, Letters, and Literary Remains of J. Henry Shorthouse.

SIDGWICK, HENRY (May 31, 1838-August 28, 1900), philosophical writer, was born in Yorkshire, the son of a clergyman who died in 1841. He belonged to the celebrated Sidgwick-Benson family which has given so many distinguished writers and clerics to England. A precocious, studious boy, with no liking for athletics, he had a brilliant career at Rugby and at Trinity College, Cambridge. In 1859 he was made fellow and assistant tutor of his college. He had by this time determined to devote his life to the study and teaching of philosophy. As part of this plan he devoted the year 1862 to studying Arabic at the University of Dresden. In 1869 he resigned his fellowship, feeling that his religious views were no longer consonant with his tenure of it; this was the last determining factor in abolishing the religious tests in 1871. He was allowed to retain his lectureship, however, and lectured more or less at Trinity all his life.

In 1875, indeed, he was made prelector of moral and political philosophy at Trinity, and in 1883 Knightbridge professor of moral philosophy. He had received an honorary fellowship in 1881, and in 1885 was re-elected fellow.

Another of Sidgwick's great interests was the higher education of women. In 1876 he had married Eleanor Balfour, sister of the Hon. Arthur Balfour, and she became first vice-president and then president of Newnham, the Cambridge women's college, in the foundation of which Sidgwick had been very active. He and his wife lived at Newnham throughout the remainder of his lifetime. He was a member of the senate of Trinity from 1890 to 1898, but resigned because the university refused to grant degrees to women.

His other chief pursuit was the investigation of psychic phenomena. He was one of the founders of the Society for Physical Research, and its president from 1882 to 1885, and from 1888 to 1893. He never became a convinced spiritualist, but held his judgment suspended to the last. This, indeed, was his habitual philosophical habit. He was a sort of liaison officer between differing schools of philosophical thought, acute, subtle, and cautious. His ethical writings were his most important work and still have value.

PRINCIPAL WORKS: Methods of Ethics, 1874; Principles of Political Economy, 1883, Outlines of the History of Ethics, 1886; Elements of Politics, 1891.

ABOUT: Hayward, F. H. Ethical Philosophy of Sidgwick; Sidgwick, A. & E. M. Memoir of Henry Sidgwick; Mind January 1900; Proceedings of the Society for Psychical Research December 1900.

SIMPSON, RICHARD (1820-April 5, 1876), biographer and Shakespearian scholar, was born in Surrey, and educated at Oriel College, Oxford, where he received his B.A. degree and was ordained in 1843. The next year he was vicar of Mitcham, Surrey; but the year following he became a convert to the Roman Catholic Church and resigned his pastorate. After several years of travel on the Continent, during which he became master of half a dozen languages, he returned to England and took up a literary career. Until 1862, when it was discontinued, he was editor of *The Rambler*, a liberal Catholic magazine. Then, with Lord Acton, the historian, who was his close friend, he founded a quarterly known as the *Home and Foreign Review*. This was attacked by Catholic prelates as unorthodox, and ceased to exist after two years. As long as Acton was editor of the *North British Review*, Simpson was a frequent contributor.

He was also a musical composer of some merit. His chief activity, however, in later years was research into Shakespearian problems; he was one of the foremost Shakespearian scholars of his age. Aside from this and his biography of the poet Campion, his principal literary service was in assisting Gladstone in the writing of his polemic *Vaticanism*; for although he remained in the Roman Catholic Church until his death (at fifty-six, near Rome, from cancer), he was always liberal and even heretical in his views.

PRINCIPAL WORKS: Edmund Campion: A Biography, 1867; Introduction to the Philosophy of Shakespeare's Sonnets, 1868.

ABOUT: Academy April 22, 1876; Athenaeum April 22, 1876.

SIMS, GEORGE ROBERT (September 2, 1847-September 4, 1922), poet, playright, and novelist, was born in London and educated at Hanwell College and Bonn University. From 1874 he made his living as a journalist, contributing a column to *The Referee*, under the pseudonym of "Dagonet," from the foundation of the paper in 1877. He was also a frequent contributor to *Fun* and to other humorous and popular magazines. His letters in the London *Daily News* on the condition of the London poor led to the formation of a Royal Commission to investigate and remedy the horrors he revealed. He was a prolific playwright, his best known work being *The Lights of London*, which survived on the stage for many years after its first performance. His novels were of no literary importance: he was primarily a good journalist, and nothing more. His verses and ballads were his most successful writing. He was married in 1901 to Florence Wykes. In 1905 he received the Royal Norwegian Order of St. Olaf.

PRINCIPAL WORKS: Dagonet Ballads, 1879; Crutch and Toothpick (play) 1879; The Social Kaleidoscope, 1880; How the Poor Live, 1883; Rogues and Vagabonds, 1885; Land of Gold and Other Poems, 1888; Dorcas Dene, Detective, 1897; Once Upon a Christmas Time, 1898.

ABOUT: Sims, G. R. My Life; Glances Back.

SINCLAIR, CATHERINE (April 17, 1800-August 6, 1864), Scottish novelist and juvenile writer, was born in Edinburgh, the daughter of Sir John Sinclair, a prominent politician. Two of her brothers became well-known divines. She was her father's secretary from the age of fourteen until his death in 1835. Thereafter she devoted herself to writing. Her first literary production was a children's book written for the entertainment of her young nephew. Her best known juvenile work was *Holiday House*. She was noted for her philanthropies, which included the setting up of seats and drinking-fountains in various locations in Edinburgh. She died, unmarried, at her brother's house in Kensington.

Miss Sinclair's stories were bright and witty, and she had a deft hand at character-drawing, especially in the depiction of her Scottish compatriots.

PRINCIPAL WORKS: Modern Accomplishments, 1836; Scotland and the Scotch, 1840; Modern Flirtations, 1841; The Journey of Life, 1847; The Business of Life, 1848; London Homes, 1853; Torchester Abbey, 1857; Sketches and Short Stories of Scotland and the Scotch, 1859; Sketches and Short Stories of Wales and the Welsh, 1860.

ABOUT: Scotsman August 7, 1864.

SINGLETON, MARY MONTGOMERIE.
See CURRIE, LADY

SKEAT, WALTER WILLIAM (November 21, 1835-October 6, 1912), philologist, archaelogist, and critic, was born in London. He was the second son of William and Sarah Bluck Skeat.

He attended King's College School. In 1854 he entered Christ's College, Cambridge, where he studied theology and mathematics. Elected fellow of his college in 1860, he took orders and married Bertha Jones of Lewisham. His first curacy was at East Dereham, Norfolk; his second (1862), Godalming. Here an illness which affected his voice made it imperative that he give up the church. He returned to Cambridge and was appointed lecturer in mathematics in 1864.

An influence which began at King's College School, where he had been under the eminent Anglo-Saxon scholar, Γ. O. Cockayne, now prompted him to study Anglo-Saxon and Gothic. He devoted his leisure to these studies with such earnestness that from 1878 to 1912 he was Elrington and Bosworth professor of Anglo-Saxon at Cambridge. For fourteen years Skeat had been editing for the Early English Text Society, to whose cause he was recruited by F. J. Furnivall. His first work for the society was *Lancelot of the Laik*. He completed Mitchell Kemble's *Anglo-Saxon Gospels* and edited Aelfric's *Lives of the Saints*. These are his two standard works, though his Chaucer texts and *Piers Plowman* are significant also.

In 1873 Skeat founded the English Dialect Society and served as its president until 1896. This society sponsored the *English Dialect Dictionary*. Skeat helped to found the Chaucer Society and the New Shakespeare Society, and was first president of the Simplified Spelling Society in England.

With the intention of sifting materials for a new English Dictionary, Skeat compiled one of his best known volumes, the *Etymological Dictionary*. Throughout his life he was an ardent and energetic worker, producing in all some sixty volumes of scholarly text, and many editions of school texts. In addition he contributed voluminously to the *Transactions of the Bibliographical Society, Notes and Queries*, and other scholarly journals. Recognition came in his election to the British Academy as fellow, and in several honorary degrees. Skeat died at Cambridge.

He was a prodigous worker, sorting glossary slips as he chatted at tea, and rigidly limiting his time and energy. Genial and kindly of manner, he had many friends and dispensed a delightful hospitality. His interests included archaeology, and toward the end of his life he devoted much time to this and the related study of English place-names.

"One of the greatest scholars in the world," was C. P. G. Scott's comment on Skeat at his death. Certainly he had done much to lay down the principles of a new philological school and to popularize the knowledge of early periods of English literature and language. His influence in philology and etymological method has been felt in other lands as well, and he has given an impetus to the study of many important and related subjects which had hitherto been totally disregarded.
D. F. A.

PRINCIPAL WORKS: *Criticism and Editions*—Songs and Ballads of Uhland, 1864; Lancelot of the Laik, 1865; Piers Plowman, 1866; Romance of Partenay, 1866; A Tale of Ludlow Castle, 1866; Piers Plowman, 1867-84; Pierce the Plowman's Creed, 1867; William of Palerne, 1867; Lay of Havelock, 1868; Moeso-Gothic Glossary, 1868; Barbour's Bruce, 1870-89; Joseph of Arimathea, 1871; Chatterton's Poems (2 vols.) 1871; Specimens of English, 1871; Anglo-Saxon Gospels, 1871-87; Specimens of Early English, 1872; Chaucer's Astrolabe, 1872; Questions in English Literature, 1873; Seven Reprinted Glossaries, 1873; Chaucer, 1874-97; Ray's Collections of English Words, 1874; Two Noble Kinsmen, 1875; Shakespeare's Plutarch, 1875;

W. W. SKEAT

Five Provincial Glossaries, 1876; List of English Words, 1876; Bibliographical List of Works in English Dialects, 1873-77; Alexander and Dindymus, 1878; Wycliffe's New Testament, 1879; Five Reprinted Glossaries, 1879; Specimens of English Dialects, 1879; Wycliffe's Job, etc. 1881; Aelfric's Lives of the Saints, 1881-90; E. Guest's History of English Rhythms, 1882; Fitzherbert's Book of Husbandry, 1882; English Etymological Dictionary, 1879-82; Concise Etymological Dictionary, 1882; Kingis Quair, 1884; The Wars of Alexander, 1886; Principles of English Etymology, 1887, 1891; A Concise Dictionary of Middle English, 1888; Piers Plowman, 1889-91; Primer of English Etymology, 1892; Twelve Facsimiles of Old English MSS, 1892; Nine Specimens of English Dialects, 1895; Two Collections of Derbycisms, 1896; Chaucer Canon, 1900; Notes on English Etymology, 1901; Primer of Classical and English Philology, 1905; Piers the Plowman Modernized, 1905; Modern English Spelling, 1906; Proverbs of Alfred, 1907; Early English Proverbs, 1910. *Poetry*—Shakespeare and Bacon, 1904. *Archaeology and Miscellaneous*—A Student's Pastime, 1896; Malay Magic, 1900; Placenames of Cambridgeshire, 1901; Wild Tribes of the Malay Peninsula, 1902; Placenames of Huntingdonshire, 1903; Placenames of Hertfordshire, 1904; Placenames of Bedfordshire, 1906; Placenames of Berkshire, 1911.

ABOUT: Skeat, W. W. A Student's Pastime; Literary Digest 45:845 November 9, 1912.

SKELTON, SIR JOHN (1831-July 19, 1897), Scottish essayist and biographer, was born in Edinburgh, son of a writer to the signet. After being graduated from the University of Edinburgh, he was admitted, in 1854, to the faculty of advocates. Although he remained as an active member of his profession throughout his life, he always preferred literature to the law. Fearing, however, that his literary appearances might detract from his legal standing, he wrote most of his non-legal work under the pseudonym of "Shirley," taken from Charlotte Brontë's novel of that name, reviewed by him on its first appearance.

Skelton was a regular contributor to *The Guardian* (Edinburgh), *Fraser's Magazine* and particularly to *Blackwood's*, for which he wrote from 1869 to his death. He also had a distinguished public career. In 1868, through the influence of Disraeli (whose biography he wrote later), he was made secretary of the Scottish Board of Supervision, in charge of poor relief and public health; and in 1894, when the board was abolished, he became vice-president of the Scottish Local Government Board, which took its place. This place he retained until ill health forced him to resign early in 1897. He was an accomplished artist and fond of moving in artistic circles. In 1867 he married Anne Adair, daughter of the professor of surgery at Glasgow University, and they had several children. He received an honorary LL.D. from Edinburgh in 1878, and was made Commander of the Bath in 1887 and Knight Commander in 1897, shortly before he died.

As a biographer Skelton is not very reliable, for he was an extreme partisan, a chivalrous defender of the historical personages who were his subjects. His work is all the more interesting for that reason, if it be considered not for authoritativeness but for readability, his quaint, eccentric style having a charm which many more sound and dependable writings lack.

PRINCIPAL WORKS: Nugae Criticae, 1862; John Dryden: In Defense, 1863; Benjamin Disraeli: The Past and the Future, 1868; Handbook of Public Health, 1870; The Impeachment of Mary Stuart, 1876; Essays of Shirley, 1882; Maitland of Lethington and the Scotland of Mary Stuart, 1887-88; Mary Stuart, 1893; The Table-Talk of Shirley, 1895.

ABOUT: Scotsman July 21, 1897; London Times April 1 and July 21, 1897.

SKENE, WILLIAM FORBES (June 7, 1809-August 29, 1892), Scottish antiquary, was born in Aberdeenshire. His father was a friend of Sir Walter Scott, and he grew up in the Scott circle. Even while he was at the High School in Edinburgh he began his study of Gaelic language and folklore, profiting by his relationship to some of the oldest Highland families. In 1824 he went with his brother to Haunau, near Frankfort, Germany, then returned to study at St. Andrews University. He was then apprenticed to his uncle, a writer to the signet, and passed to practise in 1832. He followed this profession for thirty years (until 1865 he was clerk of bills in the court of session), devoting his leisure to the history of the Highlands and to Celtic scholarship. He edited numerous Gaelic antiquities besides his independent researches. In 1879 he received honorary degrees from Edinburgh and Oxford. In 1881 he was appointed historiographer royal for Scotland. Skene was known also as a philanthropist. He was unmarried, but reared the orphan family of a niece.

Although some of Skene's antiquarian views are questioned by other scholars, and he was apt to defend to the bitter end any conviction once formed, he was a man of profound learning and his name is in the front rank of authorities on the Celtic past.

PRINCIPAL WORKS: The Highlanders of Scotland, 1837; The Four Ancient Books of Wales, 1868; Celtic Scotland, 1876-80.

ABOUT: Skene, W. F. Memorials of the Family of Skene of Skene; Proceedings of the Society of Scottish Antiquaries, 1892.

SKIPSEY, JOSEPH (March 17, 1832-September 3, 1903), poet, was born in Northumberland, the youngest of eight children of a miner killed in a strike by a special constable. He had no education whatever, but worked in the mines from the age of seven. He taught himself to read and write, the Bible being his only book until he was fifteen. In 1852 he walked to London, and got a job in

railway construction. Two years later he married his landlady, Sara Ann Hendley; they had five sons and three daughters. Soon after his marriage he went back to mining, in Scotland. A volume of poems, published in 1859 (all copies of which have vanished), attracted the attention of the editor of the Gateshead *Observer*, who got him work as under-storekeeper in a factory in that town. In 1863 one of his children was killed in an accident at the works, and he moved to New-castle-on-Tyne. After a brief and unconge-nial experience as assistant librarian of the Newcastle Literary and Philosophical Society, Skipsey went back to the mines, and worked as a miner until 1882. Then for three years he and his wife were caretakers of the board schools at Newcastle; while in this menial position he edited the *Canterbury Poets*. In 1888 and 1889 he was janitor at Armstrong College; then he and Mrs. Skipsey were made custodians of Shakespeare's birthplace at Stratford-on-Avon. They resigned in 1891, and for the rest of his life Skipsey lived with various of his children in the north of England, aided by a small government pen-sion secured through Burne-Jones, the painter. He became a spiritualist, and for a while prac-tised as a clairvoyant. He died at the home of one of his sons, not far from his birth-place.

Skipsey's poems, written in the scant leisure of a life of manual labor, display a genuine lyrical gift. Though they are not free from traces of his lack of education, they are no mere curiosities, but testify to the thwarting of a genuine talent by the economic conditions of the poet's life.

PRINCIPAL WORKS: Poems, Songs, and Ballads, 1862; The Collier Lad and Other Lyrics, 1864; Poems, 1871; A Book of Miscellaneous Lyrics, 1878 (revised as A Book of Lyrics, 1881); Carols From the Coalfields, 1886; Songs and Lyrics, 1892.

ABOUT: Watson, R. S. Joseph Skipsey.

"SLICK, SAM." See HALIBURTON, THOMAS CHANDLER

SMEDLEY, FRANK (FRANCIS ED-WARD) (October 4, 1818-May 1, 1864), novelist, was born in Great Marlow, Buck-inghamshire, of a family of clergymen and teachers long connected with Westminster School. Smedley was born with a deformed foot, and was all his life a cripple. It was impossible, therefore, for him to carry on the family traditions, and he was privately ed-ucated, at first by a tutor at home, and then by his uncle, vicar in a village near Cambridge. It was during the years with his uncle that Smedley became familiar with school, uni-versity, and sporting life, in which he could not participate, but which he could enjoy vicariously through his novels.

In 1846, encouraged by a cousin who pitied his depression at his deprivation of all active interests, Smedley began contributing to *Sharpe's London Magazine* a series of "Scenes From the Life of a Private Pupil." These, which ran for two years, were very popular, and formed the foundation of his most suc-cessful novel, *Frank Farleigh*. This book, il-ustrated by George Cruikshank, is a sort of dream autobiography of the boy and young man Smedley would have wished to be. After *Tom Brown at Rugby*, it is perhaps the best depiction of life in an English boy's school. All his novels are of this same general var-iety.

For two years Smedley edited *Sharpe's Magazine*, at first for nothing, then for a pit-tance. He also edited, in 1854, the only three numbers of *Cruikshank's Magazine* which ever appeared. But his health, which had im-proved sufficiently to allow him to go to Lon-don. failed badly from 1856, and he was no longer able even to write much. The only work he did thereafter was to edit *Seven Tales by Seven Authors* (one by himself) in 1858. The following year he bought a house near his native town, and died there suddenly the year after, of apoplexy.

Smedley's novels are full of keen observa-tion and quick, light humor. His verse, some of which was written in collaboration with his close friend Edmund Yates, is poor.

PRINCIPAL WORKS: Frank Farleigh, 1850; Lewis Arundel, 1852; The Fortunes of the Colville Fam-ily, 1853; Harry Coverdale's Courtship, 1855; Mirth and Metre by Two Merry Men (with Edmund Yates) 1855; Gathered Leaves (poems) 1865.

ABOUT: Smedley, F. E. Gathered Leaves (see Memorial Sketch by E. Yates); Illustrated London News May 14, 1864.

SMEDLEY, MENELLA BUTE (1815?-1880?), poet and novelist, was the older sister of Frank (Francis E.) Smedley, the author of *Frank Farleigh*. She was born in Great Marlow, Buckinghamshire, the daugh-ter of a clergyman, and was privately educated at home. She never married, and outside of her writing little is known of her life. She was more or less active in various philan-thropies, being particularly interested in the welfare and education of orphans and pauper children. Her stories are didactic and moral-izing, sentimental and pious. She appears, however, to have had a real if slight talent for poetry, and her shorter lyrics are described as "noble and delicate in feeling." With an unnamed collaborator, she also wrote several volumes of verses for children; and she was the author of a five-act poetic drama, *Lady Grace*, which remained unacted and is in-cluded in a volume of her poems.

PRINCIPAL WORKS: The Maiden Aunt, 1849; The Use of Sunshine, 1851; Lays and Ballads From English History, 1858; Nina: A Tale, 1861; Twice

Lost, 1863; A Mere Story, 1865; Poems, 1868; Boarding-Out and Pauper Schools, 1875.

ABOUT: Robertson, E. S. English Poetesses.

SMETHAM, JAMES (September 9, 1821-February 5, 1889), painter and essayist, was born in Yorkshire, the son of a Methodist minister. He longed from childhood to be a painter, but was apprenticed by his father instead to an architect, after being educated at a school for Methodist ministers' sons near Leeds. The architect, fortunately, was himself more interested in painting, and left the boy free to draw and study in Lincoln Minster, eventually canceling his indentures. Smetham then set up as a portrait painter in Shropshire, but in 1843 went to London to study at the Royal Academy. He seems to have had some talent as a painter—Rossetti admired his work—but he was always a failure. From the beginning also he was ambitious to be a writer as well, and in his case one ambition injured the other. In 1851 he became a teacher of drawing at the Wesleyan Normal College at Westminster, though still occasionally exhibiting, and illustrating his own (unpublished) essays and meditations. He was married in 1854, and had a large family. In 1869 he steeled himself to a final effort to overcome a life of defeat: he sent four paintings to the Royal Academy, and all were rejected. In 1877 he became insane, and remained completely irrational, in an asylum, until he died twelve years later.

Smetham's literary works were not published until after his death. They show flashes of penetration (especially in the studies of Reynolds and Blake), and occasional weird beauty, but he was not primarily a writer and was incapable of balanced judgment or sustained effort.

PRINCIPAL WORKS: Familiar Letters, 1891; Literary Works, 1893.

ABOUT: Smetham, J. Familiar Letters (see Memoir by William Davies).

SMILES, SAMUEL (December 23, 1812-April 16, 1904), Scottish biographer and essayist, was born at Haddington, one of eleven children in a family of an industrious anti-burgher, "a sort of Quaker Presbyterian . . . who was a great gardener."

When he was twenty he took his M.D. at Edinburgh, and six years later he published at his own expense his first book, *Physical Education*, which was a failure. He practised medicine for a few years in his home town and then removed to Leeds where he gave up his profession and became editor of the *Leeds Times*, secretary of the Leeds and Thirsk Railway at thirty-three, secretary of the South Eastern Railway at forty-two, and then retired in 1866 when he was fifty-four, to devote himself to writing.

SAMUEL SMILES

His first important work was a *Life of George Stephenson*, published in 1857. Two years later his position as a writer was established with the publication of *Self-Help;* a book preaching "that perseverance and courage would, in the end, lead to success of the best sort." The very title, *Self-Help*, caught the public ear, and all Europe welcomed the new "gospel according to Smiles." It was translated into all the European and many non-European languages; English parents hailed the mundane precepts as wholesome, romantic Italian youths felt the philosophy was elevating, Japanese students learned the book by heart, a Mohammedan nobleman had mottoes from the book copied on the walls of his palace along with quotations from the Koran, and thousands of people wrote to the author thanking him for stimulating them to further endeavors. He was an optimist of a new order, and to him the extraordinary success of his book was proof of the truth of his gospel.

Character, Thrift, Duty, and *Life and Labour* and many biographies, especially of engineers, followed, and in each book he repeated the simple philosophy he had expressed in *Self-Help*—"If you don't at first succeed, try, try, try again."

In his *Autobiography* he wrote of his school mates: "On the whole, provided there was perseverance, those young men succeeded best from whom little was expected." And again in the same book he wrote: "I have often been amazed and distressed to find what a number of helpless and idle creatures exist in this busy world. Some of them think that it is want of luck that attends them; but when I make inquiry, I find it is often carelessness and indifference; and very often the breakdown of character of these unhappy people comes from their devotion to drink and its sordid accompaniments." He was a great admirer of Benjamin Franklin.

An obituary in *The Athenaeum* for April 23, 1904, said of him: "The number of his years is important. For he saw the rise of railways and shared the common belief that the lines which fell on all the pleasant places of England secured prosperity for the population, that the steamships put men into touch with the Isles of the Blest, and that mechanics meant the millenium . . .

"No doubt the view of life (as expressed in *Self-Help*) was limited. It counted successes that are exceptional, as if they were normal; it knew nothing of 'the valor of the beaten host'; it was subtly open to the satire unintentionally conveyed by the thief who, when he took the book out of the prison library, said that self-help had brought him all his misfortunes . . ."

Dr. Smiles married Sarah Anne Holmes, the daughter of a contractor at Leeds, and was the father of five children. He died at the age of ninety-two.

P. G.

PRINCIPAL WORKS: *Essays—Self-Help*, 1859; *Character*, 1871; *Thrift*, 1875; *Duty*, 1880; *Life and Labour*, 1887. *Biography*—Life of George Stephenson, 1857; Lives of the Engineers, 1861-65 (5 volumes); George Moore: Merchant and Philanthropist, 1878; Robert Dick: Geologist and Botanist, 1879; Josiah Wedgwood, 1894; Autobiography of Samuel Smiles, 1904. *History*—History of Ireland Under the Government of England, 1844; The Huguenots in England and Ireland, 1867; The Huguenots in France, 1874. *Miscellaneous*—A Boy's Travels Round the World (ed.) 1872.

ABOUT: Smiles, S. Autobiography.

SMITH, ALBERT RICHARD (May 24, 1816-May 23, 1860), novelist, playwright, and miscellaneous writer, was born in Chertsey, Surrey, the son of a surgeon. He was educated at the Merchant Taylor's School from 1826 to 1831, then studied at the Middlesex Hospital, securing his licenses as surgeon and apothecary in 1838 and joining his father in practise in Chertsey. His bent away from medicine and towards writing soon became evident, when in 1840 he contributed to the *Medical Times* a long series of semi-fictional sketches. The next year he went to London to engage in the practise of his profession, but soon left it for journalism and free-lance literature. He was extremely versatile, though primarily a humorist. (He was a regular contributor to Punch.) His first play, *Blanche Heriot*, was produced in 1842, and thereafter he wrote numerous extravaganzas and adapted plays for various theatres. He also wrote the words of many popular songs. In the late 'forties, he was dramatic critic for the *Illustrated London News*, and was editor of *Puck* in 1844. From 1847 to 1849 he was co-publisher and editor of a

monthly called *The Man in the Moon*, in 1850 he edited the *Town and Country Miscellany*, and in 1851 *The Month*.

He then became a lecturer, or rather a writer and producer of "entertainments," which were vastly popular. In 1847 he had made a tour to the Near East, and in 1858 he traveled to China. From 1850 to 1858 his "entertainments" centered around the ascent of Mont Blanc, and thereafter around the Orient. In 1859 he married Mary Lucy Keeley, an actress and the daughter of a comedian. A few months later he died suddenly of bronchitis. His brother, Arthur Smith, acted as manager of his "entertainments" and was also Dickens' lecture manager for many years.

PRINCIPAL WORKS: The Adventures of Mr. Ledbury, 1844; The Natural History of the Gent, 1847; Christopher Tadpole, 1848; A Month at Constantinople, 1850; To China and Back, 1859; Wild Oats and Dead Leaves, 1860.

ABOUT: Smith, A. R. Mont Blanc (see Life by Edmund Yates in 1860 ed.); Era May 27, June 10, 1860.

SMITH, ALEXANDER (December 31, 1830-January 5, 1867), Scottish poet and essayist, was born at Kilmarnock, Ayrshire, son of a designer of patterns for lacework. In his early youth the family removed to Paisley, and thence shortly to Glasgow; and it was in a primary school in that city that Smith was educated. His biographer, Patrick Proctor Alexander, relates that his curriculum included "some tincture of Latin and mathematics." Though he did not proceed to a university his writings reveal that he acquired (probably by private reading) a wide and well-digested body of information.

Among poor parents in the Celtic countries it seemed in those days natural to train a clever boy for the ministry. Such a career was outlined for Smith, but the design was never carried out, and on leaving school he was apprenticed to his father's trade. He never regarded pattern-designing as anything but a means of getting a living, and his leisure hours were occupied in the pursuit of poetry. In 1850 his first published lines, "To a Friend" appeared in the *Glasgow Evening Citizen* under the pseudonym of "Smith Murray."

At this time there lived in Dundee a clergyman named George Gilfillan, who had somewhat more than a local reputation as a critic and publicist. He was known to be ready to look at the work of young aspirants, so in 1851 Smith sent him some poems for criticism. Gilfillan was much struck by their merit, and his praise of the young poet-artisan in the *Eclectic Review, The Critic*, and other papers had the curious result of creating a reputation for Smith before he had published anything of note.

It is said that there are more ways of killing a cat than choking it with cream; but it was a cream-choking process of excessive and untimely praise that did Smith a great deal of harm. In 1853 he collected a volume of his *Poems* and submitted them to the publisher Bogue, who published them and paid £100 for the copyright. The volume (the chief item of which was "A Life Drama") was received with universal acclamation, reprinted within the year, and reached a fourth edition by 1856. Smith's name was bracketed with the most illustrious—with those of Tennyson and Keats; and on the strength of his success he threw up his trade and went to London to live by his pen.

But, in spite of encouragement from G. H. Lewes, Sir Arthur Helps, and Herbert Spencer, he soon found it necessary to seek a regular occupation again. In 1854 he became secretary to the University of Edinburgh at £150 a year (later raised to £200). The same year a damaging blow was struck at him by W. E. Aytoun, who, as "T. Percy Jones," published *Firmilian: or, The Student of Badajoz: A Spasmodic Tragedy*. This was a parody of the styles of Smith and Sydney Dobell. The two men had not yet met, but they collaborated in *Sonnets on the War* in 1855; and Aytoun's squib had the result of attaching to both the label of "spasmodic poets," which did their reputations much harm.

City Poems (1857), like the earlier volume, was predominantly autobiographical in content, and reflected the struggles of a poetic and idealistic nature against a hard environment. But, not only did the work fall comparatively flat: it provoked accusations of plagiarism (almost certainly unfounded) which were to trouble the rest of Smith's career and which rose to a chorus when, in *Edwin of Deira* (1861) he unluckily chose a theme of chivalry at the very period when Tennyson's *Idylls of the King* were appearing. The composition of *Edwin*, in fact, substantially pre-dated that of the *Idylls*, but the flung mud adhered.

In 1857 Smith had married Flora Macdonald, of Skye, a descendant of the famous Jacobite lady. Continuous poverty, increasing domestic responsibilities, literary calumny, all no doubt played their part in turning his energies from verse to prose. His first prose volume, *Dreamthorp* (1863), contained twelve essays, some reprinted from periodicals, but mostly new. The essays were partly general and partly critical. They revealed a cultivated, humane, and surprisingly serene personality, and a nervous and resourceful prose style. They have often been reprinted, and a passage from "A Lark's Flight" has been described by Professor Hugh Walker as comparable with the knocking at the gate in *Macbeth*. In 1865 there followed *A Summer in Skye*. Smith had known the Western Isles from his youth up, and in this book he showed a Borrow-like ability to absorb and convey their mystery and charm. Apart from several editorial tasks, two novels, *Alfred Hagart's Household* and *Miss Oona McQuarrie*, both published in 1866, complete the tale of Smith's work issued during his lifetime. He died of typhoid fever a few days after his thirty-sixth birthday. In 1868 Patrick Proctor Alexander published a further collection of his essays under the title of *Last Leaves*.

There can be hardly any doubt but that Smith's career was spoiled by premature and ill-considered praise, by false accusations of literary dishonesty, and by just failing to obtain that real solid backing in London which would have enabled him to cultivate his gifts in peace. His early verse is a good deal marred by an uncurbed lusciousness, and by occasional flat passages which rival the worst of Wordsworth's. But he had a delicate and subtle imagination. Even in "A Life Drama" there are lines like—

> "I saw the pale and penitential moon
> Rise from dark waves that plucked at her, and go
> Sorrowful up the sky . . ."

which have the authentic magic. The *City Poems* show more technical agility and less autobiographical naïveté. It is in the great line of British essayists, however, that Smith is most likely to be remembered. He shows fine literary judgment, striking power of imagery and the true essayist's faculty for investing ordinary things with color and meaning. P. P. Alexander, speaking of his premature fame, wrote: "Now, as always, his

ALEXANDER SMITH

bearing was distinguished by a quiet and manly simplicity." "In prose," wrote Professor Hugh Walker, in his introduction to *Dreamthorp: With Selections From Last Leaves* (1914) "as well as in verse his work is essentially poetic. He had that insight, more penetrating than the insight of common men, which makes the true poet; and therefore his confidences are light thrown upon dark places." H. B. G.

PRINCIPAL WORKS: *Poetry*—Poems, 1853; Sonnets on the War (with Sydney Dobell) 1855; City Poems, 1857; Edwin of Deira, 1861. *Essays and Miscellaneous Prose*—Dreamthorp, 1863; A Summer in Skye, 1865; Alfred Hagart's Household, 1866; Miss Oona McQuarrie, 1866; Last Leaves: Sketches and Criticisms (ed. by P. P. Alexander) 1868.

ABOUT: Aytoun, W. E. Firmilian; Brisbane, J. The Early Years of Alexander Smith; Gilfillan, G. Galleries of Literary Portraits (Vol. I); Smith, A. Dreamthorp (see Introduction by H. Walker to 1914 edition); Smith, A. Last Leaves (see Introduction by P. P. Alexander); London Mercury 12:284 July 1925; Poetry Review 12:142, 219 May, June 1921.

SMITH, GOLDWIN (August 13, 1823-June 7, 1910), historian and miscellaneous writer, was born in Oxfordshire, his father being a physician. He was educated at Eton and at Magdalen College, Oxford, securing his B.A. in 1845 and his M.A. in 1848. In 1846 he became Stowell law professor at University College, and from 1858 to 1866 was regius professor of modern history at Oxford. He went to the United States during the Civil War, and stayed to become professor of English and constitutional history at Cornell, from 1868 to 1871. He then went to Canada, and lived in Toronto for the remainder of his life, so that he is often thought of as a Canadian.

In 1875 Smith married Harriet (Dixon) Boulton, a widow, who died in 1909. They had no children. He was by this time deep in controversial politics, and had made many enemies for himself as an outspoken advocate of political union with the United States. He had plunged into political journalism, contributing to the *The Nation, The Week,* the *Farmer's Sun* (later the *Weekly Sun*), and particularly to the *Canadian Monthly,* for which he wrote regularly for over thirty years from 1872 under the pseudonym of "A Bystander." From 1880 to 1890 he also published a magazine of his own, known as *The Bystander*.

Goldwin Smith was a brilliant stylist, and most of his books are well worth reading today. He never, however, fulfilled the exalted promise of his youth, and his immersion in journalism (besides his addiction to polemics) prevented his doing much work of a permanent nature, such as his early historical studies had led his readers to expect of him.

PRINCIPAL WORKS: Lectures on Modern History, 1861; The Empire, 1863; Cowper, 1881;

Lectures and Essays, 1881; Jane Austen, 1890; William Lloyd Garrison, 1892; The United States: A Political History, 1893; Guesses at the Riddle of Existence, 1897; Commonwealth or Empire? 1902; Irish History and the Irish Question, 1905; Reminiscences, 1912.

ABOUT: Haultain, A. Goldwin Smith: His Life and Opinions; Smith, G. Reminiscences; Correspondence (1913).

SMITH, HENRY JOHN STEPHEN (November 2, 1826-February 9, 1883), Irish mathematician, was born in Dublin, the son of a barrister. His father died when he was two, and his mother went to live first on the Isle of Man, then on the Isle of Wight. He was a remarkably precocious child, who taught himself Greek at four! He was educated first by his mother, a highly educated woman, then by a tutor. The family moved to Oxford in 1840, and the boy was sent to Rugby, but in 1843 his brother died of tuberculosis, and fearing for his health also, his mother took him from school and went with him to Switzerland. After several years on the Continent, he returned to England and entered Balliol College, Oxford, where his career was almost unequaled for brilliance. He secured his B.A. in 1850, and his M.A. in 1855, being equally distinguished in classics and mathematics. From 1850 to 1873 he was mathematical lecturer at Balliol. From 1853 he was also deeply interested in chemistry. In 1860 he was elected Savillian professor of geometry at Oxford. He was made fellow of the Royal Society and of the Royal Astronomical Society in 1861, was president of the Mathematical Society of London from 1874 to 1876, and was the first chairman of the Meteorological Council of London in 1877. The same year he became a member of the Oxford Commission. In 1874 he was made keeper of the university museum, a post which gave him a house and a small stipend, without too many responsibilities. Unmarried, he lived here with his sister after his mother's death. In 1881 his health failed from overwork, and he died two years later, at fifty-six.

Utterly without personal ambition, excessively modest, witty, gentle, and lovable, H. J. S. Smith was without question the greatest English mathematician of his time.

PRINCIPAL WORK: Collected Mathematical Papers, 1894.

ABOUT: Smith, H. J. S. Collected Mathematical Papers (see Biographical Sketches by B. Jowett, C. H. Pearson, etc.); Athenaeum February 17, 1883; Nature February 16, 1883, September 27, 1894.

SMITH, HORATIO (HORACE) (1779-July 12, 1849) and **JAMES** (February 10, 1775-December 24, 1839), parodists, were born in London, the sons of Robert Smith, custom house official, and his wife, Mary French.

The two brothers were educated at Chigwell. James entered his father's office and succeeded him as solicitor to the board of ordinance in 1812; and Horatio—or Horace, as he was better known—entered a merchant's counting house in his youth, became a prosperous stock-broker, and retired in 1820.

As young men, the brothers were attracted by the theatre, contemporary literature, and social amusements, and became known as gay wits and gentlemen about town. Horace's first published piece was a poem lauding the plays of Richard Cumberland; and James first produced, as a hoax, a series of travel letters to the *Gentleman's Magazine*. In 1802 they began their joint publication with papers to *The Pic-Nic*, and a few years later they contributed poetical imitations to the *Monthly Mirror*, which were later collected in a volume entitled *Horace in London*.

In 1812 the Drury Lane Theatre was re-opened after destruction by fire, and its managers held a competition for a poetical address to be read on the opening night. The brothers amused themselves by writing a series of addresses parodying the most successful poets of the day, and then, with considerable misgivings about offending the men they caricatured, they offered their compositions for publication. They encountered some difficulty in finding a publisher willing to undertake the venture, but when the volume appeared—entitled *Rejected Addresses*—it met with instantaneous success and was received in good humor by Byron, Scott, Southey, Wordsworth, and the other poets it parodied.

It was generally agreed that nothing of its kind had ever equaled the *Rejected Addresses* for skill, pertinence, gaiety, humor, and lightness of touch; and most critics still regard the book as unsurpassed in its field.

The two brothers realized they could not duplicate their success, and never attempted a similar venture. James, who had written most of the best parodies in the volume, produced nothing more after that but three comedies, some nonsense verse of little merit, for periodicals, and his *Memoirs*. "He wanted," said Horace, "all motive for further and more serious exertion." For the rest of his life he remained something of a professional wit and man of society. He never married.

William Maginn wrote of him in *Fraser's Magazine* for 1834: "A pleasant, twaddling, pun-making, epigram-manufacturing, extempore-grinding, and painstaking elderly joker. He made one hit and that was a good one; on the strength of which he has lived ever since, as indeed he deserved to live . . . The station which he has chosen to hold in our literature . . . is of the Smiths, Smithish."

Horace, a more humorous, kindly, and serious man than his witty brother, continued

HORACE and JAMES SMITH

to write poetry and novels, gained the lasting friendship and respect of many of the poets he had parodied, and performed many generous acts for them. Shelley wrote of him:

"Wit and sense,
Virtue and human knowledge, all that might
Make this dull world a business of delight,
Are all combined in Horace Smith."

Thackeray called him, "that good, serene old man who went out of the world in charity with all in it"; and Keats, after meeting the two brothers, spoke of how he valued humor above wit.

Of Horace Smith's later writings, *Brambletye House*, a novel in imitation of Scott, and *An Address to a Mummy*, humorous verses, are perhaps the best known, and deservedly so.

He was married and had three daughters. Thackeray, who was a frequent caller at Horace Smith's house, named his Laura in *Pendennis* after the youngest of the three.

P. G.

WORKS OF HORACE SMITH: *Novels*—Brambletye House: or, Cavaliers and Roundheads, 1826; The Tor Hill, 1826; Reuben Apsley, 1827; Zillah: A Tale of the Holy City, 1828; Walter Colyton, 1830; Gale Middleton, 1833; The Involuntary Prophet, 1835; Jane Lomax, 1838; The Moneyed Man, 1841; Adam Brown, 1843; Love and Mesmerism, 1845. *Miscellaneous*—First Impressions, 1813; Amarynthus and Nympholept, 1821; Gaietie and Gravities (3 vols) 1825; Festivals, Games, and Amusements, Ancient and Modern, 1831; The Tin Trumpet, 1836; Poetical Works (2 vols.) 1846.

WORKS OF JAMES SMITH: *Comedies*—The Country Cousins, 1820; The Trip to France, 1821; The Trip to America, 1822.

WORKS OF HORACE AND JAMES SMITH: *Parodies in Verse*—Rejected Addresses, 1812; Horace in London, 1813. *Miscellaneous*—Memoirs, Letters, and Comic Miscellanies of James Smith (ed. by Horace Smith) 1840.

ABOUT: Beavan, A. H. James and Horace Smith; Smith, H. (ed.). Memoirs, Letters, and Comic Miscellanies of James Smith.

SMITH, JOHN THOMAS (June 23, 1776-March 8, 1833), topographer and antiquarian,

was born in a hackney coach while his mother was on her way to visit her brother! His father was a sculptor who later became a print-seller. He had little formal education, but in early youth studied sculpture and engraving, then began to make typographical drawings. For a while he thought of becoming an actor, but in 1788 settled down as a drawing-master in Edmonton. In 1795 he returned to London, and set up as a portrait painter and engraver. In 1816 he was appointed keeper of prints and drawings in the British Museum, a post he retained to his death. All his numerous topographical and antiquarian books, both the technical volumes and the more popular works, are illustrated by his own drawings, for which he himself made the plates.

Smith's lighter books have much quaint charm. He was a quick-tempered man, however, more than once engaged in bitter controversy; and his life of Nollekins (a sculptor who was his father's employer and his own first teacher, and who angered him by a stingy legacy) has been called "the most candid biography ever published in the English tongue."

PRINCIPAL WORKS: Antiquities of London and Its Environs, 1800; Antiquities of Westminster, 1807; Ancient Topography of London, 1815; Vagabondiana, 1817; Nollekins and His Times, 1828; Cries of London, 1839; A Book for a Rainy Day, 1845.

ABOUT: Smith, J. T. Cries of London (see Memoir by J. B. Nichols); Nollekins and His Times (see Short Account by E. Gosse in 1844 ed.).

SMITH, REGINALD BOSWORTH. See BOSWORTH SMITH, REGINALD

SMITH, ROBERT ARCHIBALD (November 16, 1780-January 3, 1829), musical

composer and editor, was born in Reading. His father a silk-weaver, was from Lanarkshire, Scotland. The boy showed musical talent from childhood and wanted to become a musician, but his father apprenticed him to silk-weaving. In his small leisure he led a church choir and played in the band of the volunteer regiment. In 1800 the family moved to Paisley, where father and son became muslin-weavers. In 1802 he married Mary MacNicol; they had five children.

Smith's years of despondency from hatred of his work were lightened by the gradual recognition of his musical accomplishments. Finally he was able to become a teacher of music, and in 1807 was made choir leader of the abbey church at Paisley. In 1823 he became musical director of St. George's Church, Edinburgh, and held this position until his death.

He was a friend of the poet Robert Tannahill, and set to music the latter's long-popular song, "Jessie, the Flow'r o' Dunblane." He was not, properly speaking, a writer, but edited the words and music of two collections of songs and wrote a text-book on singing.

PRINCIPAL WORKS: The Scottish Minstrel, 1821-24; The Irish Minstrel, 1825; Introduction to Singing, 1826.

ABOUT: Ramsay, P. A. (ed.). Robert Tannahill's Works (see Prefatory Memoir of R. A. Smith).

SMITH, SYDNEY (June 3, 1771-February 22, 1845), satirist and divine,

was born at Woodford, Essex, the son of an eccentric man of means. Sydney and his youngest brother, Courtenay, were sent to Winchester while the other two boys went to Eton. Sydney was captain of the school when he left, at eighteen, to enter New College, Oxford, on a scholarship. This was advanced in his second year to a fellowship worth £100 annually. On this income he maintained himself for about seven years, until he received his M.A.

In 1794 he was ordained and became curate of Nether Avon on Salisbury Plain. Here the local squire became his friend and employed Sydney as tutor for his eldest son. Their plans for study in Germany were upset by war, so in 1798 they went to Edinburgh. Here Sydney remained for five very happy years. While his pupil attended the University, the tutor studied philosophy and medicine, and preached occasionally in the Episcopal chapel.

Sydney married Catherine Amelia Pybus in 1800 and the same year published his first book, *Six Sermons*. One day in 1802 Sydney suggested, in the course of conversation with his friends, Lord Jeffrey, Lord Murray and Lord Brougham, that they should start a review in which their liberal views might be aired. This was the beginning of the famous *Edinburgh Review*. Sydney acted as editor of the first issue and contributed five articles. When he removed to London in 1803 Jeffrey became editor, but Sydney continued to contribute for the next twenty-five years, publishing a total of seventy-eight articles of which sixty-five were reprinted by the author in his collected works.

Through his friend, Francis Horner, and his elder brother's wife, who was the third Lord Holland's aunt, Sydney and Mrs. Sydney (as he always called his wife) were introduced into the literary and Whig society of Holland House, where he became a great favorite. He was appointed to preach at the Foundling Hospital and alternately at two proprietary chapels in London. Here his

SYDNEY SMITH

fresh and racy style filled the pews and brought increased revenue to the proprietors. He also lectured on moral philosophy at the Royal Institution, where his success was so great that a balcony was built in the lecture hall and even then there was "standing room only" an hour before lectures began.

The Whigs came into power in 1806 and Lord Holland procured for Sydney the living of Foston-le-Clay. At first his duties there were delegated to a curate, but the Residence Act of 1808 forced Sydney to choose between the loss of his living or retirement to his parish. He chose the latter and after putting off the evil moment as long as possible he at last moved to Foston in 1814. Though he was reluctant to leave London, he undertook his duties cheerfully and became extremely popular with his rustic parishioners.

Sydney had suffered considerably for want of money until 1820, when a legacy and the addition of a second living increased his income. From that time his fortunes continued to improve. In 1829 he exchanged Foston for Combe-Flory near Taunton. In 1831 he was made canon of St. Paul's, which required annual residence of three months in London. The inheritance of £50,000 from his brother Courtenay in 1839 enabled him to take a house in London where he could resume his hospitable entertainment of friends.

With so many powerful and intimate friends, it might be expected that Sydney Smith should have had greater preferment. But his brilliant satirical wit, particularly the *Plymley Letters* in favor of Catholic emancipation, made his friends afraid of the political consequences. The direct objects of Sydney's ridicule seldom felt any resentment, but

"the honest fools," as one cabinet minister called the voters, were rabid and intolerant. Lord Dudley remarked to Smith: "You have been laughing at me for seven years and have not said a word that I wish unsaid."

As a satirist, Sydney Smith has often been compared with Swift, though Saintsbury finds him more like Voltaire. Pehaps his most remarkable quality was the overwhelming good humor, kindliness and optimism which he combined with his satire. The character of Smith's conversation, as well as his literary style and the nature of the man can be seen in his letters. Most readers will agree with George Saintsbury ". . .that here was a man who, for goodness as well as for cleverness, for sound practical wisdom as well as for fantastic verbal wit, has had hardly a superior and very few equals."

Perhaps Sidney Smith's own remarks about wit give an even clearer picture of the man's character: "When wit is combined with sense and information; when it is softened by benevolence and restrained by strong principle; when it is in the hands of a man who can use it and despise it, who can be witty and something much better than witty, who loves honor, justice, decency, good-nature, morality and religion, ten thousand times better than wit;—wit is then a beautiful and delightful part of our nature."   D. C.

PRINCIPAL WORKS: *Prose*—Six Sermons (preached at Charlotte Chapel, Edinburgh) 1800; Sermons, 1801; Letters on the Subject of the Catholics (by "Peter Plymley") 1807-8; Letter to the Electors on the Catholic Question, 1808; Three Letters to Archdeacon Singleton, 1837-8-9; Sermons, 1809; The Ballot, 1839; Collected Works (4 vols.) 1839-40.
ABOUT: Burdett, O. The Rev. Sydney Smith; Darwin, F. Springtime; Duychinck, E. A. (ed.). Sydney Smith's Wit and Wisdom; Holland, S. A Memoir of Sydney Smith; Pearson, H. The Smith of Smiths; Reid, S. J. A Sketch of the Life and Times of the Rev. Sydney Smith; Russell, G. W. E. Sydney Smith; Saintsbury, G. Collected Essays and Papers (Vol. 1); Timbs, J. Lives of Wits and Humorists.

SMITH, WALTER CHALMERS (December 5, 1824-September 20, 1908), Scottish poet, was born in Aberdeen, the son of a builder. He was educated at the Aberdeen Grammar School and at Marischal College, where he received his M.A. in 1841. He then turned from study of the law to the Free Church ministry, and entered the New College, Edinburgh. In 1850 he was made pastor of a Free Church chapel in London, but felt himself a failure and resigned. In 1853 he was appointed to a charge in Kinrossshire, Scotland, in 1857 to Edinburgh, in 1862 to Glasgow, and in 1876 to the Free High Church in Edinburgh. He was rather more of a Modernist than was common among Scotch Presbyterians of his time, and nearly came under the ban because of two sermons advocating a liberalized Sabbath. Nevertheless, he was made moderator of the general assembly in 1893, and received honorary degrees from Glasgow, Aberdeen, and Edinburgh. He was married, his wife having been Agnes Monteith, and had one son and three daughters. He retired from the ministry in 1894.

Smith's poems were written under the pseudonyms "Orwell" and "Hermann Knott." They are smooth, simple, pleasant, and unpretentious—really not so much poetry as agreeable, colloquial narrative verse.

PRINCIPAL WORKS: The Bishop's Walk, 1861; Olrig Grange, 1872; Borland Hall, 1874; Hilda Among the Broken Gods, 1878; North Country Folk, 1883; A Heretic, 1890.

ABOUT: Scotsman September 20, 1908.

SMITH, WILLIAM (March 23, 1769-August 28, 1839), geologist, was born in Oxfordshire, the son of a farmer. His father died in 1777, and his mother remarried. The boy received only such education as the village school could give but even as a child he collected fossils and speculated on geology. He taught himself surveying and became a surveyor, then a civil engineer. In 1793 and 1794 he had a position surveying coalfields, which greatly improved his knowledge of the earth's strata. He retained this coal-survey job until 1799, but meanwhile was at work on the study of the stratification of Britain, and on the classifying of the strata by the fossils accompanying them. In 1795 he moved to Bath, and gradually became known as an engineer; at the same time he attracted the attention of both scientists and men of wealth, who helped to finance the preparation of his great geological map of England (the first ever made), which in 1815 secured his permanent fame. Others did relatively little, however; Smith spent on the work every penny he possessed. By 1819 he was so far in debt that he had to sell his books and all his possessions—even his papers, which were kept for him through the kindness of a friend who bought them in. He had to give up the house he had bought in London, and the geological collection he had made. Then his wife went insane. Thereafter he had no real home, but simply moved from one engineering assignment to another. In 1824 he began lecturing on geology to eke out his livelihood. The next year over-exertion in his work caused a temporary paralysis of his legs. In 1828, no longer able to work as an engineer, he became a land steward at Hackness. Finally a £100 government pension eased his last years. He died of pneumonia on his way to a meeting of the British Association for the Advancement of Science, at Birmingham.

Smith, who was nicknamed "Fossil Smith," and who is considered "the father of English geology," was not without scientific recognition in his lifetime, in spite of his hardships. He was voted the first Wollaston Medal by the Geological Society, and he was given an honorary LL.D. by the University of Dublin. His books and maps are part of the history of geology, though history is now their only appeal to the reader.

PRINCIPAL WORKS: Observations on the Utility, Form, and Management of Water Meadows, 1806; Strata Identified by Organised Fossils, 1816; Stratigraphical System of Organised Fossils, 1817.

ABOUT: Phillips, J. Memoirs of William Smith.

SMITH, SIR WILLIAM (1813-October 7, 1893), lexicographer, was born in Enfield in a Noncomformist family. (His brother became an historian.) Smith studied first theology and then law, then was articled to a solicitor. His chief interest, however, was in the classics, and he finally prepared himself to enter University College, London, where he won prizes both for Greek and for Latin. In 1830 he entered Gray's Inn, but was never called to the bar; instead he became a master in University College School, teaching the classics. He was a contributor to the *Penny Cyclopaedia*, on Greek and Roman literature, and edited Plato and Tacitus. In 1834 he married Mary Crump.

From 1867 to his death he was editor of the *Quarterly Review*. From 1853 to 1869 he was examiner in the classics for London University, and a member of its senate from 1869. From the same year he was registrar of the Royal Literary Fund. He received honorary D.C.L. degrees from Oxford and Dublin, LL.D. from Glasgow, and Ph.D. from Leipzig. He was knighted, to his not very great pleasure, in 1892.

Although his great dictionaries, which were standards for half a century, and re-edited by him almost to the day of his death, were Smith's principal work, he also edited a series of *Students' Manuals of History and Literature*, himself writing the manual on Greece, in 1854. He also brought out a series of smaller school dictionaries, condensed from the larger works. Undoubtedly the classical and Biblical dictionaries edited by Smith were among the greatest cultural forces affecting England in the nineteenth century. They were of special value to self-taught readers and those outside the great schools and universities, and made familiar household words of the names and events of Greek and Roman history and mythology. Though superseded by later works, they are not yet entirely unused.

PRINCIPAL WORKS: Dictionary of Greek and Roman Antiquities, 1842; Dictionary of Greek and Roman Biography, 1849; Dictionary of Greek and Roman Geography, 1857; Bible Dictionary, 1860-65.

ABOUT: Athenaeum October 1893; London Times October 10, 1893.

SMITH, WILLIAM HENRY (January 1808-March 28, 1872), poet and essayist, was born in Hammersmith, his father being a barrister. He was educated at Radley School and at the University of Glasgow. With a view to following his father's profession, he was first articled to a solicitor, then read law and was called to the bar, but though he went circuit he had neither any liking for the law nor any clients, and so (since he did have an independent income) he soon retired and lived the life of a recluse, studying and writing. He emerged from his retirement briefly to help in the early editing of *The Athenaeum* at its foundation; but for the most part he was seldom seen, and his close associates, though devoted, were few.

In 1839 he began a long series of contributions to *Blackwood's Magazine*, and in 1843 his tragedy, *Athelwold*, was produced by Macready and Helen Faucit with some success. By this time he had already retired to the Lake District, where he lived thereafter. In 1858 he was offered a temporary position as professor of moral philosophy at the University of Edinburgh, but his diffidence and love of seclusion compelled him to refuse. In 1861 he married Lucy Caroline Cumming, already well known as a translator from French and German. She shared her husband's tastes, and they lived very quietly in the country. By 1869 Smith's health had broken, and from this time until his death three years later he was a recluse by physical as well as by temperamental compulsion.

Considering his retirement from the affairs of the world, Smith's interests and tastes were surprisingly eclectic. He was most deeply concerned with ethical questions, and his tragedies and novels are of the same religio-philosophical tone as are his better known volumes of essays. What chiefly distinguished all his work was his noble and grave style, which was almost classic. He is little read now, however, for although beautifully written, his books are the expression of a viewpoint long ago outmoded.

PRINCIPAL WORKS: Ernesto (novel) 1835; Discourse on Ethics of the School of Paley, 1839; Poems and Tragedies, 1846; Thorndale: or, The Conflict of Opinions, 1857; Gravenhurst: or, Thoughts on Good and Evil, 1861.

ABOUT: Merriam, G. H. The Story of William and Lucy Smith; Smith, W. H. Gravenhurst (see Memoir).

SMITH, WILLIAM ROBERTSON (November 8, 1846-March 31, 1894), Scottish theologian and Semitic and Oriental scholar, was born at Keig in Aberdeenshire. He was the son of the Rev. Dr. William Pirie Smith, a former schoolmaster, and his wife Jane Robertson.

Smith's mother is reported to have said that the first word he ever uttered was "book"; and whether this story be true or not, he was certainly a remarkable student. His father was his only teacher until his sixteenth year, in which he went up to Aberdeen, where his scholastic career was one of triumph and was especially distinguished by the winning of the Ferguson scholarship in mathematics, the highest honor open to a Scottish student. His teachers, who saw that as mathematician and physicist he was a genius, were bitterly disappointed at his refusal to go to Cambridge, which would have interfered with his plan to enter the ministry of the Free Church of Scotland. He did, however, advance his scientific studies to such a point that Professor Tait, at Edinburgh, made him his assistant.

In the summer of 1867 he went to Bonn, and spent the year 1867-68 at Göttingen University. Here he absorbed the teaching of such famous German thinkers as R. H. Lotze and Wellhausen, and came under the influence of the new higher criticism, or scientific approach to the problems and history of religion. When, despite his youth, he was appointed to the chair of Hebrew at Aberdeen in 1870, he made it clear in his inaugural address that he intended to base his teaching on the findings of the German "higher critics." These were considered little short of diabolical by the members of the Free Church, but for six years Smith taught without interference, gaining an ever greater reputation for his abilities. He was then asked to share in the revision of the Old Testament, and was invited to contribute to the ninth edition of the *Encyclopaedia Britannica*—of which he later became assistant editor and then chief editor.

WILLIAM ROBERTSON SMITH

In the first volume of the *Britannica* appeared the articles on "Angel" and "Bible" which Smith had written. Dr. Charteris, professor of Biblical criticism at Edinburgh, took violent exception to the latter and wrote a blistering review of it in a church journal, challenging the Free Church to take action against the author. A long, bitter, and useless controversy followed, lasting several years and involving all the powers of the Scottish Church in a vain attempt to convict Smith of heresy. Smith had meanwhile made trips to Egypt and Syria, and to Arabia with the famous Orientalist Sir Richard Burton; and when the final outcome of his trial was a mere admonition, he might have gone quietly on teaching as before, but for the delayed publication of the *Britannica* volume with his article on "Hebrew Language and Literature," just after he had virtually agreed to be more guarded in his statements. He was immediately accused of bad faith and was forbidden to teach any longer, though not unfrocked. For eighteen months he continued work on the encyclopaedia; he then went to Cambridge as Lord Almoner's professor of Arabic, and remained there for the rest of his life in quiet and fruitful scholarship. He held the University librarianship, which he abandoned to assume the post of professor of Arabic, and was made a member of the high table of Trinity College and a fellow of Christ's College. Besides publishing his works and collected lectures, his activities included the giving of valuable assistance to C. M. Doughty, the author of *Arabia Deserta*. Although his health failed about 1890 and the malignant nature of his illness became apparent, he remained active almost until the very last.

Smith was a splendid Orientalist, and has been pronounced one of the foremost Semitic scholars in Europe. He was an authoritative, clear, and penetrating writer too; but these characterizations perhaps fail to give an adequate conception of his extraordinary intellectual powers. His former teacher, Wellhausen, called him "the cleverest man in Great Britain"; and Donald Carswell said: "His mind seemed to be the most perfect intellectual machine ever designed by the Almighty for the equipment of a mortal." He adds that Smith "was a tiny little chap, dark-haired and dark-eyed, of swarthy, almost Oriental complexion, lively and merry as a grig and a famous judge of wine and tobacco." R. M.

PRINCIPAL WORKS: *Religious and Historical Studies*—The Old Testament in the Jewish Church, 1881; The Prophets of Israel and their Place in History, 1882; The Religion of the Semites, 1889. *Anthropology*—Kinship and Marriage in Early Arabia, 1885.

ABOUT: Black, J. S. & Chrystal, G. Life of William Robertson Smith; Carswell, D. Brother Scots; Royal Asiatic Society Journal 1894.

SMYTH, WILLIAM (1765-June 24, 1849), poet and historian, was born in Liverpool, son of a banker. He was educated at Eton and at Peterhouse College, Cambridge, where he received his B.A. in 1787, was elected fellow, and secured his M.A. in 1790. In 1793 his father's bank failed, and it became necessary for him to earn his own living. For eight or nine years he tutored the eldest son of Richard Brinsley Sheridan, the dramatist, and was one of that brilliant, eccentric, poverty-stricken, brawling household. Sometimes he received his only pay in passes to the theatre! In 1806 he escaped by being made tutor at Peterhouse, and the next year he was elected regius professor of modern history, a post he retained until his death. In 1825 he had to vacate his fellowship because he had inherited a small property, but he lived in residence at the college until 1847, when he retired to Norwich, where he died two years later.

Smyth, a bachelor, was a genial, highly sociable man. His poems were much praised, but Thomas Moore accused Smyth of parodying him and stealing his metres. His historical books are good summaries, but he was too biased and partisan to have any standing as an impartial historian.

PRINCIPAL WORKS: English Lyrics, 1797; Lectures on Modern History, 1840; Lectures on the French Revolution, 1840.

ABOUT: Smyth, W. English Lyrics (see Autobiography and Memoir by Rev. Thomas Smith); Athenaeum June 30, 1849.

SOMERVILLE, MARY (1780-November 29, 1872), Scottish author of works on science, was born Mary Fairfax at Jedburgh in Roxburgh county, the daughter of Sir William George Fairfax, vice-admiral in the British navy. She largely educated herself, taking a deep interest in mathematics and learning Latin so that she might read Newton's *Principia*. She was married in 1804 to Captain Samuel Greig and in 1812, after his death, to her cousin Dr. William Somerville, a noted physician, by whom she had two daughters. In London she and her husband were members of a brilliant intellectual group including Macaulay, Rogers, Moore, and Sir James Mackintosh. From 1838 onwards she lived mainly in Italy, and she died in Naples at the age of ninety-two. A bust of her was placed in the great hall of the Royal Society, and Oxford honored her memory with the establishment of Somerville Hall and the Mary Somerville Scholarship in mathematics for women.

Her best work, and one of the outstanding scientific works of the century, was *The Connection of the Physical Sciences*, a skilful summary of research into physical phenomena.

PRINCIPAL WORKS: The Magnetic Properties of the Violet Rays of the Solar Spectrum, 1826; The Celestial Mechanism of the Heavens, 1831; The Connection of the Physical Sciences, 1834; Physical Geography, 1848; Molecular and Microscopic Science, 1869.

ABOUT: Somerville, M. [daughter]. Personal Recollections of Mary Somerville; Quarterly Review January, 1874.

SOTHEBY, WILLIAM (November 9, 1757-December 30, 1833), translator and poet, was born in London and educated at Harrow. After a few years in the army he settled down to a literary life and became an intimate of the leading authors of the day. Scott, Wordsworth, Coleridge, Samuel Rogers, Southey, Byron, Joanna Baillie, Maria Edgworth, Tom Moore, and Hallam were among the notables who gathered at his London home. These literary friendships constitute his chief claim to remembrance.

As an author, he "ran his neck into danger of, if he did not fully deserve, the gibbeting which befell another poetaster by epics, dramas, translations, odes, and everything that readers of poetry could wish or not wish," to quote George Saintsbury. In the opinion of Sidney Lee, "Although his poems and plays were held in high esteem by his friends, his translations of Virgil and Wieland alone deserve posthumous consideration."

PRINCIPAL WORKS: Poems, 1790; Wieland's Oberon (tr.) 1798; Virgil's Georgics (tr.) 1800; Saul: A Poem, 1807; Poems, 1825; Italy and Other Poems, 1828; Homer's Iliad (tr.) 1831; Homer's Iliad and Odyssey (tr.) 1834.

ABOUT: Clayden, S. Rogers and His Contemporaries; Lockhart, J. G. Life of Scott.

SOUTHEY, CAROLINE ANNE BOWLES (October 7, 1786-July 20, 1854), poet and prose-writer, wife of the poet Robert Southey, was born at Lymington, Hampshire, the only child of Capt. Charles Bowles of the East India Company service and Anne Burrard Bowles. Her entire life, except the years at Keswick, was spent at Buckland Cottage, New Forest. From Colonel Bruce, adopted son of Captain Bowles, she received annually £150. Facing poverty, she turned to writing and sent her metrical tale, Ellen Fitzarthur, to Southey, who recommended it to John Murray. It was printed anonymously in 1820. The correspondence with the poet continued for twenty years. Her visit to Southey at Keswick led to a suggestion for collaboration upon Robin Hood but the venture failed. On June 5, 1839, she married Southey and went to Keswick. At his death in 1843 she was left £2000; this was increased in 1852 by a crown pension of £200. Hated by her step-children, she returned to Buckland where she died.

Her literary reputation is based primarily upon her intimate association with Southey, under whose influence she wrote. Her more successful work is narrative, either prose or blank-verse. As lyrist she is not notable. Tales From the Factories vigorously decries conditions of workingmen and shows a strong humanitarian interest. She is noted for the pathos of her stories. Henry Nelson Coleridge, praising The Birthday, called her "the Cowper of our modern poetesses."

PRINCIPAL WORKS: Poetry—Ellen Fitzarthur, 1820; The Widow's Tale, 1822; Solitary Hours, 1826; Tales From the Factories, 1833; The Birthday, 1836; Robin Hood, 1847. Prose—Tales of the Moors, 1828; Chapters on Churchyards, 1829; Selwyn in Search of a Daughter, 1835; Correspondence of Robert Southey and Caroline Bowles (ed. by Edward Dowden) 1881.

ABOUT: Miles, A. H. Poets and Poetry of the Century.

SOUTHEY, ROBERT (August 12, 1774-March 21, 1843), poet, biographer, historian, bibliographer, and miscellaneous writer, was born at Bristol. His father, Robert Southey, a linendraper, married Margaret Hill of a good Herefordshire family. The poet was placed at three in the care of his maternal aunt, Elizabeth Tyler, of Bath. In April 1788 he entered Westminster School, remaining until 1792, when he was privately expelled for an article on flogging in The Flagellant, the school paper. He returned to Bath until a maternal uncle, Herbert Hill, chaplain of the British factory at Lisbon, sent him to Oxford. Because of his expulsion, Christ Church rejected him and he entered Balliol in 1793.

Southey said he studied only swimming and boating at Oxford. In the long vacation he read Epictetus and fell under the Stoic influence, which shaped his life. His revolutionary sympathies soon led him to celebrate the French Revolution in an epic, Joan of Arc, but his enthusiasm cooled at the October executions of the Girondists. In June 1794 Coleridge, visiting Oxford, met Southey and converted him to Unitarianism and pantisocracy. The utopia on the Susquehanna was planned for married men, and Southey promptly became engaged to Edith Fricker, daughter of Mrs. Stephen Fricker, widow, of Westbury. The marriage (November 14, 1795) made him brother-in-law of Coleridge and Robert Lovell. When his aunt, Miss Tyler, heard of the coming marriage and of pantisocracy, she instantly ejected Southey from her house and heart. In need of money for emigration, Southey sold Joan of Arc to Cottle. Some translations from the Greek by Coleridge, Southey, and Lovell and a volume of poems by Southey and Lovell appeared the next year. Mr. Hill now invited his nephew to Portugal. He left immediately after the wedding, parting from the bride at the church-door.

In Portugal Southey gathered material for subsequent writing. Upon his return he ac-

ROBERT SOUTHEY

knowledged his marriage and sought a profession. Unitarian views made the church
impossible; medicine repelled him. At this
moment Charles Wynn, his Westminster
school-fellow, gave him an annual allowance
(Southey received this until 1806). He was
now able to study law and entered Gray's
Inn, February 7, 1797. Law proved uncongenial, and Southey moved to Westbury, then
to Burton. Illness here necessitated his moving to Bristol and taking a year in Portugal,
where he went with his wife in April 1800.
Before leaving England he completed his
edition of Thomas Chatterton, which was
intended to assist Chatterton's sister and her
daughter. Until 1801 the Southeys remained
abroad, seeking health and literary materials.
During the stay Southey finished *Thalaba*,
the idea for which he had taken from Frank
Sayers of Norwich, whom he met in 1798,
and the materials for which he gathered from
Picart's *Religious Ceremonies* in Grosvenor
Bedford's library. He also collected materials
for a projected *History of Portugal*.

Returned to England, he accepted Coleridge's invitation to Keswick. Then followed
a brief, distasteful experience as secretary to
Isaac Corry, Chancellor of the Exchequer
for Ireland. In 1803 he moved to Greta
Hall, Keswick, sharing a large double house
with the Coleridges and Mrs. Lovell. In
1809, when Coleridge practically deserted his
family, Southey took the entire house and
sheltered the Coleridge family. Keswick was
the scene of Southey's subsequent quiet life,
except for brief tours on the continent, and
in Scotland in 1805.

At Scott's instance, Southey became one
of the most active supporters of the new
Quarterly Review, to which he contributed

576

ninety-five articles, ultimately receiving £100
an article. He wrote on Spanish literature
and history, religion, poetry, and morals,
urging relief of the poor and the working-
man, and opposing free trade, Catholic emancipation, etc. Of the *Quarterly* papers, that
on Nelson is regarded as "the peerless model
of the short biography." Liberties taken with
his manuscripts and differences of opinion
with the editors annoyed Southey, but he
could not afford to drop the connection. In
these same years, 1809-16, Southey edited
and chiefly wrote the *Edinburgh Annual Register*, much of which appears in the *History
of the Peninsular War*. In the effort to
finance his large household, he wrote prodig-
ously, keeping several pieces of work on hand
always, and dividing his day among them to
provide the necessary variety.

Recognition now came to Southey. In 1813
Scott transferred the proffered laureateship
to him, thinking thereby to provide an income.
Southey accepted on condition that the birthday odes be not required, but the income was
small and his government pension only £160.
However, in 1835 Sir Robert Peel increased
this to £300. A baronetcy offered with the
increase was declined. Notoriety came soon
after these honors, the occasion being the
surreptitious publication (1817) of his *Wat
Tyler*, written in the heat of his revolutionary
enthusiasm. Southey, now the advocate of
church and state, was charged with desertion
of the liberal cause. Now and later Byron
(*Vision of Judgment*), Hazlitt (*Table Talk*),
and others accused the "ultra-servile, sack-
guzzling laureate" of political and spiritual
apostacy. Coleridge vigorously came to the
defense of his friend in *Biographia Literaria*
(1817). The sincerity of Southey's intellectual progress from stoicism through Unitarianism to orthodox Anglicanism and from
pantisocracy to toryism need not be challenged now, even though the development may
seem difficult to understand. A similar
change of views occurred in Wordsworth,
and it is entirely possible that both poets
were sincere. A final honor came in 1826
when Southey unexpectedly found himself
M.P. for Downton, Wilts. This election resulted from the impression made by his *Book
of the Church* upon the Earl of Radnor. In
December the election was voided because
Southey had not the necessary property.

The happy family life was shaken after
1816 by a series of tragedies. The death of
Herbert, the favorite son, was a terrible loss
to Southey. A daughter died in 1826, and
in 1834 Mrs. Southey was committed to an
insane asylum. She returned home in time
and died in 1837. Southey went abroad the
next year with his son Cuthbert, Crabb Robinson, and some friends. On June 5, 1839,
he married his correspondent of twenty

years, Caroline Anne Bowles. Soon he was completely broken by the long strain and the arduous work; his memory failed and he was able only to sit and fondle his books. In his rich library, second only to Richard Heber's, he took pleasure to the last. A brief attack of brain fever proved fatal. He was buried in Crossthwaite Churchyard, Wordsworth attending the funeral. Memorial tablets were placed in Bristol Cathedral and Westminster Abbey.

He left four children: Charles Cuthbert, Edith May, Bertha, and Kate.

Southey's appearance was handsome enough to draw Byron's admiration. Brilliant eyes, a beak-like nose, and a tall slender figure were his chief physical characteristics. He was exceedingly self-confident, intolerant of those whose views he did not share, and so generous and kindly in personal relationships that he never really lost a friend, although he cooled towards Coleridge and Shelley when their conduct or ideas met with his disapproval. His outlook was distinctly moral, his views on society humanitarian, his attitude to younger poets almost paternal. Working fiercely, he still gave freely of his time to many literary friends at home and abroad, of whom Coleridge and Landor influenced him most. He wrote innumerable letters.

As poet, Southey holds a medium position; certainly of the so-called "Lakers" his poetical reputation has suffered the greatest and most permanent decline. Some short poems like the "almost perfect" "Battle of Blenheim," "Inchcape Rock," "Holly Tree," and "My Days Among the Dead" show him a master craftsman. His experiments with the unrhymed stanza (*Thalaba*) and the ballad (here, in point of time, he may even precede Coleridge's *Ancient Mariner*) enriched English metrical patterns. As epic poet his function was, as Dowden says, that of *finder* rather than *maker*. He added greatly to the materials available for romantic poetry, especially through his translation of such romantic fiction as *The Cid* (1808), *Amadis of Gaul* (1803) and *Palmerin of England* (1807). His long poems (except *Madoc*) suffer from a generous inoculation of his moral concepts. But Southey the prose writer is still great. Coleridge admitted Southey's superiority in prose, and the verdict still stands. In biography, in his time, he was unsurpassed. All his prose except the *Peninsular War* and *Colloquies* was successful and has interest and merit for the curious and browsing reader of today. As bibliographer and historian he enjoyed a great reputation in his lifetime, though his historical work was often undertaken in the face of enormous difficulties and the knowledge of the amateur. As popular essayist he achieved a very pleasing combination of "wit and wisdom," which is remarkable in view of the circumstances under which this occasional work was done. As man of letters he cast a large shadow over his period.

D. F. A.

PRINCIPAL WORKS: *Poetry*—Poems, 1795; Poems of Bion and Moschus, 1794, 1795; Joan of Arc, 1796; Minor Poems, 1797; Thalaba, 1801; Madoc, 1805; Metrical Tales, 1805; The Curse of Kehama, 1811; Carmen Triumphale . . . and Carmina Aulica, 1814; Odes to . . . the Prince Regent, 1814; Roderick: The Last of the Goths, 1814; The Poet's Pilgrimage to Waterloo, 1816; The Lay of the Laureate, 1816; Wat Tyler, 1817; The Vision of Judgment, 1821; A Tale of Paraguay, 1825; Poetical Works, 1829; All for Love, 1829; The Pilgrim of Compostella, 1829; Poetical Works (10 vols.) 1837-8; The Devil's Walk, 1830; Oliver Newman (ed. by Rev. H. Hill) 1845; Robin Hood, 1847. *Biography*—The Remains of Henry Kirke White (2 vols.) 1807; The Life of Nelson (2 vols.) 1813; Summary of the Life of Wellington, 1816; The Life of Wesley (2 vols.) 1820; Life of Bunyan, 1830; Life of Cowper, 1833-7; The Lives of the Admirals (5 vols.) 1833-40; The Life of the Rev. Andrew Beel, 1844. *Letters*—Letters Written During a Short Residence in Spain and Portugal, 1797; Letters From England by Don Manuel Alvarez Espriella (3 vols.) 1807; A Letter to W. Smith, M.P., 1817; Vindiciae Ecclesiae Anglicanae, 1826; The Life and Correspondence of the Late Robert Southey (6 vols., ed. by Rev. C. C. Southey) 1849-50; Selections from the Letters of Robert Southey (4 vols., ed. by Rev. J. Wood Warter) 1856; Correspondence of Robert Southey With Caroline Bowles (ed. by Edward Dowden) 1881; Journal of a Tour in the Netherlands, 1902. *History*—History of Brazil (3 vols.) 1810-19; The Expedition of Orsua and the Crimes of Aguirre, 1821; The History of the Peninsular War (3 vols.) 1823-32. *Essays*—Omniana (2 vols.) 1812; Sir Thomas More: or, Colloquies (2 vols.) 1829; Essays on the Lives and Works of our Uneducated Poets, 1831; Essays Moral and Political (2 vols.) 1832. *Miscellaneous*—The Book of the Church (2 vols.) 1824; The Doctor (7 vols.) 1834-47; Commonplace Book (4 vols.) 1849-51.

ABOUT: Byron, G. G. N. The Vision of Judgment; Byron, G. G. N. Letters and Journals; Coleridge, S. T. Biographia Literaria; Cottle, J. Memoir of Coleridge; De Quincey, T. Recollections of the Lake Poets and Autobiography; Dennis, J. Robert Southey; Dowden, E. Southey; Hazlitt, W. Table Talk; Hazlitt, W. The Spirit of the Age; Jerdan, W. Men I Have Known; Landor, W. S. Imaginary Conversations; Robinson, C. Diary; Smiles, S. Life of John Murray; Taylor, Sir H. Autobiography; Thackeray, W. M. The Four Georges; Blackwood's Magazine 1:53, 434, 1827; Modern Language Review 29:144 April 1932; Modern Philology 30:100 August 1932.

SPALDING, WILLIAM (May 22, 1809-November 16, 1859), Scottish literary critic, was born in Aberdeen and educated at Marischal College. He was professor of rhetoric and belles-lettres at the University of Edinburgh from 1840 to 1845 and thenceforth (until his death at the age of fifty) professor of logic, rhetoric, and metaphysics at St. Andrews. By his wife, Agnes Frier, he had one daughter.

The most successful of his few works was *The History of English Literature*, which passed through thirteen editions in twenty-four years. Equally valuable was a book on Italy which resulted from his travels in that country. Of his several contributions to the *Encyclopaedia Britannica,* the most notable was an article on logic which was separately reprinted. A keen student of Elizabethan drama, Spalding contributed a series of articles on Shakespearian literature and kindred subjects to the *Edinburgh Review* between 1840 and 1849.

PRINCIPAL WORKS: Italy and the Italian Islands, 1841; The History of English Literature: With an Outline of the Origin and Growth of the English Language, 1853; An Introduction to Logical Science, 1857; Letter on Shakespeare's Authorship of The Two Noble Kinsmen: A Drama Commonly Ascribed to John Fletcher, 1876.

ABOUT: Gilfillan, G. Galleries of Literary Portraits; Spalding, W. Letter on Shakespeare's Authorship of The Two Noble Kinsmen (see Memoir by J. H. Burton).

SPEDDING, JAMES (June 26, 1808-March 9, 1881), biographer, was born in Cumberland and educated at the Grammar School, Bury St. Edmunds, and at Trinity College, Cambridge, where he formed close friendships with Tennyson, Hallam, and Thackeray. In later life Edward Fitzgerald, the translator of the *Rubaiyat,* became his most intimate friend. These literary associations gradually weaned him away from the official career which at first attracted him.

From 1835 to 1841 he served temporarily in the Colonial Office. He was secretary to the Ashburton commission to the United States in 1842, and when the civil service commission was first established he served with it for a short time in 1855.

Practically all of his life, however, was given to the study of the life and work of Francis Bacon—though he wrote occasional articles on Shakespeare, Jane Austen, Tennyson, and other writers. His complete edition of Bacon's works, brought out in seven volumes from 1857 to 1859, is still the standard, and has been called "an unsurpassable model of thorough and scholar-like editing." He opposed Macaulay's views on Bacon, and embodied the controversy in his *Evenings With a Reviewer,* which was not publicly issued until after his death. His own attitude toward the great Elizabethan, incorporated in his biography, was much more favorable than Macaulay's, though he was no blind worshiper, but displayed shrewd critical power.

Spedding was a man of indefatigable industry, immense modesty, and a certain quiet, humorous melancholy. In 1847 he declined an offer of the post of permanent secretary of state for the Colonies, and later the professorship of modern history at Cambridge, considering himself unfitted for either position. He never married. He died in consequence of injuries received by being knocked down by a cab, his last words being a statement that the accident was purely his own fault.

PRINCIPAL WORKS: Life and Letters of Bacon, 1861-74; Reviews and Discussions, 1879; Evenings With a Reviewer, 1881.

ABOUT: Spedding, J. Evenings with a Reviewer (see Life by G. S. Venables).

SPEKE, JOHN HANNING (May 4, 1827-September 18, 1864), explorer in Africa and chronicler of his own discovery of the Nile's source, was born in Jordans, Somerset, the son of an army officer. After ten years' army service in India, he went to Africa in 1854 and immediately joined Sir Richard Burton in exploring Somaliland. Three years later, following his recovery from a severe wound, he and Burton were sent by the Royal Geographical Society to explore the African equatorial lakes. Independently of Burton, who was invalided home, he discovered Lake Victoria in 1858. His theory that this constituted the headwaters of the Nile was confirmed in 1862 when he returned to the lake with James Augustus Grant and traced the river's rising from it. He and Grant were the first to cross equatorial Africa. Shortly after his return to England he accidently killed himself while hunting partridge near Bath. He was thirty-seven years old.

His candid *Journal of the Discovery of the Source of the Nile* is a meritorious contribution to the literature of exploration and travel.

WORKS: Journal of the Discovery of the Source of the Nile, 1863; What Led to the Discovery of the Source of the Nile, 1864.

ABOUT: Grant, J. A. A Walk Across Africa; Johnston, Sir H. H. The Nile Quest; see also Speke's own works; The Times September 19, 1864.

SPENCER, HERBERT (April 17, 1820-December 8, 1903), philosopher, was born at Derby, the oldest and only surviving child of nine offspring of a schoolteacher of radical social and religious views and severe, eccentric manners, and a gentle, unhappy mother. His father was so busy educating others that Spencer's early education was neglected, and he was most backward in all ordinary school subjects, while showing precocity in natural history, physics, and mechanics. In these studies he was encouraged by his father, who was honorary secretary of the Derby Philosophical Society, founded by Erasmus Darwin.

When Spencer was thirteen he was sent to his uncle Thomas at Hinton Charterhouse for further schooling. His uncle also was an advanced liberal, but so strict that the boy ran away, walking 105 miles to his home in three days. He was promptly sent back again, and finally remained three years. Then, his formal education over, he returned to Derby and for a short time acted as assistant schoolmaster. Another uncle, however (uncles came to Spencer's rescue several times at crises in his life) secured him a position as civil engineer in the London and Birmingham Railway (later the Midland), which was then under construction. He was soon promoted to a better position at Worcester, but four years later, in 1841, he was discharged, the road being finished. He went back to Derby once more, and busied himself in such incongruous subjects as mechanical invention, modeling, and phrenology.

His first publication was in 1842, a series of letters in *The Nonconformist,* organ of the advanced dissenters, which later he republished as *The Proper Sphere of Government*—practically a still-born book. From the first he showed the extreme individualism which always characterized him, and though the least gregarious of men, he became affiliated with the "complete suffrage movement," allied to the Chartists. In 1844 he became sub-editor of its organ, *The Pilot.* Some of the members, however, objected to his views on religion, and the same year he left the magazine and again, and for the last time, worked as an engineer. In 1845 this employment ended through no fault of his, and for two years he lived at home and busied himself with inventions (including one of a sort of flying machine); the only one which brought him any financial return was a binding-pin for loose leaves of manuscript or music.

Spencer's real career started at twenty-eight, in 1848, when he became sub-editor of Walter Bagehot's *Economist,* and met Lewes, George Eliot, Carlyle, Huxley, and Tyndall—the two last to be among his closest friends. George Eliot, in fact, seems to have been in love with him, but Spencer, who was practically sexless and besides that a lover of beauty, could respond with nothing but admiration.

In 1850 his *Social Statics* appeared, and he was now contributing to the *Westminster Review,* the *British Quarterly Review,* and the *North British Review.* When in 1853 an uncle died and left him £500, he decided to leave *The Economist* and to devote himself thereafter to free-lance writing. He marked the change by a trip to Switzerland, from which he himself dated his ill health, because of over-straining his heart in mountain-climbing. Actually, however, his trouble seems to have been entirely nervous.

In 1855 Spencer issued his *Principles of Psychology,* which elicited only one review, and that unfavorable. His ill health had grown acute; it took the form of cerebral congestion, which prevented him from concentrated work for more than twenty minutes at a time. If he became excited or did any

HERBERT SPENCER

serious thinking after noon he was sleepless all the following night. Nothing daunted, he nevertheless at this very time first planned the writing of an entire system of philosophy, synthesizing all that was known to his time and laying forth his own systematized views. In 1857 he drew up the plan, and in 1860 issued a program of work. The series of books was to be sold by subscription, and he secured 400 in England, while Prof. E. L. Youmans obtained 200 in America. Another uncle providentially died and contributed a legacy, and so although the payment of the subscriptions was unsatisfactory Spencer launched the scheme with *First Principles,* in 1862. While engaged on this he issued also his volume on *Education,* in 1861, with its advocacy of the teaching of science and of freedom of initiative for the pupil. *First Principles* attracted little attention, but the series went on. It continued till 1896; once Spencer was about to give up because of money difficulties (he was now supporting his aged father), but his father's death in 1866 made his way easier, and Youmans again came to the rescue, raising a trust fund of $7000 in the United States, which was presented to Spencer together with a valuable gold watch from his American admirers.

The remainder of Spencer's life, from about 1868 on, was a history of constantly issued books, of life in Bayswater boarding-houses with autumns in Scotland and occasional trips to the Continent and to Egypt, and of continually increasing invalidism. As his reputation grew he was offered many honors, most of which he refused; among them were the lord rectorship of St. Andrews, and an invitation to stand for Parliament for Leicester. An invitation to the

Royal Society he declined because it was not offered to him until all the men of his generation had long been fellows.

Spencer's peculiar ill health, combined with his growing eccentricity, made his way of work unusual. Frequently he dictated his books while rowing on the Serpentine or playing racquets or billiards. He carried ear-stoppers with him, which he put on whenever he felt the conversation would excite him— or whenever anyone opposed his opinions. As he grew older and more fixed in his ways, he became increasingly eccentric, embittered, and cantankerous. In 1882, his last public effort, he joined with Frederic Harrison and Lord Morley in forming the Anti-Aggression League against war, but the strain injured him badly. The same year he visited the United States, refusing all lionizing except for one dinner in New York.

From 1884 his health was at its worst, and his life was miserable. In 1889 he took a house in St. John's Wood with three maiden ladies, but by 1898 he had fallen out with them, and moved to Brighton, where he set up housekeeping with two other ladies, one to act as housekeeper, the other to play the piano to him—to the end he was exceedingly fond of music. There he passed his days in contention, busy correcting "misrepresentations" and claiming priority for his opinions. At 83 he began to show symptoms of aphasia, and on December 8, 1903, he died suddenly. By his will, he was cremated at Golder's Green with no religious ceremony. He was a testimonial to the possibility of combining the drug habit with extreme longevity, for in his youth he had been a morphia addict, and to the end he took a large dose of opium daily.

In person Spencer did not show his ill health, being tall, ruddy, though slender, and with such good eyes that he never used glasses. Neither had he ever had a tooth pulled or filled, but in later years this was purely through vanity and helped to increase his invalidism. He had little emotion except combativeness, though he was devoted to his father and loyal to his very few real friends. H. S. R. Elliot calls him a "heretic on principle," whose early radicalism hardened into dogma, and became inflexible. He brooked no opposition. Strangely enough, he read very little, and that only material with which he agreed; indeed he seems to have been markedly indolent, and poured forth his many books purely from a desire for self-expression. Individual freedom was his fetich and his religion; he could endure no fetters, and never wore any for long. Advanced as his views were on religion, science, and sociology, in sexual matters he was an extreme prude. It must not be forgotten, however, that these were the faults of a great thinker and a genuine philosopher.

Spencer's philosophy may be summed up by saying that it was individualistic, anti-military and anti-coercive, evolutionary, and materialistic. At the limit of knowledge, however, he posited an "unknowable." His system omitted inorganic evolution, thereby avoiding the question of the origin of life. His scheme of thought was vaster than any in England since Bacon or Hobbes, or than any since his time. Everything in it moved in the end toward "absolute ethics," which he defined as the action of a fully evolved man in a fully evolved society.

His earlier style was easy and fluent, with powerful oratorical passages and some dry humor. Later it tended to become fixed and dogmatic, and hence unbearably monotonous —as someone has remarked, it had no lights and shadows, but was all one intense glare. In spite of its defects, however, Spencer has produced a body of work which will endure as long as English is read or men devise synthetic systems of philosophy.   M. A. deF.

PRINCIPAL WORKS: The Proper Sphere of Government, 1843; Social Statics, 1850; Principles of Psychology, 1855; Essays, Scientific, Political, and Speculative (3 series) 1858-74; Education, Intellectual, Moral, and Physical, 1861; Synthetic Philosophy: First Principles, 1862; The Principles of Biology (2 vols.) 1864-67; The Principles of Psychology (2 vols.) 1870-72; The Principles of Sociology (3 vols.) 1876-96; The Principles of Ethics (2 vols.) 1879-93; The Classification of the Sciences, 1864; The Study of Sociology, 1872; Descriptive Sociology, 1873-81; The Data of Ethics, 1879; The Man vs. the State, 1884; The Nature and Reality of Religion,-1885; The Factors of Organic Evolution, 1887; The Inadequacy of Natural Selection, 1893; A Rejoinder to Prof. Weismann, 1893; Weismannism Once More, 1894; Various Fragments, 1897; Facts and Comments, 1902; Autobiography (posthumous) 1904.

ABOUT: Collins, F. H. An Epitome of the Synthetic Philosophy; Duncan, D. Life and Letters of Herbert Spencer; Elliot, H. S. R. Herbert Spencer; Macpherson, H. C. Herbert Spencer: The Man and His Work; Spencer, H. Autobiography; Thomson, J. A. Herbert Spencer; Monist 31: January 1921; Open Court 34:125 April 1920; Scribner's Magazine 67:695 June 1920; Southern Atlantic Quarterly 21:241 July 1922.

SPENCER, WILLIAM ROBERT (1769-October 24, 1834), poet and translator, was the son of Lord Charles Spencer, politician. Educated at Christ Church, Oxford, he served as commissioner of stamps from 1797 to 1826. He was a noted wit, widely popular in London society and an extravagant host to such notables as Pitt, Fox, and Sydney Smith. The last nine years of his life were spent in poverty and ill-health in Paris, where he died in his sixty-fifth year. His wife was Susan Spreti, widow of Count Spreti, who was said to have committed suicide so that she might marry Spencer. Two of his seven children became distinguished clergymen.

His light, graceful, polished society verses were fashionable in their day. Byron called them "perfectly aristocratic," like the author's conversation. John Wilson ("Christopher North") particularly admired his "Beth Gelert: or, The Grave of the Greyhound," which was long used in school readers. But later critics brand him a "twitterer" and concede his ability only as a translator.

PRINCIPAL WORKS: G. A. Bürger's Leonore (tr.) 1796; Urania: A Comedy, 1802; The Year of Sorrow, 1804; Poems, 1811.

ABOUT: Spencer, W. R. Poems (see Biographical Memoir in 1835 reprint); The Times October 30, 1834.

SPURGEON, CHARLES HADDON (June 19, 1834-January 31, 1892), Baptist preacher whose printed sermons were widely read, was born at Kelvedon, Essex, the son of an independent minister. He began preaching at sixteen, was called to a London pulpit at eighteen, and at twenty-two was the most popular preacher of his day. To accomodate the increasingly large crowds that flocked to hear him, the Metropolitan Tabernacle, seating 6,000 persons, was built. Here he preached twice weekly for a period of thirty-one years, from 1861 until his death at the age of fifty-seven in Mentone, France. Beginning in 1865 he edited the monthly *Sword and Travel*.

His sermons, issued weekly after 1854, had an average circulation of 30,000 and were collected in yearly volumes. These volumes, nearly fifty in all, were called *The Tabernacle Pulpit*. Forty years after his death, Spurgeon's sermons and sayings were still being profusely reprinted. Besides his sermons he published numerous other works, of which *John Ploughman's Talk*, a book of advice, and *The Treasury of David*, a commentary on the Psalms, were perhaps the most popular. His writings, like his oratory, had the qualities of intense earnestness and spontaneous humor.

PRINCIPAL WORKS: The Tabernacle Pulpit, 1856-92; The Saint and His Saviour, 1857; John Ploughman's Talk: or, Plain Advice to Plain People, 1869; The Treasury of David, 1870-85; Lectures to My Students, 1875-77; John Ploughman's Pictures: or, More of His Plain Talk for Plain People, 1880.

ABOUT: Shindler, R. Usher's Desk to Tabernacle Pulpit; Spurgeon, C. H. Autobiography (ed. by his wife and W. J. Harrald); Spurgeon, C. H. Letters (ed. by his son C. Spurgeon).

STABLES, (WILLIAM) GORDON (May 21, 1840-May 10, 1910), Scottish author of stories for boys, was born at Aberchirder, Marnoch, Banffshire, the son of a vintner. Educated in medicine at Aberdeen University, he cruised to various remote parts of the world as assistant surgeon in the Royal Navy from 1863 to 1871 and for two years thereafter in the merchant service. About 1875 he settled down to authorship at Twyford,

near Reading, in Berkshire. From 1886 onwards he made annual caravan tours. He died at his home eleven days before his seventieth birthday, leaving six children.

As Gordon Stables he produced an average of four books a year for thirty years. His tales of adventure and exploration, teaching resourcefulness and courage, were based on his own travel experiences. Best remembered is *The Cruise of the Snowbird* and its sequel *Wild Adventures Round the Pole*, the outgrowth of two arctic voyages made by the author in his student days. He also wrote animal books, reflecting a deep love and understanding of animals, and historical novels, dealing mainly with naval history.

PRINCIPAL WORKS: *Boys' Stories*—Wild Adventures in Wild Places, 1881; The Cruise of the Snowbird: A Story of Arctic Adventure, 1882; Wild Adventures Round the Pole, 1883; The Hermit Hunter of the Wilds, 1889; Westward With Columbus, 1894; Kidnapped by Cannibals, 1899; In Regions of Perpetual Snow, 1904. *Animal Books*—Friends in Fur, 1877; Our Friend the Dog, 1884. *Historical Novels*—'Twixt Daydawn and Light, 1898; On War's Red Ride, 1900.

ABOUT: The Times May 12, 1910.

STANHOPE, LORD (Phillip Henry Stanhope, Fifth Earl) (June 30, 1805-December 24, 1875), was born at Walmer, only surviving son of the fourth earl. Until his succession he was known, from the age of sixteen, as Viscount Mahon. He was educated at Christ Church College, Oxford, receiving his B.A. in 1827, and the same year being made a fellow of the Royal Society. From 1831 to 1832 he was a member of Parliament, as a Conservative and an opponent of the Reform Bill. In 1831 he was deputy lieutenant of Kent. His historical work was already becoming known, and he received an honorary D.C.L. from Oxford in 1834. In the same year he married Emily Harriet Kerrison, daughter of a general. She died in 1873, leaving four sons and one daughter.

During the next year Mahon, as he then was, acted as under-secretary for foreign affairs. He was particularly interested in copyright law reform, and in the promotion of interest in the fine arts, being made in 1844 a commissioner for the latter purpose. In 1841 he had been made a fellow of the Society of Antiquaries (he was president from 1846 to his death), and his public life was constantly correlated with his career as an historian. In 1845 he was secretary of the board of control for India, in 1846 he became a trustee of the British Museum, in 1855 he was elected honorary antiquary of the Royal Academy. He was one of the founders of the National Portrait Gallery, though the gallery itself was not opened until 1896. This same year, 1855, his father died and he succeeded to the earldom.

In 1858 Stanhope became lord rector of Marischal College, Aberdeen. From 1863 to his death he was president of the Royal Literary Fund. In 1864 Cambridge gave him an honorary LL.D. In 1867 he became the first commissioner to inquire into the state of the established church in Ireland. In 1869 he was active in founding the historical manuscripts commission, and was one of its first commissioners. He died at Bournemouth, of pleurisy.

Stanhope was an honest, unpretentious historian, clear and readable, though never near to greatness and with no marked originality of thought. His access to the papers of his ancestors gave him unusual facilities for his historical work.

PRINCIPAL WORKS: Life of Belisarius, 1829; History of the War of the Succession in Spain, 1832; History of England 1713-83, 1836-53; Historical Essays, 1849; Life of Pitt, 1861-62; Miscellanies (two series) 1863 and 1872; History of England: Comprising the Reign of Queen Anne Until the Peace of Utrecht, 1872.

ABOUT: Athenaeum January 1876; Spectator January 1876; Times December 25. 1875.

STANLEY, ARTHUR PENRHYN (December 13, 1815-July 18, 1881), historian, biographer, and cleric, was the son of the Bishop of Norwich. His first education was at a private school at Seaforth, where he showed precocious talent as a writer. At fourteen he was sent to Rugby, where the great educator Dr. Thomas Arnold, who was to become the guiding-star of his life, had just been made headmaster. The Rugby days were happy ones. Their story is told in Thomas Hughes' famous novel of Rugby, *Tom Brown's School Days,* in which Stanley is "Arthur," the idol of the school.

ARTHUR PENRHYN STANLEY

Stanley went on, in 1834, to Balliol College Oxford, where he won every possible prize, including the Newdigate, and in 1838 became a fellow of University College. In 1839 he was ordained deacon by the Bishop of Oxford, but reluctantly, since he shrank from the damnatory clauses of the Athanasian Creed. It was this feeling of tolerance that caused him to be known later as "the heretic dean." In 1840 he traveled on the Continent, and almost every year thereafter made a long tour somewhere outside England.

In 1841 he returned to Oxford, where Arnold had become professor of modern history. The next year Arnold died. In 1842 Stanley produced his biography of Arnold, the only one of his works of real value, and the foundation of his literary position. In 1843 he was ordained a priest and became a tutor. It was a period of religious controversy, from both sides of which he remained aloof; the consequence was that when he was made select preacher in 1845 both high and low church factions distrusted him. He did not wish to adopt the church as a profession, but in 1849 and 1850 his father and two brothers died, leaving him the sole support of a mother and two sisters, and he had to give up his fellowship because he inherited a small estate. In 1851, therefore, he accepted an appointment as canon of Canterbury. In 1856 he was made professor of ecclesiastical history at Oxford and returned there to live.

He became intimate with court circles, and in 1862 made a second tour to Palestine with the Prince of Wales (Edward VII). One of his companions was General Bruce, who died during the tour. Stanley had since 1857 been in love with Bruce's sister, Lady Augusta Bruce, daughter of the Earl of Elgin, and Queen Victoria's favorite lady-in-waiting. In 1863 they were married (both aged 41) at Westminster Abbey, and two months later Stanley was himself made dean of Westminster. When the Duke of Edinburgh, the queen's son, married Grand Duchess Marie of Russia, Stanley went to St. Petersburg to perform the ceremony. Lady Augusta died in 1876, and her husband never really recovered from the shock of his loss. In 1877 he made a tour of the United States, but traveled little thereafter. In 1881 he became ill in the pulpit, and a few days later died of erysipelas. He was buried in Westminster Abbey beside his wife.

Stanley, small, delicate, and refined, had great personal charm. He was the apostle of toleration and church unity, and abhorred factions. As a writer, he is picturesque, dramatic, and eminently fair, but only his life of his "lodestar," Dr. Arnold, a really great biography, gives him any place in literary history.   M. A. deF.

PRINCIPAL WORKS: Life and Correspondence of Dr. Arnold, 1844; Sermons on the Apostolic Age, 1845; Memorials of Canterbury, 1854; Commentary on the Epistles to the Corinthians, 1855; Sinai and Palestine, 1856; Three Introductory Lectures on the Study of Ecclesiastical History, 1857; Canterbury Sermons, 1859; Lectures on the History of the Eastern Church, 1861; Sermons in the East, 1863; Lectures on the History of the Jewish Church, 1865; Historical Memorials of Westminster Abbey, 1867; Essays: Chiefly on Questions of Church and State, 1870; Lectures on the Church of Scotland, 1872; Addresses and Sermons Delivered at St. Andrews, 1877; Addresses and Sermons Delivered in the United States and Canada, 1879; Christian Institutions, 1881.

ABOUT: Dark, S. Five Deans; Hare, A. J. C. Biographical Sketches; Prothero, R. E. and Bradley. G. G. The Life and Correspondence of A. P. Stanley.

STANLEY, SIR HENRY MORTON (June 29, 1841-May 10, 1904), Welsh explorer and travel writer, was born in Denbigh, his baptismal name being John Rowlands. (He may have been illegitimate.) His life reads like an improbable novel. His father died when he was two; his mother, a butcher's daughter, went into service in London and then married, and did not want him; his paternal grandfather, a prosperous farmer, refused to care for him. For a while his mother's brothers boarded him out; then they stopped paying for him and he was taken, at six, to the workhouse at St. Asaph, where he remained until 1856, when he was fifteen. The schoolmaster there was a savage brute, afterwards adjudged insane. The boy's life was one long series of torture, in the midst of which somehow he gained an elementary education. At last he beat his tormentor and ran away. For a while a cousin at Brynford employed him as a pupil teacher in a National School, and out of hours he studied languages and mathematics. For two or three years he went from one town and one poor and unwelcoming relative after another, working as butcher boy, haberdasher's clerk, and at similar unskilled jobs. In 1859 he shipped as a cabin boy, without pay, on a boat going to New Orleans. A kind-hearted cotton broker, Henry Stanley, picked him up, starving, on the street, cared for him, and adopted him. The boy took his benefactor's name. The next year Stanley sent him to his farm in Arkansas, to take charge of the store there. Then he died suddenly, without having made any provision for his adopted son. Young Stanley found himself stranded, and the Civil War had begun. Though his sympathies were with the Union, he enlisted as a Confederate, was taken prisoner at Shiloh, and was released from Camp Douglas, Chicago, by re-enlisting on the other side (a very discreditable performance, which he never entirely lived down.) His turn-coat tactics proved un-

necessary; he contracted dysentery, was discharged from the army, and, sick and penniless, worked his way from Harper's Ferry back to Wales. Once more his relatives threw him out, and he became a sailor. In 1864 he enlisted in the United States Navy as a ship's writer.

With this experience, he became a wandering news correspondent in the western United States. He made and saved money, and in 1866 was able to travel to Asia Minor with a friend. The next year a Missouri paper sent him to report General Hancock's Indian expedition. In 1868 he joined the staff of the New York *Herald,* which sent him to Abyssinia to report the war there.

The rest of Stanley's life belongs to Africa, where he felt he had a "mission." The famous expedition to "find" David Livingstone, the missionary-explorer, was undertaken for the *Herald,* from 1869 to 1872. For the same paper he covered the Ashanti War in 1873. He made three more African explorations—in Equatorial Africa from 1874 to 1877; in the Congo (for Leopold II of Belgium) from 1878 to 1884; and in the Soudan from 1885 to 1888. In fifteen years, without an army, this private civilian gained about two million square miles for the British Empire; and he cannot be held responsible for the atrocities later involved in Belgian exploitation of the Congo Free State. The controversies arising from the Livingstone expedition gradually died down, though they (and his quick and harsh temper) retarded any bestowal of honors on him. In 1890 he married Dorothy Tennant, and with her made a lecture tour in the United States and Australasia. He abandoned his American citizenship, was re-naturalized in England, and from 1895 to 1900 was a member of Parliament. In 1897 he made his last journey, to South Africa, just before the Boer War. He was finally knighted in 1899. He suffered a stroke four years later, and died the following spring.

Stanley as a writer was primarily a journalist, but a good one, and his books are classics of travel-writing even today.

PRINCIPAL WORKS: How I Found Livingstone, 1872; Through the Dark Continent, 1878; The Congo and the Founding of Its Free State, 1885; In Darkest Africa, 1890; My Early Travels and Adventures in America and Asia, 1895; Through South Africa, 1898; Autobiography (ed. by wife) 1909.

ABOUT: Rowlands, C. Henry Morton Stanley: The Story of his Life; Stanley, Sir H. M. My Early Travels and Adventures in America and Asia; Autobiography; Cornhill Magazine July 1904.

STANLEY, EDWARD G.G.S. See DERBY, LORD

STANNARD, HENRIETTA ELIZA VAUGHAN ("John Strange Winter") (January 13, 1856-December 13, 1911), novelist, was born Henrietta Eliza Vaughan Palmer at York, the daughter of a clergyman. She came of several generations of soldiers; her father had been an officer in the Royal Artillery before taking holy orders. At twenty-eight she was married to Arthur Stannard, by whom she had one son and three daughters. She died in Putney, a London suburb, at the age of fifty-five, following an accident.

Her short stories and novels of military life were first contributed to the *Family Herald* and other journals. She began writing in 1874, her eighteenth year, as "Violet Whyte," and in 1881, with the appearance of her first collection of regimental sketches, adopted the pseudonym of "John Strange Winter" from a character in one of her early stories. Her best known work was *Bootles' Baby,* which sold two million copies within ten years of its publication. John Ruskin praised Mrs. Stannard as "the author to whom we owe the most finished and faithful rendering ever yet given of the character of the British soldier."

PRINCIPAL WORKS: Cavalry Life, 1881; Regimental Legends, 1883; Bootles' Baby: A Story of the Scarlet Lancers, 1885; Bootles' Children, 1888.

ABOUT: The Times December 15, 1911.

STEAD, WILLIAM THOMAS (July 5, 1849-April 15, 1912), journalist and miscellaneous author, was born at Embleton, Northumberland, the son of a Congregational minister. As editor of the *Pall Mall Gazette,* from 1883 to 1889, he introduced modern newspaper methods in England and exerted a powerful political influence, notably in bringing about the strengthening of naval defenses and the passage of the Criminal Law Amendment Act of 1885, though his vice crusade ironically landed him in prison for three months as a dealer in pornography. He founded the monthly *Review of Reviews* in 1890, and its American and Australian editions in 1891 and 1892 respectively. En route to New York to attend a peace congress, he lost his life in the "Titanic" disaster at the age of sixty-two.

A keen devotee of spiritualism, he edited *Borderland,* a periodical devoted to psychical research, from 1893 to 1897, and wrote several books on the subject. The best known of these, and of all his books on varied subjects, was *Letters From Julia,* which he said he wrote involuntarily at the dictation of the departed spirit of a young American woman, Julia Ames, whom he had met shortly before her death in 1891.

PRINCIPAL WORKS: If Christ Came to Chicago, 1893; Letters From Julia (later reprinted under the title After Death: A Personal Interview) 1897; Real Ghost Stories, 1897; The United States of Europe, 1899; The Americanization of the World, 1902; Peers or People, 1907.

ABOUT: Harper, E. Stead the Man; Stead, E. W. My Father: Personal and Spiritual Reminiscences; Whyte, F. The Life of W. T. Stead; Review of Reviews January-June, 1912.

STEPHEN, SIR JAMES (January 3, 1789-September 14, 1859), essayist, was born in London, his father being a master in chancery. An attack of smallpox during his infancy made him partially blind throughout his life. Nevertheless he secured an LL.B. degree from Trinity College, Cambridge, in 1812, having been called to the bar from Lincoln's Inn the year before. The influence of his father and his father's friends helped in the young barrister's career, and in 1813 he was appointed counsel of the colonial department. The next year he married Jane Catherine Venn; they had three sons and two daughters. Two of the sons and one daughter became well-known writers.

In 1825 Stephen abandoned private practice and became permanent counsel of the Colonial Office and the Board of Trade. In 1834 he was assistant under-secretary, and in 1836 under-secretary of state for the colonies. He resigned in 1847, because of ill health, increased by grief over the death of his son. He was made a Knight Commander of the Bath and a privy councillor in recognition of his services.

An untiring worker, Stephen could not remain in retirement, and in 1849 became regius professor of modern history at Cambridge. From 1855 to 1857 he was also professor of history at the East India College, Haileybury. He wrote relatively little, though he had been a regular contributor of articles to the Edinburgh Review from 1838. A formal, talkative man, who seemed overbearing but was really painfully shy, Stephen was also extremely pious. It is said that the only time he ever "broke the Sabbath" was to draw up the bill for the abolition of slavery. Nevertheless, his early evangelical opinions gradually became so broad that he was accused of heresy. He was devoted to his family, but lived alone for years so that his children might live in Brighton for their health and in Windsor to be near Eton. He died in Coblentz, during a trip to Germany to secure medical treatment.

PRINCIPAL WORKS: Essays in Ecclesiastical Biography, 1849; Lectures on the History of France, 1852.

ABOUT: Stephen, Sir J. Letters (see Biographical Notes by his Daughter, C. E. Stephen); Essays in Ecclesiastical Biography (see Prefatory Life by his son, J. F. Stephen).

STEPHEN, SIR JAMES FITZJAMES

(March 3, 1829-March 11, 1894), historian and jurist, was born in London. His father was Sir James Stephen, the essayist; his younger brother Sir Leslie Stephen, the biographer. He was educated at Eton, King's College (London), and Trinity College, Cambridge, receiving his B.A. in 1851. He was called to the bar from the Inner Temple in 1854. The next year he married Mary Richenda Cunningham; they had two sons and four daughters.

Though Stephen joined the Midland circuit, he had little practise at first, and had recourse to journalism to eke out his income. From 1855 he wrote regularly for the *Saturday Review*. From 1858 to 1861 he was secretary to the education commission. His legal standing improved, and from 1859 to 1869 he served as recorder of Newark. He became a friend of Froude, the historian, and of Carlyle, and his literary interests grew until they competed seriously with his legal career. In any case the philosophy of jurisprudence appealed to him far more strongly than did ordinary practice of the law. He began writing for *Fraser's* and the *Cornhill Magazine*, and from 1865 was the chief contributor to the *Pall Mall Gazette*. At some periods he wrote up to two-thirds of its contents, sometimes six articles a week.

From 1869 to 1872 Stephen was in India as legal member of the council. He became professor of common law at the Inns of Court in 1875, and in 1879 was made a judge. This had been his promised reward for the immense amount of work he did in codifying the law—an enormous task which never came to fruition in his lifetime. In 1886 he was appointed chairman of a commission to inquire into the Ordnance Department. Realizing that a disease from which he suffered was gradually affecting his mind, he resigned this office in 1891. He was made a baronet in recognition of his services. He sank gradually from this time until he died, in Ipswich, three years later. Stephen was an extreme conservative, and his historical writings reflect his anti-democratic views.

PRINCIPAL WORKS: General View of the Criminal Law, 1863; Liberty, Equality, Fraternity, 1873; The History of Criminal Law, 1883; The Story of Nuncomar, 1885; Horae Sabbaticae, 1892.

ABOUT: Stephen, Sir L. Life of Sir James Fitzjames Stephen.

STEPHEN, JAMES KENNETH

(February 25, 1859-February 3, 1892), poet, was born in London, the second son of James Fitzjames Stephen, legal authority and judge, and Mary (Cunningham) Stephen. Leslie Stephen, the biographer and author, was his uncle.

His short life was one marked by many personal successes. After attendance at preparatory schools he entered Eton in 1871 on a scholarship. During the years spent at Eton he engaged in various activities and won various triumphs; and his memories of the school, reflected in the poems, "My Old School" and "The Old School List," were among his happiest. His influence upon his schoolmates was great, and few who attended Eton in the years when he was there could ever forget him. He was a contributor to the *Eton Chronicle*, and was a moving spirit of *The Etonian*, a school paper. In athletics he was conspicuous as a player in the characteristic Eton "Wall Game" of football. His tendency in his studies was to concentrate most of his energy on the subjects which interested him the most, the result being that his work in essay-writing and history outranked that in the classics and mathematics. His general scholastic standing, however, was high, and in 1878 he secured a scholarship in King's College, Cambridge.

His career at Cambridge resembled his life at Eton. He was prominent in the undergraduate body, and made a mark by his oratory in the Cambridge Union, of which he was president in 1882, the year of his graduation. While he took prizes in other fields, his scholastic success was especially notable in history; he stood in the first class of the honors examination in history in 1881; and, while he was less successful in the examination in law, in which he stood in the second class, he took the first Whewell scholarship in international law. The summer of 1883 he spent in Sandringham, as tutor in history to Prince Albert Victor (later Duke of Clarence), the eldest son of Edward VII, then Prince of Wales. His *International Law*, written as a dissertation for his fellowship

JAMES KENNETH STEPHEN

in King's College (1885), was published in 1884, and at about the same time Stephen was called to the bar.

He was not destined, however, to become conspicuous as a lawyer, for early he turned his attention to journalism, writing for *St. James's Gazette,* the *Saturday Review,* and other papers. He founded in 1888 one of his own, *The Reflector.* He hoped that this weekly, by its high literary merit and fine physical appearance, would be able to succeed without resorting to the usual advertising and the usual universality of interest and appeal. In these fond expectations he was doomed to disappointment, and the paper stopped appearing after the seventeenth issue had been distributed; but in that short time contributions by such writers as George Meredith, Edmund Gosse, Augustine Birrell, and Frederick Locker-Lampson had graced its columns, Stephen himself wrote about half of the material.

This enterprise having come to naught, Stephen again turned his attention to law, accepting a position (obtained by his father) as clerk of assize for the South Wales circuit, hoping that in the intervals between circuits he might continue literary work or acquire a legal practice. Unfortunately his health was in too precarious a state to permit much work, and he began to show signs of intermittent mental peculiarity, probably the result of an accidental blow on the head in 1886.

He resigned his post in 1890, and returned to Cambridge, accepting private pupils and giving lectures on constitutional history. His public speaking continued to command admiration, and he quickly made himself a great influence among the student body. When the proposal was made that Greek be abolished as a requirement for the degree, he defended the existing requirement in his pamphlet, *Living Languages.* In this same year (1891) he collected and published his poems in two volumes, which enjoyed a greater success than he had expected.

He was fated not to enjoy it long, for his disease flared up malignantly in November, and in the following February Stephen died, not quite thirty-three years old.

A large handsome man, with a big head, fine features, large eyes, and a strong mouth, Stephen was naturally a leader in athletics and social activities as well as intellectual ones. ". . . He was extremely good-natured, he did very little work, he defied authority, he was extraordinarily and perennially amusing, and he had the most copious and prodigious flow of elaborate bad language that ever issued from human lips," writes a school friend. His matter-of-fact way of doing unconventional and unheard-of things gave his associates intense amusement. His directness

and sweetness won him many friends, and his influence in King's College was of assistance in raising the intellectual tone of that institution. He is said to have shown considerable emotional instability and some lack of judgment in finances during the years following the accident mentioned above.

His volumes of light verse do him incomplete justice, despite the cleverness which Saintsbury has admired. An example of his humor is a well-worn couplet:

When the Rudyards cease from Kipling
And the Haggards Ride no more.

His friend Arthur C. Benson said of his poetry: "The strength of it lies in a peculiar and almost prosaic directness, a great economy of art, a saying of simple things in a perfectly simple way, and yet all leading up to a climax of humor that is the more impressive because it is so unadorned." R. W. W.

PRINCIPAL WORKS: *Educational Pamphlet*—Living Languages, 1891. *Legal Dissertation*—International Law, 1884. *Poetry*—Lapsus Calami, 1891; Quo Musa Tendis? 1891; Lapsus Calami and Other Verses, 1896.

ABOUT: Benson, A. C. The Leaves of the Tree; MacCarthy, D. Portraits; Stephen, J. K. Lapsus Calami and Other Verses (see Introduction by H. Stephen); Stephen, L. The Life of Sir James Fitzjames Stephen.

STEPHEN, SIR LESLIE (November 28, 1832-February 22, 1904), man of letters, biographer, essayist, editor, and philosopher, was born in London at a house in Kensington Gore, now 42 Hyde Park Gate, the youngest son of Sir James Stephen, Under-Secretary of State for the Colonies, and Jane Catherine (Venn) Stephen, the daughter of John Venn, rector of Lapham. For several generations both branches of his family had made their mark in the law and literature. This tradition had been continued by his father and his elder brother, James Fitzjames Stephen. Although Leslie also studied law for a time, he was destined to distinguish himself in literature alone.

He was educated at Eton and at King's College, London, which he left in 1850 to enter Trinity Hall at Cambridge. While mathematics was his chief study, he dabbled in literature, sketching, and debating, and became known as an untiring walker, runner, and oarsman.

As yet untroubled by religious doubts, he took holy orders in 1855 to retain a tutoring fellowship he had won the year before. The next ten years he spent as a don at Cambridge, teaching mathematics to undergraduates, preaching on occasion, and pursuing his studies in philosophy and literature. His first important book, *Sketches From Cambridge by a Don,* published in 1865, portrays the life there.

Throughout this period he was, according to his friends, the model of "the muscular

SIR LESLIE STEPHEN

Through his elder brother, James Fitzjames Stephen, he secured introductions to the leading literary figures of the day and to the editors of the most important journals. He proved to be as indefatigable a journalist as he was an athlete. For many years he was a regular contributor to such weekly and monthly magazines as the *Saturday Review,* the *Pall Mall Gazette, Fraser's,* and the *Fortnightly Review.* He also contributed a fortnightly letter on English affairs to the New York *Nation.* Within a short time he had won a reputation as a vigorous and judicious literary critic. The best of his essays written during this period were republished from time to time in separate volumes under the heading of *Hours in a Library.*

Stephen was appointed editor of the *Cornhill Magazine* in 1871. During his eleven years in the editor's chair, he befriended and aided many young writers who subsequently became famous, among them Robert Louis Stevenson, Thomas Hardy, W. E. Henley, Henry James, and Edmund Gosse.

The editorship enabled him to throw off the burdens of journalism and devote himself to religious and philosophical studies. The first fruits of his speculations, *Essays on Free-Thinking and Plain-Speaking,* published in 1873, made him a chief spokesman for the "agnostics," who criticized the dogmatism and spiritual emptiness of the orthodox creeds. He was largely responsible for giving currency to the name by which the school was popularly known.

In 1876 he published his most ambitious work, *The History of English Thought in the Eighteenth Century.* The enthusiastic reception accorded this history in learned circles, which had hitherto regarded him as a dilettante in philosophy, greatly increased his reputation and influence. Although they did not achieve the success of the *History,* his later philosophical writings, *The Science of Ethics* and *The English Utilitarians,* were also well received.

His fame, however, rests rather on his biographical than his philosophical works. In 1877 John Morley invited him to write the first volume in the celebrated *English Men of Letters* series, a life of Samuel Johnson. Although he finished the book in six months, it brought him more compliments than anything he had done before. He subsequently contributed lives of Pope, Swift, George Eliot, and Hobbes.

These biographical ventures were dwarfed beside his herculean labors as editor of the *Dictionary of National Biography.* This monumental enterprise, which was to include concise accounts of the lives of all noteworthy Englishmen from the earliest historical period to the present, was planned and begun under his direction in 1882, and completed eighteen

Christian," who "feared God and could walk a thousand miles in a thousand hours." After his first ascent in 1857, mountain-climbing became his dominant passion. He conquered one Alp after another, "striding from peak to peak like a pair of compasses over a large-sized map," and soon stood in the front rank of English mountaineers. He was president of the Alpine Club from 1865 to 1869 and editor of the *Alpine Journal* the following three years. Although his active mountaineering decreased as he grew older, he never abandoned his "fanatical enthusiasm" for the sport. The numerous essays on his Alpine experiences, collected in 1871 under the title of *The Playground of Europe,* are among the most charming of his writings.

The summer of 1862 marked a turning point in his intellectual development. Much reading and reflection on the writings of such philosophers as Mill, Comte, and Spencer led him to cast off his belief in Christianity and to associate himself with the English school of philosophical radicalism and liberal reform headed by Mill. One of the few men at Cambridge to side with the Union cause, he made his first visit to the United States in 1863 in order to obtain a first-hand view of the Civil War. He met the most prominent American men of letters, including James Russell Lowell and Charles Eliot Norton, with whom he formed life-long friendships; Garrison and Phillips, the abolitionists; and such political and military leaders as President Lincoln and General Meade. In 1865 he published an anonymous pamphlet in defense of the North, entitled *"The Times" and the Civil War.*

He forsook Cambridge in 1864 to try his fortune in the London literary world.

years later in 1900. Although he was compelled to relinquish his position as editor in the middle of the work, owing to ill health, he remained a chief contributor. In addition to his manifold editorial duties, he wrote a total of 320 articles, covering approximately one thousand pages. Not only was the *Dictionary* the greatest of its kind; it set a new high standard of style and scholarship.

His literary productiveness continued to the last. He wrote memoirs of his brother, Sir James Fitzjames Stephen, of his friend the economist Henry Fawcett, and edited the works of Thackeray, Fielding, Richardson, and William Kingdon Clifford. He received many marks of distinction, including honorary degrees from Harvard, Edinburgh, Cambridge, and Oxford universities, and a knighthood on the occasion of King Edward VII's coronation in 1901. He died at his home in London after two years of invalidism at the age of 68.

Stephen married twice. His first wife, Harriet Marian, the younger daughter of the novelist Thackeray, whom he married in 1867, died suddenly in 1875. Three years later he married Julia Prinsep, youngest daughter of Dr. John Jackson, a Calcutta physician, and the widow of Herbert Duckworth. Stephen left one daughter by his first wife, and two sons and two daughters (one of them now Virginia Woolf, the novelist) by his second wife.

George Meredith characterized Stephen, the original of Vernon Whitford in *The Egoist*, as "a Phoebus Apollo turned fasting friar." He was a tall, lean person with striking features. Edmund Gosse recalls: "The long, thin, bright-red beard, radiating in a fanshape; the wrinkled forehead; the curious flatness of the top of the head accentuated by the fulness of the auburn hair on either side; the long cold hands; the distraught and melancholy eyes."

He was not a profound or penetrating thinker, but he was scrupulously sincere according to his lights, daring to speak a few unpleasant truths regarding religion to his contemporaries. His literary criticism embodies the representative virtues and limitations of the Victorian era. While his balanced judgments and level tone often produce the impression that he is a book-weighing machine, automatically registering the reactions of the average reasonable gentleman, his volumes of essays can still be read with considerable pleasure and profit.   G. E. N.

WORKS: *Essays*—Sketches From Cambridge by a Don, 1865; The Playground of Europe, 1871; Essays on Free-Thinking and Plain-Speaking, 1873; Hours in a Library: First Series, 1874, Second Series, 1876, Third Series, 1879; An Agnostic's Apology and Other Essays, 1893. *Biography*—Samuel Johnson, 1878; Alexander Pope, 1880;

Swift, 1882; The Life of Sir James Fitzjames Stephen, 1895; Studies of a Biographer (4 vols.) 1899; George Eliot, 1902; Hobbes, 1904. *Philosophy*—History of English Thought in the Eighteenth Century (3 vols.) 1876; The Science of Ethics, 1882; The English Utilitarians (3 vols.) 1900. *Miscellaneous*—The Times and the American War: A Historical Study by L. S. Ridgway, 1865; Social Rights and Duties, 1896; English Literature and Society in the Eighteenth Century, 1904.

ABOUT: Benn, A. W. History of English Rationalism in the Nineteenth Century; Courtney, J. E. Freethinkers of the Nineteenth Century; Lee, S. Principles of Biography; Lowell, J. R. Letters; Meredith, G. Letters; Maitland, F. W. Life and Letters of Leslie Stephen; London Mercury 8:621 October 1923.

STEPHENS, JAMES BRUNTON (June 17, 1835-June 20, 1902), Australian poet, was Scottish by birth, having been born in Linlithgowshire, on the Firth of Forth. His father was a poor schoolmaster, who moved to Edinburgh. The boy worked his way through several years at Edinburgh University by teaching at night and during vacations, but in spite of his excellent scholastic standing he was obliged to leave without a degree. For three years he was a traveling tutor, visiting France, Italy, and the Near East with his pupils. From 1857 to 1863 he was a schoolmaster at Greenock. He started writing during this period.

In 1866 he emigrated to Queensland for the sake of his health. He worked as a tutor, first in Brisbane and then at a bush station, and in 1873 became a teacher in the public schools of Queensland, at Stanthorpe and Ashgrave. In 1876 he married Rosalie Donaldson, an Irish girl; they had one son and four daughters.

In 1883 Stephens became correspondence clerk in the office of the Colonial Secretary, and remained in this post until his death, gradually rising to be chief clerk and acting under-secretary. He was president of the Johnsonian Club of Brisbane, and the center of the literary circle of that part of Australia. He was locally known as "the Queensland poet."

Although he did not write exclusively on Australian subjects, Stephens' poems reflect Australian life in pioneer days very accurately. They are imaginative and full of whimsical humor. His position in Australian literature is roughly analogous to that of Bret Harte in the American west, though, except for one forgotten novelette, he wrote entirely in verse.

PRINCIPAL WORKS: Convict Once, 1871; The Godolphin Arabian, 1872; The Black Gin and Other Poems, 1873; Mute Discourse, 1878; Marsupial Bill, 1879; Miscellaneous Poems, 1880; Fayette: or, Bush Revels, 1892.

ABOUT: Melbourne Review October 1884; Queenslander July 5, 1902.

STEPHENS, WILLIAM RICHARD WOOD (October 5, 1839-December 22, 1902), ecclesiastical historian and biographer, was born at Haywards Field, Stonehouse, Gloucestershire, the son of a business man. Educated at Balliol College, Oxford, he served successively as curate of Purley, Berkshire (1866-70), vicar of Mid Lavant, Sussex (1870-76), rector of Woolbeding, Sussex 1876-94), and dean of Winchester from 1894 until his death of typhoid fever at the age of sixty-three. His wife, Charlotte Jane Hook, survived him with four children.

Of his voluminous works, the most notable was *A History of the English Church From the Norman Conquest to the Accession of Edward I*, the second volume in a nine-volume church history edited by himself and William Hunt. He also wrote a meritorious biography of his father-in-law, Walter Farquhar Hook, and a less meritorious biography of the historian E. A. Freeman. With Walter Hook he published a revision of Dean Hook's *Church Dictionary* in 1887. He is remembered as a painstaking scholar.

PRINCIPAL WORKS: St. Chrysostom: His Life and Times, 1872; Memorials of the South Saxon See and the Cathedral Church of Chichester, 1876; The Life and Letters of Walter Farquhar Hook, 1878; The Life and Letters of E. A. Freeman, 1895; A History of the English Church From the Norman Conquest to the Accession of Edward I, 1901.

ABOUT: Hampshire Observer December 27, 1902 and January 3, 1903.

STERLING, JOHN (July 20, 1806-August 18, 1844), poet, novelist, and essayist, was born at Kames Castle on the Isle of Bute. He was the son of Edward Sterling, a captain of reserves, and of Hester (Coningham) Sterling. Although his father's family had been originally Scottish, most of Sterling's heritage was Irish. At the time of his birth his father had recently undertaken farming after the disbanding of his regiment; they later moved to Llanbethian, Glamorganshire, Wales, and spent a year in Paris.

Sterling was first educated at Dr. Barney's school at Greenwich. He attended the University of Glasgow for some time, then in 1824 removed to Trinity, Cambridge, where his tutor was J. C. Hare, later archdeacon of Lewes, whom he afterward served as curate during his short career as a divine. At Cambridge Sterling came under the influence of Coleridge; other acquaintances included Wordsworth and Edward Irving, the religious reformer.

In 1827 Sterling, after completing his studies at Cambridge, became secretary of an association devoted to the abolition of the East India Company. In 1828 he purchased *The Athenaeum* and conducted it for half a year with Frederick Denison Maurice. He was then obliged to sell it. In 1830 he married Susannah Barton. For the sake of his health he accepted a position as manager of a plantation in the West Indies, but within three or four years was back in England, where he met Carlyle. A trip to Bonn for further study resulted in a meeting with J. C. Hare, his old tutor, now an ordained clergyman; and as Sterling had been persuaded through listening to Coleridge that he could reconcile his skepticism with service in the church, he took orders and became Hare's curate in 1834, serving in this capacity less than three-quarters of a year, and giving illness as his excuse for resigning.

JOHN STERLING

After this he traveled to France, Madeira, and Rome for his health. In 1838 he founded the Sterling Club in London. Meantime his health grew steadily worse. His mother and his wife both died on the same day in 1843, and he did not long survive the shock, but died at Ventnor the next year.

Sterling was a talented man of letters and a man of delightful character; but it is not unjust to him to say that he lives mainly as the subject of Thomas Carlyle's biography, the writing of which was a defense and a protest. J. C. Hare, four years after Sterling's death, edited his *Essays and Tales* and wrote a memoir to go with them; the memoir, however, treated Sterling chiefly as a cleric who had deserted his vocation, and dwelt at length upon this. Carlyle, irritated, replied with his *Life of John Sterling*, an eloquent and popular work, which treated the dead author as a man.

Sterling's poem, "The Sexton's Daughter," was probably his best work. His friend R. B. Ince felt that "had it not been for the many hours he wasted upon theology, Sterling would have ripened sooner and produced poems worthy to set him beside the golden names in English literature."

Of him as a man, Carlyle said that he was "good, generous, and true," and also "a more perfectly transparent soul I have never seen."   R. M.

PRINCIPAL WORKS: *Poetry*—The Sexton's Daughter, 1837; Poems, 1839; The Election, 1841. *Fiction*—Arthur Coningsby, 1833. *Miscellaneous*—Essays and Tales, 1848.

ABOUT: Carlyle, T. Life of John Sterling; Fox, C. Diary; Ince, R. B. Calverley and Some Cambridge Wits of the 19th Century; Rolli, A. Guide to Carlyle: Vol. 2; Sterling, J. Letters to Emerson; Fraser's Magazine 37:187 February 1848; Living Age 16:517 March 11, 1848.

STEVENSON, JOSEPH (November 27, 1806-February 8, 1895), historian and archivist, was born at Berwick-on-Tweed, Northumberland, and educated at Glasgow University. He was successively sub-commissioner of public records in London (1834-39), librarian and keeper of records at the University of Durham (1841-48), and curate of Leighton Buzzard, Bedfordshire (1849-62). A convert to Roman Catholicism in 1863, he was ordained priest in 1872, and devoted four years to making transcriptions of the Vatican archives for the British government. He died in London at eighty-six.

It was Stevenson who induced the government in 1856 to publish the valuable Roll Series of sources of English history, entitled *Chronicles and Memorials of Great Britain and Ireland*. "This enterprise," says the *Cambridge History of English Literature,* "has done more towards supplying a sound foundation for an accurate knowledge of mediaeval history than all preceding efforts put together." He edited several of its volumes, dealing mainly with the English in France, besides other historical works for various archaeological clubs and societies; and also published original writings.

PRINCIPAL WORKS: The Church Historians of England (ed. vols. 1-4) 1853-56; Letters and Papers Illustrative of the Wars of the English in France During the Reign of Henry VI (ed.) 1861-64; Documents Illustrative of the History of Scotland (ed.) 1870; The Truth About John Wyclif, 1885; Marie Stuart: The First Eighteen Years of Her Life, 1886.

ABOUT: The Times February 12, 1895; The Month, March-April 1895.

STEVENSON, ROBERT LOUIS (November 13, 1850-December 4, 1894), Scottish novelist, poet, and essayist, was born at 8 Howard Place, Edinburgh, son of Thomas Stevenson, civil engineer, and Margaret Isabella (Balfour) Stevenson, the daughter of Lewis Balfour, minister at the nearby village of Colinton. He was christened "Robert Lewis Balfour," but adopted the now familiar form at about the age of eighteen, "Louis" being pronounced like "Lewis." As a baby he showed signs of pulmonary trouble, probably inherited from his mother and aggravated by the dampness of a house at Inverleith Terrace, to which a move was made in 1853. He was devotedly coddled by his nurse, Alison Cunningham ("Cummy"), who indeed played a great part in the development of his childish mind, with her grim Calvinism and her stock of stories of ghosts and fairies. Both his parents came of dour Scottish Calvinistic stock; severe religion brooded over his home from the first; but he was much beloved, and apparently had a happy childhood. In later years he was to write with enthusiasm of the long periods spent at his grandfather's manse at Colinton, presided over by his aunt, Jane Whyte Balfour. He was at various private schools, and for a brief period at Edinburgh Academy, but his formal education was greatly interrupted by illness, and he was frequently taken for holidays in Scotland and abroad for the benefit of his health.

Thomas Stevenson came of a celebrated line of lighthouse-builders, and his plan was that his son should follow on as an engineer. In the autumn of 1867 he was entered at the University of Edinburgh; but he showed no application and was very irregular in attendance. He became a member of the Speculative Society (a debating club of note), helped to edit a short-lived university magazine, and was cordially received into the cultured household of Fleeming Jenkin, professor of engineering (whose biography he was in later years to write). His undergraduate life included a good deal of velvet-coated bohemianism, and in spite of the efforts of pious biographers there remain traces of a love-affair with a light lady variously called Claire and Kate Drummond. All the time he dreamed dreams and wrote, as he had done since he could hold a pen. In April 1871 he confessed religious skepticism to his father, and expressed a wish to devote himself to literature. A compromise was arrived at, whereby he was to read for the Scottish Bar, which he proceeded to do, without enthusiasm.

In July 1873 he made an acquaintance which had a powerful effect on his subsequent career—that of Sidney Colvin, fellow of Trinity College, Cambridge (later to be knighted and become keeper of prints at the British Museum). The meeting took place at the house of a relative, Cockfield Rectory, Suffolk, and there too he met Mrs. Sitwell (later Lady Colvin) who inspired some of his most brilliant talk and correspondence. It was Colvin who put him up for the Savile Club, introduced him to editors, and generally, in Louis' words, "paved my way in letters." That autumn Stevenson's lung trouble again declared itself in virulent form. He was ordered to Mentone (where he met Andrew Lang) and returned in better shape in May 1874 to Swanston, a delightful house in the Pentland Hills which his father had taken seven years before. In February 1875 he was taken by Leslie Stephen to the Old Infirmary, Edinburgh, to meet W. E. Henley, a crippled and heroically ailing man of letters, who had come there to be under the care of Joseph Lister. An intimate friendship sprang up, which was to endure until 1888, when it was broken by a misunderstanding. At Easter his cousin R. A. M. Stevenson gave him his first real introduction to Paris; and in July he passed his Bar final. But he made no attempt to practise, and in August he took up residence at Barbizon, in the Forest of Fontainebleau, where he lived happily in the artist colony. He was supported by a small allowance from his father, but had also begun to find entry in the English magazines, and in 1876 was attracting the attention of the discerning by his essays in *The Cornhill*. In September of that year he and his friend Sir Walter Simpson made the canoe journey through Belgium and France which provided the subject of his first book, *An Inland Voyage*. The next month, at Grez, he found the artist group augmented by the addition of two women, with one of whom, Mrs. Fanny Osbourne, he instantly fell in love.

Fanny Van de Grift Osbourne was ten years older than Stevenson. Unhappily married to an American, Samuel Osbourne, she had at length left him, with her three children, lived in poverty in Paris, and lost her youngest son by death. She was now, with her elder son, Lloyd, making quiet holiday at Grez. A dark, thick-set woman, with years of adventure and trouble behind her, she was forceful, imaginative, magnetic, romantic, and Louis fell immediately under her spell. One of his best-known and most deeply-felt poems is about her, beginning:

Trusty, dusky, vivid, true,
    With eyes of gold and bramble-dew,
Steel-true and blade-straight,
    The great artificer
    Made my mate.

It was several years before she was able to procure her divorce and marry him. Meanwhile he moved about between France, Scotland, and England. In April 1878, at Burford Bridge, Surrey, he met George Meredith; in September he made the journey in Auvergne which produced *Travels With a Donkey in Cevennes;* by the autumn he had, in five years, produced twenty-eight of his best essays and five stories, including "The Sire de Malétroit's Door" and "Providence and the Guitar."

During the winter of 1878-9 he was in London with Henley, working on the play, *Deacon Brodie.* Early in August 1879 he followed Mrs. Osbourne to California, where she had gone to initiate divorce proceedings. He arrived at San Francisco poor and ill; lost his road on the way to Monterey; lay out in the open for three days and nights; and did harm to his delicate constitution which made him an invalid for the rest of his days. He was at Monterey till the end of the year, working very hard, writing *The Pavilion on the Links,* drafting *Prince Otto* and *The Amateur Emigrant,* and even accepting work for a local paper at two dollars a week.

On May 19, 1880, Stevenson and Mrs. Osbourne were married. They went for a time to Calistoga, and in August returned to Scotland, where the bride, despite all fears, was kindly received by the parents. Stevenson's life for the next seven years was one of unremitting work and search for health, broken by many severe hemorrhages and monitions of death. In October 1880 the air of Davos, Switzerland, was tried. There Louis met John Addington Symonds, gloried in the keen atmosphere, and ran floor-games and a portable printing-press with the young Lloyd Osbourne. His many wanderings covered the Highlands, Davos again, Saint Marcel, Hyères, Nice, and Bournemouth—where he settled in September 1884. These seven years firmly estab-

ROBERT LOUIS STEVENSON

lished his literary reputation. *Treasure Island* was published in the periodical, *Young Folks* (as "The Sea Cook"); *Dr. Jekyll and Mr. Hyde* (1886) sold forty thousand copies in six months; and *Kidnapped* (1886) also had a great success, the austere Henry James going so far as to call Alan Breck "the most perfect character in English literature."

When Stevenson once more set out for America, in August 1887, three months after the death of his father, he was received with acclamation and booked lucrative contracts with Charles Scribner and S. S. Mc-Clure. With his wife, mother, and stepson, he spent a winter of bitter cold at Saranac, in the Adirondacks. In June 1888 he was able to gratify a long-cherished ambition, hiring the yacht "Casco" at San Francisco and sailing for the South Seas, where, though he did not know it, the rest of his life was to be spent. The voyage extended to the Marquesas, the Paumotus, the Tahitian group, and Hawaii, where a stay of six months was made. The party went as far afield as Sydney, where Stevenson was ill again. Finally, in October 1890, they settled at Apia, in Samoa, at a house which was named "Vailima," or "Five Waters." Here at last Stevenson found a climate in which he could live. The native character pleased him; he rose early and wrote industriously; and he dabbled in local politics in a way that annoyed the authorities. He was known as Tusitala ("Teller of Tales"), and his life in Samoa, surrounded by his family, had something patriarchal about it. *The Wrecker* was written with Lloyd Osbourne, and his last important books were *Catriona, Weir of Hermiston,* and *St. Ives.* On December 4, 1894, he was talking to his wife when a rupture occurred in a blood-vessel in the brain, and he died in a few hours. He was buried at the summit of Mount Vaea, devoted native hands clearing the difficult scrub on the mountainside to make a way.

"In personal appearance," wrote Sidney Colvin in the *Dictionary of National Biography,* "Stevenson was of good stature (about 5 ft. 10 in.) and activity, but very slender, his leanness of body and limb (not of face) having been throughout life abnormal. The head was small, the eyes dark hazel, very wide-set, intent, and beaming, the face of a long oval shape; the expression rich and animated. He had a free and picturesque play of gesture and a voice of full and manly fibre, in which his pulmonary weakness was not at all betrayed."

Stevenson was widely read in French literature as well as in English, and his constant and conscious striving after style is more typical of the Gallic than of the British mentality. In his own well-known phrase, he "played the sedulous ape" to one master after another, and his prose, in consequence, is often a thought mannered and over-wrought. But there can be no doubt as to his high status as a writer. His genius was many-sided. He produced not only the best boy's book in English, and several deeper masterpieces of Scottish characterization, but some of the best familiar essays in the language. His poetry had a quiet, melancholy heroism of its own, a spare sense of form, and a vocabulary never far removed from "the real language of men." He really loved and understood children, and the poems in *A Child's Garden of Verses,* in their humor, their simplicity, the quality of their imagination, are far more nourishing than the pabulum so often served out for the infant mind. The short stories in the *New Arabian Nights* series are vivid, full of action, memorable; and in mastery of the *macabre,* the eerie, the weird, not Poe himself excels "Thrawn Janet" or *Dr. Jekyll and Mr. Hyde.* Gosse, Colvin, Henley, Henry James, Meredith, and a host of other eminent friends have paid tribute to the brilliance of his conversation and the great charm of his personality. His was a heroic life, spent literally in the shadow of death; and the volume and variety of his contributions to letters are the measure of how well he fought.

H. B. G.

PRINCIPAL WORKS: *Novels and Collections of Stories*—New Arabian Nights, 1882; Treasure Island, 1883; Prince Otto, 1885; More New Arabian Nights (with Fanny Stevenson) 1885; The Strange Case of Dr. Jekyll and Mr. Hyde, 1886; Kidnapped, 1886; The Merry Men, 1887; The Black Arrow, 1888; The Wrong Box (with Lloyd Osbourne) 1889; The Master of Ballantrae, 1889; The Wrecker (with Lloyd Osbourne) 1892; Catriona, 1893; Island Nights' Entertainments, 1893; The Ebb-Tide (with Lloyd Osbourne) 1894; Weir of Hermiston, 1896; St. Ives (finished by A. T. Quiller-Couch) 1898. *Essays and Travel*—Travels With a Donkey in the Cevennes, 1879; An Inland Voyage, 1878; Virginibus Puerisque, 1881; Familiar Studies of Men and Books, 1882; The Silverado Squatters, 1883; Memories and Portraits, 1887; The South Seas, 1890; Across the Plains, 1892; Juvenilia, 1896. *Poems*—A Child's Garden of Verses, 1885; Underwoods, 1887; Ballads, 1890; Songs of Travel and Other Verses, 1896. *Plays* (with W. E. Henley)—Deacon Brodie, 1880; Admiral Guinea, 1884; Beau Austin, 1884; Macaire, 1885. *Letters*—Vailima Letters, 1895; Letters to His Family and Friends (selected and ed. by Sidney Colvin) 1899.

ABOUT: Balfour, G. The Life of Robert Louis Stevenson; Carré, J. M. Robert Louis Stevenson: The Frail Warrior; Chesterton, G. K. Robert Louis Stevenson; Hamilton, C. On the Trail of Stevenson; Hellman, G. S. The True Stevenson; Masson, R. The Life of Robert Louis Stevenson; Osbourne, L. An Intimate Portrait of R.L.S.; Steuart, J. A. R. L. Stevenson: A Critical Study.

STEWART, DUGALD (November 22, 1753-June 11, 1828), Scottish philosopher, was the only child of a professor of mathematics at the University of Edinburgh, where he was born. He was educated in the High School and University of his native city, then spent a year at Glasgow University, trying to decide on his future profession. Finally he returned to Edinburgh and became his father's associate. From 1775 his father was too ill to teach, and the son took all his classes. In 1778 and 1779 he also took over the work of the professor of moral philosophy. His day began at 3 A.M., and at its end he was often so exhausted he had to be lifted into his carriage.

In 1783 he married Helen Bannatyne, who died in 1787, leaving one son. In 1790 he married Helen D'Arcy Cranstoun, by whom he had one son and one daughter. She was a brilliant, well-educated woman, who acted as critic of all his writings.

In 1785 Stewart became professor of moral philosophy in Edinburgh University. Within a few years he was the only authoritative writer on philosophy in England or Scotland, and when the French Revolution kept English students away from the Continent, they flocked to his classes. He had an enormous influence on the young men of his time. In 1788 and 1789 he had visited France, and had been a sympathizer with the early aspects of the revolution; though he was never a radical, he refused to retract his liberal opinions, and was considered by the Tories a very dangerous person. When the Whigs came into power in 1806, he was made editor of the *Edinburgh Gazette*, a sinecure paying £300 a year, which was his for life and descended to his family after his death. In 1809 his health became so bad that he turned over all his teaching to his associate; in 1820 the associate died and he tried to return, but found himself physically incapable of the strain, and resigned. He suffered a stroke in 1822, and was an invalid until his death six years later.

Stewart was more of a philosophical commentator than an original philosopher. It has been well said that "his disciples were his best works."

PRINCIPAL WORKS: Elements of the Philosophy of the Human Mind, 1792-1827; Outlines of Moral Philosophy, 1793; Philosophical Essays, 1810; Biographical Memoirs, 1811.
ABOUT: Veitch, J. Life of Dugald Stewart (preface to Vol. 10 of Collected Works, 1858).

STIRLING, JAMES HUTCHISON (June 22, 1820-March 19, 1909), Scottish philosopher, was born in Glasgow. His father, a merchant, was a studious man and a good mathematician. His mother and three brothers died while he was very young. He was educated at Young's Academy, Glasgow, and at Glasgow University. In 1842 he became a Member of the Royal College of Surgeons of Edinburgh (F.R.C.S. 1860). In 1843 he was assistant to a physician in Monmouthshire, and in 1846 surgeon of the Hirwain Iron Works. In 1847 he married Jane Haunter Mair; they had two sons and five daughters, one of whom wrote a number of historical works.

Stirling's heart was not in medicine, but in literature and philosophy. From 1845 he had been contributing to *Douglas Jerrold's Magazine*. When his father died in 1851, he immediately gave up his profession and went to France and Germany to study philosophy. In 1867 he translated Schwegler's *History of Philosophy*. He was Gifford lecturer at Edinburgh in 1889 and 1890, and contributed frequently to the *Fortnightly Review, Macmillan's Magazine, Mind,* and other serious English and American periodicals. He received an honorary LL.D. from Edinburgh in 1867, and from Glasgow in 1901. In 1889 he was given a civil list pension.

Stirling's book on Hegel had an immense influence. It was his work which was the chief factor in turning Scottish philosophical thought and teaching into "idealistic" channels. His bent of mind was abstract and mystical, and he vehemently opposed theories which had materialistic implications, such as Darwin's theory of evolution and Huxley's premise of a universal protoplasm. A profound conservative, he also wrote attacks on the Single Tax theory. His style resembles that of Carlyle; it has the same vividness and the same peculiarities of crabbed diction.

PRINCIPAL WORKS: The Secret of Hegel, 1865; Analysis of Sir William Hamilton's Philosophy, 1865; Text-Book to Kant, 1881; What Is Thought? 1903.
ABOUT: Stirling, A. H. J. H. Stirling: His Life and Work.

STIRLING-MAXWELL, LADY. See NORTON, CAROLINE E. S.

STIRLING-MAXWELL, SIR WILLIAM (March 8, 1818-January 5, 1878), Scottish historian, was born at Kenmure, the son of a wealthy landowner and cattle-breeder, formerly a West Indian planter. His name originally was Stirling. His mother died when he was four. He was educated at Trinity College, Cambridge, where he received his B.A. in 1839 and his M.A. in 1843. He spent 1842 in Spain and the Levant, and became interested in Spanish art, of which little was then known in England.

When his father died in 1847, he succeeded to the family estates. He served as a member of Parliament from 1852 to 1868, and from 1874 to 1878, but his parliamentary career was undistinguished. On the other hand he became a well-known figure in London literary circles. In 1865 he married Anna Maria Melville, daughter of the Earl of Leven and Melville. She died in 1874, leaving two sons. In 1865 also he succeeded to the baronetcy of his maternal uncle, and added his uncle's name of Maxwell to his own.

Stirling-Maxwell was rector of St. Andrews in 1862, and of Edinburgh in 1872, and in 1876 became chancellor of Glasgow University. The same year he received an honorary D.C.L. from Oxford and was made a Knight of the Thistle. At the same time he took a great interest in his estates, bred short horn cattle and Clydesdale horses (the famous "Keir strain"), and in 1868 was honorary secretary of the Highland and Agricultural Society. He maintained a London home, which became the repository of a fine collection of objects of art. He was a trustee of the British Museum and of the National Gallery. In March 1877, he married his old friend, Mrs. Caroline (Sheridan) Norton, the song-writer; she died the following June. Stirling-Maxwell himself died in Venice the next year, of a fever.

PRINCIPAL WORKS: Songs of the Holy Land, 1846-47; Annals of the Artists of Spain, 1848; The Cloister Life of the Emperor Charles V, 1852; Velazquez and His Works, 1855; Don John of Austria, 1883.

ABOUT: Stirling-Maxwell, Sir W. Collected Works (see Biographical Note); Guardian January 16, 1878; Scotsman January 17, 1878.

STODDART, THOMAS TOD (February 14, 1810-November 21, 1880), Scottish poet, was born in Edinburgh and educated at the university of his native city. His life's main occupation was angling, in the practise of which he was expert, and he made his home from 1836 onwards in the town of Kelso, where he found excellent fishing in the conjoining rivers Tweed and Teviot. He died at Kelso at the age of seventy.

A romantic narrative poem, *The Death-Wake*, which fell still-born from the press in his twenty-first year, won the praise of Andrew Lang more than sixty years later for its passages "of poetry very curious because it is full of the new note, the new melody which young Mr. Tennyson was beginning to waken. It anticipates Beddoes, it coincides with Gautier and *Les Chimères* of Gérard, it answers the accents, then unheard in England, of Poe." But Stoddart is remembered chiefly as the Isaak Walton of Scottish fishermen, the author of angling songs which are classics of their kind.

His daughter ANNA M. STODDART (1840-1911), wrote praiseworthy biographies of her father and of John Stuart Blackie.

PRINCIPAL WORKS: The Death-Wake: or, Lunacy, 1831; The Art of Angling, 1835; The Angler's Companion to the Rivers and Lakes of Scotland, 1892; Angling Songs, 1839; Songs of the Seasons, 1873.

ABOUT: Lang, A. Adventures Among Books; Stoddart, T. T. Angling Songs (see Memoir by his daughter in 1889 ed.); Stoddart, T. T. The Death-Wake (see Introduction by A. Lang in 1895 ed.); Stoddart, T. T. Songs of the Seasons (see Autobiographical Memoir in 1881 ed.).

STOKES, SIR GEORGE GABRIEL (August 13, 1819-February 1, 1903), Irish mathematician and physicist, was born at Skreen, in county Sligo, and educated at Pembroke College, Cambridge. From 1849 until his death—a period of fifty-four years—he was Lucasian professor of mathematics at Cambridge. He was long-time secretary (1854-85) and president (1885-90) of the Royal Society, sat in Parliament for his University (1887-91), and was created baronet in 1889. Lord Kelvin was his close friend.

He made valuable contributions to the literature of science with papers describing his pioneer researches in optics, hydro-dynamics, geodesy, and pure mathematics. Of these the best known was his paper on the refrangibility of light, published in 1852; also of importance was his description—the first ever made—of the phenomenon of fluorescence, which is involved in X-ray. His writings were collected in five volumes, of which the first three were edited by himself and the last two (posthumously) by Sir Joseph Larmor.

PRINCIPAL WORKS: The Dynamical Theory of Diffraction, 1849; Light, 1884-87; Mathematical and Physical Papers, 1880-1905; Scientific Correspondence (ed. by Sir J. Larmor) 1907.

ABOUT: Stokes, Sir G. G. Scientific Correspondence (see Biographical Memoir by his daughter Mrs. L. Humphry).

STOKES, WHITLEY (February 28, 1830-April 13, 1909), Irish Celtic scholar, was born in Dublin, the son of William Stokes, a noted physician. He was educated at Trinity College in his native city. Beginning in 1855, he practised law seven years in London and twenty years in India, where, as a legal member of the viceroy's council, he revised the codes of civil and criminal procedure. Following his return to England in 1882 he devoted himself to Celtic studies which brought him fame as a pioneer in Irish literature. He died in Kensington at the age of seventy-nine.

Often in collaboration with other scholars, he edited Irish and Celtic texts, with translations and glossaries, which have been found highly useful and readable by students. He also published Cornish and Breton works. His library of Celtic books, including a rare collection of all his own writings, was presented to University College, London.

PRINCIPAL WORKS EDITED BY WHITLEY STOKES: Three Irish Glossaries, 1862; Three Middle-Irish Homilies, 1877; Irische Texte (with E. Windisch) 1884-1909; Old Irish Glosses at Würzburg and Carlsruhe, 1887; The Anglo-Indian Codes, 1887; Lives of Saints From the Book of Lismore, 1890; Urkeltischer Sprachschatz (with A. Bezzenberger) 1894; Thesaurus Palaeohibernicus (with J. Strachan) 1901-03.

STORY, ROBERT (October 17, 1795-July 7, 1860), Northumbrian poet, was born at Wark, the son of a peasant. After attending school at Wark and Crookham, he went to work as a farm laborer at twelve, taught school intermittently, and in his twenty-fifth year opened a school of his own at Gargrave in Yorkshire. This venture prospered for ten years, then ended abruptly in 1830 when Story declared his sympathy with the conservative party on the issue of reform. This stand finally brought him a minor position in the audit office in London which he held from 1843 until his death at sixty-four.

A lavish edition of Story's *Poetical Works,* issued by the Duke of Northumberland at his own expense three years before the poet's death, was praised by Macaulay, Aytoun, and Carlyle, who saw in it "a certain rustic vigor of life, breezy freshness, as of the Cheviot Hills." But a later critic, Thomas Seccombe, was "less impressed by the distinctive merit of Story's poems than by the courage and success with which he set about selling them with a view to relieve himself of the debts by which he was at all times encumbered."

PRINCIPAL WORKS: The Magic Fountain, 1829; The Outlaw, 1839; Songs and Lyrical Poems, 1849; Guthrum the Dane, 1852; Poetical Works, 1857; Lyrical and Other Minor Poems (ed. by J. James) 1861.

ABOUT: Story, R. Love and Literature; Story, R. Lyrical and Other Minor Poems (see Memoir by J. James).

STOTHARD, ANNA ELIZA. See BRAY, ANNA ELIZA

STRICKLAND, AGNES (August 19, 1796-July 13, 1874), biographer and historical writer, was born in London and educated by her father, a shipper. During an industrious literary career she devoted herself successively to poetry, to books for children (producing notably two collections of historical tales), and to a series of biographies of British sovereigns, the last being her most successful vein. Best known of these works was *Lives of the Queens of England,* from Mathilda of Flanders to Queen Ann, in twelve volumes. The biographies were entirely uncritical but full of vivid details of court and domestic life, based on unpublished official and private documents. Critics complained of their paucity of thought and style.

More than a dozen of the lives were written by Agnes' elder sister ELIZABETH STRICKLAND (1794-1875) who preferred that her name should never appear as a collaborator. She was also a silent partner in the children's books. Her style was more masculine than that of her sister.

Agnes received a civil list pension of £100 during the last four years of her life, and died at Southwold, Suffolk, at the age of seventy-seven.

PRINCIPAL WORKS (many in collaboration with Elizabeth Strickland): *Biography*—Lives of the Queens of England, 1840-48; The Letters of Mary Queen of Scots (ed.) 1842-43; Lives of the Queens of Scotland and English Princesses Connected With the Royal Succession of Great Britain, 1850-59; Lives of the Bachelor Kings of England, 1861; Lives of the Seven Bishops Committed to the Tower, 1866; Lives of the Tudor Princesses Including Lady Jane Gray and Her Sister, 1868; Lives of the Last Four Princesses of the House of Stuart, 1872. *Children's Books*—The Moss-House, 1822; The Tell-Tale, 1823; The Rival Crusoes, 1826; The Young Emigrant, 1826; The Juvenile Forget-me-not, 1827; Historical Tales of Illustrious British Children, 1833; Tales of the School-Room, 1835?; Tales and Stories From History, 1836.

ABOUT: Strickland, J. M. [sister]. Life of Agnes Strickland.

STRONG, EMILIA FRANCES. See DILKE, LADY

STUBBS, WILLIAM (June 21, 1825-April 22, 1901), historian, was born in Knaresborough. His father was a solicitor, but the family was of old yeoman stock. He was educated at Ripon Grammar School until 1842, when his father died and his mother was left in extreme poverty with six children. In 1848 he entered Christ Church College, Oxford, as a "servitor." His college life was miserable; timidity and modesty made his social position all the more painful, and he spent his spare time in the library, reading old charters and deeds. It was thus that he became one of the foremost scholars in the mediaeval history of England. He received his B.A. in 1848, but was never recognized officially as a "student" of Christ Church. However, he was elected a fellow of Trinity, and lived there until 1850.

He had entered Oxford as an evangelical, and left it as an adherent of the high church and a Tory. In 1848 he was ordained deacon, in 1850 priest, and until 1866 he served as a country vicar in a college living in Essex. All the while he studied old documents, and prepared for a career as an historian. He served also as poor law guardian, and took private pupils, one of whom was Algernon Charles Swinburne. In 1859 he married Catherine Dellar, the village schoolmistress; they had five sons and one daughter.

In 1862 Stubbs was made librarian of Lambeth, an ideal position for the sort of study in which he was engaged. The recognition of his work was very slow; it was 1863 before he was invited to edit the Rolls Series, a post he had long coveted; he was the best editor the Rolls Series ever had. Continually passed over in applications for positions, he did not dare risk another disappointment and so did not apply to become regius professor of history at Oxford when the place was vacant in 1866; it was, however, offered to him and eagerly accepted. He was professor until

1884. But the department was considered of no importance, and every obstacle was placed in his way. His *Constitutional History of England,* a landmark in history, finally brought him recognition; he was made a canon of St. Paul's in 1879, Bishop of Chester in 1884, and Bishop of Oxford in 1888. He contributed to the Dictionary of Christian Biography from 1877 to 1887, and to the Dictionary of Christian Antiquities from 1875 to 1880. In 1898 his health failed and he was about to resign his bishopric when he died suddenly in 1901.

PRINCIPAL WORKS: Select Charters, 1879; Constitutional History of England, 1873-78; Seventeen Lectures, 1886; Lectures on European History, 1904; Lectures on Early English History, 1906; Germany in the Early Middle Ages, 1908; Germany in the Later Middle Ages, 1908.

ABOUT: Hutton, W. H. The Letters of William Stubbs; Maitland, F. W. Collected Papers.

SULLIVAN, TIMOTHY DANIEL (1827-March 31, 1914),

Irish poet, journalist, and politician, was born at Bantry, County Cork. For forty-five years a contributor to *The Nation,* he owned and edited that newspaper during the last sixteen years of its existence (1884-1900), succeeding his brother. He was long a member of Parliament, sitting successively for County Westmeath, for Dublin, and County Donegal. In 1886-87 he was Lord Mayor of Dublin.

At the time of his death at the age of eight-seven he was the most distinguished figure in Irish patriotic literature. His "God Save Ireland" disputed the position of "The Wearing of the Green" as the Irish national anthem. He wrote, besides patriotic lyrics, rhythmic and humorous political satires which were widely popular. According to Stopford A. Brooke and T. W. Rolleston, his "best work is to be found in simple ballads of fatherland and home. His style when dealing with congenial themes is clear, direct and sincere."

His brother, ALEXANDER MARTIN SULLIVAN (1830-1884), Irish politician and editor of *The Nation,* wrote *The Story of Ireland* and other prose works.

PRINCIPAL WORKS: Poetry—Dunboy and Other Poems, 1861; Green Leaves, 1875; Prison Poems: or, Lays of Tullamore, 1888; Blanaid and Other Irish Historical and Legendary Poems From the Gaelic, 1891; Evergreen, 1907; Irish National Poems and Irish Prints, 1914. Prose—Speeches From the Dock: or, Protests of Irish Patriotism (ed. with A. M. Sullivan and D. B. Sullivan) 1882; A Memoir of A. M. Sullivan, 1885; Recollections of Troubled Times in Irish Politics, 1905; Bantry, Berehaven, and the O'Sullivan Sept, 1908.

ABOUT: The Bibliographical Society of Ireland Publications: Vol. 3 no. 3, 1926.

"SUMMERLEY, FELIX." See COLE, SIR HENRY

SURTEES, ROBERT SMITH (1803-March 16, 1864),

novelist, was born at Hamsterley Hall, near Newcastle-on-Tyne, second son of Anthony Surtees, a country squire, and Alice (Blackett) Surtees. After preparatory schooling at Ovingham, nearby, he went to Durham Grammar School in 1818, and in April 1822 signed articles with R. A. Purvis, an attorney in Newcastle. In May 1825 he was "further articled" to William Bell, of Bow Churchyard, in London; later establishing himself in Lincoln's Inn Fields, London, and practising (apparently not very assiduously) as a lawyer. The winter of 1829 saw his first entry into the then exclusive social circle of Brighton. In his free time he hunted enthusiastically, not only with numerous packs in different parts of England, but also at Boulogne. Gradually, from 1830 onwards, he built up a connection as a writer on sporting subjects, contributing frequent articles to *The Sporting Magazine.* His first publication in book form was *The Horseman's Manual* in 1831, a practical volume on the law relating to horses. This same year was a crucial one in his life for two reasons. First, on March 24 his elder brother Anthony died unmarried at Malta, and he thus became his father's heir. Second, with Rudolf Ackerman he started the *New Sporting Magazine,* which he edited till the end of 1836, and in which (from July 1831 to September 1834) he worked up the character of John Jorrocks, the sporting Cockney grocer, which has become famous among all those interested in hunting stories.

Surtees was no lawyer at heart, and his success as a journalist, together with the assurance of future affluence as the heir of a comfortable estate, made him give up his practise about 1835. In December 1836 he gave up his editorship also. The next year he offered himself as a candidate for Parliament in the conservative interest, but withdrew before polling-day to prevent the probable return of the sitting member in a three-cornered contest. On his father's death (March 5, 1838) he succeeded to the Hamsterley estate. Thereafter he led the life of a country gentleman, becoming a justice of the peace, a major in the Durham militia, and (in 1856) high sheriff of his county. Conservative leaders in the north hoped to find him a seat in Parliament, but it so fell out that he never renewed his candidacy for Westminster.

On May 19, 1841, Surtees married Elizabeth Jane Fenwick, who bore him one son, Anthony, who died at Rome on March 17, 1871, and two daughters. Mrs. Surtees died in 1879.

The squire of Hamsterley varied from the norm of his type, not in his pursuits, which were the usual sporting ones, but in his de-

ROBERT SMITH SURTEES

sire to depict those sports in words. Racing interested him not at all, but he knew all about horses and hunting, and produced eight long novels, all dealing mainly with the life of the hunting field. The Jorrocks papers had won immediate popularity. J. G. Lockhart, then editing the *Quarterly Review*, sent a kind message through "Nimrod" (C. J. Apperley) in 1832, and, four years later, wrote direct to Surtees asking him to produce a "cousin," and "throw the materials into light dramatic form." It was probably this encouragement that led to the writing of *Handley Cross*, which appeared in the *New Sporting Magazine* during 1838 and 1839, and came out, much expanded, as a three-volume book in 1843. Another edition was published in 1854, illustrated by John Leech, who also illustrated *Ask Mamma* (1858) and part of *Mr. Facey Romford's Hounds* (1865), this last book being completed by Hablot K. Browne ("Phiz") after Leech's death. *Jorrocks's Jaunts and Jollities* had already appeared in book form in 1838.

Surtees wrote, hunted, sat on the bench of magistrates, did political work in opposition to those who were agitating for the repeal of the Corn Laws, and varied his placid existence by visits to London, Brighton, and other places. He died at Brighton in 1864.

"Surtees," writes E. D. Cuming, "was a man of silent, almost taciturn, habit, and curiously enough, the chance acquaintance would never suspect that he was interested in any form of sport. His books furnish ample proof of exceptional powers of observation and a retentive memory. . . He was . . . a very abstemious and temperate man. . . His method of working was his own; he always wrote standing at a small desk on short legs, which was set upon a table." His novels are pre-eminent in the annals of sport, but have small claim to rank as pure literature. Despite abundant evidence of capacity in drawing the little world of the hunt, they are marred by excessive length and a somewhat irritating jocosity. All of them were first published anonymously.   H. B. G.

PRINCIPAL WORKS: *Novels*—Jorrocks's Jaunts and Jollities, 1838; Handley Cross, 1843; Hillingdon Hall: or, The Cockney Squire, 1845; Hawbuck Grange, 1847; Mr. Sponge's Sporting Tour, 1853; Ask Mamma, 1858; Plain or Ringlets? 1860; Mr. Facey Romford's Hounds, 1865. *Other Writings*—The Horseman's Manual, 1831; The Analysis of the Hunting Field, 1846.

ABOUT: Cuming, E. D. Robert Smith Surtees; Steel, A. Jorrocks's England; Surtees, R. S. Jorrocks's Jaunts and Jollities (see Memorial Preface to 1869 ed.); Times Literary Supplement March 27, 1930; Watson, F. Robert Smith Surtees: A Critical Study.

SWAIN, CHARLES (January 4, 1801–September 22, 1874), poet, was born in Manchester and lived there until his death at the age of seventy-three. Given only an elementary education, he worked as clerk in a dyehouse from the age of fifteen to twenty-nine. Thenceforth he was associated with a local firm engaged in an engraving and lithographing business, of which he eventually became proprietor. During the last eighteen years of his life he received a civil-list pension of £50. He was survived by his wife, Anne Glover, and a daughter, Clara Swain, who published four books of verse.

His own poetry, the product of leisure hours, filled a dozen volumes published over a period of forty years beginning when he was twenty-six. *The Mind and Other Poems* was the most ambitious of his works and *Songs and Ballads* was the most rapid seller, reaching a fifth edition ten years after publication. A collected edition of his verses appeared in the United States in 1857. His works were characterized by elegance and grace, but he is not ranked an important author, though Robert Southey said that "if ever man was born to be a poet, Swain was."

PRINCIPAL WORKS: Metrical Essays on Subjects of History and Imagination, 1827; Dryburgh Abbey: A Poem on the Death of Sir Walter Scott, 1832; The Mind and Other Poems, 1832; Memoir of Henry Liverseege, 1835; Dramatic Chapters: Poems and Songs, 1847; English Melodies, 1849; Songs and Ballads, 1867; Selections, 1906.

ABOUT: Manchester Guardian, December 8, 1841, September 23, 1874, February 14, 1880.

SWANWICK, ANNA (June 22, 1813–November 2, 1899), translator of poetry from the German and Greek, was born in Liverpool, She was educated at home and in Berlin, where she studied Greek and German from 1839 to 1843. The rest of her life was devoted to literary and philanthropic work. She promoted women's education, and helped to found Girton College, Cambridge, and Somerville Hall, Oxford. Her large circle of noted friends, including Crabb Robinson, Browning, Tennyson, and James Martineau, knew her as an excellent raconteuse with a fund of anecdotes of literary people. She died at Tunbridge Wells, Kent, at the age of eighty-six.

Her lively blank-verse translation of Goethe's *Faust* ran through several editions and was included in Bohn's series of foreign classics in English. It is recognized as one of the best. Also of high rank are her rhymed translations from Schiller and Aeschylus. In addition to her work as a translator she wrote several volumes of prose.

PRINCIPAL WORKS: Selections From the Dramas of Goethe and Schiller (tr.) 1843; Goethe's Faust (tr.) 1850-78; The Trilogy of Æschylus (tr.) 1865; The Dramas of Æschylus (tr.) 1873; An Utopian Dream and How It May Be Realised, 1888.

ABOUT: Bruce, M. L. Anna Swanwick: A Memoir; The Times November 4, 1899.

SWEET, HENRY (September 15, 1845-April 30, 1912), philologist and phonetician, was born in London and educated at Balliol College, Oxford. He was repeatedly unsuccessful in obtaining a professorship at Oxford and held no official position or had no regular income until his fifty-sixth year when Oxford created the position of reader in phonetics for him. He died of pernicious anemia at Oxford at the age of sixty-six, leaving no children. Independent in character, he lost many of his friends in late years.

Beginning at the age of thirty-one, he produced a series of standard works on the English language which brought him a reputation as England's greatest philologist and the chief founder of modern phonetics. His particular contribution was in establishing the sound value of words and syllables as a factor in the development of the language. His works have great originality. Perhaps best known are his *Anglo-Saxon Reader, New English Grammar,* and *History of Language.* He edited numerous Old and Middle English texts.

PRINCIPAL WORKS: History of English Sounds From the Earliest Period, 1874; An Anglo-Saxon Reader (tr.) 1876; Handbook of Phonetics, 1877; The Oldest English Texts, 1885; Elementarbuch des Gesprochenen Englisch, 1885; A New English Grammar, 1892; A Student's Dictionary of Anglo-Saxon, 1897; The History of Language, 1900; The Sounds of English: An Introduction to Phonetics, 1908; The Collected Papers of Henry Sweet (ed. by H. C. K. Wyld) 1913.

ABOUT: Modern Language Quarterly, July 1901; Oxford Magazine, May 9, 1912; see also the prefaces to Sweet's works.

SWINBURNE, ALGERNON CHARLES (April 5, 1837-April 10, 1909), poet and critic, was born during a visit of his parents to London; their home, however was on the Isle of Wight. His father was an admiral, his mother the daughter of the Earl of Ashburnham;

on both sides he came of old and aristocratic stock. His early boyhood was spent for the most part either at his father's home, Bonchurch, Isle of Wight, beside (or more frequently in) that foster-mother of his genius, the sea; or at the ancestral Swinburne estate, Capheaton, Northumberland, with his remarkable grandfather, Sir John Edward Swinburne. This old man, who lived to be ninety-eight, who had been born and reared in France, and who was a free-thinker and a republican, was one of the most formative influences on a mind singularly susceptible to impressions in earliest youth, singularly impervious after the age of adolescence. He and the rugged cliffs and clear air of Northumberland became inseparably a part of the inner being of this strange eldest child of Sir John's second son.

In 1849, just twelve years old, Swinburne entered Eton. His four and a half years there, despite his sudden and unexplained departure, were not unhappy ones. Although he was popularly known as "Mad Swinburne," he experienced no such torture as had been the lot of a boy who forty years earlier had been dubbed "Mad Shelley." He laid here the foundations of his intimacy with the Greek poets—that with the Elizabethans had already had its roots in childhood—but it is characteristic that his only honor was a modern language prize, a subject which was hardly, officially, in the curriculum. More significant is the hidden, lifelong effect on his erotic life of the public corporal punishment so much in vogue at public schools of the time.

After two years of private tutoring, and his only visit to Germany, with an uncle, Swinburne enrolled in Balliol College, Oxford, in 1856. For Eton he preserved always a tender memory; Oxford he detested and maligned. It would be excessive to say that the reason was his failure to win the Newdigate Prize, but throughout his life Swinburne hated anything or anyone who had affronted him. In any event, Oxford, though his work was unsatisfactory and he left under a cloud, gave him much: his first close friend in John Nichol; his first means of expression in the Old Mortality Club; above all, his first acquaintance with the Pre-Raphaelite poets and painters. This pale, undersized boy with the mop of flaming red hair, with nervous gestures and a voice which (again like Shelley's) broke into falsetto under excitement, this boy who played no games and was sudden and violent in speech, whose beautiful courtesy fell easily into belligerency, could hardly have fitted into the healthy mediocre fellowship of any group of young men more normal and less highly endowed. The great Jowett of Balliol, who after a time became his friend, alarmed by Swinburne's failure in his studies and his febrile dissipation, rusticated him for a while, but it was hopeless to try to adjust such a personality to the routine of a university. At the end of 1860 he left without being graduated; for eighteen years his name still appeared on the calendar, but he so loathed Oxford that in later days he refused its offer of an honorary degree.

Rather grotesquely, Swinburne had always aspired to the army; his father argued him out of that strange ambition, and after some turmoil granted him an allowance and let him live in London and—for some years without success—enter upon a literary career. There, in 1862, occurred his only known love-affair (one can hardly count the forced and artificial liaison with Adah Isaacs Menken in his middle age), and even that is veiled in some mystery. All that is known is that the girl with whom he fell in love abruptly refused him, thus giving birth to one of the loveliest of his poems, "The Triumph of Time." It was his solitary chance for a normal love-life; thereafter the echoes in his poems are only now being recognized for what they are—Swinburne yielded to the twin perverse impulses of sadism and masochism.

In London Swinburne renewed his friendship with the Pre-Raphaelites, and particularly with Rossetti. His first volume, containing "The Queen Mother" and "Rosamond," historical tragedies in verse, had been almost still-born; he had made his first visit to Italy, fruitful of so much of his greatest poetry; and he had found his first great hero (he who was peculiarly born for hero-worship) in Walter Savage Landor. From 1862 to 1864 he shared a house in Chelsea with D. G. and W. M. Rossetti and George Meredith. The experiment was not successful; Swinburne was away much of the time, at home with his parents or on the continent, and when he was in London, he and Meredith, two natures utterly unlike, grated on each other's nerves. Moreover, he alarmed his friends by the earliest of the epileptiform attacks to which he was subject under excitement, especially when the excitement was increased by alcohol. Rossetti finally terminated the arrangement.

Swinburne's first and most unqualified fame was now upon him. In 1865 appeared the magnificent *Atalanta in Calydon*, and like Byron he awoke to find himself famous. It was not good for him. His nervous constitution could not well endure the lionizing, the consequent arrogance, and disputativeness which it engendered in him, the alcoholism which came in its train. Still more disastrous was the storm which burst upon him the next year with the publication of *Poems and Ballads*. The book broke like a bombshell on the smug England of Victoria's prime. Swinburne was denounced as hotly as he had been extravagantly adulated. A wiser man would

ALGERNON SWINBURNE

have realized that the place for one of his nature and his genius was by the sea or on the cliffs which had nourished that genius in its infancy. Time and again his father was obliged to come and remove him, ill and apparently near death, from the London which was poison to him; each time he recovered promptly—and returned to his poison.

A new hero, Mazzini, and the great poems which arose from his worship of that hero, *A Song of Italy* and *Songs Before Sunrise*, saved him temporarily. Victor Hugo, the allied idol of this phase of Swinburne's thought, he did not meet until very much later, but in 1867 he and Mazzini met and sealed a connection that lasted throughout Mazzini's life. Landor he had visited in 1864, shortly before the old poet's death.

For the next ten years, Swinburne continued, amid a disordered and feverish life, to pour out poems and critical essays. He became alienated from most of the Pre-Raphaelite group, and his new friends, men like the ambiguous Charles Augustus Howell and the tragic Simeon Solomon, were far less desirable. He who was by innermost nature "courteous and affectionate and unsuspicious and faithful beyond most people to those he really loved" (Lady Burne Jones) developed under attack a readiness to invective which involved him in a series of public quarrels. In Scotland with Jowett, or at Bonchurch with his family, he was gentle, submissive, able to work in perfect health and peace; on his own in London, he was headstrong, prodigal, always keyed up to a ruinous pitch. In 1877 his father died; Bonchurch had already been deserted, after the death of a sister, for Holmwood in Sussex, and now this home too was to see him no more for a period, for he quarreled with his family over what he considered a slight in the admiral's will.

Now there was no one to watch over him and save him from himself; his worried mother was able only to fret helplessly from afar. There was no cessation in his literary production, but his health became increasingly perilous. The crisis came in 1879. He seemed to be near death when his friend and zealous man of business, Walter Theodore Watts (later Theodore Watts-Dunton), solicitor and critic of books, determined to rescue him. With the mother's approval, he established Swinburne in the famous villa, No. 2 The Pines, Putney, where he lived with his tamed poet for thirty years.

From this time on, Swinburne's outer history ceases. His life became one of the utmost regularity, carefully guarded from the associates of his former days, jealously preserved and secluded. He became half-idol and half-prisoner. However unpleasing the spectacle may be, it must be made clear that Swinburne submitted willingly, was greatly attached to Watts-Dunton, and had no regrets. In any case he could not have survived much longer without Watts-Dunton's intervention; whether the cause of literature might not have been better served had that intervention not occurred is a legitimate question; but so far as Swinburne personally was concerned, there can be no doubt that his fussy keeper was also his savior.

In 1903 Swinburne barely recovered from an attack of pneumonia, which left him susceptible in the future. At the beginning of April in 1909 he caught influenza from Watts-Dunton, developed pneumonia again, and after a few days very quietly died. He was buried near Bonchurch, in the old home on the Isle of Wight, in a grave that overlooks his "mother and mistress," the sea.

If we are to evaluate Swinburne, as man and poet, in the light of eternity, we must appraise him as he was before Watts-Dunton wrapped him in cotton-wool. In his great ruinous days, as Woodberry says, his lyre had seven strings—liberty, melody, passion, fate, nature, love, and fame. He was peculiar in that, although he showed little precocity, he was inexorably fixed, mentally and emotionally, at the age of puberty; nothing that came to him in later life could touch his inner core. He vacillated always between twin impulses of rebellion and submission. He was a republican, but no democrat. His ardor for liberty was personal and abstract far more than it was concrete or practical. Gosse's first impression was shrewd: "He was not quite like a human being." His small stature with his big head, his aureole of red-gold hair that receded to give him a strange likeness to Shakespeare in old age, his receding chin with its straggling red beard, the intent gaze of his green eyes, his twitching arms and the jerky movements of his tiny feet, even his extreme deafness in the Putney years, combined to mark him out from other men. His nerves were permanently exposed; the slightest scratch of circumstance drew blood, and often the blood was full of venom. Perhaps we should not blame Watts-Dunton entirely for all the apostacies of Swinburne's latest writings, for his repudiation of Whitman and Baudelaire, his jingoism and imperialism; perhaps all this had always lain, buried and submerged, under the highly subjective worship of liberty and passion which expressed and exalted his youth. Only one thing could not change: the deep-seated atheism (a little softened by a wistful, skeptical hankering after immortality), the aversion and challenge to Christianity, which, fresh from his Puseyite family, he had drunk in boyhood from his grandfather's full cup.

It is the fashion nowadays to depreciate Swinburne as a poet, to speak, in our later sophistication, of his dull wordiness, his meretricious hypnosis of music. It is true, to quote Mackail, that "language intoxicated him"; it is true, as Drinkwater points out, that the mystery and magic of the very greatest poets seldom descends on his "nebulous beauty." But he remains, in his rarest offerings, one of the supreme lyrists of the English tongue. His rhythm is the rhythm of the sea; sometimes the breakers are perfumed, but oftener they bear the sharp salt of authentic spray. Chew selects six poems which to him are the very wave-apex of that sea: without necessarily making the very same selection, they may well be included in any segregation of Swinburne's most early immortal works. They are "Atalanta in Calydon," "Laus Veneris," "The Triumph of Time," the Prelude to "Tristram of Lyonesse," "Siena," and "Ave atque Vale." To these every reader to whom Swinburne was the revelation of youth will undoubtedly add half a dozen more, with each of which other readers will quarrel, but which have been to him intense and unforgettable experiences.

As a critic, Swinburne was marked by sensibility, wide if not profound learning, and a partisanship which arouses interest as often as it alienates. He whose emotions and intellect were so intertangled, whose deepest experiences arose from books, could not but nail our attention when he speaks to us of his literary loves or hates. Harold Nicolson sums him up in a neat phrase: "In his early work he was a poet of amazing promise, and in his later work he was a great man of letters." In the end, even with only partial fulfilment of that promise, it is as a poet that he will live.   M. A. deF.

PRINCIPAL WORKS: *Poetry*—Poems and Ballads, 1866; Byron, 1866; A Song of Italy, 1867; Siena,

1868; Ode on the Proclamation of the French Republic, 1870; Songs Before Sunrise, 1871; Songs of Two Nations, 1875; Poems and Ballads: Second Series, 1878; Songs of the Springtides, 1880; The Heptalogia: or, The Seven Against Sense [parodies] 1880; Tristram of Lyonesse and Other Poems, 1882; A Century of Roundels, 1883; A Midsummer Holiday and Other Poems, 1884; Gathered Songs, 1887; Poems and Ballads: Third Series, 1889; Astrophel and Other Poems, 1894; The Tale of Balen, 1896; A Channel Passage and Other Poems, 1904; Posthumous Poems, 1917. *Plays (in verse)*—The Queen Mother and Rosamond, 1860; The Pilgrimage of Pleasure (in The Children of the Chapel, by Mrs. Disney Leith) 1864; Atalanta in Calydon, 1865; Chastelard, 1865; Bothwell, 1874; Erechtheus, 1876; Mary Stuart, 1881; Marino Faliero, 1885; Locrine, 1887; The Sisters, 1892; Rosamund: Queen of the Lombards, 1899; The Duke of Gandia, 1908. *Prose* —Notes on Poems and Reviews, 1866; William Blake: A Critical Essay, 1868; Notes on the Royal Academy, 1868; Under the Microscope, 1872; George Chapman, 1875; Essays and Studies, 1875; Note of an English Republican on the Muscovite Crusade, 1876; Joseph and His Brethren, 1876; A Note on Charlotte Brontë, 1877; A Study of Shakespeare, 1880; A Study of Victor Hugo, 1886; Miscellanies, 1886; The Whippingham Papers (anonymous) 1888; A Study of Ben Jonson, 1889; Studies in Prose and Poetry, 1894; Dedicatory Epistle to Collected Poems, 1904; Love's Cross Currents (novel, originally A Year's Letters) 1905; The Age of Shakespeare, 1908 (Vol. II, 1918); Three Plays of Shakespeare, 1909; Charles Dickens, 1913; Contemporaries of Shakespeare, 1919.

ABOUT: Beerbohm, M. And Even Now; Chew, S. C. Swinburne; Drinkwater, J. Swinburne: An Estimate; Gosse, E. The Life of A. C. Swinburne; Kernahan, C. Swinburne as I Knew Him; Lafourcade, G. Swinburne: A Literary Biography; Leith, Mrs. D. Personal Recollections of A. C. Swinburne; Mackail, J. W. Swinburne: A Lecture; Nicolson, H. Swinburne; Rutland, W. R. Swinburne: A Nineteenth Century Hellene; Thomas, E. A. C. Swinburne; Woodberry, G. E. Swinburne.

SYMONDS, JOHN ADDINGTON (October 5, 1840-April 10, 1893), poet, historian, and biographer, was born at Bristol, the son of a celebrated father of the same name. The older Symonds was the fifth in direct descent of a medical family, a writer and college lecturer, and an early student of and writer on psychiatry and criminal mentality.

His only son was left motherless in early childhood. His mind was the antithesis of his father's—concrete, colorful, neurotic, and unphilosophical. Yet the two earliest and strongest influences on him were those of his father and of Jowett, the famous Master of Balliol, both philosophically minded, unemotional, and highly intellectualized.

Symonds' earlier school days, at Harrow, were one long torture; he was abnormally shy, could not play games or mingle with other boys, and though he read constantly could not make headway with his studies. His beginning at Balliol, Oxford, in 1858 was equally inauspicious. But under the promptings of Jowett and Conington the boy forced himself—to his later disaster—to a feverish brilliance. He gained a double first in classics,

won the Newdigate Prize in 1860, and was made fellow of Magdalen in 1863, followed by the winning of the chancellor's prize for an English essay on the Renaissance (a prophetic subject). The result was a complete breakdown, partial blindness, and nervous exhaustion, and the first symptoms of the tuberculosis which he inherited from his mother.

He went to Switzerland, then to Italy. There rest and quiet partially restored him, and he returned to England. He settled in London, where he married Janet North in 1864. Of this marriage four daughters were born, three of whom survived him and one of whom became his collaborator. He started to study law, but the tubercular symptoms became more advanced, and for several years most of his time was spent in France or Italy. Finally, in 1866, came a crisis which approached insanity. Somehow he pulled himself out of it, returned to England, this time to Clifton, on the heights above Bristol, where his father was now living, and thenceforth devoted himself to literature. Up to that point his only published work had been some articles in the *Cornhill Magazine*. He lectured in the woman's college at Clifton, and edited the works of Conington, and those of his father, who died in 1871.

In 1873 he visited Sicily and Greece. With a feeling that his duration of life was problematical, he overworked himself constantly. In 1877 he gave three lectures at the Royal Institution, then undertook a tour of Lombardy, during which he worked at translations of the sonnets of Michelangelo and Campanella. He returned to Clifton in June, and soon after was seized by an almost fatal hemorrhage. It was a signal of extreme danger; he thought the end was at hand, and only

JOHN ADDINGTON SYMONDS

reluctantly agreed to set out for Egypt on his physician's orders. On the way he stopped to visit the tubercular sanitarium recently founded at Davos, in Switzerland, and was so taken by the place, and by the then novel treatment of open air living, that he abandoned his journey and decided to stay in Davos thenceforth. For the rest of his life this was his home.

Though his health improved immeasurably, he felt himself in exile, and considered that his days of scholarship were necessarily at an end. But he worked indefatigably, and poured out book after book. He became immensely interested in the life of the little town which was being overwhelmed by foreign health-seekers, and constituted himself the liaison officer between the old inhabitants and the alien new-comers. He became, indeed, the patriarch and patron saint of Davos; to its welfare he devoted the proceeds of his writings, keeping his inherited fortune for his family. In 1881 he built himself a house, *Am Hof,* in Davos; he took part in all its local life and fraternized with its peasants and artisans. The chief personal influence on him in this period was that of Walt Whitman, whom he never met, but with whom he cemented a long and solid friendship by correspondence. Whitman was to him the prophet of a new day; Symonds the stylist was utterly alien to the formless and inchoate poetry of the American, but to Symonds the man Whitman became in his maturity what his father and Jowett had been in his youth.

In April 1893 Symonds visited Rome with his daughter Margaret. He had been warned that any cold would be fatal; a chill turned to pneumonia, and he died a few days later. He is buried in the Protestant Cemetery there, near the grave of Shelley.

Van Wyck Brooks, Symonds' best biographer, calls him "the closest of all English equivalents of Amiel." His history is colorful, stimulating, suggestive; his writing has been called Alexandrian, and has always a faint decadence. This spontaneous, ebullient, impetuous, ardent man practically never appears in his books; Jowett did his work well, and Symonds became a true scholar, a writer of skill and richness, but essentially fragmentary and lifeless under the surface glow. Each isolated portion of his writing is picturesque and unrestricted—sometimes to the point of mawkishness—but there is no harmony; his work can never be considered as a whole. Perhaps in the end, in spite of the solidity of his study of the Italian Renaissance, he will survive as a translator—particularly for his magnificent version of the Autobiography of Benvenuto Cellini, which he has transmuted into an English masterpiece. About his own work there is always a disturbing flavor of the faintly epicene, a touch of decay. It is the work of a neurotic. Perhaps had he been allowed to develop naturally, without the formative solicitude of minds so disparate from his own, the open ardor of his personality, his "natural religion," his bent for the dramatic and picturesque, would have produced a very different body of work. On the other hand, he would not then have become the scholar, the authority in three different fields—Greek Poetry, the Renaissance, and Elizabethan Drama—which he did eventually become. His was an essentially Greek mentality forced into a Roman mold.

M. A. deF.

PRINCIPAL WORKS: *Poetry*—Many Moods, 1878; New and Old, 1880; Animi Figura, 1882; Vagabunduli Libellus, 1884; Wine, Women, and Song (Goliardic Songs of Mediaeval Students) 1884. *Biography*—Life of Shelley, 1878; Shakespeare's Predecessors in the English Drama, 1884; Life of Sir Philip Sidney, 1886; Life of Ben Jonson, 1886; Life of Michelangelo Buonarroti (2 vols.) 1892; Walt Whitman: A Study, 1893; Giovanni Boccaccio (posthumous) 1894. *History*—The Renaissance in Italy: 1. The Age of the Despots, 1875; 2. The Revival of Learning, 1877; 3. The Fine Arts, 1877; 4. Italian Literature (2 vols.) 1881; 5. The Catholic Reaction (2 vols.) 1886. *Travel Books*—Sketches in Italy and Greece, 1874; Sketches and Studies in Italy, 1879; Italian Byways, 1883; Our Life in the Swiss Highlands (with daughter Margaret) 1891. *Essays*—Introduction to the Study of Dante, 1872; Studies of the Greek Poets: First Series, 1873; Studies of the Greek Poets: Second Series, 1875; Essays Speculative and Suggestive (2 vols.) 1890; In the Key of Blue, 1893; Blank Verse (posthumous) 1894.

ABOUT: Brown, H. F. Life (based on Symonds' unpublished Autobiography); Symons, Arthur. J. A. Symonds; Brooks, V. W. John Addington Symonds: A Biographical Study.

TABLEY, LORD DE. See DE TABLEY, LORD.

TAIT, PETER GUTHRIE (April 28, 1831-July 4, 1901), Scottish mathematician, was born in Dalkeith. His father was secretary to the Duke of Buccleuch. He was educated at Edinburgh Academy, where he distinguished himself early in mathematical studies, at Edinburgh University, and at Peterhouse College, Cambridge. He took his B.A. in 1852, as the youngest senior wrangler (first in mathematics) then on record. From 1854 to 1860 he was professor of mathematics at Queen's College, Belfast; in the same period he first became interested in chemistry, then in physics, though approaching both branches of science from the mathematical angle. In 1857 he married Margaret Archer Porter, by whom he had four sons. In 1860 he was appointed professor of natural philosophy at the University of Edinburgh, at the same time being made a Fellow of the Royal Society of Edinburgh. (He was never F.R.S., though he received the Royal Society's gold medal.) His principal work, the *Elements of Natural Philosophy,* written in collaboration with William

Thomson (afterwards Lord Kelvin), was the first to argue that energy is the fundamental physical entity: it is an achievement of scientific theory that places Tait in a class with Newton, LaPlace, and Clerk Maxwell. He was, however, very devout, and an ardent anti-materialist.

PRINCIPAL WORKS: Dynamics of a Particle (with W. J. Steele) 1856; Elements of Natural Philosophy (with Lord Kelvin) 1867; Thermodynamics, 1868; The Unseen Universe (with Balfour Stewart) 1875; Heat, 1884; Light, 1884; Properties of Matter, 1885; Dynamics, 1895; Scientific Papers, 1898-1900.

ABOUT: Knott, Dr. Life and Scientific Work of P. G. Tait.

TALFOURD, SIR THOMAS NOON (May 26, 1795-March 13, 1854), dramatist, was born in Reading, where his father was a brewer. He was educated at the Mill Hill School, for children of dissenters, and at the Reading Grammar School. He then studied law until 1817. Meanwhile he became an intimate of the circle of Wordsworth, Coleridge, Godwin, Hazlitt, and Lamb (whose executor he became), and contributed to *The Pamphleteer*, the *New Monthly*, and the *Retrospective Review*, of which he was dramatic critic. He was called to the bar from the Middle Temple in 1821. The next year he married Rachel Rutt. He joined the Oxford circuit, at first supplementing his legal fees by journalism, but gradually becoming the leading member of the circuit. In 1849 he was made judge of the court of common pleas. He was a member of Parliament from 1837 to 1841, and again from 1847 to 1854; he was the father of the copyright bill, but the measure was passed while he was out of Parliament, in 1842.

Talfourd was best known, however, as a writer of tragedies. In that capacity he is usually referred to as Serjeant Talfourd, this being a legal rank which he held before becoming a judge. He died suddenly of apoplexy at fifty-eight, while delivering a charge to the Grand Jury.

As a dramatist, Talfourd is eloquent and spirited, but too florid for modern taste. His great defect was prolixity, and his characters are all loquacious to the point of garrulousness.

PRINCIPAL WORKS: Poems on Various Subjects, 1811; Ion, 1836; The Athenian Captive, 1838; Glencoe, 1840; Final Memorials of Charles Lamb, 1848.

ABOUT: Household Words March 25, 1854; North British Review May 1854.

TANNAHILL, ROBERT (June 3, 1774-May 17, 1810), Scottish poet, was born in Paisley, son of a silk weaver who owned his own mill. After a few years in the village school, where he wrote verse more than he studied, he was apprenticed to his father, continuing his education by private reading. Until 1799 he worked in the mills in Renfrew-shire and Lancashire, returning to Paisley in 1802 on his father's death, and carrying on the business with his mother. Some of his songs, set to music, became very popular. In 1805 he was one of the founders of a trades library for workingmen in Paisley. He never married because of an unhappy love affair with Janet Tennant, the original of his best known poem, "Jessie, the Flow'r o' Dunblane." This disappointment in love, together with discouragement over the reception of his poems and the physical effects of tuberculosis, drove him to melancholy which in turn led to heavy drinking. Finally he burnt all his manuscripts and drowned himself, at the age of thirty-five. From 1876 to 1883 a series of concerts was given at Paisley to raise funds for a bronze statue in Tannahill's memory.

Tannahill's best work is in his songs in the Scottish dialect. Those he destroyed in manuscript were later published from copies in the hands of friends or from previous publication in various Glasgow magazines.

PRINCIPAL WORK: Poems and Songs, 1807.

ABOUT: McLaren, W. Life of Tannahill; Ramsay, P. A. (ed.). Works of Robert Tannahill (see Life by R. A. Smith); Tannahill, R. Poems and Songs (see Biographical Sketch by J. Muir).

TAUTPHOEUS, BARONESS VON (Jemima Montgomery) (October 23, 1807-November 12, 1893), Irish novelist, was born in County Donegal, her father being a landowner named Montgomery. She was educated at home, and in 1838 married the Baron von Tautphoeus of Marquartstein, chamberlain to the king of Bavaria. She lived in Germany for the remainder of her life. She entered, in spite of being a foreigner, into the life of the people of all classes, and her novels deal entirely with the Bavarian scene. In 1885 her husband died, their only son having died two weeks earlier.

The Initials is the best of her novels. All of them, however, are brilliant, sympathetic, and full of charm. They are still good reading, and give a delightful picture of their time and place.

PRINCIPAL WORKS: The Initials, 1850; Cyrilla, 1854; Quits, 1857; At Odds, 1863.

ABOUT: Athenaeum 2:736 1893; London Times November 17, 1893.

TAYLOR, ANN (afterwards Gilbert) (January 30, 1782-December 20, 1866) and **JANE** (September 23, 1783-April 13, 1824), authors of children's poems, were born in London, the eldest and second daughters of Isaac Taylor, "the elder," a well-known artist and author of instructive works, and Ann Martin Taylor, who also wrote works of a didactic type. Two brothers also became authors: Isaac, "the younger," and Jefferys. [See sketches of related Taylors in this volume.]

ANN TAYLOR

When they were little girls, the family moved to Lavenham in Suffolk for purposes of economy, where they resided for ten years, later moving to Ongar, where their father, in 1796, accepted the ministry of an evangelical church. They were known as "the Taylors of Ongar" to distinguish them from other writing Taylors of the period.

Isaac Taylor was the son of another Isaac Taylor who had been the friend of Richardson, the novelist, and Goldsmith, the poet and novelist. He was a man of considerable miscellaneous information, with decided ideas concerning the education of the young, and saw to it that his children spent long hours in the practise of engraving, while it is said that their mother used to read aloud at mealtimes for their further instruction. Despite the severity of this régime, the two girls, if a trifle grave, seemed to be happy. Edith Sitwell thus describes them in a picture painted by their father in the year 1791: "They appear as very serious-minded, good little girls . . . each with a nosegay as bright as her cheeks."

Anne was the first to write for publication. She sent a "poetical" solution of a riddle to *The Minor's Pocket Book* when she was sixteen, and won first prize in the contest and the invitation to become a regular contributor.

Jane, a child of great vivacity, began when a small girl to amuse friends of the family with preaching and recitation. She also wrote titles, dedications, and prefaces indicative of an unusual talent. Her first appearance in print was also made in *The Minor's Pocket Book,* in the year 1804. The sisters then, upon the request of the publishers, wrote, with some help from their brother Isaac and from Adelaide O'Keeffe, *Original Poems for Infant*

Minds, receiving the sum of £75 for the work. (Adelaide O'Keeffe, born 1776, was a friend of the Taylors and the daughter of John O'Keeffe, author of burlesques and farces.) This was followed by *Rhymes for the Nursery, Limed Twigs to Catch Young Birds, Hymns for Infant Minds,* and their last joint work, *Original Hymns for Sunday Schools* (1812). In the year of this last publication, they were separated by the marriage of Ann to the Rev. Joseph Gilbert.

Jane continued to write, producing *Essays in Rhyme on Morals and Manners* and *The Contributions of Q. Q.,* a miscellany which had originally appeared in *The Youth's Magazine.* She spent the rest of her life chiefly in parish work and correspondence, and died of tuberculosis after a rapid decline in health. Ann, who survived her by forty-two years and outlived her husband by fourteen, had many children to keep her busy, but wrote hymns and other works, including an autobiography. None of the work either produced after their years of collaboration is comparable to their joint writing.

The children's poems of the sisters Taylor are still very much alive and much read. Of recent years there have been numerous new editions, with illustrations by various hands. In their own day their first work was brilliantly successful, going through fifty English editions and being translated into various European languages. There was a skill, a lightness, and a charm about these rhymes which made an immediate appeal. Edith Sitwell speaks in praise of "their fresh, elusive charm"; E. V. Lucas characterizes them as "witty and shrewd"; and Edmund Gosse said of Jane: "she is not forgotten, nor shall be, as long as the English language is in use."

It is generally felt that Jane's verses were the brighter and more original, and indeed, it is "Meddlesome Matty," "Twinkle, Twinkle, Little Star," and "I Love Little Pussy," which are now best known. However, Ann's verses were thought even better adapted for child readers. Their temperaments were rather unlike, as were their verses. Ann is said to have been sweet-tempered and thoughtful, while Jane was humorous and jolly. R. M.

PRINCIPAL WORKS: *Poetry*—Original Poems for Infant Minds, 1804; Rhymes for the Nursery, 1806; Limed Twigs to Catch Young Birds, 1808; Hymns for Infant Minds, 1810; Original Hymns for Sunday Schools, 1812.

ABOUT: Gosse, E. W. Leaves and Fruit; Knight, Mrs. H. C. Life and Letters of Jane Taylor; Taylor, A. Autobiography; Taylor, I. Memoirs and Poetical Remains of Jane Taylor; Taylor, J. Meddlesome Matty (see Introduction by E. Sitwell); Prose and Poetry (see Introduction by F. V. Barry); Walford, L. B. Twelve English Authoresses; Woolf, V. The Common Reader (1st ser.).

TAYLOR, MRS. ANN MARTIN (June 20, 1757-June 4, 1830), juvenile writer, was born at Islington. In 1781 she married Isaac Taylor, "the elder," who predeceased her by six months. She, her husband, and four of their children who became authors (the best known being the daughters Ann and Jane) are usually known as "the Taylors of Ongar," to distinguish them from another writing family of Taylors living at Norwich. Ongar, Essex, was their home from 1810. They had eleven children, of whom six grew up. Mrs. Taylor's books were an outgrowth of her correspondence with her own children after they had grown and moved away. Her didactic stories had a great sale, though they display little talent. They are distinguished chiefly by what has been called "a mild Benjamin Franklin type of morality," and are very pious.

PRINCIPAL WORKS: Maternal Solicitude, 1813; Practical Hints to Young Females, 1815; The Family Mansion, 1819; Retrospection, 1821.

ABOUT: Taylor's Family Pen—Memorials of the Taylor Family of Ongar.

TAYLOR, SIR HENRY (October 18, 1800-March 27, 1886), poet, was born at Bishop Middleham, Durham, where his father, George Taylor, had a farm. The mother, Eleanor (Ashworth) Taylor, died soon after the birth of Henry, who was the third son. After her death George Taylor, a man of literary tastes, lived quietly among his books, and managed a farm at St. Helen's, Auckland.

The boys were educated by this father; and while Henry's two elder brothers showed literary ability, Henry appears to have been rather slow. Aside from a brief experiment as midshipman in the navy he seems to have lived uneventfully enough until his going to London with his brothers in 1817 to assume a small government post which had been secured for him. All three of the young men contracted typhus fever, and the two elder boys were carried off almost at once. Henry, the survivor, lost his position in 1820, returning to his father, who had remarried, and lived in an old border tower at Witton-le-Wear, Durham.

In this quiet environment and in the society of a step-mother (of whom he later recorded that, while he supposed that she had faults, he never had been able to find them) Taylor's intellectual interests began to manifest themselves; and he studied, and wrote poetry. With an article on Thomas Moore, published (1822) in the *Quarterly Review*, he came to the attention of William Gifford, the editor; and he became acquainted at this time with the poet, Robert Southey, who was to be one of his closest friends.

In 1823 he returned to London, this time in the hopes of supporting himself by his pen. In the next year, however, he accepted an attractive offer of a government clerkship in

SIR HENRY TAYLOR

the Colonial Department, where he speedily became influential, especially in the question of slavery. He favored a policy of gradual emancipation, with financial compensation for the losses of the planters, and this was the procedure which was eventually adopted. Although disgruntled at this time by the attitude of one of his superiors (and by his own failure to secure a salary increase), Taylor remained in the Colonial Office until 1872, thus devoting about forty-eight years of a long life to government service. In 1847, for various reasons, he refused the offer of the Under Secretaryship of State, feeling that he did not wish to engage his energies to any greater extent in government work.

Meanwhile he had made many friends, and his play, *Isaac Comnenus*, had been published, with small success, in 1827. *Philip van Artevelde* (1834), issued at the author's own risk, was highly successful, and opened the way into society for him.

Not long after his marriage in 1839 to Theodosia Alice Rice, youngest daughter of Thomas Spring Rice, Secretary of State, Taylor's health gave out, and he was obliged to spend a winter (1843-1844) in Italy. From this time on, his appearances in society were less frequent. He settled at Mortlake in 1844, removing in 1853 to Sheen. He continued his writing and his official work in connection with the Colonial Office; and he was not allowed to resign the latter even after an attack of asthma had enfeebled him in 1859, making it necessary for him to do his work at home. His actual retirement occurred in 1872.

His last years were spent in an unusually happy family group and in the society of his many distinguished friends, among whom were Tennyson and Stevenson. His death occurred in March 1886 at Bournemouth, where he had spent most of his time for many years.

A handsome man, suspected of some indolence in his later years of government work, Taylor, thanks to his years of prominence as a government official, appears to have had a rather egocentric personality, which his literary successes and failures did not alter. Indeed he is said to have been so proud of the scarlet robes given him by the University of Oxford in 1862, when he was awarded the degree of D.C.L., that he made it a practise to wear them at his own table. His social popularity was hardly enhanced by *The Statesman* (1836), essays which ironically set forth the way to success as a civil servant. This work, which was misconstrued and misunderstood, was described by William Maginn as "the art of official humbug systematically digested and familiarly described."

Taylor's literary fame rests, not upon the polished essays or the interesting *Autobiography,* but upon his poetic plays, of which the best is *Philip van Artevelde,* laid in mediaeval Flanders. These works, typical of a time when enthusiasm for Elizabethan drama caused many writers to strive to imitate it, belong to "closet drama" rather than to the literature of the stage. William Macready's production *Philip van Artevelde* in 1847 was a complete failure. A disciple of Wordsworth and Southey, Taylor lacked dramatic sense, but this shortcoming is to some extent balanced by his almost forgotten talent as a minor poet.

R. W. W.

PRINCIPAL WORKS: *Autobiography*—Autobiography of Henry Taylor, 1800-1875, 1877, 1885. *Correspondence*—Correspondence of Henry Taylor, 1888. *Essays*—The Statesman, 1836; Notes From Life, 1847; Notes From Books, 1849. *Plays in Verse*—Isaac Comnenus, 1827; Philip van Artevelde, 1834; Edwin the Fair, 1842; The Virgin Widow, 1850 (also published as A Sicilian Summer, 1862); St. Clement's Eve, 1862. *Poetry*—The Eve of the Conquest and Other Poems, 1847. *Miscellaneous*—Plays and Poems, 1863; The Works of Sir Henry Taylor, 1877-78.

ABOUT: De Vere, A. Essays: Chiefly on Poetry; Taylor, H. Autobiography; Taylor, H. Correspondence; Taylor, U. Guests and Memories; Edinburgh Review 148:504 October 1878; Nineteenth Century and After 8:810 November 1880.

TAYLOR, ISAAC ("the elder") (January 30, 1759-December 12, 1829), juvenile writer, was head of the celebrated writing family, "the Taylors of Ongar." His father was an engraver in London. He was educated at the Brentford Grammar School, and then studied engraving in his father's studio. He set up for himself as an engraver at Lavenham, Suffolk, in 1786. He was also a dissenting preacher, and throughout his life combined the two professions. In 1796 he went to Colchester as pastor of a chapel there, but continued to engrave book illustrations and plates for drawings. In 1781 he married Ann Mar-

tin. He was the only teacher of their eleven children, six of whom grew to maturity. All the boys learned engraving from him. In 1810 he went as a preacher to Ongar, Essex, and remained there for the rest of his life. His books were the outgrowth of the manuals of education he wrote for the training of his own children. They included a long series of "Scenes" covering the geography of the entire globe. Many of them were illustrated by his own engravings.

PRINCIPAL WORKS: Advice to the Teens, 1818; Scenes in England, 1819; Beginnings of British Biography, 1824-25; The Balance of Criminality, 1828; Scenes of Commerce by Land and Sea, 1830.

ABOUT: Gentleman's Magazine 1:378 1830; Nation (London) May 1875.

TAYLOR, ISAAC ("the younger") (August 17, 1787-June 28, 1865), religious writer, was a son of Isaac Taylor, "the elder," usually known as "Taylor of Ongar." He was born at Lavenham, Sussex, and like his brothers and sisters, was educated entirely by his father and trained as an engraver. He illustrated many of his father's books and those of his sisters Ann and Jane, well known juvenile writers. Rossetti greatly admired his work as an engraver, but after a few years he abandoned art for literature. From 1812 to 1816, because of a tendency to tuberculosis, he was obliged to spend his winters in the west of England; during this period he turned to the study of early Church literature, and began to write on the subject; he was the inventor of the word "patristic" to describe the works of the Church Fathers. He was also an intense admirer of the inductive philosophy of Bacon, and somehow combined these two disparate philosophies in his own writings. In 1818 he became a member of the staff of the *Eclectic Review*. He translated Theophrastus, Herodotus, and Josephus, himself illustrating his translation of Theophrastus. In 1825 he moved to Stanford Rivers, near Ongar, and married Elizabeth Medland; of their large family, nine survived childhood. In 1862 he received a civil list pension. He was also known as an inventor, his principal patents being on an engraving machine and a beer tap. Although reared as a dissenter, he joined the Church of England, and was primarily, in his writing, a lay theologian. His books are full of rhetoric and "fine writing," and though many of the words he coined have survived, the books in which they appeared are no longer read or readable.

PRINCIPAL WORKS: The Elements of Thought, 1823; History of the Transmission of Ancient Books to Modern Times, 1827; The Natural History of Enthusiasm, 1829; Fanaticism, 1833; Home Education, 1838; The Restoration of Belief, 1855; The Spirit of Hebrew Poetry, 1861; Personal Recollections, 1864.

ABOUT: Gilfillan, G. Second Gallery of Literary Portraits; Taylor, I. Personal Recollections.

TAYLOR, JEFFERYS (October 30, 1792-October 8, 1853), juvenile writer, was the youngest son of Isaac Taylor "of Ongar" and his wife Ann. Like his brothers and sisters, he was educated by his father and taught engraving; like his brother Isaac, "the younger," he invented a rolling machine for engravers. In 1826 he married Sophia Mabbs; they had one son. During most of his life he lived at Brentwood, Sussex. Besides his stories for children, he wrote on geography, natural science, and religion. He is best known, however, for his juvenile books, which are whimsical and humorous, but with a lively fancy that sometimes becomes wild extravagance of imagination and expression.

PRINCIPAL WORKS: Harry's Holiday, 1818; Aesop in Rhyme, 1820; The Little Historians, 1824; The Barn and the Steeple, 1828; The Forest, 1831; The Young Islanders, 1842; A Glance at the Globe, 1848.
ABOUT: Gentleman's Magazine 2:424 1853.

TAYLOR (PHILIP) MEADOWS (September 25, 1808-May 13, 1876), Anglo-Indian novelist and historian, was born in Liverpool, the son of a merchant. In his early boyhood his father lost his fortune and the son had to go to work as a clerk for a merchant. At fifteen he was sent to Bombay, to work for a merchant there with a prospect of future partnership. Finding he had been the victim of misrepresentation, the lad enlisted as a soldier in the service of the Nizam of Bombay. In order to prepare for a civil position, he taught himself engineering, law, botany, and geology; but he was unable to make his way in civil life and had to return to the army. In 1830, as an adjutant, he made the first investigation of Thuggism, the secret terrorist movement of India. In 1840 he returned to England on a furlough, and married. For thirteen years after his return to India he was correspondent for *The Times*.

In 1841 Taylor persuaded the Rana of Shorapore to abdicate and to name him as regent of her son, who reached his majority in 1853. Taylor then became governor of one of the Berar districts, keeping perfect order without a single soldier at his command. He was in close sympathy with Indian life and character, and was much beloved. In 1858, after Shorapore had become British territory, he was its commissioner. He went back to England in retirement in 1860. His health had failed, and for a few years his mind was clouded. He recovered sufficiently, however, to continue writing, until 1875, when he went blind. At the same time his general health once more became very bad; by his doctor's advice he went to India for the winter, caught jungle fever, and died at Mentone on his way home.

Taylor's novels provide in effect a short history of India from the seventeenth century to his own time. They are reliable as history, and as fiction they are picturesque, brilliant, and lively.

PRINCIPAL WORKS: Confessions of a Thug, 1839; Tippo Sultaun, 1840; Tara: A Mahratta Tale, 1863; The People of India, 1868; A Student's Manual of the History of India, 1870; Seeta, 1872.
ABOUT: Taylor, M. The Story of my Life (see Preface by H. Reeve).

TAYLOR, ROBERT (August 18, 1784-September 2, 1844), Biblical critic, was born in Middlesex, the son of an ironmonger who died when the boy was a small child. He was reared as a ward of an uncle in Shropshire and articled to the house surgeon of the Birmingham General Hospital. He then studied at Guy's and St. Thomas's Hospitals, London, in 1805, and two years later became a member of the College of Surgeons. He did not practise, however, but entered St. John's College, Cambridge. He received his B.A. and was ordained in 1813, and for five years was a curate in Sussex. He then became a convert to deism, left the church, and for a few years alternated between recantation and attempts to re-establish himself as a clergyman, and lecturing and writing on deism. For a while his brothers gave him a remittance on condition that he stay out of England, and he worked as a private tutor, was a school assistant in Dublin (being discharged for his religious views), and was arrested for blasphemy because of an article in a paper published in the Isle of Man. About 1820 he founded the Society of Universal Benevolence, with the *Clerical Review* as its organ, and began a series of Sunday morning lectures at which he taught the higher criticism of the Bible. He went to London, founded the Christian Evidence Society, and taught Sunday morning classes. In 1827 he was sentenced to a year in prison on a blasphemy charge, and at the same time was imprisoned for debt because of a note for £100 which has been secured from him by fraud. Richard Carlile, the noted Rationalist publisher, came to his rescue, but in 1831 he was again imprisoned for two years. In 1833 he married an elderly heiress, whereupon he was sued for breach of promise by another woman. To avoid paying a judgment brought in her favor for £250, he and his wife emigrated to France, and he practised surgery at Tours until his death.

Taylor's studies led him to the belief that Christianity had its basis in a solar myth. His principal book is the *Diegesis*, written in prison, which contains much valuable material, and is still a classic of Rationalist literature.

PRINCIPAL WORKS: The Holy Liturgy, 1826; Syntagma of the Evidences of the Christian Religion, 1828; Diegesis, 1829; The Devil's Pulpit, 1831-32.
ABOUT: Taylor, R. The Devil's Pulpit (see Autobiographical Memoir); Secular Review February 15, 1879.

TAYLOR, THOMAS (1758-November 1, 1835), philosophical writer and classical translator, was born in London. At an early age he was sent to St. Paul's School, where he laid the foundation of his classical learning. He was then put under the care of a Mr. Worthington of Salters' Hall Meeting House to be qualified for the office of a dissenting minister. However, he married before he was out of his teens, and the economic difficulties arising from this early union disgusted him with his tutor and with his vocation. He became an usher in a school in Paddington, then a clerk in Lubbock's Bank.

His love of mysticism was first shown in an essay on "A New Method of Reasoning in Geometry" which he brought out in 1780. He took pupils and commenced the study of the old Greek philosophers, beginning with Aristotle and going on to Plato. He was also attracted to the works of Plotinus, Proclus, and other classical metaphysicians. The patronage of the Messrs. W. and G. Meredith made it possible for him to publish in 1787 his translation of the Orphic Hymns and some other Platonic fragments. From this time on his prodigious energy and persistence were revealed in an almost endless series of classical translations (his complete list of publications extends to twenty-three quarto and some forty octavo volumes); all rather more distinguished for enthusiasm than for scholarly exactness. He became known as Tom Taylor the Platonist because of his belief that the old polytheism or worship of many gods was, when enriched by the additions of neo-Platonic authors, the true and necessary religion.

Taylor was a poor scholar and a gullible critic. He believed Orpheus to have existed and was convinced that the mystical mathematical developments of the neo-Pythagoreans were the true science and had been corrupted by later scholars, Arab and European. His own interest in science may perhaps best be characterized by the story of his having tried to invent a perpetual lamp, which, upon his first attempt to demonstrate it, promptly exploded.

His middle and later life was devoted exclusively to study and translation of the classics. His first wife, Mary Morton, by whom he had two daughters and four sons, died in 1809, and he remarried, his second wife dying in 1823.

Critics have been more or less contemptuous of Taylor's scholarship. Horace Walpole said that his first translation of Proclus was "blundered." *Blackwood's* "Literary Idler" said: "The man is an ass, in the first place; in the second he knows nothing of the religion of which he is so great a fool as to profess himself a votary; and thirdly, he knows less than nothing of the language about which he is continually writing." R. M.

PRINCIPAL WORKS: *Translations*—The Orphic Hymns, 1787; Aristotle's Metaphysics, 1801; Plato's Works (5 vols., with F. Sydenham) 1804; Aristotle's Works (9 vols.) 1809-12.

ABOUT: Athenaeum 375:874 November 21, 1835; Edinburgh Review 14:187 April 1809; Publications of the Modern Language Association 43:1121 December 1928.

TAYLOR, TOM (October 19, 1817-July 12, 1880), playwright and editor of *Punch*, born in Bishop-Wearmouth, a suburb of Sunderland, was the son of Thomas Taylor, a well-to-do brewer of Durham who began life as a laborer. His mother was of German origin.

He was educated at the Grange School of Durham, at Glasgow University where he won three gold medals, and at Trinity College, Cambridge. He was elected a fellow and for two years served as professor of English language and literature in University College, London.

At twenty-eight he was called to the bar as a member of the Inner Temple, and went the Northern Circuit.

On settling in London, he tried his hand at journalism and worked as a leader writer on the *Morning Chronicle* and the *Daily News*; and he made frequent contributions of articles in prose and verse to periodicals. At an early date he became an active member of the staff of *Punch*, and in 1874, on the death of Shirley Brooks, he became editor of the magazine.

Taylor's great interest, however, was the theatre. From his boyhood he had written at plays, and on his arrival in London he directed most of his attention in that direction. In 1844 four of his burlesques were produced at the Lyceum Theatre. Other

THOMAS TAYLOR

plays of his followed; and in his thirty-five years of playwrighting he turned out almost a hundred plays, with but one complete failure.

The first of his many outstanding successes was a farce, *To Parents and Guardians,* produced at the Lyceum, September 28, 1845. In this, as in the majority of his plays, the construction was substantial and carefully worked out. Much of his dialogue now seems stilted; but he was a master of stagecraft, and his plays are still revived occasionally.

He attempted every type of drama and won his greatest success with domestic comedies. The two best remembered are *The Ticket-of-Leave Man* and *Our American Cousin.* The latter owes its fame principally to the fact that Abraham Lincoln was assassinated while watching a performance of it with Laura Keene in the leading rôle at Ford's Theatre, Washington, in 1865. It is generally agreed, however, that his most meritorious works were a series of historical dramas written for Mrs. Wybert Rousby, whom he introduced to London. Many of his historical pieces were adaptations from other works: *The Fool's Revenge* adapted from Victor Hugo's *Le Roi s'Amuse,* and *'Twixt Axe and Crown,* from the German, to mention two.

In 1871 an ingenious article appeared in *The Athenaeum* stating that most of Taylor's successful plays were plagiarisms or adaptations from other sources. He replied mildly that one-tenth of his plays were adaptations, but that the rest were original.

John Coleman in *Players and Playwrights I Have Known* describes Taylor as an impressive and somewhat aggressive personality: "A man of middle height, with lithe, sinewy figure, a massive brow, covered with a thatch of iron-gray hair, rugged features, a celestially defiant nose, a pugilistic jaw, bristling with a crisp beard of gray and eyes which glittered like steel, an immobile eyeglass, with stony and relentless glare, which fixed me like the bull's eye of a policeman's lantern." And Coleman added, "He was wont to maintain that had it not been for his nose he would have been a great tragedian."

In 1855 Taylor married Laura Barker, daughter of a vicar in Yorkshire; she was a skilled musical composer and contributed the overture and entr'acte to her husband's *Joan of Arc.* He died at the age of sixty-three at his residence in Wandsworth. P. G.

PRINCIPAL WORKS: *Plays*—The King's Rival (in collaboration with Charles Reade) 1854; Two Loves and a Life (in collaboration with Charles Reade) 1854; Still Waters Run Deep, 1855; Plot and Passion, 1858; Our American Cousin, 1858; The Fool's Revenge, 1859; The Ticket-of-Leave Man, 1863; 'Twixt Axe and Crown, 1870; Joan of Arc, 1871;

TOM TAYLOR

Arkwright's Wife, 1873; Anne Boleyn, 1876. *Miscellaneous*—Life of Benjamin Robert Haydon (ed.) 1853; The Local Government Act, 1858; Leicester Square, 1874.

ABOUT: Coleman, J. Players and Playwrights I Have Known; Kent, C. Personal Recollections.

TENNANT, WILLIAM (May 15, 1784-October 14, 1848), Scottish poet and linguist, was born in Anstruther Easter, Fifeshire. Both his feet were paralyzed in childhood, and he had to walk with crutches. He was educated at the Anstruther burgh school, and attended St. Andrews University from 1799 to 1801. He then became clerk to his brother, a corn factor; the brother disappeared, leaving William with a mass of debts, which led to a brief imprisonment. The Tennant home was the cultural center of the little town, and became the headquarters of an informal society which met to "spin rhymes"; at the same time Tennant studied the classics and Hebrew. In 1813, while parish schoolmaster at Dunino, he studied Arabic, Persian, and Syriac. In 1816 he became a schoolmaster at Midlothian. From 1819 to 1834 he was teacher of classical and Oriental languages at the Dollar Academy, in Clackmannanshire. He attracted the attention of Jeffrey, who had him appointed professor of Hebrew and Oriental languages at St. Mary's College, St. Andrews University. He remained in this position until 1848, when, a few months before his death, he was obliged to resign because of poor health. He never married.

Tennant was one of the most accomplished linguists of his time. A Syriac and Chaldee grammar is his chief achievement in this field. His poems were all published anonymously; *Anster Fair,* describing a country festivity, is the best known and was very popular. It is written in a stanza form invented by himself, and later used by Byron in *Don Juan*. His historical plays, though he himself thought highly of them, are feeble and melodramatic. He also edited the works of the poet Allan Ramsay.

PRINCIPAL WORKS: The Anster Concert, 1811; Anster Fair, 1812; The Thane of Fife, 1822; Cardinal Beaton, 1823; John Baliol, 1825; Hebrew Dramas, 1845.

ABOUT: Connolly, M. F. Life and Writings of William Tennant.

TENNENT, SIR JAMES EMERSON
(April 7, 1804-March 6, 1869), Irish travel writer, was born in Belfast. His name originally was Emerson; his father was a merchant. He was educated at Trinity College, Dublin, but left without a degree. (In 1861 the college conferred an honorary LL.D. on him.) In 1824 he went abroad and met Byron in Greece just before the poet's death. He was called to the bar from Lincoln's Inn in 1831, but never practised; in the same year he married Letitia Tennent, daughter of a wealthy banker, and took her name and arms by royal license in 1832. They had one son and two daughters. From 1832 to 1841, and again from 1842 to 1845 Tennent was a member of Parliament as a liberal-conservative; he was knighted in 1845. From 1841 to 1843 he had served as secretary of the India Board. He was then appointed civil secretary to the colonial government of Ceylon, serving from 1845 to 1850. In this last named year he was named as governor of St. Helena, but never accepted the appointment. Instead he re-entered Parliament in 1852. He was also permanent secretary of the Poor Law Board, and acted as secretary of the Board of Trade from 1852 to 1867. On his retirement he was made a baronet. In 1862 he became a Fellow of the Royal Society. Tennent's books, written in a dry, precise, clear style, deal mostly with his observations in Ceylon. He was also an authority on wine-making, and wrote on this subject for the *Encyclopaedia Britannica*.

PRINCIPAL WORKS: A History of Modern Greece, 1830; Christianity in Ceylon, 1850; Natural History of Ceylon, 1859; The Story of Guns, 1865; The Wild Elephant, 1867.

ABOUT: Belfast News Letter March 8, 9, 15, 1869; Illustrated London News 3:293 1843; 54:299, 317 1869.

TENNYSON, ALFRED (First Baron Tennyson) (August 6, 1809-October 6, 1892), poet, was the fourth of twelve children of a Lincolnshire rector and of a vicar's daughter. His brothers Frederick and Charles (who afterwards took his uncle's name of Turner) were also poets of some note in their day.

At seven he was sent to his maternal grandmother at Louth to attend the grammar school there, but at eleven he returned to the family home at Somersby, where his father became his tutor until he was ready for the university. The father was a man of culture, and he early recognized the remarkable promise of this boy who was an omnivorous reader and a precocious author: "If Alfred die," the father remarked when the son was only in his early teens, "one of our greatest poets will have gone." When, however, Alfred with his brother Charles published *Poems by Two Brothers* in 1827, all the outstandingly original poems which gave rise to this judgment had been carefully removed from the volume, and only the conventional Byronic imitations were allowed to remain! (It is recorded that when Byron died in 1824, his youthful admirer gave vent to his grief by carving laboriously on a rock, "Byron is dead.")

In 1828 Alfred with his closest brother Charles matriculated at Trinity College, Cambridge, where Frederick was already a student. Alfred stayed less than three years, seems not to have learned a great deal, and disliked Cambridge heartily. However, his university days gave him the greatest friendship of his life, that with Arthur Hallam, whose death gave birth to the noble lines of *In Memoriam*. One prophetic honor Tennyson attained to in Cambridge—the Chancellor's medal for English verse.

Very soon after Alfred had returned home to Somersby his father died. Alfred as the oldest and unmarried son felt himself the responsible head of the family, which was an unusually united one even for that period of intense family intimacy and loyalty. As the successor to the father's post did not wish to inhabit the rectory, the Tennysons lived there until 1837. Meanwhile Hallam had become engaged to one of the daughters, Emily. In 1832 the two friends traveled together on the Rhine, as two years earlier they had toured the Pyrenees together. Meanwhile Tennyson had published two more volumes of poetry (besides the Cambridge prize poem, *Timbuctoo*), but they attracted small attention. A scathing criticism of the poems published in 1833, made by the *Quarterly Review*, so depressed the sensitive poet that he did not publish another volume for nine years.

That same year Arthur Hallam died suddenly in Vienna, where he had been staying in company with his father, the famous historian. Tennyson's grief was dreadful. Hallam had been to him another self, a nearer being than even his beloved brothers. Although Tennyson proved himself the most affectionate and faithful of husbands and the most devoted of fathers, the romance and passion of his nature turned normally not to women, but to his men friends. He had besides a broad streak of melancholy in his personality, and for a while Hallam's sudden snatching away drove him close to suicide. The transcending of both these impulses may be traced in that monument of sublimation, *In Memoriam*.

In 1836 Charles Tennyson (Turner) married, and one of the bridesmaids was his bride's sister, Emily Sellwood. Alfred Tennyson met her on this occasion, and there seems to have been no thought from the beginning in the mind of either but that they were intended as lifelong companions. But by Victorian standards their marriage was impossible; Tennyson had no income sufficient to provide for a wife, and he was pledged to the assistance of his mother and his younger brothers and sisters. The entire family had sunk most of their funds, with the typical gullibility and improvidence of clerical families, in the "wood carving machine" of a Dr. Allen, which was a complete failure. The engagement dragged on for four years, and then Miss Sellwood's family forbade their further correspondence, in the hope that she would forget him and find a wealthier suitor. Like good Victorians, they obeyed, and lost ten years of their lives; it was not until 1850 that they met again, and that Tennyson felt able to assume the responsibilities of marriage.

The family had finally moved from Somersby, first to Epping Forest, then to Tunbridge Wells, then, for the mother's health, to Boxley, near Maidstone. Tennyson continued to write, poetry being as natural an expression to him as breathing; he published sparsely in the magazines, and in 1842 brought out a two volume collection. But the constant worry over the family's future, their straitened circumstances in the present, and what seemed his eternal separation from Emily Sellwood, worked on his nerves and he was fast becoming a thorough hypochondriac. Alarmed, his friends appealed to the prime minister, Sir Robert Peel, and secured for him in 1845 a civil list pension of £200 a year. The 1842 volume had solidly established his fame, and he was already being recognized as perhaps the greatest English poet then living—for Wordsworth, though still alive and poet laureate, had practically ceased to write.

With this change in his affairs, Tennyson began to hope again. The supersensitive, hypochondriacal young man was gradually changing into the calm, self-contained, and rather self-complacent lord of literature who is a more familiar figure. He was not yet a popular poet, though he was a recognized one. There was great controversy over his work, and he offended many readers—those who disliked his "modern" tendencies, his absorption in scientific progress, his vaguely broad religious views; and those who objected because he was unpredictable, because each volume he brought out was different in form and matter from the last to which they had become accustomed.

Tennyson's crucial year was 1850. In the spring he met Emily Sellwood again, and in June they were finally married. "The peace of God came into my life when I wedded her," he told his son many years later. In that same year he published (anonymously) *In Memoriam*, perhaps the greatest of his non-lyrical poems. And in 1850 Wordsworth died. After the laureateship had been offered to the aged Samuel Rogers, who declined it because he felt too old for the honor, it was tendered to Tennyson, who accepted it.

He was not at first a great success as poet laureate. His first offering in that capacity, the *Ode on the Death of the Duke of Wellington*, aroused much animosity because of its unconventional metre and because of the political opinions it expressed. It was not until the publication of *Idylls of the King*, in 1859, that Tennyson achieved widespread popularity, which with his later patriotic poems became adulation, and which persisted and grew until his death. Meanwhile the young couple—not so very young any more—had settled at Twickenham. In 1853 they leased and then bought the house called Farringford, at Freshwater, Isle of Wight, which became their chief home thereafter—though Aldworth, near Haslemere, built in 1868, was also their frequent residence. Their first son died at birth, and Tennyson took his wife abroad for an extended trip to ease her grief.

ALFRED, LORD TENNYSON

The remainder of his life was a placid one, made up of travel, mostly in England and France, the society of a few friends, much reading, and constant writing. His one recreation was yachting, a pleasure even of his old age. Always selective and rather seclusive in his tastes, he became more so with advancing years; there is a story, perhaps apocryphal, of an old friend who called, spent the evening in silence by the fireside, with both men smoking their pipes without a word after the first "Good evening," and then departed. "Thank you for a delightful visit," Tennyson said!

In 1855 he had received the honorary degree of D.C.L. from Oxford, and later was offered the rectorship of Glasgow University, but declined when he found that there were political implications and that he was being brought forward as the Conservative candidate. In 1873 his old friend Gladstone offered him a baronetcy, which he refused, though he was willing to accept the title for his son; the next year Disraeli repeated the offer, to meet with another refusal. In the following years he had several interviews with Queen Victoria, who approved of him all the more highly because Prince Albert was a devoted admirer of his work. Finally in 1833, through Gladstone, she offered him elevation to the peerage, and after much hesitation he accepted, becoming the first Lord Tennyson in 1884.

From 1875 onward, Tennyson began to experiment in a form entirely alien to his temperament—blank verse drama. All his plays were produced, and some had a fair success, but these are among his least happy work, lifeless and wooden imitations of Shakespeare. He had no love for the theater, and it is difficult to understand why he persisted in this field, except that he had long left behind him the lyrical impulse of his youth (his greatest lyrics were nearly all written before 1842) and that the larger epic, narrative, and dramatic forms attracted him as his singing urge lessened.

In 1886, when he was already an old man, his second and oldest surviving son, Lionel, died on his way home from India, a deep and lasting grief to his father. (The third son, Hallam, succeeded to the title and also became his father's authorized biographer.) Weakened by sorrow, in 1888 Tennyson fell prey to rheumatic gout, and came near to dying. He recovered finally, only to succumb to a bad attack of influenza in 1890. Thenceforth he was a semi-invalid, and almost a recluse. He continued to write, however, and was reading proof on *The Death of Œnone* up to a few days before his death.

This occurred from heart failure with resultant syncope. He was conscious almost to the last, and was, indeed, found in collapse with his finger still marking a passage of *Cymbeline* which he had been reading. He was buried in Westminster Abbey, in the Poet's Corner, next to Browning.

In appearance Tennyson, like all his brothers, was tall, stalwart, and handsome, and dark in coloring. He was a striking figure even at eighty-three, with his white beard, his dark cloak, and his broad-brimmed hat. In youth he had the real beauty which so often marks young poets.

He was perhaps the most entirely and typically English of any great poet since Shakespeare—more so even than Browning. His sympathies were circumscribed by his era: he voiced the prejudices as well as the virtues of the nineteenth century Britisher of the middle class. He was intensely and rather naively patriotic; but more than that he had an almost religious veneration for England itself, the physical England, the land and its people. His personal life was retired, domestic, and a bit prudish; he had all the Victorian masculine complacency—as witness *The Princess*. He believed in reform, not in revolution—the revolutionary ardor of a Swinburne he would have condemned as bad taste. He was a utilitarian, advocating slow progress, saying with Ovid, "You will go most safely in the middle." All his acceptance of evolutionary theory could not shake him from a deep, if unorthodox, religious faith, a faith in perfectability, in immortality, in a greater good above and beyond the human reason. All his youth was spent in painful inner searching for that assurance, which flowered in *In Memoriam*, with its merging of personal into the general love.

But these characteristics, which endeared him to Prince Albert, would not insure to him that permanent greatness which—in spite of a modern affectation of belittling him—is most certainly his. For he was something more than a poet of high ethical seriousness and a "prophet of immortality." He was one of the finest lyrists of the English tongue. And he was no mere accidental fashioner of beauty, but a student of form who was a superb metrist. Only Swinburne could rival him in that, and Swinburne's lush metres sometimes cloy, as Tennyson's never do. His only fault as a writer of lyrics is an occasional over-exquisite elaboration, and that is not frequent. There are besides in all his non-lyric poems passages of profound meditative music. Half at least of what he wrote the world would not willingly let die.

Tennyson in a sense is England's Virgil. He is far more Latin than Greek, and he has the Roman poet's high patriotic ardor as well as his emotional and pictorial beauty. He wrote no single British epic, as Virgil wrote the *Aeneid*. But Virgil again wrote no songs comparable to "Tears, Idle Tears," or "Marianna in the Moated Grange," or "Crossing the Bar," or a dozen others that will rise immediately to their lovers' minds. With Tennyson's death in 1892, a great epoch of English poetry came to a close.   M. A. deF.

PRINCIPAL WORKS: *Poetry*—Poems by Two Brothers (with Charles Tennyson [Turner]) 1827; Timbuctoo, 1829; Poems Chiefly Lyrical, 1830; Poems by Alfred Tennyson, 1833; Poems, 1842; The Princess, 1847; In Memoriam (anonymous) 1850; Ode on the Death of the Duke of Wellington, 1852; Charge of the Light Brigade and Other Poems, 1855; Maud, 1855; Idylls of the King, 1859; A Welcome, 1863; Enoch Arden (in first edition called Idylls of the Hearth) 1864; The Holy Grail and Other Poems, 1869; Gareth and Lynette, 1872; The Lover's Tale, 1879 (privately printed 1833); Ballads and Other Poems, 1880; Tiresias and Other Poems, 1885; Locksley Hall Sixty Years After, 1886; Demeter and Other Poems, 1889; The Death of Œnone, 1892; Akbar's Dream, 1892; Unpublished Early Poems (posthumous) 1931. *Verse Dramas*—Queen Mary, 1875; Harold, 1876; The Cup, 1884; The Falcon, 1884; Becket, 1884; The Foresters: Robin Hood and Maid Marian, 1892.

ABOUT: Fausset, H. l'A. Tennyson: A Modern Portrait; Lang, A. Alfred Tennyson; Lounsbury, T. R. The Life and Times of Tennyson From 1809 to 1850; Lyall, A. Tennyson; Nicolson, H. G. Tennyson; Tennyson, H. T. Tennyson and His Friends; Waugh, A. Alfred Lord Tennyson.

TENNYSON, CHARLES. See TURNER, CHARLES TENNYSON

TENNYSON, FREDERICK (June 5, 1807-February 26, 1898), poet, was the oldest surviving brother of Alfred Tennyson and after their father's death the head of the family. As such, he inherited a small estate at Grimsby. Born at Louth, Frederick Tennyson was educated in the Louth Grammar School, and went from there to Eton, where he was captain of the school, and then to Cambridge. After a year in St. John's College he transferred to Trinity College in the same term when his two younger brothers matriculated there. He was a fine scholar, winner of a medal for a Greek poem; he secured his B.A. in 1832.

Like his brothers Alfred and Charles, he turned early to poetry, and contributed four entries to their *Poems by Two Brothers*. Most of his life was spent abroad, chiefly in Florence, where he lived for twenty years and was an intimate of the Brownings. He married in 1839 Maria Giulotti, daughter of the chief magistrate of Siena, and his children were all born in Italy and, like their mother, were primarily Italian-speaking. His oldest son, however, eventually became a captain in the British army.

In 1859 Tennyson moved to Jersey, where he lived until 1896. His wife died in 1884, and in 1896 the old man, nearly ninety, went to Kensington to live with his son and daughter-in-law. There he died, the last of his brothers.

FREDERICK TENNYSON

Frederick Tennyson published his first volume in 1854, but was so discouraged by its critical reception that he brought out nothing more until 1890. Two more volumes appeared during his lifetime.

Frederick was the most withdrawn from the ordinary affairs of life of all the Tennysons. He was a student of art and loved music passionately, but his chief interest was given to various mystical religious movements, chiefly Swedenborgianism and spiritualism. He was also an ardent Free Mason. In his old age he reverted to the orthodox faith of his childhood.

His poems are well built, thoughtful, often lyrical, with evidence of a fine lyrical gift, but they are too diffuse by far, and suffer from abstractness and aloofness of spirit. He was a solitary soul, dwelling much on the thought of death, and his poetry, though it is sometimes tender, lacks all passion. Edward Fitzgerald admired it greatly, and preferred it to the work of its author's brother, the poet laureate. Browning said that Frederick Tennyson's poetry was "Alfred Tennyson in solution—but never crystallized." He never realized the expectations which were held of him, and virtually his only claim to the attention of posterity is that he was Alfred Tennyson's brother.   M. A. deF.

PRINCIPAL WORKS: Days and Hours, 1854; The Isles of Greece: Sappho and Alcaeus, 1890; Daphne and Other Poems, 1891; Poems of the Day and Year, 1895; The Shorter Poems of Frederick Tennyson, 1913.

ABOUT: Fitzgerald, E. Letters; Rawnsley, H. D. Memories of the Tennysons; Schonfield, H. J. Letters to Frederick Tennyson; Tennyson, C. Tennyson and His Friends; Illustrated London News 112:327 March 5, 1898.

THACKERAY, WILLIAM MAKE-PEACE (July 18, 1811-December 24, 1863), novelist, was born at Calcutta, India, the only son of Richmond Thackeray, who was descended from an ancient Yorkshire family of that name. His mother was Anne Becher, who like her husband had distinguished forebears in the Indian civil service. The beautiful young Mrs. Thackeray was left a widow in 1816 and the following year the boy was sent home to England. Here he lived mostly with his aunt, Mrs. Ritchie, at Chiswick. This lady, greatly alarmed to discover that her husband's hat would fit her young nephew, consulted a doctor. He reassured her, saying "He has a large head, but there's a great deal in it."

The nearsighted, delicate, sensitive child was not very happy in the school to which he was sent in Chiswick Mall. He continued here until 1822, when his mother and stepfather, Major Carmichael-Smythe, returned to England. The Smythes took up residence at Addiscombe College, where the major had been appointed governor, and William was put into the famous Charterhouse at Smithfield. Mellowed by time, Thackeray's account of the school with its tyrannical, fulminating headmaster, Dr. Russell, in *Pendennis* gives little indication of how miserable he was there as a boy. However, he made various friends who applauded his ability at comic verses and drawings. Here occurred the fight with George Venables, the journalist-to-be, and the "important result to Thackeray's nasal organ." He was undistinguished as a scholar and he did not care for games, but already he had begun to write for his own amusement.

Thackeray's holidays were spent at Addiscombe until 1825, when his stepfather settled down at Larkbeare House near Ottery St. Mary in Devonshire. After leaving Charterhouse, 1828, Thackeray spent some months here while his stepfather coached him for entrance into Cambridge. His university career was of short duration. He entered Trinity College in February 1829 and left at the end of the Easter term 1830, having decided that "the studies would be of no use to him." He had made such friends as R. Monckton Milnes (Lord Houghton), J. H. Kemble, Edward Fitzgerald, W. H. Thompson (afterward Master of Trinity), and Tennyson. Of Thackeray's contributions to *The Snob*, which was described as a "literary and scientific journal not conducted by members of the university," the most notable was his mock prize-poem, "Timbuctoo." Thackeray might be cited to exemplify the dictum that university contacts are more important than actual learning. Richmond Ritchie declares that "Cambridge fixed his social status. Though afterwards he was to consort with Bohemians and other strange acquaintances

into which a man is forced by adversity, he was never a Bohemian, and always faithful to the traditions of the class in which he was born and bred."

Thackeray read an immense amount of fiction, poetry, and history at Cambridge, but his activities were largely social. He lived as a young gentleman of fashion, following the hounds, attending theatre and supper parties and, considering his luck, gambling more than he should. After leaving Cambridge he traveled to Europe, visiting Dresden, Rome, Paris, and Weimar, where he met Goethe and was presented at court. Returning to London in 1831, he entered as a student at the Middle Temple, but abandoned this as soon as he came of age. Then he bought the *National Standard,* a newspaper with which Major Carmichael-Smythe was connected, went to Paris as its correspondent, and when it failed turned to the study of art. A masterly caricaturist, Thackeray's serious productions were stiff and undistinguished. Before 1835 he was contributing to *Fraser's Magazine* and in the following year occurred his well-known, unsuccessful application to Dickens to illustrate *Pickwick.*

Thackeray's problematical career as a painter was ended by another newspaper venture. This was *The Constitutional,* which Major Smythe purchased in 1836 and of which he appointed Thackeray Paris correspondent. On the strength of this position and its concomitant £400 a year, Thackeray married Isabella Gethen Creagh Shawe, daughter of Col. Matthew Shawe, in the same year. Although his patrimony was nearly gone, he was still regarded as a catch and as such he appears to have been married. His wife's mother and her behavior when she learned of the failure of *The Constitutional* are limned in *The Newcomes.* Gambling, banking failures, bad investments, and general extravagance all contributed to the dissipation of Thackeray's inheritance. And after the demise of *The Constitutional* he was definitely on his own. He returned to London (1837), established himself in Great Coram Street, and became a thorough literary hack. He contributed to *The Times* and was "a pillar of Fraser," writing reviews, articles, and various serial works like *The Yellowplush Correspondence, Catherine,* and *The Great Hoggarty Diamond.*

He wrote furiously and much, laboring under a pressure of financial adversities and domestic tragedy which would have broken a weaker man. The gay young Cambridge buck with his long-tailed coat and his monocle had become a shabby journalistic drudge. Between 1838 and 1840 Mrs. Thackeray gave birth to three daughters. The second did not live and after her third accouchement Mrs. Thackeray's mind failed. She was placed with a family in Essex and survived her husband by thirty years. Thackeray's daughters lived with his grandmother in Paris and he, himself homeless, became a frequenter of clubs. His writings developed a small following, he published several collections of earlier work, and almost from its initiation he was associated with the magazine *Punch*. He achieved a degree of security, but he had little practicality where money matters were concerned and, fortunately perhaps for posterity, there was almost never a time when necessity did not compel him to write. Without that necessity he might not have left the world much more than a collection of whimsical drawings.

Writing was always work to him. Rather socially minded, he was fond of travel, elegant surroundings, good food, and tobacco. Saintsbury, whose word is beyond dispute, says that Thackeray's "opinions on wine were singularly just and accomplished." In appearance he was extraordinarily tall, being six feet four and correspondingly broad. He had a large, well-proportioned head, leonine mane, and noble brow. The broken nose marred an otherwise handsome face.

Thackeray's connection with *Punch* lasted about ten years. He made a trip to Ireland in 1842 and stayed for a time with the novelist Lever. *The Irish Sketch Book,* which annoyed the Irish very much, appeared in 1843, and in the dedication to Lever, Thackeray used his own name for the first time. In 1844, through the influence of a friend, he obtained passage to the Far East and produced *From Cornhill to Cairo* (1846). That year he established himself, his daughters, and his grandmother at 13 Young Street, Kensington. Here he finished *Vanity Fair* and "here at last luck came to him." Ironically enough his immediate popularity was due not so much to this masterpiece as to *The Snob Papers,* appearing then in *Punch,* and the Christmas book, *Mrs. Perkyns' Ball* (1847).

Outside literary circles Thackeray was quite unknown in 1846. The first numbers of *Vanity Fair* failed to attract attention and the advisability of stopping publication was mooted. "Currer Bell's" eulogistic dedication of the second edition of *Jane Eyre* to Thackeray, an article in the *Edinburgh Review,* and *Mrs. Perkyns' Ball* all contributed to turn the tide of public opinion. Thackeray was then unaware of the identity of the author of *Jane Eyre,* but Charlotte Brontë, literal-minded and intense, had idealized Thackeray before he was personally known to her. *Vanity Fair* was followed immediately by *Pendennis,* which was interrupted by a very serious illness late in 1849. Despite his heroic size Thackeray was never very strong. It was fortunate that he had achieved

sufficient prosperity to allow the dissolution of his connection with *Punch*.

Thackeray never enjoyed lecturing and he would probably never have done so if immediate monetary considerations had not combined with the desire to leave his daughters well-provided. His two tours of the United States (1852-53 and 1855-56) were lucrative, made him many friends, and furnished him with new material. He seems genuinely to have desired some sort of civil or diplomatic post which would have assured him a regular income and leisure. His last attempt to gain it was (1854) for an appointment to the legation at Washington. Shortly before his second tour of the States he wrote, "It is quite clear neither kings nor laws can do anything so well for me as these jaws and this pen—please God they may be allowed to wag a little longer." After an almost successful foray into politics (he stood for Oxford in 1857 and was narrowly beaten by the brilliant Edward Cardwell) he commenced *The Virginians*.

At this time occurred the incident which has given rise to much discussion regarding the rivalry between Thackeray and Dickens. Thackeray's own attitude is instinct in his statement that "he [Dickens] can't forgive me for my success with *Vanity Fair*—as if there were not room in the world for both of us." From the standpoint of material returns it is difficult to understand why Dickens should have been jealous of Thackeray. *Vanity Fair,* during the time of its highest favor ran only six thousand copies the number, while some of Dickens' works went as high as twenty-five thousand. Considerations of birth are ridiculous where genius is concerned, but Dickens in his lifetime was prob-

WILLIAM MAKEPEACE THACKERAY

ably irked by comparisons of the sort credited to Theodore Roosevelt. "Thackeray," the late president is supposed to have said, "was a gentleman." Although they had many mutual friends, Dickens and Thackeray met very seldom, but there was never any trouble between them until 1858 when Edmund Yates, then a young journalist of twenty-seven, wrote a sketch of Thackeray in *Town Talk*. It was a petty, impudent, carping bit of personality of the sort that is most offensive and Thackeray, who hated personal journalism, considered the piece a gratuitous insult from a fellow clubman. He wrote Yates, censuring him severely for making journalistic use of private conversation.

Yates penned a mollifying reply which would probably have ended the matter had it been sent. Unfortunately for him he showed the epistle to Dickens, who drafted the answer which Thackeray received. Thackeray placed the whole correspondence before the Garrick Club with the eventual result that Yates lost his membership. When Dickens, evidently dismayed at the consequences of his lion-bearding, wrote to protest, Thackeray, who was well aware of his connection with the incident, referred him to the committee of the club. He admired Dickens as an author, but he obviously did not fancy the man. Thackeray genuinely hated nothing but what he considered literary dishonesty. "Lord Byron," he said, "wrote more cant of this sort than any poet I know of. Think of 'the peasant girls with dark blue eyes' of the Rhine—the brown-faced, flat-nosed, thick-lipped, dirty wenches! Think of 'filling high a cup of Samian wine': small beer is nectar compared to it and Byron himself always drank gin. The man never wrote from the heart. He got up rapture and enthusiasm with an eye to the public. . . Woe be to the man who denies the public gods."

From 1860 to 1862 Thackeray was editor of the *Cornhill Magazine*, achieving absolutely unprecedented success, but genuinely distressed by the duties involved. "How," he complained, "can I go into society with comfort? I dined the other day at ———'s and at the table were four gentlemen whose masterpieces of literature I had been compelled to decline with thanks." His strongest reason for resigning was probably the desire to put all his failing energies on *Denis Duval*, the novel left unfinished at his death. There is reason to believe he knew that his end was near. He died of cerebral hemorrhage on Christmas Eve in his new house in Palace Gardens and was buried at Kensal Green.

Thackeray, Cazamian says, never realized his genius to the full, but "when he is at his best he cannot be rivaled." Saintsbury also feels that, while Dickens "never much excelled his first distinct essay, it was years before Thackeray gave his full measure" and that *Esmond* "enshrines such studies of character . . . as not four other makers of English prose and verse can show." Master of pathos and humor, Thackeray displays a satire which is never over-bitter and his tragedy is without bombast. Whatever he did he did sincerely and he wrote as he lived, from the heart.

P. B. S.

PRINCIPAL WORKS: *Collected Sketches and Stories* (under the pseudonym of Michael Angelo Titmarsh)—The Paris Sketch Book, 1840; Comic Tales and Sketches, 1841; The Second Funeral of Napoleon, 1841; The Irish Sketch Book. 1843; Notes of a Journey From Cornhill to Grand Cairo, 1846; Mrs. Perkyns' Ball, 1847; The Book of Snobs, 1848; Rebecca and Rowena, 1850; The Kikleburys on the Rhine, 1850; The Rose and the Ring, 1855. *Novels*—Vanity Fair, 1848; The History of Samuel Titmarsh and The Great Hoggarty Diamond, 1849; The History of Pendennis, 1849-1850; The History of Henry Esmond, 1852; The Newcomes, 1854-1855; The Virginians, 1858-1859; Lovel the Widower, 1861; The Adventures of Philip, 1862; Denis Duval, 1867. *Lectures*—The English Humourists of the Eighteenth Century, 1853; The Four Georges, 1860. *Miscellaneous*—Miscellanies: Prose and Verse, (4 vols.) 1855-1857; Roundabout Papers, 1863; Early and Late Papers, 1867.

ABOUT: Chancellor, E. B. The London of Thackeray; Melville, L. The Life of William Makepeace Thackeray; Merivale, H. and Marzials, F. Thackeray; Ritchie, A. Letters of W. M. Thackeray; Saintsbury, G. A Consideration of Thackeray; Stephenson, N. W. Spiritual Drama in the Life of Thackeray; Taylor, H. Thackeray the Man of Letters and the Humorist; Thackeray, W. M. Works (see Memoir by Thackeray's daughter to 1897 ed.); Trollope, A. Thackeray; Yates, E. Mr. Thackeray, Mr. Yates, and the Garrick Club.

THIRLWALL, CONNOP (Bishop of St. David's) (February 11, 1797-July 27, 1875), prelate, scholar, historian, and theologian, was born in Stepney, and was the son of the Reverend Thomas Thirlwall, a well-known churchman. The future historian and bishop was so precocious that his training in Latin began at three years and he was introduced to Greek at four. He showed a talent for composition when he was seven, and in 1809, at the age of twelve, had the pleasure of seeing in print his first work, a collection of essays and poems with the title *Primitiae*.

At twelve he was sent to school at Charterhouse, where his mates included George Grote, the historian, and J. C. Hare, later archdeacon of Lewes. When he had completed his studies at this school, he matriculated at Oxford, where he won the Craven and Bell scholarships in his first year. Upon taking his degree, he won several minor fellowships; to round out his education he toured France, Switzerland, and Italy.

It was Thirlwall's intention to practise law, and he studied for and was admitted to the bar, his call coming in 1825. At this time he translated Schleiermacher's *Essay on St.*

BISHOP THIRLWALL

Luke, and wrote a remarkable preface to the work. He then decided upon a career in the church, went to Trinity, and was ordained in 1828. In this year he published the first volume of his distinguished translation of Niebuhr's *History of Rome,* completed four years later.

Thirlwall held various college offices at Trinity, including that of junior dean and an assistant tutorship. However, a pamphlet favoring the opening of university degrees to dissenters cost him his tutorship in 1834. Shortly afterward a living was offered him, at Kirby Underdale, and he accepted it and held it for five years.

He had now published the first edition of his *History of Greece,* which was followed shortly afterward by Grote's more famous work on the same subject. Grote generously remarked that had he known earlier of Thirlwall's history he would not have felt it necessary to write one of his own. Later editions, published in 1845 and 1852, were Thirlwall's last serious works.

In 1840 Thirlwall was created Bishop of St. David's in Wales, from which position he retired in 1874 when extreme old age compelled him to do so. Upon his retirement he went to Bath, where he died. In Westminster Abbey his remains lie in the same grave with Grote.

As a scholar Bishop Thirlwall displayed tremendous erudition. His mental powers were such that he was able to learn Welsh and preach in it within a few months after his appointment as bishop of St. David's. He knew in addition Sanskrit, Greek, Latin, French, Italian, Portuguese, Dutch, and German. He was a man without malice; a humorist; a lover of animals of all sorts; a devotee of music and the graphic arts; one of the best speakers, said J. S. Mill, that he had ever listened to. He was not a man beloved of his subordinates, who were awed by his erudition, distanced by his apparent coldness, and in deadly fear of his irony; but he was on the liberal side in every controversy.

The first definitive biography of Bishop Thirlwall was published in 1936, more than sixty years after his death. It was written by John Connop Thirlwall, Jr., an American descendant.

R. M.

PRINCIPAL WORKS: *Translator*—Niebuhr's *History of Rome,* 1828-32; *History*—History of Greece, 1835-40; *Miscellaneous*—Remains: Literary and Theological, 1877; Essays, Speeches, and Sermons, 1880; Letters to a Friend, 1881; Letters: Literary and Theological, 1881.

ABOUT: Clark, J. W. Old Friends at Cambridge and Elsewhere; Gooch, J. P. History and Historians in the 19th Century; Thirlwall, C. Letters to a Friend; Letters: Literary and Theological; Thirlwall, J. C., Jr. Connop Thirlwall: Historian and Theologian.

THOM, WILLIAM (1798?-February 29, 1848), Scottish poet, was born in Aberdeen, the son of a merchant who died while the boy was in infancy. Soon after, he was run over by a nobleman's carriage and lamed for life, the nobleman giving five shillings to his mother in compensation! After a few years at a dame's school, he was apprenticed to a weaver at the age of ten, and worked at this trade most of his life. In 1828 he was married, but when he moved to Dundee in 1831, his wife left him. Divorce being impossible, he took up housekeeping in Forfarshire with another woman (the "Jean" of most of his poems and songs), by whom he had four children; she died in 1840. During the economic depression of 1837 he was unemployed, and had to earn what he could by peddling second-hand books and by playing the flute in the streets. Later he worked again as a weaver in Aberdeen and Inverurie. Although he had written poems from boyhood, his first lyric was published in 1841, in the Aberdeen *Herald*; the attention it attracted enabled him to spend four months in London and to meet people on the outer fringes of the literary world. In 1844 he moved to London, bringing with him another girl from Inverurie; several children more were added to his household. He worked at weaving, continued to write poetry, and gradually, worn out by overwork from childhood, lapsed into inebriety. Finally he returned to Dundee, ill and penniless, and died there. He was given a public funeral.

Thom's poetry is marked by intellectual power, graphic description, and much natural beauty and tenderness. In circumstances allowing him more leisure, he might have developed into an important poet.

PRINCIPAL WORK: Rhymes and Recollections of a Hand Loom Weaver, 1844.

ABOUT: Thom, W. Rhymes and Recollections of a Hand Loom Weaver (see Biography by W. Skinner); Chambers's Journal December 1841.

THOMPSON, FRANCIS JOSEPH (December 18, 1859-November 13, 1907), poet and essayist, was the son of a homoeopathic physician at Preston, Lancashire. His parents and uncles were converts to the Roman Catholic Church, and one of his younger sisters, like two of his aunts, became a nun. Two of his uncles were writers, chiefly of devotional books; one edited a Catholic magazine.

When the child was five the family moved to a small town near Manchester. At eleven he was sent to the Ushaw School, where the teaching was mainly classical, and where the expectation was that he would be graduated into a seminary and become a priest. From early childhood, brought up in an atmosphere steeped with piety, he had been most devout. When he was seventeen, however, the headmaster sent for him and told him that he could not be considered for the priesthood; he was a fine and diligent student, but he was too dreamy, and his health was poor and gave little promise of improvement.

Baffled, his father determined that under these circumstances the best thing was to have his son trained to follow in his own profession. He sent him to Manchester to study medicine, and on his departure his adored mother gave him (prophetic gift!—perhaps a symbol of foreboding) a copy of De Quincey's *Confessions of an English Opium Eater*. The book had a lasting and appalling effect on him, though his first addiction to opium came not from experimentation, but for relief from the pain of incipient tuberculosis.

No boy could have been less fitted, either for life in an industrial town or for the study of medicine. Thompson strove manfully, but the whole bent of his mind and nature made scientific training impossible for him. For six years he stayed at the medical school, and three times he took examinations for his degree, but he always failed. During this time his mother died. Finally, in November, 1885, he suddenly deserted Manchester for London. His father, troubled and incensed, stopped his allowance, hoping perhaps to bring him back. He did not know his son's desolate pride.

Until 1888 Francis Thompson starved in the streets of London, as De Quincey had done before him. For a while he was a bookseller's errand boy, then he lost that ill-paid post and made a few pennies as best he could —by selling newspapers or matches, by calling cabs and opening their doors. He slept at night on the bare ground near Covent Garden, with other vagabonds. In the pockets of his ragged coat lay always his entire salvage from the wreck of his life—a volume of Æschylus and one of Blake. Once when he was near to actual starvation, a young prostitute, like De Quincey's Ann, pitied him and gave him help from her scanty store. A charitable shoemaker, who tried in vain to "save his soul" for evangelical Protestantism, compromised by saving his body, and took him in as an employee. He even forced a half-reconciliation between Thompson and his father, and sent him to Lancashire to spend Christmas with his family. But the father had married again, and the son felt a stranger; he went away without even divulging the kind of life he led or the straits to which he was reduced. The opium habit had full hold on him by this time; all that he had gained from six years of medical study was the knowledge of how to secure the drug for which went almost every penny that he earned.

Francis Thompson as a shoemaker's apprentice, with his weak body and his clumsy hands, was a pitiful joke. The pious shoemaker forgave many ineptitudes, but when Thompson let fall a shutter on a customer's shoulder and injured him, he was forced to discharge his protégé. Often after that he would see the pale, ragged young man wandering aimlessly near his shop, as if drawn by a magnet, but it was impossible to keep him on any longer. One thing only Thompson had taken away of value—to him: an old account book, on the pages of which he was beginning to write, sitting on curbstones or against walls.

Early in 1888, Wilfrid Meynell, editor of *Merry England*, a Roman Catholic magazine, and husband of the poet Alice Meynell, received a batch of torn and dirty manuscript, two poems and an essay, signed by Francis Thompson. The only address given was the general post-office at Charing Cross. Little did the editor suspect that the author had no other. He put the papers away in a pigeon-hole, and it was several months before he got around to reading them. Then, deeply impressed, he wrote to Thompson, but by that time the unhappy poet had long given up his hopeless visits to the post-office.

Light-headed from hunger and opium, he was beginning to see strange visions on the London streets. At last, in utter despair, he determined to end his life. He crept into a corner with what even for an addict was a lethal dose of laudanum. He had taken half of it, when another vision came to him: the boy poet Thomas Chatterton, who had killed himself at fifteen, seemed to hold his arm and bid him wait. He did not finish the draught.

A few days later he found that one of his poems was printed in *Merry England*. Unable to find him in any other way, Meynell had hoped that this would attract his attention. It did. There came to his office a haggard, filthy vagabond, shirtless and with bare feet in broken shoes.

The Meynells rescued Francis Thompson. All his life they cared for him, often an ungrateful task in his worst periods. He became an intimate of the house; he loved them all, but for Mrs. Meynell he conceived an idealistic worship. She was the only woman he ever loved, though after years he deliberately uprooted that futile passion from his heart.

They sent him to a hospital, then to a monastery at Storrington. There, in the quiet country, in the first peace of his life, he wrote his best poetry—the famous "Hound of Heaven" belongs to this period—and the iridescent "Essay on Shelley." But he was still taking opium, and the fever of London was in his bones. He came back, and once more the Meynells succored him. He met Coventry Patmore, the poet of domestic bliss who also became a Roman Catholic, and George Meredith, and he mingled with the literary groups that surrounded the Meynells. He was their children's playmate, and for the little girls he wrote *Sister Songs*.

From 1893 to 1897 most of his time was spent—again by the Meynell's management—in long visits to the Franciscan monastery at Pantasaph, in North Wales. Surrounded by rural beauty and the religious atmosphere his mystical spirit craved, his poetic genius always flowered. But it was as if he were doomed to tragedy; he could not endure very long the cessation of pain, and London, which was his nemesis, called him irresistibly and almost against his will. Most of the last ten years of his life were spent there; and after 1897 he wrote little poetry.

He became instead a hack book reviewer for *The Athenaeum* and *The Academy*, a well-known figure who trudged away with his review books in a sack over his shoulder, his old cape waving about him. He was pleased if among them was some volume on cricket, for which he had a boyish passion and on which he was almost an authority. With the Boer war he became—he, who was so unworldly—an Imperialist, and almost brought about a rupture with the anti-Imperialist Meynells. He continued to take opium, and his lifelong tubercular tendency flared up again.

In 1907 he spent the summer in the country home of the neo-romantic writer, Wilfrid Scawen Blunt, who had become his devoted friend. He was very ill, and it was plain that his end was not far off. When at last it was necessary to take him to the Hospital of St. Elizabeth and St. John, in St. John's Woods, he weighed only seventy pounds. He

died there very quietly, consoled by the rites of his church, and was buried in the Roman Catholic cemetery at Kensal Green, where his tombstone bears the quoted epitaph, "Look for me in the nurseries of Heaven."

"No one ever had so sad a life as he," Blunt said of him; and yet there was no deep sadness in his nature. He never really lived in this world. His invariable unpunctuality (an actual lack of any sense of time), his absent-mindedness, were partly the effects of opium and partly the mark of the dreamer. As E. Merrill Root called him, he was "a moth of a man." Yet he had his homely side, what he himself spoke of as his "eternal pipes, stubby beard, and shabby clothes." He suffered humanly from the failure of even the Meynells to understand fully the genius behind his careless, indolent temperament. He could on occasion become one of the world's worst bores, emerging from his habitual taciturnity to talk endlessly around and about some trifling commonplace detail. No grown man ever had so chaste a mind, almost asexual; even his spurts of jealousy of Alice Meynell were more the hurt of a boy neglected by his busy mother than the adult jealousy of a normal human being. There was in him always a streak of childishness, which lends a fatal archness to the poorest of his poems.

Thompson has always had devoted admirers, even among those who share not at all his religious viewpoint and preoccupation. (He has suffered, indeed, by too much adulation from his co-religionists, who by their emphasis on his mysticism obscure the essential greatness of his pure poetic gift.) He was at once aesthete and ascetic. At his best, his verse is pure magic, though sometimes

FRANCIS THOMPSON

the magic fails and becomes mere over-elaboration. The content of his verse was almost wholly unoriginal, but he could give it freshness by the newness of his images. If often the mystic in him limits and truncates the poet, yet it lends also a mysterious depth to the almost supernatural beauty of his finest work. He has a close affinity with the metaphysical poets of the seventeenth century: Blunt called him "Crashaw born again, but born greater." R. L. Mégroz, who called Thompson "the poet of earth in heaven" and Dante Gabriel Rossetti "the poet of heaven on earth," thought him "the greatest poet of Catholicism since Dante." He is perhaps that, but he is certainly more than that, as Dante was. He is not a major poet—his output was too small and too severely limited in theme—but he may be called (with only seeming paradox) one of the greatest minor poets in English. M. A. deF.

PRINCIPAL WORKS: *Poetry*—Poems, 1893; Sister Songs, 1895; New Poems, 1897. *Prose*—Health and Holiness, 1905; The Life of St. Ignatius Loyola, 1909; An Essay on Shelley, 1909; The Life of John Baptist de la Galle, 1911.

ABOUT: LaGorce, A. de. Francis Thompson (French); Mégroz, R. L. Francis Thompson: The Poet of Earth in Heaven; Meynell, E. The Life of Francis Thompson; Meynell, V. Alice Meynell: A Memoir; Rooker, K. Francis Thompson (French); Thomson, J. Francis Thompson: Poet and Mystic; Catholic World 139:73 April 1934; Current Literature 44:172 February 1908; London Mercury 27:58 November 1932; Spectator 149:657 November 11 1932.

THOMS, WILLIAM JOHN (November 16, 1803-August 15, 1885), antiquary, was born in Westminster, his father being a clerk in the treasury. Nothing is known of his education. Until 1845 he was a clerk in the secretary's office at Chelsea Hospital. From his earliest youth he had been interested in bibliography and in antiquarian studies. His first work in this field was as editor of *Early Prose Romances,* in 1827 and 1828. In the latter year he married Laura Sale, daughter of a well known musician; they had three sons and six daughters. During 1832 Thoms edited *The Original,* a miscellany which lived for only four issues. In 1838 he was made a Fellow of the Society of Antiquaries, and from that year until 1873 he was secretary of the Camden Society and edited numerous antiquarian works for them. In 1845 he was clerk of the House of Lords, and from 1863 to 1882 deputy librarian. His lasting claim to eminence, however, comes from his foundation in 1849 of *Notes and Queries,* of which he was editor to 1872; this immensely valuable reference magazine is still published.

PRINCIPAL WORKS: Lays and Legends of France, Spain, Tartary, and Ireland, 1834; Lays and Legends of Germany, 1834; The Book of the Court, 1838; Three Notelets on Shakespeare, 1865; Human Longevity, 1873.

ABOUT: Athenaeum 2:239, 272, 302 1885.

THOMSON, SIR (CHARLES) WYVILLE (March 5, 1830-March 10, 1882), Scottish naturalist, was born at Linlithgow, his father being a surgeon with the East India Company. He was educated at Merchiston Castle School and the University of Edinburgh, where he took a medical course. In 1850 he was lecturer on botany at King's College, Aberdeen; in 1851 professor of botany at Marischal College; in 1851 professor of natural history at Queen's College, Cork; in 1854 professor of mineralogy and geology at Queen's College, Belfast; in 1860 professor of natural science at the same institution; in 1867 professor of botany at the Royal College of Science, Dublin; and in 1870 professor of natural history at the University of Edinburgh. In 1853 he married Jane Ramage. They had one son.

Always keenly interested in oceanic life, he investigated the marine fauna and flora north of Scotland for the Royal Society in 1868, with Dr. W. B. Carpenter, and in 1869 made a similar investigation with J. G. Jeffreys off the west coast of Scotland. From 1872 to 1876, on leave of absence from Edinburgh, he served as chief of the civilian science staff of the expedition of the Challenger to Australasia and South America. On Thomson's return he was knighted in recognition of his scientific services.

Thomson retired in 1879, on account of failing health. He was the recipient of numerous honorary degrees and other honors from scientific bodies all over the civilized world. Most of his writing consisted of papers to technical journals, but his two books are in more popular vein and are highly interesting as well as informative.

PRINCIPAL WORKS: The Depths of the Sea, 1873; The Voyage of the Challenger, 1877.

ABOUT: Linnaean Society Proceedings 1881-82; Quarterly Journal of the Geological Society 1882.

THOMSON, GEORGE (March 4, 1757-February 18, 1851), Scottish song publisher and editor, was born in Fifeshire, the son of a school master. The family moved to Edinburgh in his childhood, and after an elementary education he was apprenticed to a lawyer. In 1780 he became a junior clerk with the Board of Trustees for the Encouragement of Manufactures in Scotland, and remained in this work until he retired, as principal clerk, in 1839, after fifty-nine years of service. He married the daughter of a Lieutenant Miller, and had two sons and six daughters; one of his daughters became Dickens' mother-in-law. From 1840 to 1845 he lived in London, then returning to Edinburgh.

An amateur violinist and lover of music, he decided to publish a series of volumes of old Celtic songs. He paid such composers as Beethoven, Haydn, and Weber to provide accompaniments, and disliking the words of many of the songs, he employed the leading poets of the day—Scott, Byron, Moore, Campbell, Hogg, etc.—to furnish new lyrics. His principal contributor was Burns, who wrote about a hundred and twenty songs for him. Thomson's only other work of a literary nature was his editing of the poems of Mrs. Anne Grant of Langan. He died in Leith at the great age of ninety-four.

PRINCIPAL WORKS (edited): Scottish Airs, 1793-1841; Welsh Airs, 1809-14; Irish Airs, 1814-16.

ABOUT: Hadden, J. C. George Thomson: The Friend of Burns.

THOMSON, JAMES ("B.V.") (November 23, 1834-June 3, 1882), poet and essayist, was the son of a jovial, hard-drinking officer in the merchant marine, and an intensely pious, melancholy mother. He was born at Port Glasgow, but when he was only six his father suffered a paralytic stroke (whether, as claimed, because of overstrain during a storm at sea, or as a result of chronic alcoholism is not certain), and two years later his mother died; the family in consequence moved to London, and the worse than orphaned boy (for his father never entirely regained his mental faculties) was sent to the Royal Caledonian Asylum. The eight years he passed here were relatively peaceful ones—perhaps, by contrast with his later life, his happiest time. It was determined by relatives to make an army schoolmaster of him, and in 1850 he was sent for training to the "Model School" of the Royal Military College at Chelsea.

The next year he became assistant teacher at Ballincollig, near Cork. This was the decisive year of his life, for there he met his greatest friend, Charles Bradlaugh, then a trooper in the dragoons, later the leader of Free Thought in England; and there also he met the beautiful girl, Matilda Weller, whose death two years later blasted his spirit forever. He loved Matilda at sight, and she him; they would doubtless have married had she not died at only sixteen, while he was far away in England. When he was buried nearly thirty years later, he wore a locket containing a curl of her yellow hair.

From 1854 to 1862 Thomson served as schoolmaster at barracks in Devonshire, Dublin, Aldershot, Jersey, and Portsmouth. By solitary study he gained a good foundation in English, French, German, and Italian literature, and had already published poems in the *Edinburgh Magazine*. Then, with two or three companions, he was court-martialed and dismissed from the army; the cause was merely the swimming of one of their number in a forbidden pond, and the refusal of the others to deliver their names for discipline.

JAMES THOMSON

Bradlaugh came to Thomson's assistance, took him into his home, and secured work for him, first as a solicitor's clerk and then as a journalist, on the Free Thought magazine, the *London Investigator*, and later on the newly founded *National Reformer* of which Bradlaugh eventually became sole editor. His writings in these magazines Thomson signed "B.V."—"B" for Bysshe in memory of Shelley, and "V" for "Vanolis," an anagram on Novalis, the pseudonym of the German poet and mystic, Hardenberg, whose one love also had died in early girlhood. Under this name Thomson became known not only as a poet of promise and power, but also as an effective and aggressive propagandist for Rationalism.

Thomson, however, was perhaps doomed by heredity, and was certainly doomed by the circumstances of his childhood and youth. He had twin devils to fight—his father's tendency to inebriety, which in him became a true periodical dipsomania, and his mother's melancholy, which in the son approximated melancholia. He was indeed "the prophet of despair," the most complete pessimist, perhaps, that literature has ever known. Yet in his personal associations he was genial, chivalrous, and fond of company, and even in his poetry—as in the famous "Sunday at Hampstead" and "Sunday up the River"—a note of cheer occasionally breaks the utter darkness of the scene.

His own life was hastening toward complete disaster. For the most part he earned a very precarious living by his writing, and lived in single rooms in various parts of the London slums. Bradlaugh continued to befriend him, and he had other good friends, who found him posts when they could; in

621

1872 he somehow found himself secretary of a gold and silver mining company which sent him to Colorado for several months to inspect its holdings, and promptly went bankrupt after his return; and the next year Bradlaugh got him appointed as correspondent for the New York *World* to report the civil conflict between royalists and republicans in Spain: this war was so languidly conducted that Thomson found nothing to report, and was recalled in consequence. In Bradlaugh's *National Reformer,* in 1874, was published (in serial installments several months apart) Thomson's greatest poem, the superb *City of Dreadful Night.*

But in 1875 Thomson quarreled finally with his greatest benefactor; he himself blamed Mrs. Annie Besant, then associated with Bradlaugh, for the rupture, but the probability is that Bradlaugh had reached the limit of his patience with his protégé's insane spells of drunkenness. Henceforth Thomson's essays were published in another Free Thought magazine, *The Secularist,* and in a strange journal, a house organ of the tobacco industry, called *Cope's Tobacco Plant,* which nevertheless contained a vast amount of really fine articles and literary criticisms. For this magazine Thomson wrote articles on Heine, Whitman, and others of his literary heroes.

In 1880 Bertram Dobell, who had met Thomson through admiration for his poetry, secured publication for his friend of a volume of poems, headed by *The City of Dreadful Night,* and the next year another volume, and one of essays, appeared—Thomson's only published books during his lifetime. For seven years, from 1875 until the last year of his life, he wrote no poetry at all.

There was a brief last interlude in the summer of 1881, and again in the spring of 1882, when Thomson spent happy weeks with friends near Leicester, and from internal evidence seemed to have found, in his autumn, a successor to the lost love of his springtime. But it was too late; his second visit ended in a fearful bout of alcoholic madness, which alienated his friends, and he went back to London and death. In June 1882 he appeared at the home of his friend, the blind poet Philip Bourke Marston, in a terrible condition; soon afterwards William Sharp arrived, and discovered what the blind man could not see, that Thomson was lying near death from a hemorrhage. They removed him to the University College Hospital, where a few days later he died. He was buried in Highgate Cemetery, in the grave of his friend Austin Holyoake, without religious ceremony.

All Thomson's writing is filled with his overwhelming despair. Life to him is unmitigated hell and we are a doomed race living in a world foreordained to disaster. Blind destiny is our only guide. But these overmastering beliefs are expressed in measures of firm and massive beauty. Thomson's poetry is marred by occasional carelessness and a tendency to mere rhetoric; but at its best it is a noble structure. It is to literature what Tschaikowsky's *Symphonie Pathétique* is to music. As an essayist, Thomson has not come into his own; he is indeed a critic of more than usual penetration and power. He is a minor figure; but the poignant lyricism of his best work will keep alive the name of this saddest of men on earth.   M. A. deF.

PRINCIPAL WORKS: *Poetry*—The City of Dreadful Night: With Some Other Poems, 1880; Vane's Story, Weddah and Om-el-Bonain, and Other Poems, 1881; A Voice From the Nile and Other Poems, 1884; Poems, Essays, and Fragments, 1892. *Prose*—Essays and Phantasies, 1881; Satires and Profanities, 1884; Biographical and Critical Studies, 1896; Walt Whitman: The Man and the Poet, 1910.

ABOUT: Dobell, B. The Laureate of Pessimism; Marston, P. B. Ward's English Poets (Vol. IV); Meeker, J. E. The Life and Poetry of James Thomson; Salt, H. S. The Life of James Thomson; Poetry 44:274 August 1934.

THOMSON, WILLIAM (Archbishop of York) (February 11, 1819-December 25, 1890), theologian, was born in Whitehaven of a family of Scottish descent; his father was a banker. He was educated at Shrewsbury School and Queen's College, Oxford, securing his B.A. in 1840, his M.A. in 1841. His earliest intellectual interest was in logic. He was ordained deacon in 1842 and priest in 1843, and for four years served as a curate in Surrey and near Oxford. He was then called to Queen's as college tutor, chaplain, and dean. In 1852 he became junior bursar, in 1854 bursar. He was a popular preacher and lecturer, and labored indefatigably for the welfare of the college. In 1855 he married Zoë Skeene, daughter of the British consul at Aleppo; they had four sons and five daughters. This same year he left the college to become rector of a London church, but in a few months was recalled to Queen's as provost. In 1858 he was elected preacher to Lincoln's Inn, and the next year was named chaplain-in-ordinary to Queen Victoria. At first an admirer of Benjamin Jowett and a follower of the Broad Church movement, he turned against this liberalizing tendency and in 1861 edited *Aids to Faith,* a symposium planned as the High Church rejoinder to Jowett. The same year he was made Bishop of Gloucester and Bristol, and only a year later became Archbishop of York. A liberal in economics and politics, and sympathetic with the aims of labor, he became immensely popular with the north country workers. Thomson's long years of devotion, first to Queen's College, then to his episcopal duties, left him little leisure for writing, and a volume reflecting his early interest in the philosophy of logic was the only general work he published.

PRINCIPAL WORKS: An Outline of the Necessary Laws of Thought, 1842; Aids to Faith, 1862 (in part).
ABOUT: London Times December 26, 1890.

THOMSON, SIR WILLIAM. See KELVIN, LORD

THORNBURY, GEORGE WALTER

(November 13, 1828-June 11, 1876), miscellaneous writer, was born in London, the son of a solicitor. He was educated privately by his uncle, a clergyman, and was intended for the church, but studied art instead, at Leigh's Academy. He was not a success as an artist, however, and turned to journalism. In 1850 he joined the staff of *The Athenaeum.* Later he was connected with Dickens' magazines, *Household Words* and *All the Year Round,* traveled for them and wrote several series of articles on his journeys. His most valuable work is his life of Turner, written under the direction of Ruskin. He wrote a few novels which were poorly done, really adaptations of French and German works. He was married in 1872 and had three sons. A nervous breakdown from overwork was a prelude to mental failure, and he died in Camberwell House Asylum at forty-seven.

PRINCIPAL WORKS: Lays and Legends: or, Ballads of the New World, 1851; Shakespeare's England, 1856; Life of J. M. W. Turner, 1861; Two Centuries of Song, 1867; A Tour Round England, 1870; Criss Cross Journeys, 1873.
ABOUT: Athenaeum June 17, 1876; Illustrated London News June 24, 1876.

THORNTON, WILLIAM THOMAS

(February 14, 1813-June 17, 1880), economist, was born in Buckinghamshire. His mother was a Greek. His father died when Thornton was a year old. He was educated in a Moravian settlement in Derbyshire, then spent three years at Malta with a cousin who was auditor-general there. From 1830 to 1835 he was in Constantinople, with the British consul-general. In 1836 he became a clerk in East India House, and in 1856 was put in charge of the public works department. In 1858 he became the first secretary for public works at the India Office. In 1873 he was made Commander of the Bath. His leisure was given to writing, economic questions being his usual subject. He was a close friend of John Stuart Mill and his disciple as an economist, but was opposed to Mill's utilitarian philosophy and rationalist religious views. Besides economic and ethical works, Thornton published some original verses and a literal verse translation of Horace, which is very bad, as he had no feeling for metrics or ear for beauty of language.

PRINCIPAL WORKS: Overpopulation and Its Remedy, 1845; On Labour, 1869; Old Fashioned Ethics and Common-Sense Metaphysics, 1873; Indian Public Works and Cognate Indian Topics, 1875.
ABOUT: Athenaeum June 26, 1880; Illustrated London News June 26, 1880.

TIGHE, MRS. MARY

(October 9, 1772-March 24, 1810), Irish poet, was born in Dublin, the daughter of the Reverend William Blachford and Theodosia (Tighe) Blachford.

Not long after Mary Blachford's birth her father died, and the girl received her education from her mother, who was unusually well educated for her time and her sex, and had taken active part in the Methodist movement in Ireland. Thus guided, the girl gained a knowledge of the Greek and Latin classics, and French, Italian, and German literature as well. She absorbed also the beauty of the scenery of the county of Wicklow, in which she took walks with her cousins, William and Henry Tighe. In 1793 she was married to Henry, a member of the Irish Parliament, representing Inistioge, Kilkenny.

Although her husband was described by a visitor as "the idol of his acquaintance" and as having "all the dignity and frankness of a Roman in his countenance and bearing," and at first the couple seem to have been happy, the marriage was not successful. To add to her troubles, Mrs. Tighe, about 1803 or 1804, fell a victim to consumption.

Before this she had completed (1795) and circulated among her intimates her poem *Psyche;* and the work was issued again in 1805. Its success with the public is said to have been such that Mrs. Tighe was enabled to build an addition to the orphan asylum in Wicklow, accordingly known as the "Psyche Ward." The author, however, was not allowed to enjoy her success for many years, for in 1810 she succumbed to her fatal disease at the home of her brother-in-law, William Tighe, at Woodstock, Kilkenny. Her married life had been spent for the most part

MRS. MARY TIGHE

in Rosanna, County Wicklow, and she was buried in the churchyard at Inistioge.

The records of Mrs. Tighe's life are too fragmentary to give much impression of a personality; she seems to have been beautiful and attractive. Aside from the general information that her marriage was not happy, there is no record of any quarrel or disagreement between husband and wife. With the development of her disease, however, Mrs. Tighe became afflicted by depression and decline in spirits.

Her chief poem, *Psyche,* is an allegory after the manner of Edmund Spenser's *The Faerie Queene,* and it employs the Spenserian stanza of that work. The source from which she obtained her allegory of Love and the Soul (the subject of the poem) was Apuleius' *The Golden Ass,* and she treated it in the slow, meandering style of Spenser, omitting, however, his archaisms. Her poem was praised highly in its day, and its author received tributes from Thomas Moore and Felicia Hemans. A study has been made which shows marked similarities between Mrs. Tighe's poetry (especially the vocabulary and imagery) and that of Keats, to whom one of her sonnets was, at one time, mistakenly, attributed. Whether or not Keats derived greatly from Mrs. Tighe (rather than from her model, Spenser), it is true that he admired her work. *Psyche* is a sufficient testimonial of her metrical skill and her poetic feeling. That Mrs. Tighe is so minor a figure is undoubtedly due to her early death and to the unusually great amount, in her own day and later, of poetry finer than hers. It was her fate to live in a time when England was rich in great poets; by comparison her work necessarily has suffered. R. W. W.

PRINCIPAL WORKS: *Poetry*—Psyche: or, The Legend of Love, 1795, 1805; Psyche and Other Poems, 1811.

ABOUT: Howitt, W. Homes and Haunts of the Most Eminent British Poets; Weller, E. V. (ed.). Keats and Mary Tighe; Quarterly Review 5:471 May 1811.

TOBIN, JOHN (January 28, 1770-December 8, 1804), dramatist, was born in Salisbury. His father, formerly a West Indian merchant, returned with his mother to the West Indies when the boy was five, leaving him behind. He was educated at the Bristol High School, and at seventeen was articled to a solicitor. In 1797 his employer died, and Tobin with three other clerks, took over the business. Dissension arose, and he joined another firm. From 1789 onwards all his leisure was given to the drama. He met with every delay and discouragement, many of his plays which afterwards were great successes being rejected regularly at the time they were written. *The Honey Moon,* his best known play, was the second to be performed, but the

fourteenth he wrote. Indeed, he was so disheartened that he had given up all thought of success and retired to Cornwall to edit Shakespeare when the happy news of its acceptance reached him. It was too late, however; he was far advanced in tuberculosis. On his physician's advice he set sail for the West Indies, but he died the second day out. The ship put back, and he was buried near Cork. He was not yet thirty-five when he died. He was unmarried.

Tobin's work is essentially imitative, but imitative of the best authors—chiefly Shakespeare. *The Honey Moon* remained a favorite on the stage for twenty years. His real forte was for light comedy, which he scorned. All his published work was posthumous.

PRINCIPAL WORKS: The Honey Moon, 1805; Curfew, 1807; The School for Authors, 1808; The Faro Table, 1816.

ABOUT: Benger, E. O. Memoirs of John Tobin.

TODHUNTER, JOHN (December 30, 1839-October 25, 1916), Irish poet and dramatist, was born in Dublin, the son of a Quaker merchant. He was educated at York School, a Quaker establishment, and then apprenticed to a firm of tea and sugar importers. However, in 1862 he was able to enter Trinity College, Dublin, where he studied medicine, receiving the degrees of M.D. and M.Ch. in 1867. At the same time his interest in literature is shown by his winning four prizes for English verses and a prose essay. He then studied in Vienna and Paris, and returned to practice medicine in Dublin. He soon abandoned his profession, being from 1870 to 1874 professor of English literature at Alexandra College, Dublin. After prolonged travel on the Continent and in Egypt, he settled in London in 1879. From 1886 his plays were performed frequently. Todhunter also translated Heine and wrote on the theory of aesthetics. He was a good amateur artist. He was twice married, in 1870 to Katharine Ball, and in 1879, after her death, to Dora Louise Bigby, by whom he had one son and two daughters.

Todhunter's plays (chiefly historical, and in blank verse) are all "closet dramas," better read than heard. He was a sort of minor Stephen Phillips who long outlived his time and now has few readers.

PRINCIPAL WORKS: Luerella and Other Poems, 1876; Alecestis, 1879; A Study of Shelley, 1880; Forest Songs and Other Poems, 1881; Helena in Troas, 1885; The Banshee and Other Poems, 1888; A Sicilian Idyll, 1890; The Black Cat, 1895; Three Irish Bardic Tales, 1896; Sounds and Sweet Airs, 1905.

ABOUT: London Times October 26, 1916.

TOOKE, THOMAS (February 29, 1774-February 26, 1858), economist, was unusual in both the time and place of his birth—he was born on Leap Day, in Kronstadt, Russia, where his father was chaplain of the British factory. He was reared and educated in Russia and at fifteen was put into a business house in St. Petersburg (Leningrad). The connections he formed there enabled him to go to England, where he became a partner in a London firm. The study of Ricardo, whose disciple he became, and his own business interest in the resumption of cash payments by the Bank of England, made him a writer on economics. Most of his work was an analysis of financial and commercial history. He was one of the founders, with Ricardo, James Mill, Malthus, and others, of the Political Economy Club, in 1821. In 1833 he was a member of the Factory Inquiry Commission. He retired from business in 1836, but subsequently served as governor of the Royal Exchange Assurance Corporation from 1840 to 1852. He had been married in 1802 to Priscilla Combe; they had three sons. He was made a Fellow of the Royal Society in 1821. The still existent Tooke chair of economic science and statistics at Kings College, London, was founded by public subscription in his memory.

PRINCIPAL WORKS: Considerations on the State of the Currency, 1826; The History of Prices, 1838-57; An Enquiry Into the Currency Principle, 1844.

ABOUT: Economist March 1858.

TORRENS, ROBERT (1780-May 27, 1864), Irish economist, began life as a marine officer. His exact place of birth in Ireland, his ancestry, and his education are unknown, but in 1797 he was first lieutenant of the Royal Marines. In 1806 he was promoted captain, and in 1811 major, in recognition of his services against Holland. He then became colonel of a Spanish legion in the Peninsula. Returning to the regular service, he was lieutenant-colonel in 1819 and colonel in 1837, having already been retired on half-pay in 1835. In the interludes of his service he had become a member of Parliament in 1826, but was unseated; he finally secured a seat in 1831 and held it until 1835. He was particularly interested in the colonization of South Australia and was chairman of the commission to establish provinces there. A lake and the river on which Adelaide is situated are named for him. At one time he was co-proprietor of The Traveller, and when this paper was amalgamated with The Globe he acted for a while as editor of the combined periodicals. He was an original member of the Political Economy Club, with James Mill, Malthus, Ricardo, and Tooke. He was married, his wife's maiden name having been Charity Chute; one of his sons became the first premier of South Australia.

Torrens was one of the first economists to base production of wealth on the joint action of land, labor, and capital, a theory which later became an economic axiom. In addition to his economic works he wrote two very bad novels.

PRINCIPAL WORKS: An Essay on the External Corn Trade, 1815; An Essay on the Production of Wealth, 1821; Letters on Commercial Policy, 1833; On Wages and Combinations, 1834; Self-Supporting Colonisation, 1847; Tracts on Finance and Trade, 1852.

ABOUT: Gentleman's Magazine 2:541 1840; 2:122, 385 1864.

TRAILL, CATHERINE PARR (January 9, 1802-August 29, 1899), Canadian novelist and writer on natural history, was born in London. Her maiden name was Strickland, her father being a Suffolk landowner. She was educated privately at home, and in 1832 married Lieutenant Thomas Traill. They emigrated at once to Ontario, then a wilderness. It was not until Mrs. Traill was fifty that she "arrived" as a writer—and indeed her slight previous output had been little more than a description of her new environment. She became deeply engrossed in the natural history of the region and made some valuable contributions to its literature. After her husband's death she continued to live in Canada, dying in Lakefield, Ontario, at the advanced age of ninety-seven.

PRINCIPAL WORKS: The Backwoods of Canada, 1835; The Canadian Crusoes (later called Lost in the Backwoods) 1852; The Female Emigrants' Guide, 1859; Rambles in the Canadian Forest, 1859; Studies in Plant Life in Canada, 1885.

ABOUT: Baker, R. P. A History of English-Canadian Literature to the Confederation; MacMurchy, A. Handbook of Canadian Literature.

TRAILL, HENRY DUFF (August 14, 1842-February 24, 1900), poet and miscellaneous writer, was born in Blackheath of an old Orkney family. His father was a police magistrate. He was educated at the Merchant Taylors' School, where he was head boy, and at St. John's College, Oxford, receiving his B.A. in 1865, B.C.L. 1868, D.C.L. 1873. At first intended for medicine, he changed to the law, and was called to the bar from the Inner Temple in 1869. In 1871 he was inspector of returns in the Education Office. He soon, however, turned to journalism as a career, and in 1873 was on the staff of the Pall Mall Gazette. In 1880 he went to the St. James's Gazette, in 1882 to the Daily Telegraph. Although he left this paper in 1889, to edit The Observer until 1891, he continued to write for it regularly until 1897. At the same time he was a regular contributor of articles, mostly literary in nature, to the Saturday Review. From 1897 to his death he was the first editor of Literature.

A prolific journalist, Traill also found time for much publication in book form. From 1893 to 1897 he was editor of a six-volume series called Social England. Sociological and historical writing, however, were not his forte; he had not sufficient learning for them. He is at his best as a critic and a literary biographer, as evidenced in his short lives of Sterne, Coleridge, and other authors, and particularly in his essays. He also wrote several plays, the best known being *The Medicine Man* (with Robert Hichens), which was performed by Sir Henry Irving in 1898. Most of his verse was humorous; he was a remarkable parodist. His prose style is easy and fluent. He was primarily a journalist, but an excellent one.

Traill died unmarried at fifty-seven, of a sudden heart attack.

PRINCIPAL WORKS: Recaptured Rhymes, 1882; The New Lucian, 1884; Saturday Songs, 1890; Life of Sir John Franklin, 1896; The New Fiction, 1897.

ABOUT: Literature March 3, 1900; Observer February 25, 1900.

TRAIN, JOSEPH (November 6, 1779-December 1, 1852), Scottish antiquary, was born in Ayrshire. His father, once a land steward, later became a day laborer. With very little schooling, the boy was apprenticed to a weaver in Ayr at an early age, but he was already interested in Scottish history and antiquities and used all his leisure in study. From 1799 to 1802 he served in the Ayrshire militia; a lucky chance for him, since his colonel became interested in a private soldier who subscribed for Burns' poems, and on the expiration of his enlistment secured him a position as a manufacturer's agent in Glasgow. In 1806, through the same influence, he was appointed a supernumerary excise officer. The next year he was regularly appointed, in 1820 was made a supervisor, and retired in 1836.

Train became acquainted with Sir Walter Scott about 1812, and from 1814 until Scott's death in 1832 gave up personal authorship to supply the novelist with antiquarian data for the Waverley series. He also supplied factual material to other authors dealing with the Scottish scene. In 1829 he was made a member of the Society of Antiquaries of Scotland. He was married and had five children; his wife's maiden name was Mary Wilson.

Train fancied himself as a poet, but his two volumes of verse do not justify the assumption. His real service to literature was the supplying of plots, historical facts, and antiquarian details to Scott.

PRINCIPAL WORKS: Poetical Reveries, 1806; Strains of the Mountain Muse, 1814; Historical and Statistical Account of the Isle of Man, 1845.

ABOUT: Patterson, J. Memoir of Joseph Train.

TRELAWNY, EDWARD JOHN (November 13, 1792-August 13, 1881), biographer, was the second son of a lieutenant colonel in the army and member of Parliament, and grandson of a British general in the American Revolution; on both sides he came of old Cornish families. His father was a brutal

tyrant, his home life unspeakably oppressive. From 1801 to 1803 he was sent to a school where he received more beatings than instruction; all his life his spelling and grammar were highly dubious. At thirteen he entered the Royal Navy as a midshipman. Within a year he had served on three ships, just missed the battle of Trafalgar, and attended Dr. Burney's Naval Academy at Greenwich.

In 1806 he deserted his ship at Bombay, and for six years was a privateer in the Pacific and Indian Oceans. He returned to England about the end of 1812.

There are gaps all through Trelawny's life, and the following period is one of them. All that is known certainly of his movements is that he was in Switzerland by 1820. There he met Thomas Medwin, Shelley's cousin, and Edward Williams, Shelley's friend, and first heard of the poet. He resolved to go to Italy to meet him, but was first called back to Cornwall by his father's death. Then in 1821 he went to Pisa, where he first became acquainted with Shelley and his wife.

Until Shelley was drowned with Williams in July 1822, Trelawny was constantly with him. Shelley became the object of his lifelong devotion and the mainspring of his future existence. His relations with Byron were not so happy, though they remained closely associated until Byron's death in Greece in 1824. Trelawny arranged the cremation of Shelley's and Williams' bodies on the shore at Viareggio, and himself snatched Shelley's unconsumed heart from the flames (an action often erroneously attributed to Leigh Hunt). The scar of the burn remained with him to prove it.

In 1823 Trelawny went with Byron to Greece, but parted from him at Cephalonia and attached himself to the Greek chieftain Odysseus Androutsos. The Greeks were fighting not only the Turks, but one another, and the faction to which Odysseus belonged proved to be the losing one. When Byron died, Trelawny went to Missilonghi to see his body, then returned to Odysseus and for a year lived besieged in a cave on the slopes of Mount Parnassus. There two Englishmen in the pay of the other Greek faction attempted to assassinate him; he was severely wounded and one bullet remained in his body till his death nearly sixty years later.

Most of the time until 1827 appears to have been spent by Trelawny at Zante, engaged in convalescence and a long law-suit. In the latter year he visited England briefly, then went on to Paris and Florence, where he lived till 1830. Under the guidance of Walter Savage Landor and Keats' friend, Charles Armitage Brown, he was occupied in writing the memoirs of his privateering life. In 1830 he sent the manuscript to Shelley's widow and she arranged for its publication, which oc-

E. J. TRELAWNY

curred the next year. A year later he himself returned to England, only to set sail for the United States, where he remained from 1833 to 1835, journeying all over its then territory, buying a slave in South Carolina (where he seems to have had a plantation for a while) in order to free him, and swimming the Niagara above the rapids.

For the next two years Trelawny was in London. For a short period he allowed himself to be lionized, but society disgusted and wearied him, and he could not endure it long. This period marks also the rupture of his long friendship with Mary Shelley, whom he had so greatly assisted after her husband's death, and to whom he had even half-heartedly proposed marriage in 1831. There were faults on both sides, and the cause of the break seems to have been chiefly utter incompatibility of temperament and viewpoint.

From 1837 to 1839, Trelawny was first in Cornwall, then in Putney with his friend G. Temple-Leader. Another gap in the narrative clouds the period until 1847, when he bought a farm in Wales, at Usk, Monmouthshire, where he lived for nine years. This was the duration of his fourth marriage, and marked also the writing and publication of his *Recollections of the Last Days of Shelley and Byron*. Eleven more lost years follow, until his last period finds him, in 1869, at Sompting, near Worthing (with a London home also).

His mind reverted more and more to Shelley, the idol of his youth, and he occupied himself in rewriting the *Recollections* under a new title. He died, still hale and intellectually keen, at 1881, and his faithful attendant, Emma Taylor, at his request took his body to Gotha, the nearest point where cremation could then be effected, and then buried his ashes in the grave he had bought beside Shelley's, in the English Protestant Cemetery at Rome, in 1822.

Trelawny's marital career was very complicated. In his early days in the East Indies he was married to a young Arab girl named Zela, who died. In 1813 he married Julia Addison in England, and had one daughter by her. The exact ending of this marriage is unknown, but by 1820 he was somehow free of it. In 1824, in Greece, he married Tersitza Kamenou, half-sister of Odysseus; they had two daughters, one of whom died, the other living with her father throughout parts of her childhood and youth. This marriage was ended by divorce. In 1847 he eloped with Lady Vane Goring, an unhappily married woman, and married her after her previous bonds were dissolved by special Act of Parliament. They had two sons and two daughters. In 1858 she left him when—at the age of sixty-six—he brought a mistress into their home. Until this occurred, his last marriage was happy; his wife was a highly intelligent woman who was of great help in the writing of his revised book.

Trelawny was of the great line of English eccentrics. He was of herculean stature, with a powerful voice, bright blue eyes, thick dark hair, and aquiline features. He was a born romantic, a bit of a poseur, peremptory and hot-tempered, entirely alien from conventionality of any sort; but high-minded, generous and the most loyal of Shelley's worshipers. He was all his life a rebel, an atheist and a republican, with no hardening of the mental or emotional arteries with age. His daily life was extremely abstemious; he lived mostly on fruit and bread, and never wore underclothing. From Byron on, he has been accused of untruthfulness, but the charge is baseless; he romanticized his memories, and gave voice to his prejudices, but in the main his story has fidelity to fact. His genuine talent never came to fruition, but the simplicity and freshness of his style created, as it were, two involuntary masterpieces. As H. J. Massingham well puts it: "Trelawny's contribution to the Romantic Revival is Trelawny."

M. A. deF.

PRINCIPAL WORKS: The Adventures of a Younger Son (anon.) 1831; Recollections of the Last Days of Shelley and Byron, 1858 (enlarged, as Recollections of Shelley, Byron, and the Author, 1878).

ABOUT: Edgcumbe, R. J. F. Edward Trelawny: A Biographical Sketch; Marshall, Mrs. J. Life and Letters of Mary W. Shelley; Massingham, H. J. The Friend of Shelley; Rossetti, W. M. Some Reminiscences; Sheehan, H. B. The Book of Gallant Vagabonds; Trelawny, E. J. Adventures of a Younger Son; Trelawny, E. J. Recollections of Shelley, Byron, and the Author; Winwar, F. The Romantic Rebels; Illustrated London News 79:257 September 10, 1881; Scribner's Magazine 21: 504 April 1907.

TRENCH, MELESINA (March 22, 1768-May 27, 1827), Irish miscellaneous writer, was born in Dublin. Her maiden name was Chenevix, the family being of Huguenot descent. She was left an orphan in early childhood, and was reared first by her paternal grandfather, the Bishop of Waterford, and after his death in 1779 by her maternal grandfather, Archdeacon Gervais. Her real education she gained in the latter's well-stocked library. The girl grew up to be a celebrated beauty. In 1786 she married Col. Richard St. George; he died two years later, leaving her with an infant son. Mrs. St. George spent most of her time until 1807, first in Germany, then in France. In both countries she met notables from all over Europe, and her journals (and the correspondence which later supplanted the journals) are of historical importance and are her chief passport to celebrity. In 1803 she married Richard Trench; though he was six years her junior, the marriage was markedly happy. They had three sons who survived childhood, two of whom became noted divines and authors. Early in this marriage, Trench, a barrister, was imprisoned in France by Napoleon; it was not until 1807 that the couple, with their first child, were able to escape. They went to Dublin, which was their home thereafter. Mrs. Trench continued to write, though neither her novels, her verse, nor her essays have the literary value of her unpremeditated letters and journal entries.

PRINCIPAL WORKS: Campaspe: An Historical Tale, 1815; Thoughts of a Parent on Education, 1837; Remains (ed. by R. C. Trench) 1862.

ABOUT: Trench, R. C. (ed.). The Remains of the Late Mrs. Richard Trench: Being Selections From Her Journals, Letters, and Other Papers.

TRENCH, RICHARD CHENEVIX (September 5, 1807-March 28, 1886), Irish poet, theologian, and philologist, was born in Dublin. His father was a barrister, his mother, Melesina Trench, was a writer, and his older brother also became an essayist. He was educated at Twyford School, Harrow, and Trinity College, Cambridge, receiving his B.A. in 1829, his M.A. in 1833, his B.D. in 1850. While at the university he edited and printed a little magazine called The Translator, and first became interested in Spanish literature. A period of ill health and melancholy followed his graduation. During this time he found consolation in the writing of poetry and in travel, chiefly in his beloved Spain. In 1832 he was ordained deacon, and in the same year he married his first cousin, Frances Mary Trench. They had six sons and five daughters.

The next year Trench served as curate in Hadleigh, Suffolk, then at Colchester. He was a high churchman by conviction, though a close friend of the liberal F. D. Maurice.

His health failed once more and he went to Italy; on his return, in 1835, he was ordained priest, and until 1841 served as perpetual curate of Curdridge, Hampshire. He then became curate to the celebrated Samuel (later Bishop) Wilberforce, at Alverstroke. In 1844 he was rector of Itchenstoke. In 1845 and 1846 he was Hulsean lecturer at Cambridge. From 1846 to 1858 he was professor of divinity at King's College, Dublin; after 1854 this chair was called the professorship of exegesis of the New Testament. In 1856 he became dean of Westminster, and in 1863 archbishop of Dublin. A fall on board ship in 1875 broke both his knee-caps, and he never really recovered from the shock; he was finally obliged to resign in 1884, dying in London two years later.

Trench's theological writings are no longer of interest. Though he wrote relatively little verse, he was a real poet, his sonnets and lyrics being especially fine and noble. He is best known as a philologist, his work constituting a pioneer effort in the scientific study of language. It was he who originally suggested the creation of the great Oxford Dictionary.

PRINCIPAL WORKS: The Story of Justin Martyr and Other Poems, 1835; Notes on the Parables, 1841; Poems From Eastern Sources, 1842; Notes on the Miracles, 1846; The Study of Words, 1851; English, Past and Present, 1855; Alma and Other Poems, 1865.

ABOUT: Trench, M. Letters and Memorials of Archbishop Trench.

TREVELYAN, SIR GEORGE OTTO (July 20, 1838-August 17, 1928), historian and biographer, was born in Leicestershire. His father, the first baronet, was later Governor of Madras, and Trevelyan spent part of his youth in India. His maternal uncle was the celebrated historian, poet, and essayist, Thomas Babington Macaulay.

Trevelyan was educated at Harrow and Trinity College, Cambridge. He was a brilliant student—rather too brilliant, for his light satiric poetry written while he was at the university offended the authorities, and lost him a fellowship in Trinity which would otherwise have been his.

He was first elected to Parliament in 1865, and from then until 1897, with the exception of a few years when he resigned from office because of disagreement with governmental policy, he was constantly in public life. He has been called "a first-rate writer who preferred to be a second- or third-rate statesman." A Whig of the old-fashioned, high-minded type, rigid in his ideals and unchangeable in his liberalism, he was closely associated with Gladstone and several times in his cabinets; but when he disapproved of Gladstone's attitude on public questions (notably in regard to Ireland) he promptly resigned the office he held. It is strange that Trevelyan, who is one of the most entertaining of writers and known as a witty conversationalist, should have been a noted bore in Parliament; his very insistence on accuracy and thoroughness made him long-winded and dull.

Although he was never in the first rank of statesmen, Trevelyan held numerous minor offices. He was Civil Lord of the Admiralty in 1868, Secretary of the Admiralty in 1880, Chief Secretary for Ireland (a troublesome and thankless post) in 1882, Chancellor of the Duchy of Lancaster in 1884, and Secretary for Scotland in 1886; after a few months he resigned, but was reappointed in 1892 when Gladstone was again prime minister. He succeeded to the baronetcy on his father's death in 1886. In 1897 he retired from Parliament and devoted the remainder of his long life to writing. He was a very wealthy man, owning three or four large mansions and 14,000 acres of land.

In 1869 Trevelyan married Caroline Phillips, by whom he had three sons. One of these, George Macaulay Trevelyan (born 1876), also became a biographer and historian, writing the only biography of his father.

Trevelyan was one of the original members of the Order of Merit, one of the highest honors in the gift of the British crown. He lived to the great age of ninety, dying finally from the infirmities of his many years. He had done little writing after 1914.

As both biographer and historian, Trevelyan is a splendid writer—vivid, graphic, racy, and mellow, with a strong dash of satire. His biography of his uncle, Macaulay, is among the really great, in a class with Boswell on Johnson and Lockhart on Scott. His history

of the American Revolution grew naturally out of his studies in the life of Charles James Fox, and both interests derived from his own position as a Whig and a liberal. Trevelyan, an Englishman, succeeded in writing the classic history of the momentous revolt of the American colonies. It is highly favorable to the American side—too much so, most English critics felt—and is in reality a brilliant study of the growth of civil liberty, with the birth of the United States of America serving as an object lesson. His early satires—*The Ladies in Parliament* and *Horace at the University of Athens* (later revised and incorporated into *Interludes in Prose and Verse*), which lost him his fellowship, are sparkling and acute; and his two books on Indian subjects among the best of their period. It is unfortunate that, with his great talents, he did not devote all his best years to literature instead of to politics.

M. A. deF.

PRINCIPAL WORKS: The Letters of a Competition Wallah, 1864; Cawnpore, 1865; Life and Letters of Lord Macaulay, 1876; Early History of Charles James Fox, 1880; Interludes in Prose and Verse, 1905; The American Revolution, 1909; George III and Charles Fox, 1912 and 1914.

ABOUT: Trevelyan, G. M. Sir George Otto Trevelyan: A Memoir; London Mercury 18:452 September 1928; Nation and Athenaeum 43:665 August 25, 1928; Outlook 149:699 August 29, 1928; Spectator 141:231 August 25, 1928.

TROLLOPE, ANTHONY (April 24, 1815-December 6, 1882), novelist, was the fourth son of Thomas Anthony Trollope, a barrister, and Frances (Milton) Trollope. Born at 6 Keppel Street, Bloomsbury, London, the infant was taken at the age of one year, to a house called Julians, near Harrow. The father was gloomy, ill-tempered, and improvident: his law practice gradually fell away; an expected inheritance was cut off; and the family fortunes sank lower and lower each year. In 1822 Anthony became a day-boy at Harrow School; in 1825 he was transferred to Arthur Drury's private school at Sunbury; and in 1827 he went to his father's old school, Winchester. Finally, in the spring of 1830, he went back to Harrow. Attempts at University scholarships were abortive. He was a large, awkward, uncouth boy, ill-clad and often dirty, and felt an unhappy outcast among the young aristocrats and plutocrats he met at these famous schools. At the end of 1827 his mother had gone to America with the bluestocking Frances Wright and the French painter Auguste Hervieu. Among the wildcat projects afoot at this time was the setting up of a bazaar in Cincinnati for the sale of English goods. The bazaar (a horrible architectural monstrosity) was actually built, but the enterprise failed dismally and precipitated the final ruin of the family. Sold up in April 1834, the Trollopes went to Bruges, and were now supported by the novel-writing of Fran-

SIR GEORGE OTTO TREVELYAN

ces, who had commenced authorship in 1832, with *Domestic Manners of the Americans.* Thomas Anthony Trollope died at the end of 1835.

In the summer of 1834 Anthony became an usher in a school at Brussels, hoping to learn enough French and German to enable him to take up a promised commission in an Austrian cavalry regiment. But in the autumn, by influence, he became a junior clerk in the General Post Office, London. He had seven lonely years of dingy poverty in London, making few friends and earning a reputation for insubordination, until his transfer in 1841 to Banagher, Ireland, as a deputy postal surveyor, put him financially at ease and introduced him to a larger, freer, outdoor life. His awkwardness disappeared; he took up the sport of fox-hunting (which he followed enthusiastically until 1878); and in June 1844 he married Rose Heseltine, daughter of a Rotherham bank-manager.

Trollope set himself to discover the real reasons for Irish discontent. In the autumn of 1843 he began work on his first novel, *The Macdermots of Ballycloran* (published 1847). This book and *The Kellys and the O'Kellys* (1848) were of a political cast, and are to be regarded as 'prentice work. After promotion in the Post Office and transfer to Mallow in 1845, Trollope was sent in the spring of 1851 to the west of England on a postal mission. Here in July 1852, he began *The Warden* (1855), in which he first found his *métier* as the delineator of clerical life in cathedral towns. He was in Belfast for a year from the autumn of 1853; then in Donnybrook, near Dublin. Further postal missions, to Egypt, Scotland, and the West Indies, followed in 1858-59; and in December of the latter year he settled at Waltham Cross, some twelve miles from London, as surveyor general in the Post Office at £800 a year.

He was now writing persistently. A comedy, *The Noble Jilt* (written in 1850), was set aside on the advice of an actor friend; but no less than ten new books were written or writing by the time he came to Waltham Cross. *Barchester Towers* (May 1857) showed him at the height of his powers, as the minute chronicler of events and ecclesiastical politics in the imaginary cathedral-city (founded on Winchester) and in the wider county area of Barset (Somerset) round about. The bishop's wife, Mrs. Proudie, one of the immortals of English fiction, the slimy Mr. Slope, showed him as a percipient and skilful master of characterization, and the whole scene and atmosphere of normal English mid-Victorian life in country towns was set out. *Framley Parsonage* which began serialization in the new *Cornhill Magazine* (edited by Thack-

ANTHONY TROLLOPE

eray) on January 1, 1860, consolidated his reputation and definitely made his name.

In October 1860, while visiting his mother's home in Florence, Trollope met the young American, Kate Field, who became one of his closest friends, and to whom he wrote a series of delightful letters which show the gentler and more playful side of his nature. The next year he was in Boston with his wife, on a postal mission, and the two met Miss Field. In 1861, too, he was elected to the Garrick Club, which became a favorite place of resort. He was now prosperous, famous, and sought after by publishers and literary people. His friends included such figures as R. Monckton Milnes, W. E. Forster, George Eliot, and G. H. Lewes. He had business dealings with George Smith, founder of the *Dictionary of National Biography* and partner in Smith, Elder (for whom he wrote, in 1865, some hunting sketches in the new *Pall Mall Gazette*), and with Norman Macleod, editor of that somewhat sanctimonious magazine, *Good Words*, who had to pay him £500 for breach of contract over *Rachel Ray*, which Macleod found suspect for Evangelical readers. In 1865 he sank £1,250 in the *Fortnightly Review* edited by G. H. Lewes, which went bankrupt and was bought out by Chapman and Hall. In 1866 he projected a history of English prose fiction, but abandoned it owing to the colossal labor involved. The same year occurred his first connection with *Blackwood's Magazine* in which *Nina Balatka* was serialized anonymously; and in the year following he published *The Last Chronicle of Barset*, in which he took leave of the famous imaginary county. An excursion into editorship—of *St. Paul's Magazine*—from October 1867, was soon given up, since Trollope felt unfitted for the duties. He had resigned from the Post Office in September 1867, partly from pique at the promotion of a subordinate and partly from pressure of work. From March to July 1868 he was again in the U.S.A. on postal and copyright missions; and in the autumn he stood unsuccessfully for Parliament in the Liberal interest. The novels *Phineas Finn* and *He Knew He Was Right* (both 1869) saw him at his commercial apogee; but neither repaid its cost, and he was compelled thenceforward to accept lower figures.

In May 1871 Trollope gave up Waltham House, and went on a long visit to a son in Australia. At sea as elsewhere he wrote indefatigably; on this occasion completing *Lady Anna* on the voyage out and *Australia and New Zealand* on the return journey, which he made via New Zealand and the United States. Back in England just before Christmas 1872, he settled at 39 Montagu Square, Bloomsbury, London. Here he worked, as was his habit, to a regular and rigorous schedule, assisted by his niece, Florence Bland, as secretary. Rising at 5:30, he would write till 11; then, after breakfast, he would ride or drive. Between tea and dinner a favorite diversion was whist at the Garrick Club; and at night he would dine out or entertain some of his many friends at home. This routine was interrupted (though he never stopped writing) by journeys to Ceylon and Australia (1875), to South Africa (1877), and to Iceland (1878). The *Autobiography*— a model of clear-headed modesty and frankness—was written between October 1875 and April 1876, but not published until after his death.

Advancing age brought asthma with it, and even a suspicion of angina pectoris. So, in July 1880, for the benefit of better air, Trollope moved to Harting Grange, near Petersfield, Hampshire. Three more novels were written in 1881; in May 1882, moved by the Phoenix Park murders, he went to Ireland to collect material for *The Landleaguers*. In September he left Harting and took quarters at Garland's Hotel, Suffolk Street, Pall Mall, London. Here, on November 3, while laughing at a family reading of F. Anstey's *Vice Versa*, he was struck down by a paralytic stroke; and on December 6, at a house in Welbeck Street, he died. His wife and two sons survived him.

Outwardly Trollope was a loud, heavy, booming man, partaking of the nature of British hunting squirearchy. Yet he had a reserve of sensitiveness inherited from his boyhood; he was often unacceptable to colleagues and superiors, but generosity and innate modesty made him beloved by the humble. "In personal appearance," writes Michael Sadleir, "Trollope was fresh-coloured, upright, and sturdy. Although not quite six feet in height, his broad shoulders, fine head and vigorous power of gesture gave an impression of size beyond his actual inches. Everyone who met him remarked on the extraordinary brilliance of his black eyes, which, behind the strong lenses of his spectacles, shone (as one memorist records) 'with a certain genial fury of inspection'. . . . His voice was bass and resonant. . . . His laugh was, at its healthiest, a bellow. For so large a man, he was easy of movement and could sit a horse, if not with elegance at least with monumental certainty. He was a strong walker, a good eater, a connoisseur of wine, and an insatiable disputant. . . . Extreme short sight was, indeed, his only disability." A good description (dating from 1879) and assessment of character, too long to quote here, are given by Julian, son of Nathaniel Hawthorne, in his *Confessions and Criticisms* (Boston, 1887).

After his death Trollope's literary reputation sank low, and he was regarded as something of a journeyman of letters. This arose partly from the revelation in his *Autobiography* that he treated literature as a trade and wrote by the clock. No author has been more methodical. He worked out schemes, set himself time-schedules, and rigidly adhered to them. In our own day, under the enthusiastic sponsorship of men like Michael Sadleir and Hugh Walpole, there is some small danger of praise outrunning discrimination. Trollope is, in fact, supreme in his own field, but it is a narrow field—the ordinary life of upper middle-class England (and especially clerical England) of his time. Though there is a good deal of implied satire on worldly, place-hunting clerics, there is none of the burning social indignation of a Dickens, and in humor, too, he is inferior to this master. Aphoristically, he might be described as the chronicler *par excellence* of storms in teacups. His characterization is finished but unsubtle. Mr. Sadleir speaks truly of "this queer sense of the absorbing interest of normal occupations." Trollope was not an agnostic, and was only an anti-clerical when clerics bowed to Mammon. What he attempted he did well; and his best creations are sure of immortality. A final judgment is given by Hawthorne in a letter of February 11, 1860 to his publisher Fields: "Have you ever read the novels of Anthony Trollope? They precisely suit my taste; solid, substantial, written on strength of beef and through inspiration of ale, and just as real as if some giant had hewn a great lump out of the earth and put it under a glass case, with all its inhabitants going about their daily business, and not suspecting that they were made a show of." H. B. G.

PRINCIPAL WORKS: *Novels and Short Stories*— The Macdermots of Ballycloran, 1847; The Kellys and the O'Kellys, 1848; La Vendée, 1850; The Warden, 1855; Barchester Towers, 1857; The Three Clerks, 1858; Doctor Thorne, 1858; The Bertrams, 1859; Castle Richmond, 1860; Tales of All Countries, 1861; Framley Parsonage, 1861; Orley Farm, 1862; The Struggles of Brown, Jones, and Robinson, 1862; Rachel Ray, 1863; The Small House at Allington, 1864; Can You Forgive Her? 1864; Miss MacKenzie, 1865; The Belton Estate, 1866; Nina Balatka, 1867; The Last Chronicle of Barset, 1867; The Claverings, 1867; Lotta Schmidt and Other Stories, 1867; Linda Tressel, 1868; Phineas Finn, 1869; He Knew He Was Right, 1869; The Vicar of Bullhampton, 1870; An Editor's Tales, 1870; Sir Harry Hotspur of Humblethwaite, 1871; Ralph the Heir, 1871; The Golden Lion of Granpere, 1872; The Eustace Diamonds, 1873; Phineas Redux, 1874; Lady Anna, 1873; Harry Heathcote of Gangoil, 1874; The Way We Live Now, 1875; The Prime Minister, 1876; The American Senator, 1877; Christmas at Thompson Hall, 1877; Is He Popenjoy? 1878; The Lady of Launay, 1878; An Eye for an Eye, 1879; John Caldigate, 1879; Cousin Henry, 1879; The Duke's Children, 1880; Dr. Wortle's School, 1881; Ayala's Angel, 1881; Why Frau Frohmann Raised Her Prices and Other Stories, 1882; The Fixed Period, 1882; Marion Fay, 1882; Kept in the Dark, 1882; Mr. Scarborough's Family, 1883; The Landleaguers, 1883; An Old Man's Love, 1883. *Works of Travel*—The West Indies and the Spanish Main, 1859; North America, 1862; Travelling Sketches, 1866; Australia and New Zealand, 1873; How the "Mastiffs" Went to Iceland, 1878; South Africa, 1878; *Miscellaneous*—Hunting Sketches, 1865; British Sports and Pastimes (ed.) 1868; Did He Steal It? 1869; The Commentaries of Caesar, 1870; Thackeray, 1879; The Life of Cicero, 1880; English Political Leaders: Lord Palmerston, 1882; An Autobiography, 1883; The Noble Jilt, 1923.

ABOUT: Bryce, J. Studies in Contemporary Biography; Cecil, D. Early Victorian Novelists; Cooper, T. Men of Mark (Vol. 3); Escott, T. H. S. Anthony Trollope: His Work, Associates, and Literary Originals; Friswell, J. H. Modern Men of Letters; Harrison, F. Studies in Early Victorian Literature; Hawthorne, J. Confessions and Criticisms; Heywood, J. C. How They Strike Me; Irwin, M. L. Anthony Trollope: A Bibliography; James, H. Partial Portraits; Koets, C. C. Female Characters in the Works of Anthony Trollope; MacCarthy, D. Portraits; More, P. E. The Demon of the Absolute; Nichols, S. van B. The Significance of Anthony Trollope; Quiller-Couch, A. T. Charles Dickens and Other Victorians; Raleigh, W. A. Letters; Sadleir, M. Trollope: A Commentary; and Trollope: A Bibliography; Saintsbury, G. Corrected Impressions; Sichel, W. The Sands of Time; Stephen, L. Studies of a Biographer; Street, G. S. A Book of Essays; Trollope, A. An Autobiography.

TROLLOPE, FRANCES (March 10, 1780-October 6, 1863), novelist and essayist, was born near Bristol, her maiden name being Milton, and her father being a clergyman. Her mother died early and her father remarried. Soon after this the girl, who had been educated privately at home, went to London to keep house for her brother, who was in the War Office. In 1809 she married Thomas Anthony Trollope.

Trollope was an indefatigable worker, a man of rather brilliant mind, but one of the world's foreordained failures. He failed as a lawyer, as a farmer at Harrow Weald, as an American merchant, and finally he left behind him a huge unfinished church history over which he was laboring without either adequate training or proper historical material. In 1827 the famous feminist and reformer, Frances Wright, suggested his emigrating to America. With his wife and children, he went to Cincinnati, and it was not until 1830 that he confessed himself beaten and returned to England. From this experience grew his wife's authorship. If she and her children were to live, she must support them. Her first book was her highly censorious report on American manners, which caused a furore in the sensitive United States of the early nineteenth century. Mrs. Trollope was thus over fifty when she began authorship, an almost unprecedented situation for one who became immensely popular and rich through her writings thereafter.

For several years she wrote travel books, traveling to write and writing to travel. After her husband's death she settled in Florence with her oldest son, and their house, the Villino Trollope, became a literary salon and a center for sympathizers with the Italian Revolution. This, however, was the doing of her daughter-in-law; she herself was too busy writing. She was an enormously prolific writer, and most of her immense output is pure hack work. However, she did have ability in a strange field for a Victorian lady—she was an excellent depictor of vulgar life, and had a rich vein of broad, coarse humor. She was a strong partisan and not much of an intellectual, but her best work, winnowed from mountains of chaff, is very good indeed. Two of her sons and one daughter became writers, the best known being her son Anthony. (Two other sons and a daughter died early.) She died in Florence at eighty-three.

PRINCIPAL WORKS: Domestic Manners of the Americans, 1831; The Vicar of Wrexhill, 1837; The Widow Barnaby, 1838; The Lottery of Marriage, 1846; The Life and Adventures of a Clever Woman, 1854.

ABOUT: Trollope, F. E. Frances Trollope: Her Life and Literary Work; Atlantic Monthly December 1864.

TROLLOPE, THOMAS ADOLPHUS (April 29, 1810-November 11, 1892), novelist and historian, was the eldest son of Frances Trollope, the novelist, and hence the older brother of Anthony Trollope. A sister also wrote poems and essays. Thomas was educated at Harrow and Winchester, always on the shabby edge of gentility. Already he was writing magazine articles, edited by his mother, to help make his expenses. In 1827 he went with his father and mother to New York and Cincinnati, remaining in America until 1830. On his return he entered Magdalen College, Oxford, receiving his B.A. degree in 1835. He then became a master at

King Edward's School, Birmingham, until 1839. By this time his father was dead and his mother was making money and reputation by her novels. He traveled with her, and decided to become a professional journalist. He was one of the earliest contributors to Dickens' *Household Words*. From 1843 he lived in Florence with his mother, and became deeply interested in the Italian Revolution. In 1873 he moved to Rome, as correspondent of the London *Standard*. It 1890 he returned to England permanently, settling in Devonshire.

Trollope was married twice, and both his wives were writers and extremely interesting women in their own right. His first wife, Theodosia Garrow, who was half-Jewish, was married to him in 1848. She was a linguist, a translator, and a charming essayist, and she made their Florence home, Villino Trollope, a true salon and a center of Italian and expatriate English literary life. She died in 1865, leaving one daughter.

The next year Trollope married Frances Eleanor Ternan, who survived him. She was a prolific novelist of a rather sentimental and saccharine sort. She wrote one book with her husband, and was the biographer of her mother-in-law more than thirty years after the latter's death. She too made their home, this time in Rome, a literary salon. Her books include *Aunt Margaret's Trouble*, 1866; *The Sacristan's Household*, 1869; *Homes and Haunts of the Italian Poets* (with her husband), 1881; and *That Unfortunate Marriage*, 1888.

Thomas Adolphus Trollope never attained the eminence of his famous brother or the popularity of his mother. He was afflicted with a terrible diffuseness, pouring out torrents of words as he wrote methodically at set hours every day. His novels, which he thought his best work, are uniformly dull; his essays, though ephemeral, are lively. He supplied several plots both to his mother and to his brother.

PRINCIPAL WORKS: A Decade of Italian Women, 1859; Filippo Strozzi, 1860; Marietta, 1862; Beppo the Conscript, 1864; The Papal Conclaves, 1876; What I Remember, 1887.

ABOUT: Trollope, T. A. What I Remember; The Further Reminiscences of Thomas Adolphus Trollope; Athenaeum November 19, 1892.

TUCKER, CHARLOTTE MARIA

TUCKER, CHARLOTTE MARIA (May 8, 1821-December 2, 1893), juvenile writer, was born in Barnet. Her father was an authority on Indian finance, her mother, Scottish by birth, a near relative of James Boswell, Dr. Johnson's biographer. The family moved to London when she was a year old, and she was educated at home, writing verses and plays from childhood. Her father died in 1851; he had not approved of her publishing her writings and she had made no attempt to do so before his death. From that time on she wrote books for children at the rate of at least one a year, giving all the proceeds to charity. All her work was written under the pseudonym "A.L.O.E.," meaning "A Lady of England."

In 1869 her mother died, and she went to live with her brother. She determined though nearly fifty, to become a missionary; she studied Hindustani and in 1875 went to Amritsar, India. In 1876 she moved to Lahore, where she wrote numerous tracts in the form of parables, and visited the zenanas to bring the Gospel to the secluded Indian women. She was very ill in 1885, and never recovered, though it was seven years before she died, at Amritsar. By her request, she was buried without a coffin, at a cost of five rupees.

Counting her missionary tracts, Miss Tucker wrote 142 books. All her stories for children are highly didactic and pious allegories, with a very obvious moral. She did, however, have some gift for presenting natural history in a simple and pleasant manner.

PRINCIPAL WORKS: The Rambles of a Rat, 1854; Wings and Stings, 1855; Old Friends With New Faces, 1858.

ABOUT: Gilmore, A. A Lady of England: The Life and Letters of Charlotte Maria Tucker.

TULLOCH, JOHN

TULLOCH, JOHN (June 1, 1823-February 13, 1886), Scottish theological writer, was born in Perthshire, his father being a parish minister. For some reason he was boarded out, away from his family, until he was six. He was educated at the Perth Grammar School, Madras College, and St. Andrews University, where he was a bursar and also earned part of his living by teaching. He then studied divinity at St. Mary's College, St. Andrews, and in Edinburgh, and was licensed to preach in 1844. In 1845 he was a minister in Dundee; the same year he married Jane Anne Hindmarsh, the marriage resulting in a large family.

In 1847 Tulloch studied for three months in Germany. He began to write the next year, contributing articles to the *Sacred Journal* and similar magazines. From 1849 to 1854 he was a minister in Forfarshire, and a regular contributor to the *North British Review*. In 1859 he became principal and professor of theology at St. Mary's College, a position he held until just before his death. In 1862 he was for a short time editor of the *Church of Scotland Missionary Record*. In 1874 he was commissioner of Scottish education, and in 1874 an exchange professor in the United States. He was chief clerk of the general assembly of the church in 1875, and from that time was the most prominent churchman in Scotland. His influence was a rather liberalizing one in Scottish Presbyterianism. In 1882 he was made dean of the chapel royal.

Besides being a regular writer and reviewer for many serious magazines, Tulloch was editor of *Fraser's Magazine* in 1879 and 1880.

PRINCIPAL WORKS: Theism, 1855; Leaders of the Reformation, 1859; English Puritanism and Its Leaders, 1861; Rational Theology and Christian Philosophy in England, 1872; Pascal, 1878; Modern Theories in Philosophy and Religion, 1884.

ABOUT: Oliphant, M. O. Memoir of Principal Tulloch; Scotsman February 15, 1886.

TUPPER, MARTIN FARQUHAR (July 17, 1810-December 8, 1889), poet, was born in London, at 20 Devonshire Place, Marylebone, the eldest son of Dr. Martin Tupper and his wife, formerly Ellin Devis Marris, the daughter of the artist, Robert Marris. Tupper always prided himself on the fact that his father "twice refused a baronetcy" and on the distinction of his family, which had been established in Guernsey for over three hundred years, having been driven there from Germany by Charles V for religious reasons. Martin himself was but a child when he had the honor of meeting King George III, who gave the lad his blessing.

Before he was sent to school at the age of seven to the Reverend Doctor Morris of Egglesfield House, Brentford, Martin was tutored at home by a teacher named Swallow. His next school was Eagle House, Brookgreen, where he was from the age of eight until he was eleven, when he transferred to the famous Charterhouse School, at which Thackeray, the novelist, was also a pupil. Preparatory to his entrance to Christ Church College, Oxford, in 1828, however, Martin tutored under Dr. Stocker of Elizabeth College, Guernsey. At college, he wrote, "I lived the quiet life of a reading-man." There he won the Burton prize for a theological essay, although he failed in his two attempts to gain the Newdigate prize for poetry. He took his B.A. at Christ Church in 1832 and his M.A. degree three years later.

After college he gave up all hope of entering the ministry because he had a speech impediment. He began the study of law at Lincoln's Inn, whence he was called to the bar in 1835. The day after he took his degree he married his cousin, Isabelle Devis of Calcutta, to whom he had been engaged for nine years. He hardly supported a wife on the proceeds of his law practise, however, for he never earned at it more than fifty guineas.

Indeed, it was with apparent relief that he turned to literature as a means of livelihood, for he had written verse from the age of seven, and when he was sixteen his "Rough Rhymes" came out in the *Literary Chronicle*. His first book was a collection of verse, *Sacra Poesis*, which was published in 1832. *Geraldine . . . With Other Poems* contained his addition to Coleridge's poem, "Christabel," and appeared six years later, the same year in which he began *Proverbial Philosophy* (1838), a collection of poems that made him famous. He wrote the latter in ten weeks and followed it with three other series of the same title, written from 1839 to 1876. *A Modern Pyramid*, in verse and prose, came out in 1839, while *An Author's Mind* appeared in 1841 and consisted of a series of sketches. His most popular book in America was *The Crock of Gold*, which was a novel. Other volumes of poetry appeared in quick succession, and included *War Ballads* and *Three Hundred Sonnets*. He was also addicted to publishing hymns and odes in pamphlet form, and he was the author of a trilogy of plays.

His vacations were spent in travel. He made many tours of the continent. Away for three months in 1855, he wrote a journal, which was afterwards published. During his American visits in 1851 and 1876 he gave recitations from his own works, which he repeated in his English and Scotch Reading Tours. When not otherwise engaged, Tupper dabbled in inventions. He named seven "gadgets" as the products of his toil. Among them was a kind of fountain pen. His interest in science led to his election to the Royal Society in 1845, while his efforts on behalf of the slaves brought him a visit from the King of Liberia. Oxford awarded him the degree of D.C.L. in 1847, and the Prussians presented him with a gold medal for his distinction in science and art (1844). Finally his own government put him on its pension list in 1873, after he met with financial reverses at the failure of an insurance

MARTIN TUPPER

company. He was always fond of pomp and ceremony and was often seen at St. James in a Queen Anne court suit. He also entertained frequently at his house at Albury, where he died on November 29, 1889. One of his daughters, Ellin Isabelle, was the author of several books for children, as well as translations from the Swedish.

Tupper's autobiography, *My Life as an Author* (1886), attests to his vanity, which was so much a part of everything he wrote. He even compared himself to such poets as Byron and Tennyson. His *Proverbial Philosophy* did, it is true, make an impression on a public that was fond of platitudes. In twenty-five years there were at least fifty editions of it, as well as many translations into foreign languages. With this book Martin Tupper's fame was assured, for was it not probably "the most popular book of verses of its day"? He was hailed as the "people's philosopher," but he was also termed, by his critics, the author of "superficial and conceited twaddle," of "charlatan poetry." And today his name, if it be remembered at all, is synonymous with the commonplace.

B. D. S.

PRINCIPAL WORKS: *Poetry*—Sacra Poesis, 1832; Geraldine, 1838; Proverbial Philosophy, 1838; A Modern Pyramid, 1839; St. Martha's, 1841; Proverbial Philosophy (2d. ser.) 1842; A Thousand Lines, 1845; The Loving Ballad to Brother Jonathan, 1848; Hactenus, 1848; Ballads for the Times, 1850; A Hymn for all Nations, 1850; Popery Ballads, 1851; A Dirge for Wellington, 1852; Poetical Works, 1852; A Prophetic Ode, 1852; Half a Dozen Ballads, 1853; A Batch of War Ballads, 1854; A Dozen Ballads for the Times, 1854; Lyrics of the Heart and Mind, 1854; A Missionary Ballad, 1855; Rides and Reveries, 1857; Some Verse and Prose About National Rifle Clubs, 1858; Three Hundred Sonnets, 1860; Cithara, 1863; Our Greeting to the Princess Alexandra, 1863; Ode for the Three-Hundredth Birthday of Shakspeare, 1864; Proverbial Philosophy (3d Ser.) 1867; Our Canadian Dominion, 1868; Twenty-One Protestant Ballads, 1868; A Creed and Hymns, 1870; Jubilate! 1887. *Prose*—The Crock of Gold, 1844; Heart, 1844; The Twins, 1844; Probabilities, 1846; An Author's Mind, 1847; King Veric, 1849; Surrey, 1849; The Complete Prose Works, 1850; Paterfamilias's Diary, 1856; Stephen Langton, 1858; My Life as an Author, 1886. *Drama*—Alfred, 1858; Raleigh, 1866; Washington, 1876; Three Five-Act Plays and Twelve Dramatic Scenes, 1882.

ABOUT: Cooper, T. Men of the Time (9th ed.); Lanman, C. Haphazard Personalities; Tupper, M. F. My Life as an Author; Academy 36:372 December 7, 1889; Academy 60:90 January 26, 1901; Cornhill Magazine 86:335 August 1902; De Bow's Review 11:12 July 1851; Fraser's Magazine 46:466 October 1852; Living Age 58:745 September 4, 1858; Saturday Review 62:30 July 3, 1886.

TURNER, CHARLES TENNYSON (July 4, 1808-April 25, 1879), the second surviving

of the Tennyson brothers (he changed his name to Turner on inheriting a small legacy from a great-uncle), was born in Somersby a year after his brother Frederick and a year

before his brother Alfred. After several years at the Louth Grammar School, he was tutored at home by his father, then with Alfred matriculated at Trinity College, Cambridge, where he won a Bell Scholarship (open to sons of clergymen), and secured his B.A. in 1828. He took holy orders and became a curate in Lincolnshire, and then was named as vicar of Grasby in the same county, an incumbency he held for many years.

In 1836 he married Louisa Sellwood, whose sister Emily eventually became the wife of his brother Alfred—it was, in fact, at Charles' wedding that Alfred first met her. The Charles Turners were a devoted couple, childless and inseparable; she survived him by less than a month. In late middle life, increasing ill health caused him to resign his living, and he lived in retirement in Cheltenham, where he died.

Charles Tennyson Turner was a sweet-natured, placid, amiable soul, who loved flowers and was a notable gardener, and was fond of horses, dogs, and all living things. He was the type of the country vicar of the nineteenth century, with no religious qualms and an optimistic outlook on life unmarred by the distressing changes in English life brought about by the industrial revolution. He was, however, keenly interested in theological, political, and other contemporary happenings and disputes—an interest reflected, sometimes to an unfortunate degree, in his rather undisciplined flood of sonnets on every subject under the sun.

Except for a few short lyrics, the bulk of his work is in sonnet form—nearly three hundred and fifty of them in all. Many of them are on themes hardly adapted to poetic form, and he has other faults of style and construction as well. On the other hand both Coleridge and his own brother Alfred (who collaborated with him in boyhood in the *Poems by Two Brothers*) admired his work greatly; and there is much to admire. At his best, Charles Tennyson Turner's poetry is delicate, meditative, spiritual, and imaginative. Had he been able or willing to curtail his output, or at least his published output, the body of his work would hold a higher position today. As it was, he is a sort of lesser Wordsworth, a Wordsworth transposed into a minor key.

M. A. deF.

PRINCIPAL WORKS: Poems by Two Brothers (anonymous) 1827; Sonnets and Fugitive Pieces, 1830; Sonnets, 1864; Small Tableaux, 1868; Sonnets, Lyrics, and Translations, 1873; Collected Sonnets: Old and New, 1880.

ABOUT: Lounsbury, T. R. The Life and Times of Tennyson; Tennyson, C. Tennyson and His Friends; Tennyson, H. T. Alfred Lord Tennyson: A Memoir; Turner, C. T. Collected Sonnets (see Introduction by H. T. Tennyson); Walters, J. C. In Tennyson Land.

TURNER, MRS. ELIZABETH (1774-1846), juvenile writer, is an almost entirely unknown author. Her place of birth, her exact dates, her maiden name, her education, and the circumstances of her life are alike completely forgotten and unrecorded. All that is known of her is that she died in Whitchurch, Salop, in 1846, having been the author of several moral tales in verse for children, which she called "cautionary stories." Some of these were reprinted in 1900. Their heroes and heroines are all flowers, and the verses, though bald and unpoetic, are not without a certain quaint charm. They were among the most popular of children's books in the early and middle nineteenth century.

PRINCIPAL WORKS: The Daisy, 1807; The Cowslip, 1811; The Blue Bell, 1838; The Crocus, 1844.

TURNER, SHARON (September 24, 1768-February 13, 1847), historian, was born in Pentonville. He was educated at a private academy, and in 1783 articled to an attorney in the Temple. His employer died in 1789, but by arrangement with the heirs he was enabled to carry on the business for many years. From boyhood he had been fascinated by the sagas of the Anglo-Saxons, and he spent all his leisure studying Anglo-Saxon and Icelandic philology in the British Museum. He was the first person ever to make use of these early documents, and he may be regarded in a sense as the pioneer in writing the beginnings of English history from the original records.

Turner was married in 1795; his wife died in 1843, leaving a large family of children. He had retired from his legal business in 1829, but he retained some of his clients, one of whom was John Murray, the publisher. Turner was Murray's legal adviser, and also occasionally contributed to the *Edinburgh Review*. He was a Fellow of the Society of Antiquaries, and an associate of the Royal Society of Literature. From 1835 he received a civil list pension. After his wife's death he lived with a son, at whose house in London he died.

If Turner had confined himself to the Anglo-Saxon period in English history, he would (though his work would have been superseded) have attained lasting fame as the earliest of writers in this field. Unfortunately, he felt it necessary to continue his history to the end of the Tudor Period, and his later work (written mostly in opposition to Lingard, the Roman Catholic historian) has no merit or originality. He was very orthodox and devout, and an extreme reactionary. His *Sacred History* was very popular with the devout readers of his time, but has helped to detract from his reputation as a scholar. Nevertheless, he did a valuable service to history in calling the attention of abler writers to an untouched mine of material.

PRINCIPAL WORKS: History of England From the Earliest Period to the Norman Conquest, 1799-1805; History of England From the Norman Conquest to 1509, 1814-23; History of the Reign of Henry VIII, 1826; History of the Reigns of Edward VI, Mary, and Elizabeth, 1829; (as History of England, 12 vols., 1839); Sacred History of the World, 1832.

ABOUT: Gentleman's Magazine 1:437 1847.

TWISLETON, EDWARD TURNER BOYD (May 24, 1809-October 5, 1874), essayist, was born in Ceylon, his father being the archdeacon of Colombo. His paternal grandfather was Baron Saye and Sele, who outlived his eldest son, Twisleton's father. Twisleton was educated at Oriel and Trinity Colleges, Oxford, taking his B.A. in 1829, and was a fellow of Balliol from 1830 to 1838. He was called to the bar from the Inner Temple in 1835. Until his retirement in 1870, he served on more government commissions than any man of his time; his principal posts were as chief commissioner of the poor laws in Ireland, from 1845 to 1849, and as civil service commissioner from 1862 to 1870. In 1847 his older brother succeeded to the barony by the death of their grandfather, and E. T. B. Twisleton was raised by royal warrant to the rank of a baron's son. In 1852 he married Ellen Dwight, whose father was a legislator in Massachusetts. She died in 1862; the marriage was childless.

Twisleton was never a writer in any real sense of the term. The only thing he published except his book on speech was a survey of missionary schools in Massachusetts.

PRINCIPAL WORK: The Tongue Not Essential to Speech, 1873.

ABOUT: Illustrated London News October 17 and December 5, 1874.

TYLOR, SIR EDWARD BURNETT (October 2, 1832-January 2, 1917), anthropologist, was born in London, his father being a brass founder. His brother became a well-known geologist. He was educated at Grove House School, Tottenham, a Quaker institution, his family being Quakers. At sixteen he was put into his father's business, but in 1855 his health broke down. While traveling for recuperation in Cuba, he met Henry Christy, an ethnologist, and went with him on an archaeological and anthropological expedition to Mexico. This was the spark which set off Tylor's zeal for anthropology. On his return to England he set at once to study of and writing of his chosen science, and never returned to brass founding. In 1883 he was made keeper of the university museum at Oxford, in 1884 reader in anthropology, and in 1886 Oxford's first professor of anthropology. He practically created the school of anthropology at Oxford, where he remained as professor until 1909. He also created the anthropological section of the British Association for the Advancement of Science, and acted as its president; and he was president of the Anthropological Society in 1891. In 1903 he was made an honorary fellow of Balliol, and in 1912 he was knighted. He had married Anna Fox in 1858; they had no children. After his retirement from Oxford he bought a house in Somerset, where he died.

Tylor was one of the really great anthropologists; his *Primitive Culture*, with its theory of animism, is still a classic. He was a complete Darwinian who carried evolution into human behavior, a worshiper of sound, solid fact and rigidly scientific method. He is not dull, however, for this presentation of material was made in a style simple, straightforward, and graceful.

PRINCIPAL WORKS: Anahuac, Mexico, and the Mexicans, 1859; Researches Into the Early History of Mankind, 1865; Primitive Culture, 1871; Anthropology, 1881.

ABOUT: Anthropological Essays Presented to E. B. Tylor, 1907 (see Appreciation by Andrew Lang).

TYNDALL, JOHN (August 2, 1820-December 4, 1893), physicist, was born in Carlow, southeastern Ireland, of a family which was English before the seventeenth century, and which claimed kinship with Tyndale, the religious reformer. His father was poor but well educated and intelligent, and his lessons in English and mathematics supplemented the poor teaching of the free school. The boy's aptitude at mathematics secured him a position with the ordnance survey of Ireland in 1839, and the excellence of his drawings caused him to be selected later for the English survey. For three years he acted as civil engineer at Manchester, and for three more years did engineering for railroad projects at various places in England. (This was the period of the intensive construction of railroads everywhere.) Meanwhile he read widely, and was particularly influenced by Carlyle.

He determined to become a scientist; his bent was for original research, but necessity found him a mathematics instructor at Queenwood College, Hampshire. Even in this uncongenial work his originality asserted itself—he was a most unusual teacher, who permitted the boys to choose whether they would do Euclid or make up their own problems! In 1848 he was able to leave the school, though only on promise to return, and he went to Marburg, where in 1850 he secured his Ph.D., and then to Berlin. His reputation as an investigator was established by the publication of his work on the magnetic properties of crystals.

He returned to Queenwood, as he had promised, but he was eager to find a wider

JOHN TYNDALL

field. By this time he and Thomas Henry Huxley had become intimate friends, and the two applied in vain for positions in universities in Toronto and Sidney. Both had far better fortunes awaiting them. In 1853 Tyndall became professor of physics at the Royal Institution, of which Faraday was then director. The two physicists complemented each other perfectly; they worked in the closest association ("like father and son") until Faraday died, in 1867, when Tyndall succeeded him.

Tyndall's next extended studies were in the laminated structure of glacial ice, a research which gave rise to frequent journeys to the Alps and one of his best known books. His longest and most thorough investigation, however, was in the field of radiant heat. Outside of his work at the Royal Institution he lectured often and regularly—it was the era of popular lectures—and his popularity was only second to that of Lyell. In 1872 he made a lecture tour in the United States, which netted him $13,000; he left the entire fund to be used for the benefit of science, and it now provides graduate fellowships in physics at Harvard, Columbia, and the University of Pennsylvania. One of his Alpine trips resulted in an accident and a consequent infection which interested Tyndall in studying the "spontaneous generation" of life, and in the course of this investigation he devised an improved method of sterilization, by repeated successive heatings instead of one long boiling. In recognition of this discovery the University of Tübingen gave him the honorary degree of M.D.

At fifty-five, Tyndall married Louisa, the daughter of Lord Hamilton. The marriage was most happy, his wife assisting him in all his work and accompanying him on his journeys. They built a home in Surrey, and another in Switzerland, and in 1887 Tyndall retired from the Royal Institution and prepared for a period of research and writing. Unfortunately his health gave out; constant indigestion and insomnia made him miserable, and at the end of 1893 an overdose of chloral, supposedly accidentally administered, caused his death.

Tyndall was a devoted friend—almost the only friend who never quarreled with Herbert Spencer—a man markedly chivalrous and fair-minded, irascible but tenderhearted. He has been called "a reverent agnostic," who liked to sing hymns and disliked to offend the religiously minded. (In spite of this, a mild evolutionary lecture he gave before the British Association at Belfast elicited a national clerical order of a three days' fast "to drive infidelity out of Ireland"!) Outside of his technical writing, his books are clear and competent, if not marked by any great literary talent. He was an excellent teacher, and his printed lectures are today his most readable volumes.   M. A. deF.

PRINCIPAL WORKS: Researches on Diagmagnetism and Magne-Crystallic Action, 1850; The Glaciers of the Alps, 1860; Heat Considered as a Mode of Motion, 1863; Faraday as a Discoverer, 1868; Notes on Light, 1870; Notes on Electrical Phenomena and Theories, 1870; Fragments of Science, 1871; Light and Electricity, 1871; Hours of Exercise in the Alps, 1871; Contributions to Molecular Physics in the Domain of Radiant Heat, 1872; The Forms of Water in Clouds and Rivers, Ice and Glaciers, 1872; Six Lectures on Light Delivered in America, 1873; On Sound, 1875; Lessons in Electricity at the Royal Institution, 1876; Essays on the Floating Matter of the Air, 1881; New Fragments, 1892.

ABOUT: Open Court 34:252 April 1920; Scientific Monthly 11:331 October 1920.

TYTLER, PATRICK FRASER (1791-December 24, 1849), Scottish historian, was the youngest son of Lord Woodhouselee. He was educated privately and at the Edinburgh High School, then read law at the University of Edinburgh. He was called to the Scottish bar in 1813. From 1816 to 1830 he was king's counsel in exchequer. He practised law until 1832, but never had many clients, and spent most of his time in the study of history. He was one of the earliest historians in English to use original sources and documents. Sir Walter Scott first suggested his writing a history of Scotland; the British Museum at first refused to allow him to consult its records, on the ground that he was a Scot and therefore anti-English! This experience inspired Tytler to his successful advocacy of publication of the state papers of Great Britain. In 1830 a change of ministry caused the loss of his official position, and he devoted all his time thereafter to his historical work. Although his first writing had been done for

638

Blackwood's, he now refused to write any magazine articles or reviews because they took time from his books.

In 1826 Tytler had married Rachel Hogg. She died in 1835, leaving two sons and a daughter. The widower went to live in Long Hampstead with his mother and sisters, finally settling permanently in London in 1837. In 1844 he received a civil list pension. The following year he married Anastasia Bonar, a lifelong friend of his sisters.

Tytler's is the most definite and fullest history of the thirteenth to the seventeenth centuries in Scotland, but he has been accused of a Tory, aristocratic bias which makes his picture of the period one-sided and unfair, and it is true that he is too much given to rather dubious generalizing. In his early years he was poet laureate of the Bannatyne Club, to which Scott belonged, but his topical verses written in that capacity are very feeble.

PRINCIPAL WORKS: The Life of the Admirable Crichton of Cluny, 1819; Life of Wicliff, 1826; History of Scotland, 1828-43; Lives of Scottish Worthies, 1831-33; Life of Sir Walter Raleigh, 1833; England Under the Reigns of Edward VI and Mary, 1839.

ABOUT: Buron, J. W. Memoir of Patrick Fraser Tytler; Tytler, A. [sister]. Reminiscences of Patrick Fraser Tytler.

URQUHART, DAVID (1805-May 16, 1877), Scottish political pamphleteer and diplomatist, was born at Braelangwell, Cromarty, and educated on the Continent. He performed diplomatic missions for the British government at Constantinople between 1831 and 1837, when he was recalled because of his hostility to Russia. Thenceforth, as a member of Parliament for Stafford (1847-52) and by indefatigable writing, he violently opposed the government's foreign policies, until he retired in ill health to Montreaux, Switzerland, in 1864. He died at Naples in his seventy-second year and was buried in Montreaux.

By his numerous savage treatises on international policy, he exerted a powerful influence on public opinion. Best remembered are two pamphlets expressing his anti-Russian views, which provoked a reply from Richard Cobden. As media for his opinions, he published *Portfolio*, a periodical devoted to diplomatic affairs, in 1836-37 and again in 1843-45, and in 1858 he founded the *Free Press*, renamed in 1866 the *Diplomatic Review*, to which Karl Marx contributed.

PRINCIPAL WORKS: England, France, Russia, and Turkey, 1834; The Crisis: or, France Before the Four Powers, 1840; The Progress of Russia in the West, North, and South, 1853.

ABOUT: Robinson, G. David Urquhart.

"VANOLIS, BYSSHE." See THOMSON, JAMES

VAUGHAN, ROBERT (October 14, 1795-June 15, 1868), author of historical and theological works, was born in the west of England and educated for the ministry by a Bristol preacher. He was successively minister at Worcester (1819-25) and at Kensington, London (1825-43), and president of the Lancashire Independent College at Manchester (1843-57). He founded the *British Quarterly* in 1845 and was its editor until 1867. He died at Torquay of brain congestion at the age of seventy-two. By his wife, Susanna Ryall, he had several children, of whom Robert Alfred Vaughan followed in his footsteps as an author and clergyman.

His monograph on John de Wycliffe, fourteenth century religious reformer, and his history of the Stuart period brought him a reputation as an historical writer and an appointment as professor of history in University College, London, which he held concurrently with his Kensington pastorate from 1834 to 1843. By his theological writings, both controversial and devotional, he helped to spread the literary culture of the Congregational denomination.

PRINCIPAL WORKS: Life and Opinions of John de Wycliffe, 1828; Memorials of the Stuart Dynasty, 1831; The Protectorate of Oliver Cromwell, 1838; Essays on History, Philosophy, and Theology, 1849.

VAUGHAN, ROBERT ALFRED (March 18, 1823-October 26, 1857), ecclesiastical biographer, was born at Worcester, the son of Robert Vaughan, Congregational minister and author of historical works. He was educated at University College, London, and at the Lancashire Independent College, Manchester, of which his father was president. After serving as Congregational minister at Bath (1848-50) and at Birmingham (1850-55) he spent the last two years of his life as an invalid in London, where he died of a pulmonary disease at the age of thirty-four.

He is remembered for *Hours With the Mystics*, a series of biographical studies, designed as a preface to further writings on the entire history of the church, and published shortly before his untimely death. According to Alexander Gordon, the work "has proved an introduction, of singular attractiveness and permanent value, to a class of writers and thinkers never before presented to the English mind in such lifelike tints."

PRINCIPAL WORKS: Hours With the Mystics: A Contribution to the History of Religious Opinion, 1856; Essays and Remains, 1858.

ABOUT: Vaughan, R. A. Essays and Remains (see Memoir by his father R. Vaughan); Eclectic Review, September 1858.

VEDDER, DAVID (1790-February 11, 1854), Scottish poet, was born in the Orkney Islands near Kirkwall. He was educated largely by himself. Left an orphan at an early age, he went to sea and rose from the rank of cabin-boy to that of captain. After commanding a Greenland whaler for three years and serving five years as first officer of an armed cruiser, he entered the revenue service and was for thirty-two years a tide-surveyor of customs, successively at Montrose, Kirkcaldy, Dundee, and Leith. Retiring on a pension in 1852, he died two years later in Edinburgh in his sixty-fourth year, leaving a widow and three children.

As represented in the anthologies of Scottish verse, he is remembered chiefly for his lyrics celebrating his native Orkney. Also popular were his Scottish songs and Norse ballads. "With lyric movement usually correct and fluent," wrote Thomas Wilson Bayne, "Vedder commands at once a certain frank humor, and a pathos unfeigned and manly." He was also a prose writer of extraordinary power. His memoir of Scott was widely read, and his version of the *Story of Reynard the Fox* was called "the best edition of this famous story yet presented in England."

PRINCIPAL WORKS: The Covenanters' Communion and Other Poems, 1826; Orcadian Sketches, 1832; Memoir of Sir Walter Scott, 1832; Poems: Legendary, Lyrical, and Descriptive (illus. by W. Geikie) 1842; The Pictorial Gift-Book of Lays and Lithography (illus. by his son-in-law F. Schenck) 1842; Story of Reynard the Fox: New Version (illus. by G. Canton) 1852; Poems, Lyrics, and Sketches (ed. by G. Gilfillan) 1878(?).

ABOUT: Vedder, D. Poems, Lyrics, and Sketches (see Memoir by G. Gilfillan).

VELEY, MARGARET (May 12, 1843-December 7, 1887), poet and novelist, was born at Braintree, Essex, and educated at home. She lived in her native town until 1880, then removed to London, where she died unmarried at the age of forty-four. From 1870 onwards she was a contributor to *Blackwood's, Cornhill* and other magazines.

Her output, in both prose and poetry, was small. The best known of her novels was *For Percival*, which showed a strong sense of humor not present in her later works. Most noteworthy was her verse, posthumously collected under the title *A Marriage of Shadows*. In the opinion of George Saintsbury, "her accomplishment is various and almost great. Her chief work, 'A Japanese Fan,' is really something of a positive masterpiece of quiet ironic passion, suitably phrased in verse. The title poem of her book and 'The Unknown Land' deserve an honorable place among the phantasmagorias in irregular Pindaric which have formed a great feature of later nineteenth-century poetry."

PRINCIPAL WORKS: *Prose*—For Percival, 1878; Mitchelhurst Place, 1884; A Garden of Memories, 1887. *Poetry*—A Marriage of Shadows and Other Poems, 1888.

ABOUT: Veley, M. A Marriage of Shadows (see Biographical Introduction by L. Stephen).

VENABLES, GEORGE STOVIN (June 18, 1810-October 6, 1888), Welsh journalist, was born in South Wales, the son of the archdeacon of Carmarthen. Educated at the Charterhouse, London, and at Jesus College, Cambridge, he practised law for forty-six years (1836-82). In his spare time he contributed anonymous articles to the *Saturday Review* (from the date of its first issue in 1855) and to *The Times,* by which, according to Herbert Stephen, "he probably did more than any other writer of his time to establish and maintain the best and strongest current style, and the highest type of political thought, in journalism."

He was the author of only one book, a slender volume of poems, written in collaboration with his intimate friend Henry Lushington and privately printed. His only other signed work was a biographical memoir of Lushington prefaced to the latter's book *The Italian War* (1859). He is remembered chiefly for his astute journalistic criticism and for his literary associations. He was said to have been the original of Thackeray's character of George.Warrington in *Pendennis,* and he was a friend of Tennyson, to whose poem *The Princess* he contributed a line.

WORK: Joint Compositions (with H. Lushington) 1848.

ABOUT: Saturday Review, October 13, 1888.

VERE, SIR AUBREY DE. See DE VERE, SIR AUBREY

VERE, AUBREY THOMAS DE. See DE VERE, AUBREY THOMAS

WADE, THOMAS (1805-September 19, 1875), poet, was born in London. Nothing is known of his schooling, and he was probably largely self-educated. As a young man he went to London and began to write poetic plays. Most of these were performed by Charles Kemble and other members of the famous Kemble family of actors. The first two were huge successes; the third, *The Jew of Arragon,* was howled down because it was so favorable to the Jews. Wade then published it with all suppressed passages restored, with a dedication "to the Jews of England." His next publication was of a series of poems in pamphlet form, with the intention of combining them later in one volume. For a while he was editor and part proprietor of *Bell's Weekly Newspaper.* Then he moved to Jersey, where he published the *British Press,* in which many of his poems were printed. He made in 1845 and 1846 the first English translation of Dante in the original metre. He was married, his wife being Lucy (Eager) Bridgman, a widow, a well known concert pianist.

Wade was influenced by Byron and Moore, but most of all by Shelley. An advanced liberal and a sensitive enthusiast, he displayed more feeling than he had power to express. He is chiefly important as a precursor of the neo-romantic school in English poetry, as a sort of minor older brother of Swinburne and Rossetti.

PRINCIPAL WORKS: Tasso and the Sisters, 1823; Luke Andrea, 1827; The Jew of Arragon, 1830; Mundi et Cordis, 1835.

ABOUT: Forman, H. B. Literary Anecdotes of the Nineteenth Century.

WAINEWRIGHT, THOMAS GRIF-FITHS (1794-1852), art critic and criminal, was born in Chiswick. Left an orphan in infancy, he was reared by his maternal grandfather, publisher of the *Monthly Review.* He was educated at Charles Burney's Academy, where he distinguished himself in drawing, studying later in an art studio. He then secured a commission, first in the Guards, then in the Yeomanry, but resigned and became a journalist, with art as his particular province. From 1820 to 1823 he contributed regularly to the *London Magazine* under the names of "Egomet Bonmot" and "Janus Weathercock." Through his connection with the magazine he became an intimate of Hood, Allan Cunningham, Hazlitt, De Quincey, and Lamb. Occasionally he exhibited at the Royal Academy, his pastel work being especially good. In 1821 he married Frances Ward. In 1826, hard up and living beyond his means, he forged an order on the Bank of England for half the capital of a legacy of which he was supposed to have only the interest. Escaping detection for the time, he went with his wife to live with a wealthy bachelor uncle, who died suddenly of poisoning two years later. Then he insured the lives of his mother-in-law and two sisters-in-law, all of whom speedily died of poison. The insurance company refused to pay, and Wainewright felt it wiser to move to Paris. There he sued the insurance company without result, and it is probable that during part of this period he was in prison in Paris for some unknown offense. In 1837 he ventured to return to England, was immediately arrested for the old forgery, and was sentenced to life in Van Diemen's Land (Tasmania). He died there, at Hobart Town, fifteen years later. Although he confessed the murders of his relatives, there was not sufficient evidence to try him on a murder charge.

Actually, Wainewright's literary work is feeble and pretentious, and would never have attracted the least attention had it not been for his extra-professional career.

PRINCIPAL WORK: Essays and Criticisms, 1880.

ABOUT: Allen, A. G. Twelve Bad Men; Wainewright, T. G. Essays and Criticisms (see Introduction by W. C. Hazlitt); Wilde, O. Pen, Pencil, and Poison.

WAKEFIELD, EDWARD GIBBON

(March 20, 1796-May 16, 1862), sociologist, was the son of a statistician known for his philanthropy; his uncle was a celebrated economist, his paternal grandmother a philanthropist and juvenile writer. On his mother's side he was distantly related to the historian, Edward Gibbon. He was educated at Westminster and the Edinburgh High School, which he left voluntarily at sixteen. In 1814 he went to Turin on the staff of the British envoy to the court there. Two years later he made a runaway match with Eliza Pattle, an heiress and ward in chancery. She died in 1820, leaving one son and one daughter. He returned to Turin, then was transferred to the Paris legation. In 1826 he made a foolish attempt to force, an elopement with another heiress, Ellen Turner. He and his brother were sentenced to three years in prison in consequence, and the Gretna Green marriage between the pair was canceled. It was in prison, gloomily pondering emigration as an alleviation of his disgrace, that Wakefield became interested, first in the question of capital punishment, then in that of colonization. He evolved there his colonization plan, which had as its important feature the sale of land to colonists at fixed sums, the proceeds to be used for assistance to immigrants. His articles on the subject in *The Spectator* caused the formation of the National Colonization Society and the South Australian Association. In 1837 he formed the New Zealand Association and the New Zealand Land Company, which he directed in London while his brother took charge in New Zealand. In 1838 he went with Lord Durham to Canada as unofficial adviser. He visited Canada again in 1841 and 1843, and was a member of Parliament there in the latter year. In 1846 he suffered a stroke of paralysis from overwork. On his recovery he found that he had lost his influence during his illness, and resigned. In 1850 he formed the Colonial Reform Society. Two years later he went to New Zealand to live. His final breakdown and complete paralysis occurred in 1854, and he was an invalid until his death in Wellington eight years later.

PRINCIPAL WORKS: A Letter From Sydney (published under the name of Robert Gouger, an actual emigrant) 1829; Facts Relating to the Punishment of Death, 1831; The Hangman and the Judge, 1833; England and America, 1833; A View of the Art of Colonisation, 1849.

ABOUT: Garnett, R. Edward Gibbon Wakefield.

WAKEFIELD, PRISCILLA

(January 31, 1750-September 12, 1832), juvenile writer, was born in Tottenham, her maiden name being Bell, and her family being Quakers. In 1771 she married Edward Wakefield, a London merchant. She had two sons and one daughter; two sons and a grandson, Edward Gibbon Wakefield, became well known economists. She was also the aunt of the famous philanthropist, Elizabeth Fry. Mrs. Wakefield herself was much concerned with philanthropy; she was a pioneer in the promotion of savings banks for workingmen, and also conducted a charity organization for lying-in women. She was a Quaker all her life so far as religious doctrine went, but eschewed the rules of the meeting as to clothing and amusements. She is best known as a writer for children, chiefly on travel and natural science; her books were entertaining as well as instructive, and were extremely popular. She died in Ipswich at eighty-one.

PRINCIPAL WORKS: Mental Improvement, 1794; Leisure Hours, 1794; Juvenile Anecdotes, 1795 and 1798; Introduction to Botany, 1796; The Juvenile Travellers, 1801; Domestic Recreation, 1805; Excursions in North America, 1806; Instinct Displayed, 1811; The Traveller in Africa, 1814; Introduction to the Natural History and Classification of Insects, 1816; The Traveller in America, 1817.

ABOUT: Gentleman's Magazine 2:650 1832; Ipswich Journal September 15, 1832.

WALLACE, ALFRED RUSSEL

(January 8, 1823-November 17, 1913), writer on natural history, was born at Usk, Monmouthshire, the seventh of eight children of a father who was an inefficient dreamer and had lost his entire fortune in unwise ventures. In consequence his children's education suffered; Alfred was sent to the grammar school at Hertford, but at thirteen he was already not a pupil, but a pupil-teacher. At fourteen he left for London, to learn surveying from his older brother William; in this manner he learned also the rudiments of geology. In 1838 he deserted surveying and was apprenticed to a watchmaker, but the next year William took him to Hertfordshire as his assistant. Here he first developed an interest in astronomy, agriculture, and particularly botany, and began his method of systematizing his ideas by writing them out.

The father died in 1843, but left no inheritance. Wallace became a master in the collegiate school at Leicester, where he foreshadowed the eccentricities of his later intellectual trend by experimenting in phrenology, hypnotism, and telepathy. More importantly for himself and the world, he there met the naturalist H. W. Bates, who introduced him to entomology, and there also he read Malthus —as great an influence on his life as he was on Darwin's.

In 1846 William Wallace died suddenly, and Alfred inherited his professional connections. For a while he was prosperous, but as soon as he had saved sufficient money he threw up surveying forever, and persuaded Bates to join him in a collecting trip to the Amazon, covering their expenses by the sale of specimens. They left in 1848, and parted company in 1850; but Wallace remained in

ALFRED R. WALLACE

South America for four years, and Bates for eleven. In 1849 Wallace's younger brother Herbert had joined him, but he died of yellow fever in 1851. As a crowning misfortune, the ship on which he was returning to England caught fire; the crew and passengers were rescued after ten days in open boats, but all the collections and notes not previously sent to England went down with the ship.

Nothing daunted, Wallage undertook a new journey, this time to the Malay Archipelago. He did not return until 1862, and when he did it was as co-discoverer with Charles Darwin of the theory of natural selection. Wallace did important work in the Malay Archipelago; he discovered, for example, that the archipelago is divided by a strait (now known as "Wallace's Line"), west of which the fauna and flora are Oriental in character, east of it Australian. He was gradually becoming more and more inclined to evolutionary views, but was not yet satisfied as to the causes and methods of evolution.

Suddenly, in 1858, as he lay ill with fever in Molucca, the theory of natural selection flashed upon him. He wrote his speculations and sent the paper to Darwin, already as famous as Wallace was unknown. It was the very conclusion to which Darwin had come and which, in his slow and thorough way, he had been building up ever since the voyage of the *Beagle*! It was a terrible dilemma, but Darwin solved it characteristically; on July 1, 1858, he published a joint paper by Wallace and himself, giving the younger man full credit.

Wallace's active and impatient mind, untrained in anotomy and physiology, went on to other pursuits. His particular scientific

interest was in geographical distribution, in which he did important work. Returning to England, he poured out books in half a dozen fields, and did no further research; in a sense his great discovery had been a lucky hit. In 1866 he married Mary Mitten, daughter of a botanist (he had been engaged to another—and jilted—in 1863), and for several years he kept moving continually from one town to another in the vicinity of London. A son and a daughter were born, and while they were still children Wallace speculated wildly and lost his entire fortune, accumulated at such labor. For a while he was in deep poverty, but in 1881, through the influence of Darwin and Huxley, he was granted a civil list pension of £200 a year. The same year he became president of the Land Nationalization Society; social and economic questions were increasingly engaging his attention. In 1886 he went to the United States for a lecture tour, his last trip out of England. His old age was spent peacefully in writing and gardening. He died finally of the disabilities of age at over 90.

Wallace was no mere dabbler; he had genuine scientific ability; but he lacked the necessary foundations, and he was by nature (perhaps by heredity) credulous, an eager partisan, and inclined to scatter his interests. With equal ardor he espoused phrenology, anti-vaccination, spiritualism, Socialism, the Single Tax, and vegetarianism—though only a meat diet agreed with him. He was kindly by nature, modest, and likable. He was really not a biologist, but a naturalist. And he had the naturalist's gift of apt description and vivid writing. In his last years his books became opinionated and a bit garrulous, but never uninteresting. He outlived all his great colleagues, and became a sort of monument, as the last of the Darwin circle. M. A. deF.

PRINCIPAL WORKS: *Scientific*—Travels on the Amazon and Rio Negro, 1853; Palm Trees of the Amazon, 1853; The Malay Archipelago, 1869; Contributions to the Theory of Natural Selection, 1870; The Geographical Distribution of Animals, 1876; Tropical Nature, 1878; Australasia, 1879; Island Life, 1880; Darwinism, 1889; The Ice Age and Its Work, 1894; The Method of Organic Evolution, 1896; Studies, Scientific and Social, 1900; Man's Place in the Universe, 1903; Is Mars Habitable? 1907. *Miscellaneous*—On Miracles and Modern Spiritualism, 1875; Land Nationalization, 1882; Bad Times, 1885; The Wonderful Century, 1898; Vaccination: A Delusion, 1898; My Life, 1905; The World of Life, 1910; Social Environment and Moral Progress, 1912; The Revolt of Democracy, 1913.

ABOUT: Hogben, L. T. Alfred Russell Wallace: The Story of a Great Discoverer; Wallace, A. R. My Life; Wallace, A. R. The Revolt of Democracy (see introduction Life by J. Marchant); Science ns38:871 December 19, 1913.

WALLACE, WILLIAM (May 11, 1844-February 18, 1897), Scottish philosopher, was born in Cupar-Fife, the son of a house builder. He was educated at the University of St.

Andrews and at Balliol College, Oxford, then was a fellow of and tutor at Merton, receiving his B.A. in 1868 and his M.A. in 1871, when he was librarian of Merton. In 1872 he married Janet Barclay; they had two sons and one daughter. From 1882 to his death, which came as the result of a bicycle accident, he was Whyte professor of moral philosophy at Oxford. His special field was Germany philosophy, especially that of Hegel, whose translator he was. He was primarily a clarifier and interpreter, rather than an original philosopher, and was noted for the force and beauty of his style.

PRINCIPAL WORKS: The Logic of Hegel, 1873; Epicureanism, 1880; Kant, 1882; The Life of Arthur Schopenhauer, 1890; Lectures and Essays on Natural Theology and Ethics, 1898.

ABOUT: Wallace, W. Lectures and Essays on Natural Theology and Ethics (see Biographical Introduction).

WALLER, JOHN FRANCIS (1810-January 19, 1894), Irish poet and essayist, was born in Limerick and educated at Trinity, College, Dublin, receiving his B.A. in 1831. While studying law in London he began contributing to the magazines. He was called to the Irish bar in 1833 and joined the Leinster circuit, but soon became a member of the staff of the Dublin University Magazine, of which he was later the editor, and to which he was a prolific contributor of prose and verse, especially the latter, in humorous vein, under the pseudonym of "Jonathan Freke Slingsby." He also wrote a number of popular songs. In 1835 he married Anna Hopkins; they had two sons and six daughters. In 1852 he received an honorary LL.D. from Dublin University, and he was honorable secretary of the Royal Dublin Society and, in 1864, vice-president of the Royal Irish Academy. From 1857 to 1863 he edited the Imperial Dictionary of Universal Biography; he also edited, with memoirs, the works of Goldsmith, Moore, and Swift. In 1867 he was made registrar of the rolls court, but in a few years he resigned and went to London as editor for the publishers, Cassell & Co.

PRINCIPAL WORKS: Slingsby Papers, 1852; Ravenscroft Hall and Other Poems, 1852; The Dead Bridal, 1856; Occasional Odes, 1864; Festival Tales, 1873.

ABOUT: Athenaeum 1:149 1894; Dublin University Magazine, Vol. 73.

WALPOLE, SIR SPENCER (February 6, 1839-July 7, 1907), historian, was born in London, the son of a barrister. When he was six his family moved to Ealing because of his delicate health, which was later improved by exercise in rowing at Eton. In 1857 he became a clerk in the war office, and the next year (his father being Home Secretary) private secretary to the older Walpole and then to his successor. He next returned to the war office, in 1866, emerging this time to be his father's secretary. In 1867 he was made inspector of fisheries. The same year he married Marion Jane Murray; they had one daughter. He supplemented his small income by writing financial articles for the Pall Mall Gazette. His biography of his grandfather, Spencer Perceval, in 1874, brought him a legacy of £10,000 from a wealthy distant relative, whereupon he gave up journalism and started the history of England he had long projected. From 1882 to 1893 he was governor of the Isle of Man, by Gladstone's appointment, and from 1893 to 1899 secretary to the Post Office; in 1897 he was a delegate to the Postal Congress in Washington. He was made Knight Commander of the Bath in 1898, and in 1904 received an honorary D.Litt. from Oxford. After leaving the post office he retired to Sussex, where he died at sixty-eight of a cerebral hemorrhage.

Walpole's history is clear and straightforward, detached, cool, and statistical. Its facts are sound, but it abounds in generalizations of doubtful validity.

PRINCIPAL WORKS: History of England From 1815 to 1856, 1878-90; Life of Lord John Russell, 1889; The History of Twenty-five Years (1856-1880) 1904-08; Studies in Biography, 1907; Essays Political and Biographical, 1908.

ABOUT: Walpole, Sir S. Essays Political and Biographical (see Memoir by his daughter, Mrs. F. Holland)

WARBURTON, BARTHOLOMEW ELIOT GEORGE (1810-January 4, 1852), Irish miscellaneous writer, was born in King's County, his father being a former inspector-general of the Galway constabulary. After a private education, he attended Queen's and Trinity Colleges, Cambridge, receiving his B.A. in 1833 and his M.A. in 1837. He was called to the Irish bar in 1837, but gave up the law to travel and write. During 1843 and 1844 he wrote for the Dublin University Magazine a series of articles descriptive of Syria, Palestine, and he spent most of his life in adventurous roving all over Europe. In 1848 he married Matilda Jane Grove; they had two sons. Most of his work was journalistic, though he collected material for a "history of the poor" and for an "impartial history" of Ireland, for neither of which he could find a publisher. In 1851 he was deputed by a land company to treat with the Indians on the Isthmus of Darien, with a view to peaceful trade relations, and he set sail at the end of the year. The ship, the Amazon, making her first voyage, caught fire, and Warburton lost his life.

PRINCIPAL WORKS: The Crescent and the Cross, 1844; Memoirs of Prince Rupert and the Cavaliers, 1849; Reginald Hastings (novel) 1850; Darien: or, The Merchant Prince (novel) 1852.

ABOUT: Dublin University Magazine February 1852; London Times January 7, 8, 9, 1852.

WARD, SIR ADOLPHUS WILLIAM

(December 2, 1837-June 19, 1924), historian and biographer, was born in Hampstead. His father was in the diplomatic service. He was educated at King Edward VI's School and at Peterhouse College Cambridge, being a fellow of Peterhouse in 1861 (honorary fellow 1891). After serving as assistant lecturer at Peterhouse and at the University of Glasgow, he became, in 1866, professor of history and English literature at Owens College, Manchester; he was principal of Owens College from 1890 to 1897. From 1886 to 1890, and again from 1894 to 1896, he was vice-chancellor of Victoria University. He was Ford lecturer at Oxford in 1898, and vice-chancellor of Cambridge in 1901.

Ward became a fellow of the British Academy in 1902, and was its president from 1911 to 1913. He was one of the editors of the *Cambridge Modern History* and of the *Cambridge History of English Literature,* and a contributor to the *Dictionary of National Biography.* He was best known, however, as master of Peterhouse, from 1900 to his death. He was knighted in 1913. He was married in 1879 to Adelaide Lancaster; they had one daughter.

In addition to his historical and biographical works, Ward edited many ancient authors for the Camden Society, contributed to the *Edinburgh Review* and the *Quarterly Review,* and prepared editions of Crabbe, Pope, Marlowe, and other writers. His work was sound and competent, though not of outstanding originality.

PRINCIPAL WORKS: The Counter-Reformation, 1868; History of English Dramatic Literature, 1875; Chaucer, 1880; Dickens, 1882; Sir Henry Wotton, 1897; Great Britain and Hanover, 1899; Collected Papers, 1921.

ABOUT: London Times June 20, 1924.

WARD, ROBERT PLUMER

(March 19, 1765-August 13, 1846), novelist, was born in London; his father was a merchant resident in Gibraltar, his mother of Jewish descent. He was educated at Westminster and at Christ Church College, Oxford. During the early part of the French Revolution he lived in France. He was called to the bar from the Inner Temple in 1790, and joined the western circuit, changing to the northern circuit on his marriage in 1796 to Catherine Maling. He was interested in politics rather than in the law, and, having attracted the attention of Pitt and Lord Eldon, he was through their help elected to Parliament in 1802, holding his seat until 1823. In 1805 he was under-secretary to the Foreign Office, then until 1811 on the Admiralty Board. From 1811 to 1823 he was clerk of ordnance, and then auditor of the civil list. His political diary, of great importance because of his close acquaintance with the leading politicians

of his time, was begun in 1809. In 1828, his wife having died, he married a widow, Mrs. Plumer Lewis, and added Plumer to his own name of Robert Ward. He resigned his office and moved to her home in Gilston, Hertfordshire, becoming sheriff of the county in 1830. She died the following year, and in 1833 he married another widow, Mary Anne (Anson) Okeover, an heiress. During the remainder of his life most of his time was spent abroad.

Ward's three novels are plotless, mechanical stories, but witty, and valuable because they were drawn from intimate knowledge of political society and its frequenters.

PRINCIPAL WORKS: An Inquiry Into the Foundation and History of the Law of Nations in Europe, 1795; Tremaine: or, The Man of Refinement, 1825; DeVere: or, The Man of Independence, 1827; Illustrations of Human Life, 1837; DeClifford: or, The Constant Man, 1841.

ABOUT: Phipps, E. Memoirs of the Political and Literary Life of R. Plumer Ward; Morning Post August 18, 1846.

WARD, WILLIAM GEORGE

(March 21, 1812-July 6, 1882), Roman Catholic theologian, was born in London, the son of a financier. He was educated at Winchester and at Christ Church and Lincoln Colleges, Oxford, taking his B.A. in 1834, and becoming a fellow of Balliol. He took orders in the Anglican church and became a lecturer on mathematics and logic at Balliol; he had a real genius for mathematics, and rediscovered logarithms for himself. At first inclined to latitudinarianism, gradually under Newman's influence he became increasingly sympathetic with Roman Catholicism. He did not at once leave the Church of England, but his *Ideal of the Christian Church* was so full of praise of Roman Catholic doctrine that he was degraded from his position at Oxford, whereupon he resigned from the clergy. With his newly married wife, Frances Wingfield, he was received into the Roman Catholic Church in 1845. He moved to Ware, near St. Edmund's (Roman Catholic) College, and by 1851 was lecturing there. The next year he received the position, though he refused the title, of professor of moral philosophy, and taught at the college until 1858. In 1854 the Pope conferred a Ph.D. on him. From 1863 to 1878 he was editor of the *Dublin Review,* which he made the organ of his opinions.

Ward became a dogmatic, implacable anti-liberal even within his own new religious affiliation. He was the arch-enemy of such liberal Catholics as Lord Acton, the historian, and went so far as seriously to recommend that all scientific hypotheses be submitted to the Pope for his decision before they were accepted. In philosophy he was much more moderate than in theology; he was founder and (in 1870) president of the Metaphysical Society, and in matters outside of Church doctrine he was a reasonable and kindly man, modest and congenitally melancholy by nature. Of his three sons and five daughters, one son became a priest and three daughters became nuns. Another son, Wilfrid Ward, was later a well-known essayist.

PRINCIPAL WORKS: The Ideal of a Christian Church, 1844; On Nature and Grace, 1860; Essays on the Philosophy of Theism, 1884.

ABOUT: Ward, W. William George Ward and the Oxford Movement; William George Ward and the Catholic Revival.

WARREN, JOHN BYRNE LEICESTER.
See DE TABLEY, LORD

WARREN, SAMUEL (May 23, 1807-July 29, 1877), novelist, was born near Wrexham, the son of a Methodist minister who later became a clergyman in the Church of England. Warren was reared in an excessively pious home. He studied medicine in Edinburgh, then turned to the law, and was called to the bar from the Inner Temple in 1837. In 1831 he had married a Miss Ballinger, and they had several children. From earliest youth his ambition was for literary fame, though he continued his legal career. He wrote a number of technical legal works, became Queen's Counsel in 1851, and from 1852 to 1874 was recorder of Hull. In 1853 he received an honorary D.C.L. from Oxford. From 1856 to 1859 he was a Conservative member of Parliament, resigning to become Master in Lunacy, after which time he wrote no more. His literary vanity was prodigious, though most of his novels were published anonymously; he was capable of writing his own adulatory reviews and sending them in to magazines with the suggestion that they be published! His morbid and melodramatic Passages From the Diary of a Late Physician was ascribed to a well known doctor who narrowly escaped expulsion from his profession on the charge of having betrayed medical secrets. But Warren will be remembered chiefly for his Ten Thousand a Year, one of the most sensationally popular novels ever published, though now forgotten.

PRINCIPAL WORKS: Passages From the Diary of a Late Physician, 1832; A Popular and Practical Introduction to Law Studies, 1835; Ten Thousand a Year, 1841; Now and Then, 1847; Miscellanies, 1854.

ABOUT: Blackwood's Magazine September 1877; Law Times August 4 and October 20, 1877; London Times June 10, 1853; August 1 and 2, 1877; June 7, 1895.

WATERTON, CHARLES (June 3, 1782—May 27, 1865), traveler and naturalist, was born at Walton Hall, in Yorkshire, the seat of his ancient and distinguished family. Educated at Stonyhurst College, Lancashire, he spent eight years managing family estates in British Guiana (1804-12) and thereafter made four zoological expeditions in the Demerara section of Guiana, between 1813 and 1824. The last visit was preceded by a tour of America and the West Indies. On his return to England from this journey he published a classic narrative of his travels, at once entertaining and informational. His lively account of his ride on the back of a crocodile became famous. This book was still being reprinted a hundred years after its publication.

After succeeding to the family estate in 1806, he turned its wooded park and encircling lake into a bird sanctuary. Each day he rose at 3 A.M. and read a chapter in Don Quixote. He remained extremely active and in excellent health until a few days before his eighty-third birthday when he fell from a bridge on his grounds and sustained fatal injuries; he was buried on the shore of his lake. His only child, EDMUND WATERTON (1830-1887), was an antiquary.

PRINCIPAL WORKS: Wanderings in South America, The Northwest of the United States, and the Antilles, 1825; Essays in Natural History (3 ser.) 1838-57.

ABOUT: Hobson, R. Charles Waterton: His Home, Habits, and Handiwork; Waterton, C. Essays in Natural History (see Autobiography prefaced to each ser., also Life by N. Moore in posthumous eds.).

WATSON, JOHN (November 3, 1850-May 6, 1907), Scotch-English novelist and clergyman, who wrote under the pseudonym of "Ian Maclaren," was born at Manningtree, Essex. He was the only child of John Watson, later receiver-general of taxes for Scotland, and Isabella Maclaren.

After attending the grammar school at Perth, he went to Stirling High School, and matriculated at Edinburgh in 1866. He was graduated in 1870 with the degree of M.A., having done a great deal of reading in philosophy. To please his Free Church parents, he studied for the ministry at New College, Edinburgh, from 1870 to 1874, and spent a short while at Tübingen.

He was successively assistant at Barclay church, Edinburgh, minister of the Free Church at Logiealmond, Perthshire (1875-77) and assistant, then successor, to the rector of Free St. Matthew's, Edinburgh. In 1880 he was appointed to the Presbyterian church in the Sefton Park district of Liverpool, and there spent twenty-five successful years, winning fame as a preacher. On the day of Matthew Arnold's death, the famous man of letters had attended Watson's church and had declared himself unusually impressed by the sermon. Dr. Watson built a magnificent church for his congregation, was one of the founders of Liverpool University, and was influential in transferring Westminster College to Cambridge. He received numerous honors, among them the honorary degree of D.D. from Yale, where in 1896 he delivered

JOHN WATSON

the Lyman Beecher lectures. Having resigned from his Sefton Park charge, he undertook in 1907 a lecture tour of the United States and Canada—his third—and was stricken with what appeared to be tonsilitis. Complications arising from this attack led to his death at Mt. Pleasant, Iowa, in his fifty-eighth year. He was survived by his wife, the former Jane Burnie, whom he had married in 1878, and by their four sons.

It was W. R. Nicoll, editor of *The Expositor,* who, in the search for new talent, discovered Dr. Watson and urged him to try his hand at a few sketches of Scottish country life. The clergyman had put away the thoughts of a literary career that he had entertained when younger, but he consented to make the attempt, and wrote the tales and sketches which were later published in book form as *Beside the Bonnie Brier Bush.* This, published in 1894 and followed by *The Days of Auld Lang Syne* (1895) and *Kate Carnegie* (1897) made him wealthy and famous, led to his lecture tours of the United States and Canada, and made him the chief representative of the "kailyard school." His pseudonym, Ian Maclaren, was not an effective disguise, but was probably used to differentiate the fiction writer from the author of religious works such as *The Mind of the Master* (1897), which brought him for a while under suspicion of heresy.

Maclaren was a hard-working, kindly, tolerant, and open-handed clergyman, eloquent in the pulpit and possessed of a sharp irony which he was too good-natured to employ often. Major Pond, who managed his lecture tours, described his physical appearance as that of a tall, athletic, man, with a large

head, thinning hair, clear eyes, and an expression at once shrewdly humorous and dignified; and over all, the typical Highlander.

His novels and stories have been severely criticized for their sentimentality and idyllic one-sidedness. However, Maclaren tried rather to brighten a life that was often hard and bitter, and had no pretensions toward being a realist. He understood the Scotch peasantry, knew the problems of his characters, and was interesting, witty, and colorful in his writing. He never read his own works after publication and sedulously avoided all discussion of them.

His theological works, published under his own name, are tolerant in attitude, numerous, and varied in subject matter.   R.M.

PRINCIPAL WORKS: *Fiction*—Beside the Bonnie Brier Bush, 1894; Days of Auld Lang Syne, 1895; Kate Carnegie, 1897; Afterwards and Other Stories, 1898; Rabbi Saunderson, 1899; The Young Barbarians, 1901; His Majesty Baby, 1902; St. Judith, 1907; Graham of Claverhouse, 1908. *Theology and Sermons*—The Cure of Souls, 1896; The Mind of the Master, 1896; The Life of the Master, 1901.

ABOUT: Nicoll, W. R. Ian Maclaren; Pond, J. B. Eccentricities of Genius; Bookman 29:6 March 1909; Palimpsest 7:273 July 1931.

WATTS, ALARIC ALEXANDER (March 16, 1797—April 5, 1864), poet, was born in London. He edited successively the *Leeds Intelligencer* (1822-25), the *Manchester Courier* (1825-26), and the *United Service Gazette* (1833-47). Between 1824 and 1838 he edited a series of annuals entitled the *Literary Souvenir,* which originated a fashion for similar annuals and pocket-books. Bankrupt by his various journalistic ventures, he spent the last decade of his life in a minor post in the inland revenue office and was the recipient of a civil list pension of £100 yearly. In 1856 he edited the first issue of *Men of the Time,* in which he gave himself three times as much space as Tennyson.

He is rated a poet of little merit, his chief claim to remembrance being the familiar alliterative line, "An Austrian army awfully arrayed," contained in his collection *Lyrics of the Heart.* J. G. Lockhart gave him ignominious immortality in a rhyme beginning "I *don't* like that Alaric *Attila* Watts, His verses are like the pans and the pots." To which George Saintsbury added this comment: "The pans were neatly enough polished and the pots were quite clean; but they were turned out by mould and machinery, and there was very little in them."

PRINCIPAL WORKS: Poetical Sketches, 1822; The Poetical Album (ed.) 1828; Lyrics of the Heart, 1850.

ABOUT: Watts, A. A. [son]. Alaric Watts: A Narrative of His Life.

WATTS-DUNTON, (WALTER) THEO-DORE (October 12, 1832-June 7, 1914), novelist and poet, was born at St. Ives, Huntingdonshire, the son of a solicitor named Watts. In 1897 he added to his name his mother's maiden name of Dunton; previously he had been known as Theodore Watts.

The father was keenly interested in science, and sent his son to Cambridge with a view to his becoming a naturalist. Though he retained his interest in science, he was for some reason removed and articled to his father, himself becoming a solicitor. Much of his boyhood had been spent in roving with the gypsies in the neighborhood, and he flattered himself quite without justification on having some Romany blood in his veins. He did at any rate meet and become a friend of George Borrow, the famous writer on the gypsies, and later edited his works.

After being articled as a solicitor, Watts, as he then was, came to London and began the practice of his profession. He was also inclined to journalism, however, and soon began writing anonymous critical articles, first for *The Examiner* and later for *The Athenaeum*, to which he was a lifelong contributor. It was in a professional capacity as solicitor that he first became acquainted with Rossetti and Swinburne, instituting friendships that became the chief events and achievements of his life. In both cases he came upon the poets at a time when their affairs, financial, physical, and emotional, were at their lowest ebb. Watts was ideally suited to take over from their ineffective hands the entire conduct of their lives. He constituted himself the guardian, first of Rossetti, whom he tended sedulously until his death, then of Swinburne (actually committed to him by the poet's distracted mother), whom he practically abducted to Putney. For thirty years, until he died, Swinburne lived with Watts-Dunton in their famous house, The Pines, a tame celebrity, carefully shielded from alcohol and excitement. Undoubtedly he saved Swinburne's life (it was too late to do much more than ease Rossetti's last laudanum-clouded days), but in rescuing the man he killed the poet. However, poet and man would probably have died together very soon if the little solicitor had not come to the rescue, and no one can doubt Watts-Dunton's single-minded devotion to his hero—any more than one can overlook his extreme jealously and sense of proprietorship.

Regarding his own writing, Watts-Dunton was humble, though he took a pardonable vanity in the great success of his gypsy novel, *Aylwin*. Indeed, he was sixty-five before he published any volume under his own name. And he was seventy-three before he married! His wife was Clara Reich, many years his junior, who came to live with the two old men,

THEODORE WATTS-DUNTON

her husband and Swinburne, at The Pines. She was a reverent worshipper, and adapted herself admirably to this strange marriage.

Watts-Dunton was a very small man, bald, with a heavy drooping mustache over a retreating chin. He had all the characteristics which might be assumed to go with such an appearance; he was egotistical, timid, secretly highly ambitious, ultra-sensitive and always looking for slights, and extremely jealous. On the other hand, "the stuffy little solicitor," who was cordially hated by all Swinburne's other friends against whom he built a fence around his captive, had his virtues. He was loyal as few friends are, his integrity and uprightness were unquestioned, he was a shrewd and unselfish man of business, and above all he had a genuine and rather pathetic love of literature, and was not a bad critic, with an eye for the best in art.

One may find the most contradictory estimates of him as a writer. To A. C. Benson he was "the apotheosis of the provincial amateur," while John Drinkwater praises him highly both as poet and as novelist. The truth probably lies somewhere in between. His best literary work was in the anonymous articles in *The Athenaeum*, of which he thought so little that he never collected them, and many of them are lost among other unsigned contributions. His article on poetry for the 9th edition of the *Encyclopaedia Britannica*, and on "The Renaissance of Wonder in Poetry" for *Chambers's Cyclopaedia of English Literature*, are masterly efforts. The trouble with his poetry itself is that there is too much wide-eyed wonder, too much straining after the ineffable, to the end that it becomes over-packed with thought, incoherent, and painfully diffuse. His novels (*Vesprie*

Towers was published posthumously, and he left an unfinished Hungarian novel called *Carniola*) display the same defects, and descend at times to the childishly grotesque. Yet they have passages of descriptive power and tender beauty. The fact is that the art at his command was not equal to the largeness of the design he conceived.

In the end, Watts-Dunton will live by virtue of the friends—Borrow, Tennyson, Rossetti, Swinburne—whom he attached to himself by making himself necessary to them. His volume of reminiscences, *Old Familiar Faces,* is a valuable source-book for private information concerning the great whom he knew so well.   M. A. deF.

PRINCIPAL WORKS: The Coming of Love and Other Poems, 1897; Aylwin, 1898; Christmas at the Mermaid, 1902; Old Familiar Faces, 1916; Vesprie Towers, 1916.

ABOUT: Douglas, J. Theodore Watts-Dunton: Poet, Critic, Novelist; Hake, T. St. E. & Compton-Rickett, A. Life and Letters of Theodore Watts-Dunton; Kernahan, C. In Good Company; Watts-Dunton, C. The Home Life of Swinburne; Dial 57:7 July 1, 1914; Literary Digest 49:62 July 11, 1914; Living Age 282:180 July 18, 1914; 343:531 February 1933; Nineteenth Century 76:674 September 1914; Outlook 107:378 June 20, 1914; Review of Reviews 50:105 July 1914.

WAUGH, EDWIN (January 29, 1817—April 30, 1890) Lancashire poet, was born at Rochdale, the son of a shoemaker. Self-taught while apprenticed to a local bookseller, he worked successively as a journeyman printer in the provinces and London, as head of a literary institute in Rochdale, as assistant secretary to the Lancashire Public School Association (with headquarters in Manchester), and as town traveler for a Manchester printing firm. From 1860 onwards he lived by his pen, though after 1881 his dwindling royalties were augmented by a civil list pension of £90 yearly. He died at New Brighton, Lancashire, at the age of seventy-three, and was buried in Manchester.

The best known of his works is the song "Come Whoam to the Children an' Me," which the *Saturday Review* called "one of the most delicious idylls in the world" and of which the Baroness Burdett-Coutts distributed some ten or twenty thousand copies gratuitously. His works in prose and verse dealt mainly with Lancashire life in town and country, and he is particularly notable for his rendering of the dialect of his native country. Many of his songs have been set to music.

PRINCIPAL WORKS: Sketches of Lancashire Life and Localities, 1855; Come Whoam to the Childer and Me, 1856; Poems and Lancashire Songs, 1859; Collected Works (illus. by R. Caldecott) 1881-89; Selected Works (ed. by G. Milner) 1892-93.

ABOUT: Espinasse, F. Literary Recollections and Sketches; Waugh, E. Selected Works (see Memoir by G. Milner).

WEBSTER, AUGUSTA (January 30, 1837-September 5, 1894), poet, was born Julia Augusta Davies, the daughter of a vice-admiral, at Poole, Dorset. Educated at the Cambridge School of Art and in France, she was married in December 1863 to Thomas Webster, fellow and subsequently law lecturer of Trinity College, Cambridge. They had one daughter. From 1870 onwards they lived in London, where her husband practised law. She died at Kew at the age of fifty-seven.

Her work was strongly influenced by that of Robert Browning and Elizabeth Barrett Browning, and she successfully used the form of the dramatic monologue. According to the *Cambridge History,* her verses "sometimes employed Robert Browning's licences without his justifications, and, at others, became unspeakably monotonous." She is remembered, however, as a skilful experimenter in lyrical meters, and is represented in anthologies of Victorian verse. In addition to her original poetic works, she produced commendable translations from the Greek, and wrote a novel and essays for *The Examiner.*

PRINCIPAL WORKS: *Poetry*—The Prometheus Bound of Æschylus (tr.) 1866; Dramatic Studies, 1866; A Woman Sold and Other Poems, 1867; The Medea of Euripides (tr.) 1868; Portraits, 1870; Yu-Pe-Ya's Lute: A Chinese Tale in English Verse, 1874; The Auspicious Day, 1874; A Book of Rhyme, 1881; The Sentence, 1887. *Prose*—A Housewife's Opinions. 1878; Lesley's Guardians (novel) 1864.

ABOUT: Athenaeum September 15, 1894.

WEBSTER, BENJAMIN NOTTINGHAM (September 3, 1797-July 3, 1882), actor and playwright, was born in Bath. His father, after a varied career, had settled down as a dancing and fencing master; his uncle was a theatrical manager in London. He was educated at Dr. Barber's Military Academy, but threw up a promised commission in the navy to become a dancer. He then ran away from home, and after many vicissitudes, which included marriage to a widow with several children, gradually made his way on the stage as a dancer, pantomimist, orchestra leader, violinist, and actor. He became one of the best known character actors of his time. In 1837 he became lessee of the Haymarket Theater, and in 1844 manager of the Adelphi also; in 1853 he gave up the Haymarket and managed the Adelphi alone. His best part was in Taylor and Reade's *Masks and Faces.* His last appearance was in 1875, seven years before his death. Webster founded a family of actors, two of his sons, his grandson, and his great-granddaughter all being on the stage.

In all Webster wrote or adapted (mostly from the French) about a hundred plays, for the greater part farces and light comedies. Many of them have never appeared in print; the majority of those which have been published he himself arranged for his anthology of contemporary plays. Among the best known of his own plays were *Caught in a Trap, The Man of Law,* and *The Golden Farmer.*

PRINCIPAL WORK: Acting National Drama, 1837-38.

ABOUT: Era July 15, 1882.

WEIR, HARRISON WILLIAM (May 5, 1824-January 3, 1906), artist and writer on animals, was born at Lewes, Sussex, his father being first a bank manager, then a government clerk. He was educated at Albany Academy, Cornwall, and from 1837 to 1844 apprenticed to a color printer. In 1842, when the *Illustrated London News* was started, he became a draughtsman and engraver, and remained with the magazine all his life, at his death being the last surviving member of the original staff. He did drawings also for the *Pictorial Times* and the *Field.* Occasionally he exhibited paintings of animals at the Royal Academy and elsewhere, but he was primarily a book illustrator. All of his own books, which deal with the animals with which he had such vivid sympathy, are illustrated by himself. He was also a practical horticulturist, and wrote for gardening magazines. In 1891 he received a civil list pension. He died at nearly eighty-two at his home in Kent. Weir was thrice married: in 1845 to Anne Herring, daughter of an animal painter; after her death to Alice Upjohn, who died in 1898; and then to Eva Gabell. He had in all two sons and two daughters.

PRINCIPAL WORKS: Every Day in the Country, 1883; Animal Stories, 1885; Our Cats and All About Them, 1889; Our Poultry and All About Them, 1903.

ABOUT: Daily Chronicle May 6, 1904; January 5, 1906; Field January 6, 1906; Nature January 11, 1906.

WELLS, CHARLES JEREMIAH (c.1800-February 1, 1879), poet, was born in London of middle-class parents. He was educated at Edmonton, where one of his classmates was Thomas Keats, younger brother of the poet, through whom Wells became acquainted with the latter. At first they were friendly—Wells is mentioned as the friend who sent Keats some roses and is commemorated in the sonnet on that subject—but later, owing to Wells' incurable habit of practical joking, the relationship ended.

Wells was constitutionally lazy and a poor scholar. Although he studied law and succeeded in gaining admission to the bar, he thoroughly neglected his profession and strove to earn his living by authorship. His *Stories After Nature,* published in 1822, was unsuccessful, however, and his principal work, the dramatic poem *Joseph and His Brethren,* went almost unnoticed when it appeared in 1823.

Now completely discouraged, Wells willingly accepted his friends' judgment that he had no great talent for literature, and their counsel, which was to abandon it. A short while afterward, he also abandoned his profession, and retired to the country to enjoy field sports and gardening. In 1840 he went to Brittany to live, and was afterwards professor at Quimper. His last years were spent at Marseilles.

Despite his former discouragement, Wells was unable to resist literature, and it is known that he wrote several long works, which, however, were never published, and no longer exist, for upon the death in 1874 of his wife (the former Miss Hill of Leamington whom he had married around 1835) he made a bonfire of his writings.

Just a year later Algernon Charles Swinburne, the poet, wrote an enthusiastic review of *Joseph and His Brethren,* in which he said that "a new poet was in the world, and one only lesser than the greatest of his time in some of the greatest qualities of his art. . ." With this encouragement, a new edition of the poem was brought out in 1876, with a preface by Swinburne. Dante Gabriel Rossetti, the painter-poet, was also a champion of Wells, and obliged his disciples and friends to read the poem.

There is much in *Joseph and His Brethren* of the noble and dramatic. It reproduces the Elizabethan grand manner with remarkable success, and in such scenes as those between Joseph and Potiphar's wife rises almost to greatness, but it is not the great work Swinburne and Rossetti thought it. Edmund Gosse felt that its merits were those of "rich versification, a rather florid and voluble eloquence, and a subtle trick of reserve," and Edward

CHARLES JEREMIAH WELLS

Garnett considered it undramatic, dull in subject matter, and slow in movement. After Wells' death, Harry Buxton Forman, the editor of Keats and Shelley, discovered a previously unpublished scene from the poem and it was included in *Literary Anecdotes of the Nineteenth Century* (Nicoll and Wise) in 1895.

Wells was a man of stumpy figure with a snub nose, bright blue eyes, reddish hair and a ruddy complexion. Theodore Watts-Dunton speaks of his "merry laugh with which throughout his lifetime he met every ill that life had to offer."

For the last year of his life he was confined to his bed. His exact age is not known, and he was probably older than the surmised date of his birth would indicate. He was survived, as far as can be ascertained, by one daughter, who became a nun, and by a son who rose to some eminence as an engineer, but achieved greater notice as the inspiration of the song "The Man Who Broke the Bank at Monte Carlo." R.M.

WORKS: *Prose*—Stories after Nature, 1822. *Poetry*—Joseph and His Brethren, 1823.
ABOUT: Nicoll, W. R. & Wise, T. J. Literary Anecdotes of the Nineteenth Century: Vol. 1; Wells, C. J. Joseph and His Brethren (see Introduction by A. C. Swinburne).

WENTWORTH, WILLIAM CHARLES (October 26, 1793-March 20, 1872), Australian poet and historian, was born on Norfolk Island, then a penal dependency of New South Wales. His father, an Irishman, was the government surgeon there. He was sent to England, to the Greenwich School, at seven. In 1810 he returned to Sydney, and the next year, though only eighteen, was made deputy provost marshal. In 1813 he participated in an exploration of the Blue Mountains, receiving a grant of a thousand acres of this newly discovered territory. In 1816 he went back to England, studied at Peterhouse College, Cambridge, and at the Middle Temple, and was called to the bar in 1822. He then returned to Sydney with a Dr. Wardwell, the two young men being the only barristers in the city. In 1824 they established and edited together *The Australian*, which became the organ of the "Emancipists," whose leader Wentworth then was. (This was the party of those who believed that Australia belonged to the transported convicts, and should not be made a free colony open to emigration.) In its behalf he founded the Patriotic Association, and succeeded by 1831 in recalling the anti-Emancipist governor. At the first election, in 1842, Wells was made a member of the colonial parliament, and became the leader of the Squatter Party, founding the Pastoral Association in its interests. He was never, however, a democrat; all he wanted was a self-governing state, and though the accusa-

tion that in later years he proved a turncoat may be unjustified, there is no doubt that he tried to grab for himself practically all New Zealand! His desire for the welfare of Australia was sincere, however, and he helped to found the first colonial university there in 1852. Conditions, however, did not develop in the colony according to his views, and in disgust he spent several years in England. In 1861 he returned to Sydney, but liked things no better than before, and the next year he went back to England for good. He died in Dorset, but his body was taken to Sydney for a public funeral. He was married, his wife having been Sarah Cox, of Sydney. They had two sons and five daughters.

PRINCIPAL WORKS: A Statistical, Historical, and Political Description of the British Settlements in Australasia, 1819; Australasia (poem) 1823.
ABOUT: London Times March 21, 1872.

WEST, SIR EDWARD (1782-August 1828), economist, was born in Middlesex and educated at University College, Oxford. He received his B.A. in 1804, his M.A. in 1807, was made a fellow of the college, and was called to the bar from the Inner Temple in 1814. He was soon after appointed recorder of Bombay, and became chief justice in 1823. He had been knighted the year before. He remained in India in this latter post until his death in Bombay at only forty-six. As an economist he anticipated David Ricardo, who acknowledged his debt to West in the origination of his famous theory of rent. His work was the first to state the economic "law of diminishing returns."

PRINCIPAL WORKS: Essay on the Application of Capital to Land, 1815; The Price of Corn and Wages of Labour, 1826.
ABOUT: London Times January 29, 1829.

WESTALL, WILLIAM BURY (February 7, 1834-September 9, 1903), novelist and journalist, was born near Blackburn, Lancashire. After an education at the Liverpool High School the youth entered his father's cotton-spinning business. Journalism, however, became his occupation about 1870, and he sent newspaper dispatches from Dresden and Geneva. In the latter city he came to know Russian revolutionaries, including Prince Kropotkin. These experiences and his travels in the Western Hemisphere supplied material for his many novels. Their hairbreadth escapes and other old-fashioned characteristics made them out of date by the time of the author's death—indeed, he was not at any time considered first-rate in importance—but these same traits made his stories attractive to many readers.

PRINCIPAL WORKS: Tales and Traditions of Saxony and Lusatia, 1877; The Old Factory, 1881; Her Two Millions, 1897; Larry Lohengrin, 1881; Red Ryvington, 1882; The Phantom City, 1886; The

Witch's Curse, 1893; With the Red Eagle, 1897; Dr. Wynne's Revenge, 1903.

ABOUT: London Times September 12, 1903; T. P.'s Weekly September 18, 1903.

WESTCOTT, BROOKE FOSS (Bishop of Durham) (January 12, 1825-July 27, 1901), Biblical scholar, was born near Birmingham, the son of a botanist. After a brilliant career at Cambridge he took orders and became a teacher at Harrow. His Biblical and theological studies brought him recognition; and in 1870 he became regius professor of divinity at Cambridge. In this capacity he instituted significant educational and admistrative reforms. Accepting in 1890 the bishopric of Durham, he made obvious his interest in social reform, especially problems involving labor; and he often addressed audiences of workers, among whom he was highly respected. His works include Biblical criticism and commentary, some of which has since become out of date, and an edition of the Greek text of the New Testament which was considered an epoch-making achievement. Though he was not a facile writer, his production was large. His personal influence was probably his greatest source of power.

PRINCIPAL WORKS: A General Survey of the History of the Canon of the New Testament During the First Four Centuries, 1855; Introduction to the Study of the Gospels, 1860; The Bible in the Church, 1864; The Gospel of the Resurrection, 1866; A General View of the History of the English Bible, 1868; The New Testament in the Original Greek (ed. with F. J. A. Hort) 1881; The Epistles of St. John: The Greek Text With Notes and Essays, 1883; Social Aspects of Christianity, 1887; The Gospel of Life, 1892.

ABOUT: Benson, A. C. The Leaves of the Tree; Nicol', G. W. E. The Household of Faith; Westcott, A. Life and Letters of Brooke Foss Westcott; Biblical World ns20:9 July 24, 1902; Church Quarterly Review 53:182 October 1901; Contemporary Review 80:503 October 1901.

WESTMACOTT, CHARLES MALLOY ("Bernard Blackmantle") (1787?-c. August 1868), journalist, was the illegitimate son of Richard Westmacott, a sculptor. Educated at St. Paul's School, London, and the Royal Academy, he managed by his own ability (his father's legitimate heir having left him to his own devices) to become editor of The Age, a Tory satirical paper. His criticisms made him feared and hated. Charles Kemble, the actor, thrashed him to avenge an uncomplimentary reference to his daughter, Fanny Kemble, the actress, and Edward Bulwer, the novelist, threatened horsewhipping for a similar offense. His works retail personalities and gossip, and he acquired a reputation for bullying and levying blackmail by the use of his columns. He is said to have extorted almost £5,000 from the participants in a scandalous intrigue involving members of the Court. His chief books are satirical and personal collections, rather coarse, but lively.

PRINCIPAL WORKS: Points of Misery, 1823; Fitzalleyne of Berkeley, 1825; The English Spy, 1825; The Punster's Pocketbook, 1826; The Spirit of "The Age" Newspaper, 1829.

ABOUT: Maclise, D. The Maclise Portrait-Gallery; Fraser's Magazine 9:536 May 1834; Theatre 19:289 December 1887.

WESTWOOD, THOMAS (November 26, 1814-March 13, 1888), poet and bibliographer, was born in Enfield, the son of an eccentric retired haberdasher who was a friend of Charles Lamb. Free to browse in Lamb's library, the boy acquired a taste for letters, especially for Izaak Walton; and in 1840 he issued his first volume of poems. In 1844 he accepted a position as director and secretary of a Belgian railway; and he spent most of the rest of his life in that country, collecting books on fishing and issuing exhaustive and elaborate bibliographies and catalogues on the subject which are still valuable. As a poet he has been described as "post-Tennysonian," having more polish than vigor. The poet Landor is said to have admired one of his poems. Though they were praised in the author's time for their daintiness and evidences of fine taste, they have been almost entirely forgotten.

PRINCIPAL WORKS: Poems, 1840; Beads From a Rosary, 1843; The Burden of the Bell, 1850; Berries and Blossoms, 1855; The Chronicle of The "Compleat Angler" of Izaak Walton and Charles Cotton, 1864; The Quest of the Sancgreall, 1868; Bibliotheca Piscatoria (with Thomas Satchell) 1883.

ABOUT: Miles, A. H. (ed.). The Poets and the Poetry of the Century; Academy 33:222 March 31, 1888; Notes and Queries 3s 10:221 September 22, 1866.

WHATELY, RICHARD (February 1, 1787-October 1, 1863), theologian and economist, was the son of a clergyman. As a child he was extremely delicate and very precocious. His father died in 1797. He was educated in a private school and then in Oriel College, Oxford, receiving his B.A. in 1808 and his M.A. in 1812. He won the English essay prize while an undergraduate, and was made a fellow in 1811. He then took holy orders, and in 1825 received his B.D. and D.D. degrees. As a tutor he was an excellent teacher, but most unconventional in his conduct, rough and unsympathetic and given to argument. He started his literary career during this period as a contributor to the Quarterly Review.

In 1821 Whately married Elizabeth Pope, who died in 1860, leaving one son and several daughters. Having to vacate his fellowship on his marriage, he became vicar of Halesworth, Suffolk, in 1822, also lecturing at Oxford. In 1825 he became principal of St. Alban Hall, the reputation of which for scholarship was so bad that it was known as "the Botany Bay of the university." Whately reformed it, with the assistance of John Henry (later Cardinal) New-man, who had been his pupil and became his vice-principal. From 1829 to 1831 he was also professor of political economy at Oxford.

In 1831 he was named as Archbishop of Dublin. He was unpopular in Ireland, man-aging to antagonize both the Roman Cath-olics and the Protestants. However, he worked hard in the interests of his see. He founded a chair of political economy at Trinity College, Dublin, and was vice-president of the Royal Irish Academy in 1848. Besides his many books, Whately edited Bacon and Paley. In 1856 he suffered a paralytic stroke, and though he lived for seven years more his days of activity were over.

Whately's interests were very narrow, and he was stubborn and intractable. His work is superficial and opinionated. But his mind was acute, active, and versatile, he was a marked liberal in many ways; and he was especially good at popularizing dry and dif-ficult subjects for beginning students. The *Letters on the Church* attributed to him were published anonymously and he never acknowl-edged their authorship, though he probably wrote them.

PRINCIPAL WORKS: Elements of Logic, 1826; Elements of Rhetoric, 1828; The Errors of Roman-ism, 1830; Introductory Lectures on Political Economy, 1832; Easy Lessons on Reasoning, 1843; Introductory Lessons on Mind, 1859; Miscellaneous Lectures and Reviews, 1861.

ABOUT: Whately, E. J. [daughter]. Life and Correspondence of Richard Whately, D.D.; Guardian October 14, 1863; London Times October 9, 1863.

WHEWELL, WILLIAM (May 24, 1794-March 6, 1866), scientific and philosophical writer, was born in Lancaster, the eldest of seven children of a master carpenter. His brilliant mind as a young child secured his ad-mission free to the Lancaster Grammar School, and he had a distinguished career there, particularly in mathematics. In 1810 he went to the Heversham Grammar School, and from there to Trinity College, Cambridge, taking his B.A. in 1816 as second wrangler (second highest in mathematics). After some private tutoring, in 1817 he became fellow of his college, assistant tutor the next year, and tutor in 1823. He was one of the founders of the Cambridge Philosophical Society, learned German thoroughly, and specialized in German philosophy, especially the philosophy of Kant. At the same time he did much work in physics and mathematics, being mathematics lecturer in 1820. The same year he was made a fellow of the Royal Society.

He was ordained priest in 1825, and was made moderator of his college in 1828. His vacation tours were devoted to the study of ecclesiastical architecture. In 1827 he be-

came a fellow of the Geological Society, and was its president from 1837 to 1839. From 1828 to 1832 he was professor of mineralogy at Cambridge. In 1838 he was elected Knightsbridge professor of moral philosophy. In 1841 he married Cordelia Marshall, who died in 1855. The year of his marriage he also became master of Trinity. In 1842 and 1843 he was vice-chancellor of Cambridge, and did much to help broaden the university curriculum. Three years after his wife's death he married a widow, Lady Everina (Ellis) Affleck, who continued to be known as Lady Affleck. This markedly happy mar-riage was ended by her death in 1865. His second wife's fortune enabled Whewell to found and endow a chair of international law in Cambridge. He was still active in his work at seventy-two, when he died as a consequence of being thrown by his horse.

Whewell was a critic of science rather than an original investigator. The later revisions of his *History of the Inductive Sciences* are marred by his absorption in philosophy and his failure to keep up with the changes in science. Nevertheless, it is a classic in its field, and still of value. In addition to his other writing, he translated widely from the German, in sev-eral different fields of literature.

PRINCIPAL WORKS: Treatise on Mechanics, 1819; Treatise on Dynamics, 1823; History of the Induc-tive Sciences, 1837; Philosophy of the Inductive Sciences, 1840; Elements of Morality, 1845; Six Lectures on Political Economy, 1862.

ABOUT: Douglas, Mrs. S. [niece]. Life and Selec-tions From the Correspondence of William Whewell; Todhunter, I. William Whewell.

WHITE, HENRY KIRKE (March 21, 1785-October 19, 1806), "the boy poet of Nottingham," was the second son of John White, a Nottingham butcher, and Mary (Neville) White.

He was at first destined for his father's trade, and was educated only briefly in the local schools. But his precocious intelligence began to attract attention, and at fifteen he was put into a law-office. Although the pro-fession did not appeal to him, he made such progress that within two years he was articled to a firm of solicitors. Fortunately, his em-ployers were sympathetic men who encour-aged his literary ambitions.

White's literary tastes developed early. When scarcely in his teens he was a member of a literary society in Nottingham. At fif-teen he won a medal for translations of Horace. The following year his imaginary "Tour From London to Edinburgh" won him another prize and some repute. Practical enough to see and use all literary opportuni-ties within his reach, he now began to write for the *Monthly Preceptor,* a juvenile maga-zine; he soon became a regular correspondent. He wrote also for the *Monthly Mirror,*

HENRY KIRKE WHITE

through which he became acquainted with Capell Lofft, a literary amateur of the period. In 1803 Lofft and several others interested themselves in urging publication of White's poems. These came out, before his eighteenth birthday, in a small volume, *Clifton Grove*, dedicated to the Duchess of Devonshire. It received only commonplace notice. However, Robert Southey saw and admired the book. His letter to White was the basis of a lifetime friendship.

Stirred with ambition to take holy orders, White left the law-office in 1804 to prepare for matriculation at St. John's College, Cambridge. Through the kindness of clerical friends he received a certain financial competence, but the difficulties of previous years and the limited formal education he had received now made necessary a period of most intense mental labor. Even before he entered St. John's in 1805, his health was seriously weakened by overstudy. At Cambridge the strain continued; the university, impressed by his exceptional standing in the examinations, even offered him a tutor for the long vacation. Southey said of this period of his career: "Never, perhaps, had any young man, in so short a time, excited such expectations; every University honor was thought to be within his reach; he was set down as medallist, and expected to take a senior wrangler's degree. . ."

Suddenly the strain proved too great. White collapsed and died in 1806, at the age of twenty-one. Had he recovered, it was thought probable that his intellect would have been affected. He was buried in All Saints' Church, Cambridge, at the expense of Francis Boott, an American physician and patron of the arts.

A considerable body of literary remains was presented to Southey by White's brother Neville and opened in the presence of Coleridge. The remains were edited by Southey, with a short biographical memoir, in three volumes. The remarkable scope of White's interests is immediately apparent to the reader of these volumes. Here are essays on electricity, prayer, poetry, and other topics equally diverse. Southey commented, with pardonable exaggeration, "I have inspected all the existing manuscripts of Chatterton, and they excited less wonder than these."

White was amiable, earnest, devoted to his family, deeply religious, modest in manner but aware of his abilities. He was widely read in the classical languages and knew Portuguese, Italian, and French. His intellectual curiosity was almost indefatigable.

In his day White's writings were regarded highly. Byron praised him and Southey was proud to call him his protégé. The age romanticized him as a second Chatterton, cut off prematurely, the victim of a hard and uncongenial life. This sympathetic attitude toward the person probably influenced critical judgment of the work; for modern estimates of White's importance as a writer are considerably lower than those held in his own time. He is remembered today only as the author of a few happy nature lyrics and some hymns, of which the best known are: "Star of Bethlehem" and "Oft in Danger, Oft in Woe." What his achievements *might* have been, had he lived, is another and unanswerable question.

PRINCIPAL WORKS: Clifton Grove, 1803; The Poetical Works and Remains of Henry Kirke White, 1807-22.

ABOUT: Brown, C. Lives of Nottinghamshire Worthies; Godfrey, J. T. & Ward, J. The Homes and Haunts of Henry Kirke White; Julian, J. Dictionary of Hymnology; White, H. K. Poetical Works and Remains (see Memoir by Robert Southey); White, H. K. Poems, Letters, and Prose Fragments (see Prefatory Note by John Drinkwater to Muses' Library ed.).

WHITE, WILLIAM HALE ("Mark Rutherford") (December 22, 1831-March 14, 1913), novelist and critic, was born at Bedford, eldest son of William White, bookseller and printer, and Mary Anne (Chignell) White. The father was a staunch Liberal in politics and an enthusiastic member of the dissenting sect known as the Bunyan meeting, into which the young William was initiated in 1848. After schooling at Bedford Modern School, White went in 1849 to Cheshunt College, to study theology, and thence shortly afterwards to New College, Swiss Cottage, London, a Congregationalist seminary. At the end of 1851 he and two others were expelled because of unorthodox views on inspiration. His sympathies now went out to the writings of Carlyle, Emerson, and Goethe; and his churchmanship was so broad that no ministry could hold him, though he preached unofficially for a number of years in various Unitarian chapels.

In the early 'fifties White became secretary to John Chapman, publisher, and editor of the *Westminster Review*. In 1854 he entered the Civil Service as a clerk in the Registrar-General's department at Somerset House, whence he passed four years later to the Admiralty. His father had been made doorkeeper of the House of Commons, so access to the legislature was easy for the son, and in his early years at the Admiralty he supplemented his earnings by writing London letters for *The Scotsman* and other provincial papers. But this type of journalism was for him only a means of earning money, and he abandoned it as his official emoluments increased, which they did progressively until he reached the rank of assistant-director of contracts in 1879. His more serious literary interests bore fruit in critical writings in *The Athenaeum* and elsewhere, and, quite late in life, in the production of novels. He retired from the Civil Service on pension in 1892.

White's first essay in fiction remains also his best-known work, *The Autobiography of Mark Rutherford* (1881), a sincere and deeply-pondered spiritual history. It was followed by *Mark Rutherford's Deliverance* and several other works of fiction, all issued under the Rutherford pseudonym. He was a close student of Spinoza, and under his own name translated that philosopher's *Ethic* and his *Emendation of the Intellect*. Of Shakespeare and Wordsworth he was also a devotee and rigorous textual critic, publishing a destructive criticism of Knight's edition of the latter poet in *The Athenaeum*, and, in 1898, an in-teresting *Examination of the Charge of Apostasy Against Wordsworth*. He died at Groombridge, Kent, on March 14, 1913. He was twice married—to Harriet Arthur in 1856 and to Dorothy Vernon Smith in 1911.

White has his own niche among the minor novelists as the portrayer of the spiritual history of nineteenth-century dissent. The Welsh preacher, Caleb Morris, whom he met early in life, influenced him deeply; and though he was broad enough to feel real friendship for agnostics like George Eliot and G. J. Holyoake he himself never reached the negative position, but held fast to a free and unorthodox Christianity. He had a strong ethical cast of mind, and was temperamentally a puritan. His style, wrote Robertson Nicoll, "was full throughout of the simplicity which is the first step of nature and the last of art"; personally he was reserved, dignified, and modest; his sincerity was never in question, and he was not without humor. H.B.G.

PRINCIPAL WORKS: *Novels and Journals* (under pseud. "Mark Rutherford")—The Autobiography of Mark Rutherford, 1881; Mark Rutherford's Deliverance, 1885; The Revolution in Tanner's Lane, 1887; Miriam's Schooling, 1890; Catharine Furze, 1893; Clara Hopgood, 1896; Pages From a Journal, 1900; More Pages From a Journal, 1910; Last Pages From a Journal, 1915. *Miscellaneous Writings* (under own name)—translation of Spinoza's *Ethic*, 1883; translation of Spinoza's *Tractatus De Intellectus Emendatione*, 1895; A Description of the Wordsworth and Coleridge MSS. in the Possession of Mr. T. Norton Longman, 1897; An Examination of the Charge of Apostasy Against Wordsworth, 1898; John Bunyan, 1905; The Early Life of Mark Rutherford, 1913.

ABOUT: Nicoll, W. R. Memories of Mark Rutherford; Smith, S. N. Mark Rutherford: A Bibliography of the First Editions; White, D. V. The Groombridge Diary; White, W. H. The Autobiography of Mark Rutherford (see H. W. Massingham's Memorial Introduction to 1923 ed.); Mark Rutherford's Deliverance; The Early Life of Mark Rutherford.

WHITEHEAD, CHARLES (1804-July 5, 1862), novelist, dramatist, and poet, was born in London, where his father was a successful wine-merchant. Charles was well educated, though his name is not listed at Christ's Hospital, the famous English public school, as has been supposed. He left school young and became clerk in a commercial firm.

He early showed great literary promise. In 1831 "The Solitary" appeared in *The Athenaeum*. Its Spenserianisms listed Whitehead among the romantic followers of Shelley, and the poem was praised by "Christopher North." In 1834 appeared anonymously a somewhat picaresque novel, *The Autobiography of Jack Ketch*, the joint work of Charles and his brother Alfred. Never did Charles put his name to the book. It raised a storm of mingled moral condemnation and grudging literary praise.

WILLIAM HALE WHITE

Between 1840 and 1850 Whitehead had a gay period at the Mulberry and the Grotto clubs, ruining his health and destroying his future by intemperance. A taint of insanity in the family now affected a brother and a sister, and Whitehead's own idiosyncrasies became rooted. His reputation as a humorist, after *Jack Ketch* appeared, brought him an invitation to write sketches for a humorous journal. He refused, knowing his inability to send prompt copy, and suggested his friend, Charles Dickens. To this incident we owe *Pickwick Papers*. Further connection with Dickens came in his revision of *Memoirs of Grimaldi*, edited in 1838 by Dickens. The Pickwick episode shows how talented Whitehead was thought to be and illustrates his failure to employ to the full his unusual potentialities.

His novel, *Richard Savage*, based on the life of Johnson's friend, appeared in *Bentley's Miscellany*. It used the autobiographic form of the eighteenth century and again displayed Whitehead's preoccupation with the morose and terrible. It was, however, a good novel. Intemperance in 1849 cost Whitehead his position. In an effort to recover his name he went with his wife to Australia in 1857. Here he took shelter in Melbourne at the home of an admirer. Finally escaping from this refuge, he died in destitution at Melbourne Hospital and was buried in a pauper's grave. The efforts of friends to remove the body were futile.

Whitehead was tall and dark, slightly stooped and careworn; his voice was deep and pleasant, his manner shy. In later life he was morose and very nervous.

Whitehead belongs to the mid-century transition group. His poetry has been greatly over-rated, though one or two fine sonnets were admired by D. G. Rossetti. "The Solitary" has been called "patchwork." As historian he is chiefly romancer, e.g. *The Earl of Essex*. As novelist he had talent, using with skill the burlesque and picaresque manners. He might have become one of the three or four great novelists of his time, had he not dissipated his talents. He contributed many historical and other articles to the journals, chiefly *Bentley's Miscellany*, the *Melbourne Punch*, and the *Victorian Magazine*. As dramatist he showed skill with dialogue, as in *The Cavalier* (acted by Ellen Tree and John Vandenhoff at the Haymarket in 1831). A dramatized version of *Richard Savage* later proved very popular also.   D.F.A.

PRINCIPAL WORKS: *Poetry*—The Solitary, 1831; The Cavalier, 1836; The Youth's New Vade Mecum, 1836-7; Rather Hard to Take, 1836-7; Victoria Victrix, 1838. *Novels and Stories*—Autobiography of Jack Ketch, 1834; Richard Savage, 1842; The Earl of Essex, 1843; Jaspar Brooke, 1845; The Wife's Tragedy, 1845; Smiles and Tears, 1847; The Orphan, 1852; The Spanish Marriage, 1859. *Historical and Miscellaneous*—Memoirs of Grimaldi, 1846; Memoir of Captain Marrayat, 1848; Caricature and Caricaturists, 1848; Sir Harry Smith, 1848; Life of Sir Walter Raleigh, 1854.

ABOUT: Bell, H. T. McK. A Forgotten Genius: Charles Whitehead; Caine, T. H. Recollections of Dante Gabriel Rossetti; Hodder, G. Memories of My Time; Wilson, J. Noctes Ambrosianae.

WHYMPER, EDWARD (April 27, 1840-September 16, 1911), artist and explorer, was born in London. His father was an artist, and the boy was trained to be a wood-engraver. He made a tour through the Central Alps in 1860, to make sketches for a London publisher, and in 1861 successfully made the ascent of Mont Pelvoux. In the next few years he accomplished various other feats, including ascents of the Pointe des Ecrins and the Matterhorn; in the latter exploit (1865) he narrowly escaped the death that overtook four of the party, who slipped and were killed. Continuing his travels, he made trips to Greenland, collecting trees, shrubs, and fossils, and a journey to Ecuador, where he gathered material for study of mountain-sickness and the effects on the human frame of low atmospheric pressure. His interesting narratives tell of his mountain adventures, and are embellished by his own engravings.

PRINCIPAL WORKS: Scrambles Amongst the Alps in the Years 1860-69, 1871; Travels Amongst the Great Andes of the Equator, 1892.

ABOUT: Johnston, Sir H. H. (ed.). A Book of Great Travellers; Kernahan, C. In Good Company; Popular Science Monthly 82:559-66 June 1913.

WHYTE-MELVILLE, GEORGE JOHN (June 19, 1821-December 5, 1878), sporting novelist and poet, was the son of John Whyte-Melville of Strathkinnes, Fifeshire, by his wife Catherine Anne Sarah, daughter of Francis Godolphin Osborne, fifth duke of Leeds.

After graduating from Eton, the future novelist, at the age of seventeen, received a commission in the Ninety-Third Highlanders. At twenty-four he changed to the Coldstream Guards and retired three years later with the rank of captain. When the Crimean war broke out, he volunteered for active service and was appointed major of Turkish irregular cavalry. While in the army he published some agreeable verse, and when the war ended he turned to writing fiction and to fox-hunting.

He possessed the rare advantage of writing at first hand of fashionable, military, and sporting circles; and he came to be regarded as an authority on fox-hunting. His novels appealed mainly to sporting men, and, on the whole, were written with such readers in mind; but his books, with their stamp of authenticity, their frequent poetic charm, their liveliness, and their chivalric ideals, attracted many readers of other classes. He has been

G. J. WHYTE-MELVILLE

criticized for frequenting the society of soldiers, sportsmen, and country gentlemen, rather than that of literary people, on the score that literary companionship would have helped him to address a wider public. However that may be, he could hardly have ranked higher than he did with the readers he addressed.

Most of his novels are not remarkable for plot. *Market Harborough*—to take one of the most popular as an example—is simply a series of hunting episodes strung around the central character; and it speaks highly for the author's skill that nowhere is the book dull.

In his historical novels, such as *The Gladiators*, he followed the established form of Scott. These were less popular than the stories devoted to fox-hunting, steeple-chasing, and country-house life; but are interesting for their air of reality and their faithfulness to ordinary types of character.

Whyte-Melville was inclined to underestimate his literary powers; and it is believed that had it been necessary for him to earn his living by writing, or had there been some other incentive, he might have made a greater name for himself. As it was, he devoted the rather large earnings from his books to charitable ends, mainly to providing reading and recreation rooms for grooms and stable-boys in hunting quarters.

Aside from novels, he wrote *Riding Recollections*, a valuable book on horsemanship, and some poetry. *The True Cross* is a religious poem of distinction; and in his *Songs and Verses* are several lyrics of real charm. Adam Lindsay Gordon, the Australian poet, dedicated his *Bush Ballads* to Whyte-Melville, whom he greatly admired.

Lewis Melville has written of Whyte-Melville: "He grew enthusiastic at the mere thought of noble, generous actions. . . His philosophy was not very deep, perhaps, but it was always thoroughly sound. Though he never wrote a novel with a purpose, he often inculcated a moral, always quite simple, as for instance, that earthen pots and iron pots cannot go downstream together very far, without damage to the former.

In 1847 he married Charlotte Hanbury, daughter of the first lord of Bateman; they had one daughter. His married life was markedly unhappy, and left its melancholy impress on his writings.

He was an excellent horseman, but it was on an old and favorite horse that he met his death. While hunting near his home in Northamptonshire, he started the horse into a gallop along the headland of a ploughed field. The horse fell and he was killed instantly.   P.G.

PRINCIPAL WORKS: *Novels*—Captain Digby Grand, 1853; Kate Coventry, 1856; Market Harborough, 1861; Tilbury Nogo, 1861; The Queen's Maries, 1862; The Gladiators, 1863; A Losing Hazard, 1870; Satanella, 1873; Katerfelto, 1876; Black but Comely, 1879; *Poetry*—The True Cross, 1873; Songs and Verses, 1869. *Miscellaneous*—Riding Recollections, 1875.

ABOUT: Locker-Lampson, F. My Confidences; Melville, L. Some Victorian Novelists.

WILBERFORCE, HENRY WILLIAM

(September 22, 1807-April 23, 1873), journalist and religious author, was born at Clapham, the youngest son of William Wilberforce, the Evangelical philanthropist and anti-slavery leader. He was educated at Oriel College, Oxford, where he was graduated with high standing in 1830. During this period he had made the acquaintance of John Henry Newman, at whose suggestion he took orders. Although comfortably settled in a vicarage, he resigned his position in 1850 and joined the Roman Catholic Church. He served the church of his adoption as secretary of the Catholic Defence Association and as owner and editor of the *Catholic Standard* (later the *Weekly Register*), a newspaper. His productions are interesting mainly for their religious stand; he is not an important literary figure.

PRINCIPAL WORKS: The Parochial System, 1838; Reasons for Submitting to the Catholic Church, 1851; On Some Events Preparatory to the English Reformation, 1867; The Church and the Empires, 1874.

ABOUT: Wilberforce, H. W. The Church and the Empires (see Memoir by J. H. Newman); Catholic World 88:290 December 1908.

WILBERFORCE, ROBERT ISAAC (December 19, 1802-February 3, 1857), theological writer, was born at Clapham, the second son of the anti-slavery leader and philanthropist William Wilberforce. Educated for the

most part by tutors at home, he made a brilliant record at Oxford, where he was graduated in 1824. He entered the Church, eventually (1841) becoming Archdeacon of East Riding. But, from 1843 on, his friendship with Henry Edward Manning, who seceded in 1851 to the Roman Church, exercised a powerful influence upon Wilberforce; and, despite his feeling for his brother Samuel, an Anglican bishop, he felt called upon to follow Manning in 1854. He studied at the Academia Ecclesiastica in Rome for the priesthood; and his sudden death at Albano, a few weeks before ordination, deprived his adopted church of a valuable worker. His writings, if somewhat labored, reflect his sound theological scholarship and show the development of his religious attitude.

PRINCIPAL WORKS: Life of William Wilberforce (with S. Wilberforce) 1838; Rutilius and Lucius, 1842; The Doctrine of the Incarnation of Our Lord Jesus Christ, 1848; The Doctrine of Holy Baptism, 1849; A Sketch of the History of Erastianism, 1851; The Doctrine of the Holy Eucharist, 1853; An Inquiry Into the Principles of Church Authority, 1854.

ABOUT: Ashwell, A. R. Life of the Right Reverend Samuel Wilberforce; Liddon, H. P. Life of Edward Bouverie Pusey; Mozley, T. Reminiscences Chiefly of Oriel College and the Oxford Movement; Purcell, E. S. Life of Cardinal Manning; Eclectic Review 100:734 December 1854.

WILBERFORCE, SAMUEL (September 7, 1805-July 19, 1873), bishop, was born at Clapham, the third son of the philanthropist William Wilberforce. After study with tutors he went to Oxford, graduating in 1826 with high standing. He entered the Church and soon made a reputation for eloquence as a preacher. His advancement was continuous, and in 1845 he was made Bishop of Oxford. It was due largely to his influence that the English ecclesiastical convocations recovered some of their former authority in religious matters; and, as Bishop of Winchester (1869—), he was a leading figure in the revision of the English version of the New Testament. His practical energies enabled him to perform difficult tasks, although he was not always popular or considered sincere. He was obliged to steer between Low-Church and High-Church groups. Wilberforce's greatest literary achievement was his oratory; his importance as a writer is secondary.

PRINCIPAL WORKS: Note-Book of a Country Clergyman, 1833; The Life of William Wilberforce (with R. I. Wilberforce) 1838; Agathos, and Other Sunday Stories, 1840; The Rocky Island and Other Parables, 1840; A History of the Protestant Episcopal Church in America, 1844.

ABOUT: Arnold, F. Our Bishops and Deans; Ashwell, A. R. & Wilberforce, R. G. Life of the Right Reverend Samuel Wilberforce; Burgon, J. W. Lives of Twelve Good Men; Colson, P. Victorian Portraits; Daniell, G. W. Bishop Wilberforce; Catholic World 83:721 March 1909; Temple Bar 83:246 June 1888 (also in Living Age 178:101 July 14, 1888).

WILBERFORCE, WILLIAM (August 24, 1759-July 29, 1833), philanthropist, was born at Hull. As a wealthy youth he tended to neglect his studies, although he did well at Cambridge; and as a member of Parliament (elected 1780) he became a rather fast figure in London society, coming to be a warm friend and supporter of William Pitt. His whole life was affected by his conversion, about 1784, to the Evangelical (Low-Church) religious attitude of the day. He devoted himself to social reform, especially the anti-slavery movement. From the late eighteenth century until the end of his life Wilberforce hammered, first at the slave-trade, and later at slavery, becoming, to an unusual degree, the voice of the national conscience. The Emancipation Bill of 1833 followed his death by one month. His *Practical View* was a widely popular exposition of the ideals of the "Clapham Sect" of Evangelicals, to which he belonged.

PRINCIPAL WORKS: A Practical View of the Prevailing Religious System, 1797; An Appeal to the Religion, Justice, and Humanity of the Inhabitants of the British Empire in Behalf of the Negro Slaves in the West Indies, 1823.

ABOUT: Colquhoun, J. C. Wilberforce: His Friends and His Times; Coupland, R. Wilberforce; Stoughton, J. William Wilberforce; Wilberforce, R. I. & Wilberforce, S. The Life of William Wilberforce.

WILDE, OSCAR FINGAL O'FLAHERTIE WILLS (October 16, 1854-November 30, 1900), Irish dramatist, poet, and wit, was born in Merrion Square, Dublin, son of an eminent surgeon, Sir Robert Wills Wilde, and his wife, Jane Francesca (Elgee) Wilde, a poet of some note who published under the pen-name of "Speranza."

The Dublin household was intelligent, free-spoken, and Bohemian, and Oscar shared with his mother an uncommon facility for languages. In 1864 he was sent to Porotra Royal School, Enniskillen, whence, in 1873, he went on for a year to Trinity College, Dublin. From Michaelmas term 1874 to 1879 he was in residence at Magdalen College, Oxford, taking a first-class in classical moderations in 1876 and again in *litterae humaniores* in 1878. A vacation trip with Professor J. P. Mahaffy to Ravenna provided the subject he used to win the Newdigate prize for poetry (also in 1878).

Wilde's literary career began during his undergraduate days, when his poems were published by various magazines. Also at Oxford he developed the aesthetic pose which was to contribute so largely to his fame. He wore his hair long and his dress and mannerisms were highly affected. Lucky in the occupation of some of the best rooms in Magdalen, he filled them with *objets d'art*; his rare blue china became celebrated by his expressed wish that he could "live up to it." Among the other undergraduates, needless to say, this "new aestheticism" stirred bitter controversy. At one time his antagonists wrecked his rooms and ducked him in the Cherwell; but this only increased the worship of his supporters, and a veritable cult grew up around him.

In 1879, at the age of twenty-five, Wilde settled in London and set out to impress his personality on the worlds of fashion and literature in the metropolis as he had done at the university. This might seem a more difficult task; but in a few short months his wit and brilliant conversation were legendary. Again, his success can be traced largely to his eccentricities—the product of what would today be called shrewd publicity sense. In his favorite costume of velvet jacket and knee-breeches, carrying a single flower, he was at this period the very image (as, in fact, he was the original) of the languid Bunthorne in W. S. Gilbert's comic opera *Patience*. Gilbert was not his only satirist. He was caricatured by George Du Maurier and F. C. Burnand, and scarcely an issue of *Punch* passed without some pointed jibe. This would have been humiliating to most men, but to Wilde it meant the thing he craved most—attention. (How bitterly he was later to wish that he could escape the public gaze!)

In 1881 the publisher Bogue brought out a volume of his *Poems*, his only publication of importance for almost a decade. In the following year he undertook a lecture tour in the United States under the managership of D'Oyly Carte—who was also the impressario of *Patience,* touring "the States" at the same time! In America—to quote Archibald Henderson—"he was greeted with amused incredulity, treated as a diverting sort of literary curiosity, ridiculed, satirized, caricatured. He was violently attacked in many quarters, and few cared to face the ridicule inevitably consequent to any defense of his theories and practice." None the less, he was entertained by such men as O. W. Holmes, Longfellow, and Henry Ward Beecher.

On his return to London he continued his cultivation of wealthy persons who might be supposed to be useful to him. Early in 1883 he went for some months to Paris, where he met Edmond de Goncourt, Daudet, Hugo, J. S. Sargent, and Paul Bourget. Lack of money brought him back in the summer, and later in the year he toured the English provinces, lecturing on "The House Beautiful." The considerable audiences which he drew assembled, as often as not, less to hear a discourse on practical aesthetics than to gape at the eccentric and precious Mr. Wilde.

The journalist and adventurer, Frank Harris, has left a detailed description of Wilde in the early 'eighties (in *Contempor-*

OSCAR WILDE

ary Portraits): "His appearance was not in his favor; there was something oily and fat about him that repelled me. . . He looked like a Roman Emperor of the decadence; he was over six feet in height, and both broad and thick-set. He shook hands in a limp way I disliked; his hands were flabby, greasy; his skin looked bilious and dirty." So much on the bad side. "But," Harris continues, "his grey eyes were finely expressive; in turn vivacious, laughing, sympathetic; always beautiful. The carven mouth, too, with its heavy, chiseled, almost colorless lips, had a certain charm in spite of a black front tooth which showed ignobly."

The incomings from Wilde's Irish property were sporadic and inadequate to his always extravagant and luxurious mode of living. During these years of the early 'eighties he often knew genuine poverty. But this was brought to an end in May 1884 by his marriage to a woman of fortune, Constance Lloyd, daughter of a Dublin barrister, Horace Lloyd. The couple took a house in Tite Street, Chelsea, then the heart of London's artistic quarter.

The American painter James McNeil Whistler was one of Wilde's intimates at this period; and the two wits were matched like rapiers—though Whistler usually got the better of the exchanges. A well-known anecdote relates how Wilde, after some *bon mot* of the artist, said how much he wished he had said that. Whistler's reply came swift and scathing: "Oh you will, Oscar, you will!" Small wonder is it that such a relationship should have ended, as it did, in a quarrel.

Tiring at last of his drawing room rôle, Wilde suddenly turned to serious literary endeavor. Between October 1887 and September 1889 he became a practical working journalist, occupying the editorial chair of a popular magazine, *Women's World*. In 1888 appeared his first collection of fairy-tales, *The Happy Prince and Other Tales,* not addressed to children but relying on rich imaginative description and finely-wrought style. In 1891 he published *Lord Arthur Savile's Crime and Other Stories;* a collection of miscellaneous essays called *Intentions;* and his only novel, *The Picture of Dorian Gray,* which had appeared in *Lippincott's Magazine* the year before. This remarkable book, though praised by Walter Pater in the London *Bookman,* had a "bad press" in general, and many people professed to find it immoral. It is soaked in the typical Wilde aestheticism and there are powerful undercurrents of diabolism, but the moral "lesson" (if such a term may still be used) is clear and unequivocal. This same year saw the production of *The Duchess of Padua* in New York and the publication of a second collection of fairy-tales, *A House of Pomegranates.*

In 1892 Wilde scored his first great dramatic success with the production of *Lady Windermere's Fan* at the St. James's Theatre —and appeared before the curtain with a cigarette and congratulated the audience on having admired what he himself found admirable! The play showed masterly stagecraft, and its ebullient wit and daring paradox put it into a class of comedy that had not been seen on the English stage for a century. *A Woman of No Importance,* produced at the Haymarket the next year, had similar qualities; but *Salomé* (his most powerful play, written in French) was refused a license by the Lord Chamberlain, being eventually put on by Sarah Bernhardt in Paris in 1894. January 1895 saw the production of *An Ideal Husband* at the Haymarket Theatre and February that of *The Importance of Being Earnest* at the St. James's.

Wilde was now in the full tide of social, material, and literary success. But ugly rumors of sexual perversion were abroad. In connection with these, in March 1895, he unwisely launched an action for criminal libel against the Marquess of Queensberry. Queensberry objected very strongly to Wilde's friendship with his son, Lord Alfred Douglas, and had left a grossly insulting card openly at one of the playwright's clubs. When the action was heard, Wilde was rigorously cross-examined by Edward Carson (later Lord Carson); his case broke down; and under the Criminal Law Amendment Act his own arrest followed almost as a matter of course. He was tried and found guilty at the Old Bailey and sentenced to two years' hard labor. Bankruptcy overtook him at once; and it was a ruined and chastened Wilde that emerged from Reading Gaol in May 1897. During

his imprisonment he wrote *De Profundis* (published 1905), a document concerned with his spiritual progress, under suffering, to a religious outlook. Opinion is sharply divided about it, some judges esteeming it a sincere and pathetic record of conversion and others finding it mawkish, theatrical, and full of pose.

The trial had, of course, given rise to tremendous publicity. Wilde was thoroughly vilified by the popular press even before conviction; and during a period when he was out on bail was refused admission by several hotels. Middle-class morality was shocked to the core. It had always suspected that artists were "a bad lot," and now its worst fears were confirmed by the conviction of the very *vates sacer* of art as one guilty of unnameable and beastly vice—so literally unnameable in those days that even the estimable *Dictionary of National Biography* gives no clue to what it was!

On his release, provided with funds by his friends, Wilde went to Berneval, France, living under the name of Sebastian Melmoth. There he wrote the powerful *Ballad of Reading Gaol* (1898). His wife died the same year. He was sensibly coarsened by his experiences but retained much of his old wit, and is reported to have said, when champagne was given him on his deathbed: "I am dying beyond my means." He contracted cerebral meningitis, and died at the Hôtel d'Alsace, Paris, on November 30, 1900, having been received into the Roman Catholic Church. He was buried at Bagneux. He left two sons, Cyril (born 1885) and Vivian (born 1886).

Arthur Ransome in his critical biography calls Wilde's influence on literature incalculable: "for his attitude in writing gave literature new standards of valuation, and men are writing under their influence who would indignantly deny that their work was in any way dictated by Wilde." His fame outside the borders of Britain is prodigious, and works of his have been translated into most European languages.

It is difficult to decide (as with Byron seventy-five years before) how much of this renown arises from pure literary merit and how much from his colorful and scandalous life. It is probable that his celebrity is as much a *succès de scandale* as a *succès d'estime*. Nevertheless, he takes an honored place in the history of the British drama. When he came to it, Henry Arthur Jones and A. W. Pinero were the only islands in a morass that stretched back to the beginning of the century. Wilde's plays conformed to his doctrine of "art for art's sake": they had no social axe to grind; they expounded no deep philosophy; but in sparkling wit and command over farcical situation there had been nothing like them since Sheridan. His special form of wit lay in ingenious paradox, with particular fondness for the inverted proverb, like: "Nothing succeeds like excess." In prose and verse alike he was a meticulous, if over-elaborate, craftsman, seeking out rare effects, loving to describe exotic jewels and scents and to hint at abnormal and forbidden joys.

In a sense his life was one long pose, but it was a pose that had its source in a very genuine and wholehearted love of the more artificial beauties and splendors of life. To André Gide, at Algiers in 1895, he gave a judgment that is memorable and has some truth in it: "Would you like to know the great drama of my life? It is that I have put my genius into my life—I have put only my talent into my works."

H.B.G.

PRINCIPAL WORKS: *Plays* (publication dates)— Vera: or, The Nihilists, 1880; The Duchess of Padua, 1883; Salomé (in French) 1893 (English trans. 1894); Lady Windermere's Fan, 1893; A Woman of No Importance, 1894; The Importance of Being Earnest, 1899; An Ideal Husband, 1899. *Poetry*—Ravenna, 1878; Poems, 1881; The Sphynx, 1894; The Ballad of Reading Gaol, 1898. *Miscellaneous Prose*— The Happy Prince and Other Tales, 1888; The Portrait of Mr. W. H., 1889; The Picture of Dorian Gray, 1891; Intentions, 1891; Lord Arthur Savile's Crime, 1891; A House of Pomegranates, 1891; The Soul of Man Under Socialism, 1895; De Profundis, 1905.

ABOUT: Douglas, A. Oscar Wilde and Myself; Gide, A. Oscar Wilde; Harris, F. Oscar Wilde: His Life and Confessions; Henderson, A. Interpreters of Life and the Modern Spirit; Ingleby, L. C. Oscar Wilde; Lewis, L. & Smith, H. J. Oscar Wilde Discovers America; Mason, S. Bibliography of Oscar Wilde; Oscar Wilde: Three Times Tried; Ransome, A. Oscar Wilde: A Critical Study; Renier, G. J. Oscar Wilde; Sherard, R. H. The Life of Oscar Wilde.

WILKINS, WILLIAM HENRY (December 23, 1860-December 22, 1905), biographer and novelist, was the son of a Somerset farmer. After an education for a career in the Church he was graduated at Cambridge in 1887. He had acquired literary and political interests and took up the life of a writer. Although he wrote novels and edited a monthly magazine that died a speedy death, his best work was in history and biography. Besides a memoir of Isabel Lady Burton he produced a work based on his discovery of the correspondence between Queen Sophie Dorothea, Consort of George I, and her Swedish lover, an important biography of Caroline, Queen Consort of George II, and a valuable study of the secret marriage of George IV, based on papers to which previous scholars had had no access. While his writing has been criticized for its high-flown rhetoric, he made a definite contribution to knowledge.

PRINCIPAL WORKS: St. Michael's Eve, 1892; The Green Bay Tree (with H. Vivian) 1894; The Romance of Isabel, Lady Burton (with Lady Burton) 1897; The Love of an Uncrowned Queen, 1900;

Caroline the Illustrious, 1901; A Queen of Tears, 1904; Mrs. Fitzherbert and George IV, 1905.

ABOUT: London Times, December 23, 1905.

WILKINSON, SIR JOHN GARDNER (October 5, 1797-October 29, 1875), Egyptologist, was the son of a clergyman, and inherited scholarly tastes from both parents. After an education at Harrow and at Exeter College, Oxford (he apparently was never graduated), he began first-hand study of Egyptian antiquities, passing twelve years in Egypt and Nubia and learning Arabic and Coptic. He conducted excavations and came to know noted Egyptologists of the day. His health required his return to England in 1833, and in the next few years he published popular and scholarly works on Egypt. In his later years he made travels in Montenegro, in Italy, and again in Egypt, and his studies in antiquities and art and architecture reflect his varied interests. His finest book is *Manners and Customs of the Ancient Egyptians,* which his broad knowledge and literary facility combined to make a standard authority.

PRINCIPAL WORKS: Topography of Thebes, and General View of Egypt, 1835; Manners and Customs of the Ancient Egyptians, 1837; Dalmatia and Montenegro, 1848; The Architecture of Ancient Egypt, 1850; Facsimile of the Turin Papyrus (ed.) 1851.

ABOUT: Royal Geographical Society Journal 46:1 1876; Royal Institution of Cornwall Journal 5:248 May 1876.

WILLIAMS, HELEN MARIA (June 17, 1761-December 15, 1827), poet and historical writer, was born in London. She received her education from her mother. Before she was twenty she had begun to write poetry, and her first published poem was issued in 1782. Her other early poems were successful and brought her money. About 1790 she removed to France. She plunged violently into the enthusiasm of the Revolution, was imprisoned by Robespierre, and barely escaped with her life. Her writings on the Revolution, although sincere, were so biased and misinformed that they made her enemies; and an apparently illicit relationship with an Englishman did little to help her reputation. Her works on France still have considerable interest, although they are hardly trustworthy. Her poetry, however successful in its day, has been almost completely forgotten.

PRINCIPAL WORKS: Edwin and Eltruda (poem) 1782; Poems, 1786; Julia. A Novel, 1790; Letters From France, 1792; A Tour in Switzerland, 1798; Sketches of the State of Manners and Opinions in the French Republic, 1801; The Political and Confidential Correspondence of Louis the Sixteenth (ed.) 1803; A Narrative of the Events Which Have Taken Place in France, 1815.

ABOUT: Alger, J. G. Englishmen in the French Revolution; Williams, H. M. Letters From France; Woodworth, L. D. Une Anglaise Amie de la Révolution Française; Helene-Maria Williams et Ses Amies; Unitarian Review 9:305 March 1878; 9:477 May 1878; and 10:233 September 1878.

WILLIAMS, ISAAC (December 12, 1802-May 1, 1865), Welsh poet, was born in Cardiganshire. His father was a barrister. He was educated at Harrow, where he was distinguished by his facility in Latin verse, and at Trinity College, Oxford. His winning of the chancellor's prize for Latin verse in 1823 led to his lifelong close friendship with the "Christian poet," John Keble. Overwork in attempting to obtain an honors degree caused a nearly fatal illness, so that he was obliged to aim merely at a pass degree. He took his B.A. in 1826, his M.A. in 1831, and a B.D. degree in 1839. In 1829 he was ordained deacon, and became a curate in Gloucestershire. Made a fellow of Trinity in 1831, he returned to Oxford, was ordained priest, and was curate to John Henry (later Cardinal) Newman at St. Mary's Church, Oxford. In 1832 he was made tutor and lecturor on philosophy, and was dean of the college in 1833. From 1834 to 1840 he was lecturer on rhetoric. In 1841 and 1842 he was vice-president of the college.

Williams was an active member of the high-church Oxford Movement, and wrote several of the famous *Tracts for the Times* which spread its doctrine. With Keble, Froude, and Newman, he wrote some of the poems in *Lyra Apostolica* (1836). Others of his poems appeared in the *British Magazine*. He applied for the chair of poetry at Oxford in 1841, and was an almost successful candidate. Pained at the defection of some of his friends during his campaign for the post, he left Oxford in 1842. The same year he married Caroline Champernowne; they had six sons and one daughter. Williams became curate to Thomas Keble, John Keble's brother, in Dartington. In 1846 he was very ill, for a long time at the point of death, and was an invalid, living in strict retirement, thereafter. In 1848 he moved to Stinchcombe, where for the remainder of his life he wrote, performed what church duties his health permitted, and educated his sons.

Williams' shy, modest, warm-hearted nature shows in his poems, which are sweet, gentle, and earnest, melancholy and musical, but have little life or vigor.

PRINCIPAL WORKS: The Cathedral, 1838; Hymns on the Catechism, 1843; Sacred Verses, 1845; The Altar, 1847; The Seven Days, 1850; The Christian Seasons, 1854, Autobiography (ed. by Sir G. Prevost) 1892.

ABOUT: Williams, I. Autobiography; Churchman's Family Magazine July 1865; Guardian May 10 and 17, 1865.

WILLIAMS, SARAH ("Sadie") (1841-April 25, 1868), versifier, was born in London. Her father was of Welsh extraction, and she is said to have attributed her poetic gifts to this inheritance. As an only child she was carefully educated by governesses, and later went to Queen's College, London, becoming a friend of Edward Hayes Plumptre, later Dean of Wells, from whom she received encouragement in her writing. The rest of her life is almost without incident; thanks to her father's success and her own earning-power as a writer, she was enabled to live the life of a student and an author, devoting half of her own earnings to the poor. Her poetry, including children's verses and religious writings, lacks concentrated power sufficient to make it of more than merely historical interest.

PRINCIPAL WORKS: Rainbows in Springtide, 1866; Twilight Hours: A Legacy of Verse, 1868.

ABOUT: Julian, J. A Dictionary of Hymnology (rev. ed., 1908); Miles, A. H. (ed.). The Poets and the Poetry of the Century; Williams, S. Twilight Hours (see Prefatory Memoir by E. H. Plumptre); Good Words 9:379 June 1868.

WILLS, JAMES (January 1, 1790-November, 1868), Irish poet and biographer, came of an established family, and was educated in a school at Blackrock, County Dublin, by tutors, and later at Trinity College, Dublin. He planned to study law, but reverses of fortune, due to financial mismanagement by his elder brother, left him poor. Although he took orders, the noteworthy activity of his life was literary. He contributed to periodicals, helped found the *Irish Quarterly Review*, wrote metaphysical disquisitions, and compiled a valuable collection of biographies of Irish notables. This work is his best, and contains much useful and carefully gathered material, although he was unable to do all parts with equal thoroughness. The arrangement of the book has been criticized. His poems, although they show some power of feeling, do not entitle him to a place among his great contemporaries.

PRINCIPAL WORKS: The Universe, 1821; The Disembodied, 1831; Letters on the Philosophy of Unbelief, 1835; Lives of Illustrious and Distinguished Irishmen, 1839-47; Dramatic Sketches and Other Poems, 1845; Moral and Religious Epistles, 1848; The Idolatress, 1868.

ABOUT: Wills, F. W. G. Wills: Dramatist and Painter; Dublin University Magazine 86:404 October 1875.

WILLS, WILLIAM GORMAN (January 28, 1828-December 13, 1891), Irish dramatist, was born in Kilmurry, his father being known as a poet and biographer. He was educated at Waterford Grammar School and at Trinity College, Dublin, where he left without a degree but with the vice-chancellor's medal for a poem. He was talented in art also, but had only a little very poor training. His first writing was published in his own short-lived magazine, the *Irish Metropolitan*. After a few years of idleness in Ireland, he went to London, in 1862, and led the life of an impecunious Bohemian, occasionally selling a story to a magazine. He also won his second medal—for life-saving. In 1868 his father died and he had to support his mother. He turned to portrait painting, and met with a good deal of success, which would have been greater had it not been for his extreme absent-mindedness and unconventionality, his filthy studio, and his exaggerated Bohemianism.

His first play was produced in 1865, and others also proving successful (several being played by Sir Henry Irving) in 1872 he became "dramatist to the Lyceum," on a salary. Meanwhile he kept on painting; his plays were a mere by-product, and he never attended one of them. In 1887 his mother died and he no longer needed to make any effort or exert himself; he retired to bed and did most of his writing there. In 1891, while his last play, *A Royal Divorce*, was being performed at the Olympic, he became ill in his disordered lodgings and at his own request was taken to Guy's Hospital, where he died.

Wills' plays were mostly historical tragedies in verse, or adaptations of novels. Their history was bad and prejudiced, and their verse was mostly hollow rhetoric. But he was a born dramatist, with a keen eye for theatrical effectiveness. He had some facility as a balladist, and one of the songs from his plays, "I'll Sing Thee Songs of Araby," is still heard in concerts.

PRINCIPAL WORKS: (date of performance): Man o' Airlie, 1867; Charles the First, 1872; Olivia, 1873; Eugene Aram, 1873; Marie Stuart, 1874; Claudian, 1882; Melchior (poem, published) 1885.

ABOUT: Wills, F. W. G. Wills: Dramatist and Painter; The Theatre February 1, 1892.

WILSON, HORACE HAYMAN (September 26, 1786-May 8, 1860), Orientalist, was born in London. After a medical education he became assistant surgeon for the East India Company in Bengal, subsequently holding positions in the Calcutta mint, and other important government posts. In India he became interested in Sanskrit, and in 1819 he issued the first Sanskrit-English dictionary, in its later and improved form a standard authority until the work of German scholars superseded it. In 1832 he was made Professor of Sanskrit at Oxford, and later became librarian of the East India Company and director of the Royal Asiatic Society. His contributions to Oriental scholarship are of considerable importance, although their value, like that of the work of any pioneer, tends to decrease as more modern scholars invade the field.

PRINCIPAL WORKS: A Dictionary: Sanskrit and English, 1819; Select Specimens of the Theatre of the Hindus, 1826-27; Two Lectures on the Religious Practices and Opinions of the Hindus, 1840; The Vishnú Puráña: A System of Hindu Mythology, 1840; Ariana Antiqua, 1841; An Introduction to the Grammar of the Sanskrit Language, 1841; The History of British India: From 1805 to 1835 (a con-

tinuation of James Mill's work of that name) 1844-48; Rig-Veda-Sanhitá, 1850; Works, 1862-71.

ABOUT: Royal Asiatic Society Annual Report 1860.

WILSON, JOHN ("Christopher North") (May 18, 1785-April 3, 1854), Scottish essayist teacher, and critic, was born at Paisley, near Glasgow, fourth child and eldest son of John Wilson, a wealthy gauze manufacturer, and Margaret (Sym) Wilson, who traced her ancestry back to Montrose. Like Stevenson later on, he "played preacher" in his infancy, and his early education at the hands of two private teachers had the strong religious flavor usual in Scotland at that time. He was for two years with James Peddie in Paisley and then for a longer period with the Rev. George M'Latchie, at Mearns, nearby; early in 1797 (at the age of twelve!) he entered the University of Glasgow. Obviously his course there was only of an elementary kind; the acceptance of such young boys in Scottish universities was due to the lack of sufficient high schools. At Glasgow he made a friendship which was to be of cardinal importance in his life, with Alexander Blair, who, notwithstanding his Scottish name, was an English boy from Birmingham.

In June 1803 Wilson went as a gentleman-commoner to Magdalen College, Oxford. He was rich, very strong and handsome, and intellectually well-endowed; and his vivid personality and brilliant conversational powers made him a figure of mark. He performed prodigious athletic feats, drank hard, evinced interests so varied as pugilism and ornithology, and, in 1806, carried off the Newdigate Prize for poetry. The next year he graduated B.A. in an examination described by his tutor as "glorious."

He had bought an estate called Elleray, overlooking Windermere, in the English Lake District, and shortly after graduation he went to live there, attracted partly by the superb scenery and partly by the proximity of the so-called "Lakers," Wordsworth, De Quincey, Coleridge, and Southey. He threw himself into the life of the district, organizing wrestling, cock-fighting, and regattas, mixing socially with the literary company, and at odd times writing a little verse. In May 1811 he married Jane Penny, a noted local beauty, whose family came from Liverpool. In the February following he issued his first book, *The Isle of Palms and Other Poems*, a welter of sentimentality that drew from Crabb Robinson the damning phrase, "a female Wordsworth."

During 1813 and 1814 Wilson was a good deal in Edinburgh, studying for the Bar. In 1815, through the peculation of an uncle, he lost the bulk of his large fortune at one blow, and went, with his wife and family, to live with his mother in Queen Street, Edinburgh. He was called to the Bar the same year, and with him was called John Gibson Lockhart, later to be his colleague on *Blackwood's Magazine*. In 1816 he published *The City of the Plague and Other Poems*, which, though little stronger than the first volume, drew a long and favorable review from Francis Jeffrey in the *Edinburgh*.

Wilson did little work in the courts. In Edinburgh, as at Oxford before, he was a personality, and gained some notoriety from his eccentric habit of running off without notice on walking- and fishing-tours in the Highlands. Though he was a Tory he was approached by the Whig Jeffrey to write for the *Edinburgh Review*, and actually contributed one article to it; but late in 1817 he began a close association with the new *Blackwood's Edinburgh Magazine*, founded by the publisher William Blackwood as a Tory counterblast to the *Review*.

Besides Wilson and Lockhart, prominent contributors to *Blackwood's* at this time included the Irishman, William Maginn, and James Hogg, known as "the Ettrick Shepherd." Around the figure of this last and his circle grew up the famous symposium called the "Noctes Ambrosianae." [See sketches of Hogg and Maginn in this volume.] The "Noctes" were a racy, pungent, witty commentary on life and letters. At first they were composite productions, written jointly by Maginn and Wilson, and had some relation to the real Hogg and his circle; but from 1822 they were wholly original and almost entirely the work of Wilson, under the *nom de plume* of "Christopher North." They constitute his chief claim to remembrance, and did more than anything else to establish the fame of *Blackwood's*.

In 1820 Wilson decided to put up for election to the chair of moral philosophy in the University of Edinburgh, vacant by the retirement of Dugald Stewart. He had no formal qualifications whatsoever, but succeeded in obtaining the support of Sir Walter Scott and other eminent men. The campaign was conducted with all the acrimony and unscrupulousness of an old-time political election, and was indeed nothing else; for, despite the eminent philosophical scholarship of the opposing Sir William Hamilton, Wilson was chosen by twenty-one Tory votes against nine for the Whig.

The full history of Wilson's astonishing incompetence has only recently been revealed by Miss Elsie Swann's publication of his letters to Alexander Blair. During the whole tenure of his professorship he was writing hysterical letters to Blair, begging and praying in the most abject terms for material to be incorporated in his lectures. As late as

JOHN WILSON

1850 he was writing: "Could you write to me at *some length* on *Beauty* and Sublimity and power of Piety on all that is good in our minds? Do, Socrates, philosophically. And of Socrates and the Sophists *next*. Who were the Sophists?"

To add to his troubles, he found himself compelled, in 1826, to prepare a course on political economy, a subject of which he knew even less than he did of formal ethics. With the aid of the faithful Blair he accomplished it.

Yet he retained his position for thirty-one years, mainly by a flow of picturesque eloquence which bemused the minds of many of his auditors. Henceforward Wilson was "the Professor" as well as "Christopher North"; known by his rapid stride, his athletic mien, his unkempt appearance and tattered gown.

The death of Mrs. Wilson, on March 29, 1837, threw him into such paroxysms of grief as to lead to rumors that he was mentally unbalanced. Three years later he suffered from paralysis in his right hand; and from then onward showed a gradual decline in health and productivity. He resigned his chair in 1851, was awarded a pension of £300 a year by Lord John Russell, and died of paralysis on April 3, 1854.

As a poet Wilson is negligible; as a serious critic he is prejudiced and inconsistent; his most enduring monument will remain the "Noctes Ambrosianae," in which he showed himself a brilliant journalist, a *philosophe* in the French sense rather than a philosopher, since he lacked the method, the exactitude and the speculative power to be this last. Above all he was "a character." It was impossible to be indifferent to him: he

663

was loved and revered by many and hated by not a few. He lived a full and busy life and left his mark on several generations of Edinburgh students.   H.B.G.

PRINCIPAL WORKS: *Prose*—Lights and Shadows of Scottish Life, 1822; The Trials of Margaret Lyndsay, 1823; The Foresters, 1825; The Recreations of Christopher North (3 Vols.) 1842; The Noctes Ambrosianae of "Blackwood" (4 vols.) 1843; Essays: Critical and Imaginative (4 vols.) 1866; Works (12 vols., ed. by Professor Ferrier) 1855-58. *Poetry*—The Isle of Palms and Other Poems, 1812; The City of the Plague and Other Poems, 1816.

ABOUT: Douglas, G. B. S. The Blackwood Group; Gilfillan, G. The History of a Man; Gordon, M. Memoir of Christopher North; Lockhart, J. G. Peter's Letters to His Kinsfolk; Oliphant, M. O. & Porter, M. Annals of a Publishing House; Saintsbury, G. E. B. Essays in English Literature; Swann, E. Christopher North.

WILSON, JOHN MACKAY (1804-October 2, 1835), poet and story-writer, was the son of a millwright, and was baptized at Tweedmouth, Berwick-upon-Tweed on August 15, 1804. He was trained as a printer, receiving an elementary education in Tweedmouth and serving an apprenticeship in Berwick. After a brief period of poverty in London and a rather unsuccessful career as a lecturer on literary subjects, he was made editor of *The Berwick Advertiser* (1832); and the remainder of his short life he devoted to efforts to bring about political reform, and the development of his own powers as a writer. Besides unimportant poetic and dramatic productions he issued *The Tales of the Borders,* a weekly series which reached great popularity in Great Britain and America because of the simplicity and force of the stories. This series, of which Wilson was the editor and chief author, was continued by his brother and by Alexander Leighton.

PRINCIPAL WORKS: A Glance at Hinduism, 1824; The Gowrie Conspiracy (drama) 1829; The Enthusiast: A Metrical Tale, 1834; The Tales of the Borders, 1834-40.

ABOUT: Irving, J. The Book of Eminent Scotsmen; Wilson, J. M. Wilson's Historical, Traditionary, and Imaginative Tales of the Borders (see Biographical Notices by J. Tait in 1881 ed.); Berwick Advertiser October 3, 1835.

WINKWORTH, CATHERINE (September 13, 1827-July 1, 1878), translator, was born in London, the daughter of a silk merchant. The family moved to Manchester when she was two, and she was educated there by governesses and tutors. Her mother died in 1841, her father re-married in 1845, and she was sent to Dresden for a year, to live with an aunt. She learned German thoroughly, and became especially interested in German hymnology. She is the foremost translator of German hymns, and did much to familiarize them to English readers. Her other chief interest was in the education of women: she helped to establish Bristol University College, Clifton High School, and other institutions admitting girls, and she was secretary of the Committee on Higher Education for Women. In 1872 she went with her sister Susanna (also known as a translator) as a delegate to the German Conference on Women's Work. She died suddenly of heart failure while caring for an invalid nephew in France.

PRINCIPAL WORKS: Lyra Germanica, 1853-58; The Christian Singers of Germany, 1866.

ABOUT: Shaen, M. J. Memorials of Two Sisters: Susanna and Catherine Winkworth; Winkworth, S. Letters and Memorials of Catherine Winkworth.

"WINTER, JOHN STRANGE." See STANNARD, HENRIETTA E. V.

WISEMAN, NICHOLAS PATRICK STEPHEN (Cardinal) (August 2, 1802-February 15, 1865), theological and miscellaneous writer, was born in Seville, Spain, where his father, an Irishman and a Roman Catholic, was a merchant. The father died in 1804, and the family was taken to Waterford, Ireland. Wiseman was educated at St. Cuthbert's College, Ushaw, where he decided on the priesthood as a vocation. He studied at the English College, in Rome, and was ordained priest in 1825. He was already known as a linguist, and helped to compile a Syriac grammar. In 1827 he was appointed vice-rector of the English College, and from 1828 to 1840 was its rector. During a year's leave of absence, in 1836, he founded the *Dublin Review.* In 1840 he was made president of Oscott College, and also bishop-coadjutor. He had an immense influence on the Oxford (high church) movement, and Newman and others came to him for advice and help when they determined to leave the Anglican for the Roman faith. In 1849 he was created vicar-apostolic of the London district, and in 1850 Archbishop of Westminster. Soon after, the Pope named him cardinal. This was the first appointment in the restoration of the Roman Catholic hierarchy in England, and caused great excitement, which Wiseman's skill in diplomacy helped to quell. He found time from his duties not only to write on secular as well as theological topics, but also to lecture widely on art and literature. His popular work, including his novel *Fabiola* and his play *The Hidden Gem*, has great charm and displays much natural talent.

PRINCIPAL WORKS: On the Connection Between Science and Revealed Religion, 1836; Essays on Various Subjects, 1853; Fabiola: or, The Church of the Catacombs, 1854; The Hidden Gem, 1858; Recollections of the Last Four Popes, 1858.

ABOUT: Ward, W. Life of Cardinal Wiseman.

WOLFE, CHARLES (December 14, 1791-February 21, 1823), Irish poet, was born in the County Kildare, the eighth son of Theobald Wolfe. The father died in 1799, and

the family removed to England, where the poet was reared.

Although frail in health, he was sent to school at Bath, proceeding in 1805 to a boarding-school at Winchester, where he remained until 1808. Here he distinguished himself in verse-making in Greek and Latin. In 1809 he entered Trinity College, Dublin.

His university years were the most productive of his life, and to them and the years in Dublin immediately following must be attributed almost all his poetical production. In his second year he took a scholarship, showing his abilities in the study of the classics. Despite natural disinclinations, he took high honors in mathematics. He was one of a circle of brilliant students, forming a band of kindred spirits, and his poems won him distinction in college.

He received his bachelor's degree in 1814. He seems to have considered reading for a fellowship, although his tastes did not run toward an academic career, but gave up such a prospect, apparently at least partly because of the requirement of celibacy, which would have prevented him from marrying the young lady of his choice.

His decision, if the reason was as stated, was unfortunate, for the young lady did not accept his advances. Wolfe took orders in 1817 and accepted first the curacy of Ballyclog, County Tyrone, and shortly afterward, that of Donoughmore.

The melancholy resulting from his disappointment in love and his generally hard work and poor health seem to have been too much for the poet. After a few years at his charge, in the course of which he became highly regarded by parishioners and neighbors of other denominations, he found himself a victim of tuberculosis. In 1821 he gave up his work and moved from his parish, in a belated effort to regain health. His attempts, however, were vain, and at thirty-one he died at the Cove of Cork (now Queenstown).

An extraordinary pathos clings about Wolfe's memory. Possessed of a simple and winning charm, he was sensitive to beauty, particularly in music. Palgrave compared him to Keats, "not only in his early death by consumption and the fluent freshness of his poetical style, but in beauty of character: brave, tender, energetic, unselfish, modest." Apparently not naturally vigorous or thorough in application to study (and possibly much the same in the prosecution of his love-suit), he was the most devoted of clergymen; and his friend, the Reverend John Russell, tells how the Irish peasants of his flock adored him. During an epidemic of typhus fever he faithfully visited the stricken, and it was only because of Russell's entreaties that he finally tendered his resignation, which was received with reluctance.

While he left sermons, essays, and speeches of merit, as well as winning letters, all piously edited, with most of the poems, by Russell, none of his prose writings was destined for a wide popularity. It is his poetry, and more especially "The Burial of Sir John Moore," by which Wolfe lives today. Byron praised "The Burial" as worthy of Thomas Campbell. The authorship of the poem was the subject of lively disputes, which were ended by the discovery of the poem in an autograph letter of Wolfe's. It has been described by Sir Edmund Gosse as "pre-eminent for simplicity, patriotic fervor, and manly pathos."

R. W. W.

PRINCIPAL WORKS: Remains, 1825; Poems, 1903.

ABOUT: O'Sullivan, S. College Recollections; Wolfe, C. Poems (see Memoir by C. Litton Falkiner); Wolfe, C. Remains (see Memoir by the Rev. J. A. Russell); Irish Quarterly Review 6:326 June 1856.

WOLSELEY, GARNET JOSEPH (first viscount) (June 4, 1833-March 25, 1913), Irish soldier and historian, was born in County Dublin, his father being a major in the British Army. His father died when he was seven, and the family fell into straitened circumstances. He had only an elementary education, and, desiring to follow his father's profession, he prepared himself by entering a surveyor's office. In 1852 he received a commission as second lieutenant. After serving in the Burma and Crimean Wars (in the latter of which he lost an eye), he started for the China War, but was turned back and sent to Calcutta for the Bengal Mutiny. Two years later he finally reached China, as a lieutenant colonel. In 1861 he was sent to Canada as assistant quartermaster-general. In

CHARLES WOLFE

1865 he was made colonel and deputy quarter-master-general. He had already formulated his plan of army reform, and the remainder of his life, between times of active service, was devoted to its advocacy.

In 1867 he married Louisa Erskine; they had one daughter. He served in Canada until 1871, in 1870 commanding an anti-Fenian expedition, in recognition of which service he was made K.C.M.G. and C.B. He returned to England as assistant adjutant-general. In 1873 his services in the Ashanti War, in Africa, made him G.C.M.G. and K.C.B. In 1875 he served in the Natal War. In 1878, as a lieutenant-general, he was a member of the Council of India. He then became the first British administrator of Cyprus. In 1879 he commanded the forces in the Zulu War, in 1882 was made adjutant-general, in 1882 commanded an expedition in Cairo (being made Baron Wolseley), and in 1885 commanded the army at Khartoum. In this year he was made a viscount. In 1890 he was commander-in-chief of Ireland, and in 1895 commander-in-chief of the British Army. He retired in 1899. His mind failed after 1903, and he was incompetent during his last ten years.

Wolseley practically re-created the British Army, and made it the efficient force it is today. His historical writing, like his sketching, was a mere side-interest, but he wrote with ease and was thoroughly at home in treating of military topics. His extreme piety permeates his autobiography.

PRINCIPAL WORKS: Narrative of the War in China, 1862; Life of Marlborough, 1894; The Decline and Fall of Napoleon, 1895; The Story of a Soldier's Life, 1903.

ABOUT: Arthur, Sir G. (ed.). Letters of Lord and Lady Wolseley; Wolseley, G. J. The Story of a Soldier's Life.

WOOD, ELLEN (MRS. HENRY) (January 17, 1814-February 10, 1887), novelist, was born in Worcester, her maiden name being Price, and her father a glove manufacturer. She spent most of her childhood with her maternal grandmother, Mrs. Evans, and as a child was noted for her remarkable memory. From girlhood she was deformed by curvature of the spine, and was always a semi-invalid, most of her novels having been written from a couch. In 1836 she married Henry Wood, a banker; her novels always appeared under the name of Mrs. Henry Wood. Until 1856 the couple lived abroad, mostly in France, and it was from France that she contributed her first stories to Bentley's Miscellany and the New Monthly Magazine. Her popular stories kept both magazines alive, but she received very little for them. Besides her ill health, Mrs. Wood was hampered in her work by the rearing of her several children, but she persisted in continuing her writing. Her second novel, East Lynne, launched by

an enthusiastic review in The Times, had an enormous sale; it was dramatized many times and for years was a standard melodrama in every stock company.

In 1867 she became proprietor of The Argosy, and most of her work appeared in it thereafter before publication in book form. Her husband had died in 1866, and her son Charles edited the magazine jointly with her. Very orthodox in religion and an extreme reactionary, her anti-labor novel, A Life's Secret, which appeared anonymously, caused a riot and the threat of violence to the unknown author. In spite of her frailness, she lived to be seventy-three, dying suddenly of heart failure.

Mrs. Wood had a genius for plot construction, and was excellent in her characterizations of middle class types. Her work, however, was sensational and melodramatic, and incredibly careless and inaccurate.

PRINCIPAL WORKS: Danesbury House, 1860; East Lynne, 1861; Mrs. Halliburton's Troubles, 1862; The Channings, 1862; The Shadow of Ashlydyat, 1863; Lord Oakburn's Daughters, 1864; Lady Adelaide's Oath, 1867; Roland Yorke, 1869; Dene Hollow, 1871; Within the Maze, 1872; Edina, 1876; About Ourselves, 1883.

ABOUT: Wood, C. W. Memorials of Mrs. Henry Wood; Athenaeum February 13, 1887; Illustrated London News February 19, 1887.

WOOLNER, THOMAS (December 17, 1825-October 7, 1892), poet and sculptor, was born in Hadleigh, Sussex, but moved to London as a child when his father secured a position in the post office. At twelve he became a student (taken without premium because of his talent) in the studio of the sculptor Behnes, and in 1842 he attended the school of the Royal Academy. He exhibited first in 1843. His sculptures gained him a reputation but no money, and he made his living by assisting Behnes. In 1847 he met D. G. Rossetti, and was one of the original Pre-Raphaelite group of poets and artists. The first version of his best known poems, "My Beautiful Lady" and "Of My Lady in Death," appeared in the Pre-Raphaelite magazine, The Germ, in 1850. Unable to sell any of his idealistic sculptural works, he was obliged to take to portrait painting, and in 1852, in despair, he went to Australia, to the gold-fields. But he had no luck there, and had to set up in Melbourne as a portraitist. He returned to England in 1854, to find his group attaining fame and prosperity. He too began to meet with more success, and with his bust of Tennyson in 1857 his reputation was made. Thereafter he flourished, becoming the most popular sculptor in England, and making busts of nearly all the famous men of his time.

In 1864 Woolner married Alice Gertrude Waugh; they had two sons and four daughters. He was made an associate of the Royal

Academy in 1871 and an academician in 1874. From 1877 to 1870 he was professor of sculpture at the Academy, but never lectured.

Woolner's poems show originality and power, but they have little beauty. He was not primarily a poet, but a sculptor who wrote poetry as an avocation.

PRINCIPAL WORKS: My Beautiful Lady, 1863; Pygmalion, 1881; Silenus, 1884; Tiresias, 1886; Poems, 1887.

ABOUT: Art Journal March 1894; Athenaeum October 15, 1892; Magazine of Art December 1892; Saturday Review October 15, 1892.

WORDSWORTH, CHRISTOPHER
(June 9, 1774-February 2, 1846), theological writer, was the youngest brother of the poet William Wordsworth. He was educated at Hawkshead Grammar School and at Trinity College, Cambridge, receiving his B.A. in 1796 and his M.A. in 1799. He was made a fellow of the college in 1798. He secured his D.D. degree in 1810. In 1804 he married Priscilla Lloyd, who died in 1815, leaving three sons, two of whom became bishops. The year of his marriage he became rector of Ashby, Norfolk. By the patronage of the Archbishop of Canterbury, whose son had been Wordsworth's private pupil, he was presented to various livings in Kent, Essex, and Suffolk between 1805 and 1816, and in 1817 became chaplain of the House of Commons. In 1820 he was named master of Trinity, and for a year following was also vice-chancellor of Cambridge (and again in 1826-1827). He was not a great success as a schoolmaster, but held on until 1841, when he was succeeded by William Whewell, the historian of science. Wordsworth then retired to his remaining living at Buxted, Essex, and died there five years later.

PRINCIPAL WORKS: Ecclesiastical Biography, 1810; Sermons on Various Subjects, 1814; Christian Institutes, 1836.

ABOUT: Wordsworth, C[harles]. Annals of My Early Life; Gentleman's Magazine 1:320 1846.

WORDSWORTH, CHRISTOPHER
(October 30, 1807-March 21, 1885), classicist and theologian, was the youngest son of Christopher Wordsworth, master of Trinity College. One of his two brothers became a classical scholar, the other Bishop of St. Andrews. Their mother died in 1815. Wordsworth was educated at Winchester and at his father's college, Trinity, Cambridge, where he had an almost unexampled career of prizes and honors. In 1830 he took his B.A. as senior classic, and was made fellow and assistant tutor. He spent 1832 and 1833 in Greece, then returned to Cambridge and was ordained deacon, being ordained priest two years later. In 1836 he was public orator at Cambridge and headmaster of Harrow. In the latter post, however, he was not successful. In 1838

he married Susanna Hatley Frere, who died in 1884, leaving two sons and five daughters.

In 1844 Wordsworth became canon of Westminster. In 1850 he left his difficult position at Harrow for a country living in Berkshire, where he had leisure for his study and writing. He was a remarkable linguist, and was thoroughly familiar with modern as well as ancient Greek. In 1865 he became Archdeacon of Westminster, and in 1869 Bishop of Lincoln. His episcopal career was a stormy one, involving a dispute with the Methodists and frequent attacks on the Roman Catholics. His wife's death prostrated him and actually caused his death; he resigned his bishopric in February 1885 and died the following month.

Wordsworth's principal work was the editing, with commentaries, of the New Testament (1856-60) and the Old Testament (1864-70). He was the literary executor of his uncle, the poet Wordsworth, and wrote his biography.

PRINCIPAL WORKS: Pictorial, Descriptive, and Historical Account of Greece, 1839; Memoirs of William Wordsworth, 1851; A Journal of a Tour in Italy, 1863; Church History up to A.D. 451, 1881-83.

ABOUT: Overton, J. H. & Wordsworth, E. Life of Christopher Wordsworth: Bishop of Lincoln.

WORDSWORTH, DOROTHY
(December 25, 1771-January 25, 1855), travel and miscellaneous writer, was the only sister of the poet, William Wordsworth, her senior by a year and a half. The four brothers and the sister were all born at Cockermouth, Westmoreland, where their father was steward and agent of the Lowther family.

The mother died when Dorothy was six, and she was sent to live with her mother's cousin, Elizabeth Threlkeld, daughter of a Unitarian minister in Halifax. There, with five other orphan cousins, she lived happily until 1787. For six months she was sent to a boarding school, and for the remainder of her stay in Halifax attended a day school, the sum total of her formal education.

In 1787 she was sent to live with her maternal grandparents at Penrith. They were unsympathetic, and her brothers were unwelcome visitors. Fortunately for Dorothy, at the end of 1788 her uncle William Cookson, a pleasanter person than his parents, married and secured a living (he was a clergyman) at Forncett, Norfolk, and took his niece to live with him. Here she stayed until 1794, with a year following spent in visits to various relatives, chiefly at Halifax. The dream of her life, however, was to be able to live with William, her favorite brother. In 1795 this became possible, and they were seldom separated thereafter. Through a legacy they were able to take a house at Racedown, Dorsetshire, with a child to tutor to add to their income. It was here that they first met Coleridge, and

DOROTHY WORDSWORTH

formed the close friendship which eventuated in the joint volume of poems by the two men and which crashed finally on the rocks of Coleridge's increasing deterioration through the use of opium.

The remainder of Dorothy Wordsworth's life is outwardly largely a record of travels, moves of residence, marriages and births and deaths in her immediate family, and inseparable intimacy with her brother, unmarred by his marriage, for she remained always in his household and was a second mother to his children. After a year in Germany, they settled permanently in the Lake Country always associated with Wordsworth's name, living variously at Rydal and Grasmere. In 1803 the brother and sister, with Coleridge, made the six weeks' tour in Scotland which was the theme of Dorothy Wordsworth's posthumously published book. In 1820 Wordsworth, his wife, and his sister accompanied a cousin and his bride on a six months' continental tour. Of this trip also Dorothy Wordsworth kept a detailed journal. It was, indeed, her custom throughout her life—or at least throughout her mental competency—to keep a voluminous diary of her daily doings, thoughts, and feelings, and it is from this source and from her letters that are drawn both her published writings and our chief knowledge of her history.

In 1822 she revisited Scotland, and on her return revised her *Recollections* of her previous tour, which had been widely circulated in manuscript. There was at this time, and again fifteen years later, some talk of publication of this journal, but it came to nothing; and it was not until 1874 that Dorothy Wordsworth's writings appeared in print. For nine months in 1826 she was absent on a series of visits, the longest period she and her brother were

ever separated after Racedown. Frequently, however, she left Rydal (their final place of residence) for a few weeks at a time, usually for brief visits to friends not many miles away, though in 1828 she visited the Isle of Man with her nephew.

But the end of a career poor in outward incident but rich in inner life was near. In April 1829 Miss Wordsworth was stricken with a violent illness, which seems to have been dysentery, and for a while she was not expected to live. She recovered, but never again had the strength for the long walks, the mountain climbing, the traveling, and the indefatigable attention to journals and letters which had kept her young in spirit at sixty. For several years her intense vitality pulled her out of a series of illnesses, but this alternation of ups and downs gradually became a constantly descending grade. Worse was to come. Her bodily health improved, but her mentality began to fail. For the last twenty years of her life Dorothy Wordsworth was insane, her memory gone, her nature reverted to that of an excitable child. Only one thing roused her to a brief lucid interval—the death of her adored brother in 1850. After that she lapsed once more into insensibility until she died five years later.

Dorothy Wordsworth even in her long best days was a creature of extreme sensitivity, exceedingly high-strung, passionate, ardent, full of keen zest in living, responsive to every influence. De Quincey described her as he first met her, at thirty-five; tiny, slight, already stooping, deeply tanned by the sun, quick-speaking, with "wild and startling" eyes. Her sympathy, her ardor, above all her oneness with nature, "her eager delight in birds and flowers and all common things," are implicit in every line she wrote. She had not her brother's high talent in expression, but she was in temperament far more of a poet than he. Had he not so overshadowed her, so drawn into himself, his family, and his concerns every fiber of her being, so that through the passion of her devotion she had scarcely any separate life of her own, Dorothy Wordsworth's might have been a name more famous in its own right. Even as it is, her journals, all published posthumously, are true literature, instinct with life, written with that unvolitional felicity which comes only with a naturally poetic mind married to directness and simplicity of thought. Strangely enough, the few verses she wrote are distinctly inferior to her prose, irregular, halting, and artificial. She belonged to an age of diary- and letter-writers, and she is among the choicest of her kind. No less than her inestimable services in nourishing her brother's genius, the unpublished manuscripts Dorothy Wordsworth left behind her attest her right to a place in literary history.   M. A. deF.

PRINCIPAL WORKS: Recollections of a Tour in Scotland, 1874. Journals. 1884, 1889, 1897.

ABOUT: DeSelincourt, E. Dorothy Wordsworth; Knight, W. A. Letters of the Wordsworth Family; Maclean, C. M. Dorothy and William Wordsworth; Maclean, C. M. Dorothy Wordsworth: The Early Years; Wordsworth, L. Journals; Wordsworth, W. Early Letters of William and Dorothy Wordsworth; Canadian Forum 14:185 February 1934; Catholic World 141:523 August 1935; Fortnightly Review 138:504 October 1932; New Republic 72:240 October 12, 1932; Saturday Review of Literature 10:117 January 20, 1934.

WORDSWORTH, WILLIAM (April 7, 1770-April 23, 1850), poet, was born at Cockermouth, Cumberland, second son of John Wordsworth, attorney, and Anne (Cookson) Wordsworth, of Penrith. On both sides the family was of Northern stock. There were three other brothers, and a sister, Dorothy (born 1771), who later became William's devoted companion and housekeeper. After primary instruction at schools in Cockermouth and Penrith, William was placed, in 1778, at the grammar school at Hawkshead, a village lying between Windermere and Esthwaite Water. As a boy he is reported to have been of "stiff, moody, and violent temper." The school hours were long, but, work once over, the boys (who lodged with local cottagers) were free to roam the country, and enjoyed walking, riding, and skating at will. His early reading included Cervantes, Le Sage, Fielding, and Swift; but throughout his life he learned less from books than from contemplation, and at a very juvenile age he showed that pseudopantheistic sense of union with external nature which is the most distinctive thing about him.

Anne Wordsworth died in 1778 and John in 1783. The children, none too well endowed, were scattered among relatives; and Dorothy, with her grandparents at Penrith, was to see little of William till he left college. In October 1787 he matriculated at St. John's, Cambridge, whence he graduated with a pass B.A. in 1791. His four university years, though pleasant enough, played little part in his development: his reading was desultory, and as a poet in embryo he got more from his long-vacation trips to Cumberland in 1788 and to France, Switzerland, and Germany, with a Welsh friend, Robert Jones, in 1790. On the first of these he beheld a marvelous sunrise which (as he was to record in *The Prelude*, Book IV) led him to believe that he was "a dedicated Spirit."

Wordsworth left Cambridge without any fixed notions as to a career. The obvious choices in those days, the church, the law, and the army, were all passed in review and rejected. He had a little money in hand, so, after spending a few months in London, he

determined to go to France to perfect his knowledge of the language (which, with Italian and Spanish, he had begun to learn at Cambridge). In November 1791 he went to Orleans, where he fell violently in love with Marie-Anne (Annette) Vallon, daughter of a surgeon. In the spring of 1792 Annette moved to Blois, and Wordsworth with her. An illicit relationship was in progress, and in the following December Annette gave birth to a daughter, who was christened Anne Caroline. These facts have only come to light in recent years, from the researches of Professors Harper and Legouis. It is now held, in Professor Herford's words, "that the story is substantially reflected in the more valuable parts of *Vaudracour and Julia.*" Rigidly suppressed both by Wordsworth and his earlier biographers, the episode throws new light on a character previously esteemed somewhat cold and passionless. Marriage was probably ruled out by the fact that Annette was royalist and Catholic while Wordsworth was an ardent republican and a very unorthodox Protestant, and by the Anglo-French war, which broke out in February 1793. Cordial correspondence was maintained for some years, and Wordsworth paid a small annuity from 1816 to 1835, when he commuted it with a lump sum.

The French Revolution had seemed to Wordsworth, as to many young spirits of the time, the beginning of a new era of liberty and progress. This faith was reinforced by an ardent friendship which he struck up at Blois with a republican officer, Michel de Beaupuy; and Wordsworth was probably involved in intrigues with the Girondists (the idealist Republicans). In 1793, in reply to strictures by Richard Watson, Bishop of

WILLIAM WORDSWORTH

669

Llandaff, he wrote an *Apology for the French Revolution* (not published during his lifetime), very eloquently defending his views.

Returning to England at the end of 1792, Wordsworth still had no regular employment. Next year he published *An Evening Walk* and *Descriptive Sketches*, conventional, derivative from the lesser Augustan poets; and in the summer fell in with an old school-friend, William Calvert, who took him on a tour to the Isle of Wight, which he prolonged, alone, by way of Tintern and the Wye Valley, to Denbighshire, where he stayed with Robert Jones in October. After a short visit to France he joined Dorothy at Halifax early in 1794, went with her to William Calvert's, at Keswick, and then on to Whitehaven. Thoughts of entering journalism were abandoned in 1795 when Raisley Calvert, brother of William, left Wordsworth a legacy of £900. With this exiguous capital the poet and his sister set up house at Racedown, Dorsetshire.

Among the paramount intellectual influences of this time was the individualist rationalism of William Godwin, as expressed in his *Political Justice*. Of a very different kind was the loving and understanding sympathy of Dorothy, which, until her mental deterioration, was a prop and an inspiration, and which survived not only Annette but also Wordsworth's marriage. Dorothy's life was interwoven with that of William with an intimacy unusual between brother and sister, and she was not only housekeeper and friend but in some sort collaborator. A third vital influence was the poet S. T. Coleridge, whom Wordsworth met in 1795. He paid the unrestrained homage which was so necessary to Wordsworth, but, more than this, his great and agile intellect moved with that of the other poet in deep and illuminating discussion and enabled him to rationalize and precipitate his apprehensions of the world. He introduced, too, the association psychology of David Hartley, which was very attractive to the writer of "The child is father of the man."

In July 1797 Wordsworth and Dorothy moved to Alfoxden to be near Coleridge, who then lived at Nether Stowey. In September 1798 the two poets produced a volume, *Lyrical Ballads*, which is historically one of the most significant books in the line of English poetry, and which has given rise to endless discussion since. Together they planned to produce a collection of poems of two kinds—one dealing with supernatural subjects in such a way that their reality, considered with "that willing suspension of disbelief that constitutes poetic faith," should be convincing; and the other demonstrating the poetic nature of everyday objects and incidents. Coleridge took the first group, and his outstanding contribution was "The Ancient Mariner." Wordsworth's efforts were very unequal, ranging from the memorable "Lines Composed Above Tintern Abbey" to the futilities of "Goody Blake" and "The Idiot Boy." The book, published by Cottle of Bristol, was a failure. The copyright was transferred to Wordsworth, who in 1800 brought out a revised version and added the "Preface" on poetic diction, one of the most famous pronouncements in English criticism. The gist of it is best expressed in the sentences defining the object as "to choose incidents and situations from common life and to relate or describe them, throughout, as far as was possible in a selection of language really used by men, and, at the same time, to throw over them a certain coloring of imagination, whereby ordinary things should be presented to the mind in an unusual aspect."

In mid-September 1798, the tenancy of the Alfoxden house having elapsed, the Wordsworths went to Goslar, in Germany, to spend the winter there with Coleridge. Goethe's personality was antipathetic to Wordsworth, and the German scene in general made no deep impression on his mind. Indeed it was during these months that he turned to the past in the long blank-verse poem, *The Prelude*, which was to trace the "growth of a poet's mind." This spiritual autobiography of his early years was finished in 1805 but not published until after his death, in 1850; and the successive alterations and variants, often of extreme interest. must be studied in Professor De Selincourt's critical edition of 1926. The poem, despite flat passages, is a considerable achievement in philosophic self-portraiture. It is perhaps unique in the exactitude with which it records the development of a character under the influence of environment; it has many long stretches of grave, wise, penetrating, and beautiful verse; and it is of cardinal importance in the study of this poet.

Returning to England in April 1799 the Wordsworths visited the family of Mary Hutchinson, at Sockburn-on-Tees. This girl had been at the same preparatory school as Wordsworth, at Penrith, was a close friend of Dorothy's, and three years later was to become William's wife. The brother and sister eventually settled (on December 21) at Dove Cottage, Town End, Grasmere, in the Lake district. Coleridge stayed there for a time, and then moved to Keswick, some fifteen miles away. Wordsworth wrote assiduously, tended by Dorothy. He planned a great philosophic poem on "Man, Nature and Society," to which his shorter poems should stand in the relationship of "cells, oratories, and sepulchral recesses" to a "gothic church." The cells and oratories arose indeed, and *The Excursion* ranks as "the body" of the edifice, but the cathedral as a whole was destined never to be built. He had now attained the serenity he had so long desired, and for half a century was to live chiefly in his beautiful Lakeland, growing in fame, but, after *Poems in Two Volumes* (1807), declining in power and becoming ever more conventional and conservative.

The death of Lord Lonsdale (to whom John Wordsworth had been land-agent) in 1802 brought some amelioration of the family's poverty, for the heir paid with interest a long-standing debt. On October 4, having previously, with Dorothy, spent a whole month at Calais in the company of Annette and Caroline, Wordsworth married Mary Hutchinson. The union appears to have been placid and successful, and wife and sister lived amicably together. A son, John, was born in June 1803, and four more children followed up to 1810. The next literary event was the publication of *Poems in Two Volumes* in 1807—a work containing the magnificent "Ode to Duty," "Stepping Westward," "Character of a Happy Warrior," "Sonnet Composed Upon Westminster Bridge"—and in short much of his highest and purest verse. It was vigorously attacked by Jeffrey in the *Edinburgh Review* and was widely ridiculed elsewhere. In the autumn of 1808 Wordsworth moved to Allan Bank, near Easedale, where he was much visited by De Quincey and Coleridge. In 1810 he quarrelled with Coleridge, and the friendship was not put on a firm basis again for seven years. The same year he moved to Grasmere Parsonage, and in 1813 to Rydal Mount, between Grasmere and Rydal Water, which was to be his final home. Shortly afterwards a sinecure of £400 a year, as Stamp Distributor for Westmoreland, granted by the new Lord Lonsdale, finally disposed of financial cares. A placid life now stretched out to the end. There were many long tours, several to Scotland (one of which took in a stay with Scott at Abbotsford) and several to the Continent, one in 1837 being with Henry Crabb Robinson, whose *Diary* has much of interest about Wordsworth. Durham University conferred a degree of D.C.L. in 1838; Oxford followed in 1839 with the same distinction. In 1842 Wordsworth resigned his official appointment, but Peel, at the instance of Gladstone, granted a pension of £300 on the civil list. After the death of Southey, in March 1843, he was made poet laureate. He died of a chill at Rydal on April 23, 1850.

For the tale of Wordsworth's publications between 1807 and his death the reader must be referred to the bibliography. But two volumes claim a word, representing as they do the zenith of his prose and his most ambitious attempt in verse. The first is the *Tract on the Convention of Cintra* (1809), prompted by General Dalrymple's action the year before, in allowing the French armies to retire unmolested from Spain and Portugal. It was a rapidly-written, closely-reasoned championship of nationalism as the bulwark of civil liberty, and represents Wordsworth's best advocacy of an ideal. The second is *The Excursion* (1814), which was to be part of the aforementioned great philosophic poem, called *The Recluse.* Set out with preface as an epic, its machinery was poor and its lapses from true poetry were many, so that from Jeffrey, in the *Edinburgh,* it elicited the memorable "This will never do!" Yet it has its great moments; it was praised by Southey, Keats, and Lamb; and it stands with *The Prelude* (though on a lower level) as an important autobiographical document.

Several accounts of Wordsworth's appearance are summarized in Herbert Read's book (*Wordsworth,* 1930, p. 17-25). De Quincey, meeting him in 1807, wrote that he was not well-made, that his legs were badly shaped and his shoulders narrow. But of the face— "Many such," he goes on, "and finer, I have seen among the portraits of Titian, and, in a later period, amongst those of Vandyke . . . but none which has more impressed me in my own time. . . It was a face of the long order; often falsely classed as oval. . . The forehead was not remarkably lofty. . . but it *is,* perhaps, remarkable for its breadth and expansive development. . . His eyes are not, under any circumstances, bright, lustrous, or piercing; but after a long day's toil in walking, I have seen them assume an appearance the most solemn and spiritual that it is possible for the human eye to wear. . . The nose, a little arched, is large. . . The mouth . . . composed the strongest feature in Wordsworth's face. . . "

Though probably the most unequal in performance of all the great poets, and capable at his worst of almost incredible bathos, Wordsworth maintains his position, in general critical esteem, among the most eminent of the English line, many placing him third, after Shakespeare and Milton. In his own day he was looked upon with something like veneration by Lamb, De Quincey, and his literary juniors in general. His influence was then, and has since remained, immense. He was in the first place an innovator. The *Lyrical Ballads* were a gage thrown down to the highly-mannered poetry of the previous century; and their celebrated "Preface" is a document of the utmost importance. Its dicta included the then startling doctrine of "a selection of the real language of men in a state of vivid sensation" as the poetic tongue, the eschewing of "personifications of abstract ideas" and the trite-sounding (but then significant) statement: "I have at all times endeavoured to look steadily at my subject." Among its definitions was the famous phrase that poetry "takes its origin from emotion recollected in tranquillity." Wordsworth's theories of poetry are not of universal application; nor did he adhere to them in many of his finest works; but as a well-reasoned protest against artificial and embroidered diction they are salutary.

His political development, from generous, warm-blooded enthusiasm for liberty to a cramped and crabbed conservatism, brought down on him the obloquy of Byron and Shelley and others who had retained their liberal ideals. Side by side with it went a poetic decadence covering many years, broken, however, by bright patches recalling the great days before the 1807 volumes. Wordsworth had a more vivid apprehension of the spiritual force of nature than any figure in British literature until we come to Thomas Hardy. His "Tintern Abbey" lines resume his philosophy; and exquisite short lyrics like "The Daffodils" and "To a Small Celandine" showed how simple things could form the basis of great poetry. Of a different order, Miltonic in moral dignity, are works like the "Ode to Duty." He was a master of the sonnet form, not surpassed, at his best, by Keats and Milton, and scarcely by Shakespeare; and wrote two exquisite sonnets in praise of the genre— "Scorn not the sonnet, critic, you have frowned" and "Nuns fret not at their convent's narrow room." He had a love and understanding of children and simple people the equal of which again we do not find between Blake and Hardy. His prose was stately and perspicuous, and his critical pronouncements will always command respect. "It was his mission," wrote George Saintsbury, "to reverse the general tendency of the eighteenth century by averting the attention from towns, manners, politics, systems of philosophy, and directing them upon the country, nature, the inner moral life of man, and religion." And later in his *Short History of English Literature* the same writer said: "When Wordsworth writes—

> The sounding cataract
> Haunted me like a passion;

or. . . .

> Our birth is but a sleep and a forgetting,

even Shakespeare, even Shelley, have little more of the echoing detonation, the auroral light, of true poetry."   H.B.G.

PRINCIPAL WORKS: *Poems*—An Evening Walk, 1793; Descriptive Sketches, 1793; Lyrical Ballads (2 vols.) 1798 (with Preface, 1800); Poems in Two Volumes, 1807; The Excursion, 1814; The White Doe of Rylstone, 1815; Peter Bell, 1819; The Waggoner, 1819; The Little Maid and the Gentleman: or, We are Seven, 1820[?]; The River Duddon: A Series of Sonnets 1820; Memorials of a Tour on the Continent, 1820; Ecclesiastical Sketches, 1822; Yarrow Revisited, and Other Poems, 1825; Poems, Chiefly of Early and Late Years, 1842; The Prelude: or, Growth of a Poet's Mind, 1850; The Recluse, 1888; The Poetical Works (8 vols., plus Life in 3 vols., by W. Knight) 1882-86. *Prose*—The Convention of Cintra, 1809; Two Addresses to the Freeholders of Westmoreland, 1818; A Description of the Scenery of the Lakes, 1822 (first publ. with The River Duddon, 1820); Memorials of Coleorton (2 vols.) 1887; The Prose Works (3 vols. ed. by A. B. Grosart) 1876; Unpublished Letters of Wordsworth and Coleridge, 1894; Letters of the Wordsworth Family From 1787 to 1855 (ed. by W. Knight, 3 vols.) 1907.

ABOUT: Arnold, M. Essays in Criticism (2nd ser.); Beatty, A. William Wordsworth: His Doctrine and Art in their Historical Relations; Coleridge, S. T. Biographia Literaria; Cooper, L. A Concordance to the Poems of William Wordsworth; De Selincourt, E. Dorothy Wordsworth; Dicey, A. V. The Statesmanship of Wordsworth; Elton, O. Wordsworth; Fausset, H. L'A. Wordsworth; Garrod, H. W. Wordsworth; Harper, G. McL. William Wordsworth: His Life, Works, and Influence; also Wordsworth's French Daughter; Herford, C. H. Wordsworth; Legouis, E. The Early Life of William Wordsworth; also William Wordsworth and Annette Vallon; Myers, F. W. H. Wordsworth; Pater, W. H. Appreciations; Raleigh, W. A. Wordsworth; Read, H. Wordsworth; Robinson, H. C. Diary; Reminiscences; and Correspondence; Swinburne, A. C. Miscellanies; Whitehead, A. N. Science and the Modern World; Wise, T. J. A Bibliography of the Writings in Prose and Verse of William Wordsworth; Wordsworth, W. The Excursion; The Prelude (see especially De Selincourt's variorum ed. of 1926); Wordsworth, D. Recollections of a Tour Made in Scotland; and Journals (ed. by W. Knight).

WORSLEY, PHILIP STANHOPE (August 12, 1835-May 8, 1866), poet, was born in Greenwich of a family long resident in the Isle of Wight. His father was a clergyman. He was educated at Cholmeley Grammar School, Highgate, and at Corpus Christi College, Oxford. He received both the B.A. and M.A. degrees in 1861, and while an undergraduate won the Newdigate prize for English poetry. He was made a fellow of the college in 1863.

Worsley was tubercular from youth, and his health forbade his entering any profession. Fortunately he had sufficient income to be able to devote all his time to study of the classics and to poetry. He died unmarried, of tuberculosis, at Freshwater, at thirty years of age.

Worsley's translation of Homer into English Spenserian stanzas was a remarkable achievement. It may be doubted whether the *Iliad* at least is appropriately translated into this difficult metric form, but what he set out to do he performed as well as it could conceivably be done. The *Odyssey* he completed, but of the *Iliad* he lived only to finish the first twelve books. The task was carried to a conclusion by another and inferior hand (that of John Conington); in any case the translation of the *Odyssey* is the better work of the two. His original poems are polished and pleasing, but they make it apparent that he was more gifted as an interpreter than as a poet in his own right.

PRINCIPAL WORKS: The Odyssey of Homer Translated Into English Verse, 1861; Poems and Translations, 1863; The Iliad of Homer Translated Into English Verse, 1865.

ABOUT: Athenaeum March 19, 1866.

WRAXALL, SIR FREDERICK CHARLES LASCELLES (1828-June 11, 1865), novelist and miscellaneous writer, was born in Boulogne, the eldest son of a lieutenant in the Royal Artillery. He was educated at Shrewsbury and at St. Mary Hall, Oxford, leaving without taking a degree. From 1846 to 1855 he lived on the Continent; then he served in Crimea during the Crimean War, with a Turkish contingent, as a commissary officer. In 1858 he edited the *Naval and Military Gazette,* and in 1860 and 1861 the *Welcome Guest.* In 1863 he succeeded his uncle as the third baronet. In 1852 he had married Mary Anne Herring; they had no children, and on his death, in Vienna, at only thirty-seven, the baronetcy descended to his younger brother.

Wraxall was a frequent contributor to the *St. James Magazine.* He made the authorized translation, in 1862, of Hugo's *Les Miserables.* In addition to his novels and historical and biographical works he wrote a number of books on military technicalities. His historical work (several of his novels were also historical in nature) shows the result of much industry, and his novels were entertaining, but he was primarily a journalist, and much of his production was both superficial and a mere compendium of scandalous gossip.

PRINCIPAL WORKS: Wild Oats, 1858; Camp Life, 1860; Only a Woman, 1860; Married in Haste, 1863; The Backwoodsman, 1864; The Life and Times of Caroline Matilda, Queen of Denmark and Norway, 1864; Golden Hair: A Tale of the Pilgrim Fathers, 1864; Mercedes, 1865.

ABOUT: Athenaeum June 17, 1865; London News June 24, 1865; London Times June 17, 1865.

WRAXALL, SIR NATHANIEL WILLIAM (April 8, 1751-November 7, 1831), historian, was born in Bristol, and educated in day schools there. In 1769 he went to Bombay as a civil servant with the East India Company, and two years later, at only twenty, was made judge advocate and paymaster. He resigned in 1772, and traveled in Portugal, Russia, Germany, and the Scandinavian countries. He met people of importance, and became the agent and go-between for Caroline Matilda, the banished Queen of Denmark, with her brother, George III. In 1777, with a lieutenant's commission furnished by the Prince Regent (George IV), he visited Holland, Germany, and Italy. From 1780 to 1794 he was a member of Parliament, and had a stormy career, first as a Tory, then as a Whig. After his resignation, he devoted his time to writing memoirs of his travels and political acquaintance. In 1789 he married Jane Lascelles; they had two sons, and his grandson, Frederick Charles Lascelles Wraxall, became a well known writer and journalist. He was made a baronet in 1813, by special recommendation of the Regent. The publication of the first of his memoirs, in 1815, caused a libel suit which resulted in his spending three months in prison and paying a £500 fine. He died at eighty, in Dover, while he was on his way to Naples.

Wraxall in his lifetime was undervalued by his associates, and his memoirs were attacked as garbled and untrue. He was indeed a braggart and over-ambitious, but he was an able, clear thinker, and his writing is highly interesting and frequently amusing.

PRINCIPAL WORKS: Cursory Remarks Made in a Northern Tour, 1775; Valois Kings of France, 1777; Historical Memoirs of my Own Time, 1815 (enlarged as Historical and Posthumous Memoirs, 1884).

ABOUT: Wraxall, Sir N. W. Historical and Posthumous Memoirs (see Introduction).

WRIGHT, JOHN (September 1, 1805-1843), Scottish poet, was born in Ayrshire. His father was a poor coal-driver. The family moved to Galston, where the boy had a few months' schooling, during which he learned to read but not to write. From seven he worked with his father; then at thirteen he was apprenticed to a weaver, who lent him books. At this time, his memory being prodigious, he composed in his head a long tragedy, which he kept intact until he learned to write, at seventeen! In 1824 he went to Glasgow and Edinburgh, where several influential men became interested in him and helped him to publish his book of poems, *The Retrospect.* He married Margaret Chalmers, a schoolmaster's daughter, and settled near Glasgow as a weaver. Not making a livelihood by this means, he had a second edition of his poems published and sold them himself throughout Scotland. This was his ruin: the excess of hospitality caused by his renown proved too much of a temptation; he became a drunkard, separated from his wife, and lived alone in misery and destitution. In 1843 some friends, in the hope of rehabilitating him, published his *Whole Poetical Works;* but it was too late—a few months later he died in a Glasgow hospital.

Wright's longer poems are imitative of Byron, and painfully artificial; his short lyrics, however, have much music and are instinct with the love of nature and beauty.

PRINCIPAL WORKS: The Retrospect, 1825; Whole Poetical Works, 1843.

WRIGHT, THOMAS (April 23, 1810-December 23, 1877), antiquary, was born in Shropshire. His father was a bookseller interested in antiquarianism; his paternal grandfather a pioneer Methodist and a satirical poet. He was educated at King Edward's Grammar School, Ludlow, then sent to Cambridge by a neighbor who was interested by the boy's precocious flair for antiquarian study. He entered Trinity College as a sizar (a student who pays for his keep by his services), and received his B.A. degree in 1834, his M.A. in 1837. While still an undergraduate he began contributing antiquarian articles to *Fraser's Magazine*, the *Gentleman's Magazine*, and others, and wrote a *History and Topography of Essex*. He settled in London in 1836 as a writer and editor of ancient manuscripts, his first province being mediaeval literature, and his first production an anthology of early English poetry. In 1837 he was made a Fellow of the Society of Antiquaries, and he was honorary secretary of the Camden Society and secretary and treasurer of the Percy Society. For these two societies, for the Royal Society of Literature, and for private persons of wealth he edited and published innumerable antiquarian works, and also illustrated histories of manners, dress, and social life of the past—129 volumes in all. He was made a corresponding secretary of the French Institute in 1842, and was one of the founders of the British Archaeological Association in 1842, seceding with other members seven years later. In 1865 he received a civil list pension.

Wright was married, his wife being a Frenchwoman. In 1872 his mind failed, and for the five remaining years of his life he existed in a state of imbecility.

Wright's work is often grossly careless and full of errors. But he was a pioneer in Anglo-Saxon and mediaeval English antiquarian studies, and his great enthusiasm paved the way for other more accurate scholars who followed him.

PRINCIPAL WORKS: Biographia Britannica Literaria (unfinished) 1842-46; The Celt, the Roman, and the Saxon, 1852; Wanderings of an Antiquary, 1854; Essays on Archaeological Subjects, 1861.

ABOUT: Academy December 29, 1877; Athenaeum December 29, 1877.

WRIGHT, (WILLIAM) ALDIS (August 1, 1831-May 19, 1914), Shakespearian and Biblical scholar, was born in Beccles, his father being a Baptist minister. He was educated at Northgate House Academy, Fauconberge Grammar School, and Trinity College, Cambridge. He taught in a school in Wimbledon, and was then able to return to Cambridge and (the religious tests having been removed) to receive his B.A. in 1858 and his M.A. in 1861. From 1860 to 1863 he was on the staff of William Smith's great *Dictionary of the Bible*, and this connection made Wright's name for him. In 1863 he was made librarian of Trinity, though it was not until 1878 that final removal of religious restrictions made it possible for him to be a fellow. From 1870 to 1895 he was senior bursar, and from 1888 to his death he was vice-master. He lived in the same college apartment (he never married) from 1865 until he died. Extremely formal and austere, he lived the life

of a recluse scholar. From 1863 to 1866 he was joint editor of the *Cambridge Shakespeare,* and sole editor of the second edition, 1891 to 1893. He was also editor of the *Globe* and *Clarendon Press Shakespeares,* from 1864 to 1870 co-editor of the *Oxford Chaucer,* secretary of the Old Testament Revision Company, contributor to the *Dictionaries of Christian Antiquities and Christian Biography,* edited the works of Bacon, and was literary executor of his friend, Edward Fitzgerald. He received honorary degrees from Edinburgh, Oxford, and Dublin. Wright's work is dry, but he was a true scholar, who insisted on going to the original sources for all his readings.

PRINCIPAL WORKS: (ed.) Cambridge Shakespeare (with William George Clark) 1863-66; Globe Shakespeare, 1864; Concise Dictionary of the Bible, 1865; Bible Word Books, 1866; Clarendon Press Shakespeare, 1868-72, 1874-97; Hexaplar English Psalter, 1911.

ABOUT: Cambridge Review May 27, 1914; London Times May 20, 1914.

WYLIE, JAMES HAMILTON (June 8, 1844-1914), historian, was born in London, and educated at Christ's Hospital and Pembroke College, Oxford, receiving his M.A. in 1867. From 1868 to 1870 he was assistant master at Trinity College, Glenalmond, in 1872 and 1873 inspector of returns for the Board of Education, and from 1874 to 1909, when he resigned, Inspector of Schools. From 1900 to his death he was a lecturer on English history at Oxford, which conferred an honorary Litt.D. upon him. In 1909 he became inspector of the Historical Manuscripts Commission. In 1874 he married Agnes Maclaren, of Glasgow, and they had four sons and two daughters. His historical work was useful, since he had access to and used many scarce original records, but his writing is marred by pedantry and by an attempt to include too many unimportant and confusing details.

PRINCIPAL WORKS: History of England Under Henry IV, 1884-98; The Council of Constance to the Death of John Hus, 1900; The Reign of Henry V, 1914.

YATES, EDMUND HODGSON (July 31, 1831-May 20, 1894), novelist and journalist, was born in Edinburgh during a theatrical tour of his parents, who were both actors. They were determined to keep him off the stage, and sent him away to school at Highgate, and then to Germany, in 1846, to study under a professor at Düsseldorf. In 1847, though only sixteen, he had a position in the general post office, and by 1862 had risen to be head of the missing letter department. In spite of the fact that practically all his time was given to editorial and literary work, he remained in the post office until 1872, in 1870 undertaking a special mission for the telegraph

department, to secure permission for erection of poles.

Meanwhile he had begun writing by 1850, contributing to numerous magazines and, through his father, meeting most of the literary and Bohemian lights of the day. In 1853 he married Louisa Wilkinson, and they had four sons. In 1854 Yates was dramatic critic of the *Daily News*, and remained their critic until 1860. In 1855 he edited two very short-lived humorous magazines. The same year he persuaded the *Illustrated Times* to let him conduct a column of personal gossip, the first time such a feature had appeared in any respectable periodical. He wrote several farces with N. H. Harrington, the first being produced at the Adelphi in 1857. In 1858 he became the first editor of *Town Talk*, which superseded his column in the *Illustrated News*.

This led to the most painful incident of his career: he published a scurrilous attack on Thackeray, and was expelled from the Garrick Club in consequence. Moreover, Dickens was involved in the affair, and he and Thackeray were enemies thereafter. In 1860 Yates was acting editor of *Temple Bar*, in 1867 editor of *Tinsley's Magazine*, and from 1879 to 1884 he edited a monthly called *Time*. After retiring from the post office, he made a very profitable lecture tour in America, and became European correspondent of the New York *Herald*. In 1874 he helped to found a "society magazine," *The World*, and became its editor. In 1883 an article in this magazine led to his serving seven weeks in prison for criminal libel.

Yates was indiscreet, and his journalistic writing was often in poor taste. But his novels were vigorous and well written, and his own *Recollections*, a charming book, reveals that he was as ardent a friend as he was an enemy.

PRINCIPAL WORKS: After Office Hours, 1861; Broken to Harness, 1864; Land at Last, 1866; The Black Sheep, 1867; The Rock Ahead, 1868; The Silent Witness, 1875; Edmund Yates: His Recollections and Experiences, 1884.

ABOUT: Yates, E. Edmund Yates: His Recollections and Experiences; Athenaeum May 26, 1894; Illustrated London News May 26, 1894; London Times May 22, 1894 and January 29, 1900.

YONGE, CHARLOTTE MARY (August 11, 1823-March 24, 1901), novelist and children's writer, was born and lived most of her life at Otterbourne, near Winchester. She came of a clerical line on both sides, though her father was a retired army officer who had been at Waterloo.

She was educated at home, under a Spartan system that convinced her of her "plainness and stupidity," and ordained a diet chiefly of bread and milk. She was given a thorough training, however, in ancient and modern languages, history, and literature, and continued

CHARLOTTE M. YONGE

her studies until she was twenty. The church influence was exceedingly strong in her home; she taught Sunday school from the age of seven until she died at nearly seventy-eight.

The earliest influence in Charlotte Yonge's life, aside from her family, was that of the famous theologian John Keble, who had a charge at Otterbourne and prepared her for confirmation. He and her father together edited and censored all her writings, and she obeyed implicitly every direction they gave. Through Keble she was drawn still further into interest in church affairs, and became an ardent advocate of the so-called Anglican Revival, led by Pusey and by Newman before he became a Roman Catholic. This "Tractarian" movement ultimately divided the Church of England into two schools, the Broad and the High, leaning respectively toward the Protestant and the Catholic schools of thought; and Miss Yonge was the representative of and propagandist for the extreme High Church faction.

Her life was almost without incident; her only trip out of England was a visit to Paris in 1869, and it was only after her father's death and her brother's marriage (she was the only girl) that she even moved from the house in which she was born. Her excessive shyness kept her from social life or from acquaintance with many people. For thirty years from 1851 to 1890 she edited, from Otterbourne, a juvenile magazine called the *Monthly Packet*, and most of the time edited two Sunday school papers as well. She taught daily in the village school all her mature life. Her only recreation was botany; she had an intimate acquaintance with the plant life of the neighborhood in which she lived, and though she never wrote on the subject was a real authority on it.

The Yonge family was horrified when Charlotte began in 1842 to publish articles in the *Magazine for the Young,* at the thought of a daughter and sister of theirs as a professional writer—a most unsexing occupation, they considered. But the one thing they could not suppress in her docile nature was the need to express herself in writing. It was finally agreed that she might continue her career if she never profited by it, and the proceeds from her books were always devoted to church and missionary enterprises. The two thousand pounds she earned from *The Daisy Chain* went to establish a missionary college in Auckland, New Zealand, and the still larger profits from her greatest success, *The Heir of Redclyffe,* to fit out a missionary schooner for the South Seas.

She seems never to have thought of marrying, or even to have known any men, except first cousins, of her own age. Perhaps between incessant writing, visiting the poor, and teaching she had small opportunity for the social amenities which lead to matrimony. She was distinctly an anti-feminist, though she herself had abandoned the exclusive domesticity proper to a Victorian lady; she was even very much opposed to the founding of Girton College, one of the earliest institutions for the higher education of women in England.

Though every one of her innumerable novels contains at least one chronic invalid, Miss Yonge's own health was unusually robust, and she never knew a day's illness until a few days before her death. Toward the end of her life she could not help knowing that she was a noted figure, and occasionally she received deputations of admirers who traveled to the village to testify to their admiration. But she remained completely unspoiled by any adulation, and died the same bashful, diffident person she had been as a girl.

She was, it must be confessed, a rather stuffy, prim person, a good deal of a prude, and exceedingly narrow in her views; but she was very far from a fool. She had by nature a direct and forceful mind, and she had genuine and great talent. She was sure of herself and never doubted the correctness of the ideas she held and expressed in her novels. She was fond of children, and wrote a great deal for them, mostly under the pseudonym of "Aunt Charlotte." (Her first few adult novels were issued anonymously.) She was the very type and apotheosis of the upper middle class lady of the middle nineteenth century; but all she lacked to make her a very different person indeed was a spark of the rebellion carefully trained out of her by her family in childhood.

It would be futile to attempt a full list of Miss Yonge's books; there were more than a hundred and sixty titles in all. Her historical romances are full of sound detail, and are far less didactic than her novels of contemporary life. The amazing success of these latter when they were published is beyond modern comprehension. Men and women in every walk of life wept and laughed over them, and *The Heir of Redclyffe* is even said to have had a definite influence on William Morris and others of the Pre-Raphaelite school of poets and painters.

She was the fictional historian of the Anglican Revival, and the prime chronicler of family life. The large families in her novels are appalling, especially when there is usually a poverty-stricken tubercular father or mother at their head. She has no real villians; everyone in her books is well bred; and her work is marked by the utmost smug propriety, with no slightest hint of passion. Her favorite theme is sacrifice, usually for others in the family, and submission to parental authority above all things. There are tears on every page.

And yet Charlotte Yonge just missed greatness. She had a marvelous power of characterization, and her crowded pages are alive with real persons, though not always very attractive ones to a modern eye. Her dialogue is inspired, and is infinitely better than that in the novels of, say, Anthony Trollope, with whom she may most justly be compared. She wrote entirely too much—biography, history, and fiction. In consequence she wrote herself out, and her early work is her best. But in her very limited field she is a writer almost of the first rank.   M. A. deF.

PRINCIPAL WORKS: *Fiction*—Abbey Church, 1844; The Heir of Redclyffe, 1853; The Little Duke, 1854; Heartsease, 1854; The Lances of Lynwood, 1855; The Daisy Chain, 1856; Dynevor Terrace, 1857; The Pigeon Pie, 1860; Countess Kate, 1862; The Trial, 1864; The Prince and the Page, 1865; The Clever Woman of the Family, 1865; The Dove in the Eagle's Nest, 1866; The Chaplet of Pearls, 1868; The Caged Lion, 1870; The Pillars of the House, 1873; Stories From Greek, Roman, and German History for Children, 1873-78; Magnum Bonum, 1879; Modern Broods, 1900. *Non-fiction*—Kings of England, 1848; Landmarks of History, 1852-7; History of Christian Names, 1863; Pioneers and Founders, 1873; The Life of Bishop Patteson, 1873; The Book of Golden Deeds, 1874; Eighteen Centuries of Beginnings of Church History, 1876; History of France, 1879.

ABOUT: Coleridge, C. R. Life of C. M. Yonge (includes her autobiography); Romanes, E. Charlotte Mary Yonge: An Appreciation; Bookman 13:218 May 1901; Cornhill 150:188 August 1934; Fortnightly Review 133:521 April 1930.

YOUNGER, JOHN (July 5, 1785-June 18, 1860), Scottish poet and nature writer, was born in Roxburghshire, the son of a shoemaker. He had little formal schooling, and worked at his father's trade from the age of nine. Poverty made him a skilful poacher, and incidentally an authority on angling. In 1811 he married Agnes Riddle (who died in 1856), and settled as the village cobbler at St. Boswells. The chance acquisition of Burns' poems determined him to try his own hand at poetry, though he published nothing until 1834, when he was nearly forty. At the age of sixty-two he won a prize for an essay on the Sabbath as a benefit to the working-man, and made his only trip to London to receive the award. In 1849 he was made village post-master, but disliked the work, resigned in 1856, and returned to cobbling. Like many other shoemakers, Younger was a bit of a philosopher; though he had only contempt for working-class movements, he detested the rich and everything about them, including their literature. Scott was his special abomi-nation. Yet this cranky, cross-grained old man was a natural poet, and his verses, though rough, show much real beauty. His two topics were love and fishing, and he considered him-self—and others agreed with him—an equal authority on both. His autobiography is well worth reading.

PRINCIPAL WORKS: Thoughts as They Rise (poems) 1834; River Angling for Salmon and Trout, 1840; The Temporal Advantage of the Sab-bath, 1849; Autobiography, 1881.

ABOUT: Younger, J. Autobiography; River Angling for Salmon and Trout (see biographical sketches 1860 ed.); Scotsman June 20, 1860.

ZOUCHE, LORD DE LA. See CURZON, ROBERT